THE
CHRISTIAN OBSERVER,

CONDUCTED BY

MEMBERS

OF THE

ESTABLISHED CHURCH

FOR THE YEAR 1825

BEING

THE TWENTY FIFTH VOLUME

LONDON

PRINTED BY ELLERTON AND HENDERSON
Gough Square Fleet Street

PUBLISHED BY HATCHARD & SON 187 PICCADILLY TO WHOM COMMUNICATIONS
(POST PAID) MAY BE ADDRESSED AND OF WHOM MAY BE HAD THE PRECEDING
NUMBERS OF THIS WORK EITHER SEPARATELY OR BOUND UP IN VOLUMES

SOLD ALSO

IN LONDON BY SEELEY & SON FLEET STREET AND SHERWOOD NEELY AND JONES
PATERNOSTER ROW AT OXFORD BY PARKER AT CAMBRIDGE BY DEIGHTON
AND STEVENSON AT BATH BY BINNS AT BRISTOL BY BULGIN AT EDINBURGH
BY THOMSONS BROTHERS OLIPHANT AND WAUGH AND INNES AT GLASGOW
BY OGLE AT DUBLIN, BY MARTIN KEENE AND R M TIMS

AND BY ALL OTHER BOOKSELLERS AND BY THE NEWSMEN
THROUGHOUT THE KINGDOM

1826

PREFACE

THE leading object of the Christian Observer, whatever imperfections may have attended the pursuit of it, has ever been to promote the extension of pure and undefiled religion and, believing the Established Church to be an eminent instrument in the hand of God for that purpose and cordially attached upon principle to its doctrines and discipline, the conductors of that work have conscientiously ranged themselves beneath its venerated banners and addressed their pages more particularly to its members. They have thought and maintained that to be a true Christian it is not necessary to be either an Arminian or a Calvinist, to verge towards apathy or enthusiasm, or to adopt any of the opposing extremes of doctrine which zealous controversialists have respectively insisted upon as his exclusive characteristics. They have further maintained that in order to be faithful and consistent members of the Church of England it is not necessary to anathematise their Dissenting brethren while they think it their duty not to shrink from an honest avowal and defence of what they consider valuable in the faith or discipline of their own communion. The test of a quarter of a century has proved that the plan of conducting a work on this simple and, as we think strongly Christian basis was not visionary. We could not indeed hope to unite all suffrages. Some of our Dissenting brethren have occasionally but not often we would hope or wilfully mistaken our object or assailed us with acrimony. Some ultra doctrinalists, whether Dissenting or Episcopalian it is also true have not been sparing in their censures upon us because we could not follow them to the verge of Antinomianism or fanaticism. But our most frequent and persevering and not least angry opponents have been those members of our own communion whose controversy with us has been grounded on their opposition, in whole or in part to those principles which we have ever held to be among the essentials of true religion,—such as the awfully lapsed state of mankind their utter inability to rescue themselves from their fearful condition by their own natural powers the free, and wholly unmerited nature of our justification before God by faith the indispensible necessity of the agency of God's Holy Spirit in converting and saving the soul, and the absolute obligation we are under as Christians not to be conformed to this world but to be renewed in holiness after the Divine image. To these points of difference we may add several questions connected with the practical arrangements of our common church and the operations of various religious and charitable institutions, for our attachment to which we have incurred no slight or unfrequent censure

We fully believe however that the cause of true religion, with a firm attachment to their own communion free from an intolerant or sectarian spirit, has for some years been greatly on the increase among the members of our church. For such persons especially we would wish to present a miscellany which may bring before them monthly such topics as may be found both useful and interesting. Not confining ourselves on the one side to mere sermons or points of divinity, or on the other taking up secular questions in a secular spirit. we have wished to allow a considerable latitude to our range of topics, but to imbue the whole with a Christian spirit,—not to thwart the progress of information or intellect in the vain expectation of thereby promoting scriptural piety, but rather to make every kind of talent and knowledge subserve the cause of religion.

In pursuit of this plan, our readers will find, in every Number of our volumes, several articles of a devotional, theological, biblical, or ecclesiastical kind, followed by papers more miscellaneous in their nature, but intended generally "for the use of edification," while they present to the mind many amusing or informing topics. For most of these we are indebted to our respected correspondents, to all of whom we gratefully return our best acknowledgments. Our Reviews comprise a notice of various publications, chiefly but not exclusively, theological, or connected with questions which appeared to us likely to interest or inform the friends of religion and of our church, or to give as it were a hallowed cast to matters of common interest. Our brief abstract of Literary and Philosophical Intelligence, without encroaching much upon our limits, falls in sufficiently with our general design. But no department of our work appears to us of greater moment than the monthly record of Religious Intelligence, which, owing to the vast extension of Christian and philanthropic exertion throughout the world, and without any thanks to us except for the labour of selecting and abstracting, offers a more interesting periodical mass of information connected with the progress of religion and its attendant blessings, than could ever have been presented in any other age or country. Our View of Public Affairs is designed to exhibit such a sketch of the chief passing occurrences of human society, especially in our own land, as may befit the contemplations of a reflecting Christian mind; and never was there a period which furnished more numerous or important subjects for practical inference, as well as religious and philosophical speculation.

We must leave our readers to glance over the contents of the present volume for themselves, to ascertain how far we have succeeded in our intended objects. As an illustration, we shall refer only to two or three political events, with their consequences. The first week of the year, opened with the recognition of South American Independence by the British Government; and to how many topics of interest, moral, social, political, and religious does this important subject lead! The meeting of Parliament incidentally brought before the public, in connexion with Ireland, the state of Popery; and this likewise has opened before us a wide field—unhappily a field of painful controversy, into which, as far as religion is concerned apart from politics, we have repeatedly entered in the present volume. Next followed various events connected with the state of slavery in our Western Colonies, which also have demanded from us numerous references, and we fear will often call us again to the combat with this dire curse of humanity. In other respects we have had very little in the shape of controversy in the present volume; and we would hope, from the auspicious signs of the times, that hostile discussion will become less and less a staple of Christian conversation or Christian authorship, till that blessed period shall arrive, which we devoutly trust is hastening on, when that true millennium, so largely alluded to by us in one of our recent Reviews, shall be consummated, by the banishment from among mankind of vice and ignorance, of error and irreligion, and when the kingdoms of this world shall become the kingdoms of our Lord and of his Christ.

TABLE OF CONTENTS
VOL XXV
BEING FOR THE YEAR 1825

NUMBER I

	Page
Relig Com —Scripture the Guide of Life	1
Family Sermon on Ii us ii 11—13	11
Biblical Criticism on Jer xvii 9	14
On Heb xi 1 and Acts xiii 48	15
Scriptures among the Laity	16
Miscel —Ecclesiastical Dry Rot	18
Voluntaries after Service	21
Holy Communion to Criminals	ib
Composition of Tracts	23
Cowper s Letters	ib
Version of Psalm viii	29
Rev of—Southey s Book of the Church	30
Butler s Book of the Catholic Church	ib
Cunningham s Sermons Vol II	47
Lit Intel —Great Britain — New Works Oxford Prizes Cambridge Prizes &c Royal Society of Literature Banwell Cave Egyptian Mummy Mechanics Institution Saline Bodies Sir C Wren Dew Chinese Proclamation — Tartary	55—57
New Publications	57
Relig Intel —Moravian Missions	58
Asiatic Society of Paris	60
Pub Aff —France Spain Greece United States Mexico South American Independence Irish Catholics West Indies	60—62
Obit —Wilberforce Richmond	64

NUMBER II

	Page
Relig Com —Scripture the Guide of Life (concluded)	65
Family Sermon on Psalm xxvii 4,	73
National School Tract	77
Exhortation Let us pray	78
Distributing Bibles at Confirmation	ib
Miscel —Character and Writings of Lord Byron	79
Easter	87
Violation of Sabbath	89
Rev of—Southey s Book of the Church (concluded)	89
Butler s Book of the Catholic Church (concluded)	ib
Lit Intel —Great Britain — New Works Cambridge Prizes Northern Expedition Autograph Letters Rochester Cathedral Roman Catholics Upas Poison	123
France Mortality Steam Engine	123
Spain Instruction	124
United States Emigrant Foreigners	ib
Tahiti — Chinese Entertainment	ib
New Publications	ib
Relig Intel —Ferney Voltaire	125
Prayer book and Homily Society	ib
Pub Aff —South American Independence	126
Parliament Ireland &c	ib

NUMBER III

	Page
Relig Com —The French Protestant Church	129
Family Sermon on Rom xv 5 6	137
Biblical Studies	141
Miscel —Slave grown Sugar	146
Character and Writings of Lord Byron (continued)	151
Boswell s Life of Johnson	158
Sacrament to Criminals	159
Rev of—Jerram s Parental Affection	161
Bickell s West Indies	173
Lit Intel —Great Britain — New Works Cambridge Public Buildings Chinese Secret Association British Museum Chemical Society	191
Russia Literature—India Persian Gulf—Java Steam Vessels	192
New Publications	ib
Relig Intel —Society for the Propagation of the Gospel	193
Bishop of Calcutta s Visitation	195
Serampore College	196
Calcutta School Society	ib
Calcutta Ladies Society for Female Education	197
Ohio Theological Seminary	ib
Pub Aff —France United States South America India Finance Jury Laws Cruelty to Animals Spring Guns and Game Laws Ireland	198—200

NUMBER IV

	Page
Relig Com —The Protestant Church in France	201
Family Sermon on Luke xxii 48	207
On 1 Cor ii 9 and 2 Cor v 14	212
Clerical Studies	213
Miscel —Character and Writings of Lord Byron (continued)	214
Hodgson s Letters from America	222
Church Psalmody	225
Voluntaries	226

Rev of—The Crisis by Cooper	226
Select Christian Authors	242
Lit Intel—Great Britain — New Works Chinese Language France, Fenelon Manuscript—Spain, Columbus — Greece—India—North America—South America Prison Improvements	251
	252
New Publications	254
Relig Intel—Bishopsgate Committee for Christian Knowledge	254
Church Missionary Society	256
Paris Bible Society	259
House of Reform for Children	261
Pub Aff—France Poland United States South America Burmese War Parliament	261, 262
Obit—Rev W Read	263

NUMBER V

Relig Com—Protestant Church in France (continued)	265
Biblical Criticism on Ephes i ii	274
Family Sermon on Ephes v 15, 16	276
Christian Temper	279
Miscel—Character and Writings of Lord Byron (concluded)	281
Slavery in the United States	288
Dr Johnson on Slavery	293
Clerical Non residence	ib
Rev of—Dwight's Theology	294
Lit Intel—Great Britain — New Works Oxford Rich's Collection Milton Papers Mrs H More Scripture Translations Edinburgh	321
Denmark Christians of St Thomas—Italy Palimpsest Researches—Sweden Expedition to Columbia &c—Egypt—Algiers—India—French Guiana—Mexico	322, 323
New Publications	324
Relig Intel—Church Missionary Society	324
M Peschier on Missions	327
London Hibernian Society	330
Pub Aff—France Greece La Plata Catholic Bill Corn Laws Jury Bill Game Laws	330, 331
Ecclesiastical Preferments	332

NUMBER VI

Relig Com—Protestant Church in France (concluded)	333
Genealogies in Matt i and Luke iii	338
Family Sermon on Mark xiii 37	344
Biblical Criticism on Ephes i ii	348
Miscel—Superstitions of the Catholic Church	349
Pleading by Counsel	357
Classical Parallelisms	358
Rev of—Penrose on the Navy	360
De la Beche on the Negroes in Jamaica	375
Lit Intel—Great Britain—New Works Oxford Christian Ministry Scientia Biblica Weights and Measures Burmese Articles Prayer book of Charles I MS of Homer Glastonbury Abbey Silicum Menai Bridge Church Clock	387
South Africa India North America	388, 389
New Publications	389
Relig Intel—Society for Christian Knowledge	390
Ladies Hibernian School Society	392
Pub Aff—France Spain Poland Greece Parliament Slave Colonies Chancery Burning Widows Chartered Schools Irish Bishoprics London University	393, 394

NUMBER VII

Relig Com—Philosophy of the Roman Catholic Religion	397
Family Sermon on Jer iv 14	402
Bp Jebb on Psalm i 1	406
Gregory Thaumaturgus	407
Chrysostom's Homilies De Statuis	408
Miscel—Consecration of Churches	415
Teaching Children Religion	418
Poetry—Lines to a First born the Deluge Death Lines to an Afflicted Sister Job xxxviii 7 Sonnet To a Friend with a Pocket Testament	420, 421
Rev of—Palingenesia Letters by Basilicus The Coming of the Day of God Jones on the Last Judgment Bayford's Letter to Jones Stewart's Practical View Bayford on the Second Advent Hatchard's Sermon Burton on the Jews Davison on Prophecy	422
The Loss of the Kent	435
Rev of Rev—Admiral Penrose on the Navy	441
Lit Intel—Great Britain — New Works Cambridge Inoculation	448
London University Literary Property Private Bills Silk Blood Diorama	449
France India &c America	450
United States Society Islands	451
New Publications	ib
Relig Intel—Paris Bible Society	452
Christianity in Madagascar	ib
Female Education in India	453
American Bible Society	454
Society for Education in Canada	ib
Spanish Translation Society	455
Episcopal Floating Chapel	456
Pub Aff—Portugal &c Greece United States Slavery Parliament Burmese War	458—460

CONTENTS

NUMBER VIII

	Page
Relig Com —Philosophy of the Roman Catholic Religion	461
Chrysostom's Homilies De Statuis	465
Family Sermon on Acts ix 6	475
On Psalm i 1	480
Spiritual Dangers to Students	ib
Miscel —Apocrypha	480
Conduct towards Servants	485
Cautions in Relieving the Destitute	486
Clerical Sporting	488
Rev of — Palingenesia Letters by Basilicus On the Day of God Jones on the Judgment Bayford's Letter to Jones Stewart's Redeemer's Advent Messiah's Kingdom, by J Bayford Hatchard's Sermon Burton's Sermon Davison on Prophecy Gauntlett on the Revelation Bickersteth on the Prophecies	489
Lit Intel —Great Britain— New Works &c	520
France Italy Sweden Turkey Egypt India United States Buenos Ayres Peru	521—523
New Publications	523
Relig Intel.—Society for Christian Knowledge	524
Bath and Wells Episcopal Societies	ib
Language Institution	526
London Infant Schools	527
General Knowledge Society	ib
Society for Education in Canada	ib
Letter of a Negro in Africa	528
Pub Aff —Greece Mexico Hayti Domestic	529—531
Erratum	532

NUMBER IX

	Page
Relig Com —Philosophy of the Roman Catholic Religion	533
Family Sermon on Job x 12—16	539
Chrysostom's Homilies De Statuis	543
Study of the Fathers	551
On Faith	ib
Samson not a Type of Christ	553
Miscel —Chinese Literature	554
Unitarian Chapels	557
Apocryphal Books of Enoch and Isaiah	558
Rev of—Jowett's Christian Researches	560
White on Catholicism	570
Lit Intel —Great Britain — New Works Alphabets	585
Charing Cross Library Fire Insurances Heights of Edifices	586
Prussia, Royal Edict — Poland Public Instruction &c —United States Everett's Oration—Ceylon — Mecca Pilgrims	586, 587
New Publications	587
Relig Intel —Church Building Commission	588
Missionary Seminary at Berlin	ib
Education on the Continent	ib
Naval and Military Bible Society	589
Roman Catholic Missions in China	590
Christianity in Tahiti	591
New York Episcopal Seminary	592
Ohio Episcopal Theological Seminary	ib
Poor pious Clergy Society	ib
Ecclesiastical Preferments	593
Pub Aff —Spain Greece Peru, Brazil and Buenos Ayres United States —Biblical Discussion in Ireland	594, 595

NUMBER X

	Page
Relig Com —Philosophy of the Roman Catholic Religion	597
Chrysostom's Homilies De Statuis	603
Family Sermon on Jer ii 11	609
Miscel —Jews Quarter at Rome	613
Country Wakes	616
Oratorios for Charities	617
Hints in administering Charity	618
Rev of—Osric, a Missionary Tale Douglas's Hints on Missions and Advancement of Society Thoughts on Missions Dignity of the Missions	620
Bishop of Bath's Primary Charge	633
Lit Intel — Great Britain—New Works Arctic Expeditions Knox Religions	642
France Public Schools, Children —Netherlands Spain Russia Technological Institution— Greece, Public Instruction— United States City Law Niagara Free Schools Address Tracts — Canada &c Newspapers—Society Islands	642—644
New Publications	644
Relig Intel —Society for the Propagation of the Gospel	645
Society for Conversion of Jews	646
Theological Seminary in Ohio	649
Scottish Missionary Bishop	650
Prayer Book and Homily Society	651
Sunday school Society for Ireland	652
Pub Aff —Greece Spain Hayti South America Revenue Burmese War Colonial Slavery	653—655

NUMBER XI

	Page
Relig Com —Mankind responsible for their Opinions	661
Faber on the Fathers	666
Samson a Type of Christ	670
On Religious Joy	673
Family Sermon on James i 12	680
Miscel —On Infant Schools	684
State of Religion in France	688
Rev of—Sermons of Brydayne	690

CONTENTS

Lit Intel — Great Britain — New Works Magnetic Power Paper Seatonian Prize Episcopal Professorship Perouse 710
France—Russia Schools—Sardinia, Royal Edict—New York—Brazil—India, Asiatic Society 711
New Publications ib
Relig Intel —Society for the Propagation of the Gospel 712
Church Missionary Society 714
Ladies Society for Negroes 715
Prayer book and Homily Society 717
Religious Tract Society 719
Female Education in India ib
Pub Aff—France Spain Greece United States Haytian Independence Jews — Brazil Treaty with Portugal —Combinations Weights and Measures 720—722
Ecclesiastical Preferments 723
Erratum 724

NUMBER XII

Relig Com —Mankind responsible for their Opinions 725
Letter to a Literary Friend 731
Catholic Exhortation to the Scriptures 733
Eighteenth Article 737
Biblical Criticism on Heb vii 18 19 738
Family Sermon on Ephes v 30 739
Miscel —Conduct towards Domestics 744
Relieving the Destitute 745 746
On the Fathers 747
All souls Church 748
Exhortation to Ladies on Slavery 749
Rev of—Abbé de la Mennais "De la Religion &c 751
Bishop Butler's Analogy with Wilson's Essay 769
Lit Intel — Great Britain — New Works Oxford Prizes Cambridge Prizes Chinese Language Translation of Boetius Novel Publications Westminster Abbey 777 778
France—Mathematics, Oriental MS, &c, Bridges — Italy, Memory—Russia Expedition to Siberia — United States Religion—Persia Koran—India Malabar Maxims 778—780
New Publications 780
Relig Intel —British and Foreign Bible Society 780
Fund for the Waldenses 781
National Education Society 783
Female Education in India 784
Pub Aff—France—Russia Death of Alexander—Domestic Commercial Agitation, Colonial Slavery 784 785
Ecclesiastical Preferments 794
Erratum 796

APPENDIX

Title-page i
Preface iii
Contents v
Relig Com—Mankind responsible for their Religious Opinions (concluded) 797
Rel Societies—Society for promoting Christian Knowledge — Books and Tracts and Receipts and Expenditure Office Revision of Books Amusement and Instruction Grants Sales Lending Libraries New Committees East India Mission North America and West Indies concluding Remarks 804
British and Foreign Bible Society—France &c Netherlands Switzerland Hamburg Altona, Hanover &c Frankfort Wuertemberg &c Prussia Silesia Denmark and Norway Sweden Russia Greece &c Persia India Colombo Taheita Malayan Archipelago Africa South America Jamaica North America Greenland Receipts and Expenditure 808
African Institution—Foreign Governments Memorable Judgment French Slave Trade Atrocious Cases Sierra Leone Call to the Public 816
Anti slavery Society — Second Report Order in Council Opposition to Reform Outrages West Indian Monopoly Hayti Call for Exertion 823
Prison Discipline Society—Sixth Report Tread wheel Gaol delivery Bail Ladies Committee Scotland Ireland Prison Schools Temporary Refuge Improvements 830
Church Missionary Society West Africa Mediterranean East India Missions Ceylon Australasia; West Indies North West America Summary View 834
United States Domestic Missionary Society 841
Receipts of Charitable Societies 843
Ecclesiastical Preferments ib
Index to Essays &c 845
——— Reviews 848
——— Names 849
——— Texts 851
——— Signatures 852

THE CHRISTIAN OBSERVER.

RELIGIOUS COMMUNICATIONS

For the Christian Observer

ON THE SUPERIORITY OF THE SCRIPTURES AS PRESENTING A RULE OF ACTION, THE BEST FOR THE INTEREST AND HAPPINESS OF SOCIETY

MANY of the ancients renowned for their moral regulations were pagan philosophers, and many wise and useful precepts are to be found in the stores of their learning. But, however excellent these may have been in other respects, they were in one most important particular altogether defective: they proceeded from no just or acknowledged authority. Independently of their intrinsic worth, they had nothing to recommend them to the public attention, except it were the little fame or reputation of their respective authors. Being merely the suggestions of human minds, they derived no right to command from the source in which they originated; man having no farther power over man, than what results from natural and social connexions, or from the established laws of society. They could indeed have been recommended, but not rightly or lawfully enforced. Their authors had no ground upon which to found their claim to the obedience of their fellow creatures; nor the ability to reward the meritorious or to punish the undeserving.

In this respect no small superiority belongs to the precepts of Revelation; since these are not only in themselves perfect and complete, as shall be presently shewn, but also proceed from authority, and from the highest that can possibly exist—from Him whose right to command is indisputable and extends equally to all created beings; and who regards all mankind with an eye of perfect impartiality, having no respect of persons. The Scriptures assign this pre-eminence to the Almighty; they consider this authority as vested exclusively in his hands, and announce all their commands as having emanated from this Omnipotent Being. They state also the grounds of this authority. It is founded on certain acts of the Almighty, without which there could have been no other being but himself. The great works of creation and of preservation belong exclusively to him; and, above all, the wonderful work of redemption. Being the origin and source of our existence, having "made us, and not we ourselves," he has a right to issue laws for our conduct, and to demand our obedience to them. But this right is further established by the continual exertion of his power and goodness in our preservation, in the maintenance and exercise of our faculties, and in our enjoyment of the comforts of life. The hand that made us is necessary for our continual support. And as our continuance in existence depends as much upon God, as our first introduction into being, he has the same claim to our service upon the score of what he does for us every moment of our life, as upon that of our creation. But this right receives still an additional strength—a strength which no system in the world but that of the Gospel can supply, and to which the most obdurate hearts have been known to yield, when they had long stood out against the force of every other motive—from the astonishing plan, contrived by Unsearchable Wisdom for the recovery of fallen man from that wonderful manifestation of love and mercy displayed in the redemption of the world through the mediation and atonement of the Son of God. The intention of this scheme is to bring the sinner to the acknowledgment of his obligations as a creature made and supported by the Omnipotent, as well as to compel to win and to constrain him by its own powerful claims, to restore man to his allegiance to God, and to establish him for ever under the benign influence of the government of Him who alone can bestow permanent happiness on his subjects.

Upon these grounds it is that God enforces his commands. In the first place, he asserts his right as an Almighty Sovereign who has exercised his power in bringing us into existence; in the second, as still almighty but at the same time full of goodness and as carrying on the never ceasing work of our preservation; and in the third, as a God of love who has provided the most extraordinary means of restoration for a self ruined world. Thus, his right is founded on a free exercise of power, on a continual exertion of goodness, and on a wonderful display of love. Without the first we should not have had existence; without the second we should not have been continued in existence; without the third, we should have had no happiness in it. These are the views which the Scriptures give of our connexions with the Most High; these are the considerations which they contain respecting our obligations to yield him universal obedience; and if these be not sufficient to establish a right to our obedience, the most fertile imagination may labour for ever in vain to discover any circumstances that can possibly establish such a right. But these *are* sufficient, and they appear fully so to all who have not sacrificed their reason and understanding to the sophistry of a wicked heart. Every thing in and without us, the voice of nature and of conscience, the dictates of justice, of gratitude and of love, all concur to proclaim the right of the Almighty to the unreserved obedience of all his creatures. He who denies him this obedience acts against the natural order of things, reverses the law of his being, and strives for his own ruin. He lives in God and yet disobeys him. He moves in him and yet walks in a direction diametrically contrary to his will. He has his being in God yet provokes him daily and assumes a proud independence of action as if he were his own creator. The sinfulness of disobedience is scarcely ever considered in its full extent. Were we to see it in all its enormity we could not fail to be struck with astonishment at the wonderful patience of the Almighty.

According to the Gospel representations the Divine Being may be considered in effect to address every individual somewhat in this manner:—' It was my hand that formed thee, thou art mine, obey my commands. It is my hand that supports thee every moment of thy life, thou art mine let thy life be spent in my service. It was my Son who came to redeem thee from the ruin which thou hadst brought on thyself, accept him as thy Saviour take his yoke upon thee for it is easy, love me because I have first loved thee, keep my commandments, and thou shalt for ever enjoy my favour and participate in my happiness.' Who but the Most High can use such language as this? And where can we find his will thus revealed but in the sacred Scriptures? Where else does he condescend to speak to man?

But this particular excellency of the Gospel is one only of the many excellencies which belong to it. Its precepts are the best for promoting, and exclusively those which can *effectually* promote the individual and universal happiness of mankind. They extend to all ranks, they comprehend within their scope the highest as well as the lowest, the wisest as well as the most simple and they shew partiality to none. The first and the chief principle which they inculcate equally on all is cordial love and obedience to God, which, in its extent, is another peculiarity not to be found in the codes of pagan philosophers. God being the highest, the first and the last, the beginning and the end, the centre of power, of wisdom, of goodness, of love, and of every thing great and excellent, it is but right that he should have the priority, that his will and glory should be the first object of consideration in all the actions of his creatures. Nor let it be impiously thought that there is any thing sordid or selfish in this requirement. The very nature of things cannot allow it to be otherwise, and it is nothing more than what justice demands. If God be the author of our being and of every blessing we enjoy, it is but justice that he should be recognized as such, and if all that we have is his entirely, his it is but right that we should devote our all to his service. Those who would wish the Almighty to require less than he does, would have him in fact reverse the order of his creation, violate the laws of eternal justice, and relinquish the peculiar properties of his own existence.

But besides the inherent propriety and justice of this demand on the part of God, it tends most essentially to produce unanimity and concord among mankind. The great source of dissensions is the pursuit of different or contrary interests. All the plans and proceedings of those who know not God invariably in some way or other centre in themselves. Honouring, enriching, or sensually gratifying self is the paramount object, for the attainment of which every other consideration is relinquished. What but discord can be the consequence of such a state of things? There is no co operation, no tending to one point, no gravitation to the same centre, no fellow feeling, but the very reverse, a cross marching, an advancing towards opposite directions, a motion to as many points as there are individuals, and often a reciprocal alienation of heart. To avoid these evils is impossible, unless there be established a moral system, and unless that system, like the natural one, have a grand point of attraction around which all its subjects, in their different spheres, may move with order and regularity. Some great object must be found out on which the attention of all may be fixed, an object sufficiently magnificent and interesting fully to employ the mind and engage the heart, the pursuit of which should convey present increasing and everlasting happiness and enjoyment. But what is this object? Where is it to be found? Is it that which the mere political patriot pursues, who devotes his all to the temporal good of his country? His no doubt is a noble object, yet it cannot be deemed worthy of this supreme distinction. Though it be great, yet it is not sufficiently so; 1 proposes the benefit of but one small portion of our race, and this is often attained with loss and injury to others, and even were the whole world included within its compass, it would yet be inadequate to the purpose under consideration. It could not even then secure happiness to its advocates. That measure of satisfaction which is to be derived from good intentions would no doubt accompany it, but the pleasure which results from success might often be denied, a thousand mortifications might be incurred, and the best patriot, even the patriot or the philanthropist of the universe, may die under the regrets and remorses of innumerable disappointments.

We must then search forward as our ultimate aim to some object of greater magnitude than any thing merely earthly, and which may be pursued with more certainty of success. Let us ascend higher than things seen, let us rise above mere nature, and proceed in those steps which will lead us to its Divine Author to that Being whose we are, and for whom we were made whose will brought us into existence, and whose will could reduce us again to nothing. His glory is the only object that can fully answer our expectations. The magnitude of this object is sufficient to engage the attention of the whole world, or of ten thousand worlds. its attraction and magnificence may well engross the love and admiration of all intelligent beings. its influence is so benign and powerful as to be capable of conveying pleasure and felicity, unceasing and infinite, to the utmost extent of rational existence and the interest which it excites is so varied and extensive as to afford sufficient scope for the exertions of all created minds without collision or interference. for in pursuing it, far from impeding, they mutually promote the welfare and happiness of each other. It is an object which comprehends in it every other that is good and lawful. Its promotion consists in doing the Divine will and as this refers to our entire conduct, to our duty to all with whom we are connected, and even to the whole world. we are promoting it while engaged in the performance of every branch of that duty. The glory of the Most High is advanced by every act of obedience. even a cup of cold water given from a principle of duty and love to God, shall not lose its reward. There are no circumstances under which this object may not be pursued and attained. no changes nor chances no events however untoward and distressing. no accidents however unexpected and alarming. can possibly hinder its furtherance. If our plans and endeavours to benefit our fellow creatures be unsuccessful. if the evil machinations of Satan or the world frustrate our expectations yet we shall still succeed in the main object in glorifying God by doing his will. and we shall attain this, notwithstanding all possible disappointments. And when it happens that the humble Christian is persecuted, oppressed, imprisoned degraded, or even put to death in the service of his Master, the glory of God is still promoted. when he falls, he falls only to advance the great object of his desire. and as to himself, to rise to a more exalted eminence, and to a larger participation of heavenly enjoyments. And is not this a truly glorious object. an object so elevated as to be above all the pursuits of time. so comprehensive as to include every other that is good. so peculiarly excellent that it may be prosecuted and attained under all possible circumstances. so beneficial as to convey happiness to all who aim at its promotion. and so permanent as to be pursued through eternity by men and angels with unceasing pleasure, admiration, and delight? Oh! that the world could be persuaded to relinquish their own mean, selfish, and sinful aims, and to choose this great object, and pursue it with the same ardour and diligence with which they now pursue the trifles of the present life! What union, what peace, what happiness, would be then enjoyed even here. and how abundant would these be. were all moving, as it were, around the same centre, enlightened and influenced by the great Luminary of the moral system, and aiming at the promotion of the same interest, the furtherance of the same great cause!

The necessity of this first and grand principle of moral duty for the promotion of universal peace and happiness, is incontrovertible no one who allows what every *rational* being must allow, the existence of a Supreme Being can on any fair ground dispute it. If we take away this first and great commandment, we leave no centre of union. we remove the main spring of the moral machine, which cannot be supplied by any human invention. we rob the system of that which sets it in motion, which influences all its parts, which pre serves it in order, which produces regularity and consistence in all its movements. We may as well expect the luminous and stupendous bodies in the planetary system to display their wonted splendour, and to carry on their unvaried motions without the glorious luminary of nature, as that human or rational beings should act and move with consistency and order in their different spheres of life, without living under the government, without feeling the influence, of their Creator. All the confusions and disorders, the conflicts and devastations, the bloodshed and massacres, ever witnessed in the world, are to be mainly attributed to the exclusion of this first principle of duty either from the creed or from the hearts of mankind, and the very intention of the Gospel is to restore it, to plant to engraft it in the inward parts, and to make it grow for the fructification of the earth. Its primary object is to lead the creature back to God in Christ, that he may obtain his favour, and live under his influence and to his glory, and its secondary object, to capacitate him to desire and to promote the good of others, to *love his neighbour as himself.* The means devised and prescribed for these purposes are of a very extraordinary kind, and are wonderfully efficacious for the accomplishment of their object, as numerous instances in every age of the world have proved.

Respecting the operations of this main principle but few words are necessary, the subject being very obvious. When man is brought under the controul of Him who made him, the whole character of the Divine Being exerts an influence over his mind, and fixes its own holy and glorious impression upon all his feelings and actions. As a submissive and devoted subject, he will regard the Almighty as his rightful and exalted Sovereign, as one in whose favour is his greatest happiness, in whose power and protection is his entire confidence, in whose services is his delight, and at the attainment of whose likeness he aims as the highest excellence, as perfection itself. The majesty of God will inspire him with reverence, his justice with an abhorrence of what is wrong, his holiness with a detestation of sin, his goodness with a desire to promote the comforts of others, his mercy with compassion on objects of pity, his long suffering with a patient endurance of evils, and his sovereignty with contentment in that station of life in which he may be placed. These are the natural productions of the first principle of the Divine law when "put into the mind and written in the heart," and they are visible in a greater or less degree in all those in whom this principle exists, though they are often checked and blasted by the corruption and infirmities of even the best of men in this imperfect and probationary state. In these impressions or communicated virtues is to be found every thing necessary for qualifying us to be useful members of society. We find in them the spirit of regard and submission towards those in authority, a sense of justice, to prevent oppression and wrong, a holy disposition to abstain from and abhor sin, a philanthrophic mind, to advance the happiness of others, a feeling heart, to commiserate the distressed, a patient temper, to bear with indignities, and a contented spirit, the great promoter of internal peace and comfort. What more can be required for the purpose of introducing an age of universal happiness? This ' knowledge of the Lord filling the earth' would be the only and an amply sufficient means for the attainment of that exalted end.

Descending from this first element in the precepts of revealed truth, we shall now notice some of their other properties, and point out in what manner they bear on the welfare and peace of society.

Respecting the regulation of our

conduct towards one another, nothing can be more impartial or more complete, nothing more just and more promotive of individual and universal happiness, than what the Gospel proposes. Like its Author, it shews no respect of persons, and includes within the compass of its precepts all that is necessary to be known or enjoined; like its Author also its requirements are infinitely just and tend most essentially to advance the best interests of mankind. These particulars shall be shortly elucidated.

What might be expected from him who is the common Father of all, is the enforcement of such laws as would not be more favourable to one individual than to another. Those contained in the Gospel are altogether of this kind. They allow no oppression to be exercised by any; they prescribe with equal impartiality the duty of every rank in society, and of every relation in life. No station is overlooked, no relative connexions are left without appropriate injunctions. There are directions and commands for the king and for the subject, for the powerful and for the weak, for the rich and for the poor, for the master and for the servant, in short, for all the social connexions. And there is one grand principle to be observed by all, and by which all without exception are to be regulated, the universal inculcation of which excludes all partiality; and this principle, this grand rule to which all others may be reduced, is contained in the following words:—'*All things whatsoever ye would that men should do to you do ye even so to them, for this is the Law and the Prophets*:' that is, maintain such a conduct towards others as you would justly expect from them were you to change situations, were you in their place and circumstances, and they in yours.

In the disposal of his gifts the Almighty acts according to his own good pleasure, endowing some individuals with greater mental powers than others, and also with higher advantages to improve them, and with a larger share of worldly possessions. But in prescribing the duties of his creatures he acts differently, requiring equally of all that degree of service which their state in life, their peculiar privileges and circumstances, allow. There are gradations in his gifts and there are gradations in his requirements; the former are fixed by his infinite wisdom, and the latter by his immutable justice. In his benefits he shews himself a Sovereign, acting according to his own free will and pleasure; in his enactments he shews himself a righteous Lawgiver, demanding the service which of right ought to be rendered. To make one to differ from another without doing injury to any is the usual character of his proceedings. Variety is not less visible in the mental than in the natural world; indeed, it is a prominent feature in every part of God's works. Whatever is known to us we find distinguished by variety. The vegetable creation is so greatly diversified in its productions that they are almost beyond number; the same may be said of the animal world; its inhabitants differ in size and character, they occupy different situations and are useful for different purposes, yet they have all their peculiar station, which cannot be filled by any other. Thus it is with human society; it is a world of itself diversified with as many characters as there are to be found kinds and species in the inferior productions of creation or of stars and planets in the solar system. This diversity proceeds from the same cause in all these instances, from the will of their Maker, and in common with every other feature of his works, it displays his infinite wisdom. Society receives its very being from this variety; without it no civil body could exist. Were all of the same capacity of intellect and cast of mind, of the same disposition and temper of feeling, they could not be so arranged and fitted together as to form a regular community. Instead of various articles for the different parts of the machine, there would have been only one. Instead of several members all differing from each other, yet co-operating towards one common design, there would have been only those of the same kind. All head, or hand, or foot would not form a physical frame endowed with the characteristic functions of skilful organization. Yet such a species of civil body would some wild theorist desire to form. They would construct society upon a principle different from that which prevails in every system in art as well as in nature. They would bring all men to a level, cutting off as it were the heads of some, and adding to the stature of others. To complete their scheme they should make all plants and trees of the same height, texture and strength, all animals of the same kind and bulk, all the luminaries of heaven of the same magnitude and splendour, all the parts of the machine of creation of the same dimensions, and all the members of the body of the same form, size, and vigour. They should overthrow the universal order of things, reject the lessons both of nature and art, and in fact be wiser than the Author of wisdom himself.

But will it be alleged that partiality is shewn in these appointed varieties? The supposition is not correct. Partiality is an undue leaning or improper indulgence to one side more than to another, which with regard to the abilities of men cannot be the case, for they are the free gifts of God, dispensed according to his own wisdom, for the good of the community, and ultimately for the glory of his own name, and without any partial disposition. To shew partiality in this view is indeed impossible. God forms the creature with such qualifications as seem good to him, to fit him to move in his appointed circle of life, manifesting thereby the same sovereignty as in all the works of nature: but this is not partiality. There are, indeed, conceivable circumstances under which partiality might be shewn. For instance, were rules founded on different principles, given to the different branches or ranks of the community, then its exercise would be clearly seen. But is this the case with the precepts of revelation? By no means; for they are in no way more favourable or more indulgent to one rank than to another. The great are not excused because they are great, nor the poor because of their poverty. There are limits marked out within which every individual is to move, and whenever he leaps over these boundaries, he is without respect to persons censured, and his punishment is impartially denounced. The law which regulates the conduct of all, of every one in every station and relation of life, is in principle the same; its requirements differ only in correspondence with that difference of situations and connexions which exists in society. *Love thy neighbour as thyself* is the universal law of social man. In this view all are dealt with without the least distinction, all are upon a level, equally bound to observe the same identical precept, whatever be their peculiar circumstances, however exalted or low their station, however great or small their natural endowments, however many or few their privileges. And to shew still more fully the impartiality with which mankind are treated, and to remove that objection which by some may be made on the ground of unequal qualifications and advantages, we are expressly told in Scripture that the extent of the demand will be in proportion to the extent of gifts and privileges conferred. ' *For unto whomsoever much is given of him shall much be required.* To improve then what we have is our greatest wisdom, and not to covet what we have not for to possess more would only increase our responsibility

It is a prevailing idea that the happiness of men is in proportion to the extent of their intellect or the height of the sphere in which they move but this is an unfounded opinion, and is countenanced neither by reason nor by observation. A capacious mind reason will tell us, will require a corresponding capaciousness in the objects which it contemplates a larger share of enjoyment and an extensive field of operation will demand in proportion an extensive degree of activity and exertion In perfect agreement with this view is the evidence of experience Affliction is incident to every condition and rank of life the most eminent attainments the most exalted stations will afford no exemption from it it cannot be averted by any worldly distinctions, there is no human shield that can repel its envenomed darts the poison in which they are dipped lodges within the bosom of every individual of the human race and, until that be extracted no security can be obtained against the festering wounds which they inflict The corrosions of envy the chagrins of disappointment, the mortifications of pride, the violence of appetite and passion the tortures of bodily pain, are common to all, and are perhaps more prevalent among the higher than the lower ranks of society It is not any natural endowments, or worldly eminence that can confer on us the blessing of true felicity but it is the right use of what we possess however scanty it may be the filling up that space in society which we occupy the conformity of our life to the rule of Christian duty this only, independently of any natural or artificial superiority can crown the days of man with happiness The observance of duty can lead all equally to the attainment of this, the most valuable of all possessions While God makes distinctions in other respects in this he makes none while he bestows on some more eminent talents and more worldly advantages than on others with regard to the means of being really happy he makes no difference for these are the same to all, and are as accessible to the lowest as to the highest,—they are, in short, " the way of his commandments

Again the *completeness* of the Divine precepts is no less remarkable, than their impartiality Though not very numerous, yet they comprehend the whole extent of moral duty, including within their compass all the actions of rational beings, however different in their rank circumstances, and situations, regulating the exercise of all the faculties and powers of man prescribing rules for his thoughts, for his words, and for his deeds being as extensive as the right of a Supreme Ruler would require, and the capacity of man would allow

There are two views in which the precepts of revealed truth may be considered complete namely as they embrace every kind of duty, personal, relative and social, and as they refer to every part of man, or rather to every capacity of acting which he possesses as a moral agent Changeable and varied as are our circumstances proceeding continually as we do from one stage of life to another from pupilage to manhood and thence to senescence different as our relative connexions become by various changes as from a son to a father, from a daughter to a mother from a single to a married state and multifarious as are the gradations which exist in society yet sufficiently comprehensive for all cases are the Divine commands and they are capable of affording directions for every stage and condition of life Not, indeed, that they contain prescriptions for *every* particular part of conduct but they supply ingredients, which, by variety of admixture and application, may be made suitable to all possible circumstances. The broad lineaments of duty are most distinctly drawn and from them all the minor features may be easily traced out. The fundamental principles are so simply and unequivocally stated, as to enable every 'honest and good heart' to discern the right path; and the peculiar character also of every kind of duty being clearly specified, there can be no great difficulty in ascertaining all its lesser particulars. The Divine precepts begin with what we owe to Him who formed us, and then descend to what we owe to our own species. In both instances, love is the spirit or disposition which is most particularly required to accompany our obedience: it is that indeed which is to be its influencing and predominating principle. Towards God, its exercise is demanded in an especial manner, and in a degree higher than towards any created being; and the measure of it which we are enjoined to entertain towards our fellow creatures, is the same which we feel towards ourselves. With respect to God there is nothing to oppose, but every thing to increase and facilitate, its course, he being ever infinitely worthy to be loved; and the nearer we approach him, and the larger our acquaintance becomes with his dealings and character, the greater force will be given to the current of this feeling. But with reference to mankind, there occur many impediments: the conduct of our fellow creatures, so far from being invariably calculated to conciliate affection or regard, may often tend to excite hatred or contempt. In such cases, our duty is, to consider the individual apart from his practice, and viewed as the creature of God and as one of our own brethren of the human race, he is entitled to our affectionate consideration, however unworthy he may be of personal friendship; nor are we to withhold from him every kind office, regulating our conduct in this respect by the rules of justice and wisdom, and by a regard to his ultimate good.

Commencing with this general principle, the holy law of God proceeds to particularize the distinguishing character of those duties which arise from various relations and connexions in society. For example the distinguishing or peculiar character of the duty of children to their parents, and of subjects to their rulers, is honour; *honour thy father and thy mother,—honour the king*; and the characteristic of the duty of parents and rulers in return is protection. The essence of the duty of servants is subordination; that of masters is justice or equity. The husband is to *love* his wife and the wife is to *obey* her husband. The same broad principle is suggested with regard to every other duty. And from these general and fundamental principles, are to be deduced all the subordinate rules necessary for the regulation of our conduct; many of which are indeed expressly specified in the Divine records; while others are left to be decided by these general principles, which are sufficiently comprehensive to include every possible case, and so particular and minute as to afford on all occasions a plain and unequivocal direction.

Complete too are the Divine precepts in another view. Man being capable of a threefold mode of acting; they are exactly adapted to his case, being applicable to his heart, to his tongue, and to his conduct, so that he can act in no way without coming under their controul. There are express directions for the thoughts, the speech and the actions. The spring, the channel, and the whole course of the stream are subject to particular regulations. The internal deliberation, the outward proclamation, and the execution are to be conducted severally according to specific regulations. As coming from God who is acquainted with the actings of all spirits, the Divine commands take cognizance of the most hidden workings of the heart, determining what motives and feelings ought to predominate there, forbidding the admission and encouragement of some, and requiring the reception and cultivation of others. The most important and the most excellent part of man is his mind; and upon the exercise of its faculties depends the whole of his conduct: it is therefore of the utmost consequence, and it is a most gracious dispensation, that it should be subject to the regulations of Him who is in all things perfect. But, in order to set up still another barrier in the way of evil, the employment of the tongue also is regulated. What we *think* affects only our own selves; what we *speak* affects our neighbour. The origin of what is evil is the misapplication of the thoughts; and this to the individual is the greatest part of the guilt, as forming the character of his disposition towards the Supreme Being; but the evil originating within may increase in its mischief by being communicated to others. To prevent its spread, God has charged the tongue not to give it publicity. Had all been right within, there would have been no necessity for this prohibition: its very existence proves an inward depravity; for, since *out of the abundance of the heart the mouth speaketh*, there would not have been any need of prescribing rules for the latter, had 'the abundance of the former been all good. Not that we are commanded to dissemble, but to stem the noxious torrent and to stop that wide avenue through which it so often bursts forth into the world. Yet still further do the Divine commands extend their controul: for they also decide what ought and what ought not to be *done*, distinguishing between what is right and wrong in the conduct, and inculcating the one and prohibiting the other. The action is the thought executed, the portrait completley finished, the whole man in full form: if it be good, it completes the goodness of the intention; if it be bad, it adds one evil to another. The deed makes either the good better or the bad worse: it enhances the excellence of the former and aggravates the enormity of the latter. That no means might be neglected to prevent the increase of evil, the Divine prohibitions notice and condemn it in the outward action. Thus it is no where allowed to exist, neither in the heart, nor on the tongue, nor in the conduct. God forbids its very conception in the mind; and, when conceived, he forbids its promulgation; and when promulgated he forbids its execution. But what he has issued is not only prohibitory but inculcative; he requires and enforces what is good, in the same way and to the same extent as he forbids and discountenances what is bad. Viewed in this light the Divine laws are exactly such as might be expected from a Supreme Governor and such as are fully adapted to the condition of a subject. To inspect and judge the heart and thoughts, is exclusively the province of God; to keep them under a due controul, is of the highest benefit to man; for "out of the heart are the issues of life." As the Lord of all, the God of the whole earth, it pertains to him also to establish rules for our words and for our actions: that evil should not be spread to the injury of his creatures; for besides the obedience due to God, the mutual happiness of mankind is materially involved in the proper government of the tongue and in the uprightness of the outward deportment. Hence, it appears that the Divine injunctions are peculiarly becoming the Almighty and could not in truth proceed from any other source; while they are at the same time altogether suitable to the state of man, and fully adequate to all the demands of his nature and condition.

(To be continued.)

FAMILY SERMONS.—No CXCIII

Titus ii. 11—13. *For the grace of God, that bringeth salvation, hath appeared to all men: teaching us, that, denying ungodliness and worldly lusts, we should live soberly, righteously, and godly in this present world; looking for that blessed hope, and the glorious appearing of the great God and our Saviour Jesus Christ.*

WHAT is Christianity? It is a scheme of mercy, and a code of duty. It shews us our privileges and it exhorts and influences us to the discharge of our obligations. It reveals pardon for our sins, and it promises us grace to forsake them. It bids us repair to the Saviour for forgiveness, and to the Holy Spirit for a renewal of heart. It opens to us a fountain for sin and for uncleanness; and while its language on the one hand is, " Be thou clean;" on the other it is, " Go and sin no more." This double purpose of our pardon and our regeneration, of our justification and our sanctification, is constantly kept in view throughout the Scriptures; and remarkably so in the Epistles of St. Paul, from one of which the text is taken. This passage sets before us, in a very clear manner, the nature of true religion, as we shall distinctly perceive by considering the three following particulars.

First. What is meant by the grace of God which bringeth salvation, and hath appeared to all men.

Secondly, What does it teach us: and,

Thirdly, What are the prospects and encouragements which it sets before us as motives for obeying its requirements.

First, then, by ' the grace of God which bringeth salvation and which hath appeared unto all men,' we are to understand the dispensation of God's mercy revealed in the Gospel. The Apostle calls it ' grace,' that is free favour, the unmerited love of God towards us, displayed in the atonement of Christ, and the consequences of that love in the renewed dispositions of mind implanted in us by his Holy Spirit. This " grace brings salvation." We were destitute of all meritorious claim to the rewards promised in the Gospel, we could not be saved by any works of righteousness which we had done: our only hope and trust therefore must be in the grace, the free mercy of God in Christ. Freely he provided an atonement for our sins and freely he bestows upon us the blessings of the new covenant of mercy. " It is of faith, that it might be of grace," and " not of works, lest any man should boast." No scheme of religion which human ingenuity could devise could provide for the salvation of fallen and guilty man: it was not till this grace of God appeared, that the only way of salvation became known: it was not till then that life and immortality were brought to light. Heinous were our transgressions, and imperfect and debased our best services: whither then could we have looked with any rational hope for pardon and acceptance with God, had we not been mercifully made acquainted with that blessed Name, than which there is no other given under heaven whereby men can be saved. For this grace, which bringeth salvation, does not exclude the atonement of Christ: so far from it, it was through the medium of that atonement that this grace was exhibited. God had a purpose of grace towards mankind, but he saw fit to display it through the sacrifice and death of Christ: he ' SO loved the world, that he gave his only begotten Son, that whoso believeth in him should not perish but have everlasting life.'

This dispensation of grace, it is added, has now appeared to all mankind. In former ages the knowledge of the one true God and of the way of obtaining his favour, was but partially unfolded. The whole world had thrown off their obedience to him, and in return he suffered all nations to walk in their own ways. He did not indeed leave himself without a witness in every heart, having given to all men a conscience accusing or excusing them on the commission of good or evil. He also kept up the true knowledge of himself with more or less clearness in particular families, especially that of Abraham and afterwards among the people of Israel, to whom he gave his "lively oracles," making them a peculiar nation under his own immediate and visible government. But, with these exceptions, the great mass of mankind " did not retain him in their knowledge, in consequence of which they plunged into every species of depravity, and were utterly ignorant of the means of salvation. But, under the dispensation of Christianity, the light, before obscure, and confined to a small part of mankind, became bright, and widely diffused: it was " a light to lighten the Gentiles, as well as " the glory of God's people Israel:" to no nation, to no individual, was it to be denied: it was adapted to the wants and condition of all, of ' Greek and Jew, circumcision and uncircumcision, Barbarian, Scythian, bond and free.'

Secondly, we proceed to inquire what it is that this grace teaches us. A person who did not understand the nature of Christianity, or who wished to bring a false accusation against it, might be ready to urge that a scheme of grace and mercy thus offered to mankind, ' without money and without price,' promising a favourable reception even to the greatest sinner on his return to God with repentance and true faith; and treating with us, not as just and holy beings, but as transgressors who need pardon, and freely offering that benefit to us without any claim of merit,—it might, I say, be urged by an ignorant or captious objector, that such a scheme was fraught with danger to the interests of virtue, and that it would encourage persons to " continue in sin that grace might abound." But the Apostle Paul, who was eminently acquainted with its real spirit, knew well that the lessons which it inculcates, are of a very different, and of a quite opposite, kind. The grace which bringeth salvation, far from thus leading those who truly receive it, to presume upon the mercy of God, while they harden themselves in their offences, " teaches us, that, denying ungodliness and worldly lusts, we should live soberly, righteously, and godly in this present world." This is the great lesson which the Christian has to learn: for in vain would he call himself a disciple of Christ, in vain would he profess to depend for pardon upon the atonement of the Saviour, if his heart and conduct did not bear witness to the *spiritual* efficacy of his religion.

The Apostle in the text sets before us what our holy profession teaches us to shun, and what to aspire after. We are to shun " ungodliness and worldly lusts;" we are to aspire after their opposites, namely, to live ' soberly, righteously, and godly.' These brief particulars comprehend all the various parts of the Christian character.

First, we learn what we are to deny. We are to deny " ungodliness," that is, whatever is contrary to the will of God, to his word, to his character, to his commands. The sins of the heart are particularly included in this expression, as the sins of the life are in the other expression, " worldly lusts." It is a short and most useful guide for our conduct as professed Christians to ask ourselves on all occasions of doubt, whether what we are tempted to, or wish to pursue, comes under the character of " ungodliness:" for if so, it is to be utterly denied and renounced. It may not be disgraceful to us in society: it may not be marked with the brand of the world's disapprobation: it may not lead to gross riot or excess: it may violate no human law: it may be practised by many who call themselves Christians: it may even be expected of us, or admired in us; it may appear to be the road to riches or worldly estimation; our interests or our pleasures may prompt us to it, and there may be no fellow creature who will frown upon us for indulging in it: but we must look much higher than this: to our own Master we stand or fall: God is our Lawgiver, and God will be our Judge: and if the thought, the word, the act, be "ungodly," it matters not whatever other sanctions it may boast, for it is unlawful, unchristian, and full of peril to our souls. There are many things which are "ungodly" which we might not think forbidden under the denomination of "worldly lusts;" but in order to prevent any mistake the Apostle includes both. Openly vicious pursuits all will readily acknowledge ought to be renounced; but the expressions in the text lead us to a more strict self examination; for "ungodliness" includes whatever is unlike God; and "worldly lusts," or, according to the language of another Apostle, "all that is in the world," comprise not only the grosser appetites and passions of our nature, but 'the desire of the eye,' that is, every species of covetousness, and "the pride of life," that is, vanity, self estimation, the love of worldly distinctions, and whatever is contrary to the humility and self-denial of the Christian character. These things are to be "denied."

What things the Gospel teaches us to follow after is also plainly specified. First, we are to live 'soberly,' which expression seems to relate to the duties which more immediately affect ourselves: secondly, we are to live "*righteously*," which seems to refer to the duties we owe to our neighbour: thirdly, we are to live "*godly*," which seems especially to have respect to our conduct towards our Creator. All the branches of these three classes we should diligently study with constant application to our own particular circumstances; and they are excellently summed up for our use in the Church Catechism, in the answers to the questions, What is your duty towards God? and, What is your duty towards your neighbour?

There are many ways in which the Gospel teaches us these lessons. It exhibits to us the holiness of God, who is of purer eyes than to behold iniquity. It shews us his justice, which forbids the escape of the sinner who transgresses against his laws. It unfolds what he requires of us, the perfect obedience of the heart—obedience to all his commands without intermission or exception. It shews us how fearfully we have violated these duties: it tells us of God's righteous retribution: of the evil of sin, the certainty of judgment, and the terrors of eternal wrath. On the other hand, it opens a door of hope: its language is, "As I live, saith the Lord, I have no pleasure in the death of a sinner, but that he turn from his wickedness and live:" it tells us of Him who died, "the Just for the unjust, to bring us nigh unto God:" it assures us that "through Him is preached repentance for the remission of sins;" and that whosoever cometh to God through him, shall not be cast out. It exhibits the most merciful overtures of pardon for the past, and supplies of Divine grace and assistance for the future: God's Holy Spirit is promised to them that ask him. And not only does it teach men what to deny and what to pursue, and hold forth all these motives and assistances in so doing; but by its powerful efficacy, under the operation of its Divine Author, it renews their hearts, turning them "from darkness to light, and from the power of Satan unto God;" so that there arise in the soul a love to God and a desire to obey his commands, as well as a mere knowledge of what Scripture and reason and duty require. The love of Christ shed abroad in the heart, constrains the Christian to a willing obedience to God. It is a part of his new nature to desire it, and he well knows, in the language of the Apostle in the verse which follows the text, that "our Saviour Jesus Christ expressly "gave himself for us, that he might redeem us from all iniquity, and purify unto himself a peculiar people zealous of good works."

These reflections introduce us to the third point for our consideration, and which we have in part anticipated, namely, the prospects and encouragements which the Gospel sets before us as motives for our complying with its requirements. We shall confine our enumeration to the one mentioned in the text, namely, the expectation of future glory—"looking for that blessed hope, and the glorious appearing of the great God and our Saviour Jesus Christ."

The 'blessed hope' here spoken of is the great promise of the Gospel. It is an eternal exemption from all the evils of life, the perils of temptation, and the danger of sin. It is deliverance from the wrath of God, the stings of a guilty conscience, the company of condemned spirits, the worm that never dies, and the fire that is never quenched. It is the introduction into a state of never ending happiness, an admission to the unclouded presence and favour of God and the enjoyment of his love for ever and ever.

The time at which this 'blessed hope' shall be accomplished, is at "the glorious appearance of the great God and our Saviour Jesus Christ." The awful hour of the resurrection and of judgment, so fraught with terrors to the impenitent, shall be to the humble Christian full of joy. He looks forward to it with anxious expectation, and earnestly desires so to pass through things temporal, that finally he may not lose the things eternal. If in the journey of life he often finds it difficult to keep in view and in practice the duties prescribed in the text, if the world still presents temptations which have not wholly lost their seductive powers to harass him, or the way of God's commandments should sometimes appear difficult and arduous, he calls to mind the blessed hope set before him in the Gospel, the crown of rejoicing reserved for him in heaven and the glories of that state where the toils and dangers of his earthly pilgrimage shall be for ever forgotten. Thus by the grace of God he is animated to new conquests over the temptations of the world, the flesh, and the devil, and he bears his bitterest afflictions with serenity and patience, knowing that "these light afflictions, which are but for a moment, work out a far more exceeding and eternal weight of glory."

Let us then live on earth as those who hope to live for ever in heaven. Let us wait for our appointed change, and be prepared for it. We know not when the hour of death may arrive; but if partakers of that grace which bringeth salvation, and living habitually as such in the spirit of our holy profession, we need not dread the summons. It may come in childhood, in youth, in manhood, or in old age; but arrive when it may, if it find us with our loins girded and our lamps burning, blessed to us will be its approach, for it will be to us the forerunner of a joyful immortality.

To the Editor of the Christian Observer.

EXPERIENCE has taught me to regard proposed improvements of our authorised version of the Scriptures with considerable jealousy. Many a time, after having been ready to question the common rendering of a passage, a patient investigation has convinced me that our translators were right. Your correspondent Scrutator does not appear to me to have sufficient grounds for the alteration which he has suggested in Jer. xvii. 9.

The word אנש, as will be seen by referring to the passages in which it occurs, means "*incurable*", or, as it is explained by a synonymous expression, Jer. xv. 18, that "*which refuseth to be healed*." The literal version of the passage under consideration therefore would be, "The heart is deceitful above all things, and *incurable*:" and the word appears to be figuratively used in reference to that "fault and corruption of the nature of every man, which is indeed past human aid and healing." Our translators have given in plain words what the Prophets expressed by a metaphor; and I think they could not have better conveyed the true meaning of the original than by the phrase "desperately" or *incurably* "wicked." This view of the passage is strikingly confirmed by the verse which immediately follows it; which, as it seems to me plainly shews that the incurable disease of the heart intended by the Prophet, is not frailty but depravity—not weakness but wickedness. "The heart is deceitful above all things and desperately wicked: who can know it? I the Lord search the heart, I try the reins: even to give every man according to his ways, and according to the fruit of his doings."

S.

To the Editor of the Christian Observer.

C. L.'s criticism on Heb. xi. 1, in your Number for November, seems to me more obscure than the received version of which he complains; and his explanation, in my view, weakens the force of the passage and mars its beauty. Faith "an act or the reliance of the mind," as he defines it, *lays hold of the substance of the things hoped for, and of the evidence*, or, according to C. L.'s opinion, *of the manifestation, of the things not seen.* This is his rendering. But I object to his definition of faith, and to his comment, as not giving the passage its correct import. Faith, no doubt, is an act of the mind, but not here, I conceive, in the sense of reliance: reliance is rather the effect of faith, than faith itself. What is to be understood by it in this passage is *belief*, or giving credit to a testimony. Its object is the word of God: and that word as it speaks of what is past, of what invisibly exists, and of what is to come. That it has all these things as its object appears evident from the contents of the chapter. Now, by faith it is that we give *substance* or *existence* to these things: and faith it is that affords us *evidence* or proof of them. We do not see them: and things future have no actual existence, such as the resurrection, and future glory and indeed all the unfulfilled promises of God. But faith realizes them, gives them a kind of existence, so that they operate on the feelings and conduct as if they really existed. And as to what is past, of which we have no tangible proof, such as the creation of the world by the word of God, ver. 3: and as to what invisibly exists, such as the being of God, ver. 6, it is faith or belief of God's testimony, that supplies us with the *evidence* or proof. According to this view, which I think the contents of the chapter will justify, the passage, as it is rendered in our version, which is strictly literal, is far more intelligible than the rendering offered by C. L. Faith is "the substance of things hoped for."—it gives them a reality: though future, they substantially exist to the eye of faith: and "*the evidence of things not seen.*"—it affords a demonstration of things not visible, receiving implicitly, as it does, the unimpeachable testimony of God.

There is another point which C. L. has by the way touched upon, to which I beg leave to advert. He has given an interpretation of Acts xiii. 48, which I cannot but view as a perversion. I am no systematizer, but I would not willingly see Scripture tortured from its plain and obvious meaning. He has rendered τεταγμενοι εις ζωην αιωνιαν, "disposed to receive the words of eternal life," than which a greater departure from the obvious import of the words can scarcely be conceived. Our authorised version—"ordained to eternal life"—is a fair and literal rendering, justified by the usual and current meaning of the word τεταγμενοι. We should never depart from the current import of a word, except it be for very strong reasons, arising either from the context or from some other portions of Scripture: our own peculiar system is no justification. Great disputes, I know, have been agitated respecting this passage; but the weight of evidence in favour of our present version, is, I fear not to say, tenfold greater than in favour of any other that has been offered. On the present occasion I shall do no more than quote the rendering of St. Chrysostom. He expresses the meaning of τεταγμενοι by the phrase, αφορισμενοι τω θεω—*severed*, or *separated by God*.

J. C.

To the Editor of the Christian Observer.

We are often told that the alleged uniformity of sentiment which has so long prevailed among the members of the Church of Rome is a striking proof of the excellence of its constitution as well as of the Divine authority of its doctrines. But what will 'the good Catholics of Ireland' say, when they find that their arguments against the free circulation of the Scriptures among the poor are decidedly at variance with the opinions entertained on the subject by one of the most renowned and enlightened scholars that ever professed or vindicated the papal religion? I allude to the famous Erasmus of Rotterdam; and as the passage in which he expresses his sentiments on this interesting question is extremely applicable to the present state of the controversy among the two parties in the sister island, I am anxious to see it inserted at full length in the columns of the Christian Observer. Let every unprejudiced Catholic attentively consider his words.

"Vehementer enim ab istis dissentio, qui nolint ab idiotis legi Divinas Literas, in vulgi linguam transfusas, sive quasi Christus tam involuta docuerit, ut vix a pauculis theologis possint intelligi sive quasi religionis Christianæ præsidium in hoc situm sit, si nesciatur. Regum mysteria celare fortasse satius est: at Christus sua mysteria quam maxime cupit evulgari. Optarim ut omnes mulierculæ legant Evangelium, legant Paulinas Epistolas. Atque utinam hæc in omnes omnium linguas essent transfusa, ut non solum a Scotis et HIBERNIS, sed a Turcis quoque et Saracenis legi cognoscique possint. Esto riderent multi, at caperentur aliquot. Utinam hinc ad stivam aliquid decantet agricola, hinc nonnihil ad radios suos moduletur textor, hujusmodi fabulis itineris tædium levet viator. Ex his sint omnia Christianorum omnium colloquia.*—Erasm. in Paraclesi.

* I differ entirely from those who are unwilling that the sacred Scriptures should be translated into the vulgar language and be read by persons in private life, as if the doctrines of Christ were so involved and obscure as to be intelligible only to a few theologians, or as if the security of our religion depended on its being unknown and unexamined. Earthly kings indeed may have their secrets of state, and it is better perhaps that those secrets should not always be divulged. But the mysteries of Christ's spiritual kingdom ought to be published far and wide. For my own part, it is my earnest wish that every poor woman throughout the country however degraded and despised may be able to read the holy Gospels, and the Epistles of St. Paul. May these sacred compositions be translated into all the languages of all the nations of the earth, and may they be studied and understood not only by the inhabitants of Scotland and IRELAND but even by the infidel Turks and Saracens! I am aware that many among whom the word of God shall be distributed will ridicule its truths, and treat them as idle fables; but some are likely to feel their power and to receive them with gratitude and

Had Erasmus lived in the present day and avowed such sentiments among the faithful Catholics of Ireland, he would have been denounced as an heretical enthusiast, or even as "a wolf in sheep's clothing."

But with whatever feelings the testimony of Erasmus may be regarded, I believe that most Catholics profess great veneration for the opinions of the ancient fathers, and an appeal to their authority is generally considered as decisive of the question in debate. Let us endeavour therefore to ascertain what were the sentiments of those primitive worthies on the subject now under review. The learned Casaubon in contending with the Papists of his own time observes,— Viri sancti Athanasius, Basilius Chrysostomus, Hieronymus, Augustinus et alii omnes, de majestate Divinorum oraculorum locis innumeris suorum monimentorum gravissime disseruerunt: iidem tamen omnes Christianorum unumquemque nulla sexus, nulla conditionis aut professionis adjecta distinctione, admonent, hortantur, urgent, ut sacros libros, sobrie quidem et cum timore ac tremore, sed tamen assidue legant, relegant et quantum fieri poterit, in manibus semper habeant. Sciebant magni illi viri multa esse in Scripturis difficilia, ardua, abstrusa, quæ posse intelligere paucorum sit hominum: nec minus tamen clamat Chrysostomus οι βουλομενοι σωθῆναι προσεχετωσαν ταις γραφαις, Si quis vult salvare, ad Scripturas animum applicet (Homilia sexta in priorem ad Corinth. Epist.) Sciebant malos Christianos et hæreticos in suam et aliorum perniciem Scripturis abuti: nec minus tamen clamat idem vir sanctissimus Ακουσατε παρακαλω παντες οι βιωτικοι και κτᾶσθε βιβλια φαρμακα ψυχης, Vos appello, o laici omnes, audite obsecro, parate vobis Biblia, animi remedia. Causam accipe τοτο παντων αἴτιον των κακῶν το μη ειδεναι τάς γραφάς, Malorum omnium hæc causa est, quod Scripturæ ignorentur (Homil. ix ad Coloss.) His similia passim scribit vir ille sanctus, et cum eo omnes patres.—Casaub. Exercit. xvi ad Annal. Eccles. Baron.*

As I am unwilling to weaken the force of the preceding extracts by any observations of my own, I shall conclude this paper with an appropriate quotation from Bishop Atterbury, an author against whom the Catholics themselves will not be disposed to bring the charge of enthusiasm or extravagance.

'Though there are *some* things,

joy. It is my hearty desire that the time may soon arrive when the ploughman and the mechanic shall be heard, while pursuing their respective employments, to sing the praises of God in language borrowed from the Scriptures; when the traveller shall esteem these inspired narrations as better adapted than any other to beguile the tediousness of his journey; and when Christians in general shall select their favourite topics of conversation from the same Divine materials.

* Those holy men Athanasius, Basil, Chrysostom, Jerome, Augustine, and indeed all the rest of the fathers, have, it is true, delivered the most weighty observations concerning the awful majesty of the Divine oracles; yet they all agree in exhorting and urging the whole body of professed Christians, without any distinction of sex, rank, or occupation, carefully to read the sacred Scriptures again and again; nay, they do not scruple to affirm, that we ought to have the word of God almost constantly *in our hands*: but at the same time they faithfully admonish us to examine its blessed contents with meekness, sobriety, and reverence. Those great men well knew that the Scriptures contained many difficulties which few only could obviate or explain. Yet Chrysostom declares, that if any man would be saved, he must apply himself to the diligent study of the Scriptures. They knew that heretics and hypocritical Christians would pervert the Divine records to their own destruction and to the destruction of others. Nevertheless the holy Chrysostom again exclaims, I beseech all persons among the laity to hear me, and to provide themselves with the word of God, that restoring cordial of the soul. And why is he so earnest in his appeal? Listen to his own declaration. The cause of all the evils which exist among you may be traced to your ignorance of the Scriptures. The same excellent writer and all the other fathers of the church abound in passages of a similar import.

says he, "in the Bible 'hard to be understood, yet *many*, nay, *most* things there are easy to be understood, as that very expression in St Peter intimates And how unreasonable therefore is it, to make some dark passages in holy writ a pretence of locking up all at once without distinction, from the generality of Christians because there are a *few* things there which they cannot understand, therefore to let them understand nothing at all And this is so much the harder, because all that is necessary to be understood is evidently contained in Scripture So that to deprive a man of that which he *can* understand, and which also it is necessary he *should* understand for the sake of somewhat contained in the same book, which he *cannot* understand, and which it is no matter whether he doth understand or not, is an unreasonable piece of cruelty I will be bold to say, that upon the same grounds that the Roman Church denies the people the liberty of reading Scripture, she might have debarred them also of the privilege of our Saviour's conversation while he lived upon earth For there were several things in the course of his instructions hard to be understood and therefore, for fear of misinterpreting those things it was convenient, might she have said, that all ignorant, unskilful men should utterly abstain from his company But our Saviour did not deter the common people from approaching him, because now and then he spake a dark parable And therefore neither ought they to be withheld from reading his Gospel though there be some hard things there, which perhaps they will read without understanding

PHILODEMUS

MISCELLANEOUS

To the Editor of the Christian Observer

TRAVELLING some time since in one of our midland counties and visiting as I always do those specimens of pious munificence the cathedrals and churches which fall in my way on a fine summer's evening I walked into one of those ancient Gothic structures which fill the soul with reverence, and do honour to the age in which they were built Whilst engaged in conversation with the sexton, who was directing my attention to some good family monuments, I could not but observe a sad decay in the flooring of the middle aisle, which he assured me proceeded from the inroads made by the dry rot Some of the most commodious pews had been again and again repaired, but in the course of a few years, the timbers had mouldered away so that the living had almost been suffered to mingle with the dead "Can no remedy be found for this evil? said I 'Is there no possibility of checking its progress by the introduction of a free current of air? Surely, something might be done The havock is dreadful See! it has crept under the clerk's seat! and, if my eyes do not deceive me I can trace it into the reading desk and even to the pulpit stairs! ' Why in truth, it is a strange deadly, destroying thing said the sexton "and I do not think we shall ever get rid of it We floor, and floor again and if the foundation of the church were not so sound and good as it is I do not know what would become of it

I returned to my inn, meditating upon the occurrences of the day How often, said I to myself do things which at first seem trifling and can scarcely be defined prove destructive to the finest works of nature and of art! There is a worm in the bud "The moth shall eat them up!" Lost in serious reflection, my mind wandered insensibly from the material structure in which we worship, to the Church itself, and the whole constitution of our Ecclesiastical Establishment. How good, how admirably good! how spiritual! how devotional! Surely the Reformers must have been blessed with no ordinary portion of wisdom, zeal, sound discretion, and deep Scriptural knowledge, to have ordered things as we find them. What a defence, if defence be necessary, is the Ecclesiastical Polity of the great Hooker! What sound arguments for every thing which we do in the church, may be found in our Combers and Shepherds, and other writers on the Common Prayer! And what a pattern for the ministers of religion is exhibited in 'Burnet's Pastoral Care!' It appears to me, that a conscientious churchman can not only give a reason for the hope that is in him, but, if he has deeply considered the subject and has well studied the works of those who lived nearer than himself to the time of the Reformation, he may, I humbly conceive, maintain a better argument for church government than the Dissenter can adduce for withdrawing himself from such a communion. But I leave every man to form his own opinion, only requesting the same privilege for myself.

This train of thought brought me back again to my morning's ramble. I was led to compare temporal things with spiritual. What is it, said I, 'which often weakens the hands of the clergy and renders their ministry of little use? I am acquainted with many men pleasant and agreeable in society who are yet but mere cyphers in the clerical account. If I know myself at all, I am not of the number of those who run down the clergy as a body, for I believe with Bishop Porteus that in proportion to their numbers no where shall we meet with so few glaring instances of improper conduct "That there are in ours, says this pious prelate*, 'as in every other profession, several unworthy members, it is in vain to deny; and where can be the wonder, if in so very numerous a society some apostates should be found? But take the whole in one collective view, and it may with the greatest truth be affirmed, that you will no where find, either in ancient or modern times, a body of more than ten thousand persons situated in the midst of a populous, rich, commercial, luxurious kingdom, surrounded with every temptation, and every danger to which virtue can be exposed, whose morals are so blameless, and so little injured by the general contagion as those of the English clergy." What then, where gross vice is out of the question, may be said to generate this spiritual decay? Sloth, indolence, and formality; these compose a sort of spiritual dry rot: it is not any notorious sins which shock the public eye, not any positive dereliction of duty, but an enemy which we may call a sapper and miner. The whole day (of course I am not speaking indiscriminately, and I would have my remarks applied only where they are due,) is wasted in doing nothing. The indolent shepherd gives no warning to the flock! The idle watchman slumbers at his post. These are the real enemies. These sap the foundations of the church.

Take, for example, the preaching of *Pigerrimus*. Many years since he became possessed of a box of manuscript sermons from a relative; the paper of which from old age is as yellow as the inner case of an Egyptian mummy. These manuscripts can never be creditably produced in any church with a side gallery overlooking the pulpit cushion; and it is a source of sorrow to Pigerrimus that the patent japan writing ink was not used by his deceased uncle. The old printers, indeed, (thanks to Jacob Ton-

* Sermon VII. Vol. II. p 164.

son and his contemporaries,) will ever be remembered with gratitude but the old hand writing is often equalled only by the false spelling of the seventeenth century and in the short days before and after Christmas these heir looms are apt greatly to puzzle the afternoon preacher They defy Bradbury's helpers and Dolland's clearers And even when deciphered the audience gain no new accession to their spiritual treasure for the annual text is of necessity treated in the self same manner, and the parishioners have no prospect of a sounder body of divinity, if the manuscripts hold together for another generation for the rectory is a perpetual advowson, in the gift of the family, and the eldest son is designed for the church

But this destructive propensity is not confined to the pulpit it pervades the occupations of every day in the week, and gives a death blow to spiritual improvement, as well as to active usefulness Pigerrimus is not a very early riser His breakfast and the newspaper occupy the prime of the day He strolls round his garden, and may perhaps prune a wall tree or cut the dead wood out of the holly hedge He walks to the neighbouring market town accepts an invitation to a small family dinner goes home to prepare for his friend's hospitable board praises the Madeira is thankful, that for a man at his time of life he can eat drink, and sleep well talks over the dangers which threaten the Established Church from popish machinations and active sectaries takes a hand at whist walks home again by moon light and the day is gone! Now, the question is, whether our friend ought not to exclaim,

Diem perdidi! True there is nothing essentially sinful in any particular part of the day's employments but day follows day thus spent, in quick succession and time which must be seriously accounted for is frittered away in doing nothing, or nothing to any purpose,— time, which, as Bishop Horne beautifully observes, is dealt out by Heaven like some rich, and invaluable cordial in single drops, to the end, doubtless, that not one of them should be suffered to fall to the ground!* 'Did we see the husbandman, says he "dreaming away his time while his fields lay uncultivated or the generals of an army killing an hour at cards when the enemy was preparing to storm the camp or a pilot asleep when the ship was running directly upon a rock and did all these allege as the reason of their behaviour, that they had *nothing to do*, we should think a mad house the only proper place for them —and we should think right But why do we not perceive that there is not less absurdity and madness in the conduct of that Christian who wastes his precious hours in idleness, and apologises for it by saying in the same manner, that he has nothing to do when perhaps the work of his salvation, that greatest of all works, the very work for which God sent him into the world, is not yet so much as entered upon, or even thought of? The whole of this very striking sermon, on "Redeeming the Time contains such instruction as cannot but affect the heart and conscience of every considerate reader We are sent into the world for the purpose of active usefulness When Israel had been vanquished the Divine command to Joshua was Up sanctify the people! When the Saviour of the world had completed his work of mercy in one place, he said, 'Arise let us go hence " I must preach the kingdom of God to other cities also for therefore am I sent The Apostle, St Paul dreads the very thought of idleness in his converts

Be not slothful, but followers of them who, through faith and patience, inherit the promises And at the hour of death we have many cases on record, in which, not merely actual sins but opportunities of usefulness

Vol II Sermon IX

wasted, have pressed as a heavy load upon the conscience "Time *wasted* is *existence used*, is *life*" Let the friend, but more especially the minister, of religion think upon his high calling. The crown is worth striving for. It is a crown of glory which fadeth not away. And whilst we are looking to the redemption that is in Christ Jesus, freely by God's grace, (Rom. iii. 24) for justification, let the activity, the labours, the watchings, the prayers, the acts of mercy, of the same blessed Saviour be imitated by us. For, in the language of our church, "He is not only a sacrifice for sin, but also an ensample of godly life."

R. P. B.

To the Editor of the Christian Observer.

In most of our churches where there are organs, it is customary to have a voluntary played, during the time the congregation are dispersing: the intention of which I presume is to overpower the bustle occasioned by the general rising to depart and the loud whispers which but too commonly follow the conclusion of the service. Judging however, from my own feelings, it is a custom more honoured in the breach than the observance: for, why should not an assembly of Christians accustom themselves to disperse quietly and reverently from the house of God? But, even if the ' pealing organ's lengthened strain' be admissible at the *close* of Divine service, it is surely objectionable when the service is only *partially* concluded. I refer to those occasions on which the holy communion is administered. Those who intend to participate in this sacrament, instead of being able to collect their thoughts into a holy fitness for this duty, by endeavouring to remember the suitable admonitions which may have been addressed "to all such as are religiously and devoutly disposed" to come to the Lord's Table, are not only disturbed by the sounds of the organ, but too often the very *strains* which meet the ear are calculated to inspire any feelings rather than those of devotion. Perhaps it may be urged that we should go to the house of God with hearts carefully prepared to engage in all the services of the place and that, if thus prepared, our minds would not be so easily distracted from our purpose. This indeed is true: but those who know their own hearts, are aware how difficult it is to bring them into a devotional frame, how much more difficult still to keep them so; and it is therefore of consequence that every known cause of interruption should be avoided, especially in our churches.

Sacred music is undoubtedly a most delightful and animating part of public worship, calculated to inspire holy joy and pious desires, when the strains are adapted to words becoming a Christian to use and a congregation to join in. It is not of course to this—very far from it—but only to an improper interruption to the thoughts and feelings suitable to a sacred occasion by distracting sounds *without words*, that I offer the above objections.

P. M. M.

To the Editor of the Christian Observer.

I copy the following from the public papers for the sake of grounding on it a remonstrance, which without any notice will suggest itself to every serious reader, in perusing the paragraph.

'Monday, at noon, at the accustomed place of execution on Penenden Heath, the awful sentence of the law was carried into effect on the body of Thomas Coombs, who, at the late Kent assizes, was found guilty of the murder of Thomas Morgan at Beckenham. From the first moment the prisoner entered the county gaol, the magnitude of the offence imputed to him, and the probability of his suffering the heaviest penalty the law knows of, pointed him out as an object of the more peculiar notice of the worthy chaplain, who throughout has paid the utmost attentions to him. These have been but badly received: the prisoner for the most part displayed a spirit of sullen indifference, and when questioned as to his participation in the murder of which he has been convicted, he on most occasions became violent, declaring that he had confessed the extent of his sins to Almighty God in secret, and that he was not disposed to repeat his confessions in public. Since his conviction he has slept but little, and on the last night of his existence he dozed only for about an hour. Early in the morning of Sunday he was visited by the Rev. Chaplain, who endeavoured to bring him to a suitable state of mind for the reception of the holy sacrament, and most particularly pointed out to him the necessity of making a candid avowal of his guilt or innocence in respect to the offence of which he had been found guilty. He promptly answered that he was innocent; and he was then asked, if that were the case, why he did not attempt to establish it at the trial. He replied, What would be the use when it was pre-determined that I should be found guilty? It was the reward of one hundred pounds that did for me. The strong circumstantial evidence obtained from the dove tailing of the tobacco paper was then pointed out to him, and he answered, 'What of that? It was easy to tear a tobacco paper and put part of it into the gun, and then swear that they found it so. A hundred pounds will tempt men to many acts.' Several other parts of the testimony were pointed out to him, and his reply to each was, The hundred pounds reward did for me. He was asked why he did not account for the possession of the fruit he had sold. To this inquiry he made no answer; and a little before eleven o'clock he was conducted into the chapel, where the solemn ceremony of the administration of the sacrament was performed, in the course of which he was asked by the Rev. Chaplain, whether he was innocent of the charge alleged against him. To this inquiry he returned no answer; and it was repeated, but he still remained silent. He was then asked whether he was guilty of the offence imputed to him. To which he answered, 'Don't disturb my mind by inquiries. I wish to have nothing to say to the question altogether. Do you think I would tell a lie on the subject? What! tell a lie under the circumstances of my present case? No, never.' Under all the peculiarities of the case, the sacrament was at last administered to him, and was received without an avowal of guilt or innocence; but the manner of the convict left an impression that he was in his own mind assured of the justice of his sentence, and that he was only withheld from acknowledging his guilt by a fear of what might be said of him after his death.—The culprit was a Bristol man, and served his time to a tallow chandler. About ten years ago he was married, but had not seen his wife for several years.

On what principle, I would ask, is the holy communion thus administered to condemned malefactors, often under circumstances the most painful and revolting? Is it for the supposed good of the individual, as a quietus to his conscience, or an *opus operatum* passport to heaven? Or is it for the good of society, under the hope that the solemnity of the occasion will induce the culprit to make useful disclosures, and at least to confess his own guilt, to the relief of the minds of prosecutors, judges, jurymen, and the community at large? Or is it merely because the custom has long prevailed without any due warrant of reason or Scripture? Assuredly whatever may be the cause, the effect is most unhappy. An ignorant, or thought less, or perhaps (as in the case which has given rise to these remarks) a hardened criminal, "with a lie in his right hand, is permitted, and in some instances, I fear, expected or urged, to partake of the mystical emblems of the body and blood of Christ thus outraging his Maker, and "eating and drinking his own condemnation not discerning the Lord's body." In no case ought this solemn sacrament to be administered to a condemned criminal without in the first place a strongly expressed desire on his own part to receive it and in the second a reasonable ground for hoping that he is acquainted with the nature of the ordinance and approaches it in a humble and contrite spirit with a conviction of the enormity of his offences including especially the crime for which he is to suffer and a desire to seek salvation through Him whose death he professes to shew forth.

To argue these points at length, would be utterly superfluous the only wonder to a religious mind will be by what strange conjuncture of circumstances their importance ever came to be overlooked or undervalued and most happy shall I be, if these brief hints should lead to a serious consideration of the subject, and the consequent disuse of so injurious and profane a practice.

MONITOR.

To the Editor of the Christian Observer.

IN looking over a late Number of your work, my attention was attracted by a letter on the composition of religious tracts and tales I am particularly anxious to recal the attention of your readers to that part of your correspondent's communication, in which he urges the impropriety of fabricating circumstances calculated to diminish in children those sentiments of respect which a child ought always to feel towards its parents. As an illustration of this I might mention a tract intended expressly for the instruction and encouragement of Sunday scholars, in which an actual breach of obedience on the part of the child so far from being reprobated and discouraged, is spoken of in such a manner as cannot fail of making it appear not only free from censure, but even right and commendable. The story related is this:—A poor boy in Ireland had the misfortune to have a parent who, not being very anxious for his son's intellectual improvement, or perhaps thinking according to his view of things that his child might be more profitably employed, strictly enjoined him to desist frequenting the school. In defiance however, of this injunction, the boy continued going till at length the exasperated parent had recourse to threats and punishments all of which proved ineffectual.—Now, however laudable might be this boy's attachment to his school surely a father had an undoubted right to please himself respecting his son's going and no person who has the least sense of the duties enjoined in the Scriptures, can possibly justify the boy's conduct, which was a flagrant breach of filial obedience, and a violation of the Fifth Commandment. It is the undoubted duty of every child to be subject to the will of his parent and to obey every command of his that is not plainly opposed to the will of God. I allude to this particular tract merely in illustration of your correspondent's argument. Many others more or less exceptionable might be adduced and I am happy therefore that the subject has been noticed in your pages, with a view to the cure of the evil.

W. D.

For the Christian Observer.

COWPER'S LETTERS

IN our notice of the lately published Letters of Cowper, in our last volume page 508 the discussion which we thought it right to enter into on some statements of the Quarterly Review, prevented our giving any extracts from the work itself. We, however, promised to supply this defect on some future occasion, and shall now lay before our readers a selection of extracts from the first volume, which we may probably follow up in some future Number with a few passages from the second. We have studied variety in our selection, and have included some paragraphs of a lively kind as well as others which throw a melancholy light upon the nature of that aberration of mind which embittered so many of Cowper's best years. It will be very clear to every impartial observer that his religion was not the cause of his gloom, indeed, his whole history proves that religion was his solace and delight till a deranged intellect deprived him of its enjoyments.

To Joseph Hill, Esq., Jan. 21, 1769.

"I rejoice with you in your recovery, and that you have escaped from the hands of one from whose hands you will not always escape. Death is either the most formidable or the most comfortable thing we have in prospect, on this side of eternity. To be brought near to him, and to discern neither of these features in his face, would argue a degree of insensibility, of which I will not suspect my friend, whom I know to be a thinking man. You have been brought down to the sides of the grave, and you have been raised again by Him who has the keys of the invisible world, who opens, and none can shut, who shuts, and none can open. I do not forget to return thanks to Him on your behalf, and to pray that your life, which He has spared, may be devoted to his service. 'Behold! I stand at the door and knock,' is the word of Him on whom both our mortal and immortal life depends, and blessed be his name, it is the word of one who wounds only that He may heal, and who waits to be gracious. The language of every such dispensation is 'Prepare to meet thy God.' It speaks with the voice of mercy and goodness, for without such notices, whatever preparation we might make for other events, we should make none for this. My dear friend, I desire and pray, that when this last enemy shall come to execute an *unlimited* commission upon us, we may be found ready, being established and rooted in a well grounded faith in His name, who conquered and triumphed over him upon his cross."

To the same, June 27, 1772.

"I only write to return you thanks for your kind offer—*Agnosco veteris vestigia flammæ.* But I will endeavour to go on without troubling you. Excuse an expression that dishonours your friendship. I should rather say, it would be a trouble to myself, and I know you will be generous enough to give me credit for the assertion. I had rather want many things, any thing indeed that this world could afford me, than abuse the affection of a friend. I suppose you are sometimes troubled upon my account. But you need not. I have no doubt it will be seen, when my days are closed, that I served a Master who would not suffer me to want any thing that was good for me. He said to Jacob, I will surely do thee good, and this he said not for his sake only, but for ours also, if we trust in Him. This thought relieves me from the greatest part of the distress I should else suffer in my present circumstances, and enables me to sit down peacefully upon the wreck of my fortune."

To the Rev. John Newton, May 28, 1781.

"The season is wonderfully improved within this day or two, and if these cloudless skies are continued to us, or rather if the cold winds do not set in again, promises you a pleasant excursion, as far at least, as the weather can conduce to make it such. You seldom complain of too much sunshine, and if you are prepared for a heat somewhat like that of Africa, the south walk in our long garden will exactly suit you. Reflected from the gravel and from the walls, and beating upon your head at the same time, it may possibly make you wish you could enjoy for an hour or two that immensity of shade afforded by the gigantic trees still growing in the land of your captivity. If you could spend a day now and then in those forests, and return with a wish to England, it would be no small addition to the number of your best pleasures. But *pennæ non homini datæ.* The time will come perhaps (but death must come first) when you will be able to visit them without either danger, trouble, or expense, and when the contemplation of those well remembered scenes will awaken in you emotions of gratitude and praise surpassing all you could possibly sustain at present. In this sense, I suppose, there is a heaven upon earth at all times, and that the disembodied spirit may find a peculiar joy arising from the contemplation of those places it was formerly conversant with, and so far at least, be reconciled to a world it was once so weary of, as to use it in the delightful way of thankful recollection, &c. &c. &c."

To the same, March 14 1782.

"I was not unacquainted with Mr B——'s extraordinary case, before you favoured me with his letter and his intended dedication to the Queen, though I am obliged to you for a sight of those two curiosities, which I do not recollect to have ever seen till you sent them. I could, however, were it not a subject that would make us all melancholy, point out to you some essential differences between his state of mind and my own, which would prove mine to be by far the most deplorable of the two. I suppose no man could despair, if he did not apprehend something singular in the circumstances of his own story, something that discriminates it from that of every other man, and that induces despair as an inevitable consequence. You may encounter his unhappy persuasion with as many instances as you please, of persons who, like him, having renounced all hope, were yet restored, and may thence infer that he, like them, shall meet with a season of restoration —but it is in vain. Every such individual accounts himself an exception to all rules, and therefore the blessed reverse that others have experienced affords no ground of comfortable expectation to *him.* But you will say, it is reasonable to conclude that as all your predecessors in this vale of misery and horror have found themselves delightfully disappointed at last, so will you. —I grant the reasonableness of it, it would be sinful perhaps, because uncharitable, to reason otherwise; but an argument, hypothetical in its nature, however rationally conducted, may lead to a false conclusion, and in this instance, so will yours. But I forbear. For the cause above mentioned, I will say no more, though it is a subject on which I could write more than the mail would carry. I must deal with you as I deal with poor Mrs Unwin in all our disputes about it, cutting all controversy short by an appeal to the event."

To the same, Jan 26 1783.

"It is reported among persons of the best intelligence at Olney—the barber, the schoolmaster, and the drummer of a corps quartered at this place —that the belligerent powers are at last reconciled, the articles of the treaty adjusted, and that peace is at the door. I saw this morning at nine o'clock, a group of about twelve figures very closely engaged in a conference as I suppose, upon the same subject. The scene of consultation was a blacksmith's shed, very comfortably screened from the wind, and directly opposed to the morning sun. Some held their hands behind them, some had them folded across their bosom, and others had thrust them into their breeches pockets. Every man's posture bespoke a pacific turn of mind; but the distance being too great for their words to reach me, nothing transpired. I am willing however, to hope that the secret will not be a secret long; and that you and I, equally interested in the event, though not, perhaps, equally well informed, shall soon have an opportunity to rejoice in the completion of it.

To the same. Sept. 8, 1783.

"I have been lately more dejected and more distressed than usual; more harassed by dreams in the night, and more deeply poisoned by them in the following day. I know not what is portended by an alteration for the worse, after eleven years of misery; but firmly believe that it is not designed as the introduction of a change for the better. You know not what I suffered while you were here; nor was there any need you should. Your friendship for me would have made you in some degree a partaker of my woes; and your share in them would have been increased by your inability to help me. Perhaps indeed they took a keener edge from the consideration of your presence. The friend of my heart, the person with whom I had formerly taken sweet counsel, no longer useful to me as a minister, no longer pleasant to me as a Christian, was a spectacle that must necessarily add the bitterness of mortification to the sadness of despair. I now see a long winter before me, and am to get through it as I can. I know the ground before I tread upon it. It is hollow; it is agitated; it suffers shocks in every direction; it is like the soil of Calabria—all whirlpool and undulation. But I must reel through it at least, if I be not swallowed up by the way.

To the same. Nov. 30. 1783.

"I have neither long visits to pay nor to receive, nor ladies to spend hours in telling me that which might be told in five minutes, yet often find myself obliged to be an economist of time, and to make the most of a short opportunity. Let our station be as retired as it may, there is no want of playthings and avocations, nor much need to seek them, in this world of ours. Business, or what presents itself to us under that imposing character, will find us out, even in the stillest retreat, and plead its importance, however trivial in reality, as a just demand upon our attention. It is wonderful how, by means of such real or seeming necessities my time is stolen away. I have just time to observe that time is short; and by the time I have made the observation, time is gone. I have wondered in former days at the patience of the Antediluvian world; that they could endure a life almost millenary, with so little variety as seems to have fallen to their share. It is probable that they had much fewer employments than we. Their affairs lay in a narrower compass; their libraries were indifferently furnished; philosophical researches were carried on with much less industry and acuteness of penetration; and fiddles perhaps were not even invented. How then could seven or eight hundred years of life be supportable? I have asked this question formerly, and been at a loss to resolve it; but I think I can answer it now. I will suppose myself born a thousand years before Noah was born or thought of. I rise with the sun; I worship; I prepare my breakfast; I swallow a bucket of goat's milk, and a dozen good sizeable cakes. I fasten a new string to my bow; and my youngest boy, a lad of about thirty years of age, having played with my arrows till he has stript off all the feathers, I find myself obliged to repair them. The morning is thus spent in preparing for the chace; and it is become necessary that I should dine. I dig up my roots; I wash them; I boil them; I find them not done enough, I boil them again; my wife is angry; we dispute; we settle the point; but in the mean time the fire goes out, and must be kindled again. All this is very amusing. I hunt. I bring home the prey; with the skin of it I mend an old coat, or I make a new one. By this time the day is far spent. I feel myself fatigued, and retire to rest. Thus what with tilling the ground, and eating the fruit of it, hunting and walking and running, and mending old clothes, and sleeping and rising again, I can suppose an inhabitant of the primæval world so much occupied, as to sigh over the shortness of life, and to find at the end of many centuries, that they had all slipt through his fingers and were passed away like a shadow. What wonder then that I, who live in a day of so much greater refinement, when there is so much more to be wanted and wished and to be enjoyed, should feel myself now and then pinched in point of opportunity, and at some loss for leisure to fill four sides of a sheet like this? Thus, however, it is; and if the ancient gentlemen to whom I have referred, and their complaints of the disproportion of time to the occasions they had for it, will not serve me as an excuse, I must even plead guilty and confess that I am often in haste when I have no good reason for being so.

To the same, Jan. 13, 1784.

" The new year is already old in my account. I am not, indeed, sufficiently second sighted to be able to boast by anticipation an acquaintance with the events of it yet unborn, but rest convinced that, be they what they may, not one of them comes a messenger of good to me. If even death itself should be of the number, he is no friend of mine. It is an alleviation of the woes even of an unenlightened man, that he can wish for death, and indulge a hope, at least, that in death he shall find deliverance. But loaded as my life is with despair, I have no such comfort as would result from a supposed probability of better things to come, were it once ended. The weather is an exact emblem of my mind in its present state. A thick fog envelops every thing, and at the same time it freezes intensely. You will tell me that this cold gloom will be succeeded by a cheerful spring, and endeavour to encourage me to hope for a spiritual change resembling it —but it will be lost labour. Nature revives again; but a soul once slain lives no more. The hedge that has been apparently dead, is not so; it will burst into leaf and blossom at the appointed time; but no such time is appointed for the stake that stands in it. It is as dead as it seems, and will prove itself no dissembler. The latter end of next month will complete a period of eleven years in which I have spoken no other language. It is a long time for a man, whose eyes were once opened, to spend in darkness; long enough to make despair an inveterate habit, and such it is in me. My friends I know expect that I shall see yet again. They think it necessary to the existence of Divine truth, that he who once had possession of it should never finally lose it. I admit the solidity of this reasoning in every case but my own. And why not in my own? For causes which to them it appears madness to allege, but which rest upon my mind with a weight of immoveable conviction.

To the same, March 19, 1784.

" I converse, you say, upon other subjects than that of despair, and may therefore write upon others. Indeed, my friend, I am a man of very little conversation upon any subject. From that of despair I abstain as much as possible for the sake of my company; but I will venture to say, that it is never out of my mind one minute in the whole day. I do not mean to say that I am never cheerful. I am often so; always indeed, when my nights have been undisturbed for a season. But the effect of such continual listening to the language of a heart hopeless and deserted, is, that I can never give much more than half my attention to what is started by others, and very rarely start any thing myself. My silence, however, and my absence of mind, make me sometimes as entertaining as if I had wit. They furnish an occasion for friendly and good natured raillery: they raise a laugh, and I partake of it. But you will easily perceive that a mind thus occupied is but indifferently qualified for the consideration of theological matters. The most useful and the most delightful topics of that kind are to me forbidden fruit,—I tremble if I approach them.—There are, however, subjects that do not always terrify me by their importance: such, I mean, as relate to Christian life and manners; and when such an one presents itself, and finds me in a frame of mind that does not absolutely forbid the employment, I shall most readily give it my attention, for the sake, however, of your request merely. Verse is my favourite occupation: and what I compose in that way, I reserve for my own use hereafter.

"I have lately finished eight volumes of Johnson's Prefaces, or Lives of the Poets. In all that number I observe but one man—a poet of no great fame—of whom I did not know that he existed till I found him there, whose mind seems to have had the slightest tincture of religion; and he was hardly in his senses. His name was Collins. He sunk into a state of melancholy, and died young. Not long before his death, he was found at his lodgings in Islington by his biographer, with the New Testament in his hand. He said to Johnson, 'I have but one book, but it is the best.' Of him therefore there are some hopes. But from the lives of all the rest there is but one inference to be drawn: that poets are a very worthless, wicked set of people."

To the same. March 19, 1785.

You will wonder, no doubt, when I tell you that I write upon a card table; and will be still more surprised when I add, that we breakfast, dine, sup, upon a card table. In short, it serves all purposes, except the only one for which it was originally designed. The solution of this mystery shall follow, lest it should run in your head at a wrong time, and should puzzle you, perhaps, when you are on the point of ascending your pulpit; for I have heard you say, that at such seasons your mind is often troubled with impertinent intrusions. The round table, which we formerly had in use, was unequal to the pressure of my superincumbent breast and elbows. When I wrote upon it, it creaked and tilted, and, by a variety of inconvenient tricks, disturbed the process. The fly table was too slight and too small: the square dining table, too heavy and too large, occupying, when its leaves were spread, almost the whole parlour: and the sideboard table, having its station at too great a distance from the fire, and not being easily shifted out of its place and into it again by reason of its size, was equally unfit for my purpose. The card table, therefore, which had for sixteen years been banished as mere lumber: the card table, which is covered with green baize, and is therefore preferable to any other that has a slippery surface: the card table, that stands firm and never totters,—is advanced to the honour of assisting me upon my scribbling occasions: and, because we choose to avoid the trouble of making frequent changes in the position of our household furniture, proves equally serviceable upon all others. It has cost us now and then the downfal of a glass: for when covered with a table cloth, the fish ponds are not easily discerned; and not being seen, are sometimes as little thought of. But, having numerous good qualities which abundantly compensate that single inconvenience, we spill upon it our coffee, our wine, and our ale, without murmuring, and resolve that it shall be our table still, to the exclusion of all others. Not to be tedious, I will add but one more circumstance upon the subject, and that only because it will impress upon you, as much as any thing that I have said, a sense of the value we set upon its escritorial capacity.—Parched and penetrated on one side by the heat of the fire, it has opened into a large fissure, which pervades not the moulding of it only, but the very substance of the plank. At the mouth of this aperture a sharp splinter presents itself, which, as sure as it comes in contact with a gown or an apron, tears it. It happens, unfortunately, to be on that side of this excellent and never to be forgotten table which Mrs Unwin sweeps with her apparel, almost as often as she rises from her chair. The consequences need not, to use the fashionable phrase, be given in detail; but the needle sets all to rights and the card table still holds possession of its functions without a rival

To the same, June 25, 1785

"They who have the means of grace, and an art to use them, will thrive any where: others nowhere. More than a few, who were formerly ornaments of this garden which you once watered, here flourished, and here have seemed to wither. Others transplanted into a soil apparently less favourable to their growth, either find the exchange an advantage, or at least are not impaired by it. Of myself, who had once both leaves and fruit, but who have now neither, I say nothing; or only this,—That when I am overwhelmed with despair, I repine at my barrenness, and think it hard to be thus blighted; but when a glimpse of hope breaks in upon me, I am contented to be the sapless thing I am, knowing that He who has commanded me to wither, can command me to flourish again, when He pleases. My experiences, however of this latter kind, are rare and transient. The light that reaches me cannot be compared either to that of the sun or of the moon. It is a flash in a dark night, during which the heavens seem opened only to shut again.

To the Editor of the Christian Observer

THE revival of English hexameters in Southey's Vision of Judgment and some recent minor poetical compositions induces me to send you the following antique hexameter version of Psalm viii, with a view to shew that this notable contrivance has been long tried and justly exploded. It was most affected in the age of Queen Elizabeth; but is utterly unworthy of the taste of that of George the Fourth, especially for sacred composition; in parody and burlesque it may still retain its charms. Abraham Fraunce's introduction of "Olympus" into the Psalms of David is not more inapposite than the imitation of Greek and Latin measures in English versification.

C A L

CERTAYNE PSALMS BY ABRAHAM FRAUNCE.
1591 PSALM VIII

O Prince all puysant, O K ng al mightyly ruling
How wondrous be thy works and how strange are thy proceedings!
Thou hast thy gre te name with moste greate glory eposed
Ove bove those lamps bright burning lamps of Olympus,
Ev n ery babes yong babes, yong sucking b be t y triumph t
Might set foorth to the shame of them which nju y offer
Ev n to the shame of them which damned bl sphemy utte
Wh n that I looke to the skies and lyft myne yes to the heavens
Skies thyne owne hand work and heavens fram d by thy fingers
When th t I see this sunne that makes my ght to be seeing
And th t moone her light light half darck renu ng
Sunne d ye's eye shynyng moone night's l ght che eful apearing
When that I see sweete starre through christal skies to be sprinckl d
Some to the first sph re fixt, some here nd there to b wanderyng
And yet constant course with due revolution endyng
Then do I think O Lord, wh t a thing is m n what a wonder

REVIEW OF NEW PUBLICATIONS

The Book of the Church. By Robert Southey, Esq. LL.D. Poet Laureate, &c. &c. 2 vols. 8vo. 24s. London. 1824.

The Book of the Roman Catholic Church, in Letters addressed to Robert Southey, LL.D. on his 'Book of the Church.' By Charles Butler. 1 vol. 8vo. 9s. 6d. London. 1825.

Few undertakings are more difficult than to write a just and candid ecclesiastical history of England. The bias which we receive from education, from intercourse with particular classes of society, and even from circumstances apparently of little moment at the time, has often a mighty effect upon our views in questions of religion: and, with the utmost integrity of purpose, we are apt rather to give to the scenes which pass before us the colour of our own minds, than to delineate them according to the light and shade which they actually present. So different on subjects of this nature are the statements of different writers in reference to the same periods, so discordant are their accounts concerning the same individuals, as it respects their motives, their character, and their conduct, that we cannot but wonder by what process of reasoning, or by what principle consistent with sound sense and common honesty, some of these writers can have succeeded in persuading themselves of the correctness of their own representations. There must in these cases be a great degree of self deception. If the evil were confined to the authors of these narratives it might be allowed to pass without much animadversion, or merely with that expression of compassionate concern which we feel for other mental hallucinations: but the misfortune is, that the mischief is propagated and travels far. It is pleasant to have other persons to think for us, and we readily acquiesce in the authority of those who are after the fashion of our own school, or lean towards the party to which we belong: and the errors of one age pass with a strong recommendation to the next, so that it is impossible to calculate upon the mischief produced by the prejudices of a single individual, especially if he be a man of unblemished character, and of acknowledged ability.

If, in the midst of such praise, which is due to Mr. Southey for the very entertaining volumes now before us, and for the spirit of candour which generally pervades them, we seem occasionally to discover something perhaps not a little, of that bias which we have just noticed, we would advert to it as another proof how difficult it is even for men of upright minds, to divest themselves of some feelings not favourable to sound discrimination. Of any thing like intentional misrepresentation, the author of these volumes stands perfectly clear; but some of his statements we consider as incorrect, and some of his views as by no means defensible.

The period embraced by this work comprizes the interval between the times of the ancient Britons, previously to the invasion of this island by the Romans, and the Revolution of 1688. No references are given to the authorities upon which the several parts of the narrative are founded. This is a circumstance which we greatly regret. With every feeling of respect for Mr. Southey's care in the selection of his materials and his fidelity in presenting to us the result of his best judgment in the history which he founds upon them, we cannot very readily concede to any historian the privilege of deciding for us, on many most questionable points, without furnishing the grounds of his opinion by an appeal to the writings and arguments which he has deemed conclusive. We have frequently felt the inconvenience of this omission, while perusing "the Book of the Church," and we believe that most readers will concur with us in lamenting it.

After a short introduction, remarkably well written, Mr Southey commences with an account of the Druidical religion, and with a brief notice of the Roman which succeeded it, and arrives in a few pages at the great subject of his work. Without much discussion of the question by whom the Gospel was first brought into Britain, he inclines to the opinion that this honour is due to Bran, the father of Caractacus, who having been led into captivity with his son, became a convert to the Gospel in Rome, and on his return instructed his ignorant countrymen.

For what reasons the arguments usually adduced to prove that the labours of St Paul extended to this island are altogether omitted in this chapter, we know not; they certainly carry with them some probability; and although they may not be of sufficient weight to deprive Bran of his credit, they are at least not undeserving of summary notice. The first church it is supposed was erected at Glastonbury and the first martyr to the truth was Saint Alban. Those who are not well acquainted with his story will be glad to read it in the words of Mr Southey:—

> During the tenth and most rigorous of the persecutions, which was the only one that extended to this island, a Christian priest flying from his persecutors came to the city of Verulamium and took shelter in Alban's house: he not being of the faith himself, concealed him for pure compassion; but when he observed the devotion of his guest, how fervent it was and how firm, and the consolation and the joy which he appeared to find in prayer, his heart was touched, and he listened to his teaching and became a believer. Meantime the persecutors traced the object of their pursuit to this city, and discovered his retreat. But when they came to search the house, Alban putting on the hair-cassock of his teacher delivered himself into their hands as if he had been the fugitive, and was carried before the heathen governor, while the man whom they sought had leisure and opportunity to provide for his escape. Because he refused either to betray his guest or offer sacrifices to the Roman gods, he was scourged and then led to execution upon the spot where the abbey now stands, which in after times was erected to his memory and still bears his name. That spot was then a beautiful meadow on a little rising ground, seeming, says the venerable Bede, a fit theatre for the martyr's triumph. There he was beheaded, and a soldier also at the same time, who it is said was so affected by the resignation and magnanimity of this virtuous sufferer that he chose to suffer with him rather than incur the guilt of being his executioner.—Southey, pp. 14, 15.

Christianity soon after became the religion of the Roman empire. The corruptions which prevailed at that period are well known, and the mischievous effect of them was felt in Britain. The invasion by the Saxons, who brought with them their own peculiar idolatry, proved to a great extent destructive even of the forms of Christianity; and, amidst the commotions of those disastrous times, Christianity as a public establishment disappeared from the kingdoms of the heptarchy for about 150 years.

The conversion of the Anglo-Saxons was effected by a mission during the popedom of Gregory the Great, who had been much interested by seeing some young Englishmen exposed for sale like cattle, or Africans in the West Indies, in the market place at Rome. Instead of discovering in the countenances or manners of this saleable commodity a proof that they were below the common standard of human intellect and incapable of being Christianized, the good man came to an opposite conclusion, and he determined to lose no time in obtaining leave to go and preach the Gospel in that miserable country. He set out upon the errand, but being recalled before he had reached his destination, and being subsequently raised to the bishopric of Rome* he was unable to enter upon the work in person. He dispatched, however, forty missionaries, who, with Augustine at their head, landed in the Isle of Thanet under very propitious circumstances; the Queen of Kent being favourable to the cause, and the King not indisposed to give them a hearing. A commencement being thus auspiciously made, the profession of Christianity gradually prevailed, till, in the course of eighty two years from the arrival of Augustine it became the religion of all the Anglo Saxon states.

The character of Gregory was that of a truly pious and excellent man. He seems not to have regarded power for its own sake but was anxious to fulfil the duties of his high station with faithfulness and zeal. The Church Missionary Society in this country might have adopted their excellent plan of *Christian Institutions* from the example set them by this great prelate. Certain it is that Gregory acted upon this principle. He sent an agent into France to redeem Anglo Saxon youths from slavery, and to place them in monasteries *where they might be carefully educated, and thereby trained to assist in the conversion of their countrymen.* How would this true Catholic have rejoiced could he have foreseen that future Christians of that country which he thus laboured to instruct in the Christian faith would one day adopt means of a similar nature by training young persons rescued from the holds of slave ships, to enlighten and evangelize the yet more ignorant and oppressed natives of the African continent!

Mr Southey's fourth chapter is on the causes which promoted the success of Christianity among the Anglo Saxons.

In adverting to the progress of the Gospel, we would by no means undervalue secondary causes which are so many instruments among the many employed by Divine Providence to accomplish his heavenly purposes. It is not merely *creditable* to the church, that kings should be its nursing fathers, and queens its nursing mothers, but examples of piety or even of respect for the Christian religion, when thus exhibited in the highest seats of earthly greatness, have doubtless a powerful influence upon multitudes of inferior station. We would be willing also to concede that the circumstances of the Anglo Saxons and the nature of their superstition may have held out a fairer prospect for Christian enterprise, than is to be found among the subjects of heathenism in many other countries; but the sophistries of Gibbon on topics of this sort have made us a little cautious lest we ascribe too much to secondary causes, and too little to the operation of God's Holy Spirit in the simple preaching of the Gospel; and although we by no means insinuate that Mr Southey is chargeable with this error, yet we are not sure that some of his readers may not be led to adopt it.

He assumes at the beginning of this chapter, that the introduction of Christianity into heathen countries in later ages has been found so exceedingly difficult as at one time to be generally considered hopeless and almost impossible without a miracle* Such doubtless has

---

* I cannot persuade myself says Milner to call him pope he pretended not to any thing like infallibility nor did he ever attempt any thing like a secular domination. The seeds of antichrist were vigorously shooting indeed and the reputation of Gregory doubtless contributed much to mature the poisonous plant but idolatry spiritual tyranny and the doctrine of the merit of works the three discriminating marks of the Papacy had as yet no settled establishment at Rome —Milner Hist of the Church of Christ Cent vi c 8

* The narrative of Augustine and his fellow missionaries is not without miracles which are said to have been instrumental in converting the King of Kent to Christianity Joseph Milner with a superfluity of caution does not take upon himself wholly to deny them Was this from an impression which somewhat widely prevailed even so late as his days

been the conclusion at which men of acknowledged piety, as well as those who cared nothing about the matter, have sometimes arrived but unless the attempt to introduce Christianity had been often fairly made, and had frequently failed, the conclusion was at least premature. It will scarcely be contended, except by a member of the Church of Rome that the Roman Catholics in their missions have generally proceeded either exactly in the spirit, or according to the doctrines, of the Apostles yet in many instances their efforts were attended with great success 'In opposition to the ruling powers, observes Mr Butler, in his recent work, The Book of the Roman Catholic Church, "and often under severe persecutions countless conversions have been made by Roman Catholic missionaries in Madura Cochin China Tonquin, the empire of China, the peninsula of Corea among the Hurons, Miamis Illinois, and other tribes of North America among the savages of Paraguay, Uraguay and Panama among the wild Moxos Chiquits, and Canizians All these countries have been watered with the blood of Roman Catholic Missionaries and to use the well known expression of Tertullian, 'their blood became the seed of the church' p 51

But suppose we attach little value to these conversions and in some instances we fear that it was only the exchange of one superstition for another, yet the failure of a corrupt and secular religion can be urged as no argument against the probable success of the unadulterated Gospel and so far as the great truths of Christianity have been preached in modern days, the effect has been not inferior to reasonable expectation Till times comparatively modern, the missionary spirit had not revived, or there were few

that miracles would probably yet be wrought for the conversion of heathens —See his note on this subject c vii cent 6

channels of access to pagan countries It is only within the last century that for many ages we can look to any well regulated plans of this nature really conducted upon Christian principles and how great has been the encouragement to proceed! To form a just estimate of what might probably have been achieved long ago towards enlightening the heathen world it may suffice to mention those humble men who were among the first of the non Catholic moderns, to lead the way in this labour of benevolence we allude to the missions of the Moravians or United Brethren At a period when that community was reduced to about 600 persons and had but just found a place of refuge from a wasting persecution an asylum which seemed to promise little else than a peaceful habitation and a quiet grave—instead of reposing in indolent security or desponding about their own existence as if it were a question whether their very name should not speedily become extinct they determined under the blessing and guidance of Almighty God to light up the torch of Divine truth in heathen nations They had no power to work miracles they looked not to circumstances peculiarly favourable in the countries which they visited and in some cases the difficulties were of a sort to reduce ordinary minds to despair but so little did they calculate upon this fancied impossibility to convert the heathen without extraordinary assistance from Heaven that in eight or nine years they had sent missionaries to Greenland to the Indians in North and South America to many of the West India Islands, to Lapland to Algiers, to Guinea to the Cape of Good Hope and to Ceylon—and if some of these enterprizes failed yet their success in others as for instance in Greenland and the West Indies among persons of the most hopeless description might long since have proved that the simple "preaching of the Cross is able through the Divine blessing, to reach the hearts even of very ignorant heathens. And as the miserable condition of the West Indian slaves, and of the forlorn Greenlander, has not presented an insuperable barrier to the reception of the Gospel, so neither have the vicious practices of the Otaheitans or the deeply rooted prejudices of the Hindoos. It is perfectly within our recollection with what ridicule the mere idea of giving to these heathens the knowledge of Christianity was treated by many Christians in England; but the event has proved beyond a question, that, provided the Christian teacher is permitted to preach the doctrines of the Gospel, there is no obstacle which can effectually withstand them. Not much more than a century has elapsed since a wise and good man, who was himself strongly impressed with the necessity of miraculous powers for the conversion of the heathens, and who expressed his persuasion at the same time that if the conversion of infidels to Christianity were sincerely and vigorously attempted by men of honest minds, who would make it their business to teach the pure doctrines of Christianity free from all human mixtures and corruptions, God would probably aid their endeavours in an extraordinary way, mentions as among the greatest and most splendid future triumphs of religion, the diffusion of the light of the Gospel through the vast empire of Tartary and China, and Japan and Hindostan, and the large and dark regions of the newly discovered world. We have lived to see converts to Christianity in Tartary and Hindostan; and at this moment there is much to encourage Christian zeal in the large and dark regions of North America; and there has been nothing of miraculous interposition; and why should not that simple power of the Gospel which has prevailed elsewhere, have in due season equal success in China and Japan, countries in which we know that Christianity even partially flourished, and certainly without the aid of miracles?

By the simple process of Christian education alone, when that education is free and unrestricted, the habits and principles of an idolatrous people may within the period of one century be essentially and radically changed. It appears then that the introduction of Christianity into heathen countries has not been found so difficult as to justify the conclusion which has been somewhat extensively admitted. The partial success of a corrupt system of Christianity instead of being an argument *against* the probable effects of the pure Gospel of Christ, tends precisely the other way. The experiment had not till very recently been fairly made. "It is no small reproach," says the author above cited, Archbishop Tillotson, "to the Protestant religion, that there hath not appeared an equal zeal among us (namely as amongst the Roman Catholics) for this purpose (the conversion of heathen nations) and that to our unwearied endeavours to promote the interest of trade in foreign parts, there hath not been joined a like zeal and industry for the propagating of the Christian religion, which might surely be attempted with more than ordinary advantage to those places where we have so free a commerce." It has now been made, and we see that no miracle is wanted to give it success.

The religion and conversion of the Danish settlers in this island, form the subject of the sixth chapter. We quote the concluding paragraph:

The Danes who settled in England became Christians by position and contact. Alfred with that wisdom which appeared in all his actions compelled those whom he subdued to receive baptism. They who established themselves afterwards by conquest in the island, found it politic to receive the religion of the country. The change was no doubt accelerated by propagandists from the Anglo-Saxon Church; but if there had been great zeal or great success in their endeavours, some record of it would have been preserved. The missionaries of that church were more usefully employed in medicating the bitter waters at their spring. They sowed the seed of Christianity throughout the Scandinavian kingdoms, and many of them watered it with their blood. Their holy efforts were assisted by political events. Charlemagne and Otho the Great provided for the introduction of their religion wherever they extended their conquests. They built abbeys and established bishoprics, well knowing that by no other means could the improvement of the country, the civilization of the people and the security of their states, be so materially promoted. By this policy, by the steady system of the popes, the admirable zeal of the Benedictines, and by the blessing of God which crowned all, the whole of the Scandinavian nations were converted about the time of the Norman conquest, and thus an end was put to those religions which made war their principle, and sanctifying the most atrocious and accursed actions, had the misery of mankind for their end. It was from a clear and certain knowledge of this tendency that, by the laws of Wihtræd a sacrifice to the idols was to be punished with confiscation of property and the pillory, and by the laws of our great Alfred with death. *Southey* pp 79—81.

In the next chapter, which contains the history of the Anglo Saxon Church, with the endowment of tithes, division into parishes &c., the author dwells with just encomium upon the attainments of the clergy in the first ages of that church and points out the causes of that great deterioration in learning and manners, which subsequently took place a deterioration so remarkable, that when Alfred ascended the throne there was not a single priest south of the Thames who understood enough of Latin to construe his daily prayers. The remedy projected for this great evil was the restoration of monastic establishments which, in the confusion of the times, had fallen into decay. The great champion of monachism was Dunstan abbot of Glastonbury, a personage whom Mr. Southey represents as one of the most ambitious and least ambiguous characters in ecclesiastical history.

The story of this man when stripped of the adventitious circumstances with which it is usually adorned, although very far from rescuing him from the charge of haughtiness and ambition, seems nevertheless to allow of certain feelings towards him not wholly estranged from respect. He was remotely allied to the royal family one of his uncles was primate, another bishop of Winchester. He appears to have possessed a commanding intellect and so severe in early life was his application to study as to bring on a most dangerous disease. Having attained the requisite age, he entered into minor orders in conformity with the desire of his parents, and took the clerical habit in the monastery in which he had been educated. He was now equally remarkable for diligence in his studies, for his various accomplishments, and for manual dexterity he composed music, he played upon the harp, organ and cymbals, wrought metals, worked as an artist in wood, wax, ivory, silver, and gold and excelled in design, in painting, and in calligraphy. Thus accomplished he was introduced to the palace by his uncle the archbishop, and soon attained considerable celebrity.

After a time he repaired to his uncle the bishop of Winchester and by his persuasion, contrary it should seem to his own wishes in the first instance, took upon himself the obligations of a monk. He now built for himself a miserable cell at Glastonbury, and led a life of great self denial. A widow of the royal family having at his instigation, divested herself in her last illness of all her property, left it to Dunstan the whole of it he bestowed upon the poor and the church at Glastonbury to which also he transferred his own ample patrimony. Being offered by Edred the bishopric of Crediton, he declined this promotion and recommended another person to the see. He looked forward it appears to the primacy and had already formed the resolution of remodelling the Anglo Saxon Church.

That church greatly needed re

formation the clergy were grossly ignorant, and partook of the coarse and dissolute manners of their countrymen. But whether the plan adopted to reform them were precisely of the nature which the case required, may well admit of a question. The object of Dunstan and the primate was to make the clergy put away their wives to establish the Benedictine Rules in all the monasteries, and to expel those secular priests who, according to the old custom, resided with their respective bishops, and to introduce monks in their stead. In process of time Dunstan became successively bishop of Worcester and of London, and finally reached the primacy, which he enjoyed for several years.

Now, if we form our judgment of the man from this account, it would not be very obvious what serious charge could fairly be alleged against him. His profession seems to have been settled by his parents; his mortifications were after the manner of the times; he exhibited on different occasions a noble contempt of wealth; and if it be a crime to accept a bishopric, he shares the blame with many individuals whom it has not been the fashion on that account to condemn. Should we judge of his conduct in enforcing the celibacy of the clergy from the practice of Protestant churches, or of the first ages of Christianity, he would on this ground be open to severe reprehension; but long before his time the simplicity of the Gospel had been greatly corrupted; and the course which he adopted in this instance was then generally regarded not only as consistent with good order, but almost a necessary part of ecclesiastical discipline. It was at least possible that a man of pure and upright intentions, might in all these points have resembled the abbot of Glastonbury, and if nothing farther could be alleged to justify the odium which since the Reformation has been cast upon his memory, charity would induce us to lean to the favourable side.

But there are two circumstances in the history of this man, which make strongly against him. We allude to the story of Elgiva, and to the affair of the famous synod at Calne. Those who wish to see how differently the same tale can be told by a Protestant and a Roman Catholic writer will do well, after reading the account given by Mr Southey, to peruse the statement of Mr Butler. It is a difficult task, after the lapse of so many ages, to decide which narrative is correct. Edwy was no favourite with the monks, and was not likely to receive much kindness at their hands. Dunstan is not eminently honoured by Protestants, and any violence which he might employ against his sovereign would scarcely be diminished in their report of it. We are unwilling to believe that he would offer so wanton an outrage to the king as the tale as now current, necessarily implies; but we do not imagine that he was altogether so free from just censure as his apologist would represent him.

Concerning the affair at Calne Mr Butler writes thus:—

The substitution of the Benedictine monks to the secular canons met with great opposition; two councils were held upon it. Dunstan—you (Mr Southey) intimate—*took care* that the third which was held at Calne *should be decisive*. The king, you say, was kept away on account of his youth, though he had been present at the former meetings. Beornelm, a Scottish bishop, pleaded the cause of the clergy with great ability, alleging Scripture in their behalf and custom, and arguing upon the morality and reason of the case against the celibacy to which by these new laws they were to be compelled. His speech produced a great effect, and Dunstan did not attempt to answer it; he had laid aside, says his biographer, all means excepting prayer. You endeavour, said he, to overcome me, who am now growing old and disposed to silence rather than contention. I confess that I am unwilling to be overcome, and I commit the cause of his church to Christ himself as Judge! No sooner had these words been spoken than the beams and rafters gave way; that part of the floor upon which the clergy and their friends were arranged fell with them many being killed in the fall, and others grievously hurt: but the part, where Dunstan and his friends had taken their seats remained firm.

A more atrocious crime proceeds Mr Butler, than the charge which you thus bring against Dunstan cannot be imagined. Now every canon of history, ev'n the common duty of charity requires, that such an imputation should not be brought without strong evidence. The slightest evidence neither has been nor can be produced for its support. That a council was held at Calne: that during its sitting the floor fell in: that the ecclesiastics, the nobles and the other members who attended it were cast into the ruin: that several lost their lives, or were materially injured: and that Dunstan remained unhurt, by standing on a beam: are the only circumstances which history has transmitted to us: of the diabolical contrivance of the tragedy by Dunstan, no proof whatever has been suggested. —Butler pp 66 67.

Whether the absence of such proof, under all the circumstances of the case, be not more than counterbalanced by the acknowledged facts, the reader must determine for himself. We cannot divest ourselves of a marvellous suspicion that Dunstan knew more of the matter than was consistent with his alleged sanctity.

As to the repeated miracles of Dunstan Mr Butler does not offer a vindication of them. The story of his pinching the devil's nose is expressly disclaimed, and it is not obscurely intimated that the other extravagant relations connected with the name of this saint are to be ascribed to the credulity of the age. That such stories should be propagated and believed indicates a degree of fraud on the part of some person, and of easy belief on the part of Roman Catholic England in general: which reflect no great credit either upon the church or upon the age. We take our leave of St Dunstan by requesting our readers to reconcile if they can, the following statements —

The life of Dunstan is thus given at length because a more complete exemplar of the monkish character in its worst form could not be found: because there is scarcely any other miraculous biography in which the machinery is so apparent and because it rests upon such testimony that the Romanists can neither by any subtlety rid themselves of the facts nor escape from the inevitable inference. The most atrocious parts are matter of authentic history: others which though less notorious authenticate themselves by their consistency, are related by a contemporary monk who declares that he had witnessed much of what he records, and heard the rest from the disciples of the saint. The miracles at his death are not described by this author, because the manuscript from which his work was printed was imperfect and broke off at that point: they are found in a writer of the next century who was precentor of the church at Canterbury and enjoyed the friendship and confidence of Lanfranc the first Norman archbishop. Whether therefore those miracles were actually performed by the monks, or only averred by them as having been wrought, either in their own sight or in that of their predecessors: there is the same fraudulent purpose, the same audacity of imposture, and they remain irrefragable proofs of that system of deceit which the Romish Church carried on everywhere till the time of the Reformation, and still pursues wherever it retains its temporal power or its influence. — Southey pp 116 117.

An attentive perusal of what Dr Lingard has written in his Antiquities of the Anglo-Saxon Church, and of what the same author and Mr Sharon Turner have said in their respective histories of England, and an examination of all the authorities adduced by them have convinced me that St Dunstan is entitled to the praise of probity talent and true religion. Such was the opinion of every writer whose works have reached us from the time in which St Dunstan lived till the æra of the Reformation. Then without the discovery of a single new fact that could justify a change of opinion, St Dunstan became an object of the most contumelious abuse, and since that time it has been always on the increase: you now describe him as a perfect monster. Butler p 57.

Passing over the ecclesiastical state of the country, and the encroachments of the Papacy about the time of the Norman conquest, we come in the following chapter, to the character of Anselm, of whom 'The Book of the Church' gives a representation less favourable than he appears to have deserved. We scarcely become acquainted with him here in any other character than as a warm advocate for some of the most exceptionable tenets of the papal creed, and a determined friend to the high claims of the pope's authority he was; however, something better than this, his piety, integrity, and learning entitle him to no common praise.

The subject of investitures was one at that time of vehement dispute, involving no less a question, between popes and sovereigns, than the right of appointing to vacant benefices. The exercise of this power by the crown led in many cases to very serious abuse.

It appears from the records of the exchequer, says Mr Butler, "that Henry the First of England, in the 16th year of his reign, had in his hands one archbishopric, five bishoprics, and three abbeys; in the 19th, one archbishopric, five bishoprics, and six abbeys; and in the 31st, one archbishopric, six bishoprics, and seven abbeys." "Sees were kept vacant," observes Mr Southey, 'that the kings might enjoy their revenues; they were disposed of by purchase so commonly, that Simony became the characteristic sin of the age; in all such cases, they passed into unworthy hands; and, even when they were not sold, equal or greater evils resulted, if they were given, for favour or consanguinity, to subjects who disgraced the profession by their ignorance and their habits of life.' To prevent such abuses Hildebrand claimed the right of investiture which princes had hitherto exercised as their undisputed prerogative; and had he been contented with this measure, without the publication of anathemas, which virtually rendered all sovereigns dependent upon the pope, it would be easy to defend him. To provide for the filling up of the vacant benefices was with Anselm a favourite object; and he accordingly entered heartily into the plans for transferring the right of investiture to the see of Rome, and seems not to have disapproved even of the excommunication denounced against those who should do homage to a layman for ecclesiastical honours. The marriage of the clergy he regarded also as an intolerable abuse; and, in fact, this evil had then arisen from it, that the son succeeded by inheritance to his father's church "a custom which, if it had taken root, says Mr Southey, "would have formed the clergy into a separate cast." Canons of a very severe description were passed upon the subject, compelling the married clergy to put away their wives, punishing by excommunication and loss of goods such as disobeyed, and condemning the wife to slavery if she ever held any intercourse with her husband. That Anselm lent himself in these matters to the views of the Papacy is beyond dispute; but he deserves to be placed in another point of view than merely or chiefly as an attached servant to the court of Rome; and by looking only at his public life, although fairly represented, we should be very apt to form a wrong estimate of his character. The historian of 'the Church of Christ,' a writer who, with no common powers of discrimination, has taken all due pains to examine into the character and motives of the famous men who came under his notice in the course of his work, treats Anselm with high respect. In reference to the question of investitures, whether they should be received from the king or from the pope, 'Anselm, he observes, "moved undoubtedly by a conscientious zeal, because all the world bare witness to his integrity, was decisive for the latter; and the egregious iniquities and shameless violations of all justice and decorum, practised by the Norman princes in that age, would naturally strengthen the prejudices of his education. To receive investiture from the pope for the spiritual jurisdiction, and at the same time to do homage to the king for the temporalities, was the only medium which in those times could be found between the pretensions of the civil and ecclesiastical dominion; and matters were settled on this plan, both in England and in Germany "I can easily conceive,' says he, ' that (in his strenuous support of the papal dominion) he might be influenced by the purest motives, when I reflect on the shameless and profane manners of the Norman princes But his private life was his own, originating more directly from the honest and good heart with which through grace he was eminently endowed As a divine and a Christian he was the first of characters in this century (Cent xi c 5) ' If Anselm contributed to the depression of the civil power and the confirmation of the papal he was unhappily carried away by a popular torrent which few minds had power to resist It seems certain, however that ambition formed no part of this man's character ' While I am with you he would often say to his friends, I am like a bird in a cave amidst her young, and enjoy the sweets of retirement and social affections But when I am thrown into the world, I am like the same bird hunted and harassed by ravens or other fowls of prey the incursions of various cares distract me and secular employments, which I love not, vex my soul!' He who spent a great part of his life in retirement who thought, wrote, and spake so much of vital godliness and whose moral character was allowed, even by his enemies, to have been without a spot, deserves to be believed in these declarations (Cent xi c 5) The writer proceeds to furnish strong proofs of his exemplary piety For these we refer to his work merely stating as an evidence of the enlightened humanity of Anselm, that, in a national synod held at Westminster, he forbade men any longer to be sold like cattle — a practice which had prevailed down to that time

With a view to remedy the various flagrant abuses which presently arose out of the immunity claimed and enjoyed by the clergy, from all secular punishments Henry the Second chose for the primacy his chancellor Thomas à Becket, the most confidential of his servants and the most intimate of his friends The history of this prelate is given by Mr Southey at much length, and with his usual felicity in gaining the complete attention of the reader and we see no good reason for doubting the correctness of that judgment which in common with Protestant writers in general, he has passed upon the character of Becket Mr Butler complains that this hero of the popish communion is tried in " the Book of the Church, by the present constitution, the present laws and the present manners of Christian states and by the present notions of what is fit and proper Should we not, he demands, in order to pronounce a fair judgment, transport ourselves to the middle of the twelfth century, and try him by the constitutions the laws the customs the manners and notions of his own time? And finding that the clerical immunities on which the contest in the first instance entirely turned, formed a part of the constitution of every Christian state, and that, until many centuries after this period, they had never been infringed by any whose name history has handed down to us with honour can we justly blame he asks, this illustrious prelate for his vigorous and resolute defence of rights which in his time made part of the law of England, and were an acknowledged bulwark of the English constitution? After every concession which we might, on these and similar grounds, be disposed to make to the advocates of Becket, there remains we think, in the unquestionable facts belonging to his history, sufficient to convict him of a most ambitious, domineering, and turbulent spirit In his assertion of the privileges of the church, he pursued in many cases the course which might have been adopted by Anselm but the mantle of his illustrious predecessor had not descended to him with the mitre the piety and spirit of Anselm he did not possess. The last scene of his life exhibits the same determined resolution which he had manifested on other occasions and if he had really fallen in the cause of religion and not in that of the pope, it would have entitled him to almost unqualified admiration. We say *almost* because we do not feel satisfied that the spirit in which he suffered was a Christian spirit, and because his last words were far from being in accordance with the holy Scriptures.

The four barons who bound themselves by an oath that they would either compel him to withdraw his censures against the three excommunicated bishops or carry him out of the kingdom or put him to death, if he refused to do the one and they found it impossible to effect the other, repaired to Canterbury and after some altercation with Becket, required in the king's name,—

That he and all who belonged to him should depart forthwith out of the kingdom for he had broken the peace and should no longer enjoy it. Becket replied he would never again put the sea between him and his church. Their resolute manner only roused his spirit, and he declared that if any man whatsoever infringed the laws of the Holy Roman See or the rights of the church be that man who he would, he would not spare him. In vain said he do you menace me! if all the swords in England were brandished over my head you would find me foot to foot fighting the battles of the Lord. He upbraided those of them who had been in his service as chancellor. They rose and charged the monks to guard him saying they should answer for it if he escaped. The knights of his household they bade go with them and wait the event in silence. Becket followed them to the outer door saying he came not there to fly nor did he value their threats. We will do more than threaten was the answer.

Becket was presently told that they were arming themselves in the palace-court. Some of his servants barred the gate and he was with difficulty persuaded by the monks to retire through the cloisters into the cathedral where the afternoon service had now begun. He ordered the cross to be borne before him retired slowly and to some who were endeavouring to secure the doors, he called out forbidding to do it saying You ought not to make a castle of the church it will protect us sufficiently without being shut neither did I come hither to resist, but to suffer. By this time the assailants after endeavouring to break open the abbey gates had entered under Robert de Broc's guidance through a window searched the palace and were now following him to the cathedral. He might still have concealed himself and not improbably have escaped. But Becket disdained this with all its errors his was an heroic mind. He was ascending the steps of the high altar when the barons and their armed followers rushed into the choir with drawn swords exclaiming Where is Thomas à Becket? where is that traitor to the king and kingdom? No answer was made but when they called out with a louder voice Where is the archbishop? he then came down the steps saying Here am I no traitor but a priest ready to suffer in the name of Him who redeemed me God forbid that I should fly for fear of your swords or recede from justice. They required him once more to take off the censures from the prelates. No satisfaction has yet been made was the answer and I will not absolve them. Then they told him he should instantly die. Reginald said he to Fitzurse I have done you many kindnesses and do you come against me thus armed? The Baron resolute as himself and in a worse purpose told him to get out from thence and die at the same time laying hold of his robe. Becket withdrew the robe and said he would not move. Fly then said Fitzurse as if at this moment a compunctious feeling had visited him and he would have been glad to see the intent frustrated in which his pride more than his oath constrained him to persist. Nor that either was Becket's answer if it is my blood you want I am ready to die that the church may obtain liberty and peace only in the name of God I forbid you to hurt any of my people. Still it appears that in some at least there was a wish to spare his life one struck him between the shoulders with the flat part of the sword, saying Fly or you are dead! And the murderers themselves afterwards declared their intention was to carry him prisoner to the king or if that was impossible put him to death in a place less sacred than the church but he clung to one of the pillars and struggled with the assailants. Tracy he had nearly thrown down and Fitzurse he thrust from him with a strong hand calling him pimp. Stung by the opprobrious appellation Fitzurse no longer hesitated whether to strike. A monk Edward Grimes of Cambridge was his name interposed his arm which was almost cut off by the blow. Becket, who had bowed in the attitude of prayer, was wounded by the same stroke in the crown of his head. His last words were, "To God, to St. Mary, and the Saints who are patrons of this church, and to St. Dennis I commend myself and the church's cause!" The second blow brought him to the ground, on his face before St. Benedict's altar: he had strength and composure enough to cover himself with his robes, and then to join his hands in prayer; and in that position died under their repeated strokes, each pressing near to bear a part in the murder. Brito cleft his skull; and an accursed man, the subdeacon Hugh of Horsea, known by the appellation of the Ill Clerk, scattered the brains over the pavement from the point of his sword. Southey, pp. 243—247.

The humiliations to which Henry deemed it prudent to submit in order to manifest his deep concern at this tragical event, the celebrity of the shrine of this supposed martyr, the disgraceful transfer by John of his kingdom to the pope in the person of his legate and the signature of Magna Charta, not very remotely connected with the last transaction, are well known to every reader of English history. On one of these points however Mr. Butler contends that the impression generally prevalent is erroneous: he maintains that John did not absolutely divest himself of the sovereignty of the kingdom but only agreed that he and his successors should hold it of the papal see in fee simple, by homage and fealty and an annual payment; and that standing toward the pope in the relation of a feudal vassal to his lord, he continued in reference to his subjects and their rights in the possession of the same regalities and bound by the same obligations as before. This may probably be the right view of the case: but to the transaction itself Mr. Butler is no friend; he is disposed to blame both the monarch and the pontiff, adding however, that the pontiff shares the blame with the king and his spiritual and temporal lords, and that he was less blameable than either. We cannot concur in any view of the matter which is to diminish our abhorrence of the pope's conduct, and the intolerable insolence of his legate in this base and scandalous business: they are of a piece with those other daring encroachments upon the temporal power of independent princes which have exhibited, in colours never to be effaced, the grasping ambition of the popedom.

It is due to Mr. Butler to say that he denies the right of the pope, formerly claimed to exercise temporal power over all Christian sovereigns; and we do not deny that in turbulent times that power has sometimes been exercised beneficially. The principle however is so little capable of rational vindication that Mr. Butler assures us, that no advocates for the pope's temporal power are now to be found. It is rejected, he says, 'in the Gallican declaration of 1622 which was signed by every ecclesiastic secular or religious in France. All the English Irish and Scottish Catholics have disclaimed it upon oath.'

Perhaps, adds he, it never was quite so hideous as it has been represented: perhaps we reply its hideousness could scarcely be exaggerated.

Having arrived at the period when the corruptions of the church doctrinal and practical, were at their height Mr Southey devotes a chapter to a view of the papal system. Of the general justice of his observations in this chapter as it respects the character of that system we entertain no question. It is possible that in some minor circumstances he may have fallen into error, and in one or two instances we believe this to be the case.

After stating his persuasion that the papal power was in those dark ages by no means an unmixed evil, and pointing out in a few striking particulars the occasional exercise of its beneficial influence he proceeds to the dark catalogue of its delinquencies.

Among the first of these is doubtless to be reckoned its contemptuous disregard of the holy Scriptures. The Scriptures, even in the Latin version, had long become a sealed book to the people, and the Roman see, in proportion as it extended its supremacy, discouraged or proscribed the use of such vernacular versions as existed. In maintenance of the dominant system, tradition or the unwritten word was set up, and on this ground the Romish clergy found no difficulty in defending every corruption of the truth.

The reverence which was encouraged to the memory of departed saints led naturally to the grossest worship of the creature. The church might distinguish as she pleased between the worship paid to the Supreme Being and that which was offered to a saint or angel, but the sure tendency of the system was to end in idolatry.

The prayer which was preferred with increased fervency at a martyr's grave was at length addressed to the martyr himself; virtue was imputed to the remains of his body, the rags of his apparel, even to the instruments of his suffering; relics were required as an essential part of the church furniture; it was decreed that no church should be erected unless some treasures of this kind were deposited within the altar, and so secured there that they could not be taken out without destroying it; it was made a part of the service to pray through the merits of the saint whose relics were there deposited, and the priest when he came to this passage was enjoined to kiss the altar. Southey p 299

There is, as Mr Southey observes, a natural tendency in the human mind towards this form of superstition, and the clergy of that day presumed upon human credulity to the very utmost.

The instruments of our Lord's crucifixion were shown (the spear and the cross having so it was pretended been miraculously discovered) the clothes wherein he was wrapt in infancy, the manger in which he was laid, the vessels in which he converted water into wine at the marriage feast, the bread which he brake at the last supper, his vesture for which the soldiers cast lots. Such was the impudence of Romish fraud, that portions were produced of the burning bush, of the manna which fell in the wilderness, of Moses's rod and Samson's honeycomb, of Tobit's fish, of the blessed Virgin's milk, and of our Saviour's blood! Southey pp 301 302

Hence as we have said, a very easy transition to saint worship, and to what an awful extreme was it carried! These saints were invoked as mediators between God and man; they were supposed to have special power over particular diseases; the virtue belonging to themselves they even imparted to those images in which they were really present, however distant these images from each other, and many were the memorials of their marvellous power.

Church vied with church and convent with convent, in the reputation of their wonder working images, some of which were pretended to have been made without hands and some to have descended from heaven! But the rivalry of the monastic orders was shown in the fictions wherewith they filled the histories of their respective founders and worthies. No language can exaggerate the enormity of the falsehoods which were thus promulgated nor the spirit of impious audacity in which they were conceived, yet some of the most monstrous and most palpably false received the full sanction of the papal authority, the superstition founded upon them were legitimated by papal bulls and festivals in commemoration of miracles which never happened, —nay worse than this,—of the most blasphemous and flagitious impostures were appointed in the Romish kalender, where at this day they hold their place.

While the monastic orders contended with each other in exaggerating the fame of their deified patriarchs, each claimed the Virgin Mary for its especial patroness. Some peculiar favour she had bestowed upon each. She had appointed their rule of life or devised the pattern of their habit, or enjoined them some new practice of devotion, or granted them some singular privilege. She had espoused their founder with a ring, or fed him like a babe at her breast! (it is fitting and necessary that this abominable system of imposture should be displayed)—and each of the popular orders had been assured by revelation that the place in heaven for its departed members was under her skirts. All therefore, united in elevating her to the highest rank in the mythology of the Roman Church, for so in strict truth must this enormous system of fable be designated. They traced her in types throughout the Old Testament she was the tree of life, the ladder which Jacob had seen leading from heaven to earth, the ever burning bush, the ark of the covenant, the rod which brought forth buds and blossoms and produced fruit, the fleece upon which alone the dew of heaven descended. Before all creatures and all ages she was conceived in the Eternal Mind, and when the time appointed for her mortal manifestation was come, she of all human kind alone was produced without the taint of human frailty. Southey, pp. 305—307.

That men who embraced a creed of this sort should run into the practical extremes of superstition and fanaticism was unquestionably to be expected, and accordingly we find multitudes of them, for the purpose of obtaining heaven, inflicting upon themselves the most painful and disgusting penances. To remove as far as possible in their manners from the habits of decent and civilized society was a strong evidence of saintship, and dirt, filthy clothing, self mutilation and death by lingering suicide were among the means to propitiate a holy God.

Some became famous for the number of their daily genuflections, others for immersing themselves to the neck in cold water during winter while they recited the Psalter. The English saint Simon Stock obtained his name and his saintship for passing many years in a hollow tree. St Dominic the Cuirassier was distinguished for his iron dress and for flogging himself with a scourge in each hand day and night, and the blessed Arnulph of Villars in Brabant immortalised himself by inventing for his own use an under waistcoat of hedgehog skins, of which it appears five were required for the back, six for the front and sides. Southey, p. 317.

The saints, having accumulated a fund of good works, far beyond what their own necessities required, left it of course at the disposal of the church. Now, as the redemption of mankind was only from *eternal* punishment, and sin was not, except in the case of children and distinguished saints, to go wholly unpunished, there was a place of purgatory for others, a dreadful place in which, for a time left fearfully indefinite, the imprisoned soul suffered inexpressible torments. To the relief of such persons the church, for a proper consideration, was willing to dispense part of its supererogatory fund, and, as merits were transferable by gifts or purchase, the rich were encouraged to bestow large endowments upon religious houses, and their wealth became available for them beyond the grave,—a most inviting mode to procure an abbreviation of the term of purgatory or a mitigation of its torments!

How severe these torments were to be, might in some degree be estimated by the scale appointed for those who were willing to commute at a certain rate while they were alive. The set off for a single year was fixed at the recitation of thirty Psalms with an accompaniment of one hundred stripes to each, the whole Psalter with its accompaniment of fifteen thousand availing only to redeem five years. The chronicles of the middle ages are filled with horrible legends invented to promote a superstition so profitable to the priests, and that it might be the more deeply impressed upon the people the representations of souls weltering in fire were exposed in churches and in streets and by the way side. fraternities were established to beg for them, and to give money for their use is part of the penance which is usually at this day appointed by the confessor. Southey, pp. 321, 322.

The duty of confession to the priest was represented as indispensable to salvation, the soul that departed without confession and absolution bore with it the weight of its deadly sins to sink it into perdition.

Of all the practices of the Romish Church this is the one which has proved most injurious, and if it be regarded in connexion with the celibacy of the clergy, the cause will be apparent why the state of morals is generally so much more corrupt in Catholic than in Protestant countries. This obvious and enormous mischief is not its only evil consequence. The uses of conscience were at an end when it was delivered into the keeping of a confessor. Actions then, instead of being tried by the eternal standard of right and wrong, on

---

A rude drawing of this sort was discovered some years ago in St Michael's Church at St Alban's where we believe it still exists.

which the unsophisticated heart unerringly pronounces were judged by the rules of a pernicious casuistry the intent of which was to make men satisfied with themselves upon the cheapest terms The inevitable effect was that the fear of human laws became the only restraint upon evil propensities when men were taught to believe that the account with Divine Justice might easily be settled Tables were actually set forth by authority in which the rate of absolution for any imaginable crime was fixed and the most atrocious might be committed with spiritual impunity for a few shillings The foulest murderer and parricide if he escaped the hangman might at this price set his conscience at ease concerning all farther consequences Southey pp 323 324

The doctrine of transubstantiation most absurd and unscriptural as it is was zealously inculcated by the Romish priesthood In the sacrament of the Lord s supper, an actual sacrifice was supposed to be performed, and the Saviour was again offered up in the same body which had suffered on the cross

The priest when he performed this stupendous function of his ministry had before his eyes and held in his hands the Maker of heaven and earth and the inference which they deduced from so blasphemous an assumption was that the clergy were not to be subject to any secular authority seeing that they could create God their Creator ! Let it not be supposed that the statement is in the slightest part exaggerated it is delivered faithfully in their own words Southey p 326

Towards the close of this chapter Mr Southey notices the plenitude of power claimed by the pope, and the unbounded insolence with which it was exercised he concludes by remarking, that whether the infallibility so much vaunted in the Romish Church were vested in the pope or in a general council infallible it was determined that the church must be and the key stone was put to this prodigious structure of imposture and wickedness

In stating that there are some sentiments in this chapter to which we cannot subscribe we allude particularly to the remarks (pp 310—212) concerning Pelagius and Augustine and particularly when Mr Southey says that of all those ambitious spirits who have adulterated the pure doctrine of revelation with their own opinions, Augustine perhaps is the one who has produced the widest and most injurious effects We are utterly at a loss to explain how such an observation dropt from his pen Mr Butler recommends to him the Confessions of that great man, assuring him that he will be delighted with them We beg to join in the recommendation In the voluminous works of Augustine there are many things with which we could not concur but he was unquestionably one of the best men of the times and by the blessing of God, the great instrument in a very dark and superstitious age of reviving the knowledge of evangelical truth An abridgment of the Confessions, as also an account of the Pelagian Controversy are contained in the second volume of Milner s History of the Church of Christ an invaluable work which ought to be in the hands of every one who would wish to trace the progress of real Christianity

To Mr Southey s generally excellent chapter concerning the papal power much might be added but a zealous Roman Catholic will find more in it as it stands already than he will care to admit His respectable opponent Mr Butler employs many pages on this part of the volume denying in direct terms some assertions of Mr Southey and endeavouring to weaken the effect of others by arguments which however valid on account of early prepossessions, they may appear to himself will make little impression upon the intelligent Protestant reader Whether all the intemperate and blasphemous expressions adduced by Mr Southey from Roman Catholic writers with respect to the authority of the pope can be traced to writers of credit in that community or not whether Pope Gregory the Seventh approved or disapproved of the doctrine of berenger on transubstantiation &c are matters which do not essentially affect the main question. Did not the Roman Catholic system when at its height correspond with the representation here given of it? And can such a system be defended by any rules either of Scripture or of reason?

It answers little purpose to contend that the authority of the pope was sometimes beneficially exercised, that the pope had some learning, when other sovereigns had none, that the Greek and all the other churches which separated from the Church of Rome before the Reformation, invoke the Virgin Mary, the other saints and the angels, that the Council of Trent does not ascribe any divinity or power to the images of Christ, the virgin mother of God, and the other saints, that relics &c are only *venerated*, that the existence of purgatory is an old article of belief, that Cranmer once said a mass for the soul of Henry the Second of France, that the Church of England recommends confession and authorizes the priest to pronounce absolution, that transubstantiation is founded upon the literal words of Scripture—an argument often adduced by Bishop Bonner—&c &c. We observe in general that the defence does not reach the case, the writer who would vindicate such an abuse as that of auricular confession and such a power as the absolving power of the Roman Catholic priesthood with all its train of abominations by the example of the Church of England, ought himself to suspect his own argument, and although we would not make any church or class of religionists responsible for the intemperance of all the individuals of their communion, or ascribe to them principles which they disavow, and practices which they condemn, yet is it notorious that let popes and councils define as they will, the whole system of the Roman Catholics was, in effect and in practice what Dr Southey describes it—a prodigious structure of imposture and wickedness. The corruptions of Christianity, cherished and matured by that system, corruptions which gave to it a wonderfully close resemblance to heathenism, were not unknown to the pope and his council, but what attempts were made to correct them? Was not every artifice allowed and every abuse connived at or encouraged, which could add power or endowment to the Holy See? And was it not the tendency of the entire system to destroy the intellectual energies and to subjugate the minds of the great body of the people?

In the introduction to his work, Mr Butler gives some general cautions not inapplicable to the subject which is now before us, especially laying it down as a rule to be rigidly observed *That no doctrine should be ascribed to the Roman Catholics as a body, except such as is an article of their faith*, and he refers to certain authorized documents, such as the Catechism of the Council of Trent, Bossuet's Exposition of Faith, &c &c. The rule is generally a good one, and it would be well if its principle were adopted in our day by Protestants in reference even to their Protestant brethren, one half at least of the controversial publications directed against those whom the writers denounce as Evangelical, are founded upon the most marvellous ignorance, and abound in the grossest misstatements. But, with respect to the Roman Catholics, the actual practice of that church at the time of which we speak, and the actual belief of the people had gone beyond the bounds which Mr Butler would assign for them, and had reached that dreadful deterioration to which the acknowledged principles of the church naturally led the way. Instances doubtless might be found of pious and truly excellent persons in the bosom even of that corrupt church, but they were lights in a dark place, spiritual religion was almost buried under the rubbish of a wretched superstition, papal infallibility gave full course to the system of priestcraft, and instances are not wanting so late as the period of the Reformation, even of ministers of religion who knew nothing of the New Testament.

In stating that the practice of the Roman Catholic Church had travelled beyond the principles to which Mr Butler appeals as a summary of faith, we can by no means consent to speak of those principles in other terms than those of decisive reprobation. Take, for instance, the creed of Pius IV. as given by Mr Butler page 5, addressed in the form of a Bull, to all the faithful in Christ, and acknowledged throughout the universal Roman Catholic Church as an explicit summary of their faith. It was published in 1564; but, as the Roman Catholic religion is stated to be unchangeable, it may be taken for the creed of that church, according to the suffrage of its advocates from the earliest period. To this creed, every non-Catholic, on his admission into the Romish Church, is required to testify his assent without restriction or qualification. The following is the purport of some of its articles:—

' I most firmly admit and embrace apostolical and ecclesiastical traditions, and all constitutions and observances of the same church.

' I also admit the sacred Scriptures according to the sense which the holy mother church has held, and does hold, to whom it belongs to judge of the true sense and interpretation of the holy Scriptures; nor will I ever take or interpret them otherwise than according to the unanimous consent of the fathers.

' I profess also that there are truly and properly seven sacraments of the new law, &c. namely, baptism, confirmation, eucharist, penance, extreme unction, order and matrimony; and that they confer grace.

' I receive and embrace all and every one of the things which have been defined and declared in the holy Council of Trent, concerning original sin and justification.

' I profess likewise, that in the mass is offered to God a true, proper, and propitiatory sacrifice for the living and the dead. The remaining part of this clause affirms transubstantiation.

' I confess also, that under either kind alone, whole and entire Christ and a true sacrament is received.

The next articles affirm, " that there is a purgatory; that the saints are to be honoured and invoked; that they offer prayers to God for us; and that their relics are to be venerated; that due honour and veneration are to be paid to the images of Christ, and of the mother of God ever virgin, and also of the other saints.

' I also affirm that the power of indulgences was left by Christ in the church, and that the use of them is most wholesome to Christian people.

" I acknowledge the holy Catholic and Apostolical Church, the mother and mistress of all churches; and I promise and swear true obedience to the Roman Bishop, the successor of St Peter, the prince of the Apostles, and vicar of Jesus Christ.

' I also profess and undoubtedly receive all other things delivered, defined and declared by the sacred canons and general councils, and particularly by the holy Council of Trent; and likewise I do condemn, reject, and anathematize all things contrary thereto, and all heresies whatsoever condemned and anathematized by the church.

This true Catholic faith, *out of which none can be saved*, which I now freely profess and truly hold, I N., promise, vow, and swear most constantly to hold and profess the same whole and entire, with God's assistance to the end of my life. Amen.'

Such is the Roman Catholic religion, according to the statement of one of its most able and enlightened advocates; can we wonder at the corruptions to which it gave birth?

(To be continued.)

Sermons. By the Rev. J. W. CUNNINGHAM, A. M. Vicar of Harrow, &c. Vol. II. London. Hatchard. pp. 435.

IT was the remark of one who was as distinguished for his fidelity as a minister as for his acuteness as a critical observer of mankind, that a wise minister stands between practical atheism and religious enthusiasm. And we scarcely know a better exemplification of the force of this remark than in the volume of sermons now before us. Atheism and enthusiasm are two monsters against whom every voice throughout the country is constantly lifted up. The outcry is as universal as it is vehement. They are evils, however, of a totally opposite character and, in the estimation of the complainants, indicate the one an utter absence of all religion, the other a superabundance or perversion of it. There is also this remarkable distinction between them—that whereas the former is considered as so rare that its existence might almost be questioned the latter in the sense in which it is inveighed against by the world is in precisely the same proportion common, and every individual who displays a concern in religious matters raised but in the smallest degree above the average indifference of the world around him is exposed to the charge of this exciting ingredient in the human character, and branded with it as a term of reproach. Very signal misconceptions appear in the general impression and popular clamour on both these points, and a due examination of the moral appearances of society will readily convince any man who is open to the conviction, that both atheism and enthusiasm, in the chief sense in which it is of importance to deal with them, are to be met with in a ratio the very reverse of that which is so often blazoned forth to our regard. We allude to the kind and degree of influence which they practically acquire over the heart and conduct of the individual who either puts himself forth, or is put forth by others, as their depository and defender. In our present considerations, we pass by the abstract theories which reside only in the cold brain which gave them birth nor shall we dwell upon that warmth of constitutional temperament or eccentricity of character which may lead its possessor to a few fancies, which have in them nothing essentially pernicious in their practical effect. It is with atheism as developing itself in the actual purposes and pursuits of the life and the tastes and delights of the soul, that we are at present concerned; and this *practical* atheism is *far* more prevalent than is currently imagined. With respect also to the alleged enthusiasm against which the shafts of the world are directed we apprehend from it no such mischief as is habitually and dolefully predicted. There is, however, an enthusiasm which ought to receive a check from the experience of those whom wisdom has long matured in the paths of piety and Christian zeal: we mean that enthusiasm which, in an absorbing view of one duty or one class of obligations, loses sight of some of the more obvious relative obligations, and those particularly of a quiet and unobtrusive but nevertheless an important character. It is the enthusiasm which is 'ever following' not 'that which is good, but that which is in its estimation great, which catches at every ray of new light not because it is light but because it is new, and which ' doth sit by itself and " is *not* lowly in its own eyes nor ' maketh much of them that fear the Lord."

This is the practical atheism and this the religious enthusiasm of which we speak. He is the practical atheist not who in the processes of his unintelligible and inconclusive reasoning has travelled to the mysterious conclusion that there is no God but he who in the entire possession of a self-gratulating scorn for that hardihood of spirit which can question the existence of the Creator, can yet frame his plans of business and of pleasure, and accomplish his secret gains, and enjoy his sensual delights with a determination of habit as irrespective of the laws and the will and the glory of that Creator as if he too disbelieved his being, or at least doubted his authority. Many are the men who live daily in that frame of spirit. " God is not in all their thoughts." The whole of their recognition of the Divine nature is limited to an occasional repetition of the first four words of the creed, while they evince an absolute oblivion of the comprehensive duty of acknowledging God *in all their ways*. This is practical atheism, that most common and universal of the errors and infidelities of the day. Now, between these two classes of error the author of the volume before us seems to delight to take his stand, and the subjects which he has selected are generally of a character calculated to assail these two forms of evil.

In our remarks on Mr Cunningham's former volume, we contrasted the style and character of his earlier productions with the more appropriate garb in which he appeared as a writer of sermons, and we expressed a hope, which we are glad to find now realized, that he would be spared to prepare and present an additional volume to the world. Mr Cunningham modestly calls the sermons which his volume contains, "plain and unpretending discourses," and in reply to a request which had been made to him in the strictures of a contemporary critic, that any future sermons which he might write might be of a more elaborate nature, he remarks that even if he should suppose himself capable of satisfying this wish, he should doubt, in this species of composition, the lawfulness of labouring to gratify the few at the expense of the many. We quite agree with him, that the test of the excellence of a sermon is the degree of its approach to the Scriptural model, and that it may be confidently affirmed of the New Testament that it is the simplest of all books, and of the Saviour of the world that He is the plainest of all teachers. We may observe also, that that eminent Apostle St Paul made it his boast, that, in all his communications and addresses to the churches, he had used "great plainness of speech." We have often to regret, both in reading and hearing sermons, but particularly the latter, where many of our fellow listeners are persons whose circumstances have deprived them of the benefit of a liberal education, the occurrence of terms, allusions, and ideas of a very complicated character, which demand a secret movement of the educated mind to analyse, and which must therefore be wholly unintelligible to the greater part of the auditors. How much more noble than this ostentatious parade was the resolution of a minister, celebrated both for his learning and his piety, never to employ a difficult word if he could find an easy one; because a poor but pious hearer once inquired of him who those *primitive* Christians were of whom he had said so much, and was quite astonished to find that they were only those who lived nearest to the time of our Lord. He ever afterwards called them the *first* Christians.

But it is time to examine more particularly the volume before us. It consists of twenty-five discourses, none of them long, all of them arranged with a clearness of method, and distinguished by a light and ornamental style which are characteristic of our author, and occasionally animated by a fervour which the subject has evidently kindled as the writer's meditations have rested upon it. Mr Cunningham cannot write without embellishment, even in a sermon; but, in general, his embellishments in these discourses are of so chaste and correct a character, that the graver parts of the composition cannot frown upon them. Antithesis and point are at times as useful in a moral, as they are necessary in an epigram, provided they thrust out nothing of a better stamp. In several of the discourses in the present volume texts are selected more as mottos to a particular discussion, than as integral parts of an expository address which last is clearly the most generally useful style. The other however, is not without its occasional advantages.

There is a certain class of texts of Scripture which the world seems to have claimed as its own and by a sort of prescriptive and immemorial misapplication, to have arrayed in its own ranks against the truth. We allude to such as, "Charity covereth a multitude of sins." "Judge not and ye shall not be judged" and "Be not righteous overmuch" which, in the popular application of them, are made to mean any thing rather than what the Divine Spirit intended.

With a sermon on the last of these texts the volume before us opens. We should have been glad had Mr Cunningham imparted his own view of the meaning of this equivocal passage (we use the word in reference only to its *application*) but he does not intimate an opinion whether it is to be considered as the counsel of one who objects to the strict life of the godly man, or as the admonition of the inspired penman himself and he escapes from fixing its signification to apply the caution it contains to various classes of characters who may be considered as needing it, and then details several others to whom it is *no* applicable and these last happen to be the very persons to whom it is habitually directed. This latter part of the sermon develops probably the object of the author in the selection of the subject. The former part is a direct assault on that religious enthusiasm on which we remarked in the commencement of our review and among the classes of the *excessively scrupulous*, the *superstitious*, the *turbulent*, and *rashly zealous*, and those also who, by their intense occupation with the direct employments of religion are *betrayed into a neglect of the ordinary duties of life*, Mr Cunningham finds features of that indiscretion and weakheartedness which he evidently considers as the utmost that can be deprecated in the text. Those individuals whose humility is often a main source of their extravagancies, he describes as bowing too low before the throne of justice to discover the mercy seat which is erected upon it. In describing, on the other hand, the individuals to whom the caution is not applicable, he takes particular care to rescue the passage from the use which is too often made of it and we hardly know a better mode of combating the errors of the prejudiced than by thus meeting them on their own ground, and, after conceding all that can be conceded with propriety expelling them from all the fastnesses and refuges of lies in which they have long lain secure. After proving that the passage has no reference to those whose religious habits or opinions are found to rise above the level of opinion and practice in multitudes around nor to those who carry their religion as a grand constraining principle into all the circumstances and habits of life he shews in an animated manner, that it has no bearing on the man who carries his *affections* into his religion. We subjoin the passage.—

Here as before it is to be observed that an individual may receive as true every letter of the word of God or even exhibit a devout exterior in all the public offices of religion and yet so that his religion is characterized by a rigid exclusion of feeling affection sympathy and zeal he may escape the charge of overrighteousness and may live and die the unmolested possessor of what must nevertheless be regarded as a heartless useless unscriptural faith. But if estimating the great truths and promises of the Gospel at their real value if regarding with awe the edge of the precipice to which sin has conducted him and with astonishment and delight the rescue which the free grace of the Son of God has provided any person is prompted to speak and act under the deep impression of such feelings and to call upon others in language of suitable warmth, to participate in the joys of devotion and the triumphs of the cross — am I wrong in supposing that the affectionate fervent, devoted expressions or actions of such a person will in most instances bring down upon him the charge of over righteousness? But here again I must be permitted to ask whether a mind in the state which I have described is justly chargeable with excess? Have we any scriptural sanction for branding such warmth of feeling vivacity of expression and depth and strength of emotion with the odious title of fanaticism? Does not Scripture on the contrary insist upon a religion of affection? Is it not the language of God himself My son give me thine heart? Does not Christ say Thou shalt love the Lord thy God with all thine heart? And do not his Apostles hold a corresponding language? If any man love not the Lord Jesus Christ, let him be anathema maranatha. And how strictly did the frame and character of the first and best servants of the Cross correspond with this language They loved Him because he first loved them He was precious to them that believed Believing in him they rejoiced with joy unspeakable and full of glory Is this the language of Scripture? Then is the conclusion inevitable —the love of God is not excess the love of Christ is not excess the consecration of every feeling and affection to the great Author of them and the ardent devotion of ourselves to all the duties and the eager pursuits of all the pleasures of religion— these dispositions and acts of the mind are not excess are not enthusiasm are not over righteousness Religion without love is the carcase without the living soul by which it is to be animated It is the perishable form without that imperishable essence which will alone endure the trial of the last day and survive the tempest of eternal wrath pp 15—17

In our remarks on Mr Cunningham s former volume, we expressed our regret that some of the great doctrines of Christianity did not come more fully and in detail under his consideration and we may transfer a portion of this regret to this second volume There is indeed, one sermon on 'the Doctrines of the Cross but that is not a statement of what those doctrines in themselves are, but rather an historical argument of the power of those doctrines when faithfully preached to effect the conversion of sinners, and the inefficacy of all other modes of address than such as find their materials in the Gospel of the Redeemer The appeal is made to the well known facts connected with the history of missions to the heathen those sects which deny the doctrine of the atonement having rarely undertaken any mission, as if conscious of the inefficacy of their principles for the conversion of unbelievers while the labours of the Moravian missionaries have been most successful and the efforts of the Jesuits in China altogether as fruitless

The following appeal in this sermon will be conclusive to such as can accompany the writer whilst he traces the effects of this doctrine when faithfully received in the heart of the Christian

Tell us you who feel the influence of religion upon your own souls in changing improving moralizing and sanctifying the character whether this effect has not been wrought by the power of these doctrines Tell us whether the transformation was accomplished either by the mere maxims of morality or by dry reasonings on the beauty of virtue Tell us whether it was not wrought by the tidings of your lost estate as sinners and of the full and free redemption purchased on the cross for a lost world. Tell us whether it was not on the altar on which our Redeemer was offered that you laid down if they are laid down your bad passions and tempers your selfishness and worldliness your pride and covetousness your dishonesty to the public and your unkindness in your families Tell us if conviction and experience do not constrain you to exclaim God forbid that I should glory save in the cross of our Lord Jesus Christ by whom the world is crucified unto me and I unto the world ! —As the instructors of others have not some of us ascertained the impotence of every other doctrine? As private Christians have we not discovered that although a stumbling block to some and foolishness to others this crucified Lord is to those who believe Christ the wisdom of God and the power of God? If so to us at least no demonstration can be necessary of the wisdom of the Apostle s resolution to preach Christ crucified pp 37 38.

The Apostle Paul was willing to rest his case on this single ground when he writes thus to the Galatians "This only would I learn of you received ye the Spirit by the works of the law, or by the hearing of faith?" A safe appeal might also be made to the history of the Church of England, in support of the statements advanced in this discourse. To what was to be attributed that victory over the religion of forms, ceremonies, and "carnal ordinances," which was achieved at the period of the Reformation, but to the faithful and simple preaching of "Christ crucified?" To what again shall we ascribe that cold and comfortless state into which the religion of the Church of England must be acknowledged to have sunk from the age of the Protectorate until the dawn of the present century, but to the preaching of little more than a barren system of ethics, which however it may have arisen from a dread of the excesses into which some of the Puritans had been betrayed, was abundantly demonstrated to be wholly unequal to the work of enlightening converting and saving the souls of men? When morality took the place of the doctrines of the Cross, what was the result? A second leaden slumber crept over both the ministers and the members of our communion and soon settled down into a frigid indifference to the glory of God and the good of men. That was no age for the dispersion of the Scriptures, for the ardent prosecution of missionary labours, for the extensive education of the lower orders, and the thousand other charities which now refresh the eye as it gazes on the moral aspect of England. And what is it that has brought back the fertilizing tide from its lowest ebb, and made it to pour over its banks with every blessing in its stream? What but a return (would that it were universal!) to the principles and habits of the age of the Reformers preaching as they preached and discarding all the unfruitful schemes which man's wisdom teacheth for Jesus Christ and him crucified? All other modes of preaching, however adorned by the tropes of rhetoric, or the poetical beauties of imagination, are but as the mock suns in the firmament, which have indeed a shew of power, but possess neither light nor heat while, in the preaching of the Cross, the actual Sun of Righteousness arises upon mankind "with healing in his wings"

The fifth sermon is on that fearfully instructive incident in our Lord's history—the approach of the young ruler for his counsel which counsel amiable and teachable as he appeared, he yet rejected. The sermon is entitled, "Amiableness without Piety" and it certainly demonstrates the possibility of an unqualified possession and display of the former of these characteristics, without any admixture of the latter. The narrative, as it appears in the Evangelist, is deeply affecting and Mr. Cunningham compares it to the case of one on whom at his first introduction to our notice, every eye is fixed with admiration, and to whom every ear listens with delight but from whom all this delight is withdrawn suddenly, at the intelligence that he carries about with him the seeds of some disease which is conducting him painfully and rapidly to the grave. In the amiable ruler, this disease was a self righteous spirit exhibiting the entangling snare, which even the practice of moral obligation, *if relied upon* will inevitably become ' All these moral duties he had observed from his youth'

And perhaps in his view of the law of God and looking only to the outward act there may have been a measure of justice in his reply. He had never perhaps grossly and violently offended especially against those laws which respect the conduct of man to man. It is even possible that as in the case of St Paul touching the righteousness that was in the ceremonial law he was blameless. But looking at his obedience in a scriptural point of view it is evident that he was an offender as to every one of those commandments on an implicit compliance with which he prided himself. His subsequent conduct sufficiently testifies that his obedience was rather that of the letter than of the spirit rather that of the conduct than of principle rather that of the hand than of the heart rather adjusted to his own taste than framed upon the model of Scripture Besides every act of his obedience was vitiated by the foul blot of a spirit of self justification He neither sought for pardon nor in his own esteem needed it for all these things he had observed from his youth And, my brethren to this single offence of self justification what other need be added for the conviction of the sinner? That spirit however lightly regarded by men is a temper of mind of all other the most hostile to the peculiar office of the Saviour and to the whole genius of the Gospel It was the crime probably of Cain when he offered the fruits of the earth in sacrifice instead of the firstlings of the flock It was eminently the crime of the Pharisees a body of men the most frequently and vehemently rebuked by our Lord. Nor can the offensiveness of this crime in the sight of God be a matter of surprise The object of the Redeemer and of his dispensation is to humble to exclude boasting to lead the sinner to a religion of free grace and unmerited compassion to a deep conviction on the one hand of the insufficiency of man and on the other of the all sufficiency of Christ The spirit of self justification on the contrary springs from pride and largely ministers to it claims as a right what must be received as a gift transforms the man from a lowly suppliant at the throne of compassion to the proud artificer of his own happiness and in its ultimate effects dethrones the Lord from his mercy seat and erects the sinner into his own redeemer pp 83 84.

One of the most interesting of these sermons is that on the statement of the Apostle to the Corinthians, 2 Cor x 2 "Though we walk in the flesh, we do not war after the flesh which Mr Cunningham explains (we are not clear that his exposition is critically correct) of the points in which the true Christian resembles and those in which he differs from the men of this world He takes it up as a useful consideration to oppose to the common but inconclusive apology which the latter are constantly urging to cover their own delinquencies If we sin say they, are we the only offenders? Do not the professed servants of Christ also transgress? To this he replies by marking the important distinctions which exist between the respective characters of those who only "walk in the flesh, and therefore are liable to its infirmities and occasionally successful assaults, and those who not only " walk in, but also war after or according to, its tastes, and principles, and habits

In the following correctly descriptive passage the writer shews that besides being liable to the infirmities of body and of temper, of trial and temptation the Christian is also subject to considerable fluctuations in the influence of those great principles, which are nevertheless the governing powers of his soul

What infirmity for instance is there at times in his *faith*?—Sometimes indeed it is clear and strong like the full and deep tide of the mighty river at others perhaps it is shallow irregular and disturbed, like the scanty waters of the summer stream Such indeed may be its variations that the startled Christian in some cases scarcely knows what to conclude as to the real state of his own soul and even in his best moments is disposed to pray Lord I believe help thou mine unbelief!

Look again at the *love* of the real servant of Christ At times how ardent and active are his feelings and at other times how cold and sluggish! Such is frequently the rapid descent of the corrupt heart that the man prepared to become a martyr at one moment at another is apparently immoveable and heartless indisposed to make the smallest sacrifice of self for God or for human nature

Thus also the *hope* of the real Christian is often characterized by much infirmity —To day every promise is intelligible and bright in his eyes the voice of God is in a sense audible and a strong ray of expectation and even of assurance is shed over the prospect before him the next day perhaps the consciousness of his guilt seizes upon his mind his sky is clouded he walketh in darkness and hath no light in the expressive language of the Scriptures he goes mourning all the day long

In short my Christian brethren it is not too much to affirm that there is no faculty of the inner man no power or disposition or temper or taste of the renewed soul which does not at times feel the burden of the body The flesh lusteth against the Spirit and the Spirit against the flesh and these are contrary the one to the other How powerfully does St Paul describe this conflict of the soul! To will is present with me but how to perform that which is good I find not. I delight in the law of God after the inward man but I see another law in my members warring against the law of my mind and bringing me into captivity to the law of sin which is in my members.—pp 101—103

But then the Christian is not left here—there is a very determinate line of demarcation drawn between him and the men of this world, and the very obvious distinction is pointed out, that

Holiness in a servant of God is habitual whilst sin is occasional and rare The real Christian is ordinarily right and only occasionally wrong whereas others are habitually wrong and only occasionally right. The faults of a Christian are exceptions to the general rule of his life the faults of others are conformity to the rule itself Hezekiah was betrayed into an act of vanity Herod was habitually vain p 105

The view of the Christian *mourning over sin* is truly and affectingly depicted, and also his *increasing power over it* We quote both passages.—

It is almost a folly to speak of the man of the world as mourning for sin at all but if he does grieve it is rather for property consumed for character forfeited for health destroyed than for his resistance to the will of God He stands in the midst of this garden of the Lord feeds on his hand walks in his presence rests under the wings of his tenderness and yet sins against Him without a single pang of heart The real servant of God on the contrary when he offends mourns and mourns deeply and the chief cause of his grief is the sense of his ingratitude to the Lord who made him, and to the Saviour who has redeemed him by his blood Against Thee Thee only have I sinned and done this evil in thy sight The sense of his baseness to such a Benefactor the fear of separation from the Lord of light and love and glory are to him intolerable burdens Mine eye poureth out tears unto God I water my couch with tears My tears have been my meat night and day! I am ready to halt, and my sorrow is continually before me I go mourning all the day What language is this my brethren! And when did any other penitents approach the Lord with language full of such pathos and meaning with tears drawn from a fountain of sorrow as deep and as bitter? O the anguish of a soul thus rent by the arrow of contrition! O the joy which the promises of God impart to a heart thus troubled! How natural to the man thus comforted is the language I will be glad and rejoice in thy mercy for thou hast considered my trouble The Lord is my strength and shield My heart trusted in him and I am helped therefore my heart greatly rejoiceth I will go unto the altar of God of God my exceeding joy pp 106, 107

Again

The Christian is obtaining a daily and visible conquest over his corruptions He is daily pressing toward the mark going on unto perfection abounding more and more approaching nearer to the measure of the stature of the fulness of Christ rescuing at every step of his progress a new portion of his character from the waste and clothing it with verdure and fruitfulness The corruptions of the men of the world because left to themselves or nursed up in the cradle of self indulgence are daily gaining strength and like the cloud seen by the prophet, if at first the size of a man's hand at length cover and darken the whole sky The corruptions of the Christian on the contrary are like the fig tree withering under the curse of the Redeemer Every day sees the servant of the world fitter for perdition every day sees the believer riper for glory till at last the voice of judgment is heard and the one passes away to misery and the other to unchangeable triumph and joy p 109

In the sermon on "the invisible world, Mr Cunningham has allowed his fine imagination freely to soar on the wings of a Scriptural faith and to refresh his sight with a view of those joys which fill the abodes of the redeemed With the path that conducts upwards to that world he has shewn in these discourses that he is well acquainted After the glowing language in which he describes the probable joy of a saint when actually finding himself disencumbered of " the burden of the flesh, we cannot but hope that our author may be able to feel more of sacred delight than distress in recording such allusions as are doubtless the following —

If any one of those we loved the best and who has paid the debt of nature is not now reserved in chains for the anguish of the last day if in reply to the question Your parent your child your husband your wife where are they? we may venture confidently to answer In the porch of heaven and only awaiting the judgment of the great day to establish them in all its joys and glories it is to be ascribed, first and last and altogether to the compassion and love of Him who said, Whosoever will let him take the water of life freely. p. 57.

Indeed there is no reluctance to approach even so tender a theme as this; and in the tenth sermon, which is truly beautiful, on the condescension of the Redeemer in terming his disciples, "not servants, but "friends," there is a contrast of his power with the impotence of even the closest earthly relative to effect comparatively any good for those who are the dearest to his bosom—

How little you can do for those whose interest you may be supposed to feel most deeply, the children of your bosom! You cannot stay the progress of disease; you cannot string the shrunk nerve, or give colour to the faded cheek, or perhaps even mitigate for a moment the pang which rends your own breast as much as theirs. And, even could you thus minister to the necessities of the body, what can you do for the soul? You cannot lodge the arrow of conviction in their bosom—prostrate them as sinners before God—lead them to the cross of the Saviour—fill them with gratitude for his love— pluck them as brands out of the burning, and erect them as pillars in the temple of our God. You cannot bind up the broken hearted, or let the prisoner to his corruptions go free. But hear the description which is given of our Heavenly Friend. The Lord hath sent me to bind up the broken hearted, to proclaim liberty to the captives ... to proclaim the acceptable year of the Lord, to comfort all that mourn, to give unto them beauty for ashes, the garment of praise for the spirit of heaviness. It is said of Him that he is able to succour them that are tempted, and to save to the uttermost all that come unto him; that with power he commandeth the unclean spirits and they come out; and that he shall put all enemies under his feet,— for he is Lord of lords and King of kings. pp. 177, 178.

Deeply affected by the conviction, from the painful loss of the cherished companions of former years, that friendship, like life, is but a vapour, our author breaks forth into this grateful apostrophe:—

But, thanks be to God, all is not thus fugitive and variable. If the stars shall fall from heaven and the heavens themselves be rolled up as a scroll, the Lord who ruleth these heavens shall not decay, and the star of his love shall beam for ever: I am the Lord, I change not. He hath made with his people an everlasting covenant, ordered in all things and sure. The mountains shall depart, and the hills be removed; but my kindness shall not depart from thee, neither shall the covenant of my peace be removed, saith the Lord, that hath mercy on thee. Delightful assurance to creatures navigating an ocean where from minute to minute the wind shifts and the sounding changes, and the stillest calm is but the prelude to the fiercest storm! The uncertainty of life, my brethren, is a topic upon which scarcely any man needs preach to another. I ask not what is fugitive, but what is enduring? The very bow in the heavens, which announces to us the security of the earth from one species of destruction, shall itself be dissolved—for the elements shall melt with fervent heat. Nevertheless it is your privilege as Christians to look for a new heaven and a new earth wherein dwelleth righteousness. The moment in which all things shall be destroyed is the moment which fixes the seal of permanence and perfection to the blessings of a Christian; and when time shall be no longer, he shall enter upon the unchanging glories of eternity. pp. 180, 181.

In the twelfth sermon, which is on Luke xi. 21, 22, there is a striking picture of the man who is at peace under the influence of Satan. Would that all who come under this description, might lay to heart the truth of the vivid and appalling representation!

The fourteenth sermon is on the character of Abraham, and is intended to present him to the view of the reader as an example in the character of a "father of a family." —Mr Cunningham has written it with deep and animated feeling; and we doubt not that the interesting view of the peace and joy which result from a faithful discharge of the domestic obligations, owes much of its fidelity and attraction to the opportunities which the author has had of framing his descriptions from the life. With respect to the condition of the dependents in a family, we entirely agree with him, that it is only when the state of servitude is not considered merely as an arrangement of society which binds one person slavishly to do the will of another at a certain fixed stipend, but as a scheme by which the extreme classes of society are brought together upon terms of reciprocal comfort and advantage, by which one pays with the strength of the body for the benefit of the soul, that the mutual obligations of master and servant are likely to be properly fulfilled. We particularly recommend this sermon to the attention of our readers, such of them especially as are called to sustain the responsible post of masters of families, and we think they must rise from the perusal with a deeper conviction of this fact, that when the Bible admonishes masters to

give unto their servants that which is just and due, it means much more than the faithful payment of their wages, and binds closely upon them the duty of embracing all possible opportunities of instructing and enlightening their souls.

In the remaining sermons we have found much which we think likely to minister to the edification as well as consolation of the reader. Indeed there is a far less proportion of the solemn and alarming, than of the peaceful and persuasive character of writing in this volume.— The sermon entitled "Hopelessness of Improvement exposed and condemned," and those also on "Christian membership," the desire of the servant of God," and the "prisoner of hope," are very excellent, but in that on Heb xiii. 20, 21, entitled "The God of Peace," we have dwelt with delight on some passages written in Mr Cunningham's best style. It seems to be a subject peculiarly congenial to his mind.

In the concluding sermon, on the promise of the Redeemer, in John xiv 2, Mr Cunningham has amplified, in a very beautiful manner, that consolatory declaration, 'Where I am there ye shall be also.'

It adds much to our satisfaction in this state of being to know that some dear and intimate friend has prepared the abode in which we are to dwell. We remember that he is familiar with our tastes and habits, and are sure that his large and liberal hand will spare nothing that may contribute to our happiness. Consider then the fact which is recorded in this expression of our text. Not only is the world of glory the palace of the great King, not only is it the garden of the Lord and therefore adapted to the nature of its great Proprietor, but it is an abode constructed by one familiar with your own nature, wants and capacities, devised by the mind and formed by the hand of Him who loved you and gave himself for you. He built the heavenly temple, he called the river of life from its everlasting fountains, he planted the tree whose leaves are for the healing of the nations, and when nothing of created objects remained to add splendour or worth to this invisible world he added Himself as the proper joy of his creatures to that bright habitation. I go to prepare a place for you. I go myself to shine in that temple, to walk by those fountains, to dwell in those mansions, and in my presence shall there be fulness of joy, and at my right hand pleasures for evermore. pp 427, 428

Such are the forcible and excellent sermons contained in this second volume of Mr Cunningham. They are certainly most sound practical discourses, and are enriched with many and great beauties, and we heartily commend them to the perusal of our readers, and doubt not that the Divine blessing will accompany them.

LITERARY AND PHILOSOPHICAL INTELLIGENCE
&c &c

GREAT BRITAIN

PREPARING for publication.—Memoirs of Elizabeth Stuart Queen of Bohemia Sister of Charles I. by Miss Benger —The History of the Pelham Administration by Archdeacon Coxe.—the Sydney Papers by R. Blencowe.—Memoirs of the Chevalier Bayard.—A Letter to a Sceptic,—Discourses on the Lord's Prayer by the Rev S. Saunders.— The "No Popery," to be continued monthly, price 2d. designed to expose, in a familiar manner, the fallacious principles and prejudicial institutions of Popery and the tendency of its movements at the present time

In the press.—Thoughts on the Police of England.—Travels in Greece, by Dr Bronsted.—A Tale of Paraguay, by R. Southey.—Capt Lyon's Attempt to reach Repulse Bay.—On the Advancement of Society in Science, Civilization, and Religion, by J. Douglas.

Oxford.—The following subjects are proposed for the Chancellor's Prizes for the ensuing year:—Latin Verses, Incendium Londinense anno 1666.—English Essay, Language in its copiousness and structure considered as a test of national civilization.— Latin Essay, De Tribunicia apud Romanos potestate. —Sir Roger Newdigate's Prize for English Verse not containing more or fewer than fifty lines, The Temple of Vesta at Tivoli.

Cambridge.—Sir William Browne's Gold Medals.—The subjects for the present year are—Greek Ode, Ανδρων πιφα ω πασα γη τάφος.—Latin Ode, Academia Cantabrigiensis tot novis ædificiis ornata. —Greek Epigram, Περ σσοι πάντ ς ο μέσω λογοι.—Latin Epigram, Summum jus, summa injuria.— Porson Prize, Shakespeare King John Act vi Scene ii.

"How oft the sight of means, to an innocent child"—The following will be the subjects of examination in the last week of the Lent Term 1826.—1 The Gospel of St Matthew, 2 Paley's Evidences of Christianity, 3 The First Book of Herodotus, 4 The Fourth Book of Virgil's Georgics.

The Royal Society of Literature has resumed its meetings. A number of new members have been proposed, and several important works presented by public bodies and individuals, been added to the library. At the last ordinary meeting the papers read were—by Mr Faber on the ancient Mexicans, and by Mr Tytler on the introduction of Greek literature into England after the dark ages.

Professor Buckland has published a letter relative to the cave lately discovered at Banwell, Somerset. The Professor states the thickness of the mass of sand, mud, and limestone through which the bones, horns, and teeth are dispersed to be in one place nearly forty feet. He adds— Many large baskets full of bones have already been extracted, belonging to the ox and their tribes, of the latter there are several varieties including the elk. There are also a few portions of the skeleton of the wolf, and of a gigantic bear. The bones are mostly in a state of preservation equal to that of common grave bones, but it is clear from the fact of some of them belonging to the great extinct species of the bear, that they are of an antediluvian origin.

An Egyptian mummy was lately unwrapped at the Bristol Institution. The case, which was covered with hieroglyphics, exhibited rather the copper coloured countenance of a Nubian, than the expanded forehead and wide eye-sockets of an Ethiopian. The upper part of the shell being removed, there arose a peculiar but not unpleasant odour. The skin was blackened, and the neck and one of the hands had been attacked by insects, in other respects the specimen was very perfect. It was the body of a female. The hair of the head was perfect, of a brownish auburn colour, short, but not at all wearing the character of a Negro's. The heart, lungs, and intestines were in high preservation.

The number of members of the Mechanics Institution who have paid up their subscriptions is stated in the last quarterly report to be about 750, and on the 2d of December, being the anniversary of its formation, the first stone of a building for a Theatre and Lecture room in Southampton buildings was laid by Dr Birkbeck, the president.

The boiling heats of saturated solutions of thirty four of the most important saline bodies have been determined by Mr T Griffiths, with the per centage of dry salt in most of them. The following are a specimen:

Name of Salt	Boiling Point Farnh	Dry Salt in 100 parts
Acetate of soda	256°	60
Muriate of soda	224	30
Sulphate of magnesia	222	57.5
Alum	220	52
Sulphate of iron	216	64
Sulphate of soda	213	31.5

The first and last of the salts here mentioned are also the extremes as to temperature.

When Sir Christopher Wren was building St Paul's Cathedral, he caused to be affixed to several parts of the structure the following notice, which would be very appropriate for imitation or adoption in all cases of church building.— Whereas among labourers and others that ungodly custom of swearing is too frequently heard, to the dishonour of God and contempt of authority, and to the end that such impiety may be utterly banished from these works which are intended for the service of God and the honour of religion, it is ordered, that profane swearing shall be a sufficient crime to dismiss any labourer that comes to the call and the clerk of the works, upon sufficient proof, shall dismiss them accordingly and that if any master working by task, shall not upon admonition reform the profanation among his apprentices, servants and labourers it shall be construed his fault, and he shall be liable to be censured by the Commissioners

FRANCE

The depth of water produced by dew at Vivieres in the department of Ardeche in France during the year 1823 has been carefully ascertained by M Flaugergues On 120 mornings appreciable quantities of dew fell which nevertheless amounted to only 2·42 French inches or the 1 152 5th part of the depth of rain which fell there (on 132 days) during the year and amounted to 36 90 inches The least depth of dew in March was 0·59 of a line and the greatest in October 7·49 of a line the fewest dewy mornings were, two in January and the most nineteen in October

CHINA

A singular proclamation issued by the Foo yuen or Sub Viceroy of Canton December 28 1822 translated by Dr Morrison exhibits the character of his Excellency Ching in a very flattering light The objects of this proclamation are stated in eight words Encourage Industry Establish Education Praise Virtue Repress Vice The proclamation is introduced by the following declaration —

Ancient rulers (says the Foo yuen) thought that if one man was unreclaimed, it must be some fault in the ruler I commenced life (adds h) as a Che heen magistrate and in Canton province I served twenty years I was removed to Shantung and to Honan and now I am placed here in the situation of Foo-yuen bearing also the office of Censor general General Adviser of his Imperial Majesty and a Captain empowered to call forth the army of Canton Music and women goods and gains revelry and avarice have no charms for me My only, constant, unremitted, heedful, anxious desire (which I dare not decline to cherish) is that I may look on national affairs as if they were my domestic affairs and the affairs of the poor people as if they were my own personal affairs "

TARTARY

Mr Moorcroft in a letter from Tartary says The novelties which have already met my view in natural history are so great, as to invite the introduction of details that would swell a letter to a volume One example is the Ladakh sheep This animal says he at full growth is scarcely so large as a South Down lamb of five or six months yet in the fineness and weight of its fleece the flavour of its flesh and the peculiarities of its constitution it is inferior to no race It is as completely domiciliated as a British dog In the night it shelters in a walled yard, or under its master s roof in the day it feeds often on a surface of granite rock where cursory observation can scarcely discover a speck of vegetation If permitted it will pick up crumbs drink salted and buttered tea or broth or nibble a cleanly picked bone It gives two lambs within twelve months and is twice shorn within that period A British cottager might keep three of these sheep with more ease than he now supports a cur dog as they would live luxuriantly in the day on the stripes of grass which border the roads and by keeping clean hedge bottoms Mr Moorcroft has procured some of them with a view to import them into Britain The letter contains likewise a notice of a nondescript wild variety of horse which he thinks might be domesticated for the use of the small farmer and poor in Britain It is about fourteen hands high of a round muscular form with remarkably clean limbs

---

LIST OF NEW PUBLICATIONS

THEOLOGY

Three Letters addressed to the Rev Fred Nolan on his miscriticism relative to 1 John v 7 with strictures on the vindication of the same passage by the Bishop of St David s By the Rev J Oxlee

Fashionable Amusements the Bane of Youth a Sermon By the Rev J Morrison

Helon s Pilgrimage to Jerusalem a Picture of Judaism in the century which preceded the Advent of our Saviour from the German of Strauss 2 vols 16s

Bunyan explained to a Child Part II with about 50 engravings By the Rev Isaac Taylor 4s half bound

A Reply to the Second Postscript to Palæoromaica By the Rev W G Broughton 2s

The Sabbath Remembrancer &c &c with 52 wood cuts By the Rev A. Fletcher 1 vol 12mo 5s. bound

The Evangelical Rambler Vol II 3s 6d

Twenty two Discourses on various Subjects By the Rev B S Claxson M A

A Letter in Reply to the Animadversions in the Quarterly Review on a Work entitled Divine Influence. By the Rev. T. T. Biddulph.

Literæ Sacræ, or Moral Philosophy and Christianity compared. 8vo.

MISCELLANEOUS

Cole's Bibliographical Tour. 8vo. 8s. and 12s.

Memoirs of the Life of John Law of Lauriston. By J. H. Wood, Esq. 12mo. 6s.

An Introduction to the Metres of the Greek Tragedians. By a Member of the University of Oxford. 8vo. 3s.

The Cambrian Plutarch. By J. H. Parry. 8vo. 10s. 6d.

Mounteney's Inquiry relative to the Emperor Napoleon. 8vo. 16s.

My Children's Diary, or Moral of the Passing Hour. 6s. 6d.

R. Baynes's Catalogue of Books. 8vo.

Compendium of the History of Ireland. By J. Lawless. 24s.

Memoirs of the Affairs of Europe, from the Peace of Utrecht. 4to. 2l. 10s.

Memoirs of the Life and Writings of the late Rev. E. Williams, D.D. By J. Gilbert. 8vo. 14s.

RELIGIOUS INTELLIGENCE

MORAVIAN MISSIONS IN THE WEST INDIES

WE feel great pleasure in inserting the following proposal for the establishment of a separate fund for the Moravian Missions in the West Indies. We need add nothing to the circular except our earnest wishes and prayers for the success of the object, and our gratitude to God that the unhappy condition of the Black and Coloured population of our Slave Colonies is beginning at length more adequately to awaken the sympathies of our fellow Christians of all denominations. Our own church in particular will, we trust, before long take a far more prominent part in this work of Christian mercy than she has hitherto done. There is ample scope for her exertions, and the most encouraging prospects of success to call them forth. The circular is as follows:—

Some considerations have lately presented themselves connected with the Missions of the United Brethren in the West Indies, which the Committee of the London Association in aid of the Brethren's Missions think themselves called upon to bring in an especial manner before the notice of the Christian public.

The Brethren have long observed with gratitude the general disposition which appears to prevail among the heathen in the vicinity of their various settlements to seek after and receive the Gospel. This disposition has been manifested in a remarkable manner among the Negro Slaves in the West-India islands, and there appear to be at present, some peculiar facilities for cultivating it with success in that quarter.

Notwithstanding the unfavourable feeling which unfortunately prevails in some of the islands, many of the colonial governments and of the proprietors of estates have shewn themselves much disposed to countenance, and even to invite the exertions of the Brethren, who have been domiciled among them as a Protestant Episcopal Church for nearly a century past, having no less than 28,000 Negroes under constant instruction, and the beneficial effect of whose efforts they have experienced in the improved character and conduct of their slaves. From several of these proprietors offers have been received of land for new settlements, and of other assistance in forming them. Though the Brethren will not attempt the establishment of new stations, without invitation or consent from the owners or superintendants of adjoining estates, yet where invitations are received, they are anxious to avail themselves of such openings for the further extension of the Gospel. But the present embarrassed state of the islands renders it impossible to obtain in them an adequate supply for the erection of chapels and other necessary buildings; it is only therefore by the aid of their friends in Great Britain that the Brethren can hope to accomplish the objects which they have so much at heart.

In some islands there is required more adequate accommodation for the increasing congregations in their present settlements, and greater facilities for affording Christian education to Negro children, a branch of their labours from which they anticipate the happiest effects in ameliorating the character of the rising slave population, and therein of promoting the best interests of the colonies.

Two objects connected with the foregoing views especially claim attention at the present time

At Lenox, in the parish of Westmoreland in Jamaica, a grant of land has been offered, accompanied by an urgent invitation to the Brethren to establish a new station there and not only the gentleman who has made this offer but other neighbouring proprietors are willing to supply such materials for requisite buildings as the country affords It is calculated that around this spot there are from 3000 to 4000 Negroes (besides others) who will thus be brought within the reach of the Gospel and who are at present removed to a distance of above twenty miles from the parish church and twenty five or thirty miles from any other missionary station Thus destitute of the ordinances of religion these poor creatures are sunk in ignorance and barbarism yet when any occasional opportunities for instruction have been afforded, they have shewn great readiness to attend the worship of God and have in several instances appeared to be powerfully affected by it The necessary expense of establishing this station in addition to the local supplies is estimated at more than 1200*l*

In the island of Antigua above 1800 of the offspring of Christian Negroes are left destitute of education from the want of school rooms the chapels being occupied throughout the Sabbath by successive crowded audiences of adults of whom above 12 000 attend the ministry of the Brethren in that island It is therefore earnestly to be desired that at some of the settlements school rooms should be erected and that at the principal station at St John s the capital of the island the present chapel should be converted to that use and a larger chapel erected the existing one being totally inadequate to accommodate the many thousands who attend the service there The only present remedy namely successive services throughout the day severely tries the strength of these laborious and indefatigable missionaries and prevents their paying attention to the children whom they would otherwise collect and instruct in a Sunday school Upon this object about 1200*l* might also be most usefully and economically expended and the Committee have great pleasure in stating by way of encouragement, that a few individuals of the Society of Friends have kindly contributed above 100*l* towards the erection of school rooms in Antigua

Of these openings (as well as of others in various and important quarters) for the extension of their pious and beneficial labours in the West Indies the Brethren are wholly unable to avail themselves from their own resources These resources have been long inadequate even to the ordinary expense of their various missions and they will be still further contracted by the heavy loss lately sustained through the destructive fire which has desolated their settlement at Sarepta. By the blessing of God however especially upon the exertions of their friends in this country the means have been provided of nearly liquidating a large debt which had grown up and probably of enabling them to meet the current expenses but yielding no surplus applicable to such objects as those above referred to

Under these circumstances the Committee of the London Association encouraged by the anxiety so generally prevalent in behalf of the unhappy Negro race and stimulated by an earnest desire for the wider extension of the Gospel of our Lord and Saviour in these eventful days venture to bring this case before the Christian public which they do in the confidence that the prospect of so important an amelioration will not be blighted by the want of means to carry it into effect and to satisfy the ardent desires and the extreme necessities of this hitherto benighted and degraded class of our fellow creatures

The Committee propose to open a separate subscription for the purpose of assisting the Brethren in the establishment of new stations in the West India islands with the consent or on the invitation of the proprietors or superintendants of estates and in providing facilities for the education of the children of the Negroes The plan on which this last branch of missionary labour is conducted by the Moravian Brethren will be seen in the following extract from a recent letter from the Rev L Stobwasser lately a missionary in Antigua.

It has always been the practice of the missionaries of the Brethren s Church whenever they could possibly do it, to establish schools among the Negroes It is evident what an influence may be obtained on the minds of children by means of schools especially if the sole aim of them is to procure for them a more immediate access to the sacred books of Scripture Among Negro slaves a Sunday school seems the only one practicable Our method is to give to every child a lesson pasted on a small board, which they put into a bag or pocket they have for that purpose and in which they exercise them selves in the evenings, also at noon and in the field at their breakfast time. We take care to find on every estate if possible a Negro who is able and willing to instruct them and when there are no such Negroes to be found we encourage the most able we can get to visit us once or twice a week in the evening besides Sunday in order to be qualified by us for the instruction of others. much has been done by the Brethren in this way and in our Negro congregations in Antigua, teachers are not wanting to give effect to the charity which the generous friends of missions and Sunday schools might feel disposed to exercise in this cause

When I first came to the island of Antigua, Sunday schools were generally reckoned to be impracticable though frequent and not unfruitful attempts were made especially by our truly indefatigable brother James Light (now in Jamaica) By degrees the prejudices of the planters against permitting the Negro children being taught to read which in the beginning were very perceptible wore away and we see on those estates where the children are most generally instructed the beneficial consequences of it. Quite a different generation seems there to rise and gives the prospect of happier days for the Negroes

There is now an amazing desire among the children and even among adult Negroes to learn to read and many have declared that they wish to be able to read the sacred Scriptures themselves for their comfort and instruction. An opportunity to satisfy such a laudable desire is now afforded which if permitted to pass away may perhaps not soon return but which under the blessing of God, may lead to an entire reformation of the slave population of Antigua.

ASIATIC SOCIETY OF PARIS

The Report of the Society delivered by M Abel Rémusat at its first anniversary held under the presidency of his Serene Highness the Duke of Orleans contains the following passage on the co operation of the Society with Bible Societies

I cannot but remind you gentlemen of the very particular and repeated tokens of good-will received by us from that religious and philanthropic Society which labours with zeal for the accomplishment of one only design—the highest social advancement of all nations by means of a single book—THE BIBLE. Not to speak of the interest which every Christian and we may say every philosopher cannot avoid feeling in this vast enterprise it is incumbent on the members of the Asiatic Society more particularly to take a share therein. With Bible Societies you have natural bonds of alliance and, if I may so speak, a kind of identity. The immense resources at their disposal enable them to maintain relations with the most secluded parts of the East, and to procure translations of the sacred books into idioms of which sometimes the very names are unknown to us. On the other hand, many of these translations, undertaken by persons who have not always enjoyed opportunities of acquiring a thorough knowledge of the languages require careful revision and may be greatly improved by passing under the eyes of skilful linguists such as those who are united with the Asiatic Society

Far from concealing from itself this beneficial dependence on others, the Bible Society receives with a candour deserving the highest eulogium such observations as may be made on the works which it publishes and its good will appears to be the reward of the criticisms addressed to it. Scarcely had your institution become known to its conductors when they hastened to present to you a valuable collection of versions of the Scripture in different languages of the East and I have no apprehension of going too far if I should say that their object in sending them to you, has not been merely to enrich your library with works which may assist your labours and of which they alone are in possession but still more to call your attention to these versions and to solicit at your hands the means of improving them. Noble and rare example!—worthy of being offered to learned men. Admirable love of truth! elevated by pious intentions above the vain rivalries of national or literary ambition

☞ *For a mass of interesting Religious Intelligence we refer our readers to the Appendix to our last Volume published with the present Number*

VIEW OF PUBLIC AFFAIRS

FOREIGN

FRANCE.—The session of the chambers has opened with a speech from the throne the chief topics of which are the death of the late king the continuance of internal prosperity and of pacific relations with foreign governments the convention with Spain for a prolonged occupation of that country by a part of the French troops and last not least, the intention of the king to propose measures for better securing the interests of religion and also an indemnity to the emigrants at the Revolution which the finances of the country are stated to be in a condition to allow of without inconvenience to the public. The business of the session has not sufficiently commenced to elicit as yet much debate on any of these topics; and in general both chambers seem so subservient at present to the views of the government, that much serious opposition does not appear to be apprehended. To grant a reasonable compensation to individuals unjustly and violently deprived of their property in the moment of revolutionary phrensy is doubtless simply considered an act of national justice; but the measure is too closely connected with deeply rooted associations not to be viewed by numbers with suspicion and alarm.—The proposed regulations for advancing the interests of religion, if we may judge of them from the project for securing reverence to the consecrated wafer or Host by means of the penalty of death, are likely to be more akin to the darkness of the middle ages, than to the present period of light and liberality. We may have occasion to recur to the subject when the intended measures are more fully developed; in the mean time it is painful to behold large bodies of men retrograding in the scale of civilization. In past ages we witness many fluctuations in knowledge and liberal institutions. The most refined nations of antiquity relapsed into ignorance and barbarism, and this in the midst of those vestiges of art and literature which we might have supposed would have preserved them from degeneracy. In modern times one great promoter of such retrograde movements in society has been the spirit of Popery. We cannot however believe that, with those powerful instruments for perpetuating knowledge, the press, the diffusion of education, the distribution of the holy Scriptures, and all the social and commercial relations of modern times, the gloom of ignorance can ever again become very deep or widely diffused. Still the wish to prevent even the partial return of intellectual or spiritual darkness should stimulate Christians and all who wish well to the best interests, civil or religious, of their species, to " work while it is called to-day," to labour to diffuse more widely the light of Divine truth, and in the spirit of our revered Reformers to endeavour not only in England but throughout the world to kindle a torch which shall never be extinguished.

SPAIN.—We have not much intelligence from Spain. The king continues to complain of being surrounded with a wretched set of ministers, though he has changed them often enough to suit, we might think the most capricious taste. Vengeance continues to glut itself upon its political victims; and large numbers of persons of wealth and rank, including, it is said, many not by any means prominent as Constitutionalists, are suffering the penalty of confiscation, banishment, or a dungeon, for acts committed, or for holding offices, under that system of government. The Constitutionalists thus most impolitically driven to revenge or despair are stated to be making efforts on the adjacent coasts of Africa to organise another expedition to regain their liberties.

GREECE.—The reports from Greece state that a considerable victory had been gained by the Patriots over the fleet of the chief admiral of the Porte, Ibrahim Pasha, in the neighbourhood of Candia, whither the Turkish fleet it is said was bound to take in troops to invade the Morea. Subsequent reports allege that Ibrahim was encouraged to this rash attempt in consequence of having gained over the son of Colocotroni, one of the Greek generals; but it is added that the treachery being discovered, the mutinous troops were vanquished and their leader put to death. The whole account, however, is very vague.

UNITED STATES.—The President's Speech exhibits a glowing description of the condition of the country. The native population are increasing, commerce, manufactures, agriculture and inland trade flourish, and the naval, military and financial arrangements of the Union are in the most favourable condition. The foreign relations are spoken of as pacific, though some points remain unadjusted; among which we regret to state is the treaty with this country for the suppression of the slave trade, the Senate refusing to grant a mutual right of search on the shores of America, though the clause Mr Canning states had been proposed by the American ambassador himself, and the treaty containing it, and which conceded a similar right on our part on the shores of our West India colonies, had been conditionally ratified in London. We are happy however to add, that the President does not consider the difficulty of sufficient magnitude to defeat an object so near to the heart of both nations, and so desirable to the friends of humanity throughout the world.

MEXICO.—The constitution of Mexico has been adjusted upon a plan somewhat similar to that of the United States. General Victoria is chosen President, and General Bravo Vice President.

DOMESTIC

The only domestic article of public intelligence is the gratifying announcement of the determination of Government to recognize the independence of the South American States. The recognition extends hitherto only to Mexico and Columbia, but is expected to be applied speedily to Buenos Ayres, and to the other States as soon as their stability is considered as sufficiently demonstrated.

A bill of indictment preferred by the Attorney General of Ireland against Mr O'Connell, for constructive sedition contained in one of his speeches at the Catholic Board, has been thrown out by the Grand Jury, who consisted it is said, entirely of Protestants. The prosecution is thought to have been ill advised.—The Roman-Catholic opposition to the free distribution of the Scriptures appears to become more determined and systematic, as will appear from the following passages from the Annual Pastoral Charge of the Irish Roman Catholic prelates. We need make no comment on such a document.

In this church, dearly beloved brethren, you possess the fountain of all true knowledge, *and the tribunal where God himself presides. He speaks to you by the mouths of all her pastors, whom when you hear you hear him.* Never deviate from her decisions, *they are the decisions of the Holy Ghost* who governs her, and always preserves the purity of her doctrine.

Our Holy Father recommends to the observance of the faithful a rule of the Congregation of the Index, which prohibits the perusal of the sacred Scriptures in the vulgar tongue without the sanction of the competent authorities. His Holiness wisely remarks, *that more evil than good is found to result from the indiscriminate perusal of them, on account of the malice or infirmity of men.* In this sentiment of our head and chief we fully concur, and a sad experience of its justice is found in the excesses and conflicting errors of those sects amongst whom such perusal is unrestrained. With us it is not so, and approved versions of the holy Scriptures, with notes explanatory of the text, are read by many of you with edification and advantage. We rejoice, dearly beloved, that the Word of God should dwell abundantly with you, it is useful to teach, to reprove, to correct, to instruct in justice, and when read with piety and devotion, especially in families and at the time of prayer, it assists the man of God whose heart is humble and whose understanding is captivated to the obedience due to Christ and to his holy church, to become perfect, and to be furnished unto every good work. But as heresies have arisen, and perverse doctrines ensnaring souls and precipitating them into the abyss, have been broached only when the good Scriptures have been badly understood, and when that which was badly understood was rashly and boldly asserted, it is necessary that such passages as are hard to be understood, and which the ignorant and unsettled daily wrest to their own perdition, be always received in that sense which the church of God has assigned to them, and which is the same that she has been taught by the Holy Ghost.

As to the books which are distributed by the Bible Society under the names of Bibles or Testaments or tracts or whatsoever name may be given to them, as they treat of religion, and are not sanctioned by us, or by any competent authority in the Catholic Church, the use, the *perusal,* the *reading,* or *retaining of them, is entirely and without any exception, prohibited to you.* To enter into their merits or demerits is foreign to our purpose, such of them as have come under our observation are replete with errors, many of them are heretical, and generally they abound in calumnies or misrepresentations against our holy religion; as such they are carefully to be avoided, and should any of them happen to be in your possession, they are to be restored to the persons who may have bestowed them to you, or otherwise to be destroyed, except only Bibles or Testaments which if not returned to the donors are to be deposited with the parish priest.

Such books have been, and ever will be *execrated by the Catholic Church,* and hence those salutary laws and ordinances whereby she has at all times prohibited her children to read or retain them, nay why she has frequently ordered them to be *committed to the flames.*

Two documents have been widely circulated in the public journals, to which we think it right to call the attention of our readers, especially as some of them may not have seen the official disclaimers which they have respectively called forth. The first was a petition of a Moravian missionary in Barbadoes to the House of Assembly, couched in a spirit of hostility to the anti-slavery proceedings so interesting to every true Christian and friend of humanity, and insinuating that the missionaries of other denominations had acted in a disloyal and unchristian spirit, and brought disgrace upon their profession. The second is a series of resolutions passed at a meeting of Wesleyan missionaries in Jamaica, in a similar spirit, warmly panegyrising the colonists and as warmly reprobating the conduct of the abolitionists Of the former an official disavowal has been published stating the pain of the United Brethren that other missionaries should have been disparaged or their own applauded by invidious comparisons and adding that a remonstrance had been sent out to the offending party which would be followed up by his removal The disavowal of the Methodist society is still more strongly explicit, and embraces some points which we could have wished had been touched upon in the Moravian disclaimer especially at a time when an appeal is being made to the public to contribute to a fund for enlarging their West India missions The whole document does great honour to the members of the Methodist society and we feel great pleasure in copying the following passages which we recommend to the serious consideration of all the friends of Christian missions

In particular the Committee are imperatively called upon by this unguarded and improper act of a very few of the missionaries employed by the society in Jamaica, to object:

First, to the equivocal manner in which the persons who passed the said resolutions declare their belief that Christianity does not interfere with the civil condition of Slaves as Slavery is established and regulated by the laws of the British West-Indies If no more were meant by this than that all slaves brought under the influence of Christianity are bound by its precepts to obey their masters and submit to the authorities of the state conscientiously and constantly this is no more than the missionaries have been explicitly instructed to teach and which the Committee sacredly enjoin upon them to inculcate upon all to whom their ministrations may extend but if it was intended as a declaration that the system of slavery as established in the West Indies or any where else is not inconsistent with Christianity the Committee, and the Wesleyan body whose name the framers of the resolutions have thus presumed to use without any authority whatever hold no such opinion but whilst they feel that all changes in such a system ought to emanate solely from the legislature they hold it to be the duty of every Christian government to bring the practice of slavery to an end as soon as it can be done prudently safely and with a just consideration of the interest of all parties concerned and that the degradation of men merely on account of their colour and the holding of human beings in interminable bondage are wholly inconsistent with Christianity

Secondly That the Committee feel bound in justice to disavow the sweeping charge made against persons in this country comprehended under the general term of Emancipatists and Abolitionists in the said resolutions, as written under evident ignorance of the opinions on that subject which are held in this country by those excellent and benevolent men who have of late most distinguished themselves by advocating the amelioration of the slaves in the West-India colonies with a view to the ultimate extinction of slavery The Committee conducting the Wesleyan missions take no part in such discussions as not being embraced by their one object which is to extend the benefits of Christian instruction among the Black and Coloured population of the colonies but they can never permit any of their missionaries to use their name and the name of the Wesleyan body in casting censures upon many of the most excellent of their fellow countrymen by representing them as holding sentiments on the subject of the emancipation of slaves and forming designs which if carried into effect would produce the consequences enumerated in the very unguarded and blameable resolution referred to The character and objects of the persons to whom allusion is there made are too well known by the Committee for them to suffer such unjust recollections to be given to the world in their name and not strongly to censure the said missionaries for thus adopting the language of violent party men

Thirdly That the Committee have read with great grief the very blameable language of the fourth of the said resolutions though they consider the whole to be the production of a very few only of the missionaries in Jamaica two of whom had been placed by the last Conference under censure one being recalled and the other removed from that island, for the manner in which they had surrendered themselves to the party feelings excited there in opposition to the measures of his Majesty's Government and the proceedings of the British Parliament and that so far from that resolution speaking the language of the Wesleyan body as it most unwarrantably professes that body whilst it has exerted itself for nearly forty years to promote the instruction of the Slaves of the West Indies and to render them mo ral and peaceable and has always distinguished itself at home and abroad by its inculcation of the principles of entire obedience to masters magistrates and all other legal authorities yet, after the example of its venerable founder who was among the first, by his writings to lift up his voice against that long continued national sin, the Trade in Slaves has ever regarded the system of slavery as a moral evil from which the nation was bound ultimately to free itself and throughout the kingdom has hailed with the greatest gratitude and satisfaction, the incipient measures adopted by his Majesty's Government, for ameliorating the condition of that class of their fellow subjects These are measures which as a *religious* body they have felt a deep interest in, not as connecting religion with politics as stated in the resolution but as they are essentially connected with the promotion of religion and morals, by regulations which refer to the observance of the Sabbath, to the marriage of slaves, and to their general protection.

The Committee, attentive only to the spiritual concerns of the missions confided to their management, would not have thus entered upon these topics had they not been forced upon them by the publication of the resolutions in question.

It was our intention to have offered a few observations on two recent trials in one of which an actor and in the other an actress of theatrical celebrity were conspicuous parties as forcibly shewing how little the stage either is or is ever likely to become practically what its admirers affect to call it, a school for virtue But our limits forbid the discussion and we would trust it is not necessary—certainly not to those who take the Scriptures as their standard of morals and who seriously pray not to be led into the temptations of the world the flesh and the devil

OBITUARY

WILBERFORCE RICHMOND
Died on Sunday January 16, aged 18, Wilberforce Richmond second son of the Rev Legh Richmond of Turvey He was a youth of much promise He possessed strong intellectual faculties and had acquired very considerable knowledge in various departments of study But above all he had a deep acquaintance with the word of God, which was eminently blessed to his soul and enabled him to depart in perfect peace leaving behind him a bright train of evidences that his Saviour had prepared a place for him in the mansions of his heavenly Father

ANSWERS TO CORRESPONDENTS

J S G B BLWT E G Candidus E J B Spes F R T J E O E F G H and some papers without signature are under consideration

We are very much obliged to our correspondent B G B for having drawn our attention to the terms in which in our last Number we expressed our opinion of the duty of abstinence from slave grown sugar We admit them to have been much too absolute and unqualified—much more so than we intended a circumstance which must be ascribed to the hurry of the closing hour of publication What we meant to say was this that it is the duty of Christians to do what may be in their power to put an end to slavery—that in order to effect this, it is highly expedient to discourage the use of slave grown sugar and to encourage that produced by free labour—and that therefore all practicable means should be resorted to, of carrying into effect this distinction We did not intend, by representing the use of slave grown sugar as sinful in itself to frame any snare for tender consciences but we were anxious to lead our readers carefully to consider what each in his station could do by giving encouragement to free-grown sugar and discouragement to slave grown sugar in contributing his aid to that most desirable consummation the termination of slavery in the British dominions We intend to explain ourselves at greater length on this important subject probably in our next Number

THE CHRISTIAN OBSERVER.

No. 278.] FEBRUARY, 1825. [No. 2 Vol. XXV

RELIGIOUS COMMUNICATIONS

For the Christian Observer.

ON THE SUPERIORITY OF THE SCRIPTURES, AS PRESENTING A RULE OF ACTION THE BEST, FOR THE INTEREST AND HAPPINESS OF SOCIETY.

(*Continued from p.* 10.)

THE justice of the Divine precepts comes next under notice. According to the meaning of the term in the sacred language, justice is the equal poising of a balance. It is to give a full weight, an exact compensation. There is, as it were, a balance to weigh our actions: when they are of full weight, they are just; when they are wanting, they are not just. But our present consideration is to examine whether there is justice in the injunctions of the Bible; whether the balance in which our conduct is weighed is a right balance.

To revert a moment to what has been already in a measure discussed, let the justice of the first table of the Ten Commandments be considered. Some persons complain of their strictness. But are their requirements more extensive than the just demands of a Creator, or than the just debt of a creature? Are the love of the whole heart, and the obedience of the whole conduct, more than what is due to Him whose we are, from whom we have derived our very existence? Does not an entire dependence on another most justly require an entire submission to his will? But these demands, it is alleged, are incompatible with our interest, and destructive to our happiness. If by interest is meant, what the mere man of the world understands by that term, and by happiness, that only which results from sensual and illicit pleasures, there is some truth in the sentiment; but who would admit this as a valid objection? In this world sin has evidently a wide dominion, a mighty influence; hence there prevail injustice, oppression, and a continued opposition to every thing that is good. Obedience therefore to God does not meet with popular approbation, but rather displeasure; and through the enmity of a world which lieth in wickedness, our temporal interest may at times in some degree be injured, or worldly losses sustained, for the "sake of the Gospel." But these inconveniences are, in comparison, but 'for a moment.' And is it right to violate the plainest and strongest obligations, that a temporary interest may be secured, to deny our Creator, for the purpose of conciliating the favour of sinful creatures? So much for the appeal to our supposed interest: then as to the other objection, that the Divine precepts are destructive to happiness—does not such an objection argue a state of mind utterly degraded and unbecoming a rational being? What, to love and serve the Most High injurious to the enjoyments of a creature, formed by his hands, and after his image! Has the Almighty made any thing more worthy to be loved than himself? Is there greater value, or beauty, or grandeur, in the things that are made than in Him who made them? Is there any thing or any being, which man is under greater obligations to serve than his Maker? Is there any created source from which he can derive blessings so numerous as those bestowed upon him by his Almighty Benefactor? How then is it, that to love and serve God is not viewed by him as promoting his truest felicity? There must be something wrong, something awfully defective in such a state of the understanding and affections. God is unchangeably the same, the highest, the best, the most glorious Being, infinitely good in himself, and conferring bliss on all his subjects. The defect then must be in man, and it must be a defect of a very serious nature that the only source of real and lasting happiness is not the object of his affections, that the idea of his presence, the contemplation of his character, love to his name and regard to his honour are not favourable to his enjoyments. To think it right, or reasonable, that a being endowed like man should fix on objects of delight which he cannot enjoy while retaining a sense of the Divine presence, is contrary to every notion that can be formed of the relation between the Creator and the creature, contrary to the essential properties and necessary claims of the one, and to the dependent condition and incontrovertible obligations of the other. So far is it from being unjust, that man should be required, according to revealed truth, to love God supremely and to serve him principally, that it would have been highly unjust to require less from him. There is no view of God in his character as the only God, nor any of man in his character as man, the creature and subject of the Almighty, but proves and establishes the justice of this first and great commandment. He who is the Lord of all, ought in justice to be served above all. He who is the most eminent in dignity, glory, wisdom, and goodness, ought in justice to be supremely loved; and this, not only because it is in every respect due to himself, but also because it is due to the real interest and well being of man, inasmuch as his real and permanent good can in no other way be effectually secured, God alone being capable of making him truly and lastingly happy.

The conduct of one man towards another is also prescribed in the sacred writings, and, as we maintain, with equal justice to all. Nothing more than what is just is exacted, nor will any thing less suffice. The balance between man and man is held perfectly level, with no leaning to any particular rank or situation in life. The duties imposed are reciprocal, what is required of one, is required also of another; and even where there is a difference in the station which creates a corresponding difference in the duties, reciprocity still remains. A return is to be made, though not by the performance of the same offices, yet by the performance of others suitable to individual circumstances. The rich are to be liberal, while the poor are to shew respect and gratitude. The duty of the ruler is to afford security and protection, that of the subject, to submit to lawful authority. According to the Bible there is to be an equal and mutual interchange of good offices.

The substance of our mutual obligations is contained in that single sentence, *Love thy neighbour as thyself*; and being a universal precept binding equally on all, injustice is excluded. The only conceivable objection against the strictness of the precept is, that it may be alleged to require *more* than simple justice, that to love others as ourselves is more than what is right, that it is inconsistent with our individual interest, with the duty of providing for ourselves and our families. This opinion is false as well as selfish, it proceeds from a narrowness of heart and is grounded on a misconception of the duty. A view of our connexion with one common Father and with each other as brethren, partakers of the same nature, endued with the same feelings, and possessing the same immortal principle, should surely exclude a sentiment so unworthy. Besides, the observance of the precept is by no means injurious to individual interest: to love others as ourselves does not require us to spend our time and labour as much in their behalf as in our own; but only that in all our intercourse with them, we should consult their advantage as much as our own. Every individual has a business belonging to himself to which he is more particularly to attend; a business which, while advantageous to himself, is also beneficial to society. In the prosecution of this he will come in contact with his fellow creatures, who are also engaged in concerns of their own. But whenever his affairs intermingle with theirs, an equal regard must be had to the welfare of each: it is not sufficient that no direct injustice should be offered; if the circumstances of others command a fair advantage, that advantage must be freely conceded; if by a hint or advice, or by exertions consistent with our own obligations, without a greater injury to ourselves, any loss on their part may be prevented, or any benefit obtained, that hint, that advice, those exertions must not be withheld. We are to *bear one another's burdens* while each has also a *burden of his own*. To relinquish or neglect our own affairs and to meddle unnecessarily with those of others would no doubt be exceedingly blameable; but no less so would it be to prosecute our own with no care for those of others, with no willingness or attempt to promote their welfare, and to promote it to the same extent as we would they should promote ours. Do as you would be done by, is the true meaning of the Divine precept. Had its demand been less, it would have been unjust and inconsistent with the condition of mankind.

The extent of this command may not appear to some reasonable, but it is so in the highest degree: and it is true, that it embraces within its compass the whole race of man, and every individual of that race, whatever may be his parentage, connexions, or character, whether a Negro or a White man, Jew or Gentile, bond or free, high or low, enemy or friend; and it is true, also, that in no cases are its obligations suspended, and that no pleas are allowed for neglecting the performance of them. As long as any man is our fellow creature, living in the same state, existing under the same circumstances, partaking of the same indulgences from the Sovereign of all, enjoying the gracious offers of the same blessings and of the same eternal inheritance, however unworthy he may make himself of his name and of his privileges he is still our neighbour, and we are bound to love him as ourselves. No less than this is evidently the extent of the Divine command; for, to remove every doubt that could possibly arise it is expressly enjoined, that we should *love our enemies, bless them that curse us, do good to them that hate us, and pray for them that despitefully use us and persecute us.* So that no neglect of duty on the part of our neighbour, is an excuse for neglect on ours. The reason is evident: the obligations of the command do not arise from mutuality of offices, but from an irreversible connexion or relationship, and from the expressed will of our common Parent.

The Gospel records and proposes for our imitation, a most extraordinary example of the love which we owe to one another. So great was the love of Jesus Christ to his brethren, the whole race of man, that he laid down his life for them. He laboured, he toiled, he lived, he died for their good. Following the steps of this great Exemplar an Apostle has declared, that he was 'willing to spend and be spent in the service of his brethren; and that he should joy and rejoice were he to be 'offered upon the sacrifice and service of their faith;' had he been poured out as a libation, while engaged in preparing them as a holy sacrifice unto God, rendered acceptable through the merits and mediation of his Son. Concurring with these examples are the following injunctions *Seek not your own. Look not every man on his own things but every man also on the things of others. We ought not to please ourselves let every one of us please his neighbour for his good to edification.* Are these demands too rigid? They are but the obligations which arise from the duty of doing to others what we would expect they should do unto us. Were you in distressing circumstances ready to be overwhelmed with their pressure, would you not justly expect assistance from those around you, provided they were able to afford it, though it should be in some degree to their loss and disadvantage? *Mete* therefore to others *with the same measure* with which you would have them mete to you. As we often cross our own immediate wishes for our greater benefit, we ought to do the same for the benefit of our neighbour and it is a sacrifice which never fails to bring with it its own reward.

But the enlargement which this duty has received from the Gospel, arises from the more clear and perfect views which that dispensation presents of the future destiny of mankind. It is there enforced, not merely with regard to our present, but more particularly to our eternal condition. The love required is not so much to be regulated by temporal considerations, as by those which are co extensive with eternity. To love others as ourselves demands more than the doing of such temporal good as we, in return, would expect in similar circumstances we should also regard and promote their eternal good to the same extent as we think they should regard and promote ours. The whole compass of man's existence should be always borne in mind together with his awful and hazardous destiny. Whenever these are lost sight of, there is an essential defect in our views, and, of necessity a corresponding defect in our conduct. What ought to be nearest our heart, as it is beyond comparison the greatest in importance, is the future, the eternal welfare of our species. By opening the gates of immortality the extent of this duty has been almost immeasurably enlarged. Man, as a creature that is ever to exist, is a being of the highest consideration, whose worth is incalculable. To confine his existence to the narrow span of the present life, is to reduce him to meanness and insignificance, to put him on a level with the 'beasts that perish' but to view him as destined to live for ever, is to increase his value and importance beyond all human calculation. Every office of love should be regulated by a regard, not to present merely, but to eternal things for to beings who are to exist for ever their present compared with their eternal interest is but the dust of the balance. Weighed in the scales of heaven, whatever is calculated to promote our well being only during a life which is as a vapour that vanisheth away, opposed to what is to continue for ever, or is necessary to secure our eternal well being is 'less than nothing and vanity.' This view accounts for a course of conduct which has often surprised the world, and has met with the severest reproaches and censures and been calumniated as folly and madness. There have been those to whom no worldly sacrifices have appeared too great, that they might advance the eternal welfare of their fellow creatures. Present comforts have been yielded up, temporary losses have been willingly sustained, and even life itself most freely hazarded, that they might benefit immortal souls that they might be the instruments of securing to others blessings that never fade of preventing losses not to be calculated, and obtaining life that shall never end. All this is inexplicable to one who does not comprehend in his survey the world beyond the grave. But such sacrifices are no more than are consistent with that love which is due to an immortal being. The loss of temporal life can admit of no comparison with that of eternal and the least inconvenience or trouble undergone for the preservation of the life that now is is incalculably greater in proportion than the constant labour of thousands of years for the salvation of the immortal soul. To undergo then any temporary inconvenience that may be required, to hazard the loss not only of ease and comfort, but even of life, if necessary, for the purpose of advancing the eternal good of mankind, is no more than the obvious requisition of the law of love

The last and main point for our consideration is the tendency of the Divine law to promote the peace and happiness of society. Its character, as having God for its author, and as being impartial, complete, and just fully claims for it this distinction. But let its injunctions as they tend to accomplish this end, be examined for it is the great end which all who oppose the Gospel profess to have in view

All the evils that disturb and destroy the quiet of mankind arise from causes that lodge within the heart. Oppressions and cruelty, overreaching and defamation rapacity and ambition, all the hosts of evil lusts and vile passions have their fountain in that spiritual part of man, the principles and actings of which are not subject to human laws. Now the cause must be removed, before we can suspend the effect the first bubblings of the fountain must be restrained, otherwise its waters will be sure to overflow. If the principle of evil be entertained, it will not fail to work. Let ambition for instance be the ruling passion, and the lawfulness of the means for its gratification, if free from disgrace will be a consideration of no material influence. Some subtle mode will be invented to depreciate the merits of competitors, and to raise our own. To acquire the meed of valour, and to attain a wide extent of empire, how many lives have been sacrificed, how many cities depopulated, how many fertile countries made desolate! Similar, in different proportions, are the ravages and injurious effects of every unlawful passion. Aggression is in its very nature, and its ultimate effect is misery. To destroy the germ within, the first source of evil, no human means have ever been discovered. Much has been done to hinder its growth, to repress its rankness, to prune away some of its most obnoxious excrescences but to eradicate it has baffled the genius of all the philosophic race in all ages of the world. Learning has been in a degree beneficial reasons drawn from humanity and self advantage have considerable influence but what are these in efficacy in comparison with a belief in a Supreme Being who is omniscient and fills heaven and earth whose laws reach to the inmost motives and feelings taking of all a minute account to be hereafter produced at the great audit that is to determine our eternal condition. No human consideration, no sense of propriety no sympathy of nature no honour or advantage, no prospect of superior gratifications, either of body or mind, no regard for the dictates of the wise has a power to restrain the ebullitions of evil desires and bad principles equal to the devout and habitual consciousness of the presence of the Almighty. Considerations derived from present interest and advantage operate chiefly on the outward conduct on the branches of the tree but the law of the Omniscient operates on its very root it allows not the thoughts to harbour the evil it prohibits its first risings and it comes with the authority of Omnipotence, attended by His all scrutinizing eye an advantage which no other means of restraint possesses. To detach then the creature from the law of his Maker from a belief in the superintendence and government of the Almighty, is to remove the most powerful of all checks to his passions to translate, as it were, a disorderly multitude from the jurisdiction of an energetic and vigilant magistrate to the province of one notoriously pusillanimous and inefficient; a project which but too well accords with the love of vice, and anarchy, and wickedness.

Let the Divine law be still further considered as it regulates what is due from man to man, and we shall arrive at the same conclusion, that all its requirements and prohibitions have a powerful tendency to promote the general good. What is required but that which is necessary to obtain and communicate happiness? and what is forbidden but what is injurious to it? Its inculcations are in all respects suitable to a social being who receives benefits from his connexion with others, and is therefore bound to communicate them; and the restraints it lays on the passions and appetites are rendered necessary by the general welfare. In no respect is this law either superfluous or defective. Introduce into society what the Bible enforces and dispel from it what it prohibits, and you will at once remove all disorder and misery. Lessen its injunctions and slacken its restraints, and you will in proportion contribute to the continuance of these evils. The balance is so equally held between man and man, that if you add to or take away from either of the scales, you destroy the equilibrium, and thus cause injustice and interminable confusion. Individuals, who consult merely or chiefly their own interest, may complain of or object to this arrangement; but no objection will be made by those whose minds have been enlightened and their hearts expanded by the principles of the Gospel, under the sacred influence of its Divine Author, to entertain a noble and Christian regard for the common welfare of their species. There is no virtue but what the Divine word prescribes; there is no vice but what it denounces. The characteristic of its demands is love; of its prohibitions, hatred. The one produces union and happiness; the other, disorder and misery. Let this principle prevail, and there will be an end to injuries and dissensions within the sphere of its influence.

To dilate on all the virtues which the Divine word inculcates would be beyond the limits of this essay; but it may be said of them all, as far as respects our conduct to our fellow creatures, that goodwill, beneficence and patience under evils form their character and substance; and that their tendency is union, peace and happiness. The prevailing disposition or ruling principle is good will, which is to be manifested by beneficence, or deeds of kindness and charity, and also by patience under provocations and injuries. The sum of the whole is to be found in that comprehensive and beautiful passage, "Whatsoever things are true, whatsoever things are honest, whatsoever things are just, whatsoever things are pure, whatsoever things are lovely, whatsoever things are of good report; if there be any virtue, and if there be any praise, think on these things."

The law of retaliation is wholly discountenanced in the Gospel. Evil is not to be requited with evil, but with good; which is the best means of putting a stop to its progress. Not that there should be no judicial process when justice is denied to a fair remonstrance, and when it cannot be otherwise secured; for, inferior only to the honour of God is this in importance; and not only consistent with, but promotive of, that honour is at all times its prosecution when rightly understood. But this process should not be instituted or carried on from motives of personal revenge, or for the gratification of evil feelings; but from a desire to obtain justice and to promote the public benefit.

The injunctions of the Gospel are not repugnant to the rules suggested by self-love, which in a circumscribed sense is lawful, though generally it is not confined within due limits. This agreement is an evidence in favour of revealed truth, and an enlightened regard for our own welfare would suggest the very same regulations as those contained in the Scriptures. Even had there been no conscience to accuse, no God to offend, no punishment to endure, our own comfort and enjoyment in this world would require the observance of what the Divine word prescribes. Had we millions of persons under our controul, and felt an equal regard for the well being of every individual among them, setting aside an hereafter, what laws, but those of revelation, could we venture to recommend to their attention? Should we not say to them "Let love prevail, be of one mind bear ye one another's burdens promote the interest of others equally with your own be just in your transactions oppress not revile not defraud not do good to all, and harm to none if provoked or wronged recompense not evil for evil but requite evil with good.' Perfectly consistent with all this is a legal vindication of our own rights, and the duty of reproving offenders and correcting the retractory.

The wanton exposure of private faults has ever been reprobated, as a practice condemned by the common sense of mankind and destructive to the peace of society. There are indeed cases where publicity is necessary. When for example, advice and remonstrance fail, the very interest of the individual himself may in some instances require a disclosure but always according to our Saviour's direction, first to one then to two and, if without success then at length, to the whole church to the community at large. Still the improvement of the offender, and not his degradation should be the object. Public offences must be viewed rather differently. Being already known they should for the interest of society be openly exposed their criminality and mischievous effects should be pointed out and pressed on the attention of the public. This may be done by any individual who may feel it his duty but to do it well is a task of great difficulty. It is not every man who undertakes the office of a public censor, that is capable of duly discharging its duties. Infinitely greater mischief than good is done by many empirics in this department.

To expose public offences, either of individuals or of rulers, two qualifications are indispensable,—a predominancy of love for the general good, and a large measure of judgment. Where these are wanting, there is no fitness for the office. If envy or revenge be the motive, there will be a corresponding sourness of spirit, and the object will be abuse and not remonstrance reviling and not improvement. Some justify severe and abusive censures on the ground of their necessity. The disease being deeply rooted, strong measures, they say, must be applied. But, in answer, it may be said, that they may be strong and still stronger for the purpose, without being of this character. In most instances, owing to the perverseness of our nature, a perverseness common to all, severity rather increases than lessens the evil it is intended to amend. The impression on its object will be and on others too, that malice or some other hateful passion is the fountain from which it springs and thus it will lose its good effect. Hence the little success which scurrilous writers even though their cause should happen to be right, obtain among the more intelligent part of society. Their intemperate spirit and abusive personalities though highly pleasing to rude and demoralized minds are grossly offensive to men of information and virtuous principles. Abuses of long continuance, and the moral obliquity of which does not immediately appear, are more easily tolerated than the nauseous effusions of rancour and party spirit.

It is no less contrary to the Divine word 'to suffer sin in a brother,' than to condemn it in an improper spirit. One of the special objects of the Gospel is to expose the hidden things of darkness. To reprove is one of its precepts. Its advocates are called the light of the world, the salt of the earth, to shew that it is their duty to communicate intelligence to their fellow-creatures, and to season, as it were, their morals with wholesome instructions, and with prudent, and, if there be occasion, with pungent corrections. The poignancy of reproof proceeds from two things,—from its justness, and from the spirit in which it is given. If it be unjust, or coloured with exaggerated circumstances, it loses in proportion its effect. Unless it come accompanied with the appearance of good will, unless it bear on its very front the insignia of love, it will fail of its purpose. It must also proceed from the right quarter: the reprover should be, in some sense, the superior; though an equal or an inferior may justly complain or remonstrate. Much evil unattended with scarcely any good, has frequently resulted from an inversion, in this respect, of the due order of things. There are circumstances, indeed, which justify such an irregular proceeding. When those on whom the duty properly devolves neglect the discharge of it, and thus injure the community, rather than that the evil should continue and increase, let the scourge be applied by any hand that may feel itself equal to the task: only the disadvantage arising from inferiority of station, and seeming impropriety, will require the exertion of no common degree of prudence and moderation. The public good, however, renders it necessary that every public evil should receive its corrective, either by way of reproof, remonstrance, or advice; and in gross instances, even reprobation, or indignation may be lawfully employed. Specimens of such modes of reproof are found in the Scriptures.

From this brief review the powerful tendency of the Gospel to promote the general good of the community cannot but be clearly perceived. The very springs of action are regulated. It is forbidden us to harbour a spirit of self indulgence, or any injurious propensity. The exercise of love, and of every duty which results from it, is imperatively required; while hatred, and all its vile accompaniments, are peremptorily forbidden. Reproof, remonstrance, counsel, advice, and even severe reprehension, are to be administered according to the circumstances of each particular case. And to all this it may be added, that besides entertaining good will towards all, towards foes as well as friends, the sincerity of this good will must be shewn by imploring for others a blessing from above. One of the most efficient means for destroying animosities, and for promoting harmony and peace, is prayer. The very idea of God being our common Father, must have a very powerful influence in restraining evil feelings, and generating such as are benevolent; especially as it is connected with an express command that we should pray for all men, even for our enemies. It is surely impossible to approach the Throne of Divine Mercy with any sentiment towards our fellow creatures but that of love; and, by an intercourse with the great Fountain of all that is good and amiable, this love will be increased, and rendered more active in advancing the good of others. Another advantage also which results from the discharge of this duty, is that blessings may be procured for those in whose behalf the supplication is made; which, in addition to those *spiritual* benefits which are not immediately the subject of this essay, may render them more useful members of the community, more fit to enjoy and communicate the social comforts of life. Our heavenly Father will not be entreated in vain. The request of love, especially when so disinterested as to be offered for those who are inimical to us, will surely be accepted, and answered either in blessings on the individuals prayed for, or on him who offers the petition.

But it is time to close these ob

servations, the object of which has been to develop the excellency of the Gospel, in its effects upon the interests of society. There is no other system of professed morals that can bear the most distant comparison with it in this respect, all others being miserably defective in the most essential points. Even therefore setting aside its Divine authority and its bearings on our future well being it would be both wise and beneficent to promote its dissemination. The man whose character is formed on its principles is the most efficient promoter of the public welfare, for he will be benevolent and disinterested in his actions, self denying in his indulgences, conciliatory in his spirit, firm and resolute in his principles, and diligent in the discharge of the duties of his station.

Let it not, however, be for a moment forgotten that these considerations, important as they are, are but the least part of the claims of Christianity upon our faith and love and veneration. The Christian is 'not ashamed of the Gospel of his Redeemer—not because of its moral, social and political benefits—but specifically because it is the power of God unto salvation unto every one that believeth.' This is a theme on which we might dwell with the highest admiration, the most devout gratitude, and justly has it employed innumerable tongues and pens to point out its grandeur and infinite value. The discussion of it by a mind equal to the subject—if, indeed any mind *were* equal to it—would form a most suitable counterpart to the preceding remarks; but, in an age of scepticism and proud philosophy the Christian must not disdain to exhibit to the confusion of the objector those momentous though but subordinate excellencies of the Gospel which should gain for it respect from those who are least inclined to estimate its value as the record of salvation to a fallen and guilty world.

K. G.

FAMILY SERMONS.—No. CXCIV*

Psalm xxvii. 4, 5.—*One thing have I desired of the Lord, and that will I seek after; that I may dwell in the house of the Lord all the days of my life, to behold the beauty of the Lord, and to inquire in his temple. For in the time of trouble he shall hide me in his pavilion in the secret place of his tabernacle shall he hide me; he shall set me upon a rock.*

It ought to be considered as one of the circumstances which give peculiar value to the holy Scriptures, that they unfold to us so much, not merely of the life, but of the mind of the servants of God, that they conduct us as it were, to the hidden springs of thought, feeling and action, and thus supply us with a standard to which we may bring the workings of our own souls. Such, amongst a multitude of other examples, is the character of the text which has been now read to you, and I shall proceed, in dependence upon the Divine blessing, to notice

I. The leading desire of the soul of David as here described.

II. The depth and earnestness of that desire.

III. The motive to which he traces it.

I. In the first place we are to consider the particular desire of David as stated in the text. "One thing," he says, "have I desired of the Lord, that I may dwell in the house of the Lord all the days of my life, to behold the beauty of the Lord, and to inquire in his temple."

If we have a real value for any individual, the pain of exclusion from his presence, and the joy of admission to it, are among the

---

* Our space for extracts from Mr Cunningham's interesting Discourses reviewed in our last Number having been more limited than we wished, we are happy in supplying the defect by selecting from his volume the following family sermon with only a few omissions in order to bring it within our usual bounds.

strongest emotions of the mind. And this is as true in religion as in any other affection of our nature. The man who is indifferent to his Redeemer feels no desire to approach his presence. The public and private worship of God, the study of his word, meditation upon his mercies, devout participation in his sacraments, which may be considered as so many steps of approach to the Divine presence, have no charms for such an individual. But, on the contrary, the servants of God, are said by the Psalmist, to "long after him, and to be "athirst for him,' as the "hart desireth the water brooks." And he illustrates, by an image of the greatest beauty, the joy and security of the soul which has reached this delightful presence. "The sparrow hath found an house and the swallow a nest for herself where she may lay her young, even thine altars, O Lord of hosts, my King and my God. Blessed are they that dwell in thy house, they will be still praising thee." But let us examine with more precision the object assigned in the text for this desire to approach God.

1. In the first place, it is the wish of the Psalmist, as he says, to "behold the beauty of the Lord." —And in every true servant of God the anxiety he feels thus to draw nigh to his God and Saviour is prompted in part, by a similar wish. The little which the servants of the Lord know of the Master they serve, fills them with anxiety to obtain a more intimate acquaintance with his dispensations and character. They search for him in his works—they contemplate him in his word—and charmed with the glories and beauties which develop themselves to the believing eye, they long altogether to rend away the veil which still darkens and perplexes the view and to "see as they are seen, and know as they are known."

2. But the desire of the Psalmist thus to dwell in the house of God was not prompted alone by the wish to behold the beauty of the Lord but also, as he adds, by a wish to "inquire in his temple."—In the real servant of God, the disposition to "behold his beauty" is always coupled with the wish to "inquire into his will." In all his approaches to the Throne of Grace, in taking up the Volume of Truth, in entering the courts of the Lord; in kneeling at the table of his Supper and, in short, in every moment of intercourse between Heaven and earth, he "inquires." He rejoices to escape from the ignorance and errors of man, to the wisdom of God, to learn, and to fulfil the will of Him who wheels the universe in its course, and fixes the destiny of its crowded inhabitants. Oh that such were the state of heart in every individual to whom I am speaking! that the inquiry were breathing in every soul and bursting from every lip, ' Lord, what is thy will concerning me?'—The instructions of the world will almost infallibly mislead you, the suggestions of your own heart will mislead you. God is the only safe and sufficient Guide of his creatures. The clue to all the perplexed labyrinth of duty is in his hands. Say to Him, in the words of another petitioner, "Open Thou mine eyes, that I may see the wondrous thing of thy law." and He will shed light over all your doubts, disclose to you the recesses of truth, give clearness to your views, decision to your judgment and confidence to your heart, he will stablish, strengthen, settle you, and make you his own for ever and ever.

II. But I come, secondly, to consider the depth and earnestness of this desire in the mind of David.

1. In the first place he says "One thing have I desired."—There were doubtless other gifts of God, for which as far as they were compatible with the will of the Lord concerning him the Psalmist wished. He desired health, competence, kind friends and an exemption from as many of the trials of life,

and the presence of as many of its comforts, as might be consistent with his soul's welfare. But this 'one thing,' the presence and favour of his God, a clearer view of his perfections, and a deeper acquaintance with his will, he desired with such emphasis and intenseness, that no other wish of the soul was to be compared with it. Religion was not with him one among many pursuits, many tastes, and many desires. This object he pursued the first, the last, and above all.—Can the same fact be stated with regard to any large number of those by whom we are surrounded? Most men have their one thing, their favourite object of pursuit. With some, it is money. with some, pleasure. with some, admiration. with some influence. With how few is it eternity! And yet how truly has it been said that 'nothing is of much real importance but eternity!'

2. But the strength of this desire in the mind of David, is marked by another expression of the text

that will I seek after.—If religion consisted exclusively in wishing and desiring, the number of real Christians would be greatly multiplied. Even that prophet who loved the wages of unrighteousness desired that his ' death might be " the death of the righteous, and his " latter end like theirs." But such desires may be even keenly felt without our possessing the frame of mind which is described in the text. We may covet a treasure, without setting ourselves to ' seek after it.' We may wish for the abundance of the harvest without having any disposition to cultivate the soil. How large is the number of idlers who put the wish for the act. who loiter through the stages of an unprofitable existence, and at last sink, astonished and confounded into the gulf, from which they have made no real and adequate effort to escape! ' That,' says David " will I seek after." May God put the same resolution into the mind of every individual amongst us! In that case, how many would ask for grace, who now sit idly expecting it! How many would strive to climb to heaven, who now seem to expect the heavens to bow down to them! How would the house of the Lord be thronged and our secret devotions multiplied! How would the history of the age of John be renewed, ' the kingdom of heaven is taken by violence,' — the violence of holy earnestness the violence of men who know but one object worth pursuing, and pursue that object with all their heart! How would all that is cold and dead in our nature like the bodies in the vision of bones when animated by the breath of the Lord awake and arise and go forth to the conflict with corruption and to the extension and establishment of the kingdom of God!

III. But I come now, in the third and last place to consider the motive to which the Psalmist traces this earnest desire to dwell in the house of the Lord

How distinct and beautiful is the language in which he describes the motives by which these desires after God have been mainly prompted! ' In the time of trouble he shall hide me in his pavilion. in the secret place of his tabernacle shall he hide me. he shall set me upon a rock.' David had formed too intimate an acquaintance, both with the difficulties of life and the corruptions of his own heart, to feel satisfied with a religion which did not provide for "the time of trouble" He had been persecuted by Saul. he had been driven from his throne by his own child. he had seen that child so dear to him even in spite of his rebellion, perish in the face of his enemies. he had especially, been rent to the inmost heart by the pangs of an accusing conscience, by an arrow drawn from the quiver of an insulted and angry God. Of what value, then, to him, was a Friend who could bear his burdens, draw the weapon of terror and remorse from the throbbing wound, and exchange the spirit of heaviness for the garments of joy! But all this his God had already done for him and all this he was sure the Lord would continue to do. Is there any man among us who will say he needs no defence, no shelter from the storms of life, no refuge from the guilt of sin, and the dominion of corruption? Let the individual thus exempted from the general lot and trials of his species pursue, if he sees fit, his course in proud independence of his God and Saviour. Let him go naked into the battle who needs no armour. But let us who feel and acknowledge ourselves to be weak, and guilty and miserable and lost, cry aloud, ' The Lord is my strength and shield; my heart trusteth in him, and I am helped.

Thou hast been my help, therefore in the shadow of thy wings will I rejoice.

In conclusion, if there is but " one thing," the presence or favour of God, which is worthy of eager and steady pursuit, how easily may the heart reconcile itself to the want or loss of those other things which we are sometimes disposed to covet even with feverish anxiety! Poverty or sickness, the desertion of friends, or their death, strike from under the man of the world all the props on which he has been accustomed to lean. But they cannot touch the " one thing " of the man of God, and therefore ought not deeply to affect his happiness. If you are heirs of the promises of God, it is your duty, as it is your privilege, to set the trials of life at defiance—to move in an atmosphere which they cannot reach—to live on the top of the mountain, without regarding the storm which rages beneath. Let us see in you a temper of mind corresponding with your privileges. When disappointment or affliction comes, let us see that you have entered the pavilion, or are seated on the rock; that you are calm where others are agitated, and cheerful where others are distressed. What ought to trouble the man to whom the Lord has said, " No weapon formed against thee shall prosper;" ' the Eternal God is thy refuge, and underneath are the everlasting arms?" Shall not our hearts reply, Thou hast been a strength to the poor, a strength to the needy in his distress, a refuge from the storm, a shadow from the heat; in the shadow of thy wings will I make my refuge, until the calamities be overpast?

In the next place, what an encouragement does the language of the text supply for the pursuit of that future world, which the mercy of God offers to the prayers and labours of his creatures!—When David spoke in the text of ' dwelling in the house of God all the days of his life,' it can scarcely be conceived that his view was confined to the imperfect approach of the soul to its Maker in this state of being. It is next to impossible, that, intimate as he was with the world of rest and glory, his soul should not look forward to the period when he should spread his wings, and flee away to the seats of tranquillity and joy. It is in that world alone, my Christian brethren, that we shall enjoy the presence of the Lord without interruption and without end. There, as on a height from whence all the passages of the life upon earth may be surveyed at a single glance, the triumphant Christian will discover the numerous instances in which grace has prevented and followed him, in which God has guided him by his counsel, before he " received him up into glory." There indeed, if a sincere servant of the Lord, you shall dwell in his house for ever.—dwell, not as here, in the porch of his temple, but in its deep and safe and bright recesses; not beside the throne of clouds, but the throne of glory; not in a world of probation, but of triumph, and of unmixed and unchanging joy. There our intercourse with God will no longer be fitful and transient. The spirit of devotion will never flag, or the light of love grow dim, or the sun of the Divine Presence go down. What a prospect to contemplate, and what a world to live for! May the Lord of all power and might make us meet for this bright inheritance!—Come thou "Desire of all nations, Thou in whom all the desires of thy people begin and terminate come and lift up our grovelling and reluctant souls to the world where Thou dwellest. Throw wide to us the doors of the house of many mansions so that even here we may catch a glimpse of its happy chambers and may finally take possession of them for ever. Plead for us at the Throne of Love, Thou who 'alone art worthy.' Clothe us in thy own merits, and 'present us faultless before the presence of his glory.' Help us, Thou "mighty to save" to 'overcome, and to sit down with thee in thy throne, as thou hast overcome, and art set down on the throne of thy Father.'

To the Editor of the Christian Observer.

IN your Number for December I perused with much pleasure the following passages:—

Now, assuredly there is the greatest possible difference, between *connecting* and *blending* two several operations: for, however the two operations of justification by the merits of Christ, and sanctification by His Spirit must be *always connected* together, more or less, in the same individual, yet we should object to that statement which led in any degree to *blend* them, or to make them even in appearance, one and the same act. Justification refers to the pardon of sin, and acceptance with God: sanctification is the implantation of holiness in the soul, &c. &c. But to *blend* them together we apprehend would be to compound things most essentially distinct: to lose sight, in effect, of the peculiar work of the Saviour, as a sacrifice for sin: and to depart from the clear language of holy Scripture, at least according to that interpretation which has been received by all sound Protestant confessions. We should in this case be reforming backwards, and retracing our footsteps to one of the most dangerous tenets of the Papists. Justification, in their corrupted divinity, was made synonimous with imparted and inherent holiness.

I take the liberty to refresh your memory by the above extract so perfectly consonant to the Articles, Homilies, and Prayers of our excellent church: and, having done so, I would ask, whether you have ever seen a work used all over England in our National Schools, entitled Catechetical Instruction, being an Account of the chief Truths of the Christian Religion, explained to the meanest Capacity: from the 13th page of which I extract the following question and answer:—

"Q. What are we to do on our part to *entitle* ourselves to the promises of eternal life?

"A. We must (g), by a lively faith in Christ, embrace the promises of eternal life (h), repent us of our sins and use our best endeavours to pay a constant (i) unfeigned (k) and universal (l) obedience to all the commands of GOD our Heavenly Father.

The references are excellent, and without doubt we must do all those things mentioned in the answer. But the question makes chaos come again: and in this case, as you say, sir 'are we not reforming backwards and retracing our footsteps to one of the most dangerous tenets of the Church of Rome?' ENTITLE ourselves! Surely a Papist must have written these words! They could not have been penned by any person who entered into the spirit of that truly scriptural declaration in one of our Homilies. Let us know our own works, of what imperfection they be, and then we shall not stand foolishly and arrogantly

(g) Acts xvi. 13. (h) Acts iii. 19. (i) 1 Tim. i. 5. (k) James ii. 10. (l) ii. 14 to the end of the chapter.

in our own conceits, nor challenge *any* part of justification by our own merits and works. How can any Church of England man think, that he on his part can *entitle* himself to the promises of eternal life, when he professes, and perhaps has signed his consent to, the plain and full meaning of the Article on justification, 'in its literal and grammatical sense, which says, 'We are accounted righteous before God only for the merits of our Lord Jesus Christ, by faith, and not for our own works and deservings. Eph. ii. 8, 9. Rom. iii. 20. Gal. ii. 16. The Society for promoting Christian Knowledge, in A View of the Articles of the Protestant and Popish Faith, justly says, 'The Council of Trent teaches, &c. &c. But the holy Scripture teaches, that we are justified freely by the grace of God, through the redemption which is in Christ Jesus. Rom. iii. 24. Surely sir, this venerable society will not permit our national schools unawares to be taught doctrines opposed to its own declarations, and to the Articles, Homilies, and Prayers of the Church of England, and above all, to the holy Scriptures; for instance, Rom. iii. 4. as quoted and explained by itself.

B. L. W. T.

To the Editor of the Christian Observer.

SUCH is the infirmity of our nature that it is not in our power to prevent distraction and interruptions of thought in our addresses to God. While the soul, even of the regenerate man himself, is immersed in matter, it will be sometimes too languid to raise its thoughts, or too volatile to fix them steadily upon Him who is the source of all beatitude. The Christian, therefore, should not disdain the smallest of those minor helps to devotion which good men in every age have found useful, or which the church has wisely prescribed. Of this kind is the liturgical exhortation, "Let us pray," the frequent recurrence of which, in our services, has been ofter objected to as vain, unmeaning, and tautologous. Similar exhortations have however been used and found serviceable, ever since the earliest times of the Christian Church. In the ancient Greek liturgies, the deacon was directed to cry aloud εκτενως δεηθωμεν 'Let us pray fervently.' and again, sometime after, εκτενεϲερον, 'Let us pray more fervently.' The Church of England has judiciously retained the substance of this admonition; and it would be well if every worshipper in our communion would keep in remembrance that it was inserted, as has been justly remarked "with this design, among others, to rally our undisciplined thoughts, to recal our straggling ideas, and to put us in mind, that we ought to be praying with an affectionate application.

R.

To the Editor of the Christian Observer.

DR. STEINKOPFF writes, during his late continental tour. Passing through Winterthur, I paid a visit to the principal supporters of an Auxiliary to the Zurich Bible Society and found it in a flourishing condition. On Palm Sunday the solemn ceremony of Confirmation takes place. This interesting opportunity was improved by the zealous clergyman for a public distribution of a copy of a well bound Bible to each of the young people. This was done for the first time in 1821; and it produced so good an effect, on both old and young, that they have since continued it.

Might not a similar practice be adopted with great advantage in our own country? The rite of Confirmation is exceedingly solemn; and if the impression which it is calculated to make were followed up by the gift of a copy of the sacred Scriptures, to which it would be desirable to add the Book of Common Prayer, the effect, we might hope, by the blessing of God, would be more permanent than is too often the case. The books could be furnished on cheap terms, from the Society for promoting Christian Knowledge, or from the Bible and Prayer book and Homily Societies and the expense might be paid in each parish out of the sacrament alms, which would be a much better appropriation of them than either devoting them as is too often the case at present, in such a way as to minister to an abuse of the holy communion, by inviting improper communicants for the sake of the expected gratuity, or distributing them as customary alms to the increase of the baneful spirit of pauperism, and dependence upon charity. Should, however, this appropriation be objected to, other means might easily be devised in most parishes for raising the small sum required for the purpose. All the candidates, except the poorest, might be reasonably expected to make a donation at least equal to the pecuniary value of the gift. The books might be distributed with due solemnity by the minister from the altar on the Sunday after the confirmation, with the name of the parties, the date, and the occasion inscribed in them, " for a perpetual memorial before the Lord" to themselves and their children. If the bishop himself would distribute them at the time of the confirmation, and the books were considered as his paternal gift, the impressiveness of the custom would be greatly increased.

S.

MISCELLANEOUS

For the Christian Observer.

OBSERVATIONS ON THE CHARACTER OPINIONS, AND WRITINGS OF THE LATE LORD BYRON.*

AMONG the maxims which pass current in society, without much examination, few are more common than one which prescribes that nothing

The short extracts inserted in these papers are taken either from the valuable memoir of Lord Byron by the late Mr Dallas edited by his son or from the Conversations of Captain Medwin. This last work has been convicted of a few minor inaccuracies but nothing has occurred to shake the general credit due to its contents which indeed appear confirmed by a weight of internal evidence. All allusion to anecdotes of domestic scandal and dissolute intrigue I have of course carefully avoided as well as whatever might give needless pain to a single individual. Had Captain Medwin been governed by this caution he might have rendered his work less generally entertaining but he would have made it more acceptable to the Christian reader.

Since writing the above I have seen the philippic which has been levelled by the Westminster Reviewers at the deceased Mr Dallas the living Mr Dallas and Captain Medwin. Without entering into particulars on the subject I will content myself with asking two plain questions 1 Are the alleged facts of an anonymous writer to be set above the statements of authors who give their names and who (at least hitherto) have done nothing to forfeit their characters with the public? 2 Supposing some of the alleged facts of the nameless reviewer to be real facts still are they of such a nature as to impeach the veracity of the individuals attacked? and may they not fairly be classed among those minor inaccuracies which leave the general credit due to a work unimpaired? Have the Westminster Reviewers never heard of what Paley calls "substantial truth under circumstantial variety?" Till these questions are answered I think I have a right to consider the statements of the accused persons correct at least on points in which they could not well have erred but through intention. It is singular that while the Westminster Reviewers are accusing Captain Medwin of the utmost malice against Lord Byron's posthumous reputation there are many I believe who have risen from his work with a more favourable impression of his lordship's character than they had entertained before and that this slanderous reviler (Captain Medwin) should have written of the noble

but what is favourable should be spoken of the dead "De mortuis nil nisi bonum" Dr Johnson used to express his disapprobation of this maxim, and to propose the following emendation "Let nothing but what is good be spoken of the living and of the dead nothing but what is true" But perhaps it will admit of further improvement still or rather another maxim may be substituted in its room—"Let nothing but what is at once consistent with truth, propriety, and public advantage, be written or reported of either the dead or the living"

The maxim in question evidently means, that, when we cannot speak well of the departed, we should hold our peace for to maintain that bad characters should be justified or excused, because they are no longer able to do harm, would be an outrage upon truth, virtue, and common sense The maxim itself doubtless springs from a humane and kindly feeling, and proceeds upon some one or other of the following suppositions —either that death has atoned for the evil done by the departed or that having gone to their last account, they are no longer proper subjects of human judgment or that there is injustice, and even cruelty, in speaking to the disadvantage of those who are no longer in a condition to defend themselves or, lastly, that such conduct may wound the feelings of surviving relatives and friends

With regard to the first of these suppositions, it is surely among the number of those "vulgar errors which have a dangerous tendency" That death can furnish any such atonement—(I mean, of course, *atonement with respect only to society*)—as should enforce silence respecting a person's faults or vices, seems a position equally inconsistent with reason and with Scripture An atonement is an *expiatory equivalent* and it is difficult to conceive how the mere removal of one, who has widely injured society, can operate as a compensation for the injuries he has committed In the case of enormous crimes indeed, death is the only compensation which can be given and, so far as it tends to prevent the commission of such crimes in future, may be considered as making some, though by no means equivalent, amends For not unfrequently, the vices and long impunity of the criminal while living, have done far more to corrupt or ruin others, than the recollection of his punishment, when dead, can effect towards repairing the injury

Again some appear to think that individuals, who have been summoned to their last account are no longer proper subjects of human judgment an objection which may be easily obviated The word *judgment* is here manifestly equivocal In noticing the errors of the departed, we form no judgment respecting their actual state in another world but only with regard to the general tenor of their conduct in the present and to affirm that *this* is not within the province of human judgment, or that it may not be sometimes fully justified, and even required, by the circumstances of the case, is to advance positions which surely cannot be maintained

The next supposition that the deceased is not in a capacity to defend himself has evidently no force except in those cases where the reflections on his conduct are founded on very doubtful evidence, or on vague reports to his disadvantage which might have been cleared up by further explanation on his own part It must be admitted that no observations, which come strictly under this description should be revived against the dead But, in remarks on the obvious tendency of

---

author and his works in such terms as the following — No writings tend more to exalt and ennoble the dignity of man That he was not perfect who will deny? But how many men are better? How few have done more good and less evil in their day? —If this were not written with an air of complete seriousness we might conclude this ingenious author to be an adept in irony

an author's writings, on facts which admit of no double or doubtful interpretation, on dispositions, habits, and opinions, acknowledged both by enemies and friends, there can surely be no injustice. Nor ought there to be any suspicion of improper and malevolent motives, provided the best interests of society justify such remarks. Whatever may be the case in other parts of the world,

ENGLISH vengeance wars not with the dead.

The last objection, that the revival of the errors and vices of a deceased person may wound the feelings of surviving relatives and friends, is unquestionably of great weight, and should always operate to prevent that needless disclosure of the faults of *private* individuals, which is a common meaning of the word *scandal*. Even, with regard to those whose offences are notorious it should frequently produce forbearance for a time. But were this forbearance to be extended beyond the then living generation, it would manifestly deprive us of much of the profit to be derived from good history and biography those great teachers of wisdom and invaluable recorders of the results of experience. Beyond this term the characters of *public men* at least must always be considered as *public property* and sometimes they may become so within a shorter period. This may be the case, when the probability of great moral and religious advantage, likely to be gained by proper remarks on their characters, very far overbalances that of distressing others. Where individuals have been much and justly spoken of to their disadvantage while living, the continuance of similar remarks, after death, can offer no severe shock to the feelings of surviving friends while it may often afford lessons of salutary instruction. And when their own friends and admirers come forward with a display of their characters, the public are surely warranted in drawing useful reflections and inferences from the picture. If they are exhibited in false colours of excellence, they may lawfully be stripped of the borrowed plumes and, if they are shewn to greater disadvantage than their admirers desire, they can hardly be said to be wronged, so long as the corrective remarks are conducted in a spirit of truth, candour, and charity.

This, after all, is the main point to be considered. Observations on the errors of the departed, even when justified by the end in view, must still be offered in a spirit of Christian philanthropy.

Such a disposition of mind will ever lead the Christian to regard the offences of his brother, not indeed always without some mixture of just indignation but still more in sorrow than in anger. It teaches him to look within and suspect himself, with the humble piety of the great Boerhaave who, whenever he heard of a criminal condemned to death, used to say "Who can tell whether this man is not better than I? Or, if I am better, I owe it to the goodness and grace of God. It confines itself chiefly to *facts* and *tendencies*, and always spares *motives*, except in instances where they are too plain to be misinterpreted. Above all, it presumes not to determine the *actual state* of even the most apparently criminal. It leaves men to the judgment of their God. It "hopeth all things" and would not willingly discard the possibility even against probability, that, as Cowper says, something unseen by others may have passed between the sinner and his Maker, even at the eleventh hour and that the sacrifice and merits of the Redeemer may have blotted out his offences before God though they cannot remain forgotten or unnoticed by his fellow men.

Thus, whatever respect may be felt for those particular feelings in which the maxim in question may have originated little regard is due to the maxim itself whenever the observance of it would tend to be tray the paramount interests of Christian piety and virtue.

The bearing of these remarks on the subject of the late Lord Byron's character and writings, is sufficiently obvious. He was an individual who must and will be spoken of. He performed a part so conspicuous and prominent as to have irresistibly attracted the eyes of mankind towards him. His poetry lives, and some of it will always live, the memorial of his genius, *ære perennius*, more durable than brass or marble. His character was before the world, with little attempt at concealment on his own part. So well was he known to the public during life, that he had few frailties which could be 'drawn from their dread abode in the tomb.' In short, if any man's character may be accounted *public property*, and a fit subject for general animadversion, that of the late Lord Byron may surely be so considered.

In the judgments formed respecting this extraordinary personage, two opposite errors seem to have prevailed, of which, however, the first argues the greatest want of right and religious feeling. Many have allowed their admiration of his genius to bias their opinions in favour of his general character. Without pretending to justify him, which would be quite impossible, some have been disposed to ascribe his delinquencies as an author to a partial derangement of intellect, a very convenient supposition, by which the greatest enormities may be excused and palliated as readily as the most venial faults. In first rate genius there is an overpowering splendour apt to dazzle and delude those whose Christian or merely moral feeling is less acute than their relish of intellectual enjoyment. Others there are who, looking principally to the tendency of much of his poetry, have spoken of him not as a faultless monster, but as a monster of iniquity such as the world never saw, or scarcely saw before. This too is an extreme which ought to be avoided, for, unhappily, the annals of literature exhibit individuals quite as depraved as was Lord Byron. I honour Dr Southey as much as any man, for that noble protest in behalf of religion and morality which, it is said, made Lord Byron turn pale with anger and conscious guilt; but I do not think it necessary to tie myself down to Dr Southey's taste, or to adopt all the images which his fancy may have conjured up from beneath.

That the late Lord Byron possessed some good qualities, upon which a wise and pious education might, by Divine Grace, have operated most beneficially for himself and for the world, few probably will deny; and in order that I may not be suspected of a desire to cast one needless stone of reproach at his posthumous reputation, I shall begin with noticing the fairer aspect of his character.

There is no evidence that Lord Byron originally wanted those social and amiable qualities which, under more favourable circumstances, might have rendered him an ornament to society. If he could be a bitter and implacable enemy, he could be likewise a warm and active friend. If his pride and irritability were in arms against all who disputed his real or fancied merits as a writer, he was easy, kind, and familiar with those who courted his acquaintance and acknowledged his superiority. The late Mr Dallas was, on some occasions at least, his friend in the best sense; and Lord Byron, though at last he shook him off for reasons that will be noticed hereafter, seems during much of their intercourse in this country to have treated him with kindness and respect. If he appears a misanthropist in his writings, his personal conduct frequently betokened humanity and benevolence. He is described as very kind to his domestics; and the account seems confirmed by the fidelity and affection of the servant who attended him in his last moments, and who had been long about his person. The strenuous foe of persecution, he used his utmost efforts to deliver a poor wretch at Lucca from the horrors of the inquisition. He also signalized himself by more than one bold attempt at the hazard of his life to save a fellow creature from destruction. But his support of the Greeks forms perhaps the best feature of his character. In this he rose above the influence of vanity or selfish motives, and abandoned himself to the impulse of a generous and philanthropic enthusiasm. Had his life been continued, may we not charitably conjecture that, having once found a worthy and noble object for the activity of his restless spirit to feed upon, he would have endeavoured to fix his reputation on some better grounds than those of genius debased and mental superiority perverted?

In the course of his conversations as related by Captain Medwin, we meet occasionally with gleams of benevolent feeling and a better mind. He was considerably affected for the moment by the piety of a deceased lady whose husband had sent him a prayer she had composed and offered up in her last illness for his conversion*

The circumstance here alluded to may deserve a more distinct narration. It is related in the following letter inserted by Mr Sheppard in the second edition of his excellent Thoughts on private Devotion lately published. Mr Sheppard writes as follows to Lord Byron at Pisa.

My Lord From Som t No 21 1821
More than two years since a lovely and beloved wife was taken from me by lingering disease, after a very short union. She possessed unvarying gentleness and fortitude, and a piety so retiring as rarely to disclose itself in words, but so influential as to produce uniform benevolence of conduct. In the last hour of life, after a farewell look on a lately born and only infant for whom she had evinced inexpressible affection, her last whispers were 'God's happiness!—God's happiness!' Since the second anniversary of her decease, I have read some papers which no one had seen during her life, and which contain her most secret thoughts. I am induced to communicate to your lordship

A note to one of the cantos of Childe Harold proves that he re

a passage from these papers which there is no doubt refers to yourself, as I have more than once heard the writer mention your agility on the rocks at Hastings.

'Oh my God! I take encouragement from the assurance of thy word to pray to Thee in behalf of one for whom I have lately been much interested. May the person to whom I allude (and who is now we fear as much distinguished for his neglect of Thee as for the transcendent talents Thou hast bestowed on him) be awakened to a sense of his own danger, and led to seek that peace of mind in a proper sense of religion which he has found this world's enjoyments unable to procure! Do Thou grant that his future example may be productive of far more extensive benefit than his past conduct and writings have been of evil; and may the Sun of Righteousness which we trust will at some future period arise on him be bright in proportion to the darkness of those clouds which guilt has raised around him, and the balm which it bestows healing and soothing in proportion to the keenness of that agony which the punishment of his vices has inflicted on him!' &c

Hastings July 31 1814
There is not in my lord this extract which in a literary sense can t ll interest you, but it may perhaps appear to you worthy of reflection how deep and expansive a concern for the happiness of others the Christian faith can awaken in the midst of youth and prosperity. Here is nothing poetical and splendid as in the expostulatory homage of M Delamartine but here is the sub ime my lord for this intercession was offered on your account to the supreme Source of happiness. It sprung from a faith more confirmed than that of the French poet and from a charity which in combination with faith shewed its power unimpaired amidst the languors and pains of approaching dissolution. I will hope that a prayer which I am sure was deeply sincere may not be always unavailing

It would add nothing my lord to the fame with which your genius has surrounded you for an unknown and obscure individual to express his admiration of it. I had rather be numbered with those who wish and pray that wisdom from above and peace and joy may enter such a mind.

Lord Byron's answer
Sir P Dec 8 1821
I have received your letter. I need not say that the extract which it contains has affected me because it would imply a want of all feeling to have read it with indifference. Though I am not quite sure that it was intended by the writer for me

membered Dr Drury, of Harrow with a mixture of affection and esteem and not less so, because that respectable individual had given him the most salutary though ineffectual, advice. Captain Medwin found him, one day, in a grave and melancholy mood, occasioned by a little treatise he had been reading on the evidences of Christianity. "You cannot answer this," said he, to Shelly, his atheistical associate, 'nor can I. And what is more, I do not wish to answer it.' Mr Dallas, in fact, tells us that his mind was originally 'of a devotional cast, and

yet the date the place where it was written with some other circumstances which you mention render the allusion probable But for whomsoever it was meant, I have read it with all the pleasure that can arise from so melancholy a topic I say *pleasure* because your brief and simple picture of the life and demeanor of the excellent person whom I trust that you will again meet cannot be contemplated without the admiration due to her virtues and her pure and unpretending piety Her last moments were particularly striking and I do not know that in the course of reading the story of mankind and still less in my observations of the existing portion I ever met with any thing so unostentatiously beautiful Indisputably the firm believers in the Gospel have a great advantage over all others —for this simple reason that if true they will have their reward hereafter and if there be no hereafter they can be but with the infidel in his eternal sleep having had the assistance of an exalted hope through life without subsequent disappointment since (at the worst for them) out of nothing nothing can arise not even sorrow But a man's creed does not depend upon *himself* who can say I *will* believe —this —that —or the other and least of all that which he least can comprehend? I have however observed that those who have begun life with an extreme faith have in the end greatly narrowed it, as Chillingworth Clarke (who ended as an Arian) Bayle and Gibbon (once a Catholic) and some others while on the other hand nothing is more common than for the early sceptic to end in a firm belief like Maupertius and Henry Kirke White

But my business is to acknowledge your letter and not to make a dissertation I am obliged to you for your good wishes and more than obliged by the extract from the papers of the beloved object whose qualities you have so well described in a few words I can assure you that all the

traces his moral ruin to his intimacy with a witty and clever young man at Cambridge, who was a professed atheist, and was cut off in early life This testimony comes from a respectable man, who once knew Lord Byron intimately who appears to have deeply studied his character who used repeated efforts to correct his errors, and reform his life and who at last was filled with grief and indignation at his increasing " poetic licence and the vulgar and shocking impiety of some of his later productions But *mere opinion* is not to be re

fame which ever cheated humanity into higher notions of its own importance would never weigh in my mind against the pure and pious interest which a virtuous being may be pleased to take in my welfare In this point of view I would not exchange the prayer of the deceased in my behalf for the united glory of Homer Cæsar and Napoleon could such be accumulated upon a living head Do me at least the justice to suppose that

Video meliora probo que
however the Deteriora sequor may have been applied to my conduct
I have the honour to be
Your obliged and obedient servant
Byron

P S I do not know that I am addressing a clergyman but I presume that you will not be affronted by the mistake (if it is one) on the address of this letter One who has so well explained and deeply felt the doctrines of religion will excuse the error which led me to believe him its minister

Mr Sheppard successfully combats the idea suggested by his noble correspondent that believing is an act merely intellectual and in no respect moral and clearly proves that unbelief in Divine truth whether general or merely partial is strictly connected with moral evil that there can be in truth no moral void, no blank or neutral state of mind Into the heart of man evil thoughts and principles must rush when good ones are excluded nay the former are already there generated and evolved within and to describe unbelief under the figure of a vacuum is merely to say that the mind is void of the principles of good because it is pre occupied and filled with those of evil The less there is of religious belief the more of irreligious sentiment and the greater the evolution or the influx of this by the agency of bad passions or of bad associations the more is religious faith expelled or excluded

ceived as *fact*, even when it is expressed by one who has had better means of judging than ourselves. When Mr Dallas speaks of Lord Byron's mind being originally 'of a devotional cast,' we are constrained to inquire on what grounds he rests this commendation of his friend. 'Mediocrity,' says Mr Dallas, "was out of his nature. If his pen were sometimes virulent and impious, his heart was always benevolent, and his sentiments sometimes *apparently* pious. He would have been pious, he would have been a Christian, had he not fallen into the hands of atheists and scoffers." This is far from a satisfactory account of the matter. " Evil communications, indeed, ' corrupts good manners,' nor are the greatest and best disposed minds entirely proof against its insinuating influence. But where the intellect of any particular person is certainly not inferior, but probably far superior, to that of the companions whom he selects, one should think that *a tendency to be pious* would either prevent the intimacy altogether, or would operate as some preservative against his being destroyed by the contagion. Was then the witty atheist of Cambridge—were the youthful infidels and scoffers into whose company Lord Byron fell—more acute or better informed than himself? This cannot be supposed, yet from what is said, we are left to infer that they had acquired a sort of paramount ascendency over the mind of this extraordinary genius, and made him the dupe of their wicked artifice.

The truth is, I fear, that very early in life and for sometime before the commencement of his acquaintance with Mr Dallas, Lord Byron had manifested dispositions and plunged into excesses the most opposite to "a devotional cast of mind." We look in vain even for some sparks of this celestial fire. By his own confession, obedience to parents was not one of his early virtues. The following too is his own account of his life previously to 1809 when he had not yet attained his twenty first year.—He acknowledged to Mr Dallas, " that he felt his life had been altogether opposed to propriety, and even decency, and that it was now become a dreary blank, with his friends gone either by death or estrangement." " My own master, says he, at an age when I most required a guide, and left to the dominion of my passions when they were the strongest, with a fortune anticipated before I came into possession of it, and a constitution impaired by early excesses, I commenced my travels in 1809, with a joyless indifference to a world that was all before me." Had ' the Childe Harold' really sat for his moral picture, could he have been more accurately delineated ? This ' devotional cast,' therefore, if he ever possessed any, must have worn itself out long before the period of his travels.

We should call characteristic qualities by their proper names, and beware of confounding things that differ. There is a wide dissimilarity between " an early tendency to be pious," and the occasional flight of better thoughts through the mind. When such thoughts are followed up by no vigorous efforts of amendment, when they are so many impulses knocking at the door of the heart, only to be refused admittance, when they seem constantly evanescent as the ' morning cloud' and the " early dew," when no evil passion is resisted from conscientious motives, and when, above all, no Divine help is implored, they cannot be regarded as traces of ' a devotional cast of mind.' At the same time what the present Mr Dallas has remarked, I am very willing to believe true, ' that there existed in Lord Byron, originally, that which good men might have loved.' We are informed, for example, that, hearing when abroad of the seduction of a young woman in the neighbourhood of Newstead,

Abbey, by one of his own servants his lordship ordered him to marry her, under pain of his highest displeasure. This is indeed, one of the most unequivocal traces we have yet found of Lord Byron's respect for female virtue; but, if this servant knew of his master's own laxity and licentiousness, he could hardly have allowed him much credit for his motives in issuing the command.

Among the fairer aspects of Lord Byron's character, should be placed his testimony to the misery and unprofitableness of vicious courses; for his reflections on this subject, if they produced no permanently good effect upon his own mind, nevertheless displayed the force of truth, and the upbraidings of conscience, and may afford a salutary warning to others. "I sought," said he to Captain Medwin, "to distract my mind from a sense of her desolation and my own solitude, by plunging into a vortex that was any thing but pleasure. When one gets into a mill stream, it is difficult to swim against it and keep out of the wheels. The consequences of being carried down by it would furnish an excellent lesson for youth. You are too old to profit by it. But who ever profited by the experience of others or his own?"—How then could Lord Byron's own experience prove a lesson *to youth*? He continues—'When you read my memoirs you will learn the evils, moral and physical, of true dissipation. I assure you my life is very entertaining and very instructive.' Happily for the world, these entertaining memoirs have been committed to the flames; otherwise we should perhaps have had some new supplement to the Confessions of Rousseau, or an addition to the number of those voluptuous narratives which disgrace French authorship, and operate like a moral blight and mildew on the imagination of the young. What Cowper says, and justly, of the mass of novels, is still more applicable to such works as these.

O that a word had power, and could command
Far far away these flesh flies from the land.

We have, then in the late Lord Byron another signal witness to the miseries of a life of vice and dissipation. Like the gay and witty Lord Chesterfield he had been behind the scenes; he had "smelt the tallow candles, and seen that collection of filth, rubbish, and trumpery, which is concealed from the eyes of the uninitiated spectator by the pomp and gaiety of the external show." But, alas! did not he too, like Lord Chesterfield, 'resolve to sleep in the carriage during the remainder of his journey?' When upon one occasion, Mr Dallas recommended to him the study of Christianity as 'the only refuge for fallen man,' his reply was that he would have nothing to do with the subject. 'We should all,' he added, 'go down together. Let us eat and drink, for to-morrow we die.'

It is with no feelings of proud self-complacency, far less of malignant satisfaction (this would be horrible,) that the true Christian contemplates traits of character such as these. When, as here, he observes them in an individual animated with the *mens divinior* of genius, and gifted with powers and advantages that might have qualified him for the most extensive usefulness, he is affected with lively emotions of sorrow and regret, and mourns over the desolation of so much grandeur, like the musing traveller standing by the time-worn temple of Balbec, or amidst the ruins of Palmyra.

The reflections of Lord Byron respecting a life of dissipation may prove a source of much useful instruction even to those who have been happily preserved from such a life, and whose characters are established for moral decorum, if not for Christian virtue and consistency. They should be led to feel more deeply the gratitude due to God for those circumstances and that course of education which have operated through his grace, as a salutary restraint upon their conduct. If they have escaped the rocks and quicksands themselves they should still learn to reflect, deeply and tenderly on the situation of those under their authority, who are but just embarking on the voyage of life or who from the want of early culture are less armed against its perils. Let them look well to their children and domestics. Let them govern their households with that union of prudence and piety which will be most likely to ensure success. Let them study the dispositions of their offspring and apply not the harshest but the wisest remedies to their faults and particularly in the case of such as may betray early symptoms of superior abilities and of what frequently attends them—ardent feelings and strong passions. Such a temperament requires often the nicest and most careful management and many such characters have been ruined through a want of sufficient openness and encouragement on the part of the parent leading the child to a confidential disclosure of his errors before they become so great as to drive him either into open profligacy or hypocritical concealment. If even good men would but dedicate half of that time which they are apt to bestow on comparative trifles to study the dispositions and welfare of their children what incalculable benefit might ensue! Even those who not only know but in the main practise their duty still feel the benefit of striking mementos occurring from time to time, of the miseries of sinful courses. The late Lord Byron is one of these mementos and though the circumstances of his talents and genius place him out of the range of ordinary experience it will be our own fault if we do not learn some lessons of true wisdom from his confessions of his folly.

(To be continued.)

To the Editor of the Christian Observer.

AMONG the plans for facilitating business public and private civil and ecclesiastical which have been adopted with the most beneficial effects in modern days it may perhaps excite surprise that no remedy has been proposed for the irregularities and inconveniences which arise from the moveable festivals. In our universities in the church, in the courts of law in parliament in the public offices and in innumerable details in every department of life, an almanack is often absolutely necessary before a single step can be safely taken. We must "follow still the changes of the moon" and cannot tell till we accurately consult that presiding luminary what we are to do in the church or the counting house in the senate or the college in the forum or the jail. The prisoner computes the chances of a longer or shorter confinement, the senator of his recess from public duties the parish officer of the termination of his labours, the divine the collection of his annual offerings the school boy the clerk, the academic the dates of their business and repose from a fluctuating æra never two successive years the same.

Might not these inconveniences be obviated without any offence to religion or the most cautious spirit of ecclesiastical discipline? Why might not Easter day 'on which all the rest depend' be legislatively determined to fall on a fixed Sunday in the month towards the close of March or the beginning of April within the present prescribed limits. The intention and utility of this joyful festival in which we commemorate an event most interesting to every Christian would not be in the least disturbed by making it a fixed instead of a moveable observance. Easter would still be Easter, as to all its religious and other uses, whether it began a few days sooner or later and the convenience of having the exact day fixed and invariable would be very great in the arrange ments of business, which are often seriously disturbed by the present irregularities. The clerical and legal professions, in particular, would find great advantages from such a provision; and the only persons who would suffer by it would be the almanack makers, whose commodity of "terms and returns" would thus be rendered useless to society.

I am not aware that any objection of weight can be brought against the proposed change. It may, indeed, be urged that the day ought to be the *real anniversary* of the event which it is intended to commemorate; and it must be confessed, that a devout and reverential feeling of mind is often excited by such solemn observances, which will, in many cases, be the more lively in proportion as the circumstances of the commemoration partake of a greater degree of verisimilitude. Perfect accuracy in these matters is, however, out of the question: no Protestant, for example, supposes that the 25th of December is the precise anniversary of the Incarnation, or feels his commemoration of that event to be the less profitable, on account of this ambiguity. And with regard to the celebration of Easter, every reader of history is aware how little can be boasted of uniformity or precision. The whole detail, on this point, would be too long for the purpose of the present paper; but a brief mention of a few circumstances may not be improper, with a view to inform the general reader, how little the fear of change is to be dreaded in an affair, the whole history of which has been change from beginning to end.

Even in the first ages of Christianity, there arose great disputes between the churches of Asia and other churches, respecting the day on which Easter ought to be celebrated. The Asiatic churches kept their Easter on the precise day (whether it happened to be the Lord's day or not,) on which the Jews celebrated their passover, namely, the 14th of the month Nisan, which month began at the new moon next to the vernal equinox. Other churches, especially those of the West, kept their Easter on the Sunday following the Jewish passover. Both sides pleaded apostolical tradition: the Asiatics professing to follow the example of St. John, the others that of St. Peter and St. Paul. The dispute at length became so violent that Constantine thought it necessary to interfere, and procured some canons to be passed by the council of Nice, decreeing that the 21st of March was to be accounted the vernal equinox; the full moon happening upon, or next after, that day, the full moon of Nisan; the Lord's day next after that full moon, Easter day; or if the full moon happened on a Sunday, then the Sunday after. The fathers of the next century ordered the moon's age to be calculated by Meton's cycle of the moon; and this cycle was accordingly placed in the calendar. But this cycle of nineteen years, being an hour and a half too long, in the course of time the accumulated error had amounted to about five days; besides which, there was also a solar error, the Julian year exceeding the real one by about eleven minutes; so that the equinoxes had become eleven or twelve days too forward from the time of the Nicene council. Hence, the first full moon after the 21st of March, was not always the first full moon after the vernal equinox; so that those who observed the Nicene canon in the letter, were, in fact, deviating from its express intention. The whole church was, however, very strict in adhering to this erroneous *formula*; and so tender was it of the authority of the fathers, that astronomy and the plainest matter of fact were sacrificed to it; and dire woes had betided the heretic who should have thought he saw a new or full moon in the heavens, when the Nicene canon declared the contrary. The council of Chalcedon, held about 200 years after the Nicene, issued a *formula*, grounded on the orthodox

Nicene doctrine though at war both with the sun and the moon, and declared that, whosoever celebrated Easter on any other day than that prescribed should be accounted a heretic, and punished accordingly This *formula* was religiously observed for about 534 years, till Pope Gregory XIII, in the year 1582 brought back the vernal equinox to the 21st of March and, in the year 1752, a similar reform was made in the Church of England calendar by an Act of Parliament prescribing that the 3d day of September of that year, should be entitled the 14th thereby suppressing eleven days

These, however, are but a part of the vicissitudes of this celebrated festival the rules for finding which have been repeatedly changed, and have never yet been reduced to astronomical accuracy Cycles on cycles have been, from time to time, framed such as the cycle of eighty four years, which continued to be used in the British churches long after its errors had been detected at Rome and a new cycle invented namely the Victorian cycle of 552 years, which was then decreed to be the right one, and tables were grounded upon it, which, however, were superseded, like their precursors, and so on through various other mutations and mistakes too tedious to be enumerated

After so many edicts and corrections, all in their turn duly and exclusively authorised, I trust that the charge of innovation will not be thought very weighty, in reference to the object of the present paper, which is to retain the festival in its primitive spirit but to supersede the necessity of intricate calculations by determining the observance of it to a fixed instead of a fluctuating date, and thus obviating the numerous inconveniences which have been mentioned

A B C

To the Editor of the Christian Observer

MANY strong and pointed remonstrances have appeared in your pages respecting the gross violation of the Sabbath day by public conveyances, such as coaches, vans, waggons, barges, &c ? Are Christians justified in viewing this *systematic* breach of one of the most positive and minute of the Divine commandments and of our own national laws, without offering united, vigorous, systematic and public opposition to it ? Unless immediate steps are taken to check the present extent of the crime, it will rapidly increase the projected rail road companies, for example, will of course claim the right of being on a par with other carriers no distinction will therefore be made by them between the Lord's day and other days and as the country is intended to be intersected by new lines of roads, numerous parts through which no Sunday conveyances now regularly pass, will soon witness and partake in the crime

I would most earnestly inquire, Can nothing be done to put a stop to this great and rapidly increasing evil?

SPES

REVIEW OF NEW PUBLICATIONS

Book of the Church By ROBERT SOUTHEY, Esq LL D, &c
Book of the Roman Catholic Church By CHARLES BUTLER, Esq

(*Concluded from p 46*)

THE brevity with which Mr Southey finds himself constrained to speak of ecclesiastical matters not immediately connected with the Church of England, seems occasionally to give rise to incorrect representations and the Waldenses in particular have much reason to complain of it The name of that people stands in the running title of an early page of the 11th chapter and the reader will find that they are made responsible not only for the tenets which they actually maintained, but for principles asserted by other persons, with whom they concurred in little more than in hostility to the Romish superstitions. On what evidence is it affirmed concerning the Waldenses, that, "in their condemnation of the ceremonies of the church they comprehended what was innocent and useful in the same proscription with what was superstitious and injurious; that, "because the doctrine of merits was preposterous they maintained, in any reprehensible way, what Mr Southey calls 'the not less preposterous tenet that the best works of man are sinful in themselves; and because the clergy arrogated a monstrous power that they were 'for a levelling system, which, in its direction and certain consequences, extended from religious to political opinions?' That some of the sectaries who arose about this period embraced doctrines which were highly fanatical, and conducted themselves in a manner very discreditable to religion, is unhappily a well established fact; but can this charge be justly brought against the Waldenses? Their views upon the great doctrines of religion appear to have been generally such as were adopted at the Reformation, and their lives were remarkably conformable to the purity of their faith. To the Romish Church the very name of Waldenses must be superlatively odious; and never, perhaps, were calumny and misrepresentation directed against any class of Christians with more unblushing boldness or more determined animosity. For the real character of that deeply injured people we refer to Milner's *Church History*.

As to the so called preposterous tenet that the best works of man are sinful in themselves, we have some doubt whether Mr Southey has expressed himself very happily upon the subject, and have indeed, a lurking suspicion that he has not given to this point the consideration which it deserves. On looking back to a former page, where he delivers his sentiments on the controversy between Pelagius and Augustine, we find it stated that, "through the British hierarchy, the more reasonable opinion, that the actions of good men were meritorious in themselves, obtained;" and coupling that position with the remark just noticed, concerning the preposterousness of the tenet here ascribed to the Waldenses, we feel ourselves still more confirmed in the persuasion that Mr Southey's views on these matters are by no means correct. Does he mean to contend that men possess of themselves any power to do that which is good and acceptable in the sight of God; or that either a just work or a holy desire can proceed from any other source than the influence of God's Holy Spirit? If so, whatever might be the errors of the Waldenses he is directly at variance with the Church of England. The Eleventh and Thirteenth Articles are decisive as to her judgment upon this important subject. *'We are accounted righteous before God only for the merit of our Lord and Saviour Jesus Christ, by faith and not for our works and deservings. Wherefore, that we are justified by faith only is a most wholesome doctrine and very full of comfort, as more largely is expressed in the homily of Justification.** 'Works done before the grace of Christ and the inspiration of his Spirit are not pleasant to God, forasmuch as they spring not of faith in Jesus Christ; neither do they make men meet to receive grace, or (as the school authors say) deserve grace of congruity; yea rather, for that they are not done as God hath commanded and willed them to be done, we doubt not but that they have the nature of sin.* Now so far as we can find these were in substance the very doctrines held by the Waldenses; they taught the doctrine of

---

* We recommend that homily to the attentive perusal of those who doubt the views of the Church of England on this subject.

justification by faith without human help or merit, and that of good works as the fruits and evidences of faith, in a way substantially the same with the Articles and Homilies of our church. Mosheim, whose authority in this instance Mr Southey has probably followed, qualifies his strong commendations of that people by statements which seem to justify the more general censures in the Book of the Church. He represents them as maintaining that "the rulers and ministers of the church were obliged by their vocation to imitate the poverty of the Apostles, and to procure for themselves a subsistence by the work of their hands": and, amidst other assertions about the *expiation* of transgression by prayer, fasting and alms, which it would be very difficult to reconcile with their avowed belief adds — They adopted as the model of their moral discipline the Sermon of Christ on the Mount, which they interpreted and explained in the most rigorous and literal manner, and of consequence prohibited and condemned in their society all wars and suits of law, all attempts toward the acquisition of wealth, the inflicting of capital punishment, self defence against unjust violence, and oaths of all kinds. The note subjoined to this passage might lead us, independently of other evidence, to doubt the accuracy of the text, it asserts, that ' almost all the writers of the Waldensian history are unanimous in acknowledging the sincere piety and exemplary conduct of the Waldenses, and shew plainly enough that their intention was not to oppose the doctrines that were universally received among Christians but only to revive the piety and manners of the primitive times, and to combat the vices of the clergy and the abuses that had been introduced into the worship and discipline of the church (Cent XII Part II § 12) But we have evidence more directly in point

' They are charged, says Milner (cent XIII c II), "with denying the lawfulness of oaths in all cases, without exception. This part of their history has its difficulties........ Most probably they condemned the multiplicity of oaths, with which the courts of law abounded. That they did not, however, maintain the absolute unlawfulness of oaths, is certain from the exposition of the Third Commandment in their Spiritual Almanack, in which are these words ' There are some oaths *lawful* tending to the honour of God, and the edification of our neighbours, as appears from Heb vi 16, Men swear by a greater and an oath for confirmation is to them an end of all strife Other Scriptures are alleged by them to the same purport Men who held these things should be acquitted of the charge of universally denying the lawfulness of oaths But it seems to have been one of the common artifices of the prince of darkness to calumniate the people of God in this manner He knows that, if religious men be thought wholly unfitted for this world because of certain absurd or ridiculous customs the generality of mankind will pay no great regard to their instructions concerning the right way to the next It is therefore of some consequence to clear up the character of true Christians in this respect p 487

' It was a gross calumny (proceeds Milner p 490) to accuse them as enemies to the penal power of the magistrate, because they complained of the abuse of his power in condemning true Christians to death without a fair examination when, at the same time they asserted in their own books, that a malefactor ought not to be suffered to live

" No less unjust were the charges against them of seditiousness and undutifulness to the supreme power For in the book of the causes of their separation from the Church of Rome, they said that every one ought to be subject to those who are in authority to obey and love them, to honour them with double honour, with subjection, allegiance, and promptitude, and the paying of tribute to whom tribute is due. They might possibly have condemned in their society, as Mosheim alleges, all wars and suits at law, except in extreme cases, without subjecting themselves to very serious animadversion. But on the latter subject, what do they say of themselves? Every one of us hath possessed his own at all times and in all places. In Dauphiny, and other parts, when we were dispossessed of our substance, the suits for the recovery of each estate were conducted by the particular proprietors.* The Waldenses of Provence do, at this present time, demand of the pope the restoration of the lands and estates annexed to his domain by confiscation, every particular person *making oath* of his parcel of goods and lands, which descended to him from time immemorial; for we never have had community of property in the sense objected to us by our adversaries.—Milner, cent. XIII. c. ii.

"One charge more against them is, that they compelled their pastors to follow some trade. How satisfactory their answer! We do not think it necessary that our pastors should work for bread. They might be better qualified to instruct us, if we could maintain them without their own labour, but our poverty has no remedy."—Should the somewhat indefinite animadversions of Mr Southey not meet with a sufficient answer in these extracts, we would request him to read the whole chapter from which we have selected them; he will then be disposed, we hope, to retain all his praise of the Waldenses, and to cancel the objectionable passages; and, considering how important it is

to the cause of truth and religion that the men who, in their day, were the salt of the earth, and who rendered indirectly an invaluable service to future ages, should not be made responsible for principles which they disavowed, we doubt not that in future editions he will be happy to follow these suggestions.

The comprehensive nature of Mr Southey's work must, although it has grown under his hands into a size beyond its intended dimensions, afford a satisfactory reason also for omitting many matters of comparatively inferior moment, which he would otherwise have introduced. But that, in this part of his undertaking, no notice should be taken of Grosseteste and Bradwardine, those bright stars in a dark period of our ecclesiastical history, is a circumstance scarcely to be justified even by the commendable love of brevity. Such a Bishop of Lincoln and such an Archbishop of Canterbury should have their names enrolled, with every becoming tribute of respect, in all the histories of our church, for the example and instruction of future generations.

In drawing the character of Wickliffe, Mr Southey, with a laudable partiality for that great man, has nevertheless endeavoured to judge of him with fairness, and to represent him precisely in that light in which, according to the voice of history, he ought to be viewed. When we are told, however, that the fame of that reformer, high as it is, is not above his deserts, and that it suffers no abatement upon comparison with the most illustrious of those who have followed in the path which he opened, we have considerable difficulty in agreeing with the statement. Melancthon's judgment upon him is well known. 'I have looked,' says he, 'into Wickliffe, who is very confused in this controversy of the Lord's supper; but I have found in him also many other errors, by which a judgment may be made of his spirit. He neither understood nor

---

* This appears by the legal process existing in Perrin's time, which shews that Lewis XII. condemned the usurpers of the goods of the Waldenses to a restitution. This happened about the beginning of the sixteenth century.

believed the righteousness of faith he foolishly confounds the Gospel and politics and does not see that the Gospel allows us to make use of the lawful forms of government of all nations. He contends that it is not lawful for priests to have any property. He wrangles sophistically, and downright seditiously about civil dominion. In the same manner he cavils sophistically about the Lord's supper.* Perhaps this judgment may be too severe but assuredly, for deep and solid views of the great doctrines of the Gospel, the reformers of the sixteenth century were far above Wickliffe and in simplicity of purpose, and intrepidity of character, and freedom from all artifice, they seem to have left him at an immeasurable distance Perhaps toward the close of his life he might have become more moderate in some of his political notions and possibly more scriptural in some of his religious opinions but whatever were his defects, he has left a name to which every Protestant should look with veneration and gratitude his translation of the Scriptures into the English language entitles him to no common praise and his exposure of the Romish system gave a blow to Popery which in this country it never recovered and from the writings of Wickliffe John Huss adopted those principles for which he suffered at Constance and Huss, as Mr Southey observes, prepared the way for Luther

The remainder of this chapter gives the history of the religious persecutions under the house of Lancaster This was the period of the Lollards and now, for the first time, to deny the doctrine of transubstantiation became a statutable offence, for which the punishment was death by the flames

"Undoubtedly" says Mr Southey "the Lollards were highly dangerous at this time if there were some among them whose views and wishes did not go beyond a just and salutary reformation the greater number were eager for havock, and held opinions which are incompatible with the peace of society They would have stripped the churches destroyed the monasteries confiscated the church lands and proclaimed the principle that the saints should possess the earth The public safety required that such opinions should be repressed &c

According to this report, they were a race of religious radicals differing apparently from the confiscators of church property in the present day chiefly in the circumstance that the word Saint is, with our modern plunderers, a term utterly detested

But is the representation here given of the general character of the Lollards agreeable to fact? In the absence of all citation of authorities we are not able to state with much confidence the grounds on which it rests if on the very general assertions of Mosheim, we decidedly object to them they are far too sweeping to be admitted It is not by broad assertions about Bohemia, Moravia, Switzerland, and Germany and almost every part of Europe, that we are to settle the principles and characters of those who were opposed to the Romish superstitions in England neither can any thing on this subject be inferred merely from the name Lollard for it was 'not a name to denote any one particular sect but was common to all persons and all sects who were supposed (by the Papists) " to be guilty of impiety towards God and the church, under an external profession of extraordinary piety (Mosheim) We can decide fairly concerning the character of the English Lollards, so called, only by an actual reference to their history and the result will not justify either the broad assertions of Mr Butler, or the more qualified representations of Mr Southey Let us hear the statement of Joseph Milner —

" I find that several persons who were accused of holding those speculative tenets of Wickliffe which I have allowed to be indefensible,

---

* See Milner c III cent xiv

did however, in their examinations, perfectly clear themselves of every suspicion of factious innovation. In fact, the whole body of the Lollards in general were in practice so perfectly void of offence, that speculative errors formed the only charge that could be brought against them; and, even in regard to these errors, there seems reason to apprehend that the followers of Wickliffe very much meliorated the sentiments of their master and leader. ONLY for the Gospel's sake they suffered—whatever might be the pretences of their enemies.

Of Mr Southey's admissions on these points Mr Butler has very largely availed himself, and scruples not to mention, as the acts of the English Lollards, the insurrections and murders of those distracted times. "What insurrections, what rapine, what murders, were produced by them! They murdered the Chancellor and Primate, Sudbury; the Lord Treasurer Hales; the Chief Justice, Cavendish; they sought to murder the king; to exterminate the nobility, the dignitaries and the principal functionaries of the clergy;" and then comes a quotation from Walsingham—a prejudiced and most bitter enemy of the Lollards—about a radical rout assembled under the guidance of John Ball &c. which proves nothing whatever on the point at issue. Many of those poor men were tried and executed; of what were they convicted? and how did they demean themselves? They suffered *only* for the sake of the Gospel; they were made the victims of a cruel hierarchy, and a deceived and bigoted sovereign. Mr Butler condemns, in terms that do him honour, the law which committed them to the flames; but why overwhelm the memory of these good men with charges which cannot be brought home to them, and some of which can easily be proved to be destitute of foundation? Was it for sedition that Sautre, the first victim of the new statute, was burned? or that Thorpe, the next object of Arundel's vengeance, was thrown into prison where he probably perished? or that Badby, Taylor, White and Brown were persecuted to death? Was it to root out the seditious principle that the heads of every college in Oxford were enjoined on pain of excommunication and deprivation themselves to inquire every month whether any scholars maintained doctrines against the determination of the church; and if any such were found, who remained obstinate immediately to expel them? Was it because the ecclesiastical rulers apprehended disloyalty alone that twelve inquisitors of heresy were appointed in that university to search out heretics and heretical works? The whole question was about the superstitious dogmas of Rome; and the man who believed not the doctrine of transubstantiation was to be burned.

We have, in reciting the names of several martyrs among the Lollards, purposely omitted that of Sir John Oldcastle, Lord Cobham; and we have done so with the view of meeting Mr Butler upon the only case which, apart from his sweeping generalities, he condescends to notice. His words are these:—

In the following year they (the Lollards) endeavoured to raise a rebellion in St Giles's fields where Oldcastle had appointed them to rendezvous. (p. 143.)

Before I conclude my letter, I beg leave to express some surprise at the tenderness with which you treat Sir John Oldcastle, often called Lord Cobham. You describe him as a *victim*; and when you come to his final catastrophe you tell us that the remainder of his story is perplexed by contradictory statements, from which nothing certain can be collected but the last results. Is this so? Had not his practices with the Lollards in their most revolutionary designs, and his encouragement of them been discovered? Had he not defied the process of the spiritual courts? Had not Henry V declared, in his proclamation that the Lollards meant to destroy him, his brothers and several of the spiritual and temporal lords? to confiscate the possessions of the church; to secularize the religious orders; to divide the realm into confederate districts; and to appoint Sir John Oldcastle president of the Commonwealth? On his arraignment, did he venture to assert his innocence? Did he not deny the king's title to the crown? Did not the sentence pronounced upon him declare that he should both be hanged as a traitor and burned as a heretic? It is almost ridiculous to ask—did he not impiously prophecy that he should rise on the third day? p. 145.

Now here is something tangible let us see how these assertions and interrogations accord with the facts.

When Arundel, with his ecclesiastical coadjutors, complained to Henry of Lord Cobham, the complaint was not for his disloyalty, but for his heretical practices. When Henry expostulated with this favourite nobleman it was entirely on the subject of the church. "You, says that gallant knight, in reply, 'I am always most ready to obey because you are the appointed minister of God and bear the sword for the punishment of evil doers. But as to the pope and his spiritual dominion I owe them no obedience, nor will I pay them any, for as sure as God's word is true, to me it is fully evident that the pope of Rome is the great anti Christ foretold in holy writ, the son of perdition, the open adversary of God, and the abomination standing in the holy place. Wher Lord Cobham was condemned was it not under the character of an incorrigible pernicious, and detestable heretic? and under this name was he not delivered over to the secular arm? We deny not, that instead of obeying Arundel's order to attend the process of the spiritual courts he refused the messenger admission into his castle. But has Mr Butler forgotten his own rule, which requires that men should be judged with a reference to the customs and usages of the times in which they lived? Were not feudal ideas in that day quite as fashionable as those of ecclesiastical domination? And did not Lord Cobham exercise a *right*, according to feudal opinions in standing upon his privilege, and keeping out the servant of Arundel? If that rule is to plead the apology of men who shed without mercy the blood of the innocent, let it at least be allowed some application to a Christian knight, who was acting merely on a principle of self defence, and who well knew that his appearance before that iniquitous tribunal was equivalent to the sentence of death.

As to the interrogations connected with his arraignment that is his arraignment before the Lords in 1417, subsequent to his escape from the tower, and his arrest in Wales we would ask in reply did he say any thing inconsistent with the most perfect innocence? Was not his conduct throughout that of patient silence and resignation? Was it not evident that the dominant party had pre determined his destruction and that it was scarcely possible for him to utter a word which should not be most wickedly misrepresented? And with regard to his denying the king's title, and to the foolish prophecy about rising again the third day, if Mr Butler himself believes one syllable of such matters, he is far beyond the reach of any argument of ours it was the policy of the church to blacken Lord Cobham, and they have not been very scrupulous as to the means.

The proclamation of Henry the Fifth, that the Lollards meant to destroy him &c is a document on which no stress can be laid. Henry was a brave warrior but his conscience was with the priests they had a mighty influence over him and they exercised it to the utmost. After the escape of Lord Cobham, as Henry shewed no wish to have him taken—for even according to Mr Butler's prime authority, the bigoted Walsingham, this persecuted nobleman was *for his integrity, dear to the king,*—the clergy set themselves in good earnest to exasperate the mind of the sovereign, both against the Lollards in general, and against Lord Cobham in particular. The king was no stranger to the defect of his own title to the crown, and he partook in the habitual jealousy of the house of Lancaster. It was the aim of the priesthood to avail themselves of his terrors, to fill him with apprehensions of disloyalty and treason, and to drive him on to the most furious courses. Hence that false and wicked proclamation, the work not of an enlightened prince, but of the ecclesiastics who surrounded him; men who seem not to have objected to the use of any means which could add to their influence or consolidate their power.

It was a great object with the king to put an end to the assemblies of the Lollards, who were in the habit of meeting for religious purposes. Being in a manner hunted down by the Papists, they were glad, like the primitive Christians, to meet when they could; and hence they sometimes collected in small companies, in the dead of the night. A meeting of this sort has furnished to the lovers of Popery one of the most specious grounds on which to attack Lord Cobham and the Lollards: to us, the account of that occurrence appears to be conclusive for the opposite side. We shall simply give the tale as we find it in Milner.

"St Giles's Fields, then a thicket, was a place of frequent resort on these occasions; and here a number of them assembled in the evening of January 6th, 1414, with an intention, as was usual, of continuing together to a very late hour.

"The king was then at Eltham, a few miles from London. He received intelligence, that Lord Cobham, at the head of 20,000 of his party, was stationed in St Giles's Fields for the purpose of seizing the person of the king, putting their persecutors to the sword and making himself the regent of the realm.

"The mind of Henry, we have seen, had been prepared by the diligent and artful representations of the clergy, to receive any impressions against the Lollards, which might tend to fix upon that persecuted sect the charges of seditious or treasonable practices. To his previous suspicions therefore, as well as to the gallantry of his temper, we are to ascribe the extraordinary resolution which the king took on this occasion. He suddenly armed the few soldiers he could muster, put himself at their head, and marched to the place. He attacked the Lollards, and soon put them into confusion; about twenty were killed, and sixty taken. Among these was one Beverley, their preacher, who with two others, Sir Roger Acton and John Brown, were afterwards put to death. The king marched on, but found no more bodies of men. He thought he had surprised only the advanced guard, whereas he had routed the whole army!

'This extraordinary affair is represented by the popish writers as a real conspiracy; and it has given them occasion to talk loudly against the tenets of the reformer, which could encourage such crimes. Mr Hume also has enlisted himself on the same side of the question; and in the most peremptory and decisive manner has pronounced Lord Cobham guilty of high treason.'—Milner, cent. xv. c. 1.

To those who would wish to see the whole of this matter fully and satisfactorily examined we strongly recommend the remaining pages of the chapter from which this extract is taken. We anticipate in every instance a clear judgment in favour of Lord Cobham, against all the charges, except as regards his rejection of Popery, which it has been the practice of popish persons to bring against him. We cannot but express our concern, that Mr Southey, instead of leaving the case involved in some sort of mystery, by his brief statement, in pp. 380—381, has not gone more at large into the inquiry, with Milner and Gilpin, and Rapin as his guides and rendered entire and unhesitating justice to the persecuted victims of the priesthood. That his impression generally coincides with our own on these subjects, we are well convinced for, notwithstanding his admissions, to the prejudice of the Lollards, which Mr Butler has skilfully pressed into the Roman Catholic service, he assures us, in distinct terms, that in all the records which remain of this persecution, in no one instance has the victim been charged with the levelling principles ascribed to the Lollards "In every case, they were questioned upon those points, which make the difference between the Reformed and the Romish religion in every case, they were sacrificed as burnt offerings to the mass. And with respect to Lord Cobham, personally, of whom Mr Butler and others assert that he suffered for treason, as well as heresy, Mr Southey informs us pointedly in a note, that he suffered "*as a* heretic, *not as a traitor*, and adds, with a reference to Howell's State Trials that *his indictment for high treason was a forgery*

These scenes of religious persecution were for a time interrupted by the civil wars between the houses of York and Lancaster when that struggle terminated, the intolerant spirit of the Romish Church once more commenced its fearful ministrations and the Lollards were again pursued with the utmost rigour

Among the victims was a woman of some quality Joan Boughton by name the first female martyr in England she was more than eighty years of age and was held in such reverence for her virtue that, during the night after her martyrdom her ashes were collected to be preserved as relics for pious and affectionate remembrance Her daughter the Lady Young suffered afterwards the same cruel death with equal constancy At Amersworth when William Tylsworth was burnt his only daughter as being suspected of heresy was compelled not only to witness his death but with her own hands to set fire to him! By such barbarities did the Romish Church provoke the indignation of God and man That it should have made one real convert by such means is impossible though it compelled many to abjuration In that case the miserable wretches whom it admitted to its mercy were made to bear a faggot in public while they witnessed the martyrdom of those who had more constancy than themselves They were fastened to a stake by the neck with towels, and their hands held fast, while they were marked on the cheek with a hot iron after which they were for life to wear a faggot worked or painted on the left sleeve and if they ventured to lay aside this badge which if they were in humble life consigned them to want as well as infamy they were sent to the flames without remission —so that it became a saying Put it off and be burnt keep it on and be starved Bishop Nix of Norwich one of the most infamous for his activity in this persecution used to call the persons whom he suspected of heretical opinions men savouring of the frying pan —with such levity did these monsters regard the sufferings which they inflicted! A correspondent of Erasmus wrote to him that the price of wood was considerably advanced about London in consequence of the quantity required for the frequent executions in Smithfield The statement is one of those hyperboles which in the familiarity of letter writing are understood as they are meant and convey no more than the truth Southey vol 1 pp 405—407

In pursuing the progress of the Reformation, through the reigns of King Henry VIII, Edward VI, Queen Mary, and Queen Elizabeth, the statements of Mr Southey, so far as they involve the conflicts between Protestantism and Popery, correspond generally with those of all Protestant writers and whatever might be the passions or vices of the sovereign who gave a death wound to the papal power in this country, the character of the Romish system, as exhibited during the period included in these reigns, is of a most degrading and revolting description Without an almost unqualified disbelief of the tale transmitted to us by those times, we must feel ourselves constrained to rejoice in the Reformation, as one of the greatest blessings ever conferred upon mankind and to honour with special reverence those champions of our faith, who, amidst so many difficulties and amidst circumstances so painful commenced and carried forward that salutary work Under the impression which the history of the Reformation as we find it in our most respected and accredited writers, usually leaves upon the mind, we are little prepared to hear either the usefulness of it controverted, or the character of its martyred advocates treated with contempt. We feel the value of the change, from a corrupt and idolatrous to a pure and scriptural religion; and we cannot contemplate the Ridleys and Latimers of other days, without the warmest emotions of gratitude and respect. They doubtless had their infirmities, for they were men; they had, we may reasonably suppose, many conflicts, as the light gradually broke in upon them, with the strong prejudices of early life; but there was in them such a simplicity and integrity of heart, such an undeviating love for the truth, and with a few exceptions which human infirmity will easily explain, such a Christian consistency of character and conduct, that they seem to be almost beyond the reach of sinister interpretation. We have seen however, in the case of Lord Cobham, that if hardy assertions can be of service to Popery, it will not be very backward in employing them; and he must be little conversant with the persecutors of Queen Mary's days, who would suspect them of much reluctance to defame the Protestant cause, and to calumniate its defenders by every artifice in their power. Mr Butler is a man of other times, and of a different spirit; but his attachment to Popery has a strong effect upon his judgment, and not a little influence upon his candour. Not only, therefore, have we in his work a defence of the religious orders, as they are called, but a direct impeachment of the character of our principal reformers, and a comparison highly favourable to his own church of the comparative benefits arising from the operation of the popish establishment. "Has England gained," demands Mr Butler, "by the Reformation in temporal happiness?—has England gained by the Reformation in spiritual wisdom?—was the Reformation attended by a general improvement in morals?—was the revival of letters owing to the Reformation, or materially forwarded by it? &c. On each of these points he would decide in the negative and, notwithstanding all that we know of the natural and necessary tendency of the two systems, and of their actual operation, as manifested in the history of England, and visible at this day in different countries of Europe, we are virtually invited to believe that a return into the bosom of the Romish Church would be of great benefit to this free and enlightened nation. Of a bad cause Mr Butler has probably given as fair a vindication as it will admit; but, plausible as are some of his assertions—and this is the highest praise that we can give them—there are passages in this part of his work which must satisfy even the least suspicious of his readers that his argument amounts to nothing more than tolerably good special pleading. As a specimen we will advert a little more distinctly to the section entitled "Was the Reformation attended by a general improvement in morals?" The question is one of evidence; and who are the witnesses to establish the negative? Why truly the Reformers! No Roman Catholic it seems can represent in a worse light the corrupting influence of the Reformation than the men who promoted it. We see, says Luther (as quoted by Mr Butler) that through the malice of the devil men are now more avaricious, more cruel, more disorderly, more insolent, and much more wicked than they were under Popery. "If any one wish," says Musculus, "to see a multitude of knaves, disturbers of the public peace, &c. let him go to a city where the Gospel is preached in its purity (he means says Mr Butler, a reformed city) for it is clearer than the light of day that never were pagans more vicious and disorderly than those professors of the Gospel. 'The thing,' says Melancthon, 'speaks for itself. In this country among the Reformed, their whole time is devoted to intemperance and drunkenness (*immanibus poculis*). So deeply are the people sunk into barbarity and ignorance that many of them would imagine that they should die in the night, if they should choose to fast in the day. Erasmus, a sort of non descript Roman Catholic (but allowed by the Protestants maintains Mr Butler to be impartial!) writes, And who are these Gospel people? Look around you, and shew me one who has become a better man—shew me one who, once a glutton is now turned sober—one who, before violent, is now meek—one who before avaricious, is now generous—one who, before impure is now chaste. I can point out multitudes who are become far worse than they were before. We shall not trouble ourselves to verify these passages or the others cited by our author either with respect to Germany or England we shall not occupy time by inquiring whether the Reformers in complaining of the unholy lives of many among their professed followers, might not very naturally in the anxiety of their hearts use language somewhat hyperbolical we shall not dwell upon the very obvious reflection that among the numbers who swelled the ranks of the Reformed would be found many who had left Popery from disgust at its superstitions, and had yet obtained no correct knowledge of scriptural truth we shall not insist upon this alleged deterioration of manners as exhibiting the natural result of that gross ignorance which Popery had fostered and which, when allowed to produce its genuine fruits unchecked by the terrors of the church would immediately break out into flagrant excess we will leave Mr Butler in full possession of these extracts and will simply ask in reply whether he believes that they contain a fair view of the opinions entertained by the Reformers—for, as to poor vacillating Erasmus, who, in some places has so much extolled the piety and virtue of the Reformers and in others has expressed himself in a way which certainly no Protestant can admit to be impartial * we shall say little about his testimony—of the effect of their own labours? Does he really think that Luther and Melancthon abroad or Latimer and Bishop Burnet at home, would have deemed it a just representation of their sentiments if they had found themselves thus overwhelming with disgrace the great work which they prized so highly or would have regarded this general dissoluteness and depravity as the legitimate effect of the preaching of the Gospel?

Is it indeed the persuasion of Mr Butler that Luther, when lamenting the depravity of his own heart, is to be convicted on that evidence of being a character utterly abominable and that it was by the adoption of Protestant principles that he had become thus earthly sensual and devilish? Would Mr Butler think it right that we should select from some writer on the Roman Catholic side two short passages without the slightest explanation of the subject with which they were connected and, for the purpose of condemning the man, place them in immediate juxta position? Is this the process usually followed by the lovers of truth? or will Mr Butler assert, that the effect of those particular passages, thus torn from their just connexion and forced into a new one, is not in truth entirely to misrepresent that reformer? We are the less surprised however, at these things or at any assertion contained in this book about other times, when we observe with how little regard either to candour or justice Mr Butler deals with the Protestant clergy of his own day The writer who can, in the form of a strong interrogation, publish to the world that the clergy of the Church

* See particularly his controversy with Luther as noticed by Joseph Milner

of England do not sincerely believe the doctrines of the Trinity the Incarnation, the Divinity of Christ, and the Atonement, (p 170) and who, for the purpose of debasing and vilifying the clergy, can now cite the authority of Gibbon should be apprized that any assertion which he can make, in reference to any question between Popery and Protestantism, must necessarily be viewed with at least very serious suspicion The reader will do well, in every case which affects the contending churches, to take nothing upon trust

Were it requisite to illustrate what we mean we might, in connexion with these remarks notice the assertion so positively made and not without a rebuke to Mr Southey for omitting to state it that Thomas Cromwell died in the *Roman* Catholic faith an assertion for which the only evidence adduced even by Mr Butler is his declaration on the scaffold " that he died in the *catholic* faith not doubting in any article of his faith Not the slightest hint have we from Mr Butler that this alleged fact of his attachment to the Romish Church had ever been disputed not the slightest intimation that his words in the view of most persons were intended to convey a meaning exactly the reverse of that which is here assigned to them namely, that although he had renounced the *Roman* faith the *catholic* faith he had not renounced though he doubted or denied many of the dogmas of the papal communion, he did not doubt of any article of the catholic Church We might further notice the interrogations with which Mr Butler has attempted to represent Cranmer and Latimer, as men utterly unworthy of respect interrogations which will in general be found to have no force, if a due attention be paid to the real facts of the case, and to the circumstances in which those great men were so singularly placed To go at much length into an examination of them would be tedious but it would be wrong to pass these paragraphs entirely without remark

Speaking of Cranmer, Mr Butler says,—

Although he knew Anne Boleyn was under no precontract of marriage did he not, to use Bishop Burnet s expression extort from her standing as she then did on the very verge of eternity a confession of the existence of such a contract? Was not this culpable subserviency to his master s cruelties? was it not prevailing on the unhappy woman to die with a lie upon her lips?

From this paragraph, Cranmer as it should seem, certainly knew that there was no precontract with the Earl of Northumberland How could he know this? He knew only that this was the Earl s declaration upon oath We are to suppose that Cranmer was a willing agent in persecuting the Queen Bishop Burnet himself proves the contrary he declares that Cranmer had been much obliged by her, and had conceived a high opinion of her and in his letter to the king which letter Burnet inserts in his history that he justified her as far as was consistent with prudence and charity We are given to understand further that Cranmer this willing tool of a profligate master, did according to Burnet s expression extort from her the confession of this alleged precontract This is *not* the statement of Burnet His words are these " But now she, lying under so terrible a sentence, it is most probable that either some hopes of life were given her or at least she was wrought on by the assurances of mitigating that cruel part of her judgment, of being *burnt*, into the milder part of the sentence of *having her head cut off* so that she confessed a precontract and on the 17th of May was brought to Lambeth and in court, the afflicted Archbishop sit

* In the margin we have this sentence Upon an extorted confession, is divorced

ting judge, some persons of quality being present, she confessed some just and lawful impediments, by which it was evident, that her marriage with the king was void. So far is Burnet from implicating Cranmer in the charge of endeavouring to prevail upon her to die with a lie upon her lips, that he speaks of him as *afflicted* at the scene so far is he from charging that prelate with extorting from her a confession of the precontract there is no proof that he attempted to persuade her into *any* confession and the terms of the statement imply, that this confession of the precontract was not even made in the presence of Cranmer but at some time previous to the day on which she was brought to Lambeth. The reader will see from this strange misstatement of Burnet's authority how cautious we must be in admitting Mr Butler's criminations of Archbishop Cranmer. If he can be so intrepid, and yet so incorrect, in assertion, when he cites his authority, we must be at least equally on our guard when he cites none.

We adduce another illustration of the little stress to be laid upon Mr Butler's assertions in matters which involve the interests of Popery and Protestantism and then bid farewell to this unpleasant subject —

As to Latimer whom you so highly celebrate — was he not more remarkable for inconsistency than almost any other man with whose biography you are acquainted? Was he not first known by his attack upon the doctrines of Melancthon and the other German Reformers? then by his advocation of these doctrines? then by his rejection of them in obedience to the command of Wolsey? then by his re-assumption of them? then by his second rejection of them and his craving pardon for them on his knees to soothe Henry VIII? then by his second re assumption of them in the reign of Edward VI &c. Butler p 218

Latimer it seems was originally a Papist The fact is unquestionable such were the clergy of that day before the Reformation and, so far as this involves matter of charge he shares it with them all Till better instructed, he must of necessity have been a Papist

He then became a Protestant Equally true

He next rejected the doctrines of the Reformers, in obedience to the command of Wolsey A mere gratuitous assertion. Fox says, that when called up before the cardinal for heresy, "he was content to subscribe and grant to such articles as then they propounded to him" We know of no other tolerable authority which asserts even this concession but what were these articles? The account given by Morice, a friend of Latimer, is very minute in its detail of this affair, and carries with it strong internal marks of truth and so different according to that report was the issue of the conference between Latimer and Wolsey that the cardinal expressed high approbation of his conduct assuring him, 'If the Bishop of Ely cannot abide such doctrine as you have here repeated you shall have *my* licence, and shall preach it unto his beard, let him say what he will

' And thereupon, after a gentle monition given unto Mr Latimer the cardinal discharged him with his licence home to preach throughout England —(Wordsworth's Eccles Biog Latimer)

Then by his re assumption of them No comment is necessary

Then by his second rejection of them Where and when? Before the convocation in 1531-2? It cannot be *proved* that he subscribed the articles then proposed to him Mr Gilpin thinks it past dispute that he did *not* and the reasons assigned for that opinion are exceedingly strong He possibly made *some* concession and, as Fox observes, ' no great matter nor marvel the iniquity of the time being such, that either he must needs so do, or else abide the bishop's blessing that is, cruel sentence of death which he at that time, (as himself confessed preaching at Stamford,) was loth to sustain for such matters as these were, unless it were for articles necessary of his belief, by which, adds Fox, with great candour and honesty, "I *conjecture rather* that he did subscribe at length, albeit it was long before he could be brought to do so." Fox's *conjecture*, although of little weight with us against Morice and Mr. Gilpin's arguments, is *proof* with Mr. Butler; proof so positive, as to justify the strong affirmation contained in his question to Mr. Southey, whether, even if Latimer had at that time through fear of the bishop's blessing subscribed declarations which his conscience did not cordially acknowledge, some little apology might not be found for him in the infirmity of human nature; let others judge; Mr. Butler sees nothing in it to qualify the charge of culpable inconsistency.

Then by his second rejection of them, and his craving pardon for them on his knees, to soothe Henry VIII.

We are not quite certain whether the former part of this sentence is to be taken, as we have supposed, for a detached accusation, or whether it is to be combined with the submission before the king. We have given Mr. Butler the full benefit of it as a distinct allegation; we proceed to ask then, did Latimer crave pardon for his Protestant doctrines on his knees to soothe Henry VIII.? Certainly not. The only authority on this subject is his own statement in the seventh of his sermons. It runs thus:—

' In the king's days that is dead, many of us were called together before him to say our minds in certain matters. In the end one kneeled down, —(kneeling to the King was then not uncommon)—' and accused me of sedition, that I had preached seditious doctrine, a heavy salutation, and a hard point of such a man's doing, as, if I should name him, ye would not think it.*

' The king turned to me, and said, ' What say you to that sir?' Then I kneeled down, and turned first to mine accuser, and required him, Sir, what form of preaching would you appoint me to preach before a king? Would you have me preach nothing as concerning a king, in a king's sermon? Have you any commission to appoint me what I shall preach? Besides this I asked him divers other questions, and he would make answer to none of them all; he had nothing to say. Then I turned me to the king, and submitted myself to his Grace, and said, ' I never thought myself worthy, I never sued to be a preacher before your Grace; but I was called to it, and would be willing, if you mislike me, to give place to my betters; for I grant there be a great many more worthy of the room than I am; and if it be your Grace's pleasure so to allow them for preachers, I could be content to bear their books after them. But if your Grace allow me for a preacher, I would desire your Grace to give me leave to discharge my conscience; give me leave to frame my doctrine according to my audience. I had been a very dolt indeed to have preached so at the borders of your realm, as I preach before your Grace. And I thank Almighty God, which hath always been my remedy, that my sayings were well accepted of the king; for like a gracious lord, he turned into another communication.' So little ground has Mr. Butler for the vaunting question, did he not crave pardon for them (the doctrines of the Reformers) on his knees to soothe Henry VIII.? Did he, we rejoin, ask pardon for any thing? And unless sedition and Protestantism are convertible terms, was there the remotest allusion to the principles of the Reformation?

We wish that Cranmer could be defended from the charge of having countenanced religious persecution, with as much ease as both himself and his fellow labourers in the Reformation can be vindicated from other matters of accusation brought

* Probably Gardiner, Bishop of Winchester.

forward by Mr Butler but, in the case especially of Joan Bocher and George Paris, we lament to find this gentle and amiable man deeply implicated in the guilt of shedding blood and the only plea to be offered on his behalf is one which will in some measure extend to all who were concerned in those sad tragedies The principles of toleration * were in that day, generally unknown no voice, as Mr Southey remarks had yet been raised against the atrocious persuasion that death was the just punishment for heresy and burning the appropriate mode of execution It is to the lasting honour of Martin Luther that he advanced in this respect much beyond the character of the age in which he lived The question being put to him by his friend Lincus whether he conceived the magistrate to be justified in putting to death teachers of false religion, he replied I am backward to pass a sentence of death, let the merit be ever so apparent For I am alarmed when I reflect on the conduct of the Papists who have so often abused the statutes of capital punishment against heresy to the effusion of innocent blood Among the Protestants in process of time, I foresee a great probability of a similar abuse if they should now arm the magistrate with the same powers, and there should be left on record a single instance of a person having suffered legally for the propagation of false doctrine On this ground I am decidedly against capital punishment in such cases and think it quite sufficient that mischievous teachers of religion be removed from their situations Joseph Milner from whom we borrow this passage observes — Where we are to look for examples of similar discrimination and freedom from party violence under any circumstances resembling those in which Luther was placed I know not Certainly we shall have occasion to lament, in the progress of this history, that some other reformers even of the most gentle and beneficent tempers, were of a very different opinion deceived no doubt by the perversion of the Old Testament precedents which derive their force from the Jewish Theocracy

In looking therefore at the little army of martyrs amounting to nearly 300 * who were burned in Queen Mary s reign besides those that died of famine in different prisons, we would not, in reflecting upon their persecutors leave out of sight the character of the times we would not forget that a strong case on the same ground may be made out against some of our great reformers But it is to be remembered that these were men brought up in popish habits of education and the exclusive and intolerant spirit which the creed of that church tends so directly to cherish is not perhaps to be cast off in one generation The reader of that disastrous portion of our annals cannot fail to be struck with the contrast in some important particulars between the behaviour of the reformers and that of the bigoted adherents to Popery What for example, was the conduct of Bishop Ridley while in possession of the see of London, towards the mother and sister of Bishop Bonner? They dined every day at his table And how wickedly was it recompensed by that bloody persecutor, when again in power †! Compare the

* Mr Butler holds a different doctrine and mentions (p 261) among the persons who had professed the principle of toleration Sir Thomas More he had established it in his Utopia It is to be lamented that this great man did not better understand it in practice

See Strype
† When Ridley was condemned he entreated that a supplication which he read might be presented to the Queen in behalf of some tenants to whom he had granted leases and for his sister whose husband Bonner had deprived of the provision which he had made for her and her family
The Bishop of Gloucester promised to further his request but so far was Bonner from acknowledging the beneficence which Ridley had shewn to his mother and sister that not content with depriving the martyred bishop s brother in law of his means

measures dealt out generally to the Protestant Bishops by the Romish hierarchy with that of the popish prelates to them, as each class held alternately the seat of authority, and ask whether the spirit of moderation be not incalculably on the side of the Protestant. One of the most repulsive and horrible circumstances which attended the execution of the Marian martyrs, was the delight which the wretched persecutors found in their atrocious business: they enjoyed the condemnation of the alleged heretic: they seem to have felt a barbarous pleasure in his execution: it was not in general sufficient to burn him to ashes: they loved the work as well as the wages of their iniquity: they bleated forth sounds of petty triumph and of barbarous insult: they demonized themselves, and attempted, but happily in vain, to demonize the people. Was this after the manner of Cranmer? or was there one among the Reformers who exhibited that savage disposition which has consigned to infamy the names of so many of the Marian persecutors?

As an indication of the spirit by which these barbarous men were generally influenced, we shall be contented to mark their conduct in reference to Archbishop Cranmer himself, when placed in circumstances which, whatever may have been in their estimation his previous delinquencies might, we should suppose, have awed or soothed them into decency: and that we may not appeal merely to Mr Southey, we give a short passage from Gilpin. The scene is in St Mary's at Oxford, when Cranmer was lamenting to the people his subscription to popish opinions. 'As he was continuing his speech, the whole assembly was in an uproar

of subsistence he threatened in his brutal language to make twelve godfathers go upon him: and would have brought him to the stake if Heath, in return for the kindness which he had experienced from Ridley, had not interposed and saved him. Southey p 197

Lord Williams gave the first impulse to the tumult, crying aloud, Stop the audacious heretic. On which several priests and friars, rushing from different parts of the church with great eagerness seized him: pulled him from his seat: dragged him into the street, and with much indecent precipitation, hurried him to the stake which was already prepared. Executioners were on the spot, who, receiving him with a chain, piled the faggots in order round him.

"As he stood thus, with all the horrid apparatus of death about him, amidst torments, revilings, and execrations, he alone maintained a dispassionate behaviour, &c." What indeed must have been the brutalized habits of these persecutors, when even after the death of Mary, one of them Story, 'boasted in the House of Commons of the part which he had taken: related with exultation, how he had thrown a faggot in the face of an ear-wig, as he called him, who was singing Psalms at the stake, and how he had thrust a thorn bush under his feet, to prick him: wished that he had done more: and said he only regretted that they should have laboured at the young and little twigs when they ought to have struck at the root, &c.*

It is not, however, without much confidence and all the plausibility which strong assertions can give, that the Papists complain of the persecutions endured by themselves as far exceeding those which they are charged with inflicting: and Mr Butler countenances such statements. We do not feel any disposition to vindicate sanguinary or oppressive measures from whatever quarter they may come: and it is possible that the law passed in the reign of Elizabeth for restraining and punishing those who either denied her supremacy, or who as ministers refused to use the Common Prayer or who maintained the authority of the pope, or affirmed that the queen was not a lawful sovereign or pre-

* Southey vol ii p 208

tended to have power to withdraw her subjects from their allegiance, together with the severer acts against Jesuits &c, might be unnecessary in themselves and too violent in their provisions and too rigid in their execution. But when we consider the temper of the times the circumstances under which these enactments severally took place and the general policy of Elizabeth's reign we can by no means concur in Mr Butler's unqualified statements on this subject. It was the object of the queen and her councillors to heal the unhappy divisions which existed at her accession to the throne and for some time notwithstanding the occasional violence of individual Roman Catholics that object was carefully pursued. The disposition to treat Papists with kindness and by kindness to conciliate them to the new order of things was remarkably evinced in the moderation manifested toward the popish bishops. Some of these although they refused nearly to a man to assist at her coronation were allowed to live in a sort of splendid retirement. Heath was occasionally visited by the queen in person and even Bonner had the use of the garden and orchards attached to the Marshalsea where he resided and lived as he pleased without any other privation than that of liberty, for, though he was allowed to go abroad he durst not we are told avail himself of the privilege, for fear of the people. But this calm was of no long duration. Elizabeth soon began to find, that she was made the subject of plots and conspiracies. To meet these as they successively occurred the laws to which we have just adverted were successively passed. In our days they might perhaps have been modified perhaps no government, (at least no *Protestant* government for the most modern annals of Popery show how little the spirit of its priesthood is reformed—witness the rash project just introduced into the French chambers for making disrespect to the Host, or the vessel that contains it, a capital crime,) would now have recourse to measures so revolting but, in Elizabeth's time, it was unfortunately believed that the only effectual mode of putting down the spirit of Roman Catholic hostility was by strong penal enactments and some of these were executed with unsparing severity. Whether the jealousy of the government might not, in these cases, outrun the danger must be left to every reader of English history to decide for himself but at least it must be admitted, that the conduct of the pope was of a nature to excite the worst suspicions, and to rouse into action the most tardy of the councillors of the crown. Pius V, having soon found his efforts to regain Elizabeth to the Church of Rome ineffectual, proceeded, without ceremony to instigate her subjects to rebellion

Being he said as Peter's successor prince over all people and all kingdoms to pluck up destroy scatter consume plant and build he publicly excommunicated Elizabeth whom he called the pretended Queen of England and the servant of wickedness seeing (he said) that impieties and wicked actions were multiplied through her instigation he cut her off as a heretic and favourer of heretics from the unity of the body of Christ deprived her of her pretended title to the kingdom and of all dominion dignity and privilege whatsoever absolved all her subjects from their allegiance forbade them to obey her or her laws and included all who should disregard this prohibition in the same sentence of excommunication. Southey vol ii p 266

Who that reads this Bull, and reflects upon the power and influence of the pope can doubt that the government was compelled in a manner for its own safety to act with some degree of rigour or can we be surprised, if the execution of the laws were sometimes attended in such an age by great cruelty and sometimes, perhaps by no small measure of injustice?

Mr Butler (p 219) challenges Mr Southey to compare the conduct of Latimer 'with that of More, Fisher or any of the 300 persons who suffered death under *your* penal laws and in commenting on the reign of Elizabeth, under whom most of these alleged executions took place, he asserts, that out of a given list of 204 no person is included, who was executed for any plot, either real or imaginary, except eleven, who suffered for the pretended plot of Rheims or Rome.

We were not previously aware that Protestants are responsible for the death of More and Fisher,* or that the laws under which they suffered can with any shadow of right be attributed to the Protestant church. This is one of the insinuations against which the readers of Mr. Butler would do well to be upon their guard.

It is strenuously maintained by the advocates of Popery, that the Papists who were put to death in the reign of Elizabeth, were martyrs to their *religion*; this is by Protestants as strenuously denied. They suffered, not for believing in transubstantiation, nor for performing mass, but for violating the laws which Parliament had deemed necessary for the protection of the government; for teaching that the queen ought to be deposed; that it was lawful to kill her; that all Roman Catholic subjects who obeyed her commands, were cut off by so doing from the unity of the church, &c. We have little doubt that on some occasions the blow fell upon men who may be said to have suffered for religion rather than for active disloyalty; but such was not the purpose of the government or of the laws. If Bonner was spared, what Roman Catholic had merely as a Roman Catholic any ground of apprehension? "Not one popish bishop (says Fuller) was put to death, nor peer of the realm, save for actual rebellion, in all the queen's reign. Whereas in the Marian days, we had an archbishop and four bishops burnt for mere matters of conscience." If religious persecution had been the object, would Elizabeth have overlooked such men as Bonner, to aim at inferior Papists?

The case of Campian is one which has occupied the attention of all writers on this portion of our annals; and, as might be expected, Mr. Southey and Mr. Butler differ widely in their accounts of him. By the former he is regarded as an intemperate advocate for the cause recommended by that infamous bull of Pius V.; by the latter, as one of the most innocent and excellent, as well as greatest characters, whom that age produced. He was tried and convicted of high treason; and although we would not positively affirm that he was guilty, yet both his letter to Father Edward Mercurian, as given by Fuller, and the extracts from another written by him when in concealment to the Privy Council, as adduced by Mr. Southey, scarcely allow us to regard him as an innocent man. Whether guilty or innocent, it was for alleged treason that he was condemned.

Campian and his fellow sufferers however died as martyrs according to their own views, and as martyrs they were then regarded and are still represented by the Romanists. Certain however it is that they suffered for points of state and not of faith; not as Roman Catholics but as Bull papists; not for religion but for treason. Some of them are to be admired as men of genius and high endowments, as well as of heroic constancy; all to be lamented as acting for an injurious purpose under a mistaken sense of duty; but their sufferings belong to the history of papal politics rather than of religious persecution. They succeeded in raising one rebellion which was easily suppressed; for Elizabeth was deservedly popular, and the Protestants had now become the great majority; but repeated conspiracies against the life of the queen were detected, and such were the avowed principles and intentions of the Papists wherever they

---

* In p. 217 Mr. Butler tells us that Cranmer was instrumental in bringing Lambert and Anne Askew to the stake with others both Catholics and Anabaptists. Anne Askew was one of Gardiner's victims, and Gardiner instigated the proceedings against Lambert. It is to be regretted that Cranmer, who then believed in the corporal presence, took any part in these proceedings; but over the judgment he had no controul: Henry was in person both judge and disputant.

dared avow them that Walsingham expressed his fears of a Bartholomew breakfast, or a Florence banquet. Southey vol. ii. pp. 278, 279.

We subjoin Mr Butler's view of these transactions:—

The only acts for which they suffered were those which the statutes of Elizabeth had made treasonable as denying her spiritual authority remaining in or returning to England or some other spiritual observance. Now if the priests had not remained in or returned to England, the English Roman Catholics would have been without instruction without the sacraments and without the rites of their church. To remain in or return to England was therefore the duty of the Catholic priesthood and for some act of this religious duty—but for no act of any other kind—were they executed. Then if you say they were hanged or embowelled not for being priests but for being traitors then as their being priests was the sole cause of their being traitors they were in truth hanged and embowelled for being priests.

For this last observation, Mr Butler professes himself indebted to Sir Walter Scott. It is, we think, rather too refined. The security of the state, as it was supposed, rendered it necessary to punish as offences the acts here cited, and it was not a question of religious principle at all, farther than as such acts grew out of the character of the priesthood. We would not, however, be the apologists for any species of persecution whether exercised by Papists upon Protestants, or by Protestants upon Papists or by any man whatever upon another, it is detestable in every form. Would that both the practice, and the intolerant disposition which leads to it, were banished universally from the face of the earth, and that, instead of seeking for causes of mutual exasperation men would learn at last to regard each other with the spirit of Christian charity!

The motives for this wish—we express it as a wish, rather than a consummation speedily to be hoped for—are certainly not diminished by a perusal of Mr Southey's 16th and 17th chapters including the times of James I. Charles I, and the Commonwealth. The period of religious dissension, and of civil war, however instructive in some respects, requires on the part of the historian all possible candour and moderation. It seldom happens that, amidst the confusion of the times, one party is so entirely in the wrong, and the other so perfectly in the right, as to deserve unqualified condemnation or unmingled praise, and the writer may with reason, suspect the justice of his own statements, who makes himself in such cases a determined partizan. We should rejoice to observe that Mr Southey had stood more clear in this respect than many that have preceded him,—that he had balanced with more care conflicting motives and opposing arguments that he had stated with more precision the several causes which led to the subversion of the church, and the catastrophe of the civil wars that he had avoided hard words and injurious epithets and most of all, that, by the weight of his respectable name he had not sanctioned that uncharitable spirit which at this day labours hard to exasperate on religious subjects one half of the community against the other. The tone adopted by Mr Southey, in this part of his work is alike impolitic and unjust.

The reader of this narrative, if he have no other sources of information, will rise from it with the impression that one of the main distinctions between the Puritans and the Church of England consisted in the fact of the Calvinistic doctrines being maintained by the one class and disavowed by the other. He will be taught to believe, that, with few exceptions, all was violent aggression from the Nonconformists of the day and all meekness and endurance from the sons of the Church and unless he watches both the history and his own feelings with some scrupulosity, and greater vigilance than is commonly exercised over a popular work, he will transfer the view which he takes of those times to his own. Not only will every Roman Catholic be associated with the gunpowder plot, a deed which the members of that church almost universally disclaimed, but in every Calvinist he will discover a Puritan, and in every Puritan an inveterate enemy to the civil and religious establishments of his country. We disclaim most distinctly the imputation of any such feelings to Mr Southey, but that this will be the effect of his representations, and especially of his unmeasured hostility against every thing to which fashion has attached the name of Calvinist and Puritan, and of his overweening admiration of men whose intemperate violence was scarcely less fatal to the cause of order, which they espoused, than the unwearied efforts of their opponents, we entertain not the shadow of a doubt.

Scarcely have we entered upon the history of the church in the reign of King James than Puritan and Calvinist become 'familiar to us as household words.' What then is the definition of Puritan? The strict application of it in the first instance was to those who desired to have what they conceived to be a purer *discipline* it had nothing to do with doctrines. The signification of it was gradually extended to reformers of almost every class, and, by way of odium it has now for several generations been applied to such persons as are supposed to have more religion than their neighbours.

It is little to the credit of the term, in this application of it, that it was invented by one of the worst men of the age in which he lived. 'We must not forget, says Fuller, "that Spalato (I am confident I am not mistaken therein) was the first who, professing himself a Protestant used the word Puritan, to signify the defenders of matters doctrinal in the English Church. As Spalato first abused the word in this sense, so we could wish he had carried it away with him on his return to Rome. Whereas now, leaving the word behind him in this extensive signification thereof, it hath since by others been improved to asperse the most orthodox in doctrine and religious in conversation.

It is plain, therefore, that Fuller had a strong objection to the term in its religious use. In that sense it signified nothing more than an attachment to matters doctrinal in the English Church, only it affixed upon the defender of those doctrines, as it was assuredly meant to affix, unmerited stigma and reproach. The great prelates of that day were probably not assailed by this opprobrious word, but so far as doctrines were concerned, they were in this sense as determined Puritans as the fiercest of the Non-conformists.

Next, as to the term Calvinist. This is a word of very ambiguous import. Lord Clarendon adopts it not unfrequently, as designating those who approved the Calvinistic platform of *government* and *discipline* in preference to the episcopal mode, and this without any question of *doctrine*. Mr Southey often seems to have in view the doctrines of that Reformer. We care not in what sense the term Calvinist is adopted so that there be no ambiguity in the use of it. With Mr Southey it often appears to be as indefinite a term as Puritan. His Calvinistic or Puritanical clergy are not exclusively the advocates for the platform of Geneva, let them only be Calvinistic in doctrine and for the most part the rest seems to follow as a matter of course.*

---

* This is sometimes almost directly *asserted*. When the first general synod of the Protestants was held at Dort, it was owing to the influence of the English divines that its sanction was not given to the monstrous doctrine of the Supralapsarians. The proceedings of the synod were sufficiently disgraceful without coming to such a conclusion, nevertheless the dominable doctrine that the Almighty has placed the greater part of mankind under a fatal necessity of committing the offences for which he has predetermined eternally to

If petitions tending to subvert the civil and ecclesiastical constitution were to be got up, if the subscriptions of honest men were to be obtained to a moderate paper and transferred to an inflammatory one which they conscientiously disapproved, if mobs were to be collected for intimidating the House of Lords, if a cry was to be raised for the blood of an individual whom the faction feared or hated, if the trumpet of rebellion was to be blown, the Puritanical clergy performed these services for their friends in Parliament. And it is worthy of notice that the most active in this work of wickedness were not the men who had been suspended for Nonconformity, but those of Abbot's school, who complying with the rubric as long as they stood in fear of Laud's vigilant superintendance, had hitherto enjoyed the benefices of the church, while they waited for an opportunity to pervert its doctrine, overthrow its discipline, and proscribe its forms.—vol. ii. p. 364.

In discussing questions of this sort we would look simply to historical facts. Whether the notions of Calvinism be scriptural or not, is not the question; but when the tendency of a work is to shew that doctrinal Calvinism leads to practical Non-conformity, and that a man cannot be at the same time a warm friend to the Church of England and a theological Calvinist, we assert that such a view is not borne out by the facts of the case; and Mr. Southey ought to have guarded with great care against the possibility of his readers coming to such a conclusion.

The total want of references in these volumes renders it impossible for us to state the grounds of the assertion, that 'the most active in the work of wickedness were not the men who had been suspended for Non-conformity, but those of Abbot's school, &c.' We doubt the fact; and among other reasons, we assign the following: that some of the most strict advocates of Episcopalian discipline were avowedly of the high school of Calvinism; and that among the greatest ornaments of the Episcopal bench, and the greatest sufferers for conscience sake in those disastrous times, were Calvinistic clergymen.

It is the fashion to hold up Archbishop Abbot to reprobation, as if he were the only one among the first few Protestant Archbishops who was tainted with the abominations of Calvinism. But what shall we say of the first Protestant Archbishop Parker, whom Mr. Southey himself calls (p. 253) "this excellent prelate?" Will it be denied that he was in doctrinal sentiments Calvinistic? What of that determined Supralapsarian Archbishop Whitgift, a prelate, whose discipline was so rigid that Lord Burleigh was obliged to remonstrate against his judicial and canonical sifting of poor ministers (in his Twenty-four Articles) in a letter which might be applied with not less propriety to nearly four times the number of questions proposed as a test of orthodoxy in our own times? Mr. Southey takes notice in his report of the Conference at Hampton Court of the celebrated Lambeth Articles; and were not these drawn up under the sanction of Whitgift? And are they not the very *ne plus ultra* of Genevese doctrine? The Puritans had such an affection, it seems, for these Articles, as to propose at the Conference, that the Articles of the Church should be conformed to them; happily the proposition was, after an explanation by Bancroft, rejected. But was Bancroft hostile to the doctrine of those Articles? He is mentioned by Fuller as one of the persons who concurred in them. The passage relating to this

punish them from that time lost ground. But it became the distinguishing tenet of the Non-conformists; it increased their strength, because those clergy who agreed with them at first in this point alone gradually became political as well as doctrinal Puritans; and it exasperated the implacable spirit of dissent by filling them with a spiritual pride as intolerable as it was intolerant—for fancying that they were the favourites and elect of the Almighty, they looked upon all who were not with them as the reprobate; and presuming that heaven was theirs by sure inheritance, they were ready on the first opportunity to claim the earth also by the same title.—vol. ii. pp. 327, 328.

subject is too remarkable to be omitted "Now also began some opinions about Predestination, Free will, Perseverance, &c much to trouble both the schools and the pulpit Whereupon Archbishop Whitgift, out of his Christian care to propagate the truth, and suppress the opposite errors, caused a solemn meeting of many grave and learned divines at Lambeth when (besides the Archbishop) Richard Bancroft bishop of London, Richard Vaughan bishop elect of Bangor, &c &c, were assembled these, after a serious debate, and mature deliberation, resolved at last on the following Articles (The Articles follow)— "And now, adds Fuller I perceive that I must tread tenderly, because I go not as before on men's graves, but am ready to touch the quick of some yet alive I know how dangerous it is to follow truth too near to the heels yet better it is that the teeth of an historian be struck out of his head for writing the truth, than that they remain still and rot in his jaws by feeding too much on the sweetmeats of flattery All that I will say of the credit of these Articles is this —— though those learned divines be not acknowledged as competent judges to pass definitive sentence in those points, yet they will be taken as witnesses beyond exception *whose testimony is an infallible evidence what was the general and received doctrine of England in that age about the forenamed controversies* (16 Cent Book ix)

Now that Bancroft was no lover of Puritanism, so far as that word means Non conformity, we can cite a testimony, to which Mr Southey will not object

Bancroft, who succeeded Whitgift in the primacy pursued the proper course of ejecting from their benefices all such ministers as would not conform to the rules of the church .... But Bancroft had neither the wisdom nor the moderation of Parker and Whitgift He framed canons by which all persons who spoke in derogation of the Church of England either as related to its doctrine or discipline were to be excommunicated *ipso facto*

The laws against libels were already too severe And with an impolicy gross as his intolerance when several Puritan families migrated to Virginia, that they might form a church there according to their own opinions and great numbers were preparing to follow them this imprudent primate instead of rejoicing that so many intractable spirits were willing to transport themselves out of the country obtained a proclamation whereby they were forbidden to leave it without a special licence from the king

Bancroft's rigour was less injurious to the church than the counter conduct of his successor Abbot a man who inclined to the Puritans first because he sympathized with them as a Calvinist and afterwards as a malecontent connived at Non conformity Bancroft had nearly succeeded in weeding out the discontented ministers who sought to subvert the church in whose service they had engaged under Abbot's patronage they became numerous enough to form a formidable party and to perceive that success was within reach as well as hope —Southey vol ii pp 333, 334.

Are we incorrect in supposing that Mr Southey regards Bancroft as anti Calvinistic? Yet if the Lambeth Articles, in which that prelate concurred, were now to be made the rule of admission into the church there are hundreds of her ministers, at this day branded as Calvinistic who could never have been numbered among her priests or deacons

That Abbot was a Calvinist, is, we believe, universally allowed the same concession, we presume, will be made concerning Grindall it appears, therefore, that all the Protestant archbishops of Canterbury, down to Archbishop Laud maintained those doctrinal sentiments which are tacitly and indirectly represented as exclusively belonging to the Puritans and of these archbishops some were among the strongest assertors of ecclesiastical discipline whom the church has ever beheld It is in perfect conformity with these statements that Mosheim ascribes to Archbishop Laud the considerable change which after the Synod of Dort took place in England toward Arminianism till his time the Conformists and Non conformists were in general of the same mind on the subject of Calvinistic theology.

It would be an endless task to cite all the eminent men of that period, who embraced views of doctrine similar to those which have just been noticed. We shall mention only two additional names, Bishop Hall and Bishop Davenant, both of whom officially attended the meeting of the Synod of Dort.* Bishop Hall's character was so much traduced during the time of Laud for his "too much indulgence to persons disaffected, and too much liberty of frequent lecturings within his charge, that as he says, 'he plainly told my lord of Canterbury, he would rather give up his rochet, than be subject to these misrepresentations;' yet was he one of those Calvinists against whom, as Lord Clarendon states, Laud 'entertained too much prejudice as if they were enemies to the discipline of the church, because they concurred with Calvin in some doctrinal points; when they abhorred his discipline and reverenced the government of the church and prayed for the peace of it with as much zeal and fervency as any in the kingdom, as they made manifest in their lives and in their sufferings, with it and for it.'

Bishop Davenant was summoned before the Privy Council for a sermon preached before the king, of which he gives the following account:—The text was, *Eternal life is the gift of God, through Jesus Christ our Lord*. "As in the former part I had spoken of the threefold misery of the wicked, so here I expounded the threefold happiness of the godly to be considered, first, happy in the Lord whom they serve—God in Christ Jesus; secondly, happy in the reward of their service, eternal life; thirdly, happy in the manner of their reward, χαρισμα. The two former points were not excepted against; in the third and last, I considered eternal life in three divers instances; in the eternal destination thereunto, which we call election; in our conversion, regeneration, or justification, which I termed the embryo of eternal life; and, last of all, in our coronation, when full possession of eternal life is given us,—in all these I shewed it to be χαρισμα or the free gift of God through Christ. "The last point was not disliked." "the second was not expressly taxed." "only the first was it which had the offence; not in regard to the doctrine itself, but because (as my lord's grace said) the king had prohibited the debating thereof."

Of this bishop, and his deportment in his diocese, Fuller says, "where (at Salisbury) with what gravity and moderation he behaved himself, how humble, hospitable, painful in preaching and writing may be better reported hereafter, when his memory (green as yet) shall be mellowed by time."

It is no part of our intention to *defend* the doctrinal views of these great men; with respect to the soundness of their principles in a scriptural sense, we affirm nothing; we would grant for argument's sake that the Whitgifts and Parkers, and Halls and Ushers and Sandersons and Davenants of other days could not pass the ordeal of Eighty seven Questions, or be deemed worthy of a curacy in these more enlightened times: all we contend for is, that these men were in their generation considered as lights of the church and of the world; and that the mere circumstance of a man being in doctrine a little more or a little less Calvinistic is not to be the test of dislike or attachment to the church. It was the sound opinion of Bishop Horsley as it is of some of the most distinguished prelates of the present day that the Articles of our Church embrace alike Calvinists and Arminians; both have often conscientiously subscribed them, both conscientiously

---

* Are we to infer from Mr Southey's remarks about the Synod of Dort, that those men were not Calvinists?—See a former note.

use the Liturgy, and attend the ordinances of her worship; and he is no friend to the church who would either narrow the way that leads to her courts, or close her doors against any man who loves her service and adheres to her communion.

As we conceive Mr Southey to have dealt unfairly by the Calvinists and doctrinal Puritans, and to have given a very defective account of the mixed motives which drove the kingdom into the guilt of rebellion, so must we likewise express our disagreement with him on the character and conduct of Archbishop Laud. That this prelate was an able man, and a learned man, we readily allow; but surely never was there a primate of this country less judicious in his plans, or less suited to the times in which he lived. Mr Gilpin institutes a comparison between him and Archbishop Cranmer, which seems on the whole, to be as just as it is free from all violence and party spirit. "Both, says he, were good men,—both were equally zealous for religion,—and both were engaged in the work of Reformation. I mean not to enter into the affair of introducing Episcopacy into Scotland; nor to throw any favourable light on the ecclesiastical views of those times. I am at present only considering the measures which the two archbishops took in forwarding their respective plans. While Cranmer pursued his with that caution and temper which we have just been examining, Laud, in the violence of his integrity, (for he was certainly a well meaning man,) making allowances neither for men nor opinions, was determined to carry all before him. The consequence was, that he did nothing which he attempted; while Cranmer did every thing. And it is probable, that, if Henry had chosen such an instrument as Laud, he would have miscarried in his point; while Charles, with such a primate as Cranmer would either have been successful in his schemes, or at least have avoided the fatal consequences that ensued *. The opinion of Mosheim is expressed in terms less favourable to Laud; he speaks not only of his inexcusable imprudence, but of his excessive superstition, his rigid attachment to the sentiments, rites, and institutions of former times, which made him behold the Puritans and Calvinists † with horror; and of that violent spirit of animosity and persecution that discovered itself in the whole course of his ecclesiastical administration (Mosheim, cent. xvii. sect. ii. part 2.) Warburton is still less measured in his censures. Upon the whole, little as is the satisfaction which we feel in citing unfavourable opinions of Archbishop Laud, or of any other man, we must declare that nothing could be more unpropitious to the Church of England at this day than to have prelates who should be influenced by his spirit and example. This we are not apprehensive will ever be generally the case; we believe that the views and conduct of that mistaken man are on the whole correctly appreciated by the members and rulers of the church; and we trust that the representations of Mr Southey will not materially affect them. Of Laud's sincere attachment to the Church of England, we have no question; but we trust that many years will elapse before he generally obtains the credit attached to him by Mr Southey, of being the most illustrious of its episcopal martyrs ‡.

The conclusion of the life of this excellent man was much more conformable to the Christian spirit than much of his previous conduct. There was something very noble and very Christian in his deportment after he fell into adversity, and especially as he drew near his end; the faction, which had now got the ascendency, did much to exasperate his feelings, and treated him with

* Gilpin's Cranmer.
† N.B. The doctrine of the church previously to this was Calvinistical.—Note to Mosheim, same paragraph.
‡ See vol. ii. page 347.

scandalous injustice; but he seems to have possessed his soul in patience, and probably found that it was good for him to be afflicted. Mr Southey's account of the closing scene of his sufferings will be read with all the interest which such an account is calculated to excite.

He had prepared a prayer for the occasion, and never was there a more solemn and impressive form of words: it is alike remarkable for the state of mind in which it was composed and uttered, the deep and passionate devotion which it breathes, and the last firm fervent avowal of that religious loyalty for which he was at that instant about to die a martyr. To abridge it even of a word would be injurious: for if any human composition may be called sacred, this surely deserves to be so qualified. — O eternal God and merciful Father! look down upon me in mercy, in the riches and fulness of all thy mercies, look down upon me: but not till thou hast nailed my sins to the cross of Christ, not till thou hast bathed me in the blood of Christ, not till I have hid myself in the wounds of Christ, that so the punishment due unto my sins may pass over me. And since thou art pleased to try me to the utmost, I humbly beseech thee give me now in this great instant full patience proportionable comfort, and a heart ready to die for thine honour, the king's happiness, and the church's preservation. And my zeal to this (far from arrogancy be it spoken!) is all the sin (human frailty excepted and all the incidents thereunto) which is yet known to me in this particular, for which I now come to suffer: I say in this particular of treason. But otherwise my sins are many and great. Lord pardon them all, and those especially (whatever they are) which have drawn down this present judgment upon me! And when thou hast given me strength to bear it, do with me as seems best in thine own eyes, and carry me through death, that I may look upon it in what visage soever it shall appear to me. Amen! And that there may be a stop of this issue of blood in this more than miserable kingdom (I shall desire that I may pray for the people too, as well as for myself.) O Lord I beseech thee give grace of repentance to all blood thirsty people. But if they will not repent, O Lord confound all their devices, defeat and frustrate all their designs and endeavours upon them which are or shall be contrary to the glory of thy great name, the truth and sincerity of religion, the establishment of the king and his posterity after him in their just rights and privileges, the honour and conservation of parliaments in their just power, the preservation of this poor church in her truth, peace, and patrimony, and the settlement of this distracted and distressed people under their ancient laws, and in their native liberty. And when thou hast done all this in mere mercy to them, O Lord, fill their hearts with thankfulness and with religious, dutiful obedience to thee and thy commandments all their days. Amen, Lord Jesus, Amen. And receive my soul into thy bosom! Amen. Our Father which art in heaven!

He pronounced this awful prayer with a distinct and audible voice and, giving the paper to Dr Stern who had been permitted to attend him, desired him to communicate it to his other chaplains, that they might see in what manner he left this world, and he prayed God to bless them. Observing also that a person had been writing his speech, he desired him not to do him wrong by publishing a false and imperfect copy. His countenance had all this while a ruddier and more animated hue than it was wont to have, so that his enemies, with that malignity which marked all their proceedings towards him, said he had painted it, to fortify his cheeks against discovery of fear. The scaffold was crowded with people, and when he moved toward the block he desired he might have room to die, beseeching them to let him have an end of his misery which he had endured very long, and this he did as calmly as if he rather had been taking order for a nobleman's funeral than making way for his own! Being come near it he put off his doublet and said, God's will be done! I am willing to go out of this world; none can be more willing to send me. And seeing through the chinks of the boards that some persons were got under the scaffold about the very place where the block was seated, he called to the officer either to remove them or stop the crevices, saying it was no part of his desire that his blood should fall upon the heads of the people. Never, says Heylyn, did man put off mortality with a better courage, nor look upon his bloody and malicious enemies with more Christian charity. Sir J Clotworthy now molested him with impertinent questions, and after meekly answering him once or twice Laud turned to the executioner as the gentler person and, giving him money said without the slightest change of countenance, Here honest friend God forgive thee and I do; and do thy office upon me with mercy. Then he knelt down and after a short prayer, laid his head upon the block, and gave the signal in these words, Lord, receive my soul! The head was severed at one blow; and instantly the face became pale as ashes, to the confusion of those who affirmed that he had painted it. Yet they had then the stupidity and the baseness to assert, that he had reddened his countenance, and propt up his spirit by some compounded cordial from an apothecary, so hard is the heart, and so impenetrable the understanding of the factious.—Southey, vol. ii. pp. 433—437.

The great object of Mr. Southey through the whole of the seventeenth chapter appears to be that of holding up to deserved reprobation the conduct of the factions which overturned the government and the church; and they did much to entitle themselves to the indignation of every honest mind. With many just causes of complaint against the measures of the crown, and with some ground of dissatisfaction which individuals among them received from persons of authority in the church, they proceeded to acts of violence and outrage which reflect upon them merited disgrace. Many of those who are called Puritans were probably ashamed of these excesses, but they had little power to controul them: faction and party spirit were for the time triumphant; and reason, justice, sobriety, and truth, seem, in the mixture of this religious and political phrenzy, to have been banished from the land. The few who still adhered to order, and maintained the spirit of the Gospel, were fain to retire from the scene, or to bend before the storm which they could not avert. We have complained of Mr. Southey's want of definiteness and precision as to the many causes which impelled such multitudes of persons into such violent extremes, and it would not be difficult to point out errors in his statements; but enough has been said to shew our general impression as to this part of the work, and it is unnecessary to go more into detail.

On one subject Mr. Butler supplies what he properly considers as a defect in the Book of the Church. In his seventeenth chapter, Mr. Southey has been almost entirely silent on the condition and conduct of the Roman Catholics. Their conduct appears to have in general been exemplary for loyalty; but they suffered much. The factious were keen enough to obtain liberty for themselves, but little kindness was shewn to the adherents of the pope. Of the correctness of the narrative which relates to the execution of Mr. Green, a Roman Catholic priest, we have no means of forming a judgment. Mr. Butler cites for it the authority of Dr. Challoner. If the tale be true, that transaction was a disgrace to the age and the country—a scene of brutal cruelty almost we should hope, without parallel in England.

It cannot but have occurred to every person conversant with the history of our civil wars, if he have at all attempted to compare and to balance the statements of conflicting writers, that we perhaps live at a period too near the great Rebellion, and certainly are, from a variety of causes, too much affected by the spirit of those times, to expect an impartial account of it. We apply the same observation, in all its force, to the first two reigns after the Restoration. Those were days of much conflict, debate, and mutual recrimination; and as the effects of the measures then adopted in reference to ecclesiastical matters are still sensibly perceived in different ways by different classes of the community, we feel no great surprise either at the contradictory representations on these subjects, which are given us by persons of different creeds, or at the warmth with which each espouses the cause of his favourite party. We trust that we shall not offend greatly against the rules of candour, if we say that both Mr. Southey and Mr. Butler have been too sweeping in their censures, and too strong in their approbation. Future ages will probably find that truth requires the historian to pursue a middle course, and to acknowledge that on all sides there was just ground of complaint, that the spirit of the times was ill suited for conciliation, that much injury was mutually inflicted, and that there was much to be mutually forgiven. Such was certainly the case during the reign of Charles the First, and such we believe to have been the case in the remaining interval down to the Revolution.

The Declaration of Charles II, from Breda, held out fair promises of soothing the irritations which existed on points connected with religion, by allowing freedom to tender consciences, and disturbing no man for his creed whose conduct was quiet and peaceful. But that declaration remained a dead letter; the more violent of the conflicting parties, however desirous of immunity for themselves, were not very forward to grant toleration to others; and the opinion having gained ground that the adherents of Popery, who were said to have fomented the late troubles for their own purposes, were becoming dangerous to the state, indisposed the Parliament to carry into effect the avowed wishes of the king. Mr Butler repels with some indignation the charge thus levelled at the Roman Catholics as instigators of the rebellion; and so violent was the public feeling against those persons in the reign of Charles II, that we are bound to listen with great caution to any charges which were then brought against them; and that they had increased in number during the civil wars is a statement not to be admitted upon mere authority. After a conference between some of the London ministers (Presbyterians) and the loyal clergy the king published another declaration of a comprehensive nature. Mr Southey tells us that with this the Puritanical clergy were not satisfied, and that their emissaries were employed in sowing discontent.

> These letters, he adds, were intercepted, and among many of a like tendency was one from Calamy himself to a leading minister in Somersetshire, entreating that he and his friends would persist in the use of the Directory, and by no means admit the Common Prayer in their churches, for he made no question but that they should prevail further with the king than he had consented to in that declaration. This proof of knavery in the leaders, was followed by an instance of sufficient effrontery to defeat its own purpose, the days of mob petitioning being over. A petition was presented in the name of the London ministers and many others of the same opinion, thanking the king for his declaration, and saying they received it as an earnest of his future goodness in granting all those other concessions which were absolutely necessary for the liberty of their consciences; and they prayed that the wearing the surplice and the use of the cross in baptism might be absolutely abolished, as being scandalous to all men of tender consciences. The names of those persons who had attended at the conference and requested the king to withdraw the clause were not affixed to the petition, but it came signed by those who deputed them; and after these proofs of effrontery and bad faith, it was plain that nothing could be effected with such persons by conciliatory means. Southey vol ii pp 462 463.

The alleged duplicity of Calamy on this occasion was, if true, peculiarly disgraceful, as he had been one of those who waited upon Clarendon to solicit the omission of a particular clause in the declaration, on the ground that such a clause might prejudice their exertions in gaining over the common people to the wishes of the king. The clause was at their instance omitted, and they promised that they would both use the Common Prayer themselves, and by degrees accustom the people to it. This duplicity is also noticed in a subsequent page. In the abridgment of Baxter's Life, published by Edmund Calamy the younger, it is expressly said that Calamy refused a bishoprick (Lichfield) because he could not have it upon the king's declaration. His character appears to have been generally that of mildness and moderation; he was a great enemy to the sectaries, a Presbyterian in judgment, and is represented to have been very active in order to an accommodation. The offer of a bishoprick, after the shameful duplicity ascribed to him above, seems to cast discredit upon the correctness of the story, and proves, at any rate, that he was held at court in considerable respect. Calamy was one of the ministers appointed to attend the Conference at the Savoy, for the purpose of adopting some healing measures in reference to the Liturgy. There was little prospect from the first of accomplishing that object, and the dispute ended, so far as the Non conformists were concerned, without any satisfactory or beneficial result.

The Liturgy having been approved by the Convocation and confirmed by the King, was presented to the Parliament.

An Act of Uniformity past, with some clauses which the wisest statesmen and truest friends of the church disapproved but was unable to prevent. One of these excluded all persons from the ministry who had not received Episcopal ordination,—all therefore who had received Presbyterian orders were to quit their benefices or submit to be re-ordained. Another required a subscription from every man about to receive any preferment in the universities or the church, declaring his assent and consent to every thing in the Book of Common Prayer—words which gave occasion to cavils of the same kind as had been raised against the *et cetera* oath. But the touchstone was a clause which the Commons introduced for another qualifying subscription, wherein the subscriber declared it was not lawful upon any pretence to take arms against the king, abhorred the traitorous position of taking arms by his authority against his person, and renounced the Covenant as imposing no obligation upon him or any others, and unlawful in itself. Any clergyman who should not fully conform to this act by St Bartholomew's day, which was about three months after it was published, was *ipso facto* to be deprived of his cure, and the act was so worded as not to leave it in the king's power to dispense with its observance.

It was rigorously enforced, and about two thousand ministers were deprived. The measure was complained of as an act of enormous cruelty and persecution, and the circumstance of its being fixed for St Bartholomew's day gave the complainants occasion to compare it with the atrocious deed committed upon that day against the Huguenots in France. They were careful not to remember that the same day, and for the same reason (because the tithes were commonly due at Michaelmas) had been appointed for the former ejectment, when four times as many of the loyal clergy were deprived for fidelity to their sovereign. No small proportion of the present sufferers had obtained their preferment by means of that tyrannical deprivation; they did but now drink of the cup which they had administered to others. Not a few had been deeply implicated in the guilt of the rebellion. But this ill consequence was sure to follow from a measure not otherwise impolitic and fully justified by the circumstances of the times, that while from the pride of consistency and from conscientious scruples some men of genuine piety and exemplary worth were expelled from a church in the service of which they were worthy to have held a distinguished rank, others retained their benefices who would have been a reproach to any church, and to whom it was matter of indifference what they subscribed and whether they took the Covenant or renounced it.—Southey vol ii pp 466—468

Of the measure by which 2000 ministers (the number has been much disputed) were deprived of their preferments, we are frequently reminded, but the statement is not always accompanied by the narrative of the 7000 previously cast up on the wide world, because of their determined loyalty to their sovereign and dutiful attachment to their church, neither is it always recollected that many of the ministers who resigned on account of the Act of Uniformity had obtained their preferment by the deprivation of their immediate predecessors. It is mentioned by Non conformist writers as an aggravation of their case, that in the former instance a fifth part of the income was reserved for the families of the sequestered ministers, whereas in the latter case there was no provision. Mr Southey, however, affirms, that that reservation of income was not ordered till some years after this violent measure had been executed, that it had no retrospective effect, and in most instances was disregarded. Neither can we bow with implicit reverence to the decisions of those reformers who undertook the office of purging the church of scandalous ministers. We suspect that on some occasions the circumstance of a clergyman holding a desirable living might be no mean proof that he was 'scandalous,' and that the proceedings of these judges were not seldom of a very arbitrary kind, is admitted, it seems even by Neale. There is a curious letter extant written by

Dr Owen, himself one of the tryers, giving an account of the "strangely foolish, and unjust proceedings of some of his brethren, in the instance of the celebrated Dr Pocock (See Christian Observer for 1823, p 791) Those days are not so remote but that traditions are still handed down, in different families, of the particularly hard treatment experienced, from the purgations in question, by individual clergymen of most exemplary character

It is somewhat surprizing, that certain writers, who feel so strongly for these two thousand sufferers, have little or no sympathy for those who, on one ground or another, had been deprived by the usurping authorities Dr Owen's first preferment was the living of Fordham in Essex and the tale is thus coolly told by his recent biographer, Mr Orme 'The sequestered incumbent was Richard Pully, who according to Walker, was a person of great learning, religion and sobriety but was turned out to make way for one whom he erroneously calls an Independent of New England The committee it appears, were of a different opinion The presentation was an honourable mark of their approbation and did credit both to themselves and to our author, &c There is no attempt to contradict the statement of Walker, but by an appeal to the decision of the committee as if it were not that very decision which we have a right to call in question, or as if the mere arbitrary fiat of those persons were of right to settle the question even if Mr Pully had been as scandalous as these gentry undoubtedly found him to be, one sentence of commiseration for his fate might surely have been expected in these days, even from the most determined friend of his eminent successor

We are very far from being satisfied with the remarks of the same writer in a following page, upon the conduct of the *tryers* or with the citation of Baxter's opinion to confirm them With respect to the sufferers by the Act of Uniformity, there can be no doubt that many of them were, as Mr Southey observes, persons of genuine piety and of exemplary worth and if, without any real sacrifice of the principles and order of the Church of England, that breach could have been avoided, it would on many accounts have been most desirable to prevent it Baxter's character of them, though it may be naturally suspected of a little partiality, is doubtless in the main correct It is to the following purport —" They were men that would have been highly esteemed and honoured in the primitive church, for which they who bore so hard upon them profess so great a veneration They were men of great faith and trust in God and by their integrity silenced many that apprehended religion a fancy They rejoiced in the usefulness of their brethren, when they themselves were discountenanced They prayed heartily for their civil governors and all in authority while treated as seditious persons, and unworthy of any favour They were owned of God in all their troubles, carried through a great many difficulties gained upon many of their enemies by their patience and quietness and at last were taken under the protection of the government

We have seen in a preceding quotation from Mr Southey, the provisions of the Act of Uniformity which operated with much effect upon the so called 2000 ministers The tenth chapter in Baxter's Life bears upon the same subject and it contains one or two positions, which the statement in the Book of the Church would scarcely lead us to expect We have observed nothing in the account by Mr Southey inconsistent with the supposition that the clergy when required to declare their unfeigned assent and consent to all and every thing in the Book of Common Prayer, &c, were at least acquainted with the contents of it The declaration was, according to the act, to be made on some Sunday before August 24. 1662, by all who were actually in possession of ecclesiastical preferment. Now what says Baxter? 'Very few of them could see the book, to all things in which they were to declare their assent and consent, before the time limited by the act was expired. For the Common Prayer Book, with the alterations and amendments (for so they are called, how deservedly I inquire not) made by the Convocation, did not come out of the press till a few days before the 24th of August: so that of the 7000 ministers in England who kept their livings, few, except those who were in or near London, could possibly have a sight of the book, with its alterations, till after they had declared their assent and consent to it.' This was what honest Mr. Steel and many others of the Nonconformists warmly complained of, in their parting sermons, when they took their farewell of the people at the time of their rejection. And, whatever it might seem then, when persons were in a manifest heat, at a distance it appears such a hardship, as that it is rather to be wondered that so many could act in so weighty a matter upon an implicit faith, than that such a number should in such circumstances stand out. The narrative of Burnet agrees in substance with Baxter's. 'All who did not conform at the appointed time were deprived of all ecclesiastical benefices, without leaving any discretional power with the king in the execution of the act, and without making provision for the maintenance of those who were deprived by it..... "The Book of Common Prayer, with the new corrections, was that which they were to subscribe. But the corrections were so long a preparing, and the vast number of copies, above 2000, that were to be wrought off for all the parish churches of England, made the impression go on so slowly, that there were few books set out to sale when the day came. So, many that were well affected to the church, but that made conscience of subscribing to a book that they had not seen, left their benefices on that very account. Some made a journey to London, on purpose to see it. With so much precipitation was that matter driven on, that it seemed expected that the clergy should subscribe implicitly to a book they had never seen." —Burnet's History of his own Time, 1661.

We forbear to go into the other causes which influenced, or might with their views have influenced the Nonconformists in their decision: but at any time, and especially in such feverish times, common justice requires that men should at least know what it is that they are to declare and to subscribe.

That some of the ejected ministers would have retained their situations if a little time had been allowed them, is not an unreasonable supposition: that this would have been the case with many we would not venture to affirm. The conscientious feelings of some, and the prejudices of others, would probably have disinclined them to close with any terms but such as should concede to them nearly all their objections; and, however we may condemn the harsh treatment which the Nonconformists subsequently experienced, or lament the final separation of many excellent men from our national church, it is possible that their compliance might have been purchased too dearly. Every measure in relation to them which tended unnecessarily to exasperate, deserves the strongest reprobation: but it is by no means clear, that either party expected a favourable issue to these discussions, or was very anxious to adopt the course most likely to obtain it. Baxter however is of opinion that had the king's declaration been maintained not more than 300 would have been deprived.

The trial of the bishops for their opposition to the arbitrary and popish proceedings of King James, is one of the most interesting events in the church history of England and it loses none of its interest in the hands of Mr Southey At a time when the government was availing itself of an affected liberality towards all classes of the king's subjects and by an appeal to long cherished prejudices, and to that love of power and privilege which is inherent in human nature was making the Dissenters * themselves in

Mr Southey speaks in strong terms of the apathy of the Dissenters as it respects the conflicts between Protestantism and Popery in these trying times We are not much surprised at it the very natural terms of indignation in which some of their writers at this day speak of the Oxford or Five Mile Act the Act against Conventicles &c will justify the belief that their feelings must at that time have been greatly exasperated against the clergy of the Church of England whom they regarded as their immediate oppressors and not withstanding the danger of Popery they would have two strong motives for not opposing the views of the crown namely the humiliation of the church and the accession of privileges which for the present they received from the measures of the king Baxter gives a hint at some such feeling as that last mentioned when he tells us that on the issuing of the king's declaration for liberty of conscience the Dissenters were not so fond of hard usage is to refuse a liberty so freely offered them nor did they think it good manners to inquire too narrowly how that indulgence came about so long as they were sheltered by it from oppression The indulgence of King Charles in 1672 was meant and they well knew it for the benefit of the Papists and they knew too that they should hold it no longer than the papal interest would allow it them so says Baxter yet while some applauded it, and others feared the consequences they finally concluded on a cautious and moderate thanksgiving for the king's clemency and their own liberty There was one active Dissenter however Alderman Love than whom no man was more zealous in opposing the king's declaration when it came before Parliament as illegal He said he had much rather still go without their desired liberty than have it in a way that would prove so detrimental to the nation See Baxter's Life c xiii It should be mentioned that the more reasonable Dissenters at last awoke to their danger and felt the value of that stand which had been made by the Church against the schemes of the Romanists

strumental to the re-establishment of Popery, the Church of England sustained a part which must for ever be memorable in the annals of this country The Non conformists in general stood aloof from the conflict and left the clergy to maintain the Protestant cause as if they alone had been interested in its preservation They proved themselves equal to the task and whether we regard the admirable spirit which they manifested in the whole of this arduous struggle—a spirit at once of loyalty to the king and of zeal for that religion which he was labouring to subvert —or the powerful vindications of the Protestant faith by which they enlightened the public mind both from the pulpit and the press or their resignation and readiness to suffer, when it seemed that suffering must be their lot there is a debt of gratitude and admiration due to the worthies of that age which can never be forgotten

From the time of the Revolution says Mr Southey in his concluding paragraph the Church of England has partaken of the stability and security of the state Here therefore I terminate this compendious but faithful view of its rise progress and political struggles It has rescued us first from heathenism then from papal idolatry and superstition it has saved us from temporal as well as spiritual despotism We owe to it our moral and intellectual character as a nation much of our private happiness much of our public strength Whatever should weaken it would in the same degree injure the common weal whatever should overthrow it would in sure and immediate consequence bring down the goodly fabric of that constitution whereof it is a constituent and necessary part If the friends of the constitution understand this as clearly as its enemies and act upon it as consistently and as actively then will the church and state be safe and with them the liberty and the prosperity of our country Southey vol ii p 511

Shall we be deemed hypercritical if we express a doubt about the accuracy of these expressions? We do not exactly see how IT namely the Church of England rescued us from heathenism We were rescued from heathenism first by the labours of certain teachers in the early ages of Christianity and next by the interven

In closing our remarks upon the Book of the Church, while we readily admit the many excellencies of the work, we cannot but regret, that sometimes the prepossessions of Mr Southey, and sometimes his laudable warmth of feeling, have led him, as we conceive, into statements substantially incorrect. We apply this remark especially to the history of the Lollards, and to the whole period of the Puritanical times. With as strong a dislike as Mr Southey himself possesses for disloyalty and fanaticism, we can neither admit his charges against the persecuted Lollards, nor can we join in an indiscriminate attack upon all those, or nearly all, who struggled for political freedom against Charles, or were dissatisfied with the arbitrary innovations of Archbishop Laud. We join with him to the full extent in reprobating the conduct of those factious men who shed the blood of the sovereign and the primate, and regard the execution in each case as a deliberate and atrocious murder: we are not however in examining the history of men who have filled high stations either in church or state quite to 'forget their vices in their woe,' or to leave out every qualifying circumstance in the conduct of such persons as on the whole we think it right to condemn; or because some reformers were enthusiasts and regicides, to pass this sentence upon them all. A worse race than were many of the sectaries, if Baxter's account of them is to be taken, can scarcely be conceived: yet this same Baxter speaks of numbers of the Nonconformists as persons of most estimable and excellent character. Mr Southey himself pays a handsome tribute of respect to certain of the ministers deprived by the Act of Uniformity; and towards the close of the seventeenth chapter justly remarks, that notwithstanding the hatred which the Puritans bore to the Liturgy, *none of them as yet differed in any single point from its doctrines.* Surely had he recollected these observations, he would, on revisal, have found much to qualify and something to expunge; and if his disgust had ever been excited, as it must have been, by the cant and violence of the sectaries, (to adopt Baxter's word,) and of not a few among the more reputable reformers, or by the " hard measure which, without one particle of feeling or remorse, the factious religionists dealt out to some of the best and greatest men of the age," he would have so tempered his honest indignation, and have so discriminated between the various elements of disorder, as to do justice to those better spirits, who, bearing generally the same opprobrious title of Puritans, deplored the excesses which they were not able to restrain.

We must not finish this article without adverting again to Mr Butler. In his remarks on the last chapter of Mr Southey, are many observations on the subject of Roman Catholic emancipation, on the doctrine of transubstantiation, on the charge of superstition and idolatry as levelled at the Church of Rome, &c. followed by an Appendix containing the opinions of foreign universities on the temporal power of the pope. Whatever may be the expediency or inexpediency of granting equal political rights to all classes of the community—a subject into which we shall not enter—or with whatever truth the universities of the Sorbonne, Louvaine, Douay, Alcala, and Salamanca, may have disclaimed as a principle of the Romish Church, the temporal jurisdiction of the pope in this country, we have much to unlearn before we can contemplate the doctrines and practices of Popery in any other light than that in which Protestants have generally represented them. It requires something more than the kind of argument adopted by Mr

tion of Gregory. The church at the Reformation from Popish became Protestant; and in the days of James the Second was mainly instrumental in rescuing us from the dangers of Popery.

Butler, to persuade us that the doctrine of transubstantiation differs little from our own: and it is not the dogmatism of Dr. Johnson, in his reply to Boswell's question about the mass, that will rescue the Church of Rome, as a church, from the charge of idolatry. Wickliffe's answer to those who contended "We worship not the image, but the being represented by the image," well deserves to be remembered. 'Idolatrous heathens did the same. It was not the golden calf, or the stock of a tree, to which idolaters exclusively offered their worship: it was, in the view of Dr. Johnson, to the Deity thus represented: and, on the principle here asserted by Mr. Butler, idolatry can scarcely be said to exist.

On the same dogmatical authority of Dr. Johnson, we are to believe that Roman Catholics do not worship the saints: "they invoke them: they only ask their prayers." Of course, the saints possess ubiquity, or the invocation is useless: but is not the worship of such a nature as to take away from the intercession of the Son of God? And is any thing more common in Roman Catholic countries, than to solicit the Virgin Mary to command her Son to grant the favour requested?

And as to indulgences, which perhaps we ought to have noticed in another place,—can any man read that granted to Nathan Hickman—we believe this to be the name—and to some twenty, or twenty five, other persons to be appointed at his pleasure, as it is exhibited in one of the college libraries at Cambridge, and not feel how dreadful are the perversions of Christianity, thus encouraged and sanctioned by that church?

We mentioned in our last Number the compendious confession of faith drawn up by Pius IV: to this and to the decrees of the Council of Trent, Mr. Butler would principally refer us for the doctrines of the Church of Rome: and to these as authorised* expositions of the popish creed, we should chiefly direct the attention of our readers. But we would subjoin the following observations from Mosheim:

'Those who expect to derive from these sources, a clear, complete, and perfect knowledge of the Romish faith, will be greatly disappointed. To evince the truth of this assertion, it might be observed, as has been already hinted, that both in the decrees of Trent, and in this papal confession, many things are expressed in a vague and ambiguous manner; and that designedly, on account of the intestine divisions and warm debates that then reigned in the church. This other singular circumstance might also be added, that several tenets are omitted in both, which no Roman Catholic is allowed to deny, or even to call in question. But, waving both these considerations, let it only be observed, that in these *decrees* and in this *confession*, several doctrines and rules of worship are inculcated in a much more rational and decent manner, than that in which they appear in the daily service of the church, and in the public practice of its members.† Hence we may conclude that the justest notions of the doctrine of Rome is not to be

---

* For *Protestant* authorities as to the *principles* of Popery, the following works are recommended by the Bishop of St. David's, viz. Bishop Jewell's Apology and Defence of the Apology; Barrow on the Pope's Supremacy; and the works of Bishop Moreton, Bramhall, and Stillingfleet.

† This is true in a more especial manner with respect to the canons of the Council of Trent relating to the *doctrine of purgatory, the invocation of saints, the worship of images and relicks.* The terms employed in these canons are artfully chosen so as to avoid the imputation of idolatry in the *philosophical* sense of that word: for in the *scripture sense* they cannot avoid it, as all use of images in religious worship is expressly forbidden in the sacred writings in many places. But this circumspection does not appear in the worship of the Roman Catholics, which is notoriously idolatrous in both the senses of that word.

derived so much from the Council of Trent, as from the *real signification* of those terms, which must be drawn from the customs, institutions, and observances that are every where in use in the Romish Church. Add to all this another consideration, which is, that in the bulls issued out from the papal throne in these latter times, certain doctrines which are obscurely proposed in the Council of Trent, have been explained with sufficient perspicuity, and avowed without hesitation or reserve. Of this Clement XI. gave a notorious example, in the famous bull called Unigenitus, which was an enterprize as audacious as it proved unsuccessful.—Mosheim, cent. xvi. sect. iii. Part i. c. i. § xxiv.

We are well convinced that Mr. Butler would not lend his respectable sanction to any assertions, which he believed to be unfair: but his attachment to the Romish Church is too strong to allow us to repose in him that implicit confidence which we should do in relalation to any subject in which his principles and feelings did not bias his judgment: and his incorrectness in some particulars of fact, serves to make us doubtful of most of the statements which we do not pursue to their source. Some instances of this inaccuracy we have already noticed: others might easily be adduced. For example, it is assumed, on more than one occasion, apparently as an admitted fact, that we have been twice indebted to the Church of Rome for the Christian religion. We are to suppose, of course, that the first preachers of the Gospel in this country were Roman Catholics: not, however, unless the Apostles were such, or their immediate followers; and that the religion of Gregory I. and Augustine was that of modern Rome: but this it was not: the mere fact of Gregory being a bishop of Rome, does not bear upon the point for which Mr. Butler seems to refer to him.

We are told (p. 221) that *the Irish Roman Catholics are the only sect that ever resumed power without exercising vengeance.* Yet the popish governor of King James at Dublin issued an order, that "not more than FIVE PROTESTANTS should meet together, even in churches, ON PAIN OF DEATH*."

It is asserted (p. 335), that the number of Roman Catholics who suffered death in England *for their religion*, since the Reformation, is at least 319: namely,

In the reign of Henry VIII. 59
    Queen Elizabeth 204
    King James I. 25
    Charles I. and during the
        Commonwealth 23
    Charles II. 8

We must freely admit, that if one of these unhappy persons suffered death *for his religion*, it was a deed to be utterly abhorred: but we have seen something of what is meant by the Elizabethan martyrs; and therefore, without very close examination, we are not disposed to pledge ourselves for the correctness of this report in relation to the rest.

Differing as we do on so many points from Mr. Butler, we concur with him most heartily in his remark about persecutions, that these are unpleasing topics; and in the wish which he so earnestly expresses, in the words of Fenelon, that great ornament of the Roman Catholic Church, "May the kingdom of truth, where there is no error, no scandal, no division, where God will communicate to it universal peace, soon arrive!"

* See the Jesuits Memorial for the Destruction of the Church of England, p. 54. This pamphlet is abridged from Dr. Gee's larger work, which is now very scarce. It is a most curious and interesting document.

LITERARY AND PHILOSOPHICAL INTELLIGENCE
&c &c

GREAT BRITAIN

Preparing for publication —A Manual of Family Devotion containing a Form of Prayer for every Morning and Evening —The Life and Works of Raphael translated —The Astronomy of the Egyptians —The fundamental Words of the Greek Language by F Valpy

In the press —Paley's Works with many unpublished Sermons and a Life by his Son —Sermons at the Holy Communion by the late Rev Alexander Waugh —The Opinion of the Catholic Church for the first three Centuries on the Divinity of Christ by the Rev T Rankin

Cambridge—Members Prizes —The subjects for the present year are Senior Bachelors—De statu futuro quænam fuere Veterum inter Græcos et Romanos Philosophorum dogmata? Middle Bachelors— Quantopere sibi invicem prosint populi libère mutandis inter se mercibus

Captain Franklin accompanied by Lieutenant Back and Mr Kendall with Dr Richardson and the other individuals composing the expedition are embarking for New York whence they proceed to Upper Canada, and then to Fort Chepewyan on their way to the Polar Sea, by the Mackenzie River On reaching its northern extremity Captain Franklin and Lieutenant Back with part of the expedition are to proceed to the westward in the hope of reaching Behring's Straits while Dr Richardson and Mr Kendall with the other party proceed to the eastward tracing the coast of America if possible to the Coppermine River Captain Franklin has received a message from Akaitcho the Indian chief who accompanied him on his former journey stating that he and his tribe are perfectly satisfied with the stores and additional presents which had been sent to them and are willing to accompany him on another expedition

A collection of autograph letters of distinguished persons from the reign of Elizabeth to that of James II was recently sold by auction in London A considerable number of these letters relate to Scottish history One letter of Claverhouse describing the battle with the Covenanters at Drumclog was purchased by the Duke of Buckingham for twelve guineas a letter of Mary Queen of Scots by Lord Grey for 11*l* A large portion of the letters connected with Scotland were purchased for the Advocates library There were in the whole 120 letters and they produced upwards of 270*l*

In recently taking down the Corinthian altar piece with which Rochester cathedral was deformed at the time of the Reformation a discovery has been made of three beautiful Gothic arched recesses and windows The decorations of the high altar appear in nearly all their pristine beauty consisting of birds and beasts *fleurs de lis* &c There has also been discovered a monument with a finely executed effigy of one of the early bishops of Rochester in his pontifical robes judged to be of the reign of Edward III A part of the architectural decorations of the tomb have also been found

It appears from an official statement just published that there are throughout England 256 Roman Catholic chapels 71 charity and other schools and 348 officiating priests The largest number in any one county is in Lancashire namely eighty one chapels six schools and seventy nine priests

The chemical substance called Strychnia has been lately proved to be the active principle of the Upas poison Its proportion in upas is very small notwithstanding its powerful action on the animal economy when used for poisoning arrows Silicum the metal of flint, has also been obtained in a separate state

FRANCE

At a meeting of the Academy of Sciences at Paris a memoir was lately read by Dr Villerme on the mortality in France among persons in easy circumstances compared with what takes place among the indigent In two arrondissements of Paris he makes it appear that the former which is inhabited by rich persons has a mortality of one in fifty —and the latter which is inhabited by the poor has a mortality of one in twenty four there being no other assignable cause for this enormous difference than wealth and poverty He found the deaths in Rue de la Mortellerie where the poor are crowded together in unhealthy lodgings four times and a half as numerous as in the quays of the Isle St Louis where rich persons live in large and well ventilated apartments He also shews that the mortality rises or falls with the rate of wages

The royal Academy of Paris having been called upon by the government to report on the proper means to prevent accidents from explosions of steam engine boilers have proposed that the boiler should be proved by the hydraulic press with a force five times greater than it is designed to overcome that a safety valve should be attached to the boiler and locked up and that the boiler should be surrounded by a thick wall of masonry an interval being left between the boiler and the wall and between the wall and the neighbouring buildings M Dupin proposes also a metallic plug in the boilers formed of such an alloy as should melt at a temperature a few degrees above that at which the engine is intended to work

SPAIN

The new plan of instruction organized by the council of Castile and sanctioned by the king consists of the study of philosophy theology Roman jurisprudence and medicine Those who study literature must go through three complete courses after having studied philosophy in Latin The study of the Spanish laws is also to be conducted in Latin

UNITED STATES

The National Calendar published at Washington states that in the years 1821 and 1822 there landed in the United States 20,201 passengers, of whom 3969 were citizens of the remainder who were emigrant foreigners 8284 were English 685 French 486 Germans 400 Spaniards and 112 Hollanders

TAHITI

The coronation of the young King of Tahiti Pomare III took place in April last and was made a solemn and religious festival The King is only four years of age his aunt is at the head of the government during his minority The laws of the island since it became Christianized were established about four years ago but as in the interval many things needed settling from the result of experience and unexpected circumstances a Parliament the first parliament ever held in the South Seas met in February last. It consisted of all the families related to the kings of Tahiti and Eimeo the governors of districts and provinces and two persons chosen as representatives by the people at large of every district The session lasted nine days Every thing submitted to consideration was fully discussed with calm deliberation and good breeding The members often differed much in their views but they never interrupted one another and when any found that the general sentiment was in favour of a decision contrary to their own they always yielded to the majority and their votes were thus, without exception unanimous

PENANG

The Penang Gazette gives the following description of an entertainment given by a Chinese merchant to the European residents The bird nest soup was admirable as well as the six other soups of mutton frogs and duck liver We did ample justice to an excellent hasher made of stewed elephants tails served up with the sauce of lizards eggs We also noticed particularly that some French gentlemen present seemed to eat with particular *goût* a stewed porcupine served up in the green fat of a turtle The beech de mar was excellent, as well as the fish maws served up with sea weed There was also a dish quite new to the party the expense of which was estimated at 200 dollars it consisted of a platter full of snipes eyes garnished round the border with peacocks combs and was the most delicious and delicate viand we ever tasted The dessert corresponded with the dinner We cannot pass over without remark the exquisite *gout* of the jellies made from the rhinoceros s hide

LIST OF NEW PUBLICATIONS

THEOLOGY

Sermons by the Rev Joseph Milner vol iii 12s

The Crisis by the Rev E Cooper

Thoughts on Antinomianism by Agnostos 1s 6d

A respectful Address to the Archbishops and Bishops on the Necessity of Morning and Afternoon Service &c By a Churchman

A Discourse on the Prophecies concerning Anti-Christ By Joseph Fletcher A M

Thoughts on Missions By a Missionary 6d.

MISCELLANEOUS

Domestic Duties for Young Married Ladies by Mrs W Parkes 8vo 12s.

An earnest Appeal on behalf of Hindoo Widows by Rev T S Grimshawe M A

Illustrations of Lying by Mrs Opie 2 vols 10s 6d

The Science of Agriculture by J Hayward &c 8vo 7s

Fosbroke s Encyclopedia of Antiquities complete 2 vols 4to 6l

Narrative of Lord Byron s Last Journey to Greece 8vo 12s

The History of England during the Reign of George III By William Jones 3 vols 8vo. 24s

A Vocabulary of the Greek Roots by the Rev R. Povah LL D 12mo 4s 6d

Universal Historical Dictionary by George Crabbe A M Part I 4to 9s

RELIGIOUS INTELLIGENCE

FERNEY VOLTAIRE

On the 5th of August 1823, a Bible Society was established at Ferney once the residence of Voltaire by the Baron de Stael and other friends zealous for the propagation of true religion. It is certainly one of the most memorable events in the history of Bible Societies that the antidote should thus issue from the very spot from which the poison of infidelity was so long disseminated and that the advocates of Christianity should confidently trust to the circulation of the sacred volume itself as a sufficient shield against the misrepresentations and sophistry with which in this very place it was formerly assailed

It is intended to erect a Protestant Church at Ferney which will be at the same time a monument of the triumph of Christian principles and of the progress of religious liberty. The French government has granted one hundred Napoleons for that purpose. The king of the Netherlands has given a donation of fifty Napoleons to promote the object. About 300l sterling have been collected for the purpose in Great Britain in addition to the sums raised by the Protestant inhabitants of the district who have contributed to the utmost extent of their scanty means. The sum of 200l however is still wanting to complete the church and the hope of raising that sum depends altogether on the liberality and Christian charity of this generous Protestant country

Since it has been announced that a Protestant Church is in progress at Ferney the Roman Catholics have determined to erect a splendid structure there and it is greatly to be feared that without the aid of British Christians the completion of the Catholic church will reproach the tardiness and indifference of Protestants in affording the means of completing the yet unfinished erection designed for the Protestant worship

We earnestly recommend the object to the benevolence and piety of our readers

Subscriptions will be received, by Mr Hatchard No 187 Piccadilly

We have much satisfaction in being able to promise our readers a series of highly interesting papers in our future Numbers on the history present condition and prospects of the French Protestant Church with some important suggestions for promoting its best interests

PRAYER BOOK AND HOMILY SOCIETY

We have so frequently stated the objects and proceedings of this valuable institution that we would trust they are familiar to our readers. As however its funds are by no means equal to the large prospects of usefulness which are opening before it we beg leave to impress upon the friends of religion especially those who are attached to the admirable formularies of the Established Church the urgent claims of the Society upon the support of churchmen and the public generally

I Its object is simple and strictly defined. It was instituted thirteen years since for the *sole* purpose of circulating and promoting the circulation of the authorised formularies of the Church of England. Its proceedings have been as simple as its object

II Its labours both at home and abroad are highly and increasingly useful

At Home ——*In England*—Previously to May last, 100,779 Prayer books 11 195 Psalters and 809 204 Homilies as tracts had been issued from the depository of the society at cost or reduced prices, or gratuitously as occasion required. Barracks, hospitals prisons convict-ships the hulks, &c &c have frequently been supplied with Prayer books and Homilies. Of the Homilies correct editions have been published in folio for the supply of parish churches agreeably to the eightieth canon in octavo with copious indexes and for more general circulation in duodecimo, both in a bold and in a smaller type the latter with suitable wood cuts. Editions of the Ordination Services in various types of the Articles of Religion and of the Psalter with the Epistles and Gospels have likewise been printed. But besides the publication of these various editions of the Homilies &c and supplying according to its means the destitute on shore this society has for some time past turned its earnest attention to the wants of seamen especially on the river Thames visiting ships distributing Homilies among the crews, and supplying such as are disposed to purchase with Prayer books at reduced prices. Its agent has indeed encountered many difficulties in this work, and often met with great discouragement yet the success which has crowned its efforts is of the most important and encouraging description

In Wales—the Society is circulating as occasion offers a very cheap edition of the Welsh Liturgy in an excellent type

In Ireland—one entire edition of the Book of Common Prayer in the Irish tongue and character has been prudently and gradually distributed with great acceptance, as have also very many copies of Prayers and Thanksgivings selected from the whole book, and of the Second and Third Homilies now first translated into the vernacular tongue of our sister island. A new edition of the whole Book of Common Prayer in the above named tongue and character is now in the press.

ABROAD.——*In British Colonies and Dependencies.*—In addition to supplies of English Prayer books and Homilies, this Society has printed and circulated, or is circulating at its own expense,

1 *In Hindoostanee* (assisted by means of the loan of type from the Church Missionary Society) an edition of nearly the whole of the Prayer book

2 *In Chinese* two editions of the Morning and Evening Services and Psalter, and one edition of the First and Second Homilies

3 *In Malay* an edition of the Morning and Evening Services and Psalter. And it is probable that the Second Homily (on the Misery of Man by Sin) will be soon printed in the same language

4. *In Malayalim* this society has *contributed* to the printing of the Prayer book

5 *In Indo Portuguese* the Society is about to publish the whole Book of Common Prayer

6 *In Armenian* the Second Homily is in the course of preparation for the press

7 *In Bullom* one of the languages of Africa, the Prayer book and Homily Society has printed and circulated an edition of parts of the Liturgy

In Hanover and in other foreign parts, as opportunity has occurred and expediency permitted, Prayer books or Homilies, or both, have been put into circulation in German, Dutch, French, Italian, Spanish, Modern and Ancient Greek, and Arabic. The Second Homily has been lately translated into Swedish.

The expense attending these exertions is very great, and increased means are altogether necessary to the continuance of them. The various measures adopted by the Society with a view to the extension of its sphere of usefulness, press peculiarly heavy at this time upon its funds—especially the publications above named, in Irish, Malay, and Indo Portuguese, and the most earnest and respectful appeal is hereby made to the liberality of the well disposed.

The Society offers its publications at reduced prices to sailors, watermen, &c. and has issued an appropriate recommendation to these classes to purchase them. The books may be procured at the Society's House, of Mr Courthope, Rotherhithe, and of Mr Saddington, West Street, Gravesend.

VIEW OF PUBLIC AFFAIRS

FOREIGN

No important article of foreign intelligence has been announced during the month. The almost exclusive topic of the continental journals, is the recognition of South American Independence by the British Government, which has excited the bitterest reproaches from the friends of the holy alliance. The popular continental rumour is, that a determined opposition is to be made to the decision of this country even at the risk of renewing the horrors of war. No official allusion however has transpired from any quarter indicative of such a result, and whatever be the intemperance of feeling with which certain powers may contemplate the successful resistance of our oppressed brethren in South America to their oppressors, it is scarcely to be believed that they would admit into their councils the extravagant folly of waging war with England because she has recognized the independence they have achieved.

DOMESTIC

Parliament met on the 3d of February, and was opened by commission with the following speech read by the Lord Chancellor:—

My Lords and Gentlemen,

We are commanded by his Majesty to express to you the gratification which his Majesty derives from the continuance and progressive increase of that public prosperity upon which his Majesty congratulated you at the opening of the last session of Parliament

There never was a period in the history of this country when all the great interests of the nation were at the same time in so thriving a condition or when a feeling of content and satisfaction was more widely diffused through all classes of the British people

It is no small addition to the gratification of his Majesty that Ireland is participating in the general prosperity

The outrages for the suppression of which extraordinary powers were confided to his Majesty have so far ceased as to warrant the suspension of the exercise of those powers in most of the districts heretofore disturbed

Industry and commercial enterprise are extending themselves in that part of the United Kingdom It is therefore the more to be regretted that associations should exist in Ireland which have adopted proceedings irreconcileable with the spirit of the constitution and calculated by exciting alarm and by exasperating animosities to endanger the peace of society and to retard the course of national improvement.

His Majesty relies upon your wisdom to consider without delay the means of applying a remedy to this evil

His Majesty further recommends the renewal of the inquiries instituted last session into the state of Ireland

His Majesty has seen with regret the interruption of tranquillity in India by the unprovoked aggression and extravagant pretensions of the Burmese government, which rendered hostile operations against that state unavoidable

It is however satisfactory to find that none of the other native powers have manifested any unfriendly disposition and that the bravery and conduct displayed by the forces already employed against the enemy afford the most favourable prospect of a successful termination of the contest

Gentlemen of the House of Commons

His Majesty has directed us to inform you that the estimates of the year will be forthwith laid before you

The state of India and circumstances connected with other parts of his Majesty's foreign possessions will render some augmentation in his military establishments indispensable

His Majesty has however the sincere gratification of believing that notwithstanding the increase of expense arising out of this augmentation such is the flourishing condition and progressive improvement of the revenue that it will still be in your power without affecting public credit to give additional facilities to the national industry and to make a further reduction in the burthens of his people

My Lords and Gentlemen

His Majesty commands us to inform you, that his Majesty continues to receive from his allies and generally from all princes and States assurances of their unabated desire to maintain and cultivate the relations of peace with his Majesty and with each other and that it is his Majesty's constant endeavour to preserve the general tranquillity

The negociations which have been so long carried on through his Majesty's Ambassador at Constantinople between the Emperor of Russia and the Ottoman Porte have been brought to an amicable issue

His Majesty has directed to be laid before you copies of arrangements which have been entered into with the kingdoms of Denmark and Hanover for improving the commercial intercourse between those States and the United Kingdom

A treaty having for its object the more effectual suppression of the Slave Trade has been concluded between his Majesty and the King of Sweden a copy of which treaty (as soon as the ratifications thereof shall have been exchanged) his Majesty has directed to be laid before you

Some difficulties have arisen with respect to the ratification of the treaty for the same object which was negociated last year between his Majesty and the United States of America

These difficulties however his Majesty trusts will not finally impede the conclusion of so beneficial an arrangement

In conformity with the declarations which have been repeatedly made by his Majesty his Majesty has taken measures for confirming by treaties the commercial relations already subsisting between this kingdom and those countries of America which appear to have established their separation from Spain

So soon as these treaties shall be completed his Majesty will direct copies of them to be laid before you

His Majesty commands us not to conclude without congratulating you upon the continued improvement in the state of the agricultural interest the solid foundation of our national prosperity nor without informing you that evident advantage has been derived from the relief which you have recently given to commerce by the removal of inconvenient restrictions

His Majesty recommends to you to persevere (as circumstances may allow) in the removal of similar restrictions and his Majesty directs us to assure you that you may rely upon his Majesty's cordial co-operation in fostering and extending that commerce which whilst it is under the blessing of Providence a main source of strength and power to this country contributes in no less a degree to the happiness and civilization of mankind.

The general purport of this speech (with the exception of two or three painful topics) is of a very gratifying nature. To enumerate the points which call upon us for public congratulation, and for humble thankfulness to God for our national mercies, would be to recapitulate almost every part of the speech. We are particularly pleased, not only with the assurances of existing peace and prosperity, but with the recognition and assertion of wise and enlightened principles of legislation, by which we doubt not these blessings will be extended and perpetuated. The painful topics are,—the intimation that new restrictive measures are necessary in Ireland, the interruption of tranquillity in India, the proposed augmentation of our military establishments, and the temporary impediments in the ratification of the slave trade convention with the United States.

The only one of these topics which has hitherto engrossed much of the attention of Parliament, is the restrictive enactment for Ireland. Other points, we trust, will also meet with full investigation, especially the asserted necessity for augmenting the army and the causes which have led to that necessity, whether as respects our relations in India or elsewhere. There are so few circumstances which can justify that greatest of scourges, war, that the utmost jealousy ought to be felt in examining the evidence that is to prove its dire necessity; especially as, in the case of the Burmese war, that evidence must necessarily be *ex parte*.

But passing by, for the present, the other topics of the speech, opportunities of noticing which will occur in the course of the session, we turn to Ireland, which has already occupied the almost exclusive attention of Parliament, and is likely to give rise to much further debate. The statement in the speech which alluded to the Catholic Association was followed up by the introduction, by Mr. Goulburn, of a bill for suppressing all such assemblies. An animated debate, of the unprecedented length of four days, took place upon the motion for leave to bring in this bill during which almost every public character in the house, and especially gentlemen connected with Ireland, delivered their opinions. The proposition was eventually carried by a majority of 278 to 123. We cannot undertake to give even an outline of the arguments on either side, or of those which have been introduced into various incidental discussions bearing on the same subject. It is a satisfaction to know, that the Catholic Association means quietly to submit to the intended restrictions, should they be imposed by law. We are persuaded, however, that no restrictive measures, however necessary or expedient they may be considered at the moment, are likely to give permanent peace to that distracted and hitherto ill governed country. We are happy to find that the inquiry into the state of Ireland is to be renewed and enlarged during the session. Would that we could hope that effectual measures will be devised and followed up for putting a termination to those painful scenes which it has so long exhibited.

ANSWERS TO CORRESPONDENTS

C. J. F. D. G. A Reader. L. Y. B. Olbius. An Inquirer. R. H. Σ. A Friend to Christianity. H. A Lover of Mankind. W. V. G. K. Nautilus. Philalethes. P. S. O. J. C. F. Academicus. and C. C. are under consideration. R.'s request will be complied with.

S. intended his allusion to Jer. xv. 18. to be given with the points for which the reader may refer to the passage in the original text.

The Reverend Chaplain of the County Prisons at Maidstone informs us that the account copied by Monitor from the London newspapers of the sacrament being administered to Thomas Coombs was incorrect. The Chaplain with great propriety refused to administer it. His letter was too late for insertion in this Number; but we take the earliest opportunity of giving his contradiction to the above injurious report.

THE CHRISTIAN OBSERVER.

RELIGIOUS COMMUNICATIONS

For the Christian Observer
AN ACCOUNT OF THE PROTESTANT CHURCH IN FRANCE

THERE is no fact in ecclesiastical history more fully established than that an elevated state of spiritual feeling has not continued to exist for a long period, in any place, or amongst any body of Christians. The infirmities of human nature have found a favourable soil for speedy and extended growth, even where men have met together for the best objects, and with the best desires of the renewed heart. The large experience of Baxter fixes the usual duration of a vigorous state of piety at very few years and the history of all churches, from those which our Lord more immediately addressed, to the congregations with which we ourselves are acquainted, seems to verify this position. Some bodies of Christians have indeed established within themselves a conservative principle, which, in every tendency to decay, affords the power of reviviscence and for this we are indebted, in our own Establishment to our Articles, Liturgy and forms of worship. But, under other circumstances churches which appear to have been well constructed have so entirely fallen away that their history is almost forgotten. Nor is it difficult to account for this. The generation of Christian who begin a church adapt its construction to their own standard of feeling and thus the light within and the form without are kept alive together. But the next generation who are introduced to membership by the will of others are apt, from the deadening effect of long habit to adopt a lower standard of religion than their fathers, and to carry on their worship with more formality and from not being careful to keep their lamps trimmed and their lights burning, the fire too often gradually goes out.

Sometimes again, it pleases God in his dispensations to permit opposition or persecution to arise and under the trial, the sufferers perhaps gradually yield,—or, if not are sometimes carried away by an irresistible annihilating force. The Almighty not unfrequently, sees fit thus to deal with his people in order to try their faith and promote their patience.

A striking instance of such an overwhelming dispensation is seen in the history of the Reformed Church in France. Its origin its growth, its extended influence, its purity the benefits which it conferred upon the country in which it was placed, as well as upon other lands, marked it as a building of God a part of his spiritual temple. But no church has suffered more severely from the rage of the persecutor. Many a stately monument indeed remains the proof of its excellent structure and its extended usefulness but the waste and desolation which it has experienced are almost without parallel in modern times.

It cannot but be interesting to your readers to look back on the history of this celebrated church I shall therefore lay before them some of the most remarkable particulars, appending to them such reflections as may appear suitable to the subject.

The real church of Christ seems to have had an existence in France in the time of Charlemagne at which period the purity of Christianity was zealously maintained against the idolatry of Popery.* The first dawn of the Reformation in that country appeared in the preaching of Waldo, who, in the twelfth century (1160), brought to light some truths which had been long hidden amidst the ignorance and superstition of the Roman Catholic Church. He did not propose to his countrymen any new system of doctrine, but merely complained of the degeneracy of the church, the supremacy of the pope, and various other things which he wished to bring back to primitive order. Persecution, of course, soon attended his steps. But, as oftentimes the enemies of religion, by the means which they take to crush a growing spirit of inquiry, only scatter it, as those who stamp violently upon fire in order to extinguish it, only spread it the more widely: so the opposition to the followers of Waldo dispersed the whole body of Reformers, and diffused their tenets in France and over the face of Europe. Waldo himself appears to have proclaimed his opinions in various parts of the continent. One of his disciples and ministers, Lollard, did the same in England. The Albigenses, so called from the country about Toulouse where they dwelt, embraced, in a body, the doctrine of Reform. It was carried into Calabria, Bohemia, Germany, Flanders, Poland, Spain, and even to the dominions of the Grand Sultan. Nor has this light ever been extinguished; for it was handed down to Wicliff, and by him to the Bohemian martyrs, who delivered it to the German Reformers, awakened as they were to inquiry by the remarkable circumstances which aroused the attention of Luther.—Persecution of the most determined kind attended those in France who professed the new doctrines, as they were considered; but, in truth, the old doctrines of Christianity, purified from the corruptions of preceding ages. Many however held fast to them; and in every class of society

Even in the darkest ages of Popery there were doubtless individuals who rose many degrees above the level of the surrounding corruptions; and long before Popery was known we find a Hilary giving lustre to the land of his nativity by piety and virtues of no common stamp. This celebrated man was born at Poictiers in the fourth century. He was descended from a noble family, and had received a liberal education; but he was a pagan. He tells us in his own account of his conversion, that he was led by calm reflection to perceive the vanity of idolatry; and by reading the writings of Moses and the Prophets his mind became enlightened respecting the true God. The New Testament taught him the doctrines of the Gospel; he perceived their excellence and suitableness to his condition and heartily embraced them. By the study of the Scriptures alone, says Milner, he obtained and steadily professed the Nicene faith before he had ever seen the creed of that name, or knew any thing of the Arian controversy. After his conversion he avoided the fashionable heresies of the day, and gave himself up to the promotion of true religion in himself and others. His zeal in the Arian controversy is well known. He became bishop of Poictiers; but meeting with great persecution for the sake of a good conscience, he suffered banishment for a considerable period; he was however at length restored to his see, where he died in the year 368.

Milner remarks of him that "his views of the Trinity are remarkably perspicuous and scriptural." "The Holy Spirit," he says, "enlightens our understandings and warms our hearts: he is the author of all grace, and will be with us to the end of the world: he is our Comforter here while we live in expectation of a future life, the earnest of our hopes, the light of our minds, and the warmth of our souls."— Speaking of the incarnation of the Son of God and redemption by his blood, he remarks:—"Since the Son of God was made man, men may become the sons of God. A man who with gladness receives this doctrine, renews his spirit by faith, and conceives a hope full of immortality. Having once learned to believe, he rejects captious difficulties, and no longer judges after the maxims of the world. He now neither fears death nor is weary of life; and he presses forward to a state of blessed immortality." On the subject of the Holy Trinity he remarks:—"The chief qualification in a reader is, that he be willing to take the sense of an author from what he reads, and not give him one of his own. He ought not to endeavour to find in the passages which he reads that which he presumed *ought* to be there. In such passages as describe the character of the Supreme Being particularly, he ought at least to be persuaded that God knew himself. A man who reads the Scriptures with such impressions of humility and implicit faith cannot go very far astray, even in the worst of times."

there was disseminated the information which prepared the minds of men to receive the opinions which, in the sixteenth century, were more plainly developed.

Luther preached against indulgences in the year 1517, two years after Francis the First began to reign in France. Margaret de Valois, afterwards Queen of Navarre, the sister of Francis, was a zealous friend of the new doctrines, and her influence not only softened the asperity of her brother's temper, which might have led him to measures of general violence, but protected the Reformers from the dangers to which they were continually exposed. The doctrines of Luther were, however, condemned by the Sorbonne in 1521, and the prevailing spirit of the court was that of persecution. Those who ventured the first to preach openly, were burnt alive at the stake. Fabir, Farel, and Leclerc, names dear to the lovers of the French Protestant Church, were amongst the earliest martyrs. The last of them, a woolstapler, first preached the Reformed doctrines at Meaux, and for this he was condemned to be scourged for three successive days, and then branded. The next year he was put to death at Metz. At Meaux the Bishop Bussonet, was a great favourer of the Reformation, and under his teaching many Christians were raised up, who soon after obtained, by their cruel death, the glorious distinction of the Martyrs of Meaux. During the time of their suffering in the flames, they are said to have sung a chorus of holy melody, which could scarcely be drowned in the yells of their savage persecutors.

In the year 1509, Calvin was born at Noyon in Picardy. When twenty years of age he first preached the doctrines of the Reformation to his countrymen, and seven years afterwards, in 1536, he printed his "Institutes," which contain a full, and certainly a very able, statement of his opinions. This work was dedicated, in a preface written with remarkable elegance of style, to Francis the First; but it does not seem to have produced much effect on the mind of that monarch. Indeed this could scarcely be expected, for he was at that time so given up to pleasure, to war and to the follies of the age in which he lived, that he could not have had much leisure or inclination to attend to the affairs of religion. So little did he enter into the views of Calvin that he is recorded to have assisted at Paris at the burning of six martyrs. On the whole, however, he was greatly restrained in his attempts against the Reformers, both by the influence of his sister and by public opinion, which seems very generally to have inclined towards Protestantism. Two events of considerable interest took place in his reign: the one was, the translation of the French Protestant Bible, which was published by Olivitan in 1535; the other the versification of some of the Psalms of David by Marot. Marot was the principal poet of his day. He appears to have been an inconsistent man in his moral practice, but he inclined in opinion strongly to the cause of the Reformers. His compositions, embellished by suitable and pleasing airs, were so much to the taste of the times, that they soon acquired great reputation. Both in the court and amongst the people they were in continual use, and they served to bring the Reformed religion into notice, and to give it attraction among all classes of society. The enemies of the Reformation put forth translations of the Odes of Horace to compete with the Psalms of Marot, but they did not gain their point.

The reign of Henry II., the successor of Francis, which began in 1547, exhibits much of the same spirit in the court, and much the same progress in the Reformation as that of his father. The king was engaged in burning the heretics, and the Reformers meanwhile established churches at Paris and in different parts of the kingdom. In

1553 Calvin edited an edition of Olivitan's translation of the Bible, which proved of great benefit to the church. In 1557 an attempt was made to establish an inquisition at Paris, after the plan of that in Spain to put down heretical opinions, but it did no effectual mischief. The King of Navarre, who was also a prince of the blood, and through whom the title to the crown of France afterwards descended to his son Henry IV., became about this time a convert to the Reformed doctrines. In the following year a movement took place which marked the growing strength of the Protestant cause. A number of young persons belonging to a seminary of learning in the suburbs of Paris, separating from their companions, who were amusing themselves at play, began to sing in chorus the Psalms of Marot. They were soon joined by the rest, and gradually by a large body of persons (like Saul with the prophets) who all joined in the same melody. The newness of this thing, says Burnet, 'amused many; the devotion of it wrought upon others; the music drew the rest; so that the multitude that used to divert themselves in the fields, instead of their ordinary sports, did nothing now but go about singing Psalms. And that which made it more remarkable was, that the King and Queen of Navarre came and joined with them. When the king of France heard of this Psalmody, he made an edict against it, and ordered the doers of it to be punished; but the numbers of them and the respect for the crowned heads made the matter go no further. In 1559 a small number of ministers from eleven churches under the presidency of Francis de Morell, formed at Paris the first synod of the Protestant Church. They held their meetings secretly. In this synod was laid the foundation of the ecclesiastical constitution, and of that code of doctrine and discipline which afterwards, revised by Calvin in 1566, was presented to the public. These same regulations, with occasional alterations, have been retained ever since their first promulgation, and they are the basis of the ecclesiastical law to the present day. At the conclusion of Henry's reign, which terminated in 1560, great numbers of the Reformed Church were burned at Paris; nor did this persecution diminish, but it rather increased, on the accession of his son Francis II, who being only sixteen years of age, was directed by his mother Catharine de Medicis and the family of Guise. The rising at Vassi, where the servants of the Duc de Guise assaulted the Protestants, and in which 60 were killed and 200 wounded, was the first open declaration of the views of that family towards the Reformed religion; and the hostility which they then manifested was pursued with relentless violence through those civil wars which desolated France for so many years.

In 1562 the ever memorable Charles the Ninth succeeded to his brother. As he was only nine years of age at that time, the government remained in the hands of Catharine. Two years after this period Calvin died. It does not appear that this great man, except at an early period of his life, took directly any personal part in prosecuting the Reformation in France; but it grew up under his inspection, and his authority was the acknowledged human standard of faith and duty. A number of cases which are cited in the synodal acts of the church appear to have been referred to his decision, and are published under the sanction of his name. The great learning, the uncommon acuteness, the undaunted courage, the indefatigable industry and perseverance of Calvin admirably adapted him to one portion of the duties which he was called to perform; but judging from the history of his sway at Geneva and the speedy degeneration of the institutions which he formed, it is very questionable whether his system was not one of too unbending severity to keep a permanent establishment when it was not maintained by his own personal influence

In 1571 the Protestant Church in France had reached its highest point of prosperity. A synod was held at Rochelle where the Queen of Navarre Jean d Albert her son afterwards Henry the Fourth, and two princes of the Royal family attended. At that time the Protestants had 2150 churches, some of which contained 10,000 members.

It may perhaps be as well at this point to describe the regulations by which the whole establishment was carried on. Its government was purely Presbyterian. Its synod composed of ministers and elders, deputed by different provinces, was presided over by a moderator, who, in the last mentioned synod, was no less a person than Beza and it was attended though not till after the year 1663, by an officer of the king, whose object was to see that none but ecclesiastical matters were subjects of discussion. In the synod were originated the general acts of the society. To it appeals were made by those who thought themselves aggrieved and from it issued with an equal and unsparing hand decrees against which even persons of the highest rank and most daring spirit durst not oppose themselves. A collection of the synodal acts of the church was made by Quick, after the revocation of the Edict of Nantes and printed by him in English. They are very interesting inasmuch as they afford a view of the general state of the church itself as well as its decisions upon many important questions. The representation which they give us of the church is very favourable to its general character. The ability of its members the soundness of its political constitution, the strictness with which it acted upon the principles it professed, the sobriety of its decisions in particular cases,—all commended it as well adapted for an extended and powerful hierarchy. It seemed to have nothing within it which marked decay when it pleased the inscrutable providence of God that it should be visited with a cruel and desolating persecution which entirely crippled its powers, and had nearly exterminated it altogether. This was the massacre of St Bartholomew. The deepest aversion to the views of the Protestants had long dwelt in the minds of all connected with the court except the few members of their own body. The plot for getting rid of the Reformed religion had long been meditated. To the queen mother, as one of the family of Guise, the atrocious contrivance is due of the means by which it was to be attempted. On the occasion of the marriage of Henry with the sister of Charles the Ninth, the whole body of Protestants were enticed to Paris. The mother of Henry Jean d Albert, one of the wisest and most pious women who ever adorned the high situation to which she was called had been led to consent to this alliance, from a belief that it would lay the foundation of solid peace and spiritual prosperity in the kingdom. But she was the dupe of Catharine de Medicis and she died it is supposed by poison, two years before the general massacre. After the Admiral de Coligny the champion of the Reformed cause as he was really the head of the party, was fairly in the toils the minds of the populace were exasperated against the Protestants by the contrivance of the duke of Guise and, by the command of the king, they were all given up to slaughter. The proclamation for their destruction was made at night, and at two o clock in the morning the work of death began. The king himself is said to have shot from a gallery at some of the fugitives and neither age, rank nor character, afforded any protection to the unfortunate victims. Henry of Navarre the brother in law of Charles, the

Prince de Condé his uncle, and the king's Physician, were alone exempted from destruction. Henry and de Condé were hurried from their beds and dragged, not without danger, before the king, who when they refused to be " converted," as the phrase ran, broke out into an excessive rage, declaring that he would be obeyed as the vicegerent of God; that they must teach others to submit by their acquiescence; and that it became them no longer to hold themselves in opposition to the Holy Mother. They were in consequence obliged to attend mass. The massacre was continued without cessation for three days, till the king became aghast at his own act; and his conscience was so haunted with images of murder and death, that he directed it should cease.

Amongst the victims of this destruction was the Admiral de Coligny, one of the most distinguished politicians of his day, and equally illustrious for his rank, his attachment to the Protestant cause, and his remarkable piety. He of course became one of the first victims of the savage rage of his enemies. The duc de Guise himself directed the measures for his destruction; and to verify his death to the duc d'Angoulême, who accompanied him, he commanded his body to be thrown out of the window of his house. Amidst these scenes of murder and desolation it is truly refreshing to revert to the character of this great and good man. He was the first nobleman of very high rank in France who had dared declare himself on the side of the Protestants; and this he did, not from political motives, but from the deepest attachment to the principles which they professed. Every morning and evening he is recorded to have assembled his servants for domestic worship; to have attended a daily public service, and at every repast to have implored with singing and prayer the blessing of God. He was zealous in the establishment of schools, and the extension of religion. He was indifferent to the honours of the world, and left his estate rather the worse than the better for his use of it. A few days before his death, he was wounded by a bullet fired at him from the house of the duke of Guise. In a most painful operation for the extraction of the bullet, he said to those around him, " These wounds my friends are God's blessings. The smart of them indeed is troublesome, but I acknowledge the will of my God in the dispensation; and I bless His Divine Majesty, who hath been pleased thus to honour me, and to lay any pain upon me for his holy name's sake. Let us entreat of him to enable me to persevere to the end." To his minister Merlin, who seems to have resided in his family, he said, " If God had visited me according to my deserts, he must have dealt far more severely with me. But blessed be his name, who hath dealt so mildly and lovingly with his unworthy servant." He added, " Truly from my heart I freely forgive both him that shot at me, and those also who incited him to the deed. For I know assuredly that it is not in their power to hurt me; no, though they should kill me; for my death is a most certain means of attaining eternal life." The prayer which he is recorded to have offered up has much of the force and simplicity which mark the compositions of the earlier days of the church. " O Lord God my heavenly Father, have compassion upon me for thy tender mercy's sake; remember not against me my former iniquities, neither charge me with the sins of my youth. If thou Lord, shouldest mark what I have done amiss, or shouldst impute the violations of thy covenant, what flesh could stand before thee, or endure thine anger? As for me, disclaiming all false gods and worship I call only upon thee, the eternal Father of our Lord Jesus Christ, and worship thee alone for his sake. I beseech thee, to bestow thy Holy Spirit upon me, and to give me the grace of patience I trust only in thy mercy all my hope and confidence is placed on that alone Whether thou pleasest to inflict present death upon me or to spare my life to do thee further service behold Lord, I am prepared to submit to thy will nothing doubting but if thou pleasest to inflict death upon me, thou wilt presently admit me into thine everlasting kingdom' But if Lord, thou sufferest me to live longer here grant, O my heavenly Father, that I may spend all the remainder of my days in advancing thy glory and in observing and adhering to thy true religion The Admiral was visited by the king who feigned the greatest sorrow at the atrocious attempt which had been made upon his life Many persons at the period of this attack suspected the sincerity of the king and Catharine, who made zealous professions of friendship but the Admiral full of faith and of courage, determined to wait the issue On the fatal night, his house was assaulted The staircase was so strongly barricaded that for a long time his enemies could not enter In the mean time, his minister, Merlin prayed with the whole family When he had concluded a servant coming in said 'Sir God calleth us to himself they have broken into the house and we have no power to resist His answer was very memorable and it was observed that while he uttered it his countenance was no more troubled than if no danger were at hand 'I perceive said he, "what is doing I was never afraid of death and I am ready to undergo it patiently, for which I have long since prepared my mind I bless God that I shall die in the Lord through whose grace I am elected to a hope of everlasting life I now need no longer any help of man You therefore my friends get ye hence as soon as ye can, lest ye be involved in my calamity and your wives hereafter say that I was the cause of your destruction The presence of God to whose goodness I commend the soul which will presently leave my body, is abundantly sufficient for me His enemies soon reached him and to one, who asked whether he was the Admiral, he had only time to answer, 'I am and you, young man should respect my hoary head when the swords of his enemies dismissed his spirit to its everlasting rest The persons who were with him fled in different directions Some climbed upon the tiles of the house, and others in other ways escaped Of these Merlin the chaplain was one he sheltered himself in a hay loft and it is recorded in the acts of the next synod after this event, in which he was moderator that he was supported for three days by means of a hen which deposited an egg daily near his place of refuge

Sixty thousand Protestants according to Sully, fell in this awful massacre and that it did not extend to the extermination of every individual was, under Divine Providence, to be attributed to the caution of some who left the capital in time, the intrepidity of others, and the generous feeling of many of the Catholic officers, who refused to obey commands which they said belonged rather to executioners than to soldiers

Charles the Ninth survived this event only one year He lived, however, to repent of his crimes, and to suffer for them His death was of that kind which it has pleased God often to inflict upon eminent persecutors of his church He was tormented in mind and body, and sank into his untimely grave unhonoured even by his former friends, and unregretted by every lover of his country During the concluding period of this reign, the Reformed Church was at a very low ebb There could be no security that the anniversary of St Bartholomew would not be celebrated with a recurrence of the same disasters The heads of the church were gone Henry of Navarre himself seems to have been in a sort of imprisonment and the remainder of the scattered flock could scarcely be collected together. It was not till the year 1578 that another synod was held, and then no formal notice was taken of the late events. Almost the only allusion to them is in the appointment of a general fast. " Forasmuch, it is said, ' as the times are very calamitous, and that our poor churches are daily menaced with many and sore tribulations, and that sins and vices are rising up and growing in upon us in a most fearful manner, a general day of prayer and fasting shall be published &c.

Henry the Third succeeded his brother in 1574. He had in early life displayed those qualities which afterwards distinguished him, and the Protestants therefore could expect little that was favourable from his reign. His character did not indeed lead him to those daring acts which might have hastened the ruin of the Reformed Church, but his profligacy and folly made him an easy dupe to those whose passions or whose interest led them to desire its extermination. Its destruction was carried on by a more quiet but not less effectual method than had been before employed. During his reign, the great conflict for independence and religious liberty was being carried on in the Low Countries, and the successful issue of it gave respect and consideration to the Protestant cause wherever its supporters were found.

At length, in 1589 Henry the Fourth ascended the throne. Never had a prince been nurtured amidst greater dangers, concerned in more critical enterprizes, or come to a throne more encompassed with difficulties. He had been well educated by his excellent mother, whose prudence and power he inherited, but not her piety. Gay and dissolute in his habits, he lived constantly under the influence of women of evil character. These however were in no way suffered to interfere with political matters, which he directed himself, aided by the Duc de Sully, one of the most faithful and able ministers that ever served a monarch. Henry was born in the Protestant faith, and had maintained his profession amidst the greatest temptations to abandon it. He had contended nobly against the religious faction which opposed his cause, and, although inflexibility was not one of his characteristics, he had never, except for a short time after the massacre of St Bartholomew, been tempted to relinquish his profession. His character was bold and generous, prompt and active, liberal and courteous, and a ruling passion of his mind was the good of his country. In the year 1572 he married Margaret, sister of Charles the Ninth, from whom he was divorced. He married a second time Mary of Medicis. His marriage was the first step by which he allied himself to the Catholics, and it was doubted by some whether to it may not be traced another great error of his life, his abjuration of the Protestant faith, which took place in the year 1592. The reasons which led to this change, are plainly given by Sully in his Memoirs. For twenty six years France had been desolated by civil war, arising not only from the ambition of the Guises and the queen mother, but also from party spirit, universally spread, on the subject of religion. There appeared to him no probable end of this conflict, for the league within France, and the king of Spain and the pope without, were able to have protracted the war for many years. In the mean time, the whole of Henry's life was likely to be spent in this useless struggle, which, whilst it prevented him from giving attention to the internal regulations of his kingdom, inflicted upon it all the desolation and horror of civil war. If he should succeed in the conflict it would be only by means which would leave him but half a kingdom to govern. On the other hand if he should fall in the con flict, as the cause of Protestantism in the kingdom depended upon himself he would leave the Protestants a prey to exasperated enemies without having secured for them any single advantage. His abjuration Sully thought to be a measure which promised entirely to foil his political foes, which would compose in the easiest manner the differences which existed, which offered the fewest present inconveniences, and which might, if contrary to his calculation it should bring with it any serious evil, be the most easily remedied. Besides, in Sully's opinion, to become Catholic from Protestant or Protestant from Catholic, if the alteration was made on the grounds of political expediency, was only to change for the advantage of *religion* itself, and to give it that benefit which would accrue to either profession by the more favourable circumstances in which it would be placed. Sully had, moreover, an idea that the spirit of persecution formed a component part of the Roman Catholic Religion, but would never spring up again when once his master had offered the sacrifice of his Protestant principles at the altar of the church. Henry himself also expected, by putting an end to the spirit of opposition on the ground of religious difference, that he should deserve the admiration of future ages. The avowed reasons for his change were, first The greater certainty of salvation which the one religion presented above the other, for the Protestants could not maintain with the same confidence as the Catholics, that no man could be saved out of their own pale, and therefore it was concluded that the Catholic stood on the safer ground; and, secondly The desire of embracing that mode of religion which was the most popular among his subjects. Another motive for the change is, however, suggested by Sully, which was the real predilection which Henry entertained for the doctrines of the Catholic Church. Nor was this wonderful for in proportion as any scheme of religion substituted form for spirit, external requirements for a change of heart, in the degree in which it could be made to gloss over an indulgence in habits of sin, and make some act or temporal sacrifice a compensation for transgression, would such a scheme approve itself to a man of loose character, but whose mind did not altogether approve the path he was pursuing. This was the case with Henry. Educated by a religious mother, who had placed around him men of great acquirements and piety, his conscience could not but be well instructed. His prevailing temptation was to intemperance in sensual indulgences. His Protestant teachers could offer him no salvo, whilst he continued in habits of sin, and the faithful sermons which he was called to hear must have been as daggers to his mind. But he would not be exposed to the same inconvenience in the Roman Catholic Church. Confession to a priest was an easy penance to a man whose sins were as notorious as the noon day, and after confession, he might depend upon absolution. The absolution too, which he thus obtained had no inconvenient qualification annexed to it it was absolute, and extended to every sin, and it was sure, for the alleged power of the keys is all but infinite.

(*To be continued.*)

FAMILY SERMONS.—No CXCV

Romans xv. 5, 6 *Now the God of patience and consolation grant you to be like minded one towards another according to Christ Jesus that ye may with one mind and one mouth glorify God, even the Father of our Lord Jesus Christ.*

ST PAUL in this Epistle, was writing to persons who differed greatly in many subordinate points, but who all professed to agree in one, that of being disciples of Jesus Christ. To this, as to a common bond, he appeals, earnestly desiring, that they might be closely united in spirit, avoiding both the false doctrines and the evil practices which he had exposed in the course of his Epistle and increasingly becoming partakers of those exalted privileges which he had so glowingly described. He well knew how great are the benefits to the Christian church of a spirit of union, and how hateful and dangerous is a contrary disposition. Throughout his Epistles he dwells frequently upon the necessity and loveliness of this divine badge of our holy profession. He speaks of the members of the church of Christ in all ages and nations as one body, each sympathising with each and ministering to the welfare of all: 'the whole body being fitly joined together and compacted by that which every joint supplieth, according to the effectual working in the measure of every part, making increase of the body to the edifying of itself in love.' Be therefore he says, 'of one mind and live in peace, and the God of love and peace shall be with you.' In heaven there is complete union of sentiment and of purpose, among all its blessed inhabitants. So also paradise, before the fall of man was a scene of union; but sin expelled this heavenly guest, and our corrupted earth became the seat of conflict and disorder. Christianity is intended—and would that its operation were universal and complete!—to reunite mankind in a holy brotherhood: for its proclamation as announced on the morning of the nativity was 'Glory to God in the highest and on earth peace, good will towards men.' The Saviour himself prayed that his disciples might all be one; and the promises also of the glory of the latter day point to this delightful consummation. It is the privilege then, and the duty of each individual member of the church of Christ to cherish in himself and to promote in others this spirit of unity and godly love: and with a view to assist and encourage us in so doing, we shall, from the words of the text consider,

First, The blessing for which the Apostle prays and *secondly*, Some circumstances connected with it, which may be gathered from the prayer itself.

First, We are to notice the blessing for which the Apostle prays "*That ye may be like minded, one towards another.*" Differences of opinion followed by alienation of heart deform the church of Christ, disturbing the peace of its members, and rendering it a prey to its enemies. On the other hand like-mindedness is spoken of throughout Scripture, as a blessing of inestimable value. It was the promise of God to Israel: 'They shall be my people and I will be their God and I will give them one heart and one way, that they may fear me for ever, for the good of them and of their children after them.' This blessing includes to its perfection unity of opinion and union of heart.

1. Unity of opinion. In the fundamental truths of the Gospel we have an ample basis for a common agreement, especially when we refer these truths to our own personal condition. Must we not, for instance, readily acknowledge ourselves to be the creatures of an all wise, all powerful, and infinitely good Being who hath made us and not we ourselves? As such, do we not feel that we owe to him our best and undivided services: that it is our duty to love him with all our heart, and soul, and mind, and strength, to submit to his laws, to set him always before us, and to avoid every thing that interferes with our obedience to his commands? Again does not our conscience witness that we have not done so? He has bestowed upon us favours and we have not loved him, he has held out threatenings and we have not feared him, he has offered promises which we have rejected, he has called and we have not answered, he has been patient and we have despised his long suffering and forbearance, he has warned us, and we would

not listen to his remonstrances he has soothed us, and we refused to be reconciled; he has invited us to the enjoyment of his favour, and we preferred the sins and trifles of a rebellious and unsatisfying world. Must we not then further admit the truth of those scriptural declarations which represent God as justly offended at our conduct? Can we doubt, that we have given him ample cause for displeasure? Could we feel surprised if he had at once cut us off, and 'sworn in his wrath that we should not enter into his rest?' So far then from turning with unbelief and hardness of heart from such fearful threatenings as that

the wicked shall be turned into hell, and all the nations that forget God, must we not acknowledge that they are but too justly applicable to our own case? Must not conscience confirm the record of God, and pronounce before hand the sentence of his displeasure? And further, is there any plea which we can offer, to prevent the execution of the punishment? Are we not brought in guilty and self condemned before our Maker? And even if we should now at length turn to him, what is to atone for the past, or to give us strength for the future, that we may not again offend him? Do we not then perceive the necessity for a sacrifice for our transgressions? And are we not thus led with joyful submission to receive those merciful declarations of Scripture, that 'Christ Jesus came into the world to save sinners;' that 'God was in Christ reconciling the world unto himself, not imputing their trespasses unto them;' and that 'he made him who knew no sin to be sin (that is, a sin offering) for us, that we might be made the righteousness of God in him?' Are we not prepared to embrace with gratitude of heart, the mercy thus freely offered, to believe in Christ to the salvation of our souls, and do we not learn to value the promised gift of the Holy Spirit to lead us to Christ, to enlighten our understandings, and to renew our hearts? Could we dispense with any one of the doctrines or precepts of Scripture? Do we not see the suitableness of all of them to our fallen condition? And ought we not to be devoutly thankful for such a merciful provision for our necessities? We may differ in opinion upon nice points of doubtful disputation, but upon all that involves the essentials of faith and conduct, the circumstances of our own personal cases, if we are practical Christians, and our instruction by the same Divine Spirit will lead us to no small degree of like mindedness in the opinions which we derive from the word of God. And on these we shall love to dwell, rather than on questionable controversies, which lead neither to soundness of faith nor to holiness of life.

2. The blessing of like mindedness especially includes *union of heart.*—The Christians to whom the Apostle was writing entertained various opinions respecting meats and drinks and holydays, and even in matters of faith, some of them had not yet attained to a perfect knowledge of the Gospel which they professed. The Apostle therefore prays that they might be like minded one towards another, doubtless as far as possible in uniformity of judgment; but, where this was not attainable, in union of affection, as children of the same Heavenly Parent, disciples of the same Master, redeemed with the same Blood, and professing as brethren to be travelling together towards the same heavenly inheritance. Even where they were not exactly united in opinion, they were not to hold their sentiments in a harsh in tolerant spirit, but to 'seek peace and ensue it,' not to judge one another, but 'to judge this rather, that no man put a stumbling block or an occasion to fall, in his brother's way,' to 'bear the infirmities of the weak,' to be 'of one accord, and of one mind,' 'endeavouring to keep the unity of the

spirit in the bond of peace. Errors and partial differences of sentiment might not always be avoidable, but these were not to be inflamed by unkindness and uncharitableness of heart. In their mutual discussions, they were not to advance towards their fellow Christians as warriors to the battle, but with the olive branch of peace in their hands, prepared to yield their own most cherished wishes, or interests, or prejudices in the cause of truth and charity.

But, *secondly*, there are several circumstances connected with the Apostle's prayer, which deserve our consideration. These are first, the Author of the Christian grace which he implores,—the God of patience and consolation: secondly, the law or pattern of it, "according to Christ Jesus:" and thirdly, an important end to which it conduces,—namely, "that ye may with one mind and one mouth glorify God, even the Father of our Lord Jesus Christ."

1. The Apostle reminds us of the Author of this Christian grace. It comes from 'the God of patience and consolation.'—"the author of every good and perfect gift," who alone "maketh men to be of one mind in a house." Most fitly does the Apostle address him as "the God of patience and consolation:" for not only does he bestow the grace of patience, but he exhibits it in his own character; and while we call to mind how greatly he has borne with us, we should learn to imitate his example, by bearing with our fellow creatures. We should earnestly entreat him that he would make us gentle and patient by subduing in us those proud and irritable passions which are causes of so much disturbance: and that in our humble search after truth he would bestow upon us those Divine consolations which will support our souls amidst reproach or opposition. For it is as a God of consolation as well as of patience that the Apostle addresses him when imploring the blessing of like mindedness one towards another. The reason of this will appear very clearly from the opening verses of the second chapter of the Epistle to the Philippians, where the Apostle says, "If there be any consolation in Christ, if any comfort of love, if any fellowship of the Spirit, if any bowels and mercies,"—that is, by the consolation which most undoubtedly is in him, by the motives derived from his cross, by his love and compassion, by your communion with him, by your hopes of his favour, your reliance on his Spirit, your expectations of his eternal glory,—"fulfil ye my joy, that ye may be like minded, having the same love, being of one accord, of one mind."

2. A second circumstance alluded to by the Apostle is the law or pattern of this Christian grace, namely "according to Christ Jesus," that is, according to his doctrines, and according to his precepts and example.

Our like mindedness must in the first place be according to the *doctrines* of Christ. It must not be an indifference to truth, or a sacrifice of the dictates of conscience to a false peace. We are to contend earnestly though meekly for the faith, and must give diligent search, with humble prayer to God that we may not err in it. The Bible is the great standard of agreement, and to it are we to appeal in all points of difficulty. We must "walk by the same rule, if we would truly 'mind the same thing.' It is not by our own fancies or by the opinions of others that we are to regulate our creed: these may deceive us, and our agreement may be only an agreement in error; but the word of God is infallible; and in proportion as we study and follow it, we shall obtain that like mindedness with the universal church of Christ which arises from one common appeal to the same inspired test, and one common illumination by the same Spirit: that Christian and spiritual union which the Apostle meant when he said, ' I beseech Euodias, and beseech Syntyche, that they be of the same mind in the Lord

This like mindedness is also according to the precepts and example o Christ The Apostle often appeals to this powerful argument Thus to the Ephesians he says, ' Walk in love, even as Christ also hath loved us, and hath given himself for us The whole Gospel of our Redeemer is calculated to cherish such a spirit It presents to us one body one spirit one hope of our calling, one Lord one faith, one baptism and one God and Father of all Our Lord, in his prayer, just before he was betrayed repeated again and again the petition already quoted that his disciples might all be one And in his own conduct, how careful was he to prevent among his followers every discordant sentiment and jarring feeling! How forcibly did he inculcate humility and mutual forbearance by his own spotless example! How willingly did he himself sacrifice every thing for the sake of others how cheerfully submit to every office of benevolence how meekly allure men to the reception of his heavenly doctrines how candidly listen to every objection how patiently resolve every doubt how fearlessly maintain truths the most unwelcome to the public ear yet with a meekness and a dignity which ought to have disarmed malice itself, and to have converted even his enemies into friends Surely for the professed followers of such a Saviour to be otherwise than like minded among themselves, or at the least, studious of cherishing such a spirit as tends to produce this blessed effect where it does not already exist would be a paradox indeed

3 The Apostle exhibits to us an important end to which this like mindedness conduces namely, that we may " with one mind and one mouth glorify God, even the Father of our Lord Jesus Christ The glory of God should be the great object of the Christian s desire, as it is the first petition of his daily prayer, " Hallowed be thy name' Now, in no way can we honour him more than by a devout union of heart and mind in his service While the Roman converts were eagerly disputing among themselves, they were unfitted for thus joining together in the homage due to their common Lord they had neither one mind nor one mouth so that there could be no profitable worship of a social or public nature Such a state of things the Apostle earnestly deprecates and in doing so he introduces a circumstance well calculated to effect his conciliating purpose for he speaks of the great object of worship as ' the Father of our Lord Jesus Christ, thus reminding us of those affecting motives to Christian unity already alluded to, and all of which flow from the cross of Christ As though he had said Not merely by the terrors of the law not merely by the dread of punishment but by our professed love to our dying Saviour, and by our gratitude to God the Father who freely gave him as a sacrifice for our transgressions, let us be like minded one towards another let us imitate his meek and affectionate example let us dread to violate the unity of his church let us guard against a spirit of discord or disorder and let us endeavour to grow daily in those heavenly virtues which are the bond of peace, and unanimity and joy

---

For the Christian Observer

ON THE USE AND IMPORTANCE OF BIBLICAL STUDIES

THE slight degree of attention paid by the great body of theological students in this country to the original language of the Old Testament has been often and justly lamented At different periods of our history, we have indeed had men among us who have cultivated this department of literature with splendid success, and applied it with signal ability to the elucidation of the Scriptures. But still it cannot be denied that little comparatively has been done, and that our countrymen, while they have extended their researches to almost every subject either literary or scientific, have been far eclipsed by the continental nations both in the number of those who have devoted themselves to this study, and in the extent to which their inquiries have been carried. By far the greater part even of our clergy are entirely unacquainted with the Hebrew text, and few indeed are critically versed in its niceties, though upon them, as the accredited guardians of religion, devolves the office of explaining and enforcing the truths which it contains. This circumstance will appear the more surprising when we consider the ardour with which theological studies in general have been prosecuted amongst us—the number and variety of our religious controversies, both among the members of our own church, and the seceders from her pale—and the zeal for which we have long been distinguished as a nation, for practical piety and devotion.

In the hope that some of your readers may be induced to consider this subject with the attention which it deserves and be led to the cultivation of a much neglected field of inquiry, I beg to offer a few thoughts upon the use and importance of Biblical studies. It is gratifying to witness the growing interest which they have of late begun to excite in our universities (I allude more particularly to one of them), nor can we speak too highly of those whose zeal and piety have been employed in enkindling the flame. May it spread far and wide, and be the means under the merciful providence of God of promoting in an eminent degree that " sound knowledge and religious education, for which in our university pulpits, we are statedly called upon to pray."

Much might be said relative to the advantages to be reaped from Hebrew literature, considered merely as a literary pursuit. To the antiquarian and philologist it opens a most interesting and extensive field of view. But it is in its more particular application as being the channel through which, from the earliest times the streams of Divine Revelation have flowed, that it has an especial claim to our regard. Like the Ark of the Covenant it has been for ages the depository of those sacred records, which were written with the finger of God and conveyed to mankind a transcript of his will.

As the Bible is the only source from which a knowledge of true religion can be derived, it becomes a matter of the first importance that the language in which it is written be properly explained; for any inference which is deduced from incorrect or imperfect views of it, is an inference, not from the word of God, but from the opinions of men. It is impossible to say how many false ideas have been formed upon the most momentous truths, how many unscriptural tenets maintained, how many disputes excited from the circumstance of our making a translation, and not the original Scriptures, our text book in divinity. The excellence of our English version is universally admitted, but the study of Oriental literature, and of Biblical criticism, like every other pursuit which has occupied the time and ingenuity of man, has been making continual progress since that translation first appeared. Without therefore in any degree depreciating either the labours or the learning of those excellent men who bequeathed to us this invaluable testimony of their powers of learning and sound criticism, we may fairly infer that every biblical student of the present day would derive incomparable benefit, were he to imitate their example as well as profit by their experience, and lay the foundation of his theological knowledge in an accurate and extensive acquaintance with the Hebrew text. In the case of the New Testament every sound classical scholar will be ready to admit that, although a translation may suffice extremely well for the practical and devotional study of its contents, it is only by a careful attention to the Greek original that he can become thoroughly embued with the spirit of its several authors, and enter into all those nicer shades of meaning which distinguish their respective compositions. Now whatever be the value of this argument as far as concerns the due interpretation of the New Testament, it is equally applicable to the language of the Old. We are too much in the habit of considering the Scriptures as a single and entire volume, to be interpreted throughout upon identically the same principles, without any reference to the distinguishing character of the authors of its several parts or the peculiar use of words in the ages in which they respectively wrote. The canon of Scripture being complete and our attention being habitually directed to it through the medium of a translation which being coeval in all its parts has thrown a clothing of the same texture over many things essentially distinct we forget while studying its contents, that ages intervened between the composition of its extreme books—and that the same or similar circumstances which modified the beautiful language of Greece exerted an influence of the same kind, though perhaps differing in degree, upon the vernacular tongue of the Jews. The analogy that subsists between the changes incidental to language and to the beings whose ideas it embodies holds good in this as in other instances. The golden and silver ages of Hebrew literature are perfectly distinct and a correct understanding of their varieties is essential to a full knowledge of Scripture. The language of poetry again is different in some respects from the sober livery of prose. Now all this, whatever be its value in the due interpretation of the Bible must be lost to one who is ignorant of the language employed. It is true that the less instructed may avail themselves of the light which has been thrown upon these subjects by the labours of the learned but we might as well expect to see with the eyes of another man as to reap the full advantage of another man's intellectual labours, unless our own minds be to a certain degree informed. Without this prerequisite, we have not the means of judging respecting the accuracy or even the probability of such matters as are brought before us. We cannot in short have an opinion of our own. The necessary consequence of this inability is, that our views are confined and our judgment becomes enslaved to the opinions of others, in whose assertions we have been taught implicitly to confide.

It is not intended in these remarks, to exalt above its proper rank the value of human learning as subsidiary to the study of the Scriptures—nor to place it at all in competition with that teaching of God which is indispensably requisite. Neither again is it intended to imply that it is the duty of all divines to forsake the province of expository theology and to give themselves to the critical study of divinity. Let the basis of our knowledge be laid in deep humility. Let us earnestly desire and heartily pray for the continual illumination of God's Holy Spirit, without which though we had investigated all the stores of antiquity, we should be but as the sounding brass and the tinkling cymbal. But let us at the same time open our eyes to the fact that we are living under an ordinary, not an extraordinary dispensation of that Spirit and that we cannot attain but by his blessing on our diligent research that knowledge which in the miraculous ages was conveyed by immediate inspiration. Where the degrees of piety, diligence, and all other circumstances are equal, the best theologian and most learned man will make the most useful divine. It becomes us therefore in our measure to aim at what may be extensively useful, though not to the exclusion of other things, which our particular circumstances may render more expedient.

Upon the importance of duly understanding the Old Testament, we might fairly build the necessity of Hebrew learning. But this is not all. The influence which its language has exercised upon that of the New gives it an additional importance, of which the biblical student ought not to lose sight. Without a competent knowledge of it we cannot avail ourselves of the labours of such men as Lightfoot and Schoettgen whose researches in Rabbinical literature have enabled them to illustrate its phraseology to a degree which could scarcely have been conceived. This knowledge is also necessary to enable the Biblical student duly to appreciate that irrefragable argument for the genuineness of the Christian Records which arises from the peculiar style and dialect in which they are penned. The Latinisms which a classical scholar will detect in them may convince him that the age of their appearance must have been subsequent to the triumph of the Roman arms and the consequent introduction of many of the political terms of Roman origin into the conquered lands. An acquaintance with Hebrew will give additional value to the argument. Every chapter of the New Testament affords decisive evidence, to one who is versed in Oriental idioms, that it could have been written only by a Jew. A work written in Greek, embued with the phraseology and idiomatic expressions of Palestine, and bearing distinct marks of being composed under the preponderance of the Roman power, carries along with it incontestable proof of the date to which it should be assigned. Nor amidst the mass of evidence upon which we build our holy faith is this a consideration lightly to be regarded.

Another benefit, and one of no small importance, resulting from an enlarged acquaintance with Biblical learning in its purest form is its tendency to promote peace, and to soften the asperity of religious disputation. The most vehement of all controversies are those which are founded in prejudice and contracted views. The higher we ascend in the search of truth, the more do we rise above the mists and exhalations which brood upon the valley beneath. In the progress of our inquiries, if we do not arrive at the same conclusions with others, we learn at least that there is room to differ, and can endure to see our fellow student adopt a different persuasion to our own, without feeling a conviction that ours must inevitably be correct. It is true, indeed, that knowledge puffeth up:—but it is knowledge when abused; and I must again remark that I am not instituting a comparison between piety and learning, but between a pious man who has superadded the blessings of learning to those of religion, and an uninformed though devoted servant of God. How many of the disputes and schisms which have rent the Christian church might have been avoided, but for that positiveness which is the inseparable companion of ignorance!

It has been objected to the study of Hebrew that it tends to unsettle the mind, and to involve in perplexity many points, which but for its interference would have been clear and undisturbed. It may indeed, as enlarged knowledge always will, teach us to call in question some positions which we may have imbibed in our very childhood, and from long acquaintance have learned to consider sacred. But no thinking man will allow this to be any argument against improvement in Biblical any more than in any other science. The immutable interests of truth can never suffer from knowledge well applied.

It is well known that Oriental literature has been of late years prosecuted with astonishing success upon the continent and especially in the universities of Germany. The most philosophical grammars in Hebrew as in other languages, with the most copious and accurate lexicons of the Oriental tongues have been imported from that country into our own. Happy would it have been had the knowledge so well acquired been in all instances directed to the purest ends. But this unhappily has not been invariably the case. A system of interpretation has been widely adopted by the continental theologians, which, if fully acted upon, would rob Revelation of all its peculiarities. There are indeed, even among their own body honourable exceptions of persons who have stood forward in opposition to the wild hypotheses of the German theologists; but the infection has spread far and widely, and has produced consequences which the Christian student cannot sufficiently lament. It is extremely desirable that the lovers of sound doctrine should meet such critics as those to whom I allude upon their own ground. The writings of the German divines are beginning to be extensively circulated in this country; and will undoubtedly be more so from the quantity of philological information which they convey. The only safeguard against the wild and unscriptural opinions conveyed in them, is to be found in the successful culture and proper application of Biblical knowledge. With the same weapons also must we combat as they from time to time arise, the false and injurious doctrines which the Unitarians of our own country are continually endeavouring to obtrude upon the pages of the sacred volume. The most illiterate Christian with the vernacular version in his hand, may indeed easily refute their unscriptural opinions; but as they appeal from this simple process to elaborate philological arguments, it is necessary that the sound Biblical student should be able to meet them in this arena, and thus to overturn, as has hitherto been most triumphantly done, their unhallowed speculations.

An extraordinary zeal for the diffusion of the truth in foreign lands is one of those characteristics of the present age, upon which it is impossible for a considerate and Christian mind to reflect without feelings of the most lively satisfaction. The Christian beholds in this anxiety a pledge of the reality of that principle which has given it birth. He dwells upon it with delight as affording a happy anticipation of those glorious days pointed out, as he believes in the shadowy forms and obscure though glowing language of prophecy, when the blessing which he has long considered his own will cease to be so in a peculiar and distinctive manner, the knowledge of God's word, like the light and heat of the great luminary of heaven, having gone forth unto all lands, and the sound thereof unto the ends of the earth. To both Jew and Gentile the voice of invitation is now addressed, that the wall of partition being broken down, they may all become one fold under one Shepherd. The expedients to which Christian benevolence may have recourse for the furtherance of these objects are as diversified as the various situations and circumstances of those in whose breasts it dwells. Perhaps, however, it may not be too much to say that a life devoted to Oriental studies in general, and with an especial reference to Biblical criticism and interpretation, might, by God's blessing, be a gift than which it would be impossible in the present state of the church to cast one more valuable into the treasury of Christian love. A knowledge of Hebrew and of the

Hebrew Scriptures is the only weapon wherewith we can hope to assail the Jew. Entrenching himself in prejudices which education and habit have fortified with the conviction that his has long been an injured and persecuted race, he betakes himself to a species of argument, the subtleties of which can be unravelled only by those who are acquainted with the language to which he refers, and the peculiar nature of the criticism which has been employed upon it. And who, when Egypt and Ethiopia shall stretch out their hands for the word of God, will be able to satisfy their cravings, and to impart to them the bread of life but those who possess such facilities of communication as a knowledge of their vernacular tongue can alone supply?

To the Christian who delights in the devotional study of the sacred volume and, like the Psalmist, meditates therein day and night, it must be a source of unspeakable satisfaction to have access to the original languages in which it was composed. To sing the songs of Zion in their native beauty—to enjoy communion with the saints of old—and enkindle the flame of piety upon the same altar, are privileges of high value. Nor are they mere gratifications only, but they are often productive of great spiritual benefit, opening to us unnumbered associations calculated to affect the mind, and to assist us in worshipping God in spirit and in truth. The Hebrew Psalter has been found by many Christians what there is reason to believe it was to our blessed Lord himself, a manual of devotion and praise. Bishop Horne has recorded, in the Preface to his Commentary, how rich and various were the joys which he experienced while engaged in the study of it. The pleasure of which he speaks may be that also of every Biblical student, if only his literary attainments be made subservient to the same hallowed purposes for the permission to draw water with gladness out of these wells of salvation is unlimited. Would that all felt that thirst which nothing but the water from this living spring can satisfy!

A.

MISCELLANEOUS

For the Christian Observer

SLAVE GROWN SUGAR

WE have promised to lay before our readers a full view of our sentiments on the subject of Slave grown Sugar. The following paper, recently issued by the Society for mitigating and gradually abolishing Slavery throughout the British Dominions, has so well expressed those sentiments that we shall insert it as containing a satisfactory solution of that important question.

The attention of the Committee of this Society having been called to the increasing reluctance which is felt, by many persons, to the consumption of Slave grown Sugar and numerous applications having been addressed to them for their opinion on the propriety of abstaining from its use, they have been induced to take the question into their deliberate consideration.

It will be recollected, that, in their Report delivered to the general body on the 25th June 1824, the Committee adverted briefly to this subject, intimating, that, should no effectual legislative measures be adopted for abolishing Colonial Slavery, it would still be in the power of the community at large to promote that object by renouncing the use of Sugar grown by Slaves, and using in its stead the produce of Free labour.

The Committee took the same opportunity of obviating the main objection to such an expedient which had arisen, or was likely to arise in the minds of conscientious individuals, namely, that to lower the price of Sugar would aggravate the sufferings and increase the privations of the Slaves.

They declared it on the contrary, to be and certainly it continues to be, their firm conviction, (a conviction founded in the very nature of a state of compulsory and uncompensated labour, and strengthened by all the lights of experience,) that whatever tends to raise the price of Slave grown produce tends, in the same degree to rivet the chains and to add to the labour and misery of the Slave while a material diminution in its price must operate beneficially both in relaxing his bonds, abating his toil, and enlarging his comforts. This view of the subject was briefly illustrated, in the Committee's last Report by a reference to the contrasted cases of the Bahamas and Demerara.*

Thus stood the question at the last General Meeting of the Society

As the whole of this subject is highly important the Committee propose forthwith to prepare a brief view of it for general circulation, and in the mean time they would direct the attention of their friends to the following publications as illustrative of it namely their own last Report pp 34 35 —East and West India Sugar pp 79—88 —Mr Cropper's pamphlets entitled Relief for West-India Distress A Letter on the injurious Effects of High and the beneficial Effects of Low Prices on the Condition of the Slaves and the Support of Slavery Investigated —A safe and permanent Remedy for the Distresses of the West-Indian Planters by a West-Indian,—Review of the Quarterly Review on Colonial Slavery pp 91—104 —Letter to W W Whitmore Esq M P by the Author of East and West India Sugar (in this pamphlet also the misrepresentations are exposed by which it was sought to prove that the peasantry of Bengal are slaves) —and Mr Stephen's Delineation of West-Indian Slavery pp 456—474 where the subject is most ably and conclusively treated

but the growing interest which it has excited in the public mind since that time has obliged the Committee to take a nearer and more practical view of its bearings than seemed to be then necessary

It is undoubtedly a subject of cordial congratulation, that there should have spontaneously arisen so strong and prevalent a desire to abstain from Slave grown Sugar inasmuch as it affords an unanswerable proof of the extent and force of those moral principles, on the influence of which the Committee have always chiefly relied for the final triumph of their cause On a question of this nature however they are inclined to follow rather than to lead the judgment and feelings of their friends throughout the kingdom In as far as abstinence from Slave grown Sugar may be regarded as a matter of conscience they feel that they have no right to interfere but must leave the question to be decided by each individual for himself according to the dictates of his own conscience At the same time on the supposition of the continued and effectual resistance of the colonies to the adoption of those reforms which have been proposed by his Majesty's Government they can contemplate no measure for attaining their ultimate objects more certain in its operation than the *general* substitution of Sugar grown by Free labour for that which is grown by Slaves

Such a measure however would by no means necessarily exclude the Sugar of the West Indies On the contrary the Committee hope that the course pursued by at least some of the colonies might lead to a preference of their produce founded on this very principle Those colonies which may adopt such reforms as lead to the extinction of Slavery and which should thus honourably distinguish themselves from those which persist in rejecting improvement and in seeking to perpetuate the present vicious and cruel system, would indeed establish an undeniable claim on the favour and encouragement of the British public. For who could better deserve support and countenance than those who, in spite of the example of their neighbours, the prejudices of education, and the force of habit, resolutely determine to act upon the just principles and enlightened views which have been presented to their adoption by the humanity and wisdom of his Majesty's Government? The same encouragement therefore which may be given to the produce of free labour, would without doubt be justly due to every colony which, though still involved in some of the evils of Slavery, yet should cordially embrace and honestly prosecute, effectual measures for their termination.

In drawing such a line of distinction, whenever the supposed case shall arise, the Committee believe that the friends of Negro emancipation will be promoting and not retarding those more efficient measures of direct legislative enactment which are most unquestionably the best means of attaining in the colonies at large the great ends of the recorded resolutions of Parliament on this subject. But if, notwithstanding the protracted resistance of the Colonial Assemblies, of which the latest accounts from the colonies afford but too decisive evidence, the supreme Legislature should still decline to interpose thus directly, we may yet hope that it may be induced to controul the refractory by such fiscal regulations as shall ensure a decided preference in the home market, if not to all Sugar the produce of free labour grown within the British dominions, yet, at least to that which is the produce of settlements where the recommendations of his Majesty's Government shall have been fully and effectually adopted and enforced.

Such an interference on the part of the Legislature would unquestionably be far more certain and immediate, as well as more powerful in its operation, than any voluntary efforts or sacrifices of individuals for in order to produce adequate results by these means, a more extensive concurrence of the people of this country in the plan of abstaining from Slave grown Sugar, would be necessary than can reasonably be expected to be immediately or very speedily obtained. This consideration, however, needs not cause any despair of ultimate success. On the contrary it would furnish a stronger stimulus to persevering exertions on the part of those who may be induced on conscientious grounds to adopt this plan, in order that others may gradually be wrought upon, by their influence and example to pursue the same course until the practice shall become sufficiently extended to produce the desired effect. It cannot be doubted as the Committee have already remarked, that its *general* adoption would tend powerfully to the extinction of Slavery in the British Colonies.

But although the Committee entertain no doubt that an adequate effect might thus in the course of time be produced notwithstanding the various difficulties by which such a plan would in practice necessarily be attended, they are happy in believing that there exist other means by which that effect may not only be more surely attained but by which it may be greatly accelerated as well as much more widely extended.

Unquestionably by far the most prompt and effectual of those means, as the Committee have more fully stated in their last Report, would be the repeal of all restrictive duties on the Sugars of British India and to this most important object the Committee trust that the deliberations of Parliament and the earnest prayers of the people of the United Kingdom, will be directed.

But even if this hope should fail, the Committee still believe it to be in the power of the friends of emancipation, by giving direct encouragement to the increased production of Sugar by Free labour, in no long time so to lower the cost of the article as to make it the clear interest not only of the whole population of the United Kingdom, but of all Europe to give a preference to such Sugar and thus to lead them of themselves and spontaneously to contribute their assistance in depriving the existing system of Slavery in the Foreign as well as in the British Colonies, of its main support and thus also to put a final period to that Slave Trade which to the indelible disgrace of certain European powers, and in contempt of their solemn engagements still prevails under their flags on the coast of Africa

That the labour of Free men is more advantageous than the labour of Slaves and that the produce of the former is to be obtained on cheaper terms than that of the latter are points on which this Committee entertain no doubt, and which are now admitted as axioms by every writer of authority on the science of political economy

If a proof were required of the truth of these propositions it would be found in the pertinacity with which the West Indians and their friends maintain the protecting duty against East India Sugar and the eagerness with which they have sought to increase it Notwithstanding the oppressive weight of that impost notwithstanding the aggravation of all the charges of transport by the distance of the place of its growth, notwithstanding the great imperfection and expensiveness of the rude process by which it is at present manufactured, notwithstanding the absence of encouragement from the application of British capital and skill to its production notwithstanding all these disadvantages, some descriptions of the Sugar of Hindostan come even now into direct competition with the Sugars of the West Indies in the market of Great Britain This single circumstance appears to be conclusive It appears to prove clearly that the Free grown Sugars of British India might be sold if the present protecting duty were removed, considerably cheaper than the Slave grown Sugar of the British West Indies

But this is not the only proof which may be adduced of the superiority of Free over Slave labour

Prior to the opening of the trade to Hindostan very little Cotton was brought from that country to Europe Although the protecting duty in favour of West India Cotton was small, yet East India freights were so enormous (about 32*l* a ton) that it was impossible to import Cotton thence with advantage Since the opening of the trade with India however, and the consequent reduction of freights, East India Cotton has been imported in such quantities and at so low a rate, as to reduce the price of that article all over the world to about half its former amount

A still more striking exemplification of the principle for which the Committee are contending is supplied by the Indigo Trade Forty or fifty years ago little or no Indigo was exported from British India The whole of that article then used in Europe was the product of Slave labour A few individuals in Bengal employed their capital and their intelligence in inciting the natives to enlarge their cultivation of it, and in preparing it for the European market and, though abundantly discouraged in the first instance yet the duties being nearly equalized, their efforts were at length crowned with complete success Such indeed has been the effect of British skill and capital united when employed in calling Free labour into action that notwithstanding the enormous freights which for a time the importers of it had to pay the Indigo of India has been gradually displacing from the market the Indigo grown by

Slaves until at length, with the help of the free trade, and the lighter freights consequent upon it, there is not now one ounce of Indigo the produce of Slave labour, imported into Europe while the value of the Indigo grown in British India amounts to nearly four millions sterling annually. The only existing competitors in this branch of trade are the Free labourers of Guatimala and the Caraccas and their competition which had for a time been nearly extinguished is now only reviving with the new born liberties of those regions.

Encouraged by such pregnant examples the Committee have been induced to look with much care and solicitude into the circumstances of the Sugar Trade of British India. A mass of valuable information having been obtained on the subject from the records of the East India Company, the practical result of that information has been abstracted and embodied in a pamphlet recently published for the Society by Hatchard and entitled, 'East India Sugar or an Inquiry respecting the Means of improving the Quality and reducing the Cost of Sugar raised by Free Labour in the East Indies.'

In this pamphlet the defects in the present mode of manufacturing Sugar in India are pointed out and the means are also specified by which those defects may be remedied, the quality of the Sugar greatly improved, and the cost of its production very materially diminished. And it seems now no longer a matter of doubt, provided only the simple and obvious improvements there suggested should be adopted, that it would be possible to import the Sugar of India into this country especially if the oppressive protecting duty of 10s a cwt were removed so as materially to undersell the Sugar grown by Slaves*

* It would be impossible in this brief address even to enumerate all the advantages which in addition to the annual saving to the country of at least 1,500,000*l*

In a country however circumstanced as India is, the same means of promoting the culture of Sugar must result from the removal of the bounties and restrictions on the Trade of Sugar. The experience of the past year has abundantly proved the beneficial effect of such a measure in other branches of trade. Not to mention the benefit which India would derive from the development of her resources and Ireland from the impulse which must be given to her industry and our merchants and manufacturers from the immense field which would be opened to their enterprize, the Committee on this occasion will confine themselves to the benefits which must flow to the West-Indians themselves from the adoption of this just and liberal policy. They confidently expect indeed that so soon as the West Indian planter is led to himself for relief his system will rapidly improve.

One obvious benefit which would immediately accrue to him would be that he would be induced to withdraw his poor soil from Sugar cultivation and to retain in it only those of superior fertility. Inferior soils would be employed in the growth of other articles for which they were adapted and only the best in that of Sugar. The remunerating price of Sugar would thus be lowered. A forced cultivation must always be a hazardous and expensive process and it can only be supported by a monopoly price both high and permanent.

Again the use of the plough has such obvious advantages that to a cursory observer it is wonderful that it has not been more generally adopted in West-Indian cultivation. If an English farmer were obliged to keep during the whole year all the hands that he required in harvest he too might employ them with the spade and the hoe in turning up the soil and might find less advantage from the plough. If the plough were brought into general use and cattle were therefore more generally employed the fertility of the soil by means of a change of crops of manuring and good management would be gradually improved instead of being as now continually deteriorated.

Various other suggesstions present themselves. If for example the cultivation of provisions were made universally a first and paramount object, if the women were relieved from the constant and oppressive drudgery of field labour and allowed to give an adequate share of attention to their domestic concerns as might easily be done were the plough in general use and if various other economical improvements which are obviously practicable were adopted there can be no doubt that the state of things in the West-Indies would rapidly and greatly improve. The population would increase and their con

must be resorted to, which have proved so signally successful in the case of Indigo. British capital and British intelligence must give the necessary direction and impulse to the industry of the Native Farmer. With that view, information on the subject has already been widely diffused and the Committee have great satisfaction in perceiving that attention has of late been much turned to this object, and to the means of attaining it. Still, if it should be left entirely to individual enterprize to excite the industry either of the Hindoos, or of the Free labourers in other tropical countries, the progress of things to this consummation would probably be slow. The Committee therefore will rejoice should the plans which are now on foot for accelerating it, by forming associations for promoting the growth and manufacture of Sugar by Free labour, be carried into effect. The Committee cannot but wish well to all such undertakings. Should they succeed, they must tend gradually but most effectually, to put an end to the cultivation of Sugar by Slave labour just as similar means, though much less powerfully and systematically developed have put an end to the growth of Indigo by Slave labour, not only in the colonies of Great Britain but in every other part of the world. And, when Sugar shall cease to be cultivated by Slaves, it may safely be assumed that the final extinction of Colonial Slavery is at hand. Indeed, long before that period shall arrive, it may be reasonably hoped that the planters of the West Indies will have opened their eyes to their true interests, and will be convinced, by what is passing before them, that in the present circumstances of the world, and the new state of our commercial relations, their relief from distress, the improvement of their property and their advancement in wealth and prosperity, so far from being inconsistent with the progress of emancipation, may be expected to arise, and indeed can only arise from a course of measures tending to elevate the moral and social condition of their Slaves, and to convert them into a free peasantry, labouring for their own benefit, and enjoying in common with their masters the equal protection of law, and the blessings of civil freedom and religious light

dition would gradually approach that of Free labourers. The property of the Planter would be no longer estimated by the number of his Slaves who would sink in value but by his land which would proportionably rise in value. His income would eventually be derived from a land rent paid by Black or White farmers managing their own concerns and he would then be able to compete in the sale of his produce with any other country in the world —Review of the Quarterly Review pp 103, 104

For the Christian Observer

OBSERVATIONS ON THE CHARACTER, OPINIONS AND WRITINGS OF THE LATE LORD BYRON

(Continued from p 87)

IN our attempts to analyze the characters of individuals whether dead or living considerable care and caution are requisite. The human heart, in the full extent of its windings and intricacies, is known to God only. Even, under that more limited survey which man is permitted to take of his moral nature, it is sometimes a labyrinth of perplexity, in which the most knowing and experienced are apt to be bewildered and lost. But, even where certainty cannot be secured, a high degree of probability is often attainable and 'probability' as Bishop Butler observes 'is the very guide of life'

The Westminster Reviewers tell us, that Lord Byron " rarely resisted the impulse of his feelings" undoubtedly a just remark. I cannot, however, say so much for what fol lows that "these impulses were generally of the most benevolent kind. Like all persons who unite strong passions with equally strong conceptions, and with a vivid imagination, whatever he felt at all he felt most sensibly and acutely. When minds of this cast are blessed with some proportionate counterpoise of moral and religious principle, such feelings, though they must partially influence the conduct, are still not permitted to *govern* it. But, unhappily Lord Byron wanted this ballast to keep his vessel steady under the heavy and shifting gales of passion and temptation. He therefore followed the impulses of feeling and sentiment, without inquiring whither they were likely to conduct him. Often, however, his impulses appear to have been transient, in proportion to their intensity. They roared and blustered for their little hour, and then gave place to some new gust or current, blowing perhaps from a quite contrary direction.

But the human mind may be much under the influence of sudden impulses of sentiment and passion, and yet still own the general ascendency of some one ruling or master propensity, as the various foreign effluvia which mingle under ordinary circumstances with the atmospheric air do not deprive it of that fundamental principle in its composition on which the support of life depends. Lord Byron, with all his subjection to impulses, had still his ruling passion, which developed its prevailing influence in a greater or less degree under all the changes and circumstances of his life. Perhaps it would be too much to say, in the words of a poet whom Lord Byron greatly admired, though he certainly did not copy him in manner, that

> The master passion ruling in his breast
> Like Aaron's serpent swallowed up the rest

but, if it did not annihilate occasional impulses, it controlled them, and maintained an habitual predominance in the poet's bosom. And what was that master passion? If I mistake not, it was *an exorbitant desire of intellectual and literary fame, with little or no regard to the moral feelings and characters of his admirers.* We shall find, I think, that this principle will best account for several of the most striking facts of his history, and features of his conduct.

It furnishes, for example, a clue to the display of his temper in the publication of 'English Bards and Scotch Reviewers,' one of his earliest works, composed about the time of his coming of age. It is well known that the satirical poem here alluded to was occasioned by an article in the Edinburgh Review on the "Hours of Idleness by a Minor," published two years earlier. Our great Northern Journal was at that period in the full blaze of its talents, and in the full career of its popularity, not less renowned for its wit upon matters of lighter interest, than for its power and acuteness, on graver subjects,—always excepting the subject of religion, though the gravest, the greatest, and the most worthy of superior abilities. As these formidable writers were flourishing their critical scourge, which at that time had a stinging lash appended to it, over the troop of authors who surrounded them, they found a noble minor in the throng who seemed to be pressing towards the temple of fame with more assurance than they thought became either his age or his abilities, and they could not refrain from giving him a stroke which he felt most severely. It was certainly calculated to make a youthful aspirant smart, and it happened to light upon a constitution which, perhaps, among the '*wrathful poetic tribe*,' was one of the most irascible that ever existed. Lord Byron frankly confessed that he had never been so angry in his life, either before or afterwards, though probably he said this before he had read

Mr Southey's protest twice over, and looked those unutterable things which Captain Medwin has attempted to describe. The result was, that he vented his rage in the "English Bards and Scotch Reviewers," a performance which, considering the age of the author, evinced great knowledge of mankind, correctness of criticism, keenness of satire, and in many parts a much better tone of moral feeling than is visible in his later productions. Here, I conceive, the master passion of Lord Byron rose into very conspicuous exercise. The "Poems by a Minor," though doubtless indicating a youth of superior intellect and attainments, gave no adequate promise of the "Childe Harolde" published about five years afterwards. Had then Lord Byron listened, upon this occasion, to the dictates of reason, candour, and conscience, instead of throwing the reins upon the neck of his wounded pride, would he not have contented himself with scrutinizing the matter of the review? Though he might have deemed it unfairly or even cruelly severe, would he not have waited to confute it by some subsequent performance that should have sealed his reputation as a poet, without betraying the bitterness of his resentment as a man? But angry feelings prevailed, and shewed that an attack upon his literary fame was the offence which he was least able to forgive. The same may have happened in the case of other youthful bards; but at present I have to do with Lord Byron only.

To the soreness of personal, if not intellectual, pride, must also be attributed the alteration of the couplet, in this poem relating to Lord Carlisle. Lord Byron had, in his first manuscript given this nobleman a larger dividend of praise as a poet than was ever bestowed upon him by the public. But, deeply wounded by some real or fancied neglect on the part of his noble relative, he suppressed the laudatory distich and inserted a contemptuous couplet in its place. The anecdote rests on the report of the late Mr Dallas, and I see no reason for doubting its correctness. Now, in a mind not governed by the selfishness of pride and passion, reason, if not moral principle, would surely have interposed to prevent a deviation from consistency so gross and odious as this. It may not be without its parallel in the annals of literary delinquency; but it shewed a lamentable disregard to all sense of rectitude; and, though I am not partial to certain of Mr Southey's images, I must say that it betrayed as much of the "cloven foot" of human degeneracy as could well be displayed in any single action.

The principle I have laid down, as the ruling passion in Lord Byron's character, will also account for those gratuitous and most pernicious effusions of scepticism which teem in the Childe Harolde. It was the elder Mr Dallas, as Lord Byron himself acknowledged, who first discerned the numerous beauties of this poem, a poem which the author was disposed, or *professed* to be so, to throw aside, and for which he was about to substitute a very inferior performance. In this recommendation Mr Dallas may fairly be said to have laid the foundation of his friend's celebrity, while perhaps he contributed also to that *facilis descensus Averni*—that rapidly downward course of moral feeling in the noble author—which followed the unexampled success of this poem. In his recommendation however Mr Dallas laboured, with the industry and zeal of a well principled mind, to get rid of two most exceptionable stanzas, in which a cheerless gloom of scepticism, or rather the darkness of unbelief is thrown around the awful subject of futurity. He attacked Lord Byron again and again, on this point but without success. The stanzas his lordship was obstinately bent on retaining. Do we not, here too, witness the overbearing predominance of a love of literary fame, uncombined with the smallest tenderness for moral and religious feelings? The author could not but know that the objectionable stanzas were specimens of beautiful pathos, and amongst his finest poetry. He knew also (for Mr Dallas told him so) that their insertion however objectionable, would at first rather increase than diminish the popularity of the work. At the same time he must have felt, had he felt morally at all, that they could tend to no valuable purpose but his own literary aggrandizement, and that their unavoidable effect would be to grieve the good, to confirm the scorner in his impiety, and to unsettle any feeble foundations of faith in the young, the careless, and the dissipated. But he evidently delighted in the *daring aspect* of the achievement. He was gratified with shewing the world that he was not to be terrified by the strictures of moral censors and indignant criticism. He seemed resolved to feel the pulse of the British public, on the subject of infidelity, to try what it could bear, and how far it would connive at his irreligion, from admiration of his genius. The result of the experiment was most unhappy. The poem succeeded beyond expectation, and Mr Dallas, who had good means of ascertaining the truth, informs us, that this success raised the author's vanity to a degree of confidence and presumption which led to those still grosser outrages upon piety, virtue, and common decency, that are but too well known. It is but due to the character of the late Mr Dallas to state, that he lived to repent deeply of having been so active an instrument in the publication of the Childe Harolde, and that he expressed the uneasiness of his conscience, on this account within a very short period of his death.

But perhaps some persons will say, though the staunch readers of the Christian Obsesver will hardly be of their number, "What was the mighty mischief in this case? Should we lament that one of the finest poems in the English language has not been suppressed, on account of only two objectionable stanzas? How many beauties should we have lost, in losing the Childe Harolde! Sentiments like these proceed from a cause which has been already referred to, the gratification of fancy, and the relish of intellectual enjoyment prevailing over the sense of moral duty and heartfelt religion. But, alas! weighed against these highest interests of mankind, what are the attractions of poetry but a feather in the scale? The two justly reprobated stanzas are far from constituting the whole objection of the Christian and the moralist to this fine poem. But what if they were the whole? A subtle and searching poison may be mixed in such small proportions with the sweet or innocent ingredients of the cup as hardly to be tasted by the victim, whom nevertheless it destroys.

The Childe Harolde, the Giaour, the Corsair, and some other of the first poems of Lord Byron, might be termed decorous and moral, when compared with the mingled grossness, licentiousness, and impiety of his latter productions. Yet, in these disgusting performances, strange as it may seem, he appears to have been mainly influenced by the desire of literary fame. If this motive be not admitted, his conduct, I fear, can only be resolved into something far worse—the utter depravity of a deliberate design upon the peace and morals of well ordered society. I confess that, much as I abhor the tendency of some of his poems, I should be slow to charge him with an amount of guilt that would more than justify the very worst epithets which have been bestowed on him as a writer. But how, it may be asked, could he possibly hope to establish and enlarge his reputation by works so much at variance with sound principles and sober morals as Don Juan, Cain, and the reply to Southey's Vision of Judgment? The answer is, that he thought not of the more moral and respectable, still less of the truly religious, portion of the British public. What he wanted was *the extension of a name* and this he was pretty sure of obtaining. Whether he gained it through good or through evil report appears to have been with him, latterly, a matter of much indifference. In spite of English taste and English manners, he found that his works were read. Singularity and opposition did but advance the sale of them. Numbers of thoughtless persons eagerly ran after every thing which had his dishonoured name appended to it, and openly countenanced writings which their better feelings could not but condemn; whilst many who were entire Atheists in practice, and semi Atheists in theory, were not displeased to find their views forwarded and patronised by so great a genius. The lord chancellor might refuse his injunction and the attorney general might prosecute; but the indirect censure of the one only operated to widen the circulation of the noxious work, and the more decisive proceedings of the other were not sufficient for suppressing it. In short, Lord Byron found that he was triumphing at once over public opinion, law, and equity; and he seems to have enjoyed his triumph with the spirit of one who was willing to surrender all claim to moral respectability, if he could but extend his fame as a poet, and spread around terror or amazement by the boldness and eccentricities of his muse.

Perhaps, under these circumstances, even his determination to reside abroad was more connected with the desire and maintenance of literary elevation, than may, at first view, be imagined. In his self imposed exile from his native country, there was an air of proud independence and singularity, which, while it rendered him less loved than feared made him, at the same time, more the subject of general conversation and remark. When Lord Byron had once resolved upon disregarding the advice of friends, the strictures of critics, and the voice of public opinion, as to the moral tendency of his writings, prudence clearly dictated that he ought not to reside in England. Bad as we are, in comparison of what we ought to be, there is, after all, perhaps a higher strain and standard of good feeling in this country than in any other on the face of the earth; and the liberty we enjoy affords a wider and more effectual scope for the expression of that feeling here than elsewhere. Much that will pass unnoticed or uncensured in France and Italy, is branded here with just reprobation. Even *we*, alas! may be tempted to admire and patronise genius, when abused to very unworthy purposes; but we are not easily brought to confound vice with virtue, in our estimates of the characters of individuals. Lord Byron knew this and wisely kept aloof. Unlike the objects of the material world, he shewed greatest at a distance. Greater nearness and familiarity might have lessened our admiration, and by consequence his literary eminence. In all this, I am far from meaning to deny that other motives, of a private and domestic nature, which it is not my design here to touch upon, might operate, with great force in keeping him away from his country. Still the ruling passion was, I think, strongly discernible in this circumstance of his life.

The elder Mr Dallas, who, in spite of the Westminster Reviewers, was always in intention, and often in reality the best friend of the noble bard, informs us that he had more than once urged him to occupy and adorn his proper station, as a member of the hereditary branch of the legislature. He made, I think, only one or two essays and those, though unfavourable as to manner, were highly calculated, in point of matter, to command attention. What a fine spectacle would it have been to have seen

Lord Byron, with his great powers of intellect and influence, taking his stand, in the British senate, as the firm yet temperate supporter of his country's rights and liberties,—as the consistent patron of a liberal and enlightened policy,—and as the active promoter of national improvement, in every wise, pious, and laudable undertaking! Whether this addition of the civic crown might not have shaded in some degree his poetic laurel I cannot presume to say. But if he had been somewhat less celebrated as a poet he would have had infinitely more to recommend him as a man and, if he had composed comparatively but little, yet that little would have handed down his name to posterity with far more enviable honours than it now inherits.

False conceptions of dignity and glory were the rock upon which Lord Byron split, as thousands have perished in the same way before him. Dignity and glory he made to consist, partly perhaps in personal vigour and accomplishments but chiefly in *intellectual power*. This, whether with or without the recommendation of moral and religious principle, seems to have been equally the object of his boast and admiration. He censured and almost despised Napoleon Bonaparte for condescending to survive the effects of his restless and insatiable ambition. "He ought to have gone off the stage like a hero," was the poet's observation concerning him. He remarked, that Dr Johnson "died like a coward, because he was afraid of departing in an unprepared state," and that Hume "went off like a brave man, because he danced and sported upon the edge of the tomb and dared to be jocular—to adopt the words of our great moralist— ' upon one of the few things that make wise men serious." Through the same fatal prejudice, he denied that Voltaire's end was clouded with those terrors which the Abbé Barruel has so fearfully described. We are told, that, like Alfieri, Lord Byron was "*fier, indomptable, mélancholique*" that he was "too proud to justify himself, when right or, if accused, to own himself wrong." Such are the notions of courage and dignity which the unbeliever boldly professes, and which the nominal Christian, if he be less forward to own them, still too much encourages and entertains. I need not say how totally they are at variance with the word of God. Indeed they are at variance with the simplest dictates of reason and common understanding. There is a line of Racine's 'Athalie' which ought to be prominently affixed in the study of every bold literary sceptic.

Je crains Dieu cher Abner et n'ai point d'autre crainte.

This is a better, because a more religious description of true courage than the famous passage in Shakespeare, to a like effect.

I dare do all that may become a man
Who dares do more is none.

No mind, under the influence of Christian feeling would think, for a moment, of passing judgment on Lord Byron's state, during the last hours of his mortal existence. Still, however, we may be justified in asking with deep concern, whether there be not some reason to apprehend that his ruling passion was "strong in death." As the account given by his servant cannot well be disproved, and remains uncontradicted, I suppose we may consider it substantially correct. He represents his master as having said, during his fatal illness, "I am not afraid of death I am more fit to die than many people imagine." Now, if this speech proceeded from a mere preparation of nerve and animal spirits, in what light can it be viewed but as a last effort of that false shame and those mistaken ideas of dignity by which his general character was distinguished? What does it prove, but that, like the dying gladiator, he wished to fall gracefully? If, on the other hand, it was meant to express, in any degree, a preparation of soul for his departure—the only preparation worth speaking of—then indeed we can but hope that he had some better ground of confidence than a retrospect of his life and writings was calculated to inspire.

It is a question often agitated, and of considerable importance, under what limitations, or whether under any the desire of human applause and admiration can be a legitimate principle of action, according to the morality of the Gospel. Without however attempting, in the present paper, to determine this question in the abstract, it is very certain that the desire of literary reputation—for to that I now confine myself—becomes clearly unlawful, corrupt and mischievous, when it prevails uncombined with Christian piety and principle. In this case, it addresses itself solely, either to the taste and opinions of the great mass of mankind, or to those of some particular assembly of critics who may be termed dispensers of the literary honours of their own day. Now, I hardly need say, that the opinions of such critics are not always sound and scriptural. They are, on the contrary, too often at variance with the dictates of true religion, and, even without being positively immoral or profane, may give a dangerous encouragement to what is erroneous in principle and incorrect in practice. In a word, their standard of morals too often falls short of the standard of the Gospel. And, with regard to the good opinion of the public at large, it is certain that no writer can surrender himself to the pursuit of this object, without at the same time conceding what a true Christian must ever hold most dear and most valuable. This has been strikingly exemplified in the authors of dramatic compositions, who professedly adapt themselves to the taste of the multitude, and of whom the least exceptionable, are, for the most part, miserably defective, when tried by the test of Scripture.

The desire of literary reputation, even if it were proved not to be abstractedly sinful, must at all events be an unlawful motive, when it is not kept in absolute subjection to the principles of Christianity. Not only must those principles generally prompt and influence all our actings but they should also control and govern them. They should operate so as effectually to restrain us from any irregularities and excesses which would be inconsistent with the character of a true disciple of Christ. Addison somewhere alludes to offences of this nature, as the peculiar temptations of men of wit and genius and, while he enforces the duty of overcoming such temptations, he seems to allow some merit to the sacrifice. But Addison's views of Christian doctrine and practice were, it is to be feared, not sufficiently correct and elevated. The true Christian will hardly deem the sacrifice of a loose or profane jest to be any extraordinary evidence of virtue; though he will regard the practice of such liberties as a sure proof of the want of a steady principle of religion.

A desire of literary reputation is a principle which requires to be suspected and watched over with more than ordinary care and caution. There is no instance in which the precept of the wise man is more necessary to be placed constantly before our view,—*keep thy heart with all diligence;* and there is no instance in which the danger of overstepping the limit of allowable indulgence is greater or more apparent. We are vain creatures at the best and whatever may tend to nourish our vanity, should be avoided and repressed. In opposing the temptations of undue self complacency and self applause, the man of wit, genius, or ability, has to encounter the natural frailty of his own heart, fostered by the warm praises of friends, the approbation of critics, and the flatteries of the multitude. How is he to avoid becoming oppressed, and as it were intoxicated, with the fumes of the incense which surrounds him? Only by constant vigilance, and by earnest prayer for the assistance of that Divine grace which alone can preserve him from the *pride that goeth before destruction*.

(*To be continued.*)

To the Editor of the Christian Observer.

IN taking up Boswell's Life of Johnson, I am struck with a passage in the additional part at the beginning (second edition), in which the author has volunteered, in opposition to the *dictum* of his great master, his "*magnus Apollo*," on other occasions his own private opinion, on a subject which at that time was one of eager and general discussion—the abolition of the slave trade. It may seem somewhat unkind and ungenerous to bring forward a writer's opinion, after a lapse of years, during which so complete a revolution in sentiment has taken place among his countrymen with regard to this great question. But there is so amusing an ambitiousness in the passage, such an unfortunate assumption of impregnable superiority, such a provoking "longing after immortality," that I am persuaded the author, so far from feeling himself aggrieved, would have rejoiced in the prospect, could he have foreseen that it had a chance of being embalmed in your pages. Should you be inclined to confer this honour upon it, it may serve for a specimen of the short-sightedness of man, and the unseemliness of overweening confidence in reference to questions which admit of doubt, and on which posterity is to decide. How little could Mr. Boswell imagine, that the abolition which he treats as a fanciful and wild, an inhuman and unchristian, chimera, would, at no great distance of time, not only attain the repose and dignity of a settled historical fact, but even cease to be discussed as a speculative question, as a point of history, affording sufficient play for argumentative reasoning on both sides—*ut declamatio fiat!* How little could he imagine—happily for his sensitive mind he was saved from the contemplation of so widely spread a calamity—that not only would the sounds of opposition die away in England, but the general voice of Europe, so far as the *principle* is concerned, would join in confirming our decision, and pronouncing the condemnation of their own *practice*. Nay, the day may arrive, when they will go further than this, when they will be ashamed of their inconsistency, and by the universal abandonment of this philanthropic traffic, ' the gates of mercy, in spite of Mr Boswell's prophetic deprecation, will be finally " shut on the unpitied and deserted African!

The passage is as follows:—

"I record Dr Johnson's argument fairly upon this particular case, where, perhaps, he was in the right. But I beg leave to enter my most solemn protest against his general doctrine with respect to the slave trade. For I will resolutely say, that his unfavourable notion of it was owing to prejudice, and imperfect or false information. The wild and dangerous attempt which has for some time been persisted in, to obtain an Act of our Legislature to abolish so very important and necessary a branch of commercial interest, must have been crushed at once, had not the insignificance of the zealots who vainly took the lead in it made the vast body of planters, merchants, and others, whose immense properties are involved in that trade, reasonably enough suppose that there could be no danger. The encouragement which the attempt has received excites my wonder and indignation; and though some men of superior abilities have supported it, whether from a love of temporary popularity when prosperous, or a love of general mischief when desperate, my opinion is unshaken. To abolish a *status* which in all ages God has sanctioned, and man has continued, would not only be *robbery* to an innumerable class of our fellow subjects, but it would be extreme cruelty to the African savages, a portion of whom it saves from massacre, or introduces into a much happier state of life especially now when their passage to the West Indies, and their treatment there, is humanely regulated. To abolish that trade would be

To shut the gates of mercy on mankind

But it is not merely as *a curiosity*, that I think this passage worthy of a few moments attention in the present day. A great question yet remains to be decided on which hang the destinies of nearly a million of our fellow creatures shall the descendants of the victims of a trade which has been determined to be iniquitous and proscribed as piratical, be suffered to pine under its inherited operation? Can we be said to have *abolished* it, when to these poor creatures its terrible force is the same reaching through the course of time as if they had been but yesterday torn under its gripe, from their native land and their natural liberty? The unbiassed, untutored answer of reason to this collateral question, is as plain and as short as it was to the original one, concerning the trade Abolition was the theorem emancipation is only the corollary if the former has been proved, the latter follows of course. I am not now speaking of the *time* and the *mode* but of the *duty* and *necessity*, of emancipation as a national measure. If the public mind be once strongly impressed with the obligation the means of accomplishing the object will not be wanting. Now against this assertion of the duty, do we not find a host of enemies arrayed? Are they not the same men heirs at least of the same interests and prejudices, with those who fought the battle against the abolition? Do we not see the same weapons in their hands, and the same manner of wielding them—the same undoubting confidence in their demeanour—the same flash of argument—the same shower of opprobious epithets on the wise and good of the earth—the same impatience of an appeal to the common feelings of humanity—the same deafness to the solemn and repeated protest of Religion—the same unblushing attempt to wrest the forbearance of God into a sanction to convert the " times of ignorance at which he winked, into a precedent for all times—to confound the meaning of words to put " *happiness* for slavery, and " *robbery* for reparation—to mislead the mind, to paralize the will, and to harden the heart—which we see so conspicuously displayed by Mr Boswell in the passage before us? It may serve, therefore, as an encouragement to some to go steadily and fearlessly on towards the attainment of their great object, when they perceive how vain were all these means to oppose the silent march of truth, and the *fiat* of Divine Providence and to others who have begun to waver it may be instrumental in dispelling the delusion which boldness in asseveration or ingenuity in making " the worse appear the better reason, may for a moment have succeeded in raising

B C

To the Editor of the Christian Observer

THE account of the execution of Thomas Coombs, for the murder at Beckenham, as published in the London papers having been copied by your correspondent Monitor, for the purpose of grounding on it a remonstrance on the impropriety of indiscriminately administering the holy communion to condemned criminals I think it right, in justice to my own feelings and character, to send you the true statement as given in the Maidstone Gazette, of December 21, 1824, and shall be obliged by your inserting it in your next Number From this counter statement, your readers, and Monitor among them, will see that implicit dependence ought not invariably to be placed on the rash assertions of public journalists, frequently founded on flying reports, and sometimes perhaps on their own bare conjectures. It will be seen, that Coombs was *not* conducted into the chapel on the morning of his execution, and that, for reasons about to be specified, the holy communion was *not* administered to him. Up to the last moment, I thought it my duty to pay the unhappy man the most unremitted attentions, with a sincere wish that it might please God to bless my humble endeavours for his spiritual good, and that he might be moved to make a penitent confession of his guilt but finding him, after all my efforts, obstinately determined to leave the world in circumstances very unfit for a dying man, I felt that I could not, conscientiously and safely comply with his wish and on subsequent reflection, though the propriety of my refusal has been variously spoken of among some of the clergy and others in the neighbourhood, I am still of opinion that I evinced no want of candour or charity in withholding the solemn ordinance from such a man, who not only could not " give any reason of the hope that was in him and rejected the only probable means of being enabled to learn it, but who almost invariably received my instructions with sullen indifference, and persisted in the most shocking falsehoods to the last

Our Church, in the Order for the Visitation of the Sick, expressly *recommends* nay *enjoins*, that " the person be moved to make a special confession of his sins if he feel his conscience troubled, with any weighty matter and though a clergyman ought not curiously to pry into all the circumstances of a man's life, he will not, if he really feel the weight and responsibility of his sacred office, be satisfied with a superficial confession, a confession in the gross, which has no reference to particular sins and still less, if the object of his attentions be a hardened criminal, who is convicted of murder, and has spent all his days in the most shameful and flagrant wickedness, and never cherished one serious thought of his Maker, Redeemer and Sanctifier, till sentence of death has been actually passed upon him

Monitor will doubtless be glad to find that the importance of his observations had been in a measure anticipated It may be further satisfactory to add, that the sacrament was also refused to J T Ingram, another hardened criminal, who suffered ten days after Coombs so that this holy ordinance though *too frequently* I fear, is not *always* administered indiscriminately to prisoners left for execution, without very great respect to their suitable preparation for it I should have submitted both these cases to the archbishop, for his consideration, but that his Grace s reply could not have arrived at Maidstone in time

I am, sir,
Your most obedient servant,
J WINTER,
Chaplain of the County Prisons,
Maidstone

" *Execution of T Coombs*

" Yesterday morning Thomas Coombs convicted of the murder of T Morgan, was executed on Penden heath After his condemnation the wretched man conducted himself with outward decency but, we are sorry to say he died without an explicit acknowledgment of his guilt The Rev John Winter, chaplain of the gaol, was unremitting in his endeavour to prepare the culprit for the awful change he was so soon to undergo, and the solicitude of the Rev gentleman was met by the prisoner with respectful atten tion* but it failed in eliciting from him that confession which is the only reparation that can be made to his fellow men, by a criminal about to appear before an Almighty Judge, to answer for the commission of the horrible crime of murder. But though the hapless creature faintly denied his guilt, yet he did so in a manner that shewed his words and his conscience were at variance. He wished not to be pressed on the subject, and though he said the witnesses were all combined against him, he did not attempt to contradict the truth of a single fact adduced. On Sunday night, he slept but little, and yesterday morning he wished the holy sacrament to be administered to him. Previous to complying with his wish, the chaplain again entreated him to make the only reparation in his power by a confession of his guilt, of which no man who heard his trial could entertain a doubt. Coombs appeared in some measure subdued but he declined either to acknowledge or deny the crime for which he was to die, though he confessed that he had led a dissolute and wicked life. Under these circumstances, the Rev gentleman very properly did not administer the sacrament to the culprit, who evinced no anxiety on the subject. A few minutes before 11 o clock, the under sheriff and chaplain again exhorted Coombs to make a positive declaration on the subject of his guilt, but he still refused, declaring that to press him further would drive him mad. The workings of his mind at the moment operated so forcibly upon him that he begged to be permitted to sit down, or he should sink on the ground. He was immediately seated and it was found necessary to give him some wine, to preserve him from fainting. At 11 o clock, the melancholy procession set out from the prison, in the midst of a tremendous shower of rain. On arriving at the scaffold, the chaplain ascended the waggon, and prayed with the culprit who joined him without any appearance of earnestness. The executioner then proceeded to perform his dreadful office. When placed under the beam Coombs remained unchanged he spoke not but his lips occasionally moved as if he was inwardly praying. The executioner several times asked him if he had any thing to say to the spectators of the melancholy scene but he replied that he had not, and he met his fate with a sullen composure or we may say a savage indifference, that was any thing but the demeanour of an innocent man, &c &c.

Coombs was outwardly civil, but far from shewing respectful attention to me

---

REVIEW OF NEW PUBLICATIONS

A Tribute of Parental Affection containing some Account of the Character and Death of Hannah Jerram (fourth Edition) with an Appendix, giving a short Account of the last Illness, and Death of her elder Brother. By their father CHARLES JERRAM, Vicar of Chobham Surrey. London 6s 1824.

THE present publication, in having reached a fifth edition, seems to demand of us some notice, both from its own excellence and in deference to the voice of public opinion so strongly given in its favour. To those readers who admit or require the relish of *story* to be infused into works of religious instruction as a legitimate means of superior attraction, we recommend it on a double account first, because they have here a story of a very interesting and affecting nature to arrest their attention, and, whether or not they will regard that as giving additional value, a story circumstantially and literally true: and next, because they will find in the course of its pages some highly useful observations on a taste for the perusal of such tales as are *not* true—stories founded altogether on fiction, or, what are often equally false, tales pretending to be founded in fact. We are strongly inclined to introduce the amiable and lamented Hannah Jerram to our readers by an abstract of Mr. Jerram's observations on this very subject: and we may perhaps be allowed the liberty of prefacing these by a single introductory remark of our own. The remark, then, we have to make on this confessedly hackneyed subject is, that, however paradoxical it may seem, the circumstance of a story, even a religious story, being *true*, in the proper sense of truth, is no peculiar recommendation to it in the eyes of ordinary religious story readers. As the great drawback to mere didactic exhortation is this, that there is something told us to be actually and merely *done*: so we believe a corresponding drawback to the actual verities of religious biography arises from this circumstance, that there is something to be actually and faithfully *imitated*. Now mere religious story telling is disencumbered from both these weighty drawbacks. There may perhaps be something to be *felt*, to be admired, to be even wept over, and dreamt over, but nothing to be *done*: and for this plain reason, that the thing never *was* done: and nothing to be *imitated*, for a reason equally plain, that we may, or may not, at our own option, assume the description to be *inimitable*. The religious novelist, whether writer or reader, has indeed surprising advantages. The selection of incident is left entirely to the judgment of the one as acting upon the feelings of the other. The writer has to put the reader into the newest possible and most imaginative world: to enrapture him like "the poet's eye, rolling from earth to heaven, from heaven to earth:" to make him forget, we had almost said, his own condition and proper self: and to make him appear, to his own view, the very hero, tragic or epic, which is described in the piece. Hence, in the most compendious possible way, the man is made a Christian, a Christian parent or child, master or servant, landlord or peasant, a Christian soldier, or pastor, or merchant, or missionary, according to the character assumed in the tale: without a single effort, outward or within, in heart or hand, to become what he imagines himself for the time to be. The delightful heroes and heroines "without fear or reproach" which were conjured up in the moral world in the Grandisons or the Pamelas of past ages, are not in truth converted to Christianity by the same exquisite machinery adapted to religion. Nor with regard to the reader, any more than the hero or heroine, is this desirable effect very certain: if it were, how delightful would it be to reflect upon the great increase of eminent Christian characters among the admirers of these productions! For, in imagination at least, many a sickly sentimentalist becomes self invested with the sturdy virtues of a veteran missionary: whilst perhaps the robust and Herculean contemplatist may be most meritoriously dreaming over the peaceful duties of a cottage maid. Such portraits as that one traced in the affecting pages of Mr. Jerram from real life, possess none of these recommendations. The writer, for the most part, here delineates not for the imagination but the conscience of the reader: and his business is not to make the most agreeable composition but the most faithful portrait: a portrait so faithful as to apply itself to the circumstances and feelings of fellow probationers in this mortal state. And hence, to the mere imaginative reader a faithful biographical memoir is not so at tractive as a highly wrought fiction. This or that circumstance might have been modified, or might have been omitted, the exhibition might have been a little differently dressed, and the real state of the case needed not have been fully exposed. The virtues above humanity, the imperfections but too consistent with it, form not the *beau ideal* of imagined perfection, or something in the Christian experience happens to be inconsistent according to our views with the Christian character that is pourtrayed. In short what we are, what we may be, what we ought to be, and what we must stand prepared to do, to suffer, to experience in the Christian life are lessons of too serious import to be learnt in the exact position of novel readers, and indeed to such persons even an interesting biographical detail will appear perhaps scarcely relieved from the wholesome dryness of mere instruction.

This, however, which is the very charm of Scripture itself—namely that it pourtrays things and characters as they really are—is that which we consider the recommendation of the little work before us. And now that we may sanction our own observations, which we fear by some may be considered as rather of an invidious and carping nature against the very innocent race of story readers, we shall proceed, as we promised, to give a very important passage from Mr Jerram, on the same subject. It occurs in his mention of the *classical* pursuits of his beloved and regretted Hannah, and comprises in its extent a general review of the various classes of fictitious tales, beginning with those of the ancient poets, proceeding to those of the moderns, dismissing at once those wretched tales, whether in verse or prose, which are written in professed opposition or professed indifference to moral instruction, and tracing the line through every higher department of moral intention, till we arrive at that very point of direct religious novel with which it has been our object to confront the more chaste and severe muse of faithful and legitimate biography. Having justly contrasted in their respective effects in the nursery the tales founded on mere general morality with those in which every principle is placed and retained in its proper situation, Christ being made the centre, and attracting, enlightening, beautifying, animating and fructifying every part, Mr Jerram proceeds as follows in reference to this last and least exceptionable of all modes of fiction.

This system of education I am happy to observe has been advocated and supported by numbers of individuals of both sexes and of the first order of talents, and it affords me a sincere pleasure to have an opportunity of offering my tribute of respect to those numerous females who have brought their excellent abilities to bear on the best interests of the rising generation. It is impossible to mention the names of More and Trimmer and Sherwood and Taylor and several others without associating with them a wide diffusion of Christian principles, a large increase of domestic happiness, and much of that active zeal which has been recently displayed and especially by females in support of the great institutions which are spreading throughout the world the knowledge of our Lord and Saviour. They have smoothed the rugged course of education by their appropriate and lucid elementary books. They have furnished us with the best materials embellished with all the ornaments and attractions which the subject will admit for storing the memory and forming the character of our youth; and they have illustrated their precepts by such a variety of interesting examples that they can scarcely fail to make an indelible impression wherever they are read. It is not easy to conceive any thing more sound in doctrine, more pure in morals, more rich in variety, more perfect in execution, or more beautiful and elegant in form than the library with which their united efforts have supplied the younger branches of our families; and I am persuaded that at this moment thousands of parents and children are reaping an abundant harvest from their labours.

After bestowing this justly merited praise, it may appear somewhat ungracious to say any thing which may seem to detract from the value of their performances; and yet I have my doubts whether some inconvenience may not arise both from the continually increasing number of these publications and the style and nature of their composition. Scarcely a month passes, without some addition being made to the already abundant stock; and it is easy to perceive that invention is somewhat tortured to find any thing in the shape of novelty. The result is what might be naturally expected. Many of the recent performances are considerably inferior to those which first appeared; the reader feels a diminished interest in what is put into his hands; and there is some danger of the most valuable of these publications thus falling into discredit.

But it is from the nature and style of these compositions that I anticipate the principal mischief. For the sake of illustrating principles and giving the weight of facts to lessons on virtue and vice imaginary characters are introduced with great effect, and no doubt make a more lasting impression on the mind and memory than abstract rules and dry lectures upon morals. But there is some danger even in this. Imaginary characters seldom bear an exact resemblance to real life. They are generally highly wrought and wound up to a pitch of excellence or depravity which have rarely any counterpart in fact. Hence real occurrences make a feebler impression than they would have done from their falling short of what we had previously read in books; ordinary virtue passes as of little worth; and common suffering produces scarcely any sympathy. The feelings having been frequently and powerfully excited require a continually increasing stimulus to keep up their tone; and from the difficulty of obtaining this the mind at length sinks into listless apathy from which the customary events of life are incapable of arousing it. A habit also is acquired of overstating facts in order to excite interest. Perceiving that what appeared important to ourselves excites but little attention in others, we are tempted to set things out with a false colouring and give them an appearance with which the facts themselves have scarcely any correspondence. Every person who pays a scrupulous regard to truth has often been exceedingly distressed at hearing statements which he is sure are any thing but correct; and it is not unreasonable to suppose that this inattention to strict veracity may be owing at least in part to the circumstance on which I am animadverting.

There is also so close an affinity between works of this nature, and the common class of novels, that there is some danger of gliding imperceptibly from one to the other; and thus acquiring a taste for those pernicious publications which have poisoned the minds and corrupted the hearts of so many of our youth.

It will not have escaped the notice of many of my readers that among many professing Christians a sort of sentimentalism has usurped the place of experimental religion. The sober views and feelings which the facts of our case and the nature of the Gospel, might be supposed to occasion are superseded by sensations of a more exquisite and inexplicable nature and by undefined and romantic notions of imaginary excellence and enjoyments. May not this evil also have some connexion with the writings which we are now considering? pp 51—56.

We shall dismiss this subject with so far qualifying both our own and Mr Jerram's observations, as to say, that no imputation can be intended on the legitimate exercise of one of the most valuable and most operative faculties with which the Almighty Creator has graced our nature. And it is impossible not to concede the greatest weight to the example set by the first of all teachers in his own powerful appeals to the imagination, through the medium of his divine parables. We only add, in reference to this great example of perfect instruction that as the Parables of our Lord establish the lawfulness of a fictitious assumption of facts, for the purpose of illustrating moral truth, so they assign its best possible limit: they place the imagination in direct contact with plain palpable truth, and borrow their highest interest from the doctrine they illustrate.

We shall now pass to a brief notice of this interesting little memoir of real life, which, with no fictitious appeal whatever to the imagination will, we are fully assured, speak loudly to the heart and to the conscience and will combine, for the lover of real instruction, all that is interesting in family or personal detail, with all that is edifying in solemn practical appeal.

The subject of the memoir, Hannah Jerram seems to have been one of those early and rare productions of a superior nature which are seldom found to join a long duration with intenseness of excellence, and having been shewn to the world for the instruction of survivors are removed from its contaminating influence for their own higher blessedness and perhaps for the real, though mysterious, benefit of those also who might have leaned too fondly on their presence amongst them. She was the daughter, the only and beloved daughter, of Mr. and Mrs. Jerram; the name and qualifications of her father as Vicar of Chobham, Surrey, and now Minister of St. John's, Bedford Row, being too well known to need any further designation. Her short earthly career was comprehended within the limits of April 4, 1800, the day of her birth, and May 9, 1823, the day of her death. But, in point of many useful and invaluable attainments, of much happiness enjoyed and diffused, and of large attainments of piety made and perhaps imparted, it was a long life. Too short indeed to the natural feelings of the bereaved parent: the recollection of it, as expressed in the early pages of his memoir seems to have reproduced what we read of the ancient parental grief in recording its losses,

Ter patriæ cecidêre manus

yet, for relief of his own mind, for a memorial to the family bereaved, and for profit to mourners under similar afflictions, he proceeds. The first anecdote he records in proof of the early interest which his daughter had engaged in his parental care, is as follows:—

The only time, as far as I recollect, when I had occasion to use any thing like severity was when she was in her second year; and I record the circumstances of it as exemplifying my views of an important preliminary step in the training of children. We had a family party. Her grandfather and grandmother, her uncles and aunt were dining with us, and our little Hannah was permitted to be seated at the table. On something being presented to her by one of her relatives she was desired to say "Thank you," a sentence which she had but recently learned to pronounce: but upon this occasion she was too eager to enjoy the kindness to acknowledge her obligation to the hand from which she received it. I repeated the injunction, but without the desired effect. The affair then assumed another aspect, and an important *principle* was in agitation. Excuses were offered by her fond relatives, and the tears of the child appealed to my feelings: but I considered that a compromise in this case involved future consequences, and that the point between us must sooner or later be decided. I knew that the victory of the child would lead to fresh attempts upon her yielding parents; and thus I should hereafter with a much greater expense of feeling, and to a greater disadvantage, have to renew the contest. I therefore took the child into another room, and desired her to say "Thank you," which she did immediately. I supposed from this that the conquest was complete, but to my surprise, on returning to the dining room, she had lost the power of uttering this short sentence. I had again to retire with her, and administer a slight correction for the disobedience; and again, when alone with me, she repeated the difficult words: but being a second time placed at the table, the task became insuperable, and she said, "I tan't say so." Her relatives too, whose feelings overcame on this occasion their good sense, joined in thinking the child could not repeat the words, and some of them united their tears with the child's in urging me to proceed no further. The duty now became difficult. The yearnings of my own heart, the entreaties of those around me, and the sobs of the sweet child, were all on one side, and only a sense of duty on the other. I stifled however my feelings, and again retired. I had no doubt of the ability of the child to pronounce the words, because she had done so every time of my withdrawing with her; and I was determined to go through with my task. After four or five attempts I at length succeeded, and with a throbbing heart and flowing tears, the little creature sobbed out "Tank you." Every thing now was properly settled. The victory was on the side of the parent, who knew how to make a suitable use of it, instead of the daughter, who would have abused it: the tears were soon dried up, our friends were satisfied that all was right, and the dear child never made another attempt with papa for the mastery. pp. 14—17.

Mr. Jerram dwells on this little incident, and proceeds to some further observations, with some minuteness, and even exultation at remaining master of the field on so important an occasion: but as reviewers are not parents *ex officio*, we shall leave to those who are so to fix their own limits as to the imitable or inimitable nature of this parental act of authority.

The reminiscence of those amiable and endearing qualities which marked the mind of his daughter in her adolescent state, naturally calls forth the fullest and strongest expressions from the father. He knew at once the source of all true excellence in man and woman kind, when he sums up all that was moral in her disposition in those few expressive words 'It is difficult to conceive a character more DIVESTED than she was OF SELFISHNESS' A proof of this immediately follows in an affecting anecdote which is connected with the mention of her uniform desire of making others happy under whatever languor of spirit, or even acute pain of body she might have been herself suffering

About two years ago she was on a visit to some of her most beloved friends at Southampton The disease which probably terminated her life had already commenced its attack Her friends could not help seeing at times by her countenance that she was far from being in the health they could wish and they were extremely anxious on this account but they were not aware of the extent of her malady She afterwards told her mother that she frequently retired into her room as if for the purpose of dressing writing letters or other indifferent affairs but with the real intention of rolling on the carpet (for if she had done so on the bed it would have probably led to inquiries about her health) to obtain a little ease of her acute pain and when she appeared again in the parlour she threw herself on the sofa for the apparent purpose of playing with a favourite little girl upon it but with the real object of obtaining if possible some mitigation of suffering pp 25 26

Her powers of intellect at least of intellectual acquisition which seem to have been accompanied by those of very lively communication, are exhibited by our author in a statement of her talents and acquisitions The legitimate deduction to be drawn from the history of her studies by the conductors of youth is the necessity for inculcating a wise and enlightened moderation on the youthful mind, whether of male or female and the importance of taking all imaginable care not to sacrifice the very power of usefulness itself to an undue pursuit of the means for acquiring it The "times, both of old and young are in that "hand which does always what is wisest and best And this consideration truly a consideration which, we doubt not, has long assured the bereaved parents of the 'needfulness of their loss at the very moment it happened, is sufficient to withhold from us the observation that the amiable Hannah Jerram might now have been diffusing cheerfulness around the family circle or even instruction around her little pupil table had she been induced to make her bodily health and her actual powers the strict limit of her exertions or *could* her parents have applied to their eldest child that experience in management which is for the most part the product only of repeated experiments subsequently made on other children

The placing of his daughter at the boarding school of (the present) Mrs Bowden, in Kensington, leads Mr Jerram to some valuable observations, as the result of his own mature experience in the proper management of youth under a course of scholastic education We must refer those whom they may more especially concern to his work passing on ourselves to the point of Miss Jerram's first clear manifestation of a religious character

It was to the pious and affectionate but firm and prudent, management of her excellent governess that I attribute under God much of the character for which she was afterwards distinguished Early impressions of the best nature had undoubtedly been previously made and the good seed had taken some root but as yet nothing decisive of character had taken place The mind was flexible evil tendencies were strong and pious habits were yet unformed Much depended on the individual to whom she was now to look not only for instruction but example whether her previous impressions should be deepened and become permanent or whether they should be entirely effaced whether the seed should produce fruit or be choaked with weeds and happy was it both for our beloved daughter and ourselves that we had not mistaken the character to whom we had intrusted her education The instructions of her early infancy were ably seconded and an example as amiable as it was correct and as prudent as it was Christian was constantly before her The result was such as might be anticipated the suitable means had been employed in hope of God's blessing upon them and that blessing was abundantly bestowed Our dear daughter was at length restored to the bosom of her family to our mutual joy not only with a mind well stored with the most useful and ornamental elementary knowledge which was a matter of great importance but what was paramount to every thing else with a heart duly affected towards God and religious truth prepared to advance to higher attainments in the divine life and ready to take an active part in promoting whatever might bring glory to God, or good to man pp 69—71

Mr Jerram gives proof of a candour and moderation which we always find most congenial to minds of a settled piety, and habitual separation from the dust and tumult of earthly parties and adhesions, in his historical description of a pious clergyman, to whom, under God, he avows his obligation for his first distinct religious impressions. We shall not go much further into the subject, than to give the following explanation by Mr Jerram, of certain imprudences alleged against the gentleman in question and his remarks on the consequences with which these imprudences were attended. After describing fully a change of religious views in this gentleman, Mr Jerram proceeds —

At length he found himself as it were in a new world and the Apostle s observation was exemplified in him If any man be in Christ Jesus he is a new creature old things are passed away and all things are become new This change of sentiment was accompanied with an ardour of feeling in some degree corresponding with the magnitude and importance of the truths he had recently been taught and under the strong influence of this new impetus he was sometimes carried beyond the limits which a cold and calculating prudence would have prescribed Nor do I intend to justify all his measures I well recollect several things which were far from being discreet and which were calculated to excite a strong prejudice against him and I the more readily pass this opinion on part of the conduct of an individual whose memory I shall ever revere because more than once afterwards I heard him express his regret on account of these imprudences p 104

After stating that the whole of the opposition this clergyman met with ought not to be charged to the score of religion, Mr Jerram proceeds —

I would take this opportunity of urging upon every zealous advocate of the peculiar truths of the Gospel the necessity of caution lest by any indiscretion he excite unnecessary prejudice It is of the last importance clearly to distinguish between what is *essential* and what may be only *expedient* In the former no compromise can possibly be made The truth in a Christian spirit and in its just proportions must be delivered fearless of all consequences But there is much scope for deliberation as to the extent to which *improvements* ought to be pushed A minister may discharge his own conscience and his flock may be saved without adopting them at all and it becomes a simple question of ultimate advantage or disadvantage whether they should be introduced Taken by themselves the question is decided at once but taken in their necessary connexion with other things they require a sound judgment to determine their expediency The benefit expected may be purchased at too high a price and the price should be ascertained to its full extent before any experiment be made If some good men had previously calculated the degree of irritation and the party spirit which a change in modes of singing or in the usual version of the Psalms or in times of performing Divine service and other innovations on long established customs were likely to produce they would have hesitated before they adopted the obnoxious measure and at least have waited till a fair opportunity had occurred of making the alteration with the least possible violence to inveterate prejudices Rashness in these respects, has frequently excited strong opposition and sometimes led to the removal of valuable men from important stations In such cases it is unjust to attach these consequences to a faithful discharge of pastoral duties they ought rather to be ascribed to a want of judgment and an ill disciplined mind in the individual who forced his plans and could brook no opposition to his wishes I say nothing of those measures which some would adopt in direct opposition to the usages and discipline of the church to which they belong because it seems to be a violation of the principles of common honesty to trample upon the regulations to which they had voluntarily bound themselves No man can have received a dispensation to set at nought his own vows as well as the decent order which the wisdom and piety of the best of men had prescribed and when after having done this he charges those whose duty it is to guard the institutions of the church against innovation with persecution for righteousness sake for having discountenanced his irregularities and appeals to the public on the hardship of his case he merits any thing rather than that Christian sympathy to which he lays claim and which he is sometimes fortunate enough to obtain pp 107—109

We shall only observe, that these

qualifying observations proceed from a writer who to the full admits the necessity of clear scriptural views, and of a bold and zealous avowal of Christian doctrine and that we have therefore here a further confutation of those objectors who would lower every thing within their reach to a worldly level, and consign every thing beyond it to the charge either of blind enthusiasm or blank imposture. The testimony of such men as Mr Jerram to this point is invaluable. We thank God that we have amongst us a zeal tempered with knowledge, and a knowledge working by zeal a knowledge ever sought from those pure fountains "fast by the Oracles of God" a zeal ever intent on the best method of opening the streams of instruction and grace to the whole world.

But we can no longer suffer Mr Jerram to lead us astray into his own pleasing digressions, and must now confine our further observations to the closing scene of his beloved daughter's life to which will be also found a most important appendage, in the subsequent death bed of his eldest son. It is a very true definition of religion, that it is the art of dying well. On this, as well as on every other account, we are not surprised, and we still less regret that Mr Jerram has dedicated so large a portion, a full third, of his miscellaneous little volume to the important scene. A death bed unveils often what is obscure defines every feature, and heightens every colour. Holy dying is the completion of holy living and though we are fully aware that many deceptions may arise in the last scene where the former life has not been under the influence of true piety, yet, where holy living has been witnessed, and nothing peculiar supervenes to darken the closing scene, no spectacle can be more truly worthy of interest and sympathy than the dying Christian. It is here, however, that our observations on biography, as distinct from tale telling may be brought especially to bear. The fictitious and the real death bed may have the greatest possible dissimilitude. In the one case, it is as *we* please in the other case, it is as *God* pleases. In the one case, it may be just as we expected it would and ought to be in the other, it may be quite the reverse. The lessons to be learnt from a true obituary may be no less surprising than true, and in appearance even contradictory, though, in the result, most important. Under such impressions, Mr Jerram seems to have transcribed from the life the last days of his beloved daughter's earthly sojourn the circumstances of which were deeply painful. Seldom indeed have we read a relation of the kind more distressingly interesting associated as it is with the knowledge that "*it is all true*" Miss Jerram—of the most blameless and unoffending life fraught with good deeds the fruits of faith and knowing that her whole claim to acceptance lay in the merits of her Saviour's obedience unto death—does not yet appear to have enjoyed that full assurance of hope, or even that entire peacefulness of mind, except quite at the last, which we might have anticipated. Such a circumstance must have inconceivably aggravated the feelings of her afflicted parents, overtaken as they had been by utter surprise with respect to the actual nature and danger of her bodily disorder. The contrast between this first surprise and their former blissful intercourse with this idolized object of parental attachment, is most deeply affecting. And when the heart rending disclosure was made both to parents and child the additional conflict of feeling from a near and a religious view of the rapid approach of the king of terrors combined to produce a tale of anguish which can scarcely be exceeded. No party had been sufficiently prepared for an event which possibly might have been to be feared many weeks before. And the sudden transition from all the pursuits, and innocent *pleasures* shall we call them? or *duties* of life, for with Hannah Jerram they were but one, to the immediate work of preparation for the last so lenn close, was sufficient to have overpowered for a moment the strongest mind and best regulated heart. The tender spirit of Miss Jerram sank at first under the pressure, and she fell into a state very natural to her own habitual humility and jealousy over herself—a state of doubt as to her *fitness* to appear before the tribunal of God, and by a deduction not remote from that feeling of doubt also as to her *personal interest* in the merits of her Saviour. Nothing that we can see from first to last in her education or her present treatment could be fairly alleged as tending to create such apprehensions. They seem as far as appears to us the simple result of circumstances occurring under God's high permission, and perhaps the only exception we should take at the affecting narrative of Mr Jerram is the weight of concern he expresses at so probable an occurrence, and his evident labour to guard against an impression as to the incongruity of such feelings with such a life. To our minds we must say, the circumstances related by Mr Jerram if not such as might have been expected before hand, yet *when* related appear beautifully illustrative of the history which had preceded. On the one hand the careless in life will be careless in death. There are no bands in *their* death, but their strength is firm; whilst on the other, the careful, the anxious the tried servant of God will often have to complain that every day has he been plagued, and chastened every morning. The stake he will feel to be infinitely important, and while the lot is still lying in the lap he may even fearfully await the disposing thereof by the Lord. In short, we are not to expect miracles at any period of this dark earthly scene and very generally, as a man has lived, in point of concern for his everlasting interests so will he die. But it will be needful to give an extract bearing upon this portion of the interesting history before us, together with a part of Mr Jerram's excellent observations on the difference between *faith* and *hope*.

There was such a *predominance* of what was truly Christian moral and amiable in her character as clearly to shew that she had been renewed in the spirit of her mind and was an ornament to her Christian profession. It might therefore be expected perhaps that in her case death would have been divested of his terrors and that she would have passed through the mortal conflict if not with triumph at least with calmness and composure. But the contrary of this actually took place. When the king of terrors first presented himself she was filled with dreadful consternation and shrunk back with horror from the awful conflict. She was agitated with such an internal tempest as I had never before witnessed and no sinking mariner ever clung to the last plank with so much eagerness as she did to the cross of Christ. All around her seemed a wide waste of desolation. The billows rolled. Deep called to deep and all hope that she should be saved was taken away except as this cross afforded her a stay. Never can I forget this awful moment. We were like persons standing on the shore beholding the storm but incapable of affording any assistance. All that we most loved and cherished and almost adored was tossed on the tempestuous waves. Our hearts failed us. We directed we encouraged we exhorted. We pointed to the hand of Omnipotence stretched forth for her deliverance and said Be of good courage! We entreated her to take fast hold of it and assured her she was safe. We pledged our life that there was no danger and told her it was impossible she could perish—that she was just on shore and that angels were waiting to welcome her arrival in the haven of rest! But—O the infinite stake she had in the event of a single moment!

pp 140 141

Passing over some very striking observations in explanation of this distressing case we proceed to the following remarks.

It is at times like this that the importance of a close and somewhat familiar acquaintance with the kind and compassionate character of Jesus Christ and a persuasion of an interest in his merits is chiefly seen. There may be a firm reliance on the atoning sacrifice, a sincere devotedness of heart to the service of God and an habitual predominance of holy af fections towards him, and yet such an awful perception of the distance between the humble individual and the infinitely glorious God, as to preclude all joy and peace in believing. And when a natural timidity of disposition and a keen perception of religious deficiencies are connected with this profound reverence, there must necessarily arise great doubt and distrust in peculiar emergencies, and especially in the near prospect of dissolution. Nothing, we know, is so suitable to a weak and sinful being as the humble and contrite heart which trembles at the Divine word, and such we are assured are the peculiar objects of God's favour; but yet there is a close affinity between this state of mind and anxious fear, and nothing but a most vivid perception and persuasion of our personal interest in the sufferings of Christ for the sins of mankind can overcome the feeling of personal guilt and unworthiness. When therefore these things do not accompany each other (and there is no *necessary* connexion between them,) the most excellent Christian may be brought into great doubt and even despondency, whilst at the same time he may be in perfect safety and high in the favour of God.

The difference between *faith* and *hope* is not always sufficiently attended to, and much presumption on the one hand, and despondency on the other, have arisen from confounding them. One person considers himself a believer of high attainments because he entertains no doubt of his being in a state of salvation, and another doubts whether he be a believer at all, because he cannot persuade himself that his sins are forgiven. But it is obvious that two distinct and very different acts of the mind are here confounded and blended together:—one which assents to the fact of Jesus Christ being the only and all sufficient Saviour of sinners, and which places a reliance on the atoning sacrifice for pardon of sin and acceptance with God, which is the province of *faith*, and another which appropriates to itself the blessings of this salvation and confidently expects a future state of felicity which is the province of *hope*. Now it is clear that these persuasions of the mind may exist separately from each other, and that one of them may be very strong whilst the other has scarcely any existence at all. St. Paul clearly recognises this distinction when he offers up a prayer for the church at Rome (xv. 13) that the God of *hope* would fill them with all *joy* and *peace* in *believing*. It is here implied that genuine faith may exist without either *joy* or *peace*, and by addressing his prayer to the God of *hope* he intimates that *joy* and *peace* are the fruit of *hope* and are distinct blessings and to be superadded to the grace of faith. Faith then may not only be unaccompanied by hope, but remain without any joy or even consolation, and the person possessing it may continue under great dejection of mind. Nor is it, in point of fact, uncommon to find Christians who have no doubt whatever of the ability and willingness of Christ to save sinners and who come to him alone for salvation, and yet are subject to distressing fears lest they should not be partakers of the blessings of the Gospel. I recollect a striking instance of the truth of this remark in the case of a late eminent Christian minister. For a long time previous to his death he laboured under a morbid affection of the nerves which sometimes brought him to the very verge of despondency, and on one occasion he said to me, My conviction of the truth of these things (laying his hand on the Bible) is stronger now than it ever was, but I have no interest in them. Had this excellent man died in this state of mind, no one could have reasonably doubted of his safety, for the obvious reason that he exercised the fullest faith in Christ, and had shewn its genuine character in a holy and most useful life, though he denied that he had any hope of ultimately sharing in the blessings of salvation. The full assurance of hope is indeed an invaluable privilege and cannot be too earnestly desired, but it is nowhere stated in Scripture as being essential to our future happiness as faith is, and a person may be a genuine Christian without the former though not without the latter. (Mark xvi. 16.) pp. 147—151.

Mr. Jerram, with a faithfulness which reflects the highest credit on himself and gives true value to his work, unveils many a heart rending scene which follows, more especially after some faint interposing hopes magnified into a momentary expectation of the recovery of his beloved child. These favourable symptoms afforded a crisis at once corporeal and mental. No material struggle of mind appeared subsequently to that change. A merciful preparation for the last scene seems to have been provided in this intermediate stage. The nascent hopes as to her recovery were, it is true, soon nipped, and the afflicted parents became partakers of the trying experience of the Psalmist, Thou hast lifted me up and cast me down. But the daughter seems to have insensibly passed into a state of calm contemplation and silent devotion, from which no alarm at the final advances of her disorder aroused her; she lay in a frame of peaceful recipiency as the blessed truths of the Gospel were occasionally presented to her her affectionate attention to the feelings of her weeping parents shewed itself to the last and she at length breathed her latest breath without struggle or sigh and with those words dying on her lips in reference to the all atoning Sacrifice I have no other hope

It seems to have been a mercy singularly appropriate to the overwhelmed survivors that a few hours after her death the following admonitory and most seasonable lines were found apparently recently copied on a blank leaf in a pocket Bible which was her constant companion

With peaceful mind thy path of duty run
God nothing does nor suffers to be done
But what thou wouldst thyself couldst thou but see
Through all events of things as well as He p 224

The lessons of consolation which the subsequent pages of the narrative afford to the afflicted on the one hand and the warning voice which on the other they address to *the young* and inexperienced cannot be too often turned over or too highly prized May such lessons have their effect! May they teach an early and decisive detachment from a world which we all love too well indeed from every object terminating in this life and even from merely earthly views of those blessings which are given us to carry forward our hopes to an eternity of bliss —We consider as highly important the observations in which Mr Jerram enlarges on the possible effects of some supposed neglect in not availing himself of all opportunities for spiritual conversation with his beloved daughter when in health with close application to her own case And happy would it be were we induced to converse more with each other as fellow citizens of a heavenly state fellow travellers to an everlasting home It might serve doubtless to relieve much of that surprise which too often is induced by the sudden irruption of the last enemy and might alleviate the painfulness of those last disclosures which few perhaps had less reason to fear than the gentle and faithful spirit of Hannah Jerram

The same volume which in its first three editions narrated only the true and affecting details above mentioned adds in its fourth a new and striking instance of ' God s moving in a mysterious way To the heavy weight of preceding trials it adds the death of an eldest son Yet the pressure which might have seemed severe beyond all common endurance, appears in fact to have been medicinal It wounded and it healed It stands with a most important bearing on all that preceded in the volume before us, as well as on all that had passed in the dark volume of parental feeling It opened fully those views of life which we had almost said nothing but deep affliction can disclose It operated in appearance to take off the mind from every human rest and sublunary stay and to fix it upon that which is alone stable and divine—even on " that which is within the veil So at least we collect from the sentiments of Mr Jerram It was on the 18th of September 1824, one year and four months after the death of Hannah, that her brother C S Jerram, was taken ill It was however not till the morning which preceded his death on the 26th that any serious alarm was felt Mr Jerram writes,

Being under the necessity of going to town on Thursday the 23d and being assured by one of his medical attendants that there was no apparent cause for expecting an unfavourable termination of his malady I spoke to my son of my intention and asked him a few questions on the state of his mind He said his faith and entire confidence were placed on Jesús Christ and he asked me as I *then* thought to pray *for* him though it afterwards appeared that he meant I should pray *with* him After he found I was gone he expressed much uneasinesss and was particularly grieved that I had not prayed with him This indeed I should have done notwithstanding my mistaking his request had I not been afraid lest under the circumstance of my going away for that and the following day it might be too much for his feelings. I regret, however the omission and I hope I shall hereafter think less of momentary emotions and take the opportunity when it occurs of discharging every Christian duty pp 257 258

On the Saturday however symptoms had arisen which rendered necessary the painful disclosure of his son's extreme danger and this with an exemplary firmness to be expected from such a father as indeed generally due from all friends in similar circumstances was communicated to the patient himself

He received the intelligence without any apparent alarm and intimated that he was not surprised at the information but had himself suspected that his case was dangerous From this time till that of his death I scarcely ever left his bed side Indeed if I were absent for a moment he immediately inquired Where is my father? and seemed uneasy till he saw me return At one time when I had been directing his views to the all sufficiency of the Saviour and said he is able to save to the uttermost all that come unto God by him he replied with emphasis Yes and he is also *willing* to save and on my adding O yes he is indeed willing to save and that the greatest of sinners he rejoined If it were not so what must become of such poor wretched sinners as we are? He then said if it should please God to restore him to health he trusted he should be more diligent in his service than he ever had been and I may here remark that it was chiefly the sins of *omission* that most grieved him He thought he might have done more in the cause of religion than he had done and he determined on a life of greater zeal and devotedness if he were permitted to return to health pp 259—261

The intercourse which subsequently took place was such as might have been expected between such a father and such a son 'I love to lean upon my dear father said the dying son on one occasion when requiring support ' because it reminds me of leaning upon my heavenly Father." And on another occasion he evinced the same affectionate tenderness, when, on hearing from his mother the expression of kindness from a near friend he exclaimed, " Stop!—do not say any more such kindness quite overpowers me and he burst into tears

When it is understood that the general disposition of this youth then twenty one years old, was of this kind so formed by nature and so renewed by Divine grace, we seem prepared for that which did take place in him whilst it was in part mysteriously withheld from his Christian sister namely, an uninterrupted flow of joy and unclouded serenity of hope from the earliest to the latest period of his short mortal disorder The bearing of these scenes on those which had preceded in the same family sixteen months before, will be most fully understood by the last extract we shall give from this memorial and which will leave room for but few of our own closing observations After remarking, that notwithstanding the assured confidence of his hope as on a rock that had long been tried

nothing could well exceed the humility with which he viewed his own character but he was mercifully enabled (as far as any one could ascertain the fact) during the whole of his illness and especially the last day of it to turn his thoughts from himself to the all sufficiency and willingness of the Saviour to save the greatest of sinners p 276

Mr Jerram proceeds

And herein I cannot help thinking that the rough passage which his beloved sister had experienced during a part of her voyage to the haven of rest had smoothed the waters for him for he evidently had her frequently in mind he quoted most of the passages of Scripture as actually affording him comfort which were presented to her with a view to bring consolation and as though he had begun in his sickness where she appeared to leave off Enjoying from the first a full confidence that he should be accepted for the sake of the Saviour he seemed never to have had this confidence shaken and the enemy was not permitted for a moment apparently to harass his mind If this were the case how can I be sufficiently thankful for the events of my dear daughter's last few days and for having been enabled to record them! pp 276 277

Thus have we brought our extracts and notice of this double memoir to a close and our readers, we think will agree with us in thinking we have not dwelt on it too long The experience of two highly interesting and Christian death beds and the bearing of each on a surviving Christian family whose living feelings could scarcely have met with a more vivid and faithful painter than the present devout and talented author form independently of all other matter in this volume, a subject for contemplation alike interesting to the public instructor and the private Christian The mixture of sobriety in principle with fervour in feeling, of practical circumspection with sublime contemplation, of self renouncing faith with self denying holiness and the truest obedience this handed down from parent to child, and beautifully displayed in either generation and surmounted by a really magnificent exercise, under most trying circumstances of Christian resignation and triumphant patience both in the living and the dying —all this we say forms together a phenomenon which if uncommon amongst Christians, ought surely to be exhibited for its instructive novelty but if *not* uncommon, then still more deserving publication for the credit of our blessed religion, and for being one case only of many to prove that to be most excellent which lifts us far above the waves of this troublesome world, and that to be divine which actually raises us up together, and makes us sit together in heavenly places in Christ Jesus

———

The West Indies as they are or a real Picture of Slavery but more particularly as it exists in the Island of Jamaica By the Rev RICHARD BICKELL a Member of the University of Cambridge, late Naval Chaplain at Port Royal some time Curate of that Parish and previously of the City of Kingston, in the aforesaid Island London Hatchard 1825 8vo pp 256

SOME of our readers we fear begin to be tired of the subject of slavery Its enormities, however, still exist ing in almost undiminished force and malignity, notwithstanding all that the government and the parliament, and the public have laboured to effect for its mitigation and final extinction we are compelled by a sense of duty still to recur to the painful topic and to reiterate our calls on the Christian world to persevere in their efforts on behalf of the oppressed slaves We have endeavoured to make our readers acquainted with the real nature and effects of Negro bondage Still we fear that the general impression of the iniquity and wretchedness of the system is far less deep and vivid than the truth of the case if it were fully understood would justify On this account we hail with satisfaction the appearance of the present volume, which is the work of a clergyman of the Church of England who resided for about five years in the West Indies, chiefly on the island of Jamaica We cannot it is true, speak in very high terms of the work as a composition It abounds in faults of style and is expanded to very undue dimensions But, though it might have been contracted with advantage into a much smaller space and might have been divested of many blemishes which diminish its value as a literary production it is nevertheless a most important as well as seasonable accession to our stock of information on a subject of peculiar interest The writer is evidently a fair, upright and unbiassed witness who describes plainly and distinctly and we would add fearlessly, the scenes which have recently passed under his own eyes and no one can peruse his observations without an irresistible impression of the fidelity with which it is his purpose to execute the task he has undertaken He paints the West Indies as they are in the eye of an impartial Christian observer and his testimony has this peculiar recommendation, that it is given by one who is uninfluenced by party feelings, and exempt from controversial asperity

Mr. Bickell is a moderate man, by no means disposed to go all lengths in vituperating those whose practices he feels himself compelled to condemn. He sympathises with his West Indian friends in the difficulties of their situation, and is solicitous both for their personal safety and for the security of their property. The tale at the same time which he has unfolded is a tale of horror. We refer to it with confidence as establishing in their full extent the specific charges which have been preferred against the West Indian system. If Mr. Bickell is to be believed, and his book bears every mark of truth, then is the indictment against the colonies not only found to be a true bill, but a verdict of guilty must be recorded, and condemnation we trust will follow.

In the course of the last year the Anti-slavery Society published a sheet for general circulation throughout the country containing 'A Brief View of the Nature and Effects of Negro Slavery, as it exists in the Colonies of Great Britain.' This statement has been vehemently attacked by different advocates of the colonial system, as false and calumnious, and particularly by Mr. Gladstone in his correspondence with Mr. Cropper, published by the West Indian Committee of Liverpool, and by Mr. Macqueen of Glasgow. In order that the reader may judge of its correctness, we shall transcribe a part of it for the purpose of more easy comparison with the statements of Mr. Bickell.

"In the colonies of Great Britain there are at this moment upwards of 800,000 human beings in a state of degrading personal slavery.

"These unhappy persons whether young or old, male or female, are the absolute property of their master, who may sell or transfer them at his pleasure, and who may also regulate according to his discretion (within certain limits) the measure of their labour, their food, and their punishment.

The Slaves being regarded in the eye of the law as mere chattels, they are liable to be seized in execution for their master's debts, and without any regard to the family ties which may be broken by this oppressive and merciless process, to be sold by auction to the highest bidder, who may remove them to a distant part of the same colony, or even exile them to another colony."

Now let us see what confirmation these statements of the Anti-slavery Society's *Brief View* derive from Mr. Bickell's book.

Slavery is undoubtedly and confessedly one of the greatest evils that ever was inflicted on the human race, and has been considered as the greatest curse by all nations in all ages of the world. (p. 1.)

It was reserved for modern times for men calling themselves Christians and nations professing the religion of the meek and lowly Jesus, to carry this heaviest curse inflicted on the human race to its highest pitch. (p. 3.)—Of this system some of the harsher and more cruel features may have been done away. Still however much remains to be done both in a physical and religious point of view, before the Negroes can be said to approximate to even the lowest and worst paid poor of the British islands. (p. 4.)—

The great body of the colonists with very few exceptions look upon the Negroes as beings every way inferior to the Whites, and this is one great cause of their ill treatment, and being deprived of many little privileges which I think might with perfect safety be granted them. (p. 8.) They look upon the Blacks as much beneath themselves as the brutes are beneath the Negroes; they think them hardly capable of religious impressions, and almost insensible to punishment. This is one great reason of their depressed state and frequent rigorous treatment. (p. 197.) These illiberal opinions, he adds, I can positively assert, are adopted and held by a great part of the colonists of the present day.

Another of the evils of slavery is that the slaves are so degraded and depressed in the eye of the law as not to be considered persons but mere animals or chattels, so that they can be sold not only at the will and pleasure of their masters or owners to any other person at any part of the island, but can be seized and sold for debt by a writ of execution and exposed for sale at a public auction to the best bidder. Many a bitter cry is heard when the marshal's deputies (dogs as they are emphatically called) are sent to hunt down and seize the victim or victims, and drive or drag them away to the workhouse or gaol till the day of sale arrives which is to deprive them of their little homes the gardens they have cultivated the acquaintances they have made and all the little comforts which make even slavery in some measure tolerable This hardship is much increased when slaves are married or have families as the woman may be separated from her husband or parents from their children for here the tenderest ties of nature are broken in an instant and the wife's or mother's or children's cries would not be in the least attended to nor heeded any more than the moans of so many [brute] animals pp 16 17

The distress and terror among a gang of Negroes, when the marshal's deputy with his dogs and other assistants comes to levy in a large way cannot be conceived by those who happily for themselves have never been spectators of such scenes and can scarcely be described by those who have witnessed them I was once on a coffee mountain (staying for a few days with a brother clergyman who had permission to reside there) on which were about seventy or eighty Negroes The proprietor was much in debt and was aware that one or two of his largest creditors had for some time wished to make a levy on his slaves to pay themselves but by keeping his gates locked and the fences round the dwelling house and Negro houses in good repair he had hitherto baffled the Argus eyed deputy and his deputies The night after I arrived on the property however I was awaked about an hour before daylight by a great noise as of arms with cries of women and children In a few minutes a private servant came to my window and informed me that it was the marshal's deputies making a levy on the Negroes and that the noise proceeded from the clashing of weapons for some of the slaves he said had stoutly resisted I then alarmed my friend and we determined to go out to see that no improper use was made of the tremendous power given to these Cerberuses By the time we arrived at the Negro houses the resistance had ceased for the Negroes being divided had been overcome by the myrmidons of the law One poor fellow however was being dragged along like a thief by a fierce and horrid looking Irishman who had been one of M Gregor's freebooters and who when we came near grasped his victim more tightly and brandished his broadsword over the poor creature with the grin and growl of a demon

Many of the men escaped from the property and some few others with some women secreted themselves among the coffee trees till the party had gone off with their prey They secured however ten or twelve men and many of the women and children amounting in the whole to between thirty and forty who were huddled together on the outside of the principal fence and presented such a heart-rending scene as I never witnessed before and should be very sorry ever to witness again Some of the children had lost their mothers and some of the mothers had been torn away from a part of their children for some of the little urchins also escaped One woman in particular a housewoman had six or seven children two or three of them were seized and the others escaped but the youngest an infant had been caught and she wept aloud and very bitterly for it saying that she must give herself up if the child was not got back for she could not live separated from it There were many a bitter cry and sad lament among the women and children for they loved their master who was kind and had excellent provision grounds for them but most of the men were dogged and sullen and only wanted arms to obtain their freedom from the savage Whites and their associates, who now guarded them As it was two or three of the poor fellows were wounded and I was assured by a free Brown man, who was looking after the property in the master's absence that had the proprietor been there there would have been sad work and very likely murder for it was an illegal levy and the resistance would have been desperate under their master's eye and voice They were tied together or hand cuffed and driven off the same morning to Spanish Town gaol a distance of twenty miles but as they had been seized before sun rise and the fence had been also broken through both of which are illegal the owner obtained their enlargement shortly after and they were allowed to go back to the spot they loved I might here remark that the labour is much lighter on a coffee mountain than on a sugar estate and that the Negroes are not required to be up so much *at night* to pick and cure coffee as they are to make sugar where therefore they have good provision grounds as they had on this mountain I have been speaking of they are much more comfortable and less harassed than on a sugar estate p 19–23

Has any thing ever been written by Mr Cooper or Mr Meabry or has any thing ever been asserted by Mr Wilberforce or Mr Buxton more damnatory of the slave system than the above simple narrative of a respectable eye witness?

We could not without quoting nearly the whole of Mr Bickell's book adduce any passage which is directly in point as to the absolute right of property in his slaves possessed by the West India planter That right however is assumed throughout the work, as well as in all the arguments of West Indians on this subject. In the absence of Mr Bickell's direct testimony upon it, we shall be excused for referring to authority at least equally unquestionable.

The Report of the Committee of the Privy Council, made in 1789 states, that the leading idea in the Negro system of jurisprudence was " that Negroes were property."

" The numerous laws passed in the different islands " had uniformly this for their object." This principle has been at the root of all the laws of slavery which have prevailed in all our colonies without exception, and it has hitherto undergone no modification. Nor is it merely tacitly assumed as the basis of legislation, it is fully recognized in many recent acts of the colonial assemblies.

The practice is in strict accordance with the law. It is impossible to look into a West Indian newspaper without seeing advertisements by proprietors of the sale of Negroes, or by the marshals or under sheriffs, and by the collectors of the revenue, of slaves levied upon either for debt or for taxes. For example, in the Royal Gazette of Jamaica, of June 15, 1823 —

" For sale Charlottenburg estate, in the parish of St Mary's, consisting of 982 acres of land, about 86 head of working stock, and 89 Negroes."

April 26, 1823. 'For sale 15 valuable young Negroes together or *singly* to suit purchasers.'

May 10, 1823. Notice is hereby given that on Tuesday next I will put up to public sale, a Negro woman named Violet, a Creole, accustomed to all sorts of work, levied upon for taxes due by G H Swift.

April 26, 1823. For sale under a writ of venditioni exponas. Charles James, a Black, a waiting boy, aged 6 years, belonging to M Freeman.

' William, a Black, a waiting boy, age 8 years, belonging to M Muir.

" Tom, a Black, a waiting boy, age 18 years, belonging to S Bowen.

" Frances, a Black, a field Negro, age 34 years, belonging to C Cole.

" Quasheba, a Black, a drudge, age 28 years, belonging to Solomon Isaac.

" George Frazer, a Black, a carpenter, age 35 years, belonging to M Gowrey."

Such extracts might be indefinitely multiplied. These will suffice to shew that men, women and children are regarded absolutely as property, and are seized and sold as unceremoniously as cattle or household goods for the payment of debts or of taxes, or are disposed of by proprietors in gangs, or singly, as best suits their interest.

It has indeed been confidently affirmed that the law of Jamaica forbids the separation of families, by sale. There is, however, no such law. And if there were, yet in practice it is obviously violated every day. There is a law indeed that when persons of the same family are seized by the marshal, they shall be sold together. But what law can ensure their being *seized* as well as *sold* together? And even this law is no restraint on the power of the proprietor. He may sell *fifteen young Negroes either together or singly*, as best suits his interest. And then to look at the sales by the marshal or tax gatherer, had Quasheba or Violet no relations or connexions, their ties with whom were torn asunder? Had the infants of six and eight years sold singly, no parent, no brother, no sister? These facts speak volumes.

Nothing can shew more strongly, the extreme vigilance with which this right of property is guarded in the West Indies, than the fact that when Colonel Arthur had communicated to Earl Bathurst the details of a most atrocious series of barbarities exercised by one Carty upon a female slave, his lordship was compelled thus to write in reply.

' The cruel conduct of this inhuman wretch could not fail to excite feelings of pity and commiseration, and I immediately submitted your letter &c to the law officers of the crown to know how far I was authorized to direct you to manumit the unfortunate woman. But they report, that Carty is indictable only for the cruelty committed *that as she is his property there is no power to take her away*, consequently none for her manumission. I can only therefore express my concern that such a wretch should remain unpunished.

Now, if the absolute and uncontrollable right of property vested in the slave holder be such as to force his Majesty's Government to declare their utter impotency to redress such grievous wrongs, it will follow as a matter of course that the master's discretion will regulate within certain limits the measure of a slave's labour, as well as of his food and punishment. To what privations and sufferings would not a mother submit before she would expose herself to the exercise of the master's power of separating her from her children? The following occurrence related by Mr. Gilgrass, a Methodist missionary, speaks volumes on this point.

'A master of slaves who lived near us in Kingston, Jamaica exercised his barbarities on a Sabbath morning while we were worshipping God in the chapel, and the cries of the female sufferers have frequently interrupted us in our devotions. But there was no redress for them or for us. This man wanted money, and, one of the female slaves having two fine children, he sold one of them, and the child was torn from her maternal affection. In the agony of her feelings she made a hideous howling, and for that crime was flogged. Soon after he sold her other child. This 'turned her heart within her, and impelled her into a kind of madness. She howled night and day in the yard, tore her hair, ran up and down the streets and the parade, rending the heavens with her cries, and literally watering the earth with her tears. Her constant cry was, '*Da wicked massa Jew, he sell my children. Will no Buckra massa pity Negar? What me do? Me no have one child!*' As she stood before the window, she said, lifting up her hands towards heaven, '*My massa, do, my massa minister, pity me! My heart do so* (shaking herself violently), '*my heart do so, because me have no child. Me go to massa house, in massa yard, and in my hut and me no see em.*' And then her cry went up to God.—(Watson's Defence of Methodists, p. 26.)

The principle developed under this head, will receive a farther illustration as we proceed with our review.

"Many of the slaves are (and all may be) branded, by means of a hot iron, on the shoulder or other conspicuous part of the body with the initials of their master's name, and thus bear about them in indelible characters the proof of their debased and servile state.—Brief View.

With respect to this horrid custom of branding the slaves, observes Mr. Bickell, it is not so common now as it was before the abolition of the slave trade; for then it was customary to brand the greater part, that they might be known in case of running away. The Creoles, or those born in the colonies, are not so apt to desert, though many of them are branded when they are inclined to wander, as may be seen by consulting any of the work house lists that are published in some of the weekly newspapers of the islands. It is a horrid practice, for it must be attended with very acute and lasting pain, besides the disgraceful and disgusting appearance of seeing a human being marked like or worse than a horse, because that principle, that unconquerable desire of freedom or liberty implanted in every mind, has tempted the unfortunate being to quit a place of ill treatment, for they seldom run away unless they have been ill used in some way or other. p. 37.

Mr. Bickell confirms this statement, by a long list of instances occupying nine or ten pages, taken from the Jamaica newspapers. We shall extract only a very few specimens.

John Stevens, a likely young Creole Negro man, 5ft 6¾in, marked MI on left shoulder, has a large scar on the left side of his throat, and other scars between his shoulders and neck, to the estate of Mr. Mark, of Black River, dec.—Aug. 5 1823. p. 39

Philip, a Creole Sambo man, of Carthagena, 5ft 5in, marked ICD on left, and

LH apparently but blotched on right shoulder to Charles Newman Esq. Manchester.—Sept. 10. 1823. p. 39.

Richard a Creole 5 ft. 5¾ in. marked apparently CC and CA on shoulders and CA on left cheek to Syssons estate.— Sept. 29. 1823. p. 43.

William Nelson alias Thomas Mole an Eboe 5 ft. 5½ in. marked ASIA on shoulders, breasts and cheeks to Mr. Holmes of Vere.—Oct. 17. 1823. p. 44.

The Slaves, whether male or female, are driven to hard labour by the impulse of the cart-whip, for the sole benefit of their owners, from whom they receive no wages; and this labour is continued (with certain intermissions for breakfast and dinner) from morning to night, throughout the year.

In the season of crop, which lasts for four or five months of the year, their labour is protracted not only throughout the day, as at other times, but during either half the night, or the whole of every alternate night.

Besides being made to work under the lash, without wages, during six days of the week, the Slaves are further obliged to labour for their own maintenance on that day which ought to be devoted to repose and religious instruction. And as that day is also their only market day, it follows that Sunday shines no Sabbath day to them, but is of necessity a day of worldly occupation and much bodily exertion.

The colonial laws arm the master, or any one to whom he may delegate his authority, with a power to punish his slaves to a certain extent without the intervention of the magistrate, and without any responsibility for the use of this tremendous discretion; and to that extent he may punish them for any offence, or for no offence. These discretionary punishments are usually inflicted on the naked body with the cart-whip, an instrument of dreadful severity, which cruelly lacerates the flesh of the sufferer. Even the unhappy females are equally liable with the men to have their persons thus shamelessly exposed and barbarously tortured at the caprice of their master or overseer.—Brief View.

On these several heads Mr. Bickell is clear and copious in his statement.

The universal custom in Jamaica, he observes, is not to allow the slaves any wages (except a few domestics in the towns where they are allowed from two shillings and three pence to three shillings sterling per week*) but to each slave is apportioned a piece of land which he is to cultivate at the portions of time allowed him, and on which he raises roots and other vegetables such as yams, cocoas and plantains for himself and family if he have any; the females have portions of land as well as the men and provide for themselves when single, but when married or living constantly with a man they often unite their grounds and conjointly labour for themselves and families till the children arrive at a certain age when they must provide for themselves. The vegetables provisions as they call them they commonly boil in an iron pot (sometimes they roast them) in the open air, and to qualify them they are allowed a few salt herrings each, not always of the best kind, and they are served out to them once a week or fortnight, most commonly the former; but at Christmas on most estates and plantations they have an extra allowance of salt cod fish which they use in like manner. p. 9.

All the field slaves are allowed by the law of the island every other Saturday out of crop time, and some extra days after crop to make up the number of twenty-six days in the year when they are to labour in their grounds to raise provisions for their subsistence. Crop time means the time that the mill is at work for grinding canes to make sugar, and this generally lasts from Christmas to June or July, so that the slaves get only from fourteen to sixteen days in the year, besides a few extra days after crop, in which to work their grounds; and on many estates and plantations they get no extra days at all, so that these few days being wholly insufficient, the Sundays are intruded on, and the Sabbath therefore is with most a day of labour instead of a day of rest.

---

* Mr. Bickell is usually very accurate in his statements. Here he has committed a slight mistake. He calls the money allowed to domestic slaves in towns wages, whereas it is not wages, but merely the subsistence money allowed by law in lieu of the produce of provision grounds—in fact board wages, which is quite a distinct thing from wages. The law on this subject will be found in the 6th clause of the Slave Code of Dec. 1816, and it ordains that where there are not proper lands, each slave is to have provision equal to 3s. 4d. per week, which is equal to 2s. 4d. sterling.

This is certainly a hardship and shews that the object of the planters is to obtain the greatest quantity of labour possible up 11 12

This is also a principal cause of one of the greatest hardships in West-Indian slavery I mean the constant use of the whip for seeing that work is their only portion they are as I before observed inclined to be indolent and a driver is continually after them in the field to flog them with his heavy whip if they do not work so hard as he thinks they ought It is certainly a most degrading sight to see one fellow creature following twenty thirty or forty others and every now and then lashing them as he would a team of horses or mules but this is not all for it any one offends more than ordinarily master driver who has almost unlimited power takes him or her from the ranks and having two or three strong Negroes to hold the culprit down lays on twenty or thirty lashes with all his might Thirty nine is the number specified by law beyond which even a White man cannot legally go in one day but I have seen a Black driver lay on most unmercifully upwards of forty at one time whilst his fellow slave was crying out for mercy so that he could be heard a quarter of a mile from the spot pp 12 13

I once saw it done in the mountains of Port-Royal on a property belonging to a Mr Regnier I was walking out with a Mr Jackson the custos of the parish who had a coffee mountain near when we heard the cries of some one as being punished and the sound of a whip On looking down from the mountain where we were we saw a Negro on the side of another mountain held down on his stomach and the driver flogging him with all his strength Curiosity led us to see how many lashes he would lay on before he stopped and he had exceeded forty before I called out aloud to him to desist He then ceased and I asked what had made him flog the other so severely when he replied that the offender had been set to watch his master's provision grounds last night and had suffered some of the plaintains to be stolen or had stolen them himself

Though this driver had exceeded the number which even a White man can inflict by the laws of Jamaica I never heard that he was degraded or punished for it and yet the chief magistrate in the parish witnessed the illegal stripes pp 197 198

I do not think he adds that the whip can be entirely laid aside whilst slavery exists — but the present use of it should be abolished and no punishment should be inflicted even by order of an overseer but of some neighbouring magistrate for most of the overseers are too fond of flogging and feel no more for the cries of a Negro than they would for the howling of a dog Those daily punishments of the present horrid system for indolence or other trivial faults lose more over their intended effect for the frequency hardens the poor wretches and makes them less willing to exert themselves for after all their endeavours they are not certain of giving satisfaction

On every estate or plantation there are also stocks in which a proprietor or overseer can place any of the Negroes for real or supposed faults as often as he pleases When a slave has offended more than commonly he is placed in them for a considerable time day and night but sometimes he is sent to the field to work under the inspection and charge of another in the day and sent back to the stocks again at night This is often done when they are given to running away or after a severe flogging when they are suspected of being inclined to desert Sometimes for greater safety and an increase of punishment they are sent without the interference of a magistrate to the parish workhouse or gaol where they get a severe thirty nine at going in and coming out and are worked in pairs chained together by the neck in this manner they go out to work on the roads or in the streets with a workhouse driver after them who lashes them pretty sharply to urge them on I have been told that in a certain parish they were marched in this heart rending state to church though I never saw it myself pp 14 15

Just before I left Jamaica I was very credibly informed by a respectable White person who lived near the scene of this tragedy in Kingston that a Negro had died a few days before from severe flogging and that the poor fellow had been buried without any inquest having been held or scarce any notice taken of it for it was not generally known The case was this The Negro had done something wrong and the master fearing to give him all the intended punishment at once had him severely punished three several days following the consequence was that the man was unable to do any thing more but lingered a short time and died undoubtedly from the cruel and repeated floggings

It may be objected that thirty nine lashes or stripes inflicted on a man for three days following would hardly cause death but I can assure my readers that the whip in a strong man's hand is a severe instrument of torture I had once occasion to send a stout servant boy or hired slave of my own to the workhouse for punishment (on account of stealing from a shopkeeper who complained to me) and I desired he might be given only two dozen Though he richly deserved the flogging yet I was sorry to see him when he returned for he crept and rolled about the yard for some time crying aloud and was so much marked that he could scarcely sit or walk for several days

The power which every owner or every overseer or other deputy possesses of flogging the slaves daily is indeed a dreadful engine of oppression, and cannot, in my humble opinion, be too soon abolished. It is not enough to say that very few take advantage of that power given them by the law. I would reply, it is neither fit nor just that one single person should be able to do so; for as long as the present law exists, there will be found too many hardhearted and unfeeling masters and mistresses and overseers to put the whip in frequent requisition. I have heard of a White lady of good property of the parish of Westmoreland, who was accustomed to send her female slaves to a large pond, a cattle pond, to wash themselves, whilst she herself would be mounted on a charger, and would point out to a driver or some flogging assistant such and such females as were to be flogged in their naked state!!!

I knew another lady in the parish of Port Royal, who had a female slave of Colour, of whom she was rather jealous (perhaps not without reason, for the poor slave could not long resist the entreaties and presents of her master,) and was in the habit of punishing her severely with her own hand, till the unfortunate creature, like Hagar the Egyptian of old, wept aloud for the hardness of her bondage. She was allowed to go out as a servant, and a gentleman of Kingston hired her, and was much pleased, as I heard him say, with her industry and attention to his domestic affairs. The mistress however was not content, but thought her too happy and too well off, so she ordered her back again to her own residence where the horrible scene of jealousy and consequent flagellation was renewed.

I am not ignorant of an island law which professes to protect the slaves from severe and cruel punishment, and authorises magistrates to impose a fine on the offender or even to manumit the slave or slaves for very ill usage, upon complaint being made and due proof of the fact. But it must not be forgot, that those magistrates to whom complaints are made are themselves slave owners, and are not over anxious to interfere in such matters. It must be a very strong case indeed, and the Negro must have influenced some lawyer through interest or some other White man, from ill will or revenge to this owner or deputy that has ill treated him, or he must have used some other means to make it notorious before he can have much chance of redress.

I was once present at a sitting of magistrates at Port Royal, when a complaint was laid by several female Negroes and children who through ill treatment had run away from a certain coffee mountain and had come to the magistrates for redress. The complaint was that they had not enough to eat, and had been cruelly punished, for being domestic slaves they had pilfered a little provision, to the best of my recollection a little biscuit and a few plantains or a yam or two from the store. For this they were severely punished by their mistress's order, by a stout male slave who beat them with a stick or flogged them more than once. Young mistress also, two of them said, had helped to punish them. Whether this last were true or not I will not pretend to say, but this I know, that the two women who were the principal complainants looked as if they had been half starved, and their backs were most cruelly mangled from their shoulders downwards. They were in such a state that I could not bear to look at them after the first sight, but turned my face away while the examination went on.

The above cause of their being punished was elicited from themselves, and from their miserable and pitiable appearance it must have been sheer want and keen hunger that drove them to take a little food to satisfy craving nature. That their punishment had been much too severe was manifest to every one, but the principal examining magistrate had been appointed by the Custos of the parish, (the owner of these slaves being a relation,) and was completely his creature, he was therefore inclined to throw a veil over the affair, and for this purpose questioned a Jew, the deputy president of the workhouse and flogging master general, as to the severity of the beating and flogging. Do you think, said this magistrate and president of the workhouse, do you think Mr B—— that a person receiving thirty nine lashes would have his back injured as much as the backs of these women? The poor Jew having some little feeling left, was almost ashamed to say Yes, and did not dare at the risk of his situation to say No, so he looked very queer for a short time and at last said, I don't know sir, but some people shew marks much sooner than others. I have seen some that appeared but little injured after the punishment that the law allows, but others whose backs are soft, I think might be as bad or nearly as bad as the backs of the complainants. Ah! replied the justice, you think so? and after a few more words, for there was very little consultation, the other magistrate not caring to support a farce which he could not well prevent, they were ordered back to gaol again, with the understanding that their mistress should be spoken to. This was an atrocious case, for these Negroes were cruelly maltreated and by the slave laws of Jamaica they ought to have been emancipated, or at least, their owner ought to have been heavily fined, but no redress was obtained, and this too frequently being the case the poor wretches do not very often lay their complaints before the partial justices for legal redress, (as they get an additional flogging for bringing such a charge if not well proved) but weep over and lament their hard and degrading lot in secret. *pp 25—31*

The time of labour for the slaves, generally is from sunrising to sunsetting viz. from five o clock to seven one half the year and from six to six, or thereabout the other half They are generally summoned from their slumbers by the cracking of the driver s whip about half an hour before daylight which whip as it is pretty long and heavy makes the valleys resound and the welkin ring with its alarming sounds and woe be to the hapless slave who does not lend a willing ear and speedy footsteps to its repeated calls

If he be absent at roll call the judge juror and executioner all stand by him in the shape of an inexorable driver and without any defence or leave of appeal he is subjected to the lash Nor will a trifling excuse serve the Black female she makes the best of her way to take her place her unequal share of the task by the strong armed and stout-made man in the well dressed up rank of the gang Should she be too late her sex and slender form or gentler nature will not avail but, as if devoid of feeling she is laid down by force and punished with many stripes on those parts which shall be nameless for me but which in women for decency s sake ought never to be exposed Surely nature is outraged at such devilish indelicacies

Out of this time is allowed half an hour for breakfast and two hours for dinner but many overseers have the first shell blow for dinner at half past twelve o clock, and the second at two to go to the field again as they are not very particular when they are busy in crop or wish to have a certain quantity of work done Independent of this also in crop time the gangs are divided and one half must work at night whilst the other half sleeps though on some estates where they have great strength as they term it (viz where the Negroes are more numerous than strict necessity requires for the quantity of land in cultivation) the whole number is divided into three parts; so that on most sugar estates the slaves work one half the year three nights in the week independent of the days and on the others two nights a week With respect to the hardness of the labour it is not greater than (perhaps not so great as) our husbandmen are accustomed to in England nor do I think it possible for any men to work so hard in a tropical climate as they could in a cold one but the length of time that they are employed (viz eleven or twelve hours besides the night work) is more than was intended for man to bear and must hasten debility and old age For the poor women it is a great deal too much, as their frail frames cannot stand it many years pp 47—50

I am aware that there is a law in Jamaica, imposing a fine on proprietors or overseers for compelling the Negroes to do certain kinds of labour on the Sabbath but it is notorious that this law is altogether a dead letter and that with respect to their grounds, the Negroes not only go of their own accord to work there as not having sufficient time allowed them otherwise but if they are found inattentive it is a custom to send one of the book-keepers on that holy day to see that all the slaves are at work and to watch them a certain time that there may not be a want of food

For putting the mill about (viz for making sugar) on a Sunday there is a fine of 50*l* one half of which, I believe goes to the informer but though this is done in defiance of law in almost every if not every parish in the island I never heard of an information being laid for that offence as those planters who do not put their mills about wink at it in others and no clergyman or other religious person would venture I think, to inform as he would be sure to meet with insult, or some worse injury for his conscientious interference

A short time before I left Jamaica I was in St Thomas in the East the most religious parish in the island (Kingston perhaps excepted) and on one of the Sundays I was there several overseers put their mills about, in the afternoon and the whole or greater part of the gangs were busy at work but where the mills are not put about they work so late on most estates, on Saturday nights that the Negroes and even the Whites belonging to the boiling house department, are employed all the forenoon of the Sabbath potting sugars &c so that they are prevented from going to church

I will record one instance of this as coming more particularly within my own knowledge it was on a large estate in the parish of St David belonging to a gentleman who wishes (as I have been informed) to afford his people every facility that they may attend to religious duties and encourages them to go to church as often as possible I had been staying a week with the rector of the parish and on my return to Kingston on a Monday morning called with a friend at Albion, the estate alluded to it was about breakfast time and the head book keeper invited us to breakfast of which we gladly accepted We remarked to rather a fine young Irishman who had been only a few months in the country that we had not seen him or any of the others at church yesterday he replied that he used to attend regularly in his own country but having been generally engaged of a Sunday morning since he came upon that property he had not been able to attend church and that yesterday in particular he was in the boiling house till twelve o clock superintending the Negroes whilst they were potting sugars, as the mill had been kept about late on Saturday night The young man seemed to have a sense of religion and spoke with regret of his inability to attend a place of worship On this estate there were six or seven White men, and four or five hundred Negroes, scarcely any of whom attended the parish church, which was only about three miles distant, and the rector of which parish was most anxious to instruct those who would attend. pp. 71—73.

The goodness of the Almighty in ordaining every seventh day a day of rest from labour, was of the greatest consequence to man, even in a temporal point of view, as most of the human race are labourers; for by ceasing from work on that day, man is cheered and invigorated, and goes to his labour or business the following morning with a willing mind, and his sinews full of strength. That Omniscient Eye which looks into futurity, and has weighed the hearts of all men in a balance, foresaw that when men multiplied upon the earth, the powerful would oppress the weak, and that the rich would require perpetual labour from the poor; that this fatigue of the body would weigh down the soul, and destroy or very much diminish the powers of the mind; he therefore in his own time commanded the Sabbath to be kept holy, that man who is in part an immortal creature, might reverence and worship his Creator, learn the nature and value of his being, and with fear and trembling, but in humble reliance, prepare for that never ending state of eternity for which he was at first destined.

By the Israelites under the covenant of works, the seventh day was very strictly kept, and the Sabbath breaker was commanded to be stoned to death, by a statute of Levitical Law. The Ten Commandments have lost none of their force under the covenant of grace, or Christian dispensation, and the Sabbath has been kept strictly and religiously by most Christians in all ages of the church of Christ; yet in the West Indian colonies planted by Christian nations, and particularly in Jamaica, the largest colony of highly favoured and Christian Britain, the Sabbath is worse kept than by Turks themselves. It is not enough that most of the Slaves must work in their grounds a part of that holy day, but to add to the abomination, a market must be kept also on the Sunday for the sale of provisions, vegetables, fruit, &c. It is the only market day fellow countrymen and fellow Christians which the poor Negroes and Coloured Slaves have, and instead of worshipping their God, they are either cultivating their portions of land to preserve life, or trudging like mules with heavy loads, five, ten, or even twenty miles to a market, to sell the little surplus of their provision grounds, or to barter it for a little salt fish to season their poor meals, or what is much worse, to spend very often the value in new destructive rum, which intoxicates them and drowns for a short time the reflection that they are despised and burthened Slaves.

I shall never forget the horror and disgust which I felt on going on shore for the first time in Kingston, in the month of August, 1819, it was on a Sunday, and I had to pass by the Negro market, where several thousands of human beings of various nations and colours, but principally Negroes, instead of worshipping their Maker on his holy day, were busily employed in all kinds of traffick in the open streets. Here were Jews with shops and standings as at a fair, selling old and new clothes, trinkets, and small wares at cent per cent to adorn the Negro person; there were low Frenchmen and Spaniards, and People of Colour in petty shops and with stalls, some selling their bad rum, gin, tobacco, &c. others salt provisions and small articles of dress, and many of them bartering with the Slave or purchasing his surplus provisions to retail again; poor free people and servants also from all parts of the city to purchase vegetables &c. for the following week. The different noises and barbarous tongues recalled to one's memory the confusion of Babel; but the drunkenness of some, with the imprecations and obscenities of others, put one in mind rather of a pandemonium or residence of devils. Surely the gates or entrances to this city, instead of being entrances which lead to solemn temples or gates of heaven, as they should be in a Christian country and on a Christian Sabbath, are much more like gates directing to the broad way that leadeth to destruction, that leadeth to hell itself. pp. 64—67.

" Marriage, that blessing of civilized and even of savage life, is protected in the case of the Slaves by no legal sanction. It cannot be said to exist among them. Those therefore who live together as man and wife are liable to be separated by the caprice of their master, or by sale for the satisfaction of his creditors.

" The Slaves in general have little or no access to the means of Christian instruction.

' The effect of the want of such instruction, as well as of the absence of any marriage tie, is that the most unrestrained licentiousness (exhibited in a degrading, disgusting, and depopulating promiscuous intercourse) prevails almost universally among the Slaves, and is encouraged no less universally by the debaucheries of their superiors the Whites.—Brief View.

I have resided, says Mr Bickell, nearly five years in Jamaica, and have preached two or three sermons almost every Sunday, many other clergymen have also exerted themselves, but to very little purpose as far as the slaves are concerned, those horrid and legalized scenes are just the same; for this Sunday market is a bait of Satan to draw away the ignorant Negro; his temporal and pressing natural wants are set in opposition to his spiritual ones; and the former prevail to that degree that most of the churches in the island are nearly empty. pp. 67, 68.

The White inhabitants who were baptized in their childhood or youth and promised obedience to the Divine law have forsaken the covenant made with their God in baptism, have broken and despised his Sabbaths, have built other altars than those of prayer and praise, and compel poor ignorant Negroes, whom it is their duty to instruct and reform, to do the same.

It is chiefly owing to the institution and due observance of the Sabbath, that true religion and morality are kept alive in the world; and I would lay it down therefore as an axiom, that before the great body of Negro and other Slaves can have any proper ideas of the Christian religion, the Sunday markets must be done away with, the labouring in their grounds on the Sabbath must be forbidden; for to pretend to make them moral and religious, and to cause them to break the Sabbath at the same time, is not only highly offensive to Almighty God, but is grossly insulting to the correct feeling and common sense of a truly Christian people. pp. 68, 69.

In some of the parishes a considerable number of marriages have taken place.

The same parishes where religion has made the greatest progress, there also the greatest number of marriages have been solemnized amongst the slaves. In Kingston and St. Thomas's in the East in particular a great number of couples have been married; in the former parish about 2000 (one third perhaps from Port Royal St. David's and other parishes,) and in the latter 1500 within these last seven or eight years. In Spanish Town, (or St. Catherine's) St. Andrew's and St. David's a good many have been married also, and a few in some other parishes; but in several others none at all. In the small town of Port-Royal, which is quite separated from the other part of the parish, during the two years and three months that I served it, I married twelve or fourteen couple, free people and slaves; and several more were about to be married when I quitted the parish in April 1823. This is not a great number to be sure, but more than had been married there for twelve years previously to my taking the cure. Two or three of these couples had lived together in a state of concubinage for many (I believe nearly twenty) years, and married I can confidently say from religious motives, as did some of the others. In two instances free men of Colour married Black women, and in one particular case the man, a very decent mechanic applied to me for advice; as he said he had lived with the woman many years, and knowing now that it was wicked to live in that way any longer, they wished to be married; but that he had been much laughed and scoffed at by many in the town for his good and virtuous intentions, as the woman was older than himself and had had a child by some other man before she lived with him. Having ascertained that it was not his intention to desert her, whether they were married or not, I advised him by all means to marry, and not to mind what irreligious and wicked people said. They came to my house to have the ceremony performed, and such was the crowd of low and noisy persons around it, that I was obliged to send for a constable to keep the peace. After the ceremony was performed the rabble followed shouting and jeering as if the newly married pair had committed some dreadful crime. I was obliged in two or three instances to have recourse to the constable on these occasions when they first began to marry, so rare a thing was it in Port Royal; but I am happy to say that before I quitted the parish I could throw open the doors and allow them to look on, which they did with much propriety and attention. pp. 91—93.

The evils of slavery, great as they have already been shewn to be, would yet be less lamentable than they really are, if they affected the slaves only; but truly distressing to an awakened and well regulated Christian mind is it to witness the demoralizing effects brought on the White part of the population also; nearly the whole of whom live in a state of open and acknowledged and even boasted fornication. It is a well known and notorious fact that very few of the White men in the West Indies marry, except a few professional men and some few merchants in the towns and here and there in the country, a proprietor or large attorney. Most of the merchants and shopkeepers in the towns, and the whole of the deputy planters (namely overseers,) in all parts of the country have what is called a house keeper who is their concubine or mistress, and is generally a free woman of Colour; but the book keepers, who are too poor and too dependent to have any kind of establishment, generally take some Mulatto or Black female slave from the estate where they are employed, or live in a more general state of licentiousness.

This is so very common a vice and so far from being accounted scandalous, that it is looked upon by every person as a matter of course, and if a newly arrived young man happens to have brought a few moral or religious ideas with him from Great Britain he is soon deprived of them by taunt and ridicule, and is in a short time unblushingly amalgamated into the common mass of hardened and barefaced licentiousness. This does not depreciate the privileged White men even in the eyes of most Creole White ladies for they often pay visits to the mistress of a relative and fondle and caress the little ones; nay I have known some married ladies pay visits to the kept mistresses of rich men who were not relatives, though they would not look upon a more respectable woman of the same colour who might be married to a Brown man.—pp. 104, 105.

What a horrible picture is this! In Jamaica alone there are seven or eight thousand White men, nearly the whole of whom live in this wicked state, in defiance of the commands of God, and in spite of the examples and precepts inculcated upon their minds in the mother country.—p. 106.

This unchristian way of living, this almost total absence of the sacred rite of marriage amongst the Whites has been productive of that numerous and intermediate race between Whites and Blacks commonly called People of Colour.—p. 111.

The greater part of these live also in a state of fornication; many are condemned to do so by their poverty and a total want of employment for the poor females are brought up to no business, with very few exceptions, nor is there any demand for their services as servants. Except then their parents have left them sufficient to live upon (which is but seldom the case,) they must prostitute their persons or starve; for such is the contempt with which the men of Colour are treated (even by the lowest of the White men,) and such is the poverty of many of them that most of the Brown women prefer being kept by a White man to being the wife of a man of her own colour and rank, though it can scarcely be said that they have any rank at all. Such were the disadvantages that the Brown men laboured under, that till within these last few years marriage was seldom solemnized between two People of Colour; but of late, and particularly in Kingston and two or three other parishes where the doctrines of Christianity have been most propagated, a considerable number have been married and live in an exemplary and respectable manner. Many more would follow these praiseworthy examples, were it not for the White man's gold and fine promises, connected with the idea in the female mind of having a fairer offspring; for such is the disgrace and disadvantage attached to colour that the greater part of the females take a great pride in seeing their children progressively advancing to the privileged colour and cast.—pp. 112, 113.

The following anecdote will aptly shew the difficulties with which missionaries have to contend, even on estates where absentee proprietors are most desirous of affording them every requisite facility. Sir George Rose's zeal in the cause of religious instruction is well known, and yet it is on one of his estates that the following circumstances took place.

I know one instance in the parish of St Thomas in the East, on an estate belonging to Sir George Rose, where one of the Wesleyans, a very correct and zealous man, had been in the habit of attending, and from what he had taught them, several of the Negroes were in the habit of meeting in the evening in one of the Negro huts to offer up a few short prayers and to instruct each other as well as they could. This however displeased the overseer, and they were ordered not to do it again. They then I believe complained to their minister of the hardship of not being allowed to worship their Maker in the inoffensive way he had taught them; and he represented the innocence of the practice and impossibility of any danger arising to the property; but the overseer, instead of being persuaded, was enraged the more, and took an early opportunity of punishing the complainants for some pretended fault and said tauntingly (whilst the whip was being applied to their backs by a stout driver,) You'll go and tell the Methodist parson again, will you? I'll make you tell him for something. And they were punished more than usual for having complained to one whom they considered a friend, and who they thought would be able and willing to protect them from the cruel and cutting lash of the whip for merely worshipping their God and innocently perusing his holy word.

When the missionary was informed of the unjust floggings and unfeeling taunts he remonstrated with the overseer upon his unreasonable conduct, and remarking that he was allowed and encouraged by the proprietor to instruct the Negroes, further observed (on finding that he could do no good with the deputy,) that he should represent the matter to the attorney, and in his warmth said (to the best of my recollection,) if the attorney did not countenance his teaching the slaves in a proper manner it should be represented to the proprietor Sir G. Rose himself. The cunning and revengeful overseer, however, anticipated him and went to the attorney with a woeful tale of the dire intentions of the poor preacher against them both. The consequence was that he was very nearly being brought into serious trouble, for the attorney represented the case to some of the vestry and they talked of calling a meeting to take the affair into consideration. It was however hushed up (I was informed) by the senior missionary of the connexion going up from Kingston and making some kind of apology for the humane and worthy, but (as the planters thought) too zealous interference of his fellow minister.' pp. 210, 211.

'In none of the colonies of Great Britain have those legal facilities been afforded to the Slave to purchase his own freedom, which have produced such extensively beneficial effects in the colonial possessions of Spain and Portugal, where the Slaves have been manumitted in large numbers, not only without injury, but with benefit to the master, and with decided advantage to the public peace and safety. On the contrary, in many of our colonies, even the voluntary manumission of Slaves by their masters is obstructed, and in some rendered nearly impossible by large fines.'—Brief View.

In the same strain Mr. Bickell observes, that

'The obstructions thrown in the way of emancipation are also a very great evil. It is provided at the same time that every proprietor or owner should give a bond to the proper authorities in the sum of 100l. for every slave he might emancipate to be claimed from him or his executors in case such slave should become chargeable to the parish. I do not mean to say that every slave made free is likely to become chargeable; but I am convinced that it has acted as a very great and insurmountable check to the liberal intentions of many owners, and has kept many a slave in bondage who would otherwise have been enjoying his freedom. To make the best of it, it is but half a boon.

But to other modes of emancipation there are still greater obstacles; for if an industrious Negro in a favoured situation saves a little money, the sum demanded for his freedom is in most instances so enormous that it is but seldom effected. In many cases where free Brown or Black men have been connected with female slaves, they have had a wish to purchase their freedom out of love to the wife, as she is called, or if she be a mother, perhaps to the child or children also; but so much has been demanded that they have been obliged to relinquish the generous idea. With one instance of this kind I was well acquainted, as it happened in the city of Kingston. A decent free man, a tradesman, had lived with a Black female slave belonging to a certain White lady (whose name I shall not now mention) and much desired to purchase her, that he might give her her freedom and marry her. He applied to the mistress, who did not altogether object to selling the young woman, but demanded so great a sum for her that the poor fellow could not raise so much even by selling all he had. The common price for a good domestic female slave was then from 100l. to 130l. currency; but how much dost thou think, gentle reader, that this virtuous and humane White lady asked for this her female slave, who wished to be freed and married to the man she loved? Why, the small sum of 200l. currency!! at least 70l. more than she was worth; nor could she be prevailed on to sell her for less, although assailed by the prayers of the free lover and the tears of his enslaved mistress; so that she was neither emancipated nor married, for the man did not like to marry a slave; but she was allowed to live on in the same wicked way; though had a moderate and equitable sum been demanded, she would have been emancipated, and her children (now being slaves and bastards) would have been free and legitimate. This is not a solitary case, it often occurs; and in many instances they will not sell a valuable slave on any terms. I became acquainted with a case of this last kind just before I left Jamaica, where a Mulatto slave was not allowed to be sold, though a good price, more than her full value, was offered for her.

There is a much greater liberality in this respect in the Spanish colonies, where emancipation cannot be withheld from slaves on certain sums being offered, and on other certain conditions, there being fixed laws on this head.

But in our colonies there is no inducement held out, for the slave is a complete chattel, a mere machine impelled by the whip, as the master has the power of perpetual possession. However deserving or fortunate the slave may be in being steady and industrious, and having friends and a little money, it avails nothing; for if the owner choose, he or she must die in bondage. Indeed being good and industrious would, in nine cases out of ten, rivet his chains more tightly, for the more he does the more valuable he is, and therefore the less likely to be parted with. Go to any estate or plantation in the British West Indies and offer a fair sum for a worthless Negro, he or she would be readily and gladly sold to you. Offer a good price for an ingenious tradesman, a hard working steady field Negro, or an interesting young female, and say that you wish to make them free, the owner or manager would reply, "No sir, these are some of my most valuable slaves. I would not part with either of these men for more than his value. And as to that young woman, sir, she will work as well as any man I have got; she is likely also to have a large family; I cannot spare her for any sum!"' pp. 32—37.

Mr. Bickell tells us that although he has confined his observations to Jamaica, yet that, having visited some of the other colonies, he can safely assert,—

That the picture drawn of Slavery in Jamaica, will pretty faithfully delineate its features its actual and present state in all the other Slave holding islands and colonies belonging to Great Britain There may be and is a variety of shades some darker and some brighter but as a whole it will be found tolerably correct p 119

In some colonies however as Demerara, Berbice, and St Lucie,

The evils and hardships of the Slaves are even greater than in Jamaica particularly in the two former for the fatness and abundant goodness of the soil has augmented the cupidity of the planters there to that degree that the poor Negroes are very much over worked to increase the enormous produce and to cause their masters pockets to overflow with money pp 119 120

Were the colonists inclined of themselves to make any material and beneficial changes in their Slave Code neither the British government nor British people would think of interfering but experience teaches us that their professions with respect to their Slaves are unmeaning and empty and that even the few concessions that have been wrung from them are not *bona fide* fulfilled Witness their compelling them to labour in their grounds and permitting them to make sugar on Sundays Witness their not allowing them time to attend the places of worship (the pretended chapels which were never built) for moral and religious instruction Witness the non redress of their just complaints for severity and cruelty of punishment Witness their throwing numerous obstacles in the way of individual emancipation Witness their preventing those of the curates who wished to attend on some of the estates to preach and catechise from doing so and thereby shutting the doors of instruction on the poor Slaves altogether !

It must be plain to every impartial person indeed that the colonists do not wish or intend to lighten the hardships of their Slaves or grant them any privileges if it be likely to lessen their income their principal object is to keep them in total ignorance and to compel them to raise the greatest possible quantity of produce for they calculate thus— If we do away with the Sunday market there must be more time given to the Slaves and our crops will fall short if we allow them to be instructed it will take a little more time and the Negroes will also know too much to be content They therefore do and will oppose all interference by the British Parliament because they wish and intend at all hazards to keep the Slaves and their descendants in perpetual bondage It will be for the British Government to determine if such a cruel and impolitic system shall be allowed to go on to the shame and outrage of religion and humanity and to the risk of so great a loss to the British crown pp 137 138

The following passages will serve to counteract some of the prevalent notions so industriously propagated by West Indians of the enviable comforts of the Negro slave comforts which we are unblushingly told place him above the British peasant

Of the great care taken of the Slaves in sickness and of the boasted and frequent attendance of the medical men on the different properties I have never seen any very flattering specimens though I have been on a great many plantations and have seen plenty of doctors Their hot houses or hospitals are generally speaking filthy receptacles they are very happily styled hot-houses for they are hot enough as the hospital is on most estates a confined room very often an earthen floor in this is a platform of boards raised two or three feet high like the soldier s guard bed on which the sick lie down in their own clothes covered sometimes with a blanket and sometimes not on some large estates they have a superior kind of hospital on a first floor with better accommodations The hot-house is often the place where the Negroes are also confined in the stocks so that it is both hospital and gaol pp 52, 53

The feeding and clothing of the Slaves have been much over rated by the colonists and on the other hand somewhat depreciated by the advocates of the Africans or abolitionists for what can be more absurd than to hear it constantly reiterated that the Negroes in our colonies are better fed and better clothed than the British peasantry? If the quantity of food be meant, the favour is even then very frequently I might say generally with our own poor but in the quality there is no comparison —for none but a bigotted and low minded planter or some interested professional resident, who cannot return to reside in this country would compare the coarse yams and cocoas and the stringy indigestible plantains with a few bad or rotten herrings to the wholesome bread of this country and to potatoes and other fine vegetables with a small portion of fresh meat or bacon, which the English cottager enjoys I have seen a good deal of the state of the English poor having served curacies in Somersetshire Gloucestershire Monmouthshire and Wiltshire besides having an intimate acquaintance with Devonshire and I can conscientiously say that I never saw any one even a pauper who lived in the mean hoggish way that the Slaves in the West Indies do and moreover that if such coarse food as the Negroes generally eat were offered them they would reject it (at least much dislike it) as thinking it hardly fit for human and rational beings English stomachs could not well digest it three times a day. I know mine could not, and I can assert with much truth that the coarsest Irish potatoes with a little milk or buttermilk and salt are preferable to the Negro yams and green plantains at least, I would sooner have them and I think most of the British poor would approve of my taste, had they an opportunity of judging.

The English poor are also much better clothed, for where is there a poor cottager that has not a decent cloth or fustian coat, of any colour he pleases with other parts of his dress suitable independent of good and warm stockings and sound shoes to keep his feet from the gravel and dirt? But what has the Slave? He has for his best (from his master as I before observed) a large baize surtout which hangs about him like a sack and would as well fit any person you please as himself and moreover a pair of coarse trowsers and coarse shirt of Oznaburgh which with the coarsest kind of hat is his whole wardrobe, for this is the general livery or badge of Slavery. The female Slaves are clothed as much inferior to our poor women, and both Negro men and women are without stockings and shoes and generally go in a half-dressed state viz without coats or gowns, the women's petticoats up to their knees, and very often before fresh supplies are given out many of them are in a ragged state and some almost in a state of nudity, and yet it is said they are better off than the poor in Great Britain!

On the other hand however they are not so badly off as to food, as many people in this country imagine, for as I before remarked the quantity in most cases is sufficient, and as to clothes they have no need of such warm garments as the poor in this our happy island. It cannot be expected they should be so well off even in these respects, but if they were they have not the comfortable cottage and warm bed with decent furniture and the snug chimney corner of the English peasant, which no one not even a lord or a prince dares to enter into without permission. No in his mud built and straw covered hut without a window or a chimney on two or three boards raised a little above the floor or on the floor itself the Negro Slave lies down on his mat very often uncovered, and if he wants a little fire as in the mountains they sometimes do he must light his few sticks in the open air and like an animal I could mention sit upon his heels shivering by it. It is painful indeed to carry on the comparison, but independent of all this is it nothing that the peasant's son is most commonly sent to school and taught to read his Bible and oftentimes to write and cypher and when grown up can travel to any part of this free country to better his condition none molesting him or daring to make him afraid? pp. 56—59.

More might be quoted to the same effect, but we must give a few lines as to the state of the clergy. Many of them, Mr Bickell observes, are anxious to advance the knowledge of religion, but are prevented through the general profanation of the Sabbath, and the labouring and marketing of the Negroes on that day. Some who have attempted to introduce reforms have been stigmatised as Methodists and it is scarcely safe for them to venture to preach against such vices as fornication, Sabbath breaking, &c. One consequence of this intolerance of zealous and pious clergymen is that many have been ordained both as rectors and curates who are but little qualified and less disposed to contend with the prevailing evils. One of these curates is stated to have been owner of a small trading vessel passing between Kingston and Cuba. On one occasion

He went on board of her himself, made a voyage in her to Cuba, and returned safe and prosperous with an assorted cargo, some part of which (I was credibly informed) was exposed for sale in his own parish, not in his name but for his account. The only punishment he incurred for this disgraceful conduct was the loss of his salary for the time he was absent through the vestry of the parish. This thoughtless Creole was only in deacon's orders though he managed after some time to get testimonials signed to enable him to take priest's orders also and was on his passage home for that purpose but the vessel in which he embarked never reached England as it was wrecked and the poor young man I am sorry to add perished with nearly all the others on board. pp. 98, 99.

Another of these clergymen a rector of a large parish was exposed very lately in one of the public or island papers for his indecent observations on some Coloured females at a funeral where he officiated.

Another who had hesitated between an ironmonger's shop and the church and who had been appointed curate to a large country parish which was partially disturbed about Christmas last was (instead of being at his post where it may be supposed a clergyman might have been of some service) strutting about Kingston and Spanish Town in large spurs *a la militaire* idling away his precious time and taking his fill of pleasure. Can a serious man who wishes well to the cause of religion in general and to the Church of England in particular, see such things without thinking of the words of the prophet Ezekiel, chap. xxxiii?" pp. 100, 101.

Mr. Bickell supposes an objector to blame his exposure of the Jamaica clergy as unnecessary, bishops having been appointed to remedy all defects; he might without injury have omitted it. His answer is, that though he rejoices in the appointment of West Indian bishops, he is sure they will never see what he has seen. Even if they were to visit different parts of the colony, they would not be admitted, as he had been, behind the scenes.

"A veil would be studiously thrown over the most prominent parts of the evils of the system by every person with whom they might converse and on every estate they might choose to visit. There would be no floggings, nor even a single stroke of the whip in a bishop's presence; no indecency to shock his sight, nor any thing said to offend his ears; and if he attended at any church it would be crowded by design and order for that time; every thing in fact would be acted so as to deceive and make a favourable but false impression." pp. ix, x.

Our author's remarks on the oppressions and disabilities of the free People of Colour, notwithstanding their many claims to favour, are peculiarly just and seasonable.

"It has been asserted that nothing but coercion can induce a Negro to labour more than barely to raise enough for his subsistence. This is extremely erroneous; witness the great number of free Blacks in the towns of Jamaica: in Kingston they are most of them good mechanics and work as regularly and as hard as White men in this country; they also conduct themselves as well; can read and write many of them, and are more respectably clad than White men of the same class in England. In Port Royal just the same; they are industrious and intelligent, and several of them (to their credit be it said) have more, much more religion than the low White men there, who affect to despise them." p. 16.

"A great part of the People of Colour in the towns are constant attendants at places of worship, and many of them both men and women possess respectable property in houses and Slaves:—for a considerable part of the houses in Kingston belong to Coloured females. In different parts of the country also many of the men and some women have small coffee mountains and some few have them of a large extent. Of late years a few privileges have been granted them, such as their being permitted to give evidence in courts of justice and to hold property to any extent, but no Brown man is allowed to serve on juries, to be an overseer or book keeper, to fill even the low office of constable or beadle, or (whatever property he may have) to vote for a member of Assembly; but although he cannot save deficiency on any White man's plantation (viz. though he cannot on any estate or plantation fill any low office of a White man, either as carpenter or smith or book keeper, so as to assist in making up the number that must be kept according to law in proportion to the quantity of Slaves, except it be on another Brown man's property), yet he is obliged to turn out in the militia and to clothe and accoutre himself at his own expense, which expense is more than some of them can well bear." pp. 114, 115.

"It is very evident therefore that it is not to the Negroes as Slaves only that the colonists have objections, for when they are free they are considered equally beneath the favoured Whites; even those descended from them on one side only, however far removed, are treated with contempt and disdain, for they are not accounted worthy to sit in their presence, nor hardly to pick up the crumbs under their table.

"Colour therefore, colour is the mark of disgrace; colour is the stain for which those who have the least of it pay so dearly and suffer so much from those who call themselves Christians." pp. 116, 117.

"Some years ago a gentleman in the parish of Clarendon married a respectable and well educated Brown lady, and as he was a proprietor and therefore admissible into genteel society, he went with his wife to an assembly which was held at the court-house in the parish, but such umbrage was taken at their presence by all the others assembled there, that he was desired or ordered to take his wife out of the room, which of course he hastily did after such an insult, but this and other neglect and insult so much overwhelmed them with grief that they both shortly after died of broken hearts.

"In the parish of St. Thomas in the East also a few years ago a respectable man holding an office of trust and profit, married a woman of Colour as privately as possible (by licence) for he and the rector (the late rector Mr. West) well knew the deep rooted prejudices of the Whites in the island. By some means or other it got wind and came to the ears of some of the vestrymen, when the rector was asked if it were true; he however not choosing to satisfy them, the parish register was demanded of him by the magistrates and vestry, but he refused to shew it them, as wishing to preserve his friend from injury for doing so praiseworthy a thing as preferring to marry the woman of his affections rather than live in open and barefaced fornication. At last however the churchwardens obtain d a sight of the register and when it was ascertained that the marriage had taken place he was not only shunned by h s former friends and acquaintance but was soon deprived of his situation and was nearly ruined. The worthy rector also incurred a good deal of odium and they thwarted and injured him in all that they could because he had so properly morally and religiously discharged his duty to God and his fellow man. pp 225, 226

In our present Number we have inserted a circular communication of the Anti slavery Society in which the injurious effects of high prices of produce, and the beneficial effects of low prices, on the comfort and well being of the slaves, are maintained. Without the slightest apprehension that he is illustrating this hypothesis Mr Bickell states some facts which bear directly upon it. Speaking of jobbing gangs or gangs of Negroes consisting usually of from twenty to forty stout male and female slaves who are hired out to perform some of the heaviest labour of estates he observes

They work very hard and before sugars were depressed in price three or four years since their masters were paid ten pounds per acre for digging cane holes when each Negro could earn them a dollar a day but for the last two or three years the jobbers have got only six or eight pounds an acre and can with difficulty find employment for their gangs at that rate. These jobbers used to make fortunes in a short time as a slave by his labour would in three or four years gain for his owner more than his prime cost But it may be supposed that the Negroes have a great antipathy to being sold to these jobbing gentlemen for independent of the continual heavy labour they are obliged to be almost altogether away from their own huts (which though poor are far better than the temporary ones) and grounds except a few Saturdays and the Sundays their poor children also must be neglected and their little stock lost or gon astray So great is the objection they have of being sold to jobbers that I have known many of them run away to avoid it a long time often intervenes before they can be recovered and it is not a trifle that will make a Negro run the risk of getting imprisoned with two or three floggings into the bargain or perhaps get transported from the island for life These jobbing gangs have been compared, very aptly to over wrought or over driven horses the poor slaves composing them may certainly without exaggeration be compared to the London hacks A double price is paid for them and they are worked so very much that they do not last long. It is *gold* versus *life*. pp 51 52

This statement shews us clearly, how it is that high prices operate in increasing the labour and diminishing the comforts of *jobbing gangs* The price of their labour being raised by temporary and accidental circumstances, their owner is tempted to comprise more of that labour into a small space—*in short to make hay while the sun shines*—even at the expense of over driving his slaves and exposing to risk both their health and life Estimating the work of a gang at an acre per day, the income of a single year, at 10*l* an acre would be 3,000*l* at 6*l* an acre 1800*l*,—the difference being no less than 1,200*l* And, if by additional exaction and the abridgment of the time usually allowed the slaves, the jobber had it in his power to add fifty acres more to the tale of their labour he would thereby raise his income to 3 500*l* whereas at 6*l* the same degree of exaction could only raise his income to 2,100*l* He could obviously, therefore, afford to kill more slaves in the former than in the latter case and would therefore be more strongly tempted to overwork them, especially as he would fear the higher rate might be but temporary And is not this exaction of labour a direct effect of high prices?

And let it not be supposed that this effect is confined to jobbing gangs It extends to the slaves universally The proprietor of a sugar estate is just as much tempted to overwork his Negroes when the price of sugar is high, as the jobber is when the price of holing an acre of land is high while, on the contrary, when prices are low, and little or no profit is to be made by overworking his slaves, as compared with the loss of health or life which may be the consequence, he will feel it to be his interest rather to spare his Negroes, with a view to their increase and improvement than to hazard the loss caused by overworking them, without an equivalent. There may, doubtless, be benevolent individuals whom no temptation would induce to oppress their slaves. But we cannot doubt, that, in the mass of instances the effect would be as we have stated it.

This view of the subject which it would be easy to establish even to demonstration if our limits would permit, shews the pernicious operation on the comfort and well being of the slaves of that system of bounties and protecting duties on the sugar grown by slave labour which prevails in this country. We object to this impost not merely because the sum of a million and a half which in this way is exacted from the people of this country is a most unnecessary and oppressive burden, nor merely because by these restrictions our trade with other parts of the world is cramped and fettered. We object to it mainly because it adds to the misery of the slave, and because it tends to prolong and to embitter his bondage.

Accordingly in the Bahama islands, where no sugar is grown and where no impulse is given to slave labour, by bounties and protecting duties on that article, the slaves increase at the rate of about $2\frac{1}{2}$ to 3 per cent per annum; whereas in Demerara, where the largest quantity of sugar is made in proportion to the population, and consequently the sum received in bounties and protecting duties is in the same proportion the largest, the slaves decrease still more rapidly than they increase in the Bahamas. In Jamaica, the proportion of sugar to the slave population is smaller than in Demerara, and the decrease of the slaves is smaller, being about one per cent instead of two and a half. In Barbadoes the proportion of sugar is still smaller than in Jamaica, and there there is a small increase of the population. In short, the principle will be found to hold good universally in slave colonies that the wretchedness and decrease of the slaves are aggravated by the larger profits of the planter, whether these larger profits are the effect of natural causes, such as comparative fertility of soil, or of artificial encouragement by bounties and duties. The slaves, let it be always remembered, receive no wages. They stand on the footing of cattle or machinery, with this difference, that when the demand for the produce of the labour of cattle or machinery increases, the number of cattle or of machines may be proportionably increased; whereas in the case of slaves, the slave trade being prohibited, the increased demand can only be met by an increased exertion of the muscles of the existing stock of slaves, extracted from them by an increased use of the cart whip.

What measures Government mean to pursue for the extinction of slavery, we know not; but it is obvious that if while they profess to seek its amelioration, with a view to its final extinction, they at the same time, continue those bounties and protecting duties which tend, as we have seen, to aggravate its severity, they are undoing by one set of measures what they propose to effect by another. It is highly important therefore that both parliament and the public should attain to right views on this subject. No mere enactments can avail much in diminishing the evils of slavery while solid rewards are attached to the unmeasured exaction of slave labour.—while a high premium continues to be paid by the public of Great Britain for every ton of sugar which is produced by the blood and sweat of the slaves. And are the people of this country guiltless in silently permitting this system to be prolonged in going on, without complaint or remonstrance, to reward the slave driver for every ad ditional severity of exaction of which he is guilty? The average annual sum which each proprietor of a sugar estate in the West Indies has been receiving from the people of this country, in bounties and protecting duties, has been about 800*l.* This is neither more nor less than our eleemosynary contribution to the support of the whips, and chains and stocks, and gibbets which grind down the poor Negroes to the dust, and which have converted into a charnel house one of the fairest portions of the globe. This state of things cannot last. Indeed, it only requires the concurrent exertion of the people of England to put an end to it for ever. That exertion, we are confident, will be made and when made, it must succeed. Reason, justice, humanity, policy, and the sacred voice of religion all plead for it, and they will not long plead in vain.

LITERARY AND PHILOSOPHICAL INTELLIGENCE, &c. &c.

GREAT BRITAIN

PREPARING for publication.—No. I. of the Christian Repository.—Lingard's History of England, vol. VI. containing the Reigns of James I. and Charles I.

In the press.—History of the Protestant Church of the United Brethren, by the Rev. J. Holmes.—The History of the Dominion of the Arabs in Spain.—The Life of John Chamberlain, late a Missionary in India, by Mr. Yates of Calcutta, republished in England, edited by the Rev. F. A. Cox, A. M. Hackney.—A Practical View of the Redeemer's Advent, in a Series of Discourses, by the Rev. J. H. Stewart, M. A. of Percy Chapel.

Cambridge.—The following is a summary of the Members of all the Colleges in 1824.—Trinity College 1222, St John's College 1015, Queen's College 221, Emmanuel College 218, Christ's College 210, Jesus College 204, Caius College 201, St Peter's College 169, Clare Hall 139, Trinity Hall 135, Corpus Christi College 130, Pembroke Hall 125, Catharine Hall 118, King's College 108, Sidney College 101, Magdalen College 95, Downing College 53, University Officers 11—4489. Comparative View—1748, 1500; 1813, 2805; 1823, 4277; 1824, 4400.

The House of Commons Select Committee on the Public Buildings report that with regard to public buildings in general this vast metropolis presents a much smaller number of those which can be denominated grand or ornamental than its extent and opulence would induce a stranger to expect, for with the exception of the two cathedrals, of three of the stone bridges over the Thames, and some very few other structures, it offers but little that deserves admiration. This deficiency the Committee state arises not so much from cost having been spared as from good taste having been wanting; and they strongly impress the importance in a national point of view of paying great attention in future to the public edifices which may be required. They regret that architecture has not kept pace with our other advances towards perfection, and that we are still obliged to look for examples of excellence in this art either to times that are past or to other countries rather than to our own.

At a late meeting of the Royal Asiatic Society, the secretary read a paper from Dr Morrison respecting a remarkable secret association which has been discovered to exist in China, and to prevail among the Chinese at Java, Malacca, Singapore, Penang, and other places. This association is known by a term equivalent to the Triad Society from the three objects (heaven, earth, and man) of their veneration. The paper furnishes an investigation of the name, character and government of this secret band, which under the mask of philanthropy and social principles and objects, Dr Morrison says, conceals very dangerous and immoral designs.

During the year 1824, there were admitted into the British Museum 112,840 persons. The estimated expense for the current year is 15,416*l.* Amongst the items of approaching charge are for Drawings from the Athenian Marbles, 350*l.* Engravings from ditto, 1,300*l.* 'For the purchase of Foreign Books and continuing the works in progress in the Library of Sir Joseph Banks and MSS 1000*l.* Towards printing the Alexandrian MS there were last year expended 391*l.* and the sums already expended in the printing &c of this MS amount to 8,877*l.* The printing of the whole of the text, and of the greater part of the notes is completed. The remaining portion of the notes and of the Prolegomena will amount to about 300*l.* Sir R. C. Hoare has presented his valuable collection of Italian Topography amounting to 1700 articles to this national institution.

Dr Birkbeck who has shewn himself most anxious for the advancement of useful knowledge and for the welfare of our working mechanics and artizans has been induced by the success which has attended the Mechanics Institution to form The London Chemical Society the regulations of which are in circulation.

RUSSIA

Previously to the year 1817 the number of works printed in Russia did not exceed 4,000 about the same number as is annually contained in the catalogues of the fair at Leipzig. This number is now augmented to about 8,000. There are at Moscow nine literary and ten printing establishments; at St Petersburgh, nine of the former and fifteen of the latter and in various other towns one of each. In the whole empire there are nine letter founderies. There are at present fifteen periodical papers in the four provinces of the Baltic.

INDIA

Two vessels lately left Bombay to continue the survey of the Persian Gulf. Until the year 1821 that coast was comparatively unknown. The late survey terminated at the island of Bahrein and the whole line of coast was laid down by a continued series of triangles verified by celestial observations. The space between Bahrein and the mouth of the Euphrates is to be completed by the close of the next cool season.

JAVA

Mr Burgess a merchant at Batavia, has obtained a licence for four and a half years to build steam vessels to navigate on the coast of Java. They are to be built in the Netherlands and during the term of the licence may go from Europe to India.

LIST OF NEW PUBLICATIONS

THEOLOGY

Sermon for the Irish Society of London by the Rev. H. M. Neile. 1s 6d

A Discourse concerning Transubstantiation, reprinted by Admiral Bullen

The Christian Ministry by the Rev. W. Innes. 8s

A Manual of Family Prayers by the Lord Bishop of Chester

The Essentials of Religion by the Rev. H. F. Burder. 9s

A Farewell Sermon by the Rev. J. Leifchild. 1s 6d

Impressions of the Heart relative to the Nature of Genuine Religion. 3s 6d

Discourses and Evening Thoughts by S. Burdett. 4s 6d

Sketches of Prophecy by the Rev. A. Keith. 4s

MISCELLANEOUS

Life of the Rev. P. Henry by J. B. Williams, F.S.A. 1 vol. 15s

Life of the Rev. J. Wesley by the Rev. H. Moore. Vol. II. 10s 6d

Memoirs of the late E. Williams, D.D. by J. Gilbert. 14s

Memoirs of M. Mendelsohn by M. Samuels. 7s 6d

Historic Defence of Experimental Religion by T. Williams. 7s

Visions of Hades. 6s

A Visit to the Sea Coast

Remarks on Volney's Ruins of Empires by W. Hails. 10s 6d

Correspondence relative to the Progress of Christianity in India

Journal during a Residence at the Red River Colony and Excursions among the North American Indians by the Rev. J. West. 8vo. 8s 6d

Memoirs of Canova by J. S. Memes. 8vo. 15s

Practical Observations on the Education of the People by Henry Brougham, Esq. 6d

The First Principles of the Differential Calculus by the Rev. A. Browne. 8vo.

Sonnets and other Poems by E. L. Richardson. 8vo. 5s

A new and faithful Translation of Bishop Jewel's Apology for the Church of England by Rev. S. Isaacson. 8vo. 14s

The Plenary Inspirations of the Scriptures asserted by the Rev. S. Noble. 8vo. 14s

The Harmony of the Law and Gospel with regard to a future State by T. W. Lancaster, M.A. 12s

A Visit to Greece by G. Waddington. 8vo. 8s 6d

Narrative of Lord Byron's last Journey to Greece by Count Gamba. 8vo. 12s

Travels in South America in 1819-20-21 by A. Caldcleugh, Esq. 2 vols. 8vo. 30s

Travels in Russia and the Krimea, the Caucasus and Georgia by Robert Lyall, M.D. 2 vols. 8vo. 30s

RELIGIOUS INTELLIGENCE

SOCIETY FOR THE PROPAGATION OF THE GOSPEL

Our readers are aware of the exertions which were made by this society in urging the necessity of an Episcopal establishment for the West Indies with a view as the Report presented by them to Earl Bathurst on the subject mentioned to the instruction and conversion of the Slaves and improving the condition of the Coloured population as well as those other excellent purposes which they justly considered would result from such a measure. The greater part of the annual sermon preached by the lord Bishop of Exeter before the Society and prefixed to their last Report is devoted to this important subject. The following are extracts from it

After sketching the state of the population in the West-India settlements the Bishop urges the duty and benefits of uniting them in one body by the influence of Christianity —

In such a frame of society if society it can be called where the materials are so heterogeneous and the parts so fundamentally disproportionate what cement is there sufficiently binding to hold the building together? Where the property the power the intelligence and the liberty all in short that gives dignity and moral strength to man is on the one side and mere numbers on the other what is there to determine the rights of each?

I may be thought perhaps that law or at least a sense of natural justice would be sufficient to define and to secure them But the law is unwilling to interfere in the disposal and management of private property and the selfishness of the human heart is apt to extinguish all sense of equity where there are no public rights to enforce it So long therefore as the master shall command and the slave obey without question or resistance there may be peace and in some degree there may be kindness between them but there will also be pride and contempt in the one party and undoubtedly meanness and debasement in the other In such a state of things there may be the fallacious appearance of security but in reality there will be constant danger

Some common principle therefore which law cannot infuse—some common bond which society itself cannot supply—must be found to interpose and to unite these unequal and discordant parties or a field will undoubtedly be open for the display of every bad feeling and the exercise of every evil propensity which unrestrained power in the few or the keen sense of degradation and injury in the many may give rise to

Now Christianity is the only bond sufficiently comprehensive to effect this It embraces equally the freeman and the slave and while it permits and sanctions the inequality of their stations it acknowledges them both as equal objects of its regard It tells them that they are all the children of one common Father and the heirs of one common promise partakers of the same heavenly grace and candidates for the same heavenly reward As brothers in the eyes of God it bids them meet together in the same house of prayer and join in the same service of praise and thanksgiving while abroad and at home it still equally impresses upon them their relative obligations and inculcates equally the duty of kindness and compassion in the master of good will and obedience in the slave

On the subject of an Episcopal establishment for the West Indies his lordship remarks The influence of such an establishment in our West-Indian islands, circumstanced as they are will be most extensively and beneficially felt It will be felt by the planter in the support which it will lend to legitimate authority by the Negro in the check which it will oppose to the abuse of power and by all in the wholesome strength which it will give to public opinion and the lasting energy which it will impart to morality and religion

The present state of affairs in those islands is one which compels the attention of all classes of our fellow citizens it concerns the commercial no less than the ecclesiastical orders of the community the statesman no less than the missionary For the changes which a few years have brought about in the condition of the Negro population are in every point of view of the greatest moment The decline if not the extinction of their popular superstition the decrease of promiscuous intercourse and of the crimes which arose from it the growing inclination to marriage and the careful nurture of their progeny occasioned by the improved system of their management and education their increased numbers their increased knowledge and consequently their increased power the abolition of the trade which made them Slaves by our own Government and its denunciation as piracy by that of America [and now by our own] the example of the empire founded by their brethren in St Domingo and the question constantly agitated among ourselves concerning their own emancipation—all these circumstances have conspired to awaken hopes expectations and desires which must materially affect their ardent character. It is impossible now to quench those hopes or to check entirely those desires. Indeed so far as they may urge them to the acquisition of sound knowledge and the practice of pure religion they are rather to be fostered than discouraged but then in order to preserve the equilibrium of the community a countervailing power must be exerted to balance the increased weight in the scale of the Negro. And where can this power be placed? It cannot be intrusted directly to the planter because it would add not to his strength so much as to his invidiousness nor to the colonial government alone for it would require another and a higher sanction than that of human laws to support its influence. Where then can it be confided so safely or so advantageously as to the hands of a regular church establishment whose duty and interest it will be—to assist the local government in calming the fear and allaying the ferment of the times and to reconcile the planter to the propriety of granting and in due time to fit and prepare the Negro for receiving that liberty which with religion and the love of order will be really a blessing to him but without them will infallibly prove a curse.

A greater necessity exists for the judicious combination of all ranks and orders in the church than ever existed before. It will also I trust be allowed that present circumstances open a great door for the propagation of the Gospel and one that may be rendered effectual by the establishment of local episcopacy.

On the opposition which may be anticipated, his lordship remarks:—

Let not the number of our adversaries alarm us nor their enmity deter us from the prosecution of the great work which we have in hand. Opposition must always be looked for and may often be converted into an instrument of good for if the spirit which it produces be but free from personal animosity and the uncharitableness of party its effect must ever be to purify our motives and inflame our zeal. And in the present instance we have strong allies in the roused attention of the nation at large in the redoubled exertion of all good men in the bright example of the East, and in the general feeling of those connected with the West, both at home and abroad—the feeling that their cause is the same with ours that the propagation of the Gospel is the best means of securing the integrity of our colonial empire and that Christianity by equalizing and conciliating the whole island population will be the best defence against invasion from without and insurrection from within.

This conviction will give us auxiliaries numerous powerful and indefatigable this will unite the intelligent planter the zealous missionary and the true because judicious friend of humanity this will give to the cause of the Gospel the support of the merchant and the protection of the government.

Opposition however it may deter the lukewarm or the fainthearted affords no just ground for inactivity or despondency in the great task of preaching the Gospel to all nations. We have the example of the Apostles we have the conclusions of reason we have the lessons of experience to convince us that resistance and difficulty are among the appointed means of stimulating and concentrating our efforts for its propagation.

And with this conviction on our minds we may behold not indeed with unconcern but with less uneasiness and sorrow the occasional failure of our warmest hopes and hear without impatience or mistrust the sneers of our adversaries when they point to the continued blindness of the Jew or the unyielding abominations of the Gentile. Like the remnant of the Canaanites in the holy land the Jew the Gentile and the Mahomedan are left perhaps to prove our virtue and to perfect that which is lacking in our faith.

Meanwhile however there is much to console and encourage us. There are many circumstances in the present day which justify the expectation that the great impediments to the propagation of the Gospel will in some degree at least and in some parts of the earth be speedily overcome. We may survey with increasing hope the gradual removal of heathen darkness and rejoice with growing joy at the dayspring of the Gospel as it breaks through the mists of superstition and idolatry. It may be long indeed before the Sun of Righteousness shall shine forth in his meridian strength on the benighted regions of the East and of the South but we may hail the dawn of that everlasting light, which shall one day equally illuminate the isles of the Gentiles and the city of our God.

BISHOP OF CALCUTTA'S VISITATION

On last Ascension day, after a sermon by Dr Parish at the cathedral Calcutta, the lord bishop took his seat near the altar, and the clergy being assembled near him, his lordship delivered his charge. After some remarks upon the ecclesiastical establishment in India, his lordship adverting to the backwardness of the English clergy to enter upon their calling in India, remarked, "Those indeed would be much mistaken who should anticipate in the fortunes of an Indian chaplain a life of indolence, of opulence, of luxury. An Indian chaplain must come prepared for hard labour in a climate where labour is often death; he must come prepared for rigid self denial in situations where all around him incites to sensual indulgence; he must be content with an income, liberal indeed in itself, but altogether disproportioned to the charities, the hospitalities, the unavoidable expenses to which his situation renders him liable. He must be content to bear his life in his hand, and to leave very often those dearer than life itself to His care alone who feeds the ravens, and who never or most rarely suffers the seed of the righteous to beg their bread. Nor are the qualifications which he will need, nor the duties which will be imposed on him, less arduous than the perils of his situation. But to the well tempered, the well educated, the diligent and pious clergyman who can endear himself to the poor without vulgarity, and to the rich without involving himself in their vices, who can reprove sin without harshness, and comfort penitence without undue indulgence, who delights in his Master's work even when divested of many of those outward circumstances which in our own country contribute to render that work picturesque and interesting, who feels a pleasure in bringing men to God proportioned to the extent of their previous wanderings, to such a man as Martyn was—I can promise no common usefulness and enjoyment in the situation of an Indian chaplain. I can promise in any station to which he may be assigned an educated society and an almost unbounded range of usefulness. I can promise him the favour of his superiors, the friendship of his equals, and affection strong as death from those whose wanderings he corrects, whose distresses he consoles, and by whose sick and dying bed he stands as a ministering angel. Are further inducements needful? I can promise to such a man the esteem, the regard, the veneration of the surrounding Gentiles; the consolation at least of having removed from their minds by his blameless life and winning manners, some of the most inveterate and injurious prejudices which oppose themselves to the Gospel; and the honour, it may be, of which examples are not wanting among you, of planting the Cross of Christ in the wilderness of a heathen heart, and extending the frontiers of the visible church amid the hills of darkness and the strong holds of error and idolatry."

His lordship then adverted to the great assistance afforded to the ministers of the Gospel in India by the parental care of Government, the bounty of individuals, and the labours of the Society for promoting Christian Knowledge, in the establishment of schools, the distribution of religious tracts, and the management of lending libraries, which his lordship wished to become universal. The missionaries who attended the visitation were then addressed by the Bishop, who alluded to the object and importance of their labours, and this led his lordship to the consideration of the great question of the conversion of the heathen, and to some remarks on the late publication of the Abbe Dubois. His gross mis statements were confuted by an appeal to the Protestant converts of Agra, of Benares, of Meerut, and of Chunar. "Bear witness," said his lordship, "those numerous believers of our own immediate neighbourhood with whom, though we differ on many and doubtless on very important points, I should hate myself if I could regard them as any other than my brethren and fellow servants in the Lord. Let the populous Christian districts of Malabar bear witness, where believers are not reckoned by solitary individuals but by hundreds and by thousands. Bear witness Ceylon, where the Cross has lost its reproach, and the chiefs of the land are gradually assuming without scruple the attire, the language, and the religion of Englishmen; and let him finally bear witness whom we have now received into the number of the commissioned servants of the church, and whom we trust, at no distant day, to send forth in the fulness of Christian authority to make known the way of truth to those his countrymen from whose errors he has himself been graciously delivered."

The concluding passage relates, we believe, to the Rev Christian David, who was baptized at Tranquebar many years since, and has lately been admitted to holy orders at Calcutta by the bishop of that diocese. He has since preached at

Calcutta in the English language and his discourses are said to be highly appropriate and affecting

SERAMPORE COLLEGE

The following passage from the last Report of this institution seems to indicate an increasing abatement in the prejudices of the natives and their confidence in the good will and intentions of the Missionaries

The Brahman Class—On the hypothesis of some it might have been expected that when it is known to be so much the design of Serampore College to spread the knowledge of Divine revelation no brahman would ever have entered within its precincts with the view of receiving instruction This however facts completely disprove In the last Report it was mentioned that there were seven brahmans studying in the college This year there have been no less than twelve and several others are earnestly pressing for admission Among these are three from the most respectable brahman families for rank and wealth in Serampore who felt so desirous that their sons might enjoy the advantages of the institution that they entreated the Governor of Serampore to interest himself in their behalf engaging that if they were permitted to enjoy the advantages of instruction in the college for five years they would furnish them with board and clothing themselves and put the institution to no farther expense than that of instruction and books This desire manifested by the respectable native inhabitants of the town in which those who conduct the college have resided nearly a fourth of a century and where of course their conduct and views must be so thoroughly known requires no kind of comment

CALCUTTA SCHOOL SOCIETY

The last annual examination of the more advanced boys of the Calcutta School Society was held at the house of a native gentleman in the presence of a large number of Europeans friends to the education of the natives

The examination consisted first of the boys from the indigenous schools of the Society in Bengalee secondly of its preparatory English schools and schools at Arpoolee supported by a number of the committee in English and lastly of the boys educated at the Hindoo college at the expense of the Society in English also

The indigenous schools are those under native masters in various parts of the city in which the parents of the boys pay for their education the School Society furnishing each master with instructive books, and examining the progress of his head pupils These examinations are held thrice in the year according to the proficiency made the master is rewarded with a small gratuity Of these schools there are seventy six under the patronage of the Society each under the immediate superintendence of a Bengalee gentleman residing in the neighbourhood The total number of boys under education in them exceeds 2,800 Their progress is highly gratifying

We were much gratified writes a Calcutta journalist by the examination in English both of the select boys in the Arpoolee and preparatory school and of those at the Hindoo College altogether amounting to about sixty The correctness of pronunciation and spelling and the knowledge of the meaning and grammatical construction of what they read was evident in almost all but particularly so in those of the Hindoo College whose improvement of their superior advantages was very honourable to themselves and their teachers The cordial friendship of our host and his son (Baboo Radacant Deb the native secretary of the Society) the sight of at least thirty native gentlemen of the first respectability and learning uniting with their European friends in approving and supporting the education of their countrymen the spectacle of more than two hundred pupils in general neatly and in many cases elegantly dressed (proving them to be of the middle and higher ranks of the native population) the recollection of the correct ideas as to morals and science imbibed by these and their companions—combined to give us the most pleasurable emotions Whatever may be the impressions of the Abbé Dubois it is evident to *us* that intellectual and moral as well as religious improvement is on its march in India For proof of the former we can refer to the success of this Society and of the latter to the account lately received from Ceylon by which it appears that in the schools superintended by the American Missionaries there more than one hundred pupils and two schoolmasters voluntarily and openly expressed their conviction of the superiority of the Christian Religion and their desire publicly to profess it Let the friends of native improvement but continue and enlarge their labours and with the blessing of God they must effect an important, extensive and blessed change in the face of society generally

CALCUTTA LADIES SOCIETY FOR NATIVE FEMALE EDUCATION

At a meeting of ladies friends to the education of the female natives of India held in the Church Mission Library Mirzapore the Right Hon Lady Amherst in the chair it was resolved as follows — That the education of native females is an object highly desirable and worthy the best exertions of all who wish well to the happiness and prosperity of India That the system introduced into India by Mrs Wilson has been pursued by her under the patronage of the Church Missionary Society with a degree of success which could hardly have been anticipated by those who were aware of the novelty and apparent difficulty of the undertaking and is capable of an extension and improvement only limited by the want of sufficient funds for its prosecution on a scale commensurate to its object That it appears to this meeting that there are at present twenty four schools under her superintendance attended on an average by 400 pupils That females of the most respectable caste and station in society have both sent their daughters and in some instances have themselves expressed an anxiety to obtain instruction and that the system of instruction pursued has met with the expressed concurrence and approbation of some of the most distinguished among the native gentry and religious instructors and lastly That in order to render Mrs Wilson s labours yet more effectual and to meet the feelings of the respectable natives of India by rendering the establishment more exclusively female it is expedient that the affairs and government of these schools now existing or hereafter to be established in connexion with them in Calcutta and its vicinity be placed under the superintendance and controul of a certain number of ladies as patronesses and visitors who may be inclined to give a portion of their time to this interesting and laudable object and it being understood that the Church Missionary Society are willing to relinquish the entire management and direction of their Female School in Calcutta, and its vicinity to a committee of such a description the following ladies hereby undertake that office under the designation of the Ladies Society for Native Female Education in Calcutta and its vicinity

Lady Amherst is the patroness of the institution and Mrs Heber with several other ladies of distinction are vice-patronesses

OHIO THEOLOGICAL SEMINARY

We have received the journal of the proceedings of the seventh annual convention of the Protestant Episcopal Church in the State of Ohio, held at Chillicothe last November

Bishop Chase s address to the convention is such as might be expected from the lips of that revered prelate Having alluded with pious resignation to the decease of his lamented son and other local circumstances in his diocese he passes on to the auspicious result of his late visit to this country When says he a famine of the means to sustain our church threatened us with desolation there was a blessed land to which a man of God might fly —a land in which though continually munificent to all the barrel of meal and the cruse of oil had never failed

To this land were we directed and to this land our Missionary Society resolved to send a messenger and make known our wants The circumstances which prevented the person appointed from proceeding on the mission and my own determination to supply his place are well known to you all as also the unexpected objections urged against the measure by many of our eastern brethren and the obstructions and difficulties thrown in our way But of these I will not speak further they are passed they have been happily surmounted the errors in which they were founded have been dissipated and I trust we shall no longer remember them except as chastening afflictions permitted only for our spiritual good

When a resolution is once formed evidently in accordance with the word of God and sustained by a consciousness of Divine direction it is no subject of regret that the efforts to carry it into execution are surrounded with apparent difficulties It makes us feel our dependence to be on God alone and when crowned with success it makes the glory more conspicuously His

With this simple and undisguised dependence on God was the mission to Old England undertaken and most signally has our trust in Him been crowned with success That great and generous people from whom the most of us derive our origin and who are spreading the Gospel throughout the world received your messenger with kindness heard the story of your wants with compassion investigated your plans with candour examined carefully the objections urged against you and finally determined in your favour and munificently contributed to your relief

"My powers are not equal to an enumeration of all the instances of kindness which were showered upon me; far less is it within the reach of my abilities to give a full estimate of that *fellowship* which, in the bonds of our common church, accompanied the rich gifts to our infant western Zion. Very pleasant however is the recollection thereof; their memory is embalmed in my heart, and it is a delight more than a duty thus officially to acknowledge them. Never was benevolence more disinterested; never was Christian zeal more active. Delicacy as well as generosity was the characteristic of our benefactors. The task of solicitation being assumed by the most respectable characters, the rich feasts of intellectual intercourse and Christian courteousness were every where spread before me. I deny to myself the pleasure of pronouncing, and to you that of hearing, the names of our benefactors in this address, because I cannot without offending their delicacy speak of them as my heart prompts and they deserve.

Wherever I went, one continued succession of hospitality, beneficence, and Christian communion cheered my heart and elevated my opinion of my fellow men. God is merciful unto me, thought I, in giving me grace in the eyes of this people whose God is the Lord, and whose kindness to me is the fruit of the Gospel of peace.

The amount of donations I had reason to believe before I left England nearly equalled 20,000 dollars. This may not be exclusive of expenses and specific liberalities. Among the latter are a set of plate for the holy communion already alluded to, and another set of smaller size for the use of the bishop and his successors, presented to him by a select number of his most affectionate friends.

The stereotype plates for the Common Prayer Book were nearly finished before I left London. The value of the books contributed is not exactly known; their number before I returned was about five hundred.

That interesting part of our plan through which so much good is anticipated, the design of having a printing press attached to our Seminary, met with such general and cordial approbation in England, that separate funds for it also were set on foot. And though the amount of each subscription was limited to a guinea, yet a generous anxiety to subscribe made the sum in a few weeks nearly equal to our wants.

The avails of the subscriptions in England are deposited in the hands of trustees, the Right Honourable Lords Kenyon and Gambier, the Rev. Dr. Gaskin and Henry Hoare, Esq. and are not to be drawn for but upon certain conditions, and by the proper authorities. What these are you will perceive by attending to the deed of donation dated London, 27th November 1823. By that instrument it may be seen how foreign from my mind it has ever been to create any division in our church by making our institution in any way independent of the constitutional and canonical authorities. To the superintending control of the General Convention and House of Bishops, all our institutions of this nature ought to be subject. In case there is a departure from our landmarks, the Articles and Liturgy of our primitive Zion, a controuling power must be acknowledged in those to whom God in his providence hath committed it.

We most earnestly unite our prayers with those of the bishop and episcopal clergy and laity of Ohio for the abundant blessing of God upon this important institution, in the success of which every friend of the Church of England must take a deep and permanent interest.

VIEW OF PUBLIC AFFAIRS

FOREIGN.

FRANCE.—The proceedings of the chambers on the indemnity and sacrilege bills continue to form the chief subject of French public affairs. Both measures appear likely to pass, though not without having excited warm discussions. The more liberal members of the house of peers have in vain endeavoured to moderate the ruthless character of the sacrilege bill during its progress through their chamber, by proposing hard labour for life instead of the penalty of death for the profanation of the consecrated elements, and for a limited time instead of for life for the profanation of the vessels containing them. To the disgrace however of French legislation in the nineteenth century, the bill has gone down to the lower chamber enacting the punishment of death for the profanation of the sacred elements if committed publicly, and of the vessel containing them, if committed publicly or in a public place before several persons Where one of these incidental aggravations is wanting a sneer at the pyx or chalice will cost the offender only the mitigated penalty of captivity and hard labour for life It is deplorable to see an enlightened and high minded nation thus reverting to the legislative barbarisms of the darkest ages

UNITED STATES.—Mr Adams is nominated President for the ensuing four years after a warmly contested election Great efforts were made particularly in the Western States to return General Jackson but it is perhaps for the peace of the world that this important post has been reserved for a less violent spirit

SOUTH AMERICA.—Advices received from Peru during the month detail the complete success of the liberating army over the remnant of the Spanish forces The whole of this vast continent may now be considered free and if considerable advances have already been made in the science and practice of wise and just principles of legislation, and in the promotion of arts, commerce agriculture manufactures education and the public and private welfare of mankind amidst these long and arduous struggles for liberty and political existence what may we not hope for under the blessing of Divine Providence, now that these impediments have as we hope for ever ceased The Christian, no less than the politician and the man of business, (would that the characters were more constantly united!) must feel deeply interested in the rising prospects of this new world The various nations of central and Southern America present an almost unlimited sphere for the exertions of British and North American Christians and though all difficulties are not yet surmounted in opening this extensive continent to Protestant exertion, yet, from the generally liberal nature of its public institutions, we indulge sanguine hopes that they will not long continue The decay of some of the worst features of Popery may be hoped for and it will depend in a large degree on the zeal and wisdom of pious and liberal minded Protestants, whether the blank thus left shall be filled by spiritual ignorance and infidelity or by the pure doctrines and precepts of the word of God We should scarcely know where to begin or to end if we were to undertake to enumerate all the auspicious circumstances which rise before us in reference to those new States, with the exception (temporary only, we would hope) of the Brazils In Columbia especially colleges public libraries, and the circulation of periodical publications and works of standard literature are all rapidly on the advance Every village has already a school, and the law of the land requires that after the year 1840, no person who cannot read and write shall have a voice at public elections Protestants may hold any civil office in common with Catholics In the province of Buenos Ayres during last year the legislature voted no less a grant than 21,000 dollars for public schools besides 18,480 for the support of young men at the University and various other large sums for other truly wise and valuable objects In Peru notwithstanding Catholic prejudices, and the checks interposed in the way of improvement by the war much has been done and in particular a pressing demand is being made for the sacred Scriptures the translation of which into the ancient Peruvian language now completed, will be of incalculable value to that extensive country We mention these only as individual illustrations of the general spirit and to them we cannot forbear to add the truly politic as well as Christian and humane determination to extirpate slavery and to elevate the long degraded Negro to his just rank as a man, a citizen and a brother and this not with a stinted dole of partial rights but with the fullest permission for him to rise to any office, however high in church or state, which his character and abilities may merit The temporary sacrifices, public and private which have been made in the execution of this act of justice, may well shame the tardiness of our own enlightened and Protestant nation and we cannot forbear quoting from the Report of the Columbian Minister of the Interior for 1823 a passage relative to this subject, which shews at once the inflexible integrity, and the prospective wisdom with which the plan of emancipation was conceived and is upheld

'It seems says the Minister "that, in certain provinces of the Republic an apprehension exists that by the gradual extinction of slavery the productions of the soil and the working of the mines will be diminished This is an event that may happen but it is unquestionably a minor evil to the inhabitants of those provinces compared with that of living amidst a volcano ever ready to explode with dreadful effect it is better that their agriculture and mines should suffer partial ills to which gradual remedies may be applied, than by continuing the former personal slavery insensibly to heap up combustibles for a terrible conflagration It is well known that in this particular our legislators have been animated by the most profound foresight and justice'

When nations are guided by principles

such as these we may confidently hope for the special blessing of God upon their measures and with this persuasion we hail the rising prospects of the American continent as among the brightest that await the future generations of mankind

DOMESTIC

Intelligence has been received from India, of some partial reverses sustained by a detachment of our forces in Ava, followed up, however, by a detail of subsequent successes in driving the enemy from a number of posts in the vicinity of our head-quarters at Rangoon and taking various forts on the coast of Siam. The Siamese have received our troops rather as friends than enemies. We are concerned to state that a mutinous spirit had broken out in a native regiment at Barrackpore, near Calcutta, which was not quelled but with the loss of many lives of the offenders. The disturbance arose, it is said, from discontent at the withdrawment of some customary allowances. No investigation has hitherto taken place either in parliament, or in the court of proprietors of East India stock respecting the necessity or the objects of the war, or the causes that have led to the insubordination of the troops but we trust that both points will yet be strictly inquired into.

The proceedings in parliament have been of a highly momentous and, in numerous instances of a most gratifying character. The chancellor of the exchequer's exposition of the state of the finances, exhibits a progressive increase of national prosperity. He calculates upon a surplus of revenue, to the amount of a million and a half, which is to be applied to a reduction of the imposts on hemp coffee rum British spirits and cider wines and foreign iron, with some small reductions on parts of the assessed taxes, chiefly affecting persons of the poorer classes. These repeals are calculated to increase commerce curtail smuggling and encourage good will and reciprocity among the great commonwealth of nations. The above measures have been followed up by a bill for removing many of the remaining restrictions on the commerce of the West-Indies, to the whole world, and allowing the import of corn from Canada into Great Britain, at a duty of five shillings a quarter. We are sorry that any duty should have been imposed. Various other relaxations of our prohibitory laws are about to be proposed by Mr Huskisson but we greatly fear that he means to stop short of the most important and beneficial relaxation of all namely the removal of the restrictions on our trade with India.—Mr Peel has introduced a most beneficial and popular bill for consolidating, and amending the laws (no less than eighty five in number) respecting the impannelling of juries so as to put an end to the abuses which have been long complained of in the existing practice. He strongly recommends also a general consolidation of all the statutes beginning with the criminal code. The country must feel for ages to come deeply grateful for these highly beneficial measures. The cause of humanity also has found powerful advocates in parliament as well as that of an enlightened political economy.—Mr Martin, though with a temporary failure of his object has widely inspired a determination to prevent the exercise of cruelty towards the inferior animals.—Lord Suffield has carried through the house of peers a bill to abolish the use of spring guns and Mr S Wortley, through the commons, an important amendment of our sanguinary game laws, making game a vendible article and giving every man leave to kill game on his own estate.

The state of Ireland has been undergoing a minute and highly useful investigation by committees of both houses Sir F Burdett, has carried a motion for a bill for catholic emancipation. The proposed provisions are to be discussed on the 19th of April. The bill for the suppression of illegal associations has been passed, and the Catholic Association of Dublin has in consequence closed its sittings. The Government have expressed a determination to do all in their power to repress associations calculated to produce irritation whether called by the name of Orange, or Catholic or any other denomination.

ANSWERS TO CORRESPONDENTS

R D C F P , S R A constant Reader J B C J S H—; L Y T B H F B T S J D E P Clericus Cornubiensis G B H S. B D. Truth N H , An old Correspondent A Friend to Ireland Mercator T F J R. P B and Indagator, have been received and are under consideration

Anonymous had better consult some judicious clergyman

We refer Monitor to our Preface for 1821

CHRISTIAN OBSERVER.

APRIL 1825.

RELIGIOUS COMMUNICATIONS

AN ACCOUNT OF THE PROTESTANT CHURCH IN FRANCE

(Continued from p 137.)

I HAVE mentioned the reasons which induced Sully to lead Henry IV to abandon the Reformed Church. The change was expedient in his view of politics, and he looked upon every other point as of little importance. He thought that whatever was lost to the Protestants would be gained to religion itself, which would profit by having more power set to work on its side, whether by Protestants or Catholics. This was obviously a false position, for one religious profession might not tend as much to the advancement of true religion as another, it might indeed act in direct opposition to the progress of truth, and thus become an instrument for promoting irreligion. It is so in the present times, when the influence of the Roman Catholic Church is employed in shutting out scriptural light and knowledge from mankind. Sully's calculations moreover as to the causes of the past

> The following is part of a curious letter from Queen Elizabeth to Henry IV on the occasion of his leaving the Protestant Church.
>
> Mon Dieu qu'elle cuisante douleur! très-ai-je pas ressentie au récit que Morland m'a annoncé! Où est la foi des hommes! Quel siècle est celui-ci! Est-il possible qu'un avantage mondain vous ait obligé de vous départir de la crainte de Dieu? pouvons-nous attendre une bonne issue d'une telle action? Ne pensez-vous pas que celui qui vous a conservé jusqu'ici par sa puissance, vous abandonnera maintenant? Il y a une multitude de dangers à faire du mal afin qu'il en arrive du bien. J'espère pourtant qu'un meilleur esprit vous inspirera une meilleure pensée.

disasters of France and the consequences which would arise from the change of religious profession which the king contemplated, seem to have been very doubtful even in a political view. If it was true that for twenty-six years a dreadful conflict had been maintained, the massacre of St Bartholomew and the convulsions necessarily attendant upon a great national change of religion, were sufficient to account for it. But that these dissensions would have continued, seems improbable, for Henry had now arrived at the height of his power, he had an indisputable claim to the crown, he was supported by an excellent and victorious army, his chief enemies were dead, and the religious profession of the court he might have concluded would have soon become the religious profession of the people. It has been so in all ages. Besides all this, if he had felt that he contended for the cause of truth, he might have trusted the providence of God to vindicate its own cause, and it would have prevailed in spite of the opposition of man. The affairs of Henry had prospered during the whole period he had continued faithful to his principles. He had been delivered in a very remarkable manner from many difficulties into which he had been brought by his connexion with the Protestants, and he might have rested assured that the same power which had protected him hitherto would protect him to the end. Certain it is, that after his abjuration, he had no reason to feel more confident of his personal protection. The Catholics, jealous of the liber ties which he had given to his Protestant subjects or suspicious of himself after three different attempts, effected his destruction. The arm of an assassin put a period to his existence in 1610.

After Henry had quitted the Protestants he always behaved towards them with the greatest kindness and they had no reason to complain as long as he lived. In 1598 he gave them what is called the Edict of Nantes, an edict which confirmed all the privileges they had ever enjoyed, allowed them free admission into public employments, and secured them liberty of religious worship, and power to educate their children. He also permitted them to open a church at Charenton, within two leagues of Paris where as before there was none allowed within five leagues of the capital. During the last twelve years of his reign, the Protestants with the rest of his subjects enjoyed perfect peace. The defection of the king from their cause had indeed made a great difference in their power and political importance. The nobility, in general, followed the court, and the Protestant cause seemed every day to be losing ground. In the year 1598 they had only 706 churches, the small remnant of the 2150 which twenty seven years before had flourished amongst them.

Louis the Thirteenth succeeded his father in 1610. The government, during his minority, was conducted by Mary of Medicis the queen mother. In 1616 the Cardinal de Richelieu became prime minister. One of the first objects of his policy was to abase the power of the Protestants and this he effectually accomplished. Rochelle, where their strength principally lay and which under their influence, defended itself against the king, was at length taken, and its fortifications razed to the ground. The outward defences of the Protestants were thus lost, and the popular voice was turned against them. They did indeed obtain a pardon from the king whose views were at that time directed another way but their power was circumscribed, and their movements became an object of continual jealousy. Their great defenders with the exception of two or three were gone. The abandonment of the Protestant cause by Henry the Fourth had so effectually served as an example to others that scarcely any person possessing political power stood by it. The Protestants themselves, however were numerous but they were principally amongst the middle and lower classes of society. In 1637 the number of their churches had increased to 806 and they reckoned amongst them 641 ministers including some individuals of remarkable erudition and talents. In 1634 began the celebrated controversy about the doctrines of grace of which Moses Amyraut appears to have been the originator. He, as well as many other divines did not approve of the doctrine of reprobation, as it was inculcated in the Calvinistic school and he therefore attempted in the first instance to prove that Calvin taught the doctrine of universal grace, and then he gave out a creed of his own in which he endeavoured to reconcile the general doctrines of Calvinism, with the free invitation to sinners to return to God and obtain salvation. In his opinions he was seconded by Mæstrezat, Faucher Daille, and Du bosc. Their doctrine may be justly compared to what is called moderate Calvinism in the present day. A short account of it is given by Mosheim as follows:—

"That God desires the happiness of all men and that no mortal is excluded *by any Divine decree*, from the benefits which are procured by the death sufferings and Gospel of Christ. That however, none can be made a partaker of the blessings of the Gospel, and of eternal salvation, unless he *believe* in Jesus Christ. That such indeed is the immense and universal goodness of the Divine Being, that he refuses to *none* the power of believing though he does not grant to all his assistance and succour that they may wisely improve this power to the attainment of everlasting salvation and, That in consequence of this multitudes perish through their own fault, and not from any want of goodness in God

How much farther off than it was before this interpretation places the difficulty I will leave your readers to determine and, without entering into the discussion of doctrines which on various occasions have been noticed in your work, will proceed to a statement of facts The doctrines of Amyraut were ably and vigorously assaulted by Rivets Spanheim and Desmarets who took the higher ground of absolute decrees At length it was determined in the synod at Alençon that silence should be kept on these points of doctrine No recommendation could be more wise than this but at the same time, none when the passions of the combatants were warmly engaged in the controversy was less likely to be attended to The disputation was carried on in a variety of forms till the revocation of the Edict of Nantes put aside all question of difference on these points by involving the debaters in a common ruin

The history of this remarkable and afflicting period is briefly as follows.—Louis the Fourteenth began to reign in 1642 The regency during his minority was in the hands of Anne of Austria In the contests in which the government was engaged during the minority it stood in need of the assistance of the Protestants and the bribe offered to them was that of edicts which cost little to the givers, and with which the receivers were constrained, in the absence of any surer pledge, to be satisfied From the year 1660, when the ministry of the Cardinal de Mazarin ceased the persecution of the Protestants began in a direct and alarming degree Louis the Fourteenth might, when he was young, have possessed that portion of benevolent feeling which would have led him to tolerate his Protestant subjects but as he advanced in life every thing concurred to spoil the better dispositions of his mind His was the age of the revival of arts and literature and in this revival his own talents and taste may have considerably assisted But it was also the age of corruption, of inordinate flattery of unbounded profusion and all these ministering to his selfishness, made him careless of the wants and sufferings of others The cruel and exterminating wars in which he was engaged, added to the idolizing admiration of his own subjects had so hardened his heart that it was almost relentless to any suffering of his people which did not at the same time interfere with his own popularity He was totally unlike Henry the Fourth in this respect It has been a common course with men who have sat down fatigued with the infliction of human misery, and which has turned rather to their own loss than profit that they have yielded themselves to idle superstitions, or to the direction of a confessor Thus did Louis and his confessor was a Jesuit, a bitter foe to the Protestants The king was by this man, the Pere De la Chaise led to the commission of an act which scarcely a bigot will deem praiseworthy, and which has been branded by every wise and virtuous man as one of the most wicked and impolitic measures which ever disgraced a professedly Christian and enlightened government I allude to the revocation of the Edict of Nantes by which the Reformed Church as a body, was nearly annihilated in France Every Protestant was either outlawed or compelled to renounce his religion The ministers who would not consent to abandon their faith, were sentenced to be banished, together with their people the former at one, the latter at six months notice. But when the unhappy victims endeavoured to take advantage of the permission to expatriate themselves they were stopped by the way; for their industry was found necessary to the prosperity of the nation, and they were therefore driven back again to their homes. Those who forced their escape and were afterwards taken were sent to the galleys; those who succeeded had their property confiscated; and those who remained at home were subjected to the visitation of the dragoons, by whom they were cruelly tormented, and in the end either ruined or forced to apostatize. The Protestants were forbidden by express edicts to follow any branch of the medical or legal professions, to fill any public office, or to enter into trade as silversmiths, printers, or booksellers; they could obtain no rank in the army; their marriages were annulled, their children were declared illegitimate, and their wives concubines. By this act 800,000 useful members of society were lost to France, and they carried with them branches of the arts and manufactures which were henceforth to give prosperity to other and rival countries. England and the German States, in particular, were great gainers by this fatal impolicy in the French government.

As this act was most unjust and impolitic, so it was entirely unprovoked. Since the year 1628 the Protestants had possessed no power which could be troublesome to the government. They had lost all their aristocratical supporters, and most of their landed influence, and they existed only as a large body of respectable, industrious, quiet and orderly citizens, employed chiefly in the laborious branches of the mechanical arts and in agriculture. They might be said to be the salt of that kingdom, in which superstition, profligacy, and infidelity so remarkably abounded. If the ruin of the Protestants did not bring down a curse upon the guilty government which directed it, and draw upon it a portion of those horrors to which it was afterwards subjected, their banishment unquestionably entailed upon France many obvious and positive evils. Not only did the loss of so many industrious subjects diminish the wealth and proportionably weaken the resources of that country, but the materials of disorder, which had existed for a long time among its population, being by this act of signal injustice and impolicy set in motion, finally produced the most disastrous results. If ever national crime called for national retribution surely it might be expected to follow in this instance. The massacre of St Bartholomew, and the revocation of the Edict of Nantes, as they have been among the worst acts ever perpetrated by a government calling itself Christian against a Christian and unoffending people, so they may well have brought down upon the government which directed them, the judgments which are appropriated to those who are chargeable with " the blood of the prophets and of the saints and of them that are slain upon the earth."

During the hundred years which followed the revocation of the Edict of Nantes the Protestants continued under persecution, which however varied in activity according to the circumstances of the times and the bigotry or forbearance of the different governors under whose superintendence they lived. The chief part of those who remained in France were obliged either to fly to the mountains, and carry on their worship in seclusion, or to conceal their real opinions or to apostatize from the faith. Many acts of great cruelty are recorded to have taken place, in the interval before the re-establishment of the rights of different denominations of Christians by the States General. There were some terrible executions at Toulouse; and, even in the year 1767, the parliament of Grenoble condemned a minister to death, for having preached in the open air, and burnt him in effigy. As toleration was not granted by law it was of course precarious, and depended upon the willingness of the provincial governors to evade existing statutes. At the same time the Protestants, if they were tolerated, were still outlaws; they received no public protection, could possess no property, and partook of no privileges. They had no power legally to baptize their children, to enter into the married state, or to join in public or social worship. It was not till the reign of Lewis XVI during the ministry of Malesherbes that any disposition was discovered in the government to alter the law which respected those who were called Non Catholics. In 1787 Rabaut de St Etienne was at Paris. From circumstances which occurred he was led to suppose that something might then be effected in the relaxation of the laws which had been enacted against the Protestants. He applied to the minister and received immediately a favourable answer. He was soon after invited and received in public, as a Protestant clergyman and obtained an edict favourable to the body to which he belonged. The Reformed Church being thus again acknowledged a great number of persons ranged themselves under its banners. Nearly a million of people came forward to profess their faith and to register before the local governments the baptisms and marriages which had been secretly performed. At the meeting of the States General in 1789, some Protestants were returned as representatives and a decree was passed that no one should be interrupted in his religious opinions, if the manifestation of them did not break in upon the public peace. Soon after all Non Catholics were permitted to hold civil and military employments in common with other citizens. In 1790, that portion of the confiscated property of Protestants which had remained unsold after the re____ __ _ __ in the hands of the government, was restored to the heirs of the former possessors. The government of the National Assembly, which usurped the authority in 1792 declared itself hostile alike to all ministers of every religious persuasion, who would not join with it in the desecration of the profession to which they were attached and would not assist in the establishment of Atheism, pronounce death to be an eternal sleep and partake of those diabolical acts which characterized the age of terror. It was not till the year 1802 that Christianity could be said to be publicly recognized by the Government of France. Till that time the decades took the place of the Sabbath and the altars of God lay in ruins. It was in the consulate of Bonaparte that the churches were repaired and religion publicly re established. Whatever might be the character, and whatever the political views of that remarkable man religion and especially the Reformed Church was greatly indebted to him for its revival. Reports upon this subject were, by his direction presented to the different members of the state and upon them was founded a religious establishment which, of course, gave to the Catholics a pre eminence in the state, but which afforded also to the Protestants a free worship and equal political rights. The day which brought in the re establishment of religion was hailed with joy by many faithful servants of God, who had survived the storm which for twelve or fourteen years had been desolating that wretched country. Nothing was wanting on the part of the Government to justify the expectation that it intended to fix the institutions of religion on a solid and permanent footing. The First Consul went in state to Nôtre Dame, from which the altar of Theophilanthropism had been removed the statue of Mars was taken from the temple of the invalids churches were re-opened, chapels were consecrated, the Sabbath day had its old place assigned to it, and obtained the same homage, scanty and imperfect indeed, which it now has in that country.

When Bonaparte received the address of the Protestant ministers he made them an answer which spoke a spirit of ample toleration, while it was couched in that peculiar style by which so many of his edicts and dispatches were distinguished. It will not perhaps be an uninteresting record to present to your readers.

"Je vois avec plaisir rassemblés ici les pasteurs des églises Reformées de France. Je saisis avec empressement cette occasion de leur temoigner combien j'ai toujours été satisfait de tout ce qu'on m'a rapporté de la fidélité et de la bonne conduite des pasteurs et des citoyens des différentes communions Protestantes. Je veux bien que l'on sache que mon intention et ma ferme volonté sont de maintenir la liberté des cultes. L'empire de la loi finit où commence l'empire indéfini de la conscience; la loi, ni le prince ne peuvent rien contre cette liberté. Tels sont mes principes et ceux de la nation, et si quelqu'un de ceux de ma race, devant me succeder, oubliait le serment que j'ai prêté, et que, trompé par l'inspiration d'une fausse conscience, il vînt à le violer, je le voue á l'animadversion publique, et je vous autorise à lui donner le nom de Néron."

A code of discipline for the Reformed Church was next drawn up. It is founded upon the ancient synodal acts, and partakes of what its author, M. Portalis, calls the "forme severe" of those acts. The articles of faith are not stated in it, nor is there any clear reference to the doctrines held by the ancient church, except in the appointment of ministers and professors, who are required to acknowledge what their forefathers believed. Although, under all the circumstances of the case, the government could not be expected to enter into minute distinctions of doctrine and discipline, yet the code was on the whole well framed. It is divided into fourteen parts.—As a specimen, I will select a few passages from the first portion, which is on the character and office of the ministry, and which is divided into fifty-seven heads. Those which I shall transcribe are on the *examination of candidates* and the *manner of preaching, catechising, and writing.*

"The examination of the candidate shall begin with a theme in French on certain texts which shall be given him from the Scriptures, and another in Latin, if the conference or synod shall judge it to be expedient; for each of which discourses twenty-four hours shall be allowed for preparation. If the Company are satisfied with these, they shall examine him in a chapter of the New Testament, to ascertain how far he understands and can interpret Greek; and in the Hebrew language they shall examine whether he knows enough of it to enable him at least to make use of valuable works to assist him in understanding the Scriptures. To these shall be added a trial of his knowledge of the most necessary parts of philosophy; but all in a spirit of kindness and without aiming at thorny and useless questions. Finally he shall make a short confession of his faith in Latin, and shall be examined on it by oral discussion.

"Those who shall be elected shall subscribe the confession of faith agreed upon amongst us, and also the code of ecclesiastical discipline in the churches in which they shall be elected, and in those to which they shall be sent.

'The duty of ministers is chiefly to preach the Gospel and declare the word of God to their people. They shall be exhorted to abstain from every mode of instruction which is not conducive to edification, and to conform themselves to the simplicity and general style of the Spirit of God, taking care that there shall not be any thing in their discourses which can detract from the authority of the holy Scriptures, which they shall generally follow, and from which they shall take a text which they shall explain to the best of their ability abstaining from all unnecessary amplifications, from long and irrelevant digressions, from quoting a mass of superfluous passages, and from a useless repetition of various interpretations. They shall quote the writings of the ancient doctors but sparingly, and still less profane histories and authors. They shall not treat of doctrines in a scholastic manner or with a mixture of languages: in short they shall avoid every thing which may lead to ostentation, or excite a suspicion of it.

"The churches are enjoined to make more frequent use of the catechism, and the ministers to explain it by succinct simple and familiar questions and answers, adapting themselves to the ignorance of the people, without entering upon long discussions of common place subjects. It will also be the duty of ministers to catechize every individual of their flocks once or twice a year, and to exhort every person to come carefully to the examination.

Those to whom God has given talents for writing are exhorted to do so in a modest manner, becoming the Majesty of God; consequently not to write in a light and injurious strain; which propriety and gravity they shall also maintain in their ordinary style of preaching.

When the Protestant Church was re-established in France the dominion of that country extended to far wider limits than those of the old or the present government. It included a vast population of Protestants principally of the Confession of Augsburg, and also of the Reformed Church belonging to the city of Geneva and the valleys of Piedmont. In the registry made of the ministers in the empire, it was found that there were 557 attached to the Reformed, and 481 to the Lutheran Church. They were spread over the whole empire from Brussels to the Pyrenees, and from the utmost west to Turin. During the reign of Bonaparte the Protestants received the protection and encouragement of the Government. Many of the old and dilapidated churches which had belonged to Catholics before the Revolution were given for the Reformed worship. As numbers were gathered into their communion principally from the scattered remains of those who had survived the persecutions to which the church had been subjected, new ministers were appointed and paid by the Government. The number of these both in France itself and in other parts formerly dependent upon it but now separated from it have since the year 1802, very much increased. No other change of importance has taken place in the situation or circumstances of the Reformed Church since the time of Bonaparte. The provisions which had been adopted for its support and security were included in those fundamental laws which formed what is called the Charter, and which were solemnly recognized when the Bourbons reascended the throne. This, it is to be hoped, will experience no material abridgment or violation. In the mean time, the church experiences a state of peace, and not only have its numbers been enlarged but a sounder bulwark is every day erecting for its permanence and prosperity in the character of its members. It may be hoped indeed that a church which it has pleased Providence to preserve through so many extremities of danger will still be upheld by the same Almighty power and be made a burning and a shining light to illuminate the moral darkness which surrounds it.

(*To be continued.*)

FAMILY SERMONS.—No CXCVI.

Luke xxii. 48. *But Jesus said unto him, Judas, betrayest thou the Son of man with a kiss?*

Of the miserable and wicked man whom our Lord addressed in these words, nothing is known except what is recorded in the Gospel narrative. Respecting his education, his early history, and habits of life before his call to the holy office of the Apostleship, from which he so awfully revolted, we are not informed. He is first mentioned on occasion of our Lord's choosing twelve individuals from among the multitudes which attended his ministry: the three Evangelists who give us an account of that transaction all concluding their catalogue with the name of "Judas Iscariot, who also betrayed him." Some time after this we find him endued, in common with the eleven, with the power of working miracles, and commissioned to go and preach the Gospel to "the lost sheep of the house of Israel." The next time we hear of him is on that memorable occasion when many professed disciples having forsaken our Lord, he put the question to his Apostles, "Will ye also go away?" and received from the lips of St. Peter the reply of every heart but that of Judas, "To whom shall we go? Thou hast the words of eternal life, and we believe and are sure, that thou art that Christ, the Son of the living God." In answer to which Jesus replied, "Have I not chosen you twelve, and one of you is a devil?" that is, as the term literally signifies, an accuser: alluding, says the Evangelist, to Judas who should betray him. We next hear of him when the box of precious ointment was poured upon our Saviour's head shortly before his agony. He affected to be indignant that the ointment had not been sold, and the money given to the poor: not adds the sacred historian, 'that he cared for the poor, but because he was a thief, and had the bag, and bare what was put therein.'

These brief events in this wicked man's life prepare us for the dreadful deed which blackened his closing days, and has consigned his memory to eternal infamy. We shall not dwell upon the particulars of this awful narrative. Behold him contracting with the priests and leaders of the people to betray the Innocent Blood; yet afterwards sitting at the table of his Master, listening to the prophetic declaration of his own treachery, witnessing the overwhelming grief of his fellow disciples at the dreadful thought, hearing their impassioned exclamation 'Lord, is it I?' daring even with a hypocritical hardihood himself to utter the same condemning question, and receiving from the Searcher of all hearts, the fearful reply, 'Thou hast said: what thou doest do quickly.' See him in the hour of his Master's agony in the garden at the foot of the Mount of Olives, advancing with an armed band to seize the guileless victim of his perfidy: pointing him out by the kiss of pretended friendship: then with bitterest remorse returning to his employers, casting down at their feet the base reward of his treachery; and plunging himself in despair into eternity with all his aggravated transgressions on his head! Many and awful are the reflections to which the particulars of this narrative may well give rise; but we pass them by to allude more particularly to that part of the transaction mentioned in the text; and this not for the purpose of venting our grief and indignation upon the traitor Judas, but of applying the subject to our own hearts: asking ourselves whether we too have not betrayed the Lord of life and glory by a spirit and conduct unbecoming those who profess themselves his disciples; and whether we also have not too often, like Judas, wounded him in the house of his friends; yea 'crucified him afresh, and put him to an open shame.'

There are four circumstances connected with the crime of Judas which greatly aggravate his guilt. *First*, The character of Him whom he betrayed, called in our text "The Son of Man." *Secondly*, The despicableness of the inducement for so doing. Thirdly, His neglect of the warnings he had received, and which ought to have put him on his guard against temptation; and, Fourthly, The base treachery under which he perpetrated his crime, and which is so affectingly referred to in our Lord's expostulation in the text, "Betrayest thou the Son of man *with a kiss?*" These several circumstances we shall briefly refer to, adding to the consideration of each a few applicatory remarks by way of warning to ourselves.

I. The first aggravation of the crime of Judas was the character of the sacred Personage whom he betrayed.—When our Lord, in the passage under consideration, spake of himself so emphatically as the "Son of Man," Judas could not but have recollected that remarkable conversation, in which his Divine Master had twice used this very expression with a prophetic reference to the crime of his betrayer. "The Son of man," said he, "goeth as it is written of him; but woe unto that man by whom the Son of man is betrayed." This was the title by which our Lord habitually spoke of himself; and Judas well knew its import. 'Betrayest thou Him who has ever been to thee so kind a master, so faithful a friend? Him whose whole course of life thou knowest to have been pure and blameless, full of mercy and good works? Him whom thou hast seen going about doing good, comforting the afflicted, and healing the sick; restoring sight to the blind, hearing to the deaf, and life to the dead? Him, above all, who is the promised Messiah, the Lord of life and glory, the eternal Son of God, the omnipotent Saviour of the world?' Had not Judas been fearfully hardened by the deceitfulness of sin, how deep must have been the emotions of penitence and remorse which this tender expostulation must have awakened! For his offence was committed against the greatest and best of Beings, against Him "in whom dwelt the fulness of the Godhead bodily, but who had assumed our frail and degraded nature, though without sin, from a disinterested love to mankind, that in that nature he might expiate our transgressions by the sacrifice of himself, and redeem us to God by his own most precious blood.

Let us learn, each of us, to view our transgressions in their true light, as offences against God himself. Besides any injury that may arise to ourselves or to our fellow creatures from our conduct, every evil thought, and word, and work, is a violation of the law of our Creator, whose we are, and whom it is our duty and privilege to serve. 'How shall I do this great wickedness,' said Joseph, "and sin against God?" In like manner, said David, "Against Thee, Thee only have I sinned;" not that he had not deeply injured his neighbour, but he felt that in addition to this, his crime had the greatest of all aggravations, that of being an offence against the Majesty of heaven itself. He whose laws we break, and whose threatenings we despise, is not a man like ourselves, who may be deceived by artifice, or overcome by force, or appeased by bribes; but the Most High, who is infinitely wise, and must know all our offences; infinitely just to punish them, and from whose omnipotence there is no escape. He is also our father, our benefactor, our friend; he gave his Son to die for us; he freely offers to pardon our sins through faith in this all-sufficient sacrifice; and all he asks in return is, that we should yield our hearts to him, and live to his glory. Such is the character of that gracious Being whose service we are so ready to neglect, whose cause we are so prone to betray!

II. But, secondly, the sin of Judas had the aggravation of being committed for a most despicable inducement.—It was not in a moment of terror, in order to escape the pains of martyrdom, or from some violent impulse of passion or temptation. No, it was a mere calculation of covetousness, which, for the sordid bribe of thirty pieces of silver, led him to commit the most atrocious crime which stains the annals of human history. He might doubtless indeed be incited in part by a hatred of that immaculate sanctity which was a constant reproof to his own corrupt dispositions and practices; he might dread the detection of his hypocrisy and theft; he might be stung by disappointment at finding that the kingdom which the Saviour had to offer was not, as he had probably expected, a splendid earthly dominion; and he might feel resentment on account of the prophetic declarations which our Lord had uttered of his intended perfidy; but whatever other motives might concur in stimulating his mind to this deed of wickedness, the love of money was the root of the evil. "What will ye give me," said he, "and I will deliver him unto you?" and "they covenanted with him for thirty pieces of silver."

And here again let us apply the subject to ourselves, with the heart searching question, 'Lord, is it I?' Base and despicable as was the inducement of Judas to betray his Divine Master, what are the inducements of thousands who virtually tread in his steps? Would it be credited, were it not a matter of every day experience, that men will break the most solemn commands of God, not once or twice, but all their lives through, at the impulse of the most trifling temptations? that they will risk their immortal souls for the gratification of a momentary appetite or passion? that a despicable bribe of money or pleasure or vanity outweighs in their estimation all the laws, the promises, and the threatenings of their adorable Creator? that for a fraction perhaps of Judas's gains so many who call themselves Christians will break the Sabbath of the Lord their God, by devoting it to their worldly concerns? that others will take his name in vain for a mere idle exclamation, or profane it to call down vengeance on their fellow creatures? that for the bait of worldly estimation, or to escape the sneers of the wicked, so many will sacrifice their conscience and make God their enemy? In short, so weak and corrupt is the heart of man since the fall, that there is no sin into which, but for the restraining grace of God, we may not fall, even to that of denying, as did Peter, the Master whom we profess to worship; or, like Judas, betraying him by immorality, profaneness, or unbelief.

III. A third aggravation of the crime of Judas, was his neglect of the warnings which he had received, and which ought to have put him on his guard against temptation.—The traitor did not rush suddenly and without opportunity for reflection into his dreadful career. His Master had spoken plainly to him on the subject; yet he did not avail himself of this miraculous discovery of what was passing in his heart, to own his guilt, and to pray that he might be kept from perpetrating his intended crime. So far from this, he deliberately brooded over it, till the evil dispositions which he had cherished in his heart "brought forth sin; and sin, when it was finished, brought forth death." His own conscience witnessed against him; for, as he confessed in his remorse within a few hours after, it was innocent blood which he had betrayed. Though tempted by the hopes of reward, he could not make any one discovery unfavourable to the character of his Master; and his awful end shews what opinion he had throughout entertained on the subject; for no new warning or disclosure had taken place to urge him to that desperate course; all that he knew, when he cast down the reward of his treachery and went out and hanged himself, he had known from the first, so that he was utterly without excuse. His crime was committed not ignorantly or hastily, but against knowledge and warning, and with every circumstance to increase its heinousness.

And, though by the mercy of God, we may have been preserved from gross vice and profligacy, have we not, alas! reason to confess, with deep humiliation, that our sins, whether of thought or word, or deed, have partaken of this aggravation, that they have been committed against the checks of conscience, the admonitions of God's word, and the secret strivings of his Holy Spirit in our hearts? We have not, indeed, had any particular offence foretold by an express voice from Heaven; but has not the Bible "told us all that ever we did?" Are not its warnings adapted to our case, as clearly as though they had been written for us alone? and are not its declarations respecting the sins and temptations which assail our fallen humanity a transcript of what is passing in our own hearts, and in the world around us? We cannot plead that we have not had sufficient information; we cannot complain of want of warning. Life and death are set before us; the consequences of our choice are plainly pointed out; we are invited to forsake sin and turn to God; the most merciful promises of pardon and eternal life are made to us, and the Holy Spirit is promised to give effect to our humble resolutions. How then shall we escape, if we despise so many warnings and neglect so great salvation?

IV. The last aggravation of his crime was, the treacherous manner in which it was effected. "Betrayest thou the Son of man *with a kiss?*" Must the badge of affection, the ordinary salutation of friendly intercourse in the age and country in which these words were spoken, be the signal for treachery and bloodshed? Judas had professed himself a disciple of Christ; he had been admitted as his friend and follower, to his social and domestic circle; and now, under the garb of respect and affection, he determines to betray him into the hands of his bitterest enemies. They indeed sought his life; but they pretended to no attachment. Their crime was great, unspeakably great, in "crucifying the Lord of life and glory;" but Judas added to this the guilt of broken vows and perfidious hypocrisy.

And may we not in some measure continue to apply the parallel? The atheist, the scoffer, the professed unbeliever, the notorious profligate, openly oppose the cause of Christ; they are his avowed enemies; and it is said of all such, "Thou shalt break them with a rod of iron; thou shalt dash them in pieces like a potter's vessel." But there are others who may be said to betray him; namely, those who call themselves his disciples, while they "crucify the Son of God afresh, and put him to an open shame." There are many ways in which persons may do this to a greater or less degree. They may do it by false doctrines, or by an unholy and inconsistent life. Suppose that professing to believe the Divine mission, the spotless character, and the perfect doctrines and precepts of Christ, we should deny his claim to be equal with the Father, as touching the Godhead, though inferior to him as touching his manhood; should we not, while calling ourselves his disciples, rob him of his highest honour, and, as it were, take part with those who thought it blasphemous that he made himself equal with God? Again, if acknowledging his Divinity, we virtually set aside his atonement by a proud trust in our own merits, are we not undermining the foundations of the religion we profess, and reducing the Divine Saviour to the level of a mere teacher and example instead of a sacrifice, the only sacrifice, for the sins of the world? Again, if professing to trust alone in his atonement and perhaps vaunting loudly of the efficacy of faith, we slight either in word or practice the obligations of his law, are we not betraying him under the pretence of friendship, setting his commands at variance with his promises, and virtually maintaining that his Gospel leads to that most unscriptural conclusion, " Let us sin that grace may abound?"

In short, the neglect of prayer, the allowed indulgence of evil thoughts, a worldly spirit, all false, corrupting, or uncharitable conversation, and every sinful course of life, in those who profess and call themselves Christians, are a tacit abandonment and betraying of Christ. Who indeed can say that he has been duly faithful to him? There is, however, an essential distinction between the treachery of Judas and the fall of Peter. It is to our shame that we have so often proved weak, timid, or inconsistent disciples, as in a memorable instance was the latter: but let us most of all dread lest we become final apostates, like the former; and the most effectual way to guard against this is, to watch and pray against every temptation to evil, and to beware of the first approaches to coldness or infidelity in the cause of our professed Lord.

To the Editor of the Christian Observer.

A CORRESPONDENT who signs himself *a Constant Reader*, in your Number for December last (pp. 740, 741), thinks that "a complete misapprehension exists generally with regard to the subject of which the Apostle speaks in 1 Cor. ii. 9. *Eye hath not seen*, &c. namely, in its being " commonly applied to the state of the people of God in a future world of happiness, instead of to " the glory of the Gospel revelation upon earth." As far, at least, as commentators and ministers are concerned, I conceive him to be quite mistaken as to the general existence of such a misapprehension. Whitby expressly says, " These words do not immediately respect the blessings of another world, but are spoken by the prophet (from whom the Apostle quotes them) " of the Gospel state, and the blessings then to be enjoyed by them that love God:" and the reader who shall consult Scott, Doddridge, &c. with this particular question in his mind, will, I think, perceive that they had the same view of the passage. " St. Paul," says Mr. Scott on Isa. lxiv. 4, " quotes the sense (though not the exact words) with reference to the blessings of redemption by the death of Christ." The mistake of your correspondent probably arises from his having frequently heard preachers quote or allude to the words, when speaking of the heavenly state. I myself have often done so, though aware, for at least twenty years past, of the circumstance to which our attention is now called. Nor can I see any reason for relinquishing the practice; for, though the ' immediate' reference may be, as Whitby justly observes, to "the blessings of the Gospel state," yet is it possible, in contemplating a passage which speaks generally of "the things which God hath prepared for them that love him," to *confine* our views to the present world? Surely not. No, they are blessings of which we have the earnests, indeed, here upon earth, but which reach forward into eternity, and there only are *fully* known and enjoyed: they form "a well of water" even now "within us, but " springing up into everlasting life." Even including those with which we are "blessed" on earth, they seem to be called " blessings in heavenly places" (Eph. i. 3) because that is their proper seat and home: thence they issue, thither they lead, and there only are they consummated. Great reason indeed have we to exclaim with holy ardour of gratitude, "Oh! how great is thy goodness, which thou hast laid up for them that fear thee, which thou hast wrought for them that trust in thee, *even before the sons of men*, and in this world (Psalm xxxi. 19. see Prayer book version): but I need not observe to your correspondent, that the devout contemplation of these will ever bear our minds away towards the future rather than fix them upon the present.

There is another passage to which I should be glad to draw the attention of your critical readers. The words occur 2 Cor. v. 14. Ει εις υπερ παντων απεθανεν αρα οι παντες απεθανον and they are thus rendered in the authorised translation ' If one died for all, then were all dead.' That is, previously to his dying for them and considered without respect to that event, they were all under condemnation to death. This is the view of the passage taken by Whitby, Doddridge, Macknight, and Scott. But there appear to me to be two objections to it. 1. The different rendering of *the same word* in the two clauses. " If one *died*... all *were dead*.—namely *previously* to his death. and 2. I feel considerable doubt whether απεθανον can express simply *the state of being dead*, as contradistinguished to *becoming dead*, or *the act of dying* which it seems requisite that according to the received interpretation, it should do in this place. There are indeed several passages in the New Testament in which it is rendered *is dead*, or *was dead*, but I question whether they might not all be rendered *died*, or *has* or *had died*, which would not answer the purpose in the present case. I am inclined to think, that simply the *being in a state of death* requires to be expressed by an adjective with the verb ειμι. Thus Luke xv. 24 and 32, "This my son was dead, νεκρος ην. Rom. vii. 9, χωρις νομου ἁμαρτια νεκρα. see also viii. 10. Eph. ii. 1 and 5, υμας οντας νεκρους. Ja. ii. 17. 20, and 26, πιστις νεκρα εστι. Rev. iii 1, το ονομα εχεις οτι ζης και νεκρος ει.

Keeping then to the same rendering of the verb in each clause— If one died for all, then all died.—I would suggest the following interpretation. That the death of Christ was taken and considered as the death of those on behalf of whom it was undergone: the death of the Surety was virtually, that is, as to its effects, the death of those who were represented by him; by his sufferings for them, justice was satisfied and they were freed. In short, it will express the *acceptance* of that atonement, the offering of which the adjoining clauses describe. That this is agreeable to " the analogy of faith," and the tenor of Scripture, will, I apprehend, not be denied: that it is a novel interpretation, I till very lately suspected; and I feel a repugnance to obtruding novel interpretations of Scripture; but on turning to Poole's Synopsis, I find it supported by one, if not two, of the authorities adduced by him. " Omnes mortui fuerunt [died], sub intellige *una cum ipso* says Zegerius—a name unknown to me.—and Piscator more fully ' Perinde ac si illi omnes essent mortui [had died], et moriendo pro suis peccatis satisfecissent. (See also Christian Observer for 1821, p. 409.)

In proposing this view of the passage for consideration I have no system to support: if I have prejudices they are rather in favour of the common interpretation. I only wish the true sense to be ascertained.

J. S—H.

To the Editor of the Christian Observer

THE defective preparation for the peculiar duties of the ministry in the Established Church is an evil extensively felt and frequently complained of. The subject has latterly engaged a certain degree of the public attention: and while some individuals have proposed, others have put into practice, plans for the better conduct of clerical education. Great good, it is to be hoped, will result from attempts of this nature, both as it respects the advantages immediately to be derived from them, and as they may lead to the establishment of more enlarged and publicly authorised institutions.

There is, however, a class of persons to whom such schemes and institutions, whatever excellence they may possess, can now be of no service. I allude to those who have already obtained admission into Holy Orders, and have entered upon the discharge of clerical functions. Many such persons painfully experience the defectivenes of their preparatory education. The whole circle of ministerial duties is new and strange to them, and many are placed in situations where there is no affectionate counsellor to advise, or helping hand to assist them, and they feel, in consequence, their comfort disturbed and their usefulness circumscribed by their want of knowledge and experience. Of the responsibility of their office they are deeply sensible; they are inspired with an earnest zeal conscientiously to discharge its duties, and they are not unacquainted with the *general* means to be adopted for that end. But this is not sufficient either for the comfortable or the profitable performance of their duty. They want something more *specific*, something which they may lay hold of, and immediately act upon. They would be glad to be advised respecting the best means for the attainment of sound theological knowledge, and of the best methods of executing some of their essential occupations. They are desirous of being informed *in detail* of the most profitable method of studying the sacred Scriptures, distinguishing between that reading which is practical and common to every Christian, and that which is necessary to give a *minister* a sound and extended acquaintance with the word of God. They wish also to know whether any other and what kind of theological reading would be eligible. They would be glad of *particular* information relative to the composition of sermons, and of the best means of conducting their pastoral communications with their people, as well as what portion of the week, and what times of the day, would be recommended for these several occupations.

It has struck the writer of this communication that much benefit might be conferred on the class of persons in question, as well as upon the church at large, if some faithful and experienced minister would, through the medium of your pages, convey the information required on these several topics. He might favour the inquiring party with the actual details of his own practice; and while considerable advantage could not fail of being derived from such minute information, the most scrupulous modesty would be screened under the veil of an anonymous communication.

OLBIUS.

MISCELLANEOUS

CHARACTER, OPINIONS, AND WRITINGS OF LORD BYRON.

(Continued from p. 158.)

LORD BYRON was accustomed to say of himself, that his "character required a long plumb line," and perhaps this ought to deter an ordinary writer from the attempt to fathom it. But the soundings vary in characters, as well as in channels; some parts, in both, lie nearer the surface than others, and I may still touch the ground sufficiently for useful purposes, though I should miss of finding the greatest depth.

Much has been said of the misanthropy of the noble bard; but, in the full sense of that term, it may well be questioned whether such a charge has ever been strictly applicable to any considerable number of human beings. Many individuals doubtless have existed in every age, whose opinions and lives have operated little less unfavourably for the well being of society, than if they had been really deliberate enemies of their species. But a conscious and intentional hater of his fellow creatures is assuredly, a monster of iniquity seldom seen. Deeply as mankind have fallen, (and with respect to God their fall has been low indeed,) they are not accustomed to exhibit traces of malice so diabolical as this. Conscious enmity is often directed against individuals: but not, I apprehend, often levelled at society in general.

There is, accordingly, no ground for believing that Lord Byron was a moral chimera of this description. His actual burden of guilt will be found sufficiently heavy without any needless or imaginary aggravation.

His general love of liberty, and especially his zeal in the cause of the oppressed Greeks would alone prove that so far as the interests of the present life are concerned, he was no systematic hater of mankind. Nor did he manifest any general abhorrence of society. With his few intimate acquaintance, unworthy as some of them might be, he was kind, easy and familiar. He deeply regretted the early loss of some of them, and the unexpected coolness of others. When about to take his seat in the senate, we find him bitterly lamenting the solitude of his condition. The repulsive coldness with which, as Mr Dallas informs us, he received the hearty welcome of the chancellor on his first appearance in the House of Lords, is to be attributed, not to misanthropy, but to wounded feelings and disappointed pride. When he was prompted, partly from the influence of these motives, to abandon his native land, he did not lead the life of an ascetic or an anchorite. His passions, on the contrary, plunged him into company of a certain class: the company of the dissipated and licentious, from which, by his own confession, he derived at the time no substantial enjoyment and which left behind it, as does all vicious pleasure, a drawback of weariness, vexation, and woe. As Mr Dallas remarks, he had chiefly frequented that kind of society which was calculated to inspire him with contempt for human nature. "Disgust of life, observes the same writer, "leading to scepticism and impiety prevailed in his heart, and embittered his existence. Perhaps, however, it would be more correct to consider his disgust of life not so much the cause of his scepticism as the effect of it, united to immorality of conduct: and both these concurred to render him a misanthropist in the common acceptation of the term. Ill at ease with himself, with his own reason and his own conscience, he vented his uncomfortable and irritated feelings in frequent expressions of disgust at the general spectacle of life, and complained of it as a scene of littleness, vanity, corruption and sorrow. He was too penetrating not to see the deep depravity of human nature; while his sceptical principles, by keeping out of his view the great remedy for our lost estate, only added darker shades to the picture which observation and experience had sketched out. He confessed in a letter to Mr Dallas that he "considered human nature as every where corrupt and despicable." Yet, in another place, he attempts to apologize, in some degree, for his sentiments, by assuring us that "his was not a *sneering*, but a *desponding* scepticism."

The fact seems to have been that the expression of his infidel opinions varied with the state of his animal spirits, and assumed the form of levity or sadness as this ever shifting barometer happened to be high or low. Another of his moral reflections may here be noticed. He expressed himself 'convinced that mankind did more harm to themselves than satan could do to them, and acknowledged that God arranged the best for us all.' The former member of this sentence, though probably the writer did not seriously believe in the existence of the evil spirit, contains a most im portant truth for satan could never injure us, if our own hearts were not prone to yield to temptation. The latter part may have been nothing more than a careless remark, savouring rather of deistical than of Christian optimism.

If all painful views of human nature are to be indiscriminately branded with the appellation of misanthropy, every consistent believer of the Bible not to say every thinking person, must be implicated in this odious charge. Misanthropy is a term of reproach with which the gay and thoughtless are but too forward to attack those whose observation of life is more conformable to reality than their own. But this reproach, as applied to the well informed believer, is utterly without foundation. The Christian and the cynical philosopher may indeed seem, at first view, to be setting out together in their speculations but they are soon found to part company, and to pursue very different roads. The one, in tracing the sources of human depravity, wanders without a guide the other goes directly to the true origin of the calamity. The one abandons himself to gloom, to levity, or to indifference as his humour may dictate, with little consideration of consequences the other, as he looks back to the sources, looks forward also to the awful results, of sin. The one is doomed to struggle with his distemper, devoid of help or hope the other knows of an adequate remedy, endeavours to make it his own, and earnestly recommends it to others. The one contemplates mankind with deep emotions of pity the other with indifference or contempt. The one exerts himself by all possible means to mitigate the evil the other is content to sit still, and do nothing but scoff, or murmur perhaps he even does far worse, and is mischievously industrious in aggravating the moral malady of which he so loudly complains. Which then of these two characters is open to the charge of misanthropy? he who, convinced of the common evil and the common danger, exhorts me to escape, and points me to a place of refuge or he who tells me that my state is deplorable and then leaves me without the hope of cure, or even the poor comfort of sympathy? he who dwells upon an awful and humiliating truth, in order to avert the fatal consequences of disregarding it, or he who conceals the precipice by drawing a flattering veil of self delusion before the eye? It is then the sceptical philosopher, and the careless worldling, who stand chargeable with the guilt of being enemies to their species not the sober the serious, the sympathising Christian.

The opinions and conduct of Lord Byron with regard to the female sex, form certainly one of the most revolting features of his character. Upon this subject he displayed a mixture of levity and inconsistency, not unusual among men of lax principles and dissolute habits. At one moment we find him indulging in the most contemptuous reflections upon the understandings of women —the next, perhaps, giving a loose to expressions which savour of all the homage of gallantry, falsely and absurdly so called. From an unhappy concurrence of circumstances, his early youth had been spent in comparative solitude with regard to pleasing female society. He had no quiet domestic circle no sisters, no female relatives with whom he associated. Mr Dallas informs us that "he thought lightly of family ties. He was little acquainted with those examples of modesty, simplicity, delicacy gentleness and discretion, which, amidst all the avidity for flutter and display, may still not unfrequently be found it is to be hoped in the higher walks of life. Only a few such acquaintance would have taught him more respect for the female character, though his early habits might still have been licentious. But unfortunately he derived his estimate of that character from very partial and inadequate knowledge. It was from the frivolous and the dissipated—too large a class, it must be admitted,—that he formed his opinion of the whole sex. If there were any exceptions, he seemed to think that they were to be found only in the ranks of female scholarship, mental acquirements, and literary taste. Such ladies he constantly dressed up before his imagination in *blue stocking* costume; and having thus arrayed them, he disliked them still more than he despised the thoughtless and the dissipated. In short, he looked upon women, for the most part, as mere toys and trifles; instead of regarding them as beings endued with the same faculties as men, subjects of the same moral probation, and hastening to the same issues of final happiness or misery. Meanwhile, he forgot to inspect his own side of the account, and never appears to have duly considered the reciprocal influence of the two sexes in forming that specific character, whatever it be, by which each is chiefly distinguished, in any particular age or country.

It may be remarked, in connexion with this topic, that the satirical sport of poets, novelists, and dramatists, on the vices and follies of the gentler sex, has probably done more, upon the whole, to check their improvement than to promote it. As the object of such writers has been to produce rather a strong, than a natural effect, they have usually coloured their pictures too highly. They have sometimes also, given us an individual for a species, forgetting that moral and intellectual character admits of and exhibits as many gradations and varieties as form and colour. Their careless and not very good natured merriment has been productive of mischief in two ways. It has irritated women, instead of reforming them; and it has tended to confirm the gay and dissipated of our own sex in that contempt for the other which any unhappy examples within their own knowledge might have originally led them to entertain. I am far from meaning to include all satirists under this reproach. Cowper is a splendid exception, and perhaps Young is another; but the charge applies to some names of the highest celebrity. How frequently do we find Pope diverting himself at the expense of the female character! Boileau too has an outrageous satire upon women, which, like his other satire upon human nature in general, for which he was censured by Addison, is never likely to answer one useful purpose. In fact, it is calculated to do much harm; as it is neither more nor less than a satire upon wives, and a dissuasive from marriage. It may well be doubted whether a single French lady has become a better woman, or a better wife, in consequence of this celebrated invective, though composed upwards of a century ago. All such undistinguishing severity is no less absurd than the opposite extreme of unmeasured compliment and chivalrous homage. Both are unworthy of the male sex; and both tend to the degradation of the female, though in different ways. The blandishments of the flatterer blind and corrupt the weak, and the unsparing lash of the satirist fails of reforming the wicked; while the truly modest, sensible, and virtuous portion of the female world regard both the one and the other as equally insulting and injurious.

How admirably do the doctrines and precepts of Scripture, particularly those of the New Testament, guard us against extremes upon this subject! There we do not find one of the sexes exalted at the expense of the other. In the conjugal union, indeed, it seems absolutely necessary, for preventing the conflicts and contentions of a never ceasing rivalry, that pre-eminence should be given to one of the parties; and that pre-eminence Scripture has conferred upon the man, as due to his priority of creation, and to his general superiority of corporeal and intellectual power. But his moral dignity apart from which his other advantages are worthless, must always depend on his care to keep within the well-defined circle of his duty. To each sex the Bible has allotted specific and appropriate obligations, and in the due discharge of those obligations it makes the whole honour and happiness of each to consist. It assumes that there is a moral reciprocation established between them, in consequence of which the characters of both are in a great degree formed by the example of each continually acting and reacting upon the other. Were all this properly considered we should no longer hear of " tyrant man cruelly adding contempt to injury, and proudly despising the weakness of which he is often too ready to take advantage. Did he make any account of *moral strength*, he would perceive that the charge of weakness may be retorted upon himself, and that he degrades himself to a far lower level than that upon which stands the object of his unfeeling merriment, and perhaps the victim of his arts.

There is no feature of Lord Byron's character more prominent than what has been termed, with as much propriety as point, his 'restlessness of rest.' The greater part of his waking hours was spent in a state of high excitement. Not that this excitement was necessarily unnatural and pernicious. It would prove beneficial or otherwise, as it was directed to useful and innocent, or unworthy and vicious pursuits. It was not to be expected that a genius of his order should display the calmness and composure of an ordinary mind. A still fire may impart the most lasting and comfortable warmth but the blaze, that enlivens and exhilarates, is always aspiring and in motion. We must therefore make all due allowances for that elevation of mind which was connected with the inspiration of genius strictly and properly so called. We must also, I suppose, extend the customary courtesy to one who is born a poet, of not being too severe upon him, if he occasionally manifests some impatience of the routine of ordinary life, and the number of low and little circumstances to which the present condition of human nature condemns us, and which, it seems, operate as a clog and encumbrance on his ethereal spirit. But the duties which depend on this dull uniformity of existence, as a poet might call it, cannot be disregarded with safety, even by the greatest minds. They are of imperious obligation, though they have no charms of novelty or sublimity to recommend them. Even if a dull road, they are still a straight and a sure one. Genius, not under the controul of religious discipline, may find and call it a drudgery; but enlightened piety, looking forward to the end of the journey, will account it, though not strictly upon all occasions, *a way of pleasantness*, yet always *a path of peace*.

Lord Byron, when not in a state of elation and excitement, was liable to be proportionably depressed. His fever or tension of animal spirits, left him a prey to subsequent languor and this was one, though by no means the only, cause of that mental dejection of which he sometimes complained. What he termed his indolence, probably had reference to his state of mind at these intervals for he certainly cannot be accused of either bodily or mental inactivity strictly so called. His lowness he endeavoured to dissipate by his favourite amusement of riding in which he excelled, and by shooting at a mark. A little matter, we are told, such as success in his shots, would restore him to his previous elevation. By filling him with a high degree of momentary self complacency, it banished for a short season, the sense of ennui and depression. But his constitution was impaired and, young as he was, his intervals of melancholy probably increased in duration and intensity. During his residence at Pisa, he sat up studying or writing till two or three in the morning, and roused his inventive faculty by the use of ardent spirits. These, he told Captain Medwin, were "the true Hippocrene." They certainly must have been the fount of inspiration whence some of his later compositions flowed. To suppose that his muse was a *Bacchante* when she gave a loose to those vile performances, would be the most charitable conclusion that could be formed respecting her. Good poetry has no necessary, no natural dependence on such helps. Waller never drank any thing but water, though perhaps it may be said that he is hardly an example in point. Cowper, however, we know, was lavish in praise of the tea table, and he was no flat or feeble poet. It was Pope, if I am not mistaken, who used sometimes to exalt his imagination with cups of coffee. The laureates indeed have, from time immemorial, "addicted themselves to sack," but the general character of their verses has done no honour to this beverage. The poet who requires strong or lengthened potations to stimulate his muse, may well doubt whether her most successful strains are not purchased at too dear a rate. We have no proof, however, I believe, that Lord Byron was ever addicted to inebriety: and, with respect to eating, he appears to have practised at some periods of his life, great abstemiousness.

His infidelity, or at least his scepticism, which in its operation and effects amounted to the same thing, appears to have consisted very much in a mixture of pride and levity. With an understanding naturally powerful, great miscellaneous reading, and extensive knowledge of life, he possessed admirable qualifications for the investigation and discovery of important truths, had he added to them candour, caution, and humility. But without these moral regulators, the highest endowments of intellect can no more produce a beneficial effect, than the best constructed machinery can perform its intended operations, unless it be set in motion by an impulse acting in a right direction. The machinery, indeed, may stand still, and do neither good nor harm; but the moral agent, if not usefully employed, will commonly be active in the work of mischief and destruction. A superior mind, turned to the observation of human life, is very apt, without some counterpoise of moral and religious principle, to engender infidelity; because, though many are the aspects of the living world which irrefragably confirm the representations of Scripture, yet there are unquestionably some which, when taken apart, may tend to infuse doubts into a merely speculative mind. It was a colloquial remark of the late Mr Cecil, a man of much observation and sagacity, that a Christian may see more to exercise his faith, in what he beholds between Charing Cross and Temple Bar, than in the whole space from Genesis to the Book of Revelation. A pointed remark in casual discourse should not be over nicely criticised; but his meaning evidently was, that the manifold apparent inconsistencies which present themselves on the surface of the living world, are sometimes more calculated to perplex us than any difficulties we meet with in Scripture. Every thinking person has probably experienced this in a greater or less degree. Lord Byron then, with a strong early leaning to scepticism, engendered by his very independence of mind and proud confidence in his native talent, beheld as others have done much in the scenes around him to excite his astonishment. He probably gazed on the picture sometimes with disgust at its deformity, sometimes with amusement at its variety, and sometimes with wonder at its strangeness; while every fresh observation only served to add to the force of that unfavourable impulse which had been early given to his thoughts. But why was this? Only because he took a partial and unfair survey of the world. Only because he refused to examine the contents and evidences of Scripture with due candour and attention. Whether the Bible were true, false, or doubtful, was at any rate a question of the greatest moment. Had he then been influenced by that proper seriousness which the love of truth inspires, he must have seriously applied himself to the solution of it; and, as Johnson observes of Gilbert West and Lord Lyttleton, both at one time unbelievers, " his inquiries, being honest, would have ended in conviction." That merciful Being, who has promised to " guide the meek in judgment," and to " direct the path" of those who " lean not to their own understandings," would have crowned his efforts with success. But he appears to have treated the subject of religion with habitual levity. I do not allude simply to the infidel tendency of his writings. The anecdote already mentioned, of his perusing a little treatise on the evidences of Christianity, which he acknowledged himself unable to answer, is itself a proof of his criminal indifference in this respect: for, had his mind been in a fit posture for the investigation of truth, would he not have perceived immediately that his very consciousness of inability to confute the essay, furnished, of itself alone, the strongest reason for sober and persevering inquiry?

Lord Byron had looked a good deal into the Bible, but with a merely curious, or a poetical eye. He observed of the Book of Job, that " it was the first drama in the world, perhaps the oldest poem, and that no poetry was to be compared to it." He read Scripture, therefore, rather to be amused than instructed: to see what he could glean for intellectual and literary purposes, not to examine whether it contained any thing that might throw light upon his doubts respecting the great subject of futurity. Hence it was that he found nothing in the narrative of Cain and Abel, but matter for a poem of the most profane tendency, in which the mouth of the evil spirit is studiously " filled with arguments," for the sole purpose of uttering blasphemies against God, while little or nothing occurs in the remainder of the piece to counteract the pernicious effect of this horrible representation. This surely is as unlike Milton as any thing can well be, though Lord Byron attempted to justify himself by the example of that sublime and Christian poet.

He seemed to betray at times a kind of lurking suspicion that the Bible might, after all, be true. Upon one occasion, we find him expressing a wish, " that the Reformers had retained something like Purgatory:" not considering that, as honest inquirers after truth, they could retain nothing which Scripture had not revealed. The feelings which may have prompted this wish, if indeed it were any thing beyond a careless observation, are sufficiently apparent. He could not but be conscious— indeed he confessed the fact—that much of his life had been utterly at variance with the dictates of virtue and religion. Neither could he deny the *possibility* at least of such a state of future punishment as the word of God describes. But then the doctrine of eternal condemnation appeared to him revolting in the extreme. It would have been comfortable to think that the worst to be dreaded hereafter, was a place of temporary suffering, issuing either in the purification of the soul, preparatory to its final happiness, or in a total and irrevocable dismission from existence itself, with all its joys and sorrows. Thus the dream of purgatory would have laid " a flattering unction" to his soul: and his remark upon it may seem to denote the operation of a mind generally and habitually settled in unbelief, but rendered uneasy at intervals, by a suspicion that the Gospel might be true. He should have reflected, according to the language of the powerful and eloquent Dr Barrow, that " if it be true, the unbeliever acts most absurdly; if probable, very imprudently; if only possible, not wisely.

Lord Byron is another instance of the union of unbelief and scepticism with a tincture of superstition and credulity; though in him these propensities were not nourished by fear (an emotion of which he seems hardly to have been conscious,) but were connected with certain loose notions of fatality. He had faith in omens, and entertained, it is said, some respect for a fortune teller, who informed him, when a boy, that there would be certain periods of his life, recurring within equal intervals, which would be marked with some calamitous event. If he had come into the world only a century earlier, he might perhaps have been as firm a believer in astrology, and as great a caster of nativities, as Dryden himself. Homer has an admirable line, proving how much he could rise superior to the gross superstitions of his age, where he tells us, that *the most favourable omen for our country is the union of all hearts and hands in its defence.*

Εις οιωνος αρισος, αμυνεσθαι περι πατρης.

How happy would it have been for the noble English poet, and his readers, had he improved upon this reflection of his great predecessor, and duly considered that the surest augury of happiness consists in early moral discipline, and religious self denial!

As I am on the subject of Lord Byron's infidelity, this paper may be not improperly concluded with a few remarks on his intimate friend and associate, the unhappy Shelley. Nothing could be more inconsistent than the opinions which Lord Byron expressed, at different times, respecting this author's poetry. At one moment, it was "baseness and bigotry not to admire his verses:" at another he speaks of him as one who could judge of poetry, but could not produce it. Shelley was not devoid of feeling and imagination, but they were both buried under a heap of the vilest jargon of metaphysical impiety that ever offended the taste of a critic, or the seriousness of a Christian. He is happily, however, too unintelligible to attract many readers. The very best that can be said for him, as a man, is, that he was partially insane; and assuredly the youth, who could sit down to compose a formal treatise in favour of Atheism, and then circulate his pamphlet among the bishops, and propose to discuss the question with the examining masters at Oxford, must have made, to say the least, some approaches to derangement of intellect. Not that this supposition will wholly excuse him; for he may still have retained, generally, such a power of self controul as to constitute him a responsible agent. And, even in the case of decided mental aberration, great guilt may be incurred by that original neglect of moral discipline which may have contributed to produce it; as the law renders men in some degree punishable for crimes committed during a state of intoxication. The catastrophe and obsequies of this wretched individual have about them an air of horror. It is well known that he was drowned on a pleasurable excursion, and that his body, having been recovered from the waves, was solemnly burnt by Lord Byron upon a funeral pile, in the presence of some other friends. The ceremony, as described by Captain Medwin, seems to have blended the rites of paganism in strange conjunction with the gloom of infidelity. No service was said—no dirge was sung over the departed. The professed Atheist had "died, and made no sign." Leigh Hunt lay almost fainting in a carriage. In front of the pile stood Lord Byron with a fixed but not unfeeling eye, marking the gradual consumption of the poor remains, and only breaking the solemn silence by a low muttered remark, seeming to proceed from the idea that both body and spirit were alike reduced to nothingness. Altogether it was a scene of sadness, apparently unrelieved by the feeblest ray of hope or consolation: a scene worthy of the muse of a Byron, or the pencil of a Fuseli.

(*To be continued.*)

To the Editor of the Christian Observer.

I HAVE just been reading with renewed pleasure Mr. Hodgson's two interesting volumes of "Letters from North America," the substance of which first appeared in your pages. These volumes are represented by American writers generally as containing the most candid and impartial view of the state of society and manners in the United States which has yet appeared. They are therefore highly deserving of public attention. I have been particularly impressed with his truly graphic sketches of slavery; the misery and impolicy, as well as the iniquity, of which he has most ably delineated. There is also a candour in his remarks on this afflicting subject, which gives the greater force to his statements. Warm and honourable as is his zeal in the cause of humanity and freedom, he is ever willing to give full prominence to whatever mitigation he can discover in the abhorrent system which he condemns; and to arrive at as hopeful a conclusion as possible amidst the most unpromising premises. It is, however, the singular fatality of the slave system, that nothing can be uttered either by hope or charity as the slightest fraction of compensation, but what, when re-considered, assumes other aspects so distressing and gloomy that the mind refuses to indulge the pleasure resulting from the alleged partial mitigation in the overwhelming painfulness of positive and present misery. Mr. Hodgson will allow me to adduce the following illustration. Speaking of the practice of letting out slaves on hire, or sending them out to find employment where they can, the master expecting a certain proportion of their gains, or exacting a fixed sum per week, and allowing them the remainder if any, Mr. Hodgson remarks, that 'the system of allowing the slaves to select their own work, and to look out for employment for themselves, *notwithstanding the frequent hardship attending it,* is a great step towards emancipation, and an admirable preparative for it: and may we not regard it as one of the avenues through which the African will ultimately emerge from his degraded condition?' 'Surely, continues he, "the warmest advocates of perpetual slavery, (if there be any, which I greatly doubt,) will not contend that a man who is capable of taking care of his family while compelled to pay his owner a premium for permission to do so, will become less competent to manage his concerns when exonerated from the tax, or that he will relax in his efforts to improve his condition, because a stranger no longer divides with him the fruit of his toil. The truth of this inference is undeniable: and the mind is for a moment almost inclined to indulge some charity towards a system which is to produce such happy results; a system which teaches the slave those habits of diligence and forethought which it is the almost inevitable effect of his servile and dependent condition to eradicate, and which, while it thus prepares him for emancipation, has the superadded merit of stopping the mouths of those who would deny his competency to make his labour when untaxed as valuable to himself as when subjected to a heavy impost. But miserable are even the compensations and mitigations of slavery. The natural way in which the system of letting out slaves may eventually issue in their freedom, is by accustoming them to feel their strength and self-dependence, which may, sooner or later, lead them to achieve their independence, amidst those horrors which Mr. Hodgson so feelingly deprecates, and which he wisely exhorts the masters to prevent by a timely emancipation beneficial to both parties. But in the mean while how dreadful is such a system to the poor slaves! Mr Hodgson even in taking the most hopeful view of the case, tells us that 'frequent hardships attend it, that 'in the Charleston and Savannah jails, *besides numerous pirates*, there were many *slaves* in confinement for not giving their masters the wages they had earned.' But what proof is there that (in *every* case at least) they *had* earned these wages? The most diligent labourer may sometimes fail of meeting with work, and it is painful enough for him to lie down at night faint and famishing, without the misfortune of having to make up to an inexorable master a sum which he has not had it in his power to earn.* Mr Hodgson incidentally throws some light on the practical working of this system when he says "You will be surprised to learn that children who are thus situated generally prefer chimney sweeping, as they can earn more by this than by any other employment." I confess that I see nothing "surprising" in this selection. The child no doubt knows full well the miseries of chimney sweeping, but finding that it best enables him to meet the exactions of his employer, and preferring on the whole the lacerations and suffocation of this toilsome and unhealthy employment to the angry lash of his owner, or the severe inflictions of 'the Charleston and Savannah jails,'

he adopts it as the less painful alternative. I will not waste a single line in arguing on the manifest cruelty and the injustice of this system, but will present to your readers, without note or comment, a passage from "Lieut Shillibeer's Voyage to Pitcairn's Island, including a Sketch of the present State [anno 1817] of the Brazils and Spanish South America." I by no means wish to adduce what I hope is a rare example as a general specimen, but the incident shews at least what hardship may arise from the system in the hands of an unrighteous master, and adds one proof more to the innumerable ones already on record of the manifold atrocities of slavery. Speaking of Rio de Janeiro, he relates the following affecting incident.

"A man possessing a few slaves may be considered of good property, particularly if he bought them when young and has brought them up to trades. With a man of this kind I am acquainted who is as barbarous and remorseless a wretch as can be conceived. He has several slaves and, as they have all been taught some trade or other, he sends them forth to earn, according to their occupations, certain sums, and their food, which must be completed under a penalty (which is seldom remitted, even to the most industrious or lucky,) of a severe flogging. One of them was a barber, and for a considerable period shaved me every morning he was a quiet man, and of great industry and, as far as came under my observation, always on the alert for his master's interest. For several days I observed he bore a gloomy and melancholy appearance I asked him the reason, and was informed he had been unsuccessful, and could not render to his master the sum required that he had little hopes of being able to raise it, and as little doubt of being punished. I gave him something towards it. When he came again, he informed me, that out of thirteen or fourteen, he alone had escaped the lash but, if

---

* A very respectable and humane West India slave proprietor lately observed to the writer of these remarks. 'The slaves are very happy and some of them earn and lay by considerable sums. A slave of mine a cooper made a great deal for persons were always glad to get him for their jobs because free workmen expected regular wages which are very high whereas they could give this man just what they pleased often a mere trifle and if he was not satisfied *they had only to give him a box on the ear and send him about his business*.' If the Savannah and Charleston slaves are paid in the same manner no wonder they are often in confinement for not giving their master the wages they had earned [query received?] not including I suppose a moiety of the gratuitous cuffs. And this is being very happy!

he did not make up the deficiency, his would be of greater severity than had been inflicted on his companions. As the time approached when he must render to his master an account, he became greatly distressed, and despaired of accomplishing his promise. He went with tears in his eyes, tendered what he had gained, and assured him of having used every means to raise the specific sum, and implored a remission of punishment, or a suspension until the following Monday, which at length was granted him; but not without threats of many additional stripes in case of failure. The time fast approached, when he must return. He was still deficient. He reached the door of his master's house, when, in despair of being forgiven, and dreading the ordeal he had to undergo, he took from his pocket a razor, and with a desperate hand nearly severed his head from his body. I saw him several days after, lying in this mangled state near the place where he had perpetrated the act. This horrid deed had no other effect on the master, than to increase his severity towards the others, on whom he imposed heavier burdens, to recompense him for the loss he had so recently sustained. — *Shillibeer's Voyage to Pitcairn's Island*, pp 16—18.

There is another passing remark of Mr Hodgson's, to which, for the sake of the great cause which he has so ably advocated, I beg leave to add two partially counter statements. He says (vol i p 310,) " The Black children, when very young seem to mix almost indiscriminately with the White children, who however occasionally demonstrate their acknowledged superiority, *though less frequently than I should have expected*, at least as far as fell under my observation." What Mr Hodgson " expected," may easily be supposed; for history and philosophy alike shew that nothing more certainly, or more early in life, ruins the character of a human being than the unchecked power of domineering; and it is among the worst evils of slavery in all ages and countries, that it generates almost from infancy in the privileged classes those unjust despotic, and often positively cruel dispositions and habits which are a curse alike to the individual, to the community, and to the unhappy victim of his unbridled caprices. It seems, however, that Mr Hodgson's experience did not go to the full length of his philosophy on this subject; but then he intimates that his opportunities of forming a judgment were but partial; for he adds, " at least as far as fell under my observation," and, at all events, he saw and heard enough to convince him that the White children do " occasionally demonstrate their acknowledged superiority." It would be, so far as it extends, a mitigation of the evils of the system of slavery, if its direful effects either on the dominant or the oppressed party were postponed to the meridian of life; but I am persuaded that Mr Hodgson did not intend to convey any such impression. Long before manhood, the habit either of enduring or inflicting wrong, must have stamped a corresponding and most baneful impress upon the character. To grow up under the system must almost inevitably be to become the victim of its injurious influence. If an authority of great weight, and on the very spot where Mr Hodgson wrote this observation, be necessary to decide the point, I may refer to that shrewd and philosophical observer Mr Jefferson, whom, in the next leaf to that in which the observation occurs, we find Mr Hodgson visiting. He speaks in the highest possible terms of the powerful conversation of that statesman, from whom he elicited much valuable and interesting information. Had he chanced to put to him the question, what effect has the system of slave holding on the character of the younger and ultimately on the adult part of the community, the answer would have been decisive. Indeed, it happens that I can supply Mr Jefferson's answer, in his own words for, in his Notes on Virginia, I find him thus strongly expressing himself:—

"There must doubtless be an unhappy influence on the manners of the people, produced by the existence of slavery among us. The whole commerce between master and slave is a perpetual exercise of the most boisterous passions the most unremitting despotism on the one part and degrading submissions on the other. *Our children learn this and imitate it* for man is an imitative animal. *The parent storms the child looks on, catches the lineaments of wrath, puts on the same airs in the circle of smaller slaves, gives loose to the worst of passions and, thus nursed, educated, and daily exercised in tyranny, cannot but be stamped by it with odious peculiarities.*"—Jefferson's Notes on Virginia, pp 270, 271, London edition

Such is the opinion of this North American statesman to which I beg leave to add the following observations from Stewart's 'Present State of the West Indies'

"Wherever slavery exists there must be many things attending it unfavourable to the improvement of the minds and manners of a people arbitrary habits are acquired, irritation and violent passions are engendered—partly, indeed, by the perverseness of the slaves,—and the feelings are gradually blunted by the constant exercise of a too unrestrained power, and the scenes to which it is continually giving birth. *The very children, in some families, are so used to see or hear the Negro servants whipped for the offences they commit that it becomes a sort of amusement to them.* It unfortunately happens that the females as well as the males, are too apt to contract domineering and harsh ideas with respect to their slaves—ideas ill suited to the native softness and humanity of the female heart.—so that the severe and arbitrary mistress will not unfrequently be combined with the affectionate wife, the tender mother and agreeable companion,—such is the effect of early habits and accustomed prejudices, suffering qualities so anomalous to exist in the same breast. A young lady, while yet a child, has a little Negress of her own age pointed out to her as one destined to be her future waiting maid *her infant mind cannot conceive the harm of a little vexatious tyranny over this sable being who is her property and thus are arbitrary ideas gradually engrafted in her nature.* Such is the power of habit over the heart, that the woman accustomed to the exercise of severity soon loses all the natural softness of her sex. Nothing was more common formerly than for White mistresses not only to order their slaves to be punished, but personally to see that the punishment was duly inflicted.

In truth looking at slavery in what aspect we may, it is one entire system of pure and uncompensated evil. I am glad to hear from Mr Hodgson, that it has no "warm advocates" would that it had no practical upholders! and would that all who profess to believe its enormities would heart and hand, unite for its extinction!

A B C

To the Editor of the Christian Observer

I AM a layman of the Church of England resident for the most part in the country, and have been accustomed to great disappointment in the character of the music used in many of our churches, as well as in the selection of the words appropriated to the tunes. The venerable Society for promoting Christian Knowledge, with a view, I presume to remedy the latter defect circulates a selection of stanzas from the new version of the Psalms and I beg to suggest for consideration the propriety of adding to its list of books, a corresponding selection of our best church tunes. Such a selection would be of great utility in promoting a solemn and edifying discharge of this much neglected part of public worship, especially in country congregations, and being afforded at a cheap price, would also probably be in extensive demand in National and Sunday schools, and in private families.

A READER.

To the Editor of the Christian Observer.

YOUR correspondent P. M. M. in your Number for January objects to the use of voluntaries upon the organ at the conclusion of the church service. I would ask, however, is not this the least exceptionable mode of dismissing a congregation, with a view to counteract the noise and confusion *unavoidably* attendant upon the dispersing of a large assembly? and may it not operate as a means of *silencing* those unseemly whispers so justly complained of by your correspondent? In some churches the difficulty is attempted to be obviated by a method which appears highly exceptionable, namely by ordering a Psalm to be sung while the congregation are dispersing. By this mode of proceeding, persons are obliged either to remain in church against their inclinations, after the service is concluded, or to shew disrespect and be guilty of irreverence by departing while others are employed in singing the praises of God.

As a matter of personal feeling, my experience differs entirely from that of your correspondent. I conceive that the solemn tones of the organ, introduced at that particular moment, so far from disturbing the thoughts or unfitting the mind for the continuance of devout speculations, rather assist it in the attainment of that desirable object, and elevate still more the pious affections which may have been raised by the preceding service. Much doubtless will depend on the skill and judgment of the performer, and the selection of pieces; but these ought always to be under proper regulations.

With regard to the introduction of a voluntary after the sermon when the sacrament of the Lord's Supper is to be administered, it should doubtless be dispensed with, if it should prove to be in reality a source of disturbance to those who remain for the purpose of communicating. This however, I conceive needs not be the case; or at all events, there will not arise from this quarter a greater interruption than would necessarily take place if there were no voluntary. It must also be remembered, that to the larger part of the congregation the service is then actually concluded; since, even in these days of increased attendance at the table of the Lord, it is to be feared that those who remain for the purpose of performing that sacred duty will still be found a minority in the congregation.

P. S. O.

REVIEW OF NEW PUBLICATIONS.

The Crisis; or an Attempt to shew from Prophecy, illustrated by the Signs of the Times, the Prospects and Duties of the Church of Christ at the present Period; with an Inquiry into the probable Destiny of England during the predicted Desolations of the Papal Kingdoms. By the Rev. E. COOPER, Rector of Hamstall Ridware and Yoxall. 7s. London. 1825.

WE began our critical intercourse with Mr. Cooper in the very first year of our literary existence, when his eldest born production, (his Visitation Sermon preached at Walsall,) so deservedly attracted public attention, and prepared the way for his subsequent and successful appeals to the patronage of the Christian world. On the present occasion he has discovered what many will term a spirit of adventure and almost daring enterprize. He has opened and worked a new vein in the dark and mysterious depths of prophecy: and whatever be his ultimate success, or whatever the value of the ore brought by his industry, to the surface, for the analysis of our chemical divines, his efforts merit much gratitude: neither can they fail to be beneficial, as in their *practical* bearings at least, they are directed to the advancement of man's everlasting interests. So that even if his leading theory be found on examination, like most of those which have preceded it, to be untenable, no question will arise as to the utility of the cautions thence induced, which will be duly estimated by every one who reads the volume with seriousness. Its monitory portion is indeed the application of the writer's long text; but it is one of those addresses to the present generation of mankind, which may be studied to high advantage, though entirely separated from the context, and, independently of any interpretation of prophecy, either fanciful or indisputable, it is calculated to administer alarm, conviction, persuasion, and consolation as the spiritual exigencies of its various readers may demand.

The present work, as we understand from the preface, was not despatched to the press before it had received the virtual *imprimatur* of some competent judges, who admitting that Mr Cooper had made out a strong case, recommended the publication, and, as we should farther infer, were anxious not to deprive the religious community of a solemn warning distinctly addressed to themselves. The suffrage of Mr Cooper's private critics is altogether in his favour. The value of *their* opinion is obvious. A new hypothesis on the prophecies, while it dazzles a novice, brings the student to a pause. With the first of these, it has the glare of a vision: with the other, a vision's indistinctness and unreality. In the instance immediately before us, it is however, so far accredited by those who have already examined it, as that they deem it deserving of the patient investigation of the student of *prophecy*.

No mention is made in Mr Cooper's title page, of one leading object of his inquiry,—the identity of the king ' who should do according to his will,' (Daniel xi. 36,) with none other personage than the late Napoleon Bonaparte! We anticipate the surprize of the generality of readers at this unexpected illustration of prophecy; and as it must necessarily communicate to them a startling sensation, it may in an equal degree, awaken their curiosity,—using that term, not in its idle vulgarity of meaning, but as indicating a spirit of serious investigation on a point of highly momentous import: and certainly if we could believe the writer's reasonings to be just and well founded, the results drawn from them would tend to impress a deeper sense of the responsibilities and awful aspect of the times, and would seem to connect them more closely with our eternal apprehensions and hopes. Mr Cooper writes:

It is well known to the student of prophecy, that both Daniel and St John agree in predicting a remarkable period in which, during the space of 1260 years, the church of Christ, throughout the western part of the Roman Empire under its last divided form, would be oppressed, corrupted, and persecuted by the civil and ecclesiastical powers, bearing the name of Christ and professing to act by his authority. It is no less clear that the same inspired writers unite in predicting a second period, which shall commence at the expiration of the former, and in the course of which these tyrannical powers, after being wasted by a series of desolating judgments, shall at length be utterly broken, and the church being by degrees emancipated from bondage shall make a rapid advance to millenial glory——— Daniel tells us by implication that the period in question will occupy a space of seventy five years for blessed is he that waiteth, and cometh to the thousand three hundred and five and thirty days (Daniel xii 12) This period thus defined the prophet farther calls *the time of the end* a name descriptive of the nature of those events by which it will be distinguished for it is within this period that God will gradually put an end to the triumphs of his enemies to the sufferings of his church and to the dispersion of the Jews —The writer fully concurs in sentiment with those who date the beginning of this period that is the *first* of 1260 years from the year A D 533 when the Emperor Justinian by his memorable edict, formally delivered the saints into the hands of the little (papal) horn and who consequently following the usual mode of scriptural interpretation (by incomplete and current time and not by time complete and past,) assign the termination of the period in question—an event which synchronises with the sounding of the seventh trumpet in the Revelation of St John—to the year 1792 The arguments in favour of this interpretation adduced by Mr Cuninghame appear to the writer conclusive on the subject It is with this interpretation that the views exhibited in the following pages are intimately connected, and should they be established they will place it beyond dispute pp 1—3, and xiv xv

On the assumption, therefore, of the accuracy of these dates, a point on which we do not pretend to decide, Mr Cooper places the chronological corner stone of his interpretation And *if* the year 1792 was indeed the close of the great prophetic period, and *if* the " wilful king" was really then to commence his mighty career, the most sceptical and severe student of prophecy would of course pause, before he ventured to pronounce the author's hypothesis visionary It is no part of our plan to revive the controversies involved in these preliminaries of Mr Cooper's performance We shall proceed directly to state, that, in his view, the eleventh chapter of Daniel, from the thirty sixth to the forty fifth verses inclusive, is a prediction of the character, exploits and end of Napoleon For the illustration of this opinion the reader must be referred to the work itself What may be the effect on his mind of a careful examination of the validity of the author's argument, we know not For our own parts however plausible may be his elucidation of the verses under his consideration we cannot regard it as altogether satisfactory We do not deny, indeed, that, darkly as the character of Bonaparte has been painted in the progress of Mr Cooper's parallelisms, the shades might have been even deepened without exposing the artist to any charge of exaggeration or malignity The character of the late Emperor of France may be contemplated under two aspects Individually he deserves to be a forgotten man But, as a being, if not actually brought within the awful sphere of prophecy, yet certainly acting as a scourge in the hand of God, to punish a guilty world and, as such, occupying a distinguished station among the executioners of the Divine wrath he may already be too much forgotten He fixed and retained the attention, and kept alive the fears, of the world for the long space of more than twenty years and almost every year a season of bloodshed and despondency He was the king maker of Christendom and it is not always now recollected, that four monarchies of this adventurer's own founding yet remain, and are recognised among the legitimate thrones of Europe ! We mean those of Saxony, Bavaria, and Wirtemburg, (the princes of which were elevated, by his arrangements, from the inferior rank of electors,) and the new dynasty which holds the sceptre of Sweden In the fulness of his power, Napoleon married the near relation of the consort of Louis XVI and, like her a descendant of the Cæsars and he allied his family to other royal houses of Europe Neither did he seem to confine his ambition to be the *Emperor* of the West but as many sagacious observers believed, he aspired to be also the western *prophet* Being all this, and more than this, he was doubtless a king who for a time at least was permitted " to do according to his will!" "The Revolution, says Mr Southey, "had given the government absolute command over the whole physical force of France and this prodigious power was at the disposal of an individual unchecked by any restraint, and subject to no responsibility Perhaps it would not have been possible to have selected, among the whole human race any other man to whom it would have been so dangerous to commit this awful charge Napoleon Bonaparte possessed all the qualities which are required to form a perfect tyrant His military genius was of the highest order his talents were of the most imposing kind his ambition was insatiable his heart impenetrable he was without honour, without veracity, without conscience looking for no world beyond the present and determined to make this world his own at whatever cost He regarded his fellow creatures merely as instruments for gratifying his lust of empire,—pieces with which he played the game of war in the presumptuousness of his power he set man at defiance and in his philosophy God was left out of the account * These reminiscences of this extraordinary man tend, we admit, rather to confirm Mr Cooper s estimate of the external splendour of his name, exploits, and pretensions He certainly gathered around him, in his day, the applause or the dread of a vast portion of the inhabitants of the earth Little minds vainly endeavoured to sustain against him feelings of contempt their efforts of this kind, in despite of themselves, were perpetually absorbed into fear At the same time, wise men, while they detected the inherent vileness of his character, were also awed by its power, which, in a human sense, was irresistible, devising and executing his mighty projects with an almost superhuman energy But his own forced pleasantry, when a fugitive from the climate and armies of Russia "From the sublime to the ridiculous there is but a step, was marvellously realized in his deposition and deportation The god was rapidly changed into the worm The Exile of St Helena, (such was he called in the sentimental phraseology of his adherents,) sank almost to a deeper degradation than would have been prepared for him by his bitterest enemies His last days were sadly

* See Southey s History of the Peninsular War pp 15—18 In a subsequent passage Mr Southey referring to the Jewish Sanhedrim held at Paris in 1807 writes — When in their hall of meeting they placed the Imperial Eagle over the Ark of the Covenant, and blended the cyphers of Napoleon and Josephine with the unutterable name of God impious as this was it was only French flattery in Jewish costume But when they applied to him the prophecies of Isaiah and Daniel when they called him the Lord s anointed Cyrus — the living image of the Divinity — the only mortal according to God s own heart to whom he has entrusted the fate of nations, because he alone could govern them with wisdom these things resembled the abominable language of his bishops and of his own proclamations too much to escape notice And when they reminded him that he had subdued the ancient land of the eternal pyramids the land wherein their ancestors had been held in bondage that he had appeared on the banks of the once sacred Jordan and fought in the valley of Sichem in the plains of Palestine such language seemed to indicate a project for resettling them in the Holy Land, as connected with his views concerning Egypt Nay as he had successively imitated Hannibal and Alexander and Charlemagne just as the chance of circumstances reminded him of each was it improbable that Mohammed might be the next object of his imitation? that he might breathe in incense till he fancied himself divine that adulation and success and vanity utterly unchecked as they were having destroyed all moral feeling and all conscience should affect his intellect next and that from being the Cyrus of the Lord he would take the hint which his own clergy had given him and proclaim himself the temporal Messiah? Nothing was too impious for this man nothing too frantic —and alas! such was the degradation of Europe and of the world England alone excepted that scarcely any thing seemed to be impracticable for him pp 63 64

disgraced, and chiefly by the indulgence of a certain sordid querulousness on matters of mere personal inconvenience. He became the politician of the kitchen, the cellar, the bath, the larder, and the laundry; so that, instead of performing the last act of the drama in the costume and attitudes of philosophy or of heroism, he expired all but a driveller and a shew. "He came to his end, and there was none to help him!"

Mr Cooper is quite aware of some of the objections which may be raised against his theory, and he has attempted to anticipate and rebut them. But, leaving this portion of the work in our rear, we march forward to the results from Mr Cooper's interpretation. He writes,—

As the 1260 years expired in the year 1792, so the 1290 years (a period prolonged from the former by the intervention of Bonaparte's career) were concluded in the year 1822, and consequently *this* was the precise year which the angel predicted Michael then stood up (Daniel xii. 1.) for the children of the Jews. And how remarkably does this hypothesis accord with the statement already given! It was in the year 1821 that Napoleon came to his end, in the year *immediately* preceding that in which the 1290 years terminated. pp. 78, 79.

It is then argued, that two events took place in 1822—namely the proceedings of the congress at Verona, and the matured state of the Greek insurrection—which may be severally instrumental in effecting great changes in relation to the papal kingdoms, and also to the restoration of the Jews. A second result refers to what the angel says (Daniel xii. 1.) respecting the then coming days of unprecedented trouble. On this subject Mr Cooper speaks a language which, whatever may be its prophetic accuracy, will seem to many much more gloomy than is warranted by the political appearances of the current period. He remarks—

There is indeed at present an apparent calm upon the face of the earth but it is only a deceitful calm, the earnest and precursor of the more dreadful storm. The peace which seems to reign is merely superficial. Beneath the surface the most hostile feelings are at work, the most hostile preparations are at hand. Never were there so many disposing causes to confusion. This is not the language of conjecture and exaggeration. Those persons who possess the most efficient means and opportunities of ascertaining the real political state of Europe know that the view here given of it is correct. The parliamentary declarations of senators and even of statesmen are continually confirming this representation. Nay, every attentive observer must be aware that the three great principles of Infidelity, Despotism, and Popery, those three unclean spirits which, about this time, like frogs coming out of the mouth of the dragon, the beast, and the false prophet, are to go forth unto the kings of the earth and of the whole world, to gather them to the battle of that great day of God Almighty, are now busily at work throughout the papal kingdoms and preparing the materials for some prodigious explosion. pp. 91, 92.

These are certainly strong uncompromising assertions, and they shew at least the unhesitating confidence of our author in his own views of prophecy; but, except in a single point, we cannot see that his delineation would not have been more strictly and strikingly applicable to the first years of the French Revolution than to the present day. The single point to which we allude is the difference between the depressed state of the Roman Catholic Church at the former period, and its recent restoration to power and influence. At the close of something like a profound and lengthened repose, the Roman Catholic system appears now to be rising 'as a giant refreshed with wine.' One cause of this renovation of its energies may be found in the correspondent spirit of exertion, which of late years has developed itself in the rival communion of the Protestant Church. As long as the two grand opposing divisions of Christianity, though in different degrees slumbered and slept, the pontiff and his cardinals with their prelates *in partibus infidelium*, were content to perform the ancient routine of rite and ceremony, unobserved and unmolested. For, as their yet surviving sagacity taught them, Protestantism was troublesome only when it ceased to be formal. The Reformed congregations of the continent, with some exceptions, had become either too unimportant or too quiescent, to attract more than, now and then, an idle and transient expression of dislike. The religion of England was locally too distant to be seen, and it was also confined within our own island. But the recent invasion of the continent by British zeal, and especially the rapid and widely diffused effects of the Bible Society summoned to arms as with the shrillest clarions of alarm the entire soldiery of the kingdom of Antichrist; and we once more repeat, in this place, our conviction, that the present war raging from the head quarters of Mohammedanism itself to the western division of the British empire, and to aid which too many professed Protestants have joined the unholy alliance, is practically, a gathering together of the nations against the Bible. This indeed is its one distinct, avowed determinate object. It is not an expedition fitted out at Constantinople or Rome, or at some subordinate arsenal and port of the Antichristian empire against any specific fortress of the Reformation, but the point of attack is THE BOOK which, according to its various enemies, contains the elements of universal mischief. As once at Ramoth Gilead the king of Syria commanded the captains of the chariots, saying, Fight ye not with small or great, save only with the king of Israel; so in the present thickening conflict, the instructions delivered to the commanders and subalterns of the forces in array against us, when divested of the formalities of office, are — Oppose not specifically the consistories of the Lutheran Church, the hierarchy of England, the General Assembly of Scotland, or even the conventicles of Independency, Methodism, Unitarianism, or Antinomianism, but *fight only* with the volume containing the professed foundation of these multiform heresies, lest this charter of evil should be yet farther disseminated, and ultimately shake the authority of the conclave and the divan, refute the infallibilities of the koran and the missal, and involve in one common ruin the holy places of St Peter and St Sophia.

Without, however, meaning to identify the interests of the Roman and Mohammedan communions, and of the other parties hostile to the Bible, we speak the sentiments of every *true* Protestant, in asserting that the court of the Vatican feels the utter impossibility of suffering its divinity and modes of worship, to establish their claims by a reference to the holy Scriptures; and therefore between an unreserved study of the Bible and the Catholic population, a great gulph must be fixed. It is a matter admitting no compromise; the separation must be complete and absolute. Let no one stigmatize our periods as positive, or as intemperate, till he has read, among other documents, the circular letter of Pope Leo XII to the patriarchs, primates, archbishops, and bishops of the Roman Catholic Church, the bull of jubilee for the year 1825, and the annual pastoral charge of the Irish Roman Catholic prelates. Extracts from the last appear in our Number for January, p. 62. A translation of the two former, with notes, was recently published by Messrs Butterworth. Parts of these documents are inserted in Mr Cooper's volume, as justifying the solemnity of his appeals to the original principles of Protestant readers. For the conclusion to which *he* comes is, that the spirit of Popery survives at this moment as it existed in the pontificate of Leo X, and that its superiors have never recanted any single dogma established by the decrees of the Council of Trent. We admit that whoever has seen with his own eyes and heard with his own ears the visible and audible mysteries of the Latin Church as they are *now* practised in St Peter's and the favourite basilicas of the 'eternal city,' or in Naples, Madrid, Vienna, and the principal cities under papal influence, must be convinced that, even were its creed, or doctrinal system, pure as the aspirations of a seraph, still the actual ritual of their worship must, to a Scriptural Protestant, appear to be a continual insult to the common sense of mankind. Were indeed this all, one plea might perhaps be urged in its favour, that the delusion and corruption of the heart are not necessarily combined with the errors of the understanding. But Popery levels its devices at *the heart*, and, through the affections, degrades and enslaves the judgment. The Roman Catholic religion is indeed sometimes called a corruption of Christianity, and at others, Paganism in a Christian guise; but whatever its designation may be, it is, in naked reality, the religion or irreligion of the world fighting against the genuine Gospel of Jesus Christ. It is so constructed as to be found an opiate for the guilty conscience; the refuge of man, obscurely conscious of his own sinfulness, and of his consequent exposure to punishment,—yet unwilling to submit to "the righteousness of God, and to become in heart and life" a new creature in Christ Jesus. This adaptation of religion to relieve men from their natural fears; this release of the soul—with what ease and rapidity!—of its burden, by the apparatus of the confessional, mass, and other similar externals of the system, is the true secret of its ascendency over the mind. It is the human road to heaven; and what man makes for his own track of salvation is sure to run in an opposite direction to the narrow way which alone leads to eternal life.—We are not writing a regular essay against Popery; but the subject of the work before us necessarily points to what is now in full action on the seven hills. Mr Cooper refers us to the undesigned and concurrent testimony of the numberless tourists * who, within these few years, have described the abject idolatry and incredible ignorance of the population, noble and plebeian, of the papal kingdoms and particularly the elaborate mystifications which awe and delude our young compatriots; thinking, as some of them do, that the animal emotions created by the contemplation of the transfiguration, and of the heathen statuary converted into the images of saints and martyrs, created also by listening to the overwhelming pathos of the *misereres* of the Sistine chapel, are devotion! These were indeed the arguments which wrought conviction in the mind of Kotzebue, and in the end effected his conversion to the Roman Catholic religion. Many others will probably undergo a similar process. 'Gods such as guilt makes welcome' are too often, we fear, the real divinities of Catholic mythology. They are not God the Father reconciled, in Jesus Christ, to such as are partakers of the Holy Ghost; for though these names and ideas remain in their formularies, and sometimes in connexion with strains of fervid and sublime devotion, yet *in practice* too frequently all is lost, or is hidden under the superincumbent pollutions. Many of these abominations are the worse for the exterior of taste, beauty, and majesty with which they are invested; and, to reverse a well known position, in this view vice itself augments its evil by losing its grossness. The victim perishes by a draught of secret poison administered from a crystal vase. But it is time to introduce to the reader Mr Cooper's inquiries on this subject.

What have been the marks and fruits of national reformation and improvement which since the restoration of peace have characterised the kingdoms of the beast? What proofs have they manifested of an amended and ameliorated state on the great subjects of religion and morals? Have the kings and potentates of the papal earth so wonderfully and almost miraculously reinstated in their ancient thrones, testified their gratitude to God, by endeavouring to promote among their subjects a purer worship and a holier knowledge of Him, their gracious Benefactor? Penetrated by a sense of his goodness and power

* Mr Cooper (p 253) particularly recommends a popular and, we believe accurate work, called Rome in the Nineteenth Century, published at Edinburgh (1820) in 3 vols 12mo.

so strikingly displayed towards themselves, have they suppressed with abhorrence the mummeries and abominations of Popery and renounced the idolatrous worship of the Virgin? Have they anxiously sought to enlighten the minds of their people and to deliver them from the bondage of error and infidelity by aiding every effort to dissemi nate among them the unadulterated word of God? Have they discountenanced the violation of the Sabbath and endeavoured by legislative enactments and by the in fluence of their own example to introduce a more scriptural observance of that sacred day in the place of the heathenish and licentious profanation of it which previous ly had so generally disgraced the papal kingdoms? Has any large portion of the community throughout any of these king doms expressed any desire for alterations and improvements of these descriptions? In the dissatisfaction and opposition which the people have so generally manifested in regard to those who have authority over them is it the reluctance or supineness of their rulers as to purifying the national religion or correcting the public morals which has formed any part of their com plaints? Have they in these things set an example to their rulers and by any out ward improvement in their own conduct have they given evidence of an amended principle within? Has a more elevated tone and line of moral policy marked the nations in question? Have they displayed a more sacred attention to the rights and feelings of other nations? Have they been distinguished by a stricter regard to justice humanity and fidelity in all their political transactions? Alas! we are surely con strained to reply in the negative to all these questions Public events and private in formation unite in compelling us to con clude that one great use which the papal potentates have made of their recovered sceptres has been to restore and re establish the corruptions of Popery to bind in still stronger fetters of ignorance and superstition the minds of their subjects and to extinguish those sparks of liberty and right feeling which had been excited among them which had inspired some hope of an amended state of things and which if cherished and encouraged, might have been kindled into a flame of moral and religious improvement —that the population of the papal kingdoms however in some instances they may have endeavoured to oppose the revival of political grievances have in general acquiesced without any expressed disapprobation in every attempt to resist the progress of moral and religious ame lioration and that consequently from the influence of these combining causes the actual state of the papal countries in general so far as the interests of religion and morals are concerned is at this moment in a re trograde condition and exhibits a far more gloomy and awful aspect than it did even at the termination of the revolutionary war Witness in support of these con clusions the principles of despotism so openly avowed, so unblushingly record ed, and so practically developed in the un justifiable invasions of Naples and Spain. Witness the systematic opposition in most of the papal countries and especially in the dominions of Austria, to the free cir culation of the word of God Witness the revival by papal authority of the order of Jesuits the most experienced and inde fatigable emissaries of the Church of Rome their restoration to all their former privi leges and the renewed and recognised acceptance of their services by the Holy See Witness the Papal Bulls repeat edly issued against the principle and the objects of Bible Societies and conveying their animadversions in language little dif fering from that of profaneness and blas phemy Witness the revived sufferings and difficulties of the Vaudois churches struggling anew in the valleys of Piedmont, with Roman Catholic oppression and tyran ny Witness in every town of Italy the idolatries and abominations of Popery universally practised, and exclusively sup ported to the extinction of pure religion and worship Witness the intolerance and bigotry of Spain and Portugal who in their new modelled conceptions and codes of liberty and of the rights of man could find no place for religious freedom nor could grant to any others than to Papists, the right of serving God according to their conscience Witness in France the restless and unceasing endeavours of the court to revive the spirit of Popery and to re establish the follies and pageantries of the Roman Catholic church Witness in that country (as in every other country of the beast) the allowed habitual desecration of the Lord s day and the profane application of it to purposes far less congenial with its instituted design then even worldly labour and secular occupations Witness in that country the continuance of the licensed abominations of the Palais Royal and the moral degradation of the capital Witness in that country the monstrous iniquity of the slave trade revived and pursued with renovated vigour under circumstances of very aggravated guilt in the face of a direct recognition of its enormity in a de fiance of national engagements in a viola tion of national honour Other testimonies of a similar kind might be adduced and observation will abundantly supply them But these are sufficient for the purpose of supporting the conclusions before us Let us only bear in mind the additional weight which these testimonies derive from the consideration of the time in which these things are doing and of the situation of the parties who are doing them It is in the nineteenth century of the Christian era it is when the full blaze of pure Christianity is illuminating the mists of papal darkness and even in some places notwithstanding every precaution to the contrary is pene rating the dense and obscure mass and pouring its light and heat into the very centre of it it is at such a time that these things are perpetrating by those very nations and governments which have recently experienced in the most signal manner the severity and the goodness of the Lord which having for a season been visited with some of the heaviest dispensations of his providence were suddenly by his interposition delivered from the calamity of war and blessed with returning tranquillity and peace but which now forgetful alike of their mercies and their judgments are thus requiting the Lord a foolish people and unwise * pp 209—220

* But are there not among ourselves and in situations of high pretension and ostensibly connected even with the government influence of the country writers who insidiously aid the worst errors of Popery by their manner of treating the subjects connected with it? A leading periodical publication thus supports the Abbé Dubois and the abettors of the papal system in opposition to the Protestant Missionaries in India The Roman Catholic ritual, says the reviewer would appear to be of all others best calculated to make an impression and to gain proselytes It has as the Abbé well observes a *poorga* or sacrifice it has processions images statues *tirtan* (or holy water) fasts *tittys* (or feasts) prayers for the dead invocation of saints &c all which practices bear more or less resemblance to those in use among the Hindoos yet it failed altogether What chance of success then have the rash unconciliating evangelical Missionaries pouring forth (says the Abbé) in their blind zeal anathemas and indiscriminate abuse both *of* the nations, and *to* the nations?

Nor are their hasty versions of the Scriptures much calculated to raise the sacred writings in the opinions of the Hindoos The language is low and vulgar utterly destitute of the majestic simplicity of the original and of our own excellent translation A Vakeel attached to one of our corps having in possession a copy of these versions was asked by the colonel what he thought of it the answer was short —

Very ill written much I don t understand some good stories some bad a great deal of nonsense (Quarterly Review July 1823, p 411) The infatuation of this Protestant critic in thus virtually *preferring* the papal system as the instrument of converting the Hindoos to Christianity is really extraordinary Nor less fatuitous is the Abbé himself in *owning* the similarity between the Catholic and Hindoo modifications of idolatry in the profound simplicity of his wonder that still no union could be effected between them and in thus frankly implying that the two parties had no real obstacle to a junction in itself so mutually easy

To the great cloud of witnesses brought forward, in the preceding citations, to deliver their testimony against the governments and subjects of the continental nations Mr Cooper opposes (pp 225—230) by way of auspicious contrast, the existing state of moral and political feeling among ourselves Here, however, we only partially agree with Mr Cooper and while we admit that we have cause above all the nations of the earth for gratitude to the Giver of all our national blessings we yet have considerable doubts respecting the general correctness of Mr Cooper's inferences from the inquiry and comparison he has instituted We will state our reasons somewhat at large

We admit then that there is much truth in this powerful appeal It appears to us however, much as we dislike Popery, to be far too unqualified and exclusive in its application to that erroneous system Some of Mr Cooper s questions, indeed, go simply to this point and beneficial His degradation of the Church of Rome is in this singular instance so humiliating that the most bitter enemy of his communion could scarcely have sunk her lower —As to forming an estimate of the reviewer's share in the Abbé s vituperation of the Missionaries the reader will need no assistance of ours The attack on the Serampore translators we shall repel by the evidence of a witness who delivered his testimony in the Quarterly Review for Feb 1809 (p 225) Nothing *says the Reviewer* can be more unfair than the manner in which the scoffers and alarmists have represented the Missionaries We who have thus vindicated them, are neither blind to what is erroneous in their doctrine or ludicrous in their phraseology but the anti-Missionaries cull out from their journals and letters all that is ridiculous sectarian and trifling call them fools madmen tinkers Calvinists and schismatics and keep out of sight their love of man and their zeal for God their self devotion their indefatigable industry and their unequalled learning....In fourteen years these low born low bred mechanics have done more towards spreading the knowledge of the Scriptures among the heathen than has been accomplished, or even attempted, by all the princes and potentates of the world, and all the universities and establishments into the bargain

Have Papists ceased to be Papists? Now, it is evident, that while they continue to be professors of Popery, they will of course retain much of what we may justly designate as mummery, and they will still address their prayers absurdly enough to the Virgin Mary. But this is a charge which, be it remembered, no less affects the Greek than the Romish Church, and which no less affects five sixths of the population of Ireland, (about a third of the whole population of the United Kingdom), than it affects Italy, France, Spain, or Portugal. But with all her revived mummery, it may surely still be a fair question whether France be not now in a better state in respect to religion, morals, and government, than during the closing decade of the last century, or at any preceding period. And even in Italy, Spain, and Portugal, there has not, we apprehend, been any deterioration in these respects, but rather an improvement. Is it no improvement, for instance, that Protestantism should be tolerated in France that Bible Societies should be allowed to exist there? That in Spain the Inquisition, instead of being a secret tribunal, should have been converted into an open court? That in Portugal, the Inquisition should have entirely ceased? That in the colonies of Portugal, and even in Lisbon itself, Catholic churches should have been appropriated to English Protestant worship? That in Leghorn, for instance, and even in Rome itself, such worship should be allowed by authority?

Again while we fully admit that many of the continental governments are justly charged with not having laboured to enlighten the minds of their people, with not having aided in disseminating the word of God and with not having framed laws to prevent the desecration of the Sabbath, yet, we would ask, is no part of this serious charge applicable to our own Protestant realm? And in so far as it is applicable, is not our guilt, considering our superior advantages, of a more aggravated character than theirs? Have our rulers in church and state, (speaking of them generally, for there are doubtless bright exceptions,) given their support and countenance to that part of our clergy who have been labouring most assiduously to enlighten the minds of the people? Or have they not rather in too many instances regarded and treated these devoted servants of their Lord with marked dislike and discouragement? Nay, do we not owe it to the freedom of our political institutions, rather than to the anxiety for the diffusion of religious light which is prevalent among them, that the men to whom we allude are even tolerated? Then have we nothing to complain of on the score not merely of supineness in disseminating the word of God, but of active opposition to those who are zealously engaged in that work? And, with respect to the Sabbath, have not some good men laboured in vain for the last thirty years to obtain some legislative correction of the abuses and profanations of that sacred day, which abound among us? The very intimation of such a purpose has been met on more than one occasion only by scorn and derision and Sunday newspapers continue to multiply, and the ordinary occupations of life to be pursued, on that day, in open defiance of the Society for the Suppression of Vice, and of the ineffacious enactments which it vainly endeavours to enforce enactments which, however they may prove the piety of our forefathers, are now become ridiculously impotent.

In the popular discontents which, during the period that has elapsed since the return of peace, have prevailed both in Ireland and in the manufacturing districts of England and Scotland, there certainly have not been visible many traces of that high moral feeling, the want of which among continental malcontents Mr Cooper regards as one of the symptoms which mark out the kingdoms of the beast for judgment. They were, on the contrary, distinguished by violence and outrage, and by an extensively combined and determined spirit of resistance to the constituted authorities, maintained by unlawful oaths and fostered by those infidel and seditious writings, which have been multiplying with a most alarming profusion among us.

No one can reprobate more unreservedly than we do the profligate and tyrannical conduct of the great continental powers, in relation to those countries which have attempted to shake off the galling yoke of the despotism that weighed them down to the ground. But let us not forget that Russia and Prussia were parties in this unjust and faithless confederation against freedom, as well as France and Austria. Nor let us forget, that many of the spoliations which have furnished a ready and recent precedent for their atrocious acts, were sanctioned by us. Genoa, despoiled of her independence, and annexed as a province to the most tyrannical and blindly papistical government in Europe. Protestant Saxony, the cradle of the Reformation, abridged of her territory, to gorge the cravings of Prussia and Austria. Norway forcibly transferred like a bale of goods from one power to another. the Belgic Provinces compelled to submit to a government, and to unite with a people, they detested as heretical, and contemned as an inferior race. were all transactions in which Great Britain was a party. We were parties, that is to say, in these instances, to the recognition of those very principles of action, setting at nought the rights and feelings of other nations, which have been pleaded as a justification for the subsequent outrages in which we have happily refused to join. We rejoice in believing that these principles have been renounced, and that for ever, by the government of this country; but still it is unquestionable, that much of the evil we have now to deplore, and which we have endeavoured in vain to prevent, may be traced to our guilty and inconsiderate acquiescence in their application, at a moment when it was unhappily conceived to be our interest, for the sake of the cession of a few wretched and pestilential slave colonies, to acquiesce. Demerara, Essequibo, Berbice, St Lucia, Trinidad, the Cape of Good Hope, and the Mauritius, with their more than 200,000 slaves, still held by us in a miserable and deathful bondage, were the price we received for our dereliction of principle, in shutting our eyes to the spoliation and oppressions of Europe. Nay, does not Mr Cooper well remember, that we, we ourselves, were among the prime agents in re-establishing the papal power itself, with all its corruptions, and in opening again that fruitful source of all the evils which he so feelingly deplores? And are not we, is not Great Britain, thus chargeable with a full measure of the guilt of " binding in still stronger fetters of ignorance and superstition the minds of men, and extinguishing those sparks of liberty and right feeling which had been excited among them?" It is most obviously then not to the papal powers alone that we are to attribute these lamentable retrogradations. Russia, Prussia, Sweden, Holland, and Great Britain are no less involved in this awful responsibility than are Austria, France, Spain, and Portugal. Our consent was indispensable, and it was not withheld: it was freely given.

We greatly question also whether Mr Cooper is right in considering the aspect of affairs in Europe to be more awful and gloomy at the present moment, than at many former periods. The principles of despotism were at least as unblushingly acted upon by Peter and Catherine, in Russia, as they have since been by Alexander,—by Frederick the Great in Prussia, as by the existing ruler of that kingdom;—by former emperors of Austria, as by the present,—and by Louis the Four teenth, and Napoleon Bonaparte, as by any one of their successors. The invasions of Naples and of Spain, unjust and profligate as they were, do not exhibit a more atrocious consummation of cruelty, faithlessness, and oppression than the partition of Poland, by the combined forces of Austria, Russia, and Prussia, or the seizure of the Spanish crown by the Emperor of France.

As to the opposition made to the free circulation of the word of God, which Mr Cooper seems to consider peculiar to the present times, we see nothing in it but the application of the unchanged principles of Popery to the new circumstances of the present day. Forty or fifty years ago no attempts were made by Protestants, to distribute Bibles in Catholic countries. There could therefore have been no opposition made to their circulation. Had the same means been employed then as now, they would doubtless have excited the same resistance as now, and probably one much more sanguinary. Indeed had Bible Societies existed then to the same extent as now, the measures employed to counteract and crush them, we apprehend would have been far less mild and measured than the worst expedients of the kind which we have recently witnessed. And, whatever may be said with truth of the bigotry and intolerance of Italy, Spain, and Portugal, we can have no doubt whatever that these evils have greatly diminished of late, as compared with their intensity at any preceding period. We lament, in common with Mr Cooper, every residue of bigotry and intolerance which deforms the fair face of Christianity in this or in any other country,—but what we maintain is, that these evils have not increased, but that on the contrary they have decreased, during the last fifty years. And even the pomp and pageantry of Popery, as exhibited in the court and capital of France at the present moment, cannot be greater evils than that unbridled profligacy, and the deadly poison of those infidel principles, which pervaded the courts of Louis the Fifteenth and Sixteenth, and which attained their height during the first years of the revolutionary phrenzy. Bigoted and intolerant as Portugal also may be, yet she has permitted of late what she would not have permitted at any former period. English Protestant churches, as we have already remarked, have been opened in her dominions. and even Portuguese churches have been appropriated by the government for the purposes of Protestant worship.

With respect to the Palais Royal, it is we readily believe a very wicked and licentious place. but many who have frequented it have assured us, and we might add our own testimony, that in as far as vice is obtruded on the eye, more of it may be seen in a short walk along some of the streets of London than in a day's sojourn in the Palais Royal. And as for the abominations of the latter being licensed, that is no new regulation. they have always been licensed—as they are also licensed in Protestant Amsterdam.

But we come now to what may appear a less questionable topic—the Slave Trade. We shall not be suspected of any intention of palliating the conduct of the French or of the Portuguese government in respect to this enormity. It has been marked by the grossest hypocrisy and by a disgraceful indifference to the most sacred engagements. And yet have we ourselves given no countenance to their crime? have we afforded them no plea in our own example? When pressed upon this point, their defence is to this effect. ' You, Great Britain, professed to investigate the nature of this traffick. Having investigated it in 1792 you pronounced it, by a solemn resolution of Parliament, to be impolitic, inhuman, and unjust. and yet in the face of this public and solemn recognition, you retained it for sixteen years longer, during which time about half a million of wretched Africans were torn from their native soil and transported to chains and death in the West Indies. You then indeed abolished the trade, but you retain in your hands its guilty fruits. You preach abstinence to us; but the victims of your own cruelty and injustice, those of them who survive their sufferings, still languish out their miserable lives in an oppressive and depopulating bondage, while their children and their children's children, instead of having any reparation of their wrongs, are born only to the wretched heritage of their parents,—compulsory labour, brutal debasement, bodily anguish, and mental darkness. You have at length indeed resolved to bring this inhuman and profligate system to a close. But what has been the effect of this resolution? Has it not hitherto been barren of good? Two years have elapsed since it was adopted, and what has been done to carry it into effect? Who are more highly favoured by your laws and your financial regulations than the holders of slaves? You protect their produce by duties; you encourage it by bounties; you aggravate by these means the sufferings of the slaves, while at the same time you depress by restrictions and exactions the produce of free labour. You violate all your recognized principles of commercial policy, rather than deprive that system, which you hypocritically condemn in abstract resolutions, of the distinguishing privileges which alone uphold it.—In this appeal there may be some exaggeration; but is there no truth in it? do we not in point of fact allow our slave holders to bully us out of our feeble purposes of humanity? Are we not even now at this moment shrinking from the prosecution of our own admitted obligations? What subject is so decidedly unpopular at the present moment in the House of Commons as the cause of the Negroes? What party distinct from the government is so decidedly influential in that place as the West Indian body, the holders of these Negroes as slaves? Does this indicate that loftiness of principle and correctness of feeling for which Mr Cooper would give us credit? But the nation, the people at large, we shall be told, are on the side of humanity and justice. We trust they are; but still we long for the proof that their interest in this question is something more than a passing sentiment, an evanescent impression. A general election cannot be far distant, and we shall rejoice to see the eulogy of Mr Cooper receive its confirmation in the determined stand which they shall then make against all who shall refuse to maintain the rights of outraged humanity, and to put a final period to this monstrous evil.

We have thus ventured to express our dissent from Mr Cooper's general views, not because we do not entirely concur with him in reprobating and condemning the errors and the mischiefs of Popery and despotism; not because we do not admit the force of his representations with respect to the prevailing tendency of the conduct and policy of the continental powers, and the prevailing evils which characterize the state of society among their subjects; but because we cannot assent to the hypothesis which he founds upon these facts. Taking into view all the circumstances of the case, and especially the superior light and freedom of Britain, as contrasted with the state of other nations, we cannot discover any such peculiar and appropriate grounds for her exemption from suffering as Mr Cooper would flatter us with. And again, if we compare the present period of the world with the times which have preceded, we cannot perceive any such extraordinary deterioration in the moral and political principles and conduct of the continental powers, or even of such of them as are Roman Ca tholic, as would seem to us to justify the speculations of our author with respect to their approaching fate. On the contrary, in the midst of much which is most deeply to be deplored, we think we see a visible and progressive improvement in the state of Europe. We perceive a recognition, tardy and reluctant indeed but still influential, of better principles both in religion and in the science of government, than would have been formerly admitted —a greater deference on the part of crowned heads to public opinion,— and a wider diffusion among their subjects of light and knowledge — while we witness on the western side of the Atlantic a happy and rapid enlargement of the boundaries of religious and intellectual as well as political freedom, and in the East, at the same time, the dawning of a brighter day.

But, supposing Mr Cooper to be right in his conjecture that a period of great temporal calamity is approaching and we do not venture to deny it, yet, as far as this anticipation is expected to influence human conduct, we feel some doubt of its efficacy. If the more awful and unquestionable terrors of the future and eternal world will not deter men from sin, and lead them to repentance and amendment of life, what effect is to be looked for from vague apprehensions of some impending worldly evil? The heaviest calamity which can befal an individual unprepared to stand before God, is the summons to appear at his tribunal, in whatever form that summons may be conveyed in comparison of this, all worldly losses and afflictions sink into absolute insignificance. And although it be true that the actual presence of affliction is often made instrumental in turning the heart to God, yet the doubtful apprehension of it, in minds unaffected by the great and certain realities of death and judgment, we should fear would exert on most men but an extremely feeble influence.

A subject of some moment, already alluded to, is the secession of the members of the Holy Alliance from the principles laid down in their first declaration on the 25th of December 1815, at least as those principles were naturally to be gathered from the language of that declaration. It will be recollected with what warm enthusiasm this professed recognition of pure Christianity as the basis of all future proceedings in government, was received by the majority of our countrymen. Others, however, discovered in this treaty the elements of concealed mischief, as they observed the union of a Roman Catholic Emperor, an Emperor of the Greek church, and a Lutheran king and their conviction was, that the foundation of such a system of incongruities must be unsound. A late respectable writer on prophecy, Mr Bicheno*, went so far as to denounce the alliance at once, as the germ of a conspiracy against the liberties of mankind and if his work were unnoticed or despised by many, it offended or, at least, surprized numbers of religious persons, who blamed the author's forebodings as premature, unprovoked, and an act of ingratitude towards the liberators of a lately enslaved world. Subsequent events have, however justified his suspicions. The conferences of Laybach and Verona decided the question against the allies and the invasions of Naples and Spain were the practical comments. In refe-

---

* The title of Mr Bicheno's book is "The Fulfilment of Prophecy farther illustrated by the Signs of the Times or an Attempt to ascertain the probable Issues of the resent Restoration of the old Dynasties of the Revival of Popery and of the present mental Ferment in Europe as likewise how far Great Britain is likely to share in the Calamities by which Divine Providence will accomplish the final Overthrow of the Kingdom of the Roman Monarchy London 1817. Mr Bicheno is one of those writers on prophecy who think that the 1260 years terminated at the beginning of the French Revolution.

rence to these points Mr Cooper writes —

The connexion between the rulers and their subjects which had been violently rent asunder by the arms of Napoleon was as suddenly renewed by his defeat and deposition and thus a pledge might seem to have been given of returning tranquillity and repose But the result was otherwise The rulers and their subjects were not now in a situation to coalesce on the same terms and in the same manner as they had done before their temporary disunion The people under their new masters had become too enlightened not to see something of the iniquity and oppressions of their ancient governments and too strongly attached to the novel idea of liberty which they had learned to admire patiently to acquiesce in the re establishment and continuance of former abuses while the rulers had so little profited by the salutary lessons which they had received, and were made so little wiser by the chastisements which they had undergone as not to perceive that it was only by some concessions to the newly-acquired views of their subjects that they could reasonably hope to resume their sceptres with benefit to them or with comfort and security to themselves Such concessions, however ill accorded with the principles and prejudices of those who had no conception of any law but their own will, nor of any government but such as is arbitrary and despotic Hence has arisen a continual system of mutual mistrust and dissatisfaction of suspicion and jealousy of aggression on the one side and of resistance on the other which amidst the semblance of peace has generated and maintained a spirit of secret hostility and in some instances as in the cases of Naples and Spain has actually produced a state of undisguised and open warfare In the last of these two countries it is notorious that nothing but the overawing presence of the French troops has restrained it from bursting forth into the most unbridled anarchy and confusion while in nearly all the other kingdoms of the beast, the struggle for political power when it is not actually suppressed by the immediate operation of military force is venting itself in unceasing contentions divisions and intrigues Such is the agitated and tumultuous state of the papal earth and the injurious tendency of such an unsettled state and its baneful effects on the power and prosperity of the countries where it prevails must be too obvious to require a proof Let us but cast our eyes over the countries in question and we shall perceive that instead of exhibiting those marks of renovated vigour and political reviviscence which so long an interval of peace might have been expected to produce, they are, for the most part, in a less formidable, and, if possible in a more enervated condition than they were even at the termination of the war So true it is that neither in peace nor in war is it given to them any longer to practise and prosper pp 200—203.

This language, we conceive, can scarcely be applied with strict propriety either to Austria or to France, which are the two greatest of the papal powers With respect to Spain and Portugal, they are suffering from causes which are producing propitious results in other parts of the world The detachment of their colonies cannot but issue in good and, even from the spirit of restlessness and dissatisfaction which agitate them internally, we are disposed to hope for the most beneficial effects If the people were dead and torpid under the pressure of the despotism to which they are subject, their case would be hopeless indeed

We now pass on to the portion of the volume which contains its author's monitory cautions to his countrymen, founded on the parenthetical admonition, "Behold I come as a thief Blessed is he that watcheth, and keepeth his garments, lest he walk naked, and they see his shame To impress on his readers the lessons deducible from this passage, was avowedly the writer's ultimate design If his hypothesis be tenable, (a point which we shall not profess absolutely to decide,) the inhabitants of this Protestant empire, are standing within sight of the spot where the coming storms will arise, to vex and desolate the papal earth At this "*crisis* according to Mr Cooper, we are nearly arrived What ever may be the feelings of the thousands of our inconsiderate countrymen, who are only nominal members of the Christian church, an appeal is here made to such among us as look towards future years with a consciousness of their own responsibility The most tranquil periods are certainly seasons of self vigilance and circumspection to all the followers of Jesus Christ but when, in the higher sense of prophecy, "coming events cast their shadows before," their estimate of the spiritual character will rise with the increased solemnities of the approaching season, and they will feel themselves called upon to be ready to *stand in the evil day, and having done all to stand.* Thus far we cordially unite with Mr Cooper. We wish to find him a correct interpreter of prophecy when he so far tranquillizes our national apprehensions as Britons, as to anticipate for our country a refuge from the storm, in the day when God arises to shake terribly the earth. Or, if there be not an absolute refuge, he yet argues that we shall be swept only by the skirts of the tempest, and be thus, comparatively, safe and prosperous. Not that this supposed exemption from wrath is represented by him as in any degree merited by this our insular division of a guilty world; but he casts a retrospective glance at what God *has* done for us, and thence the prospect appears to him to brighten with hope and confidence. He also regards and perhaps justly this island as the secondary fountain, itself supplied by the streams proceeding out of the throne of God and of the Lamb, whence the whole world is copiously deriving divine and eternal truth. And it does not appear to him to be a part of God's providential dispensations to mankind that the instruments of good to others will themselves be destroyed, so long as the current of blessing is unimpeded and fertilizes where it flows. At the same time the hour of punishment to Antichrist, and his adherents, he conceives, may be an hour of peculiar trial to the really faithful among ourselves. They may be taken by surprise, though not by a snare; and the degree of surprise may be such as may at the moment, cause something like sensations of confusion and of being not entirely prepared for the pressure and alarm of the crisis. Now the object of our excellent author is to prevent Christians from being taken thus unawares. If his calculations be correct, he urges upon them the paramount necessity of looking well to their own state and character. If his scheme be visionary, still they will never regret any efforts made, on their parts to be found in an attitude of watchfulness. In either case, they will be gainers. We confess ourselves that independently of any scheme of prophetic interpretation the existing condition of Christendom, both ecclesiastical and civil, including the state of things in the sister kingdom, is itself a crisis and a crisis indicating, to all serious minds the necessity of diligent prayer, exertion, and vigilance. The increase of national prosperity appears to be rising to a flood tide; but the contemplation of this will naturally impart to the retired and thoughtful Christian emotions not unmixed with apprehension. Such a man is not satisfied with the most solid worldly prosperity of the nation, unless its possessors have also a reversionary interest in the kingdom of everlasting glory. There is indeed this difference between his feelings and those of the shrewd and calculating worldling, that while the latter secretly laughs at the follies of human speculation, and selfishly congratulates himself on his own prudent security, the genuine Christian regards mankind with the most tender compassion, and breathes out the aspiration, "Oh! that they were wise, that they would consider their latter end; and that they would turn from idols to serve the living God!" In these sentiments we are persuaded that Mr Cooper will entirely concur. They are indeed only the echo of his own, and are offered to our readers, as wishing without pronouncing upon his specific anticipations grounded on prophecy to be his co-operators in his great and patriotic object. We hope that he, in the pastoral retirement of a village, and ourselves, surrounded by the restless swarms of this gigantic metropolis have one and the same end in view, the diffusion of the pure and perfect Gospel of Jesus Christ more immediately among our countrymen at home, and from them extending to the unknown millions of mankind, whose unchangeable condition must speedily be decided. As far as we write under the influence of this hope, we shall find every day, and every hour a crisis. *Ab hoc momento pendet eternitas!* With a maxim so applicable to our condition, mortal and immortal, we bid farewell to the subject of these remarks; and if, in any degree, they aid the monitory counsels of Mr Cooper, we shall be grateful to him for the opportunity of thus addressing those readers who honour our pages with their perusal.

---

1. *Payne's Translation of Thomas a Kempis on the Imitation of Christ, with an Introductory Essay by the Rev. T. Chalmers, D.D.* 3s. 6d.
2. *The Works of the Rev. J. Gambold, with an Introductory Essay by T. Erskine, Esq.* 3s. 6d.
3. *The Redeemer's Tears over lost Souls, by the Rev. J. Howe. Essay by the Rev. R. Gordon, D.D.* 3s.
4. *The Life, Walk and Triumph of Faith, by the Rev. W. Romaine. Essay by Dr Chalmers.* 2 vols. 7s.
5. *Treatises on Justification and Regeneration by the Rev. J. Witherspoon, D.D. Essay by W. Wilberforce, Esq.* 3s. 6d.
6. *An Alarm to unconverted Sinners by the Rev. J. Alleine. Essay by the Rev. A. Thomson.* 4s. 6d.
7. *Private Thoughts on Religion, by the Rev. T. Adam. Essay by the Rev. D. Wilson.* 3s. 6d.
8. *The Christian Remembrancer, by A. Serle. Essay by Dr Chalmers.* 3s. 6d.

THE above publications form part of an intended series of reprints of valuable and popular works in divinity, with Introductory Essays by living writers whose names are calculated to give renewed sanction and circulation to the works which they recommend. Several other treatises have appeared in continuation of the plan; but the present are all we have hitherto seen, and are indeed as many as we could conveniently notice in a single article. Our publication not being a retrospective review, we shall not think it necessary to discuss the merits of the works themselves which are all, or almost all of them well known to the readers of religious treatises: but shall confine ourselves almost entirely to a few extracts from the Introductory Essays, which form the distinguishing feature and intended attraction of the series. The respective authors having long since gone to their reward, the only parties among whom we are called upon to distribute critical justice are the publishers the prefacers, and the readers. With regard to the first it is not, we presume, uncharitable to suppose that the project originated in the ordinary motives that give rise to other commercial transactions. The publishers might justly calculate upon the large existing demand for some of these works; and the probable demand for others which only needed to be better known to be extensively sought after; and might fairly hold out the *bonus* of an introductory essay from an influential pen to allure the public to their own edition. We should not, however do justice to these bibliopolists if we did not add that they have not sacrificed their Christianity to commerce; but, on the contrary have chosen in these volumes such a line of publication as does them credit, especially at a time when so many of their fraternity are employing their wits and their capital in very different speculations. With regard to the prefacers, their object is to recommend to the increased attention of society works which they consider of great importance for the spiritual and eternal welfare of mankind, and at the same time to prefix such brief cautions or explanations as the works respectively recommended may seem to require. In some instances, this latter province must be a most requisite part of such an undertaking; for it is not every popular, or even in the main good and valuable, treatise that is equally meritorious throughout, or calculated for the specific edification of all classes of readers. The result then, as it affects the third party, the purchaser, is that, at a charge which the expected demand enables the publisher to render very moderate, he has a neat and correct copy of the work he wishes, with a preface which in many instances greatly enhances its value; the whole series forming a cheap and uniform edition of popular religious publications. In this age of embellishment, the publishers might perhaps find their account in adding to each work a portrait of the author, where procurable.

The preface to the first publication, Thomas a Kempis, is from the pen of Dr Chalmers; and it bespeaks the enlarged and liberal mind of the prefacer, and his abstinence from the vice of doctrinal favouritism; that he should have selected for his eulogies the De Imitatione of à Kempis and the Life, Walk, and Triumph of Faith of Mr Romaine. These two writers may be considered in some important respects as almost antipodes to each other; and yet a mind like that of Dr Chalmers well knows how, in the main, to reconcile them. Of à Kempis he says

We have sometimes heard the strenuous argumentation of the author of the following treatise in behalf of holiness excepted against on the ground that it did not recognize sufficiently the doctrine of justification by faith. There is in many instances an over sensitive alarm on this topic which makes the writer fearful of recommending virtue and the private disciple as fearful of embarking on the career of it—a sort of jealousy lest the honours and importance of Christ's righteousness should be invaded by any importance being given to the personal righteousness of the believer as if the one could not be maintained as the alone valid plea on which the sinner could lay claim to an inheritance in heaven and at the same time the other be urged as his indispensible preparation for its exercises and its joys

It is the partiality with which the mind fastens upon one article of truth and will scarcely admit the others to so much as a hearing—it is the intentness of its almost exclusive regards on some separate portion of the Divine testimony and its shrinking avoidance of all the distinct and additional portions—it is in particular its fondness for the orthodoxy of what relates to a sinner's acceptance carried to such a degree of favouritism as to withdraw its attention altogether from what relates to a sinner's sanctification—it is this which on the pretence of magnifying a most essential doctrine has in fact diffused a mist over the whole field of revelation and which like a mist in nature not only shrouds the general landscape from all observation but also bedims while it adds to the apparant size of the few objects that continue visible   pp v vi

We like not that writer to be violently alleged against, who expounds and expounds truly the amount of Christian holiness because he says not enough it is thought of the warrants and securities that are provided in the Gospel for Christian hope We think that to shed a luminousness over one portion of the Divine testimony is to reflect at least if not immediately to shed a light on all the other portions of it The doctrine of our acceptance by faith in the merits and propitiation of Christ, is worthy of many a treatise and many are the precious treatises upon it which have been offered to the world But the doctrine of regeneration by the Spirit of Christ equally demands the homage of a separate lucubration which may proceed on the truth of the former and by the incidental recognition of it when it comes naturally in the way of the author's attention marks the soundness and the settlement of his mind thereupon more decisively than by the dogmatic and ostentatious and often misplaced asseverations of an ultra orthodoxy   p xvii

A Kempis does not argue or dwell upon (some readers would add, that he does not even clearly recognize) the doctrine of justification freely by faith but in the exhibition of the Christian graces and practical virtues which flow from a true and lively faith his treatise is incomparable and it has the superadded merit that while it enforces the imitation of Christ, even with much self-denial, it shews the blessedness which results from such a course of conduct

Such a work remarks Dr Chalmers may be of service in these days of soft and silken professorship—to arouse those who are at ease in Zion to remind them of the terms of the Christian discipleship as involving a life of conflict, and watchfulness and much labour to make them jealous of themselves and jealous of that evil nature the power of which must be resisted, but from the besetting presence of which we shall not be conclusively delivered until death shall rid us of a frame work* the moral virus of which may be kept in check while we live but cannot be eradicated by any process short of dissolution p xvii

Lest any over scrupulous reader, after perusing these remarks, should be afraid that the reverend prefacer may be in danger of becoming too much *legalized* by his contact with à Kempis, we shall ease his mind by turning at once to the fourth treatise on our list, where he will find him advocating with equal zeal the writings of a divine of a very different school Mr Romaine has been frequently accused of constant iterations and reiterations of the same topics this Dr Chalmers defends, from the example of the Apostle Paul, as " safe, and undertakes to shew that it ought not to be wearisome or " grievous

The doctrine says he of Jesus Christ and him crucified which forms the principal and pervading theme in the following treatises possesses a prominent claim to a place in our habitual recollections And for this purpose ought it to be the topic of frequent reiteration by every Christian author and it may well form the staple of many a Christian treatise and be the leading and oft repeated argument of many a religious conversation It is this which ushers into the mind of a sinner the sense of God as his Friend and his reconciled Father That mind which is so apt to be overborne by this world's engrossments or to lapse into the dread and distrust of a conscious offender or to go back again to nature's lethargy and nature's alienation or to lose itself in quest of a righteousness of its own by which it might challenge the reward of a blissful eternity stands in need of a daily visitor who by his presence might dissipate the gloom or clear away the perplexity in which these strong and practical tendencies of the human constitution are so ready to involve it There is with man an obstinate forgetfulness of God so that the Being who made him is habitually away from his thoughts That he may again be brought nigh there must be an open door of entry by which the mind of man can welcome the idea of God and willingly entertain it—by which the imagination of Deity might become supportable and even pleasing to the soul so that, when present to our remembrance, there should be the felt presence of one who loves and is at peace with us Now it is only by the doctrine of the Cross that man can thus delight himself in God, and, at the same time be free from delusion This is the way of access for man entering into friendship with God and for the thought of God as a friend entering into the heart of man And thus it is that the sound of his Saviour's love carries with it such a fresh and unfailing charm to a believer's ear It is the precursor to an act of mental fellowship with God and is hailed as the sound of the approaching footsteps of him whom you know to be your friend pp xi xii

We know of no treatises where this evangelical infusion so pervades the whole substance of them as those of Romaine Though there is no train of consecutive argument—though there is no great power or variety of illustration—though we cannot allege in their behalf much richness of imagery or even much depth of Christian experience And besides though we were to take up any of his paragraphs at random we should find that with some little variation in the workmanship of each there was mainly one ground or substratum for them all— yet the precious and consoling truths which he ever and anon presents must endear them to those who are anxious to maintain in their minds a rejoicing sense of God as their reconciled Father He never ceases to make mention of Christ and of his righteousness—and it is by the constant droppings of this elixir that the whole charm and interest of his writings are upheld With a man whose ambition and delight it was to master the difficulties of an argument or with a man whose chief enjoyment it was to range at will over the domains of poetry we can conceive nothing more tasteless or tame than these treatises that are now offered to the public

But to a regenerated spirit, that never can be a weariness in time which is to form the song of eternity pp xix xx xxi.

Dr Chalmers proceeds to shew that " the theme on which Mr

---

* We have so often commented on the peculiarities of Dr Chalmers's stile that we consider ourselves privileged to pass them by on the present occasion otherwise we should be inclined to ask what is meant by such expressions as keeping in check the moral virus of a frame work.

Romaine so much loves to expatiate is a purifying as well as a pleasing theme. He continues,—

We are aware of the alleged danger which some entertain of the tendency of such a full and free exhibition of the grace of the Gospel to produce Antinomianism. But the way to avert this is not by casting any part of Gospel truth into the shade. It is to spread open the whole of it, and give to every one part the relief and the prominency that it has in Scripture. We are not to mitigate the doctrines of a justifying faith and an all perfect righteousness because of the abuse that has been made of them by hypocrites—but, leaving to these doctrines all their prominency we are to place by their side the no less important and undeniable truths that heaven is the abode of holy creatures and that ere we are qualified for admittance there we must become holy and heavenly ourselves. Nor is there a likelier way of speeding this practical transformation upon our souls than by keeping up there through the blood of Christ, a peace in the conscience which is never truly done without a love in the heart being kept up along with it. pp. xxi. xxii.

Every reflecting Christian will admit the truth of these statements, as well as the correlative, not contrary statements in the preface to à Kempis. They prove that writers of very different complexions may yet be respectively useful to the world as advocating important *parts* of the great code of Divine revelation; but in our idea, and we are sure also in that of Dr Chalmers as shewn both by his own example and by the very two prefaces now under consideration, it is not desirable nor is it always " safe that a Christian divine or laic should indulge a spirit of exclusion or favouritism. His effort should be to " go through the good land in the length thereof and in the breadth thereof: partial views will afford but an incorrect notion of its extent and fertility. And in this view, while we fully admit all that Dr Chalmers has said, and most justly, in praise of the writings of Mr Romaine, we could wish that that divine and others of various schools had somewhat enlarged their range of topics, or at least have given greater prominence to some which they have partly slighted so as to afford a full and consistent view of the Gospel in all its bearings. Why should the latter part of the Epistle to the Ephesians or the Colossians be ever separated from the former, as if the union of the two involved a sort of inconsistency: as if the privileges of the Gospel would deter men from its duties, or its duties render them incapable of appreciating its privileges? Dr Chalmers advocates à Kempis and Romaine respectively but it is the praise of his own well balanced mind that he knows how to unite the characteristic views of both, and thus to avoid those opposite mistakes which it is the tendency of partial and confined systems of divinity to generate or foster.

The second publication on the list comprises the works of Gambold, with an Introductory Essay by Mr Erskine the justly celebrated author of an Essay on Faith and " Remarks on the internal Evidences of revealed Religion. The object of this essay is to apply the often alleged maxim, that man is the creature of circumstances, to the *religious circumstances* of his being. The disquisition is too closely woven to allow of our abridging its argument, but the following passages will shew its practical bearing.

If the circumstances of this highest relation (our relation to God) be wrong all is wrong. They may be wrong and often are without being felt to be so. There are many who have not set down their relation to God in the list of their relations who have never regarded his favour or displeasure as circumstances of their condition and who have never looked into eternity as their own vast, untried dwelling place destined to be either their heaven or their hell. And yet this is the chief relation and these are the chief circumstances of their being. The very root of the moral existence of such persons is dead. Their circumstances are in truth most deplorable and their insensibility to pain from them arises from palsy not from health. But in some just so much animation remains, that these mighty circumstances are felt to be unfavourable and then they blacken existence and convert it into anguish. They poison every other relation and paralize action in every other duty.

Escape is impracticable. The only remedy lies in having these circumstances altered. But who can command these circumstances? Can man command them? pp. ix. x.

God alone can command these circumstances: no one but God has authority to say that our offences and failures in that relation are forgiven—that a full satisfaction has been made on our behalf to the broken laws of the universal government—that the gates of the family of God are thrown open to us, and that we are invited every moment to speak to him as to a Father, and lean upon him, as on an almighty and faithful and tender Friend—and that the unending duration to which we are advancing is safe and peaceful, full of bliss and full of glory. The circumstances of that highest relation have been most particularly and fully made known to us in the Bible, that we might have happiness, even the joy of the Lord, which, if really attained by us, will supply strength for the cheerful and affectionate and diligent performance of every duty springing from every relation in life, and will be our comfort and hiding place in every sorrow. p. xi.

Mr Erskine proceeds to argue, that the freedom of the mercy of God as made known to us in the Gospel, far from having a tendency to relax the Christian's discharge of moral obligations, has the direct contrary effect. Love, gratitude and joy he shews to be far more influential on the character than mere delineations of duty.

Do we wish to perform fully the duties belonging to our various relations? Then joy must be infused into the circumstances of those relations. But how is this to be done? Who can command the gifts of fortune or nature? Who can stay the approach of sickness or death? Aye, and what are we to do for the other world? Will the joy of these temporary relations, supposing that we obtain it, carry us forward in healthy and cheerful action through another state of being? Let us be wise in this inquiry, and beware of wasting our time and our strength in vain attempts. Joy infused into the circumstances of any passing relation perishes when that relation perishes. But there is a permanent relation, and it also is the root from which all other relations grow. Oh how desirable to have joy infused here, that it might, like living sap, circulate through the whole tree of human relations, and bring forth much fruit on every branch! And praised be our God who hath shed forth joy abundantly on the circumstances of this relation, even joy unutterable and full of glory. pp. xv. xvi.

The argument is applied as follows to the writings of Gambold.

We know no author who has illustrated the origin and tendency of the joy of the Lord so simply, so beautifully, or so strikingly. His mind was evidently of a very fine order. In his youth he had mixed philosophical mysticism and theology together. He had formed an elevated and pure and holy idea of perfect goodness—he felt his obligation to attain to it—he attempted it long—and at last sunk under the mortifying and heart-chilling conviction that he was only adding sin to sin without advancing a single step towards his high object. Whilst he was in this melancholy condition it pleased God that he should meet with one of the Moravian brethren, who declared to him the simple Gospel, that Christ is made of God unto us wisdom and justification and sanctification and redemption—that the only atonement that ever could be made for sin was already made and accepted—that we neither could take away our guilt by any scheme of our own, nor was it necessary, for Christ's blood had done it—and that now we are called on and invited as blood-bought and well beloved children, to follow him who had so loved us, to keep near to him as the fountain of our life and happiness, and to testify our gratitude to him by obeying his commandments. Pardon is proclaimed through the blood of Christ, and sanctification is the fruit of faith in that pardon. Mr Gambold gave up his laborious and unsuccessful efforts, and he walked by faith in humble and peaceful holiness, rejoicing in him who is the strength of his people. The simple child-like joy for sin blotted out, did for his soul what all his efforts and sincere efforts they were could never accomplish. This joy is his great theme. But we cannot rejoice by endeavouring to rejoice, any more than we can love by endeavouring to love. It is by keeping the glorious and blessed circumstances of our relation to God before our mind that we shall feel and continue to feel a natural and unforced joy, which will produce a natural and unforced walk in the way of God's commandments. pp. xix. xx.

Mr Erskine goes on to prove that the doctrine for which he contends does not lead to licentiousness, by shewing that Christian joy is not merely a joy for deliverance from misery, but that it is a joy for a deliverance effected through the atonement of Christ, that it has respect to the attributes and perfections of God, and to the object of the Gospel, which is to conform us to the will of God, and that it is the companion of love, gratitude, and sacred endearments, which purify while they elevate the soul. Every true Christian will cordially enter into the spirit of this glowing argument, though unhappily truth obliges us to add, that there are those who, if works are a test of faith, are *not* true Christians, who will yet contend for this doctrine in a manner which Mr Erskine would be among the first to condemn, so as absolutely to nauseate every other topic, to admit of nothing in the shape of exhortation and remonstrance, and to turn from every expostulatory suggestion with some semi Antinomian remark, as if joy and 'comfort' were all that a Christian needed for 'doctrine, reproof, correction, and instruction in righteousness.'

As we do not profess (our limits forbid it) to discuss the merits of the various works in this series, we purposely abstain from inquiring whether the respected prefacer has not spoken somewhat too strongly on the subject of Gambold's talents, at least his poetical talents. The popular hymn beginning with

O tell me no more
Of this world's vain store

which is one of two hymns introduced into the present volume, we have long reckoned among the veriest pieces of well meant doggerel in the language. Mr Erskine certainly does not praise it, and those pieces which he *does* praise are undoubtedly of a higher order. But these points are not to our present purpose, nor, we may add, are the peculiar sentiments of the writers whose works are comprised in the series; otherwise we should ask why Mr Gambold might not have arrived at scriptural ideas of justification and sanctification, and lived in love to God and usefulness to mankind without giving up his post in the Anglican church, and joining the Moravian brethren?

An interesting and appropriate Essay from the pen of the Rev Dr Gordon of Edinburgh, ushers in the powerful and affecting treatise of Howe on "the Redeemer's Tears wept over lost Souls," with two discourses of the same author on self dedication and yielding ourselves to God. Dr Gordon's object in these preliminary observations is

to remove if possible from the plain and impressive language of Scripture that indistinctness in which we are so apt to envelop it, and which so frequently prevents it from making its way to the heart—to place distinctly before the sinner's eye the fact recorded in the Gospel history that the Saviour wept over the ruin of those who lived and died in a state of unbelief—to shew that in as far as the Divine compassion is concerned it is still the same as that which dictated the pathetic lamentation over Jerusalem—and to bring the persuasive influence of this simple fact to bear on the affections of all of those who have, as well as those who have not yet yielded to the constraining power of the love of Christ. pp xx xxi

For the further illustration of this subject, and as exhibiting in a most impressive manner the persuasiveness of the arguments derived from the compassion of God towards sinners for subduing the most obdurate heart, Dr Gordon confidently refers to the treatise which it is his object to recommend. He says

It would be difficult indeed to point out any work in which so much important matter has been condensed into so small a compass. Within the limits of a few pages the reader will find exhibited in a very striking and impressive light the true state of the controversy which sinners are maintaining with God—the nature of faith and genuine repentance—the responsibility of those who live under the Gospel dispensation as enjoying a day of grace which may in various ways terminate while they are still in a state of alienation from their Maker—the folly of the arguments by which the unregenerate will sometimes seek to justify their indolence and indifference on the ground that no anxiety or efforts of theirs will avail any thing till God is pleased to put forth upon them the efficacious influences of his Holy Spirit—the unreasonableness as well as the mischievous tendency of those painful suspicions by which the awakened sinner sometimes permits himself to be perplexed when he sets about determining whether his day of grace may not already be over—and a vindication of the rectitude of the Divine procedure in those cases where in consequence of the sinner's obstinacy the influences of the Holy Spirit are withheld, or finally withdrawn. pp. xxviii. xxix.

And should any such begin to feel uneasiness, on the recollection of the ingratitude and neglect with which they have treated the mercy and forbearance of God, we would earnestly recommend to their serious perusal the discourses on Self-dedication and Yielding ourselves to God. p. xxix.

Dr. Witherspoon's well known and valuable treatises on justification and regeneration are introduced to the reader by an essay from the pen of the revered author of the "Practical View of Christianity;" an individual of whom it would be difficult to say whether his writings or his example, his public life or his private virtues, have most illustrated and adorned the doctrine of God our Saviour; an individual, one of the very few perhaps whose names will be handed down to posterity, of whom it may with perfect justice be said, that he retired from the ordeal of public life after a long and intimate acquaintance with its most arduous scenes, not merely intact and uncorrupted, but brighter from the flame, with a character as it were purified and burnished by a collision so often fatal even to men of far more than average strictness of principle; and carrying into his retirement the affections of the good, the admiration of the gifted, the imperishable gratitude of the afflicted and oppressed, the sympathies of his friends, the involuntary homage of his enemies, if indeed such a man can have enemies—enemies not personal, but rendered such as the opponents of those projects of justice and mercy of which he was the eloquent, the disinterested, and the successful champion,—and the esteem of all. But we will not digress from the immediate object before us to express the respect we feel for those eminent talents and still more eminent virtues which have so long rendered this revered individual the idol of his country, and which, now on his retirement from the senatorial duties which he has so long and faithfully discharged, will, we are sure, call forth the most gratifying sentiments of affection and regret from men of all opinions and parties in that dignified assembly where he is so well known and highly esteemed. Our present purpose is only to give a short specimen of the prefatory remarks before us. The following passage is of great practical importance.

But it is not merely by his obtaining credit with the irreligious world that the Christian is in danger. Perhaps he has even more to dread from becoming popular among those who profess a more than ordinary respect for religion. We all for the most part naturally associate with those who agree with us substantially in opinion. With them we form our intimacies and our friendships; their applause is the fame we covet. In truth, to all men, the world may be said to consist of those with whom they are chiefly conversant, and whose good opinion they hold in habitual regard. The world of the professing Christian therefore consists mainly of those whose opinions and conduct are formed on a principal of respect for the doctrines and precepts of Christianity; and he cannot but be habitually conscious that he would lose his credit with them if he were openly, or to any great degree, to violate the proprieties of his assumed Christian character. But this habitual reference to the opinions and feelings of others, though it may sometimes supply a counteracting influence against open vice, and an additional security against the suddenness or force of temptation, especially of temptations to actual sin, is yet but too apt insensibly to become the main spring, the actuating principle of our conduct. But alas! we may be popular among our fellow Christians from the exterior of our Christian character, while the inner man may all the time be growing weaker and weaker. The true Christian therefore, conscious of the corruption and deceitfulness of his own heart, will be constantly on his guard against the delusion to which he knows himself to be prone. He will be afraid of having the respect and attachment of his fellow Christians chiefly at heart, while he professes to be supremely actuated by love and gratitude to his God and Saviour. He will therefore be endeavouring to fix and habitually to maintain in his mind, a strong impression of the nature and effects of true spiritual religion; and having ascertained beyond dispute his own title to that blessed character, he will strive to keep the evidences of this title to the name of Christian continually present to his view, remembering the Apostle's declaration, that as many as are led by the

Spirit of God they are the sons of God. pp. vii. viii. ix.

Mr. Wilberforce speaks in very high terms of Witherspoon's treatises on Regeneration and Justification, as useful not only to the more advanced Christian, but also to all who are in earnest on the subject of religion. He concludes his remarks with impressing on the reader the way in which alone the study of the most valuable exhortations, or even of the holy Scriptures themselves, can be really useful.

But it is only by accompanying our study of the Scriptures with constant humble and fervent prayer that we can hope to draw down those blessed influences which alone can enable us to feel the truths of Christianity in all their vital power, and can maintain the life of religion in the soul. Such, alas! are the depraving tendencies of the moral atmosphere of this world, that Christianity itself, though heaven descended, experiences the deteriorating effects of its corrupting qualities. It is the object of Dr. Witherspoon's excellent work to detect and extirpate some of those corruptions. May the Divine blessing abundantly attend its perusal, and render it eminently successful in vindicating the claims and establishing the dignity of that Christianity which alone deserves the name. May all who recognize the truth of the doctrines, and who admire the excellency of the lessons which it contains, endeavour to let their light shine before men, and to compel them to acknowledge the superior value of true Christian principles from the superiority of its practical effects. "Herein," said our blessed Lord, "is my Father glorified, that ye bear much fruit,—so shall ye be my disciples." pp. xv. xvi.

Mr. Thomson has introduced Alleine's Alarm with a discussion, in which he shews that, however painful may be the faithful representation of " the terror of the Lord," it is a necessary and highly important part of the office of the Christian instructor. In proof of this he urges five unanswerable arguments; namely, that the terror of the Lord constitutes an essential part of Divine truth; that it is necessary for understanding and appreciating the Gospel; that the exhibition of it for the purpose of persuasion is in just accommodation to the principles of human nature and the practice of mankind in concerns of far inferior moment; that the example of the inspired teachers of religion justifies a recurrence to this argument; and lastly, that the declarations objected to on the score of harshness are in truth dictated by and fraught with the most exalted mercy. We cannot follow the prefacer through his exposition of the various heads of his discussion, and it is the less necessary, as the various positions of the argument will be readily allowed by every reflecting reader. At the same time Mr. Thomson is no advocate for always or too frequently dwelling on the terror of the Lord, nor does he vouch for every sentiment or expression in Alleine's treatise; which, however, he maintains, and justly, to be on the whole most striking, impressive, and scriptural in its statements. We detach the following passage from his course of argument.

Even those terms which are employed in speaking of Christianity and our use of which is never objected to, have no meaning but what they derive from the terror of the Lord. Christianity is distinguished by mercy: but what is mercy? Mercy is the exercise of goodness towards those who are in circumstances of danger and misery. Take away these circumstances, or keep them out of sight, and you deprive the word mercy of its true import, and render it wholly inapplicable to the case of man. But let his danger and misery be acknowledged—let them be unfolded in all their certainty and extent—let those consequences which must ensue if they are not averted be exhibited without disguise —and then mercy becomes a significant and appropriate word, and we are able not only to perceive its meaning but in some measure to scan its vastness and to rejoice in its triumphs as these are displayed in the Gospel.—Christianity is a plan of salvation; and salvation is a word which every one repeats with pleasure and delight. But can any one repeat it with understanding and with a proper sense of what renders it an object of complacency, or a source of joy, who thinks not of the terror of the Lord? It is impossible; for salvation irrespective of those evils in deliverance from which it mainly or altogether consists is but a sound to which no precise idea is annexed. You exult in the salvation of the Gospel; but is not your exultation groundless and absurd and delusive, unless your attention has been directed to the calamities out of which it rescues you; and will not your exultation be rational and lively in proportion to the clearness and the interest with which you have realized these calamities in your imagination? pp. xviii, xix.

The Rev. Daniel Wilson introduces the seventh work on our list, with the following just and characteristic description:

The Private Thoughts on Religion of the late Rev. Mr. Adam of Wintringham, which are here republished, are inestimable. They are the produce of a very pious, a very acute, and a very honest mind. It is not a volume which charms by the force and purity of its style, by the closeness of its reasoning, or the tenderness of its persuasion. It is not a detail of evidences, nor a series of discourses. It was not even designed for publication, and partakes therefore of the disadvantages inseparable from merely private papers. The language is plain and sometimes coarse. The topics are detached and unconnected. Some of the expressions are brief and even obscure, and others strong and unguarded. But with all these and perhaps some other defects, the thoughts are so acute and penetrating, they spring from such a mature knowledge of the holy Scriptures, they open the recesses of the human heart with such skill and faithfulness, they lift up so boldly the veil which conceals the deformity of our motives, and the whole conception of Christianity which they exhibit is so just and so comprehensive, as to render them a most valuable monument of practical and experimental divinity. Such a writer as Mr. Adam takes us out of our ordinary track of reading and reflection, and shews us ourselves. He scrutinizes the whole soul, dissipates the false glare which is apt to mislead the judgment, exposes the imperfections of what is apparently most pure and inviting, and thus teaches us to make our religion more and more spiritual, holy, solid, practical, humble, sincere. pp. v, vi.

On the necessity of deep and enlarged views in religion, Mr. Wilson has the following useful observations:

At a period when, by the mercy and grace of God, an extensive revival of pure Christianity is taking place, it is more than ever important that a solid and adequate knowledge of Christian truth should be cultivated. For in proportion as religion is more widely spread, the corruption of man will mingle with it in various ways; and nothing can so directly tend to correct errors as they arise, as a full and really Scriptural knowledge of religion—truth accompanied with all the attributes and guards, with all the consequences and uses, with all the bearings and proportions which surround it in the holy Scriptures. p. x.

The pious and zealous author strikingly exemplifies the importance of a clear and thorough knowledge of religion, by selecting one fundamental truth, the doctrine of the fall and the corruption of our nature, and shewing how it affects the whole detail of faith and practice. We regret that we cannot follow up the able sketch which he has presented of the way in which the Christian student, setting out from one important principle, may and should advance to a full and mature knowledge of Christianity, as opposed to mere hasty, partial, and inaccurate notions seized upon at random, espoused in a spirit of obstinacy, and defended before they are understood.

Serle's Christian Remembrancer is the last volume on our catalogue, prefaced by an essay from the pen of Dr. Chalmers. The work itself being well known, and our limits being exhausted, we shall content ourselves with one or two extracts from the Introductory Essay, the object of which is to shew the importance of frequently and habitually calling to our remembrance the truths of Christianity which we admit into our acknowledged creed.

It is quite possible that a doctrine may at one time have been present to our minds, to the evidence of which we then attended, and the truth of which we did in consequence believe, and yet in the whole course of our future thoughts may it never again have occurred to our remembrance. This is quite possible of a doctrine in science, and it may also be conceived of a doctrine in theology, that on one day it may have been the object of faith, and never on any succeeding day be the object of memory. In this case the doctrine, however important, and though appertaining to the very essence of the Gospel, is of no use. It is not enough that we have received the Gospel, we must stand in it. And it is not enough that we barely believe it, for we are told, on the highest authority, that unless we keep it in memory we have believed in vain.

This may lead us to perceive that there is an error in the imaginations of those who think that after having understood and acquiesced in Christian truth there is an end of all they have to do with it. There is with many a most mischievous repose of mind upon this subject. They know that by faith they are saved and they look to the attainment of this faith a. a terminating good with the possession of which could they only arrive at it, they would be satisfied; and they regard the articles of a creed in much the same light that they do the articles of a title deed which may lie in their repository for years without once being referred to: and they have the lurking impression, that if this creed were once fairly lodged among the receptacles of the inner man, and only produced in the great day of the examinaton of passports, it would secure their entry into heaven—just as the title deed in possession, though never once looked to, guarantees to them a right to all that is conveyed by it. pp. v, vi.

To rectify this wrong imagination let it never be forgotten, that every where in the Bible those truths by the belief of which we are saved, have this efficacy ascribed o them, not from the mere circumstance of their having once been believed, but after they are believed, from the circumstance of their being constantly adverted to. p. vii.

It is from these considerations that we estimate so highly the following valuable treatise of Mr Serle, The Christian Remembrancer; in which the great and essential truths of Christianity are exhibited in a luminous and practical manner. But it is not merely those more essential truths of the Gospel which form the foundation of a sinner's hope that he brings to our remembrance, the operative nature of these truths as inwardly experienced by the believer in the formation of the spiritual life—the sanctifying influence of Christian truth over the affections and character of the believer—the whole preceptive code of social and relative duties to which, as members of society, Christianity requires our obedience—in fine, the whole Christian system of doctrines and duties is presented in a plain and practical manner, well fitted to assist the understanding in attaining a correct and intimate acquaintance with the truths of Christianity; while the brief but distinct and impressive form in which they are presented is no less fitted to assist the memory in its recollection of them. pp. xxiii, xxiv.

LITERARY AND PHILOSOPHICAL INTELLIGENCE
&c. &c.

GREAT BRITAIN

PREPARING for publication.—A Sequel to Evelyn's Memoirs, by Mr Upcott.—Hints to Churchwardens on the Repairs of Parish Churches.—Expedition to St Peter's River, Lake Winnepeek, by W Keating.—The Life and Administration of Lord Burleigh, by the Rev Dr Nares.—A Journal across the Andes, by R Proctor.—The Public, the Mystical and the Philosophical Religions of Ancient Greece, by W Mitford.

In the press.—The Religion of the Patriarchs illustrated by an Appeal to the subsequent Parts of Divine Revelation, by the Rev T T Biddulph.—Memoirs of Elizabeth Stuart, Queen of Bohemia, by Miss Benger.—Classical Disquisitions and Curiosities, by Dr Malkin.—Pompeiana, by Sir W Gell and J Gandy.—An Expostulatory Letter to the Rev E Irving occasioned by his Oration for Missions, by the Rev W Orme.

Dr Morrison attends at No 26 Austin Friars London on Mondays Wednesdays and Fridays from 11 till 2 o'clock to communicate elementary instruction in the Chinese language and to confer with persons who may be desirous of acquiring some knowledge of it whether for religious purposes or for objects of general knowledge and literature. He justly considers that human nature in different nations is greatly improved by an amicable interchange of thought and sentiment of which letters must generally speaking be the medium and that not only Christian truth but much useful knowledge subversive of hurtful superstitions might be conveyed to the eastern hemisphere were the language of China more studied in the United Kingdom. The written medium of thought employed by the Chinese is legible to the people of four other nations making collectively a fourth part of mankind. A considerable part of the population of the five nations alluded to namely those of China, Corea, Japan, the Loochoo Islands and Cochin China are able to read but they have little on which to exercise their faculties except their own pagan literature. The number of Christian books in the Chinese language is hitherto very limited. Although the several countries just named are not open to living teachers of Christianity, they are accessible by books which may be written and printed in Christian states or colonies, and conveyed by natives returning from those states to their respective countries; and thus Christian knowledge may be gradually spread throughout the continent and islands of eastern Asia.

FRANCE

It is stated that an unedited manuscript of Fenelon has lately been found buried among the archives of the establishment of St. Anne in the town of Cambray. It is said to have been composed by Fenelon in the year 1702 and is entitled, Reponse de l'Archeveque de Cambrai au Mémoire qui lui a été envoye sur le Droit du Joyeux Avenement.

SPAIN

The Spanish journals announce that the Autographic Journals of the voyages of Columbus and of several other illustrious navigators which have been preserved in the Escurial, and which up to the present time no person has been allowed to inspect, have been ordered, by the king, to be published.

GREECE

Two Cypriot youths redeemed from slavery and sent to England in 1823 were trained by the British and Foreign School Society as schoolmasters, and the elder of them is gone to Greece to impart instruction to his countrymen. Nine others have been since admitted for the same purpose, and the Society earnestly solicit contributions to this department of their benevolent exertions.

Mr Waddington says in his recent Visit to Greece that, in the midst of so many circumstances of devastation, very trifling injury has been sustained by the remains of antiquity. The Parthenon has been the severest sufferer. The Turks having expended all their balls, broke down the south west end of the wall of the Cella in search of lead, and boast of having been amply rewarded for their barbarous labour. But this is the extent of the damage; no column has been overthrown, nor have any of the sculptures been displaced or disfigured. All the monuments except two have escaped unviolated by the hand of war.

INDIA

At a late meeting of the Calcutta Asiatic Society the secretary read an analysis of the Vishnu Purana, the most famous of all the Puranas, and a plan is in progress for analysing the whole of these celebrated compositions. The collective works called the Puranas hold an eminent place in the religion and literature of the Hindoos. Inferior in alleged sanctity only to the Vedas, and like them possessing the credit of an inspired origin, they exercise a much more practical influence upon the Hindoo community, regulate their ritual, direct their faith and supply in popular legendary tales materials for their credulity. They are of two classes, principal and subordinate. The eighteen great Puranas are said to contain 1,600,000 lines of verses. The Vishnu Purana appears designed to inculcate the adoration of Vishnu. It is considered not to be older than the tenth century, but it is avowedly compiled from older materials and refers the historical portion to ancient and apparently traditionary memorials.

At the same meeting of the above Society the Rev Mr Mill communicated a notice of a Christian community in Persia, which is stated to have escaped the observation of European travellers. These Christians are said to occupy a small town near Tabreez called Khosraven, but have churches and bishops at Jerusalem, Diarbeker and Mousel. They are distinguished from other oriental Christians by their professing to be of Jewish descent and by their forming an independent community regulated by a patriarch and bishops unconnected with any other establishments. It is added that there may be amongst them other peculiarities, but the information yet received is of an imperfect nature and it was chiefly with a view to call attention to excite further inquiry that the notice was communicated to the society.

NORTH AMERICA

Mr West in his very interesting journal of his residence at the Red River Colony, lately published, relates the following tradition current among the North American Indians; it seems however to bear marks of modern interpolation. They spoke of an universal deluge which they said was commonly believed by all Indians. When the flood came and destroyed the world, they say that a very great man, called Wæsackoochack, made a large raft and embarked with otters, beavers, deer and other kinds of animals. After it had floated upon the waters for some time, he put out an otter with a long piece of shagganappy or leathern cord tied to its leg, and it dived very deep without finding any bottom and was drowned. He then put out a beaver which was equally unsuccessful and shared the same fate. At length he threw out a musk rat that dived and brought up a little mud in its mouth which Wæsackoochack took, and placing in the palm of his hand he blew upon it till it greatly enlarged itself and formed a good piece of the earth. He then turned out a deer that soon returned, which led him to suppose that the earth was not large enough, and blowing upon it again its size was greatly increased, so that a loon which he then sent out never returned. The new earth being now of a sufficient size, he turned adrift all the animals that he had reserved.

SOUTH AMERICA

Among the improvements in the internal affairs of South America we observe with great pleasure the great attention which is devoted to the regulation of the prisons The following facts we doubt not, will interest our readers

In the prisons of South America till lately were to be found prisoners of every description the innocent and the guilty the young and the old men and women all confounded together and shut up in dark damp and unwholesome dungeons Torture was employed to oblige them to confess imaginary or imputed crimes and severe punishments were made use of such as whipping to maintain order and humble the unfortunate prisoners An American writer after the Revolution in 1817 describes as follows the pernicious effects of such a system of prison discipline With us a man is imprisoned—not that he should be corrected but that he should suffer not that he should labour but that he should be in total idleness not that he should receive a warning but accumulated misery If we enter one of these prisons we behold hundreds of men covered with rags or in a state of nakedness we observe them emaciated and looking like spectres loaded with chains trembling at the presence of an insolent guard who delivers them their pittance of food and treats them with insult Many were stripped of every thing and shut up in noisome dungeons for a period almost forgotten The business of the gaoler was to load the condemned prisoners with heavy chains by which means the insecurity of the buildings was to be compensated for he was to keep them totally secluded and to introduce at his own will and pleasure such articles of food as the friends of the prisoners or other charitable persons presented at the prison Prisoners who had no relations or who were not fortunate enough to excite the commiseration of their companions have been known to die from want In Lima there were only two prisons calculated to hold about two hundred individuals at a time when the population of the city amounted to 52 627 souls The capital of Chili the population of which exceeds 50 000 inhabitants contained but one and that a very bad prison At Buenos Ayres amidst 60 000 inhabitants there were two prisons and in other places the proportion was also very deficient in consequence of which the prisoners suffered greatly At the commencement of the Revolution the dungeons of the Inquisition were destined to contain persons suspected of treason The punishments inflicted by this diabolical institution were also, extensively adopted in the civil prisons In those of Lima Abascal the Spanish viceroy established subterranean dungeons (called Infiernillos or little hells) which were so constructed that a person when shut in them could not sit stand, or lie down or place himself in any natural position Into these dungeons were thrust the victims of despotism and if ever they came out of them it was only to mourn over their existence being rendered helpless for the rest of their lives crippled or subject to the most acute and generally incurable diseases

In October 1821 General San Martin visited in person the prisons of Lima accompanied by the ministers of state the judges and various other persons calculated to give solemnity to the occasion Upon carefully investigating the state of the pending causes several prisoners were set at liberty others were relieved from their heavy fetters and directions were given that the trials of the remainder should be brought to a conclusion in the space of twenty days The General also abolished all kinds of torture and prohibited the use of the horrible *Infiernillos* He further gave orders for the introduction of useful labour that the criminal might be converted into an industrious and useful member of society Even in the midst of the clamour of arms and when all disposable resources were scarcely sufficient to secure their own existence the government have made great efforts to improve the construction and discipline of the prisons

The following are a few of the beneficial arrangements which have been recently enacted in several South American States

The city of Buenos Ayres now contains five prisons one for debtors exclusively a second of the police a third for military and marines a fourth for untried offenders a fifth for persons convicted and condemned to the public works In Chili in 1818, it was established that no citizen shall be confined in fetters In the same year the senate resolved that weekly visits shall be paid to every prison and accounts of the results of such visits transmitted to the court of justice In March 1822 the government of Peru established a most useful and humane code of rules for the regulation of all the prisons of the state Every prison is to have four separate departments the first division to contain those accused of criminal offences the second females the third prisoners under the age of 15 and the fourth those committed for debt Each prison is to have an alcaide and an adjutant one of whom shall constantly attend at the prison and be subject to the strictest responsibility In the course of every twenty four hours the prisoners shall be visited by the surgeon in order that if any be ill they may be passed without delay to the infirmary The doors of the wards are opened at six in the morning in summer and at seven in winter the prisoners attend to the cleanliness of their respective wards and are occupied in useful employments Any prisoner who conducts himself improperly is punished by solitary confinement. The constitution of Columbia, promulgated in October 1821, lays down as a rule that every man shall be presumed to be innocent, until declared guilty by due process of law. The 162d article expresses that no gaoler shall receive any person without an order signed by the proper authorities setting forth the reasons of imprisonment, a copy of which shall be given to the detained person. Article 163 forbids the alcaide or gaoler to prohibit the prisoner from having communication with any person except in cases where the order of commitment contains a clause for seclusion, and this is not to be continued longer than three days. The 168th article declares that any kind of treatment which aggravates the punishment determined by the the laws is a crime. It is also directed that the prisons shall be regularly visited.

LIST OF NEW PUBLICATIONS

THEOLOGY

A Collection of the Promises of the Gospel, arranged under their proper Heads, with Reflections and Exhortations deduced from them, by John Colquhoun, D.D. Minister of the Gospel, Leith. 4s.

Hints on Christian Experience, by the Rev. Charles Watson, Minister of Burntisland.

Regard to the Affairs of Others, A Discourse, by the Rev. R. Morrison, D.D. of China.

A Funeral Sermon for the late Rev. S. Parr, LL.D. by the Rev. S. Butler, D.D. Archdeacon of Derby.

Memoir of Catharine Brown, a Christian Indian, by R. Anderson. 1s. 6d.

Beneficial Influence of Knowledge, by the Rev. R. Keynes. 8vo. 1s.

The Progress of Dissent, by a Nonconformist. 8vo. 2s. 6d.

Scientia Biblica, 3 vols. royal 8vo. 5l. demy 8vo. 3l.

A History of the Christian Church, from its Erection at Jerusalem to the present Time, on the Plan of Milner, by the Rev. John Fry, B.A. 8vo. 12s.

Calvinistic Predestination repugnant to Scripture, by the Very Rev. Richard Graves, D.D.

A Caution to Protestants and Warning to Catholics, a Sermon, by the Rev. W. Marsh. 1s. 6d.

An Inquiry into what it is to preach Christ, and the best Mode of preaching Him, by the Rev. R. Lloyd. 8vo. 9s.

The Liturgy of the Church of England considered as a Summary of Religion, a Course of Instruction, and a Form of Devotion, by the Rev. Basil Woodd. 6d.

MISCELLANEOUS

Historical Outline of the Greek Revolution. 8vo. 5s.

History of Napoleon's Expedition to Russia, by General Count Segur. 2 vols. 8vo. 30s.

The present Laws relating to Saving Banks in England, omitting repealed Clauses, with Notes, Forms, &c. by a Barrister. 12mo. 3s.

Tables of the New System of Weights and Measures. 5s.

Going too Far, 2 vols. 12mo. 12s.

Jerusalem regained. 8vo. 8s.

Cavendish's Life of Cardinal Wolsey, with Notes, by S. W. Singer, Esq. 2 vols. 8vo. 30s.

Life of Schiller, with an Examination of his Works. 10s. 6d.

Memoirs of the Countess de Genlis, 9 vols. 8vo. French 16s. English 18s.

Account of the Life and Writings of Thomas Brown, M.D. by the Rev. D. Welsh. 8vo. 14s.

Itinerary of a Traveller in the Wilderness, by Mrs Taylor. 8vo. 6s.

The Death of Absalom, a Seatonian Prize Poem, by the Rev. H. S. Beresford. 2s. 6d.

The Lay of Truth, a Poem, by the Rev. J. Joyce. 6s.

Remains of the Rev. C. F. Schwartz, consisting of his Letters and Journals, with a Sketch of his Life. Part I. 8s.

RELIGIOUS INTELLIGENCE

BISHOPSGATE DISTRICT COMMITTEE FOR CHRISTIAN KNOWLEDGE

We have much pleasure in noticing the First Report of this highly useful local institution, the plans and proceedings of which we strongly recommend, especially to our clerical readers, as an excellent model and incentive in their efforts to establish parochial or district committees in connexion with the Society for promoting Christian Knowledge.

Prefixed to the Report is a list of resolutions passed at the first annual meeting, the lord Bishop of Chester, rector of the parish and president and treasurer of the institution, in the chair. The addresses delivered on that occasion are not prefix ed to the Report but we have understood that they were highly interesting and well calculated to promote the excellent designs of the institution. The zeal and unwearied diligence of Bishop Blomfield in promoting education and the circulation of the Scriptures the Prayer book and other religious publications in his parish and diocese have met with their best reward in the practical benefits which by the blessing of God have followed his exertions

The Report commences with a brief sketch of the plan and proceedings of the Society for promoting Christian Knowledge the particulars of which are too familiar to our readers to need transcription. The Report then adverts as follows to the operations of the Bishopsgate Auxiliary

It is with much pleasure that the Committee request the attention of the subscribers to a detail of those operations in which they have a more immediate and local interest and the good effects of which are not to be judged of simply and entirely by the number of books which appear to have been distributed. An opinion was expressed at the first formation of this Committee that the gratuitous distribution of Bibles Prayer books and Religious Tracts was less desirable than the sale of them at very reduced prices for it is well known that the poor set a greater value upon that which they have purchased out of their honest earnings than upon that which comes to them perhaps unasked but at all events unbought. Add to which that their readiness to buy even at a low price proves their desire of possessing. At the same time regarding the word of God as absolutely necessary to every Christian who can read it your Committee by no means approve of exacting from the poor a greater price for Bibles and Prayer books than is sufficient to give them a certain feeling of property in the books which they buy and therefore it was recommended at the commencement of this undertaking that the reduced prices of the books on the Society's catalogue should be still further reduced for sale amongst the poor of this district, by means of a fund formed by donations. The result has been very encouraging. The poor have evinced great alacrity in purchasing the books offered to them on these terms and the whole number of Bibles Testaments and Common Prayer Books which your Committee have distributed with the exception of two Bibles and two Common Prayer Books have been sold at the reduced prices. The smaller tracts have been in some instances sold and in many given to the purchasers of Bibles and Prayer books. The following is the account of books which have been issued from the Committee's depository within the last year —Bibles 215 Testaments 126 Common Prayer Books 355 Books and Tracts 890 forming a total of 1586. Of these one Welsh Testament and four Welsh Prayer books have been sold four Testaments have been sold to Roman Catholics and two Prayer books to a Roman Catholic for his Protestant wife and child. Two hundred and eighty three of the tracts have been issued to the Sunday schools now established in this parish for the reception of those children who are not able to attend the daily National Schools and the Committee may be excused for taking this opportunity of expressing their anxious wish that these Sunday chools which are at present wholly conducted by gratuitous teachers may be more generally known and better supported

In stating the number of books which have been distributed in a district of limited extent the Committee wish to remind the subscribers that independently of the good which must always result from placing the word of God in the hands of a person who is desirous of receiving it a great advantage accrues to the cause of religion through its ministers when the clergy are made the instruments of conveying that blessing to the poor. While prosecuting an inquiry into the spiritual wants of their flock they become acquainted with many interesting and important facts and find many unlooked for opportunities of doing good. The very circumstance of their being seen so employed, is a sensible proof of the concern which they feel for the welfare of their charge as they that must give account' a proof which is generally appreciated as it deserves to be. It is matter of fact that in this district many poor persons while taking in religious books have directed the attention of their clergyman to cases of distress and sickness in their neighbourhood and what is more important still many who had never attended any place of worship having been induced to purchase a Bible or a Prayer book have ever since gone regularly to church indeed there has been a sensible increase in the attendance of the poor at church since the institution of this Committee. Being made acquainted with the testimonies of the Lord they have learned to love the courts of his house Were there only one well-attested instance of this sort it might justly be considered as a sufficient return for the bounty of those who support this institution and for the labours of those by whom that bounty has been dispensed

It must not be forgotten that while it was one object of this Committee to provide for the spiritual wants of their immediate neighbourhood another was to contribute to the general designs of the Society itself to throw its mite into that treasury the contents of which may truly be said to be dedicated to the service of the Lord's house Accordingly the sum of 76l has been paid to the Society's treasurers being one third of the donations and subscriptions received by the District Committee and in addition to this the sum of 16l being one third of the money for books sold within the district —The donations and subscriptions for the year amount to 228l and the sales of books to 48l

Most earnestly do we wish that an institution such as this were in operation in every parish in the kingdom The plan of offering books to the poor at a cheap rate instead of bestowing them as a free gift, is most wise and we are glad to find the members of the Society for promoting Christian Knowledge adopting this among other improvements in the machinery of benevolence Formerly with the most pious and charitable intentions a notice was affixed to the books issued by the Society entreating that no person would sell its publications The Bishopsgate Committee receive and invite annual subscriptions or occasional contributions however small so that besides their more wealthy contributors their list of subscribers contains many who give from 2s 6d to 5s annually And why we would ask in spite of the charge of meanness and cruelty which has been so strangely urged against receiving small gratuities should not the alms even of the labouring classes themselves be welcomed when thus bestowed for their own benefit and the benefit of others? Why should a subscriber of half a crown yearly or as is a common practice in some other institutions of a weekly penny (according to the apostolic injunction 1 Cor xvi 2) be deprived of the luxury of casting his mite into the treasury of Christian benevolence in behalf of a cause equally dear to the rich and the poor the young and the old to male and to female if they alike feel as they ought a personal concern in the religion which they profess? Most justly does the Report before us remark that it will be the constant prayer of all who feel the power of the Gospel in their own hearts that he who gave himself for us that he might redeem us from all iniquity and purify unto himself a peculiar people zealous of good works may bless the labours of his servants in the work of converting souls and day by day enlarge the boundaries of his kingdom upon earth

Fully concurring in this devout aspiration we earnestly pray for the blessing of God upon this institution and upon those who have conducted its concerns with so laudable a spirit of wisdom conciliation and zealous piety

CHURCH MISSIONARY SOCIETY

The Twenty fourth Report of the Society having been lately published we are enabled to lay before our readers as copious a summary as our limits will allow of its proceedings during the year

West Africa Mission

Of the West-Africa Mission the Committee know not whether to speak with joy or sorrow In no one year has it ever suffered a greater loss in its friends and labourers—while in no one year has there been a more evident blessing on their labour Those who have died have died in the Lord thanking God for calling them to this work and glorifying his holy name in the midst of their sufferings The surviving missionaries seem to have had their faith elevated above the trying circumstances in which they have been placed and to have become more entirely united and devoted to their work

An extract of a letter from the Rev G R Nylander dated July 21 1823, very feelingly details the destitute state of the colony and of Freetown in particular in respect of religious instruction — By the removal of so many of our number places have become vacant and others that were vacant before remain still unprovided for Freetown is almost destitute Two simple hearted and pious chaplains are much wanted in Freetown and two missionaries of the same description will find plenty of employment There is a congregation of about 200 disbanded soldiers in a place called the camp these people and about 200 more near the camp have no teacher One Sunday after having attended to the duties of the church at Freetown I called at the camp and saw about 100 people assembled in their little church—a wattled house with grass roof one of the soldiers had acted as minister In subsequent letters the destitute state of several of the country towns is forcibly depicted

The late Sir Charles MacCarthy also pleaded earnestly for further aid As long says he as I have my health and his Majesty may require my presence on the coast I shall promote to the utmost of my power the religious instruction of this part of his dominions and more particularly so of the liberated Africans who from the forlorn condition in which they are landed more peculiarly call for assistance Here as every where assistance and means are required otherwise all must end in unavailing wishes I shall end this letter by again expressing my sincere thanks for the aid which I have obtained from the Society and leave it to the liberality of your own feelings to be thoroughly convinced that in regretting the want of a sufficient number of zealous missionaries I am thus bearing the strongest and most positive testimony to the value which I set upon the labours of those whom I have had

The Committee were anxious not only to supply the colony with teachers in its present state of urgent need but to make the best arrangements in their power for the future In reference to this subject they determined to propose to his Majesty's Government that the Society should take on itself the preparation and support of all the English clergymen which were found necessary for the service of the colony whether in Freetown or in the towns of the liberated Africans—these clergymen to be approved by his Majesty through the Secretary of State for the Colonial Department—the Society having the power of placing them with the concurrence of the Governor as local circumstances may require It was proposed that Government should provide in each of the country parishes for the education of its inhabitants and for their civil superintendance under the authority and direction of the clergyman This arrangement has been since settled and will regulate the future measures of the Society

Considerable difficulty has arisen in conducting the Adult Schools among the liberated Africans It appears however that in proportion as religion influences the people a desire of knowledge and diligence in attaining it discover themselves

To native teachers the Committee look under the peculiar circumstances of Africa with earnest hope that while special attention is paid to their due instruction and preparation the blessing of God will be granted and they adduce satisfactory proof of the competence of the natives to acquire all needful knowledge

The Committee trust that the arrangement with Government in connexion with the supply of labourers by means of the Institution at Islington will enable the Society to pursue its objects in Sierra Leone on that scale which is required both for the good of the colony itself and for its efficient influence on the surrounding tribes for both these objects are comprehended in the Society's design

To instruct the many thousands of natives who were liberated from slave vessels was a task of peculiar difficulty under the circumstances of a climate so unfavourable to Europeans Before any considerable progress could be made these natives speaking many different languages and dialects were to be made acquainted with the English language as it was most important to melt them down as soon as possible into one community The Christian Institution also was established in order to train native teachers not only for the service of their countrymen in the colony but to convey the knowledge of Christianity to their own tribes whenever a way should be open to them

The Committee continue to avail themselves of every opportunity in their power to obtain accurate information relative to the mission from unbiassed persons A Naval Officer on the station thus writes on this subject — Regent and the other liberated towns have surpassed my most sanguine expectations in all points of view and I trust this good work will prosper If God is on its side who can be against it? And that His Spirit has wrought wonderfully in the hearts of hundreds I think there are evident marks Indeed I myself found such in the visits which I made to their huts Their conduct at church is beyond every thing good I had the pleasure to see about 1700 in the church at Regent and to join with them in praising God from whom all blessings flow My feelings on this occasion were more than I can express I was present, most likely at the liberation of many of these people when I was on this station some years ago Then the place was an impenetrable wood the haunt of wild beasts and now to find myself in a good church with so large a congregation offering up my humble prayers and thanksgivings to that God who has been pleased hitherto so mercifully to preserve me—you may better conceive than I can express the feelings of one so situated. The children's improvement astonished me much. I passed four days in the mountains. Regent was my head quarters and I did all in my power to elicit truth and you may judge what delight I have experienced from finding every thing so much surpass my expectations.

We cannot follow the Committee through the details from all the stations but we shall select as a specimen a few particulars respecting the interesting settlement of Regent. The report of the late Mr Johnson written about a month before his lamented decease gave the following particulars.

As it respects Regent's Town the work of the Lord is proceeding as before. Divine service has been regularly attended by the communicants and the other inhabitants. The schools continue to improve. We have had several additions to our congregation and the schools by the arrival of slave vessels and our population now amounts to upward of 2000 persons. The people behave quietly and orderly. The youths in the seminary continue to *walk worthy of the high vocation wherewith they are called*. They have made considerable progress in their studies and promise well for future usefulness.

The number of scholars is 1079. There are 710 persons who can read. The number of the communicants including 48 candidates will be about 450. Our last anniversary of the Regent's town Branch Missionary Association was very interesting. The collection after the meeting amounted to 10*l*. Since October last, 7470 bushels of cassada and 1421 bushels of cocoa have been issued and there is now enough in the people's farms to supply them with half rations throughout the year. The new road to the sea is nearly completed. Some of the people have begun to trade in the country one canoe has been purchased and another hired for that purpose. One man has already delivered two tons and sixteen bushels of rice. The fishery has commenced and promises to become a permanent benefit to the town.

From Sherbro country Mr Nylander reports well of the continued endeavours of the brothers George and Stephen Caulker to instruct the natives under the authority of their family. Divine service is regularly performed in Bullom. They read prayers and sing hymns and read portions of Scripture of George Caulker's translation when he addresses the people on the passage read. G Caulker anxious for his own improvement that he may be the better able to instruct his people, has applied to the Society for a small library which the Committee have readily presented to him. The Committee continue to afford every assistance in their power to this first attempt of native chiefs to benefit their own country.

The cause of true religion remark the Committee cannot indeed but have to contend with many and serious impediments in a station surrounded as this is on every side by the empire of those antichrists which God has in inscrutable wisdom permitted to degrade and oppress the church.

Mediterranean Mission

A printer has been sent out for the service of this mission who took with him founts of Greek and Arabic types. Mr Jowett had determined on a visit to Syria in order to carry his researches into that part of the surrounding shores which he had not before explored. He was well furnished with the Scriptures and tracts. His purpose was to reach Jerusalem with all convenient speed and to spend about six months in Syria. At Alexandria he had the pleasure of meeting Mr Salt. Here he received an application by the British inhabitants requesting the assistance of the Society in obtaining for them a stated English minister. Many circumstances concurred in rendering such an appointment highly important and a clergyman so situated might render most valuable aid to the objects of the Society. The Committee promised the assistance desired as soon as might be in their power.

Of the general state of things in that part of Egypt Mr Jowett writes It has been a matter of great joy to me during these few days to compare the present state of things with what it was five years ago. God has certainly blessed and is still blessing His cause in these parts. It is impossible to say to whom or to what in particular this is owing it is the result of a series of impulses which have from year to year been communicated to Egypt. May the Church Missionary Society have the means promptly to meet the wants of the people! But my mind is more deeply impressed than ever with the need which we have of more labourers.

Having availed himself of the opportunity of entering afresh into many interesting topics relative to Egypt and Abyssinia Mr Jowett left Alexandria for Syria. In this visit he collected much interesting information on various points connected with the future objects and operations of the Society.

(*To be continued*)

PARIS BIBLE SOCIETY

We have received the monthly Bulletins of the Paris Bible Society up to a recent date and wish that our limits allowed us to translate very largely from these interesting documents. Feeling as we do most deeply interested in all that concerns the promotion of true piety in France, and specially in the religious prosperity of our fellow Christians of the Protestant communion, we have learned with the greatest satisfaction the success with which it has pleased God to bless the operations of this most important institution. For the present we must content ourselves with the following passages from the documents before us, to which we may find another opportunity of again adverting.

The Society most properly lays down as the foundation of all its proceedings that truly Protestant and Scriptural maxim, that the sacred books of the Old and New Testament contain the foundations of our faith, all the principles which should guide us in the present world, and all those truths which lead to happiness in that which is to come. Hence the primary duty of a Christian is to read and meditate upon the Bible, and the greatest blessing which man can offer to his fellow creatures is to place this Divine book within their reach.

Speaking of the success which has followed the exertions of the British and Foreign Bible Society, the Committee justly remark: It would be a great mistake to imagine that these magnificent results are due principally to the richer classes of society. For in the first place the English Government has no connexion with the Bible Society, although the princes of the royal family, the ministers of state and the nobility may individually be members of it. More than two thirds of the sum it has received proceeds from the voluntary contributions of artisans, mechanics and labourers; it is the produce of their savings; it includes even the mite of the widow and orphan.

The Committee proceed to point out the great importance of a Biblical Institution with reference to the peculiar circumstances of their own communion.

The French Protestants have not been strangers to the general feeling which is bringing evangelical Christians back with renewed ardour to the regulating code of their faith. To the reasons which their fellow Christians in other countries had to promote this object, their peculiar situation added others still more urgent. It was necessary to supply in the bosom of their own families the loss of those Bibles which were destroyed at the period of the suppression of the Reformed Church, a loss which could be but very partially repaired during the years of revolution and war which succeeded without interruption from the re-establishment of their rights till the restoration. It was necessary also to provide for replacing those Bibles which, although they had escaped destruction, were no longer fit for use, the language not being sufficiently intelligible. It was necessary to supply the increasing wants of successive generations, to whom the improvement in intellectual education, which is generally perceptible in the most numerous classes of society, renders reading at once more easy and more necessary. The importance of the measures which supply this deficiency appear with an increased weight of evidence when it is considered that the Protestants are scattered in the midst of a large Catholic population, and that they are destitute in many places not only of public worship, but also of every means of religious instruction. Must not this motive render the possession of the Bible even more indispensible (if we may so speak) to them than to their fellow Christians in other countries? And if it be recollected again that France is deprived of all those public and private institutions which, since the time of the Reformation, have in Protestant states supplied the ordinary demands by new editions of the sacred Scriptures, is it not absolutely necessary for the French Protestants to establish among themselves a special institution which alone is capable of supplying wants so various and so calculated to affect every benevolent heart?

It must be truly gratifying to British Protestants to witness the zeal with which the cause of Bible Societies is espoused by the members of sister communions on the continent. With few exceptions, remark the Committee, all the Reformed consistorial churches possess biblical establishments, which proves that their ecclesiastical authorities unanimously acknowledge their necessity and utility. In the small number of those churches which are still deprived of Bible Societies, measures are being taken to establish them as soon as possible.

The parent and auxiliary committees have wisely taken every opportunity of giving the utmost publicity to their proceedings.

Independently, they remark, of the wish which the several Committees felt to give an account to the subscribers of the disposal of the funds which were intrusted to them, they resolved to under take this task from the conviction which they feel, that the prosperity and even the support, of the Bible Society in France absolutely requires that its object, its principles, its constitution, its labours, the amount and expenditure of its funds, the names of the persons who compose it, and of those who manage it in all its departments, shall be made as public as possible, and that it is by this publicity that every effort that malevolence or ignorance may direct against the simple and eminently religious object of this institution will be defeated.

The Society have distributed directly or indirectly more than fifty thousand copies of the holy Scriptures. Without such an institution it would have been difficult, not to say impossible, to supply a very small part of the necessities which existed in France.

Among the Bibles printed under the direction of the Society is a stereotype impression in large octavo according to the version called Ostervald's, of which 4,000 Bibles and 2,000 Testaments are already struck off, and a new impression is going to be put to press. The Society is making preparations for publishing Bibles in various sizes, among others a Bible in folio or in quarto for the use of families and for public worship, and pocket Testaments.

In order to offer to the French Protestants a constant supply of Bibles and Testaments of the two versions of Martin and Ostervald, the Society requires very considerable funds, which the Committee remark, depend principally upon the support of female Bible Societies and the numerous Bible Associations which are already formed in Paris and in other parts of the kingdom. Some of these latter are composed of artisans and mechanics, others of agricultural labourers, and many even of children at school. These, as well as the female societies, are established, the Committee state, upon the model of those with which England abounds; their object is to collect weekly and monthly contributions either to procure Bibles for those of their members who are still destitute of them, or to increase the general funds of the Society, and to enable the central Committee to meet its official expenses, to procure new stereotype plates, and to make gratuitous grants of Bibles for Paris and the departments. These last amounted, last year, to the sum of more than 28,000 francs, without reckoning the depots of Bibles and Testaments which have been established in different parts of the kingdom.—The Committee attest that the Bible Societies and Associations have already produced the most beneficial effects in France. They have reanimated Christian piety; they have brought the members of the two Protestant communions, formerly too much dispersed, nearer together, and have formed a new bond of union between the Reformed Churches. They have exhibited to all classes of society Protestants zealous in the cause of religion, which is also that of good order and good morals. And they add: The purity of the Bible Society's objects, and the publicity given to all its operations, which their very nature exposes openly and renders incompatible with any design foreign to the simplicity of its aim, in short, intentions so perfectly upright and so benevolent, cannot fail of conciliating the good will of Christians not of our communion, and ought to secure to us more and more of the high protection of a government which justly considers the support of religion as among the first of its duties. But the most solid support of our confidence and the only immoveable foundation of our hopes is in that Divine Providence which, in the sight of the principal nations of the five divisions of the globe, has already impressed upon the labours of the Bible Society the seal of its august sanction, by granting to them a protection which may justly be compared to that with which it surrounded the first heralds of the Gospel and the enterprises of our glorious Reformers.

The Committee give the following striking epitome of the rapid advances of the Biblical cause. In 1804, a small society of friends to the Bible is formed in England; in 1824, three thousand Bible Associations, more or less numerous, are employed in distributing it in every part of the globe. In 1804 the parent Society receives contributions to the amount of six hundred pounds for the promotion of its object; in the beginning of 1824 its receipts have amounted to more than a million sterling. In 1804, measures are taken for printing some thousands of copies of the Bible in English and Welch; in 1824 more than five millions of copies of the sacred Scriptures in an hundred and forty languages of every part of the habitable globe, had been dispersed by the exertions of Bible Societies. Who can calculate the amount of good which has hence resulted? God only knows it, but eternity will reveal it. But does not this unexpected success prove that God favours the efforts of associations employed in the distribution of his word?

HOUSE OF REFORM FOR FEMALE CHILDREN

The following benevolent proposal has been issued for instituting a house of discipline and school of reform for viciously disposed and neglected female children

Many calls have been of late made upon the public attention to institute societies for checking various species of crime but as it is still more desirable to *prevent* than to *remedy* an evil it is respectfully submitted to the benevolence of the British public—1st That as yet no institution has been formed for the specific object of arresting the progress of vice in the minds of female children already contaminated by actual guilt—2d That the experiment has been tried with great success in the case of boys by the Philanthrophic Society the Refuge for the Destitute and other establishments where by their valuable exertions many have been checked in their career of wickedness and instead of becoming amenable to the offended laws of their country are now restored to the community useful and respectable members of society—and 3d That it is a lamentable fact, that there are now (January 1825) four female children under thirteen years of age in Newgate two of whom are under sentence of death unavoidably associating with the numerous old offenders and habitually vicious inmates of that prison It is therefore proposed that an institution should be formed for placing under strict discipline and wholesome restraint female children of vicious habits to correct them in their evil ways and to prevent the confirmation of those practices which in all human probability must terminate in their destruction

The necessity of such an establishment has presented itself very forcibly to the minds of those who have given much of their attention to the subject of female prisoners and finding upon inquiry that none of the societies at present in existence can lend their valuable aid towards the reception of such objects it is earnestly hoped that this appeal to the British public will not be made in vain but that a sufficient number will be found ready to contribute towards forming supporting and perfecting a system from which it is reasonable to expect with the blessing of God who alone can give the increase that the amount of crime will be lessened and the aggregate of good materially augmented

It is intended that this establishment should be under the care of a Schoolmistress with such other assistants as may be requisite that the children be carefully instructed in the holy Scriptures reading spelling and needlework also, that they be employed in household labour in proportion to their strength and that plain clothing be provided for them during the time they remain in the institution

Subscriptions are received by Sir John Perring Shaw & Co Bankers 72 Cornhill

---

VIEW OF PUBLIC AFFAIRS

FOREIGN

FRANCE—There appears to be great public discontent at the line of policy pursued by the government and the legislature especially respecting the reduction of the *rentes* the indemnification to the emigrants and the disgraceful sacrilege bill which has passed both chambers The commercial part of the community are also complaining of the injury inflicted upon the country by the refusal of the government to acknowledge the independence of South America—Sixty of the first banking and commercial houses in Paris have presented an address to the king urging his majesty to follow the example of England and secure to his country its due share of the trade of that rising continent Happy would it be for France and the world if the French government could be induced to retrace its steps and to adopt both in its political and ecclesiastical arrangements those enlightened and Christian principles which alone can secure peace and prosperity to its subjects—Great preparations are being made for the coronation

POLAND—A proclamation has been issued by the Emperor Alexander for convoking the third Diet, under the provisions of the constitution or charter The emperor bitterly complains that in the Diet of 1820 there was displayed a most grievous spirit of disputation to prevent which he has decreed that the public shall be excluded from the chambers, in order that the speakers may not be seduced to court an ephemeral popularity to the destruction of that tranquility and expected unanimity which his majesty considers ought to prevail in their deliberations His majesty also takes the opportunity of reminding them that it was of his own free will, and paternal sentiments that he bestowed a constitution upon his Polish subjects Yet amidst this mockery of a constitution we would not despair of good being ultimately effected Our own parliament was once equally abject and with far fewer opportunities of information from without especially by means of the press than may now be enjoyed even by a Polish senator or deputy, who seriously turns his thoughts to the business of legislation and the welfare of his country The intercourse and collision of mind with mind among persons of intelli gence and influence, chosen from every part of the country, will almost necessarily in the end favour the cause of public liberty nor can the chambers be made so completely air tight by an imperial decree as to prevent the sentiments and discussions of the members having some considerable influence upon the minds of their countrymen at large

UNITED STATES.—Mr Adams on taking the oath of office as President delivered an inaugural address in which he depicts as follows the advances made by his country since the establishment of its independence

The year of jubilee since the first formation of our Union is just elapsed that of the Declaration of our Independence is at hand Since that period a population of four millions has multiplied to twelve a territory bounded by the Mississippi has been extended from sea to sea new States have been admitted to the Union, in numbers equal to those of the first confederation treaties of peace amity, and commerce have been concluded with the principal dominions of the earth the people of other nations inhabitants of regions acquired not by conquest, but by compact, have been united with us in the participation of rights and duties, of our burdens and blessings the forest has fallen by the axe of our woodmen the soil has been made fertile by the tillage of our farmers our commerce has whitened every ocean the dominion of man over physical nature has been extended by the invention of our artists liberty and law have marched hand in hand all the purposes of human association have been accomplished as effectively as under any other government on the globe and at a cost little exceeding in a whole generation, the expenditure of other nations in a single year Such is the unexaggerated picture of our condition under a constitution founded upon the Republican principle of equal rights'

Mr Adams admits that there have been shades in this picture, caused by differences of opinion upon the theory of Republicanism, the policy of America towards other states, and jealousies of sectional interests All these, however, he states are now at an end and he exhorts his countrymen to discard from their hearts every remaining vestige of political hostility We feel much more inclined to congratulate our Transatlantic brethren upon the substantial realities of this picture than to protest against any partial exaggeration of the colouring otherwise we might justly urge some abatements from these glowing descriptions, and not least that 'plague spot" of slavery which still infects so large a portion of the domestic soil of this land of freedom

But we forbear long may Great Britain and these flourishing States continue in sisterly amity, benefiting each other by their mutual intercourse and reciprocation of commerce and promoting throughout the world those civil and religious blessings which each so richly enjoys

SOUTH AMERICA.—The current intelligence from the whole family of the South and Central American States Brazil partially excepted continues to be of a gratifying character Our readers will have seen in another department of the present Number some interesting details relative to the improved criminal jurisprudence and discipline of the jails in several of the new States The message addressed by the Vice president of Colombia (the President Bolivar being absent with the army) to the Congress of 1825 is marked by great wisdom liberality, and firmness and though at that period neither the decision of Great Britain to acknowledge their independence nor the mortal blow to the power of Spain in Peru was known the executive government seemed perfectly confident of the stability and rapid prosperity of the Republic —A letter has appeared in the journals from Mr Joseph Lancaster dated Carraccas in which he states that he is forming a school and a seminary for schoolmasters and that a desire for education is very prevalent The same remark applies to the other new States The British and Foreign Bible Society is sending out an agent to forward its benevolent designs in this vast continent

DOMESTIC

Intelligence has arrived from India of a series of decisive military successes in the contest with the Burmese The whole Burman coast from Rangoon eastward was subject to the British arms The native forces amounting to fifty or sixty thousand men had been defeated with a loss of five thousand men killed and wounded and re-collecting their strength to the number of twenty or twenty five thousand were again completely routed We trust that a decisive issue has been thus put to the war and we would hope that in the end these unhappy pagans may reap some solid advantages from the new relations which may be formed with an enlightened and Christian country but we stand appalled at the fearful sacrifice of human life, British, Indian, and Burman, which has attended this sanguinary contest, the causes and objects of which still remain unexplained

The proceedings in parliament have been interrupted by the Easter holidays since which the subject of Catholic emancipation has been the chief topic of discussion. The bill for annulling the civil disqualifications of the Catholics has passed the second reading in the house of commons by a majority of twenty seven. Other bills have been introduced for raising the scale of the elective franchise in Ireland and allowing stipends to the Roman Catholic clergy, which provisions it is contended are politically necessary to lessen the influence which the abolition of civil disqualifications may throw into the popular scale and to give the government a counterpoising weight. The former measure is advocated by its friends on the ground of simple justice, as well as of absolute necessity; the two latter are urged as matters of expediency and chiefly with a view to quiet the fears of those who from *political* views, object to the bill for emancipation. We forbear entering into any discussion of the subject, especially as the details of the proposed countervailing plans are not before the public while this sheet is going to press.

The government measures for relaxing the restrictions on commerce have been fully detailed in parliament, but we have no space for the particulars. They are however liberal and leave but few relics of the prohibitory system and its attendant evils. Foreign corn and free grown sugar are however still most impolitically kept out of the British market, but it is admitted that such a system cannot last much longer. Mr Whitmore is about to propose some measures respecting corn this session, and the king's ministers have pledged themselves for a full parliamentary inquiry into the whole question next session.

OBITUARY

REV W READ

The uncertainty of life and the consequent necessity of being constantly ready for the summons of death, are subjects constantly illustrated and enforced; there are however some instances of sudden death which seem to proclaim these truths with a voice peculiarly audible and emphatic. Of this kind is that which I am about briefly to detail. I refer to the lamented death of the Rev William Read, A M formerly of St Edmund Hall, and late Curate of Stone Easton Somersetshire. The calamity which terminated his valuable life, took place on the 14th of August last but it is only recently that it has occurred to the writer to offer this brief memorial to the readers of your publication, who will feel interested in the deceased, as the writer of the affecting little memoir of Thomas Hogg the Scottish wanderer which was inserted in your Number for January 1823, and has since been presented to the public in tracts of various forms.

The facts to which I allude, were these.—Mrs Read was recovering from a transient indisposition when her affectionate husband took advantage of a bright day to propose to her the benefit of air and exercise. Their eldest little boy, a child of more than ordinary promise, accompanied them, and also a faithful man servant. They took their drive, happy in each other's society, and hailing the smiling sky and luxuriant fields as in unison with the joyful and grateful emotions of their hearts. How fair the prospect, but how soon to fade! we may apply to it the Psalmist's words—" The wind passeth over it, and it is gone." Their morning's excursion was nearly completed and they drew nigh to their home, when the horse set off at full speed, and became ungovernable. Could they have kept the main road they might have yet escaped but the horse having been accustomed to a short cut down a lane, turned quickly round and rushed into it. The vehicle was dashed against a wall, and every individual in it severely injured. Mr Read was taken up insensible. Mrs Read's skull was fractured, and her arm broken the child's skull was fractured and the servant's shoulder dislocated! It is not easy to conceive a scene more heart rending than that which presented itself on the return of the party all of whom had but three hours previously left home in health and spirits. How forcibly does it inculcate the sacred admonition " Be ye also ready, for in such an hour as ye think not the Son of Man cometh!" Mr Read remained in the same state of insensibility till the morning of the 16th when his happy spirit, freed from the burden of the flesh returned to God who gave it. The little boy recovered his faculties for a short space only, and was then observed to clasp his feeble hands and utter, (though indistinctly,) the Lord's Prayer, adding, "I am going to heaven." His gentle spirit joined that of his father at the distance of only one hour. That so young a child should spontaneously commend his soul to God in prayer, in the hour of extremity, and under the pressure of such a weight of suffering is worthy of being recorded, as affording encouragement to parents to bring up their offspring in the nurture and admonition of the Lord.

Mr. Read was called from his labours at the early age of thirty four, before he had borne much of the heat and burden of the day. No interval of returning reason occurred during which he might bear his dying testimony to the truths which in the faithful discharge of his ministry it had been his constant endeavour to inculcate. The truly Christian spirit and happy consistency of his conduct engaged the love and reverence of the poor, and commanded the respect and esteem of all. Even those who thought his principles too uncompromising respected him for his consistency and loved him for his exemplary conduct. What those principles were, may be collected by your readers from the little memoir already mentioned.

Having a numerous family (eight children under eleven years of age) Mr. Read had undertaken the instruction of pupils by whom he was affectionately loved and honoured and who can testify to the parental kindness with which he studied both their temporal and spiritual benefit. The afflicted widow is, through Divine mercy, after a long and painful illness, restored to her little family.

Mr. Read passed his life in so retired a manner that though all who knew him loved him, yet their number was but small. Divine grace had adorned his character with many beautiful traits, but these excellences were as unobtrusive as they were lovely, furnishing little upon which the pen of the biographer could dwell, though much upon which the recollections of friendship and affection cannot but expatiate. His piety too was of the like unostentatious kind. There are indeed records of it. It stands recorded in the language with which he was wont to commune with God and pour out his heart in secret. It stands recorded in the published production of his pen above mentioned. It stands recorded, it is trusted, in the memory and in the hearts of some who drank in lessons of heavenly wisdom from his lips and are following him as he followed Christ. But its chief record is on high, and not to be divulged till that day when God shall judge the secrets of men by Jesus Christ.

Up to the period of Mr. Read's ordination his time was passed at school and the university, at neither of which places did any thing remarkable occur, except indeed the most important of all events, and that on which he ever reflected with devout feelings of gratitude, namely his being brought to a knowledge of the truth as it is in Jesus. This took place at the early age of fourteen, in consequence of which he was preserved from falling into many of the sins peculiarly incident to youth.

Mr. Read served the curacy of Midsomer Norton, Somerset, seven years, and during four years of that period the cure of the neighbouring parish of Holcombe was added to his ministerial duties. It is not too much to say that no individual in either of these parishes saw him depart without regret. The last four years of his ministry and of his life, were spent at Stone Easton and terminated in the manner which it has been my painful office to record.

J.

ANSWERS TO CORRESPONDENTS

W R I, D G L S, J B, and I M W are under consideration

CHRISTIAN OBSERVER.

No. 281.] MAY 1825. [No. 5 Vol. XXV.

RELIGIOUS COMMUNICATIONS

AN ACCOUNT OF THE PROTESTANT CHURCH IN FRANCE

(Continued from p. 207.)

I WOULD now proceed to advert to some circumstances in the present condition of the French Church, which seem to afford a reasonable prospect of its increase and improvement.

1. The first point which I shall notice on the state of the Protestants of France is, the comparative toleration in which they are now permitted to exercise their religion.* No interruption is offered them in the exercise of public and social worship. Proselytes may be made to the Protestant Church, and any means be used to extend its boundaries which do not offend against the public peace. Protestant schools and universities may be instituted, and Protestant ministers have the privilege of teaching members of their own body in the different prisons and hospitals of the kingdom. There will of course occur, and especially amongst a people who are not as practised in toleration as we are in this country, many instances of attempts to restrain the liberty of the Protestants, and to prevent what may be regarded as the usurping influence of a falsely called Reformed Church. But this is not the common state of feeling; indeed, indifference to all religion is at this period too prevalent in France. Protestantism is therefore, tolerated as much by public opinion as by the law of the land. The distribution of useful books and tracts therefore is not prevented; and, in short, good may be done by any means which do not affect the public tranquillity. It is incumbent upon the Protestants of France not to permit their present advantages to remain unimproved, but to employ them zealously in extending the influence of true religion throughout their whole community, not knowing how soon a conjuncture may arise of evil influences, by which their means of beneficial exertion may be greatly abridged.

2. Another favourable circumstance in the present state of the Protestants of France is, the increasing distribution of the word of God among them.—By means of the exertions of the Bible Society most of the urgent applications for the Scriptures have been answered, and in general those individuals alone are without them who, like many in this country, have not learned their inestimable value, or who have not the power of reading them. There are two versions of the Bible made use of by the Protestants of France, those of Martin and of Ostervald. The former is grounded upon the oldest translation originally patronized by Calvin. It is sound in its construction, and forcible in its style, although it is ancient and somewhat obscure. The version of Ostervald is of more recent date than that of Martin, which appeared about the time of the revocation of the Edict of Nantes, but it is more paraphrastic and less vigorous. Two other versions have

---

* The two Confessions, that of Augsburg and the Reformed, have the same privileges both in the establishment of their worship and the support of their ministers.

a partial circulation, but principally amongst the Swiss population speaking French. One is that of the modern school of Geneva made about twenty years since which, with the exception of twenty or thirty capital errors, fatal to its character for orthodoxy is not a bad translation but it has now fallen almost wholly into disuse beyond the city which gave it birth. The other is that of the Canton de Vaud, published at Lausanne, in the year 1821. This is even more paraphrastic than that of Ostervald upon whose model it has been constructed. These two last mentioned versions will probably have but a small circulation amongst the French. The attention of all classes in France is however every day more and more directed to the word of God. By means of the energetic labours of the Bible Society in that country and of the notoriety which Bible institutions have acquired in consequence of the labours and reports of the Protestants and the bulls of the Pope, public attention even among Catholics, has been remarkably directed to this subject and some priests themselves have been induced to read the Scriptures and to distribute and expound them to their people. The young are becoming acquainted with the sacred volume, through the medium of schools in which the Testament is freely distributed and, whilst a knowledge of the word of God is thus gradually diffusing itself over the population, the ponderous works of the fathers and schoolmen which issued from convents and were patronized by bishops are now scarcely to be found. The avidity with which copies of the Scriptures are received by the people when offered to them, is remarkable and those who have made the trial will bear witness that they have never experienced, in the conduct of those to whom they have been presented, any thing but respect for the book and gratitude to the giver. Much benefit must result to the cause of truth from the general perusal of the word of God. A more elevated standard of practice is thus insensibly erected the pernicious influence of Neologism among Protestants is gradually counteracted and the grosser errors and superstitions of the Romish creed and ritual are found to have no foundation in Scripture. But whatever may be the effect among the Roman Catholics, it cannot be doubted that a solid foundation is laid for improvement among the Protestants by the free distribution among them of a sound and popular version of the Bible which I trust that all classes of society will gradually be brought more and more to make a lamp unto their feet, and a light unto their path

3. A third feature which I shall notice in the state of the French Protestants, is a soundly constructed church.—I have before spoken of the Edict of Bonaparte by which public worship and an established order of church government were restored to the Protestants. The internal regulations of their church the code of discipline to which the Protestants had themselves assented I have also mentioned. The Reformed and Lutheran churches have of course different governments but in their practical proceedings the same observations are applicable to each. The relaxation of discipline in their administration is not that point of which the members of our own establishment have any right to complain. Their state of discipline only partakes of the common defect which most unhappily belongs to the principal churches of Christendom. The Liturgy used by the Reformed Church has been handed down with little variation, since the time of Calvin and it seems as far as it goes to be unexceptionable. The sacraments are rightly and devoutly administered. In many of the Protestant churches especially in Switzerland the preparation for receiving what is called the *premiere communion*, that is, the first attend

ance at the Lord's table, is not the almost negative preparation which is usually judged to be sufficient before Confirmation in this country, but it consists in two or three regular courses of religious instruction upon a basis something like the Assembly's Larger Catechism, and these are gone through with real seriousness, and in many cases with an almost exclusive attention for a time to this subject. Many persons from this country who have attended the services at the French places of worship, have been struck with the decency and good order, the simplicity and outward reverence, with which the whole has been conducted. Sermons are regularly preached, and the Scriptures are publicly read, although this last part of the service is generally performed in a very slovenly and indevout manner. The old Psalmody which used to revive the hearts of the faithful, is still partially in use. Those very Psalms which once arrested the attention of the whole French Protestant Church (now indeed considerably altered to suit the taste of the times, and still very much behind modern compositions in style and elegance,) are sung; and those who think upon their forefathers and sympathize in their distresses, may raise their voices in the very melodies which cheered them on their way. I do not apprehend that under the existing circumstances of the Protestants any better mode of administration could be devised than that under which they are at present placed. They possess a constitution already made and fixed by law, which, supposing them to be actuated by a spirit of genuine piety, is well adapted to render their church a source of unspeakable blessings to their country.

4. A fourth point to be noticed in the state of the Protestants, is the large body of ministers attached to their churches.—I have before observed that at the period of the re-establishment of religion by Bonaparte, 1038 ministers of the two communions were registered in the books of the government. This number however included all that were scattered over the whole French empire. Although much dominion has been detached from France by the late political changes (as the city of Geneva and the valleys of Piedmont,) in these particular places the number of pastors greatly exceeds the estimate of 1802, and in France itself the number has much increased. These ministers are dispersed over the north, the east, and the south of France, and they are generally at a distance from each other. They are usually poor in their circumstances, but not uninstructed in general literature, nor unmindful of the high trust placed upon them. The effect of the original outlawry under which some of the ministers were born, and of the forty years political convulsions in which they have lived, their separation for a long period from pious individuals of other countries, the want of books, and therefore the difficulty of acquiring any deep theological knowledge,—these and other circumstances have served to prevent their maintaining that distinguished place in the Christian ministry which was formerly held by their predecessors. But these hindrances to their advancement having been in some degree removed, it may be hoped that the Protestant ministry of France will rise again to its original level, and exhibit that ability, that learning and that theological knowledge for which at one time it was so eminent; so that we may again hope to see amongst its members sermon writers like Mastuzet, Amyraut and Daillé, Supuville, Claude, and Saurin; and commentators as illustrious as Calvin, Beza and Desmarets. Of the present race of Protestant ministers it may be truly said, that, in general, they are solicitous to do all they can for the benefit of their people, but they have scanty means and little influence. Those means, however and that influence, they are

disposed zealously and faithfully to employ in carrying forward any designs of piety and benevolence, which are consistent with the peculiarities of their faith, and which will not compromise them with the government

5 A fifth point to be noticed in the present state of the French Protestants is, that their population amounting, it is supposed, to upwards of a million, some say a million and a half is spread over the whole kingdom In some cases discoveries have been made of considerable numbers secluded at a distance from the common haunts of men whose ancestors had hid themselves in the remotest and most inaccessible corners, that they might escape the ruin which fell upon their brethren The First Report of the Paris Bible Society contains an interesting account of some of this class of French Protestants "Many small tribes of Protestants, scattered over the surface of France, appeared worthy of the attention and care of the Society Some are without pastors, and without public worship The department de la Somme alone counts about six thousand individuals in this state of abandonment and religious privation yet among these reformed Christians, so long forgotten, the faith of their fathers has been preserved in all its purity For want of sacred books of which violence had deprived their obscure families, and from replacing which, either fear or poverty had prevented them, oral traditions have transmitted from generation to generation the most interesting narratives, the most important lessons and the holiest precepts of the Bible Passing from the father to the children prayers and hymns, the most fervent and the most proper to nourish faith and hope have never ceased to resound in their cottages and the paternal benediction has stood in place of that of the minister of the Lord —In some instances a sufficient number of these interesting individuals have been brought together, to constitute a church, and to claim an allowance for the payment of a minister In other cases this would have been effected but for the want of suitable ministers to take the charge of congregations

The Protestants are dispersed about France much in the same way as the society of Friends are in England and those who know the value of this body of Christians, and the diligence with which they give themselves to works of practical utility —indeed, in many districts, they are the main stay upon which certain institutions of benevolence depend,—will see how important the Protestant body in France may prove if actuated by a spirit of Christian piety and zeal There are generally a few of them in all the great towns and many divisions of the kingdom are well sprinkled with them What invaluable instruments might they not therefore become not only in plans of general benevolence but in diffusing more widely the blessings of moral and religious light

6 A sixth point to be noticed, is the general character of the Protestants —It is true that there may be much of ignorance amongst them but there is not perhaps more than their unfavourable circumstances both before the Revolution and since that period will account for There is also amongst the less instructed part of them a mistaken feeling which leads them to identify their zealous opposition to Popery with real religion They are in this respect like men who should value the casket more than the jewel which it contains Considering what they have suffered from Popery with the recurrence of St Bartholomew's day upon their annual calendar with the tombs of their forefathers almost fresh before their eyes and with an apprehension that Popery is Popery still and that the upholders of that system if they had the power, might not

want the disposition which would lead to the destruction of every other mode of worship, and perhaps to their own proscription surrounded too as they are by the revived mummeries of popish worship by follies which speak to their senses, can we wonder that the Protestants, convinced that the Catholics are totally wrong, should be too easily led from their opposition to them, and from that circumstance alone, to conclude that they themselves are entirely right. The very strength, however, of their prejudices in favour of their peculiar principles, is likely to prevent their being seduced to participate in the prevailing superstitions, and will come in aid of more scriptural and really efficacious means of confirming them in the faith and practice of the Gospel. The reviving spirit of religion amongst them may be seen in the progress of the Bible Society, and in the monthly publications of the Missionary Society of that country. The word of God has been eagerly welcomed amongst them the voice of praise for the progress of the Gospel amongst the heathen, now resounds in France and the Society established in Paris receives contributions from a variety of quarters, and is aided by those prayers for promoting the extension of the Gospel in other countries, which are calculated to bring down a blessing upon their own. Education, moreover has within the last few years much enlightened the body of Protestants. The report of the proceedings in other countries has provoked them to emulation. Religion has been brought before them, not merely as the watchword of a party but as a living principle of action which is able to make them wise and happy and the effect of this change has become visible in the body at large.

7 The only other point I shall notice as encouraging in the existing state of the Protestants, is the able instruments for doing good raised up by Providence among themselves — I have frequently alluded to the Bible Society, which incidentally subserves many most valuable purposes besides the distribution of the word of God. One of these is the union of all the Protestants in a common object of interest and exertion. In the large and scattered population of the Reformed and Lutheran churches, a common tie was wanting and this has been found in the Bible Society, which unites them notwithstanding their shades of difference, and I trust will continue to unite them. The Paris Society has regular communication with the different Bible Associations throughout France. In that city, therefore the circumstances of the whole body may be known and thence in cases of difficulty the requisite aid and counsel and encouragement may be obtained — The Missionary Society, though a small, is a most interesting institution. It was observed by the late Mr Owen that till the Bible Society in England entered into foreign labours its efforts were small, and the interest excited by those efforts was feeble. But when it extended its exertions to distant parts of the world, a powerful reaction was immediately felt in this country and a much more lively and effective zeal was created. In the French Protestant Church they have acted upon this principle. Although their means were scanty, they desired to shew that they were willing, out of their poverty to aid the cause of God in heathen lands and it has pleased God to favour their institution. The funds have increased and the spirit which has been excited promises a rapid enlargement of Christian feeling in the minds of the people in general. One missionary has already been sent into the field and a seminary has been established at Paris to educate missionaries at the head of which has been placed the eminent minister of the Reformed Church at Berne M Galland —A third means which has been set to work in France, is a Tract Society. Many

tracts had for several years past been distributed in that country, but they were translations indifferently executed, and were not generally popular. The tracts at present made use of are either original or well prepared translations.—A fourth means which has been set on foot to extend religious information, and to communicate intelligence as to the progress of religion in France and in other countries is a monthly publication somewhat resembling the Christian Observer. It is called the "Archives du Christianisme," and it is edited by that valuable minister of the Gospel, M. Monod, junior, who visited England three years ago. This work conveys the principal religious intelligence of England and Germany, through the body of Protestants wherever the French language is spoken. By this means great good is effected. The recital of the labours and success of others serves to confirm the zealous, and inform the ignorant, to encourage the weak, and to lead all who hear it to feel a portion of that glow which is seen to arise from the intercourse and communion of kindred spirits in a good cause.— Lastly, amongst the instruments for doing good which are now in operation, I must mention the zealous, laborious, faithful ministers who are labouring for the cause of God in France. It is scarcely possible to mention any in preference to others, without seeming to be invidious. But I must still be allowed to speak of two or three persons who, as ministers and as men, would do honour to any cause but that to which they have devoted themselves, and in which it is honour enough to be permitted to serve.

I will mention first of all the pastor Oberlin, of the Ban de la Roche, the first foreign correspondent of the English Bible Society, described in so interesting a manner by Mr. Owen who visited him in the year 1818. This individual early in life left the refinements of the city where he was born, and where he might have obtained a high situation to which his rank and talents entitled him. Led, as he conceived, by the hand of Providence, he took his station amidst a cluster of villages, in a cold comfortless situation, nearly at the top of the Volges. From that place he has scarcely ever removed, except, during the Reign of Terror, to the prison of the Republic; nor has he been tempted to emigrate but by one offer which was made him to settle in a more desolate place, on the continent of North America. In the Ban de la Roche this *Cher Papa* as he is there universally called, has raised up a people as remarkable for their intelligence as their practical piety. He has established schools, built school houses, constructed roads, and promoted civilization: so that, in spite of cold and damp, and soil and situation, the population of this place may justly be regarded as objects of envy by the inhabitants of more fertile and genial regions. So distinguished is the character of the pastor Oberlin, that the Government of his country have placed him in the ranks of the legion of honour. Mr. Owen says of him in his Letters, (Bible Society's Fifteenth Report, p. 11.) "The first foreign letter which awakened an interest in our minds, the letter which made its way most directly to our hearts, and which at our first anniversary produced the strongest, and, if I may judge of others from myself, the most lasting impression upon us all, was that of this venerable pastor." "The reception he gave me was such as, from the profound humility of his character, might be anticipated." He adds afterwards 'The appearance of his congregation, their neat and becoming costume, their order and their seriousness, together with the fervour, tenderness, and simplicity with which the good minister addressed them, both in his sermon in the morning, and his catechetical lecture in the afternoon, conveyed to my mind the most delightful impression—that of a sincere and elevated devotion.—The Ban de la Roche is without doubt advantageously situated for the morals of the people, and the minister, a man of uncommon powers, has been for half a century sedulously and almost unremittingly engaged in his work but perhaps there does not exist in Europe a village of the same extent of population, where the fruit of religion is more fully developed and where it is seen in so beautiful and interesting a form I need only appeal to the character of some of the poor people given in the History of the Bible Society vol 1 p 151 and the statements there made have been fully verified by other persons who have subsequently visited the Ban de la Roche

The next individual I shall mention is the minister of Toulouse M Chabrand If a distinguished piety a sound judgment a warm affection to the cause of his Master and a laborious devotedness to his service should give credit in our estimation to a faithful servant of God it is due to M Chabrand—I would also mention M Lissignol whose zealous attachment to the cause of the Gospel has been known and felt not only by the Protestant but the Catholic population of that vast country His writings, his translations, and his various labours will long remain a testimony of his faithfulness to his Master, and of his importance to the church

The last name I shall mention, and I stop here because my enumeration would lead me too far is that of M Monod, junior, the pastor adjoint of the church at Paris a gentleman distinguished by his arduous and persevering efforts to do good not only at home but abroad With small means a weak constitution a young family, incessant duties as an author and a minister he has never ceased to labour in his Master's service The societies, the prisons the hospitals, have alike witnessed his zeal and whatever he has not undertaken has only been neglected because his time, his health, or his necessary duties have prevented him

The picture which has now been laid before your readers of the present state of the Protestant Church in France, surely encourages a lively hope respecting its future prosperity and that hope is greatly strengthened by recollecting how marvellously it has been preserved It has indeed been assailed in every possible way The fury of persecution the more paralyzing influence of long continued neglect, the follies of superstition the demon of anarchy the horrors of a state in which all religion was rejected the world and the devil, seem to have set all their array against it but still it has maintained its ground and now we cannot but hope, nay expect not only that it will maintain its ground, but that it will increase and flourish Its toleration by law, the soundness of its institutions, the number of its adherents the zeal and piety of many who are connected with it the prayers which are daily offered for its prosperity all these afford good ground to expect its future security and improvement Still it becomes an inquiry of deep interest to the cause of true religion, what are the means which may be advantageously pursued by the Protestant Church in France for insuring its permanence and stability and for ameliorating its condition My French friends, I am sure will excuse me if I venture to offer a few hints on this important subject

First, I should say that all the benevolent institutions already established in France require to be zealously supported The means by which in any country the greatest good can be effected are generally speaking those which have had the warrant of successful experiment If such means have moreover eminently prospered in other countries this is an additional argument for their support and encouragement

It is impossible, in this view, to estimate too highly, or to promote too zealously, the Bible or Tract Societies of France, the means of diffusing religious information, and of cementing the union of the Protestants as a body. Much good will undoubtedly be attained by every effort to that end. But still there are other expedients which may come in aid, some of which I shall now proceed to suggest.

In the first place, considering the ignorance which still prevails among Protestants, and the comparatively uninformed state of many of the ministers, and at the same time the extensive and increasing distribution of the word of God in that country, it seems of great importance that there should be brought into general use some sound commentary upon Scripture. This is of peculiar importance in France with a view to the errors of the Arians on the one hand, some of whom have taken possession of the Protestant altars, and of the Roman Catholics on the other. The original confession of faith which is still understood to be the standard of doctrine in the Reformed Church, and which its ministers and professors are required to subscribe, provides for the recognition of the main truths of religion. It secures the church from the two classes of errors to which I have adverted, and all ministers who are not orthodox according to this creed, must take and hold their situations in spite of solemn declarations which are at variance with their real sentiments. But still there is no direct comment on the word of God suited to popular use. The commentaries which have been published in France are now so out of date that it would be of little use to reprint them. Neither Calvin, Beza, Desmarets or Martin, afford what would be pronounced to be a commentary on Scripture both sufficient and adapted to the present times. There needs a fair full exposition, critical, devotional, and practical, bringing together all the aids of modern criticism and information, and which is in unison also with the acknowledged creed of the Reformed Church. It is with this view of the subject that a plan has been devised for translating a part of Mr Scott's Commentary on the Bible, and placing it as a specimen before the French public, in order that, if approved, the ministers of the church might continue and complete the translation. If not, some good may be done by distributing even a part of this valuable work. Objections may probably be taken to this design, even by some strenuous friends of religion. Some may object that in all points Mr Scott's opinions are not those of the French Protestants, and others may doubt the possibility of transfusing with advantage so cumbrous a work as that of Mr Scott (the style of which, even in English, is not always lucid) into another language. As to the first objection, whatever may be the judgment formed of Mr Scott's theological opinions by persons in England, any competent judge will, I think, determine that there is no great discordance betwixt them and those which are contained in the confessions of the ancient Protestant churches. The ministers of the present day are not, as were their predecessors, obliged to sign the Articles of the Synod of Dort, and it is probable that the great mass of them would object to those Articles; yet I apprehend that, as far as the particular religious opinions of the ministers of the French Church have been investigated, all those whose character is distinguished by piety and energy will be found to accord in opinion, much more with Mr Scott, than with those who differ from him. I would venture at least to say, that his commentary is most likely to meet the views of a majority of those who would read any commentary. But in order to ascertain this point more accurately, a number of copies of that publication have been distributed in France amongst persons who were likely to take an interest in the subject, and their judgment of the suitableness of the work to the object proposed has been obtained. Private communications have been made by some, and the heads of both the Protestant communions established in Paris have published a recommendation of Mr. Scott's work, which has been circulated, and which is affixed to a prospectus of the work itself and a specimen of the translation. From this document, to which the names of MM. Stapfer and Keiffer of the Lutheran Church, and those of M. Monod junior and M. Juillerat of the Reformed Church is affixed, I will take the liberty of laying before your readers a few extracts.

Il n'existoit pas, avant ces derniers temps, d'ouvrage d'une étendue bornée, qui offrît une interpretation continue de tous les Livres Saints, où le lecteur qui veut les comprendre et en tirer le parti le plus fructueux pour sa propre edification fut sûr de rencontrer, unies à tous les eclaircissements nécessaires à l'intelligence du texte sacré, des réflexions judicieuses et de tendance pratique, fécondes en applications usuelles, mais également eloignées de recherche et de trivialité.

Les seules gloses qui depuis la revocation de l'édit de Nantes aient été imprimées en langue Françoise pour faciliter aux fideles l'intelligence et l'application salutaire des Livres Saints ont paru à l'etranger. Sans doute nous devons beaucoup de reconnoissance aux Martin, aux Ostervald, aux Beausobre; leurs travaux ont efficacement contribué à l'édification et à l'instruction de leurs co-religionnaires en France et dans les pays qui leur ouvrirent un asyle. Mais leurs notes, ou ne s'étendent pas à toutes les parties de la Bible, ou n'ont qu'un but special, tendent principalement à nourrir des sentiments de pieté et de soumission à la volonté Divine, sans s'occuper des difficultés du texte.

Le projet de mettre les Eglises Protestantes de France en possession de ce precieux recueil d'éclaircissements et de réflexions sur les Saintes Ecritures a reçu l'approbation des personnes les mieux placees pour juger des besoins de ces églises et des dispositions qui accueilleroient son execution. L'usage de lire la Bible comme acte de dévotion privée ou dans des réunions de fideles plus ou moins nombreuses reprend graces à Dieu, de plus en plus, et reclame comme aliment et subside le secours d'une exposition telle que l'offre le beau travail de Thomas Scott. Cet ouvrage etant un dépot des observations les plus judicieuses et les plus utiles qu'une saine critique et le savoir guide par une pieté eclairée aient reunies sur l'ensemble des Livres Saints et sur tous les passages diversement expliqués, nous sommes en droit d'assurer qu'il pourra tenir lieu de bibliotheque exégétique aux candidats du saint ministere, et qu'il les dispensera jusqu'à un certain point, de l'acquisition dispendieuse de beaucoup de livres réputés nécessaires à leurs études. Ils y trouveront un tresor de pensees religieuses et d'idees fecondes en applications usuelles, presentant au predicateur d'excellents materiaux pour les compositions auxquelles ses fonctions l'appellent. Quelle que soit la page du commentaire de Thomas Scott que le ministre de la parole de Dieu comme le simple fidele soit conduit à consulter, il se sentira partout excité à reflechir sur le sens spirituel de l'Ecriture et penétré de ces sentiments de foi, de resignation, d'humilité, de joie et d'amour que respirent tous les écrits de ce grand theologien.

Le commentaire de Scott se distingue encore par deux qualités précieuses, l'originalité et la conséquence. Mais qu'on ne se méprenne pas sur le sens de cet éloge. L'originalité est plus dans l'indépendance de l'auteur et dans la franchise de sa manière, que dans la nature de ses idées ou les tournures de son style, toujours mâle, vigoureux, mais simple et libre d'affectation et de recherche. La parfaite conséquence de charactère, de conduite et de doctrine que présentent la vie et les écrits de Scott, est empreinte dans toutes les parties de son immense travail biblique. Mais cette harmonie, cette absence de contradiction n'est point le résultat d'un systéme, ou le fruit de l'application d'une analogie de foi, devant laquelle le commentateur fasse fléchir les regles d'une interpretation loyale et d'une saine critique. La probité la plus scrupuleuse ne le quitte jamais.

Should this work approve itself to the French people, and become popular, it would not only be of great use to ministers, but to the heads of families, who have at present no publication which is calculated as this is to assist them in domestic worship and instruction. Many of the Roman Catholics also might be glad to satisfy their inquiries in the interpretation of Scripture by those numerous and well selected marginal references with which Mr. Scott's work is replete, as well as by his sober and devout criticism. I would therefore venture to anticipate, from the publication, a great increase of Biblical knowledge among both the Protestants and Catholics of France.

(To be concluded.)

To the Editor of the Christian Observer.

THE divisions of the chapters in our Bible are generally allowed to be in many instances exceedingly improper: they even occur often in the middle of a paragraph. There is one instance which I shall now notice, and shall at the same time suggest an alteration in our version, on which I wish to have the opinion of some of your critical readers. The passage I refer to, is the latter part of the first chapter of the Epistle to the Ephesians and the beginning of the second.

The paragraph, as the sense seems to require, begins in verse fifteenth of the first chapter, and ends with the tenth of the second. There is a parenthesis, as I conceive, commencing in the middle of the twentieth verse, after the words "when he raised him from the dead," and extending to the end of the chapter; so that the beginning of the second chapter is connected with the words just quoted. "You" in the beginning of the first verse, is joined by "and" to "him" in the twentieth verse of the former chapter, governed by the verb "raised." So that instead of borrowing a verb, as in our present version, from the fifth verse of the second chapter, I would borrow it from the twentieth verse of the first, and would thus render the passage—'And *when he raised* you, who were dead in trespasses and sins.'

There are reasons which induce me to think that this view of the passage is correct.

First, the import of the whole paragraph seems to favour this rendering. The Apostle's prayer for the Ephesians was that they might know, among other things, what is 'the exceeding greatness of God's "power towards them that believed," verse 19. Then he specifies the instances in which that power had been manifested. One was the resurrection of Christ from the dead; another their own resurrection from a death in trespasses and sins; and in verses third, fourth, and fifth of the second chapter, he adds as an instance of the same power, the resurrection of the believing Jews as well as of the believing Gentiles; and, in verse sixth, he mentions not only their conjoined resurrection, but also their conjoined exaltation to privileges and blessings in Christ. These were clear and manifest instances in which God exhibited his great power and which he prayed God that the Ephesians might know or fully comprehend.

Secondly, The construction of the twentieth verse seems to favour this view. "When he raised," is in the original a participle, εγειρας and "set him" is a verb, εκαθισεν so that they cannot be connected with each other, as our version seems to shew, nor can εκαθισεν be well joined to the verb "he wrought," in the beginning of the verse, the objective case being necessarily different. This leads me to think that the whole from this verb to the end of the chapter, is parenthetical, especially as by considering it so, the resurrection of Christ, and that of believers, are brought into close connexion with each other. It is true, that the Apostle in the second chapter, mentions not only the *resurrection* of believers as being a similar instance of God's power to that of Christ, but also their *exaltation* as being a similar exhibition of the same power, which may seem to require, that the one should have the same prominence in the context as the other. Yet I conceive, that the passage, without admitting the parenthesis I have mentioned, would be very obscure. The Apostle clearly states, in the first instance, the *whole* case of Christ, and then without employing either a verb or a participle, introduces the Gentile believers, and, as he proceeds, connects the Jewish believers with them, and instances the same particulars as he before mentioned with respect to Christ. The compound verbs, in verses 5 and 6, chap ii, *quickened together, raised together*, and *made to sit together* evidently refer to Jews and Gentiles as being connected in those gracious and powerful acts of God, and not so much to Christ, in the similarity of whose resurrection and exaltation they were also indeed raised and made to sit in heavenly places.

If any of your correspondents should be able in any other way to clear this involved paragraph of its obscurity, I should feel thankful to him for his information.

G. K.

FAMILY SERMONS.—No. CXCVII.

Ephes. v. 15, 16. *See then that ye walk circumspectly, not as fools but as wise, redeeming the time, because the days are evil.*

THE Apostle, in this short but most animated and affecting Epistle, exhibits to the Ephesians their privileges and their obligations as Christians. In several of his other Epistles, he was led by the doctrinal errors or inconsistencies of life of those to whom he was writing to reprove and rebuke as well as exhort, and to dwell largely upon points of controversy which were necessary to be settled before he could profitably advance to the more direct topics of consolation and instruction. But, with the Ephesians, who appear to have been a remarkably pure and spiritually minded church, he enters at once upon the doctrines and duties of Christianity. He applies himself to the establishment of these converts in their holy profession,—by exhibiting to them the love of God in making them partakers of the blessings of the Gospel according to his eternal purpose of grace in Christ Jesus; by praying that they might obtain a more clear knowledge of the great objects of their hope and faith, and of the power and love of God exhibited in the work of their redemption; by leading them, to this end, to consider that wretched state of spiritual death and alienation from God in which the Gospel found them, and that unmerited mercy by which they had been raised to newness of life, and the exalted privileges of the Christian dispensation, being made members of Christ, and heirs of eternal salvation; and lastly, by various exhortations for the conduct of their lives, with motives and encouragements to the discharge of their several duties, among which he enumerates unity, purity, truth, gentleness, love, and then, in our text circumspection; after which he branches off to the relative duties of parents and children, masters and servants, and concludes with a general exhortation to boldness and constancy in their Christian warfare.

The particular duty, then, immediately under our consideration is that of walking circumspectly, a duty most important, and which the Apostle impresses upon the Ephesians as 'children of the light,' 'risen with Christ,' followers of God, and 'having no fellowship with the unfruitful works of darkness.' Now, walking circumspectly implies, first, that we ascertain that we have entered the right path; next, that we proceed cautiously in it; and, thirdly, that we do not turn aside from it. Each of these particulars is highly important for the purpose of determining our character in the sight of God, and the foundation of our prospects for eternity.

I. In the first place, then, we should ask, Have we entered the right path? There are many ways which may seem right to a man, the end of which is death; and therefore the professed Christian traveller must direct his primary attention to this essential inquiry. If he has chosen the wrong path, no care as to other particulars will be sufficient; so that he must exert himself to ascertain from the sacred Scriptures, with the diligent use of all the assistances which God has mercifully bestowed upon him, what is that narrow way described by our Saviour, which leadeth to life everlasting. The ways of sin and error are numerous, and some of them are even specious and tempting; in selecting his path, therefore, the follower of Christ must be on his guard against the evil example of others, and the corrupt wishes and delusions of his own heart. He is not to ask what is the most easy or the most frequented way, but what is that which alone will lead him to the place of his proposed destination. To ascertain this, he must carefully examine the map of his journey traced out for him in the word of God. 'Having a sure word of prophecy,' he must take heed to it, as to a light shining in a dark place. He must not be content to be guided by his own imperfect reason, or deceitful feelings; but he must ask, What are the declarations of God himself? how is my case described in his word? what are the hopes of salvation held out to me in that infallible page? and how may I become a partaker of eternal life? The way of salvation by human merit he will find to be delusive and unscriptural: he must therefore be justified freely by faith, through the redemption that is in Christ Jesus. On the other hand, the hope of enjoying this inestimable blessing, or of his faith being genuine, while his heart and actions contradict his professions, is equally delusive and unscriptural: so that he must also have evidence that he is 'renewed in the spirit of his mind:' he must be walking in that 'highway of holiness' which alone can lead to the kingdom of God. Thus must he combine the doctrines and the precepts of the Bible, and have set out in that heavenly path which the word of God describes; the way opened by the blood of the Saviour, a way of repentance and faith, of holiness and self-denial, of love and charity, and not less certainly of pleasantness and eternal peace. By nature, such as our nature is in our present fallen condition, we follow a very different course to this: we study our own ease or pleasure, and the gratification of our pride, or covetousness, or evil passions. God at least is not the great object of our affections: his ways are not our delight: and it is not, as it ought to be, our chief effort to live to his glory. From this broad frequented track, fatal to the souls of all who tread in it, we must by the mercy of God have been turned and led into the way which our baptismal vows and our obligations to God enjoin: renouncing the devil and all his works, the pomps and vanities of this wicked world, and all the sinful lusts of the flesh believing, not in profession only, but in truth, the articles of the Christian faith and keeping God's holy will and commandments, and walking in them all the days of our life

II. And this leads us to the consideration of the second particular of Christian circumspection namely that having ascertained that the path in which we are walking is the right one, we should take heed how we walk in it. We must not proceed incautiously, as if no difficulty or danger was nigh nor must we slumber when we ought to be diligently pressing forwards on our journey. We need unrelaxing vigilance, unceasing prayer and the constant direction of God's Holy Spirit, that we may pursue our course aright. Circumspection means looking round on every side and this we are to do in order to discover what snares or impediments are in our path and from what quarter the tempter is most likely to assail us, and to prevail against us. Our spiritual career is spoken of in Scripture as a race which we are to run what care, then, is necessary that we do not loiter by the way, or stumble at the obstacles in our progress. The great work of making our calling and election sure is no indifferent or trifling object it demands the most watchful attention it calls for the exertion of our will, our understanding and our affections it is, in short, the great business of human life and though it interferes with no other call of duty or with our lawful worldly occupations it is infinitely more important than any thing that can be put in competition with it. And can such a concern be attended to with too great circumspection? Shall we handle with negligence that on which depend all our hopes for time and for eternity? No let us 'keep our hearts with all diligence, for out of them are the issues of life' let us foresee the danger of negligence, and avoid it and especially let us "walk in the Spirit, that we may not 'fulfil the lusts of the flesh'

III. But, thirdly, having ascertained what is the right path, and how we ought to walk in it, we must employ the most diligent circumspection that we do not turn aside from it. There will be many temptations to wander into paths less arduous or more pleasing to the evil inclinations of our corrupt nature so that, like the Galatians, we may 'run well for a time' and then be 'hindered that we should not obey the truth' It becomes us, therefore, to give "earnest heed" not only that "the things which we have heard are according to sound doctrine" but that "we do not let them slip" We should "look diligently, lest we fail of the grace of God and lest any root of bitterness springing up trouble us and thereby we be defiled" We 'should fear lest a promise being left us of entering into God's rest, we should come short of it' We should ever remember that it is those only who 'endure to the end' that "shall be saved" that it is those "who faint not" that "shall reap" that it is 'those who are faithful unto death' that shall receive a crown of life. How many alas! after imbibing impressions of religion in their childhood or youth, utterly neglect them in after life, and perish in their transgressions! How many form the most devout resolutions in the house of God, and then return to the world to forget or despise them! How many whose conscience was once susceptible have suffered it to become torpid whose heart was once tender have allowed it to be hardened by the deceitfulness of sin whose principles were once correct, but now are utterly sapped whose doctrines were once scriptural but now are perverted whose life was once exemplary, but is now at war with every dictate of their discarded Christian profession Surely such examples should inspire us with an earnest desire to walk cir cumspectly, "lest, being led away with the error of the wicked, we fall from our stedfastness." And at the same time, knowing our own insufficiency, to our diligent exertions we should add our humble prayers to Him whose strength is made perfect in human weakness, that 'he would keep us from falling, and present us faultless before the presence of his glory with exceeding joy.'

Having thus urged the duty of walking circumspectly, the Apostle illustrates his exhortation by adding, "not as fools but as wise." In Scripture sin is frequently spoken of as folly, and righteousness as wisdom. And surely no folly is so great as that of forgetting the chief purpose of our existence; walking in paths which must inevitably lead to destruction; refusing to accept of the offered mercy of the Gospel, wilfully offending our Creator, calling down upon ourselves the just inflictions of his violated law, and preferring darkness to light, death to life, and hell to heaven. On the other hand, to be a devoted servant of Jesus Christ, is to be truly wise: "the fear of the Lord is wisdom, and to depart from evil is understanding." "The testimonies of the Lord make wise the simple;" or, in the corresponding language of the New Testament, "the Scriptures are able to make us wise unto salvation through faith which is in Christ Jesus." To be wise, therefore, in the highest sense, is to follow their dictates; and this can be done only by constant circumspection and prayer, that we may neither mistake the path which they point out, nor swerve from it when it is known.

In conclusion, the Apostle, in the text, lays before us a practical direction for discharging this duty of circumspection, with a most solemn reason for so doing.

First, we have a practical direction for the discharge of the great duty of circumspection—*redeeming the time.* Much of our short period of life is already past; and it has been perhaps wasted, or worse than wasted, as respects the great purpose for which it was bestowed. Christian wisdom and circumspection therefore dictate that we lose not another moment of our brief space. We cannot live the past over again; but let us not neglect the present; the future may not be ours. 'The time past should suffice to have walked according to the course of this world;' let the remainder of our days be devoted to higher purposes; to the service of God and the salvation of our souls. We know not "what shall be on the morrow; for what is our life? it is even as a vapour, that appeareth for a little time and then vanisheth away." Let us then redeem the passing moment from sin, from ignorance, from unbelief, from practical ungodliness; and employ it in "making our calling and election sure." To whatever else our life may have been dedicated, if this be neglected, it will have passed away as a dream, and leave in remembrance only the bitterness of everlasting regret.

But, secondly, the Apostle specifies a most solemn reason for thus redeeming the time; namely, that *the days are evil.*—He, doubtless, referred chiefly to the peculiar circumstances under which the early Christians were placed, being surrounded by heathens, and exposed to powerful temptations on the one hand, and to bitter persecutions on the other. But the spirit of the passage applies in every age, and to every individual; for "few and evil" are the days of our earthly pilgrimage; and most important therefore is it that we should "walk circumspectly, redeeming the time." We live in a world which abounds with snares and dangers; most necessary then is it that we should "look well to our ways," and pray that we "may be kept holy and blameless to the coming of the Lord Jesus." If life were im measurably long, if there were no possibility of wandering, or if our wanderings were attended with no evil consequences, we might more safely relax our diligence but not so in a deceitful and uncertain world not so with a heart prone to evil, and exposed to be allured by the most specious but dangerous baits not so while " our adversary the devil as a roaring lion goeth about seeking whom he may devour The Christian, in this evil world is situated like the Israelites among the idolatrous nations and he has need of the warning given to them, " Take heed to thyself lest thou make a covenant with the inhabitants of the land lest it be a snare in the midst of thee but thou shalt destroy their altars, break their images, and cut down their groves for thou shalt worship no other God, for the Lord whose name is Jealous, is a jealous God We are not to be conformed to any unscriptural principles or practices which we may find current in society and we are to use our utmost circumspection in avoiding them praying always thereunto and watching with all perseverance Our chief peril lies in our want of vigilance, in our not reflecting on the dangers that threaten us or not using the means given us of guarding against them May the considerations presented to us in the text by the blessing of God, stir us up to renewed caution, and may we henceforth proceed in our Christian course under the influence of those inspired exhortations " Watch ye, stand fast in the faith, quit you like men, be strong

---

To the Editor of the Christian Observer

A CHARGE is sometimes brought against religious persons, which if it could be substantiated, would tend greatly to their disparagement It is sometimes said by men of the world, when they are pressed by fair argument to embrace the peculiar doctrines of the Gospel, to withdraw themselves from the follies and vanities which surround them, and to act up to the promises and vows which they made in their baptism, " We do not see that the most precise and scrupulous are always the most amiable and best tempered The conversation imperceptibly grows warm living instances are adduced on both sides, and friends and relations in town and country made auxiliaries in the contest The skirmish begins conduct is closely sifted, and the discussion perhaps concludes with some such observation as the following " Well! the persons you mention may be very good in public but I have seen them so hasty in their own families, that I cannot take them as patterns for imitation

Now, as a general charge I firmly believe that this allegation is, for the most part, false —but even an unfounded aspersion should make the Christian doubly watchful—since more is expected from a tree planted on a rich luxuriant soil, and carefully trained, than from one upon which less cultivation has been bestowed

There are graces and virtues, with their opposite vices and evil qualities which meet the eye at every turn and do good or harm on a public and widely extended scale There are others of a more retired nature and it is upon these that the enemies of religion delight to dwell The lover of scandal holds up to the world the failings of some well known pious individual and blows a trumpet in the streets, that the sin of his neighbour may be known of men Happy are they whose reputation falls not into such hands in which it fares like a sufferer racked upon the wheel, or the victim of the butcher bird affixed to a thorn to be torn limb from limb These public executioners of character might almost be subjected to the penalties which attach to the inflictors of wanton cruelty Of the graces which appear chiefly in private life, I know not of any one which affects domestic happiness so closely as the tempers of the various members of a family. In this small circle the tenderness and kindness and willingness to oblige, of each individual, act as a fragrant balm of solace to all around. On the other hand the petulant, the hasty, the irritable embitter the lives of all who come within the range of their influence. Surely they will not say, "We suffer our passions to reign ungovernably to try your patience and long suffering." If they should, their victims might reply, "We would have our trials and our crosses apportioned by One who better knows our wants and our necessities."

A family is a little kingdom—a little world. In it, there are those who rule, and those who are to submit to authority. But, as the mild yet resolute conduct of a king will always advance the prosperity of his subjects, so the sound judgment and impartial authority of a father will have great influence over his children. Good temper and affectionate regard are the bonds of union. When the manners of such a family are described by those who do not love order and good government, we must allow for strong colouring and exaggeration. But still the interior of the building should bear inspection. Such was the household of Mr Stanley in Cœlebs. There may be occasionally a glow of somewhat too ardent feeling, or a momentary chilling of tenderness yet, after all the thermometer stands pretty generally at temperate, and the summer heat is soon regulated by genial showers.

The world forms its estimate of religious persons, as indeed it has a just right to do by their fruits but it is apt to be censorious and hypercritical in its censures when it does not love the subject of its inquiry. The world will 'love its own' and it is the natural effect of party spirit to bear tenderly upon one of its own fraternity when he falls under its stroke and to put a new lash to the scourge, when persons not so nearly allied are the subjects of the infliction. But, if the temper of any one who professes to be not of the world brings disgrace upon his high calling, how great is the mischief, how fatal are the consequences! In this point of view it is painful to observe what trifles, what mere shades of opinion, will sometimes produce an undue warmth of expression from the lips of persons who ought to prove themselves better taught. How much more admirable that genuine religious deportment which silently and gently suffers many a winged shaft, shot from a bow at a venture, to pass by unheeded and disregarded! The arrow grazes the mark will it be sent back again? No! the Christian temper gains the victory first over self, and then over the adversary.

But what shall we say in a Christian point of view, to the temper of the bitter controversialist? He indeed shoots with poisoned arrows. What shall we say to the man who, because his fellow man does not precisely accord with him in sentiment upon some doubtful point, in the very act of dipping his pen loses his temper and sends forth a volley of canister and grape, of quartos or octavos, to overwhelm the enemy? And usually the controversialist takes the very way to confirm his opponent in his preconceived opinions. He spoils the temper of his weapons by the heat of his furnace. Above all, he forgets that he is a professed disciple of the Prince of Peace of that blessed Saviour who, when he was asked to command fire to come down from heaven to consume the Samaritans who would not receive him said 'Ye know not what manner of spirit ye are of for the Son of Man is not come to destroy men's lives, but to save them.'

Every careful observer of mankind who in a good sense, knows the world, and has watched the habits of society, is well convinced that a temper easily provoked, does the greatest possible injury to the Christian cause. "We will not receive your doctrines, says an opponent, "if you do not prove that your principles control your conduct." Discordant notes never vibrate so painfully on the ear as when proceeding from an instrument professedly attuned to heavenly melodies. Kind words flowing from benign and holy tempers, will convince the most obstinate gainsayer, that the Christian is walking in the footsteps of his blessed Master.

The Apostle St. Paul evidently knew the provocations to which the early Christians would be exposed when he said to the Ephesians, Be ye angry, and sin not. Let not the sun go down upon your wrath neither give place to the devil. By nature the several Apostles and Evangelists of our Lord were very differently constituted in the temperament of their minds; but their patient continuance in well doing proved that the courageous and the timid may alike be servants of God. Indeed, the whole Christian building would not perhaps be so fitly framed together, if there were not this variety in its component parts. The difference between the Christian and the man of the world is this: the Christian wishes to see every faculty and power sanctified and devoted to the service of God. Whatever may be his besetting sin, he prays that it may be restrained. If his hand offends him, he would cut it off. If his eye, he would pluck it out. If his temper be rebellious and his will perverse he would seek for peculiar grace to restrain, and to correct them. The man of the world lives by the maxims of the society in which he is placed. He calls things by false names. He puts darkness for light, and light for darkness; bitter for sweet, and sweet for bitter. And he must be taught by a Divine agency before he can see things as they really are in the sight of God.

I would urge upon every Christian an impartial examination of his own heart in reference to his habitual temper. Let him in every capacity either of parent, husband, child, master, servant or friend, ascertain whether by an evil temper, he is giving just occasion to the world to doubt the sincerity or the value of his religious principles. If he needs any present inducements to the good regulation of his temper, I would mention from long experience the three following.—1st. His own comfort tranquillity, and peace of mind. 2dly. The satisfaction with which he will be met in the best private society, as a lover of peace. 3dly. The good he may do, in every public capacity by arguing with mildness upon the most important subjects. His opinion will be asked and his judgment valued because from experience his friends will know that he can hold the scales with an even and impartial hand. And on many nice and delicate occasions when a rough demeanour would counteract every effort to do good, his name will stand with the names of those of whom it was said by the lips of unerring Wisdom. Blessed are the peace makers, for they shall be called the children of God.

R. P. B.

MISCELLANEOUS

CHARACTER OPINIONS AND WRITINGS OF LORD BYRON
(Concluded from p. 222.)

THE *political opinions* of Lord Byron are too notorious to require much observation: every one knows that he was at all times the professed enemy of despotic governments and slavish principles; but in this, as in other parts of his character, great inconsistency sometimes prevailed. His admiration, or rather his idolatry of commanding intellect seems to have blinded him in some degree to the unmitigated despotism of Bonaparte, who, though he might occasionally favour liberal principles, was ready, like all conquerors that ever were or will be, to sacrifice the rights and independence of nations to his inordinate ambition.

The *critical opinions* of an eminent poet can never be uninteresting, and a few of these opinions, though a very few, have been noticed by Capt. Medwin. He was hardly, I think, so warm an admirer of Shakespear as the majority of his countrymen. He praises the French and Italian dramatists at the expence of the bard of Avon, of whose want of taste and decorum he vehemently complains. I have no desire to cover Shakespear's gross moral offences; and with regard to want of decency, in the proper sense of that expression, no excuse can be admitted either for him or for any other poet. So far however as mere taste is concerned, he ought in common fairness to be judged by the character of the age in which he lived, and which in this country was the infancy of polite literature. He should not, in this respect, be weighed in the same balance with Racine or Moliere, who wrote at a later period, and in a country which had made earlier advances towards elegance and refinement. But is it not an indelible stain upon the literary character of Lord Byron, that in unseemly description—the most pernicious form of indecency—and sometimes even in grossness and disgusting details, he has outstripped in the nineteenth the old bard of the sixteenth and seventeenth centuries?—Lord Byron, like every judge of poetry, knew how to appreciate the pre eminence of Milton, but he seems to have thought that he is shamefully neglected by the present generation of readers. 'Who now,' said he, "reads Milton?" This, however, is an exaggerated censure of the age. In spite of our poetical novelties, which like the new charities, rise up in such abundance that we are apt sometimes to overlook the old, Milton can never cease to be extensively read and admired. There is reason to believe that in France, and other continental nations, his fame is on the increase in proportion to the growing acquaintance of foreigners with the English language, and their power of enjoying his beauties in the original. Many too, who dip into him at first as a sort of duty, doubtless find his writings really delightful when they have once surmounted the Latin peculiarities and sometimes obscure transpositions of his verse. It will not soon be forgotten that the present lord chancellor, after having during one of his summer recesses read the Paradise Lost, not of course for the first time, and partly in order to form a proper judgment of Lord Byron's Cain, intimated in open court the exquisite pleasure he had derived from the perusal.

Pope was a favourite poet with Lord Byron. He seems to have entertained an opinion concerning him, in which I believe many good judges will coincide, that as he was too much idolized during his life, he has been too much depreciated since his death, and particularly since the rise of the Scotts, the Southeys, and the Wordsworths of the present day. Amongst Lord Byron's compositions, his satirical poem is the only one which at all reminds us of the school and manner of Pope. By this work he has proved that he was gifted with a versatility of talent, of which, from the too uniform matter and manner of his other poetry, we might hardly have conceived him capable.—The noble bard observed of Dr. Johnson, that 'he looked upon him as the profoundest of critics.' This will appear an important admission on the part of Lord Byron, when it is considered how extremely different were the cast of mind, the opinions the principles the tastes, and the characters of these two writers. The criticism of Johnson though sometimes too careless, sometimes too meagre, and sometimes too severe, is indeed, upon the whole, what he has called Butler's wit—'weighty bullion.' The more closely and impartially it is examined, the more will it compel our acquiescence, and call forth our admiration. If we except the critiques on Gray and perhaps on Collins and on Dyer, there are I think hardly any in which he will not be found substantially in the right, and in which his sentence will not be confirmed by the verdict of impartial posterity.

One instance of Lord Byron's careless inconsistency in his opinions has been given in the different judgments which he passed, at different times, on the poetry of his friend Shelley. Another passage of his conversations will serve to exemplify his occasional negligence of remark. What poets, he once observed, "had we in ninety five? Hayley had got a monopoly such as it was." Did he then forget Cowper? or had Cowper not established his reputation as a poet, before the year ninety five? It must be admitted indeed, that at first he was not read, relished, and admired as he was afterwards. The public were not altogether prepared for his novelty and peculiarity both of matter and manner. His too is one of the very few reputations which rise higher with the lapse of years. But surely all judges of vigour, originality, care, and nature in poetry, must have ranked Cowper far above Hayley, before the year ninety five. The latter was himself at that time fully sensible that he was in the descending and his amiable and powerful brother poet in the ascending scale.

It is far from my design to enter upon an examination of Lord Byron's several compositions. I am not ashamed to say, indeed I am very thankful, that there are some of them with which I am not sufficiently acquainted for the purpose, even were my critical abilities equal to the task. But a few additional remarks on the turn of his genius and the tendency of his poetry will not be out of place here, though perhaps this is a subject upon which it will be difficult to say any thing that may not have been already better said elsewhere.

Lord Byron certainly exhibits some of the features of a commanding genius, formed for great and lasting celebrity. The sublime and the pathetic were equally within his reach, and in each department he aims at producing nothing short of the most powerful impressions. In the sublime however it was not so much the vast, the lofty, the majestic, and the magnificent that he affected, as the terrific, the mysterious, and the horrible; nor does he shew himself capable of combining the grand and the dreadful with the skill which Milton has displayed in the first two books of the Paradise Lost. In regard to the pathetic also, he delights and excels not so much in what has a tendency to excite soft emotions, or kind commiseration, as in images of heart rending affliction or mute and morbid despondency. To this turn of genius his subjects are well adapted. The melancholy of a contemplative and sentimental profligate who wanders to amuse a mind divided between remorse and scepticism,—the reckless intrepidity of a corsair who, destitute of moral principle, is fired with all the ardour of the passions,—the mysterious inmate of a lonely tower,—the sack, of strange and questionable appearance, in which Turkish jealousy consigns its victim to the waves,—the adventures of a wretch bound to a wild horse, and left to his mercy till both horse and rider are ready to expire with terror and exhaustion,—the woes of shipwreck,—the fearful expedients and resources of famine,—the awful repose and chilling calm of death,—such are the pictures which the sorcery of his imagination calls up, and presents before the mind under every form and circumstance of horror. He had much of that sort of power which appears in his favourite Danté; but he was less qualified for displaying his "Paradise" than his "Hell" or his "Purgatory." If the story of Count Ugolino had been reserved for him, he might perhaps have surpassed even Dante himself in the description.

None of Lord Byron's compositions display the peculiar features of his genius in a stronger light than the little poem of Mazeppa. The subject, novel, eccentric, and horrible in itself, was precisely suited to his turn of mind, and is wrought up with the most forcible and tremendous effect. That very carelessness and rapidity which occasionally strike us as a fault in his performances are here in character and keeping with the principal, and almost the sole, figure of the piece. What, within the range of real and possible calamities, can be conceived more strange and terrific than the condition of a wretch, bound naked upon a wild horse, and struggling in vain to extricate himself, while the furious animal rushes with his helpless load through entangling thickets, and across deep and dangerous streams, over moor, and rock, and fen, and every variety of country, plunging continually under the mingled operation of rage and terror, till he wears out himself and his rider to a state of utter exhaustion? The scene where a troop of wild horses rush out upon their fellow brute, and, after gazing and wheeling about at his strange appearance, fly off with the rapidity of lightning, is inimitably described, and is one of the finest conceptions that ever occurred to the imagination of a poet. In short, I look upon Mazeppa as a masterpiece of Lord Byron's genius. It appears as though it had been conceived and executed during some single uninterrupted heat of the imagination; and the chief figure of the piece may perhaps remind us a little of parts of his own career—a mad and wretched whirl of dissipation, in which life was embittered, and in some degree worn out, before the usual limit allotted to human existence.

The "Hebrew Melodies" are almost the only instance in which Lord Byron has tuned his harp to the serious celebration of a Scriptural theme; for the drama of Cain seems to have been composed to bring the Old Testament into contempt and obloquy. But, in his imitations of passages from this portion of the sacred volume, though he availed himself of some of the richest sources of poetical inspiration, he has not, as it appears to me, displayed his accustomed vigour. And if his wonted power forsakes him upon the threshold of the sanctuary, such a result is surely attributable to the defects not of the subject but of the writer. The poet who would do justice (so far as any imitation can do justice) to the poetry of Scripture must first cordially embrace its principles, and practically imbibe its spirit. Even a very inconsistent believer, if a poet, may have occasional, though transient movements of a sort of religious feeling that will animate and elevate his muse; but a determined sceptic or infidel must always find himself out of his element, in endeavouring to transfuse into his lines, the pure, heartfelt, and sublime devotion that distinguishes the poetry of the sacred oracles. The short pieces of the Hebrew Melodies seem to have been the hasty effusions of a vacant hour; and, though necessarily containing much that is beautiful, they sadly disappoint the reader upon the whole. His favourite measure also is too light and airy for the subject; and this fault is particularly observable in his imitation of the 137th Psalm. That sacred ode, even if we look at it merely as a human composition, will be found to rival the most exquisite productions of the lyric muse of Greece and Rome. Its grand characteristic is an inimitable union of the tenderest pathos with the noblest spirit of patriotism; yet by Lord Byron it is rendered in a jigging measure which rather reminds us of the song and the dance, than of that scene of exile where the captives sat down and wept at the remembrance of their lost and beloved Zion.

Lord Byron often spoils the effect of his pictures by a perverse mixture of the horrible and the ludicrous, by attempts to relieve and diversify his scenes with flashes of merriment which can only disgust every reader of taste, feeling, and delicacy; and as it were damming up or diverting the proper channel and stream of thought by a vile collection of mud and rubbish. This is something like throwing up squibs and sky rockets amidst the roaring of a tempest or the eruption of a volcano. It might have been supposed that one who was so good a judge of human nature as Lord Byron has proved himself on many occasions to have been, would have carefully avoided this absurd and disgusting expedient to gain attention. It reminds one of some old paintings of the last day—a subject to which neither painting nor perhaps poetry can do the smallest justice—where, amidst much fine drawing, grouping and colouring, a corner of the piece presents us with some ludicrous image of a pitchfork or a wheel barrow, utterly at variance with the general effect intended to be produced. The only instance, I think, in which Milton has offended in this way is by the punning of the fallen angels, in his sixth book, a blemish for which he has been often condemned. Shakespear's mixture of tragic and comic scenes in the *same drama* cannot be excused, and only admits of palliation from the very imperfect taste of the period at which he wrote. But even Shakespear has not often united grave and ludicrous images in the *same scene*.

If we look at the best parts of Lord Byron's poetry, we must admit his literary merit to be of the very highest order; if we look at the worst, we shall be obliged to confess that hardly any true poet ever descended lower. I am not now speaking of his moral delinquencies, as an author. If he have some beauties which call up to our remembrance the sublimities of Dante and Milton and the passions and characters of Shakespear, he has many lines where he sinks into prosaic tameness, and the most careless and unmelodious versification; and several in which he has degraded himself to the doggerel, without aspiring to the wit, of Hudibras. He was assuredly an ardent lover and admirer of the grand and beautiful scenes of creation; and he has sometimes caught and collected the most expressive features of nature, at a glance, and copied them with a union of vigour and precision which communicates the most picturesque effect to his descriptions. But at the same time he is frequently not a little harsh and obscure; partly from carelessness, partly from too much condensation of his thoughts, and partly also from an eccentricity of genius or an ambition of novelty, I cannot decide which, that makes him speak not like a man of this world. He is too uniform in the plan and perhaps in the execution, of his pieces. He seldom writes in any other form than that of a descriptive and sentimental tale; and his tales all come from the same quarter, and exhibit for the most part, similar manners and characters. It is not true that his several heroes are nothing more than fresh exhibitions of the 'Childe Harold,' under different aspects and circumstances; but he has not sufficiently attended to variety: while gloom, melancholy, scepticism, pride, discontent, and contempt of human nature, are in all his writings prominently conspicuous. I may just observe that Capt. Medwin seems under a mistake in telling us that his composition was accompanied with very few alterations and corrections. Mr Dallas, who had good means of information, gives a different account. But his lordship's poetry would have been much improved, even in a literary aspect, by more erasures and corrections: and, while he disliked and almost despised what has been called "the Mosaic work" of Gray, he erred himself in the opposite extreme of carelessness.

But his literary faults, whatever they are, might easily be forgiven for the sake of his many beauties. It is his delinquency in a moral and religious sense which forms "the head and front of his offending," which has made much of what he has written pernicious, and which ought to brand some of his later performances with a stamp of lasting infamy. His scepticism and impiety have been already noticed: his licence of remark and improprieties of description constitute another charge against him, of the most serious nature. In truth, the sins of indecency and profaneness are not seldom found associated in the same writer. It is grievous to reflect that the poet who in one of his first performances had blamed a brother poet, though far too tenderly, for his polluting strains, should afterwards pursue the same course, and lend himself to the same species of corruption. Upon this subject, however, I shall not detain your readers long: this is a vice which has been exposed and reproved with such just severity, in one of the most powerful passages of the "Rambler," that, instead of any remarks of my own, I shall here take the liberty of extracting it.

"The wickedness of a loose or profane author, says Dr Johnson, 'is more atrocious than that of the giddy libertine, not only because it extends its effects wider, as the pestilence that taints the air is more destructive than poison infused in a draught, but because it is committed with cool deliberation. By the instantaneous violence of desire, a good man may sometimes be surprised before reflection can come to his rescue; but for the frigid villainy of studious lewdness, for the calm malignity of laboured impiety, what apology can be invented? What punishment can be adequate to the crime of him who retires to solitudes for the refinement of debauchery, who tortures his fancy and ransacks his memory only that he may leave the world less virtuous than he found it? that he may intercept the hopes of the rising generation, and spread snares for the soul with dexterity? What was his motive, or what his excuse, is below the dignity of reason to examine. If, having extinguished in himself the distinction of right and wrong, he was insensible of the mischief which he promoted, he deserved to be hunted down by the general compact of mankind, as no longer partaking of the social nature; if, influenced by the corruption of patrons or readers, he sacrificed his own convictions to vanity or interest, he was to be abhorred with more acrimony than he that murders for pay, since he committed greater crimes without greater temptations.'

It may be observed, upon a general review of Lord Byron's poetry, that its moral aspect and tendencies have spoiled, to every reader of proper feelings, those attractions which the superiority of his genius has created. No poet ever knew better how to display the grand and picturesque of nature in a striking light; but the chilling gloom of his half sneering half desponding scepticism, descends at intervals upon the prospect, and, like clouds and rain sweeping over some rich valley after the brightness of sunshine, buries all its beauties in mist and mournfulness. What are the glories of creation to one who beholds them without any reference to a wise, merciful, and 'faithful Creator,' who looks around upon this scene of wonder and magnificence without ever having his thoughts lifted up in adoration of the great Being

> Who fills who bounds connects and equals all

who is warmed into no devout gratitude for the bounties of nature, and derives no comfort from reflections on the government of Providence who, in short gazing at the natural world with the Bible for its interpreter, knows not what to make of it and sees in it nothing but a chaos of doubt difficulty, and inconsistency? Such a spectator may indeed from the mere workings of taste and imagination, glean a certain portion of enjoyment in ranging over this field but how poor is his relish, compared with that of another man who, gifted with the like perceptions can look upon the scenes around him in the confidence of holy faith and love and can whisper to himself in a spirit of admiring and adoring piety — *My* Father made them all! Such was Cowper in his happiest moments and such might Lord Byron have been, but for the corrupting and baneful influence of his scepticism and irreligion The association of ideas, produced in the reader's mind by this unseemly mixture of the graces of poetry and the gloom of infidelity, throws a deadening shade over his pictures, and takes something from our enjoyment of his finest passages

A few words must be added respecting his powers of conversation, so far as they can be collected from Captain Medwin's account Of course the full effect of this rare and influential talent depends so much on the tones, the looks the manner and the gesture of the speaker, that no discourses set down from memory can ever do justice to the living original Still much effect may be produced, as we see from Boswell's picture of Johnson, and as appears though in an inferior degree from this portrait of Lord Byron These colloquial memorials *must* be substantially correct. The relater could not have produced them, though we should suppose him more addicted to such a species of forgery than we have any right to imagine The character and manner of the poet appear throughout his boldness of intellect, his licence and carelessness of remark, his contempt for human nature, his indifference about religion, his mixture of force point and levity We observe in these conversations a natural flow, ease and readiness marking a powerful mind in full play and capable of producing something striking or powerful, upon any subject that might be started in discourse I should call this a most enviable talent, if it were not so frequently abused if it did not, perhaps, lay a man more open to the snares of flattery than any other talent which he can possess and if it did not too often also operate unfavourably for that love of truth and that accuracy of examination which seldom thrive without the retirement of the study and the cautious employment of the pen The aphorism of Lord Bacon is well known, that 'reading makes a full man writing a correct man and conversation a ready man

Lord Byron's reading had been considerable in certain departments of literature He tells Mr Dallas, in a letter written I think from college that he had looked through history from Herodotus to Gibbon He probably collected his knowledge very rapidly and preserved it by a retentive memory But all was poisoned by his early and most unhappy prejudices on the subject of religion To adopt a scriptural image the wholesome *meat was turned* and was *the gall of asps within him*

When we consider the mischief which has accrued, and which is likely to accrue from a large portion of Lord Byron's writings we may well be justified in wishing both for his own sake, and for the sake of his readers that he had not been born a poet The loss of a poet, is trifling indeed compared with the loss or decay of Christian faith and virtue in the mind of a single individual I will not undertake to say which of Lord Byron's poems may or may not be read without danger but of all works palpably evil or even doubtful the duty of the Christian is clear, to abstain from familiarity with them. Let then every one, who professes the smallest regard for morals and religion, abstain from the gross inconsistency of encouraging publications which have a manifest tendency to overturn them. Want of serious consideration, as to this particular, sometimes produces the worst effects that could ensue from total want of principle. Were all decorous and respectable persons—to say nothing of sincere Christians—to concur in a determination of this nature, the result would be most salutary. Their conduct would operate as a strong expression of public opinion, and as a happy restraint upon the polite literature of the present, and perhaps of future ages. It would be the means of gradually consigning to oblivion what ought never to have seen the light. It would shew that with a British public no superiority of rank or intellect can screen an impious and licentious author from the just punishment of being reprobated and consigned to oblivion. And let me add that the warmest friends and admirers of the deceased poet cannot by any other means so effectually benefit his memory as by suppressing those at least of his works or parts of them, which, whatever be his condition now, whether happy or miserable, he must wish that he had never penned.

T.

To the Editor of the Christian Observer.

A WORK has recently appeared from the pen of " an English Gentleman," entitled "an Excursion through the United States and Canada in the Year 1822-23," which contains some incidental notices of Negro Slavery, fully confirmatory of those views of the subject which you have uniformly promulgated. I inclose a few extracts from that work, which seem well calculated to increase the just detestation in which Negro Slavery begins to be held in this country. I leave it to you to insert them or not, as you think proper.

S.

'A Missouri planter, attended by two slaves, a man and woman, was travelling to St. Louis in a small wheeled carriage called a Dearborn, and had stopped at Vincennes to rest his horses. Now the day before I arrived both his slaves had run away. Trying to travel all night when nearly bare footed, the man had both his feet so severely frost bitten, that he could not proceed. Consequently he was overtaken by some people sent after him by his master and was brought back to Vincennes the very evening after my arrival. When I got up early the next morning, I saw the poor old slave, who had passed the night in the kitchen, with a heavy chain padlocked round both his legs. A man from North Carolina, who had ridden in company with me from White River, where he had been delayed, came into the room at the same time I did; and, although a slave holder himself, was touched with compassion at seeing the miserable state of this old Negro. Having procured the key, he took off one of the padlocks, and desired the unhappy being to come towards the fire in order to warm his frost bitten legs and feet which were much swollen and were no doubt very painful. The poor slave was so lame he could hardly move, but managed to come and sit down by the hearth. The Carolinian then said to him, You have committed a great crime, as you must be well aware; how came you to do it? The Negro replied, Master, I am an old man upwards of sixty years of age and I have been all my life in bondage. Several White men told me that as this was a free State, if I could run away I should be free and you know, master, what a temptation that was. I thought if I could spend my few remaining days in freedom, I should die happy. But, replied the Carolinian, 'You were a fool to run away: you know you are much better off as a slave than if you were free.' 'Ah! master,' said the poor old Negro, 'no one knows where the shoe pinches but he who wears it.'

'Just at this time in came the master of the slave, and, after swearing a terrible oath that he would punish him, desired him to go and get ready the carriage. The poor old man answered that he was in too great pain even to stand upright. Upon this the brute, saying 'I will make you move, you old rascal,' sent out for a 'cowhide.' Now the sort of whip called by this name is the most formidable one I ever saw. It is made of twisted strips of dried cow's skin; and from its weight, its elasticity, and the spiral form in which the thongs are twisted, must, when applied to the bare back, inflict the most intolerable torture.

"The wife of the tavern keeper coming in, and hearing that the Negro was going to be flogged, merely said, 'I would rather it had not been on the Sabbath.' For my part, I thought it signified very little upon what day of the week such an atrocious act of wickedness was committed; so, after trying in vain to obtain a relaxation of the punishment, I called for my horse, determined not to hear the cries of the suffering old man. Yet even when I had ridden far from the town, my imagination still pictured to me the horrors that were then being performed; and I should have thought myself deficient in human kindness if I had not cursed from the bottom of my heart every government that by tolerating slavery, could sanction a scene like this.'

"The constitution of this Republic would be, if it were not for Negro slavery in the southern States, a spectacle for gods and men to rejoice at. It must however be confessed, that slavery is a blot of such magnitude and enormity as greatly to diminish our admiration for the whole system.

"The traveller, in crossing from Kentucky into Ohio, sees at once the marked difference between a slave and a free State: for though Ohio is by much the younger State, he will there find a far greater degree of comfort and cleanliness, in both the interior and the exterior of the houses and taverns. This arises from the habits of industry necessary in a new State, where that moral pest Slavery is not tolerated."

America, this traveller tells us, furnishes a practical demonstration of the truth of a noble sentiment of Mr Fox, "that what is morally wrong, cannot be politically right;" and he thus illustrates it:—

"Slavery is a complete check to the building of towns and villages, because it almost entirely prevents any demand for labour or merchandize. Say a man possesses forty slaves. All these unhappy beings are clothed and fed in the coarsest and cheapest manner, generally on a little salt fish and Indian corn. They live in huts on the estate of their master, and, having nothing to sell, can buy nothing. Each proprietor has his shoemaker, tailor, carpenter &c. on his own estate—all slaves. These are either taught by other slaves, or are, when young, sent by their masters as apprentices to a White artisan at some large town.

"If, therefore, a White settler should go to one of the slave States, what could he do? He could not, if an artisan find any employment for there is no demand for it. If he should buy land, he could not cultivate it without becoming a slave holder; and this would require considerable capital. Hence in the slave States, the *towns*, as they are called, consist of little more than a tavern, a small store, and a blacksmith's shop. I speak, of course, of the towns in the interior, where there is no foreign commerce. The truth of this statement is fully proved by examining the census

"The White population of the slave States increases a little in the sea port towns, but scarcely at all in the interior. The mixed breed, however, is constantly becoming more numerous; for the young men of a family are allowed to cohabit with the female domestic slaves who, from being Mulattoes, are in general preferred to the pure Negresses.

'All these spurious generations are slaves liable to be sold, and often actually sold to Negro drivers, who again sell them to some one else, for mistresses. Indeed, in the southern States, the ladies would be very angry, and turn any one out of society who kept a White woman for his mistress; but would not scruple even to marry him, if he had a Coloured one, and a whole family of children by her. But what should we say in Europe if a man sold his own natural son, brother, or sister? This however takes place quite commonly, and as a matter of course. I could mention the name of a lady, not a hundred miles from Washington, who lets out as a servant her own natural brother, a good looking Mulatto.

"The further to the south, the worse the slaves are off. This is particularly the case in those States that do not produce food for them. In the more northern slave holding States, as Delaware, Maryland, Virginia, and towards the west, in Kentucky, where Indian corn and other sorts of grain abound, the slaves are somewhat better provided for. But in the more southern where little else is raised but cotton, sugar, coffee, and tobacco, the food of the slave (which must be bought) is an object of greater consequence to the master, and consists of little but Indian corn and salt fish. Moreover, in these States, the slaves are kept together in much larger gangs, and with a much smaller admixture of Whites; consequently, there are fewer of the domestic slaves, who under a humane and kind master are not much worse off than the lowest order of domestic servants in Europe, always however excepting their liability to be beaten or sold.

The following paragraph copied from a Charleston paper of 1823, will give some idea of the enlightened spirit existing among the slave holders:—

"'The Grand Jury of Charleston present as a nuisance the numbers of schools which are kept within the city by Persons of Colour, and believe that a city ordinance prohibiting under severe penalties such persons from being public instructors would meet with general approbation.

'As the Blacks are most carefully excluded from all schools kept by *White* persons, where their presence would be considered as a sort of contamination both by the master and scholars, this bill of the Grand Jury will deprive them at once of all instruction. This indeed although they do not avow it, (for even the most hardened are sometimes sensible to public shame) is their real object and intention.

It is curious to see how fearful all despots are, that mankind, and particularly those under their own immediate rule, will ultimately become enlightened.

'That great man the Emperor of Austria, when inspecting a certain University, is reported to have said, 'I do not want learned, but loyal subjects!' which being interpreted, means—I do not want men of enlightened understandings but slaves.—He, in common with the aforesaid Grand Jury of self styled Liberals, is aware that despotism can only be maintained by keeping the mass of the people in ignorance. Let any one contrast the anxiety of the State of Connecticut for the extension of knowledge, in their admirable system of obliging, under penalties, every child in the State to be taught to read and write, with the Austrian like conduct of the Grand Jury of Charleston. He will then be convinced, if indeed he ever doubted it, of the vast moral superiority of the Nothern over the Southern States

"The moment any one hints at emancipation, all the slave holders cry out about 'their rights, and property' It has been well observed in our House of Commons

The horrible injustice and monstrous crime of kidnapping the father and mother has given you no right to enslave the child If it do, why may not a man say, ' I have murdered this child s father and mother, and therefore I have a right to murder him also ?

I in common with every Englishman rejoice that my country, which was the first to abolish the Slave Trade, is now also leading the way in the abolition of Slavery Notwithstanding however it has been declared in Parliament, that measures are contemplated for gradual emancipation in our West India islands, yet the planters still display a violent and determined spirit of opposition

"Whoever considers how ungraciously they have received Lord Bathurst s circular, in which he humanely orders them to abstain from flogging women, must be convinced, that, if those humane and good men who advocate emancipation deserve the name of 'saints' the planters deserve that of ' devils' Instead of sending out Missionaries to instruct the poor Slaves, I would advise subscriptions for sending out Teachers, who might convert the devils to Christianity for certainly those who speak and act like the planters cannot be said to believe in that religion, the leading tenet of which is ' Do unto others as you would they should do unto you

In despotic governments which maintain the right divine to govern wrong one would not be astonished to hear Slavery advocated The United States, however, have denied this *right* and maintain that ' rebellion to tyrants is obedience to God' a somewhat different doctrine They have it is true abolished the slave trade but they have a little Africa within themselves It is computed that every year from 10 to 15 000 slaves are sold from the States of Delaware, Maryland, and Virginia, and sent to the south I have seen a gang of these poor people chained to one another, walking on foot while their White drivers rode by their side armed with whips and pistols When they arrive at the town at which they intend to stop, the slaves are confined in the jail, while their drivers go to the tavern

" A slave auction is also a common thing of every day occurrence I will not attempt to describe the scenes that take place at them, or the cries and shrieks of fathers, mothers, and children, sold to different and distant States The Blacks are in general very quiet people, and are uncommonly fond of their children Let any one imagine how a father must feel at these auctions of human flesh ! That they do feel may be proved by the following extract from a Maryland paper —

Cumberland Oct 27 1829

Mr W Polling of this country was shot on Sunday night last about seven or eight miles from this place by a Negro man belonging to Mr Stewart of Virginia The wife and children of the Negro had been sold by their master and Mr Milbourne of this place, accompanied by Mr Polling, were going to the house for the purpose of bringing them away The Negro fellow awaited their approach, and immediately lodged the contents of a musket in the side of the unfortunate Mr Polling who survived but a few hours The murderer has been committed to the jail at Romney to await his trial '

" In 1790 the whole number of slaves in the United States was only 694 480. In 1820 they amounted to 1,531 436 In addition to these there were 233 398 free Coloured Now can it for a moment be suppo sed, that this enormous and rapidly increasing mass of population will long remain in bondage,—when they hear their masters talking of nothing but liberty, the rights of man, &c.,—when they see processions and rejoicings every year on the anniversary of national independence,—when they hear that Bolivar, as well as the Mexican government, has entirely abolished Slavery.—when they see how the Blacks of St. Domingo opposed 25,000 veteran French troops? When all these examples are held up to their eyes, will they, can they remain slaves? Impossible.

"The desire of freedom is already beginning to manifest itself in those parts where the slaves are most numerous. In 1820 there was a conspiracy at Charleston in South Carolina, which was only discovered a few days before it was to have been carried into execution, and which ought to have opened the eyes of every slave holder who was not wilfully blind.

"The conspirators were headed by a free Black named Denmark Vesey who was a working carpenter in the city, and was distinguished for his activity and strength. His being a free Black demonstrates, what indeed I believe has never been doubted, that, in the event of an insurrection the slaves would be joined by their free Coloured brethren, who, finding themselves despised by the Whites, and treated as a degraded caste, would gladly take part in any scheme tending to ameliorate their condition.

"It was perhaps *alone* in Denmark Vesey's power, to have given us the true character, extent, and importance of the correspondence which it was afterwards proved was carried on with certain persons in St. Domingo. But these men mutually supported each other, and died obedient to the stern and emphatic injunction of their comrade Peter Poyas. '*Do not open your lips! Die silent, as you shall see me die!*'

'They in fact died like heroes, and in a better cause they could not have yielded up their breath. They were executed for wishing to emancipate a million of their brothers from merciless bondage. Yet how much better to die, even thus, than live a life of slavery!

Who, though they know the riven chain
Snaps but to enter in the heart
Of him who rends its links apart,
Yet dare the issue—blest to be
Ev'n for one bleeding moment free
And die in pangs of liberty!

"The Southerners turn a deaf ear to every thing that reminds them of their danger, saying, that the Whites are so much more numerous in the United States than the Blacks, that an insurrection could not be attended with any very fatal consequences. But surely the people of the Northern and New England States would be very slow in assisting the slave holders: for so much do they abhor slavery, that I am myself convinced they would take no part whatsoever in the contest. The Blacks would say to them ' This is the cause of Washington! will *you* hinder us from becoming free, *you* who made such efforts in that cause, *you* who threw off your allegiance to England because she wished to make you consent to some trifling taxes on tea and stamps? Only look at the beginning of your Declaration of Independence!' "We hold these truths to be self-evident—That all men are created equal: that they are endowed by their Creator with certain unalienable rights: that among these are life, liberty, and the pursuit of happiness. Will you then, because we differ from you in colour, aid our tyrants in reducing us again to slavery? Or do you say, that "all men" means only those whose skin is white? If so why not enslave the Spaniards and the Portuguese whose skin is darker than your own? The army of the United States, in all 6,000 men, scattered over their immense frontier from Maine to the Gulf of Mexico, and in posts on the St. Lawrence, the great lakes, the Missouri and Mississippi, would be quite unable to take any efficient part in the contest, which therefore would only exist between the slaves and their masters. The Blacks would have every thing for them that can animate men to great deeds.

To the Editor of the Christian Observer.

A CORRESPONDENT, in your Number for March (p. 158), having raised the ghost of Boswell, to listen to the inglorious tale of the biographer's defence of Slavery, it may not be useless to remind the reader of the circumstances whence Boswell's rebellion against his master's authority originated. The case was this.—In the year 1776 a Negro, named Joseph Knight, having been purchased in Jamaica, attended his owner to Scotland, where he was told that he was free. The question came before the Court of Session, and the man formally obtained his liberty. The proceedings and the decision of the court on this occasion tempted Boswell to break *his* fetters also, and to disown the right of Dr Johnson to hold him, on that point at least, any longer in bondage. But it is highly gratifying to observe the warm interest taken by Johnson in the issue of the pending inquiry. He writes (Dec. 21, 1776),—" Is the question about the Negro determined? Has Sir Allan any reasonable hopes? What is become of poor Macquarry? Let me know the event of all these litigations. I wish particularly well to the Negro and Sir Allan."—Boswell answers (Feb. 14, 1777), " The Negro cause is not yet decided. Maclaurin is made happy by your approbation of his memorial for the Blacks." In July, Johnson is again impatient.—" I long to know how the Negro's cause will be decided. What is the opinion of Lord Auchinleck or Lord Hailes, or Lord Monboddo?"—Dr Johnson formally dictated an argument in favour of this slave. Portions of his paper are copied, as follows.—" It is impossible not to conceive, that men in their original state were equal, and very difficult to imagine how one would be subjected to another but by violent compulsion. An individual may indeed forfeit his liberty by a crime, but he cannot by that crime forfeit the liberty of his children.—" The sum of the argument is this. No man by nature is the property of another: the defendant is therefore by nature free: the rights of nature must be some way forfeited before they can be justly taken away: that the defendant has by any act forfeited the rights of nature we require to be proved: and if no proof of such forfeiture can be given, we doubt not but the justice of the court will declare him free." It is impossible either to refute this reasoning or to confine the spirit of it to particular parallels of latitude or longitude. If it holds good in Great Britain, why should it not hold equally good in the Carolinas or Jamaica?

AN ABOLITIONIST.

To the Editor of the Christian Observer.

THE evils attending the non-residence of the clergy have frequently engaged your attention since the commencement of your labours. There is, however, one point of view in which I am not aware that this subject has been (at any considerable length) brought before your readers, and which, I cannot but think deserving of the most serious attention. I allude to the frequent changes of ministers necessarily attendant on this pernicious system.

I have been led to trouble you with this hint, from the recent perusal of a remark in one of the biographical sketches contained in an early volume of your work. " We are informed, says the writer of the article to which I refer, speaking of the subject of it—the Rev. Josias Shute—" that he was often offered a better living, which he as often refused; being unwilling, as he said, when he had brought the souls of his neighbours part of the way to heaven, to leave them to a new convoy." "This sentiment," the biographer adds, 'seems not to have arisen from an overweening opinion of his own parts or piety; but he knew his own motives; he was aware that there were many of his profession ill qualified to be spiritual guides, and as his income probably was sufficient (for he had no children) he would not quit the flock committed to his care, lest it should fall into unfaithful hands.' We should not be prompt to censure those ministers whose lives are broken by frequent removals, as such changes may arise from necessity, or a sense of duty, rather than from any censurable inclination: but *assuredly it must be allowed, that the advantages of long continance in the same post of service, exemplarily occupied, are very great; and it is devoutly to be wished, that when once a minister is settled with a charge of sufficient extent to employ his time and attention, he should be disposed to continue there for life, and never suffer his thoughts to waste themselves in the ideal recommendations of another situation* (Christian Observer, vol. for 1804, p. 5.) If this concluding reflection be just, and as such I am certainly disposed to regard it, there can be no question as to the desirableness, in a spiritual point of view, of a minister's being enabled to regard the flock among whom he labours as his own—and of his not considering himself, as merely hired to discharge the duties of the sacred office, among a people who are the flock of another. Viewing the subject in this light, it matters little or nothing even though the whole income of the living should be given to the curate—the people are not his, and he is not their primarily appointed guide—he is a substitute, and a substitute only; and if he should imagine that there is no difference as to the good which he may (I speak of course, instrumentally,) under these circumstances, effect and that which he might accomplish were he actually in possession of the real charge, he will scarcely fail of being in the end experimentally taught his mistake. But on the other hand, if he regard the charge of souls, free from the authority of a primarily appointed incumbent, as a situation offering greater opportunities to do good and to glorify God, even should pecuniary remuneration be diminished, his thoughts will be too apt to waste themselves in the recommendations; and these not merely ideal but real, of another situation than that in which he is placed. Is it not also a grievous circumstance, both for the parish and the individual, that a curate who for years has been discharging with exemplary diligence and success his functions amongst an affectionate people, should be liable to be immediately dismissed in the event of any of those contingencies to which his precarious appointment is always exposed?

D. G. L. S.

REVIEW OF NEW PUBLICATIONS.

Theology explained and defended, in a Series of Sermons. By Timothy Dwight, S.T.D., LL.D., late President of Yale College, Connecticut. With a Memoir of the Life of the Author. 5 vols. 8vo. 2l. 10s. Reprinted London. 1824.

"The people of the United States," says one of our own ardent countrymen, "find themselves in a condition to devote their whole energies to the cultivation of their vast natural resources; undistracted by wars, unburdened by oppressive taxes, unfettered by old prejudices and corruptions. Enjoying the united advantages of an infant and a mature society, they are able to apply the highly refined science and art of Europe, to the improvement of the virgin soil and unoccupied natural riches of America. They start unincumbered by a thousand evils, political and moral, which weigh down the energies of the old world. The volume of our history lies before them: they may adopt our improvements, avoid our errors, take warning from our sufferings, and, with the combined lights of our experience and their own, build up a more perfect form of society. Even already they have given some momentous, and some salutary, truths to the world. It is their rapid growth which has first developed the astonishing results of the productive powers of population. We can now calculate with considerable certainty, that America, which yet presents to the eye, generally, the aspect of an untrodden forest, will, in the short space of one century, surpass Europe in the number of its inhabitants. We even hazard little in predicting, that before the tide of civilization has rolled back to its original seats, Assyria, Persia, and Palestine, an intelligent population of two or three hundred millions will have overspread the new world, and extended the empire of knowledge and of the arts from Cape Horn to Alayska. Among the vast mass of civilized men there will be but two languages spoken. The effect of this single circumstance in accelerating the progress of society can scarcely be calculated. What a field will then be opened to the man of science, the artist, the popular writer, who addresses a hundred millions of educated persons! What a stimulus given to mental energy and social improvement, when every new idea, and every useful discovery, will be communicated instantaneously to so great a mass of intelligent beings, by the electric agency of the post and the press! Imagination is lost in attempting to estimate the effects of such accumulated means and powers. One result, however, may be anticipated. America must then become the centre of knowledge, civilization, and power.*

The prophetic vision created by this zealous writer would have brightened into more radiant splendour, had he not entirely omitted to anticipate the future triumphs of the Cross, and in regions where it has already begun its conquest. Among the ten millions † of the inhabitants of the United States, there are computed to exist eight thousand Christian congregations; and, in some divisions of the Union are to be found the efficiency and importance of an established church, though without an exclusive hierarchy. The proportions of truth and error, and of faithful and faithless shepherds, may be much the same as among ourselves. There are many circumstances which, God be praised! most tenaciously bind together the continental, and the insular Christians of the old and new countries. They use, for example, the same Bible, and in the same translation: their libraries are alike enriched by the approved writings of British and American divines: their ecclesiastical ceremonies and liturgy are substantially the same: the plans of their religious societies are similarly arranged: the missionary systems of both countries proceed with an identity of spirit, perseverance and success: and the parallel might be extended with such minuteness as to shew, that when English Christians

* Mr. Maclaren, in the Supplement to the Encyclopædia Britannica.

† The inhabitants of the Union, by the census of 1820, amounted to 9,638,226 persons. The population of England and Wales, in 1821, was 12,218,500 souls; and the ecclesiastical benefices, in these divisions of the British empire, are in number 11,342.

nite in worship, with the correspondent communions to their own in America, they recognize even the very same hymns and tunes; and, if Episcopalians, the same liturgical formularies, which solemnize or animate the public assemblies of Britain. To these points of similitude ought to be added the fact, that in some instances, the encouragement given in the United States, to our religious publications has been warmer even than our own; although the fervid patronage afforded by our countrymen to these works at home, is become one of the distinctive marks of this age and nation. In illustration, in this respect, of American superiority, may be mentioned, that, of Mr Scott's Commentary on the Bible eight editions were printed at Philadelphia, New York, Boston and Hartford, from the year 1808 to 1819, amounting to twenty-five thousand two hundred and fifty copies; besides an edition of the sacred text without notes, but with Mr Scott's references, contents of chapters, and introductions to the several books of Scripture. The retail price of these copies was 132,000*l*.* During the same period, the number of copies sold in Great Britain was only twelve thousand and the retail price was about 67,000*l*. The reader will compare this account with the respective populations as enumerated in the note in our preceding page. We have mentioned Scott's Bible, as from its extent and the number of copies disposed of, it is the most splendid illustration of our argument; but, in fact, there is scarcely any new work of celebrity, either theological or otherwise, that is not reprinted and largely disposed of in America. Among others, Bishop Mant and Dr D'Oyley's Bible has been, for the last year or two, in a course of publication at New York. Among religious periodical publications, our own miscellany as our readers are aware, has been widely circulated in two rival reprints from the presses of New York and Boston; and it is, we hope, no discredit to us as Episcopalians, and certainly it is none to us on the general ground either of Christianity or of literature, that it was Dr Dwight who first and most warmly introduced us to his compatriots. His opinion will be found in our volume for 1815, p 838; see also volume for 1816, p 642. Of our Episcopalian friends in America, we say nothing as we might more naturally calculate upon—though we do not feel the less obliged for—their kind suffrages.

If the above statement disclose a highly honourable proof of the value attached by trans-atlantic Christians to the productions of their father land, we may advert, in the next place, to the beauty and richness of various specimens of their own indigenous produce; one of which stands at the head of this article, in the "Theology of a writer,

European travellers in America, on the language learning morals, religion, and manners of the people of New England, and on the prospects of the United States, are particularly valuable and we strongly recommend them to those of our countrymen who see nothing amongst their brethren in the United States but matter for ridicule or vituperation.

---

* The booksellers of London would appear to have displayed a generous imitation of their brotherhood in America by publishing, and we believe within the course of one year three editions of Dr Dwight's Theology in 8vo 18mo and 24mo. The octavo impression is stereotyped being with the exception of Scott's Bible the largest work in divinity yet submitted to the stereotype process. The small edition is very cheap. There is also a good abridgment, entitled, Beauties of Dwight in four small volumes price 12s (Westley 1823) In 1823 appeared from the London press a reprint of Dr Dwight's Travels in New England and New York, in four closely printed volumes, price two guineas undoubtedly the most elaborate and accurate description extant of the scene of his travels. The work is tedious for current reading; but, omitting the minuter statistics and details, it is an interesting book especially in its narratives and incidental disquisitions. An excellent paper from it on 'Fashionable Education' appeared in our volume for 1823, p 289. The discussions in the last volume on

deserving a very exalted station among the moral and religious benefactors of his country, and of mankind. This munificent contribution to the literature of the Christian church is presented to us by a genuine native of America. He died only so lately as the year 1817, yet his efforts in the cause of Christianity seem already to have secured for this his great work a place among the established classics of our divinity libraries; and it will certainly descend to posterity, as a monument of its author's genius, of the philosophical precision and comprehensiveness of his mind, and of his devotion to the purest principles of the Gospel of his God and Saviour. The volumes immediately under consideration are to the doctrinal and ethical portion of Scripture in some respects what Mr. Hartwell Horne's "Introduction" is to the illustration of the sacred volume by criticism and Biblical erudition. Both authors collect, digest, and arrange the widely diffused labours of preceding writers, and communicate to the result an air of reviving freshness and novelty. From the nature however, of the two works, President Dwight has, of course far higher claims to the celebrity of an original thinker. Never did a theologian measure the length and breadth of the expanded regions of revelation with less need of dependence upon the achievements of his predecessors in the same department of spiritual science. If there have been, like Pascal, mathematicians by intuition, there was also in the author before us, a certain ability not indeed to make any discoveries in religion by the force of his own genius, but a power of mind capable of proving, illustrating, applying, and decorating all that he himself and others long before him had found in the Scriptures, and in the argumentation and eloquence of such as loved the Scriptures, with an energy and a beauty which would seem to be almost exclusively his own.

Bodies of divinity, like bodies of men, are usually composed of discordant elements, repelling and repelled. Thence the frequent complaint, that such compilations can only be safely studied by selecting their sound parts. Some divines, for example, are unexceptionable in their proofs and elucidations of the external evidences of Christianity; but the moment they retire from these outworks towards the citadel, they darken its great and holy cause by the frowns of hostility. Instead of strengthening the interior defences of truth, they weaken the object they profess to defend, dishearten its real supporters, and betray them into the hands of their enemies. To illustrate, with all plainness, the direct meaning of these remarks,—will it be denied, that many able and even triumphant opposers of infidelity have been unable to answer that most urgent of all human inquiries ' *What must I do to be saved?*' And, what is more lamentable, there are not wanting instances, among the eloquent and learned apologists for the Gospel, who when approached with this question, have repelled the inquirer with the cold sneers of irony and derision, and have thus left men, convinced of the truth of Revelation, to perish in an utter destitution of its beneficial, healing power. On the other hand, we have also witnessed numbers of genuine and exemplary believers in Jesus Christ, who could acquaint others with the practical efficacy of religion, with its ability to communicate peace, serenity of mind, and the brightest hopes of eternal life, and could do this, not merely from their accurate knowledge of the Scriptures, but from their own personal acquaintance with the energy and consolations of Christianity; and yet were easily embarrassed, and puzzled by the sophistries of an unbeliever. So that *they* also, in *their* way, have surrendered the bulwarks of truth; and this at the onset of an enemy whom they would have courageously met, had they been furnished with the *whole* of the panoply treasured up in the arsenals of heaven. Few, comparatively very few defenders of the faith have been completely equipped for their great conflict. We have no need however to embark for America in search of theologians who have put on the whole armour of God. We have had warriors among ourselves fully appointed with arms, both of protection and of active warfare, prepared to struggle alike with the open enemy, and with the traitor within the walls. But the nineteenth century has opened, in the western hemisphere, with a system of theology, which without rendering obsolete similar attempts in Europe must be considered as at least their equal, and, in respect to many their superior. It is indeed a work which as it were synchronizes with the character and necessities of the age.

Whatever truth may be in the remark, that authors and their books are two things, the observation is completely neutralized in the present instance. The character and life of President Dwight were a transcript of his writings. He was the evidence, and the brilliant illustration of his own system. He was one of those extraordinary men who combine in the same person, eminent powers of mind with an expansive persevering activity in doing good. He was a philosopher in his habits of intellect, and a Christian philanthropist in the daily routine of benevolence. He could demonstrate with the mathematician, refine and subtilize with the metaphysician, and in the same hour, assist at the committee of a missionary society, or with all simplicity preach the Gospel to the poor in their cottages and attend at the bedsides of the sick and the dying. We state the diversified excellences of this great man's character by way of preliminary to such extracts from his publication and his life as the limits of this article permit. A student of these volumes might, it is true, be forgiven if he judged from the extent and elaboration of their contents, that their author was a divine, absorbed in books, a stranger to every apartment but his library, and with a pen perpetually under the pressure of his fingers. He would yet at the same time feel his suspicions awakened by the internal evidence of the work itself, that its writer was quite as familiar with the living world out of doors, as with the silent and meditative employments of learned and devotional solitude. The suspicion is far more just than any reader would at first calculate. The writings of the President when compared with a life almost entirely spent in active duty, are only an offset, not the parent stem of his renown. His biographer writes—

In the prosecution of his duties as professor of divinity he early began to deliver the lectures in these volumes. His practice was to preach one on the morning of each Sabbath in term time. By this arrangement he finished the course once in four years. Thus each student who completed his regular collegiate period had an opportunity of hearing the whole series. He first conceived the plan of the work at Greenfield. While there he completed it in short notes in about one hundred sermons, and delivered them twice to his people before his removal. At Newhaven he twice went through with them in the same state, frequently however adding to their number, and altering their arrangement. In 1805 when he was permanently appointed Professor of Theology, the corporation allowed him fifty pounds per annum to employ an amanuensis. Though the compensation was trifling yet the place was coveted and regularly applied for, a length of time before it became vacant. He began immediately to write out these lectures, and wrote one a week during term time, or forty a year till they were completed. If not prevented he commenced this task on Monday morning. His progress depended, with the exception of casual interruptions, on the rapidity of the amanuensis, which always fell short of the rapidity with which he dictated. Sometimes though rarely the sermon was finished in a single day, usually in the course of the second day. The remainder of the week was employed in writing his travels and occasional sermons. When interrupted by company, if propriety did not forbid, he would proceed with two trains of thoughts by the hour together, conversing with the company, and also dictating to his amanuensis." Vol. I. pp. xlix. l.

When engaged in the composition of sermons, or any other literary performance, not only did the conversation of those around him not interrupt his course of thinking, but while waiting for his amanuensis to finish the sentence which he had last dictated, he would spend the interval in conversing with his family or his friends, without the least embarrassment, delay, or confusion of thought. His mind took such firm hold of the subject which principally occupied it, that no ordinary force could separate it from its grasp. He was always conscious of the exact progress which he had made in every subject. When company, or any other occurrence compelled him to break off suddenly, it would sometimes happen, that he did not return to his employment until after the expiration of several days. On resuming his labours, all he required of his amanuensis was to read the last word or clause that had been written, and he would instantly proceed to dictate, as if no interruption had occurred. In several instances he was compelled to dictate a letter at the same time that he was dictating a sermon. In one, a pressing necessity obliged him to dictate three letters at the same time. He did so; each amanuensis was fully occupied, and the letters needed no correction but pointing.

A single fact will exhibit in a striking light the comprehension of his mind, and the admirable method of its operations. The reader is requested to examine the analysis at the close of this Memoir, and to observe how extensive, and yet how logical is the plan of his lectures. This analysis was formed from the lectures themselves since his decease. He wrote no plan of them himself, but in completing them relied exclusively on the scheme of thought which existed in his own mind. We have rarely seen any work, even of much less extent, unless some treatise on mathematical or physical science, in which the perfection of mathematical arrangement is so nearly attained. It ought to be added, that the following volumes are published as they were dictated to the amanuensis, with almost no corrections except those which were owing to the mistakes of the penman or the illegibility of his hand.

To conceive, to invent, to reason, was in such a sense instinctive, that neither employment appeared to fatigue or exhaust him. After severe and steady labour, his mind was as prepared for any species of exertion, as if it had done nothing for the activity and sprightliness of conversation, or for the closer confinement of investigation, or for the excursive range of poetry. Almost all his poetry written subsequently to the age of twenty three was dictated to an amanuensis, after the unintermitted application of the day. Not unfrequently in an autumnal or winter evening would he compose from fifty to sixty lines in this manner. The first part of his 'Genius and Common Sense' is in the stanza of The Faery Queene, the most difficult stanza in English poetry. Repeatedly has he been known to dictate four of these stanzas, or forty four lines, in the course of such an evening, and chiefly without any subsequent corrections." pp. lxxv.—lxxx.

By those individuals who are in full possession of the visual sense, the mental strength of Dr. Dwight will be estimated with infinite difficulty, when they are informed that he was obliged almost to depend upon the eyes of others for whatever, after a comparatively immature period of life, he gathered from the treasures of literature. What in this state of deprivation he lost was, however, in a considerable measure regained in the concentration and vigour of a mind compelled to collect its own sustenance, and to impart to others from its own resources. The following quotation from the Memoir will in this connexion be read, we conceive, with peculiar and serious interest.

"The loss of the use of his eyes at the early age of twenty three is to be regarded not merely as a calamity by which he was deprived of the capacity for reading and study, but in connexion with the fact that it constantly subjected him to severe and almost uninterrupted suffering. With this insurmountable embarrassment he was obliged to struggle through life. During the great part of forty years he was not able to read fifteen minutes in the twenty four hours, and often for days and weeks together the pain which he endured in that part of the head immediately behind the eyes amounted to anguish. His life, it will be remembered, was devoted to a learned and laborious profession, and to literary and scientific pursuits. The knowledge he gained from books after the period above mentioned was almost exclusively at second hand, by the aid of others, a process slow, tedious, and discouraging." pp. lxxv. lxxvi.

We think that the extraordinary air of originality diffused in his Theology over many of the beaten and worn subjects of divinity, may readily be accounted for, by the peculiar circumstances under which the work was thought out and dictated. Mingled with much modesty, and with very humbling views of the abject state of the human mind, as degraded and enfeebled by sin there is in these pages, nevertheless, a general consciousness on the part of the author of the superiority of his own understanding of the prodigious affluence of his materials and of his ability to use them in the order and proportion required in the magnificent structure which he undertook and completed. Such students as are able to read for themselves, and who fill their memories to the brim from the inexhaustible reservoirs of libraries incur, at least the danger of becoming nothing better than the channels of their predecessors opinions. Dr Dwight was so far preserved from this peril that as his reading was confined it was also select. He was a great adept in the art of condensation. His discourse for example on heathen Jewish and ancient Christian testimonies to the doctrine of the Trinity is a digest of the materials furnished by Bishop Bull Doctor Jamieson, Mr Maurice, and the writers in the Asiatic Researches and in summing up the concurrent testimony of these witnesses he displays his unvarying address and precision. But whatever skill is exhibited by the author in instances of this nature, the general execution of his Theology is that of a master builder who works after his own design. Former compilers of similar systems found themselves, as they imagined compelled to labour chiefly as copyists of a prescriptive model. Instead, for example, of proceeding directly with their subjects, they were always stepping aside to confute the heresies on the left and right which appeared to embarrass their progress. All the *isms* of error, fatuity and wickedness which, under the names of innumerable sects from the first century of Christianity, have arisen to disturb the peace of the church to shelter bad men from the alarms of their own consciences to convert the Gospel into a minister of sin and to destroy all sense of human responsibility for the blessings of revelation,—"all these and more came flocking' when the theologians of former days sat down to their books and tablets, to tell mankind the meaning of the New Testament Ecclesiastical history itself was little better than a calendar founded on the lives and adventures of fanatics lunatics, and impostors till Milner arose and, for the first time endeavoured to convince the world, that the history of imposture was not the true account of a religion meant to produce, among men, righteousness and peace, and joy in the Holy Ghost. Not that the efforts of this historian have cured the evil Even in smaller circles when the aberrations of an individual however insignificant and unmeaning may be himself and his heresy, communicate to him a sort of dark inspiration to meddle with established truth, how often does it occur that, for a season the whole system is thrown into confusion not so much perhaps by the new theory, as by the opposition of those who raise it into an absurd importance when they vouchsafe to it the dignity of public notice and refutation! By doing this they only retard the natural process of dissolution. Dr Dwight was too sagacious not to mark this and he has escaped the impending mischiefs He never condescends to interrupt the course of his argumentation and instructive discussions by calling off the reader's attention to trivial obstacles scattered along the line of march but leaves these in their own nothingness, and marshals the way onward to truth and holiness. He is, at the same time a most uncompromising opponent of the leading heresies prevalent in various degrees, among the professors of the Christian name His discourses, in these volumes, on the Unitarian controversy, for example are worthy the purity of his principles, and exemplify their practical influence on his character. His knowledge of divine philosophy taught him to observe, that in confuting what is become too extensively an American as well as European heresy, he should gain very little by proving the Divinity and atonement of Jesus Christ and by leaving the discussion at this point With him, the direct result of Unitarianism was to release insincere believers or infidel Christians, from the spirituality and humiliating obligations of the Gospel. The debate in his view, was not a philological disquisition upon texts but a question addressed to the conscience. He did not wish so much to ascertain what his adversaries *thought* as to persuade them to ask themselves what they *were*. He discerned that the heresy was indeed a degrading opinion respecting the attributes of the Son of God, but that it was much more a struggle to avoid his yoke. We particularize thus his mode of controversy (and in this he had been nobly preceded by the late Andrew Fuller) from a painful conviction that theological disputes are generally managed as though religion were nothing higher than a series of correct opinions, and especially on the doctrines in question. We have, accordingly defenders of Athanasian and Nicene Creeds who compile their octavos receive the congratulations of their party set themselves at rest and think that all is right. We have also anti Athanasians, pursuing precisely the same course retiring also into winter quarters, and reposing on the fame of their conquests. Alas! it occurs to neither of the belligerents, that an opinion, whether established or questionable is, *per se*, barren and useless. All hypothesis not ripened into a vivific principle of action all conviction never transferred from the understanding to the affections, is a shadow and a sound. No patient in the vast infirmary of this world, is ever cured of his moral sickness by forming grand estimates of his physician's skill, so long as he submits not to his regulations. He thinks, and may think well but there is no movement towards an actual application for the remedy, and he dies!

Before we proceed with our review, we think it will prove interesting to our readers to become better acquainted with the history of this truly eminent man we therefore need offer no apology for devoting a few pages to a sketch of his interesting life.

Timothy Dwight was born at Northampton, in the county of Hampshire, in the State of Massachussetts, on the 14th day of May, A D 1752. The first ancestor of his father's family in America came from Dedham, in England, and settled at Dedham in Massachussetts, in 1637. The subject of this Memoir was able to look back on each individual in that line including five generations as spiritual members of the church of Christ. His father received his education at Yale College and was by profession a merchant. His mother was the third daughter of Jonathan Edwards, the celebrated President of Nassau Hall. She devoted herself to the instruction of this son with the most assiduous attention, without however neglecting the several claims which her numerous rising family had upon her care. She began to instruct him almost as soon as he was able to speak and such was his eagerness as well as his capacity for improvement that he is stated to have learned the alphabet at a single lesson and before he was four years old was able to read the Bible with ease and correctness. He continued the pupil of his mother till he arrived at the age of six years. She also instilled into his opening understanding those principles of piety and virtue which combined with the influence of his father's example, under the blessing of Divine Providence, laid the foundation of his future eminence.

At the age of six, he was sent to the grammar school, and pursued his studies with such alacrity that, at the age of eight, he would have been prepared for admission into college had not the discontinuance of the school interrupted his progress, and placed him again under the faithful tuition of his affectionate mother. This domestic education rendered him fond of home, and led him to feel a livelier interest than is usual with boys of the same age in the conversation of those who were older than himself. His father's hospitable house was the well known resort of men of intelligence, and even at this very early period of his life, while listening to their conversation on the character of the great men of the age, both in the colonies and in Europe, a deep and lasting impression was made upon his mind, and he then formed a resolution that he would make every effort in his power to equal those, whose talents and character he heard so highly extolled.

In his twelfth year he went to Middletown to pursue his studies under the Rev. E. Huntington, a gentleman of high classical attainments. Not content with the time regularly allotted to study in the school, he spent most of his leisure hours at home in intense application. His conduct continued to be marked with the strictest propriety, and his manners were amiable and affectionate.

When he had just passed his thirteenth year, he was admitted as a member of Yale College. Here he had the misfortune to break his arm, and for several months he was prevented by sickness from pursuing his studies; which circumstances, together with the irregularities which at that time unhappily prevailed in the college, tended much to impede his advancement in knowledge. He however gained considerable reputation for genius and acquirements, and his information and address rendered his society generally pleasing.

In addition to his ordinary pursuits, he attained such a degree of excellency in penmanship, that his writing was with difficulty distinguished from engraving. He was also skilled in poetry and music, particularly sacred music.

While at college he formed a resolution to which he adhered during the remainder of his collegiate life, to employ fourteen hours each day in close application to his studies. At that time college prayers began at half past five o'clock in the morning in the winter, and at half past four in the summer, before which hour he regularly construed and parsed a hundred lines of Homer. This lesson, which formed no part of the regular college exercises, was of course, acquired by candle light. As he advanced it was gradually increased to a much larger quantity. By this incessant application to study his eyes became seriously affected, and a foundation was thus early laid for that weakness in them which caused him so much distress during the remainder of his life. He received the degree of Bachelor of Arts in the year 1769, when he was a little past seventeen years of age.

A short time after leaving college he was employed to take charge of a grammar school at New Haven. This was the commencement of that course of life which, with very little interruption he pursued for nearly fifty years, a course of life in which Providence had peculiarly qualified him to excel.

In 1771, at the age of nineteen, he was chosen a tutor in Yale College. In this situation he remained for six succeeding years, performing its duties with distinguished success and reputation. His associates were men of eminent talents, and by their united efforts the institution soon acquired considerable celebrity. It was in the first year of his tutorship that he commenced writing his 'Conquest of Canaan,' a regular epic poem. About this time he was inoculated for the small pox, by which, and too early a return to study, his eyes were so seriously injured as to cause him, through life, a great degree of pain and embarrassment

In the year 1772, he received the degree of Master of Arts. On that occasion he delivered as an exercise his 'Dissertation on the History, Eloquence, and Poetry of the Bible' which was afterwards published, both in America and in Europe. It unfolded, at that early age, the bolder features of the author's mind and evinced great maturity of judgment and taste. The field of thought was new in that country. The style is described as dignified and manly, and formed by a standard truly classical. At a subsequent period, during his residence in college as a tutor, he engaged deeply and with great success, in the study of the higher branches of the mathematics.

During the second year of his tutorship, he attempted by a very restricted and vegetable diet to remove the necessity for bodily exercise, and yet to secure himself from the dulness incident to a full habit and inactive life; but his health rapidly declining, a physician whom he consulted recommended to him among other things, a daily course of vigorous bodily exercise as the only means of restoring his constitution to its primitive vigour. He followed his advice and within twelve months, walked upwards of two thousand miles, and rode on horseback upwards of three thousand. To his perseverance in this system, he was probably indebted for his recovery, as well as for the uninterrupted health and vigour of constitution which he enjoyed for the ensuing forty years.

In 1774, Mr Dwight united himself to the college church. At this time it was his expectation to pursue the practice of law, and his studies were directed towards that object. In March 1777, he married Miss Woolsey of Long Island. They had eight sons, of whom six survived their father. Mrs Dwight is still living.

In May of the above year the college was broken up by the war, and the students left New Haven, and pursued their studies under their respective tutors, in places less exposed to the sudden incursions of the enemy. Early in June he was licensed as a preacher in his native county of Hampshire, in the State of Massachussetts. Soon after he was appointed chaplain to General Parsons' brigade, which was part of the division of General Putnam, in the army of the United States. He joined the army at West Point, in October. The troops, who composed the brigade, were principally Connecticut farmers, men who had been piously educated, and who were willing to listen to the truths of the Gospel, even in a camp. On the Sabbath, they heard him with profound attention. During the week they saw him exerting himself as far as lay in his power to instruct them in morals and religion. Several of his discourses delivered to the whole army, owing partly to their intrinsic merit, and partly to the feelings of the times, gained him high reputation with the American public. He also wrote several patriotic songs, which were universally popular among his countrymen. His connexion with the army enabled him to form an extensive acquaintance with many officers of distinction, and, among others, General Washington who honoured him with flattering attentions.

He remained in the army a little more than a year when the news of his father's death rendered it necessary for him to resign his office, in order to console his mother and to assist her in the support and education of her numerous family. Mr Dwight had left a widow and thirteen children, ten of whom were under twenty one years of age. The subject of this memoir was the eldest and on him devolved the care of the family, at a period when the circumstances of the country rendered the task peculiarly difficult. In this situation he passed five years of the most interesting period of his life performing in an exemplary manner the offices of a son and a brother. The government and education of the children, as well as the daily provision for their wants, depended almost exclusively upon his exertions. To accomplish these objects he postponed his own establishment for life, and a provision for his family. Though destitute of property, he relinquished his own proportion of the family estate, in favour of his brothers and sisters. His mother was accustomed to acknowledge, in language of eloquent affection and gratitude, his kindness, faithfulness, and generosity to her and her children. The respect which she manifested towards him, though perhaps not his inferior in native powers of mind, resembled the affection of a dutiful child towards a father, rather than the feelings of a mother for her son.

During this period he laboured through the week upon the patrimonial farm, and preached on the Sunday to several destitute congregations in the neighbouring towns. He also established a school at Northampton, for the instruction of youth of both sexes, which was almost immediately resorted to by such a number of pupils, that he was under the necessity of employing two assistants. A part of one of the classes in his college repaired to Northampton, and placed themselves under his care as their preceptor. The compensation which he received for preaching, as well as the profits of his school, were all expended in the support of the common family.

A strong disposition was manifested by the inhabitants of Northampton to employ him in civil life. In the county conventions, he repeatedly represented the town; and, in connexion with a few individuals, met and resisted that spirit of disorganization and licentiousness which was then unhappily prevalent. Twice he consented to serve the town as their representative in the State Legislature. This was in the years 1781 and 1782, just before the close of the war of Independence. When subjects of an interesting and perplexing nature, growing out of the great controversy in which the country had so long been engaged, extensively agitated the public mind, and engrossed legislative attention. Every thing was unsettled. The war had sundered not only the cords which fastened the colonies to the mother country, but those also which bound them to each other. The old foundations were destroyed, and new ones were to be established. In this situation, inexperienced as he was in the business of a politician or a legislator, he at once became one of the most industrious and influential members of that body, and was greatly admired and distinguished for his talents and eloquence. All his exertions were on the side of good order and good morals, and indicated a steady attachment to the principles of rational liberty, and a decided hostility to licentiousness.

On one occasion he was enabled to prove his devotion to the interests of learning. A petition for a grant in favour of Harvard College was before the Legislature. At that time such grants were unpopular. During his occasional absence from the House, the petition had been called up; and, after finding but few, and those not very warm, advocates, had been generally negatived. On taking his seat Mr Dwight learning what had occurred, moved a reconsideration of the vote. In a speech of about an hour in length, fraught with wit, with argument, and with eloquence, and received with marked applause from the members and the spectators, he effectually changed the feelings of the House, and procured a nearly unanimous vote in favour of the grant.

At this period, he was again earnestly solicited to quit the clerical profession and devote himself to public life; and some flattering proposals were made him in the event of his so doing; but nothing could change his resolution. In May 1783, he was ordained according to the rites of the community to which he belonged, to the pastoral charge of the parish of Greenfield but the stipend, which consisted of five hundred dollars, the use of six acres of parochial land, and twenty cords of wood, did not allow, with the many claims on his purse, of his relinquishing tuition. During the twelve years of his residence at Greenfield, he instructed upwards of one thousand pupils. Besides the instruction of his school, he preached twice every Sunday, and regularly visited his people. He also cultivated with his own hands a large garden. Having numerous family connexions and friends, he entertained an almost uninterrupted succession of company greater, it is said than any individual in the State. Greenfield was the resort of learning of talents, of refinement and of piety and his own hospitable doors were ever open to welcome the stranger as well as the friend. He was the centre of such extensive attractions as entirely to have altered the aspect of society in the regions around him.

Being unable, from the weakness of his eyes, to write, he very early discovered that he must either preach unwritten discourses, or abandon his profession. Few men have been so well qualified to adopt the former course and he pursued it for many years almost exclusively, till the assistance of an amanuensis enabled him to have his sermons written out for him at full length, which he preferred when practicable, partly for the sake of fulness and correctness, and partly the better to check a floridness of style, which he regretted to see becoming popular among his college pupils.

In 1787, Mr Dwight received the degree of Doctor of Divinity, from the college at Princeton, New Jersey. He was then thirty-five years of age.

Among other subjects which engaged his attention, was that of a more intimate union of the Congregational and Presbyterian churches throughout the United States and his efforts were in several instances successful, even during his life.

In May, 1795, the Presidency of Yale College becoming vacant, Dr Dwight was appointed to fill that station. The people of his parish with whom he had lived for twelve years in uninterrupted harmony, heard of his appointment with extreme regret, and did not surrender him without great reluctance. We are now entering upon a very interesting period of his life. The state of Yale College, at the time of his accession to the office of President was most unhappy and one of the greatest evils under which it was suffering was an extensive prevalence of infidelity among the students. This pernicious spirit had been derived from the circumstances of the country, at the close of the preceding war. As was natural, it found easy access to the minds of a collection of youths, who were fascinated with ideas of mental as well as political independence, and who were easily induced to shake off what they considered to be the shackles of habit and superstition. The degree to which it prevailed may be conjectured from the fact, that a considerable portion of the class which Dr Dwight first taught had assumed the names of the principal English and French infidels and were more familiarly known by them than by their own. To extirpate a spirit so fatal, he availed himself of an early and decisive opportunity. Forensic disputation was an important exercise of the senior class. For this purpose they were formed into a convenient number of divisions and it was the practice for each division to agree upon several questions and then refer them to the President to select which he thought proper. Hitherto the students had not been allowed to discuss any question which involved the inspiration of the Scriptures, from an apprehension that the examination of these points would expose them to the contagion of scepticism. As infidelity was extensively prevalent in the State, and in the country the effect of this course upon the minds of the students had been unhappy. It had led them to believe, that their instructors were afraid to meet the question fairly and that Christianity was supported by authority, and not by argument. One of the questions presented by the first division was "*Are the Scriptures of the Old and New Testament the word of God?*" To their surprise the President selected it for discussion, told them to write on which side they pleased, as he should not impute to them any sentiments which they advanced as their own, and requested those, who should write on the negative side of the question, to collect all the facts and arguments which they could produce, enjoining it upon them, however to treat the subject with becoming respect and reverence. Most if not all of the members of the division, came forward as the champions of infidelity. When they had finished the discussion, he first examined the ground they had taken, triumphantly refuted their arguments, proved to them that their statement of facts was mistaken, or irrelevant and to their astonishment, convinced them, that their acquaintance with the subject was wholly superficial. After this he entered into a direct defence of the Divine origin of Christianity, in a strain of powerful argument, and animated eloquence, which nothing could resist. The effect upon the students was electrical. From that moment infidelity was not only without a strong hold, but without a lurking place. To espouse her cause was now as unpopular, as before it had been to profess a belief in Christianity. Unable to endure the exposure of argument, she fled from the retreats of learning ashamed and disgraced.

Dr Dwight's system of discipline was peculiarly his own, and commanded universal approbation. His mode of instructing was also equally excellent. His long experience in this employment had made him thoroughly acquainted with the youthful character, and enabled him to teach, as well as to govern young men, with extraordinary success. In the year 1795, when he entered upon the duties of his office, the whole number of students was one hundred and ten. Almost immediately after his accession, they began to increase, and in the course of his presidency amounted to three hundred and thirteen, an increase unexampled in any similar institution in the United States. It was never any part of his plan merely to discharge his duty, he did it with his whole mind and heart, and thought nothing adequately done till all was done that the case admitted of. "The public says Professor Silliman, have been little aware of the extent and diversity of the labours of President Dwight in this institution. He has in fact discharged the duties of four offices either of which is, ordinarily considered as sufficient to engross the time and talents of one man." "His object was not only to instruct the young men under his care, in the particular sciences which came before them, but to fit them by repeated counsels, and by information pressed upon them with parental solicitude for the various scenes into which they were to pass in life. He encouraged the students, especially those of the senior class, in all their difficulties and troubles to come to him for advice and assistance. In every such case, the instructor was forgotten in the friend and the father. His pupils familiarly spoke of him as "the young man's friend."

At the commencement of his presidency the Professorship of Theology was vacant. The Corporation proposed to appoint him in form to the office, but for the first ten years he would consent only to an annual appointment. In 1805 it was made permanent, when, as we have stated, he was allowed an amanuensis.

None but his intimate friends knew how great at this period, were his sufferings from weakness of sight. For years it was with extreme difficulty that he could read or write even a sentence. He was greatly alarmed, for a long period, with the symptoms of an approaching *gutta serena*. Repeatedly the pressure on the brain was so great as to produce momentary blindness and apparently to threaten apoplexy. Occasionally, for weeks together, the anguish of his eyes was so intense, that it required powerful exertion to draw off his mind to any other subject, and often, after attempting in vain to sleep, he has risen from his bed, and, to promote a free perspiration, has walked for miles in the middle of the night.

In the year 1796 he commenced journeying on horseback, or in a vehicle called a 'sulky' during the college vacations. This practice he continued through the remainder of his life, except the last year, and in these various journeys, it is computed that he rode about twenty thousand miles. His excursions were chiefly confined to the New England States and the State of New York. He experienced the highest gratification from the beauties of scenery, and scarcely a spot can be named within those limits where these beauties are to be found in high perfection, which he did not visit and describe. For his own amusement, he took notes of the most material occurrences of his several journeys, and afterwards wrote them out for the gratification of his family. This suggested to him the idea of collecting materials for one or more volumes of travels, in which should be comprised not only an account of the climate, soil, mountains, rivers, scenery, curiosities, and general face of the country over which he passed, but of the state of society, of manners, morals, literature and religion, the institutions, civil, literary and religious, and the character of the governments and laws of the above mentioned States. In these journeys, he visited great numbers of the most intelligent and respectable inhabitants of those tracts of country over which he travelled, and derived from his conversation with them a large collection of facts relative to the general state of morals, manners and religion. The information thus gained was arranged, reduced to writing and prepared for publication, and has since been printed on both sides of the Atlantic. No work has appeared, which contains so much correct information, concerning the subject of which it treats, as this.

To enumerate the various literary, charitable, and pious institutions which Dr Dwight was active in founding or assisting, would be a laborious employment. He was particularly interested in the Connecticut Academy of Arts and Sciences, the Missionary Society of Connecticut, to whose funds he was a liberal contributor of upwards of one thousand dollars, the Society for Foreign Missions, established in the year 1809 at Boston, Massachussetts, the Theological Seminary at Andover in that State, and above all the British and Foreign Bible Society. From the time of the establishment of that most illustrious and sublime charity which has ever engaged the attention, or drawn forth the exertions and the wealth of the pious and benevolent, it was the ardent wish of President Dwight to see a similar institution established in the United States, and it was a consoling consideration to him, that he lived to see it accomplished. In addition to these institutions, a long list of more confined but active societies had the benefit of his influence and patronage.

At the age of sixty three, owing to his regularity, temperance, and exercise, he had become more active and energetic than most men of forty. No apparent declension was discernible in the powers either of his body or his mind. About this time, however he was seized with the first attack of a disease to which he finally became a victim. That attack was most severe, and it made fearful ravages on a constitution which had increased in strength and firmness for more than sixty years. Amidst his extreme sufferings, not a murmur, not a repining expression escaped from his lips. His mind was perfectly clear, and his reason unclouded. Patience under suffering, and resignation to the will of God, were exhibited by him in the most striking and exemplary manner. His conversation was the conversation of a Christian, not only free from complaint, but at times cheerful and animated. His prayers were fervent, but full of humility, submission, and hope.

At the end of twelve weeks, his disease assumed a more favourable appearance, so that he was able, through the summer, to preach in the chapel, to hear recitations, and to attend to a class of theological students, who were pursuing their studies under his direction. He also wrote, during this season, several Essays on the Evidences of Divine Revelation, and on other subjects: the whole forming matter for a considerable volume. The last of these Essays was finished only three days before his death. He also wrote the latter half of a poem of about fifteen hundred lines, on " Genius and Common Sense." Other works also were begun or projected: but he was now drawing fast towards the close of his earthly labours.

He met his senior class for the last time, on Wednesday, Nov 27th, when he took cold, was worse from the exertion, and did not go out again. He still, however, continued to hear the theological class at his house. Their last recitation was only a week before his death. his sufferings at the time were extreme, and his debility scarcely permitted him to speak at all: but his mind abstracted itself from its sympathy with an agonized frame; and in a discourse for one hour and a half on the doctrine of the Trinity, he reasoned upon and illustrated it in the most cogent and interesting manner, and left an indelible impression on the minds of his pupils.

He continued in a state of great suffering till Tuesday the 7th of January, 1817, when his disorder assumed a most alarming aspect, and terminated his life on the Saturday following. On the Thursday of that week he got out of his bed, was dressed and sat in his chair till evening. He answered questions put to him, with clearness and promptitude, inquired with affection respecting his friends and neighbours, and in the evening attempted to conduct family prayer, and proceeded for a few minutes with clearness and propriety but a paroxysm of pain rendered him incapable of utterance, and he desisted. On Friday, it being apprehended by his family that he was not aware of his approaching dissolution, the fact was announced to him. He received the intelligence with great calmness, and at short intervals through the day, when his sufferings permitted, he conversed on various topics in his usual manner. Subjects connected with the great objects of his labours, his desires, and his prayers through life; the effusion of the Spirit of God, revivals of religion, the propagation of Christianity, and the dissemination of the Scriptures, were not only near his heart, but, when mentioned, kindled his feelings and awakened his devotion. In the course of the evening, at his request, the eighth chapter of the Epistle to the Romans was read to him. He listened to it with great attention, remarked upon a mistranslation in one or two places, spoke with much fervour of pious emotion on the subject of the chapter, and at the close of it exclaimed, " O what a glorious apostrophe!" He also made a number of remarks on the opinions and sentiments of some of the English divines, particularly Clark and Waterland, respecting the doctrine of the Trinity. Upon being reminded that his religious friends would be gratified to learn his views and feelings at the prospect of death, he began to make some remarks upon the promises of the Gospel, when he was seized with a paroxysm of distress, which prevented him from proceeding. A few hours before his death, the subject was for the last time, mentioned. He appeared to comprehend the object in view, and, though he spoke with difficulty, he answered with clearness, that in the extreme sickness with which he was visited in the spring during some weeks of which he had no expectation of recovering, he had experienced more support and comfort from religion, and the promises of the Gospel, than he had ever realized at any former period of his life. "Had I died then," he said, "that fact would doubtless have been considered as affording strong evidence of the sincerity and reality of my faith; but, as I recovered, it probably made but little impression." It was a sentiment often inculcated by him, that it was more safe to rely upon the tenor of a person's life, as evidence of the true state of his religious character, than upon declarations made upon a death bed. In the above mentioned remark, there is little reason to doubt that he alluded to that subject, and intended that it should apply to his former sentiments. After this he requested his brother to read to him the 17th chapter of St John. While listening to the latter verses of the chapter, he exclaimed, "O! what triumphant truths!" Afterwards the 14th, 15th, and 16th chapters were read to him. He listened attentively, and spoke with lively interest on various passages. His mind however began to wander while the last chapter was being read, and it was not completed.

For several of his last hours, his organs of speech were much affected, but his mind was unclouded, and his thoughts were fixed on death and heaven. He was occupied a great part of the time in speaking, sometimes in an audible voice, and sometimes in a whisper. His language, though inarticulate, was evidently that of prayer and adoration. His eyes appeared to be fixed on that celestial world whose gates were just opening to receive his departing spirit into the mansions of everlasting rest. He did not appear for several hours previously to his death to suffer much pain, but continued to breathe more and more shortly, until a few minutes before three o'clock, on Saturday the 11th of January, when he expired in perfect peace.—His death caused deep and general sorrow, not only through the State of Connecticut, but through New England, and extensively through the Union. Beloved by his relatives, esteemed by his friends, revered by his pupils, and highly honoured by his countrymen, his loss was universally considered as a great public as well as private calamity, and the expressions of veneration for his memory have been increasing rather than diminishing up to the present period, and are not likely to be soon forgotten. To New England he was "a father, her moral legislator, and his life is an era in her history."

Thus lived, and thus died, the lamented author of the valuable work now before us. We must leave his character to speak for itself. Those who knew him have spoken in high terms of eulogy of his native powers of intellect, his extraordinary assiduity, his entire command of his thoughts, and his large attainments in science and literature. Still more highly have they spoken of his moral and religious virtues, and especially of his disinterestedness, his charity, his hospitality, his habitual Christian cheerfulness, his warmth of friendship, his domestic virtues in his own happy circle; and, above all, of his patience, his meekness and his humility. How he wrote, the discourses before us shew; how he preached, is described, by those who knew him, as follows:—

"As a minister and preacher of the Gospel, it is not easy to convey an adequate idea of his characteristic excellence. His pulpit efforts possessed every characteristic of animated and powerful eloquence. Many instances of its effects upon large audiences are remembered, and might easily be mentioned, which were most striking proofs of its power over the feelings and the conscience. To simplicity in manner and matter, he added dignity; to ease he added energy; to fervour he added humility. He preached as a sinner and dying man himself; he preached as in the presence of God, and of the spirits of just men made perfect; he preached as though he saw his crown of glory ever before him.

It is impossible to attempt any thing like an analysis of the Theology, and it is difficult to know what ought to be the selections, under the usual form of a reviewer's extracts, from a work of such extent and exuberant excellence. We shall however copy the following paragraphs. They refer to one of the most common of all divinity topics; and on this very account, we prefer giving them, in order to exemplify what has been advanced respecting Dr Dwight's talent in communicating to a familiar subject, characters of freshness and originality. He is enforcing the doctrine of man's universal apostasy from God; and, having previously argued the matter as a theologian supported by Scripture, and by immediate deductions from various texts and scriptural facts, he extends the illustration by an appeal to the audible, visible, tangible evidences which surround us in the world, and are confirmed by the past history of mankind.

The laws of all nations are a strong proof that the human character is universally sinful.—Human laws are made only to repress and restrain sin; are derived only from experience and are forced upon mankind by iron handed necessity. They exist in every country and restrain sin of every kind which human laws can affect or human tribunals can prove and punish. The penalties by which they attempt this restraint are various and dreadful; are the most efficacious which experience can suggest or ingenuity devise; and are changed continually as they are found to fail of their effect, by the substitution of others which promise greater success. Still they have always fallen short of their purpose. The propensity to evil in the heart of man has defied all their force and terror; and boldly ventured on the forbidden perpetration in the sight of the pillory and the prison, the gibbet and the rack. No ingenuity on the one hand, and no suffering on the other has in any country been sufficient to overcome this propensity, and so far to change the character of man as to exterminate even a single sin.—To this head ought to be referred all the means furnished by law of safety to our persons and our property; the bolts, bars and locks, by which we endeavour to defend our houses and their contents, our persons and our families, especially in the night against the inroads of theft and violence; the notes, bonds and deeds by which we endeavour to secure our contracts, prevent the mischiefs of fraud and compel dishonesty to fulfil its engagements; the jails and dungeons, the chains and galleys by which we endeavour to confine villains and prevent them from disturbing by their crimes the peace of society; the post, the pillory and the gibbet by which we punish some culprits and labour to deter others from repeating their perpetrations;—all these and the like things are gloomy and dreadful proofs of the corruption of the world in which they exist. They exist wherever men are found of sufficient capacity and in proper circumstances to attempt a regular opposition to crimes, a continual preservation of peace and a general establishment of personal safety. The sinfulness therefore which they intend to resist is equally universal. In a world of virtue they would have no place, because they could not be of any possible use; the spirit of the inhabitants supplying infinitely better the peace and safety which they so imperfectly secure.

2d. *The religion of all nations is a forcible proof of the same doctrine.*—The religion of every nation has been expiatory; that is, it has been so formed as intentionally to make satisfaction for sin and to obtain reconciliation with a God acknowledged to be offended. Of this nature obviously are *sacrifices*. The victim was always intended to be an offering for sin and the means of regaining forfeited favour. The more valuable the victim the more efficacious was supposed to be the atonement, and the more certain the favour solicited. Accordingly when inferior offerings were found or believed to fail, human sacrifices were substituted for them; and these not unfrequently of the highest estimation; youths nobly born, possessed of eminent endowments and educated in the manner most advantageously fitted to insure mental distinction. Sacrifices of this general nature were offered by all the ancient heathen nations and have been offered by many still existing. In Hindostan they appear to be offered at the present time. Nor did the other offerings of the heathen speak any other language. The fragrance, the beauty, the costliness, the frequency, and the multitude of these were plainly intended to conciliate the good will of the god who was supplicated: a good will confessedly estranged but supposed to be capable of being acquired anew. According to the same scheme also were formed their *prayers* which either implicitly or explicitly acknowledged the sins of the suppliant and besought the restoration of the favour which he had forfeited. On the same principle tedious *pilgrimages* consuming at times a length of years and traversing no trifling part of the breadth of the globe were undertaken and executed. The burning heat, the parching drought, and the excessive perils of an Arabian or a Nubian desert were quietly and even cheerfully sustained by hosts of wanderers who had voluntarily exiled themselves from their friends, families, and country with the hope of obtaining the remission of sin considered as absolutely necessary and supposed to be unattainable by any means less dangerous and distressing. *Ablutions* speak the same design in a manner still more direct and unequivocal. To wash away his guilt the Egyptian plunged himself in the Nile and the Hindoo in the Ganges. From these waters, invested by popular superstition with the transcendent power of removing moral pollution, each expected to come out cleansed from all his turpitude and entitled anew to the complacency of the god whom he was conscious of having offended. On this ground the holy streams were resorted to by immense multitudes with incredible eagerness and anxiety and were supposed to furnish a certain passport to future blessings. To ablution was added *penance* as a very hopeful means of obtaining the same desirable object. This unnatural resort existed in a great variety of forms all of them humiliating, forbidding, and dreadful. Hunger, thirst, the heat of summer and the frost of winter, nakedness, weariness, extreme want, and excruciating pain have been undergone by millions of the human race without a groan, a murmur, or a sigh from an expectation that this voluntary suffering would shelter the criminal from the demands of future justice. It ought to be remarked that the length to which this self denial has often proceeded, shews in the strongest manner not only the reality but the intense degree of guilt with which the subject of it supposed himself to be stained. All these were regarded as essential duties of religion and as indispensably demanded of every man. In performing them, every man confessed he was stained with the common guilt, and that he needed an expiation.

3d. *The same doctrine is proved by the writings of all nations among whom writings are found.*—The history both of nations and individuals is professedly a true account of their actions and characters. It is also rarely written by men who are not at least candid towards those concerning whom they write and often by those who are strongly prejudiced in their favour, men of the same nation or party or for some other reason partially inclined towards the individual or the cause which is the subject of their history. There is also in most historians a strong prevailing inclination to cover the defects and crimes of those whose actions they record; lest by a full disclosure of them they should render the history less entertaining than they wish to their readers. From all these causes history is often a mere panegyric and almost always perhaps always a much more favourable account of the conduct of men than truth would warrant. The history of the Bible being dictated by inspiration presents its subjects more generally darkened and deformed in a great proportion of instances, both because it was designed to unfold the *moral characters* of men in an especial manner and because it is true. Hence we commonly suppose the people of Israel to have been more depraved than other nations. This however is an erroneous opinion, as any man who reads the first chapter of the Epistle to the Romans will easily discern. Had prophets written the history of the rest of mankind there is but too much reason to believe that nations and individuals generally who have been the subjects of history would have presented features equally disgusting and monstrous with those of the Israelites. But favourable as all these causes are to the human character, powerfully as they have influenced writers to present and that with many adventitious ornaments only the bright and to conceal as much as possible the dark side of man, history is still a satire upon our race scarcely less severe than any of those professedly written under this name. Should we contrary to all probability or in better language to absolute certainty acknowledge the portrait to be an exact unflattering likeness we must still be obliged to confess the whole aspect to be misshapen and monstrous without symmetry, beauty, or loveliness. Man as described by history is undeniably and always has been an evil odious being, disobedient and ungrateful to his Maker, unjust, insincere, and unkind to his fellow man, and far removed from the character which the Scriptures demand, which conscience approves, or which even in our opinion God can be supposed to love.

With history *moral and philosophical things* have abundantly concurred.—I will here pass all those which have been immediately directed to the point in question and have either declared or argued it in form their aid being unnecessary for the present purpose. Those which have been conducted with other designs, nay those which have intentionally opposed this doctrine have nevertheless served to establish it. This they have done in many ways, particularly by the feebleness of their arguments advanced in opposition to it, by the pains which they have taken to disguise human turpitude by fair names, flattering ascriptions, and false justifications, by the gross moral sentiments which they have abetted, and by the deformed dispositions which they have thus disclosed to the public view. Their very confessions also of what they in vain attempt to deny furnish no small evidence of its truth, while their efforts not unfrequently wear the appearance of a concerted design to carry a point scarcely supposed to be tenable, of an artful and insidious struggle to gain converts and achieve a victory rather than an honest endeavour to establish a truth of which the author is sincerely convinced. Upon the whole, in spite of all the exertions made to cover this humiliating truth, and hide from the perception of man an object so offensive, the fœtor still escapes and forces itself upon the senses in a manner so disgusting as to compel a conviction of its existence.—Poems, plays, novels, and other books of entertainment, written professedly only to amuse and please, are necessitated to unfold the same truth in a still clearer manner. All the characters almost, are characters mixed with sin, and the few unmixed ones which they have attempted are perceived by mere taste unaccompanied with intellectual examination to be dull, lifeless, and unnatural. Accordingly rational criticism has every where condemned them as improperly introduced, because they have no originals in fact. The sentiments also thrown out in these productions, are evidential of the same truth. In innumerable forms they declare and appeal to the universal corruption of mankind, as the object about which they are extensively occupied, and the only source, in a great multitude of instances, from which they are derived. Were not human nature corrupted, a great part of them could never have had either existence, or meaning. Vol. I. pp. 469—474.

In our strenuous recommendation of this work to the theological students of the Established Church, there must be, of course, a point of reservation, as Dr Dwight is an opponent both of Episcopacy, and of liturgical worship. That he was justified in such opposition, will naturally be allowed by the members of the Presbyterian and Congregational churches of the two countries, and especially by those of America, where the Presbyterian and Congregational modes of discipline are the prevailing systems — including of course the Baptists, who outnumber all the rest, and are congregational in their discipline. On the other side, Episcopalians and Liturgists might hail with the purest satisfaction such an enemy, if enemies they must have, as Dr Dwight, who opposes them without the spirit of enmity, and without a tincture of sectarian feeling.* He is indeed firm in his general conviction of the human origin of diocesan bishops, and of the inexpediency of forms of worship, or, at least, of their being not more advantageous to devotion than the usages of his own church. He is also aware of the difficulties attendant on all subjects where Christians, otherwise united in doc-

---

* The following is the close of the President's disquisition on Episcopacy —

From all these considerations it is clearly decided to my apprehension that diocesan bishops are not of scriptural, but of human origin, introduced either casually or from considerations of a prudential nature only. Christ has established pastors in his church, the church itself has constituted its bishops, and this, to a great extent, has been acknowledged by the bishops themselves. Such clearly appears to me to be the truth concerning this so much debated question. Still I have no disposition to contend with those Christians who are attached to Episcopacy, and who think they find any peculiar advantages in that form of ecclesiastical administration. Nor can I willingly adopt the same aspersions sometimes thrown upon it by individual Presbyterians. I cannot but remember, and remember with emotions of gratitude and respect, the very great and beneficial exertions made by the English church in the cause of Christianity, and made in many instances by the dignitaries of that church. Butler, Berkeley, Jewel, Beveridge, Bedell, and Wilson were bishops. Cranmer, Leighton, and Usher were archbishops. Cranmer, Latimer, and Ridley were martyrs. In that church also real religion has at times flourished to a great and very desirable extent. Like other churches, it has had its bright and dark days, but it has undoubtedly sent multitudes of its members to heaven, and at the present time is fast rising in the gradations of piety

trine and holiness of living, have for centuries disagreed and regards the actions fought on debateable ground, as something like drawn battles or as skirmishes, where each side alternately assumes the credit of victory He is farther onscious, that among these amicable quarrels, the best informed disputants are always the least bitter half knowledge being uniformly more positive than solid learning and that, in journeying through the wilderness of life, the Christian traveller has more serious work to do than to impede his neighbour's progress—and we may add his own—by attempting to determine what will never be determined Not that we undervalue questions of ecclesiastical polity neither do we forget with what promptitude, when required the advocates of Episcopacy and liturgical worship can bring forward replies rejoinders, and all the machinery of powerful controversy in their own defence We only wish that, on such occasions men would not merely use the lawful weapons of warfare, but use them lawfully There is such a thing as fighting the battles, both of the cathedral and of the conventicle with weapons furnished from the arsenals of rancour and practical irreligion The combatants meet, and finally separate but not perhaps till they have given some reason to the scoffers and infidels who witness the combat to urge, that there is often an approximation between a fiery zealot, whether for bishops presbyters, or itinerants, and the cold hearted unbeliever who stands by to watch and report the event

We feel with the greater force the truth implied by these remarks during the existing ferment of Christendom in relation to the struggle between Protestantism and Popery In its real essence, for we speak not of nominal national Protestantism it is not a question of discipline or of economy or of doctrine but it is the irreconcileable feud ever raging between the kingdom of this world, and the kingdom of our Lord and of his Christ How superficial and fatal is the notion of those persons—and some of them we believe to be, if not sagacious Christians yet humble and sincere—who dream, that the matter in debate merely refers to the resolution of such abstract questions as transubstantiation, monachism, penance, and the power of the keys and that if these things were conceded, the current of the Christian church would thenceforward roll on, in all its deep and pacific majesty increasing towards its estuary, till absorbed into the mighty ocean of eternity! Nothing like it the religion of mankind would never cease to molest the religion of the Gospel, so long as the latter exhibited the real influence and the former the mere shadow of Christianity The advance of the Evangelical system (using the term, not as a technical, but as an intelligible one) awakens perhaps the jealousy of some nominal *Protestants* and causes them to look towards the hitherto rival and opposing church as an ally in repelling the incursions of that purer form of Christianity, which disowns on the one hand, the pretensions of the Papacy, and, on the other the profession of all nominal religion whatever In fact, the strong hold of Popery is the asylum it affords to such religionists as want a protection from the demands made upon their hearts and lives by the Gospel itself As things really are, the exterior of the Church of Rome is the veil by which she conceals the necessity for spirituality and holiness Rites and ceremonies preoccupy the place of personal religion and the more gorgeous they can be made the more irresistible is their potency They become not the outward and visible means of devotion, but devotion itself Neither is this substitution of external things for inward holiness confined to this corrupt communion It is a distemper incident to all human minds and affects variously the *mere* Churchman, and the *mere*

Dissenter, in our own enlightened country. Each of them finds his consolations, although in the absence of crucifixes and relics, one within the walls of his parish church, the other in his meeting house; and *not* in the instructions delivered by their respective ministers, but in the scanty ceremonials allowed in either case, by the severe simplicity of a Protestant ritual.

Now, the evangelical scheme knows nothing of an individual's religion, unless it is rooted in the affections, and exemplified in practical obedience. The first point is to ascertain the aspirant's sincerity, and his personal acquaintance with "the excellency of the knowledge of Christ Jesus his Lord." This indispensable qualification being produced, as far as man can read the heart and observe the conduct, all other points are secondary and subordinate. But nominal Christianity, whether at Rome or Canterbury, in Essex street or in Moorfields, inverts this order; or rather, is quite satisfied with its followers' submission to ecclesiastical regulations, and concerns itself no farther. On this account, the Evangelical requisitions are exceedingly repulsive to all formalists of whatever communion; and at this point Popery comes to their aid. They are precisely in the state of mind prepared to welcome its assistance. The parties, by an instinct common to both, soon understand each other. Preliminaries of peace, after a little diplomatic etiquette, are readily signed and exchanged; and the religion of human nature, as modified at Rome, receives a fresh accession of converts, once formal Protestants, and now become formal Papists. Or, if these nominal Lutherans have too much pride to change their religion, they practically unite with their Papal co-adjutors, in opposing the incursions of pure Christianity. They are alike jealous of the Bible, and of the institutions which circulate the Bible; they both insist upon some authorised interpreter of its doctrines: they quote the self-same texts in support of exclusive churches; and their final determination is, that whatever either party allows, or disallows, *must* be enthusiasm—and they perfectly know what they mean by that word—and *must* be put down. In direct terms, you may join what communion you please, whether in England, Connecticut, Switzerland or France: *but you shall not be a practical Christian.* You may use the liturgies of the Anglican or Reformed continental churches, or you may sign the Congregational confessions of faith in America; but you shall not do these things except with the lip and the pen. You may be any thing, *provided only you know nothing of the spirit and power of the Gospel.*

The connexion of these remarks with the name and performances of Dr. Dwight is this; that *he* treats theology not as a national creed, or as the formulary of any particular church, but as a matter of every man's personal, individual concern. He considers that Christianity is, distinctively, the religion of private life, of the closet, the fireside, the exchange, the office, the farm, the house of merchandise; and that so far, and only so far, as its professor exhibits the influence of his principles, as thus particularized, is he at all likely to be accounted worthy " to obtain the joyful resurrection of the dead," and " to stand before the Son of Man." He is also quite as spiritual in his estimate of the inward character, as he is uncompromising in his views of holy obedience. The cross of Christ is his glory, the foundation of his hope; as the blood there shed is the price of his redemption. No part of his system assumes that gregarious character which equalizes the pretensions of men to piety, without scrutinizing their claims one by one. He is perfectly aware, that on earth the foolish and the wise both continue to bear their lamps; while the folly and the wisdom of the several parties will, at the bridegroom's appearance, prove the visible church to be a mingled and anomalous assembly.

We have thought it right to caution the Episcopalian, and the friend of precomposed liturgies, of Dr Dwight's opinions upon these topics. There are also necessarily various other points in the course of the innumerable subjects discussed in these volumes, on which pious and well judging persons may and will differ. We shall not however enter upon any of these litigated questions, so calmly and uncontroversially handled by our author; but we must just apprize our readers, with respect to one class of them, that Dr Dwight (see his discourses on the decrees and sovereignty of God,) is decidedly though modestly and candidly, Calvinistic in his sentiments. His Calvinism is not, however, very harsh or dangerous, as explained in the following passages.

The conduct of God is sovereign in this sense, that he does according to his will independently and irresistibly without giving an account of any of his matters any further than he pleases; but that he wills nothing without the best reason, whether that reason be declared to his creatures or not: that real glory to himself and real good to his creation, not otherwise attainable, are universally the objects to which his pleasure is directed, whether it respects the existence and motions of an insect, or the salvation of a man. God never acts arbitrarily; and to say that he wills a thing because he wills it, is to speak without meaning. All his pleasure, all his determinations are perfectly wise and good, founded on the best of all reasons, and directed to the best of all purposes. Vol I p 246.

If we please to be saved, we shall now be saved: this is one great part of the Divine pleasure. There is nothing which prevents us from being saved but our own inclinations; and this would as effectually prevent us in any supposable circumstances. Nor could we in any circumstances possess a greater freedom of choice or action with respect to this or any other subject than we now possess. Nor is there, so far as I know, any influence from God which at all hinders us from choosing salvation with all that freedom of action which moral beings can possess. It will be observed I speak not here of persons punished for their incorrigible obstinacy with judicial blindness and hardness of heart; though it is to be questioned whether even in this case God does any thing more than leave them to themselves. The language of God to every sinner is, As I live, saith the Lord, I have no pleasure in the death of a sinner, but would rather that he should return and live. His invitations to sinners are,

Ho, every one that thirsteth, come ye to the waters; and he that hath no money, yea come buy wine and milk without money and without price; and whosoever will, let him come and take the water of life freely. This language is perfectly sincere and exactly descriptive of the disposition of God. Vol I p 240.

We will now offer to the reader's perusal, a citation from the author's conclusion to his great work, lamenting that we cannot find room for more than this fragment, and which we are compelled to begin, and to terminate abruptly. Should any person be startled at the use of the term *virtue*, in the following extract, it may be expedient to inform him, that it is employed, in the "Theology," as synonymous with holiness.

The science of Theology is capable of yielding more PLEASURE *to the mind than any other.*—The pleasures which science is capable of yielding to the mind, are addressed both to the *imagination* and the *understanding*. Of both these kinds of pleasure theology is eminently productive. The pleasures conveyed to the mind through the *imagination* are derived from such objects as are new, various, beautiful, refined, great, and noble; and the more these attributes prevail, the more capable are the objects in which they are found of yielding this species of pleasure. But in no field of human pursuit are objects found in such numbers and of such uniformity, which are invested with these attributes, or possess the power of yielding this pleasure in the same degree. In vain will you search for objects equally beautiful with multitudes which are presented to you in the Scriptures; with paradise and its inhabitants; with the innumerable and most delightful variegations of excellence which adorn the angelic character; with the endless diversified, manifestations of kindness, compassion and good providence of God towards his children; the grateful and unaffected effusions of their piety to him; the delightful scenery, if I may so style it, of the millennial world, drawn with such unrivalled elegance by several of the prophets, and particularly by the pencil of Isaiah; the charming features of a virtuous character depicted by Christ and his apostles; and the wonderful exhibition of the future prosperity of the church, arrayed in glory and beauty by the hand of St John. The Scriptures are the native region of *sublimity* both *natural* and *moral*. The single volume of the Scriptures, says Sir William Jones, one of the best judges whom the world has ever seen, contains more and higher specimens of this excellence than all the remains of Grecian and Roman antiquity united. The God of the Scriptures is an object infinitely sublime; and wherever he appears, whether his character is exhibited, or his actions are recited, he appears with power, wisdom, and goodness, glory and majesty, to which nothing is equal, nothing second. The works of God here recounted are possessed of a splendour suited to his character. The creation, the deluge, the wonders of Egypt, the wilderness and Canaan, the miracles attendant upon the death, resurrection and ascension of the Saviour, the resurrection, the conflagration, the future judgment, and future existence of the righteous and the wicked, are objects compared with which all other events which have entered into the conceptions of man shrink into nothing. In moral beauty, greatness and glory the Saviour stands alone. — On this divine subject I have no room to expatiate, and shall only observe that the Scriptures themselves have done more justice to it than can within the same compass be done a second time, when they inform us that Christ is the light of heaven, and the effulgence of the Divine glory. Not less distinguished is this science for the power which it possesses and the means which it furnishes *for refining the views and the taste of man*. On the one hand, the Scriptures forbid every thing which is impure and licentious; and on the other effectually discourage every thing which is gross and grovelling. To accomplish this combined purpose they commence their efforts in the only efficacious manner, namely, by *purifying the affections of the heart*. Wherever these are gross and debased, the imagination will be gross and the taste debased. So universally is this true that no advantages of education, no superiority of talents, no acquisition of learning, no refinement of society, hitherto have sufficient power to purify the fancy and the taste where the affections had been yielded to licentious indulgences. A gross heart will delight in gross objects, and on these objects so long as they are relished the imagination will love to dwell. Elegance of mind grows out of the refinement of the heart. It is hence that the sentiments of Paul and John, of Peter and James, their images and their language are immeasurably removed from the gross efforts of heathen antiquity. Had Cicero's oration for Cœlius or the third eclogue of the polite and elegant Virgil formed a part of the sacred volume, either would have furnished an argument against its inspiration which all succeeding ages could never have refuted, and infidelity would long since have gained a final triumph over the Gospel. In the Scriptures we are presented every where with those objects which more incomparably than any other originate and establish refined affections, spotless views, and dignified excursions of the imagination. By a continual correspondence with the precepts of the Gospel the affections are gradually and in a sense instinctively purified. By a frequent recurrence to its sentiments and imagery the imagination is exalted and the taste wrought into elegance as silver is beautified by the hand of the burnisher. By conversing with noble objects the mind is ennobled in a manner and to a degree which will admit no parallel, is estranged from every thing low and little, assumes insensibly a portion of the celestial character, and directs its flight unceasingly towards heaven. On the variety and consequent novelty of objects every where presented by the Scriptures to the imagination it is unnecessary here to expatiate. Both are unceasing, both are endless; and as they are successively unfolded to rational beings will regularly enhance their enjoyments throughout the ages of eternity.—There is another and very important view in which this subject demands our consideration. *Theology spreads its influence over the creation and providence of God, and gives to both almost all their beauty and sublimity.* Creation and providence, seen by the eye of theology and elucidated by the glorious commentary on both furnished in the Scriptures, become new objects to the mind, immeasurably more noble, rich, and delightful than they can appear to a worldly sensual mind. The heavens and the earth and the great as well as numberless events which result from the Divine administration are in themselves vast, wonderful, frequently awful, in many instances solemn, in very many exquisitely beautiful, and in a great number eminently sublime. All these attributes however they possess, if considered only in the abstract, in degrees very humble and diminutive compared with the appearance which they make when beheld as the works of Jehovah. Mountains, the ocean, and the heavens are majestic and sublime. Hills and valleys, soft landscapes, trees, fruits and flowers and many objects in the animal and mineral kingdoms are beautiful. But what is this beauty, what is this grandeur compared with that agency of God to which they owe their being? Think what it is for the Almighty Hand to spread the plains, to heave the mountains and to pour the ocean. Look at the verdure, flowers, and fruits which in the mild season adorn the surface of the earth; the uncreated Hand fashions their fine forms, paints their exquisite colours, and exhales their delightful perfumes. In the spring his life reanimates the world, in the summer and autumn his bounty is poured out upon the hills and valleys in the winter his way is in the whirlwind and in the storm and the clouds are the dust of his feet His hand hung the earth upon nothing lighted up the sun in the heavens and rolls the planets and the comets through the immeasurable fields of ether His breath kindled the stars his voice called into existence worlds innumerable and filled the expanse with animated being To all he is present over all he rules for all he provides The mind attempered to Divine contemplation finds him in every solitude meets him in every walk and in all places and at all times sees itself surrounded by God —How superior are the works of creation and providence when considered in this manner to the highest conceptions formed by a worldly mind which merely looks at the things themselves and with a folly a stupidity which is extreme stops short of their author How enhanced is their beauty! how exalted their sublimity! The pleasures yielded by science to the *understanding* are derived extensively from the same sources which furnish so much delight to the imagination for the understanding also finds exquisite pleasure in that which is new beautiful and sublime At the same time it is peculiarly delighted with such views as expand the intellectual powers and with such objects as are seen to possess fitness for valuable purposes the symmetry of parts happily arranged in a system the rectitude apparent in their own nature and their utility to moral beings and to the universe Many sciences are without a question sufficiently extensive to employ and exhaust all the efforts of the intellect This is true of mathematical and metaphysical science of natural philosophy and astronomy medical science law and civil policy It is hardly necessary to observe that this is eminently true of theological science which has for its object the character word and works of God the nature of man his apostasy his restoration to the Divine kingdom his virtue existing as a principle and operating practically in all his duties to God his fellow creatures and himself the character offices and kingdom of the Mediator the character of the Holy Spirit and his agency in renewing and sanctifying man and in conducting him to endless life and that boundless scheme of dispensations which controls all human concerns in the present world and beyond the grave directs the existence of men and angels their employments and their allotments for ever —At the same time theology is conversant, more than all other sciences with that which is beautiful and that which is sublime I mean with that which is seen to be such by the intellect and not merely that which is felt to be such by the imagination The truths of theology are without limit conversant with moral excellence and are extensively employed in unfolding to man whatever is lovely and dignified in the intellectual nature There is no beauty or dignity of mind but virtue and there is no virtue but that which is evangelical It is noble and lovely when in its fairest forms, it is seen in such beings as we are In angels it is sublime and wonderful In Jehovah it is exalted not only above all conception but above all blessing and praise a summit which receding beyond the utmost reach of finite minds will as they ascend through the endless succession of ages rise higher and higher and higher for ever Vol V pp 547—552

This is indeed an exceedingly imperfect and unsatisfactory specimen of quotation as the current of the author's eloquence suffers a sudden interruption If the extract has awakened in the reader such an interest as causes him to desire its continuation and thence to study the work itself our own wishes will be so far satisfied A Christian journalist ought to have only one end in view and this will be obtained in proportion as he succeeds in diffusing confirming and defending truth —whether by the direct efforts of his own pen, or by introducing the attempts of others to the observation of mankind

Whatever may ultimately be the public decision on the theological importance of these volumes, they will at least tend to reduce to reason some persons who have indulged a spirit of scepticism, not so much on the moral as on the mental excellence of their relations on the other side of the Atlantic It will, we think, be at length conceded, that man in America as well as in Europe is a reading writing and even thinking animal This by many, will be deemed a liberal concession There are those among us from whom it will, however and must ultimately be extorted, in despite of what they have spoken and written to the contrary Our Quarterly Reviewers and similar writers should be aware of the recoil of their vituperation upon themselves if in no other point yet in this, that the people of the United States are ' bone of their bone and flesh of their flesh descendants from a com mon ancestry, and substantially British in their civil and ecclesiastical institutions, literature, science, domestic habits and entirely one with them in language. But thus it is that even handed justice bestows its impartial decisions, and chastises the abettors of family quarrels, by causing them to expose their own shame. We wish that certain of our countrymen remembered, and imitated in the spirit of their conduct the dignified consistency of his late Majesty, when he received the first ambassador of the new Republic with this address,—" I was the last man, sir, to consent to the independence of America, and I shall now be the last man to violate it." Those who recollect the manner and graceful elocution of George the Third, in the moments of royal etiquette, will imagine the effect of these manly expressions; and indeed it is, we believe, on record, that the ambassador, on this occasion, was completely overpowered, and returned to his government under the full conviction of the king's determination to maintain the relations of peace and amity.

If America exhibits the vices of a young nation, she should not gratuitously retaliate upon the alleged infirmities of her aged and still surviving parent: though as Americans seem to think, under the pressure of years, and still suffering from various domestic troubles. One of these, so at least it appeared at the time, was the desertion of a favourite daughter on the 4th of July, 1776. Greybeards perfectly well recollect the consternation of the family at that trying moment, especially the shrieks and hysterics of the mother. They remember too, that for several tedious years the strongest measures were adopted to effect the child's return; but all in vain! A compromise at length took place in 1782, and since that time, (with one unpleasant exception of recent date,) things have been tolerably quiet. Why then, not " *let well alone?*"—If we continue to complain, in our quarterly reports, of the disorderly behaviour of backwoodsmen, squatters, rowdies, gougers, and other persons designated by appellations of similar elegance, we must not be angry, if we are reminded in return of Thurtells, Proberts, Fauntleroys, radicals, agitators, St Giles's and Wapping, and of the thousands classed and described by Mr Colquhoun, Mr Pierce Egan—we beg pardon for coupling the names,—and by " the gentlemen of the press" in their " reports of the ring," and the Westminster pit, and in their elaborate details of " sporting and pugilism," and the existing morals of the theatres. Above all, let no American spy be suffered to take the steam boat some summer morning at Holyhead, and land the same afternoon at the Pigeon house: otherwise there will be some danger, lest, in an evil hour for us, he should *progress slick right away* through the emerald isle, *guessing* his route from county to county, and favour the world next season with two *lengthy* octavos from his publisher's *store* at New York, describing the state of our sister kingdom, which, for centuries, had possessed a vice regal court, a peerage, parliament, university, and, lastly, an established church, with an independent and numerous clergy: yet, notwithstanding all these advantages, presents every fearful sign of insubordination, misrule, and of the most abject and gloomy superstition. We are now, indeed, treading on tender ground; and we can only bring ourselves to the mention of Ireland, on this occasion, to demonstrate the infatuation of such persons as find in America nothing better than " a den of thieves," without adverting to the state of things at home.*

* Very, very far indeed are we from viewing the state of Ireland with the feelings generated by party questions. Our only intention in the above remarks is to illustrate the unfairness and suicidal folly of declaiming against the United States of America, on points where the

Steering a middle course between adulation and contumely, we cannot for a moment doubt that the United States are rapidly rising in the scale of civilization, science, general literature, and moral vigour. In naval architecture, in steam navigation, in certain branches of engraving, in amplifying the powers of machinery, in the construction and extent of canals, in the appointments both of their military and mercantile marine, and in various practical applications of art and science, they are already either our superiors or our rivals. Their diplomatists have contrived to meet the practised statesmen of Europe on tolerably equal terms; while Mr Washington Irving occupies a conspicuous rank, even in our own cherished island, among the elegant, refined, and polished writers of the day. They regularly republish all our popular works, and, among these, the Edinburgh and Quarterly Reviews, and some other British periodical publications; our own, as we have stated, among the number. Some of their own periodical works also, especially of a scientific kind, are in good repute. We have therefore only to give our cousins a little time; and in their turn, they will perhaps produce a Bacon and Newton, a Locke and Butler, a Milton and Shakspeare; as they have already, in the emergency of the war of independence, shewn their Washington, and other chiefs of the armies, which after a severe struggle with the disciplined veterans of Europe, established a new empire. In the mean time, we are quite as fully aware, as Mr Fearon, Mr Howison, and Mr Cobbett, (for even he felt the grievance,) of the frequent coarseness of American manners; and we are also conscious of the darkness overshadowing those divisions of the States which, with all their republican intolerance of despotism continue to legalize slavery. This black spot *must* be expunged, before America can be selected as the only land of liberty on the surface of a bondaged world. But here we pause; as, on this perilous topic, it becomes us to beware of the recoil!

It is, however, chiefly to British Christians, that the increasing importance of the United States discloses the opening visions of future times. We have mentioned, in an early paragraph of this article, the identity of religious feeling which binds together the spiritual philanthropists of the two countries. The principle thus brought into exercise, and receiving perpetual accessions of vigour, by the plans of co operation constantly passing and repassing between us, will outlive all such international arrangements as terminate on this side the grave. Religion, pure, un sectarian religion, is the golden chain, reaching from heaven to earth; and extending itself throughout the communion of saints, wherever its members can be found, which, at this moment, reunites, and will hereafter retain in the most intimate combination the followers of Jesus Christ scattered among the millions of Great Britain and America; and will, we are convinced, do more in effecting the continuance of a pacific system, than all the stratagems and elaborations of mere politicians. These wise men of the world have indeed very slender conceptions of the national utility of their Christian fellow subjects and fellow citizens. They are the salt of the earth, the means of preservation to a sinful world; although all the gratitude they receive, in return, may too ge

---

parent country feels itself vulnerable and feeble. The time was when Dr Johnson himself who was a *good hater* of the daughter thus sung of his favourite metropolis:—

London — the needy villain's general home
The common shore of Paris, and of Rome!

What the capital is become now should in justice be left to the determination of its visitors from the banks of the Seine and Tiber and in default of their reports to the wanderers from Philadelphia, Charleston and Washington

nerally be the same world's derision, scorn, and neglect. Such preservatives were, once, less than ten righteous persons in a city devoted to destruction: and to one of whom, at the moment of the impending storm of fire and brimstone, it was said, 'Haste thee, escape: for I cannot do any thing till thou be come thither:' that is, till he ceased to be, (if we may adopt the term,) the palladium of the guilty inhabitants, whom his presence protected. We well remember, during the late war, the solemnity of the appeal to his countrymen made by an eminent American minister (Dr Morse), with regard to a contest at once so unnatural and peculiarly anti-Christian: when he considered the religious character and obligations of the belligerents, and the spiritual injuries each might sustain by the calamities incident to a state of hostility. Yet such was the elastic, irrepressible, invincible energy of religion, that the *golden chain* was never broken asunder. Our institutions for the diffusion of the Scriptures, of education, and of missions, pursued their uninterrupted course. There was tranquillity in the midst of the tempest. Surely this was a strong collateral proof of the reality of the religion of Jesus Christ: a sensible evidence of its greatness, and of its indestructible excellence and power. We have since seen, at the anniversaries of our own societies, our brethren in the highest sense, from America, standing forward, and speaking in our own tongue, and in theirs, the wonderful works of God. We have lately had the gratification of receiving two of their bishops, and assisting by our contributions in some of their plans of piety and benevolence: thus reviving a reciprocity of esteem and affection.

The great writer: for such he is, whose work primarily has given birth to these observations, was one who, before he departed from this earthly scene, beheld the horizon already glow with the bright promises perhaps of millennial glory: or if not of an era so supremely blessed, yet of one when God, as we trust, will visit the earth with an unmeasurable plenteousness of grace and truth. He was the cordial and efficient friend of the magnificent schemes of good now in full action among all our religious communities. He was also alive to the injuries intended against the moral and intellectual credit of his country, and repelled them, not with the irascible temper of a partizan, but with the strength of a warrior capable of resisting aggression, and, if necessary, of rolling back the tide of war upon the aggressor. He also discerned that, in proportion as every species of hostility was discountenanced, the two countries would obtain mutual benefit. He identified their interests: and he scarcely wished his own America to possess any source of prosperity, unless the consequences could be equally shared by the land of his fathers. If this be not an enlarged and enlightened patriotism, let the word henceforth lapse into desuetude. *He* loves his country who loves mankind,—those of mankind, especially in whom he can confide, as heirs of the same promises: and such as these, if to be found any where, are numbered among the inhabitants of our own island, and of her original colonies. We conclude, by citing, in reference to our kinsmen dispersed or dispersing over the wide regions stretching from the Atlantic to the Pacific, a passage, which also closes one of Mr Washington Irving's conciliatory efforts, — 'For my brethren and companion's sakes, I will now say, Peace be within thee. Because of the house of the Lord our God, I will seek thy good!'

LITERARY AND PHILOSOPHICAL INTELLIGENCE,
&c &c

GREAT BRITAIN

PREPARING for publication.—The whole Works of Archbishop Leighton, with his Life, by the Rev. J. N. Pearson.—Historical Notes respecting the Indians of North America, and the Attempts to civilize and convert them.—The Parish Church, or the Religion and Customs of the Ancient Britons, by the Rev. T. Wood.—No. I. of the Christian Examiner and Church of Ireland Magazine, to be continued monthly.

In the press.—The Works of Dr. Lightfoot, edited by the Rev. J. Pitman, 13 vols. 8vo.—Sermons by the Rev. H. M'Neile, 1 vol.—Nine Sermons intended to illustrate the leading Truths contained in the Liturgy, by the Rev. F. Close.

Oxford.—Four University Scholarships have been instituted by the munificence of the Dean of Westminster, for the promotion of classical learning and taste. The candidates are to be Undergraduate Members of the University, without regard to place of birth, school, parentage, or pecuniary circumstances, who shall not have exceeded their sixteenth term from their matriculation. The first election on Dean Ireland's foundation takes place next term.

A Professorship of Political Economy has been founded on the endowment of Henry Drummond, Esq. The Professor is to be elected by Convocation, and to hold the professorship for the space of five years, being capable of re-election after the lapse of two years. He is to read a course of nine lectures at the least during one of the four academical terms in every year, and to print and publish one of the same lectures. Three persons are to be considered as forming a class, and if the Professor neglects so to read or to publish according to the intention of the founder, he forfeits all claim to the salary during the period of such neglect.

The late Mr. Rich's valuable collection has been purchased for the British Museum: it consists of Arabic, Persic, Turkish, and Syriac manuscripts, gems and other antiquities from Babylon and Nineveh, and coins, Oriental, Greek, Roman, &c. The report of the parliamentary committee gives the opinions of various learned men as to the value of the collection. Professor Lee states that the manuscripts are the best he has seen collected by any one man. The Syriac consist of sixty-eight volumes; there is one copy of the Philoxenian version of the Gospels which is valuable. Mr. Lee knows of only one other copy, which is at Oxford. There are copies of the Nestorian and Jacobite editions of the Peschito version of the Scriptures; there is no other complete copy of the Nestorian edition in any of our libraries. The Nestorian and Jacobite sects separated as early as the year 500, and continued their editions in their own churches; the collection of them may therefore be important on certain disputed passages. Some of the copies are a thousand years old. There is a History of the Persecutions of the Nestorians which Mr. Lee believes to be unique. Among the coins and medals there is one coin, a Kufic Derham, represented to have been struck in the 79th year of the Mohammedan era, considered worth 100*l*.; there being only one similar one known, belonging to the Royal Academy of Sweden. Among the Babylonish and Nineveh antiquities is a cylindrical brick covered with arrow-head characters. The house of commons have voted 7,500*l*. for the whole collection.

Since the discovery of the Milton manuscript among the state records in the Tower of London, several other papers have been rescued from oblivion, which give information hitherto unknown relative to the official situation and family affairs of that celebrated man. They have been put into the hands of Mr. Todd, who is about to incorporate them in a memoir of the poet.

A contemporary periodical work, the Gentleman's Magazine, notices Mrs. Hannah More's late publication entitled The Spirit of Prayer, in the following terms. We copy the passage not only to introduce to our readers this excellent little publication (which being a compilation from the author's works already reviewed, and recommended in detail in our pages scarcely comes within our critical department) but to express the pleasure which we feel in observing the merited eulogy paid to the writings and character of that revered Christian instructress, by the conductors of a respectable and widely circulated miscellany usually perhaps candid but not always so correct or fortunate in its theological decisions. We were not however aware nor do we think upon reconsideration that Mrs More has pushed some devotional points further than either Scripture or the formularies of our church warrant. The reviewers say

This is a sacred and a beautiful work sacred as being the dying legacy of a pious Christian whose life has finely illustrated the important truths she has uttered beautiful in the correct purity of its taste and in the lucid arrangement of its matter. To no female writer of the present age has the Christian world been so largely indebted as to Mrs Hannah More. We say this deliberately and we are aware at some hazard but if she may have pushed some doctrinal points further than many sincere persons are disposed to go with her still we affirm that those subjects on which all sincere believers are agreed have been enforced and treated with a strength of argument a felicity of style and a masculine energy of thought which we should in vain look for in any contemporary female. Of the instructive tenor of her conversation let those who have enjoyed the happiness of an introduction to her society at Barley Wood speak. No one ever yet left her uninstructed by her conversation or unaffected by her cheerful piety and her devout resignation. To a friendly intercourse with the young she always was partial and she never failed almost in an instant to remove those impressions of *awe* which would naturally steal upon their minds from the consideration of her superior talents such was the suavity of her manners and the gentleness of her heart.—The present little volume contains the collected thoughts of the writer upon the subject of prayer which were hitherto scattered throughout her numerous works. These reflections have been arranged under their several heads and the whole form a manual worthy the attention of every pious mind

At a late meeting of the Asiatic Society Mr Platt the Librarian of the British and Foreign Bible Society presented on their behalf copies of the translations of the holy Scripture into various languages made under the auspices or at the expense of the Society. This magnificent donation amounted to upwards of one hundred volumes handsomely bound. The Secretary also read a communication from Mr Platt accompanying copies of certain Abyssinian MSS relative to the constitution and condition of the Christian church of Ethiopia and including a calendar of its saints obtained by the Bible Society by means of the Rev Wm Jowett.—The Abyssinian devotional works contain page after page of prayers and ascriptions of praise to the Virgin Mary and various other objectionable particulars but Mr Platt has translated several prayers of a much higher and more excellent character. We give the following example.— O my Lord and my God Jesus Christ Son of the ever living Jehovah I entreat and beseech thee that thou wouldst pardon my sin and my transgression—thou whose mercy is unbounded! What man is he that sinneth not? Where is the wood that burns not? and who is he a man the son of a woman that doth not commit sin? Unto whom wilt thou look O Lord Jesus Christ? There is none good and pure besides thee. And now O Lord pardon my sin and transgression and blot out the hand writing of my debt that is against me according to thy mercy and compassion for thou art merciful and compassionate to thee be glory and praise! to the Father to the Son and to the Holy Ghost in heaven and on earth always and for ever and ever. Amen

The clerks and apprentices of the woollen drapers haberdashers and some other tradesmen in Edinburgh lately addressed a representation to their employers requesting that the shops might be shut at such an hour as to enable them to attend the School of Arts or other institutions from which they might derive the means of improvement. The representation was immediately attended to and nearly all who are engaged in these branches of trade now shut their shops at eight o clock. Most of the tradesmen of Glasgow have followed the laudable example of those of Edinburgh so as to allow their apprentices to attend Mechanics Institutions and Reading Rooms

DENMARK

A work has recently been published at Copenhagen entitled De Originibus et Fatis Ecclesiæ Christianæ in India Orientali by Matthew Haquin Hohlenberg. It is well known that when the Portuguese arrived in India they found there certain Christians of the Nestorian sect who were afterwards denominated Christians of St Thomas according to a tradition that St Thomas preached the Gospel to the Hindoos. This tradition has been treated by some writers as a fable but M Hohlenberg agrees with Dr Buchanan who has defended the truth of the tradition in his Christian Researches. The

Danish author examines the arguments against the tradition and labours to prove that the Apostle was really the founder of the Christian church in India. He then traces the history of this church up to the arrival of the Portuguese. The inscriptions which Dr. Buchanan has preserved but which have not been decyphered it is said might probably throw some light upon the subject.

ITALY

It is stated in some of the periodical publications that Angelo Maio pursuing his palimpsest researches has discovered voluminous fragments of Polybius and Diodorus, an entire book of the latter containing details of the Phœnicians and numerous fragments of Menander.

SWEDEN

The first expedition to Columbia, from Sweden sailed last October freighted with Swedish iron and steel.—A project is afloat at Copenhagen to introduce Macadamization into Holstein.

EGYPT

Mohammed Ali Pacha, the Viceroy, among his other projects for the improvement of his states has lately established telegraphs from Alexandria to Cairo and relays of horses for the despatch of couriers. He has also founded a college supported by himself at a short distance from Cairo in the palace of his son Ismael Pacha; it already contains one hundred students. Some of the students are studying the European languages for the purpose of translating the works which Ali Pacha intends to introduce. He has also established a printing press and published an Arabic and Italian Dictionary with some military works translated from Italian into Turkish. It is his intention to build an hospital for persons infected with the plague, and by the precautions he prescribes it is hoped that Egypt may be freed from this distemper. French and Italian physicians are sent all over the country to vaccinate the children, a measure the more extraordinary as it opposes the strongest religious prejudices of the people. The country is making rapid advances in agriculture and commerce, particularly in the culture and exportation of cotton.

ALGIERS

The city of Algiers and its neighbourhood were visited with a tremendous earthquake on the 2d of March which continued at intervals for the five following days. It has totally destroyed the town of Blida burying in its ruins nearly all the inhabitants. Out of a population of 15,000 souls chiefly Moors, Jews and Arabs it is asserted that about 300 only have been saved and those in a sadly mutilated state.

INDIA

Semaphoric telegraphs are about to be introduced into Bengal by means of which it is calculated communications can be made between Calcutta and Madras in forty eight hours.

The car of Juggurnauth is kept at Chandernagore which belongs to the French. This huge car used to be dragged along the main road leading to Ildanga but the road having undergone repair the French authorities sent word to the proprietors of the Ruth that as the wheels of the car would tear up the road they could not suffer it to be dragged over it unless they consented to pay five hundred rupees for its repair in consequence of which the Ruth was not allowed to be drawn in spite of the earnest entreaties of the Hindoos. The conduct of the French remarks the Calcutta Missionary Herald has not created any spirit of rebellion among the Hindoos. O that the rulers would exercise their authority in abolishing the burning of widows! And that they might do it without causing any stir among the people the prohibition of the removal of Juggurnath's car fully testifies.

The importation of cotton wool from the East Indies which in 1792 was only seven pounds weight now amounts to upwards of ten millions.

FRENCH GUIANA

Baron Milius the governor of Cayenne has sent an expedition up the country composed of two scientific men, a physician and a missionary, with a view partly to examine the soil and its productions and to complete the topography and geography of Guiana but especially to open a communication with the natives and to lay a foundation for their civilization and conversion to Christianity.

MEXICO

The American journals state that the President of Mexico had published a decree of the Sovereign Congress authorizing him to receive proposals for cutting a communication between the Pacific and Atlantic oceans by the isthmus of Tehuantepec.

LIST OF NEW PUBLICATIONS

THEOLOGY

A Catechetical Exposition of the Apostles Creed, by J. T. Law, A.M., Chancellor of Lichfield and Coventry. 1 vol. 8vo. 9s.

Sermons, by the Rev. J. E. N. Molesworth. 1 vol. 8vo. 10s. 6d.

Supplement to the Protestant's Companion, by the Rev. C. Daubeny, LL.D., Archdeacon of Sarum. 1 vol. 8vo. 6s. 6d.

Formularies of Faith in the Reign of Henry VIII. 8vo. 7s.

A Collection of Passages from the Holy Bible which combat the Errors of the Church of Rome. 1s.

The Bible prohibited, a Dialogue between a Roman Catholic Priest and a Roman Catholic Layman. 4d.

Reflections on the Word of God, by W. Ward, of Serampore. 6s. 6d.

Rickard's Hymns for Private Devotion. 3s.

A Letter to R. Wardlaw, D.D. on Infant Baptism, by John But.

Calendarium Palestinæ, comprising the Natural History of Syria, and the Jewish Fasts and Festivals, on a large sheet, by William Carpenter. Also an Edition in 12mo. with a Dissertation on the Hebrew Months, from a Tract of Michaelis.

Letters to C. Butler, Esq. on the Roman Catholic Church, by the Rev. H. Phillpotts, D.D. 1 vol. 8vo.

The Doctrines of our Saviour in Harmony with those of St. Paul, the Hulsean Prize Dissertation for 1824, by J. A. Jeremie, B.A.

The Doctrine of the Church of Geneva illustrated in a Series of Sermons preached by the Modern Divines of that city, edited by the Rev. J. S. Pons. 8vo. 10s.

MISCELLANEOUS

A Picture of England from the Arrival of the Saxons down to the Eighteenth Century, by J. Aspin. 7s. 6d.

The Negro's Memorial, or the Abolitionist's Catechism, by an Abolitionist. 8vo. 2s. 6d.

Travels among the Arab Tribes inhabiting the Countries East of Syria and Palestine, by J. S. Buckingham. 4to. plates. 3l. 15s. 6d.

The Dublin Philosophical Journal and Scientific Review. No. 1. 7s. 6d.

The Century of Inventions of the Marquis of Worcester, from the Original Manuscripts, with Notes and a Biographical Memoir, by C. T. Partington. 12mo. 7s. 6d.

The Philosophy of Trade and Manufactures, by J. Fontaine. 1s.

The Poetical Works and Letters of Thomas Gray, with a Memoir of his Life and Writings, and a Portrait of the Author. 2 vols. crown 8vo. 15s.; large paper 21s.

An Attempt to establish the First Principles of Chemistry by Experiment, by T. Thomson, M.D. 2 vols. 8vo. 30s.

A Reply to Mr. Brougham on the Education of the People, by the Rev. E. W. Grinfield. 8vo.

Appendix to the Report of the Trial of Lieut. Dawson, R.A. being an Appeal to the Lords Archbishops of Canterbury and York, and to the Lord Bishop of London.

The History and Antiquities of Bath Abbey Church, by J. Britton, F.A.S. Royal 8vo. 1l.

The History and Antiquities of Wells Cathedral, with 24 engravings, by J. Britton, F.A.S. Medium 4to. 2l. 10s.

The History of Paris from the earliest Period to the present Day. 3 vols. 8vo. 2l. 2s.

The Historical Works of Sir J. Balfour of Kinnaird. 4 vols. 8vo. 3l.

Origines, or Remarks on the Origin of several Empires, States and Cities, by the Right Hon. Sir W. Drummond. 2 vols. 8vo. 24s.

The History of Italy from the Fall of the Western Empire, by G. Percival. 2 vols. 8vo. 30s.

RELIGIOUS INTELLIGENCE

CHURCH MISSIONARY SOCIETY

In proceeding with our abstract of the last published Report of the Society we arrive at the

Calcutta and North India Mission

The appointment of Dr. Reginald Heber to the See of Calcutta is an event of the greatest promise to the cause of Christianity in the vast regions of the East connected with the United Kingdom. In reference to this Society the Committee warmly congratulate the members on his lordship's appointment, having long been its zealous friend and able advocate; his countenance and support in its enlarging concerns in India was confidently anticipated.

It was stated in the Twenty-second Report that the Committee had placed the sum of 1000l. at the disposal of the late Bishop of Calcutta, for the use of Bishop's College this was to be considered as a grant for the year 1822 and a confident expectation was expressed that the liberality of the members of the Society would enable the Committee to appropriate a like sum annually to the benefit of the College. The Bishop's lamented death occurring, no further steps were taken in India in reference to the grant. On the appointment of the Rev. Dr. Heber to the vacant See, the Committee placed at his lordship's disposal this sum, with a request that he would be pleased to appropriate it in such manner as might seem most expedient, and would apprise the Committee in what way, in his lordship's judgment, the Society could hereafter most effectually render assistance to the college—the statutes having been framed with a wisdom and liberality which afford opportunity both to the local governments and the religious societies connected with the United Church of co-operating with the College to the attainment of its great ends. His lordship at a monthly meeting of the Committee stated that he had reason to believe that the sum might be most advantageously applied in placing the printing department of the College on an efficient footing. His lordship had appointed the Senior Chaplain the Rev. Daniel Corrie, a warm and steady friend of the Society, to the Archdeaconry of Calcutta. In reference to the Society's operations in *Calcutta and its vicinity*, the Corresponding Committee report the arrival of several new missionaries and the useful employment of others. The native female schools had increased to twenty-two, and of the persons who were first admitted to the schools three young women had made sufficient proficiency to be employed as teachers. They have each charge of a school containing from fifteen to twenty-five girls, and acquit themselves with much credit. Many other women who were under instruction would soon be able to engage in similar undertakings. The Marchioness of Hastings had rendered important aid to the female schools especially by visiting them in person. The parents were much attracted by her ladyship's visiting lanes and gullies where Europeans are seldom seen, and by her condescension to their children. The Corresponding Committee had circulated proposals for the erection of a central school for the especial improvement of the first classes of all the other schools. Very considerable contributions were in a short time collected for that object and the general support of native female education. The press also has been entirely employed, no less than 17,150 tracts and school books having been printed for the use of schools and missionaries. The Society's affairs in the north of India, had been placed under the charge of an Auxiliary Society, and the Bishop of Calcutta had lent his powerful sanction in placing them in a relation to the Episcopate which gives the best promise of usefulness.

On a review of the different stations of the North India Mission, it appears that there were employed in it 12 Missionaries, two of whom are natives and the rest Europeans. These are assisted by 10 Europeans of whom six are females, and by 75 native men and youths and 28 native females—making a total of 125 agents in this mission. The schools of the mission were in number 65, and there were under instruction in these schools 2453 boys 520 girls and 65 adults,—making a total of 3038 scholars.

The expenditure from the 1st of July 1822 to the 31st of August 1823, amounted to 84,588 rupees or about 10,573*l.* reckoning the rupee at 2*s.* 6*d.*

Madras and South India Mission

The Corresponding Committee at Madras had continued with the best effect their vigilant superintendance of the Society's concerns in the south of India. In the different stations of this mission there are employed 9 European Missionaries, assisted by 8 Europeans of whom 7 are females and by 143 native men and youths—forming a total of 160. The schools at the last returns amounted to 119 and contained 4287 boys 40 girls and 45 students at Cotym College—making a total of 4372 scholars. The Corresponding Committee had collected a mass of information relative to the state of the natives in some of the chief districts of the Madras Presidency which cannot fail to afford most valuable aid to the Society. Protestant and Roman Catholic Missions had been established at different periods in several parts of the countries composing the southern portion of the Indian peninsula. Brahminical influence is generally on the decline—and there is no aversion on the part of the people to receive books or to listen to discourses on religious subjects. Every year witnesses increased proofs of the value and importance of missionary establishments in this country and their growing efficiency and utility.

Various works had issued from the press at Madras in Tamul during the year and among others 7000 copies of the Gospels. Of the female school at Tinevelly a Missionary writes— Our native girls give us much satisfaction and encouragement. We have now twenty three consisting of one Soodra four Shanars and the others of low caste but as our views respecting the unreasonableness of the distinction of caste have been fully explained to the parents the little girls eat together in one room without hesitation and live together like members of one family. It is astonishing how quickly they improve. At Cotym Cochin and Allepie among the Syrians and their neighbours Mr Bailey Mr Fenn Mr Baker and Mr Norton had pursued their steady course when not interrupted by sickness. Mutual confidence and regard continued unimpaired, between the Syrian Church and the Missionaries and the improvement of that interesting body of Christians under their devout and exemplary Metropolitan and the fostering care of Colonel Newall the British Resident was proceeding steadily by the blessing of God on the assiduous labours of the Missionaries. The Rev Mr Mill principal of Bishop's College Calcutta in a journey which he took round the peninsula in the year 1822 spent some time among the Syrians. He bears ample testimony to the right spirit and measures of the Missionaries. The College had forty five students. When the Scriptures or some parts of them are printed the Catanars would read them regularly to the people on the Sabbath day at least the Metropolitan is most anxious for them to be printed and circulated among his people. In the preparation of the Malayalim Version for this important end Mr Bailey had proceeded as far as the eleventh chapter of the Epistle to the Hebrews.

Bombay and Western India Mission

The Rev Richard Kenney continues his schools at Bombay. They were four in number and contained 110 boys. He is also engaged in translating the Liturgy into Mahratta. The Corresponding Committee urge the appointment of more missionaries on this side of India. The Scriptures and elementary books are in a great measure prepared in the chief native languages.

Ceylon Mission

To the two stations before occupied among the Cingalese Kandy and Baddagame two others had been added namely Cotta and Nellore. To these four stations twelve Europeans have been sent out from this country. They are assisted by twenty four natives and have opened twenty four schools. Of the scholars at Cotta no return had been received but at the other stations there are 724 boys and 141 girls. It was resolved that a Christian Institution should be formed for the advancement of the general objects of the Mission.

Australasia Mission

Sir Thomas Brisbane continues to cooperate with Mr Marsden in promoting the interests of this Mission which gives better promise of an ultimate reward to patient labour than at any time since its establishment.

At Rangheehoo Mr W Hall and Mr John King continue to reside and, at Kiddeekiddee Mr Kemp and Mr Shepherd. The Rev Henry Williams and Mr Fairburn were forming a new station at Pyhea on the south of the Bay of Islands. Mr and Mrs Clarke were to join Mr Kemp and Mr Shepherd at Kiddeekiddee. Rangheehoo is near a large and populous native town called Tapoonah. Within seven miles there are eight or ten villages and in each a number of children and adults may be daily collected together for instruction. The natives about this settlement have made considerable advances in civilization. Of Kiddeekiddee Mr Leigh a missionary of another society writes — Kiddeekiddee resembles a neat little country village with a good school house lately erected in the centre. We may see cattle sheep goats pigs and horses—houses—fields covered with wheat oats and barley—and gardens richly filled with all kinds of vegetables fruit trees and a variety of useful productions. The settlement altogether forms a most pleasing object and especially in a heathen land. Within twenty miles of it, there are several very populous native towns and villages in which are hundreds and thousands of inhabitants ready to receive useful instruction and I hope even the word of life from the servants of God. Mr Leigh also remarks I have no doubt but these Christian settlements will stand for ages to come as a proof of the charity and liberality of the Church Missionary Society and of the British public. That society has had discouragements but the cloud has in a measure disappeared and now greater light begins to dawn. A number of native youths in these stations can repeat the Creed Ten Commandments the Lord's Prayer and several hymns in their own tongue and can unite in singing the praises of the Lord Any person visiting these stations may soon perceive that civilization has made considerable advance and that they are stations which hold out great prospects of usefulness to the Christian Missionary Mr Marsden observes — The minds of the chiefs are much enlarged and a way is gradually preparing for the Gospel Nothing has happened since the establishment of the mission to the present time but what might have been expected, especially from the natives As Shunghee justly observes We have made no new laws we have established no new customs we are only following the institutions of our forefathers which we cannot as yet relinquish our forefathers ate human flesh and taught us to do so Many of their superstitions are however giving way I am surprised—not at the number and greatness of their public crimes—but that they govern themselves so well without laws When the light of Divine Revelation once shines upon them it will be like the sun rising upon the benighted world

West Indies Mission

This field of the society's labours remark the Committee may be considered as connected with that in West Africa the objects in both being the same—the remuneration by the blessings of the Gospel of Africa and her children for those enormous wrongs which they have suffered at our hands for wrongs they are and wrongs they will continue to be how many ages soever have passed since they were first inflicted, and whatever may be the period which must elapse before they can be done away If blind self interest or the exercise of cruel authority over human beings have disqualified any persons from cordially entering into the just and humane views which now actuate the government and the country we may well hope from the success which the question of the abolition of the Slave Trade obtained by the patience and perseverance of its friends over feelings and opinions even still more hostile that a steady course of wise and humane proceedings will carry with it at no great distance of time the whole mind and conscience of the country

The Society's labours in this quarter have hitherto been limited to education In the islands of Antigua Barbadoes Dominica and St Vincent it had fourteen schools which contained 2172 scholars Many applications having been made to the Committee by proprietors of estates to supply their slaves with teachers and liberal offers having been made to assist in their support the Committee had pledged themselves to do all in their power to second these just and benevolent views

North West America Mission

Mr West had exerted himself indefatigably in establishing schools and had placed them on such a footing as to secure the benefit of them not only to the Indian children whom the Society has primarily in view but also on the payment of a small sum annually to the children of the settlers Fifteen Indian boys and fifteen girls were to be received for maintenance and education at the Society's charge, as soon as they could be collected from the Indians Eight Indian boys and two Indian girls were under the care of a half breed woman The day schools were attended by seven children of settlers and the Sunday schools had an average attendance of sixteen boys fifteen girls and eight adults

Mr West has just given to the public a very interesting account of his proceedings in a volume entitled Substance of a Journal during a Residence at the Red River Colony and frequent Excursions among the North West American Indians

M PESCHIER'S DEFENCE OF INDIAN MISSIONS

The following is an extract from a discourse by M le P Peschier President of the Missionary Society at Geneva delivered at the general meeting We present it to our readers for the purpose of shewing the bright aspect which our Bible missionary and educational exertions in India assume in the eyes of a pious and intelligent foreigner as well as for the sake of the refutation given to the statements of the Abbe Dubois After succinctly sketching the history of India, M Peschier proceeds — The fall of Tippoo Saib in 1799 corroborated the English power and thenceforward the peaceable ruler over sixty millions (now over one hundred millions) of men she begins to vindicate its colossal greatness by the benefits conferred by a just and happy government It is from this period also that modern missionary societies date their establishment and from which they recommenced the holy labours so long interrupted during wars and troubles This brief sketch superfluous to those well informed persons who listen to us will assist you in forming an idea of this immense population consisting of aboriginal inhabitants of the country some attached to the Brahminical superstitions, others to the crescent of Mahomet; of native people of European origin tarnishing by their ignorance, or dishonouring by their manners the worship they profess; of men, likewise more occupied with projects of gain than the advancement of religion, enervated by the climate, distracted by luxury and the indulgence of great cities. What a field is this! And how often must the seed of the word fall amongst rocks and thorns! What difficulties, what contentions, what obstacles, what subjects for lamentation and prayer! The missionaries do not practise dissimulation; their letters, full of candour and humility, acquaint us with the real facts more fully than all their adversaries together. One of the most grievous oppositions to their work is doubtless that which they meet in some of the southern provinces on the part of other Christians, whose form of worship and maxims of government are incompatible with the doctrines they preach. Nevertheless they very rarely speak of it; they delight in doing justice to whatsoever they recognize as useful and respectable; they even propose as examples, expedients for the dissemination of truth, the model of which they find in a different communion; they mildly complain of not experiencing the same fairness, and they deplore an assimilation of ceremonies between Christian worship and idolatrous superstition. We might be tempted to apprehend that there was in these complaints a leaven of antipathy and some slight disregard of Christian charity. But lo! a voice (alluding to the work of the Abbé Dubois) is raised to justify them; it boldly avows this assimilation, in accusing those who send missions to India of aiming at an absolute impossibility, and proposes to make Christians by concealing the holy word. This voice, issuing from the south of the Indian peninsula, has been heard in England, has echoed in France, and has penetrated even hither.

We are asked for facts, and it is by facts alone that the practicability of an undertaking is to be demonstrated. But what facts are required? That every year we should announce the conversion of an entire Otaheite to Christianity? If we spoke, as the adversary of evangelical missions often, of a hundred thousand conversions in one single city, we should be taxed with exaggeration and fable. And if we say that the Gospel makes itself known by means of diligent preaching, by elementary treatises, by the distribution of the sacred volume; that prejudices diminish, that curiosity is roused to listen; that the benefits of education are preparing the rising generations to receive the truth; that already it has disciples every where; that the edifice of superstition begins to totter by the very hands interested in sustaining it,—men of too impatient tempers tell us that we possess no facts, and conclude that nothing can be done. A person who has sojourned thirty years in India preaching to unbelievers, declares to us that he has not been able to work a single conversion. We do not question the veracity of such an acknowledgment; it must have cost him much to make; but how long is it since the inutility of one man's labours in a given career is allowed to prove the impossibility of success by other men and other means? It is doubtless extremely easy in a combination of good and evil to develop only the latter, in order to conceal the knowledge of the good operated. If Celsus and Porphyry had lived in the time of St Paul, would they not have been able to record that the Apostle had been obliged to fly from Iconium and was stoned at Lystra by the populace? Would it therefore have been less true that the churches were established in the faith and increased in number daily? Tacitus wrote of the first Christians that they were condemned by the universal hatred of mankind; yet Christianity has vanquished the world by the charity of its disciples and by the courage of its martyrs.—We are asked for facts; we reply, Behold them, come and see! We are asked for witnesses; we exhibit the missionaries; read their narratives, and tell us if you can withold your confidence from them. They revisit Europe to recruit their strength and then return to their post; is it to renew unprofitable toils? We are asked for other witnesses; well then we shew an entire nation, its travellers, its traders, its officiating ministers in India, its prelates, nobles, military commanders, legislators, and princes. Reflect, gentlemen, upon the constant intercourse between England and her Indian empire, upon the thousands of vessels annually passing to and fro. We may consider that Bengal is to the English of all ranks accustomed to the sea, what a country house a few miles from the capital is to the inhabitants of our own country; can they be ignorant of what passes there? But we are called upon to produce witnesses who, besides possessing a knowledge of the truth, are interested in speak ing it we adduce the numerous auxiliary societies the committees of correspondence who are employed even in India, in biblical and missionary labours and the establishment of schools and seminaries who are continually adding their donations and subscriptions to the treasures accumulated in Europe. We are required to produce witnesses inaccessible by their character to deceitful illusions. I find this species of evidence in what we know of the progressive march of the English Government in Bengal. At first the projects of the Bible Societies and Missionaries excited alarm, it seemed as if millions of Hindoos were about to rise and overwhelm an insignificant number of Europeans. Mildness and prudence in the expedients employed to propagate the doctrine of charity and salvation dissipated apprehension. The missionaries have been protected, schools, Christian congregations, missionary houses have occupied ground granted by the local authority and ships offered by their commanders. In the early part of the present century Dr Buchanan lamented to observe idolatrous ceremonies protected protected as it were by a Christian nation, the police then attended upon the odious rites of Juggernaut and the funeral piles of widows. At the present day Government is gradually advancing towards an object which heretofore we dared not even hope to reach. After the sacred drownings at the Isle of Saugor suppressed by the Governor General Lord Wellesley after the cessation of infanticide obtained by Col Walker from a tribe under his controul after that of the judicial proofs known under the name of Ordeal the Government have set limits to the sacrifices of widows burnt or buried alive, and the English Society at the head of which is a list of forty three peers and eminent members of the lower house of Parliament do not hesitate to declare publicly their anxiety to see these sacrifices soon entirely prohibited as being not strictly required by the most ancient laws and primitive religion of the Hindoos. Can we doubt that these acts of Government are consequent upon the weakness observed in the superstitious opinions of a vast people? And the shadows of night having thus commenced their departure, can the twilight which appears be other than that proclaiming the rising of the Sun of Righteousness bringing health in its beams?

You will hear ladies with congenial satisfaction that the fate of the Indian women has interested in a lively manner the ladies of England and that a benevolent society has been formed amongst them for the especial purpose of labouring in Bengal for the education of young women. It is to this portion of the human race so degraded and so wretched under the influence of false religions that the wives of the missionaries devote their attention not disdaining the humble office of school mistress. Miss Cooke arrived at Calcutta with this view she announced her design Indian mothers with their daughters flocked around her they required her to explain her motives You perform then said they an act agreeable to your God here are our children we resign them to you Our husbands says one treat us a little better than brutes and they indulge the hope of becoming their partners and companions. This Christian lady's ambition when she quitted England was to collect 200 children and she soon had more than twice that number.

We might easily reckon thousands if we united in one sum the children in all the different schools (at Burdwan alone their number is nearly a thousand) and there would be no bounds to the enumeration of what has been done in this way the details in respect to the diversity of the forms and the extent of instruction would be infinite. Large colleges are building at Cotym in Malabar for the ecclesiastical education of the Catanars or Christian priests of that ancient church at Madras Calcutta and at Serampore a small district of the Danish territory which has become celebrated by the labours of Baptist missionaries.

I would speak of those versions of the sacred volume in twenty different languages accomplished with the aid of the most skilful interpreters which the country afforded with so much care labour and expense and revised so scrupulously and to which ten others are to be added I would tell with what religious distrust with what hesitation and with what precautions the missionaries admit their pupils to Christian baptism and more tardily still their adult converts to the holy Supper what joy is theirs what fervour of gratitude towards God when they believe they are able to discern the sincerity of a soul called into light and what triumph for the faith when the Almighty changes an adorer of idols into a preacher of the Gospel such as was Anund whom death snatched away last year Abdoul Messeeh and Bowley all deemed worthy of divine ordination

Christianity we have been presump

tuously told has become odious in India! And he who so speaks has inhabited the very land where lived that genuine man of God, Schwartz whose rare virtues made him be honoured as a father by the Rajahs of that country whom the people blessed to whom the East India Company erected a monument which is resorted to with respect whose memory the first bishop of Calcutta found still surviving when he visited the provinces and who according to the testimony of a person of high respectability left as the fruit of his labours ten thousand converts from paganism. The names of Macaulay of Munro are affectionately repeated in the south of the peninsula where they exercised with impartiality an extensive influence over the Hindoo Princes the Syriac Christians the evangelical churches and those which belonged to the see of Rome. Even Rome herself has cherished and manifested towards them a sentiment of gratitude and esteem. The Christian converts are exposed to persecutions but they support them for the love of Jesus for they constitute the touch stone of their sincerity and the sign of the children of God.

LONDON HIBERNIAN SOCIETY

This Society was established in London in the year 1806 for the purpose of diffusing religious knowledge in Ireland. A deputation was sent in 1807 to ascertain the state of that country and the result of their report was a determination on the part of the Society to confine their operations to the establishing of schools and the circulation of the holy Scriptures. During the last year the number of schools amounted to 1072 containing 88,000 scholars receiving religious instruction and there had been circulated 16,300 Bibles and Testaments in the English and Irish languages. The Society has 188 schools in connexion with resident noblemen and gentlemen 274 under the care of Clergymen 26 under Roman Catholic priests and 10 under Dissenting ministers

---

VIEW OF PUBLIC AFFAIRS

FOREIGN

FRANCE.—The proceedings of the chambers continue to be nearly barren of subjects of great public interest. The only novelty of the month has been the presentation to both chambers of an able and spirited petition from forty two of the first merchants and bankers of Paris, of whom thirteen are members of the chamber of commerce complaining of the shameful extent to which the slave trade is carried on under the flag of France, and of the just imputations of bad faith or supineness to which this state of things exposes the French government, and calling on the legislature for new and stronger laws of repression against this odious and disgraceful crime. We hail this petition as a proof of the rising interest which exists in France on this subject and we particularly rejoice that this first public symptom of feeling upon it should proceed from the mercantile body. The committee in the house of peers, to whom the petition was referred recommended simply that it should lie on the table. This however was opposed by the Marquis de Marbois the Viscount Laine the Count de Segur the Baron Mounier, (the Duc de Broglie unfortunately was absent) who insisted on the necessity of referring it to the government with a view to the consideration of the subject, and the proposal on their part of a new law if necessary and this course was finally adopted

The chief topic of the month has been the approaching coronation, which is to be celebrated at Rheims, on the 29th with the utmost splendour. The ecclesiastical arrangements in particular, are most pompous and exhibit the prominence which the ritual and spirit of Popery have of late been so rapidly and ominously acquiring in that country at least in its public and official proceedings.—The court the missionary Jesuits, and the time-serving part of the bishops and clergy with perhaps a comparatively few genuine devotees have succeeded in fencing in some of the veriest mummeries of Popery by sanguinary enactments at a time when the great majority of the people are probably sceptical as to the Divine authority of the first elements of the Christian faith. These things are deeply afflicting to those of the French nation themselves who are anxious for the promotion of true religion and its attendant blessings as well as those numerous spectators in other countries who witness with grief whatever wears a contrary aspect

GREECE.—Intelligence from Greece states, that a considerable victory had been gained over a body of Egyptian troops which had been disembarked at Modona, and that the Greek fleet had sailed to intercept the invading expedition

UNITED PROVINCES OF LA PLATA.— The first treaty of friendship, commerce, and navigation between this country and an independent State of South America has been concluded with the Government of Buenos Ayres who are charged with the general authority of the newly formed nation of " the United Provinces of the Rio de la Plata " It stipulates perpetual friendship, reciprocal freedom of commerce the abolition of the slave trade and perfect liberty of conscience British subjects are not to be disturbed on account of their religion the forms of which they may celebrate either in their own houses or in churches and chapels which they shall be authorised to build in convenient situations This is a most important concession indeed the foundation is laid for a full and adequate recognition of the rights of conscience throughout South and Central America and ultimately, we doubt not throughout the world

DOMESTIC

The most important occurrence of the month has been the proceedings in parliament on the Catholic relief bill The result we need not inform our readers has been, that after passing the house of commons it was rejected by the house of lords 130 peers having voted for it, and 178 against it It would be quite impracticable for us to attempt a sketch of the protracted debates which took place on the occasion or of the chief arguments employed by the numerous speakers on either side

Among the leading memoranda of the debates we may mention the introduction of the measure into the house of commons on the second reading by Mr Brownlow the member for Armagh who had hitherto been warmly opposed to further concessions.—and a temporary dislocation of parties in consequence of the bills for disfranchising the forty-shilling freeholders, and paying the Catholic priests several members voting out of their usual line both as respected the main bill and its appendages Among the cabinet ministers no change has taken place in their respective sentiments and the report that Lord Liverpool, in particular had determined to vote for the measure was strongly contradicted by his lordship's speech which considering that nobleman's usual temperament was somewhat remarkable for its warmth

The corn laws have undergone some discussion in both houses and his majesty's government have stated their conviction that they cannot remain on their present footing and have pledged themselves to a full inquiry into the subject next session To say nothing of other circumstances or of past times it is very clear that now that the restrictions on commerce have been so liberally thrown off the British workman is placed under a most serious disadvantage if while his goods are unprotected he pays a monopoly price for the corn with which he has to support himself and his family We shall be tempted in that case either to recur to the old restrictive and ruinous system of commerce or to follow up what has been so wisely commenced by further reformations which in the end must benefit all parties whether commercial or agricultural.—While on this subject we cannot but add our deepest regrets that while Government has so vigorously opposed monopolies in general and has now even publicly proclaimed that the great monopoly of corn itself must be examined into and a better system devised it should still be afraid to advance a single step towards the extinction of that worst of all monopolies the West India monopoly which in addition to all the other evils of monopolies is the almost sole support of the horrors and atrocities of slavery But we do not despair the death blow we are persuaded has been struck and slavery however long it may writhe and linger in convulsive efforts to extract the shaft that rankles in its vitals must ultimately sink beneath the wounds inflicted upon it no less by political expediency than by humanity and religion

We rejoice to state, that the house of commons is zealously adopting and maturing the details of Mr Peel's admirable jury bill.—The chancellor of the exchequer has brought in a bill to prevent the judges receiving fees and to assign a suitable salary in place of them.—Mr Peel has pledged himself to look into some additional points connected with the administration of justice which are susceptible of improvement We trust that, among many others which suggest themselves to our minds, the three following will be considered first, the propriety of extending the privilege of pleading by counsel to all classes of offence secondly, of securing to the public the services as jurors and witnesses in all cases of a class of men who have taken a most zealous and useful part in the reform of prison discipline and numerous other objects of enlightened benevolence—the Society of Friends who are now excluded by conscientious scruples respecting oaths from sharing the duties of their fellow countrymen in criminal and partly in civil courts of justice: thirdly, of abolishing the absurd and most injurious practice of making an arraigned person plead *guilty* or *not guilty*, one among many instances of the evil effects of which has just occurred in the case of Mr Savery of Bristol, who refusing, whether from conscientious motives or from hopes improperly held out by a magistrate, to plead not guilty, was condemned without trial. Why should a prisoner be constrained either to add a solemn falsehood to his other crimes, or be adjudged guilty of an offence which cannot perhaps be proved? Instances may even occur of persons either through ignorance or conscientiousness pleading guilty to crimes of which, technically speaking, they are not guilty. For example, deep remorse may induce a person to plead guilty to an indictment for murder, and he may in consequence suffer the penalty of death without a trial under circumstances which, had witnesses been called, would have reduced the offence to manslaughter, and have saved his life. Indeed in the official form in which a charge often appears, in order to adapt it to particular statutes, it is perhaps not possible for an illiterate person to know whether he is really guilty of the exact offence specified in the indictment, though he is morally guilty of a certain act which he knows to be wrong and illegal, and is willing to confess. But we forbear to enter further upon the subject, and we only suggest these remarks in passing as illustrative of some of the points to which we wish that legislative attention were directed, in order to the improvement of our written and practical jurisprudence.

We grieve to state that the game-laws bill, after passing the commons, was thrown out of the house of lords. Another year must therefore elapse under the evils of the present mischievous system.

ECCLESIASTICAL PREFERMENTS

Rev J M Turner M A to the Prebend of Lafford at Lewes near Sleaford Lincoln *vice* George Turner deceased

Rev Jos Cross Rev Ames Hellicar Rev Frederick Rouch and Rev Mr Lambert elected Minor Canons of Bristol Cathedral

Rev Henry Parr Beloe Trinity and St Mary RR Guilford *vice* Dr Weller res

Rev J Bardgett Broughton V Yorkshire

Rev J Brasse B D Stotfold V Beds

Rev Wm Carwithen Allhallows on the Wall Exeter and Manaton RR Devon

Rev Liscombe Clarke Downton V Wilts *vice* Lear resigned

Rev E B Elliot Tuxford V Notts

Rev Asgil Colville Market Harboro Perp Cur co Leicester

Rev Nathaniel Colville Great and Little Livermere united RR Suffolk

Rev David Davies Llanboidy V Carmarthen

Rev C J Davies Marfleet Perp Curacy Holderness

Rev J Fellowes Beighton R Norfolk

Rev Charles Griffiths Trentishoe R Devon

Rev O W Kilvington Snaith V co York

Rev J Milne Swine V Holderness

Rev J Procter D D Conington R Hunts

Rev Phil Nic Shuttleworth D D Foxley R Wilts

Rev Geo Uppill Hornbloton R Somers

Rev J Digby Wingfield Geashill Living King's County Ireland

ANSWERS TO CORRESPONDENTS

ARTHUR N J B C I A LAYMAN AN OLD WOMAN F M B D P D R N R H W I OUT H T S SEPTUAGENARIUS and T P are under consideration

The half of a Bank Note No 7007 for 100*l* (anonymous) has been received by the British and Foreign Bible Society

THE CHRISTIAN OBSERVER.

No. 282] JUNE, 1825. [No 6. Vol. XXV

RELIGIOUS COMMUNICATIONS

AN ACCOUNT OF THE PROTESTANT CHURCH IN FRANCE.

(Concluded from p. 274.)

A SECOND plan which may be suggested for the improvement of the Protestant body, is the more extensive promotion of religious instruction and information.— Much has already been devised for this purpose: schools have been established and besides this, the general plan of education in France has hitherto admitted the instruction of the Protestants with the Catholics. The Tract Society which has been established has put a number of useful works into circulation. The monthly papers issued by the Bible and Missionary Societies are also extensively read. I have already mentioned the Archives du Christianisme, the circulation of which deserves every encouragement. It has moreover been proposed to reprint some standard works of divinity, and to translate others from the English and German languages. With this view, a publication called the "Conservateur Chretien" edited by M. Perrot Droz, of Geneva, has been published periodically. Its first Number contains an old and valuable account of the death of Duplessis, Mornay and four other Christians of the same period, together with the account of M. Rieu who died two years since in Denmark. The last mentioned memoir is one of the most interesting obituaries of a Christian Minister, taken from the conflict whilst "standing and clothed in all the armour of God, that has appeared before the public for many years. The express object of this publication is to reprint parts or the whole of works original or translated, all having a moral or religious tendency. The character of the excellent individual who edits the Conservateur Chrétien will be a security for its orthodoxy, its sobriety, and its genuine piety. This publication, if conducted as there is reason to hope it will be, will prove of great value. With similar views, a translation of Milner's Church History has been set on foot. No work can be better calculated than this to teach most important lessons to the Protestants of France for it will serve to shew them, not only how the Almighty can and will preserve his true church from all the storms as well as hidden difficulties through which it must pass, but also what are the means by which the decay of religion among a people may be checked, and its revival promoted. Translations of other works are from time to time announced at Paris and at Geneva. Dr. Chalmers's Commercial Discourses have been translated by M. Pons. Mr Wilberforce's Practical View, by M. Froissard. Mrs Barbauld's Hymns, by M. Coquerel. Beattie's and Erskine's works on the Evidences of Christianity, by M. Jaquier and the Duchess de Broglie. And Mrs. Hoare on Nursery Education, &c. The more translations of this kind that are made the better. The knowledge and experience of one country will thus be given to the other; and the bonds which hold together Christians in each country will be strengthened.

A third object of great import

ance is the education of ministers. The number of pastors is at present insufficient to provide for the vacant charges, and many districts have no pastor nor any spiritual instructor whatever. Whence does this deficiency of ministers arise? One cause is that in France the Protestant clergy are very poorly paid, and those persons who look to the Church for support can scarcely obtain it. The allowance made to each minister by the government does not exceed forty, sixty, or eighty pounds a year, and in the capital one hundred and twenty pounds; and they derive very little in general from voluntary contributions to supply the scanty allowance of the state. This condition of things not only produces a want of ministers, but it tends to prevent men of superior talents and learning from engaging in the important office of the ministry, which is thus apt to be occupied by persons but ill fitted, not only to maintain with advantage the interests of religion against the enemies of the faith, but to enlarge the numbers for enlightened and pious attendants at their places of worship. It is true that there are many distinguished ministers in the French Church, but they stand in need of help; they are in general encumbered with a weight of occupation, and although the influence of their character is powerfully felt in their own circle, their exertions can reach but a little way. The remedy for these evils would be to educate young men of talent to fill up the vacant offices in the ministry, and to gather into the fold the scattered Protestants. These when educated might be first placed as curates to the older ministers. They would thus prepare themselves for their work, and set those ministers whom they assisted at liberty for more extensive usefulness. An attempt to educate a body of young men has been made, but serious difficulties have arisen in the way of the undertaking. But these difficulties I trust may be obviated. It is evident that such a measure would prove a great and lasting blessing to the Protestant community.

The last expedient I would venture to suggest by which the cause of religion may be advanced in France is by abating or counteracting as much as possible the various hindrances of real vital religion which prevail in that country. I here allude not merely to those public amusements which are pursued with such avidity by the mass of the French nation, but also to the violation of the Sabbath, whether by open dissipation as amongst the French, or the more concealed though scarcely less dangerous, practice of holding Sunday evening societies as amongst the Swiss. Neither do I mean to dwell on the multitude of bad books which are circulated in France, to say nothing of the works of Voltaire which alone are enough to stock a library, and which are stereotyped and sold in every shape and every size, as well as those of Rousseau and the encyclopedists and novelists in general. But I would speak of a still more formidable enemy prevailing within the church itself, which under the most specious subterfuges, eats out the very heart's core of vital religion. I mean the Arian or Socinian heresy. A large majority of La Compagnie de Pasteurs at Geneva has shewn itself Arian in its profession, and as the election of ministers is by vote, it is to be feared that no candidates for orders will be admitted in future but such as agree in opinion with the majority, and that in a few years, therefore the pastors will be unanimous in their religious tenets. The University of Geneva has from the beginning been accustomed to furnish ministers to the churches of France, as well as to the French Churches in various parts of Europe. As the number of regular appointments in its own canton is very limited, and there is always a considerable number of candidates for ordination a disposable body of ministers is generally to be found in that place for any service which may present itself. The Genevese character is marked by intelligence and activity, and in these qualities the Company of Pastors are by no means deficient. They exercise a considerable influence in various parts of Europe, and even in this country. In proof of this, the London papers have announced the publication of a second edition of the Geneva Catechism translated into English, and recommended for the use of schools. In this catechism it is needless to say that the doctrines of the Divinity of Jesus Christ, and the personality of the Holy Spirit, are passed by without notice, and in fact disowned. In France a monthly publication is printed under the auspices of persons connected in principle with the Compagnie at Geneva, and these persons omit no opportunity by means of the press or by influencing the appointment of professors to foreign universities, of propagating their mischievous and heretical doctrines. The readers of advertisements will have observed that in the course of last year in the Monthly Repository of Theology and general Literature, a Socinian work published in London, an attack was made by the professor of divinity at Geneva, M. Chenevière, upon the Christian Observer, the Archives du Christianisme, and on all the promoters of orthodox knowledge and religious improvement, as Mr. Haldane, Mr. Drummond, &c. as well as upon a little regiment of middle aged ladies armed with pocket Bibles, and upon a host of Methodists of both sexes, all of whom appear to be particularly obnoxious to M. Chenevière. Only Mr. Haldane seems to have thought the professor's work worth a public answer. The remaining objects of his displeasure have treated his animadversions with entire disregard. It is, however, evident that publications of this description, if conducted with a less outrageous violation of common truth and honesty, than is conspicuous in the writings of M. Chenevière, and with less of that profane mockery which must offend every pious mind, may do great injury amongst the Protestants of France. Means therefore should be taken to check them, and to protect the Protestants of France from the pernicious influence of the Arian Church of Geneva, which, by means of its vigilance and activity and its juxta position to them, is certainly an object of serious alarm to every sincere friend of vital religion.*

To the means which I have now enumerated as likely to be productive of good to the Protestant Church of France, I would only briefly add in conclusion one more, that of earnest and continual prayer for the influences of the Holy Spirit to render those means effectual. Without this aid we well know that all efforts will be in vain!

After this review of the state of

---

* Our correspondent does not seem to be aware that in addition to the reply of Mr. Haldane the Rev. J. P. Smith, D. D. addressed to the Editor of the Monthly Repository a series of letters in reply to M. Chenevière with a rejoinder to Mr. Bakewall which have since been reprinted in a pamphlet. Dr. Smith had alluded in very strong terms to the lamentable relapse of Geneva in Christian doctrine in his highly valuable and interesting Scripture Testimony to the Divinity of Christ. Some of the individuals whom M. Chenevière had rudely and calumniously attacked, addressed letters to him which though they were not printed were freely circulated in Geneva and some of which exhibit in glaring colours the wilful misrepresentations of this theological professor and mark him with the indelible characters of an equivocator and slanderer. The whole of the Genevese controversy as well as the infamous persecutions which have taken place in the Canton de Vaud—persecutions worthy of the middle ages or of the Spanish inquisition though carried on under the authority of a Protestant Council of State—will form the subject of future articles. The annals of Romish tyranny furnish no more striking exemplification of bigotry and intolerance than has been exhibited by this petty government, reigning over a district not half so large as many an English county.—Ed.

the Reformed Church of France it is impossible not to feel a more than usual interest in a body of Christians whose history presents so many points calculated to excite every sympathy of our nature and to associate us with them by every humane and generous feeling We cannot hear how nobly the ancestors of these poor sufferers gave up their lives for the truth, or were content to abandon all they possessed, to save their consciences from shipwreck we cannot contemplate the act of one monarch ordering all his Protestant subjects to be massacred, or that of another compelling them to sacrifice their religion or every possession and comfort of their lives, and not feel, in the unhappy objects of this oppression, a more than common interest And when we look farther, at these sufferers as our associates and brethren victims in a cause most dear to ourselves,—that of religious liberty, to the establishment of which in this country we owe most of our public blessings when we see them, in their lives and sufferings and death, exhibiting such courage in resisting the arm of oppression, such zeal in the cause of God, and such patience under the most afflictive dispensations when we know that the cry of their calamities has been the lesson which has prevented tyrants of later times from entering upon the same work of persecution with their prototypes of old when we remember the claim of the offspring of these martyrs as the oppressed and destitute and fatherless —all these views of the subject will give the Protestants of France a peculiar claim on our regard, and cannot fail to enlist our best and warmest feelings in their cause

The Protestants of France are still surrounded, as formerly by an immense population, professing the same principles of Popery which led their forefathers to light the flame of persecution And, although the Papists generally are restrained by the temper of the times, the principles by which many of them are actuated probably remain the same. When we see, therefore, how small a spot the Protestants occupy in that kingdom, and how soon they may be assailed, if not by open violence, yet by secret and silent opposition, we should not consider their state as perfectly secure The situation of France may not, even now, be very stable A few years have seen a rapid succession of different governments in that country and the people readily acquiescing in them all Its future governments may not pursue an equally liberal policy as it respects religion with some of those which have preceded them, and days of darkness may hereafter arise It is therefore the truest wisdom of the Protestant Church to employ the present season of tranquillity, in planting deeply and widely that knowledge which is power and cannot be eradicated from the minds of the people and in sowing that seed which, even amidst the persecutions of the world, may still spring up and flourish The time may be short in which an opportunity is allowed of labouring in this field let them therefore work whilst it is called to-day

The Protestants of France however, I trust have a still higher destination to fulfil than that of merely keeping alive the knowledge of religion among themselves They will feel themselves called upon to do much, and to become instruments of diffusing the light of the blessed Gospel all around them A great part of the inhabitants of the continent of Europe, though long favoured with evangelical light, are now living in a state of deplorable darkness The light in them may be said to be darkness How urgent then should be the endeavour of all Christians to convey to them the light of life! and how important an instrument for effecting this object is presented to us in the Protestants of France! They afford a lever by which the sacred enginery of Christianity is to be set to work. The pure doctrines taught in their churches, their numbers, their established places of worship, their voices, their hands, their hearts, would powerfully aid in fighting the battles of the Lord, whether against the seductive superstitions of the Greek and Romish Churches, or against the Arian and Socinian heresies, or against the general lukewarmness and indifference of a worldly spirit, or against the scarcely more dangerous assaults of infidelity itself. So that, even if circumstances should arise to prevent *our* intercourse with the continent, the Protestants of France may still find the means of carrying forward plans of benevolence and of religious improvement.

It must ever be regarded as an evident display of the almighty power and providential care of God, that this church, after losing eight hundred thousand of its best members, and passing through an almost exterminating persecution for one hundred years, during which time it was scarcely known to exist, should at the end of that period be numerically almost as large as at first. Does not the same Providence which has protected it mark it out as an object of no ordinary interest, a bulwark against the progress of error, a rallying point of religion in the vast regions which surround it?

If such be the prospects of usefulness which open to the Protestant Church of France, her obligations must be considered as commensurate with them. I trust her members will rise to the measure of her high destination, and that they will not disdain, in the prosecution of it, to call on their fellow Christians of Great Britain for such aid as it may be in their power to afford. The relative circumstances in which they are placed may not perhaps allow of that efficiency of co-operation which could not but prove mutually advantageous; but in every effort they make, they may rely on the cordial concurrence and ready pecuniary aid of British Christians, so far as these could be usefully bestowed or properly accepted. And in any case they may count on the affectionate sympathy and fervent prayers of all who love their common Lord.

The foregoing narrative, with the observations which accompany it, present to us many instructive lessons.—We may learn in the first place a lesson of gratitude. We must acknowledge in the peculiar protection which has been afforded to our own church, the mercies of Divine Providence. If the reign of Queen Mary had continued as long as that of her father or her successor, or if the Queen who came after her had been educated in the same principles; if the schemes of King James the Second and of his son had been conducted with more wisdom and discretion, it is probable that our Established Church had again been subjected to papal dominion, and we ourselves, if not universally Catholics by profession, yet in the situation of the Protestants in France. But these evils have been averted, not by human sagacity, but by the direction of Him who putteth down one, and setteth up another.

But if we learn from the history of the French Church a lesson of gratitude, we may learn also a lesson of warning.—The light of the Gospel, although placed in a nation by the hand of Omnipotence, may by the same hand be removed. It becomes us then vigilantly to attend to the means of our own security; to take care that spiritual religion, the best bulwark of any church, be kept alive; that established forms do not degenerate into empty ceremonies; that our zeal be not so much to make converts to a party, as to the truth; and that we are not satisfied with dependence upon the riches or political power of an Establishment, which may in fact in the end only become the occasion of our decline and downfal. " Remember, therefore, how thou hast received, and heard, and hold fast and repent. If thou shalt not watch I will come upon thee as a thief, and thou shalt not know at what hour I will come upon thee.

We are taught also by this history, not to calculate too much upon remote contingencies in human affairs. It has been a line of argument made use of in this present day, and employed against various institutions which are allowed on all hands to be doing great good in the world, that the result of our proceedings may, in future generations, be productive of evil to our church. The history of the French Church teaches us, that other circumstances than those we apprehend may be the causes of ruin; that, if our efforts are directed to Christian ends, and are governed by Christian principles, we must leave distant events to Providence, and that in the meanwhile we must go on labouring in the path of duty whilst time is granted to us, and looking only to be found to have been faithful in the use of all our talents when our final account is given up. We may, for example, be well satisfied to aid one society which has distributed six millions of Bibles and Testaments in one hundred and forty languages, or another which has sent four hundred missionaries to preach the Gospel, or to instruct the heathen of twenty different languages, without looking to immeasurably remote evils, or shadows of evil, conjured up by the morbid apprehensions of the lukewarm and the timid. The word of God teaches us to work whilst it is called to day, and whilst we have the opportunity to do good unto all men.

I would in conclusion urge upon all who are interested in the various objects to which I have drawn their attention the duty of being prepared to forward them by all the means in their power. They may obtain at the publishers of this work information respecting the channels in which any funds they may wish to contribute to those objects (and funds are what is chiefly wanting) may be advantageously applied.

But, above all human aid, I would again exhort the friends of religion earnestly and perseveringly to pray that the Almighty would pour out his Holy Spirit upon the Protestant Church of France, that he may again raise it up, and make it what it once was,—a gem of glory in the Redeemer's crown, and the nursing mother of a numerous and holy people.

To the Editor of the Christian Observer.

THERE is often reason to complain that modern commentators are too intent upon novelty and invention, and suffer old but important matters to become obsolete. Having lately had occasion to examine the genealogies of our Lord in the Gospels of St. Matthew and St. Luke, and the methods proposed for reconciling the apparent differences between them, I have been forcibly impressed with this remark. In the pursuit of this inquiry I found nothing satisfactory, until I had recourse to writers who, though frequently named, are too little read. Some passages however in Lightfoot and other authors to be mentioned hereafter have removed most of the difficulties which at first appeared to be interwoven with this subject; and as these writers are not in the hands of every person, it has appeared to me that I shall not waste my time or trouble in drawing up a brief epitome of their most important suggestions.

In the time of Julius Africanus, who wrote during the early part of the third century, the differences between the genealogies had already become a matter of serious inquiry; the authentic records and national archives of the Jews had long before that time ceased to exist, and recourse could no longer be had to original documents. We have in the Ecclesiastical History of Eusebius a letter of Africanus containing his opinion on this subject and the mode in which he re conciled the genealogies his hypothesis was generally adopted by the church in the following centuries It is given by Africanus as an account received by him from persons who were regarded as relatives of our Lord and is founded on the position that both the Evangelists have given the genealogy of Joseph Matthew the natural or true genealogy and Luke the legal one, following the line of those who stood as legal fathers in succession

The first observation that occurs on this hypothesis is that it affords no account of the ancestry of the blessed Virgin which was the real ancestry of our Lord Jews who perhaps considered pedigrees only in a particular point of view and regarded not the order of natural generations but merely looked for legal or putative successions might be satisfied with such a scheme But Christians expect to find a proof that our Lord was really of the seed of David this if the hypothesis of Africanus be admitted, cannot be obtained from these tables Accordingly, some of the fathers have endeavoured to deduce this important fact from inferences and it may be worth while to consider what these inferential proofs amount to

1 Chrysostom Cyril and Isidore conclude that the mother of our Lord was of the same family with Joseph because it was not permitted to a Jewish heiress to marry out of her own tribe and kindred but there were exceptions which prevent our drawing any positive conclusion that is satisfactory from this circumstance (See Levit xxii 12 Dr Barrett prefat ad Cod Rescript S Matthæi p 45)

2 Others have inferred that the blessed Virgin must have been, as well as Joseph of the house and lineage of David from the fact that she went up with her betrothed husband although then great with child to be taxed or registered in Bethlehem where the family of David resided " Joseph went up with Mary his espoused wife to be taxed in the city of David Hence it seems to follow, that she was of the same lineage Tertullian says, ' Christum intelligere debebis ex Davide deputatum carnali genere, ob Mariæ virginis censum Ambrose says, ' Censas tempore ascendit Joseph de domo et patria Davidis ut profiteretur cum Mariâ. Quæ professionem defert ex eadem domo et patriâ utique ejusdem tribus se esse designa

3 The terms of the annunciation see Luke i 32 appear to shew that the blessed Virgin was of the house of David The angel announces to Mary then betrothed to Joseph that she shall, though still a virgin bear a son, to whom shall be given *the throne of his father David* Would not these expressions have immediately suggested in her mind the inquiry, how David could be the father or progenitor of her son, had she herself been an alien to the family of David? These expressions used on such an occasion seem plainly to imply that the blessed Virgin was herself descended from the royal stem

So much for the inferential proofs that the mother of Christ was of the house of David admitting that both the genealogies relate to Joseph but after all it must be allowed, that this supposition is a very improbable one That both the Evangelists should have confined themselves to the genealogy of Joseph, and which in reality was not that of our Lord would be a thing very difficult to account for and can only be received on strong and unsuspected evidence now the fact is that such evidence does not exist for it The statement of Africanus was only received during an *uncritical* age and it has been rejected by modern times not merely from a dislike to the consequences but from the witnesses not being entitled to belief Relatives of our Lord according to the flesh, if such there were in the time of Africanus, might indeed claim some regard, but who knows that the informants of this compiler had any fair pretensions to such a title? Africanus indeed so terms them, but he immediately calls in question their credentials. They relate as follows η φανητιῶντες η εκδιδασκοντες—either pretending to know more than they really knew, or having obtained correct information.—however, in this instance, he says 'they tell the truth.' It is evident that Africanus believed their account, because it afforded him what he thought a satisfactory solution of difficulties, and not at all by reason of the credit of the narrators. Then as to the explanation itself, there are in it, when narrowly examined, the strongest reasons for concluding the whole to be a forgery. A complex and intricate scheme of intermarriages is adduced, some of them contrary to the Jewish ordinances, in order to account for the double genealogy of Joseph. In addition to all this we have a story respecting the birth and education of Herod, which is contradictory to Josephus, and seems altogether so apocryphal as to throw discredit on the whole narrative with which it is connected. On the whole it appears, that Africanus was imposed upon, and that those who have followed him have in this instance been wanting in circumspection.

Most modern writers have accounted for the discrepancies between the genealogies in a different way. They suppose that Matthew has delivered the pedigree of Joseph, who, though not the father, stood, in the opinions and legal customs * of the Jews, in the relation of father to our Lord: and they understand the genealogy given by Luke to be that of the Virgin Mary, supposed to be the daughter of Heli: whose name stands second in the series, her name being omitted, because those of women were never inserted in the Jewish genealogies. This opinion is maintained, among other learned writers, by Lightfoot; and I shall now cite his comment upon this genealogy, which begins by stating Jesus to have been the Son (as it was supposed, or as the law accounted him) of Joseph, of Heli, of Matthat, &c. of Adam, of God. "There is not the least cause or necessity for having recourse to imaginary relationships and intermarriages, in order to remove difficulties from this part of Scripture, where in fact there exists no difficulty at all: for, in the first place, it is not Joseph who is here termed the son of Heli, but Jesus. The word Jesus, or υιός—filius, (not υιου filii) is to be understood, and in the mind of the reader to be supplied before each turn in the series of this genealogy, as follows: Jesus, filius Josephi (ut existimabatur), filius Heli, filius Matthat, and at last filius Adami, filius Dei. For it was not the purpose of the Evangelist, either to deduce the genealogy of Joseph from Adam, or to declare Adam to be the Son of God: this indeed would appear not only harsh and abrupt, but, in the present connexion, unnatural and almost blasphemous. For after Luke had just informed us, in verse 22, that a voice from heaven had proclaimed *Jesus* to be the Son of God, is it to be supposed that the *same writer* would have chosen immediately to pronounce *Adam* to be the Son of God? The context itself plainly shews what the Evangelist proposed to himself in inserting this genealogy: namely, that he might prove that that Jesus who had received a testimony from God in heaven, ' This is my Son,' was the same who had been promised to Adam from the seed of the woman. He accordingly drew out his genealogy by the female: namely, by his mother the daughter of Heli, con-

---

* On this subject Lightfoot has some important observations. It is also ably considered in a work entitled, The Genealogies of our Lord and Saviour Jesus Christ, as recorded by St Matthew and St. Luke critically examined &c. by Edw. Yardley, B.D. London, 1739.

tinuing this as far as Adam, to whom the promise was given. Now this being remarked concerning the last link in the genealogical chain, it will be more sufficiently evident from this last, in what sense the first is to be understood: namely, that Jesus, *and not Joseph, is called the son of Heli*, as Jesus and not Adam, is the Son of God. And so likewise in every intervening link we must understand: Jesus was the son of Matthat, he was the son of Levi, he was the son of Melchi, and so of the rest.

'And the construction of this genealogy exactly coincides with that of Moses, in Genesis xxxvi. 2. If you render the words *Abo libamah beth Anah beth Zibeon* by Abolibamah filia Anæ filiæ Zi beon, that is Abolibamah daughter of Anah *which was* the daughter of Zibeon, (as the genealogy in St. Luke has commonly been understood,) you make Anah to have been a female: whereas this Anah was in reality a man, and the father of Abolibamah (see ver. 24, 25.)

"Secondly, even if it were allowed that Joseph is here called the son of Heli, which is by no means granted, still there would then be no solecism in the case, since Joseph as the husband of Mary, the daughter of Heli, would stand in a legal sense in the relation of son to Heli.

'In 2. Hieros Chagigah fol. 77. 4, mention is made of a certain religious person, who in a vision beheld the punishments of the condemned. Among other expressions the following remarkable ones occur. He saw Mary the daughter of Heli in the shades. Rabbi Lazar bar Josah says, Hanged up by her breasts. Rabbi Josah bar Haninah says, A bar of the gate of hell was fastened upon her ears. If there is any meaning in these words (and I believe that there is a very clear one) it agrees with the testimony of the Evangelists in so far as to declare that Mary was the daughter of Heli: and who will not suspect the remainder to be said in order to throw insult on the blessed Virgin, who under the name of Sarda, is not unfrequently the object of contumely*?

Thus far Lightfoot and I think his remarks under the first head are quite sufficient to prove that the construction of St. Luke's genealogy of our Lord is in style and manner similar to that of Abolibamah in the passage above cited from Genesis, which passage is in itself a proof that such a method of construction was not foreign to the customs of the Hebrew genealogists.

The Abolibamah mentioned in the preceding passage, was one of Esau's wives: she is said, in the genealogy alluded to, to have been the daughter of Anah the daughter of Zibeon the Hivite. It appears from verse 24 of the same chapter, that Anah was a man, and the son of Zibeon, and therefore the word daughter must of necessity be referred in both places to Abolibamah; and the construction is this: 'Abolibamah was the daughter of Anah (she was) the daughter of Zibeon.' Exactly similar is supposed to be the genealogy of our Lord in St. Luke. Jesus was the son (according to putation or legal descent) of Joseph, (he was) the son of Heli, (he was) the son of Matthat, &c. (he was) the son of Adam, (he was) the son of God.

As this is proved to be a mode of expressing the series of a genealogy in use among the Hebrews, we are at liberty to presume it to be the one adopted in this place by St. Luke, if only the context agrees with that supposition: and surely Lightfoot has proved this by the remarks above cited. It is very unlikely that the Evangelist, immediately after saying that a voice from Heaven had proclaimed Jesus to be the Son of God, should choose

---

Lightfoot, Horæ Hebraicæ in Evangelium Lucæ ad cap. 3. v. 23—27. p. 504, tom. 2. Operum in edit. Rotterd. 1686. I have translated from the Latin edition where this passage is given much more fully than in the English.

to embarrass his readers, by styling Adam the son of God in a different sense, and in one remote from the common use of words. I say it is particularly improbable that he should choose to go out of his way in order to select expressions unusual, and strained aside from the common meaning, (though not altogether unauthorised) especially when his doing so would have no other effect than to lessen the force of that expression which had been so emphatically pronounced by the miraculous Voice. Now this improbable supposition is quite unnecessary, since it has been satisfactorily shewn, that there is another way of reading the genealogy which is clear of every such difficulty.

But what is gained if it is allowed that the construction of this genealogy is such as Lightfoot, and as Usher before him supposed it to be? It will follow that it is the genealogy of our Lord, by his mother, the blessed Virgin, up to Adam to whom an Avenger, of the seed of the woman, was first promised. This inference may be collected from the following circumstances:—In the first place the words (ὡς ἐνομίζετο) — "*as was reputed*, must refer either to the first link in the genealogical chain merely, or they must refer to all. They do not refer to all, because it never could be St Luke's intention to style our Lord the *putative* Son of God. Therefore these expressions belong only to the first link, namely to Joseph, and Christ is termed the *real descendant* of Heli, which he could only be through his mother. Secondly Joseph was not the son of Heli, because he was begotten, as St Matthew has informed us, by Jacob. Therefore our Lord must have been the son, or offspring of Heli through his mother.

Such are the inferences which the internal evidence of the case, or the analysis of this genealogy itself, presents to our consideration. Even if we do not adopt the conclusion that the scheme of generations is contrived according to the method of which an example has been cited from Genesis, it will still be most probable that St Luke has given us the ancestry of Mary, and that on account of the anomalous appearance which the name of a female would present in a Jewish pedigree, that of her husband has been substituted in the first place for her own, with a distinguishing expression.

As for external and independent evidence on this subject, we can hardly expect to find any considering the speedy destruction of the Jewish state and the consequent confusion or obliteration of the memorials of families. Perhaps more remains than might be expected. The following hints appear to me chiefly deserving of consideration under this head.

1. There was a tradition very prevalent in the primitive ages of the church that the parents of the blessed Virgin were named Joachim and Anna. This appears to have been founded on the testimony of the Aprocryphal Gospels, which, though uncanonical and even full of false and absurd inventions, are, on account of their antiquity, regarded as authorities of some importance. The tradition was generally received by the fathers, as it has been by modern writers of great learning, particularly the elder Vossius Mill and Barrett. These writers as we must further observe, consider it as a confirmation of the opinion above stated, refuting St Luke's genealogy and the relation of Heli to our Lord. They observe that the names of Eliakim and Joachim were not only equivalent in Hebrew, but are known to have been not unfrequently interchanged for each other among the Jews the same person having been called, on different occasions, by either, and it would appear that they were used almost indifferently as two forms of the same appellation.* Again

* Nomina enim Eliakim et Joachim tanquam synonyma permutari satis docet non modo commutatio nominis Joa

Vossius supposes, with great probability, that Eli is a contracted or abbreviated form of Eliakim. On this subject he makes the following remark: 'Eli esse ex Eliakim, verisimile facit, quod in cunctis pene gentibus, et olim, et hodie, studere soliant propriorum nominum brevitati nisi personæ admodum forent illustres. Sic Herodes rex, qui dictus Αντιπατρος is dum privatus foret, Αντιπας orabatur. Etiam ex Κλεοφιλος, fecêre Κλεοφας, ex Επαφροδιτος, Επαφρας.

These considerations are strongly confirmed by the Rabbinical author cited by Lightfoot in the passage before inserted, where it appears evident that Mary is termed expressly the daughter of Eli or Heli.

2. A passage has been cited from Justin Martyr's Dialogue with Trypho, which plainly indicates that this Father regarded the genealogy in St Luke, as that of our Lord through his mother the blessed Virgin. Now if we consider that Justin was a native of Palestine, that he was a man very inquisitive and learned, that he lived very soon after the apostolic age, when the memory of the events recorded in the New Testament was yet recent, that during most of his life he was contemporary with Polycarp the friend and disciple of St. John, and that these two excellent men were together for many years principal leaders of the Christian Church, we can hardly persuade ourselves that any considerable innovation in doctrine, or any great mistake in a prominent point of evangelical history could be introduced at this period, and especially by such a person as Justin. This, if allowed, will lead to important consequences, inasmuch as Justin is a strenuous maintainer of the Divinity and incarnation of our Lord, and seems in a singular manner to have anticipated and in his replies to his Jewish disputant to have refuted all the principal objections which have been urged by the Socinians of latter times. However, not to wander from the particular point at present under consideration I shall merely extract the passage from Justin in which he alludes to the genealogy and with it bring these observations to an end, leaving the reader to adopt what opinion he prefers on the application of the passage.

"Christ has revealed to us," he says, 'all those things which we have learnt from the Scriptures, through his grace, that he the first begotten Son of God, before all creatures, before the patriarchs afterwards becoming incarnate by the Virgin, who was of their race, even endured to be born as a man destitute of external beauty and honour, and capable of suffering: wherefore in his conversations when he discoursed concerning his *future sufferings*, he said that it behoved the Son of Man to suffer many things, and to be rebuked by the Pharisees and Scribes, and to be crucified, and to rise on the third day. He termed himself the Son of Man, either on account of his birth by the Virgin, who was, as I have said, from the race of David and Jacob and Isaac, and Abraham; or on account of Abraham (perhaps we should read Adam) being the father of *those enumerated as the ancestors* of Mary; for we know it to be customary to term those who have begotten daughters the fathers of the children which are born to their daughters*

---

cim regis filii Josiæ in Eliacim 2 Reg xxiii. 34. sed et collatio Vulgatæ Versionis Latinæ cum Græco textu Libri Judith cap. iv. Nam qui tribus illic in locis Græcè dicitur Joacim Latine vocatur Eliacim et sic cap. 15. Milln Prolegom — Yardley on the genealogies &c.

Justin Dialog. e Triphone 327. Dr. Barrett suggests that there is in this last sentence a particular allusion to Heli as the father of Mary and therefore termed the father of Christ. See Barrett Cod. Rescript Matthæi Prolegom p. 42. He supposes with great probability that by *those enumerated as the ancestors of Mary* Justin Martyr meant the names in the genealogy given by St Luke.

FAMILY SERMONS.—No CXCVIII

Mark xiii. 37. *And what I say unto you, I say unto all, Watch.*

Our Lord, in this chapter, was foretelling the destruction of Jerusalem and pointing out the signs and afflictions which should go before, and accompany that calamity. In order that they might be prepared for the fearful occurrences about to ensue, he especially urges upon his disciples the duty of constant watchfulness; and this in terms which most aptly apply to all mankind, in reference to a far more important and awful event; the coming of the Son of Man at the last day to judge the world. "Of that day and that hour knoweth no man: therefore, "take ye heed, watch and pray, for ye know not when the time is:" 'what I say unto you, I say unto all, Watch.' We are not to be inquisitively curious to find out the date of the end of the world: God has not revealed it, and prophecy itself has cast a veil around it which cannot be penetrated by our dim conjectures: but the event itself is certain, and requires on our part constant vigilance, that we may be prepared for it. Indeed, the whole of the Christian life is an exercise of watchfulness; which is a duty incessantly and most urgently impressed upon us in Scripture. It may be arduous, and by no means agreeable to our natural love of ease and self indulgence: but it is not the less commanded; and when we become really anxious respecting our salvation we must and shall earnestly endeavour to practise it; and in so doing we shall find our safety and our happiness equally united: for to neglect it is to expose ourselves to certain destruction.

In order to assist our minds in gaining right views of the duty of Christian watchfulness, and to impress its importance upon our hearts, we shall make the following inquiries: first, who are commanded to watch; next, when they are to watch; thirdly, why they are to watch; and lastly, how they are to watch; and may the Holy Spirit give us so to feel the necessity of this great Christian duty, that if we have never yet practised it, we may begin now: and that if we are already familiar with it we may estimate its importance anew, and perform it henceforth with greater care and humility and with more fervent prayer than we have ever yet done.

I. Who are commanded to watch? —Our Lord leaves us no room to doubt on this point: for he says, 'What I say unto you, I say unto all.' The command is universal: the young must watch amidst the snares of youth; the adult amidst the busy scenes of manhood; the aged amidst the cares and infirmities of age; the rich man because he is exposed to the dangers of wealth; the poor because he is assailed by the temptations of poverty; the timid and feeble Christian, lest he be overtaken by despondency; the bold lest he fall into presumption; the inexperienced, that he do not mistake the way; and the advanced that he do not wander from it. Should any one imagine that he is exempted from the necessity of watchfulness, that his repentance has been so deep, his faith so firm, his progress in holiness so decided, his spiritual enjoyments so vivid, that he no longer needs to be addressed in the language of precaution; he of all men most requires it: let him that thus "thinketh he standeth take heed lest he fall." If even the great Apostle of the Gentiles, after his miraculous conversion and his eminent advances in the Christian life, after his toils and perils in the service of his Redeemer, after supernatural gifts and manifestations such as in the present age we are not to expect, found it necessary to be constantly impressing on his own mind as well as on his less established converts the duty of vigilance; if he could humbly say, "I keep under my body, and bring it into subjection lest that by any means, when I have preached to others I myself should be a cast away, which of us may safely think that we need less caution of spirit which of us may venture to neglect any of those merciful assistances in our Christian course which were intended at once to remind us of our frailty, and to lead us to an Almighty arm for strength and support?

II The duty being thus shewn to be universal in its application, we inquire, secondly when it is to be put in practice.—Some commands refer chiefly to select times and seasons they rise with the occasion and with the occasion expire But not so the duty of watchfulness it applies to all times and under all circumstances We are travelling through a world of snares and dangers, and must not relax our vigilance till we have arrived at the end of our journey The first moment of fancied security may be that which our spiritual enemy may select to effect our destruction We must watch so long as any possibility of danger exists till the world has ceased to spread its snares till our own hearts are no longer capable of temptation to evil till the last enemy is slain till the final victory is won in short till we have escaped from this preparatory scene to a world of eternal safety and repose Watch ye, says our Saviour 'and pray always not merely in moments of peculiar difficulty not merely in the stated exercises of devotion and self examination but "always at home and abroad in the secrecy of retirement, and the public walks of life from the first waking thought in the morning to the last conscious thought at night not indeed always expressly or directly—this would be impracticable amidst the various occupations of life—but habitually and with a fixed purpose of taking heed to our ways so that when we are not at the moment thinking of the command our heart, and lip and life may still be under its settled and powerful influence

III Our next inquiry is, *Why* we are to watch.—If the duty appear difficult it is equally important and it concerns us most seriously to attend to it Our merciful Father in heaven lays upon us no obligation which it is not for our own highest interest to perform Our repentance our tears our self denial, our sacrifice of our corrupt will and evil tempers, are not commanded in order to appease a stern and vindictive being who delights in human mortification and misery but because they become us as offenders against the Divine Majesty, and as creatures in a state of probation and responsibility because they are connected with our spiritual advancement,—our growth in faith and holiness, in peace and joy and because without them we must every moment fall into those snares and temptations which would cause our eternal ruin

The necessity of watchfulness will strikingly appear from two considerations first the infinite importance of the stake at issue and secondly, from the danger of losing it

1 And what in the first place is the stake at issue? Is it some temporal good something valuable to us only as inhabitants of the present world? If it were so, then we should little need to be thus earnestly exhorted to watchfulness, for in the concerns of this life how anxious are men accustomed to be how incessantly do they meditate and contrive and toil for a comparatively small portion of worldly affluence, or some other object that presents itself as worthy of their cares and ambition ! The Apostle, in speaking of the watchfulness and self government of the Olympic candidate says, " Now they do it to obtain a corruptible crown how much more earnest then he infers should be the vigilance of those who seek for the inestimably higher prize of ' an in

corruptible crown, "a crown of glory that fadeth not away." In the case of the disciples, whom our Lord was addressing in the chapter before us, in immediate reference to the destruction of Jerusalem, we see the importance of watchfulness: a fierce invading army, it was predicted, should besiege the city in which they dwelt; destruction was to overtake that devoted place; their only hope of escape was by timely vigilance, by keeping in constant remembrance the warning prophecy which had been given them, and preparing for their escape at the first moment of alarm. And is watchfulness less necessary in reference to an infinitely more awful day, that day when our eternal condition shall be irrevocably decided, and when we shall receive the award either of never ending happiness or never ending misery? Yet, while men will watch with sleepless vigilance where their worldly interest is concerned, how little do they think of devoting their attention "to making their calling and election sure;" to obtaining the pardon of their sins freely offered to them in virtue of the obedience unto death of Christ; to enjoying true peace of conscience, grounded on faith in the Saviour, and acceptance with God through him; to walking in the light of God's countenance upon earth, regenerated, sanctified, and supported by his Holy Spirit; and at length to becoming partakers of his everlasting glory in heaven! But, surely, if any thing be worth an effort or a wish, it is to secure blessings like these, in comparison with which all earthly pursuits are less than nothing and vanity.

2. But secondly, the necessity of watchfulness will appear, not only from the magnitude of the stake at issue, but from the danger of losing it.—The prize of eternal glory, though freely bestowed, not on account of human merit, but as the gift of God through Jesus Christ, is not the reward of the careless, the indifferent, the Christian merely in name and profession. We have a race which we must run, a warfare which we must wage, and watchfulness is needful that we lose not the prize. Consider the dangers which assail us in our path to heaven. Have we not at all times an enemy who goeth about like a roaring lion seeking whom he may devour; and ought we not therefore to be vigilantly on our guard against his devices? Does not the world also present its ever varying temptations; and, what is worse than all, are not our own hearts treacherous and prone to evil, so that if no other danger were nigh, we should still be in constant peril from our own innate corruptions? But there is yet another reason for watchfulness, which is particularly dwelt upon by our Lord in the chapter before us, and in various other places; namely, the uncertainty of the time of the day of judgment, or, what in our own particular case, amounts to the same, of the hour of our death. "Take ye heed," says he, "watch and pray, for ye know not when the time is. For the Son of man is as a man taking a far journey, who left his house, and gave authority to his servants, and to every man his work, and commanded the porter to watch. Watch ye, therefore, for ye know not when the master of the house cometh, at even, or at midnight, or at the cock crowing, or in the morning; lest coming suddenly he find you sleeping." In the corresponding chapter in St. Matthew, our Lord dwells upon this point still more largely. "As the days of Noe," says he, "so shall also the coming of the Son of man be. For, as in the days that were before the flood, they were eating and drinking, marrying and giving in marriage, until the day that Noe entered into the ark, and knew not till the flood came and took them all away; so also shall the coming of the Son of man be." Our Lord further illustrates the subject by the comparison of a man who would have

been upon his guard, had he known at what hour the thief would have broken into his house: and again by the comparison of a servant, whose lord had left him in a responsible station, while he went on a journey, but who, not knowing the hour of his return, abuses his confidence, till 'the Lord of that servant cometh in a day when he looketh not for him, and in an hour that he is not aware of, and shall cut him asunder, and appoint him his portion with the hypocrites.' What striking representations are these of our present condition, and how forcibly should they urge us to the great duty of constant watchfulness!

IV. The necessity of watchfulness being thus proved, we proceed in the last place, to give some directions for the due discharge of the duty, in reply to the inquiry, How must we watch?—We must watch then as feeling the great importance of circumspection, but not to the neglect of other means of spiritual stability. Sensible of our own weakness to watchfulness, we must unite constant prayer for the blessing of God, who alone can grant us good desires, or holy resolutions, or an obedient life. By his arm must we be supported, and looking up to him we cannot fall. We must further diligently study his word, that we may know what are our dangers and how we may obtain deliverance from them. We must exercise self-examination, in order to learn what are those particular sins and infirmities to which we are most strongly inclined, and where we are most likely to be overtaken by temptation. If a traveller had frequently mistaken his way at a particular part of his journey where the track was more than usually intricate, or if he knew by fatal experience some dangerous spot where he had often been attacked by robbers and been plundered of his property, and with difficulty escaped with his life, how watchful would he be not to venture unnecessarily near the scene of peril, or if he had occasion to pass it, not to be off his guard at the moment of danger. And thus should the Christian traveller watch in reference to the sins that most easily beset him. He should be especially prepared against the particular temptations most incidental to his age, his natural disposition, and his station in society. He should place, as it were a barrier at every inlet to evil. He must shut his ears to all unchristian and corrupting conversation: he must pray that God would turn away his eyes from beholding vanity: he must shun the book, the scene, or the company which would cause him to err from the path of holiness and obedience to God. And while he thus watches against the entrance of the enemy from without, he must guard, if possible, with still greater vigilance against the enemy within. He must "keep his heart with all diligence, for out of it are the issues of life." True conversion of the heart to God is the necessary foundation of all Christian virtues. He must also guard his lips that they corrupt not both himself and others according to the holy resolution of the Psalmist, "I will take heed to my ways that I sin not with my tongue:" "I am purposed that my mouth shall not transgress." He must put a constant guard also upon his actions, remembering ever, "Thou, O God, seest me:" "Thou compassest my path and my lying down, and art acquainted with all my ways." And especially he must cultivate habitual communion with God. He must be strong in the strength of his Saviour, animated by his love, guided by his example, and sanctified by his Spirit. Thus will he be found habitually prepared for death, and judgment, and eternity: the Son of man, come when he may, will find him waiting for his advent, and will welcome him with those blessed words, "Well done good and faithful servant, enter thou into the joy of thy Lord."

To the Editor of the Christian Observer.

I BEG to offer a remark or two upon the criticism of your correspondent G. K., in your last Number, on Ephes. i. 11.

There can be no doubt that the paragraph begins, as he states, at the fifteenth verse of the first chapter, and ends with the tenth of the second. The argument of the Apostle sufficiently establishes this point; and in Knapp's edition of the New Testament (ed. 3, published at Halle 1824,) it is so distinguished from the context. But I cannot think that either the import of the paragraph, or the construction of the twentieth verse, favours the view which he has taken of the passage.

With regard to the latter, it may be urged, that the aorist indicative εκαθισεν is used for the participle καθισας by an idiom of the Hebrew language, which not unfrequently expresses by a participle and verb the sense of two participles—thus, in 1 Sam. ii. 5, we have שאול ויעל מוריד properly rendered in our version 'He bringeth down to the grave and bringeth up.'

A construction not unlike this is used in the Epistle to the Hebrews viii. 10. διδους νομους μου εις την διανοιαν αυτων και επι καρδιας αυτων επιγραψω αυτους where the Apostle deviates from the original passage in Jeremiah. Probably an attentive examination of his writings would supply further instances of this peculiarity of idiom.

The import of the passage I take to be as follows. Having expressed his earnest desire that the Ephesian Church might be led to a still greater acquaintance with the riches of the Gospel and power of God that they had hitherto experienced, the Apostle adduces a twofold illustration of that power, namely the resurrection of Christ from the grave, and the spiritual resurrection of believers from a death in trespasses and sins. Upon each of these thoughts he dilates in his usual manner, seeming for a while to break the thread of his argument, but he returns to it after he has given vent to the warmth of his feelings, and embodied those vivid conceptions of the grace and goodness of God which the subject had suggested to his mind. Thus in the 20th verse, having occasion to allude to the resurrection of Christ, he pursues and expatiates upon the glorious subject, describing in glowing terms the consequences of that great event, the mention of which though not essentially necessary, could not fail to impart a greater degree of force to his illustration: this and the succeeding verses are therefore to be considered rather as an amplification than a parenthesis. In the beginning of the second chapter he returns to his subject, intending to advert to the change which *they* had undergone as a further instance of the power of God. Struck however, with the thought, that this although a surprising proof of the point in question, fell far below the reality, inasmuch as they all, both Jews and Gentiles, had been children of wrath, he again diverges from his immediate topic and enlarges upon it in such a manner as to take in the whole of the case. When therefore he returns to his argument in the fifth verse he adopts the pronoun of the *first* instead of the second person, intending thereby to include both Jews and Gentiles in his remark και οντας ημας νεκρους τους παραπτωμασι συνεζωοποιησε τω χριστω. I cannot therefore but think that our translators are correct in pointing out a connexion between the first and fifth verses, and that if any alteration be required it is only that the compound verb should have been supplied instead of the simple, in order to mark it with still greater precision.

A. O.

MISCELLANEOUS

To the Editor of the Christian Observer

I BEG leave to lay before your readers, as illustrative of the practices of the papal kingdoms, a series of detached extracts from a work entitled "Rome in the Nineteenth Century," and which well deserves the attention of Protestant readers. Its writer tells, it is true, a thousand times repeated tale; but it is here related with considerable spirit and graphic effect. I wish it could be added that the work merited the far higher commendation of describing the mummeries and superstitions of that corrupt church with feelings of compassion and sorrow. But this is not the case. There is throughout its pages too much of the spirit of irony and satire; and in some passages, the reader is offended with indications of levity inconsistent with the profession of a purer faith, and I regret to add, not entirely suitable to the station and sex of the writer. With these large deductions from her claims to unreserved approbation, Miss —— has still made an honourable addition to the elegant literature of her country. As a traveller and an observer, wandering among the basilicæ, galleries and ruins of Italy, she creates and sustains an interest far superior to that produced by Mr Forsyth and Mr Eustace; and her exposures of ecclesiastical imbecility, profaneness, and fraud, are a complete refutation of the last named gentleman's indirect apologies for his church. The following passages appear to me among those most likely to interest and inform your readers.

J

Rome 1817-18

"In our impatience to secure places for the first Miserere in the Sistine chapel, we went at three o'clock, and sat waiting nearly an hour and half before the service commenced. Even at that hour, however the gentlemen had difficulty enough in finding standing room, so great was the pressure in the confined space allotted to them. Many were unable to get in from want of room, and many were turned back from going in boots or trowsers, instead of silk stockings; for no man may attend this service of religion and penitence, unless he be dressed as if going to a ball; and if he has any description of military uniform, it is highly expedient for him to wear it. When at last the service did commence, nothing could exceed my disappointment. It was in no degree superior to the most ordinary chant of a Catholic church; and, finding nothing in it to occupy me, I amused myself with watching the ill concealed drowsiness of many of the cardinals, who, having just risen from dinner, seemed to have the greatest difficulty in refraining from taking their customary *siesta*. Though broad day light there was a row of candles of *mourning* wax, (of a dark brown or purple colour,) ranged upon the top of our grate; the utility of which was not very apparent, as they were extinguished before it grew dark. There were also fifteen similar mourning candles erected on high beside the altar, which, I was given to understand, represented the Apostles and the three Maries, rising gradually in height to the central one, which was the Virgin. As the service proceeded, they were put out one by one, to typify the falling off of the Apostles in the hour of trial; so that at last they were all extinguished, except the Virgin Mary, who was not under the altar. The shadows of evening had now closed in, and we should have been left almost in total darkness, but for the dull red glare which proceeded from the hidden lights of the unseen choristers, and which, mingling with the deepening twilight, produced a most melancholy gloom.

After a deep and most impressive pause of silence the solemn Miserere commenced and never by mortal ear was heard a strain of such powerful such heart moving pathos. The accordant tones of a hundred human voices—and one which seemed more than human—ascended together to heaven for mercy to mankind—for pardon to a guilty and sinning world. It had nothing in it of this earth—nothing that breathed the ordinary feelings of our nature. It seemed as if every sense and power had been concentered into that plaintive expression of lamentation, of deep suffering and supplication which possessed the soul. It was the strain that disembodied spirits might have used who had just passed the boundaries of death and sought release from the mysterious weight of woe, and the tremblings of mortal agony that they had suffered in the passage of the grave. It was the music of another state of being. It lasted till the shadows of evening fell deeper and the red dusky glare, as it issued stronger from the concealed recess whence the singing proceeded shed a partial but strong light upon the figures near it. It ceased a priest with a light moved across the chapel and carried a book to the officiating cardinal who read a few words in an awful and impressive tone. Then, again the light disappeared and the last, the most entrancing, harmony arose, in a strain that might have moved heaven itself—a deeper, more pathetic, sound of lamentation than mortal voices ever breathed. Its effect upon the minds of those who heard it was almost too all powerful to be borne, and never—never can be forgotten. One gentleman fainted and was carried out and many of the ladies near me were in agitation even more distressing, which they vainly struggled to suppress. It was the music of Allegri, but the composition however fine is nothing without the voices which perform it here. It is only the singers of the papal chapel who can execute the Miserere. It has been tried by the best singers in Germany and totally failed of effect. There is never any accompaniment though at times the solemn swell of the softened organ seemed to blend with their voices. This music is more wonderful, and its effect more powerful, than any thing I could have conceived. At its termination, some loud strokes that reverberated through the chapel, and are intended, I was told to represent the vail of the Temple being rent in twain, closed the service.

On the morning of Good Friday we resumed our labours by going to the Sistine chapel. About ten o clock the pope appeared and after a long service the crucifix over the altar which had been covered up all the week with a violet or purple coloured cloth, (which is the mourning of crosses and cardinals here) was uncovered. This is called the discovery of the cross and then after a great deal of fuss and mummery, it is laid on a napkin on a stand before the altar, and after some charting, and much loss of time, the pope comes to it, kneels to it prays or seems to pray over it and goes away and all the cardinals come one by one, and do the same. And this is called the Adoration of the Cross. Then they all set off upon the usual procession to the Paulina chapel the only difference being that the pope walks without any canopy over him and uncovered. The doors of the Paulina chapel were closed upon them and what they did there I do not know only I understand, their business was to take up the Host which they had deposited in the sepulchre yesterday. Certain it is they came back just as they went except that the pope wore his mitre. As soon as this was over without waiting for the long mass which was to follow, I went to the service of the *Tre Ore*, the three hours of agony of Christ upon the cross which lasts from twelve to three. It is a complete drama, and is performed in several churches. I attended it in S. Andrea delle Fratte, which, before I arrived, was crowded almost to suffocation; but a chair, in a commodious situation, and a soldier to guard it, had been kept for me by the attention of the priests, who had been apprised of my coming. The upper part of the church was arranged like a theatre, with painted trees, and pasteboard rocks and thickets, representing Mount Calvary. A little way, two Roman centurions, large as life, dressed in military uniforms, and mounted on pasteboard horses, were flourishing their pasteboard swords. Higher up on the Mount, on three crucifixes were nailed the figures of Christ and the two thieves, so correctly imitating life, or rather death, that I took it for wax work. Catholics say Christ spoke seven times upon the cross, and at every saying a dagger entered the heart of the Virgin, who is therefore painted with seven daggers sticking in her breast, and adored as *Nostra Signora* de sette dolori.—Our Lady of the seven sorrows. The service of the *Tre Ore* is therefore divided into seven acts, between each of which there is a hymn. In every act one of the seven set dissertations upon the " sette parole" of Christ is read, or begun to be read by a priest, who goes on until his lecture is interrupted by the preacher, who breaks in upon it at whatever part he pleases with a sermon (as they call it) or rather a tirade of his own, which seems to be extempore, but I am told is previously learnt by rote. A fat Dominican filled the pulpit on this occasion. He opened his seven sermons by a preparatory exhortation, inviting us to come to listen to the last accents of Christ, to witness his dying agonies. Then he burst forth into a string of apostrophes to Christ on the cross, being an incessant repetition of interjections and vocations, interlarded with a few metaphors, most of which I hold to be perfectly untranslateable. The following, which I took down verbatim from his mouth, were uttered without the smallest interruption or pause.— ' O my Jesus! O most beloved Jesus! O brother Jesus! Most beloved brother! O Jesus of my heart! O most suffering Jesus! O Jesus afflicted! O Jesus crowned with thorns! O dear Jesus! O my Jesus! O most sweet Jesus! O most sorrowful Jesus! O most benign Jesus! O our beloved Jesus! whose burning love the waters of so much cruelty and tribulation could not extinguish!'—During his last discourse, which in vehement emphasis, ejaculation and gesticulation far exceeded the six preceding ones, he continually importuned Christ for one sign, one look; then he said he had given him one look full of mercy, and he asked for another. At length the discourse was drawn out to the right instant of time—the three hours were expiring—' *Ecco il momento!*' he cried, and every body sunk prostrate on the ground in tears, and sobs, and groans, and cries, and one loud burst of agony filled the church. I believe mine was the only dry eye in the church, except the priest's. The sobs of the soldier who leaned on his firelock behind my chair, made me look round, and I saw the big tears rolling down his rugged cheeks.—At length the preacher cried ' Here they come— the holy men—to bear the body of our Redeemer to the sepulchre;' and from the side of the scene issued forth a band of friars, clad in black, with white scarfs tied across them, and gradually climbing Mount Calvary by a winding path amongst the rocks and bushes, reached the foot of the cross, unmolested by the paper centurions. But when they began to unnail the body, it is utterly impossible to describe the shrieks and cries and clamours of grief that burst from the people. At the unloosening of every nail, they were renewed with fresh vehemence, and the sobs and tears of the men were almost as copious as those of the women. Five prayers, separately addressed to the five wounds of Christ—first, the wound in the left foot then that of the right foot and so of the two hands, and, lastly, of the side, were next repeated. They were nearly the same, and all began, *Vi adoro, piaga santissima*—(I adore you, most holy wound). The body of Christ being laid on a bier, decked with artificial flowers, and covered with a transparent veil, was brought down Mount Calvary by the holy men, as the preacher called them, who deposited it on the front of the stage; where all the people thronged to kiss the toe through the veil, and weep over it. I was conducted round to it, along with some Italian ladies of my acquaintance, through a private passage, by one of the civil priests, and so escaped the crowd. Upon close inspection, I found that the body was made of pasteboard, extremely well painted for effect. It had real hair on the head, and it was so well executed, that even when closely viewed, it was marked with the agony of nature, and seemed to have recently expired. The congregation consisted of all ranks from the prince to the beggar, but there was a preponderance of the higher classes. Some ladies of the first rank in Rome were beside me, and they were in agitation the most excessive.

"There is in Rome a convent, called, and justly called, the *Sepolto Vivo*, in which are buried contumacious, or fanatic nuns, from all convents—females condemned by the inquisition for too little or too much religion—and wives and daughters, whose husbands and fathers have the means to prove they deserve, or the interest to procure the order for, such a dreadful punishment. Instances have occurred, where mere resistance to the will of a parent, or causeless jealousy conceived by a husband, have been followed by this horrible vengeance. What may pass within its walls can never be known: none but its victims may enter, and none of them may quit it. They see no human being, excepting once a-year, when, in the presence of the abbess, they may have an interview with their father or mother; but they must not tell the secrets of their prison house. They hear no tidings of the world that surrounds them, nor even know when the friends dearest to them are removed by death.

'Within this little month three great miracles have happened in Rome. The last took place yesterday, when all Rome crowded to the capitol to see an image of the Virgin opening her eyes. Unluckily we were in the country, and did not return in time to witness it; for as this miracle was thought a very improper one by the higher powers,—who would rather she had winked at certain practices which, it is thought, she had not only opened *her* eyes upon but those of other people,—she was carried away, and certain priests, who are supposed to be in her confidence on this occasion, have been shut up in prison. Two officers of the *Guarda Nobile* are also in custody in the state prison at the castle San Angelo, for expressions which implied no extraordinary admiration of the present state of things. It is so nearly impossible to get at the bottom of any thing in Rome, that both these disgraced military and clergy may have given much more reason for their enthralment than we hear of. 'The last miracle was of a much more orthodox description. The miraculous Madonna in this case, opened her mouth instead of her eyes and spoke to an old washerwoman, to whom she imparted her discontent at being so much neglected, and her chapel left in such a dirty and ruinous condition, while so many other Madonnas, no better than she, had theirs made as fine as hands could make them. The Madonna spoke no more, but the old washerwoman proved a very loquacious reporter of her wishes and sentiments. The news of the miracle spread like wildfire: thousands (I am not exaggerating) may be seen every day crowding to this little old chapel, near St. John Lateran's, about four in the afternoon, the hour at which the Virgin addressed the washerwoman, it being supposed that this is her favourite time for conversation; but I have not heard that she has made any new observations. Not only the lower orders but crowds of well dressed people and handsome equipages of all sorts, daily throng the door; and the long green avenue that leads within the walls to the Porta San Giovanni, instead of an unbroken solitude now wears the appearance of a cried fair. At the corner of every street you stumble over a chair set out with a white cloth, a little picture of the Madonna, and a plate for collections to beautify her chapel. You are assailed on all sides with little begging boxes for the Madonna's beautification; and even the interests of the holy souls in purgatory are forgotten in the pious zeal to make her fine enough.

'One would have thought there had been miracles enough of late in Rome to have satisfied any reasonable people; but the pope, and a detachment of cardinals, are going about every day after dinner in quest of more. They visit all the Madonnas in town in regular succession. They began with Santa Maria Maggiore, who takes precedence of all the rest here; and they will not leave one unapplied to, till they get what they want,—which is rain; for the country, with the unexampled cold and drought of the spring, is dried up—vegetation is pined and withering—and there is but too much reason to dread that the miseries which the poor have suffered during the last dreadful year of scarcity will be increased ten fold in the next. " I understand not one miracle happened during the whole reign of the French and that it was not until the streets were purified with *lustrations* of holy water, on the return of the pontiff, that they began to operate again. Private miracles, indeed, affecting individuals, go on quite commonly every day, without exciting the smallest attention. These generally consist in procuring prizes in the lottery, curing diseases, and casting out devils.

There is certainly more superstition in the south of Italy than in the north, because there is more ignorance. In Milan, and in most of the cities of Lombardy, it is rapidly disappearing with the diffusion of knowledge and science. Yet Florence, enlightened as she is, has a reasonable share; and miracles, and miraculous Madonnas abound nearly as much in Tuscany as in the estates of the church; as I have good reason to know. Even the liquefaction of St. Januarius's blood, which is generally quoted as the *comble* of superstition, is not without its parallel. At Mantua, a bottle of the blood of Christ is liquefied every year, to the great edification of the countrymen of Virgil. The bottle, containing this *real blood* of Christ was dug up at Mantua, in a box about two hundred years ago, with a written assurance, that it had been deposited there by a St. Longinus, a Roman centurion who witnessed the crucifixion, became converted and ran away from Judea to Mantua with this bottle of blood; and after lying sixteen centuries in the ground, the box, the writing and the blood, were as fresh as if placed there only the day before!

We were present to day at one of the most ridiculous scenes I ever witnessed even in this country. It was St Anthony's blessing of the horses; which began on that saint's day and I understand lasts for a week; but as this was a *festone*, I rather imagine we saw it in its full glory. We drove to the church of the saint, near Santa Maria Maggiore, and could scarcely make our way through the streets, from the mul titude of horses, mules, asses, cows, sheep, goats and dogs, which were journeying along to the place of benediction; their tails, heads and necks, decorated with bits of coloured ribbon and other finery, on this—their unconscious gala day. The saint's benediction though nominally confined to horses is equally efficacious and equally bestowed upon all quadrupeds; and I believe there is scarcely a brute in Rome, or in the neighbourhood that has not participated in it. An immense crowd were assembled in the wide open space in front of the church; and from the number of beasts and men it looked exactly like a cattle fair. At the door stood the blessing priest dressed in his robes, and wielding a brush in his hand which he continually dipped into a huge bucket of holy water that stood near him, and spirted at the animals as they came up, in unremitting succession, taking off his little skull cap, and muttering every time 'Per intercessionem beati Antonii Abbatis hæc animalia liberantur a malis in nomine Patris et Filii et Spiritus Sancti Amen.' The poor priest had such hard work in blessing that he was quite exhausted and panting, and his round face looked fiery red with his exertions. The rider, or driver of the creature always gave some piece of money larger or smaller, in proportion to his means or generosity, and received an engraving of the saint and a little metallic cross. However all animals might be blessed gratis. Several well dressed people in very handsome equipages attended with out-riders in splendid liveries drove up while we were there, and sat uncovered till the benediction was given. Then having paid what they thought fit they drove off, and made way for others. One adventure happened which afforded us some amusement. A countryman having got a blessing on his beast, and therefore putting his whole trust in his power set off from the church door at a grand gallop, and had scarcely cleared a hundred yards before the ungainly animal tumbled down with him, and over his head he rolled into the dirt. He soon got up however, and shook himself, and so did the horse without either seeming to be much the worse. The priest seemed not a whit out of countenance at this catastrophe, and some of the standers by exclaimed with laudable stedfastness of faith, that but for the blessing they might both have broken their necks.

By far the most valuable relic brought from Palestine by that indefatigable collector Santa Helena is the Holy Staircase, the very same on which Christ descended from the judgment seat of Pilate. It is certainly somewhat singular that it should have escaped the total destruction of Jerusalem,—but here it is. It is likewise strange that its merits should have been overlooked for so many centuries during which it was permitted to rest in the obscurity of the old Lateran palace, and people walked up and down it with the most irreverent insensibility. But when Sixtus V rebuilt the palace he brought its forgotten virtues to light, and raised for it an erection of its own opposite the church in which it is now placed; and these holy steps are now never ascended but on the knees and are never descended at all, four parallel staircases are provided in the same building which are not holy and by which the penitents descend. These holy steps that pious knees have worn till they are almost worn away have now been cased in wood, and so great is the passage upon them that except on a grand festa—a festone —you cannot fail to see various sinners creeping up them on their knees repeating on every step a Paternoster and an Ave Maria. On the Fridays during Lent crowds go up. I have myself more than once seen princes of royal blood slowly working their way up on their knees, their rosary in their hands—

I am told, the ascenders of this Holy Staircase gain three thousand years indulgence every time of mounting but what temptation is that in a church, where indulgences for thirty nine thousand years may be bought on the *festa* of the patron saint?

'I was surprised to find scarcely a church in Rome that did not hold up at the door the tempting inscription of 'Indulgenzia Plenaria.' Two hundred days indulgence I thought a great reward for every kiss bestowed upon the great black cross in the Coliseum but that is nothing to the indulgence of ten twenty and even thirty thousand years that may be bought at no exorbitant rate in many of the churches. You may buy as many *masses* as will free your soul from purgatory, for twenty nine thousand years, at the church of St John Lateran on the *festa* of that saint at Santa Bibiana on All Souls Day, for seven thousand years at a church near the Basilica of St Paul, and at another on the Quirinal Hill, the names of both of which I have unluckily forgotten for ten thousand and for three thousand years and at a very reasonable rate. But it is in vain to particularize—for the greater part of the principal churches in Rome and the neighbourhood are spiritual shops for the sale of the same commodity. The indulgence they hold out was perhaps at first confined to exemption from fasts and other ordinances of the church or exemption from the ecclesiastical penances imposed as atonement for sins. But they soon extended to liberation from the pains of purgatory for a stated period so that those who during their lives buy or earn indulgences for one hundred thousand years will have credit for it in the next world and be released from its purifying fires so much the sooner. The priests say it is the pains of purgatory only not the pains of hell that can be thus commuted for fines. And yet if the pains of hell be not merited for such offences as the records of the Roman Chancery prove to be commutable for money I know not how men could incur them. Murder fratricide parricide, incest, and every crime that can disgrace our nature, have here their stated price upon the payment of which their commission is not only pardoned, but pronounced compatible with holding holy orders. In proof of this monstrous fact, I shall pollute my page with a few extracts from these foul laws or records of licensed profligacy. (It is not necessary to copy these disgusting recitals two may suffice.) 'The absolution of him who has murdered his father, mother, sister, or wife from five to seven gros. The absolution and pardon of all acts of impurity, committed by any of the clergy in what manner soever *together with a dispensation to enable them to take* and hold holy orders and ecclesiastical benefices costs thirty six tournois, nine ducats. Many more instances might be adduced and those above might be mentioned with minute particularity tending to authorize the commission of every sin, on payment of certain fines, and may be found in Bayle's Dictionary, article Banck Laurence or in Laurence Banck's Taxa S Cancellariæ Romanæ from which the above is copied. The book was published by authority at Rome Venice Cologne and Paris and the editions of all these places are still extant, though they are now becoming rare for it was prohibited and its future publication stopped immediately after the Protestants assigned it as a reason for rejecting the Council of Trent. The latest edition is of Paris 1625

The old church of Santa Maria in Ara Cœli crowning the summit of the Capitoline Hill, and supposed to occupy the site of the splendid temple of Jupiter is adorned on the outside with a flight of 124 steps of marble said to have formed the ascent to the temple of Romulus Quirinus. Up these Pagan steps, I have frequently seen good Christians painfully mounting on their knees — a method of locomotion they seem to think more to the taste of the Virgin who lives at the top of them, than the vulgar mode of walking: and it is either practised, in order to repay her for some benefit already received, or to obtain some desired gratification. One woman told me she had gone up on her knees, because she had made a vow to do it, if the Madonna would cure her of a bad sore throat: in this case, it might be termed a debt of honour. Another performed this exploit in order to prevail upon the Madonna to give her a prize in the lottery. Nineteen centuries ago Julius Cæsar, at his first triumph, ascended on his knees, the steps of this very temple, (that of Jupiter Capitolinus.) Strange! after the lapse of ages, to see on the same spot the same superstitions infecting opposite faiths, and enslaving equally the greatest and the weakest minds! The last time I visited this church, it was crowded almost to suffocation by peasants from remote mountain villages, arrayed in their grotesque and various holiday costumes, who had performed this festive pilgrimage, in order to see the *Bambino*, the new born Jesus, and pay their respects to the Virgin.

The upper part of the Church around the great Altar, was adorned with painted scenes, and converted into a stage, in the front of which sat the figure of the Virgin, made of wood, with her best blue satin gown, and topaz necklace on...... There lay, the new born *Bambino* rolled in rich swaddling clothes, and decked with a gilt crown: beside him stood St Joseph, and the two Maries: and at a little distance were seen two martial figures who, we were given to understand, were Roman centurions, made of pasteboard, and mounted on white horses. Near them projected from a side scene the head of a cow.

"We paid a visit (when at Sienna) to the house of St Catherine, where is still to be seen the stony couch on which the poor saint used to sleep at nights, and the identical spot where our Saviour stood when he espoused her, and put the wedding ring on her finger! My astonishment was unutterable. I have seen the marriage of Christ and St Catherine a thousand times, in painting; but I always concluded it to be metaphorical, or thought at most, that credulity had magnified some accidental dream into a vision sent by Heaven: but it never once entered into my head, that any human being had ever imagined or pretended, that such a marriage really did take place. Yet here I was repeatedly and most solemnly assured by every body present,— consisting of a priest, a lacquey, a tailor, and two women,—that our Saviour actually appeared on this spot in his own proper person, invested her with the ring, and declared her his spouse: notwithstanding that he had been crucified several hundred years before St Catherine was born! Nay, they declare that he carried on a most affectionate correspondence with her, and that many of his letters of conjugal love are still extant. Of these, however, I could not obtain a sight: but I saw in the public library in this city, several epistles on her side, to her dear husband Jesus Christ, and her mother in law the Virgin Mary. That such a legend ever should have been accredited in the darkest ages of extravagant fanaticism, I could scarcely have believed: but that it should have been gravely repeated as authentic, in the nineteenth century, nothing, I think, short of the evidence of my senses, could have convinced me.*

It is not without extreme hesitation that I have copied this last extract, nor should a recital so painful and revolting have been transferred to your pages, but for the important purpose of revealing the practical deformities, loathsome and impious as they are, of the papal system. I would only add one inquiry: does the Roman Catholic Church, or does it not, authorize, encourage, or defend such

To the Editor of the Christian Observer.

THE following observations are submitted, on the subject of the wish expressed by you, in your last Number, "to have the privilege of pleading by counsel extended to all classes of offences with a view to qualify your decisive opinion on that subject *

The well known practice at present is this, so far as respects cases of felony counsel *are* allowed on both sides,—for the crown, to open the nature of the case and to examine witnesses; for the prisoner to examine and cross examine on his behalf that is they have that liberty but there are cases where no counsel is engaged on either side Prosecutors, however, have *this* advantage, that it is in the discretion of the judge to allow them reasonable costs including those of counsel In that opening, candour and humanity are the prevailing features so much so that a counsel would forfeit his respectability, both

practices as are here detailed? for setting aside every question purely doctrinal such rites and legends are surely the invention and in their practical influence on the minds of the papal populace the triumph of the powers of darkness over the pure and undefiled religion of Jesus Christ They effect under the mask of Christianity what Voltaire and Condorcet endeavoured to accomplish by the weapons of infidelity

* Our correspondent will perceive on referring back to the passage, that we expressed no decisive opinion even if we had one on the subject we merely stated that as Mr Peel intended to look into various circumstances connected with the administration of justice with a view to such improvements as may appear expedient we could wish that among other points he would consider of the propriety of extending the privilege of pleading by counsel to all classes of offences We insert G s arguments without comment leaving the discussion open so far as suitable for our pages to our correspondents We forbear also to embark on the consideration of some other points to which our attention has been summoned especially that of the uniformity required in *every* case of jurymen which certain of our correspondents consider as irrational in its principle and highly injurious in its operation leading often to the grossest perjury

to the bar and the public, did he indulge in a different strain On the other hand, the counsel for the prisoner is left to the fullest liberty of cross examination which is often exercised to a pitch of severity, even beyond the latitude taken in civil causes Then again where the prisoner has no counsel, which on the proposed plan must still often be the case, the *judge* becomes his counsel and this in many instances much more to his advantage, than were a counsel to act for him It must not also be omitted to be observed, that the prisoner s counsel is at full liberty to state and argue points of law on his behalf

Under these circumstances it is not easy to discover what advantages a prisoner would derive from this supposed privilege of pleading by counsel The following are some of the *disadvantages* if not to himself, yet to the courts of judicature and even it may be to the perfect administration of justice which might result from allowing such a practice

1 The trouble and inconvenience to judges and jurors An assizes or commission of oyer and terminer, would last at least twice as long as it now does, were counsel to be heard at length for and against the prosecution and this being a case of life or death the prisoner s counsel would feel bound for his own credit, perhaps also urged by his feelings to expatiate to the utmost his opponent, of course to resist his arguments at equal length as in fact is already observable in cases of treason

2 The passions would be attempted to be unduly worked upon And in cases of this nature a counsel would scarcely be restrained by the court, from any length he might choose to go, though in a civil cause he might be subject to some check

3 Criminals, both those who were tried and those who were waiting for trial in court, would be apt to derive encouragement to crime,

from the specious colourings and reasonings of an ingenious barrister in favour of their innocence.

4. The jury, who in crown cases (for the best reasons) generally consist of plain men, would be not assisted, but confounded and embarrassed, by the addresses in defence and in reply; and though they would have the resource of the judge's opinion (without which in civil cases they would often be lamentably bewildered,) yet that resource would be likely to be much more simple and serviceable without those wearisome and extraneous appendages of pleading and argument.

In answer to this surmise of inconvenience and even mischief, from introducing the practice alluded to, it may be replied, that the accused ought at least to have equal measure with the accuser in such serious circumstances: but *has* he not already equal measure, if not by the express provisions of the law, yet in the sanction of public feeling, established now so firmly, that neither a judge nor an opening counsel would be under any temptation to violate it?

Nor does the change appear to be called for on constitutional grounds. If it were; if every subject had a *right* to be defended by counsel; and to this extent, provision should be made by law, *in forma pauperis*, that every culprit, unequal to the expense, should have an attorney assigned him, to draw up his case, and inquire out his proofs, and a counsel to hold a brief for him: yet this very impression of "equal rights" is the one likely to carry over many in favour of the present idea, for want of cool investigation: and indeed unless we are on our guard, other plans of reform of the present day might, at first sight, appear corrections of abuses, which yet, on re-consideration, would be found to militate against usages founded in wisdom, and matured by experience.
G.

To the Editor of the Christian Observer.

No employment perhaps has so strong a tendency to weaken the impressions of religion as mental pursuits, whenever they become the main occupation of life. The thoughts of the practical mechanic may range to a certain degree at will, over spiritual subjects, in his busiest hour: but the scholar must bend earnestly and constantly every faculty of his mind to the one object immediately before him. To the evils which such an absorption is liable to induce, the experience of every Christian student will bear witness. How often may progress in earthly knowledge be measured by retrogression in heavenly wisdom. How often have the fascinations of literature chilled the ardour of devotion, opened a way to vain glory and ambition, and gradually brought on a grievous decay in every part of the spiritual life. To check such a tendency, to avert such consequences, one would catch at any thing which promises, however indirectly, to break the continuity of this abstraction, and to recal the ideas though but for a moment, from Parnassus to Sion. With this view the writer would recommend to the classical student, in the midst of his daily labours, ever to have his Bible within reach. Let him, as a philologist or antiquarian, remark and compare whatever parallel phrases, sentiments, imagery, customs, or incidents may occur: and they are neither few nor uninteresting. This habit of reading, with the eye perpetually glancing off to the pages of Scripture, could not fail of being attended with happy effects. Not to mention the value of the illustrations so derived, he would thus be brought into a closer and more frequent intercourse with the repository of his faith, and imperceptibly be led to identify it with every object of his study.

By way of following up the suggestion, a few instances of such parallelism, (the best the recollection of the moment can adduce,) shall close this communication.

1. ' It is turned as *clay* to the seal.' Job xxxviii. 14.

This use of *clay*, where we employ wax, is incidentally noticed by Herodotus, Euterpe 38. where, speaking of the examination of the victims by the Egyptian priests, he says, " If the animal is found unblemished, the priest marks it by twisting a slip of byblus around the horns and then having spread thereon *sealing* CLAY (γην σημαντριδα) he impresses his signet."

2. " After that I was instructed, I *smote upon my thigh*. I was ashamed, &c." Jeremiah xxxi. 19.

This expression of violent emotion is mentioned in Homer. Iliad xii. 152. " Then Asius uttered a piercing cry, and *smote upon his thighs* (ω πεπληγετο μηρω)." And so Mars, Iliad xiv. 113.

3. ' My *net* will I also spread upon him and he shall be taken in my snare.' Ezek. xii. 13. referring to Zedekiah.

"Who didst cast thy *net* (εβαλες δικτυον) upon the towers of Troy." Æschylus Agamem. 348.

4. " I will sweep it [Babylon] with the *besom* of destruction, saith the Lord of hosts." Isaiah xiv. 23.

" O Jove, what meanest thou to do? Lay down the *besom* (το κορημα) sweep not (εκκορει) Greece." Aristophanes Par. 59.

Æschylus furnishes a somewhat similar instance. ' Having rased Troy with the *spade* of Jove (Διος μακελλη).' Agam. 508.

5. ' Many also which used curious arts, brought their *books* together and burned them before all men.' Acts xix. 19.

So Horace, (Epod. xvii. 4.) addressing the enchantress Canidia conjures her " by the *books* (libros carminum) of incantations, potent enough to call down the stars from heaven."

6. ' In the shadow of thy *wings* will I make my refuge.' Psalm lvii. 1, &c.

The same image is used to denote protecting power and guardian care, by the classical writers, as Æschylus (Eumen. 1004.) " Dwelling beneath the *wings* (πτεροις) of Pallas the sire respects them."—And Euripides (Heracl. 10.) " Keeping his children under my *wings*, I protect them, &c."

7. " For this cause the king was angry and very furious, and commanded to destroy all the wise men of Babylon." Daniel ii. 12.

Thus, Astyages, the Mede, when his army was defeated by Cyrus, " First of all *impaled the interpreters* of dreams, who had formerly persuaded him to let Cyrus go free." Herodotus Clio 128.

9. " There is yet one man, Micaiah the son of Imlah, by whom we may inquire of the Lord: but I hate him; for he doth not prophesy good concerning me, but evil." 1 Kings xxii. 8.

So the son of Atreus indignantly addresses the seer Calchas. " Prophet of wars, never yet hast thou once declared aught prosperous for me. Thy delight is ever in predicting misfortunes; and never hast thou delivered a prophecy of good." Homer, Iliad i. 106.

10. " Lo, children are an heritage of the Lord. Happy is the man that hath his quiver full of them: they shall not be ashamed, but they shall *speak with the enemies* in the gate." Psalm cxxvii. 3. 5.

" For this reason men pray for children *that they may repay their enemy with evil*." Sophocles Antigone, 643.

Ουτις

REVIEW OF NEW PUBLICATIONS

Observations on Corporal Punishment, Impressment, and other Matters relative to the Present State of his Majesty's Navy. By Sir C. V. PENROSE, K.C.B., Vice Admiral of the Blue. Bodmin, 1824.

WE rejoice to observe that a very large share of public attention has of late been increasingly devoted to various points connected with the well being of seamen, both in the king's and the merchants' service. Too long have seafaring men been considered as little better than mere machines or animals, incapable of being regulated by those higher motives and principles which influence, or ought to influence, other classes of mankind; and as it were naturally destined to be governed by slavish severity in this life, and to be almost excluded from all practical acquaintance with a life to come. The scene happily has changed; our maritime population are at length acknowledged to be human beings, responsible beings, immortal beings; beings whose stock of necessities is not confined to eatables, drinkables, and inflammables, shot and gunpowder for their enemies, and rum and rope's end for themselves. The British public have ascertained that sailors have souls as well as bodies, and are beginning, very insufficiently indeed, but still hopefully, to act upon that discovery. Hitherto this benevolent agency has been chiefly voluntary and of an eleemosynary kind; but we despair not of its becoming, rapidly we would hope, but ultimately we cannot doubt, national, official and co-extensive with the moral, physical, and religious wants of this large and interesting class of our fellow-subjects.

The sum of what has been done, or is in progress, by voluntary agency for our seamen, is chiefly as follows. The Naval and Military Bible Society, and the Merchant-Seamen's Bible Society, have extended the circulation of the Scriptures among them; the Prayer book and Homily Society is diffusing among them the formularies of the Church of England, so far as its very insufficient funds will allow; tract societies are sending them their "winged messengers;*" and on every side are arising, in various parts of the world, but chiefly under the auspices of different bodies of Dissenters, "floating chapels," "mariners' churches," and "mariners' libraries." The Church of England has not yet come forward with sufficient activity in this great service of humanity, religion, and true patriotism. Ireland, however, has set us a most honourable example in her noble marine institution in the port of her metropolis under the zealous patronage of the Arch-

---

The venerable Society for promoting Christian Knowledge has long been engaged in its measure in the important object of circulating the Bible, the Prayer book, and Tracts among our seamen. It is most justly remarked in one of the tracts of that institution.

The miscarriages of too many of our seamen have occasioned great reproach to us abroad, and have been the cause of great damage to us at home. No sufficient remedies can be provided for these mischievous disasters till there be particular care taken for the good education and religious instruction of such as are designed for a sea-faring life; and till constant prayers and good government be generally set up in our ships. Human nature is a corrupt and degenerate thing, and will bring forth nothing but wickedness and ill manners without diligent education and careful conduct; and therefore where the name of the great God is not mentioned but in order to blaspheme and profane it, it is no wonder if all the mischief abound that the devil can suggest and men can commit;—for it is religion only that makes the world habitable, which would otherwise be as a wilderness of savage beasts, and a universal den of robbers, as among the uncultivated Caribbees.

bishop of Dublin and from some arrangements now in progress, we have reason to hope that London, and other parts of England will not long be without similar establishments. It is certainly not much to our credit, that while our Presbyterian friends on the Forth, and our fellow Episcopalians on the Liffey, have nobly taken up this great object, the Thames should so long have been destitute of a chapel in connexion with the Established Church. But we write not to reproach our countrymen, private or official, landsmen or connected with maritime life, for past deficiencies, but to stimulate them to future exertions; we therefore add no more at present on this topic, except the following overwhelming statistics, for those who may need them in order to inform their minds of the magnitude of the object, and to excite their commiscration, and arouse their consciences to assist in its accomplishment.—It has been computed that the total amount of property shipped and unshipped in the port of London, in one year, amounts to nearly seventy millions; that there are employed about 8000 watermen in navigating wherries and craft; 4000 labourers, lading and unlading ships; 1200 revenue officers constantly doing duty; besides the crews of the several vessels, occupying a space of nearly five miles. On an average there are 2000 ships in the river and docks, together with 3000 barges and other small craft employed in lading and unlading them; and 2000 barges engaged in the inland trade; and 3000 wherries or small boats for passengers. The exports and imports employ about 4000 ships whilst the cargoes that annually enter the port are not less than 11,000. From a return lately printed by order of the House of Commons, it appears that the imports into London in 1822, amounted to eighteen millions sterling; and the exports to nearly twenty two millions, of which sum eight millions were foreign and colonial merchandize. The number of vessels that entered the port in 1822, was 3648 British, and 865 foreign. The total number of vessels that had moored between Limehouse and London bridge was, in 1822, 13,112, exclusive of ships or vessels which had entered docks and canals. In 1823, the arrivals of steam vessels were 945, and the departures 915. The lineal frontage of wharfs and quays extends to 6451 feet; and 141 vessels of 100 tons and upwards, may discharge their cargoes at the same time in different places.

We do not attempt to estimate the amount of the benevolent exertions above alluded to, or of other highly useful efforts for the extension of schools, savings banks, hospitals, and other valuable institutions among seamen. It is obvious, however, that most of what is effected, or to be effected by voluntary efforts has relation more particularly to merchant seamen; his Majesty's navy being placed under peculiar circumstances, which bring it more immediately within the scope of legislative and official regulations. And, what renders it most strongly the duty of Government of Parliament, and of the public to look with a jealous eye to themselves, and with a most humane and disinterested aspect towards this vast national service is, that to a great extent it is an involuntary service. The merchant must submit to pay the just price of labour according to the circumstances of the market; but the public fixes a lower rate of wages for its sailors, and forces men to accept it whether they will or not; and the press gang and the magistrate's warrant are appended to the system, to prevent that depopulation of the navy which would be the obvious consequence of this national parsimony and injustice. But low wages are not the only or the chief source of the unpopularity of the navy; for the severity of discipline which ever attaches to involuntary service, and the general degradation of character consequent upon every step in the whole process make it a most obnoxious line of life to moral, respectable, and religious men. Here then is a most powerful reason for the increased attention of every wise and benevolent mind to exert itself for the welfare of our national seamen. If the merchant fails in his duty, if his wages are too low, or his demands too great, or his captain's discipline too severe, his ship may remain unmanned till he reforms his regulations; but the royal seaman is a sort of maritime slave, (we do not use the word offensively,) he cannot quit his post if he is ever so justly dissatisfied, and therefore it becomes the nation, as a humane and enlightened master, to do for him what he cannot do for himself,—to teach him as well as to feed him,—to give him medicine for the soul as well as for the body, and to watch over his morals and best interests, as well as to look to his mere professional ability in his occupation.

We should scarcely know where to begin or to end, if we attempted to give a sketch of what we understand to be the actual condition of our navy in those points which, as Christian Observers, would particularly excite our attention, or if we attempted to detail all that may be necessary to render that service what every friend of Christianity would wish it to become. Indeed we feel our incompetence to such a task; nor is it necessary to undertake it with a view to our present object, which is rather to excite a spirit of serious inquiry into the whole subject, than to pretend to enter upon the details of it ourselves.

There are, however, three particular points connected with the present administration of naval affairs which have of late excited considerable attention; we mean, the three noticed by Admiral Sir C. Penrose, in the pamphlet before us—namely, corporal punishment, impressment, and some immoral customs to which we have before had painful occasion to allude. We shall confine our remarks to these three points, on all of which our opinion is well known to our readers; but the modest, frank, and we are persuaded ingenuous, pamphlet on our table summons us briefly to notice them anew, especially as the gallant writer has seen fit to refer to our publication, and to blame us for our former remarks, relative to the third point above noticed. We have ever been of opinion, that the reform of any community must ordinarily come from without its immediate members, even though persons of sound judgment and honourable minds, will usually have grown up so familiarised with the abuses incrusted on its surface, or, perhaps penetrating to its very core, as either not to perceive them or not to be sensible of their enormity. Anglo-Indians deprecated, and many of them, we doubt not, with honest and unaffected forebodings, the extension of a Christian establishment, and Christian missions to India: slave traders knew of no atrocities in man stealing and piracy: the receivers in this nefarious commerce, while they now universally condemn the thief, see no moral invalidity in the bargain, and urge, that there is little or nothing to amend in the existing state of slavery. We might proceed further, but we forbear; our only inference is, that while the public ought to listen with the most respectful attention to facts proved by professional persons, and to their details of practical routine, they are at liberty to dissent from their principles, and also to apply as far as may be expedient sounder principles in the regulation of their particular profession, even at the risk of running counter to certain prejudices, of which it may not be easy for the existing functionaries to divest themselves, but which will not be known to their successors under a better regulated system. In effecting all such reforms, the remonstrances and forebodings of those who have been matured under the repudiated tactics, may be expected but these, in the end, will usually have a beneficial tendency, by leading the public soberly to examine both sides of the question, and to determine on the comparative strength of evidence. If written in a harsh and angry spirit, they injure the cause which they are meant to defend; if in a candid and temperate vein, they clear the way for those reforms of which their partial concessions unintentionally shew the need. The refutations also which they call forth promote an enlarged acquaintance with the subject; and in a few years the only point for wonder is, that the abuse could have been so long tolerated, and that well principled persons were found to defend it. We are persuaded that such will ultimately be the result as respects the three practices noticed in the present pamphlet.

The object of Admiral Penrose's remarks is thus described by himself:—

I have endeavoured in my observations, to shew that the declamations which have appeared plausible are certainly erroneous; and to prove that the crews of our ships of war, which the declaimers would make appear as if dragged on board by violence, to be as violently punished while they are at the same time permitted in all manner of excess, are treated with such liberal kindness as might well induce them to volunteer to receive it; and that their comforts and morals are by no means neglected, but on the contrary are increased and increasing, are improved and improving, as much or more than in any other portion of our community. pp. v. vi.

We fully believe with our respected author, that very great attention is paid to the wants and comforts of our seamen, both by individual officers and the public authorities; and we have noticed from time to time, various beneficial regulations which do great honour to the promoters of them; and especially the excellent orders issued last year, which embrace some of the chief points which Admiral Penrose had wished to find accomplished. (See Christ. Observer for 1824, pp. 461, 462.) But every community must judge of its own feelings; and it is not for us, or for the gallant Admiral, or for Parliament, or Government, to say, that the treatment is such as "*might well* induce men to volunteer to receive it" if in point of fact they are not found to do so. The best proof of its being adequately "liberal" is not that persons "might well," but that they actually *do*, "volunteer to receive it." So long as compulsatory means are found necessary to secure "volunteers" the service cannot be viewed as desirable. The food, the clothing, and the medical attendance may be excellent, and yet there may be other circumstances which counteract the effect of these comforts; and in truth, if the service is so desirable, why is it held out as a punishment by the magistrates, and considered such by those on whom it is inflicted? A service is never truly liberal or just till the employer can say with effect, "If you do not do your duty, you shall lose your appointment." Is this the state of the navy?

The first point upon which Admiral Penrose touches is the infliction of corporal punishment, respecting which he remarks:

I am, and have always been, an earnest adviser of and advocate for the most cautious use of corporal punishment, fully aware that it has been often injudiciously and sometimes harshly inflicted; but I know also that it has been often injudiciously and weakly refrained from. I have maintained and believe that the advance made in the habits of reflection and exertion of the kindlier feelings in the higher classes, and of improved decency and morality in the lower, are fast blending in that happy harmony which will render corporal punishment of rare occurrence, under the strictest discipline; but if there were only one dozen lashes in a year inflicted throughout the navy, I would not withdraw the power of infliction.

I am most fully aware of the greatness of the charge and responsibility lying on those who are invested with this power; and I have felt this charge and responsibility which the declaimers never did.

A late noble admiral before alluded to, whose heart was as humane as his professional skill was eminent, has often assured me, that although ardent in the feelings of honourable ambition and, of course, desirous of enlarged command, yet that the greatest pleasure he derived from his promotion to a flag was the thought, that it relieved him from superintending punishments at the gangway. I most cordially agree with my lamented friend, and I believe all that is wanted to prevent any improper use of the power complained of is, that all who are entrusted with it should really feel the very serious responsibility attached to it. I do not think I have here used too strong a term as what situation can be more seriously responsible than that which puts a man not only in the place of judge and jury in hearing evidence for and against a fellow creature under his command, passing judgment, and superintending punishment awarded by himself, but having also the power at the latter period still to make the punishment more severe, to lessen its severity, or to remit its execution altogether. Surely there cannot be many who will use this power without mercy, and who would not gladly embrace the means of mitigation and remission when their duty admits.

I allow then the magnitude of the power, the great responsiblity of those on whom the execution rests, with the duty imposed upon them of most serious deliberation and of feeling a due sense that mercy should always temper justice.

But not in the smallest degree do all these weighty considerations shake my firm opinion that the existence of the power is absolutely requisite for the well being of the navy, and necessarily for the safety of the nation. pp 6, 7

We are happy to learn from this extract, not only that our gallant admiral is hostile to severity, but that he considers that the advances made in habits of reflection, and in decency and morality are greatly curtailing and fast banishing, the infliction of corporal punishments, a fact which we so fully believe that we are convinced the good habits of which he speaks will, before long, reform the code itself, as well as the actual practice.* But the power, it seems, must be retained, even if not used, and this at the fear-

* While this sheet is going to press, a proposition has been made in the House of Commons by Mr Hume for some reforms in the navy, particularly as respects impressment and arbitrary flogging. The proposition has failed; but we cannot forbear saying that though the majority of votes was on one side, the preponderance of sound argument was on the other. This is a subject on which the spirit of party ought to have no influence.

ful risk, and we may add, on our author's own shewing, at the absolute certainty, of its being abused. We agree with Sir C Penrose, that if all who are entrusted with the power would duly consider the serious responsibility which attaches to it, it would not be *wilfully* abused; though even in this most favourable case, mistake, haste, or momentary excitement of temper, might have much of the effect of deliberate severity.—But *will* persons in any station always cherish, this sense of responsibility, responsibility not only to man, but to God? Will arbitrary power always be exercised under this salutary and conscientious feeling? If it will, abolish at once as useless all laws, all restrictions, upon the actions of one man towards another, and give to every judge, every magistrate, every master of a family, the power of life and death upon his own irresponsible arbitriment. Our respected author will not say there is sense or reason in such a proposal; but absurd as it is, the cases do not differ in reason, but only in degree, from the peculiar circumstances under which a ship's company at sea are placed. Our author's own admissions prove that both philosophy and fact are against him; for does he not, in this very extract, admit that corporal punishments are often injudiciously and sometimes harshly inflicted; and does he not, in his very exhortations to leniency, in his advice to captains not to direct the infliction of punishment for an offence, "till their pillow has been their counsellor," and in his own candid acknowledgment, that at the moment when a fault has been reported to him, he has himself resolved to award "a much more severe punishment" than he found it either just or his duty to inflict on a subsequent day.—does he not in all these admissions, unintentionally prove, that the power of inflicting instant, summary, and arbitrary punishment, is unwise, and open to the most flagrant abuses? Let the reader judge by one fact, as a specimen from our author's own pamphlet. It is introduced by him incidentally, not in reference to the point which we are considering, but merely to illustrate a technical question respecting the relative powers of a captain and his flag officer. It however applies very particularly to the point under discussion.

When reefing topsails some unusual delay or slackness was shewn on a topsail yard arm. The admiral on deck was very angry, and said to his captain, before many officers and men, I desire that every man on that yard arm may be flogged to-morrow. The captain who did not consider that every man on the yard was in fault, made very properly a respectful bow without remark. The following day the captain reported to the admiral that punishment was about to take place, to which the latter replied, Very well. The captain had found on strict inquiry that the fault lay entirely on two men who had *sulkily disobeyed the orders of their officer* and hindered the other men in their duty. These two men received some punishment. The admiral afterwards asked the captain what he had done about the men who had been so long about reefing the topsail. He replied, I found on inquiry that two men were very much to blame and alone prevented the others from doing their duty, and those two have been punished. You have done very right, was the admiral's reply; but had he persisted in his directions given on the evening before, could the captain have obeyed them, and punished men he knew to be not guilty? pp. 18, 19.

It was well for the unoffending portion of this yard-arm party that it was the admiral and not the captain who happened to have taken the offence; otherwise, without witnesses or jury or court martial, and before their judge could 'consult his pillow' to calm his bilious ferment, they must have submitted — the most respectable man amongst them — to the severe and disgraceful punishment which he might have ordered and seen inflicted on the spot. And yet, when even the long tried coolness of a British admiral can be thus betrayed into an act of the most detestable tyranny and injustice, our gallant author has no hesitation in committing this arbitrary power to mere boys — we beg their pardon for, by a recent and excellent regulation, they cannot arrive at the power of commanding a ship of war till they are, at least, *twenty two* years of age, — having, he says, "too high an opinion of the mild and liberal feelings of a well educated British youth to fear that such a one will err on the side of severity." We confess we could wish that our gallant veterans had some better guarantee, as both justice and policy demand.

We are so unfortunate as again to differ from our author where he laments that, owing to the number of hands through which the quarterly returns of punishments, now happily required from every ship, have to pass, secresy has been impossible though doubtless it would have been desirable; and where he suggests that with a view to promote a greater uniformity of discipline in our ships of war, in some of which punishments are much more numerous, arbitrary and severe than in others, there should be drawn up and transmitted to each commander from the Admiralty *private*, admonitory, and explanatory instructions. In our view the chief existing evils of the system arise from the *unavoidable* privacy which attaches to a service in which the captain and his crew may be separated for months or years from intercourse with their fellow subjects; and where, consequently, many an undue exercise of power may pass unpunished which on land would have called down the vengeance of the laws; and the best way to avoid this evil, and also to gain the uniformity which Admiral Penrose desires, would be an increase of publicity to the regulations and results of the whole system. The sailor ought to know under what instructions his captain acts in a matter which so nearly concerns himself; and the captain ought to feel that he is amenable to the bar of justice and public opinion for the due discharge of his functions. We wish that these very quarterly returns, which Admiral Penrose laments should be known, even by the transcribers and transmitters were regularly laid on the tables of both Houses of Parliament. We are far from thinking that they would prove dishonourable to the navy; but whether they would or not, the knowledge even of an evil is better than ignorance, and is the first step to a cure. The plan of secresy, both as to regulations and punishments, which our author recommends, is better fitted for the court of an inquisition than for that noble and generous service in which he holds so honourable a rank. And it is the more unaccountable in him to recommend it, as he elsewhere justly finds fault with an opinion ' entertained by some very respectable officers, that no *reasoning communications* should ever be made to seamen,' and shews, by his own practice on some trying occasions, that the adage is unfounded.

We have contended, that whatever be the mode of punishment in our navy, it should not be rash or arbitrary in its infliction. As for the particular mode of punishment more immediately in question, we think it about the worst that could be devised. Even as respects the point of disciplining notoriously ' bad men,' it does not seem to be very efficacious: for, says our author,

' The great proportion of punishment falls on a few hardened individuals: and this experience shews the little effect it has in reclaiming such offenders.' p. 15.

And as to its effect on less hardened offenders, it is still worse: for he remarks, that

There are men who will strive long to avoid the shame as well as pain of a public exposition and flogging, who when that shame and pain has been once surmounted care much less for a repetition. p. 11.

And are there not punishments sufficient of other and more humane kinds? Does not our author himself further on, recommend for example withholding the pay for a time, or advancing it according to the men's conduct, which he thinks would naturally tend to render corporal punishments needless?

The subject of impressment next follows. This also our author considers necessary: it is an evil, but it is unavoidable. In our code, nothing that is wrong is necessary, nothing that is unjust is really expedient. Sir C. Penrose begins with affirming that " no man is a more sincere friend to the true liberties of a British subject than he is; but that ' there are circumstances which may allow the warmest advocate of those liberties to consider impressment without all the horrors some pretend to.' For ourselves, we can assure him our share of this " horror" is no " pretence;" and it is not with our author's wonted urbanity of style thus to insinuate, that those who feel deeply on this painful subject are but pretenders to humanity and the love of ' true liberty.' We have looked in vain throughout his pamphlet for any of the alleged circumstances which diminish this " horror:" all that we learn is, that seamen consider it as

a common and *necessary* chance of their line of life, which does not abate one atom from its injustice or its severity: and again, that it is " a *necessary* power:" and a third time, that ' it is necessary for the public safety and honour:' neither of which do we believe, for surely a fleet of high spirited volunteer sailors, preferring the service on the ground of their own interest, in addition to all the other motives which at present actuate our seamen, would not be less " safe" than a company of reluctant impressed men bribed by spirits and kept in order by the lash, or less " honourable" to the nation who had the generosity to devise, even at some pecuniary sacrifice, a more liberal system. Government has already done much, but much remains to be effected. Our author himself complains, and justly, that ' the service is deficient in the means of rewards and encouragements:' and why might not these be adequately supplied?

Our author augurs much, and we most heartily concur in his opinion, for the benefit of seamen from " the irresistible but quiet impulse now in progress from the character of the times" but he adds ' I should like to see this impulse farther and more visibly aided by those in authority,' —a wish in which we heartily join, and this not hopelessly or ungratefully when we remember the great improvements lately introduced and which we trust will before long be followed up by some others equally, or more than equally necessary and useful

We cannot forbear quoting from our author the following interesting sketch of the highly improved moral and intellectual condition of our national seamen within the period of his own recollection We fully believe that the extension of education and the efforts of our Bible societies and other kindred institutions have had a principal share in effecting this auspicious amelioration

We have to consider whether there remain any disadvantages which could be safely removed or any additional advantages or indulgences which might be beneficially granted and whether justice and policy require any alterations which could render the navy still more desirable and, of course more effective and which would tend still more to lessen the necessity of recurring to corporal punishment or to impressment In short have the modern naval regulations adequately met the great changes of the times the progress of education and consequent improvement of the human intellect? It is my firm belief that there is no class of men whatever in which there has been a greater advance in the reasoning powers than among our seamen From fifty two years experience of the naval service I could point out many extraordinary variations to shew that the general character of the crew of a ship of war has been materially changed and with this of course the whole mode of life and discipline has undergone as great alteration Many distinct causes concurring to one end have occasioned this change besides the powerful effects of general education The agitations occasioned by the French revolutionary horrors the very long war the mutinies of 1797 —all led to anxious inquiries and communications and I am of opinion that the present system of numerary and telegraphic signals has also greatly tended to enlarge the reasoning and comprehending faculties of our seamen

When I mention the powerful effects of general education I do not allude merely to the increased number of those who have been taught to read and write, but to think to the impulse which has been given to reflection and combination of ideas The modern school system of mutual instruction is (if I may so say) the most powerful engine of thought which has ever been brought into moral action and the communication which has taken place between the higher and lower classes of society in consequence of the benevolence of the former seeking to administer both to the bodily and mental wants of the latter has mutually opened the manners and characters of each to the other and certainly advanced the latter to a higher degree in the scale of intellectual being

Perhaps the following short digression may in some degree elucidate this idea In 1781 or 1782 I first saw the plan of numerary signals on board a Swedish frigate these had been introduced by French officers into the Swedish marine and I was much struck with their comprehensive simplicity I was at that time first lieutenant of a frigate whose captain had a small squadron under his orders With his approbation I made out a code sufficient for its guidance adopting the numerary system instead of the tabular plan of superior and inferior flags we had before used Two officers then commanding brigs now old and distinguished admirals were the first to whom my captain and I explained them and both these excellent officers *then* declared it as their opinion that the difficulty of comprehending the numerary combinations was so great that they did not think they could ever be brought into use *Now* how many seamen marines and boys are masters of all our signal and telegraphic practice! And to equal extent has their intellect improved in other respects

During my early experience it would have been deemed an extraordinary thing for even a quarter master to use a spying glass and now what confidence do we often place in our signal and look-out men!

Another vast improvement has taken place from the unwearied attentions of officers seconded by the most liberal support from the Admiralty and which if foretold in my early days I should have doubted the possibility of what I now see,—very many of the messes of our seamen and marines sitting at their meals with far more decency cleanliness and comfort than warrant and petty officers and I may add some ward room messes formerly did

A great change in the language and

manners of seamen has also kept pace with the advance of other decencies of life thanks to the example as well as precepts of their officers and I believe I may say with truth that within the memory of old seamen many officers made use of more coarse and blasphemous expressions than are now to be heard between decks in the births of the ship's company

To make the most of this change all parts of the system should as much as possible glide on in equal progress and it would be ingratitude in an old seaman not to acknowledge the bountiful increase of pay the beneficial improvement of the diet the humane and liberal supply of medicine and encouragement of medical officers the system of allotment increased pensions and many other attentive indulgences which have already aided this progress pp 30—33

Our author greatly laments the proverbial improvidence of seamen and this not merely on the score of waste but from the moral evils connected with it He says

I was once paid off in a seventy four gun ship at Plymouth and many of her crew had never set foot on land for six or seven years except in the dock yard at Jamaica. Entirely exclusive of commissioned and warrant officers the payment exceeded twenty two thousand pounds and in a few hours some and in a day or two many of these valuable men were as pennyless as if they had shared between them as many shillings And where was this large sum of money transferred? Just where its amount multiplied profligacy disease want and bodily and mental misery! When no moral or religious pleas were allowed to be entered on this subject it was said that the nature of seamen was such that thus it must be and that the sooner they threw away their money the better as it left them no resource but to enter again in the service But when ships are paid off at the end of war very few of these poor ruined men are wanted for the naval service and they go on board merchant vessels with their minds and bodies contaminated from the means of excess which such great payments have led them into and many a master of a merchant vessel will speak of the restless insubordination these habits have occasioned p 36

The best remedy for these evils he considers to be the system of short payments, which familiarize the seamen with the legitimate uses of money to which we would add, the universal introduction and encouragement of savings banks in our ships and ports, under the auspices of Government itself

We are most happy to find our gallant author protesting against privateering All reflecting to say nothing of religious persons allow the enormity of the practice but it may add to the public detestation of it, to hear from the testimony of a veteran British admiral that it is the lowest degradation of character to which seamen ever sink We venture to hope that in the present state of public feeling and after the humane and enlightened representations of the United States to our Government on the subject this atrocious practice will never again be resorted to We could wish however that Parliament would effectually guard against the hour of temptation before it arrives, by making the practice illegal

But we turn to the third part of our author's work, relative to the immoral practices to which we have alluded in a former review (Christian Observer 1824 p 28)

The author mentions that the pamphlet entitled ' Statement of certain immoral Practices in his Majesty's Navy had been put into his hand more than two years before his work was written (that is, three years from the present date) but that he did not reply to it in order that he might not give greater publicity to the charges made in that publication, and also not knowing whether those to whom it was addressed wished to have any naval notice taken of it He was however induced to alter his determination from the following circumstances —

I have learnt, with a considerable degree of concern that they (the charges) have made a very deep impression on the minds of many respectable people and British gentlemen have been heard to declare that after reading the pamphlet in question nothing could ever induce them to send a son into the navy Thus a most unfavourable and I will add most unjust opinion of naval officers has been largely disseminated and it is not long since that the pamphlet has been reviewed at considerable length in a highly popular monthly publication thus renewing and spreading the stigma to a great extent as this periodical work is regularly reprinted in the United States and has I believe a very considerable sale on the continent of Europe

The opinion I first held after the perusal of the pamphlet (a second edition) was that it was ill judged to publish it at all. If the writer felt on the subject as I doubt not he did all the regret and disgust he evinces in his book his feelings may very naturally have led him to call the attention of those in power towards the practices he so justly laments and condemns with the respect due to his superiors in means of information as well as rank, but I regret that he thought proper to lay his charges before the public at large.

For the reasons he himself assigns he must be very sure that the highly respectable tribunal to which he addresses himself and appeals would earnestly desire to abolish usages which are contrary to religion and good morals and highly inconvenient to the naval service whenever the power to effect the change was adequate to its beneficial accomplishment and the time served for its being carried into execution unless as may possibly have been the case it was considered that the wished for reform is gradually advancing on more certain grounds towards final success than an immediate intervention of power would effect. pp 52 53

We have reason to believe that the periodical publication alluded to is our own. We think it right, therefore to state to the gallant admiral our reasons for having noticed the subject. This we may very briefly do in two words —duty and utility. We did not invent the evils complained of, we found them existing, we knew that private remonstrances had been made in the proper quarter repeatedly without producing any effect. The writers of the very pamphlet reprehended by our author had long silently waited in vain for a correction of the abuse by the official authorities, and before they laid the abuses in question before the world were given to understand that nothing would be done. The unchristian disgraceful and most pernicious scenes detailed by them were made known to the proper authorities and were going on without any official attempt to repress them, nay, with an understanding that nothing official would be done to repress them. Every year the sons of moral and virtuous families were entering this pest house of contagion while those already initiated were adding evil to evil and there appeared no prospect of the nuisance being abated. Was it not then our duty as Christian Observers, and could we in conscience neglect in a country where public opinion is the grand effective instrument of reformation to make the public acquainted with this evil, with a view to its correction? Our chief difficulty was, that the guarded and domestic character of our pages prevented our exposing it so fully as appeared necessary to shew its enormity and even now, those who have occasion to follow up the subject must refer from us to the pamphlet above mentioned. So much for the plea of *duty*.—With regard to that of *utility*, our author's own observations and the deep impression which he states to have been made on so many respectable people particularly British gentlemen by the circumstances alluded to prove that the public discussion of the subject was highly useful indeed indispensable. Would British gentlemen determine never to send a son into the navy, if they had not found the dangers adverted to to be real and most perilous? Would mere declamation or exaggeration have thus changed the views of well judging men respecting an honourable and favourite service to which the sons of our nobility and gentry are wont to crowd with avidity and the truth or falsehood of which they might have ascertained by a visit to Portsmouth or Plymouth? Must they not have inquired into the facts of the case, and have found the statements of the pamphlet to have been notoriously true and the evils to their sons most fearful before they would have made up their minds to so unwelcome a resolution? But, in sooth does our respected author himself venture to deny a single particle of those statements? does he not most distinctly admit and lament the evil? Yes but still, 'why make it public?' Because, we reply, publicity had become essential to its being eradicated. Other means of repression had been perseveringly tried, and had failed: and, in every department of life, so long as the system of "secresy" is persisted in, with reference to abuses the knowledge of which is to be prudently confined to those who are familiar with them, but have not corrected them, though they had the power to do so, so long in most instances will the abuse be suffered to continue. But let it not be supposed that either we, or the authors of the pamphlet who are reprehended by Sir C. Penrose, or any living individuals, have been the first to notice these immoral practices. Every member of the service who has passed through the ordeal without being wholly hardened by the corrupting scenes around him, cannot but have felt shocked and disgusted at the enormities complained of. Time was not wanting to introduce an amended system: for the evil is not of recent standing. The celebrated Skelton, whose excellent works, especially his "Deism Revealed," have long been among the classics of our divines*, gives the following relation respecting the wreck of the Royal George. We do not willingly quote the passage, but duty compels us. Poor honest Skelton thought that the report was "too ugly for credibility:" but the late discussions shew that it was unhappily far too probable: and we know not how sufficiently to express our grief, that the evil should still remain uncorrected. "It is a current report," says Skelton, "but on what authority grounded I know not, that *three hundred lewd women* were, like other stores, shipped on board the Royal George, sunk near Portsmouth, and that the divers, who went down to rummage the wreck, found them and the sailors in pairs." "Whoever," continues Skelton, "believes this, ought always to remember, that God is on land as well as at sea: and if here he hath water, there he hath fire at all times ready, as an instrument of justice and vengeance. I doubt however, he adds for reasons which he gives, "the truth of this ugly report." (Skelton's Senilia, No. 127, Vol. VI. p. 128 of Lynam's edition of his works.)

But we return to our author, who gives us the following intended expurgation of the public authorities.

The question has been further agitated whether or not measures should be taken by those in authority to ameliorate an evil which they cannot hope to suppress: and it has been truly answered that it is an unpardonable weakness when such persons neglect to use endeavours to lessen such enormities as they cannot hope wholly to eradicate. But in the present instance surely this has been already done: for the laws and regulations for naval government are strong and explicit against all vice and immorality. The articles of war begin with a forcible injunction for the due and reverent observance of Sundays, and the second article decrees punishment for all actions in derogation of God's honour and corruption of good manners. The twelfth article of the captain's instructions directs the utmost attention to prevent swearing, drunkenness and every other immorality: and the thirty seventh article is equally express in directing him to prevent every thing which may tend to the disparagement of religion, or to the promoting of vice. The lieutenants are enjoined to watch over the conduct of the divisions of seamen more immediately under their controul and observance. The chaplain is directed to instruct in the principles of the Christian religion, not only all such young gentlemen as the captain shall put under his care, but all the boys in the ship. He is to hear them read, and to explain to them the Scriptures and Church Catechism, &c. He is also enjoined to be very assiduous in his attendance on any of the sick * to prepare them for death, and to comfort or admonish them as the state of their minds or other circumstances may require.—I have selected these few extracts to shew my countrymen on shore that the religion and morals of those employed in the naval service of our country have been by no means abandoned to chance; but that

---

* We are happy to state that the complete works of this powerful writer now first collected have been recently published in six closely printed volumes octavo price 3l. 12s. by the Rev. R. Lynam, assistant Chaplain of the Magdalen Hospital, with Burdy's life of the author, one of the most interesting and entertaining pieces of biography in the English language.

those in authority have openly and powerfully inculcated all those principles which do honour to human nature, and lead not only to happy lives but happy deaths. pp. 53, 54.

On this paragraph we remark, first that we concur with the writer, that it is "an unpardonable weakness:"—we would use still stronger language; for it is a flagrant dereliction of duty—in public functionaries, to neglect to use endeavours to lessen such enormities as they cannot hope wholly to eradicate: and from this most blameable 'weakness' we fear that the official directors of our navy cannot be exculpated. But, next, we differ from him in opinion, that the evil might not be "wholly suppressed*," as far as *the service* is concerned: for we do not of course apply our remarks to those immoralities which do not fall under official inspection. These two points, however, only in passing: the remainder of the paragraph is more important. It is clear that both the articles of war and the captain's instructions, (all of which, by the way, are quoted by the authors of the pamphlet to prove the failure of duty on the part of the executive authorities,) are most direct and praiseworthy as respects every kind of immorality and irreligion: but the inference we should deduce from this is the very contrary to that which our author derives; not that the commissioners of Admiralty have acquitted themselves of their obligations when they have issued the usual routine regulations, but that they have thereby increased their responsibility, and have only failed the more in their duty from not seeing them adequately carried into practice. Had no such articles or instructions been given, they might have pleaded that such matters were foreign to their province; that provided our sailors duly worked and fought their own ship, and took the ships of their enemies, they had nothing to do with their " swearing, drunkenness, or *other immorality:*" that the ' derogation of God's honour,' " the disparagement of religion," " the promoting of vice, except it interfered with business," ' explaining the Scriptures and the Church Catechism,' ' preparing the sick for death,' &c. were subjects which they could not officially recognize. But having for years, and for aught we know to the contrary, their predecessors for centuries, issued, and most properly issued, instructions, comprising moral as well as technical regulations for the service, it has surely been a double crime not to see that these orders were obeyed: and though the crime is not new, so far as the offence was known by former Boards, it is more particularly chargeable now that it has been regularly promulged and substantiated. If such instructions are improper or extra-official, let them be repealed; but it is a mockery to public decorum to plead as a sufficient apology that such instructions are issued, when it is notorious, as respects the great point in question, that they are not enforced. Let us hear our author's own description of the existing practice; for, guarded as it is, we need go no further either for fact or for authority to prove the enormity of the evil complained of.

The custom of allowing such women to be with the seamen when in harbour is I believe as ancient as the navy itself; *always forbidden* either by general or particular instructions, but *always allowed*—always considered as an evil of no small magnitude, but as a necessary or rather unavoidable evil. It has arisen from the idle habits of seamen when on shore, and the difficulty of getting them on board again when allowed to go there.

To keep the seamen contented on board, then, has been the chief cause why women have been allowed to remain with them there; and such is habit, that in most instances perhaps this permission has been granted with as little reference to the moral or religious view of the subject, as when any other indulgence has been requested after a long voyage: and so powerful is this habit, and so much had the custom become a matter of course, that it has been acquiesced in by officers

---

* We understand the author as so saying, though we know not how to reconcile this assertion with his statements hereafter, that it might be suppressed without difficulty.

of the most moral and serious conduct. p. 55.

We learn then, that it is an evil, a great evil, but an old evil, an 'unavoidable evil,' and an evil arising from the bad habits of sailors on shore, and the difficulty of getting them on board again. This last statement indirectly lets out the whole fact: men are unwillingly forced into the service, and can only be kept from desertion, even at the risk of their life, by being confined to their ship; even if married, they cannot, as much as they reasonably ought and might under a better system, visit their families and homes; and, therefore, must be kept "contented on board," at whatever sacrifice of health or morals. Its being an old evil does not prove that it is unavoidable, even under the present mode of manning and disciplining the navy; but it would certainly be most readily avoidable if a more liberal system were adopted, by which ill conduct or desertion would become its own punishment. The men would not desert the service any more than their officers, if it were placed on the footing of a voluntary avocation.

But let us see further our author's own statements with respect to some of the evil effects of the immoralities to which we allude.

It is granted that, independent of the superior considerations of moral and religious obligation, it is a great and absolute evil to have these unfortunate women on board; and it is well stated that two thirds of a ship's company without them are more efficient than the whole complement with them. p. 55.

'The permission for women of bad character to reside on board ought not to be termed an indulgence to a ship's company, but the contrary. It may possibly be considered as a temporary indulgence by a few, but is the reverse of indulgence to the majority. p. 65.

Almost all would be glad to be rid of these troublesome inmates in a day or two, if they had the means of paying them. But our payments in general being made only at the moment of a ship's sailing, these unfortunate wretches are consequently kept on board till that period, when their presence is an intolerable nuisance.

All those of the crew who have wives on board, all who, whether married or not, have no female companions, must be in many ways dreadfully annoyed by the presence of this degraded class of human beings, whose depravity is in many cases still farther augmented by the practice in question. p. 64.

The evil which all are desirous to put an end to is, in the words of the articles of war, 'in derogation of God's honour and corruption of good manners,' avowedly detrimental to the comfort of the seamen themselves, injurious to their health, a powerful enemy to good discipline, and a great impediment to the exertions of the officers, frequently when most materially called for. p. 57.

We need not state what our readers will have perceived in the whole tone of the gallant admiral's remarks, that he is deeply anxious for the abolition of this disgraceful custom, and we are most happy to be able to report his deliberate opinion, that not the smallest difficulty exists as to *the immediate* stop of the practice in its full extent, and that 'the great majority of a ship's company would be glad to see the practice put a stop to.' He reports, as the sum of his observations, that

There is at present no reason whatever why the regulations against such an immoral and inconvenient practice as admitting abandoned women on board our ships of war should not be strictly obeyed; but if the boon of short payments should be ever granted, and more leave to go ashore allowed, it is not, I think, too much to say that a breach of these regulations would be inexcusable, considering the case either by the military or moral duties of the officers concerned. p. 66.

Our author offers several suggestions which may deserve consideration. Among others, he says,—

I have long thought that, under certain regulations, a proportion of the married seamen and marines might be advantageously permitted to have their wives with them both in port and at sea. Of course they must be of irreproachable characters; they should be allowed provisions, and be made well acquainted with the rules to which they are to be amenable, one of which would be dismissal from the ship for any improper conduct. p. 66.

We do not know to what extent this plan might be conveniently carried into practice; but we have no doubt, from the concurrent testimony of all nations and ages to the good effect of a mixture of well-regulated female society in softening the ferocity of the less gentle division of our race, that the presence of the wives of our seamen, if practicable, would tend materially to improve their character.

Sir C. Penrose wishes that instead of an appeal to the Admiralty the writer of the 'Statement' had applied his arguments to those who are guilty of the immoral practices described, and to those under whose more immediate care they are placed. He justly thinks that 'the common imperfection of human nature is as fully perceptible on shore as afloat, and afloat as on shore; and that hence arises the neglect of the excellent instructions issued for the moral discipline of our seamen.' He further considers that a written order on the enforcement of military discipline will not suddenly generate morals, by which word he adds, "I always mean *Christian* morals in the minds and habits of mankind." We so fully agree with him in these observations that though we do not think that private exertions supersede, or can be adequately efficient without, good official discipline and authoritative regulations, we should be glad to see much more of the former in operation. The field is large, and it is also most promising. Many of our author's own statements respecting the improved and improving character of our seamen are most cheering; and his exhortations to his professional brethren to do all in their power to promote this much wished for amelioration, and to carry into effect the letter of their instructions, in all that relates to the moral as well as physical condition of their men will, we trust, meet with that respectful attention and concurrence which the age, and rank, and benevolent intentions of the gallant writer demand.

Notes on the present Condition of the Negroes in Jamaica. By H. T. DE LA BECHE, Esq. F.R.S. London. Cadell. 1825. 8vo. pp. 63. Price, 3s.

Two publications have recently appeared, giving an account of the island of Jamaica; one written by the Rev. Richard Bickell, who resided nearly five years as a clergyman in that island, and which we have already reviewed, in our Number for March last; the other, which stands at the head of this article, by Mr. De la Beche, the proprietor of a sugar estate in the parish of Clarendon, called Halse Hall, and who resided there during the whole of 1824. The latter gentleman appears to feel a natural leaning in favour of the community of planters to which he himself belongs; and yet his statements wonderfully confirm those of Mr. Bickell, and of the Abolitionists generally, in all essential points. The account, indeed, which Mr. De la Beche gives of the management of his own estate, and which we assume to be correct, evinces a more than usual portion of consideration for the well being of his Slaves. Accordingly the decrease which took place during the year of his residence was very small. In March 1823, the number returned as being then on his estate was 208. When he quitted the island in December 1824, he states the number to have been 207, (96 males and 111 females), being a decrease of only one in about twenty-one months. It would appear, however, that previous to 1823 the decrease had been much more rapid. The return made in March 1820, states the number at that time to have been 233. Between March 1820 therefore, and March 1823, the decrease must have been no less than 25, being nearly eleven per cent in that time. This decrease may possibly admit of some satisfactory explanation; but none is given in the pamphlet before us. The author merely states, in general terms that there had been "a decrease of his Negroes until the year ending in March 1824, but without any specification of its amount. It would have been useful, however, to have pointed out the causes which had produced such a ruinous depopulation previously to his own visit to the island, and the nature of the changes which had arrested the course of that depopulation during the year when he himself was present, and when he appears to have paid that laudable degree of attention to the temporal and spiritual interests of his Slaves, which it were to be wished he could have said had been imitated by the planters generally. This however he gives his readers to understand, was by no means the case. On the contrary almost all the assertions made by the Anti Slavery Society on the subject of the state and condition of the Slaves are fully borne out by the statements of this writer, notwithstanding the caution and reserve with which they are obviously given.

In the Second Report of the Anti Slavery Society just published is the following passage:—

'The depopulation of our Colonies is proceeding at a rate which can be explained on no principle but that of the severity of their treatment. They still labour under the whip without wages. They are still chattels. They are still not the subjects of law, but of individual caprice. They are still without any civil or political rights. Even their marriages are still unsanctioned and unprotected by any legal recognition. Their evidence is still generally inadmissible. Their manumission is still obstructed, and even after being made free they are still liable to be reduced again to Slavery if unable to produce proof of freedom. The master may still sell or transfer them at his pleasure, without any regard to family ties. He alone still regulates the measure of their labour, their food, and their punishment. He may still brand them, whether men or women, in any part of their bodies, with a heated iron, confine them in the stocks, load them with chains, strip them naked and cartwhip them at his pleasure. He may still deprive them of half their night's rest, and leave them no alternative, with respect to the employment of Sunday, but that of toiling for their subsistence or carrying their produce to market, and he may still shut them out from the means of religious instruction. He may thus and in a variety of other ways make their lives bitter with hard bondage.

It may prove useful to take the propositions contained in the above passage in their code, and to compare them with this gentleman's statements. This, therefore, we shall now proceed to do.

Mr De la Beche admits that his own Slaves had hitherto decreased, and authentic documents make that decrease, previously to March 1823, to have been proceeding at the enormous rate of nearly four per cent per annum. He admits also (p 17) that a decrease of Negroes is *very common* on Jamaica estates, and that in some instances this may be owing to ill treatment, but he endeavours to account for it by assigning other causes such as polygamy, promiscuous intercourse, licentiousness, and voluntary abortions. It is very easy to excuse the planters by calling abortions voluntary. But let it be remembered, that the women work in the field and under the whip, as long and as laboriously, as the men, not even pregnant women being excused from their full proportion of labour, until their pregnancy is visible to the eye of the overseer. It is well known however, that most of the abortions take place (the liability to them being then greatest) in the early periods of gestation, and long before any external marks of it are perceivable. And as for their licentious habits, have not these been promoted not merely by the utter neglect of their moral culture but by the profligate example as well as by the seductions of their su periors? There exists not to this hour, in Jamaica a single law encouraging, legalizing or protecting the marriages of Slaves. What can be a more decisive proof of ill treatment than this? Even in Africa, though polygamy prevails, yet the institution of marriage is anxiously maintained and protected; while in the West Indies, Africans and their descendants rank in this respect with the brutes. What signify the Methodist marriages of which this gentleman speaks? These have no legal sanctions; neither indeed have even marriages of Slaves by the established clergy. Admitting therefore all Mr. De la Beche's explanations respecting the causes of depopulation to be just, they still resolve themselves into that grand cause assigned by the Abolitionists —*the ill treatment of the Slaves, and the state of brutish degradation in which they are kept*.

2. They still labour under the whip without wages.

Mr. De la Beche says that he has abolished the use of the whip as a stimulus to labour on his own estate, and that Mr. Hibbert has also abolished it on Albion estate. He adds "Our Negroes have been quite as orderly, if not more so, since the carrying of the driver's whip has been discontinued; and our work is as well done, though I was gravely warned that such innovations would cause every species of insubordination" (p. 17). He does not state however what it is which he has substituted in the place of this stimulus. Had he given wages, it would doubtless have been mentioned. This is a point on which he ought to have been more clear and explicit for the sake of his brother planters, who deny that the whip can be dispensed with. But what is Mr. De la Beche's account of the general practice in this respect? The most common mode of calling the Jamaica Negroes to their labour, (and also from their labour to breakfast, p. 19) is by the cracking of the driver's whip—a "barbarous practice" which he wishes might be discontinued. 'It is much to be regretted,' he adds, "that considerable *martinetism* exists on some properties with regard to the time when the Negroes ought to assemble in the morning; *then it is that the Negroes suffer most from the driver's whip; for he unfortunately can upon his own authority inflict punishment on those who are not in time** thus making him the judge of an excuse that might appear quite valid to the overseer —though I by no means wish to state that the overseers always lean to the side of justice, believing that *not above one half of them are qualified to wield the power that under existing circumstances, must necessarily be entrusted to them*" (p. 19). So that even by the frank admission of this planter, one half of the overseers of Jamaica who have the destiny of the Slaves in their hands are unfit to wield the unlimited authority confided to them. But he goes on 'With very few exceptions the drivers on Jamaica estates carry either whips or cats; on some they are little used, but I am afraid they are not always mere symbols of authority. ' On estates where the whip is permitted as a stimulus to labour, the driver stands near the Negroes when at work *and has the power of inflicting punishment at his own discretion upon those who may to him appear idle; a power, as may easily be imagined, liable to much abuse and which should be abolished* (p. 21). This is decisive language on the part too of one who attributes to the Abolitionists the use of unmeasured invective.

3 "They are still chattels. They are still not the subjects of law, but of individual caprice. They are still without any civil or political rights. Even their marriages are still un-

It will be remembered with what clamour and invective the Rev. Mr. Cooper was assailed as guilty of falsehood and calumny when he made precisely the same statement in the pamphlet entitled *Negro Slavery*

sanctioned and unprotected by any legal recognition.

This last evil has been already adverted to. Mr. De la Beche does not say, that marriage is even now encouraged. All he says is, that "I have never heard or known of a late instance in Jamaica where it was discouraged." And he goes on to account for its infrequency by observing that "the *mass* of the Black population have still a very great objection to this state." Undoubtedly they have; and so would the population of England if the state of the law and of manners was the same in England as in Jamaica. Who would marry in England if there were no law to protect marriage; if the marriage bed could be violated with impunity; if an attempt to resent or punish the violation might be visited, as rebellion, with stripes or with death; if the conjugal tie might be abruptly torn asunder by the will of either party, or by the arbitrary will of third parties, or by their insolvency or death; if the married pair had no interest in their children, they being as much the property and at the disposal of another as the calves or the lambs of the grazier; and above all if no disgrace or discredit or disqualification of any kind attached to either women or men on account of their living in illicit and unrestrained concubinage? Who would marry in England were such the case there? And yet such is the case in Jamaica. Now, surely Mr. De la Beche might have accounted for the objections of the Blacks to marriage on better grounds than that of their non advancement in civilization. Does he mean then to say, that they are not as far advanced in civilization as the Africans are in their native land; as the Hottentots, for example; or as the Indians in North America; or as the Esquimaux, or as the New Hollanders? The near approximation of the Slaves to civilized Europeans, or rather their domestication with them, must, in that case, have operated inversely to its more natural and obvious tendency. But in what nation savage or civilized, except among the Slaves of polished and enlightened Europeans, can he point out so singular a brutishness and debasement of the human nature as is implied in the non existence of marriage among them?

The other evils mentioned above are rather implied in the general tenor of the pamphlet than expressly mentioned in it. They are so obvious however as not to have required any direct recognition; or they will be found involved in the point which follows.

4. 'Their evidence is still generally inadmissible against free persons.'

This is admitted by Mr De la Beche (p. 49) and the utmost he can say is, that some persons in Jamaica and himself among the rest are favourable to the principle of Negro evidence being admitted. But what a total destitution of all civil and political rights, and what an exposure to individual caprice is implied in the inadmissibility of their evidence!

5. 'Their manumission is still obstructed.'

In Jamaica, a bond for 100*l.* was required on the manumission of every Slave; and in a variety of cases of mortgaged or contested property, or where the owner was a minor, manumission was not practicable. The necessity of giving the bond in question Mr De la Beche says has recently been dispensed with; although it would appear from the act of which he gives an abstract, that even this dispensation is partial. That act professes to give facilities to manumissions; but it does so very ineffectually; indeed it is little better than a mockery. What is chiefly wanted is not a law enabling *Masters* in certain specified cases to *grant* manumissions; but entitling the *Slaves* to *claim* and to *obtain* their freedom whenever they have the means of paying for it at a fair and equitable appraisement.—

On this point, Mr De la Beche contrary to his usual candour is so far infected by West Indian prejudices, as to object to giving to the Negro a power of purchasing his own freedom, or that of his wife and children. And the reason he assigns for entertaining this objection is not a little singular. 'To those who possess local knowledge*, or have made themselves acquainted with the Negro character difficulties will present themselves which if not guarded against by some regulations, might involve the planter in great embarrassment; for his best and most industrious people are alone likely to avail themselves of this right, and he therefore would be saddled with the worthless and unprofitable, with whom he would be unable to cultivate the property.' (p. 50.) Now let any man weigh this mode of reasoning—and it is one which it is to be feared prevails very generally in the West Indies—and what will he find to be its result but the condemnation of the whole Negro race to perpetual and irreclaimable Slavery? The industrious and deserving are too good to be parted with, even at their fair price; and of course the worthless and unprofitable are never likely to obtain those means of redemption which must be the fruit either of their own industry, or of their master's favour. What a system must that of West India slavery be which could even suggest to the mind of a benevolent man such an objection as this, and still more which could induce him seriously to entertain and publicly to urge it! If a proof were wanting of the absolute necessity of parliamentary interference, to remove the obstacles to manumission, it would be found in the view taken of the subject by Mr De la Beche.

* This gentleman's local knowledge was not very extensive. But even had it been much more so, there often exists along with it such a thing as local prejudice which is apt to grow in a like proportion.

6. 'Even after being made free they are still liable to be reduced again to slavery if unable to produce proof of freedom.'

Mr De la Beche says nothing on this enormity. Had it ceased to exist he would doubtless have stated the fact. But there is abundant proof of its continuance at the very time he himself resided in the island. In the Jamaica Gazette of July 3. 1824 there appears the following advertisement:—

Kingston Workhouse, May 28. 1824.

Notice is hereby given, That unless the undermentioned Slave is taken out of this workhouse prior to Monday the 26th day of July next, he will, on that day, between the hours of ten and twelve o'clock in the forenoon, be put up to public sale, and sold to the highest and best bidder at Harty's Tavern, in this city, agreeably to the Workhouse Law in force, for payment of his fees.

William Hall, a Portuguese African Negro man, says that he was sold on the coast when a boy to a Captain Roper, who commanded a ship called the Eliza, with whom *he went to England twice,* and *finally ran away from him while there,* and came to Jamaica in the ship Duke, Captain Smith, as a servant in lieu of passage money, and has ever since been here.———By order of the Commissioners.

" Henry Broughton, Supr."

Now, here we have a Negro man claimed as a Slave by no one, accused of no crime, but who is seized as a runaway, put in jail, and at last sold for the payment of his jail fees. Where is he now, and what is his condition? He had been twice in England. The last time he was there he quitted the only person who could claim any title to him, and asserted, as he had a good right to do, his liberty; but going to Jamaica, and living there for some time, he is at length, in that Christian land, in that land which boasts its free, its British constitution, seized and sold as a Slave. What worse could have happened to him at Algiers or Tunis? But ought not the Secretary of State for his Majesty's Colonies to interfere in a case of this atrocious nature, where under the pretended operation of law administered in the King's name, men entitled to his protection are thus made the subjects of the most odious and brutal oppression? What signify our Abolition Laws if such scandalous acts of kidnapping and Slave trading can take place *openly* and *legally* too (if the word *legal* will admit of such a prostitution,) in the largest city in the British West Indies, and within a few miles of the residence of a British governor? If a foreign state were thus to treat a British subject, it would be regarded as justly furnishing a cause of war. But here, in one of our own colonies, the local authorities have the audacity to seize and enslave, and in open day and by public auction vend for his jail fees a man who by the laws of England had obtained his freedom and was as fully entitled to preserve it unimpaired as the superintendant of the workhouse or as the Duke of Manchester himself. Is there no process by which such an atrocious transaction as this can be brought before some competent tribunal?

But to take another instance no less flagrant. In the Royal Gazette of Jamaica, of the 18th September 1824, is contained the following advertisement:—

Manchester Workhouse, Aug. 4, 1824.

Notice is hereby given, That unless the under mentioned Slaves are taken out of this workhouse prior to Wednesday the 29th day of September next, they will on that day between the hours of ten and twelve o'clock in the forenoon be put up to public sale and sold to the highest and best bidder, at the *Court House* Mandeville agreeably to the Workhouse Law now in force for payment of their fees.

Fearon Davidson, a Creole, 4 feet 11 inches. She has a little girl with her, and has been delivered of a male child since she has been in this workhouse, says she is free and that John Davidson, a free Brown man of Kingston, is her father.——By order of the Commissioners.

John Hollingsworth, Supr.

It was only in September last that this outrageous violation of humanity and justice was perpetrated under the operation of what in mockery is called *law* in the island of Jamaica, and that not covertly but openly. A female, the mother of two children, one recently born, is confined in jail without a pretext of any kind for her arrest and imprisonment, and without a single reason being assigned for it, is doomed with her children to perpetual slavery. Much has been said of the violence and acrimony which mark the writings of the Abolitionists towards the West Indians. It may be, and certainly is, unjustifiable to employ violent or acrimonious language towards the West Indians themselves. But it would be something less than human to contemplate such fruits of the system which they administer as this, without horror and indignation. It is impossible not to press these matters on the attention of the Secretary of State for the Colonies. Can it be that such transactions as these do not meet the eye either of himself or of those who are employed under him? Is there no one to be found who will direct a moment's attention to the observation of our authorities? They have only to cast an eye over the Jamaica newspapers in order to discover them. After all that has been made known of the abuses of the West Indian system, and after the solemn pledges given by Government and Parliament, must it be left to accident to detect and expose such crimes as these, crimes of the very worst description under the colour of law,—of law, however, which is such an outrage on all law as could not be tolerated by any set of men not previously prepared for them by the presence and influence of Negro Slavery?

7. 'The master may still sell or transfer them at his pleasure without any regard to family ties. He alone still regulates the measure of their labour, their food and their punishment. He may still brand them, whether men or women, in any part of their bodies with a heated iron, confine them in the stocks, load them with chains, strip them naked and cartwhip them at his pleasure.'

Now it has been positively asserted by various writers on the side of the Colonists, that the laws of the West Indies do not permit family ties to be broken. Such assertions only prove either the gross ignorance or the wilful falsification of fact on the part of such writers. Mr De la Beche is superior to practising any such deception, he says, 'Families ought *never* to be separated, nor is it by any means *so* common a practice *as formerly*, still however laws cannot be too soon enacted (they are not then as yet enacted) 'to prevent the possibility of this being done.' Are such things then actually done, or is the absence of law supplied by a sense of humanity in practice? Let the recent Gazettes of Jamaica answer the question. In that of the 16th October, 1824, stand the following advertisements:—

Deputy Marshal's Office, Kingston Oct 9 1824.

'VENDITIONIS returnable October Grand Court 1824

'Campbell Alex esquire exor, vs Thos Hardy free Black

'Hamilton Robert esquire vs Same Fishley & al esquires admors vs Same

'James, a Black, a mason supposed age 30 years

'Jack ditto ditto supposed age 36 years

Billy ditto ditto supposed age 34 years

Hale & al merchants vs Anthony Gutzmer jun esquire

"Maria, a Black, a waiting girl supposed age 13 years

Chamberlain & al practitioners, vs Michael Hughes mason

"William Gilbert, a Black, a mason, supposed age 35 years

'*Bravo Abraham merchant vs Edward Boyden Gent*

'Joe a Black a waiting boy supposed age 12 years

Glen Frances of colour vs Robt Chamberlain esquire

Betty a Black, a drudge supposed age 32 years

Barclay Andrew druggist vs Abraham Alex Lindo esquire

Edinburgh a Black a labourer supposed age 50 years

George ditto a waiter supposed age 26 years

Take notice, That I shall put up to public sale at Harty's Tavern on Monday the 25th inst between the hours of 10 and 12 o'clock in the forenoon the above Negroes, levied upon under and by virtue of the foregoing writs of *venditioni exponas*

Also the following five Convicts to be sold for transportation

'Betsy Morgan, Nick *alias* Edward Bartly, William Bond, Prince, and Chance

Wm Rose, D M

Deputy Marshal's Office Kingston Oct 2 1824.

VENDITIONIS returnable October Grand Court 1824

M Bayne & al, vs John Orr dec in hands of Joseph Donnell esquire admor

'Susanna a Black a washer supposed age 45 years

Stephen (her son) ditto a waiting boy supposed age 12 years

Allick (ditto), ditto, ditto supposed age 6 years

George (ditto) ditto supposed age 3 years

Nancy (her daughter), ditto supposed age 1½ year

Duffus Wm Gent, vs Winckworth Tonge dec in hands of Wm James Murphy admor

John Young a Black a field Negro supposed age 35 years

Salentin, L. L. merchant, vs John B. Cadou, Gent.
Jane, a Black, a drudge, supposed age 34 years
Louisa (her daughter), ditto supposed age 3 years

Mois, John, esquire, vs Mary Marquis of colour
Prudence, a Black, a drudge supposed age 35 years

M Mickan, Gilbert Gordon, vs John Lodge of colour
Bella, a Black, a drudge supposed age 33 years

' Bogle, Janet, of colour vs Wm. Henry Sowley, Gent.
" Joe, a Black, a sailor, supposed age 30 years

Millward & al, attorneys at law vs Wm. Geo. Mowatt, of colour
George, a Black, a waiting boy supposed age 6 years

Rieusett, Leonora Sarah, widow vs Elizabeth Crichton, widow, in hands of Edward and Joseph Boyden, exors.
' Henry, a Black, a waiter, supposed age 30 years

Henry Peter, Gent., vs James M'Queen, of colour
A Cart and three Chaise Bodies

' Muler, Alex., merchant vs Frances Woollery, of colour
' Benjamin, a Black, a hair dresser, supposed age 20 years

Miskelly, John, Gent., vs Robert Rainford, Gent.
' A Dun Horse

' Grant, Alex, & al exors vs James Oughton
A Bay Horse

' Take notice, That I shall put up to public sale, at Harty's Tavern, on Monday the 18th inst. between the hours of 10 and 12 o'clock in the forenoon, the above Negroes, Cart, Chaise Bodies and Horses levied upon under and by virtue of the foregoing writs of *venditioni exponas.* William Rose, D. M.

Portland, Sept. 28, 1824.

Notice is hereby given, That on Tuesday the 12th day of the ensuing month of October, between the hours of 10 and 12 in the forenoon, I shall set up to public sale, at the Court House of this parish the following Negro Slaves distrained on for taxes and arrears of taxes against Charles Bernard, Esq. and Mill Bank, namely,
Samuel Cochran, a field man
' Isabella Bernard, a field woman
Flora Bernard, ditto
Frances Bernard, ditto
Judy Bernard, ditto

John Steel, C. O.

St. Andrew's, Oct. 6, 1824.

Take notice, That on Wednesday the 20th inst. I shall put up to public sale at Harty's Tavern in Kingston, between the hours of 10 and 12 o'clock in the forenoon, a field Negro boy named Amos, levied on for taxes due by Mr. Joseph Fry.

P. Pinnock, C. C.

Deputy Marshal's Office, Kingston, Oct. 16, 1824.

' VENDITIONI S returnable February Grand Court, 1825

' Desgouttes, Lewis, esquire vs Peter De Gourney, planter
Same vs Same
Same vs Same
Eliza, a Black, a drudge, supposed age 30 years
Mary, ditto, a field Negro, supposed age 38 years
' Thomas, ditto, a carpenter, supposed age 34 years
' Charles, ditto, a cartman, supposed age 30 years
' Moss, ditto, ditto, supposed age 30 years
Antoine, ditto, a mason, supposed age 30 years
' Terrice, ditto, a waiting girl supposed age 25 years
Thomas (her son) ditto, a waiting boy, supposed age 7 years
Benjamin, ditto, a driver, supposed age 35 years
Gillott, ditto, a car man, supposed age 30 years
Gabriel, ditto, a waiter, supposed age 24 years
La Croix, ditto, a carman, supposed age 30 years
' Charlotte, ditto, a cook, supposed age 50 years
" Edmund, ditto, a muleman, supposed age 20 years

'John, ditto, a field Negro supposed age 30 years

'Eleanor ditto, a grass cutter; supposed age 35 years

'Cudjoe, ditto, a cartman supposed age 35 years

VENDITIONI returnable Nov. Court of Common Pleas, 1824.

"*Bravo, Abraham, merchant*, vs *John Ashburn, of colour.*

"Hagar, a Black, a drudge supposed age 18 years

Take notice, That I shall put up to public sale, at Harty's Tavern on Monday the 1st day of November next between the hours of 10 and 12 o'clock in the forenoon, the above Negroes, levied upon under and by virtue of the foregoing writs of venditioni exponas

Wm. Rose D. M.

St. Andrew's Oct. 9. 1824

'Take notice. That on Monday the 25th inst. I shall put up to public sale, at Harty's Tavern in Kingston between the hours of ten and twelve o'clock in the forenoon, a Negro girl named Olive, a house servant, levied on for taxes due by Mullet Hall Plantation the property of the late Robert Chamberlain Esq. dec. P. Pinnock C. C.

Now all these advertisements occur in a single week in the Royal Gazette of Kingston. What further advertisements of the same descriptions in the same week might be found in the newspapers of Spanish Town and Montego Bay, it is impossible to say. But here, in this one paper is enough for our present purpose—is enough to furnish the most conclusive evidence of the fact of the frequent disruption, by sale, of the nearest and dearest family ties. The instances of a contrary kind are rather the exception than the rule

But it would be altogether to misapprehend the extent of the evil which arises from the transferable nature of this species of property to suppose that the above advertisements comprise all the transactions even of that one week which go to attest that Slaves are chattels, the mere objects of an unceremonious and brutal traffic, literally ranking them with the beasts of the field. Taking this same one week's Gazette of the 16th of October 1824, besides the sales already enumerated, there may be found in it advertisements for the sale of about 1,900 Negroes, chiefly under decrees of the Court of Chancery. These are advertised to be sold either together or in families, and with or without the land. For example:—

Portland Aug. 24, 1824

'To be sold Mount Oakley including Lydart 322 acres and three rods with the buildings, 60 Slaves, 23 cattle and 57 sheep or, if more agreeable a part of the land and Negroes as may be most desirable to a purchaser. Time will be allowed for the payment, by instalments on giving good and sufficient security. This property is well known to be a very healthy and pleasant residence.—Apply to the proprietor on the property

"Thomas Oakley

Oct. 16. 1824

"For sale, Twickenham park, in the parish of St. Ann on which there is a spacious dwelling house, out offices, barbicues &c. &c. The situation is very healthy, and is a most desirable residence for a family. The property contains 400 acres of land cultivated in Guinea Grass subdivided in pastures and pimento walks. It has two springs of water one of which has supplied the neighbourhood in the late drought. There are 50 able Slaves, who are also for sale and if not sold with the property, they will be disposed of in families to suit purchasers. Application to be made to James Betty Esq. Crescent Park, St. Ann's Mr. Netlam Tory Kingston or to the subscriber, on the property. John Williams

Let any one conceive the dismay and devastation which the sale of such gangs in lots must produce. What becomes now of their houses their provision grounds*, their former associates? And what a gloomy and uncertain futurity awaits them! Death may have deprived them of a kind and indulgent master whose very kindness may now serve no other purpose but to embitter their present destiny. They may be doomed to form part of a jobbing gang, the only consideration with the master of which may be, how many doubloons he can extract from them by the power of the cart whip, before they are ground down to their native dust. Of jobbing gangs Mr De la Beche himself observes, that their lot is worse than that of the plantation slaves, having generally hard labour to perform, and frequently far from their own homes, when they are obliged to take up with the temporary huts which have little appearance of comfort (p. 34.)

Then as to the other parts of the picture, there cannot surely be a more decisive witness than Mr De la Beche. Though the drivers on Halse Hall are not permitted to carry whips, neither are they allowed to punish of their own authority (p. 5.), yet even there the Slaves may be punished at the will of the master, or in his absence, of the overseer, by the stoppage of extra allowances, by confinement in the stocks, by switching, and, in bad cases, by the whip. Though *he* has abolished the whip as respects women, yet he is obliged to express his " surprise " at the continuance of a practice so revolting (p. 45.) And he admits, as has been already seen, that, ' with very few exceptions, the drivers on Jamaica estates carry either whips or cats, and

We hear much of the rights of property *practically* allowed to the Slaves. What becomes of their property in cases like this, cases too of continual recurrence? In a single week we find in one newspaper of one island about 2,000 Slaves advertised for sale, and thus exposed to be torn from their domiciles and to lose in a moment much if not all of what they had been collecting around them, perhaps during their whole lives.

that, when they do, " *the driver has the power of inflicting punishment, at his own discretion, upon those who may to him appear idle* a power, he adds, liable to much abuse (pp. 20, 21.) ' The usual method of punishing Negroes is by the whip, cat o' nine tails, and switch*, or by confinement in the stocks. This last he thinks should be generally adopted as far as respects women, instead of the *present* disgraceful custom of flogging them. And though he thinks this custom not now common, yet he says there is no excuse for not doing it away entirely (p. 33.)

Again, though on his own estate he gives his people an allowance of food, yet he ingenuously adds that it is only in a few lowland districts that the people have such allowance; elsewhere the people supply themselves with the produce of their own labour (p. 23.) When the proprietor is an absentee, he gives a power of attorney to some gentleman in whom he has confidence. The attorney then occupies the situation of the proprietor, and directs the management of his property, appointing overseers &c. Some gentlemen are attorneys for many properties. (p. 36.)

" These arrangements, observes Mr De la Beche, ' would not affect the comforts of the Negroes, IF the attorney took the same interest in them that the proprietor must necessarily do; but *here matters become altered for the interest of the attorney* (he being paid a percentage on the produce) " *is to make as much as possible from the estate, and the Negroes become only a secondary consideration* Attorneys having the management of many estates, can seldom inspect them. " They are in consequence often entirely left to the overseers, with the exception perhaps of a yearly or half yearly

* This switch which is spoken of in such modest terms is usually an ebony bush full of small prickles, and if smartly applied draws blood from the posteriors at every stroke.

visit. Another evil arises from this system. The overseers look up to this person for patronage, and seldom or never trouble their heads about the proprietors; they study his interest before that of the proprietors, and think more of making large crops to benefit their employer, than they do of improving the condition of the people (p 37.) The comforts of the Negroes depend therefore greatly on the overseers (of whom he had before said, that not more than one half were fit for their situation,) for these persons constantly reside among them, and have it in their power to exercise a petty tyranny over them. It is true they can and do complain to the attorney, for which purpose they undertake long journeys; yet I am afraid there is sometimes a leaning to the side of the overseer from an idea of supporting the White people on the estate. 'For any serious act of injustice (what would be considered in Jamaica as a *serious act of injustice?*) the Negroes complain to the magistrates, who, it is but fair to state, most commonly see them righted. The comforts of the people may still however be seriously affected by the conduct of the overseer, should he not be a humane man; a circumstance not always sufficiently attended to in his appointment (p 38.) Upon many properties even the book keepers (generally raw lads from school) 'are permitted to order punishment; a practice that should not be allowed (p 39.) And besides all this Mr De la Beche states that at the various workhouses (there is one in every parish) 'Negroes are often sent by individuals to receive punishment which ought never to be done but under the authority of the magistrates; implying that it is now done without that authority (p 46.)

But before we conclude this head it will be necessary to say a few words on the practice of branding. Mr De la Beche does not deny its prevalence. On the contrary, he has the candour to admit that, on his own estate three were branded so recently as 1822 or 1823. He adds "it was wished to punish the overseer who had caused them to be branded but *as the operation had been performed by heating the small silver brand in burning spirits and had been applied only for an instant to the back it was by no means certain that we could do so.* And yet, by way of palliating the practice he gives the particulars of three convictions for *cruel* branding. One man, Joseph Boyden, was charged with cruelly, maliciously and wantonly maltreating, by flogging, and marking in five different parts of her body with the initials of his name and that of his estate, a Sambo Slave named Amey. He was found guilty. He was sentenced to *six months imprisonment* and the Slave was made free. In another case, the same crime is stated to have been perpetrated with a *hot iron* probably such an iron as when heated red hot is used to brand casks with. The culprit, a black smith of the name of Lee was sentenced to four months imprisonment and a fine of 100*l*. and the girl was declared free and entitled to an annuity of 10*l* a year for life. In the third instance a female was branded on the breasts probably in the same horrid manner by a wretch of the name of Cadore who got off for a fine of 100*l*., the sufferer being manumitted. In these cases there must have been some circumstances of peculiar atrocity which ensured conviction and a measure of punishment but for branding with a silver brand heated with burning spirits, though described by Mr De la Beche as 'an abominable practice' there is it seems no punishment. It may legally be inflicted by any ruffian on any man woman or child placed under his authority and 'brutal characters when possessed of power will abuse it' (p 27.) There is at least no law against *branding*, unless it is accompanied by such wanton cruelty as a jury will be found to regard and to punish as a nuisance. Mr De la Beche thinks that instances of branding are now rare. He is mistaken, and the Jamaica newspapers prove that he is so.

Let him only look at the Royal Gazettes of Jamaica, that, for example of the 19th to the 26th June 1824, while he himself was in the island, and abundant proof will there be found of the frequency of the practice, at least at no distant period. The following are notices of Slaves advertised, either for sale or as runaways:—

" Elizabeth Francis, a Creole, marked G F, G F below, not plain on the right shoulder.

' William Bullock, a Creole, marked T S, heart on top, on left shoulder.

' Fin, a *young* Creole Negro boy, marked S on right shoulder.

" Edward Frazer, a Mulatto Creole man, marked R S on shoulder.

" William *alias* Harry, a Creole, marked apparently I A on right shoulder.

" William Slater, a Creole *boy*, has blister marks on the left, and marked A S on the right shoulder.

" Frank, a *young* Creole Sambo man, mark not plain on right shoulder.

" Robert Henry, a *young* Creole man, marked M R *about* the shoulders.

' Sam, a *young* Creole Negro man, marked G J on right shoulder.

" Robert, a *young* Creole Negro man, marked apparently T R P on left shoulder. &c. &c.

8. " He may still deprive them of half their night's rest, and he may leave them no alternative with respect to the employment of Sunday, but that of toiling for their subsistence, or carrying their produce to market, and he may still shut them out from the means of religious instruction."

On the subject of night work, Mr De la Beche is very frank and explicit. ' During crop time, he says, " which generally lasts about four months, the Negroes are, in consequence of being but comparatively few on this estate, divided into two spells, which relieve each other, thus allowing half the night for work and half for rest, besides be it remembered, working all day. The law forbids working the mill on Sunday night, or after a certain hour on Saturday night."

Mr De la Beche appears to entertain a most honourable solicitude for the religious instruction of his own Slaves, and he engaged one of the Wesleyan Missionaries to attend them once a fortnight in the evening. The Jamaica markets however, are still held on Sundays, but he says that a Saturday market is beginning to grow up in Kingston, owing greatly to the exertions of the Baptist and Wesleyan Missionaries. The only measure which the legislature have taken in the way of encouraging the change has been to avail themselves of the circumstance to prevent their Slaves from being levied on for debt on the Saturday as well as on the Sunday. This however is still more for their own benefit than for that of the Slave.

The religious and moral instruction of the Negroes Mr De la Beche admits, has been very little attended to until lately. The curates appointed some years ago have done little, generally speaking, in this way. Indeed little religious improvement among the Negroes has been effected by the Established Clergy, except in two or three districts. ' Hundreds of Negroes have no doubt been baptized, but the ceremony seems to have been considered as sufficient, no religious instruction having been afforded either before or after. The common though not perhaps the universal, practice has been, to assemble numbers of the Negroes together, they are merely asked what their names are to be, and are then baptized *en masse*, the rector receiving half a dollar for each (p. 27.)—" It is only justice to add, that instances have occurred in which the offers of some of the clergy to instruct the Negroes, have been very ungraciously received, and even refused by the managers of estates. A different spirit he says, *begins* now to prevail: and he hopes that *ere long* all the Negroes will be instructed—much being expected from the bishop.* (p. 28.) Mr De la Beche ascribes whatever progress Christianity is now making to the Wesleyan and Baptist Missionaries: the former of whom especially he represents as a highly useful body of men. The supineness of the clergy he does not consider however, as a ground of blame on the people of Jamaica: who, he says, have nothing else to do with their appointments, than to pay the salaries attached to them. And yet he admits that the services of the clergy have often been refused: nor does he say that any effort has been made to stimulate their exertions, except the questionable one of giving them half a dollar for each act of baptism.

Mr De la Beche, it will be allowed, after this detail, is an important witness in confirmation of almost all that the Abolitionists have affirmed or sanctioned on the subject of Negro Slavery. His book however contains further matter which calls for some remarks: and these the respectability of the writer makes it the more expedient not to withhold. He meant doubtless to be fair and candid: but then he must, as a planter, naturally wish to convey as favourable an impression of his own occupation as possible: and his opportunities of accurate observation, during the twelve months he was in the island, with much to employ him on his own estate, could not have been such as to exempt him from error. He must have depended much on the information of others: and that information was not likely to be quite impartial. It is probably to this cause that the mistakes into which he has fallen in some instances may be ascribed.

In fairness he ought to have distinctly informed his readers that his description of the state of things on his own estate had little or no application to plantations generally: and he ought to have afforded some explanation of the causes of the large decrease of his own Slaves which had preceded his arrival.

Mr De la Beche concurs with every other writer in representing the labour of sugar planting as greater than that incident to every other species of culture. 'On cattle farms and coffee plantations they have no night work: neither have they cane holes to dig, which is hard labour when the land has not been previously ploughed.' He ought to have added, that the plough is scarcely ever used in Jamaica.

He states, that the labour of the Negroes begins at five in the morning during half of the year: and at half past five during the other: and continues till seven or half past six in the evening: with an interval of half an hour for breakfast, and two hours for dinner—so that their actual work in the field, independently of the labour of going to it and returning from it, is protracted from ten hours and a half to eleven hours and a half. He entirely omits, however, all mention of the heavy task which is further imposed upon them after the labour of the day is over, of collecting grass for the horses and cattle on the estate, and which occupies at

* Two circumstances serve to damp this expectation. The first act of the bishop's administration was to appoint the Rev. Mr Bridges his chaplain: a man notoriously opposed to all reform: and the thorough going advocate of a system of which Mr De la Beche though no clergyman has exhibited so dark a picture. The second was to give, probably under Mr Bridges's dictation, a somewhat repulsive answer to a very respectful address of the People of Colour of Kingston. To these may be added, a most extraordinary official despatch addressed by him to Lord Bathurst, which has been laid before the House of Commons.

least an hour more of their time making it eight o'clock before they can get to their huts, or set about preparing their supper,—all this too being exclusive of the night work of crop time. There are, besides, in his detailed statements certain little unintentional inaccuracies which serve to produce a false impression, such as —" their breakfast has been prepared and brought to the field by cooks" whereas it is first brought to the field by the Negroes themselves, and there prepared by cooks —Again " from choice they defer their principal repast till the evening" Not from choice but necessity, the interval allowed at noon being wholly insufficient to go home light a fire, prepare a comfortable meal and eat it before they must be again in the field. He labours also to prove that Negroes prefer bad houses to good ones (p 26). He bears a remarkable testimony, however, to the voluntary industry of the Negroes, which dissipates at once all the calumnies on that score of which they have been made the victims. He represents them, after having been toiling in the field, under a tropical sun, from five in the morning until half past twelve, seven hours and a half, as devoting the interval of rest to the cultivation of their provision grounds which in his case (a very rare one) happen to be near their houses while their children are employed by them in collecting food for their pigs although they also form a gang (from six to nine years of age) which is at work, like their parents, during the day (p 7)

' It is generally agreed' says Mr De la Beche, ' that punishment is by no means so common as it used to be and that the general improvement in the treatment of the people is considerable (p 34) This is possible and yet it is remarkable, that such has been the uniform language of planters from the year 1787 to the present day All admitted the badness of the treatment at some preceding period, and maintained the existence in their own day of great improvement And yet the Slaves still decrease they are still chattels, they are still without marriage, they are still driven at their work, they are still cart whipped, and they are still subject to the arbitrary power of overseers not more than one half of whom, M De la Beche allows, are fit to be trusted with the care of them These are not very pregnant proofs of improvement But he would infer from the familiarity with which they are often treated by their masters and mistresses, and the gaiety they exhibit in their dances and on their festivals that the statements given of the unhappiness of Slavery are exaggerated and that it is not that depressing institution which many suppose There cannot however, be a more unwarranted inference and it is precisely what has deceived many who have had only a passing glimpse of West Indian Slavery But when we contemplate even Mr De la Beche's own admissions with respect to their state, in what light can we view their joyousness on certain occasions but as marking the obtuseness of feeling which Slavery never fails to engender? It resembles the revels of London during the plague, or the Saturnalia of the Romans and is so far from proving that the Slaves are not a depressed race that, under all the circumstances of the case it is one of the indications of their extreme depression

It is due to Mr De la Beche to state, that he cordially approves of almost all the reforms proposed by Government and that he condemns the Jamaica Assembly for having refused to adopt them On the whole the public are greatly indebted to him for his seasonable publication

LITERARY AND PHILOSOPHICAL INTELLIGENCE,
&c. &c.

GREAT BRITAIN

Preparing for publication.—A Commentary on the Psalms, by Mrs Thompson.—Miscellaneous Writings of Evelyn, by Mr Upcott.—Documentary Supplement to "Who wrote Icon Basilike?" by the Rev. Dr Wordsworth.

In the press.—A full Answer to the Rev. T. Baddeley's "Sure Way to find out the true Religion," by the Rev. J. Richardson.—Annotations on the Gospels and Acts of the Apostles, by the Rev. W. Wass, M.A. F.S.A.

Oxford.—Convocation has accepted a proposal from the Rev. Dr Ellerton to found an annual Prize of Twenty Guineas for the best English Essay on some doctrine or duty of the Christian Religion, or on some subject of theology which shall be deemed meet and useful.

The prizes for the year 1825 have been awarded to the following gentlemen:—Latin Verse, "Incendium Londinense anno 1666," E. P. Blunt, of Corpus.—Latin Essay, "De Tribunicia apud Romanos potestate," F. Oakley, B.A. Christ Church.—English Essay, "Language in its copiousness and structure considered as a test of national civilization," J. W. Mylne, B.A. Balliol.—Sir Roger Newdigate's Prize English Verse, "The Temple of Vesta at Tivoli," R. C. Sewell, of Magdalen.

A volume has been published by the Rev. W. Innes, entitled "The Christian Ministry," consisting of extracts from the works of Baxter, Watts, Alleine, Witherspoon, Dr Erskine, Henry Martyn, Brainerd, Cecil, and Robert Hall. Most of our clerical readers are doubtless acquainted with the valuable collection of treatises on the pastoral charge, collected by the late Bishop Randolph, and printed at the Clarendon press, in a volume entitled "the Clergyman's Instructor," containing Herbert's "Priest to the Temple," Jeremy Taylor's "Rules and Advices," Burnet's "Pastoral Care," with treatises on the same subjects by Bishops Sprat, Bull, Gibson, and Hort. Mr Innes's extracts form a highly valuable companion to this work, and they enter, as might be expected from the names of the respective writers, with great earnestness into the most intimate *sacra privata* of the subject, as respects the state of mind of the minister himself, and his spiritual preparation for the right discharge of his arduous office.

A work highly useful to Biblical Students has just been published, in three closely printed volumes, price 3*l.* entitled "Scientia Biblica," containing the New Testament in Mill's edition of the Greek text, and the authorised English version, with a copious and original collection of parallel passages printed at length. The parallel passages which have been collected with great care and application, are particularly adapted to the use of the clergy, for quotation, comparison, or selection, in the composition of sermons, without the labour and distraction of mind of turning to scores and hundreds of passages from the usual marginal references.

The act for regulating weights and measures, which was to have come into operation on the 1st of May, is deferred to the 1st of January 1826.

At a late meeting of the Asiatic Society of London, several Burmese articles were presented. Among others, a Burmese sabre of a very rude and awkward shape, and a copy of a curious Burmese book, the letters of which are in mother o' pearl. It is of an oblong shape, and composed either of wood or pasteboard lackered.

The Prayer book of Charles I. used by him at his execution, was lately sold by auction for one hundred guineas. The work is folio, partly black letter, bound in Russia, originally purple, but now much faded, with arms and cover in gold. On the leaf of the preface is written, "King Charles the First's own Prayer book;" and "Ex Libris Biblioth. Presby. Dumf. Ex dono Joan. Hutton, M.D. 1714." On the title page of the Psalter is "Carolus R." supposed to be the autograph of the unfortunate monarch. This book is reported to have been given by the king at his execution to Dr Hutton, and presented by him as a relic to the Presbytery of Dumfries. It is stated that it afterwards became the property of a gentleman named Mair, and at his death was put up for sale, but the Presbytery of Dumfries declared that it had been surreptitiously removed from their library, and threatened proceedings at law to recover it, and were only deterred from instituting them by their inability to shew how they lost the possession, the law of Scot land requiring that as the first step towards regaining possession of any moveable property

Captain Clifford has brought to England a most valuable manuscript upon Papyrus of a portion of Homer's Iliad belonging to Mr Bankes the Member for Cambridge University. The MS was discovered in the island of Elephantina, in Upper Egypt by a French gentleman travelling for Mr Bankes. It is written in Uncial letters and is ascribed to the age of the Ptolemies. It is alleged to be by many centuries the oldest classical writing in existence

A curious antiquarian discovery was lately made within the ruins of Glastonbury Abbey by a party of gentlemen engaged in searching after the hitherto unexplored antiquities of that consecrated monastery. On sinking a pit four yards square to the depth of 5 or 6 feet, they found the crown of a nearly semicircular or Anglo Norman arch of beautiful and elaborate masonry similar in pattern to the lozenge like ornaments of the windows of St Joseph's chapel. They also found a flight of winding steps leading to this subterraneous arched recess and a small well overhung and protected by the costly arch that rose above it. This secret chamber and sacred well seem to have been used for the purposes of miraculous cure for tradition speaks of the holy water as well as the holy thorn of Joseph of Arimathea but no visible evidence of its existence was known to remain till the development of the crypt in question. Mr Reeves, the recent purchaser of the Abbey domain has directed the subterraneous chamber with its staircase arch well and pavement to be cleansed and restored as nearly as possible to its primitive condition

Silicum the supposed metal of flint has been obtained in a separate state and proves to be of a dark nut brown colour without the least metallic lustre

The first chain of that stupendous work the Menai Bridge near Bangor has been thrown over the straits. The extreme length of the chain from the fastenings in the rocks is about 1600 feet. The road on the bridge is to consist of two carriage ways of 12 feet each with a footpath of four feet in the centre

The face of a church clock may be easily rendered as legible in the night as in the day. This has for some years been exemplified at the Tron Church in Glasgow. A gas lantern is supported at several feet distant from the upper part of the clock face on which side only it is glazed. A gas pipe supplies the lantern and another is used for lighting it. It effects this by means of a row of small holes along its whole length from the ground. The lamplighter by means of cocks within his reach in the street turns the gas into both these pipes and after waiting a proper time for it to ascend to the lantern he applies his flambeau to the jet of gas issuing from the lowest of the holes in the subsidiary or flash pipe, the flame from which instantly communicates to the jet next above it and so on until in a few moments this chain of flame enters the lantern and lights the burner of the main pipe which being perceived by the illumination on the clock face the flash cock is then turned off and no further attendance is needed

SOUTH AFRICA

The South African Advertiser contains the following extract from a letter from Graaf Reinet — This morning several of the inhabitants were attracted by a cloud which had made its appearance about a mile eastward of the town and it was soon ascertained that this phenomenon was occasioned by a vast swarm of migratory locusts the first which have made their appearance in this neighbourhood since 1808. They are still young and though their numbers in comparison with the immense swarms with which some of us have had formerly to contend may be termed few they are sufficiently numerous to astonish those who have lately come among us and they cause no small degree of anxiety to the farmer who knows by experience what they may become in a season or two, if Providence be not pleased to arrest so dreadful a visitation

INDIA

Private letters and the public journals from India continue to teem with such accounts as the following. When will the arm of authority interpose as so easily and effectually it might its benign efforts to abolish this inhuman custom?

Sulkea Dec 31 1824 —Yesterday a suttee took place near the godowns of the late Mr Jones. A gentleman hearing of the circumstance proceeded to the spot in hopes of preventing it but was unfortunately too late. On inquiry he was given to understand that the victim was a fine young woman about sixteen. No intoxicating drugs were administered to her at the pile but they had been given at the house of the deceased. She was obliged to walk round the bier of the deceased and as soon as she fell down exhausted the vile Brahmins secured her with bamboos and prevented the possibility of escape There was a man present enjoying the sight, with a spear in his hand who called himself a chowkeydar by him the gentleman who inquired for the order of the magistrate was referred to the darogah who was represented to be near at a subordinate police station Thither the gentleman went and found the darogah enjoying a chillum who on being asked for a sight of the perwanah said that he had received one authorizing the sacrifice but that he had left it at Sulkea! All the Brahmins but one skulked away on hearing the gentleman making inquiries and it is worthy of remark that the man only died in the morning nevertheless a report must have been made to the magistrate permission granted and intimation thereof sent across the river within the space of about four hours Credat Judæus!

A subscription is in progress amongst the Unitarians in India and in England towards enabling Ram Mohun Roy and Mr Adam a Unitarian missionary to build a chapel at Calcutta This coalition seems to speak as little in favour of the Christian complexion of modern Unitarianism as did the celebrated letter and epistle dedicatory to the Mohammedan ambassador from Morocco to the Unitarianism of the age of Charles the Second

A Roman Catholic priest of the name of Stabellini has been consecrated Portuguese Bishop of Dorilea, and Apostolical Vicar General, in the dominions of the Great Mogul, Idulshaw Golconda, and in the island of Bombay at the mother church of De Esperanca at Bombay The ceremony was performed by the Bishop of Antiphila, and two Vice Bishops

NORTH AMERICA

The temperature of newly killed animals was on sixteen different occasions noticed by Captain Lyon, during the severity of the Arctic winter of 1821 2 The greatest heat observed that of a fox, was $106\frac{3}{4}$ deg of Fahrenheit when the surrounding air was 14 deg below zero The mean of fourteen Arctic foxes a white hare and a wolf gave 102 deg of animal heat, at extreme depressions of the thermometer in the surrounding air How wonderful this provision of an all-wise and merciful Creator!

LIST OF NEW PUBLICATIONS

THEOLOGY

A History of the Christian Church from its Erection at Jerusalem to the present Time by the Rev John Fry B A 8vo 12s

The Fifth Volume of the Village Preacher by a Clergyman of the Church of England 12mo 5s

Davison s Primitive Sacrifice 8vo 7s 6d

Groser s Lectures on Popery 12mo 5s

Evidence against Catholicism by the Rev Blanco White 8vo 9s 6d

Death Bed Scenes by the Author of the Evangelical Rambler 7s

Letters to Mr Butler on his Book of the Roman Catholic Church by the Rev H Philpotts D D

Defence of Religious Liberty by the Author of Letters on Prejudice 8vo 3s 6d

St Paul s Visitation at Miletus a Visitation Sermon preached at Ipswich by the Rev J Wilcox M A

A Charge delivered to the Clergy of the Archdeaconry of London by Archdeacon Pott 1s 6d

An Essay on the Absolving Power of the Church by the Rev T H Lowe M A

The Primer or Book of Private Prayer authorised by Edward VI edited by the Rev H Walter

Thoughtful Hours devoted to the interests of Youth

A Practical View of the Redeemer s Advent in a series of discourses by the Rev J H Stewart M A

Osric a Missionary Tale by C Elizabeth

A Sermon on the Vice of Gaming by the Rev B Sandford

MISCELLANEOUS

History and Antiquities of the Tower of London by J Bayley F R S Part 2 4to 3l 3s

Dr Young s and M Champollion s Phonetic System of Hieroglyphics by Henry Salt F R S 8vo 9s

Maps to Herodotus 10s 6d

Maps and Plans to Thucydides 10s 6d

Geographical Memoirs of New South Wales by Barron Field Esq F L S

The History of Wales by J Jones LL D 8vo 20s

The Sydney Papers Edited with Notes &c by R W Blencowe 8vo 10s 6d

A Table of the Mineral and Vegetable Poisons with the Symptoms Treatment and Re agents from the French of De Salle by W Bennett M D 4s 6d

Thompson s First Principles of Chemistry 2 vols 8vo 1l 10s

Mineralogy by F Mohs of Freiberg Translated by William Haidinger 3 vols post 8vo 1l 16s

Elements of Chemistry by W Weldon. 8vo 12s

Recollections of Foreign Travels by Sir E Brydges Bart 2 vols 18s

The Vision of Hades To which is added the Vision of Noos Foolscap 8vo 6s

The Lost Spirit, a Poem by J Lawson 1 vol 18mo

The Life of J Chamberlain by Mr Yates and re published and edited by the Rev F Cox A M 1 vol 8vo.

Juvenile Prize Essays with a Preface by the Rev H F Burder 2s

Affectionate Advice to Apprentices and other Young Persons by the Rev H G Watkins 6d

Isabella a Moral Story by the Daughter of a Clergyman 2s 6d

Inaugural Discourse of Henry Brougham Esq M P on being installed Lord Rector of the University of Glasgow 2s 6d

Excursions in Maderia and Porto Santo by the late T E Bowdich Esq 4to 2l 2s

Brazil by Maria Graham 4to 2l 2s

Journey across the Cordillera of the Andes by R Proctor 8vo 12s

RELIGIOUS INTELLIGENCE

SOCIETY FOR PROMOTING CHRISTIAN KNOWLEDGE

The last published Report commences with stating that the progress of the Society's affairs during the year is such as to afford general satisfaction The number of subscribing members amounts to about 15 000 of whom 621 have been elected since October 1823 A considerable increase is found in the receipts and expenditure and the circulation of religious books has been greater than in any former year The whole number of books and tracts delivered from the Society's stores, between the audit in 1823 and the audit in 1224 amounted to 1 454 818, exceeding the issue of last year by 54 107 The increase in the single article of Bibles was 5031 and in Common Prayer books no less a number than 22 605

The demand for the family Bible continues to increase Three editions comprising together 26,000 copies have been printed

The rules and orders of the Society have been revised during the past year The form of recommending new members has been shortened and whether the parties reside in London or in the country the signature of a single member only is required Ladies are again admitted as annual subscribers upon payment of the usual benefaction and subscription without ballot as was the ancient custom of the Society The annual Report is in future to be laid before the General Meeting of the Society in the month of June The house in Bartlett's Buildings not affording sufficient accommodation for the general meetings or for the Society's increasing business, a house in Lincoln's Inn Fields has been purchased and is now occupied by the Society

The Report next adverts to the appointment of two bishops for the West Indies

While the duty say the Board of communicating religious instruction to the slaves was felt more irresistibly from day to day the Society for promoting Christian Knowledge was convinced that no exertions could prove extensively successful until the Government led the way by the formation of an enlarged and sufficient church establishment An increasing sense of what is due to the temporal and spiritual welfare of the Negroes led to the adoption of the long desired measures The Report adds further on this subject — The bishops will be accompanied by the archdeacons and by a large number of highly respectable clergymen whose duty it will be to administer to the spiritual wants of the Negroes In addition to the clergy appointed by his Majesty's Government the Incorporated Society for the Conversion of the Negroes have recently made a considerable increase in the number of their missionaries to the West Indies Under such favourable circumstances while the efficiency of the existing parochial clergy in the islands can not fail to be incalculably increased by the blessings of Episcopal superintendance their duties will be shared among an additional number of labourers The Board would have deemed it incumbent upon them to make especial exertions in this great cause had not the work been already auspiciously commenced by the Incorporated Society for the Conversion of Negroes an institution which is conducted upon principles in no respect dissimilar from their own

A translation of the First Homily into modern Greek having been sent to the Board by the Rev Mr Leeves Chaplain to the British Factory at Odessa, who expressed an opinion that the circulation of the Homily would be highly useful in some parts of the East, and the translation having been carefully examined the Board resolved to print 5000 copies. These copies were forwarded to Mr Leeves without delay.

Communications have been received from clergymen resident in Wales recommending the Society to encourage the translation of a number of tracts in addition to those already on their catalogue into the Welsh language. the Society determined to adopt the measure and have obtained the services of three gentlemen who are now actively engaged in procuring the translation of the tracts.

Since the publication of the former Report the Society has been deprived of a zealous friend and most munificent benefactor by the death of Archdeacon Owen The fund of Clericus which was established by this benevolent individual for the supply of the soldiers of the regular army on foreign stations with Common Prayer Books and religious tracts amounted previously to the decease of the founder to 5,743*l* stock 3 per cent annuities and the Archdeacon bequeathed to the Society the sum of three thousand pounds to augment this fund.

The Diocesan and District Committees continue to prosecute their labours with unabated spirit Several new Committees have been added to the former list.

The foreign operations of the Society are briefly as follows In Nova Scotia and Quebec the Committees have succeeded in acquiring a pretty extensive sale for their books. In Bengal the designs of the Society are prosecuted with activity and success. The Calcutta Diocesan Committee had distributed during the year 12,286 books and tracts in which number are included 445 Bibles 1117 Prayer books. A printing press and 1000*lbs* of English type have been consigned to the Madras Committee for the use of the mission press at Vepery The general information from this presidency is highly satisfactory. It was determined that a new mission church should be built at Vepery and the congregation and schools had so rapidly increased that it was found necessary to erect a building of much larger dimensions than had been originally contemplated. The church will now be large enough to contain 1000 persons. The Society's books it is stated are in great demand in this part of India In addition to those sent out from England a supply is constantly issuing from the mission press at Vepery During the last year a large proportion of the Old Testament has been printed in Tamul and many school books in Tamul and English A Tamul and English Dictionary compiled by the Rev Mr Haubroe is now passing through the press. The number of scholars in the school at Vepery is 383 of whom 41 are heathen and a new school has been opened. The Rev Mr Wright the Company's chaplain at Trichinopoly has instituted a small circulating library for the use of soldiers at his own expense From Bombay the Society has received intelligence that the general distribution of the Society's books and tracts is usefully pursued and that several of the chaplains have expressed their sincerest thanks for the great assistance afforded them through the Committee In some of the larger and distant stations in this archdeaconry have been formed depots of books from which the chaplains make issues at their discretion under the general instructions of selling at prime cost to such as are capable of purchasing and at reduced prices to those who are not so capable so that gratuitous issues are limited as far as may be practicable to those who from special circumstances are unable to purchase or are otherwise particularly deserving of the Committee's assistance The several schools under the Bombay Education Society and the regimental schools are supplied with all the tracts used in the National system The number of children in these schools may be estimated at about 1000 The Committee have printed the Chief Truths of the Christian Religion in Mahrattee and have agreed to print the History of Joseph in Persian taken from Mr Robinson's translation of the Book of Genesis The series of the National School Tracts now completed both in Mahrattee and Guzerattee are made great use of in many of the native schools and a considerable number has been distributed by some of the missionaries Large consignments of books had been received in Jamaica and books had been issued to every parish in the island and distributed either gratuitously or at reduced prices at the discretion of the incumbent In conclusion the Board earnestly solicit the prayers of all the members for the Divine blessing on the Society's endeavours to promote the glory of God and the best interests of mankind

LADIES HIBERNIAN FEMALE SCHOOL SOCIETY

A statement of the establishment and objects of this highly useful institution will be found in our vol for 1823 p 805 From the First Annual Report of the Committee we collect the following particulars relative to its proceedings during its first year which has been employed chiefly in forming connexions and laying the foundation for the future operations of the Society No other institution had been previously founded for the exclusive education of Irish females and considering how greatly the state of society is influenced by the wives mothers and sisters of families such a society appeared to be of great value for the welfare of that long neglected country

The nature of the Society's present connexions in Ireland and its progress in forming schools may be ascertained by tracing its operations through the several provinces The following are a few cursory memoranda

In Ulster a general desire has been expressed and manifested by the Society's correspondents to promote the wishes of the Committee The inspectress has hitherto been employed here and six schools have been arranged by her Six other schools have been promised aid in this province and the inspectress is proceeding in their formation

In Leinster the schools await the arrival of the inspectress for regular formation Six are quite ready for her visits In two instances the commencement of schools is suspended merely till the houses designed to receive them shall be completed Much has been done in the way of commencement extensive promises of co operation have been given and it remains only to realize the hopes held out during the past year

The Committee have received from every county in Munster earnest solicitations for assistance and promises of co operation Little has yet been effected but they trust that much has been begun in Cork They have already assisted three schools and it is hoped that a fourth will very soon be opened

In endeavouring to form a just conception of the state of those parts of the province of Connaught which have come under their observation the Committee while deeply affected by the representations of their correspondents as to the ignorance poverty and want of cleanliness which too commonly prevail in that district of Ireland and especially among the lower classes of female peasantry are encouraged by the accounts which continue to arrive of the great and increasing desire for instruction of the eagerness with which the children flock to the schools already formed in connexion with the Society and the applications which are constantly made for new schools Four large schools have been established in the county of Sligo and to another assistance is promised and to several others in other counties of the province

Seven Associations in aid of the Society have been formed in England at Clapham Walthamstow Cheltenham Brighton Clifton Exeter and Sheffield Several associations have also been formed in Ireland

The following is a standing rule of the Society The books used in schools deriving assistance from the Society shall be the Scriptures, and approved Spelling books Employment in needle work and what belongs to an exclusively female education shall be considered a prominent and necessary part of the system Various other excellent regulations have been adopted

We select the following passages from the recent correspondence of the Society From a Lady in the county of Donegal

The only circumstance which causes any difficulty in the school is providing materials to keep the children in work We are also desirous of rewarding the poor girls by distributing some cloaks and stuff coats for the winter as many of them live three or four miles from school and have no covering fit for the cold of winter It is hard to relieve *all* their wants they *all need* instruction and with a few exceptions all need clothing and many alas want food some few even want the shelter of a home but thanks be to God, the prospect is brightening for the peasantry of Ireland We held our quarterly examination the first week in this month and I have great pleasure in communicating the progress evident in all the classes Fifteen girls repeated from the 14th chap of St John's Gospel to the 20th chapter perfectly correctly The plain work was beautifully done though on coarse materials From a Clergyman in the county of Down

The establishment of a school for the specific object of instructing the rising female generation in useful industry is extremely desirable and the more especially since many of the lower class of females enter upon the duties of domestic life without being able in any degree to provide for their own or their children's temporal comfort

VIEW OF PUBLIC AFFAIRS

FOREIGN

FRANCE.—The coronation seems to have gone off somewhat heavily notwithstanding the great anxiety displayed to render it attractive to the public. The king is said to be unpopular in consequence of the favour he has shewn to the views of the priests and Jesuits, and his partiality for the system of ultra royalism. The chambers have closed after a session marked by very few debates of much interest or importance, with the exception of those on the law of sacrilege and of indemnity to the emigrants. The power and influence of the popular branch of the legislature seem to be increasingly on the decline and new measures it is rumoured, are in contemplation against the next session for abridging the liberty of publishing their debates.

SPAIN.—The misfortunes of this ill governed country continue to thicken around it. The native soldiery on whom since the evacuation of the garrisons by the French the maintenance of the public peace has devolved have evinced great discontent at the tardy payment of their wages and are preying in a disorderly manner upon their fellow subjects. The government seems also to be greatly alarmed and not without cause, for their favourite colony of Cuba. In addition to these misfortunes Columbian privateers have found their way into the very ports of old Spain and the government has neither money nor influence to repress these retaliations for the injuries committed on the western side of the Atlantic. Every new negociation for a loan meets with the most peremptory denial and all parties seem to be awaiting in languid exhaustion the occurrence of some fresh convulsion.

POLAND.—The Polish chambers have met but their deliberations are greatly restrained by the arbitrary dictations of the emperor of Russia who has also forbidden the publication of their speeches. The emperor promises to approve whatever they may propose of a beneficial kind but to reject whatever would be injurious to their prosperity of which he constitutes himself the sole judge. A committee has been chosen by his direction to revise the regulations which exist with reference to religion but it is not stated what are the specific objects in contemplation. It is well however to have even the form of a popular assembly. The Polish legislature is probably as unshackled in its deliberations as was the parliament of England under Henry the Eighth or Elizabeth.

GREECE.—The most important intelligence from Greece is the report, that the patriots have captured and burned the whole of the remainder of the Egyptian fleet in the port of Navarino, and also put to flight the Egyptian army a few fugitives only escaping in safety to Modon. The public is waiting with much anxiety for a confirmation of this intelligence.

DOMESTIC

The attention of Parliament has been directed to complaints of illegal and oppressive transactions in three of our colonies—all slave colonies. Those against the government of the Cape of Good Hope we pass over as they are founded on ex parte statements which are to be investigated in the next session. Those from Jamaica and Barbadoes are of a less dubious character and involve abuses of singular atrocity and of most momentous import.

With regard to the first of these islands our readers cannot have forgotten the cruel and illegal proceedings detailed in our last volume (p 221 &c) respecting the apprehension of two free persons of colour named Lescesne and Escoffei, against whom the governor of the island issued a warrant for their deportation as aliens, though they were well known to be and were afterwards judicially proved to be British subjects and this without any form of trial without even any specific charge being made against them, and although each of them had wives and families dependent on them for their support. Their real offence was that they had promoted a petition to the insular legislature by the free coloured population for the removal of the disabilities under which they most unjustly labour. Time however, was fortunately allowed them to sue out a writ of Habeas Corpus and they were liberated by a decree of the Court of King's Bench in Jamaica, as having proved themselves to be British subjects (as stated in our volume for last year). A few weeks afterwards, however they were again seized and hurried on board a king's ship. No time was now allowed them to appeal to the laws or even to bid adieu to their families or to settle their affairs and they were put ashore in a state of destitution in St Domingo whence, with difficulty they made their way to this

it urged, strangely enough, that even Lancastrian schools and Infant schools are but parts of a system for abolishing a truly religious education among the people. With regard to the former (Lancastrian schools) as we have National schools in abundance which as church men we prefer we shall not undertake their defence, except so far as to say that no one who has ever visited one of them would, we think, be able to urge that he found the children ignorant of the leading points of Christian faith or duty. With regard to the latter (Infant schools) we reject the charge as wholly unjust, for whatever may have been the particular practice at one private institution, the children of the schools conducted by the friends of the Infant School Society display a remarkable, we might say a precocious acquaintance with the precepts and declarations of holy writ, and, what will not be thought of less importance, a most pleasing early exhibition of them in the little details of infant conduct. But we did not purpose to go so far at present into the subject, our only intention being to urge upon every truly Christian member of the community the necessity of watching the aspect of the times on the important subject of public education, and to consider the peculiar duties which devolve upon himself individually towards securing the benefits and preventing the evils which may respectively arise from a right or wrong application of this vast machine.

ANSWERS TO CORRESPONDENTS

A Protestant; Z Y; T W; Educator; S; Scholasticus; A B C; D S W V; and Anonymous, are under consideration.

The circumstance alluded to by J B has been frequently mentioned in our pages.

We perfectly concur with J P as to the duty of British Christians availing themselves prudently but most zealously and by the blessing of God efficiently of the present facilities for extending the pure light of the Gospel in South America both among the Pagan and the Roman Catholic part of the population and he will find that we have already frequently urged the subject upon the notice of our readers.

The remaining half of the anonymous Bank note for 100*l*. has been received by the Bible Society.

If M W P will carefully refer to our Family Sermons he will find his wish anticipated in fact, though not in name. With regard to his first query, we reply that the Church intended nothing but Canonical Scripture to be used for Sunday Lessons; on the subject of the second, he had better consult his proctor.

F C will find an account of the opening of the Missionary Institution at Basle in our volume for 1820, p. 847. We are much obliged by his communications.

We are requested by some friends of the Hibernian Society to state that Mr O Connell having publicly alleged against the Society that it had misapplied its funds, including 26,000*l*. of parliamentary grants; that it had published false statements and that not a child was under education by its means in all Munster; a correspondence ensued in which Mr O Connell was unable to adduce a shadow of proof in favour of his assertions. The Committee, on the other hand, affirm that the funds of the Society have never been applied to any other purposes than those pointed out by its laws and regulations, which have now for many years, limited its operations to the establishing of schools and the reading and circulating the holy Scriptures in Ireland; that the Society has never received any assistance from Government and therefore could not misapply the parliamentary grants; that it has been always and it now is supported entirely by the private and voluntary contributions of benevolent individuals to whom it delivers an Annual Report, and publishes the same for their information; that it has never calumniated the people of Ireland nor misled the people of England but has confined itself to the publication of events and circumstances founded as the Committee believe, on unquestionable evidence; and that it has instructed and now instructs in its schools in the province of Munster as well as in the other provinces of Ireland many Roman-Catholic as well as Protestant children. Respecting one county of this province, Kerry of which Mr O Connell says "In your 17th Report, you charge for six hundred children in Kerry, six hundred children educated by your Society in the county of Kerry!!! Oh monstrous!"—Why any person, who knows the county of Kerry and could swallow the assertion that the London Hibernian Society educated in the year 1822 six hundred children in Kerry would actually swallow the children themselves clothes and all! the Committee state, that, in the year 1822 there were in the county of Kerry in connexion with this Society *four schools* containing *six hundred and three* children; that in the year 1823, there were in the same county *five* schools, containing *seven hundred and forty-three* children; and in the last year *twenty-two* schools containing *two thousand six hundred and forty-one* children.

THE CHRISTIAN OBSERVER.

RELIGIOUS COMMUNICATIONS

For the Christian Observer

THE PHILOSOPHY OF THE ROMAN CATHOLIC RELIGION

No. I

THE usual resources of controversy appear to have been long since exhausted in the disputes between Romanists and Protestants. What at an earlier period of discussion was advanced and received as original argument has now degenerated into wearisome and powerless repetition. The inquiry is notwithstanding once more revived and it is urged, perhaps with greater fervour than has been exhibited at least in this country since the Revolution at the close of the seventeenth century.

Every person, conscious of the incurable diversity of human opinion on all points incapable of absolute demonstration, must be aware of the difficulties of a subject so extensive and diversified as the one in question for, as the materials of the controversy have rapidly increased with time, it seems, at this late hour of the discussion, to defy compression. The combatants are now required to take the field, not barely to argue direct questions of divinity but to deliver in their theses on metaphysics, physics, chronology, language, history, bibliography, and a variety of other subjects diffused over the accumulations of literature and science. All this is an involution of what, in its abstract nature, is a matter of plain argumentation. The majority of our opponents divert us from the straightforward track into the bordering thickets of uncertainty and as long as we steal after them to practise the bush fighting of irregular warfare, the contest will be desultory and endless.

If the solution of the question can only be effected by years consumed in examining the evidence deposited in the Vatican, Bodleian and British Museum or even by weeks devoted to the study of recent publications on the controversy it is utterly impossible for the bulk of the persons interested in the result both for time and eternity to become acquainted with the truth farther than as what professes to be such is delivered out to them, at second hand by persons who may or may not, have discovered the truth for themselves. In the concerns of the life to come, every man is bound to search on his own separate account. It is criminal to attempt this by a substitute. Christianity is a religion addressed, indeed, *ad aulam*, and *ad clerum*, but also *ad populum* and to the last as inviting and requiring all individuals to be, in one sense, their own instructors. Such is at once the obligation and the privilege of our own countrymen. As the subjects of the British crown, they have been for upwards of two centuries, in possession of the canonical Scriptures provided for their express use in the shape of an authorised translation executed by royal mandate, confirmed as a national right by successive acts of the legislature and recognized by all our ecclesiastical formularies as their basis and criterion. In this view, there is only one portal into the temple, to be entered alike by priests and people.

Grounding our estimate on this undeniable statement, it is asked, whether the investigation at issue may not be confined within definite and manageable limits accessible to men of plain understandings, and educated *without* the pale of theological erudition? And may not this be accomplished by examining the subject in its primitive elements? The present writer aspires to attempt this. He by no means professes to have gone through a regular course of study on the points before him. It will appear, in the sequel, that his plan is formally opposed to such a procedure. He would endeavour to analyse the controversy on the principles of sound philosophy, under the guidance of the written revelation of God illustrated by appeals to the general sense of mankind, and to the experience and observation of all such as observe with discrimination, the passing events of the world. It must further be distinctly understood, that, though he is a member and minister of the national established church, he does not approach the arena, on the present occasion, either under the banner of his own confession, or that of any other Reformed communion whatever. He cannot, as a consistent Protestant, concede, that even the purest assembly of Christians is to be regarded as the sole accredited interpreter of the general charter of the church. The debate must never be lowered from the lofty scriptural position already taken, into an effort to establish the superiority of any single branch of the Reformation, to the disparagement of the rest. Matters of eternal importance involve struggles, not for rivalry, but for the salvation of souls. The writer would urge this, without in the least impeaching his own attachment to our public establishment. It would be offering a degrading compliment to the Church of England, as the eldest daughter of the Reformation, to press claims in her behalf far higher than she ever herself preferred. She is not answerable for the adulation of friends whose false zeal is more adverse to her prosperity than the attacks of her confessed opponents. Enemies, in the guise of flatterers, have beset her in every period of her history. Some of these have exerted themselves to force her back almost to the intolerance and despotism of the times of darkness. Such injudicious advocates should be apprised that the church will prosper or decay not by reviving among us the principles of the hierarchy which we so justly deserted, but by our consistency or inconsistency with our original doctrine and discipline. We do not oppose the papal scheme of Christianity, in order to substitute the Confession of Augsburg, or our own Articles, or any human formularies, however excellent, for the decrees of the Council of Trent. From the earliest dawn of the Reformation, it has been a current head of impeachment against the pontiff and his conclave, that *they* limit the faith by the boundaries of the Latin Church, and thus reduce religion, I might say, to a question of geography. Let therefore those who persevere in the accusation, beware of the extent of the charge, of its powers of recoil, and of their own exposure to the stroke of its reaction. The friends of pure and undefiled Christianity, must suspend their inter ecclesiastical dissensions, while they agitate questions of more pressing interest. They must agree, in the interval, to fight in the same ranks: and, for the time, cease to quarrel on the subordinate distinctions of uniform, accoutrements, and discipline.

It should be ever recollected, that Cramner, Ridley, Hooper, and Latimer, no farther died for the Anglican Church than Huss and Jerome of Prague suffered for the congregations of Bohemia. They were, severally, martyrs for the faith of Jesus Christ; as that faith existed then, and exists now, independently of its connexion with any human system. No church, as such, is at all dependent upon its martyrology, for the support of its legitimacy. To say nothing of various modifications of heathenism itself, which have had their willing victims to what they considered to be truth, Catholicity arrays its army of Elizabethan martyrs, to confront the rival line of the Marian witnesses and, if an almost superhuman fortitude, and endurance of anguish and agony, could establish its later pretensions, the *convulsionaires* of Paris, so recently as the close of the last century, might be adduced as undeniable evidences of the truth they aspired to confirm. But the argument might prove too much. For, what shall we call, in this relation, the self torture of the Hindoo devotees, the sacrifice of widows, so far as voluntary and all such acts as inflict, upon their victims, mutilation, protracted torture, and death? Whatever the value of the induction derived from martyrdom, in the opinion of religionists of any denomination, I only advert to it now as a *specimen*, in passing, of convertible arguments: those, it is intended, which are open to all parties, and conclusive to none. As an opponent of the Romanists on this occasion, I will suppose myself a member of no existing church; but beg to be considered as a neutral observer, independent of educational and social prejudices, and coming as it were, fresh and new to the discussion, with the Bible in my hand, and with an intellect capable of exercising itself unaided by any servile submission to borrowed opinions.

These papers then are an essay towards explaining the philosophy of Popery, including a view of its origin, genius, and responsibilities and illustrating also its identity with every Protestant form of merely nominal Christianity. My object is to give what may be termed the natural history of the system, and to furnish an hypothesis accounting for its appearance and success.

Whence originated Catholicity?

In endeavouring to solve this inquiry, the reader's attention is requested to the following detail of the reception of Christianity among mankind.—The religion of Jesus Christ soon irresistibly established itself among the inhabitants of the earth numbering, in the crowd of its adherents, a mixed body of sincere and false disciples. The quick-sighted world not only discovered the power of this early influence of the Gospel, but calculated upon its increase and perpetuity. Its adversaries also acknowledged the impracticability of effecting its destruction. At the same time, the new religion was found to bear, with intolerable severity, on the then living idolaters, sophists, and esoteric professors of wisdom; on the covetous and the sensual; on the tyrannical and the selfish: and these, as in all ages, formed the general aggregate of mankind. They tried, individually, to despise the doctrine and practical requisitions of the Cross; but felt themselves defeated, and stung to the quick, by the mortification of the overthrow. They hated the Gospel; but their hatred was less than their fear. They witnessed, with awe, the appearance on earth, of a new and mysterious power. "Herod was troubled, and all Jerusalem with him." Some of them, indeed, affected to join the new party; but their hypocrisy, already known to themselves, was either detected by their sound associates, or, in most cases, terminated in speedy desertion. In every manner, therefore, the Gospel was so far inaccessible to human interference. Yet mankind distinctly foresaw that it would go on, and prosper. They discerned, as by a kind of unconscious instinct, its ability to bid defiance to all opposition. They were driven to a difficulty of no common magnitude.

What was to be done? The world's answer to this inquiry was, practically at least, this:—"We must appear to submit to Christianity; but, in effect, apply the energy of this mighty engine to our own purposes: we must press the Gospel into the service of its enemies. Its name and credit shall be identified with a scheme subservient to our own vanity ambition, lust and avarice By flattery or compulsion, by manœuvre or violence we will ultimately convert the doctrines of its Founder into a system directly opposed to his own principles A shew of his doctrine, sufficient to blind suspicion, and to confront his own party, shall be retained, and exhibited on the surface while all beneath gradually restores the power and glory of the world under the name and pretensions of Christianity ——Avowals such as these did not indeed proceed from the lips of men but they were developed in their industrious efforts to secularize an unworldly religion Efforts of this kind—rather these very attempts themselves, not indeed in a preconcerted form and system but gradually developing themselves as occasion arose—I call the ORIGIN of the Roman Catholic Religion They are the germ indeed of *all* the corruptions superinduced, in the lapse of centuries, upon the faith of Jesus Christ

Now with the Scriptures in his hand, and with the comments supplied by a competent knowledge of mankind, painfully confirmed by self acquaintance I think that any person, of a philosophical cast of mind would anticipate the result here described He would argue that such would be the certain consequences of a pure and holy religion being proposed to the acceptance of mankind and when such a system was delivered into their external possession The career thus pursued by the world was precisely according to the constitution and course of human nature as vitiated and perverted by sin

The calculation receives force from our familiar remembrance that the Christian church itself even in all the freshness and comparative innocence of its infancy, was polluted by its own professed members and, in not a few cases, by some among them who, although in reality sound in heart, did yet become the grief and shame of their society by aberrations in judgment obstinacy in minor points of importance, indulgence in favouritism and in attachment to an obsolete dispensation The proverbial purity of the primitive church is not borne out by the inspired writings which record the imperfections and stains of the communities established, for example at Corinth and in Galatia, and at many other stations of the Apostolic mission And what shall we say of the lamentable state of the seven Asiatic churches affording examples of Christian societies spiritually dying, or on the verge of death notwithstanding only sixty three years had elapsed since the Saviour had been crucified and risen and ascended ? But that same Saviour himself had warned his earliest disciples of the approaching corruptions in his church There shall arise false Christs and false prophets and shall shew great signs and wonders insomuch that (if it were possible) they shall deceive the very elect *Behold I have told you before* Nor less observable were the subsequent predictions of St Paul and St Peter ' For I know this that after my departing shall grievous wolves enter in among you not sparing the flock Also of your own selves shall men arise, speaking perverse things, to draw away disciples after them " There shall be false teachers among you, who privily shall bring in damnable heresies, even denying the Lord that bought them and bring upon themselves swift destruction And many shall follow their pernicious ways

While desperate wickedness was thus intruding itself into the very fold of Christ and confounding the wolves with the sheep we may ask what was the world doing *without* this sacred inclosure ——I mean, the world who abstained, at that period, from any general union with Christianity in its then purest form? Why—it was doing this,—it was exulting over the crimes and divisions of the infant church and gathering thence many a lesson on the art of leading on its own designs beneath the shadow of the Cross. It was maturing its plans watching the movements in the enemy's camp and learning gradually how to accomplish a plausible compromise between God and the world. The conspiracies of the first century were thus the radical principle of the highest triumph since achieved by any form of antichrist.

Electrified and confounded therefore, as a Christian philosopher of the present day might at first be, could he be transported, instantaneously from the seclusion of his closet to the basilica of St Peter's, during the pageantries of a festival,—yet, how rapidly would his astonishment subside into the calms of contemplation when he could recal to his mind the simple circumstance that, for eighteen centuries mankind had been employed in elaborating the stupendous spectacle before his eyes, with all its adjuncts, out of the Gospel of Jesus Christ. Their success is indeed great and overwhelming but not greater than the urgency of the case prompted. It is the natural inevitable result of the world's endeavour to darken the effulgence of truth and to divert its rays in such a manner as might seem to light up its own inventions. Men whose minds as instructed from above look before and after would wonder if things were otherwise. They are not strangers to the maxim, that in proportion to the excellence of any thing is its capacity of abuse. In the same proportion, is it found necessary to impose upon human ignorance by dazzle and glare, that is, with such an exterior as overpowers men too much to allow of their investigating what it conceals.

The above hypothesis surely reduces the question, Whence originated Catholicity within definite limits. It exhibits a creative, restless principle, always in action, and quite sufficient to explain all the mysteries of paganized Christianity. Where then exists the necessity of dilating the subject according to the immeasurable scale usually adopted? Fathers, councils schoolmen, cardinals are not only without authority but their interference is positively superfluous. We can anticipate all they can advance since whatever they allege is comprized, in its elements in our present theory.

Neither does it more efficiently determine the debate when Protestant disputants, on the other hand, bring forward counter statements from the same fathers and councils, and turn the ordnance of these artillerists upon themselves. On the principle I assume it can be of no avail when they allege, for instance that Paschase Radbert invented the real presence Ignatius Loyola the order of Jesuits Dominic the Inquisition and Benedict a certain order of Monachism. We are concerned immediately, with the doctrines and observances which we *find* and not with the dates of their appearance. It matters not in this view, what sides Radbert and Berengarius took in the controversy of the Eucharist. The invention itself like every superaddition to papal despotism was only a step found to be necessary in the progress of a system intended to enslave mankind.—To illustrate the postulate of my argument, I would in this place ask whether, in the ferment excited among us by the question of the abolition of slavery, we are anxious to ascertain, at the present hour what individuals have rendered their names illustrious, in colonial history by the discovery of the cart whip, the iron collar and the brand. No! our undivided aim is the ultimate annihilation of sanguinary oppression. The system may have its own accurate and undisputed chronology of cruelty and avarice but this part of the investigation is remote, and practically useless. The mere annalist of guilt and misery may, indeed, busy himself with the arrangement of dates and events occurring in West India history as they who compile the memoirs of the age of Louis the Sixteenth may find it expedient to detail the invention of the guillotine, and the organization of the Revolutionary Tribunal. But if your friend be assassinated, do you ask, except perhaps for the purpose of fastening upon the murderer his guilt when and where he purchased his dagger?

The moment we are beguiled into the mazes of dates and the distant ramifications of a subject so near to us as the one in discussion, we become detached from its pressing importunities. The substance of the inquiry is forgotten in the examination of its accidents. Catholicity is indeed so affluent in the materials of debate that an adventurer into the controversy may exclaim, *Inopem me copia fecit!* I feel the appositeness of this confession, in the difficulty of restraining myself within the limits prescribed at the outset of these papers. With whatever inconsistency, I beg to proceed, in the next Number, with a wider extension of the subject or rather, with an attempt to illustrate the application of the principle, already developed to some of the leading particularities of the Roman Catholic religion. In the mean time let me record the honest confessions of a great man —" My censures of the Papists, said Baxter, " do much differ from what they were at first. I then thought that their errors on the doctrines of faith were their most dangerous mistakes. But now, I am assured that their mis-expressions and misunderstanding us, with our mistakings of them, and inconvenient expressing our own opinion, hath made the difference in these points to appear much greater than they are. But the great and irreconcileable differences lie in their church tyranny and usurpations, and in their great corruptions and abasement of God's worship, together with their befriending *vice* and *ignorance*. At first I thought that Mr Perkins well proved, that a Papist cannot go beyond a reprobate but now doubt not but that God hath many sanctified ones among them, who have received the true doctrine of Christianity so practically, that their contradictory errors prevail not against them, to hinder their love of God and their salvation but that their errors are like a conquerable dose of poison which nature doth overcome — (*Reliquiæ Baxterianæ*, London, 1696.)

(*To be continued.*)

FAMILY SERMONS.—No CXCIX

Jer. iv. 14.—*O Jerusalem, wash thine heart from wickedness that thou mayst be saved. How long shall thy vain thoughts lodge within thee?*

WHEN we read passages of this kind, we should ever remember that they are not of private interpretation for, except as respects the peculiar circumstances of the times in which they were written, or the persons to whom they were first addressed, they apply to all mankind. The declarations, the promises and the threatenings, of the Old Testament have not lost their force and they are unchangeable in their spirit. The warnings to repentance scattered throughout this prophecy and in this very chapter, and the multiplied assurances of the mercy of God, and his willingness to receive the returning penitent, still speak forcibly to every heart. Oh that each of us may duly consider their importance and apply them personally to our own case, while we proceed from the text to shew,

First. That the heart of man is the seat of wickedness and vain thoughts and

Secondly. That it must be wash

ed from that wickedness, and its vain thoughts be dislodged before we can be saved

I. First, then, we are to shew, that the heart of man is the seat of wickedness and vain thoughts and most important is it, that we should be well acquainted with this lamentable truth, in order that we may be aware of our danger, and be led to seek for and apply a remedy, the remedy offered in the word of God. Now, the declarations of our Creator, and our own individual knowledge of ourselves, to say nothing of the experience of all ages and countries, equally prove this melancholy fact.

1. In the first place, how is it that the moral and spiritual condition of mankind is spoken of in Scripture? It will not be said that God does not understand the character of us his guilty creatures how then does he describe it? At a very early period after the Fall (Genesis viii. 21) he saw that "the imagination of man's heart was evil from his youth or, as it is still more strongly expressed in the sixth chapter, that "the wickedness of man was great in the earth, and that every imagination of the thoughts of his heart was only evil continually" A deluge of waters was in consequence sent upon the earth, by which all the race of mankind, except the few who found safety in the ark, perished but the succeeding generations of our fallen race continued inheritors of the same corrupt nature, and followed the same evil courses. The Psalmist represents the Almighty, ages after, as "looking down from heaven upon the children of men, to see if there were any that did understand and seek God and the result of this inspection was, that they had "all gone aside, and were altogether become filthy, and that there was none that did good no not one." The testimony of Solomon, who had large personal experience of mankind, as well as the gift of wisdom and inspiration from God, was to the same effect; that "there is not a just man upon earth, that doeth good, and sinneth not." "The heart of the sons of men, said he, "is full of evil" The declarations of the inspired writer from whose prophecies our text is taken, are in the same afflicting strain "The heart, he declares, "is deceitful above all things, and desperately wicked who can know it? He indeed who made it, and made it for far other and holier purposes, knows it and such are his declarations concerning it. These declarations were further repeated from the lips of the Divine Saviour himself when upon earth and well did he prove that "he knew what was in man, when he said, that "out of the heart of man proceed evil thoughts, adulteries, fornications, murders, thefts, covetousness, wickedness, deceit, lasciviousness, an evil eye, blasphemy, pride, foolishness all these things come from within and defile a man" The Apostles of our Lord continued to give the same account of human depravity both in its evil and its universal extension "Are we,' said St. Paul, speaking of himself and his countrymen who had been favoured with peculiar privileges, and comparing their case with that of the Gentiles, 'Are we better than they? No, in no wise for we have before proved both Jews and Gentiles, that they are all under sin. As it is written, There is none righteous, no not one there is none that understandeth, there is none that seeketh after God."

After these declarations of the great Searcher of hearts himself, speaking either directly or by his inspired servants, we need not appeal to any inferior testimony. For his attestation is grounded on full and unerring knowledge the human soul is open to him, in all its darkest windings and intricacies he cannot be deceived respecting it "Man looketh on the outward appearance, but the Lord looketh on the heart, and this he does that he may give an equitable decision upon the case of every individual. "I the Lord search the heart, I try the reins, to give every man according to his ways, and according to the fruit of his doings."

2. But still, secondly, we may bring the subject home to ourselves by personal inspection. Stronger proof we need not and cannot have, than the declaration of God; but individual application to our own case will abundantly shew us its truth. Even if, by the restraining mercy of God, our lives have been respectable and moral, do not our hearts still testify to the corruption of our nature? Are there not innumerable sources of wickedness within us? Does not the state of our affections, our will and our understanding itself, shew the effects of our fallen condition? Do not vain thoughts lodge within us? If we retrace our thoughts but for a single day or hour, do we not discover that this is their character? Even when not what the world considers 'wicked,' are they not too often vain? What idle imaginations, what false judgments, what selfish plans, what proud ideas of our own importance, what undue concern for our own ease, or interest, or pleasure, what frivolous excuses for our neglect of God, what conscious deficiency in the love which we owe to our neighbour! Measured by the standard of Scripture, our thoughts may be habitually vain where we least suspect it. For what is the great concern of human life, what is that most pressing avocation compared with which all other things are less than nothing? Is it not to secure an eternity of happiness in the world to come? And, if so, what shall we say of those thoughts and hearts from which all that relates to this chief object of human concern is habitually excluded? If we are living without deep repentance, without a lively faith in the Saviour, without love to God, without true prayer, without self examination, without Christian watchfulness, without holy affections; if our thoughts, even when not employed upon things wrong in themselves, are still destitute of all spiritual and heavenly direction, are confined to the business, the cares, or the gratifications of this life; if 'God is not in all our thoughts;' if our affections are not set upon things above; if the knowledge and the practice of our obligations, as servants of Christ, are not familiar objects of our study,—then whatever we may be in other respects, in the sight of God our hearts are wicked and our thoughts are vain; and it is necessary to our eternal safety that a complete change of character should take place in us before we can enter into the kingdom of God. Our personal experience of ourselves thus agrees with the estimate given of us by our Creator; and then how seasonable the exhortation in the text, 'Wash thine heart from wickedness, that thou mayst be saved. How long shall thy vain thoughts lodge within thee?'

II. We proceed, secondly, to shew that this exhortation must be complied with; that our hearts must be washed from wickedness, and our vain thoughts be dislodged, in order that we may be saved.

There is no truth of the word of God more clearly revealed or more frequently repeated than that the wicked cannot be saved. "The wicked, it it said, ' is reserved to the day of destruction; they shall be brought forth to the day of wrath.' 'The heavens and the earth,' says St. Peter, 'are kept in store, reserved unto fire against the day of judgment and perdition of ungodly men.' Every species of sin is included in these denunciations. St. Paul, in the sixth chapter of the first of the Corinthians, enumerates various kinds of evil doers, none of whom, he says, 'shall inherit the kingdom of God.' He gives in the fifth of the Galatians a similar catalogue, with the same declaration. Another similar catalogue occurs in the twenty fifth chapter of the book of the Revelations. In all these, and various other passages of the same kind, we see the displeasure of God both against sin generally, and against particular sins by name. Nor are gross transgressions or outward vices only mentioned: for we are told, that for every "idle word we must give an account:" that "the wrath of God is revealed from heaven against "all ungodliness and unrighteousness:"—that even sins of negligence and omission are included, as well as actual transgressions: for it is said, "Cast ye the unprofitable servant into outer darkness:" and again, "Every tree that bringeth not forth good fruit is hewn down and cast into the fire."

It is necessary, then, to salvation that our hearts should be washed from our wickedness, and our vain thoughts be dislodged. The character of God demands this: for he is just and holy, and of "eyes too pure to behold iniquity," and is "angry with the wicked every day." The nature of heaven also requires it: for into its sacred regions can nothing enter that defileth. Our qualification also for that world of purity depends upon it: for so long as we continue the willing servants of wickedness and vanity, we can have no taste, no aptness for the service of God or spiritual enjoyments upon earth, or for the divine employments of the celestial world.

But what, it may be asked, is meant by this washing of the heart, this dislodgment of vain thoughts? More is intended than breaking off from openly vicious pursuits if we have been addicted to them. The purification must be as deep as the defilement: the heart, the first springs of thought and action must be cleansed. The hypocrite would deceive mankind, and the pharisee endeavour to propitiate God, by an outward shew of religion, while the heart remains unchanged: but not such is the purification required in the word of God. To dislodge our vain thoughts, is no slight or superficial process: it is the business not of a day or an hour, but of our whole life. The heart hardened by the deceitfulness of sin, is not easily softened; the corrupt imaginations entrenched in the inmost recesses of the soul, are not readily expelled. There is need of many warnings, many instructions, often of many deep afflictions, to complete this necessary transformation. Above all, there is need of an Almighty Agent, the Holy Spirit, to influence and direct this spiritual preparation for the unseen world. But he addresses us not as passive machines, but as reasonable and responsible creatures. His exhortation is, "Wash thine heart:" his expostulation, "How long shall vain thoughts dwell within thee?" Too long have they dwelt within us: too often have they been indulged: too often have his converting and sanctifying influences been repelled. It is therefore to our own neglect and obstinacy that we must attribute it if we are still in our sins. God has mercifully provided the means for our purification, and his grace is promised to render those means effectual. The "blood of Jesus Christ cleanseth from all sin:" it is "a fountain opened for sin and for uncleanness:" but we must betake ourselves to it, or it will not profit us. Those who are now before the throne of God, are such only as have accepted the offered mercy: who ' have washed their robes and made them white in the blood of the Lamb.' Let us then follow their example: let us, deeply feeling the necessity of the pardon of our sins, and of being cleansed from their defilement, repair to Him who "gave himself for his church, that he might sanctify and cleanse it," meritoriously "by his own blood," and instrumentally " with the washing of water by the word: that he might present it to himself, a glorious church, without spot or wrinkle, or any such thing; that it should be holy and without blemish." Let us seek to be "washed, and sanctified, and justified in the name of the Lord Jesus, and by the Spirit of our God, and then to all eternity shall we have reason to join in that grateful expression of praise and adoration, 'Unto him that loved us, and washed us from our sins in his own blood, and hath made us kings and priests unto God and his Father, to him be glory and dominion for ever and ever. Amen.'

To the Editor of the Christian Observer.

IN your review of Bishop Jebb's "Sacred Literature" (Christ. Obs. Dec. 1821) you express your persuasion that the aim of the learned writer has been, to excite others to assist him in the search of truth rather than to urge his own view of any particular text upon his readers.* His lordship will therefore, I am sure, allow a reader of his interesting volume to make a remark upon a passage which does not appear to me to have been written with sufficient reference to the original. In page 41 Psalm i. 1 is quoted as an example of a gradual rise in each line, not merely in the general sense, but specially in each line of the triplet.

> Oh the happiness of that man
> Who hath not walked in the counsel of the ungodly,
> And hath not stood in the way of sinners,
> And hath not sat in the seat of the scornful!

'The *counsel* implies the ordinary place of meeting or public resort; the *way* the select and chosen foot path; the *seat* the habitual and final resting place.' I think the correctness of this remark may be questioned; but the author proceeds—'the *ungodly* negatively wicked; *sinners* positively wicked; the *scornful*, scoffers at the very name or notion of piety and goodness.'

The words *ungodly* and *sinners* favour this idea, which is followed by many commentators. Mr. Scott for instance considers the former to be those who however moral and virtuous live as unconverted men do; the latter those who add to their ungodliness gross immoralities and vices.

The words in the original are רשעים and חטא. The former translated *ungodly* certainly implies *positive* wickedness, and answers to πονηρος ασεβης impious, Gen. xviii. 23, Psal. ix. 17. In *hiphil* the verb signifies to *condemn*.

The word translated "sinners" is derived from a verb signifying to miss the mark, Judges xx. 16, and answers to the Greek word αμαρτανω, and although very frequently used to denote positive sin, signifies less heinous sin, and is certainly inferior in degree to the former verb; and hence Kimchi applies it to childhood when the knowledge is imperfect. In Piel it signifies to expiate, to purify. St. Paul, referring to the sin offering חטאת which was offered, if a soul sin through ignorance, &c. Lev. iv. 1, employs the word αγνοηματων, the *ignorances*, errors of the people (Heb. ix. 7.) To this idea of error the Psalmist alludes when he uses the word in Psal. xxv. 8 and li. 13, "He will

---

* As our correspondent has alluded to our review of his lordship's elaborate work, it may be worth while, though somewhat out of date, to remark that another correspondent has recently blamed us for admitting in our last volume, p. 338, an alleged injurious garbling by a correspondent of the bishop's exhibition of the remarkable parallelism in Psalm ii. and Acts iv. The writer of the passage objected to, ought certainly to have recollected, that in the fourth chapter of the Acts the passage from the Psalms had just been cited, so that the two passages were contiguous instead of being separated by nearly half the Bible; a circumstance which materially strengthens his lordship's reasoning; but we do not think that the omission was intentional, and least of all ought we to be accused of wishing to invalidate the learned prelate's exhibition of the parallelism; when in our critique above referred to (vol. for 1821 p. 774) we had copied the passage as it stands in the Acts, and had given his lordship's own argument at great length in his own words, and had spoken of it as a most instructive sample of the valuable results which might arise from the learned author's discoveries.

teach *sinners* in the way." "All the *paths* of the Lord are mercy." "Sinners shall be converted unto thee;" and in our Church Service we confess "we have *erred* and *strayed* from thy ways; but thou, O Lord, have mercy upon us miserable sinners." Christ was made "sin or a sin offering (αμαρτια) for us," 2 Cor. v. who knew no sin. I should have been almost inclined to think that the climax had risen the contrary way. "Who hath not walked in the counsel of the ungodly" (positive sinners), "nor even stood in the way" (a less intimate term) "of sinners" (negatively wicked); but that the latter clause will not agree with this idea.

I offer these remarks with the greatest deference. The system of Bishop Jebb cannot suffer by objections to one example; but the distinctions in the original language are important to be observed.

N. J. B.

To the Editor of the Christian Observer.

GREGORY THAUMATURGUS was a bishop of Neo Cæsarea in the third century. He is said to have bequeathed the creed which bears his name as a valuable legacy to his church; and we are told that a hundred years after his death the autograph of it was extant. The original Greek of this creed has been preserved to posterity by Gregory Nyssen his biographer; and a translation of it will doubtless be acceptable to your readers. The following is the version of Mr. Boyd, as given in his recent publication on the Catholic faith. Mr. Boyd remarks that venerable as are the Apostles', the Athanasian, and the Nicene creeds, the creed of Gregory Thaumaturgus is in some sense entitled to still greater deference. We know not when or by whom the creed called the Apostles' was framed; and though of the others we can point out the dates of the composition and the writers' names, yet Gregory's has the advantage of having been drawn up more than a hundred years before them. The circumstance that this creed was composed fifty or sixty years before the Council of Nice, points out the gross incorrectness of the allegations that the Christians of the first three centuries were Unitarians, or at least Arians, and that the doctrine of the Trinity sprung up in the fourth. The creed of Gregory, though not so copious and precise as the Nicene and Athanasian, the false doctrines to which they refer not having arisen, is yet very clear in its specifications of the essentials of Christian doctrine respecting the Holy Trinity.

C.

The Creed of St. Gregory Thaumaturgus.

There is one God, the Father of the living Word, of the subsisting wisdom and the power and the eternal impression, the perfect generator of the perfect, the Father of an only begotten Son.

There is one Lord, the alone of the alone, God of God, or the impression and image of the Godhead, the energizing Word, the Wisdom which devised the systems of the universe, the Power which effected the whole creation, the true Son of the true Father, the invisible of the invisible, the incorruptible of the incorruptible, the immortal of the immortal, and the eternal of the eternal.

There is one Holy Spirit, from God deriving his subsistence, who by the Son shone forth upon mankind, the perfect image of the perfect Son, the life which gives existence to the living, the holy fountain, the sanctity and the dispenser of sanctification; by whom God the Father is revealed, who is over all, and in all; by whom God the Son is manifested, who is through all. A perfect Trinity in glory and eternity and sovereignty, indivisible, and unalienable!

To the Editor of the Christian Observer.

FAMILIAR as are the name and history and character of St. Chrysostom to every theological student, his works not having been translated into our language, the English reader has no opportunity of becoming acquainted with them. It has occurred to me, therefore, that a few samples might not be unacceptable for insertion in your pages, and I therefore send for your inspection a translation of three of his Homilies, being part (about the fifth part) of the series entitled Ανδριαντες, which is reckoned undoubtedly genuine, and is a good specimen of his works. Two or three Homilies thus entire will present a better idea of the manner in which this celebrated man was accustomed to write, and, it may be added, of the writings of the Fathers in general, than a selection of detached passages. It needs scarcely be remarked, that they must not be weighed by the rules of modern composition, and much less considered as always perfectly correct in doctrine or illustration. The first Homily may be conveniently disposed of in two successive Numbers, and the other two, if thought sufficiently interesting, inserted at a future period.

R.

The First of the Homilies, entitled Ανδριαντες, *or Sermons, preached when the Statues of Theodosius at Antioch were thrown down.*

Homily of Chrysostom, delivered in the old Church at Antioch, where he was a Presbyter, upon that passage of the Apostle (1st Ep. to Tim. v. 23), "Use a little wine for thy stomach's sake, &c.—(containing also an admonition) to those who are offended at the misfortunes of the righteous and the prosperity of sinners, and against those that dare to blaspheme.

Ye have heard the voice of the Apostle, the trumpet from heaven, the spiritual lyre: for as a trumpet uttering a terrible and warlike sound, it confounds enemies, and revives the depressed spirits of his friends; and, infusing much fortitude, makes those who attend to it impregnable against the assaults of the devil. Again, as a lyre delighting and enchanting the soul, it suspends wicked thoughts and passions, and administers at once both pleasure and edification. Ye have heard him then to-day discoursing about many necessary things to Timothy: for he wrote to him about ordinations, saying, "Lay hands suddenly on no man, neither be partaker of other men's sins:" and he shewed the extreme danger of such a transgression, declaring that these transgressors will undergo the punishment of offences committed by others, along with the offenders themselves, because, by electing and ordaining, they gave a sanction to the iniquity (of the persons so distinguished). Then again he says, "Use a little wine for thy stomach's sake, and thy frequent infirmities:" also concerning the obedience of servants, the madness of the covetous, the folly of the rich, and many other things he has this day discoursed of to us.* Since then it is impossible to go through them all, which of these subjects would you have us select to treat of before you, my beloved brethren? For I see, as in a meadow, many and various flowers of speech, and many a knot of roses, many violets, and as many lilies, and various fruits of the Spirit, scattered every where in abundance, and great fragrance: yea, rather not a meadow only, but a garden also is the reading of the Divine Scriptures; for these flowers have not barely fragrance, but fruit that is able to nourish the soul. Which then of the things spoken by the Apostle do you wish me to bring forward this day? Do you choose that we should now take in hand that which seems the cheapest of all, and the most intelligible to the common people?

---

* These are the subjects of 1 Tim. v. and vi. which had been read in the church that day.

I think (we should), and I am persuaded you will be of the same opinion. What then is it that is plainer and easier than other things? What else can it be but that which appears, to a man of ordinary judgment, easy and perspicuous: and what is that? 'Use, says he, "a little wine for thy stomach's sake and thy frequent infirmities." Let us then spend the whole discourse upon these words—and we do it, not out of vanity, nor from a desire of displaying rhetorical powers, (for the things spoken are not our's: they are what the grace of the Spirit may inspire,) but that we may rouse the most sluggish of our hearers, and may convince them how great is the treasure of the holy Scriptures, and how unsafe and perilous it is to disregard them: for if this plain and simple text which seems to many to have nothing in it of any necessity or use should appear to furnish us with valuable matter and to be an incidental source of Divine philosophy: much more will those passages, which display at once their own inherent affluence, supply the attentive with vast treasures. Let us not then negligently pass by even those sentences of Scripture which are considered to be trite and unimportant: for these also proceed from the grace of the Holy Spirit, and that grace is never of small value, but (always) great and admirable, and such as becomes the munificence of the Giver. Let us not then hear carelessly, since even they who melt the metallic ore, when they cast it into the furnace do not only take up the large masses, but also gather small particles with great exactness: and since we also are founders of golden ore, extracting it from the apostolic mine, not casting into a furnace, but letting it down into the cogitations of the soul, not lighting a fire, but kindling the fire of the Spirit,—————let us collect even the small fragments with great care. Though the sentence be short, yet the power is great: since pearls derive their value not (merely) from their bulk but from their specific beauty, so also (is it with) the reading of the Divine Scriptures: for pagan education displaying many fooleries, and deluging the hearers with many subtleties, (yet) sends them away empty handed, without either much or little of solid fruit: not so (η $\chi\alpha\rho\iota\varsigma$ $\tau\upsilon$ $\pi\nu\varepsilon\upsilon\mu\alpha\tau\circ\varsigma$) the grace of the Spirit but altogether the contrary: by little words it infuses wisdom into all who attend to it: yea one word is often sufficient to supply those that receive it, with adequate provision for the whole journey of life.

Such being the riches (of Scripture) let us rouse ourselves from slumber, and, with wakeful minds, receive what is spoken: for I intend that my discourse should descend to the very bottom (of the subject) for to many this admonition appears to be redundant, and to be something superfluous. They say, Could not Timothy of himself see clearly whatever was proper for him to make use of? did he wait to be informed of it by a preceptor? and must that preceptor not only lay the injunction upon him, but also commit it to writing, as if he would engrave it on a brazen pillar (by its insertion) in this Epistle? and, was he not ashamed to give a charge about such things, when writing publicly to the disciple? Wherefore, in order that you may learn that this admonition is not only not superfluous, but necessary and most useful, and that it is not Paul's, but is graciously communicated by the Spirit—I do not mean to say, merely spoken, but also written and delivered to posterity by this Epistle—I will presently proceed to the proof.

But besides these points just now stated, some have proposed a doubt, different indeed, but not of inferior moment, putting this question to themselves, For what reason did God permit a man having such great and well founded confidence whose bones and relics have driven away evil spirits, to fall into a state of so great infirmity? for he was not only ill, but always (so,) and perpetually, and with successive and continual illnesses, such as did not allow him any respite * whence does this appear? from the very words of Paul for he did not say, on account of infirmity but infirm*ities* and, more than that, he signifies the continuance of them ' thine *often* in firmities Let them hear (this) who are given up to a long disease, and sink into grief and despondency But this is not the only thing that is called in question that one so holy should be sick, and that continually but one entrusted with affairs of the utmost concern to all mankind for if he had been one of those who retire to the tops of mountains, or patch up a cabin in a desert and consume life in inert seclusion, this question had not (then) been so perplexing but that one whose lot was cast in public life and was entrusted with the care of so many churches and regulated (the ecclesiastical † affairs of) whole cities and nations and even all the world, with so much forwardness and zeal (that such a man) should be constantly harassed by infirmities is of all things the most likely to perplex and trouble the inadvertent for they would say if not for his own sake, yet for the sake of others, he ought to have been in good health he was an excellent general war, say they, was levied against him, not only by the infidels but evil spirits also, and the devil himself all the enemies pressed (him) closely with much vehemence ravaging the camp and making prisoners and he was capable of bringing back many (of them) to the truth *but* he was sick wherefore if no other detriment to their affairs resulted from his illness this alone were sufficient to make believers more inert and careless for if soldiers when they see the general confined to his bed, are more inactive and less disposed to fight much more was it probable that the faithful should then be overcome by human infirmities, when they saw their instructor who had wrought such great miracles continually sick and afflicted with corporeal maladies

But besides these objections, another question is started by these doubtful (disputants) Why did not he cure himself or why did not his master cure him when thus laid up by sickness? They had raised the dead, they had cast out devils, they had triumphed over death abundantly and could they not restore one infirm body? Could not these men, who in their life time and after their death had shewn such great power in the bodies of other men, so much as invigorate a weak stomach? And what is more, Paul, after so many great miracles wrought by a bare word is not ashamed when writing to Timothy to have recourse to the drinking of wine for a cure not that drinking of wine is dishonourable (by no means for that is the doctrine of heretics), but (I mean to say) that Paul did not consider it any dishonour to him that he was unable to cure this one organ (the stomach) of its morbid affections without the help of wine but so far was he from being ashamed of it that he has made it manifest to all posterity You know we proposed thoroughly to investigate the subject (and to shew) how that which is apparently trifling and minute is (nevertheless) replete with a variety of topics Let us proceed then to the solution for we penetrated to the very foundation (of the subject) for this reason that we might by stimulating your minds (to attention) lay up thoughts in a secure repository

Now give me leave, before I solve these questions to say something of the virtue of Timothy and

---

* Here surely we are obliged to say fallitur vir egregius for the whole Epistle supposes the contrary e g Be instant in season and out of season &c

† This parenthesis is not in the original but it seems necessary for what had Timothy to do with the government of cities &c ? Even *with* the parenthesis the language is very hyperbolical

of Paul's solicitude (for his welfare) for who could be more affectionate than he, when from such a distance and surrounded as he was with so much business, he shewed so provident a regard for the health of the disciple and gave particular directions for rectifying his stomachic disorder? And what can equal the virtue of Timothy who so despised luxury and derided expensive entertainments, that he fell into an infirm state of health from excessive rigour and intense fasting for that he was not originally infirm but destroyed the strength of his stomach by fasting and drinking water may be learnt from the Apostle himself who signifies as much very clearly, for he did not simply say 'use a little wine' but premised 'drink no longer water' and then added this advice about drinking wine and the word, 'no longer' signifies that up to that time he did drink water and for that reason was become infirm Who can avoid being struck with his ascetic and strict life? He grasped heaven itself and rushed to the very summit of virtue his master bears this testimony of him when he says (1 Cor iv 17) 'I have sent unto you Timotheus who is my beloved son and faithful in the Lord' and when Paul calls him son and faithful and beloved son these words are an adequate description of all his virtues for the judgments of the saints are not grounded in partiality or enmity but are free from all prejudice Timothy would not have been so much regarded if he had been Paul's son by birth nor so admirable as he is now that being no relation to him he has by a kindred piety advanced himself to be his adopted son, preserving in all respects the lineaments of his divine philosophy with great exactness—for as a steer and bull harnessed together so they jointly drew the (Gospel) yoke in every part of the world and he was not at all inferior notwithstanding inequality of age but his zeal qualified him to grapple in the labours of his master and this also is attested by Paul himself in these words (1 Cor xvi 10 11) "Let no man therefore despise him for he worketh the work of the Lord, as I also do" You see how he bears witness to his zeal and constancy then that he may not be thought to say these things from partial affection he makes his hearers themselves become witnesses to the virtue of his (adopted) son saying, 'Ye know the proof of him that as a son with the father he hath served with me in the Gospel (Phil ii 22) Ye, says he have yourselves had experience of his virtue and tried activity of mind but though he had risen to such a height of piety, he did not grow confident upon it but was anxious and fearful therefore he fasted even with strictness and he was not of the same mind as many are who after they have given themselves to fasting for ten days only or perhaps twenty, then immediately break loose (or perhaps destroy all the benefit και αλυσσιν απαντα,) from all (restraint) but he was not of such a disposition, nor did he say to himself any thing of this kind 'What need have I to fast any more? I have obtained the victory I have subdued my lusts I have mortified my body I have struck terror into evil spirits I have expelled satan (himself) I have raised the dead I have cleansed lepers I am formidable to all adverse powers how can I any longer need fasting and the stability resulting from it? No such thing did he speak or (even) think but the more he abounded in good works, so much the more he feared and trembled and this spiritual wisdom (φιλοσοφιαν) he learnt from his master for even he who was caught up into the third heavens and transported into paradise and heard unutterable words and had such great mysteries imparted to him and traversed the whole world like a winged (messenger) even he when writing to the Corinthians said (1 Cor ix 27) I fear " lest that by any means, when

I have preached to others, I myself should be a cast away. And if Paul feared after such great attainments (in the Christian life), he who could say, "To me the world is crucified, and I unto the world:" much more does it become *us* to fear: and the more we have abounded in good works, the greater reason there is for this fear, for then the devil is more exasperated: then he is more incensed when he sees us regulating our lives carefully: when he sees grace and virtue accumulated, like bales of merchandize of great magnitude: then he is eager to effect a shipwreck, that will be more than commonly ruinous: for an abject person of little worth, if he be supplanted and fall, doth not inflict so great an injury upon the community: but he that stands conspicuous upon an eminence, on the pinnacle of virtue, known and marked by all men, and held in great admiration: when *he* is assaulted and falls, (he) makes a great downfal and damage, not only because he has fallen from a high station, but also because he has made many of those who looked up to him decline in zeal and piety: and as in the body when some other (inferior) member is destroyed, the damage is not great: but when the eyes are blinded, or the head wounded, the whole body becomes useless in future, so may we say of those saints who had made great attainments in righteousness: when (their light) is extinguished: when they stain their high reputation: they inflict on the rest of the body an universal and intolerable injury.

Wherefore Timothy, being aware of all these things, secured himself on every side: for he knew that youth is intractable [or atrocious χαλεπον], unstable, easily deceived, slippery and needs a strong curb: it is as a pile of wood lying exposed, and easily taken [by every passenger], or quickly set on fire: for which reason he fenced it on every side, that it might submit to coercion, and diligently endeavoured by all means to slacken this flame, and checked with much vehemence this horse so impatient of bit and bridle: till he had repressed its sallies: till he had made it tractable, and delivered it up into the hands of reason: to hold the rein and exercise a vigorous authority over it. He said, "Let the body be weak, but let not the soul be weak: let the flesh be curbed, and let not the progress of the soul towards heaven be impeded." And, besides all these things, this circumstance in particular must raise our admiration of him: that though so ill, and struggling with such great infirmity: yet he never neglected the things of God: but with more (speed) than men of vigorous health, he flew about every where,—one while to Ephesus: then to Corinth: in Macedonia: often in Italy, in every part of the earth and sea he appeared with his master, and shared all his conflicts and dangers. The infirmity of his body did not damp the piety of his soul—so powerful is Divine zeal, with such swiftness does not wing the soul! For as they who have a sound and healthful frame, will derive no profit from it if the soul be abject, inert, and sluggish, so will the infirmities of the infirm be no injury to them if the soul be strenuous and alert.

But this admonition and counsel may to some appear to countenance immoderate drinking of wine: but it does no such thing, for if any one weighs the expression itself carefully. (he will observe) that the admonition supposes a case of fasting rather (than intemperance) for take notice that Paul did not give this advice in the beginning: in the outset, but when he saw all his strength thoroughly impaired, then he advised it: and then not absolutely but with a certain limitation, for he did not say positively, Use *wine*: but a little wine: not because *Timothy* needed such (cautious) exhortation and counsel: but because *we* do: for this reason it is that when writing to Timothy, he assigns to us the just measures and bounds in drink ing of wine, bidding (him) drink as much as would relieve his weakness, as would impart health and not another disease for immoderate drinking of wine produces disorders of mind and body, no less than too much drinking of water yea more numerous and more grievous disorders, for it introduces into the mind a conflict of passions and a storm of absurd and wicked thoughts, and makes the body weak tumid and watery For the texture of the earth when infested by a watery deluge, is not so rapidly and constantly dissolved as the strength of the body is when it is relaxed slides away and disappears by being exhausted with continual ebriety Let us therefore avoid extremes on either side let us both take care of the health of the body and also restrain its exorbitance for wine was given us by God not that we should be intemperate, but cautious (in the use of it) that we should be exhilarated not oppressed (by it) for he says (Psalm ciii 16), 'Wine maketh glad the heart of man whereas you make wine the occasion of depressing it for intemperate drinkers are clouded by heaviness of heart much darkness overspreads their intellect it is an excellent medicine if it be tempered with an excellent moderation — And this passage is of use to us against heretics, who disparage the things which God has created for if it were one of those which are prohibited Paul would not have allowed it he would not have said that he should use wine And not only against heretics (is this passage applicable) but also to some more abstemious persons among our own brethren, who when they see men that are inebriated behaving indecently instead of censuring *them*, throw the blame upon the fruit (of the vine) which God has given us saying 'Let there be no wine —' and we may reply, Let there be no drunkenness for wine is the work of God but drunkenness is the work of the devil Wine is not the cause of drunkenness, but it is man's intemperance produces it Blame not the creature of God, but blame the phrenzy of thy fellow servant but you [here Chrysostom again speaks προς τυς αφελεςερυς those simple persons above mentioned who argued from the abuse against the use,] instead of punishing and reclaiming him that commits a sin reproach him that confers a benefit When therefore we hear men saying such things as these let us stop their mouths for not the use (of wine) but the immoderate use produces drunkenness drunkenness that root of all evil Wine was given to relieve the infirmity of the body not to destroy the strength of the soul to remove the sickness of the flesh not to injure the health of the spirit Do not then by an immoderate use of this gift of God afford a handle to the simple and foolish for what is more wretched than drunkenness? A drunkard is a breathing corpse he is become a devil by his own choice it is a vice that excludes from pardon a transgression destitute of excuse the disgrace of human nature for the drunkard is not only useless to society, both in private and public affairs but barely as an object of sight he is of all things the most unpleasant, exhaling offensive effluvia The eructations and yawnings of the inebriated and their grating discordant yells fill the beholders and attendants with extreme disgust And what completes the mischief this vice renders heaven inaccessible and excludes from eternal felicity besides ignominy here intolerable punishment hereafter awaits those that are infected with it Let us then extirpate this evil habit and give ear to the Apostle when he says Use *a little* wine for even that little he permitted on account of infirmity insomuch that if the disciple had been troubled with no malady, he would not have enjoined him to take a little for in the use of those gifts of God which are the necessaries of life, meat and drink, we are bound to regulate the proportion by the season, and by our own want of them, and by no means to exceed what is requisite and useful, nor to do any thing without reason, in (a rash and foolish) simplicity

Having enlarged upon the virtues of Timothy, and Paul's solicitude for his welfare let us proceed to the solution of the questions (which were previously stated) What then are they? for it is necessary to repeat them, that the solution may be the clearer Why then did God permit so great a saint, and one who had the management of such important affairs, to decline in his health, so that neither he himself nor his master could cure the disease, but must have recourse to the aid of wine? This was the question the answer ought to be adapted not only to the case of disease and infirmity but also poverty hunger, imprisonment, torture, injuries, false accusations, and whatever sufferings of the present life may befal men of admirable piety and goodness that such persons may be enabled to derive from what I shall this day speak a full and clear answer to those who are disposed to accuse them For I hear many putting such questions as these How is it that every day such or such a man, so moderate and equitable, is dragged before a court of justice by another who is lawless and wicked, and undergoes many grievous sufferings, and God permits it? How is it that another is put to death unjustly, by a false accusation? one man is cast into the sea, another down a precipice And we might produce many instances, both in our own times and in those of our forefathers, of saints who have sustained many and various afflictions Wherefore, that we may see the reason of all these things, and not be ourselves distressed by them, nor negligently pass over the stumbling block which they present to others, let us attend diligently to what shall now be said (upon the subject), for I propose, my beloved brethren, to set before you eight reasons for the multifarious afflictions of the righteous wherefore let us all exert ourselves with close application of mind, considering that in future we shall have no excuse or apology for being (offended and) scandalized at such events, if, when so many reasons may be alleged for them, we will nevertheless be as much troubled and alarmed as if there were none

The first reason then is this God suffers these (righteous persons) to be afflicted, that they may not be suddenly elated by the greatness of their virtues and miracles The 2d is, That other men may not have a greater opinion of them than comports with human nature, and may not think them gods rather then men The 3d, That the power of God may be made manifest by its prevailing and getting a victory and propagating his religion by (such incompetent instruments as) sick men and prisoners The 4th, That there may be a more conspicuous exercise of patience in the persons themselves, as not serving God for the sake of the reward, but discovering such constancy of mind as even after great afflictions to shew the same attachment as ever The 5th, That we may exercise our thoughts upon the subject of the resurrection (and the rewards of the life to come) for when you see a just man who abounds in all virtues suffering an infinite number of afflictions, and departing this life in the midst of them, you will be altogether constrained, even against your will, to form some conception of a judicial sentence (to be pronounced) elsewhere for if men do not let those depart without a recompence who have suffered for their sake, much less would God ever think of dismissing uncrowned those who have endured such great conflicts (for him) and if he would not choose to deprive them of the reward of their labours, then it is quite clear that there must be, after their departure hence, some other opportunity of receiving the reward of these labours of the present life. The 6th, That all who are involved in great afflictions, may derive sufficient consolation and encouragement from looking at these (eminent saints), and remembering the evils which have befallen *them*. The 7th, That when we exhort you to (the imitation of) their virtues and say to each of you, Emulate Paul, emulate Peter, ye may not be backward to this imitation, from imagining that they who were so eminent in righteousness must have been partakers of a different nature. The 8th, That when we have occasion to decide the question of any man's felicity or infelicity, we may (hence) learn who ought to be considered as (really) happy, and who wretched and miserable. These then are the reasons, and we ought to prove all of them by the Scriptures, and accurately demonstrate, that these assertions are not the inventions of human reason, but the declaration of the Scriptures: for so will our discourse be more deserving of credit, and be more deeply impressed upon your minds.

(*To be continued.*)

MISCELLANEOUS

To the Editor of the Christian Observer.

At a time when so many ecclesiastical structures are being erected, and solemnly set apart from all secular uses for the worship of God, it may be interesting to your readers to peruse the usual Form of Consecration, which all who have witnessed the dedication of any of our new churches or chapels must attest to be exceedingly solemn and appropriate. The following is copied from the Bishop of London's Registry in Doctors Commons, and is given as used in his lordship's recent consecrations. There will of course be a few alterations according to the character of the particular edifice to be consecrated. In the following form there is no allusion to baptisms, marriages, or funerals; but I believe there are appropriate clauses for one or all of these, where they are intended to be solemnized.

P.

The bishop, attended by his chaplain, goes to the church, and is received at the door by the chancellor, registrar, minister, and vestrymen; and being shewn into the vestry room, he there puts on his episcopal robes, and from thence proceeds to the front of the altar, where the minister presents to him the petition, which the bishop receives, and orders the registrar to read; and the same being read, the bishop declares that he is ready to consecrate the church according to the prayer of the petition; and he then proceeds to the consecration and dedication thereof; and, with the clergy and others attending him, walks in procession down the church and back, alternately repeating the twenty-fourth Psalm—the bishop beginning thus:

1. The earth is the Lord's, and all that therein is: the compass of the world, and they that dwell therein.

2. For he hath founded it upon the seas, and prepared it upon the floods.

3. Who shall ascend unto the hill of the Lord? or who shall rise up in his holy place?

4. Even he that hath clean hands, and a pure heart: and that hath not lift up his mind unto vanity, nor sworn to deceive his neighbour.

5. He shall receive the blessing from the Lord: and righteousness from the God of his salvation.

6. This is the generation of them

that seek him, even of them that seek thy face, O Jacob.

7 Lift up your heads, O ye gates, and be ye lift up, ye everlasting doors, and the King of Glory shall come in.

8 Who is the King of Glory? It is the Lord strong and mighty, even the Lord mighty in battle.

9 Lift up your heads, O ye gates, and be ye lifted up, ye everlasting doors, and the King of Glory shall come in.

10 Who is the King of Glory? even the Lord of Hosts, he is the King of Glory.

Glory be to the Father, and to the Son, and to the Holy Ghost.

As it was in the beginning, is now, and ever shall be, World without end. Amen.

The minister then presents to the bishop the Act of Parliament for building the said church, and the deeds of conveyance, which his lordship places on the communion table, and standing on the north side thereof, turns himself to the congregation and says—

Dearly beloved in the Lord, forasmuch as devout and holy men, as well under the Law as under the Gospel, moved either by the secret inspiration of the blessed Spirit, or by the express command of God, or by their own reason and sense of the natural decency of things, have erected houses for the public worship of God, and separated them from all profane and common uses, in order to fill men's minds with greater reverence for his glorious Majesty, and affect their hearts with more devotion and humility in his service, which pious works have been approved and graciously accepted by our Heavenly Father:—let us not doubt but he will also graciously approve this our godly purpose of setting apart this place in a solemn manner to the performance of the several offices of religious worship; and let us faithfully and devoutly beg his blessing on this our undertaking, and say—

Then the bishop kneeling down says the following prayer:—

"O eternal God, mighty in power, and of majesty incomprehensible, whom the heaven of heavens cannot contain, much less the walls of temples made with hands, and who yet hast been graciously pleased to promise thy especial presence in whatever place even two or three of thy faithful servants shall assemble in thy name to offer up their supplications and their praises to thee; vouchsafe, O Lord, to be now present with us who are gathered here together to consecrate this place with all humility and readiness of heart to the honour of thy great name, separating it from henceforth from all unhallowed, ordinary, and common uses, dedicating it entirely to thy service, for reading therein thy most holy word, for celebrating thy holy sacrament, for offering to thy glorious Majesty the sacrifices of prayer and thanksgiving, for blessing thy people in thy name. Accept, O Lord, this service at our hands, and bless it with such success as may tend most to thy glory, and the furtherance of our happiness, both temporal and spiritual, through Jesus Christ our blessed Lord and Saviour. Amen."

Then the bishop standing up, turns towards the people, and says the following prayer:—

Grant, O Lord, that whosoever shall receive in this place the blessed sacrament of the body and blood of Christ thy Son, may come to that holy ordinance with faith, charity, and true repentance, and being filled with thy grace and heavenly benediction, may, to their great and endless comfort, obtain remission of their sins and all other benefits of his passion. Amen.

Grant, O Lord, that by thy holy word, which shall be read and preached within this place, the hearers thereof may both perceive and know what things they ought to do and may have grace and power to fulfil the same. Amen.

'Grant we beseech thee blessed Lord that whosoever shall draw near unto thee in this place to give thee thanks for the great benefits they have received at thy hands, to set forth thy most worthy praise, to confess their sins unto thee humbly to beg thy pardon for what they have done amiss, or to ask such other things as are requisite and necessary as well for the body as the soul, may do it with that stedfastness of faith, that seriousness of attention, and devout affection of the mind, that thou mayest accept their bounden duty and service, and vouchsafe to them whatsoever else in thy infinite wisdom thou shalt see to be most expedient for them, and this we beg for Jesus Christ his sake, our blessed Lord and Saviour. Amen.

After which the bishop being seated directs the sentence of consecration to be read which being done his lordship signs and promulges the same and commands it, together with the petition and other instruments to be recorded and registered in his registry among the other records.

Then the minister begins morning prayers, and Psalms and Lessons suitable to the occasion (to wit) the 84th 122d and 132d Psalms First Lesson 1st of Kings the 8th chapter, from verse 22d inclusive to verse 62d. Second Lesson, Hebrews the 10th chapter from verse 19th inclusive to verse 26th. After the collect for the day the minister who reads the service stops till the bishop hath said the following prayer—

"O most blessed Saviour, who by thy gracious presence at the feast of dedication didst approve and honour such religious services as this which we are now performing unto thee, be present at this time with us by thy Holy Spirit, and because holiness becometh thine house for ever sanctify us we pray thee, that we may be living temples, holy and acceptable unto thee, and so dwell in our hearts by faith, and possess our souls by thy grace, that nothing which defileth may enter into us, but that being cleansed from all carnal and corrupt affections we may ever be devoutly given to serve thee in all good works who art our Saviour Lord and God blessed for evermore. Amen."

Then the minister who officiates goes on with the morning service to the Prayer of St Chrysostom and The grace of our Lord Jesus Christ and the 6th 7th, and 8th verses of the 26th Psalm are then sung with *Gloria Patri*

COMMUNION SERVICE

The bishop standing on the north side of the communion table, as before reads the Communion Service. After the collect for the king he says the following prayer

"O most glorious Lord God, we acknowledge that we are not worthy to offer unto thee any thing belonging unto us. Yet we beseech thee in thy great goodness graciously to accept the dedication of this place to thy service, and to prosper this our undertaking receive the prayers and intercessions of us and all others thy servants who either now or hereafter entering into this house shall call upon thee and give both them and us grace to prepare our hearts to serve thee with reverence and godly fear. Affect us with an awful apprehension of thy Divine Majesty, and a deep sense of our own unworthiness that so approaching thy sanctuary with lowliness and devotion, and coming before thee with clean thoughts and pure hearts with bodies undefiled and minds sanctified we may always perform a service acceptable to thee through Jesus Christ our Lord. Amen."

The Epistle—14th verse to 17th inclusive of the 6th chapter of 2d Corinthians—to be read by the bishop's chaplain, as follows

"Be ye not unequally yoked to

gether with unbelievers: for what fellowship hath righteousness with unrighteousness? and what communion hath light with darkness? and what concord hath Christ with Belial? or what part hath he that believeth with an infidel? and what agreement hath the temple of God with idols? For ye are the temples of the living God: as God hath said, I will dwell in them, and walk in them; and I will be their God, and they shall be my people. Wherefore come out from among them, and be ye separate, saith the Lord, and touch not the unclean thing; and I will receive you."

The Gospel—verse 13th to verse 18th inclusive, of the 2d chapter of St. John—to be read by the bishop's chaplain.

"And the Jews' Passover was at hand, and Jesus went up to Jerusalem, and found in the temple those that sold oxen, and sheep, and doves, and the changers of money sitting: and when he had made a scourge of small cords, he drove them all out of the temple, and the sheep, and the oxen, and poured out the changers' money, and overthrew the tables; and said unto them that sold doves, Take these things hence; make not my Father's house an house of merchandize. And his disciples remembered that it was written, The zeal of thine house hath eaten me up. Then answered the Jews, and said unto him, What sign shewest thou unto us, seeing thou doest these things?"

Then the bishop reads the Nicene Creed, and notice is given for the celebration of the holy communion on the following Sunday; after which the 100th Psalm is sung.

THE SERMON.

The sermon being ended, the bishop reads the prayer for the church militant; and immediately before the final blessing, says the following prayer:—

'Blessed be thy name, O Lord God, for that it pleaseth thee to have thy habitation among the sons of men upon earth, and to dwell in the midst of the assembly of the saints upon earth: bless, we beseech thee, the religious performance of this day, and grant that in this place, now set apart to thy service, thy holy name may be worshipped in truth and purity to all generations, through Jesus Christ our Lord. Amen.

'The peace of God, which passeth all understanding, keep your hearts and minds in the knowledge and love of God, and of his Son Jesus Christ our Lord: and the blessing of God Almighty, the Father, the Son, and the Holy Ghost, be amongst you and remain with you always. Amen.'

To the Editor of the Christian Observer.

I KNOW of no subject of greater importance to the character of a country, than the religious education of its youth; and I have in consequence observed with peculiar pleasure that the pages of your publication are sometimes devoted to this interesting topic. Having myself had considerable experience in education, and having, I trust, been animated with the wish of instilling into the minds of my pupils, not only the knowledge which might be of service to them in this life, but also that which will stand them in good stead as respects the life to come, I trouble you with a few remarks, in the hope that what I shall say may meet the eye of others engaged in education, who may be induced, if they have not already done so, to commence a regular system of religious instruction. I will just hint at a few of the general principles which might be adopted in all schools, whether public or private; and the more numerous the establishment the more requisite is religious improvement.—A proper observance of the Sabbath, is one of the *first principles* and habits to be insisted on. This ob servance, in many schools, is confined to an attendance at church, once or twice on the Sunday; but to instil a due reverence for it, *no part of the sacred day should be spent in secular employment*; it should be wholly " sanctified to the Lord." Serious conversation, pious books, instructive lectures, and above all, the reading of the Scriptures, may most profitably fill up the intervals of Divine service at church. All plays and games on that day should be strictly forbidden.

Another point to be observed is bending classical studies to religious improvement. The constant repetition in the study of the classics, of the power of Jupiter, Neptune, or Pluto, the deification of the worst passions of our nature, intermixed as they are with the beauties of eloquence and poetry, although they may have no visible effect on the belief of the young student, will naturally tend, unless carefully watched, to make him forgetful of the *one true God*, in whom we live, and move, and have our being. An essential point then in religious education is to display the absurdity and the immorality of the Polytheism of the ancient classics; to shew its follies, as a religious system, its vices as a practice. To exemplify my meaning on this head, Homer tells us that when Thetis had promised to represent the hardships of Achilles to Jupiter, she informs her son, that she cannot at present address the king of all the gods, as he was gone on a visit. Upon this absurdity, what an account might be given of that God, whose ears are *ever* open to our prayers, who never slumbers nor sleeps, and without whom not a sparrow falls to the ground!

A third point which I would enforce, is this: a watchful care over all the amusements, relaxations, and pursuits of the pupils; that they should be uniformly directed by the injunctions of the Bible; no other standard should be appealed to. The false notions of human honour, too often instilled into the mind at school, tend, in after life, to form a duellist; while the indulgence of immodest conversation or conduct leads, in manhood, to corresponding evils. Nor is restraint of this kind, upon the relaxations of the pupils, so difficult as may be imagined by some persons: the master is often appealed to, and he can, if so disposed, answer that appeal from Scripture. If a word of indecency should reach his ears, he can reprove it by the awful threat of our Saviour, that for every idle word that men shall speak, they shall give account thereof in the day of judgment. In short, the fear of God and the love of Christ should be made the ground work of every thought, word, or action.

The last and most important point to which I will now advert, is the proper reading of the holy Scriptures: *no day should be begun or ended* without the perusal of them; attended of course with simple and earnest prayer. To infuse a habit of constantly reading the Bible, as a duty incumbent on every one through life, will be furnishing the young with a most powerful antidote against all the temptations of the world. I will only add, that every one concerned in education—to say nothing of that powerful inducement, the happiness, temporal, and eternal, of his pupils—will find, in his own comfort and interest, a rich reward for instilling sound influential religious principles into their minds: and to no class of men do those beautiful words of the Preacher more aptly apply: ' Cast thy bread upon the waters, for thou shalt find it after many days,' than to those intrusted with the education of youth.

T. S.

POETRY

WE have so many urgent demands for poetry, that we greatly regret we have it not in our power more liberally to oblige our readers with this article. We select from pieces which have reached us the following compositions

LINES TO A FIRST BORN AND BELOVED CHILD

Child of my earliest care whose opening
  buds
Of richest promise to the prescient sense
Told of the fragrance of thy riper years!
How fondly had I hoped with thee to tread
Once more the realms of fancy and of
  song
Mid gales that breathe of paradise and
  sounds
That speak to us of heaven! Vain fruit
  less hope!
Fancy and song *were* thine but they are
  quench d
In the cold grave while nought remains
  for *me*
But the faint echo of that dearest voice
Which I must hear no more Then fare
  well song
And farewell all that on my youthful ear
Poured its unreal witchery My child!—
Thy infant eyes had traced the page of
  God
And at the fountain of eternal truth
Had quaffed its purest stream Oh! to
  that page
From all that once allured my charmed eye
For ever may I turn! And though I fling
A mournful chaplet o er the lonely tomb
Where yon loved relics moulder though
  I pour
A sad and solemn requiem o er the spot
Those dear remains have hallowed shall
  my view
Look forward to the realms of brightest
  day
Where fancy s meteors play not but where
  truth
With stedfast lustre beams There dear
  est child!
We yet will live to poesy and song
To all heaven s harmonies Thy voice
  which here
Warbled in native sweetness there shall
  learn
A wider compass more ennobling strains
As round the throne of God and of the
  Lamb
We raise the song celestial ——
Then shall it grieve me not that here the
  buds
Of richest promise withered and that
  hope
Which fondly spake of happiness to come
Shone but the day dream of an earthly
  mind
Which sought for *he* the triumphs of an
  hour
For whom the eternal gates of heaven
  flung wide
Their golden splendour and for whom
  the harps
Of plumed seraphs struck the chords of joy
Which hail a saint s beatitude

D S W

THE DELUGE

The cups of gold were spread
  The goblets foam d with wine
And curses deep were heard instead
  Of melodies divine
The viol harp and lute
  To idols praises rang
And mingled with the breathing flute,
  In hymns profanely sung

But hark! the rush of waters loud
Shakes with affright the joyous crowd
Dread thunders pealing from the skies
With flashing glare ot lightn ngs rise
The mountain to its centre shakes
The world in horrid movement quakes
The ocean yielding up its stores
O er the wide world destruction pours
From heaven s high vault the storm im
  pends
And wing d with death to earth descends

Too late the fated race of men perceive
The vengeful bolt of wrath too late they
  grieve
In hopeless agony each foul offence
That urged the thunders of Omnipo
  tence
In vain the rock the lofty tower they
  seek
Frail is the mound the marsy bulwark
  weak
O er loftiest crags the gathering storm is
  hurled
And waters tell where stood yon late fair
  world

H W Y

DEATH

The time must be when I shall lie
  The prisoner of the tyrant death
His frown must glaze this sparkling eye,
  His voice arrest this vital breath

A friend of earthly mould may smooth
  The brow *that* mortal touch hath prest
May ease life s pangs —but can he sooth
  The anguish of a guilty breast?

The solace of a loftier power
  That raging fever must control
And in the frame s dissolving hour
  Say to this breaking heart Be whole

Jesus! reveal thy blissful face!
  Let welcome accents greet this ear
Of peace and joy and conquering grace
  Till rapt I soar to yon bright sphere

TIRO

LINES ADDRESSED TO AN AFFLICTED SISTER

Bereft of health of ease bereft
Is there for thee no solace left
  No balm to heal the ills of life?
Forbid the thought—thy Saviour near
Shall strength supply and banish fear
  And calm thy spirit s inward strife
On Him in life in death depend
The faithful never failing Friend

O love! beyond the reach of thought
That from the realms of glory brought
  The Lord of life with men to dwell!
For men to die!—the crimson stream
Flow'd from his body to redeem
  Our souls from sin and death and hell
O then to Him thy soul commend,
The faithful never failing Friend

Now thron'd on high and Lord of all
Bright angels at his footstool fall
  Or tune their harps to Jesus' name
Yet saints on earth with those above
His pity share and praise his love
  Who is from age to age the same
Mercy and truth their steps attend
And He will be their faithful Friend

If gathering clouds around thee roll
And sorrow's night oppress thy soul
  Yield not to unbelief or fear
The morning hours are on their way
And with the sweet return of day
  Shall hope and joy again appear
And songs of gratitude ascend
To thy unfailing faithful Friend

Kindly he chastens whom he loves
'Tis thus the faith of each he proves
  And purifies from sin the heart
The path thy weary feet have trod
So long though rugged leads to God
  Then bid thy every fear depart
Soon shall the mortal conflict end
And thou, with joy behold that Friend
                        LYSIAS

---

*When the morning stars sang together
and all the sons of God shouted for joy*
                  JOB

Creation's task completed to the heights
Of heaven the Everlasting bent his way
While from unnumbered and harmonious choirs
Of cherubim and seraphim and thrones
The loud hosannahs pealed — Twas thus to harps
Of gold, ethereal sang the angelic throng

He comes! he comes! The glorious work complete
Heaven's Potentate assumes his lofty seat!
  Through all the worlds around
  Let heavenly anthems sound
And grateful each existence tune his praise;
Let the bright morning stars together sing
And lauding him their sweetest concert raise
  While listening hosts proclaim
  With reverence his blest name
And with enraptured awe their fervid homage bring

Let all the sons of God in brilliant throng
Proclaim his glory with celestial song
  The wisdom of his deeds,
  The highest praise exceeds
That loftiest, brightest angel knows to give

Another world created by his might
Another creature formed by him to live
  So far his wondrous name
  Is above angel's fame
As from the depths of hell is the pure æther's height

In light ineffable he takes his place!
Rejoice rejoice ye pure angelic race!
  In awful state alone
  Girt round with princedom throne
Archangel angel cherub seraph power
Virtue and domination far as heaven
In vast expanse outspreads its brilliant bower
  He reigns the King supreme
  Each seraph's endless theme
While to him wisdom honour glory might are given
                        H W

SONNET
Imitated from the Italian of Michel Angelo

How sweet shall be the incense of my prayer
  If gifted from on high with power to pray
I may draw near and bring those spices rare
  That spring not forth from my unfertile clay
Source of all perfect gifts! ah who shall lay
Aught at thy feet, unless by Thee bestowed?
Thine are the softening dew the quickening ray
And thine the right to reap where thou hast strowed
Forerunner to the purchased abode!
  Oh shed thou then upon me—e'en on me
Thy light to find thy strength to tread the road
To where the pure in heart shall dwell with thee
Take all thine own —inspire enkindle raise
My thoughts—my tongue—my life to thy immortal praise!
                        S M W

TO A FRIEND WITH A POCKET TESTAMENT

Say! wouldst thou live? this hallowed page shall tell
Where life's best joys and holiest pleasures dwell
Say! must thou die? ah prize this sacred lore
That points to worlds where death can wound no more
Living or dying this shall sooth each pain
Whispering To live is Christ, to die is gain
                        G

REVIEW OF NEW PUBLICATIONS

1. *Palingenesia The World to Come* Paris and London 1824
2. *Letters by Basilicus* Reprinted from the Jewish Expositor for 1820, 21, 22
3. *The Coming of the Day of God &c* By an humble Expectant of the Promises Dublin and London
4. *Scriptural Doctrine of the Last General Judgment* By J E JONES M A Gloucester 1823 2s
5. *Letter to the Rev J E Jones occasioned by his Sermon on Modern Millenarianism* By JOHN BAYFORD Esq F S A Author of Messiah's Kingdom
6. *Practical View of the Redeemer's Advent* By Rev JAMES HALDANE STEWART M A &c 1825
7. *Messiah's Kingdom a Brief Inquiry into the Second Advent* By JOHN BAYFORD Esq London 8vo 10s
8. *Predictions and Promises of God respecting Israel a Sermon on the Baptism of Mr Alexander late Reader in the Jewish Synagogue* By the Rev J HATCHARD A M, Vicar of St Andrew's Plymouth 1825 1s 6d
9. *Conversion of the Jews a Sermon delivered in All Saints Church Manchester after the public Baptism of a Jew and his two Children* By the Rev C BURTON 1824
10. *Discourses on Prophecy* By the Rev JOHN DAVISON late Fellow of Oriel College Second Edition London 15s

ONE of the great evidences for the Divine origin of revelation may be considered to be its prodigious variety of topics in correspondence to that endless versatility with which He who framed the mind of man knew it to be endowed To the simple and contemplative mind the holy Scriptures open sublime descriptions of the works of nature, and through nature lead to nature's God Again the beauties even of poetry and composition are afforded as if to direct the most elegantly moulded mind to a consideration of those truths which the poetry illustrates or the eloquence enforces Others more studious of *man*, the proper study of mankind find an allurement to the doctrines and precepts of Scripture in the details of character which it presents in the course of histories most stupendous which it unfolds and none it must be owned can have a fuller claim on the attention and admiration of mankind than those histories which exhibit the personal character and office of the Son of God himself To some and those perhaps the wisest and best of our species the simple view of the mercies of God as revealed in the Gospel will have afforded the highest motive and guide to action Their aim will have been deeply to impress upon their own minds, and the minds of others those blessings of salvation which are beyond all price as preachers to urge without ceasing that incessant call to sinners Be ye reconciled to God and as Christians of whatever rank to press forward the great designs of benevolence peace on earth and good will to men, of which they find every variety of example in the character of our Great Exemplar

But there is one department more the department of *prophecy*, which possesses with some persons a charm superior to all others, and indeed it must be owned of the most edifying kind Their evidence for Christianity is not so much its other miracles whether of mercy or power, as that which has doubtless the highest claim to be called miraculous the delivery and fulfilment of Divine prophecy The correspondence of prediction and event presents a line of investigation, and an order and force of conviction to their minds which they feel perfectly irresistible. And it is not to be questioned, that the Almighty framer of worlds and of his own blessed word has in a singular manner consulted and gratified this very taste in his rational creatures. Prophecies of successive temporal events have been concurrent with the Divine dispensations in all ages. The great predictions respecting the Messiah himself were delivered with a view to the striking effect to be produced by their accomplishment. The glow of expectation previous to his predicted coming, was at once important and salutary. Other prophecies likewise previously or subsequently delivered of glories yet future, which are to signalize the Messiah's reign, have awakened, and do still awaken in the hearts of many, the same glow. And that nothing in this department might be wanting to complete this effect, even on minds the most variously constructed, the circumstance of exact numerical calculation has been superadded, so that neither imagination shall exceed nor exact judgment despair in investigating times and seasons, so far as those times and seasons are put within our own power of inquiry.

Far be it from us to condemn that which God approves. We dare not pass the slightest censure on that which has evidently been the employment and the solace of many faithful and sincere Christians in every age. The sober and serious investigation of prophecy is even more than a help, it is according to our means and opportunities a duty. It tends to raise the mind to heavenly things. It works a separation from earth and earth born speculations. It produces a holy disinterestedness as to objects of mere secular worth. It arms the mind against the influence of passing events. It relieves it of many uneasy and doubtful apprehensions. It teaches it reliance on an unseen but infallible Providence, ordering all things in heaven and earth. It both results from, and promotes a strength of faith, a brightness of hope and a fitness of acquiescence in the Divine proceedings. It is greatly serviceable in producing a minute attention to the word of God. No student of prophecy can fail of close and realizing views of some parts at least of Scripture. And the study of prophecy has then produced its full measure of benefit when it is connected with a study *as* attentive of the doctrines and morals of the sacred code, and has formed as it were a bridge or a portal into the sacred inclosure of Divine love, Christian tempers, and a holy practice.

We say thus much, to justify our early resumption of the subject of prophecy after having so lately reviewed the interesting Crisis of Mr. Cooper. And perhaps if monitory notes were not required to mix in the general accordance of our feelings with the prophetic commentators we should not have so soon again invited our readers to similar discussions. We hold that prophecy should be made strictly subsidiary to its *two* proper and intended purposes, one that of *affording evidence to the sacred and saving doctrines of Divine writ* the other that of *furnishing an incentive to present duty by a consideration of future prospects*.* But

Mr Davison the eminent author of a very distinguished work at the head of our article to which we hope more particularly to allude in our continuation of this review in a future Number, has hinted at what might be considered another distinct end of prophecy more especially as viewed in connexion with the sublime moralities with which it is ever accompanied in the sacred code. Let the predictions of prophecy he says for a time be put out of our thoughts and let the prophetic books be read for the pure theology which they contain. With what feelings of conviction they are read by the religionist it is not hard to tell. He perceives that he is instructed and elevated by the discoveries made to him of the Supreme

this study, like every other, may be perverted from its purpose, by the pride and perverseness of man. It may become the minister of mere curiosity, or of mere presumption. It may be made an arena for the display of dexterity in the use of intellectual weapons. It may be made the watchword of party. It may sound the note of discord and turbulence. And the very discussion of the signs and modes of the Lord's approach may be amongst the means used by the great enemy of souls for rendering us unmindful of his approach, or at least unprepared to meet our Lord.

And this is a danger more particularly imminent in the discussion of prophecies of which the fulfilment is wholly future. Here one great object of prophecy is not yet developed. It affords no evidence to the truth of Divine writ. Revelation itself is, on the other hand, compromised, or at least suspended in its authority, till the accomplishment arrives. The mind undrilled by patient investigation, and slow comparison of predictions with their supposed events, has only to invent facts in correspondence with supposed predictions. In this process, the imagination has clearly the upper hand of all the other faculties. It is that faculty most needed in the pursuit of oracles as yet hidden in the roll of futurity. But it

Being and of the kind of worship and obedience required from himself—and these discoveries made with an authority and a commanding power which argue them to be what they are given for a law of life and practice doctrines not of theory but of self government and direction the most useful therefore to himself and the most worthy of the source from which they profess to come On this head I cite the words of Origen who does not overstate this persuasive force of the prophetic writings when he says of them that to the meditating and attentive reader they raise an impression of enthusiasm (a true and rational enthusiasm like a spark of their own inspiration) and by his perceptions convince him as he reads that these compositions can be none of the works of men which have obtained the credit of being the oracles of God

is that faculty which is of all others the most liable to lead astray the decisions of the understanding and to warp the affections and tempers of the heart. Hence erroneous judgments maintained with warmth, are always the rock of which such expositors have to beware. The check which others find in the stubbornness of facts, compared with their commentaries on prophecy must with those persons be derived from within their own breast. One great benefit, as we have observed being necessarily absent from their investigations, (namely, that of strengthening the evidences of our holy faith by the correspondence of fact with prediction) they must doubly regard the remaining benefit they have to offer which is timely to warn mankind of their duties, to control their conduct in preparation for the future, and to lead them to circumspection watchfulness, and prayer. They are to ' stand upon the tower and watch to see what God will say unto them not indeed as prophets, but as sincere though fallible expositors of his word " and what they shall answer when *they* are reproved.

On this account, we regard the volume of Mr Stewart which stands No 6 on our list as deserving notice and commendation. It assumes the very ground we are speaking of. It goes upon what is future but it goes upon it for the sole and exclusive purpose of preparing its readers for the advent of their Lord. It guards, whilst it assumes the supposition of his near approach, and makes the time and the manner of the event in every way subservient to the great practical consideration, ' Who may abide the day of His coming? who may stand when He appeareth?' We shall reserve room for some practical extracts from this interesting and important volume important from the time of its publication, and interesting from the matter it contains, and the spirit in which it treats it

The direct subject of this, and

most of the other works before us, is the second coming or advent of our Lord and, viewed in connexion with that most true, but as yet future and most mysterious of all periods in the annals of prophecy the MILLENNIUM. And the first particular observation we feel it strongly our duty to reiterate upon the minds of considerate Christians is this, that it *is* future and that being so, it is unquestionably in some sense hidden from our eyes. There can be no analogy sensible to us between events that are future, and events that are past in the evolutions of prophecy. The view that we have of the past is and must be, of a totally different kind from that which we can form of the future. The prophetic commentator may write a very interesting and edifying history of past events, in connexion with predictive declarations witness Rollin Prideaux above all Newton and other direct commentators on prophecy. But it would be unreasonable to look for any such delineations of the future. It would be presumption to anticipate even the political course of the world for a single day and how much less its spiritual or providential course for unknown years to come! The prophecies never in the nature of things could have been intended for an orderly journal of futurity. And, whatever, in explaining them tends merely to captivate the imagination and gratify curiosity, may be considered like one of the prophetic almanacs, as carrying *ipso facto* its own contradiction along with it

Not only is the manner, but the *time* also, of future events hidden from our eyes. It is, and it never can be for us to know future times and seasons which God hath put in his own power. And it is not a little remarkable as applied to this view of the case that periods so well defined in themselves as those severally of the 1260 the 1290, the 1335 years in the roll of prophecy, should yet, at this late period of the world, remain unsettled with respect to their actual place in the map of time. Reasons respectively alleged to be the most cogent are offered for their commencement and consequent conclusion at very different eras. Certain *limits* are laid down it is true by the all wise Disposer of prophecies and their events, *within which* it might appear that all parties have strong reasons for agreeing to place those periods. But it would be impossible for the careful and judicious reader not to allow that within these limits much uncertainty prevails and that humility and patient waiting, with respect even to those more obvious calculations is at present our safest course and highest duty. It was probably under some such general impression that a very sanguine expositor of future prophecies the author who stands *first* at the head of our article—and who has as we think with singular infelicity embodied a very extended series of prophetic arrangements in a running page of measured lines—has endeavoured to fix the difference between offering diagnostic symptoms of our Lord's approach, and the presumption of defining the actual time of his arrival in the following specimen of his versified prose. The instances, however, which he adduces appear to us to be at least questionable in their application. Abraham, Moses and Daniel were themselves the subjects of direct and immediate inspiration

Behold! a woman travaileth—
Fit emblem this!
And prominent in holy writ to mark
The period of the world's deliverance
From groaning of corruption—day and hour
Unknown to man or angel—previous signs
And diagnostics so discernible
That hypocrites alone regard them not!
Such was the Saviour's language yet his church
Professing to believe and follow him
Deem it presumptuous to watch the times
And ascertain the seasons though the Lord
Hath said he will do *nothing* upon earth
Without a previous warning —Thus a time

Known to the Father only, and concealed
E'en from the Son, on earth to him made known
By revelation more express, and sent
And by his angel signified to John
Of things which are and shall be. Moses knew
According to the promise sworn of God
To Abraham, and by the covenant
Of circumcision ratified, how long
His seed should sojourn in a foreign land
Subject to bondage. When four hundred years
The time of their deliverance drew nigh,
The people grew and multiplied, when he
Full forty years of age, and conversant
In all Egyptian wisdom,—trained up
And nourished by the daughter of the King,
Refused to be called her son, and chose
Affliction with his people, knowing well
That God would by his hand deliver them
Howbeit disobedient, for at first
It came into his heart to visit them
By secret meditation, till at length
His inward purpose and intent of mind
Was outwardly confirmed by flame of fire
And voice in Sinai, sending him forthwith
With full commission and express command
To shew great signs and wonders in the land
And bring them forth from Egypt.—Daniel
First set his heart to pray, and learnt in books
The computation of another time
Set and determin'd for deliverance
From Babylonian bondage. So may we
By patient observation of the word
Written for our instruction, upon whom
The latter days are fall'n and evil times,
So may we judge redemption to be nigh,
And lifting up our heads, run to and fro
In search of knowledge, till the measure full
Words once shut up, and sealed books appear
Open to view.

pp. 103—105.

And here we must once more take leave to premise, that we consider *accuracy of definition*, in regard to future events, as not at all necessarily involved in *certainty of expectation*. No doubts respecting the mode of the Millennium, whatever that Millennium be, no difficulties respecting its time, its course, its duration, whether for 1000 or 365,000 years, or its termination, can for a moment shake in the mind of the believer the clear testimony and sublime assurance of the twentieth chapter of the Revelations respecting its reality. After the account of binding Satan for a thousand years, the Apostle continues in his sublimest strains,— AND I SAW THRONES, AND THEY SAT UPON THEM, AND JUDGMENT WAS GIVEN UNTO THEM, AND I SAW THE SOULS OF THEM THAT WERE BEHEADED FOR THE WITNESS OF JESUS, AND FOR THE WORD OF GOD, AND WHICH HAD NOT WORSHIPPED THE BEAST, NEITHER HIS IMAGE, NEITHER HAD RECEIVED HIS MARK UPON THEIR FOREHEADS, OR IN THEIR HANDS; AND THEY LIVED AND REIGNED WITH CHRIST A THOUSAND YEARS. BUT THE REST OF THE DEAD LIVED NOT AGAIN UNTIL THE THOUSAND YEARS WERE FINISHED. THIS IS THE FIRST RESURRECTION. BLESSED AND HOLY IS HE THAT HATH PART IN THE FIRST RESURRECTION: ON SUCH THE SECOND DEATH HATH NO POWER, BUT THEY SHALL BE PRIESTS OF GOD AND OF CHRIST, AND SHALL REIGN WITH HIM A THOUSAND YEARS. AND WHEN THE THOUSAND YEARS ARE EXPIRED, SATAN SHALL BE LOOSED OUT OF HIS PRISON.

What can we say after reading this decisive and sublime testimony to the fact of the Millennium but, in prior language of the same inspired writer, Blessed is he that readeth, and they that hear the words of this prophecy, and keep those things which are written therein. Can any question after this remain, but an inquiry only *how far* we may humbly investigate, within what limits of *time* or under what course of providential *circumstances* this animating prophecy is finally to be accomplished, *if not accomplished already*. We add this last clause of exception because we know it to have been the opinion of some that the Millennium has passed already, and Vitringa has been at some pains to confute the various suppositions that it actually took place, either counting the thousand years from the first coming of our Lord, or from some period intermediate between that and the reign of Constantine or finally from Constantine himself It is remarkable that Grotius and many other intelligent and learned commentators should have been numbered amongst these premature Chiliasts whose opinion was, in truth near that of all the interpreters of the middle ages, and perhaps may account for the prevalence of a very general expectation that the end of the world was come about the thousandth or eleven hundredth year of the Christian era

We stay not now to refute or even to detail these exploded and impossible suppositions which are in truth resolvable into this a determination to get rid at all risks of so to speak a *more impossible* as these writers thought, and more ill favoured position the position of the elder and truer Chiliasts These elders all agreed in placing the Millennium where the most just and latest views of prophecy seem finally to agree in placing it at the conclusion of the present order of things after the judicial destruction of Anti Christ and during a reign of Jesus Christ far more universal than any hitherto manifested and enfolding alike both Jew and Gentile within its wide embrace This must now be felt to be the only basis on which the question can rest the only principle on which it can be argued And this we imagine being fully conceded by all who deem it necessary to cast a single glance towards the Millennial controversy added to what we have before offered, renders superfluous for the purposes of that controversy, any consideration of *the exact time* in which it is to take place

The question then is thus narrowed to a very simple but very important inquiry by what *course of providential circumstances* we are to define the plain and undeniable declarations by the Apocalyptic Prophet of the yet future glories of the millennial kingdom? And here before we pronounce on the possibility of coming to any distinct definition at all, it will be necessary to glance again at the opinions that were held on this subject by the elder Chiliasts before alluded to in making which appeal, however, it will be fully understood, that we are far from feeling a spirit of entire submission to the commentators, even of the *first two centuries* The interpretation even of a prophet himself were it Isaiah Daniel or John, would not be conclusive on his own prophecy unless his comment as well as his prediction, were given by inspiration for we know, on the best authority that not unto themselves but unto us they did minister *these* things, when the Spirit by them testified beforehand the sufferings of Christ and the GLORY THAT SHOULD FOLLOW Any indirect and traditional report of their views respecting their own prophecies, must of course be very uncertain, and of little or no value And we must say that their immediate, uninspired successors seem to have been remarkably we might say almost providentially defective in the work of a just and *authoritative* interpretation of Scripture of that very Scripture to the authenticity and genuineness of which they bear so invaluable and irrefragable a testimony Be this however as it may, the appeal to antiquity is important on many accounts and it would seem in this point to be almost wholly in favour of *a literal interpretation of the promised glories of the Millennium* Justin Martyr stands at the head of all the early advocates for this doctrine for distinctness of statement having been converted to Christianity, not more than thirty years after the demise of John the Divine His testimony but for the inconvenient omission of a certain negative particle which Joseph Mede is for restoring against the faith of all manuscripts and as Whitby strongly contends against the force of the passage itself would make *all* pious and pure Christians of his age, to hold this interpretation. But even, though *some* pious and pure Christians might have doubted, still he unquestionably maintains, that *all* truly *orthodox* and absolutely *correct* Christians did hold it: namely that "at the period of the Millennium *Jerusalem* is to be rebuilt, adorned, and enlarged: that the nations of Christians are to be gathered together into it: that the race of the Jews, converted to Christ, are to return and repeople their ancient city: that a resurrection of all the saints departed, whether in the Jewish or Gentile churches, is to take place: and that all, together with Christ himself and the holy patriarchs and prophets of old, are to rejoice and reign upon earth a thousand years." To this view of the Millennium Tertullian some years after is made to add the notion of a gradual resurrection, during its course: but only of the saints, according to their respective *merits*, sooner or later, till the very end of the destined period: when eventually *all* the dead, small and great, are to stand before God. This last he calls the judgment *de libris*, out of the *books*; as the other and first resurrection had been *de solus*. I saw *thrones*, &c.—Long however, before either Justin or Tertullian we find that Papias, an undoubted contemporary with the surviving contemporaries of the Apostles, had written concerning the Millennium, that 'there shall be a thousand years after the resurrection of the dead, wherein the kingdom of Christ shall corporally subsist upon this earth.' 'which opinion, I suppose,' continues Eusebius as quoted by Lardner, 'he was led into by *misunderstanding the apostolical narrations*, and for want of seeing into those things which they spoke *mystically* and in *figures*: for he was a man of no great capacity, as may be conjectured from his writings.' Yet he gave occasion to a great many ecclesiastical writers after him to be of the same opinion, who respected the antiquity of the man as Irenæus, and the rest who have maintained that opinion. The truth is, Papias seems to have been the medium of conveyance to later writers, not only of Apostolical but Jewish and Rabbinical, traditions on this subject. And accordingly, not singly in his own pages, but in those of many even wiser writers of these earlier ages we find such a mass of unworthy stuff: such a *farrago* of secular and corporal ideas heaped up upon the original and well meant interpretation of the millennial prophecy, as to bring the whole into utter discredit, nay contempt, and final rejection, very early in the Christian church. Whoever has a taste for such details, for we confess we have none, may see them given at full length in Whitby's discourse on the Millennium, at the end of his Commentary on the New Testament: and given, we must say, very much *invidiæ causa*, and without any very *strong* bearing on the question itself.* It is much more to the point of mere authority that the names of Origen, Jerom, and

* The Jewish and even Rabbinical origin of many millennian notions will not, we believe, be discovered by some who consider the ancient Jewish Commentators as not wholly unenlightened in their own Scriptures. We shall only give one testimony to these Judaical tendencies of the elder Millenaries, as found in Lardner from Basil. Speaking of Apollinarius bishop of Laodicea A.D. 362. Basil says 'He is chargeable with the mystic or rather Judaic doctrines respecting the resurrection in which he says that we are to return again to the services of the law, again to be circumcised, to observe Sabbaths, abstain from meats, offer to God gifts and adorations in Jerusalem, in attendance on the temple—in short from Christians to become Jews.' Lardner's Credibility chap 95 p 11.—We quote Basil the rather as we find him ranged in Palingenesia, amongst the friends of the Millenaries, as also Origen whom Whitby and Lardner repeatedly quote against them: as also Austin of whom *we* too shall have a word to say hereafter. Eusebius likewise is claimed, whose account of Papias given in our text is any thing but favourable on this head, and who is considered point blank against the opinion in question. These things, till explained, must very much tend to weaken our confidence in the *authorities* of Palingenesia.

Austin, those great pioneers of antiquity and immortal, though doubtless *human* guardians of scriptural truth are mainly ranged against the Chiliasts other great names might be added. And we think we shall better gratify our readers by extracting the account of a friendly episcopal conference, holden on this very subject so early as about A.D. 250 than by retailing any angry or splenetic effusions only tending to darken counsel on either part. The account is given by Lardner from a fragment preserved by Eusebius of a work of Dionysius, bishop of Alexandria a prelate of very distinguished talents and piety in the third century. A book had been written by Nepos, another Egyptian bishop in favour of the literal Millennium and against the *allegorists* (as their opponents were termed) And 'when, says Dionysius in this fragment I was in the province of Arsinoe where you know this opinion has for some time so far prevailed as to cause divisions and apostacies of *whole churches* having called together the presbyters and teachers of the brethren in the villages admitting likewise as many of the brethren as pleased to be present I advised that this opinion should be publicly examined into. And when they produced to me that book as a shield and impregnable bulwark I sat with them three whole days, successively from morning till evening discussing the contents of it. He goes on highly applauding the good order of the dispute the moderation and candour of all present their willingness to be convinced and to retract their former opinions if reason so required. With a good conscience he says and unfeignedly and with hearts open to the sight of God embracing whatever could be made out by good arguments from the holy Scriptures. In the end Coracio the chief defender of that opinion engaged and promised, in the presence of all the brethren that he would no longer maintain or defend, or teach, or make mention of it, as being fully convinced by the arguments on the other side. And all the brethren who were present rejoiced for the conference, and their mutual reconciliation and agreement. Lardner's Credib. of Gosp. Hist. part ii. ch. 42 a place in which much curious matter will be found on the subject of the Apocalypse in general.

That the opinions of these Allegorists or Antichiliasts alluded to in the above authorities were worth having or inquiring after on the other side we cannot very well imagine. They were content with very vague and general interpretations having evidently none or very slender means of ascertaining the prophetic current of mere inchoate times and seasons, or of gathering any conclusion from past events and developments of prophecy to illustrate the future. The Chiliasts themselves occasionally apprehended the Millennium to be about immediately to appear at the very latest says Lactantius a warm advocate for the doctrine two hundred years hence. And the Antichiliasts who spoke of resuscitations of doctrine and the general extension of Gospel truth under the notion of having part in the first resurrection had nothing certain to fix their foot upon, in the history of the church to warrant such an application. St Austin, in his Civitas Dei seems to regard the first resurrection as the restoration of the dead soul to spiritual life and attempts amidst many strange labours, a mystical resolution of the number thousand into a cube of perfection from that of ten. Thus he would intimate a large reach of time for the prevalence of Christian doctrine, as we are promised to receive a hundred fold more in this present life. He speaks out however explicitly in the same chapter of those who suspect the passage in Rev xx to mean, a *corporeal* resurrection on the ground more especially of the thousand years falling in as a sabbatical millenary, after the 'six thousand years of sorrow and of labour,' which opinion, says he 'would be how soever tolerable (utcunque tolerabilis) if spiritual pleasures were to be the result to the saints of this personal presence of the Lord, *for once we ourselves were even of the same opinion.* But since they attribute to the risen saints such immoderate grants of good eating and drinking, as not only exceed temperance, but even belief, such things can only be credited by carnal men. Those then who are spiritual, call those others marvellous believers, Chiliasts.' De Civitate Dei lib. 20 chap. 7.

To this may be added, as below, from Lardner, the remarks of Andrew bishop of Cesarea, about the year 500, whose prudent conclusion from the whole matter in commenting on the Apocalypse seems to be this: 'Whether the thousand years here spoken of denote exactly that term or only a long duration God only knows!'* Credib. part ii. ch. 146.

In short it might justly seem to have been the will of the Supreme Director of events and Great Dispenser of prophecy, that the doctrine of the Millennium, after having run a short course of unintelligible or untenable interpretation in the earliest ages, should lie in abeyance till later ages; and that men, discouraged by the impotent attempts of themselves or others, should contentedly defer the fuller and more intelligent examination of the prophecy to periods long subsequent, and furnished with means of illustration and investigation far more copious and effective. We may conclude this reference to antiquity with the short but appropriate introduction to the comments of latter ages by Burnet, the great theorist on all the several stages of subsistence belonging to this our lower planet. 'In latter ages,' says he, speaking of millennial writers, "they seem to have dropt one half of the doctrine, namely the renovation of nature, which Irenæus, Justin Martyr, and the ancients join inseparably with the Millennium; and by this omission the doctrine hath been made less intelligible, and one part of it inconsistent with the other. And when their pretensions were to reign upon this present earth and in this present state of nature, it gave a jealousy to temporal princes, and gave occasion likewise to many fanatical spirits under the notion of saints to aspire to dominion &c. This I reckon as one great cause that brought the doctrine into discredit. All of which the author hopes himself to rectify and to reduce the question to its true state.'

And here the true state of the question meets us for discussion, as found in still more modern times, even in 'these *last days*.' Beginning afresh with the great names of Mede and Burnet on the one side, and those of Whitby and Vitringa on the other, we cannot but confess it has had since their time full opportunity for growing up to a measure of importance which it could never have gained of old, even from

---

* Some confine the above mentioned hundred years to the short period of our Lord's ministry from his baptism to his ascension to heaven, being no more than three years or three and a half years. Others think that after the completion of six thousand years shall be the first resurrection from the dead which is to be peculiar to the saints above who are to be raised up that they may dwell again on this earth where they had given proofs of patience and fortitude, and that they may live a thousand years here in honour and plenty, after which will be the general resurrection of good and bad. But *the church* receives neither of those interpretations, for we remember what our Lord said to the Sadducees that the righteous shall be as the angels which are in heaven, Mark xii. 25, as also the words of Paul who says, The kingdom of heaven is not meat and drink, Rom. xiv. 17. By the thousand years therefore we understand the time of the preaching of the Gospel in the time of the Gospel dispensation.—Andrew bishop of Cesarea in Rev. xx. 7. Lardner's Credibility part ii. ch. 146.

the labours of a Papias or a Justin Martyr, a Jerom or an Austin. We see it is very true, under different names, something very like a revival of the old controversy between the Chiliasts and the Antichiliasts, the Millenaries and the Allegorists; only there is this great difference and great improvement. The advocates for a literal Millennium have brought themselves to speak in a much more guarded and modest manner of that mysterious period and to affix more spirituality to its *sensible* imagery. Their opponents on the contrary, the spiritualisers have learned to affix a definite period to their Millennium, to make it absolutely coincident with the millenarian scheme, in point of time and many of its circumstances, and only to demur on one or two points very material, it must be owned; but we trust in a kindred spirit of forbearance and humility. And must not, indeed, each party, after their full measure of experience from all that is past, say, from the depth of their soul in the solemn view of an undefined futurity, "Secret things belong unto the Lord our God?"

Here then finding ourselves at present shut out by our limits from a further prosecution of the subject in the present Number, we should very contentedly leave it altogether, did our duty to our readers excuse us from a resumption of it at a point where we must be more immediately drawn ourselves into the controversy. In the mean time however we shall satisfy ourselves with taking our leave under cover of Mr. Stewart's Practical View, who avails himself of his privilege in leaving the grand question wholly undecided. His little preface on the subject of the second coming of the Redeemer contains what we believe all parties will now subscribe, as it must be admitted to be much in confirmation of our own historical sketch above.

There appears to be a studied obscurity in the sacred writers in their manner of speaking of his advent, as the attentive reader will perceive; so that in some passages it is difficult to ascertain whether we are to understand his coming to be by his Spirit, by his providence, or by his personal appearance. This obscurity seems to have been designed, that his church might ever be allowed to exercise the hope of his glorious manifestation, not knowing the day nor the hour wherein the Son of man cometh.

This hope was the animating principle of the first Christians. They are represented as waiting for his Son from heaven, as looking for the blessed hope and the glorious appearing of the great God and our Saviour Jesus Christ, and were distinguished from the world around them by this character, that they loved his appearing.

As the love of the church waxed cold, this hope very much declined. Individual believers doubtless were still using the prayer of the Apostle, Come quickly, even so come Lord Jesus; but the great apostacy almost entirely obliterated the expectation of a coming Saviour. A purgatory after death, which might allow a longer period to cleanse the souls of the wicked, was far more agreeable to such a system, than the near approach of an Almighty King, who was coming to take vengeance on them that know not God and that obey not the Gospel of our Lord Jesus Christ.

At the era of the Reformation however this hope which had been so long buried in oblivion was again revived. Our Reformers commenced their ecclesiastical year by a reference to the coming of our Lord, framing the collects of our church and selecting the portions of Scripture to be read for her occasional services in reference to this event, and this not for one Sabbath only but for four successive weeks, as if they wished at the outset of the year to restore her worshippers to the position of the first church.

Notwithstanding this return of our Reformers to the principles of the early Christians, the second advent of our Lord is a practical operative principle is in the present day almost entirely lost to the church of Christ, so much so that if Christians in general be asked, Are you waiting or do you hope for the coming of the Lord? their answer is, I expect to go to him, but I have no expectation that he will come to me. They have ceased to look for his appearing.

It is evident there must be some error in this; for if any truth should become more influential by the lapse of time, the near approach of the Saviour is that truth. If the early Christians nearly eighteen hundred years since were waiting for him, surely we who live in the latter days should be earnestly expecting him.

It is easy however to account for the

progress of this error. Soon after the revival of this animating doctrine by the Reformers, it was abused by various crude and fanciful, and indeed carnal and wicked opinions upon the Millennium—a subject quite distinct from the advent—opinions that tended to overturn civil government and to introduce worse than heathen licentiousness. This discouraged many from referring much to this subject. The day of death has been practically considered as the period of the believer's felicity, rather than that great day when the trumpet shall sound, and death shall be swallowed up in victory.—Preface, pp. ix—xi.

The laudable attempt of Mr. Stewart, in the subsequent pages, is, "entirely distinct from all sentiments respecting the Millennium, upon which he offers no opinion; to place before the Christian church the substance of that which is revealed in the Scriptures upon the second advent of our Lord. It is done with no design of establishing a mere theory or fanciful opinion, but with a view to Christian edification in these remarkable days."

The general plan of the work is a division into four parts; the first containing four discourses, on The Redeemer's Advent desirable to his Friends; the second containing two discourses, on The Redeemer's Advent terrible to his Enemies; the third containing two discourses, on Reasons for expecting the Redeemer's Advent; the fourth containing ten discourses, on The Course and Conduct becoming an Expectation of the Redeemer's Advent. The whole is written in Mr. Stewart's well known style of deep piety and affectionate tenderness, with some felicity of illustration, much fulness of matter and clearness of arrangement, and is altogether creditable as a work composed and delivered, as it appears, during a single season for the benefit of the congregation of Percy Chapel. We shall give a few extracts somewhat bearing upon our present subject. The first descriptive of that glorious appearing of Christ so desirable to his faithful followers betrays the impossibility of confining our more general and congregational descriptions of that event, to the *measured* glories of a mere millennial state.

The glorious appearing! And if you examine the particulars, you will find it well merits this title. For he comes himself the incarnate God; his seat a great white throne, a throne so filled with majesty, that at its appearance the heavens and the earth flee away, and their place is no more seen.—He comes attended by myriads of angels. As kings in visiting their subjects have a numerous train with them, when the King of kings appears ten thousand times ten thousand of angels form his train. All the host of heaven accompany him. The mighty angels which excel in strength, the seraphim which surround the throne, the archangels—none will be wanting; all these happy spirits with joy attend their King.—The voice which will proclaim his advent will heighten the solemnity. On great occasions heralds are sent before to proclaim the coming of a judge or the near approach of a king; in that day when the Judge of all the earth draws nigh, archangels will be the heralds. The trump of God will sound, and that with so loud a voice that the whole creation will return the echo. For all that are in their graves will come forth———the sea will give up its dead, and death and hell will give up the dead that are in it.

Such in a few words will be the glory of his advent.

Here bearing in mind, my Christian friends, what was mentioned in the first discourse, that ere the terror of this scene commences, you will have an assured proof of his favour by your bodies having been caught up to be with the Lord, let me request you to pause for a moment and behold his glorious epiphany. Will you not, when you see him thus exalted, break forth in some such strain as this?

Is this he who was a worm and no man? whom man despised, and whom the nations abhorred? Is this he who agonized in Gethsamene, and whose blood was shed on the mount of Calvary? Yes! mine eyes see it is the same Jesus; the marks of his love are still fresh upon him; but, oh how gloriously transfigured! That head which was swoln by thorns is now arrayed with many crowns; that countenance which sorrow had marred more than any man's now shines like the sun in his strength; that face which was defiled with shame and spitting is now the seat of loveliness and consummate beauty.—Is this he again, you will say, who was deserted by all his disciples? who in that trying hour had no friend or acquaintance, lover and friend put far from him? Yes! it is he; but now how numerously attended! Thousands of angels are ministering to him, and ten thousand times ten thousand are standing around him.—Is this he who appeared to be left of his

Father and who in the agony of his soul cried out, My God my God why hast thou forsaken me? Yes! I see he is the same, but, O how marvellously changed! He now appears in the glory of his Father. All his love is made manifest and he seems to say to the whole creation

This is my beloved Son in whom I am well pleased.

O that these and far far higher thoughts may possess your souls in that day! pp 49—51

The same train of description accompanies Mr Stewart to his new heavens and new earth. To his rather infelicitous expression of 'happy negatives' in that state he subjoins in a dactylic stanza not very worthy of such a subject as the crowning felicity of the blessed inhabitants, that

Their foreheads proclaim his ineffable name
Their bodies his glory display
A day without night they feast in his sight
And eternity seems as a day. p 68

They shall reign for ever and ever. It is not for a limited time that the happy occupants of this city are to enjoy their privileges. It is for eternity, an eternity so absolute that when the myriads of stars which deck the heavens shall all have been counted, when the sands that lie so thickly on the shores of every ocean and of every sea shall have been slowly reckoned one by one, when language shall have lost expression and the powers of numbers ceased, this eternity shall still appear in all its youthful vigour, shall commence its course anew, till other stars and other sands shall have again and again been told and still this unbounded eternity remain. This shall be the duration of their blessedness. They shall reign for ever and ever.

They go out no more.—Not like our first parents—who for a short season enjoyed their paradise but were then driven by sin into the region of thorns and briars—for ever they abide enjoying FOR EVER the happy reign of their Lord and King. I mention this the more particularly *as it puts an end to the question which has been raised whether these chapters describe the millennial state or the final state of bliss in heaven.* For what further can be desired than to dwell where whatever occasions distress or misery shall be absent, where God and the Lamb shall dwell, where his servants shall serve him and see his face and reign with him for ever and ever? pp 73 74

The terribleness of Christ's coming to his enemies, is dismissed by our affectionate preacher in two discourses, one on the temporal precursors of vengeance, the other, on that vengeance itself, which equally leave undecided the period respectively of each, and gather strength in our judgment from that very indecision.

From the two discourses which follow on "Reasons for expecting the Redeemer's Advent," we think the following extract from Discourse VII contains an original and interesting remark. After shewing that our Lord's object evidently appeared to be always that of keeping up expectancy on the part of his church, he continues—

I would notice another forcible argument to prove this important doctrine. It is this. The manner in which the Apostles comforted believers under their trials. This can only be accounted for from the authorized expectation of the advent of the Lord Jesus.

Our great consolation to distressed Christians is the comfort that death will relieve them from all their sorrows and bring their happy spirits to the presence of the Lord. This is our constant course of alleviation. If some sudden reverse in his pecuniary circumstances happens to a sincere Christian what is our language? Mourn not my dear friend, the loss of your property, death will soon put you in possession of far greater treasures. If we visit a Christian suffering under acute disease how do we address him? Be patient my afflicted brother, death will soon come as a welcome visitor and release you from all your pain. So if we are called to sympathize with the widow or the orphan we say, Dry your tears, in a little moment you will follow him for whom you mourn, pursue but his steps and death will come and take you to the land whither your friend is gone. This is the mode in which we—I mean Christians in modern times—console our afflicted brethren. But this was not the Apostolic mode. We may not perhaps have noticed this, but such is the fact that death is very rarely introduced by the Apostles in the way of consolation, their comfort was the coming of the Lord. Thus St Paul when addressing the Christians at Rome says, If so be that we suffer with him that we may also be glorified together. For I reckon that the sufferings of the present time are not worthy to be compared with the glory which shall be revealed in us. Not that our present sufferings are not worthy to be compared with the felicity we shall enjoy at death but with the glory that shall be revealed in us or that shall be made manifest at the fulfilment of that blessed promise When Christ who is our life shall appear, then shall ye also appear with him in glory." So when he writes o the Hebrews, who took joyfully the spoiling of their goods, knowing that in heaven they had a better and an enduring substance, he does not refer to their death as the short interval only for which they were to wait: he says "For yet a little while, and he that shall come will come, and will not tarry." I have also already shewn that it was in this manner he consoled those who mourned over the death of their Christian friends: "Them which sleep in Jesus will God bring with him: therefore comfort one another with these words" —with the hope of the coming Saviour. pp 134—136

Mr Stewart's prophetic interpretations in regard to the present outpouring of the sixth vial on the nations, as warranting an expectation of the near approach of our Saviour's advent, will be found in Discourse VIII pp 159 et seq. We do not ourselves pretend to form any decisive opinion on such questions, and therefore pretermit them. Subjoined are the following encouraging details of the missionary progress as indicative of the present times

We live in so extraordinary an age that marvellous events make but little impression upon us, or otherwise we should be deeply affected with the facts of the day. It is not that one particular body of Christians has formed a plan for preaching the Gospel, the whole church of Christ is at this time in motion. Thirty years since missionary exertions were confined principally to our two venerable institutions, the Society for promoting Christian Knowledge and the Society for the Propagation of the Gospel, to the Moravians, and to some other small societies. During the whole of the last century, though that which the Lord effected by their instrumentality is a cause of great thankfulness, the visible results of their labours were comparatively small. This is attested by the reports of the patient endurance of the United Brethren on the coast of Labrador, and by the accounts of the missions in India of our venerable Society for promoting Christian Knowledge. But mark the change. There are at present no less than forty one public societies in our own and other Protestant countries formed for the single purpose of spreading the kingdom of our Saviour. An annual revenue of above four hundred thousand pounds is collected for this purpose, and daily additions are making to these revenues. An institution connected with the cause of Christ is planned, and funds and agents are almost immediately raised to commence and carry forward its object, and this without injuring other institutions, but on the contrary benefiting them. There are now either ministers of the Gospel or the holy Scriptures translated into one hundred and forty four languages, or Scriptural tracts as silent preachers going into all parts of the world. Africa, Asia, North and South America, the isles afar off, some of them not even known to our ancestors, have all their preachers. And such has been the success which by the Divine blessing has attended these exertions that whole islands have renounced idolatry. Untutored Africans also, who a few years since were in the lowest state of barbarism, literally worshipping devils, have been converted, and are now manifesting the power of Christianity by the exemplary discharge of the duties of civilized life

Some idea of the rapidity of these movements may be formed from the following short sketch of the progress of the Church Missionary Society. During the first ten years that society had but one mission, it has now nine missions. The clergy who were supporters of its objects were during the first year 50, at the end of the first ten years 260, they are now about 1500. The whole income for the first ten years was 15 000*l* for the last year alone it was above 40 000*l* There were none or few converts who were communicants at the end of the first ten years, there are now above 1000. There were then few hearers, there are now several thousands. Then it had but four schools and two hundred scholars, now it has two hundred and thirty one schools and 13 200 scholars

Is there not upon this point a great similarity between the prophetic marks and the actual occurrences before us? Must we not be almost compelled to say, It does indeed appear very like the Lord sending out his angels with the great sound of a trumpet, to gather in his elect from the four winds, from one end of heaven to the other? pp 171—174

We should have pleasure in continuing our extracts through the remaining series of ten discourses on the Conduct becoming the Redeemer's Advent, but our limits forbid, and we shall take our leave for the present of our readers, and finally of our excellent instructor Mr Stewart, by giving the summary of the last discourses from which our readers may themselves conjecture the instruction they would derive from their perusal

Ten Discourses —Readiness for his Coming. The Necessity of Inward Meet ness—Assurance of Readiness—Holding Fast our Profession—Earnest Prayer for Divine Aid—Active Zeal in Spreading the Gospel—Vigilance against Satan—Watchfulness against the Dangers of the Present Times—Dwelling in Love—Patient Waiting for Christ. p 184

(To be continued.)

Narrative of the Loss of the Kent East Indiaman by Fire in the Bay of Biscay on the 1st of March 1825, in a Letter to a Friend. By a Passenger. Edinburgh. 2s 6d.

THE leading circumstances connected with this painfully interesting narrative were detailed in the public journals at the time; but the appropriately serious and religious tone which pervades the little publication before us, and the information not however alluded to in the work that it is published for the charitable purpose of assisting the widows and destitute children of the sufferers induce us to notice it, and indeed it is well worthy of the attention of our readers both for the sake of its remarkable narrative and for those moral and Christian reflections which arise out of it. Our notice will necessarily consist chiefly of a few extracts from the publication itself. The writer of the letter gives the following statements

The Kent, Captain Henry Cobb, a fine new ship of 1350 tons, bound to Bengal and China, left the Downs on the 19th February with 20 officers, 344 soldiers, 43 women and 66 children belonging to the 31st regiment, with 20 private passengers and a crew (including officers) of 148 men on board

With a fine fresh breeze from the north east the stately Kent in bearing down the channel speedily passed many a well known spot on the coast dear to our remembrance, and on the evening of the 23d we took our last view of happy England and entered the wide Atlantic without the expectation of again seeing land until we reached the shores of India

With slight interruptions of bad weather we continued to make way until the night of Monday the 28th when we were suddenly arrested in lat 47 deg 30 min long 10 deg by a violent gale from the south west which gradually increased during the whole of the following morning

The activity of the officers and seamen of the Kent appeared to keep ample pace with that of the gale Our larger sails were speedily taken in or closely reefed and about 10 o clock on the morning of the 1st of March after having struck our top gallant yards we were lying to under a triple reefed main top sail only with our dead lights in and with the whole watch of soldiers attached to the life lines that were run along the deck for this purpose The rolling of the ship which was vastly increased by a dead weight of some hundred tons of shot and shells that formed a part of its lading became so great about half past eleven or twelve o clock that our main chains were thrown by every lurch considerably under water and the best cleated articles of furniture in the cabins and the *cuddy* were dashed about with so much noise and violence as to excite the liveliest apprehensions of individual danger

It was a little before this period that one of the officers of the ship with the well meant intention of ascertaining that all was fast below descended with two of the sailors into the hold where they carried with them for safety a light in the patent lantern and seeing that the lamp burned dimly the officer took the precaution to hand it up to the orlop deck to be trimmed Having afterwards discovered one of the spirit casks to be adrift he sent the sailors for some billets of wood to secure it but the ship in their absence having made a heavy lurch the officer unfortunately dropped the light and letting go his hold of the cask in his eagerness to recover the lantern it suddenly stove and the spirits communicating with the lamp the whole place was instantly in a blaze pp 4—7

Every possible effort was instantly made to repress the flames but this being found impracticable Captain Cobb directed the lower decks to be scuttled and the lower ports to be opened so as to admit a free passage of the waves into the vessel The immense body of water thus introduced into the hold checked the flames but the danger of sinking now became imminent and it seemed doubtful by which of the two instruments of destruction the unhappy company of human beings congregated in the vessel would perish that they must perish by the one or the other, appeared inevitable

The scene of horror which now

presented itself is described as follows by the highly respectable and pious author whose modesty has prevented his putting his name to his narrative; but if any of our readers in perusing it should be surprised, that, while the merits of various other individuals on this trying occasion are so warmly eulogized, those of Major M'Gregor, which are known to have been highly praiseworthy, are wholly passed over, and should be inclined to suspect the cause, we take the liberty of informing them that their conjecture is well founded. But to proceed with our extract:

"The upper deck was covered with between six and seven hundred human beings, many of whom, from previous sea sickness, were forced on the first alarm to flee from below in a state of absolute nakedness, and were now running about in quest of husbands, children, or parents. While some were standing in silent resignation, or in stupid insensibility to their impending fate, others were yielding themselves up to the most frantic despair. Some on their knees were earnestly imploring, with significant gesticulations and in noisy supplications, the mercy of Him whose arm, they exclaimed, was at length outstretched to smite them: others were to be seen hastily crossing themselves and performing the various external acts required by their peculiar persuasion; while a number of the older and more stout-hearted soldiers and sailors sullenly took their seats directly over the magazine, hoping, as they stated, that by means of the explosion, which they every instant expected, a speedier termination might thereby be put to their sufferings. Several of the soldiers' wives and children, who had fled for temporary shelter into the after cabins on the upper decks, were engaged in prayer and in reading the Scriptures with the ladies, some of whom were enabled, with wonderful self possession, to offer to others those spiritual consolations which a firm and intelligent trust in the Redeemer of the world appeared at this awful hour to impart to their own breasts. The dignified deportment of two young ladies in particular formed a specimen of natural strength of mind finely modified by Christian feeling, that failed not to attract the notice and admiration of every one who had an opportunity of witnessing it.

"One young gentleman of whose promising talents and piety I dare not now make farther mention, having calmly asked me my opinion respecting the state of the ship, I told him that I thought we should be prepared to sleep that night in eternity; and I shall never forget the peculiar fervour with which he replied, as he pressed my hand in his, 'My heart is filled with the peace of God,' adding, 'yet though I know it is foolish, I dread exceedingly the last struggle.'

"Amongst the numerous objects that struck my observation at this period, I was much affected with the appearance and conduct of some of the dear children, who, quite unconscious in the cuddy cabins of the perils that surrounded them, continued to play as usual with their little toys in bed, or to put the most innocent and unseasonable questions to those around them. To some of the older children, who seemed fully alive to the reality of the danger, I whispered 'Now is the time to put in practice the instructions you used to receive at the Regimental School, and to think of that Saviour of whom you have heard so much'; they replied, as the tears ran down their cheeks, 'O sir, we are trying to remember them, and we are praying to God.'

"The passive condition to which we were all reduced by the total failure of our most strenuous exertion, while it was well calculated and probably designed to convince us afterwards that our deliverance was effected not by our own might or power but by the Spirit of the Lord, afforded us ample room at the moment for deep and awful reflection, which it is to be earnestly wished may have been improved, as well by those who were eventually saved as by those who perished."—pp 9—12.

It is not often that we have an opportunity of learning from competent sources of information, the moral and spiritual phenomena of a scene like this. Few persons in such a situation could sufficiently calm their minds amidst their individual danger and individual duties to notice the minute varieties of so terrific a scene. Our author's calmness clearly arose from that source which alone can give true repose in the hour of expected death, an habitual and well grounded hope of a blessed immortality, through the merits of the Redeemer, accompanied by that "peace with God which follows upon being justified by faith," and proved to be solid by the scriptural fruits of a renewed and regenerate heart. Thus supported himself, it was our author's privilege at this solemn hour to have been enabled to warn and comfort others; and we would humbly trust that his pious efforts, and those of others like minded among his fellow sufferers may have left a deep and salutary impression on the minds of many—would we could hope of all!—who were mercifully permitted to survive the catastrophe. May the perusal also of these pages call to their recollection and renew upon their hearts those holy resolutions of dedicating themselves, should they be spared, to the service of their Almighty Deliverer, which doubtless in some if not many instances were formed during those awful moments of suspense. Nor will the narrative be lost upon the public at large, if, while it adds another most impressive illustration to the solemn truth that in the midst of life we are in death, it leads its readers seriously to ask,

"Of whom may we seek for succour but of thee, O Lord, who for our sins art justly displeased?"

The experience of Major Macgregor on this fearful occasion corresponds with what we believe is the melancholy testimony of most clergymen and others who are in the habit of visiting the beds of the sick and dying, that the vast majority of mankind live in habits of indifference or practical scepticism, which render them wholly thoughtless or careless respecting eternity.

> I should apprehend that a large majority of those men whose previous attention has never been fully and fairly directed to the great subject of religion, approach the gates of death, it may be with solemnity or with terror, but without any definable or tangible conviction of the truth that after death cometh the judgment. Several there were indeed who vowed in loud and piteous cries, that if the Lord God would spare their lives, they would then afterward dedicate all their powers to his service; and not a few were heard to exclaim in the bitterness of remorse, that the judgments of the Most High were justly poured out upon them for their neglected Sabbaths and their profligate or profane lives; but the number of those was extremely small who appeared to dwell either with lively hope or dread on the view of an opening eternity. And as a farther evidence of the truth of this observation, I may mention that when I afterwards had occasion to mount the mizen shrouds, I there met with a young man who had brought me a letter of introduction from our excellent friend Dr. G——n, to whom I felt it my duty, while we were rocking on the mast quietly to propose the great question, "What must we do to be saved?" and this young gentleman has since informed Mr. P. that, though he was at that moment fully persuaded of the certainty of immediate death, yet the subject of eternity in any form had not once flashed upon his mind, previously to my conversation. pp. 13, 14.

Most unexpectedly and providentially a small brig was discovered at a distance, which proved to be the Cambria, of 200 tons burden, bound for Vera Cruz, having on board twenty or thirty Cornish miners and other agents of the Anglo Mexican Company, commanded by Captain Cook, with a ship's company of only eleven men. The length of time the Kent had been burning, the tremendous sea that was running, the extreme smallness of the Cambria, and the immense number of human beings to be rescued, rendered it very improbable that many could be saved; but by the great exertions and good conduct of all parties, the majority of the crew of the Kent excepted, no less than five hundred and fifty-seven persons escaped. The perilous circumstances which attended the rescue occupy the chief part of the narrative. The women and children were first put into the boats; next followed the various classes of men on board, the officers themselves remaining to the last, and preserving order to a degree not to have been hoped for, but which materially facilitated the perilous operation, and was the means of saving many lives. The rescue of the first boat full is thus described:—

> Arrangements having been considerately made by Captain Cobb for placing in the first boat, previous to letting it down, all the ladies and as many of the soldiers' wives as it could safely contain, they hurriedly wrapt themselves up in whatever articles of clothing could be most conveniently found; and I think about two or half past two o'clock, a most mournful procession advanced from the

after cabins to the starboard cuddy port outside of which the cutter was suspended. Scarcely a word was uttered—not a scream was heard—even the infants ceased to cry, as if conscious of the unspoken and unspeakable anguish that was at that instant rending the hearts of their parting parents—nor was the silence of voices in any way broken, except in one or two cases where the ladies plaintively entreated permission to be left behind with their husbands. But on being assured that every moment's delay might occasion the sacrifice of a human life, they successively suffered themselves to be torn from the tender embrace, and with the fortitude which never fails to characterise and adorn their sex on occasions of overwhelming trial, were placed without a murmur in the boat, which was immediately lowered into a sea so tempestuous as to leave us only to hope against hope that it should live in it for a single moment. Twice the cry was heard from those on the chains that the boat was swamping. But he who enabled the Apostle Peter to walk on the face of the deep, and was graciously attending to the silent but earnest aspirations of those on board, had decreed its safety. The tackle, after considerable difficulty, was unhooked—the boat was dexterously cleared from the ship, and after a while was seen from the poop battling with the billows —now raised in its progress to the brig like a speck on their summit, and then disappearing for several seconds as if engulfed in the horrid vale between them. The Cambria having prudently lain to at some distance from the Kent, lest she should be involved in her explosion, or exposed to the fire from our guns, which being all shotted, afterwards went off as the flames successively reached them, the men had a considerable way to row; and the success of this first experiment seeming to be the measure of our future hopes, the movements of this precious boat—incalculably precious without doubt to the agonized husbands and fathers immediately connected with it—were watched with intense anxiety by all on board. In the course of twenty minutes it was seen alongside the ark of refuge, and the first human being that happened to be admitted out of the vast assemblage that ultimately found shelter there was the infant son of Major Macgregor, a child of only a few weeks old, who was caught from his mother's arms and lifted into the brig by Mr Thomson, the fourth mate of the Kent.

I have been told by one abundantly capable of judging, that the feelings of oppressive delight, gratitude, and praise experienced by the married officers and soldiers on being assured of the safety of their wives and children, so entirely abstracted their minds from their own situation, as to render them for a little while afterwards totally insensible either to the storm that beat upon them, or to the active and gathering volcano that threatened every instant to explode under their feet. pp. 17—20.

The perils of the remainder were far greater, as the boats could not again come alongside the Kent, and the women and children were obliged to be lowered by ropes from the stern, and were often plunged repeatedly under water before they could be dropped into the boat. None of the women ultimately perished under this dangerous operation; but great numbers of the younger children were drowned. Many affecting proofs occurred of parental and filial affection, which shed a momentary brightness round the gloomy scene.

Two or three soldiers, to relieve their wives of a part of their families, sprang into the water with their children, and perished in their endeavours to save them. One young lady who had resolutely refused to quit her father, whose sense of duty kept him at his post, was near falling a sacrifice to her filial devotion, not having been picked up by those in the boats until she had sunk five or six times. Another individual, who was reduced to the frightful alternative of losing his wife or his children, hastily decided in favour of his duty to the former. His wife was accordingly saved, but his four children, alas, were left to perish. A fine fellow, a soldier, who had neither wife nor child of his own, but who evinced the greatest solicitude for the safety of those of others, insisted on having three children lashed to him, with whom he plunged into the water; not being able to reach the boat, he was again drawn into the ship with his charge, but not before two of the children had expired. pp. 21, 22.

We throw together two opposite traits of selfishness and generosity, as illustrative of the anomalies of the human heart.

Three out of the six boats we originally possessed were either completely stove or swamped in the course of the day; one of them with men in it, some of whom were seen floating in the water for a moment before they disappeared; and it is suspected that one or two of those who went down must have sunk under the weight of their spoils, the same individuals having been seen eagerly plunder in the cuddy cabins. p. 24.

Towards evening, when the melancholy groupes who were passively seated on the poop, exhausted by previous fatigue, anxiety and fasting, were beginning to ex perience the pain of intolerable thirst, a box of oranges was accidentally discovered by some of the men, who, with a degree of mingled consideration, respect, and affection that could hardly have been expected at such a moment, refused to partake of the grateful beverage until they had offered a share of it to their officers. p. 27.

We pass by our author's testimony to the ability and presence of mind of Colonel Fearon of the 31st regiment, who, under the complicated anxiety of a commander, a husband, and a father, inspired composure and fortitude in all around him, in order to give the following passage respecting our author's own sensations in the immediate prospect of eternity. Let our readers contrast the feelings with which this pious and 'gallant' officer gazed on that setting sun which appeared about to be his last, with the celebrated death-bed scene of Rousseau. "Open the window," said that unhappy man to his wife in his expiring hours, "that I may see the verdant meadows once more. How beautiful is nature! How wonderful is yon splendid orb! [the sun was setting at the moment in all its glory on the Lake of Geneva] behold its glorious light! The Deity summons me! How delightful is death to a man who is unconscious of a crime! [On which point consult *passim* his own infamous Confessions.] O God I surrender to thee my soul pure as it came out of thy hands, crown it with thy heavenly bliss."—Now let us see a truly Christian contrast under far more appalling external circumstances.

"Some of the soldiers near me having casually remarked that the sun was setting, I looked round, and never can I forget the intensity with which I regarded his declining rays. I had previously felt deeply impressed with the conviction that that night the ocean was to be my bed; and had I imagined sufficiently realized to my mind both the last struggles and the consequences of death. But as I continued solemnly watching the departing beams of the sun, the thought that that was really the very last I should ever behold, gradually expanded into reflections the most tremendous in their import.—It was not, I am persuaded, either the retrospect of a most unprofitable life or the direct fear of death or of judgment that occupied my mind at the period I allude to, but a broad illimitable view of eternity itself altogether abstracted from the misery or felicity that flows through it,—a sort of painless, pleasureless, sleepless eternity. I know not whither the overwhelming thought would have hurried me, had I not speedily seized, as with the grasp of death, on some of those sweet promises of the Gospel which give to an immortal existence its only charms; and that naturally enough led back my thoughts, by means of the brilliant object before me, to the contemplation of that blessed city which hath no need of the sun, neither of the moon to shine in it, for the glory of God doth lighten it, and the Lamb is the light thereof.

"I have been the more particular in recording my precise feelings at the period in question, because they tend to confirm an opinion which I have long entertained—in common I believe with yourself and others—that we very rarely realize even those objects that seem in our every day speculations to be the most interesting to our hearts. We are so much in the habit of uttering the awful words—Almighty, heaven, hell, eternity, divine justice, holiness, &c. without attaching to them, in all their magnitude, the ideas of which such words are the symbol, that we become overwhelmed with much of the astonishment that accompanies a new and alarming discovery if at any time the ideas themselves are suddenly and forcibly impressed upon us; and it is probably this vagueness of conception experienced even by those whose minds are not altogether unexercised on the subject of religion, that enables others, devoid of all reflection whatever, to stand on the very brink of that precipice which divides the world of time from the regions of eternity, not only with apparent, but frequently, I am persuaded, with real tranquillity. How much is it to be lamented that we do not keep in mind a truth which no one can pretend to dispute, that our indifference or blindness to danger, whether it be temporal or eternal, cannot possibly remove or diminish the extent of it." pp. 29—31.

We subjoin the following graphic delineation, for the sake of the memento which it suggests to the reader to be habitually prepared for that great and solemn change which cannot be far distant from any, and which may be much nigher than in the hour of health and vivacity usually appears probable. Whether on land or at sea, how soon may all our earthly plans and projects be effectually and for ever put an end to, when we least think it, and "the place that knew us, know us no more!"

Some time after the shades of night had enveloped us, I descended to the cuddy in quest of a blanket to shelter me from the increasing cold; and the scene of desolation that there presented itself was melancholy in the extreme. The place which only a few short hours before had been the seat of kindly intercourse and of social gaiety, was now entirely deserted, save by a few miserable wretches who were either stretched in irrecoverable intoxication on the floor, or prowling about like beasts of prey in search of plunder. The sofas, drawers, and other articles of furniture, the due arrangement of which had cost so much thought and pains, were now broken into a thousand pieces and scattered in confusion around me. Some of the geese and other poultry escaped from their confinement were cackling in the cuddy; while a solitary pig wandering from its stye in the forecastle was ranging at large in undisturbed possession of the Brussels carpet that covered one of the cabins. Glad to retire from a scene so cheerless and affecting, and rendered more dismal by the smoke which was oozing up from below, I returned to the poop, where I again found Captain Cobb, Colonel Fearon, and the few officers that remained superintending with unabated zeal the removal of the rapidly diminishing sufferers as the boats successively arrived to carry them off.—pp. 31, 32.

The interval of nearly three quarters of an hour which elapsed between each trip of the boat, and during which nothing could be done but to remain tranquil and ' see the salvation of God,' was a truly fearful pause, especially to those who still remained on board when the shades of evening began to advance. On one of these occasions an officer was entreated by his companions in danger to pray with them, and his prayer was frequently interrupted by exclamations of assent to some of its confessions on the part of the afflicted auditors. Similar acts of devotion seem to have been solemnly conducted during the whole of these intervals, and the effect was very striking in the order and composure which they secured in the most perilous moments. The author assures his readers, that if any persons should be disposed to despise as unsoldierlike or contemptible these humble exercises of devotion, there were no indications of ridicule even by the most profligate among those who were the subjects of this awful visitation.

Captain Cobb was the last person to quit the vessel, with the exception of a few individuals either intoxicated or struck powerless with apprehension and dismay, and who could not by the most earnest entreaties, be persuaded to risk the perilous plunge into the boat. Of these however fourteen were picked up by another vessel, the Caroline, Captain Bibbey, three having perished. The officers had only just preceded Captain Cobb, beginning with the juniors, the superiors remaining to the last. The vessel was seen to blow up at half past one in the morning.

We must pass over the scene of hope and fear, of joy and sorrow, which in the mean time was occurring on board the Cambria, as the successive parties arrived; the meeting of husbands and wives, parents and children, friends and companions, or the fatal intelligence of the separation of these and all other human ties by the stroke of death. We shall only state that after great fatigue and suffering, and no slight peril from the over crowded state of the ship,—600 men, women and children on board a brig of 200 tons, and several hundred miles from any accessible port,—the Cambria arrived in safety at Falmouth, where the whole party were received with a truly humane and charitable assiduity which reflects the greatest honour upon the inhabitants. No labour or expense was spared to supply their necessities and promote their comfort; and the author utters a warm effusion of gratitude in particular for the strenuous efforts made by the members of the Society of Friends on the occasion. On the first Sunday after their arrival Colonel Fearon, and his officers and men, with Captain Cobb, his officers and private passengers, repaired to the temple of God to pour out their thanksgivings for their great and providential deliverance. Indeed from first to last there is more of a religious spirit mixed up with the events of the narrative than we remember to have read of in any similar catastrophe. In particular the letters of gratitude from the officers of the 31st regiment and the private passengers to Captain Cook and Captain Cobb, Colonel Fearon's letter on behalf of himself and officers to the Falmouth Committee, and Captain Cook's reply, are marked by a strain of truly Christian sentiment, incomparably more scriptural and affecting than the usual common places on such occasions. The coldest heart, the most sceptical mind, could not indeed fail to have paid some passing acknowledgment to Divine Providence for such a deliverance; but we are pleased at witnessing in the religious allusions in all these communications far more than this barren homage; and if we may take these documents as indicative of a widely extended feeling, we have ample reason to be grateful to God for the great progress which true religion is evidently making, with whatever painful drawbacks, among all classes of our fellow subjects; and for which, to quote the words of Captain Cook, we shall not cease to offer up our grateful acknowledgments at the Throne of Grace.

We must not omit to add, in conclusion, that the East India Company, the Commander in Chief, and other public bodies, have united in testifying their admiration and gratitude for the highly honourable conduct of Captain Cook, his passengers and crew; and various pecuniary and other rewards have been conferred upon them. Their best reward is the pleasing consciousness of the signal benefits which they have been the instruments in the hands of God of conferring upon their fellow creatures.

REVIEW OF REVIEWS.

WE most readily insert the following candid and conciliating remarks of Admiral Sir C. Penrose, in reply to some passages in our review of his pamphlet in our last Number. Most honourable would it be to individuals, and most beneficial to society, if all discussions which involve difference of opinion were conducted with the truly Christian courtesy and ingenuousness which characterize the communication of this gallant and venerable writer. We do not think that his reply affects the substance of our argument; but as it may "tend to useful elucidation," while it does honour to the writer, we record it in our pages, with the addition of a few running notes, leaving the general balance between the gallant admiral and ourselves to be adjusted by our readers. We must not, however, fail to add our best thanks for the obliging manner in which he is pleased to speak of our labours, and for the several documents with which he has favoured us, and which abundantly prove how long and zealously the writer has exerted himself for the promotion of education, Christian morals, and the circulation of the sacred Scriptures among our seamen.

To the Editor of the Christian Observer.

Ethy Lostwithiel, July 16, 1825.
Sir,

I have only been just enabled to read carefully your indulgent review of my little pamphlet on the state of the Navy; and, in offering you my thanks for the manner in which you have remarked on my observations, whether in concur rence or the contrary, I beg leave also to notice a few points on which I am desirous of being clearly understood, or which may tend to useful elucidation

Though very averse to appear again before the public, yet the zeal you have evinced on a very interesting subject which is so much and so variously agitated and in my opinion so little understood, almost *compels* me to address you You will I am certain consider it right, when we feel what is desirable to take into consideration also *what is practicable**, and the contents of your columns are important as they will guide the opinions of so many

I think it right to premise, that I have possessed and perused your valuable work from its first Number the gradual accumulation of your columns in my library, forms a range as highly prized as any on its shelves and I have sometimes been flattered by your admission of some of my observations on passing subjects Our principles therefore, cannot be at variance and if we differ on any point, I flatter myself, that it arises only from our seeing the object in, or from, a different point of view

I am aware of the danger, when writing to a *Christian Observer*, that slips of the pen may possibly subject me to a charge of making principle subservient to practice, unless a previous charitable impression is formed Aware how the term 'morals might be differently understood by different people I explained in my pamphlet briefly but I trust distinctly, how I wished it to be understood when used by me namely, Christian practice from Christian motives I now request you to do me the justice to believe* that keeping in view these great moral principles my desire is to make all practice harmonize with them as quickly and as perfectly as human nature and human means will allow these principles to act happy if we can approximate uniformly without any retrograde movement or the incurring a greater evil in the removal of a lesser

In page 362 you say, that I have seen fit to refer to your publication and to blame you for your former remarks relative to the third point noticed in my observations I do not recollect having found fault with your remarks which I deem perfectly consistent with your plea of duty and utility in page 369 I thought and still think that the zealous advocate for the wished for reform had not used the properest means of attaining the desired end and my regret was that your very generally extended publication should have made what I deemed that writer's errors more publicly prejudicial to the character of the naval service

I admit that my long professional career may have engendered habitual modes of thinking which may be considered as professional prejudices but in forming such habits, the bias of which I have lived too long not to observe in others and to allow may also influence myself I have gained a considerable degree of experience, which may excuse my obtruding my opinions

I allow, as a general principle that the reform of any community must ordinarily come from *without* yet I am sure you will admit on your part, that those who reform from *without* should be intimately acquainted with the nature and ex

---

* We are happy to learn from Sir C Penrose's own pamphlet that the prompt and total abolition of one at least of the three evils complained of the admission of immoral females on board is perfectly practicable We continue to think the same of the other two indeed as respects impressment (except in a few emergencies) our author appears to agree with us that it might be and ought to be abolished though he modestly concludes that as the proper authorities have not abolished it its retention for reasons which he cannot divine is necessary

We certainly do the author the full justice to believe that such was his wish and intention and we endeavoured most explicitly to state this in our review

tent of the errors which exist *with in*, and that with respect both to causes and effects. To the honour of my profession however, I may state that the very extensive reform which has of late marked its progress, has originated and been so far perfected from *within*. The operative and executive departments have been equally alert; the former vigilant in detecting errors and suggesting improvements; the latter prompt, liberal and judicious in banishing the defects from, and incorporating the amendments into, the system.

I will also venture to assure you sir, that the practical regulations of a ship of war, to be understood, must be practically known; for you have on shore nothing wherewith any comparison can be formed, or which can usefully aid the comprehension; of course no subject is so little understood by a landsman. As an inexperienced eye may deem that a blemish in a work of art, which in the eye of science may be known as an excellence, so may honest zeal labouring in ignorance fall into as great an error in the attempt to reform a community without being minutely acquainted with all its principles and practices and their mutual and relative bearings. *

In page 364 you allude to a proposition of reform which has been made in the House of Commons respecting impressment and *arbitrary* flogging. There have been propositions made in that House, and much declaiming elsewhere, and there are threats of future propositions, by persons who however pure in their intentions are to the best of my honest and deliberate judgment very deficient in the requisite knowledge which could entitle them to be proper judges of the subject.

What these gentlemen cannot but know is that there never was a period in which more earnest attention was paid by an able and zealous naval government and by the officers of the navy whether to its mechanical or moral state, than the present.* They must know, if they have inquired and they are inexcusable if they have not so done, that the progressive improvement is rapid yet they repose more confidence in their own comparative ignorance, (for such must unavoidably be the case,) than in the long tried experience and equal zeal of those who earnestly desire the same results wherever they are practically attainable. I lament this, Mr Editor, because I believe that such indifference paralizes more useful efforts, and tends to foment discontent, where it otherwise would never have existed and which in fact has no other origin. Excuse a little professional

We admit the truth of these observations so far as they relate to every thing technical and professional; but of moral principles an exoteric may judge as well as the initiated, and it was to the application of these that we chiefly confined our remarks. If impressment be inevitably an act of injustice and the admission of lewd women on board our vessels a gross immorality no induction of professional experience can sanction the practice. And even with regard to starting and flogging, knowing that human nature is the same afloat as on shore, we see not why a landsman may not form as accurate an opinion respecting their propriety as a seaman. At least he has not to contend with that prejudice in favour of the practice which arises from having both administered it, and experienced its unquestionable efficacy when cautiously applied in maintaining discipline.

* We expressly alluded several times in our review with the utmost gratitude both to our able and zealous naval government and to the officers of the navy as the authors of the great improvements which have taken place in the service and we should deeply regret if in pressing the importance of further ameliorations we should appear insensible to the value of those which have been already adopted. We have heard with great satisfaction that the excellent Port Admiral of Devonport Sir James Saumarez has given orders to limit the admission of females on board the ships under his controul to married women. But with still higher satisfaction have we witnessed the formation under the patronage of the Admiralty of a Society for establishing floating churches in every part of the kingdom. This is a measure eminently calculated to benefit our seamen and most honourable to Lord Melville. An account of it will be found under the head of religious intelligence.

warmth, and it is all professional; but in truth some speeches as I have seen them recorded reminded me of Tom Paine's days, when his admirers, if a man was hardy enough to confess to them that he was contented and happy, very benevolently volunteered to prove to him, that he was in duty bound to be miserable.*

In page 363 you remark that "a service is never truly liberal or just till the employer can say with effect, If you do not do your duty you shall lose your appointment." Is this the state of the navy? It certainly is not so; including every description of persons, which compose its crews, and until such an improvement can be suggested and acted upon, as will admit of a fleet or a ship being managed without great deprivation and restraint, it never can be. A *thousand men* on a floating area of two hundred feet by fifty five, requires some different government from that which may suit a *mixed population* of little more than two hundred in a square mile; and those who are only used to the latter have much to learn as to the management of the former. Nature is against us; and it is a common expression among sailors when talking of the tediousness of a long voyage, and a longing that it was at an end, *I was born on shore,* and it will be a long time before a return to that shore will be deemed a severe punishment by some parts of our crews. I have heard a well re-

* Far from accusing our correspondent of warmth, we greatly admire his uniform candour; but the allusion to Paine's agents is somewhat out of place; for it is not landsmen who persuade our sailors that they are not "perfectly contented and happy;" but their own officers would seem to intimate that they are not so, in proportion as impressment is alleged to be necessary for keeping up their numbers, or severe regulations to preserve discipline or confinement to their ship to prevent desertion. We are however as remote as our respected correspondent from justifying those who either in parliament or elsewhere give vent to exaggerated and inflammatory statements on this or any other subject.

gulated ship of war defined as "the noblest work of man, directed by the noblest work of God:" still though it is man's greatest triumph over natural impediments, it is but the work of man, and in all avocations on shore the works of nature are more blended—men *are* where they were born; at sea, men *wish to be* where they were born. Even if means could be devised to substitute punishments in all respects better than those in use, to do away the necessity of impressment, and to make our crews as moral as can be hoped for, even then I doubt whether your query could be answered affirmatively.*

There are many causes which prevent seamen from volunteering to ships of war in preference; but I do not believe that the fears of ill treatment or the system of corporal punishment deter them. I believe I have stated fairly the circumstances which operated against the navy; but we have besides a constant and powerful rival using every effort to keep volunteers from us. In peace we have indeed volunteers enough; we must therefore shortly look to a state of warfare. Merchant ships must be manned, as well as ships of war; if 5*l.* bounty is offered to volunteers for the navy, more must and will be offered for the merchant service. Whatever daily pay is given to naval seamen, it will be found that merchant seamen must have at least double, to prevent them volunteering into the navy; and so much more to counteract the hope of prize money, the enjoyment of many advantages when on service, and the hope of a good pension when the service is

* Our author in this paragraph does not deny the truth of our statement, but doubts whether under any circumstances the service could be rendered just and liberal, according to *our* notions of justice and liberality. It is, it seems, an unnatural mode of life, and must necessarily involve some degree of compulsion. But if so, how are the officers retained in the service, or how are merchants' ships manned?

ended. Thus, the system of the two services out-bidding each other might be carried to a ruinous extent, and fail again at last, as it has done before.*

I will not conclude this part of my subject, without giving it as my firm *opinion* that, generally speaking, the life of a seaman in a ship of war, is a much happier one than that of a seaman in the merchant service. He has less labour, he is *better* fed, there is less irritation, there are more comforts, more decency of manners, and more attention shewn to the moral and religious duties.†

I am anxious to remark on a use you make of the quotation from my pamphlet, in your page 365. How far it was quite legitimate to make that use of it I am not critic enough to determine; but as you allow that I introduced the anecdote "to illustrate a technical question," you will be aware that if I had brought it forward for moral elucidation, some additional remarks would have accompanied it. I notice it particularly, as some of my readers may have known the officers alluded to; and I confidently assure you that so far from the seamen running any added risk, had the power been vested in the admiral, he was the very last man in the world to have inflicted punishment, without most strict inquiry and most humane consideration. A hasty threat in a moment of disappointment and difficulty, probably of danger, to be warded only by dispatch and skill, may very possibly, as in this instance, fall from the mouth of a man whose heart was feelingly alive to the most benevolent sensations.*

Page 366. No man, I trust, exists, who will disagree in the opinion, that punishment should never be *rashly* inflicted. To punish rashly, I consider a much greater crime than any which is likely to be brought before a captain's tribunal for punishment. I believe it is thought by many persons, that when a fault is committed, or supposed to be committed, it is usual for the captains of his Majesty's ships to be rash enough to order immediate corporal punishment, and that rashly both as to manner and degree. But as far as my experience goes, such is not the case. Evidences are fairly examined, and acted upon, so that "mercy tempers justice," and the time of infliction is marked by much solemnity.†

If by *arbitrary* is meant that discretion vested in the captain, to

* We are at issue with the gallant admiral on the whole of this statement. The price of labour at sea could not rise permanently above that on land, except to that degree, be it what it may, in which naval employments are less desirable than those on shore; and this reasonable addition, if such an addition there be, ought not in fairness to be witheld. There are many employments far more irksome and unwholesome than that of a mariner, for which there is no dearth of candidates, because the remuneration is graduated accordingly. If the wages of seamen rise above the level of other businesses, landsmen will soon flock on board ship and reduce it to that level.

† We are most happy in perusing this gratifying statement; yet how, we would ask, is it that under such circumstances the press-gang should be alleged to be necessary? Are men in any other department of life accustomed thus blindly to refuse good fortune?

* This paragraph seems to us to make strongly in favour of our argument; for we have no doubt as to the humane consideration and benevolent sensations of the officer alluded to: but *a fortiori*, if *such* a man could be provoked, in a moment of disappointment and difficulty, probably of danger (though by the way no such palliation appears in the narrative), to order a party of men, two only of whom were guilty, to be flogged, what must be the case where such power is consigned to less humane and considerate hands? Our author speaks of the command as a hasty threat; but in truth it was an official order; and the very point for which the incident is introduced in Sir C. Penrose's pamphlet is in reference to a disputed question in the profession, whether the captain, even after the innocence of several of the party had been proved, could legally disobey it.

† We do not for a moment think that it is usual with the officers of this honourable profession to be unjust or severe; but why should not the possibility be as much as possible guarded against?

punish, according to his judgment, as guided and limited by the naval laws. I trust such power will never be changed. If some of the plans I have known suggested in theory, for the internal discipline of a ship of war, had been attempted in practice, no experienced officer would have risked his character in the command, and our fine fleet had, in such case, be better continued in ordinary.

I doubt, Mr Editor, if there are punishments of other and more humane kinds which would prove *really* humane in the practice and effects. Solitary confinement is almost impracticable, and in some climates much more severe than the lash. To reserve men to the end of a voyage, to be then tried by a court martial, would add long imprisonment and apprehension to much more severe punishment than could, or would have been inflicted by a captain; and I have not yet heard of a proposed alteration in our code, which would not effectually be a harsh one. Let us war against ignorance and vice, by suitable instruction and the encouragement of all good conduct, and it will have a much more beneficial effect, thus to do away the necessity of any punishment, than to dispute about the nature of punishment itself.

The sentence in the same page, 366 for which I justly incur your mildly given reproof will be however found to insinuate no unmerited censure. I most sincerely believe there is no 'pretence' in your expressions of horror at the practices in question; and I have many valuable friends, genuinely impressed by the same feeling. Yet, in the midst of human imperfections may not some persons be found who do pretend to more horror than they really feel? It is doubtless possible, and it is made to me probable, from my observance of time, place and manner, aided also by the clear general purposes of some of those whose talents are used to produce a powerful effect on that stage on which popularity is courted. If I could not truly say that I not only do not bear ill will to any individual in the world, but that I feel goodwill to every such individual, I would not have ventured to give this public opinion of public conduct. The impression has been forced upon me, and I hope it is erroneous. My remark applies not to the sincere; and if there are no pretenders it applies not at all. I confess, however, with regard to the sentence itself that, on perusal after publication, it pleased me less (how numerous soever may be the passages in which alterations would be great improvements, and perhaps omissions still greater,) than any other in my little work, from the fear that it might merit the character you have justly assigned to it.

With regard to punishment I have, I trust, sufficiently expressed my opinion that it should be applied most cautiously, and I have also admitted its general inadequacy to the end designed, though no one will deny the necessity of a power of punishing, or that necessity is the only plea for punishment. Whatever may be the faults of the nature of naval punishments, I have never yet heard of a plausible, much less an adaptable, substitute.

With respect to impressment, does it not *as yet* resolve itself into the following queries? If Great Britain is at war, is it necessary that her fleet should be manned? Can it be manned without impressment? Which evil must we submit to,—to leave our commerce unprotected, and our enemy triumphant, or impress men to complete our ships crews? Long before any of your valued pages went to the press, I had been earnestly endeavouring to discover means to do away the necessity of impressment, and I have formed an opinion, as I have always declared, that means could be adopted which might prevent that necessity, except upon urgent and tem porary occasions, and I have never ceased to consider the subject with anxious solicitude. This I have no doubt, is also done by those who have means of information which I do not possess; and I must therefore conclude that there are obstacles which I cannot perceive.

In page 369, you say of those gentlemen who would not send their sons to sea, after reading the anonymous pamphlet in question, ' Must they not have inquired into the facts of the case, and have found the statements of the pamphlet notoriously true?' In the cases I referred to, the resolution was formed from reading the pamphlet, which was deemed sufficient evidence. Had the gentlemen inquired, they would doubtless have found the *particular* statements true; but the impression made on many, that such was a *general* case in the navy, would have been found very incorrect. I have, before and since I wrote my pamphlet, made diligent inquiry from many respectable officers, who all declare they never heard of such atrocities elsewhere, and considered the writer must have been peculiarly unfortunate in having been himself acquainted with them.*

In reply to this statement, we might oppose the notoriety of the facts in our sea-port towns. It so happens that the very day we received the gallant admiral's letter, we received a packet inclosing several little pamphlets (dated Devonport June 28, 1825,) which are at this moment widely circulating in Plymouth and its neighbourhood, with a view to urge the inhabitants to subscribe for a mariner's chapel. The author is said to be a Dissenting minister, and he states himself in one of these tracts to have been once an officer in the naval service. The merits of his plans or tracts it is not necessary that we should here discuss, but we presume that his personal testimony as to facts will not be impeached. At the very time then that Admiral Sir C. Penrose is stating, and we are convinced most ingenuously his belief that the immoral practices alluded to are very rare, the following statements are widely circulating in Plymouth without any attempt that we have heard of to impeach them, and merely as incidental and average facts not selected for the occasion, but which happened at the moment to be passing under the writer's own eye and in the cognizance of the whole fleet and neighbourhood.

I inclose a little tract written by me for private distribution a few

The writer has visited the Carnation sloop of war; she has been in the West Indies about four years; one hundred and one officers and men sailed in her, and only about thirty-four have returned. The mortality of the Pyramus lately paid off at Portsmouth is reported to be much greater. The remnant of sickly sailors and the remainder of the crew made up from sickly ships in the merchant service or drafted from ships of war, say that the most awful deaths took place with what they term the black vomit; they declare also that they witnessed the most distressing and agonizing scenes continually. What is the return made for the goodness of God on their arrival at this port? A whole host of the most infamous characters have been admitted on board; these agents of hell have filled the ship with ardent spirits, drunkenness, insubordination, and almost open mutiny, with every other vice have followed; and last Sabbath day (one of the crew assured the writer) the most guilty scenes and the most extraordinary profanations abounded. Some were flogged, but others still revelled in wickedness defying God and man, and they were led on by the most depraved dregs of North Corner. Thus as the poor wretched man expressed it, the Sunday being a leisure day they kept it up, and had a good blow out of every thing, that is every vice. Why do we talk of the wickedness of the Hindoos and the crimes of their temples? Why do we send missionaries at an immense expense to warn them of the consequences of their wickedness, and point them the way to salvation? Why do all this for the heathen, and yet not do the same for our sailors? Alas! England in the very eye of God Almighty—in the broad light of meridian day in the eye of Bible, Missionary, Village School, and Tract Metropolitan Anniversaries—England with all her bishops, Bibles, churches, meeting houses, profession, societies, and zeal, negligently and awfully gives up those poor sailors after all their calamities and miseries, to perish by the hands of vile prostitutes!

Let but an Hindoo or an Asiatic go on board the Carnation, *or any other ship that comes in to be paid off,* and will he not stand amazed, saying to England, You send missionaries to my country, but physician heal thyself? What if he were told the officers and men and women were Christians! What if he were informed the king's proclamation was against this immorality, and yet all hands despised it with impunity! What if he were informed also, that in matters of naval duty, years since, when it was the fashion among seamen to ' *pretend* (see page 13 of the tract) to a dislike to the navy it will shew you my disobedience and contempt to royal edicts or Admiralty orders might be punished with death but in cases of morality or religion it was of no consequence!

The appearance of the Carnation on the Monday afternoon was almost too bad for description A great exhaustion of spirits appeared among the wretched seamen and mariners a general languor prevailed fore and aft among those who were below and such as were above unrigging the ship did not appear more lively excepting the officers Many of the unhappy females were sleeping in the greatest wretchedness some on tables others on lockers and others on the decks The Sabbath Bacchanalian revel and festival had subsided and God s air was polluted no longer with the horrid oaths and blasphemies of this den of desperadoes against all laws human and divine Nothing can describe the lower deck of this ship and all other ships where such sinners dwell more powerfully than the picture of Babylon in Rev xviii 2 The habitation of devils and the hold of every foul spirit and a cage of every unclean and hateful bird

Every commanding officer who has the least regard to conscience to God to death judgment or eternity should at once say No I dare not comply You would make me render useless all the chaplain s labours disobey the king s proclamation and sin most awfully against God A regard, therefore to your welfare and my peace forbids it If you rush into this practice on shore I cannot help it—I am not responsible

good will, at the same time with my want of ability to give it effect, and also some of my opinions as to the condition of a naval seaman Were I to address my brother sailors at present, I should have still more advantages to point out to them in consequence of those truly beneficial regulations mentioned in my introductory remarks The benevolently useful and boldly extensive operations of these regulations may well convince all us naval reformers, that the interests of British seamen occupy a large portion of attention, guided by no common talent and the time has been so well chosen for doing what has been done, that we may confidently rely that whatever more is useful and feasible will also follow

I beg leave to repeat my thanks for the manner in which you have reviewed my pamphlet many parts of which review as to the principles inculcated would lead me into cordially concurring observations, longer than the pamphlet itself if I did not value your time more than my own

That the operations of genuine Christian motives may lead to genuine Christian practice, both afloat and ashore is the sincere wish of your constant reader,

C V PENROSE

LITERARY AND PHILOSOPHICAL INTELLIGENCE,
&c &c

GREAT BRITAIN
PREPARING for publication —Archdeacon Jortin s Sermons abridged by the Rev G Whitaker —Sermons by the Rev D Gordon

In the press —The Forest Sanctuary a Poem by Mrs Hemans —History of India during Lord Hastings s Administration by H Prinsep

Cambridge —The Porson Shakespeare prize is adjudged to J Hodgson of Trinity College and the Members prize for the best dissertation in Latin prose, to J Buckle of Trinity College

The following statements have been published in the town of Cambridge by Mr J J Cribb —More than 300 individuals have probably died in Cambridge of natural small pox in the course of twenty five years preceding the summer of 1824—i e 1 in 7 of those who have had the disease Ten have died in the same period of small pox from inoculation—i e 1 in 113 Three have died of small pox after vaccination or

1 in 1318 vaccinated. From the joint influence of vaccination and small pox inoculation it is very probable that 713 deaths from natural small pox have been prevented. If all who have been affected, within the given period with either of these diseases (namely inoculated small pox, and natural small pox, or cow pox) had been inoculated with small pox 64 only would have died. Had all undergone vaccination five or six only would have died of small pox. Where one person has died of small pox after vaccination 11 or 12 have died of inoculated small pox. In several parishes of Cambridge in proportion to the diffusion of vaccination has been the prevention of small pox. Two hundred and twenty four cases of small pox have occurred after supposed vaccination. In these cases the disease was slight in 163 more severe but not dangerous in 33 dangerous in 9 and fatal in 3. The supervention of small pox in persons previously vaccinated has been incomparably more frequent of late than in former years. The lapse of time does not impair the protecting influence of cow pox in the persons of those who have once undergone the disease. The vaccined virus has lost none of its efficacy from the time which has transpired and the number of individuals through whom it has passed since it was first taken from its original source.

The following is the substance of the Prospectus of the London University.

The object of the institution is to bring the means of a complete scientific and literary education home to the doors of the inhabitants of the metropolis so that they may be enabled to educate their sons at a very moderate expense and under their own immediate and constant superintendance. The whole expense of education at the London University will not exceed 25l or 30l a year (this supposes a student to attend five or six of the general classes but the medical education is necessarily more expensive from the costs of the anatomical department) including the sums paid to the general fund and there will not be more than ten weeks of vacation in the year.

A suitable piece of ground for the buildings and walks and in a central situation is now in treaty for and it is expected that the structure will be completed in August 1826 and the classes opened in October following. A fortnight's vacation will be allowed at Christmas and Easter and six weeks from the middle of August to the end of September. The money being raised by shares and contributions each holder of a 100l share will receive interest at a rate not exceeding four per cent and be entitled to send one student to the University. The shares will be transferable by sale and bequest. No person can hold more than ten shares. Each contributor of 50l will have all the privileges of a shareholder during his life except that of receiving interest and transferring his rights.

Each student is to pay five guineas a year to the general income besides one guinea to the library museum and collection of maps charts drawings and models.

It is proposed to vest the government of the institution in a Chancellor and Vice Chancellor and nineteen ordinary Members of Council chosen by the shareholders a certain number of the Council to go out every year. The emoluments of the professors will be made to depend on the fees received from students with the addition of very moderate salaries.

A decision has been lately given in the Court of Chancery connected with the question of literary property and the right of publication. The proprietors of a medical work called the *Lancet* which is published weekly obtained an exact copy of Mr Abernethy's lectures (which are delivered not from a written paper but orally) and inserted them in their publication. Mr Abernethy applied to the Court of Chancery to stop the publication by summary injunction but was unsuccessful, because as the identity of the lectures could not be proved by any copy or manuscript no legal evidence of property could be shewn. Mr Abernethy then made a fresh application to Chancery on the ground that an implied contract existed between himself and those to whom the lectures were delivered and that consequently a trust became vested in the hearers. The Chancellor has issued his injunction to restrain the publication thereby establishing the rule that individuals who attend a lecturer to whom they pay a fee have no right to publish what they hear.

The private bills brought before Parliament during the late session amounted to the unprecedented number of 383. In the four years ending with 1794, there were only 112 bills on the average. Only a small proportion of the several hundred proposed joint-stock speculations have been hitherto brought before the Legislature.

A company is announced for raising silk in this country and forming planta tions of mulberry trees. One individual at Camden town has already planted eight thousand of the trees.

The quantity of blood taken into the heart, and expelled therefrom into the arteries, in the course of twenty four hours has been lately estimated by Dr Kidd at 24¾ hogsheads in a man, and 8,000 hogsheads in a whale! The whole mass of blood therefore, reckoning it at thirty five pints, passes 288 times through the heart daily, or once in five minutes by 375 pulsations, each expelling about 1¼ ounce of blood.

A patent has been taken out by Mr Arrowsmith for his Diorama, the principle of which consists in a new mode of throwing the light upon or through painted scenes, and of varying the brilliancy of the light. In the diorama in the Regent's Park the pictures are transparently painted on canvas hung before large windows, at sufficient distances to admit of screens being occasionally let down or drawn aside, as often as a changing scene is intended to be represented. In the roof there are large sky lights furnished with transparent-coloured screens, so as to modify the light on the front of the picture.

FRANCE

The Society for the Encouragement of National Industry has adjudged a gold medal to M. Crespel for the manufacture of red beet sugar. This gentleman annually disposes of 150,000 lbs of this sugar; his factory is open to all who wish to examine its regulations, and he supplies workmen acquainted with all his proceedings. A prince of the Ukraine left his country to put on a labourer's frock and learn of M. Crespel to make beet sugar.

INDIA &c.

It is highly pleasing to perceive that the benevolent spirit which so honourably characterizes Great Britain and Ireland extends itself more or less throughout our colonies. We subjoin in confirmation of this remark the following list of religious and charitable institutions established at Calcutta. *Religious Institutions*—Auxiliary Bible Society, Bible Association, Committee of the Church Missionary Society, Church Missionary Association, Diocesan Committee of the Society for promoting Christian Knowledge, Auxiliary Missionary Society, Baptist Missionary Society, Bishop's College, Bethel Union, and Seamen's Friend Society. *Benevolent Institutions*—Government Sanscrit College, Madrissa or Government Mohammedan College, Committee of Public Instruction, Government Chinsurah Schools, School Book Society, School Society, Female Juvenile Society, Ladies Society for Native Female Education, Benevolent Institution for the Instruction of Indigent Children, Military Orphan Society, Military Widow's Fund, Lord Clive's Fund, King's Military Fund, Marine Pension Fund, Civil Fund, Mariners and General Widows Fund, Presidency General Hospital, Native Hospital, Hospital for Native Insanes, Government Establishment for Vaccination, School for Native Doctors, United Charity and Free School, Charitable Fund for the Relief of Distressed Europeans and others, European Female Orphan Asylum.

Communications from India continue to abound with such melancholy facts as the following:—Vizier Singh died at Nepal on the 3d of last December. The following day the body was burned, and along with it two of his wives and *three slave girls*; the latter however had not the honour of being burned on the same pile with their master, but had a pile to themselves. The brother of the deceased, with his nephew in his arms, lighted the funeral fires—such being the custom. Suttees are not unfrequent in the valley. One took place some months ago of a woman burning herself with her seducer, who had been killed by her own husband.

AMERICA

M. Humboldt has published a statement respecting the population and languages of America, of which the following is a summary.

Population

Roman Catholics—		
Spanish Continental America		
White	2,937,000	
Indian	7,530,000	
Mixed Race &		
Negroes	5,518,000	
		15,985,000
Portuguese America		
White	920,000	
Negro	1,960,300	
Mixed Race &		
Indian	1,120,000	
		4,000,000
United States Lower Canada		
and French Guiana	536,000	
Hayti, Porto Rico & French		
West Indies	1,656,000	
		22,177,000
Protestants—		
United States	9,990,000	
Upper Canada, Nova Scotia		
and Labrador	260,000	
English and Dutch Guiana	820,000	
English West Indies	741,500	
Dutch & English West Indies	80,500	
		11,237,000
Independent Indians not Christian	820,000	
Total Population		34,234,000

M. Humboldt divides this population in respect of languages as follows:—English 11,297,500; Spanish 10,174,000; Indian 7,800,000; Portuguese, 3,740,000; French 1,058,000; Dutch, Danish, Swedish, and Russian 214,500.

UNITED STATES

The sudden development of commercial power in the United States is unprecedented in the annals of civilization. Discovered only about 330 years ago, this immense territory remained for years the abode of savages and beasts; a few wandering and half starved hordes possessed the land which now supports 10,000,000 civilized beings. In 1778, the *capital* of this country might be roundly stated at between two and three millions sterling: in the short period of half a century this sum has been increased to no less an amount, it is calculated, than nearly a hundred and forty millions.

SOCIETY ISLANDS

In these now Christian islands rapid improvements are going on in the arts of civilized life. At Otaheite a sugar manufactory has been established, where sugar is made from the native cane. At Eimeo a building designed for a cotton manufactory has been erected; the machinery for spinning and weaving was imported from England, and was to be put in motion by water power. Cotton grows spontaneously in abundance.

LIST OF NEW PUBLICATIONS

THEOLOGY

Discourses on the Lord's Prayer, by the Rev. S. Saunders. 8vo. 10s. 6d.

Seventeen Sermons, by the Rev. H. M. Neile. 8vo. 12s.

Death Bed Scenes, by the Author of the Evangelical Rambler. 7s.

Remarks on applying the Funds of the Bible Society to the Circulation of such Foreign Versions as contain the Apocrypha, where no other Version will be generally received.

Essays and Letters, by John Kitto, with a Memoir of the Author.

Six Sermons preached at Cheltenham, by the Rev. J. W. Cunningham. 3s. 6d.

Guthrie's Christian's Great Interest, with an Introductory Essay by Dr. Chalmers. 12mo. 3s. bds.

Butler's Analogy, Essay by the Rev. Daniel Wilson. 12mo. 6s. bds.

Rutherford's Letters, Essay by T. Erskine, Esq. 12mo. 4s. bds.

The Christian, by the Rev. Samuel Walker, Curate of Truro, Essay by the Rev. C. Simeon. 12mo. 3s. bds.

Treatise on the Religious Affections, by Jonathan Edwards, Essay by the Rev. D. Young. 12mo. 7s. bds.

Pascal's Thoughts on Religion, a new Translation with a Memoir of his Life by the Rev. E. Craig. 6s.

The Importance of a full Exhibition of Scriptural Truth, a Sermon preached before the University of Cambridge, by the Rev. T. Webster, M.A.

The Parish Church, containing the Religion of the Britons, the Errors of Popery, the Reformation and Revolution, by the Rev. T. Wood, A.M. 8vo. 10s. 6d.

Gesenius's Hebrew Lexicon to the Books of the Old Testament, including the Geographical Names and Chaldaic Words in Ezra and Daniel. Translated into English from the German by Christopher Leo. 1l. 4s.

A Sermon preached at St. Michael's, Bath, on the Death of the Rev. John Richards, A.M. by the Rev. James Pears, B.C.L. 8vo. 1s. 6d.

Sermons by the Rev. Thomas Frognell Dibdin, M.A. F.R.S. 8vo. 15s.

Sermons on various Subjects, by the Rev. Thomas Rennell, B.D. F.R.S. 8vo. 12s.

Sermons on various Subjects, by the Rev. J. Hewlett, B.D. F.A.S. 8vo. 10s. 6d.

Aids to Reflection in the Formation of a Manly Character. By S. T. Coleridge, Esq. 10s. 6d.

MISCELLANEOUS

Nichols's Progresses and Entertainments of James the First. Part I.

The Commercial Power of Great Britain, by the Baron Dupin. 2 vols. 8vo. 1l. 8s.

Miscellaneous Writings of J. Evelyn. 4to. 3l. 10s.

Classical Disquisitions and Curiosities, by B. H. Malkin, LL.D. and F.S.A. 8vo. 12s.

Essays on Landscape Gardening, by R. Morris, F.L.S. 1l. 11s. 6d.

Poems, the early Productions of William Cowper, now first published. Foolscap 8vo. 3s. 6d.

The Negro's Memorial, or Abolitionist's Catechism, containing a Compendious Analysis of Arguments relative to the Slave Trade and Negro Slavery. 8vo. 2s. 6d.

RELIGIOUS INTELLIGENCE

PARIS BIBLE SOCIETY

At a meeting for the formation of a Ladies Bible Association at Sommières as a Branch of the Auxiliary Society at Nismes, M. Marignan, a small country farmer, one of the collectors of the Milhaud Bible Association, rose and in a simple but very feeling and expressive manner delivered an address in which he remarked—

I am, gentlemen, but in an humble station, you will excuse me if I do not speak with eloquence, it is the love which I have to my religion that induces me to address you on this occasion. M. Borrel, the pastor of our church, proposed to me to become a collector of a Bible Association, and obtain subscribers of one penny weekly, with the design of employing the sums raised in the purchase of Bibles and Testaments, in order to present them to newly married persons at the celebration of their marriage, and also to those poor persons who had not the means of procuring them for themselves.

I will not attempt to describe the joy which I felt, when this excellent servant of Christ offered me this employment. I opened a list of subscriptions in conjunction with my colleagues and friends. Scarcely was the first stone of our undertaking laid, when a considerable number of persons became subscribers, declaring themselves happy in being able to co-operate in a work so excellent, and we have the delightful satisfaction of seeing this number increase daily. Thus our enterprise is as a small grain of mustard seed which we have sown, but if all Christian churches acted thus, the tree would attain to its perfect height and cover with its shadow many of our brethren who are living without God and without hope in the world, and who, destitute of the light of the Gospel, walk according to the course of this world and the desires of the flesh, not knowing that the goodness of God leadeth them to repentance.

Many of our brethren, desirous of possessing the Book of Books and not having the means of obtaining it, loudly call for our assistance. How affecting is this spectacle! Shall we be indifferent to it? No, we will open our hearts to the first of Christian graces—*charity*, and our continued exertions will, I trust, bring multitudes to the obedience of Christ, happy if we may attain that end without at the same time attributing to ourselves the glory.

After this address and another delivered by a person of the same class, M. Vincent, pastor of St. Mamert, addressed the meeting on the influence of Bible Societies in reference to the religious knowledge which they have already been the means of diffusing among the humbler classes of society, and added—

Experience here comes in to the support of argument. It says more upon this subject than all our discourses. Two men born and brought up in the country, accustomed from their childhood only to the laborious employments of agriculture, having entered upon no studies which could enable them to express themselves correctly before a large assembly, have eagerly accepted a place among the members of the Bible Society. They have read and meditated on the holy Scriptures. By this pious employment their minds have been enlightened—their zeal has been excited—their tongues are unloosed—they have become eloquent. You have seen it, you have heard it, gentlemen. They have edified us, and the sentiments with which their hearts were overflowing have deeply penetrated our own.

PROGRESS OF CHRISTIANITY IN MADAGASCAR

The following is an extract from a letter of a missionary at Madagascar.

It is with inexpressible joy I inform you that I have important and very encouraging information to impart. The mission at Madagascar now wears a most pleasing and promising aspect. There are fourteen schools established in which are taught about one thousand two hundred children, and were we furnished with sufficient means, many, very many more might be formed, as applications for teachers have been made from various quarters which we have not, as yet, been able to meet. Many of the youths in the Royal School have made commendable progress in learning, can read the Bible with facility, write a fair hand, are far advanced in arithmetic, and have acquired a general knowledge of the principles of the Christian religion. It is from this school that the villages have been supplied with teachers. The in struction of native females is likewise attended to. Mrs Jones and Mrs Griffiths have more than 100 under their care. The children who have been with them from the beginning are become very clever at their needle. Messrs Jones and Griffiths have commenced preaching in the native language. The number of people who attend is considerable. The prejudices of the natives are stronger and their superstitious observances more numerous than persons in England are aware of; but blessed be God they perceptibly lose ground.

The following is an extract from a recent letter from another missionary.

I have the pleasure to inform you that this mission has never worn a more promising aspect than it has since last May. The King continues his protection to us and gives us encouragement to labour with assiduity. We have twenty two schools established since last April under his patronage, in which more than 2000 children are instructed. Our first scholars teach at the different villages, and their ardent pursuit after knowledge and their unceasing assiduity in communicating instruction to others affords us great satisfaction and encouragement. Those villages that have above eight scholars have four teachers; two to teach every other week by turns while the other two are learning in town, so that they are one week learning and the other teaching. The scholars both in town and the country have learnt almost the whole of a large catechism which I have translated and formed for the use of the schools.

I have a chapel built annexed to my house. Mr Jones and myself preach by turns when we are in town, one in English and the other in Malagash. About two months ago Mr Jones and I commenced visiting the villages where schools are established, to preach and catechise; we go by turns every Sunday. We have thronged congregations on the Sabbath; our chapel in town is crowded and the doors and windows lined. We have three or four and sometimes 5,000 hearers in town and often 2 or 3,000 in the country besides the assembling of three or four schools. We catechise them first and then we sing and pray and preach often in the open air. We ask them to repeat what they remember of the sermon and we propose to them any question that may occur to us. The talents they display on these occasions would put many in England to the blush.

I have translated the Book of Exodus and the Gospels by Mark and Luke, and also part of the Psalms as far as the 50th and the first three chapters of the Epistle to the Romans. I have also prepared a course of plain discourses. Mr Jones has finished translating the Book of Genesis and the Gospel by Matthew and is far advanced with the Gospel by John and the Acts and with the First Book of Samuel &c. He has prepared a series of discourses on the work of creation and is also preparing discourses on the Divine attributes. Every thing is going on in union and peace.

FEMALE EDUCATION IN INDIA

The Committee of the Church Missionary Society have issued an Appeal to the Ladies of the United Kingdom in behalf of the Native Females of British India, from which we copy the following passages, most earnestly recommending th object to all our readers.

The deplorable state of ignorance and degradation under which females in heathen countries labour has long excited the compassion of those Christians who have witnessed their situation and who feel as they ought for this branch of the great family of man. Several attempts were made from time to time to remedy this flagrant evil but they were not successful. The prejudices and apprehensions of the men and the apathy of the females themselves defeated the plans pursued.

In the autumn of 1820 a fund was raised for the purpose of sending out to the Calcutta School Society a lady duly qualified who would undertake to superintend a school for training native female teachers who might be fixed after proper instruction as school mistresses in suitable stations. On her arrival in Calcutta in November 1821 she was greatly concerned to find that the Committee of the School Society to whom she had been recommended composed partly of native gentlemen was not at that time prepared to engage in any general plan of native female education. At this juncture the Corresponding Committee of the Church Missionary Society who had for seventeen years been watching every opportunity of meliorating the condition of the heathen thought that they could perceive among the natives generally the growth of more liberal habits of thinking. They devoutly hoped that the time had arrived when the heathen youths who had been instructed in their schools and had grown up to manhood, began to appreciate the positive benefits which they had derived from their education and they trusted that the confidence reposed in themselves by the natives would greatly facilitate their plans to impart instruction to the females. Under this impression they undertook to provide for the support of Miss Cooke (who has since been married to the Rev. Isaac Wilson one of the society's missionaries in Calcutta) and to promote the objects of her mission. The result has surpassed their most sanguine expectations. In three years the number of girls under instruction in the society's schools in Bengal alone has exceeded 800 and that number may now be enlarged to a very great extent when adequate funds shall be provided—so rapidly is this happy change of sentiment in regard to females taking place among the natives.

With a view to meet the wish of some ladies of high consideration in Calcutta as well as the feelings of native gentlemen well disposed to promote the education of females the society's female schools in and near Calcutta were in March of last year placed under the direction of a special institution (See Christian Observer for March p 197) For the present that institution confines its operations to Calcutta and its more immediate neighbourhood if it should be deemed expedient it will endeavour to extend its influence to other parts of India. Its Church Missionary female schools are rapidly increasing not only in parts of Bengal beyond the present range of the Calcutta Ladies Society but in its missions in the South of India and in Ceylon. The Committee have made a grant of five hundred pounds to the Calcutta Ladies Society and they hope to be enabled by enlarged contributions effectually to cultivate this new field of labour.

AMERICAN BIBLE SOCIETY

The last Report states that there have been printed at the depository during the year 48,550 Bibles and Testaments including 2000 Spanish Bibles —making a total in the nine years of the Society's existence of 451,902 Bibles and Testaments and parts of the latter printed or otherwise obtained by the Society. Stereotype plates for a pocket Bible are casting and are expected to be completed by the ensuing autumn. There have been issued from the depository in the course of the year 63,851 Bibles and Testaments and the Gospels in the Mohawk language making a total since the establishment of the Society of 372,913 Bibles and Testaments, and parts of the latter exclusive of the number issued by the Kentucky Bible Society. The managers have been recently engaged in contributing to the supply of penitentiaries and prisons with the Scriptures and the troops stationed at remote posts of the United States the army and navy both being now furnished with Bibles from the same source. The managers have granted 500 dollars to assist in the translation and publication of the Scriptures in some of the languages of the native tribes of Peru one of which tribes contains a million of people. Gratuitous donations of the Scriptures for distribution principally in the new territories of the Union have been made during the year to the value of 10,447 dollars. The number of new auxiliaries recognized during the year has been 45—making in the whole 452.

The following simple facts connected with the distribution of the Scriptures by the Philadelphia Bible Society shew the importance of the Society's operations. The copies adverted to were in the German language.

I have been said a poor man expressing his thanks to the distributor,— I have been for a long time contriving many plans to get a Bible I have never yet been able at last I saw a notice in the paper that the poor would be supplied.—What a fine thing it is that the poor can get Bibles! I have said another but one quarter of a dollar but I want a Bible badly and if that will be of any service I willingly give it. It was accepted and a Bible given. The poor man went away rejoicing.—Another observed Now you see that the English people are friendly to the Germans if they were not they would not send them Bibles. Another writes as follows —

Friend I wish to inform you that I have been so long sick now more than a year and I want a Bible and cannot pay for one. If you would be so good as to send me one I will thank you and God also for it. This note was accompanied with 25 cents which were received and a Bible sent. Another said he had never had a Bible nor his father before him nor his wife's father.

SOCIETY FOR PROMOTING EDUCATION AND INDUSTRY IN CANADA

An institution has been formed under this appellation the object of which is to train up teachers and assist in the establishment of schools of industry among the Indians and settlers in such parts of the provinces of Upper and Lower Canada as are destitute of the means of instruction. The reading of the Scriptures and some useful manual labour are to constitute parts of the daily exercise of the pupils.

Mr. Osgood, who has been itinerating seventeen years in the provinces of Canada, and on the frontiers of the United States distributing Bibles, Testaments, and elementary tracts, giving moral and religious instruction to the poor, establishing schools, particularly Sunday schools, and setting up small libraries wherever practicable, visited England in the year 1813 under the patronage of the Governor in Chief Sir George Prevost, and collected 1,800l. partly for an asylum for the poor and partly for the instruction of orphans and destitute children. Though it was thought adviseable that the interest only of the money should be used, so pressing have been the importunities in behalf of the poor in Canada that more than half of the original fund has been expended, but it is added not in vain, for in consequence of this effort it is calculated that more than 2000 children have been brought under elementary and moral instruction, and assistance has been granted to two masters versed in the system of mutual instruction, who were sent out to organize and conduct schools in Canada. In these schools a number of young men have been qualified to become teachers, two of whom are sons of an Indian chief. So anxious are some of these natives of the forest to receive instruction that one of the chiefs offered to give up his own house for a school room.

Mr. Osgood has again visited this country bringing with him most respectable testimonials, with a view to obtain funds for civilizing and christianizing the Canadian Indians and training teachers for the new settlements, many of which are in a most deplorable condition with regard to the means of instruction. The time is fast approaching when these Canadian Indians must either be civilized and christianized, or extirpated; for their means of subsisting by the chace must soon be entirely cut off, their reservations being almost surrounded by the White people.

In order effectually to promote the intended objects a society has been instituted, among the first contributors to which are the names of the Earl of Liverpool, the Earl of Harrowby, Lord Bexley, Lord Calthorpe, the Bishop of Salisbury, Joseph Butterworth, Esq. M.P. and various clergymen and gentlemen. The following gentlemen have agreed to take charge of the funds collected, and to superintend their application:—Mr. Mortlock, Mr. Hankey, Mr. Allen, Mr. Howard, Mr. Reyner, Mr. Haslope, Mr. Mills, Mr. Steven, and Mr. Pellatt.—The trustees will receive donations for the object; also the following Bankers: Messrs. Hankey and Co. 7, Fenchurch street; Sir John Perring and Co. Cornhill; Sir Peter Pole and Co. Bartholomew lane; Messrs. Drummond, Charing Cross; Messrs. Lees and Co. Lombard street; also Messrs. Hatchards, 187, Piccadilly.

SPANISH TRANSLATION SOCIETY

We have great satisfaction in recommending to the notice and patronage of our readers this newly formed society, the chief object of which is the religious improvement of the rapidly augmenting population of Spanish America,—of sixteen or eighteen millions of our fellow men, professing Christianity indeed, but strangers in a great degree to its real nature and effects. To communicate to this vast population just views of revealed truth must be considered as an object of very high interest. The political revolution they have recently undergone has awakened amongst them a spirit of free inquiry, which in its excursive range is beginning to be eagerly directed to the subject of religion. Should they, however, be left to form their ideas of Christianity from that exhibition of it which alone they have hitherto witnessed, there is reason to fear that they will too much confound it with the errors, superstitions, and corruptions with which they have unfortunately seen it associated, and thus be led to reject it as unworthy of their belief and acceptance. Such has been the result which has attended similar revolutionary movements in Europe, and such is likely to be the result in Spanish America, without a vigorous and seasonable effort to prevent it.

In this point of view, the most important measure is undoubtedly the general circulation of the holy Scriptures, as contemplated by the British and Foreign Bible Society, from which the happiest effects may be fairly anticipated. But next to the holy Scriptures, the exposition of Christian truth by works of acknowledged excellence is perhaps the most important means that can be employed. And this is the design of the present society, which proposes to print in the Spanish language and circulate by sale or otherwise works which shall exhibit genuine Christianity to the opening minds of the Spanish Americans—which shall set forth the irrefragable proofs of its Divine origin, which shall detail the commanding doctrines of redemption in all their simplicity and fulness, which shall shew the indissoluble connexion of those doctrines with purity of heart and conduct, and explain and enforce the various obligations resulting from a Christian profession. This the Society proposes to accomplish either by the translation of suitable works of undoubted merit, or by the republication of such works already existing in the Spanish language.

The residence in this country of many expatriated Spaniards of great talents and acquirements affords at the present moment peculiar facilities for such an undertaking, which it would be ungrateful not to acknowledge, and criminal to neglect. Other circumstances may be mentioned as affording the strongest encouragement to the adoption of the proposed plan, such as the tolerant spirit which has been manifested by the different Governments of Spanish America, the reform already began in the affairs of the church, the rapid extension of education among the people, the eager thirst for knowledge which has been excited among them, and the fact that wherever either the holy Scriptures or religious books have been accessible, they have been sought for with an eagerness and received with a gratitude which afford pledges of the most important and beneficial results.

The Society however, though directing its views chiefly to Spanish America, would by no means overlook the spiritual interests of Old Spain, which it is obvious may be essentially promoted by the same means which are calculated to benefit her former dependencies.

The following extract from a speech of Sir James Mackintosh in the House of Commons, gives us a striking idea of the general extent and importance of the Spanish American States.

Spanish America lies on the western coast from the northern point of New California to the utmost limit of cultivation towards Cape Horn. On the eastern it extends from the mouth of the Mississippi to that of Orinoco, and after the immense exception of Guiana and Brazil, from the Rio de la Plata, to the southern footsteps of civilized man. The prodigious varieties of its elevation exhibit in the same parallel of latitude all the climates and products of the globe. It is the only abundant source of the metals justly called precious, the most generally and permanently useful of all commodities except those which are necessary to the preservation of human life. It is unequally and most scantily peopled by 16 or 18 millions whose numbers freedom of industry and security of property must quadruple in a century. Its length on the Pacific coast is equal to that of the whole continent of Africa from the Cape of Good Hope to the Straits of Gibraltar. It is more extensive than the vast possessions of Russia or of Great Britain in Asia. The Spanish language is spoken over a line of nearly 6000 miles. The state of Mexico alone is five times larger than European Spain. A single communication cut through these territories between the Atlantic and Pacific would bring China 6000 miles nearer to Europe, and the Republic of Columbia or that of Mexico may open and command that new road for the commerce of the world.

Subscriptions and donations are received by the members of the Committee which consists of Lord Calthorpe, the Hon. F. Calthorpe, P. Aiken Esq. John Green Esq. Rev. C. Jerram, Rev. W. Marshall, Z. Macaulay Esq. T. Marshall Esq. John Mortlock Esq. Colonel Powan, R. P. Staples Esq. C. Stokes Esq. Rev. Dr. Thorpe, Capt. Vernon, Rev. D. Wilson, Rev. Basil Woodd—by the Treasurers Henry Drummond Esq. Charing Cross, John P. Robertson Esq. 16 York Place, and by the Secretary Rev. George Lawrence, 22 Colebrook Row, Islington.

The Society is already engaged in translating and printing Bishop Porteus's Evidences, Doddridge's Rise and Progress, and the first part of Milner's Church History. Translations from the works of Archbishop Leighton, Bishop Hall, Bishop Hopkins, Bishop Beveridge, Hooker, Baxter, Witherspoon, Scott, &c. will probably follow, together with republications of the Imitation of Christ, Pascal's Thoughts, some of the writings of Nicole, &c. which already exist in the Spanish language.

EPISCOPAL FLOATING CHAPEL SOCIETY.

A society has been formed under the above title, the objects and encouraging prospects of which are described in the following circular. We take the earliest opportunity of bringing before our readers its powerful claims to public patronage. The sanction and liberal assistance pro mised by Government in aid of the objects for which it is instituted demand the gratitude of all who have at heart the moral and religious welfare of our seamen and by the blessing of God, the benefit will return tenfold to the nation at large from the improved character and habits of that long neglected portion of the community. The Society has been formed under the most respectable sanction and must commend itself to all who value our holy religion and the best interests of their fellow creatures.

It has long been a subject of regret that the variety of benevolent efforts to improve the moral condition of the lower classes in society should have effected so little in behalf of seamen and this indifference to the discharge of an important national and Christian duty has of late years been particularly felt by such as were anxious to promote their religious instruction in connexion with the Established Church.

A very superficial acquaintance with the moral character of seamen will be sufficient to discover that the credit of such qualities as generosity and heroism is not necessarily associated with the possession of Christian virtue. It is the misfortune of these men that they are doomed to early and in too many instances to habitual separation from those opportunities of religious improvement which are common to society at large and the effect of such privation combined with the force of depraved example is too frequently a habit of indifference and moral insensibility which is not to be corrected by an influence so distant and unconnected with their situation as that which is exerted by the regular parochial churches. But if any thing in addition to extreme ignorance were wanting to repress an occasional inclination among seamen to frequent the ordinances of public worship in the Establishment it would be the conviction that they do not come within the scope of church provisions. A sailor is impressed by the belief that he possesses no claim to accommodation in a church and he is too frequently the victim of professional vanity to think of intruding himself in any situation where he cannot establish the title of undisputed right. Such feelings in the bosom of seafaring men are powerfully aided by a reluctance to expose themselves to the observation and fancied contempt of a genteel congregation and the concurrent influence of these and similar causes will be sufficient to account for the fact, that an average of probably not fewer than ten thousand seamen in the Thames alone will not in ordinary cases present two hundred in attendance upon the national forms of worship.

This apathy and misconception can only be overcome by an arrangement which shall carry the principles and the ritual of the Church of England to our seamen in a shape calculated to awaken attention and accommodate the ordinances of public worship to their professional condition their stated habits and even their prejudice.

This has been attempted in the case of other denominations and a number of zealous individuals acting under the influence of a religious concern for the spiritual improvement of seamen have succeeded with the establishment of Floating Chapels in several of the principal ports. The result of the experiment has in most instances surpassed reasonable expectation affording satisfactory evidence that there is nothing repellant to the seamen in the sanctities of congregational devotion and that these interesting but neglected objects may be collected in attendance upon religious worship with probably greater facility than any other class of the community.

Having ascertained the peculiar adaptation of such institutions to the end in view it was proposed to constitute an Episcopal Floating Chapel Society for the object of promoting their establishment in connexion with the Church of England. Lord Melville upon the part of his Majesty's Government has most liberally promised the grant of as many vessels as may be required for the principal ports of the empire including the expense of alteration and outfit necessary to accommodate them to purposes of congregational worship. Nor will the bounty of Government be restricted to the donation and equipment of the necessary vessels it is intended to comprehend the salary of clergymen regularly approved by the bishops in those particular cases where the want of means or other circumstances of a local nature may render it desirable that the Admiralty should undertake the appointment.

The design has also met with the approbation and concurrence of several distinguished prelates who have already favoured its application to their respective dioceses and the Committee have every reason to believe that the same liberal and satisfactory arrangement as it respects the appointment of the clergymen will be effected in every port to which it may be necessary to extend the provision. The chapels will be granted by Government to gentlemen or societies appointed on behalf of particular ports to present the application, and it is proposed that they shall severally be placed under the direction of a local committee, which is to charge itself with the responsibility of the superintendance, the provision of the clergyman's salary, and whatever may be essential to the promotion of the general design.

An object intimately connected with the religious improvement of seamen is the care and instruction of apprentices; and the same provision which afforded the advantages of a chapel to the one would supply the accommodation of a school to the other. In seminaries so intimately connected with the profession the juvenile part of its members might be collected from those scenes of depravity and vicious example where they are ordinarily scattered during the continuance of their vessels in port, and introduced to such an acquaintance with the principles of the Christian religion and the elements of practical navigation as should constitute the foundation of a moral worth and nautical superiority honourable to the individuals and beneficial to the country. A lending library and depository for the Scriptures, Prayer books, Homilies, and judiciously selected Tracts might also be annexed to each chapel, and placed under the direction of the clergyman, who must in every case be appointed with the approbation of the bishop of the diocese.

VIEW OF PUBLIC AFFAIRS.

FOREIGN.

PORTUGAL, &c.—This country may now be added to the list of those which have begun to imitate the enlarged policy of Great Britain with regard to restrictions on commerce. A duty of thirty per cent has been imposed in place of prohibitory imposts on a multitude of articles, and the export duty on wine is reduced to one half. The edict states, that however beneficial the old laws might be when enacted, they are quite incompatible with the exigencies of modern times. We scarcely know an instance in history in which sound principle has had a more striking triumph over ignorance, prejudice, and mistaken self interest, than in the introduction of this new system of commercial policy, which must soon become the settled code of nations. We rejoice at the change on higher grounds also than mere fiscal considerations; for the new system has a tendency to bind together the whole world in the ties of brotherhood, rendering them mutually dependent and obliged, opening new facilities for the promotion of knowledge, civilization, and the arts which contribute to the well being of individuals and nations, giving new currency to the circulation of the sacred Scriptures and promoting the universal study of those sacred oracles, and cutting off many of the sources of war and disunion, by making it the mutual interest of all parties to live at peace. Great Britain has begun the system (and we hope before long will be able to complete it in some important branches yet untouched). In the mean time let British Christians avail themselves of the advantages which it affords for extending as far as possible to the whole world the blessings which they themselves enjoy. We perceive with great delight that a desire to do so is widely prevalent. We may mention another instance of it in the formation of a society (see our Religious Intelligence, page 455) for translating and circulating valuable religious works in the Spanish language, more immediately with reference to the wants of Spanish America. We however allude to it under the present head, as these new facilities, and others which may be hoped for, are materially connected with those liberal views of international interest which the Portuguese edict shews to be rapidly gaining ground throughout the community of nations. Considering the vast number of foreign vessels which visit and are likely still more to visit, our own ports in consequence of the new system, it might perhaps be useful if a society or board were formed expressly for devising and carrying into effect in the most judicious manner, the best plans for the religious welfare of our foreign visitors of all nations, according to their various wants and prejudices which ought of course to be consulted and respected. Individual societies are already laudably and usefully engaged in the object; and all the needful apparatus and machinery, so to speak, might be derived at compa ratively little expense or inconvenience from existing sources; but a Board directing its whole attention to this one point, with agents suitably qualified, understanding the habits, languages, and creeds of different nations, and corresponding with our Bible, Missionary, Educational, Marine and other charitable societies, might be able to act with greater effect than individual institutions, though by no means to their exclusion; and the good thus effected in this country, as a central point, would radiate on every side throughout the world.

GREECE.—The recent reports from Greece confirm the accounts of the success of the Egyptian army at Navarino, and the progress of the Turks in the Morea, balanced however by a defeat of the invading fleets. If these partial reverses should teach the patriots the useful lesson of the necessity of merging their mutual differences, and postponing the settlement of their respective pretensions till they have achieved their common freedom, it were well. It augurs favourably that Colocotroni and his companions in exile have been recalled, and are now fighting the battles of their country.

UNITED STATES.—The differences between the Northern and Southern States comprehended in the American Union, which have been thought to threaten future disruption, seem to be becoming more serious than at any former period. The chief source of difference is that foul stain on national honour, slavery, of which the slave states exultingly and most offensively make their boast. The contest between the New England States, strengthened by the friends of humanity and religion generally throughout the Union, and the slave-holders in the South and West, is an exact counterpart to that which is taking place between the legislature and government and people of Great Britain and Ireland, and their foreign dependencies in the West Indies. A committee of the state legislature of Georgia have drawn up a parliamentary report which can only be matched by the official manifestoes of our own islands. They talk of the 'snivelling insinuations' urged against them, and recommend their northern brethren to bask in their own self-righteousness and elysium. They then exclaim, As Athens, as Sparta, as Rome was, so will we be! *They* held slaves, we will hold them; that is, We, like them, will be heathens, and not Christians, professed imitators of three states, the first of which was one of the most profligately licentious,—the second the most barbarous, brutal, and inhuman,—the third the most unjust, tyrannical, and sanguinary, of all whose names and atrocities have blotted the page of history. Yet these Georgian legislators, after their pagan protest, affect to quote Scripture to their purpose, and to look up to the Great Author of justice and of mercy to smile approvingly upon that most audacious outrage on his laws which is involved in the maintenance of slavery. 'In the simplicity,' say they, "of patriarchal government we would remain master and servant, (are the committee, then, after all, secretly ashamed of the odious sound of SLAVE?) "under our own vine and fig tree, (a most suicidal allusion: see the passage, Micah iv. which describes a scene of peace and humanity, when swords shall become ploughshares, and 'every man, slaves as well as others, shall sit under his *own* vine and fig tree "*none daring to make him afraid*;' and when those who are now so driven out and afflicted and cast off shall be made ' a strong nation.') ' and confide for safety upon Him who, of old time looked down upon this state of things without wrath."—a palpable misstatement, for the Bible is full of denunciations against this and every other species of oppression, and it is expressly said, Jeremiah xxxiv. 17 in reference to this very subject. 'Thus saith the Lord, Because ye have not hearkened unto me in proclaiming liberty every one to his brother and every man to his neighbour, behold I will proclaim a liberty for you, saith the Lord, to the sword, to the pestilence and to the famine.' So far from the Almighty looking down upon this state of things without wrath, he provided means for its instant amelioration, and for its ultimate extinction, under the influence of our mild and holy religion —that most perfect contrast to the codes of Athens and Sparta and Rome." The allusion to the patriarchal ages is quite absurd: there is something far more like it among the savage Indians, with whom the Georgians are at perpetual war, than among themselves; but whatever it might be, it was at least such a system of comparative mildness and mutual confidence that the master felt no scruple in putting arms into the hands of his slaves ' (see Genesis xiv. 14. xxxii. 6. xxxiii. 1) and in some instances under the ancient slave system he even gave his daughter in marriage to his slave (see for example 1 Chron. ii. 34, 35). Is any thing like this the state of things in the South-western parts of the Union, or in the British slave-colonies? Would the pa triarchs of our plantations feel secure in the volunteer arms of their primeval servants, against an army of freemen? The people of the free states of America have nothing to fear from their brethren of the south till slavery ceases to pollute their soil, and, whenever that happy event takes place they will be too much brethren' in truth and in mutual interest to render war either just or necessary.

DOMESTIC

The session of Parliament closed on the 6th. The speech delivered by Commissioners, was very brief, stating the continuance of peace with foreign powers, the improved and tranquil condition of Ireland, a hope that the Burmese war might be speedily and satisfactorily terminated, and a congratulation upon the late enactments relative to commerce.—The session has produced many highly beneficial statutes, and has been characterised by a remarkable and most pleasing unanimity on some of the most important measures (on a few there has been an unusual warmth of debate) between the leading parties in Parliament. The commercial and colonial regulations so far as they go have elicited the eulogies of the Opposition, and Mr Peel's Jury Bill is such a liberal concession of power in the executive branch, for the sake of justice and the public good, as does the greatest honour to the administration that planned and promoted it. We may have an opportunity of noticing the chief provisions of this and some other recent acts, and also some of the interesting reports laid before both Houses in future Numbers, now that the pressure of parliamentary topics has subsided. One of the most litigated enactments of the session, the act more immediately framed for suppressing the Catholic Association in Ireland, is likely to prove a nullity. Mr O'Connell and his friends having formed a new board in such a manner as they consider will legally evade its provisions.—One of the last acts of the session was an excellent measure for adjusting the mutual rights of masters and workmen, by continuing the permission for workmen to combine as they please for their own interest, but to prohibit their molesting their companions who may not choose to conform to their regulations.

The last dispatches from India give very favourable accounts of the progress of the Burmese war. Assam has submitted to our arms, and the people of Pegu seem inclined to join us. The causes of the war are still an enigma to the public.

ANSWERS TO CORRESPONDENTS

Q U A, A Constant Reader, M S, E F, A Close Observer, G W, Y Z, Miles are under consideration.

The passage sent by Δ from Montesquieu has already appeared in our pages. It is strange that our correspondent should not have perceived that the sarcastic Baron was writing ironically.

Our American (U S) friends do not seem to be aware that owing to the different regulations of the Post offices of the two countries we cannot correspond with them on reciprocal terms. They can send a considerable packet to every part of the Union at a very trifling charge, and are not aware that for every letter we remit to them we pay on putting it into the Post office 2s 2d if single, 4s 4d if double, and so on for every additional inclosure. Two or three letters addressed by us by desire to American gentlemen in London and containing papers inclosed have been returned to us with the postage, the parties not being known or having left this country, and we did not think that our correspondents wished us to burden ourselves with an onerous export postage to forward them to the United States. On the other hand, their communications to us, even when intended as they usually are to be free, come often very heavily laden with inland carriage or postage. This very month the number and names of the students &c at the Presbyterian seminary at Philadelphia, with an accompanying paper cost us a heavy postage, and four newspapers just received from New York with the request of the editor to exchange publications were charged with a postage of 1l 5s 4d, whereas the whole charge of his paper for a year is but three dollars. In several cases an U S report, pamphlet or sermon costs us several times what we could order it for at an American bookseller's in London. We enter into these trifling details, only for the purpose of requesting our United States friends not to impute our silence to neglect of their favours, and to accept this notice that we have been obliged to direct our publishers to decline receiving packets unless delivered at their store free of these incumbrances.

THE CHRISTIAN OBSERVER.

No 284] *AUGUST* 1825 [No 8 Vol XXV

RELIGIOUS COMMUNICATIONS

To the Editor of the Christian Observer

THE PHILOSOPHY OF THE ROMAN CATHOLIC RELIGION

No II

THE first application of the hypothesis, generally developed in my former paper shall be directed to an elucidation of the origin of that system of ecclesiastical authority which has long borne the comprehensive appellation of INFALLIBILITY

It is utterly immaterial to my argument to ascertain whether this attribute—whatever be its meaning—be vested exclusively in the sovereign pontiff or in general councils or in the concurrence of both of these portions of the papal legislature It is sufficient that the thing is inherent in that metaphysical entity which under the name of *the church* has hitherto eluded the grasp of definition The power in question resembles an unwritten law delivered from human lips like the responses of an oracle, with an air of mysterious and irresponsible authority incapable of being privately examined but possessing far more than the force of a statute actually recorded and open to public inspection Or, it is analogous to a corporation composed of innumerable and separated individuals all of them asserting the supremacy of the general body but no one able to define in what or in whom the power resides, or whence such power is derived Neither does any individual though forming a part of the aggregate, hold himself to be answerable for what has been done, or will be done by——he cannot tell whom or what, except that it is *the church* In an age less enlightened than our own, Lord Coke said that ' corporations have no souls Whether he meant that the proceedings of these bodies subject none of their members to individual responsibility, or that they frequently act, in their collective capacity as though they feared no reckoning in a future state may be known to the jurists In either case the ecclesiastics of Rome might perhaps be aware of parallelisms in their own practice

As to this infallibility itself, few mysteries are, in my opinion more palpably open to the penetration of sound philosophy than this secret of the papal cabinet It evidently originated in the necessity felt by its hierarchy of establishing a high, commanding absolute authority, for bidding all scrutiny and essential as the grand moving power of its whole machinery To effect this it sagaciously calculated upon the incredible credulity of mankind, and the disposition of common minds to be mystified and silenced by a look and tone of decision It knew well, that, with few exceptions—too few to spoil its projects—men are passive machines, obeying an exterior impulse like the pistons and wheels of a steam engine on the application of fire The only caution necessary to be observed in working human mechanism is, that you must beware, in the operation of obstructing the immediate gratification of men's passions or, if this must be done to a certain degree, you must allow them afterwards some compensatory indulgence, such as may not disturb your present process In the mean time, let not the en gineer overload the safety valve. The doctrine of ecclesiastical compensations shall be illustrated in its proper place. Let it now be observed, that the court of Rome has always uttered its decrees with the tact of a dictator, completely satisfied with his own decisions, and with a manner triumphantly anticipating submission. It does not offer a doctrine referable, for proof, to a higher criterion, but to be received implicitly, instantaneously, finally. All this in its exterior is magnificent, but in essence it is nothing but the vulgarity of what the world calls *quackery* invested with the pretensions and splendour of the Vatican, as a coward might wear the costume and brandish the sabre of a hero.

Infallibility, or an assumption of power bordering upon such a name, is quite necessary to the existence of the entire system. It is the main spring of a despotism affecting to derive its sovereignty from Heaven. In this instance, as in all others of papal usurpation, it is perfectly needless to consult the chronological tables of Christendom, in order to discover whether the occupier of St Peter's chair reached his extravagance of power under the pontificate of an Innocent or a Boniface! Whoever, whatever first scaled this summit, the enterprize and success gained a natural and necessary point in the progress of spiritual tyranny advancing with the lapse of time in regular progression, and attaining its present eminence. Whoever has seen in St Peter's itself at Rome, or even in the magic illusions of a diorama, the inscription circling round the lower part of the dome of the Basilica TU ES PETRUS ET SUPRA HAC PETRA ÆDIFICABO ECCLESIAM MEAM ETC ETC, in its splendid and gigantic proportions, may have felt how irresistible such a motto so appropriated and so *interpreted* by the surrounding majesty of the edifice must be to those whose faith so it is called, is derived to them and strengthened by the external sense, and with whom the gorgeous vision has more than the force of argumentation.

But the authority of the triple crown cannot be sustained, even among its most abject devotees, without the perpetual motion of the under works of the system. We must therefore pass onward to the consideration of the SACRIFICE OF THE MASS, TRANSUBSTANTIATION AND PURGATORY.

No human scheme of religion has ever been constructed without a recognition of the universal fact that mankind in whatever degree are conscious of guilt, that they are obscurely aware of there being *something against them* an accusing spirit being lodged in every bosom, and that they are consequently fearful lest, in an after state of existence they should be obnoxious to punishment. The religion of all nations is *expiatory*! The splendid polytheism of Greece and Rome in various measures of obscurity adverted to this fact. The comparatively civilized millions of Hindostan connect it with their redundant superstitions, and savages abject as the Esquimaux, exhibit some traces of it in the penury of *their* systems. Papal sagacity on this occasion also, discovered the policy of meeting the world's prevalent suspicion of its own pravity. It acknowledged the justice of the suspicion, and availed itself of the circumstance in providing a ceremonial by which the sin struck conscience might be soothed and its alarms silenced and tranquillized. But the experiment was critical. Men if they knew any thing whatever of Christianity were aware of that leading fact in its history, that Jesus Christ died, and their notion, however confused was a certain conviction that his death was a sacrifice for mankind. The least ignorant knew, farther, that it partook of the nature of an atonement for human transgression. At this point the commander of the papal legions took up one of his all but impregnable positions. As the sacrifice of the New Testament was made only once, it was found necessary to invent a perpetual repetition of this one great oblation in order to divert men from the Cross to the crucifix from the blood shedding on Mount Calvary to the altar within the rails of a Roman Catholic chancel

———Hic illius arma
Hic currus fuit———

A visible sacrifice it was foreseen, would act as a continual appeal to the senses Then came the wafer the chalice the representatory, the thurible—prostration, genuflexion, elevation—whispers, intonations and all the visible, audible tangible signs meant to persuade the devotee of the efficacy of this grand process A vast collateral advantage also was here derived to the church in the increase of influence thus obtained by the priesthood *They* alone could transmute the sacramental symbol into an atonement Hence the unknown value of *tran substantiation* It was an exclusive and permanent patent to counterfeit it was so to speak, parricide, treason, or deicide It perpetually strengthened in the popular mind, the conviction of the immeasurable power of spiritual superiors

But who discovered the name and pretensions of the Mass? Many a theological book worm could muster a numerous host of authorities in reply to this inquiry and I may have often read myself the tale in a variety of ecclesiastical annals sleeping at present on the shelves now opposite my writing desk But, in connexion with the leading hypothesis of this paper, the investigation becomes useless and insipid May we not be satisfied with a recurrence to the philosophy which grounded upon the Scripture and thought out on the acknowledged principles of the human mind, informs us with so much clearness that the service of the Mass is only a necessary link in the fetters forged by antichrist, to retain its victims in bondage? By whom and at what period this specious delusion was imposed upon human credulity may be left to the compilers of ecclesiastical history As to the ceremony itself it is long elaborate diversified, and splendid Yes! It is a veil hung over the true mystery of the Cross It is made of costly materials and of a texture impenetrable by the vulgar eye It is ample in its drapery and folds richly embroidered with representations of the crucifixion cyphered and inscribed with the titles and attributes of The Crucified exhibited in the solemn gloom of temples, echoing at the time music such as might seem to emulate the strains of the cherubim displayed and explained by attendants, in vestments and attitudes correspondent to its magnificence —and the success of the illusion is triumphant! It is this veil which hides the Gospel from a miserable world,—from the miserable millions, before whom Jesus Christ is thus literally, but oh how unscripturally! set forth crucified among them The actors in this scene never directly inform the spectator, that all true penitents have *boldness to enter into the holiest by the blood of Jesus!*— Alas! the veil is suspended before the holy of holies, and conceals the blessing within Yet such is the exquisite artifice employed in this mysterious ceremonial, that the whole exhibition appears, all the while, to honour the very Saviour whom it degrades, and would force from his throne The Missal is not deficient in the language of penitence and in ascriptions of glory to the *Agnus Dei, qui tollit peccata mundi* In many places it rests the hope of man's salvation on his death and sacrifice It recognises his godhead, his love, his grace his truth and this in terms sometimes of exalted devotion, and then in language approaching to fondness and impassioned affection But all is neutralized by something which throughout contradicts the first principles of redemption by Jesus Christ Its practical effect tends therefore to persuade men that they are saved, not by the one oblation once offered, but by the succession of sacrifices repeated daily within the consecrated enclosure of a Catholic altar.

Purgatory * is a continuation of the self same system. It defrauds the Son of God of the sufficiency of his atonement, attributing a share of every individual's salvation to a process distinct from the death of Christ. It divides the glory of the event between a punishment borne for man by a Redeemer, and a punishment inflicted upon man, as though the last were necessary to fill up the deficiencies of an infinite merit. The *origin* of purgatory is readily detected—apart from the self righteousness connected with the process—in the vast superaddition it confers upon the sacerdotal prerogative. Did the doctrine imply that the dead could release themselves from posthumous penalties, or, that the purificative fires raged for a season and then spontaneously subsided, it would have been without any assignable value. It never would have caught the attention of a hierarchy which monopolizes all spiritualities capable of imparting influence and of exuding silver and gold. In the natural course, therefore, of the policy pursued by the papal cabinet the invention of masses for the dead lengthened out the chain of masses for the living and, after this fashion, bound together the lucrative concerns of time and eternity. It is thus that the ministrations of the Church of Rome descend, as it were into *hades* professing to loose the spirits in prison, not from any anxiety to diminish their sufferings, farther than may consist with an augmentation of the power and affluence of the church.

I would remark by the way that the doctrine of purgatory is extremely inconsistent with the idea of a happy death, for who can expire in peace with the assurance, that he directly passes into a region of penal fire? Yet I have read of devout Papists—for such there are—who have approached the confines of the unseen world, not only with tranquillity but with confidence. Had they forgotten the terrors of the middle state? or, in the midst of many speculative notions had they *practically* looked to the sacrifice of Christ, and to this alone, for salvation? Most serious Christians will answer both questions, I believe in the affirmative, and will exult in the conviction, gathered from an unexpected source, that the Gospel is the power of God unto salvation to every one that truly believeth, notwithstanding he may have been surrounded, all his days by the most impure corruptions of Christianity. From such circumstances the religion of Jesus Christ seems to derive another collateral evidence of its vitality and identical nature.

I have frequently observed, in the course of my own ministry, the natural appetite of the human mind for a something which in an after state, is to purify such persons as are, to vulgar apprehension, too wicked to be directly saved, and too good to be eternally lost. Such a sentiment seems to have floated even in the lofty imagination of Lord Byron, and its philosophy is justly considered by a correspondence in your journal (for April 1825 p. 220). Similar expressions of fear manifest themselves, in more humble guise, at the death beds of our village poor. On such occasions men, if they say any thing speak out their meaning and certainly,

---

* There is a purgatory in the theology of the Esquimaux. The first three stages in the progress of departed souls ' are bad uncomfortable places and the good soul, in passing through them sees multitudes of the dead who having lost their way or who not being entitled to the good land are always wandering about. (Capt. Lyon's Private Journal pp. 373, 374.) Whether by this state is meant a place of temporary or permanent punishment does not appear. But it will be observed that the innocent souls *pass through it*. How forcibly does this article in the polar confession held most probably as pertinaciously as the kindred dogma in the Tridentine creed remind one of some expressions in the sixth Æneid!

it is an affecting consideration to observe the ignorance, even in the ory of our population, concerning the nature of the Gospel, as a remedy all sufficient for the spiritual distempers of mankind. They seem, as by a kind of depraved instinct, to reject the notion of a freely offered complete and unbought salvation and would seem solicitous either to plead their innocence of any indictable offence, or, if sin must be confessed, to seek for its pardon between the cross of Christ and some degree of merit furnished by themselves. The wisdom of the papal world is fully aware of this confusion of mind, as it universally exists among the children of Adam and the doctrine of purgatory was easily invented, in aid of our self righteousness and of our antinomianism,—the two pillars on which we all naturally support ourselves, in prospect of the hour of death, and of the day of judgment. Our self righteousness is our protection against the charge of demerit and our antinomianism relieves the conscience from the obligations of practical religion, and therefore hides the terrors of a future day of reckoning. But as apprehensions may yet linger in the mind, as to our final safety, notwithstanding *we have done no harm*, and are also deficient in active virtue the fires of purgatory—and oh how awful is the responsibility of those who uphold *such* a supplemental salvation!— are ready to burn up the remaining dross and in the end, THESE are to concur in presenting us faultless before the presence of God with exceeding joy!

(*To be continued.*)

CHRYSOSTOM'S HOMILIES.—NO I DE STATUIS

(*Continued from p. 415.*)

1 (namely, of the eight reasons.) Now that afflictions are allotted to the righteous, and that God has permitted them to happen *for this purpose*, to preserve moderation and humility, and to prevent their being puffed up by their miracles and good works, let us hear (proved) from the Prophet David and from Paul, who both speak to this effect. The former says, (Psalm cxix. 71) 'It is good for me Lord, that thou hast humbled me—[in our translation, that I have been afflicted]—that I might learn thy statutes' the other, after having said, I was caught up into the third heavens, and translated to paradise, proceeds thus (2 Cor. xii. 7) 'And lest I should be exalted above measure through the abundance of the revelations, there was given to me a thorn in the flesh, the messenger of Satan to buffet me, lest I should be exalted above measure' What can be more clear than this? That I might not be exalted for *this* reason, says he, God permitted the messengers of Satan to buffet me. By messengers of Satan, he does not mean evil *spirits*, but *men* who were subservient to the devil,—unbelievers, rulers, Greeks, who continually troubled him, and continually harassed him. What he is here saying is this God could have hindered these persecutions and successive afflictions but since I had been caught up into the third heavens and taken into paradise, in order to prevent my being elated by these abundant revelations, and becoming high minded, he permitted these persecutions and let loose these messengers of Satan to buffet me by persecutions and afflictions, that I might not be exalted. For since these holy and admirable men Paul and Peter, and all such persons, in whatever state they be, are still men, and need to be strongly guarded against presumption and spiritual pride so none (need to be so fortified) more than persons of great sanctity for nothing is so apt to intoxicate the mind and breed a vain confidence, as a consciousness of many virtues and good works, and an energetic and lively spirit of devotion. Wherefore, to obviate such

ill consequences, God has permitted those temptations and afflictions which may operate as a restraint upon them and produce moderation in all things

2. That this same (dispensation) does also much contribute to make manifest the power of God hear (the proof) from the same Apostle, who maintained the former position That you may not say as the unbelievers do that the God who permits these things is defective in power and that because he is not able to rescue his friends from dangers therefore he allows them to be continually ill treated consider well how Paul has cleared up this point and shewn that these events so far from disparaging the power of God, do more effectually make it manifest to all men for, after saying " There was given me a thorn in the flesh, a messenger of Satan to buffet me"—meaning thereby a succession of temptations—he added, " For this thing I besought the Lord thrice that it might depart from me and he said unto me, My grace is sufficient for thee for my strength is made perfect in weakness He means to say, My strength is then made manifest when you are in weakness when by instruments such as you manifestly destitute of power, the word preached increases in efficacy, and is every where disseminated When therefore after receiving many wounds, he was confined in gaol, he (himself) bound the gaoler His feet were in the stocks his hands in chains yet the prison was shaken at midnight, whilst they were singing hymns Do you see how the power of God was made perfect in weakness? If Paul had been set at liberty and had shaken that dwelling house, the event would not have been so wonderful therefore he said Continue in bonds, and let the walls be shaken on every side and let the prisoners be loosed, that my power may thus the more clearly appear by their being all released by you their fellow prisoner you that are confined and fettered like themselves This it was that so deeply impressed the jailor that one under such close confinement should be able by prayer alone to shake the foundations, throw open the prison doors, and unbind all the prisoners And not in this instance only but in the case of Peter and Paul and the other Apostles, we may see the same thing happening continually God's grace ever flourishing in persecutions, becoming conspicuous in afflictions and so making his power more publicly known therefore he said, ' My grace is sufficient for thee for *my power* is made perfect *in weakness*

3. If men had not seen the Apostles suffering these great afflictions they would have often suspected that they were more than mortal Observe how Paul expresses his fears on this subject, 2 Cor xii 6 For though I would desire to glory I shall not be a fool but now I forbear lest any man should think of me above that which he seeth me to be, or that he heareth of me What is this that he says? " I might have spoken of much greater miracles, but I do not choose to do so lest the greatness of those miracles should give men too high an opinion of me For this reason, Peter and his companion (John) when they had cured the lame man, and all the bystanders were looking at them intently, checked (their eagerness) and assured them it was no power of their own that they had displayed Why look ye so earnestly on us as though by our own power or holiness we had made this man to walk? And again, at Lystra the people were not only struck with astonishment but brought victims crowned with garlands and attempted to offer sacrifice to Paul and Barnabas Observe the craftiness of the devil by those very men by whom God was endeavouring to purge the world of impiety by them the devil endeavoured to introduce it which he also did in former times, persuading (the people) to take men for gods and it is this

chiefly which became the origin and root of idolatry for many who had successfully carried on war, and erected trophies, and built cities, and had been benefactors in other respects to their contemporaries, were accounted gods by the multitude, and were honoured with temples and altars and the whole catalogue of the gods of the Greeks is composed of such men Wherefore that this might not be the case with the saints, he permitted them to be continually assaulted, to be scourged, to be encompassed with infirmities in order that extreme bodily weakness and a multitude of temptations, might convince the beholders that the workers of these great miracles were (really) men, and did nothing of themselves, but grace alone wrought the whole by them for if they reckoned *those* as gods who had performed but small and trivial services, much more would they have imagined these (to be gods) who had done such things as no one ever saw or heard of, if they had been exempted from the sufferings to which human nature is liable If even now that (on the contrary) they have been scourged thrown down precipices, cast into prisons harassed, and every day exposed to danger, some have notwithstanding fallen into this impious error, what (idolatrous) imaginations would they not then have formed respecting them, had they been free from calamities? This then is the third * reason for the afflictions (of the righteous)

4 The fourth is that the saints may not be thought to serve God from the hope of temporal prosperity For many men of licentious lives when they meet with much reprehension and frequent exhortations to virtue and self denial, and hear the encomiums bestowed upon the saints for their fortitude in affliction endeavour to cast some reflections upon them, drawn from this source And not only have *men* (adopted this method of recrimination), the *devil* himself hath conceived the same suspicion for whereas Job was possessed of great riches, and enjoyed much prosperity this evil spirit, having been reprehended by God in a way of reference (or contrast, to that patriarch), and having nothing to say in his own defence or against the integrity of that just man, immediately resorts to this apology, saying, Doth Job fear God for nought? Hast thou not made a hedge about him.....on every side? This man, says he, is godly for the sake of the reward because he (thereby) enjoys such great prosperity —What then does God? Being desirous to shew that the saints do not serve him for the sake of the (temporal) reward he stripped him of his wealth and reduced him to poverty, and permitted him to be afflicted with a grievous disease Then reproving the adversary, as having suspected (Job of) these (motives) without just cause, he says (Job ii 3), ' Still he holdeth fast his integrity, although thou spakest * (to me) to destroy his substance without cause For the service of God is itself a sufficient requital and recompence to the saints since, even in human friendships, a reciprocal regard is esteemed an adequate recompence (for affection) nor is any other sought for, or any greater imagined and if with men it be so, much more with God God being desirous of shewing (that Job served him with) this (disinterested affection) granted to the devil more (power against him) than he required for *he* said, " Put forth thine hand, and touch him (v 5) but God said ' I deliver him up to thee For as, in the wrestling matches of the heathen, those wrestlers who are in luxuriant health and have a bodily structure firm and compact, do not appear such whilst their anointed bodies are enveloped in thin (loose) garments

---

It was the second in the general enumeration but the order of the second and third is inverted in the detail

Chrysostom follows the Septuagint which differs a little from our translation

but when these are thrown off, and they step forth unclothed into the area, *then* more especially they strike the spectators with admiration by the symmetry of their forms there being no veil to conceal it so it was with Job when he was invested with affluence on every side, it did not appear (so clearly) to the world what manner of man he was but when he was stript of this (veil of prosperity) like the wrestler divesting himself of his garments, and entered the lists of this spiritual combat undisguised—when thus bare and destitute, he impressed the beholders with admiration, so that not only the men that were present, but the angelic spectators, when they witnessed the constancy of his soul applauded the victor with loud acclamation for, as I before observed, he was not so fully discovered to mankind while his great abundance encircled him, as when he had thrown it off like a garment, and was exhibited bare and defenceless upon the stage of the world, and all men admired the athletic vigour of his soul

Now (Job's eminent virtue) was discovered not only by his being stript of his property, but also by his great patience in sickness for, as I before observed, God did not *himself* smite him, lest the devil should reply, " Thou hast spared him thou hast not exposed him to a temptation sufficiently great ' but he permitted the devil to be the executioner, both in the destruction of the cattle and in his personal affliction He said, I have confidence in this champion involve him in whatever struggles you please I do not forbid it But as wrestlers of established reputation, who can rely with confidence on their own skill and strength frequently decline grappling with their antagonists in a direct manner and upon equal terms and suffer themselves to be laid hold of by them, in order to make the victory the more conspicuous, so God gave up this saint into the hands of the devil, that when, after so great inequality between them, he nevertheless prevailed and overthrew him (at last) the crown of victory might be the more brilliant It is gold that has been assayed try it as you please said he rack it as you will you shall find no dross or blemish in it And he does not only shew us the fortitude of others, but also furnishes another great consolation for what says Christ (Matt v 11) ' Blessed are ye, when men shall revile you and persecute you and shall say all manner of evil against you falsely for my sake rejoice and be exceeding glad for great is your reward in heaven for * so did their fathers to the prophets Again Paul, desiring to comfort the Macedonians says (1 Thess ii 14) " For ye brethren became followers of the churches of God which † are in Judea for ye also have suffered like things of your own countrymen, even as they have of the Jews   And he comforts the Hebrews in a similar manner, by making a catalogue of righteous persons who had lived some in furnaces others in pits (and mines) some in deserts, others in mountains and holes of the rocks some in hunger others in (various) distresses for a community of sufferings administers some consolation to the afflicted ‡

5 That this point naturally introduces some mention of the resurrection, hear from the mouth of Paul himself " If after the manner of men I have fought with beasts at Ephesus what advantageth it me, if the dead rise not ? (1 Cor xv 32) And again (ver 19) ' If in this life only we have hope in Christ we are of all men most miserable We suffer, says he, a vast

---

* Here he quotes from memory or his copy of St Matthew varied from all others

† In Christ Jesus is left out

‡ The latter part of this paragraph would appear to belong to the sixth head which is scarcely touched upon in its right place We might almost suspect that here and there a page of the manuscript had been transposed by careless or ignorant transcribers

number of afflictions in the present life wherefore, if there is no hope of another life, what can be more wretched than we? whence it is clear that our concerns are not confined within the limits of the present life our temptations make it evident [that they are not] for God can never forbear requiting with gifts much greater (than their sufferings) those who have endured so much, and spent the whole of the present life in temptations and in dangers innumerable and if he cannot forbear (rewarding them), then it is manifest that he must have provided another life better and brighter (than the present) in which he intends to crown the champions of piety, and to proclaim (their victory) before all the world Wherefore, when you see a righteous man afflicted, injured, terminating the present life in sickness, poverty, and a thousand other evils, say to yourself, Had there been no resurrection and future judgment, God would not have permitted a man who suffered so much for his sake to depart this life without having had any enjoyment in it it is clear, therefore, that he has provided for him another life more pleasant than this, and much more advantageous Had there been no such provision, he would not have permitted many of the wicked to spend their lives in continual enjoyment, and left many of the righteous in the midst of troubles but because there has been prepared a future state, wherein he designs to render to every one a recompence suitable to his wickedness or his goodness (as the case may be) for this reason he endures (for the present) the sight of afflicted virtue and prosperous iniquity

7 I will endeavour to produce out of the Scriptures another *

reason (for the afflictions of the righteous) and what is that? That when we are exhorted to lead the same holy lives (as these primitive saints), we may not put off the exhortation by saying that they were of a different nature from ourselves, or were not men—[i e they suffered these afflictions in order that they might appear mere mortals, and therefore imitable examples] wherefore one saith, when discoursing about the great Elijah, " Elias was a man subject to like passions as we are (James v 17) You see it is from a community of sufferings (or infirmities) that he denominates him a man like ourselves And again*, " For I also am a man of like passions with you —and this is a sufficient pledge to assure us that the nature is the same

6 That this (subject) teaches us to pronounce those blessed, (and those only) who ought to be so accounted, you may evidently infer from the following considerations for when you hear Paul saying (1 Cor iv 11), " Even unto this present hour we both hunger and thirst, and are naked, and are buffeted, and have no certain dwelling place and labour and again, (Heb xii 6), " Whom the Lord loveth he chasteneth, and scourgeth every son whom he receiveth, (if we duly weigh these words of the Apostle), it is manifest that we shall eulogize, not those who enjoy

---

* Here he passes over the sixth reason which was for the encouragement of those who should suffer in future times and proceeds to the seventh which is to prevent our saying that the great saints we are exhorted to imitate were more then men The two specific points to be shewn were (6) that if we are afflicted so were they and (7) that if our nature is weak and frail so was theirs the first part of which two fold intercommunity he passes over unless there is some mistake in the manuscript from which his works were printed See preceding note

* This second quotation is referred to Wisdom vii 1 but it may be Acts xiv 15 or even Acts x. 26 may be glanced at The two meanings of παθος—affections of the mind and external sufferings—seem rather confounded but the general meaning of the passage is plain namely that the usual infirmities and sufferings of humanity proved the Apostles to be mere men and their example applicable to ourselves in a way of exhortation

themselves in undisturbed tranquillity, but those who are in straits, those who are afflicted for God's sake, and we shall admire and emulate those who devote their lives to piety and virtue. And to the like effect does the Prophet speak (Psalm cxliv. 11). 'Their right hand is a right hand of iniquity. Their daughters (are) beautiful, richly adorned after the similitude of a temple; their storehouses are full, pouring forth (abundance of all things) from kind to kind; their sheep prolific multiplying as they range about; their oxen full of flesh; there is no gap in their hedge (for an enemy to break in at), nor any going out (or desertion of their own people); no cry (of distress) in their * streets. Men who are in such a case are (usually) pronounced blessed: but what say you, O Prophet? "Blessed (says he) is the people whose God is the Lord:"—not the man who abounds in wealth, but him who is adorned with piety, do *I* pronounce to be blessed, even though he should be suffering ten thousand evils.

† 9. If I might mention a ninth reason it should be this. That affliction makes men more thoroughly approved [having given proof of their genuineness by passing through the ordeal]: for Tribulation, says the Apostle, 'worketh patience, and patience experience, and experience hope, and hope maketh not ashamed.' You see that the experience derived from afflictions inspires us with the hope of the blessings (of the world) to come. Wherefore I did not say without reason (namely under fifth reason) that these afflictions indirectly suggest

* Πλ τ α ς in Septuagint παυλ σ. This is the only variation from the Septuagint which differs from our translation, but is countenanced by the Syriac and Arabic, as Pool says in Synopsis, &c. and the sense appears much improved.

† The ninth, tenth, and eleventh reasons seem to have occurred to the writer in the course of his composition, as they were not mentioned in the enumeration of his intended divisions.

to us the hope of a resurrection, and they make the afflicted persons themselves become better; for as Gold [here φησιν occurs referring to Ecclus. ii. 5. and it must be acknowledged that Rom. v. 4. is introduced by the same word φησιν] is tried in the furnace, so is an approved person in the furnace of humiliation.

10. I may also add a tenth reason: and what is that? That which I have before mentioned often, that if we have any blots these we here [I suppose he means in this furnace of affliction] get rid of; and the Patriarch (Abraham) signified as much to the rich man, when he said, "*There* Lazarus received evil things and *here* he is comforted."

11. And in addition to this tenth we may find another reason (for the afflictions of the righteous); and what is that? That we may have a more abundant reward and a brighter crown. For in proportion to the intenseness of our afflictions will be the increase of our reward,— or rather in a much greater proportion; for, says (the Apostle) ' the sufferings of this present time are not worthy to be compared with the glory which shall be revealed in us.' Rom. viii. 18.

Having then so many reasons to assign for the afflictions of the righteous, let us not be cast down in temptations, nor be perplexed, troubled, and oppressed with grief; but let us ourselves admonish our own souls, and teach others also the same (lesson). Should you see a man leading a virtuous life, one much occupied in devotion, one that pleases God, suffering various afflictions, let it not be a stumbling block to you, my beloved (brother). Should you see one who is intent on spiritual affairs, when he is just on the point of accomplishing some useful work, at that very moment supplanted and defeated, do not be troubled (at it); for I have known many frequently raising questions (and complaints) on this subject. Such a one, say they, went abroad to visit the tomb* of a martyr carrying with him money for the poor, was shipwrecked and lost all another, engaged in the same work fell among thieves, and with difficulty preserved his life, was stript of his property and took to flight. And what reflection should we make (on such events)? That we ought not to be depressed by them for though the man was shipwrecked, he possesses nevertheless the reward of his charity complete and without diminution for he fully performed his own part he collected the money and laid it by he took it (with him) and departed he executed his design of setting out for a foreign land the shipwreck which ensued did not result from his will and intention But why did God allow it to happen? That he might make him a man accepted and approved, (one that had stood the test and scrutiny of affliction) But the poor you may say, were deprived of the money You do not provide for the poor, as God their Maker does—[perhaps he means to say God does not need your aid in providing for them] What though they were deprived of this supply he is able to furnish them with more ample means of abundance from another quarter. Let us not then demand of him reasons for his proceedings but in all of them let us praise and glorify him for it is not at random, and to no end, that he permits these things frequently to happen besides that he does not neglect those who should have been relieved by the money (that was lost), but provides other means of sustenance in its stead, he also makes the man himself, who suffered shipwreck become more confirmed and established in virtue, and procures for him a larger reward for when a man is involved in such calamities *then* to offer thanksgiving unto God is a greater thing than bestowing alms for it is not what we give in charity, but what we lose with religious fortitude, that yields us an abundant increase That this is greater than the other, I will prove from the case of Job he while he retained possession of his wealth opened his house to the poor and distributed his property among them but he was not so illustrious when he opened his house to the poor, as when he heard of the destruction of that house without emotions of grief and impatience he was not so illustrious when he clothed the naked with the fleeces of his sheep, nor so thoroughly approved, as when he heard that fire from Heaven had consumed his flocks—heard it, and gave thanks *Before*, he was humane *now* he is devout he *then* gave alms to the poor *now* he offers thanksgivings (the most grateful and sublime oblation) unto the Lord of all He did not make such reflections as these within his own breast Wherefore is all this befallen me? The sheep are destroyed which supported many thousands of the poor for their sakes they ought to have been spared notwithstanding I was myself unworthy to enjoy such great abundance But he neither said nor thought any thing of the kind he knew that God arranged every thing so as ultimately to produce a beneficial result Now that he inflicted a greater wound on the adversary when he gave thanks in the midst of his severe losses, than he did when he gave alms in his prosperity, you may be convinced by this consideration that in his prosperity the devil was able to forge and publish some insinuation against him and though it was a groundless one, still he had some pretence for saying ' Doth Job serve Thee for nought ?' but when he was stript of every thing, and preserved notwithstanding the same love towards God as ever then at last the mouth of this bold (calumniator) was stopped, and he had nothing more to say For this just man was a more eminent cha

---

* I have so rendered Ε ς μαρτυρ ο απ δη μησ but should prefer if correct went abroad to be a witness of the Gospel

racter after the expiration of his antecedent prosperity; for to bear the privation of all things with fortitude and thankfulness, is a much greater attainment than to be charitable in the midst of abundance, as has been (before) declared with reference to this (same) just man. Then his benevolence to his fellow servants was great, but *now* he discovered such (exalted virtues) as gained him the love of their common Master and Lord. It is not without reason that I enlarge upon this subject, since many persons of habitual generosity, such as maintained the widow and the destitute, have been robbed of all their property; others have lost all by fire; others have been shipwrecked by false accusations, and by injuries of a like nature; other charitable men have been reduced to the lowest poverty, to infirmity, and to disease, and have found none to relieve them.

Wherefore, that we may not say, as many often do, No one knows anything [the affairs of the righteous and the wicked being in such inexplicable confusion], the observation already made will be found sufficient for us, to obviate the disturbance of mind (which such sentiments are apt to create). It may be said, the man who performed great acts of charity lost his all; but what if he did? if he gives thanks for this loss, God will extend his beneficence to him in a much higher proportion; he shall receive not twice as much as before, as Job did, but in the life to come a hundred fold. If he suffer here, his bearing it with fortitude will make his treasure *there* the greater; for it was in order to call him to a more arduous conflict that God made him descend from affluence to penury. Have repeated conflagrations dissipated your whole property? remember what befel Job; give thanks to the Lord, who could have prevented those disasters and did not; then you shall receive as great a reward as if you had bestowed all upon the poor. But you live in poverty, hunger, and innumerable dangers—remember Lazarus, who had to struggle with disease, poverty, desertion, and a multitude of similar evils; and that after (a life of) such great virtue; remember the Apostles, who lived in hunger, and thirst, and nakedness; the prophets, the patriarchs (yea all) the righteous; and you will find them not among the rich, not among those who live delicately, but among the poor, the afflicted, and the distressed. While you reflect upon these things, give thanks to the Lord for having assigned you the same lot—not in hatred, but out of abundant love—for he permitted these to undergo such great sufferings not because he hated them, but because he greatly loved them; he sent them afflictions, to make them the more illustrious. Nothing is so good as thanksgiving, just as nothing is worse than blasphemy. Let us not be surprized if many grievous sufferings overtake us as soon as we devote ourselves to spiritual things; for as robbers dig and watch assiduously, not where hay and stubble, and straw, but where gold and silver (are deposited), so is the devil peculiarly intent on those who are attached to the pursuits and treasures of a spiritual life. Where virtue is, there are many snares; where charity is, there is envy; but one mighty weapon we have, able to defeat all his machinations; and that is, to give thanks to God in every thing. Did not Abel fall by the hand of his brother, when he was offering the firstlings of his flocks to God? yet God permitted it to be so; not because he hated the man that honoured him, but because he greatly loved him; because, in addition to the recompence and crown due to that most excellent sacrifice, he intended to provide for him another still more ample,—the crown of martyrdom. Moses attempted to succour an injured man, and it brought him into imminent danger of his life, and made him an exile from his native country and God permitted it (so to be), that you might learn the patience of the saints (from his example) for if we devoted ourselves to the labours of a spiritual life with a clear foresight that no evil would befal us, we should not appear to do any thing great, being in possession of a pledge to assure us of our safety whereas, now, they who adopt that course may very justly attract admiration, on this account, because they foresee dangers, and losses, and deaths, and evils without number, yet are not diverted from their righteous undertakings, nor slackened in their pace by these alarming anticipations For as the three children said, Daniel iii 18, "There is a God in heaven able to deliver us and if not, be it known to thee, O King, that we do not serve thy gods nor worship the golden image which thou hast set up Whenever, therefore thou art preparing to do any thing for God, foresee many dangers, many losses, many deaths and be not startled at such events, as if they were strange and unusual, neither be troubled for, says (the Son of Sirach, ii 1), "My son, if thou come to serve the Lord, prepare thy soul for temptation No one who chooses to be a pugilist (at the public games) expects to be crowned without receiving wounds thou, therefore, beloved, who hast undertaken to enter the lists with the great adversary in every species of combat, think not to lead a life of security, delicacy, and indulgence for no recompences, no promises here but every thing glorious in the world to come, has God pledged himself to bestow upon thee When, therefore thou hast thyself done good and received evil (in return), or hast seen another so treated, be glad and rejoice, for it will be the occasion of a greater reward Desist not, neither abate thy zeal, nor become more inactive but rather apply (to thy work) with greater zeal than ever, since even the Apostles, when they preached, were scourged, stoned, and frequently imprisoned, and yet continued to publish the truth with still greater zeal, not only after they were delivered from danger, but in the very midst of danger so may we behold Paul in prison, even in chains, instructing and initiating in the sacred mysteries still prosecuting his work, though before a tribunal, in a shipwreck, in a storm, or amidst various perils

Emulate, O beloved, these holy men devote thyself to good works while life yet remains draw not back, though Satan raise a thousand obstructions against thee Perhaps thou wast shipwrecked when carrying abroad money (that was to have been expended in charity) but Paul, when he had set out* to carry to Rome what was far more valuable than money, the word (of God), did both suffer shipwreck and sustain a variety of other afflictions he expresses as much in these words, 1 Thess ii 18, 'We would have come to you once and again but Satan hindered us —and God permitted (such impediments) for weighty reasons, since he thereby discovers his power, and shews, that, notwithstanding Satan should raise ten thousand obstacles, the preaching (of the Gospel) would not be diminished and obstructed on that account Wherefore Paul gives thanks to God in all events of this nature, inasmuch as he knew that he was thereby rendered a more thoroughly tried and acceptable person, and that the stedfastness of his zeal became more manifest when none of those impediments could divert him from his purpose Whenever therefore, we meet with disappointments (in any pious undertakings), let us increase our application to sacred subjects, and not say, why did God permit these obstacles (to prevail)? for this reason he permitted them, that he might make thy zeal, and

---

* Acts xix 21 shews that St Paul went to Jerusalem with the intention of going thence to Rome and in his way thither he suffered imprisonment as well as shipwreck

the greatness of thy love towards himself, conspicuous in the sight of many. For it is one of the principal signs of sincere affection, never to desist from any thing which is acceptable to the beloved person: for an empty, listless man shrinks immediately at the first assault; but one who is stanch and vigilant, though defeated a thousand times, will apply to Divine things so much the more; fulfilling the part which depends on himself, and in all (other) things (whether adverse or propitious) giving thanks. Now let us* do the same: for thanksgiving is a great treasure, great wealth, a benefit inexhaustible, an instrument of great efficacy; even as blasphemy (or arraigning the equity of God's proceedings) aggravates any misfortune, and makes us lose still more than we already have. You have *lost money*: if you give thanks, you have *gained* with respect to the *soul*; you have acquired greater wealth, being advanced to a higher degree of favour with God: but if you blaspheme, you have lost, besides, your own salvation: those other things you have not recovered, and *that* you have utterly sacrificed.

And, now that I have mentioned blasphemy, I have one favour to beg of you, in return for this public address and discourse,—that you would reprove for me the blasphemers in this city. If you hear any one in the street, or in the market place, blaspheming God, go up to him and rebuke him: if it be necessary to add blows, do not forbear: smite him on the face, crush his mouth, consecrate thine hand by the blow. If some men charge you with it as a crime, if they drag you before a court of justice, follow them (without making resistance); if at the tribunal, the judge inflict a penalty,

---

* Chrysostom was an eminent example himself of thanksgiving in adversity: for when he was in exile, guarded by fierce soldiers, and hurried by them from place to place in extreme bodily weakness and hourly expectation of death, he concluded his last prayer with these words: Glory be to God for all events.

boldly say He blasphemed the King of angels: if the blasphemers of an earthly king ought to be punished, much more ought those who insult Him: it is a crime committed against the community, an injury to the public at large: it is lawful for every one that will to denounce it.* Let the Jews and Greeks be made to understand that the Christians are the preservers of the city, its guardians, patrons, and instructors. Let the incorrigible and perverse be taught to fear the servants of God, that, whenever they choose to utter any such thing, they may look round them on every side, and be afraid of their shadow, apprehensive lest some Christian should hear, and spring upon them, and punish them severely. Have you not heard what John (the Baptist) did? He saw a king violating the laws of marriage, and he boldly said, in a public assembly, "It is not lawful for thee to have the wife of thy brother Philip." But I have not urged you on against a king, nor against a magistrate, nor respecting the subversion of connubial laws, or any injury done to your fellow servant; but for this drunken fury against the Lord (himself) I wish you to admonish one who is only your fellow servant (of the same rank with yourself); and to reduce him to sobriety. If I had said to you, Coerce and correct kings and governors, would you not have pronounced me mad? yet John did this: wherefore even this is not above us. Now, however (I have only said) if he be your fellow servant, one of the same rank with yourself, correct him; though you should die for it, shrink not from the task of admonishing your brother: to you this is (equivalent to) martyrdom; since John also was a martyr, though he was not called upon either to sacrifice or to worship an idol, yet in defence of those sacred laws which had been contemptuously broken, did he resign his life. strive you too for the

---

* But to strike is going further and usurping the magistrate's office.

" truth unto death, and the Lord shall fight for you: and do not make me this lukewarm reply, 'What concern is it of mine? I have no connexion with him, nothing in common:'—only with the devil have we nothing in common: with all mankind many things they are partakers of the same nature as ourselves: they inhabit the same earth, and are sustained by the same nourishment: they have the same Lord, have received the same laws, and are invited to participate the same blessings as ourselves: say not then that we have nothing in common with them: it is satanic language, inhumanity diabolical. Let us not then say such things: but shew a becoming concern for our brethren: and I do positively undertake to say and pledge myself to you all for the truth of it, that if you that are here present would all contribute to the salvation of the inhabitants of this city, it would be speedily and generally reformed: though the smallest part of the city is here present: the smallest in number, yet with respect to piety it is the principal part: let us then contribute to the salvation of our brethren, [or let us each take his share in this good work]. One man inflamed with zeal is sufficient to reform the whole people: but when there is not one, nor two or three, but so great a multitude, able to attend to the reformation of these neglected men, it can be from no other cause but our cowardice, not weakness: that the greater number fall and perish. For how absurd is it, that we can come up and part combatants whenever we see them fighting in the forum: and what is more, if we only see an ass fallen down we can make haste to assist in lifting it up: and yet when our brethren are perishing pay no regard! The blasphemer is one of these beasts of burden, sunk under the insupportable load of his own anger:* go and lift him up, both by words and actions, both by gentleness and by vehemence: let various remedies be applied: since we use this dexterity in our own affairs, let us assist in like manner in the rescue of our neighbours: and to themselves, to as many of them as are happily reclaimed by the admonition, we shall soon become objects of esteem and affection; and, what is far greater than all, we shall enjoy the blessings that are laid up (in heaven): which may we all attain, by the grace and beneficence of our Lord Jesus Christ: by whom and with whom unto the Father be glory, with the Holy Spirit, for ever and ever. Amen.

FAMILY SERMONS.—No. CC.

Acts ix. 6.—*And he trembling and astonished, said Lord, what wilt thou have me to do?*

SUCH was the earnest inquiry of Saul of Tarsus, afterwards the great Apostle of the Gentiles, when, on his way to Damascus: breathing out threatenings and slaughter against the infant church of Christ: he was arrested by an Omnipotent aim, and accosted in words which penetrated with conviction to his heart: by that Almighty Saviour whom, in the persons of his faithful followers he had so bitterly persecuted. How altered that fierce aspect! how quelled that haughty self conceit! how changed those cruel threatenings! He trembles and is astonished: and, prostrate before his offended Creator, his hitherto unknown and slighted Saviour: he submissively inquires,

What wilt thou have me to do?

As the first sin of mankind, that which expelled our fallen race from Paradise: was an act of deliberate opposition to the will of God: so the first trace of a desire to return to our spiritual allegiance is the wish to know and to do his will. This was the turning point in the conversion of the Apostle. He was not yet enlightened with a clear

* [Or literally thus: The blasphemer is an ass and not bearing the burden of anger is fallen down.]

knowledge of Christianity, but he was prepared for its reception by a sincere desire to obey the will of God. The seed of the word, afterwards sown, did not fall upon stony ground, but in "an honest and good heart the fallow ground had been ploughed up penitence had softened the stubborn soil so that, watered by the dews of God's blessing, and fertilized by the genial rays of the Sun of Righteousness, the heavenly plant took deep root, and brought forth fruit, thirty, sixty, and a hundred fold According to our Lord's own declaration, wishing to "do the will of God, he had the promise that he should "know of the doctrine, and means were accordingly provided for his instruction "And the Lord said unto him, Arise, and go into the city, and there it shall be told thee what thou must do

Many of the circumstances connected with St Paul's conversion were miraculous, and are recorded, not as illustrations of the usual process by which men are brought to the knowledge and obedience of the faith, but chiefly perhaps as connected with the remarkable history of this great Apostle and of the early church and as affording a strong testimony to the truth and power of the Christian religion but the anxiety of the Apostle to know what God would have him to do, is a common, a never failing characteristic of true religion in every age and as such deserves our serious consideration We, like Saul of Tarsus, must each one of us solemnly inquire, ' Lord, what wilt thou have me to do? and this with an earnest desire, first, to know the will of God, and, secondly, to do it We shall endeavour to illustrate the operation of this two fold desire, with a view to shew when it may be considered as sincere, and, as such indicative of true repentance toward God, and faith in our Lord Jesus Christ

I *First*, then, there must be an earnest desire to *know* God's will — Faith, love, obedience, and every good fruit, are grounded on scriptural knowledge we must know in whom we believe, what he requires of us, what he has promised to the obedient, what he has threatened against the disobedient Now we may judge whether we really feel this desire to know God's will, by examining whether we are willing to surrender our own will to it—whether we are using the appointed means for coming to a knowledge of it—and whether we are making use of this knowledge with a practical reference to our own particular circumstances

1 The first token of our sincerity in wishing to know the will of God, is a willingness to surrender our own will to it, so far as it is known This was strikingly displayed in the case of the Apostle His own will had been strongly bent towards his favourite object of extirpating Christianity he was pursuing his journey with alacrity, charged with a commission from the high priest for that purpose but now he renounces his own plans and projects, and, like his great Master, the wish of his soul is "Not my will, but thine, be done "I am willing, as though he had said, "to abandon my own schemes, and my most fondly cherished opinions I ask not what would be most agreeable to myself, or what would be most applauded by my fellow creatures but what thou, O Lord—*thou*, who art my Creator, and hast a claim to my fullest obedience thou O Saviour, whom ignorantly I have persecuted—wouldst have me to do Speak Lord, for thy servant heareth Command me what thou wilt for thy commands must be holy, just, and good Thou art infinitely wise, and canst not mistake thou art supremely good and what thou willest must be best for the happiness of thy creatures It is thine to command be it mine to listen and to obey

2 A second token of our sincerity in wishing to know the will of God, is our diligent use of the

means which he has provided for our coming to an understanding of it. The means in the Apostle's instance were, to repair to a particular place, where an instructor was divinely appointed to receive him and to tell him what he should do. To have asked the question in the text, and not to have availed himself of the source of information pointed out in reply to his petition, would have shewn great hypocrisy and contempt for the command of God. Yet such is the conduct of many who esteem themselves to be Christians: they pray daily "Thy will be done," but they seek not to know what God demands: especially, they consult not the Scriptures, which are the record of his will; or, if they peruse them, it is only perhaps for the sake of form or amusement, without any serious desire of learning what he requires. Too many persons follow the dictates of their own fancy, or the current opinions of the world around them, instead of "inquiring at the mouth of the Lord." Now, this is quite inconsistent with a sincere use of the petition in the text. The man of Ethiopia, wishing to know the will of God, diligently perused the Scriptures, and entreated Philip to explain them to him: Cornelius was not contented indolently to say, "What is it, Lord?" but in compliance with the answer to his inquiry, he sent immediately to Joppa for the Apostle Peter, and summoned his kinsmen and friends reverently to hear "what was commanded of God." We have not indeed, in the present age, the same special and miraculous manifestations of God's will, because they are no longer necessary, since we have his revealed word, and various assistant means of religious edification and instruction. If we diligently use these, with humble prayer for the guidance of his Holy Spirit, we shall not go far, and, above all not fatally, astray. The page of Revelation plainly declares what is God's will—not, indeed, all those mysteries of his secret counsels which our curiosity might wish to fathom, but all that concerns ourselves, so far as is necessary to be known by us for our present or eternal welfare; especially our duties and obligations towards God; the way to obtain the pardon of our sins through faith in the atonement of the Saviour; the virtues and graces which become our holy profession; and the rewards and punishments reserved for the righteous and the wicked in the unseen and eternal world. In that sacred page we are instructed in various branches of that will; different parts of it being at different times more particularly specified, but all combining in one consistent whole. Thus it is said, "This is the will of God, that ye believe on Jesus Christ, whom he hath sent:" and again, "This is the will of God even your sanctification:" and again, "In every thing give thanks, for this is the will of God in Christ Jesus:" and again, "What doth the Lord thy God require of thee, but to do justly, and to love mercy, and to walk humbly with thy God;"—all of which are comprised by our Saviour in the two golden precepts of loving God with all our heart, and our neighbour as ourselves. In an especial manner is unfolded to us that part of God's will which relates to us as sinners: thus faith in the Saviour is spoken of as the will of God in the first of the texts just quoted; holiness, in the second; and in numerous other passages, repentance, contrition for sin, prayer, humility, and all other particulars comprehended in the Christian life.

3. But it is not a mere general inquiry into points of Christian doctrine or duty that is sufficient to shew that we are in earnest in wishing to know the will of God, unless also we apply the investigation to our own particular case. The inquiry of St. Paul was strictly personal: "What wilt thou have *me* to do?" And similar is the language of every sincere penitent: he hears the word of God speaking

to his own heart, pointing out his own sins, urging upon him his own duties. Every discourse he listens to seems to say, "I have a message from God unto thee, and it finds an echo in his heart, Thou art the man." He is not satisfied with general principles but brings them practically to bear upon his own character and conduct. Is repentance enjoined? Have *I* repented? Is faith essential? Do *I* believe? Is holiness indispensable, Am *I* renewed in the spirit of my mind? am I living as a servant of God, a disciple of Christ, a candidate for heaven? And besides the application of such general principles he will seek to know the will of God as referable to his own individual circumstances: he will consider what are the sins, the duties, the difficulties of his particular age or calling: what God seems especially to require of him at that very time —the daily trial, the daily duty, the neglected command, the besetting sin, to act, or to suffer, to learn, or to teach, in short whatever may direct him to a perfect knowledge of the will of his Father which is in heaven. The man whose speculations are merely general and barren, who does not, by prayer, by self examination, and by the application of Scripture to the discipline of his own heart and life enter into the details of his own circumstances before God, cannot be said sincerely to offer the petition in the text.

II. But *secondly*, our inquiring into the will of God must be accompanied with a wish and endeavour to *do* it. This is in truth the best, the only test of our sincerity. True Christianity is ever practical in its effects: if, therefore, our faith be a mere creed or system of opinions, it profits us nothing. The inquiry of the Ruler in the Gospel, Good master what must I do to inherit eternal life? appeared as sincere as the question of Saul of Tarsus in the text: but how different the result!—the former, when he learned that the will of God towards him was, that he should sell all that he had, and take up his cross and follow Christ, would not obey it: whereas the latter repaired to the appointed instructor, received in faith the doctrines and commands of his Saviour, and followed his blessed steps, amidst a series of persecutions and afflictions, such, perhaps, as no other apostle or martyr of Jesus Christ was ever appointed to endure. Our knowledge of God's will will only aggravate our punishment, if we do it not. True we never can do it perfectly or meritoriously: at best we are unprofitable servants not entitled to the rewards of unerring obedience, but looking solely for the pardon of our acknowledged disobedience for the sake of the infinitely meritorious obedience of our Divine Surety: yet, still, the very test of our sincerity, the proof of our conversion, are the desire and effort to act up to the knowledge we possess. When St Paul asked the question, What wilt thou have me to do? it was his earnest resolution to do whatever might be commanded. He did not stipulate for an easy task: he did not wish to consult his own natural inclinations or partialities, but was willing, by the grace of God, to yield a *universal* and *voluntary* obedience to the Divine command.

1. His desire to obey was *universal* in its influence —This is a conspicuous mark of true devotion of heart to God. It is not enough that we select a few favourite points of doctrine or duty as our standard: that like the rich man before mentioned we profess to be willing to keep all other commands, if we may only be covetous, and decline self-denial and bearing our allotted cross: that, like Saul, we slay the Amalekites and spare Agag their king. No, the true standard of our submission to God, according to our daily prayer, is, that his will may be done upon earth as it is done in heaven, and there it is done *universally* and *most willingly* We must act with singleness of

heart, and "have respect to *all* God's commandments." We must carry this desire into the whole course of our spiritual life and our secular conduct. There must be no reserved corner of the soul where God is not to reign; where some favoured sin is to remain secure in its entrenchments, and some neglected duty to seek in vain for admittance. Even if the will of God towards us should be that we should bear many heavy afflictions, or make many painful sacrifices — and who had more to endure or to give up than St. Paul?—we must not hesitate to submit to it.

2. And this submission must further, be *voluntary*.—It is not a code of reluctant duties, that God requires. He would hear from us the language of cheerful self dedication. "I delight to do thy will, O my God; yea thy law is within my heart." And such will be our feeling, if our desire to do his will be duly grounded on *faith*, and *love*, and *gratitude*, as well as on a mere general sense of obligation and responsibility. On *faith*—for we shall thus trust him in the darkest hour of affliction, and in the most difficult path of duty. On *love*—for thus will our compliance with his commands be prompt and cordial: like the Psalmist, we shall rejoice in his testimonies; our affections will go before, and open the way for our actions: to know what is God's will, will be to make it our own; while to do any thing contrary to that will, would be to wound our own bosoms, as well as to offend the Great Object of our reverence and supreme regards. On *gratitude*—for the love of Christ will constrain us: we shall love him, because he first loved us; and, loving him, we shall seek to know and to perform his commands: we shall co operate as it were with him: we shall not willingly resist or grieve his Holy Spirit; but shall pray for and value his sacred influences: and to do God's will will be to us, as it was to our Great Example, our meat and our drink, the object of our desires, our prayers, and our unceasing solicitude.

In conclusion, let me ask, Are we seeking to know and to do the will of God?—Some, perhaps, are not seeking this at all: and others are not seeking it as conscience dictates and God commands: to each of these classes does the subject apply with fearful interest—and oh that it may be impressed upon their hearts by the Holy Spirit to their eternal welfare! But others, perhaps, doubt whether they know the will of God aright; or, where they know it, they feel their inability to do it as they ought, and would desire. To each of these classes also, which include the true penitent, the sincere believer, our subject speaks in suitable words of hope and encouragement. If only they are honest in their inquiries, and act up to their convictions, they have the promise of God that 'the meek will he guide in judgment, the meek will he teach his way.' "If thou incline thine ear unto wisdom, and apply thy heart to understanding; if thou seekest her as silver, and searchest for her as for hid treasures: then shalt thou understand the fear of the Lord: for the Lord giveth wisdom; and out of his mouth cometh knowledge and understanding." Nor must this effort to know and to practise the will of God be confined to the first stages of our religious progress, but must continue and increase through life. It constitutes our highest advancement: it is our preparation for that heavenly world where the will of God is done perfectly and without reserve: it befits us as the creatures of God and especially as redeemed by the blood of Christ and professing to be dedicated to his service: and it is also our privilege as well as our duty, for to submit to the will of God, lightens all the cares of life, while it opens to us the prospect to a blessed immortality.

To the Editor of the Christian Observer.

A CORRESPONDENT, N. J. B., in your last Number, in the respectful observations which he has offered upon the Bishop of Limerick's remarks upon Psalm i. 1, considers that the word translated 'ungodly' implies *positive* wickedness, answering, he says "to Πονηρος, ασεβης, impious." It so happens, however, that two of the synonimes which he himself brings forward are, as to grammar, clearly *negative*—α σεβης, im pious—but not so their application, which is positive indeed; negative terms often convey the most positive ideas: as, an impious man, means not merely a person negatively wicked, but one far gone in actual ir religion, in justice, and im piety.

Whether your correspondent is right or wrong in his criticism I shall not undertake to decide; but I beg leave to notice the foregoing distinction, as, for want of it, an unfounded objection may be urged against his argument. I quite agree with him in his opinion of the highly valuable and interesting nature of the learned Prelate's volume.

R. L. G.

To the Editor of the Christian Observer.

It would be a great favour conferred upon many of your readers, if some of your experienced correspondents would furnish a reply to the following query: "What are the prominent sins, temptations, and spiritual dangers peculiarly incident to religious students; and how may they best be avoided?"

G. F.

MISCELLANEOUS.

To the Editor of the Christian Observer.

IN referring to your volume for 1822, my attention has been recalled to the papers on the "Apocryphal New Testament;" the re publication of which called forth several most convincing and decisive refutations of any claim to Divine inspiration in favour of the long exploded compositions in that volume. Some recent circumstances having summoned the attention of the public to the consideration of the Apocryphal Books of the Old Testament, I should be glad, for the benefit of those who have not access to the many learned dissertations which have appeared at different times on the canon of Scripture, to see in your pages a brief popular notice of the character of those books, and of the arguments which prove their palpable want of authenticity as Divine records. The following remarks, extracted chiefly from Dr. Ranken's excellent 'Institutes of Theology,' (published at Glasgow in 1822), will perhaps be sufficient for this purpose. Further particulars may be obtained by consulting Blair's Lectures, Gray's Key, Arnauld's Commentary, Dick on Inspiration, and numerous other works *passim*; but, above all, Jones on the Canon, or, for a brief epitome of the argument, Mr. Hartwell Horne's valuable and justly popular "Introduction."

G.

OF THE APOCRYPHAL BOOKS OF THE OLD TESTAMENT.

The apocryphal books are so called from the Greek word, which signifies 'hid,' or 'concealed,' because their origin, their real authors, times, and places of residence, of writing, and publication are unknown. They are undoubtedly of great antiquity; are admitted by some Protestant churches into the same volume, though carefully distinguished from the canonical and sacred Scriptures, and not regarded as inspired: but by many of the Roman Catholics they are believed, with some exceptions, in consequence of the decree of the Council of Trent, to be of equal authority with the inspired books

They are entitled to respect on account not only of their antiquity, but of the historical information which they convey, of the wisdom of many of their doctrines and practical observations on human conduct and of that general simplicity yet sublimity and eloquence, in which they often much resemble the books of Divine inspiration

But they do not claim to be *, and have no title to be considered, inspired. The Jews never admitted them into their canon. They appear, indeed, to have been composed after the age of Ezra, and even of Simon the Just, when, we have reason to believe, the canon was completed. They were never quoted by our Saviour and his Apostles. The coincidences which have to some appeared like quotations or, at least, allusions, may be fully accounted for from the resemblance of style to that of the sacred books generally, both of the Old and New Testament, and from accidental associations of the same ideas, sentiments, and even expressions, which we may find even in heathen writers

It is no wonder that they abound in phrases of Hebrew idiom, having been composed most probably by Jews, and being designed imitations of the style of the Hebrew Scriptures. But none of them seem ever to have been written in Hebrew nor did they ever constitute a part of the collection of the Septuagint version, formed in the reign of Ptolemy Philadelphus. Subsequent to that period, they seem to have been received by the Hellenistic Jews, and by them communicated to the Christian church, not as canonical, but as venerable books. Accordingly, we do not find them in any of the early catalogues but, on the contrary, they are declared, by the Greek and Latin fathers of the first four centuries, to be excluded from the sacred canon. They call them Ecclesiastical but not Divine. After the fifth century, they began to be held sacred in a secondary sense—" we read them for example of life, says Jerome, " and instruction of manners, but not to establish any doctrine."—till at last the Council of Trent pronounced them Divine, excepting, however, the Prayer of Manasses and the third and fourth books of Esdras. The internal evidence is strongly against them. They contain many things fabulous, contradictory, and at variance with the canonical Scriptures many that are absurd and incredible and some that are inconsistent with the narrative of accredited historians

First and Second Books of Esdras

The first book of Esdras is believed to have been written by a Hellenistic Jew, but when is unknown. It is thought to have been before Josephus wrote his history, as he relates the same facts, probably taken from it. It never was in the Hebrew canon, but has been annexed to some copies of the Septuagint. On this account it was read in the Greek church, and received by the Council of Carthage into the canon. It was quoted by St Austin and others as ecclesiastical, but not canonical and in this sense it seems to have been marked even by the Council of Trent, with a *non legitur*, as not authorized to be read publicly in the churches

The venerable name of Ezra, which it assumed, acquired for it much credit. But while it repeats many of the facts recorded in the canonical books of the Chronicles, and of Ezra and Nehemiah, it contradicts many others the story of the three competitors for the favour of Darius is trifling and fabulous and most of the circumstances added to the facts related in the canonical books, appear improbable, and intended as mere embellishments

---

* Indeed, the writers of some of them virtually acknowledge the contrary See prologue to the book of Ecclesiasticus 1 Mac iv 46, and ix 27 and 2 Mac xv 38

The second book of Esdras is written in a style altogether different from that of the first book, and most likely, therefore, by a different person. It may have been written originally in Greek, but it is not contained in the Septuagint, and there is now no Greek copy of it. Its author and date are totally unknown; but there is reason to believe that it was written after the propagation of Christianity, and perhaps by a Christian.

It is remarkable for a spirit of piety and seriousness throughout, and contains much useful instruction, and many animated exhortations. It assumes the prophetic character and strikingly describes the ruin of empires, and the coming and design of Messias; the latter is done so clearly, and circumstantially, as to excite a strong suspicion that it was written some time after the promulgation of the Gospel. It was never received as canonical by any father, church, or council. It is venerable for its antiquity and good spirit, and may be useful, when read with caution; but as a counterfeit of prophecy and of Divine authority, it is disgusting.

Book of Tobit

The book of Tobit may have been founded on the memoirs of real persons, such as are celebrated in the story, and arranged or filled up, afterwards by another author. It was probably Hebrew or Chaldaic originally; but the oldest copy of it now extant is the Greek version of probably an Hellenistic Jew, some time previous to the age of Polycarp, who quotes it.

It was never admitted into the Hebrew canon. It seems not to have been known or respected by the historians Philo, or Josephus, for they have taken no notice of it. It is not to be found in any of the catalogues of the sacred books; yet it has been referred to with much respect, both as ancient and useful, by many of the fathers, and some councils have reckoned it canonical.

Tobit does not pretend to prophecy, but rather to found his remarks on the predictions of the prophets. The historical facts which he records have not been questioned; and the instructions which his book conveys are serious and impressive. But some of the circumstances, as the cause of his blindness, are ludicrous. The agency of angels and the miracles which it details, are improbable, and give to the whole story the air of fiction. The moral is good, however, even considering it as fictitious, and in this view may be read with pleasure and advantage; with this exception, that any counterfeit of things sacred—any false assumption of Divine authority or power—even an awkward imitation of holy Scripture—shews a want of reverence, and certainly tends to diminish our veneration for the sacred writings. Such a fiction as that in chap. v. 12, will be readily discredited. The angel Raphael is there represented as assuming the appearance of a man, and feigning a name, in order to become the guardian of young Tobias; and as discovering a ridiculous drug or perfume, to frighten demons, and another to cure diseased eyes.

Book of Judith

The author and age of the book of Judith are equally unknown. It is unnecessary to inquire concerning them, because it is vain to mention the mere conjectures of learned men. It is uncertain whether there ever was a Hebrew copy. The Greek one is referred to by Clemens Romanus, and therefore must be still more ancient; whether as an original, or as is generally supposed, a version from the Chaldee original. Philo and Josephus take no notice of it, nor of its subjects. Yet many of the facts and circumstances which it narrates are agreeable to the accounts of Herodotus, and other writers; and it was received as authentic history, both by Jews and early Christians. The period to which it refers is involved in much obscurity, which renders it difficult to ascertain what is or is not truth—

to distinguish real history from embellishments—extraordinary events and incidents from hyperbolical fiction. There is an appeal at the conclusion to the evidence of contemporaries, and to a sacred festival annually celebrated in memory of Judith's triumph. Were this ascertained, it might serve as a voucher for the reality of the facts. But the passage referred to, chap. xvi. 31, which is the last verse in the Vulgate is not to be found in the Greek, Syriac or ancient Latin versions; nor is the festival noticed in any of the authentic Hebrew calendars. It has been received as canonical by the Council of Trent; but it was accounted apocryphal by the Jews; it was never acknowledged by Jesus, nor his Apostles, nor any of their immediate successors, nor admitted into the early catalogues of the canonical books.

The spirit of the book is pious, and may have been well intended by its author, either to record an illustrious fact, or to encourage and animate the people not to despond in any extremity, but to cherish a daring and adventurous mind. Yet the moral cannot be held good, if the example exhibited tends, in any respect, to encourage the use of improper means in order even to a good end.

Additional Chapters to Esther &c.

The *rest* of the chapters of the book of Esther are not to be found in either the Hebrew or Chaldee tongues, and never were admitted into the sacred canon, or received as canonical by the Christian fathers, though accounted such by the Council of Trent.

The canonical book of Esther itself appears complete, and needed no addition. These chapters are therefore superfluous. They appear mean and insignificant. The first chapter is sufficient to satisfy any judicious person, that the writer is fanatical and absurd; but if he proceeds, he must be convinced that he is reading an awkward abridgment of Esther, and a silly romance, and not by any means a sacred book.

Book of the Wisdom of Solomon.

This book assumes to have been written by Solomon; for the author speaks in his name and person, and endeavours to imitate his style and sentiments, transcribing many passages or the substance of them, from the real writings of Solomon. But it must have been composed long after Solomon's death, probably about the time of the Maccabees. It contains quotations from Isaiah, and from other books of the Septuagint. It never was admitted into the Hebrew canon, nor into the earlier catalogues of the Christian church.

The antiquity and excellence of the book have excited and maintained the highest respect for it, as a common composition, approaching, in internal evidence, according to some, very near to the importance and authority of revelation. But, according to others, the style and method are less simple than those of the sacred books, and partake more of the art, and even mythology, of Greek heathen writers. The author seems particularly to have been familiarly acquainted with the writings of Plato. It rather breathes a spirit of philosophy, falsely so called. Some things are added of an historical kind, which seem fictitious. Its political lessons to rulers are interesting, and its doctrines in general are good and edifying.

The Book of Ecclesiasticus.

This book, though ascribed to Solomon by some writers, because it resembles his Proverbs and book of Ecclesiastes, yet must have been written long after him, and nearly as late as the Maccabees, since it mentions names and circumstances of the preceding age. Jesus, the son of Sirach the professed author of it, may, like others in the time of Solomon, have been a collector of proverbs and wise sayings, which, with those of his own invention, he published in that book. Some of the most ancient of this collection might be in Hebrew, and be translated by the grandson of the collector, also named Jesus son of Sirach, probably about the 3835th year of the world, and about 170 years before Christ

It abounds in the most just and admirable observations on human life, and directions for human conduct. By an attentive imitation of the spirit and style of the sacred writers there is often a striking coincidence of thoughts and expressions between it and passages both of the Old and New Testament.

But it was always accounted uncanonical, both by Jews and Christians, till after the fourth century, and even afterward was held inferior in authority, until it was absolutely received as canonical by the Council of Trent.

The Greek version of it is considered as the best but it is understood not to have been happily translated in this country. Our English version is in many places inaccurate, and in some erroneous.

Twenty four chapters of it contain the proverbial and wise sayings. Wisdom there personified utters her instructions they are followed by a pious address or hymn, in praise of Divine wisdom and after a panegyric on some characters of the Jewish nation, the book concludes with thanksgiving for some personal deliverance. It is certainly one of the best human compendiums of moral duty and virtue.

Book of Baruch

From the book itself, the author appears to have been a person of high rank, and a friend of the Prophet Jeremiah. There may be no reason to dispute this, as far as the first five chapters of the book the style is full of Hebraisms there is no anachronism, nor inconsistency. But it was never held canonical, and even the Council of Trent hesitated about admitting it, because it had not been received by the Councils of Laodicea and Carthage, nor by the Roman pontiffs. Yet they gave it a place in the canon, as some parts of it were read in the service of the church.

The sixth chapter has been generally considered as spurious. So is the epistle ascribed to Baruch, which bears the marks of acquaintance with Christianity, and consequently of a late age.

Song of the three Children, Susannah, and Bel and the Dragon.

It is wonderful that the Council of Trent included even these in their decree, as canonical parts of the book of Daniel. It is very uncertain when they were composed. They are in the Arabian and Syriac versions, and are mentioned early by Christian writers, but were never in the Hebrew copy. Incorporated, by some means unknown, with the book of Daniel, they were admitted, under the sanction of that name, into some copies of the Septuagint. But they were easily discriminated from the genuine writings of that prophet, and readily and uniformly rejected from the canon.

The first is a pious expression of gratitude and devotion in imitation of some of the Psalms, and might have been composed on some interesting occasion or was afterwards adapted to it. But there is sufficient evidence that it did not originally belong to the book of Daniel, and was never held to be canonical.

The other two carry internal evidence of their fictitious and absurd nature.

Prayer of Manasseh

The Prayer of Manasseh was rejected as apocryphal even by the Council of Trent. It is said to have been composed by Manasseh during his captivity in Babylon, in the 22d year of his reign, A. M. 3227.

It contains nothing inconsistent with either history, piety, or propriety. But it was never deemed canonical, and is supposed to have been inserted by some zealot, to supply the place of the prayer which that king is said, in the book of

Chronicles (2 Chron. xxxiii. 19) to have offered up

The Maccabees

The first book of the Maccabees contains historical facts relative to the Jews, from the beginning of the reign of Antiochus Epiphanes A. M. 3829 to the death of Simon the high priest, A. M. 3869. John Hyrcanus, the son of Simon, is generally supposed to have written it, in the Chaldee or Syriac languages, as used by the Jews on their return from Babylon. It was then a part of the office of the high priest to write the annals of the nation. The Greek version from which our English translation was made, has named the book from the persons whose actions chiefly are celebrated in it.

It was never esteemed canonical, nor admitted into the Christian catalogues of the Scriptures by the fathers or councils, until it was decreed in all respects canonical by the Council of Trent. Yet it has been always read and referred to as a respectable history. It is lively, accurate, and like an account of facts which the author himself had witnessed. Josephus had approved of it, for he copies the most of it into his history. It relates the wars of the Jews, under Mattathias and his family against the kings of Syria, until they recovered their liberties and re-established their religion.

The second book of the Maccabees is a compilation of history, relating chiefly to the persecutions of Epiphanes and Eupator against the Jews for about fifteen years, from A. M. 3828 to 3843. It begins earlier than the preceding book and is generally an abridgment or repetition of it. It is in a very different and less simple style. It is not so accurate, and in some things inconsistent.

The author whoever he was, for it is in vain to conjecture, speaks modestly of himself, disclaiming all title to inspiration, or Divine authority. Nor was it ever received into the list of sacred books by Jews or Christians, until it was canonized, like the other apocryphal books, by the undiscriminating decree of the Council of Trent. The account of the martyrdom of the woman and her children, is lively and interesting. The views given of their faith and hope, shew the opinions in those times, respecting a resurrection and future state, to have been clear and well established.

The silence of Josephus with respect to these martyrs, the omens, and visions, and other superstitious circumstances related in it, tend of course, together with its unsound doctrine, to diminish the credibility of the author, and would serve as conclusive arguments to prevent its being received as canonical, were there any disposition to admit it to that honour. They may caution us, too, against implicit reliance on the author's statements, as they shew him to have been credulous. But they do not affect his principal facts, more than Livy's credulity and prodigies do the general truth of his history.

To the Editor of the Christian Observer.

THE importance of Christian conduct in the professed disciples of Christ can scarcely be estimated too highly. To let our light shine before men, has a powerful efficacy in recommending religion to the notice and estimation of the world; while to fail in this duty, produces the most deleterious effects. The success of the Gospel in every age has been connected in no small degree with the conduct of its professors, and the neglect of a holy and amiable life has always been, in a great measure, the cause of its unsuccessfulness and decay. I have been led to these remarks by the following circumstance.

While on a visit some time since to a professedly religious friend, I had occasion to notice, with much grief, a want of Christian like conduct towards his domestics. In stead of a becoming kindness of manner and of language, there was a tone of harshness and tyranny in every thing he said to them. They were treated more like vassals than fellow Christians. Peremptory and authoritative, vituperative and commanding, peevish and displeased at almost every thing they did, he seemed as if no person's comfort and convenience were to be consulted but his own. The effect of this conduct was very visible in the countenances of the servants. Sometimes they appeared mortified, at other times indignant, and at no time in a pleasing happy mood. In the evening we had family prayers. The servants came in, and I noticed particularly their physiognomy, and I thought I could trace sentiments of this kind in their countenances— "You read a good book, and pray well, but you do not behave to us accordingly. You read and speak of, and pray for, brotherly love and sympathy and kindness; but you do not shew much of them in your conduct. We cannot receive any good from your prayers and instructions; for you give the lie to all we hear at this service." I suspected that something of this kind was passing through their minds; certainly at least it passed through mine; and I could not but reflect on the indescribable injury done to their minds by this manifest inconsistency. If they had no religion, what a barrier must such conduct have raised in their minds against it! What unfavourable ideas of it must they have formed!

This is, no doubt, a glaring case; but there are others less glaring, which yet are very reprehensible. The situation of masters and mistresses, it must be allowed, is frequently very difficult. Provocations from servants are often many and great; their neglect, idleness, or disobedience, is not a little vexatious; and to exemplify daily and on all occasions, and under all these and similar circumstances, the true spirit and character of a Christian towards them, requires no common vigilance. But what should be constantly had in view, is the spiritual and eternal good of those connected with us. In proportion as this is regarded, will our conduct be Christian like, and beneficial to them, and eventually to ourselves. The question to be asked, under every circumstance, is, What will promote the good of their souls? and whatever militates against this, does not become us as Christians. A mere regard to what the world considers right and wrong, in dealing with them in cases of impropriety and bad conduct, is not sufficient, and will often fail to produce any beneficial effect. Many things must be quietly borne with and passed by in servants, as well as in other people. I am not pleading for undue indulgence towards them; but I think, in general, they do not share our sympathy so much as they ought; and we do not treat them with that kindness and love which we should expect from them, were we to exchange places. Perhaps in no particular are respectable persons, professing religion, more defective, than in the general tone of their behaviour towards their servants. They follow the conduct of the world too much in this respect. This subject deserves the attention of your readers; for, apart from other considerations, without good, kind, and judicious masters and mistresses there will never be affectionate, faithful, and useful servants.

M. S.

To the Editor of the Christian Observer.

A DESIRE to do good belongs to the very essence of Christianity; but this desire is in some minds too greatly separated from the fear of doing evil. Many persons satisfy themselves with endeavouring to promote the benefit of others whilst they disregard the duty of endeavouring to suppress those evils which, in the ordinary course of things, are almost certain to cause their bene volent exertions to prove abortive. I propose to confine myself to an illustration of these remarks in reference to the subject of affording relief to individuals apparently in distress.

Who has not heard the trite observation, that 'it is better to relieve ten worthless impostors, than to suffer one really afflicted supplicant to pass by unassisted?' and yet we profess a religion which teaches us 'not to do evil that good may come.' Many a benevolent man has felt his mind deeply wounded because perhaps in his haste, he has improperly refused to listen to the plea of some object of distress, who yet never experienced a moment's uneasiness at having been the cause, by ill judged liberality, of ten fold greater miseries—perhaps of having heedlessly aided in promoting the vice, and pauperism, and intemperance, with which his own neighbourhood was already almost overwhelmed and adding to the afflictions of deserted wives and forsaken families, by encouraging idle and profligate mendicants to revel in public houses, and other scenes of vicious indulgence.

The frequency of this almost incomprehensible conduct, in persons of benevolence and piety, probably springs from the neglect of considering *the special duties of their own age and country.* The times may have been when there was comparatively little need to enforce on Christians the duty of watchfulness against imposition or to guard them against the evil which indiscriminate liberality might produce. This may have been peculiarly the case in the primitive church, when the disciples of Jesus Christ could often give little to the afflicted but their tears and the men of the world preferred a religion which knew nothing of 'bowels of mercies.' * Then the precept which it might be needful almost exclusively to enforce, on such a subject as this, was, that men should be 'ready to distribute, willing to communicate.' But great is the change which, in this respect has taken place in the world now called Christian, at least in our own land.* From the most benevolent, but ill judged, motives, we have institution upon institution for the relief of the poor until at last we have some that actually and obviously hold out a premium to indolence and vice † besides many that practically, though less glaringly, have the same effect. If the millions of our poor's rates could be increased ten fold and the overseers rendered as numerous as the applicants, we should still have the poor with us, and, without doubt, the objects of *real* charity, rendered such by a false and injurious system, would rather be increased than diminished.

Let it not, however, be supposed that there is no room for the exercise of benevolence in affording succour to the destitute and afflicted far, very far from it but it must appear, to every reflecting mind, that the circumstances of our age and country render it a duty which

---

* It is not however clear that even in very early ages the evils alluded to were not felt and in the primitive church of Christ itself some commentators have thought they discerned traces of it in the conduct of Ananias and Sapphira, who they conjecture by pretending to throw their all into the common stock hoped to be maintained for life out of the charitable funds of the religious community to which they hypocritically attached themselves. Indeed, unless they had some such interested motive it may be difficult to account for their conduct vanity and ostentation alone not appearing to have been adequate inducements for selling their estate and giving away even a part of the produce especially in minds in which avarice had evidently a dominant sway.

I confine my remarks to our own land my paper being addressed practically to my own countrymen and countrywomen but justice demands that I should add that we are much less assailed by clamorous mendicity in this than in many other countries though if our *legalized pauperism* be taken into the account, we shall I fear have no reason to boast of our superiority but very much the contrary.

† It is the rule for example of some Benefit Clubs to allow so much a-week to any member whilst imprisoned for debt

to discharge aright requires the utmost discrimination, and is of no easy performance. Every true Christian therefore, should avoid countenancing in however slight a degree those evils which wrongly directed charity has already brought in some places to an alarming height. It is, no doubt exceedingly troublesome to investigate the cases of strangers who apply with a piteous tale of sorrow for relief, and it is often difficult, with much exertion to discover the real extent of distress even when the applicants for assistance are in some measure known. Genuine charity will, however bear in mind, that one case thoroughly examined into is an evidence of more real benevolence than a multitude carelessly relieved. Let it be remembered also, that the ability to do good and to communicate even where it is most extensive has its limits, and it will not surely be difficult to answer the question, whether that man best employs what he has to give who bestows more liberally and to the full extent of his resources on the few cases which he can thoroughly investigate, or he who gives a careless gratuity, in a more indiscriminate manner to a larger number, as much perhaps to get free from their importunity as from a hope that his bounty is well bestowed.

O U A

To the Editor of the Christian Observer.

THE impropriety of Clerical Sporting, has been so often animadverted upon, and is so generally allowed by all seriously reflecting persons, that I know not that I could add much, if any thing to what has already been so frequently and so well said upon the subject both in your own pages and elsewhere. But as the season for the destruction of game will have arrived on the day in which your next number will salute the eyes of the public, permit me to discharge one straggling September shot, in hopes it *may* at least graze some of these thoughtless delinquents. Happy should I be, if it might strike them so deeply as to deter them in future from the practice! At all events, even a slight annual remonstrance may be of use to confirm those who have somewhat waveringly discontinued the practice, and to determine others who are hesitating whether or not to adopt it.

Let me then, caution my Reverend brethren against the idle habits which the seductive practices of hunting and shooting too frequently induce. Let me caution them against entering into competition with the lay inhabitants of their neighbourhood. A Clergyman cannot be too circumspect in his appearance, in his conversation, and in his conduct. It is not decorous to behold the man who sustains this solemn office in an uncouth dress, and accompanied by his dogs trespassing on the lands and rights of others. It is not becoming a Clergyman that his conversation should be principally about dogs and game, or that he should value himself more upon his being a good shooter or hunter than a good divine. Roving pursuits lower the dignity of those who follow them, most of all of the ambassador of Christ. Clergymen, who become professed sportsmen, too often forget that they are Clergymen; they are so much engrossed by their low concerns that they have no leisure for the high duties of the clerical profession. Let me advise my elder brethren especially to set becoming examples to the younger clergy by a sedulous and punctual discharge of their parochial duties.

The time of a Clergyman may be sufficiently taken up in visiting the sick, consoling the distressed, relieving the poor and superintending parochial schools. If however he should consider much exercise in the open air to be conducive to his health, no amusement can be better suited to a Clergyman than that of horticulture.

A CONSTANT READER.

REVIEW OF NEW PUBLICATIONS

1. *Palingenesia, The World to Come.* Paris and London. 1824.
2. *Letters by Basilicus.* Reprinted from the Jewish Expositor for 1820, 21, 22.
3. *The Coming of the Day of God, &c.* By an humble Expectant of the Promises. Dublin and London.
4. *Scriptural Doctrine of the Last General Judgment.* By J. E. JONES, M.A. Gloucester. 1823. 2s.
5. *Letter to the Rev. J. E. Jones, occasioned by his Sermon on Modern Millenarianism.* By JOHN BAYFORD, Esq. F.S.A. Author of Messiah's Kingdom.
6. *Practical View of the Redeemer's Advent.* By Rev. JAMES HALDANE STEWART, M.A. &c. 1825.
7. *Messiah's Kingdom, a Brief Inquiry into the Second Advent.* By JOHN BAYFORD, Esq. London. 8vo. 10s.
8. *Predictions and Promises of God respecting Israel, a Sermon on the Baptism of Mr. Alexander, late Reader in the Jewish Synagogue.* By the Rev. J. HATCHARD, A.M., Vicar of St Andrew's, Plymouth. 1825. 1s. 6d.
9. *Conversion of the Jews, a Sermon delivered in All Saints Church, Manchester, after the public Baptism of a Jew and his two Children.* By the Rev. C. BURTON. 1824.
10. *Discourses on Prophecy.* By the Rev. JOHN DAVISON, late Fellow of Oriel College. Second Edition. London. 15s.
11. *Exposition of the Book of Revelation in Forty four Discourses.* By the Rev. H. GAUNTLETT, Vicar of Olney. Third Edition. London. 8vo. 1822.
12. *Practical Remarks on the Prophecies.* By the Rev. EDWARD BICKERSTETH, Assistant Minister of Wheler Chapel. London. 1824. 12mo.

(*Concluded from p. 435.*)

WE have already noticed the improved state of the Millennial question within the last two centuries, and shall accompany our readers through such remarks on intermediate writers as our limits may afford, down to the present *revivification* of the subject in a spirit, perhaps, not quite such as we could have wished and expected. It is a curious fact, that the two great contemporary commentators, Grotius and Mede, should have been penning, perhaps at the same moment early in the seventeenth century, the opposite representative sentiments of all former ages respecting the Millennium.—Grotius with the Allegorists of old tying down its nature and meaning to the successful establishment of Christian doctrine and Christian practice, which event *he* dates from the era of Constantine, though some writers place it earlier and others later; whilst Mede, on the other hand, stands forth as the representative of the little band of ancient Millennaries, and leads the modern ones, first in placing the commencing *date* of the 1000 years at the conclusion of the other Apocalyptic periods, after the destruction of the Dragon, the Beast, and the False Prophet, and synchronically with the out pouring of the seventh vial and the sounding of the seventh (or third woe) trumpet * and next in asserting the actual resurrection of the dead in Christ

To this very period indeed Tertullian nearly approximates in a passage partly referred to by Mr Davison (in our ed. Lutet. 1675 p. 339, or p. 297 in Mr Davison's ed. Lutet.) as a proof of the exactness and comprehensive views of that father upon the great New Testament prophecy of the coming of Anti Christ during this blessed period and the welcome union of Jews and Gentiles as one body in him, settled in the ancient capital of Judea, the long lost city of holiness, Jerusalem—Jerusalem, however in a very different condition from what it once was or indeed can now be conceived to be. In truth the once Holy Land would now be very far from a desirable inheritance—nor could it well become so without a miracle; and when the Jews are converted to Christ, we doubt not that having found a spiritual Salem and High Priest, and an endeared brotherhood in the whole family of Christians, they will not be anxious for returning to a literal Jerusalem, but will cheerfully content themselves with the stations and the places in which it shall please God to call them. But this by the way. Mede further, throws some blame on Tertullian for seeming to put off the work of conflagration and renovation till the *end* of the Millennium and the final Judgment; and rather apprehends with other ancients, that a purifying fire is to *commence* the Millennium; and that the Lord Jesus will even then " be revealed from heaven in flaming fire, such as may properly beseem a commencing fire of judgment, for the burning out of all the stubble of wickedness and the establishment of a new heavens and a new earth, wherein dwelleth righteousness.

And here Dr Thomas Burnet in the beginning of the last century comes in to seasonable aid, by providing his exquisitely wrought and highly eloquent description of an actual renovation of all things by fire, and a universal conflagration of the whole globe itself and all the works that are therein. Imagination we may truly say pants and toils under the glowing figures with which this great theorist introduces us to his new creation; and *that* creation he follows Mede by name and the elder Chiliasts, in peopling with risen saints, and planting with his new, and after all highly figurative, Jerusalem. The *personal* appearance of Christ upon earth during this sabbatical Millennium seems indeed by these writers though not by modern Millennaries confined to a Divine schekinah, or cloud of glory, similar to that in former periods of Jewish history; but from this happy state are to be gathered away all things that offend, and they that do amiss. ' Disease is none and the whole series of " happy negatives" delineated in Rev xxi and xxii will have their full place. Upon the question of a succession of generations by marriage and by death there seems to be small agreement; only so far as we can trace it this succession is denied with regard to saints actually recalled to life during this interval and is confined to such survivors according to Mede, after the fires of the first judgment as are thought worthy of this first resurrection. This is, in truth that great that " ONE *day of the Lord,* which is as A THOUSAND YEARS" during the whole of which time the process of judgment is to be virtually regarded as proceeding, and the King continuing to sit on the throne of his glory. His reign now substantially commences. His saints now inherit the earth. His foes are made his footstool and the prophecy now is satisfied, that ' God will bruise Satan under your feet shortly.' Satan is, in truth bound for a thousand years. He is loosed after, but for a little space. He then proceeds to his accustomed work of deceiving the earth and with his armies Gog and Magog dares the very camp of the holy city. But all is security and peace within. The fire from God comes down out of heaven, and devours leader and army. And then the mystery of God is fully accomplished by that same fire preluding the awful and terrific blaze of eternal judgment itself. The 'great white throne' is then set; the "books" are then opened; " earth and heaven, that is our lower atmosphere " fly away"—become according to Dr Burnet, *a bright star* —and the dead, small and great, alike stand in one grand contemporary multitude before the throne of God, and are judged out of the things written in the book The saints formerly risen, and all who had part in the first resurrection become assessors at the dread tribunal and the eternal future which then ensues as distinct from the Millennial blessedness detailed in the twenty first and twenty second chapters of Revelation is now hidden from our eyes The hell and heaven of Christian expectation remain a sort of unfigured blank under this hypothesis,—a portion of the " colourless ether which cannot better be described than in a quotation we shall now introduce from Palingenesia in order to verify much that we have stated on the Millennarian scheme and to bring it down to modern times

> Think not—O ! vain objector we disclaim
> As inconsistent with this world to come
> Or hell or heaven—we of either speak
> According to the oracles of God
> As far as they have spoken —We believe
> Eternity but do not use the term
> With reference to time and circumstance
> Of limited duration and the course
> Of this or any world that hath an end
> Ages of ages without number roll
> Before the face of their Eternal King
> The great incomprehensible I AM
> When this world s transitory stage and earth
> And heavens that succeed are fled away
> And found no place for them and thus the soul
> That seed of immortality a germ
> Of amaranthine bloom transplanted there
> Where first it grew will bear immortal fruit
> According to its properties —We leave
> The veil where it is plac d beyond the throne
> White with excess of brightness as the beams
> Of solar radiation merg d in one
> In sight are colourless —The second death
> Sufficeth us to know will be the lot
> And portion of impenitence —The just
> Whose names are written in the Book of Life
> Can die no more but what those words imply
> God will be all in all we are not wise
> Above that which is written to unfold
> Paling pp 173 174

We interrupt the quotation to remark, that the *soul*, " that seed of immortality, is here put in *contra distinction* to St Paul s simile in 1 Cor xv which has respect to the *body*, and which here is solely applied to the revivification of the body for the Millennium This is but one example of the too many instances in which we find Revelation misconstrued to suit the views of *modern* Millennarians and can only be referred to similar sentiments in the discourse (No 3 on our list) by " An humble Expectant of the Promises, who says, p 36, " It should be remembered, that if the Scriptures reveal something short of what some have expected [with regard to *the glory attending on salvation*], they should submit Our quotation from Palingenesia, however, proceeds, with a view to explain that the new heavens and earth we look for have reference *only* to the Millennium on earth, not to any ulterior bliss in heaven itself, according to the usual, and we think scriptural and legitimate, ideas of heaven

> Reason and revelation each forbid
> A renovated earth in heaven plac d
> According to that strange hypothesis
> Which contradicting all analogy
> The laws of nature and the lapse of time
> Can find beyond all sublunary state
> Remains of time and sense e en death itself
> Crying and pain and sorrow kings of earth
> And national distinction former things
> No more to be remember d—wrath fill d up
> Pour d out again in judgment, within view
> Of beatific vision ! and no more
> Curse where it never occupied a place
> In the third heaven ! paradise of God !
> Such inconsistency the consequence
> Of transposition in prophetic terms
> Clear in themselves and obvious although couch d
> In language highly figurative—true—
> Yet figures bear analogy to things
> And none but crazy brains could take the toes
> Of Daniel s metal image for the head !
> Such were a transmutation strange enough
> Turning man upside down and causing time
> With all political vicissitude
> To roll upon his axle back again
> But all relation and conformity
> Must suffer violence to square with scheme

Of that inverted order under which
The glorious holy city goeth up
Which to the sight of John in spirit borne
Unto the mountain by his angel guide
  Descended out of heaven Coming down
Prepared as a bride and having on
The glory of her God when He will come
To tabernacle once again with men!
Transpose the terms—as commentators do
Wresting this scripture from its obvious sense
And things already hard to understand
Concerning the last days by Peter's own
Acknowledgment confessedly obscure
Assume another character and form
Delineate such who will—we freely grant
Our common liability to err
But claim our Christian liberty of thought
Of speech and conscience if in fear of God
And jealous for the honour of his word
We venture thus to differ—nor would add
Or take away one word of prophecy
Remembering that awful penalty
Denounc'd on such presumption—God forbid!
And guide us by his Spirit, for we know
All may be liars but he must be true
Truth is our end not argument we mean
Offence to none whom truth would not offend
Fools we would gladly be for sake of Christ
Despising shame and when defam'd intreat
And when reviled bless—and warned warn
Absolving thus our conscience from the charge
Of having hid our talent or conceal'd
That candle in a bushel which we trust
Hath been committed to our care to set
Upon a candlestick—that other eyes
Not purblind may behold but prejudice
Hath neither eye nor ear a ready tongue
To speak at large in generals it shuns
Particularity as prone to lead
To nice investigation and the test
Of open evidence—it swallows down
As doth an ostrich iron—lays an egg
Upon the sand and leaves it, stalks away
Full of its own importance or stands still
And slumbers in suppos'd security
Hiding its head and thinking none can see! Paling pp 175—178

There is something *objurgatory* in the style and tone of these remarks towards those "ready tongues to speak at large in generals, which we think they by no means deserve, and which such authors as those we have quoted (we would speak without offence) are not entitled to assume. If the persons they reprove, really, as they tell us, swallow down, as doth the ostrich iron, their present sentiments, they should have some credit for so doing in order as *they* think, to avoid other materials of no very easy deglutition or digestion, which to *them* appear involved in the above Millennarian scheme, and which *seem* to require both Scripture and reason to be swallowed into the same gulph

But, having brought down this scheme from antiquity to its last and most modern use, we shall proceed to perform the same service for the opposite class of opinions

We observed, that Grotius seems to us, in the line of commentators to represent the Allegorists, "the speakers at large in generals, of antiquity and although we apprehend all moderns are agreed in rejecting entirely the notion of Grotius and his constituents as to a Millennium commencing from Constantine or we know not what other past period in the Christian history, and terminating according to Grotius when a respect for the memory and the *relics* of the martyrs ceased in the church still we think it important to remark, by the way that the *general notion* of a figurative, or rather constructive Millennium consisting in a *general diffusion of Christian doctrine and supreme reign of Christian principles over the nations of the earth*, certainly derives strength from the sanction of those great and inquisitive minds which understood it of a period either passed or passing —Durham who places it *after* the period of the 1260 years, but antedates that period so as to place us at present in the third or fourth century of the Millennium, has some very striking and copious observations on its nature, for the express purpose of rescinding marvellous and vain expectations of a partial and unknown futurity Bishop Horsley also might be read with advantage, by those who defer greatly to his powerful name—excellent, however, sometimes as Mr Davison remarks rather " in force of style than severity of reasoning, (Discourses, Notes, p 532)—in order to appreciate duly the real and effective nature of the kingdom of Christ, as *already* set up in the world, and begun to be set up from the earliest periods of the Christian revelation Such a reign universally extended, and blessed by peculiar interferences of Divine Providence, would, in sober truth, fall little short of all that is really *spiritual* in the anticipations of Millennial glory The reader may refer to the admirable sermons on Psalm xlv, in which the Bishop describes the Psalmist as "proceeding to the second great period in the Divine history of Christianity the successful propagation of the Gospel, and our Lord s *final victory* over all his adversaries a work *gradually accomplished and occupying the whole interval of time* from his ascension to the epoch, not yet arrived, of the fulness of the Gentiles coming in — with much more to the same purpose of the *present* reigning and judging power of Christ We must remark, in passing, that Bishop Horsley, though very confidently quoted by the Millennarians—

Prelate of Rochester! whom Asaph claim d
Worthy of such translation ! Pioneer
Of that great army of evangelists
Since call d to fight the battles of the Lord — (Paling p 253)

is either not at all, or a very inconsistent, advocate of their favoured Millennium

It is, in truth, some modification of this spiritual reign of Christ and his doctrines upon earth, which constitutes the Millennium of Whitby and Vitringa, whose opinions, delivered early in the last century—a full century after those of Joseph Mede —we think are most worthy of note on the opposite side These writers are very naturally startled at the difficulties of the ancient doctrine,— difficulties, indeed *inexplicable* and *insuperable* till the day shall reveal the truth and, therefore, difficulties which leave us quite as unresolved as those on the opposite side could do and this class of writers consequently, satisfy themselves with adhering to what is plain and palpable to our present conceptions, and carrying on the present kingdom of the Messiah to the utmost perfection of which it is now sensibly capable, and which, we must with grief confess, it is far, very far, from having hitherto attained To the eye of faith, a most stupendous change was introduced into the history of the world, though mainly consistent with the present order and course, or at least *face*, of nature, at the day of Pentecost Miracles of mercy and power were then wrought, as if to shew what wonders are consistent with the wisdom and providence of God as displayed even in this lower world, in subservience to the everlasting kingdom and gospel of our Lord and what imagination can set a limit to the exercise of the same power, in a natural course of providence, for restraining the acts of the great deceiver and establishing the glories of eternal truth ? A veil is yet upon the heart, both of Jew and Gentile who can tell what shall be the effulgence of that spiritual light which shall one day pierce it or, rather which shall burst upon the enraptured eye both of Jew and Gentile when they shall turn to the Lord, and the veil itself shall be taken away ! We are told very plainly, or very figuratively—which shall we say? —that *this* event shall be 'AS *life from the dead* And even before we come to ask whether this be indeed what is meant by *the first resurrection*, we may still clearly perceive that it would be *a resurrection* When the Gospel preached first for a witness to both classes, to all the world, to every creature, shall subsequently take effect as far as its witness shall have extended —when principles of universal toleration (we use the term in no stinted or merely negative and grating acceptation) shall become as extensive, as now the almost universal reign of contrary principles or, rather, when tolerance shall scarcely be needed, because "error shall be none, deserving of the name:—when nations shall come to the light of Divine truth, and kings to the brightness of its rising,—and when, by the adoption of the true principles of " light and love (may we not, in some cases be even *now* making advances toward such a state?) all the kingdoms of this world shall become the kingdoms of our God and of his Christ and he shall for a time reign in the full completion of his earthly power, as he shall hereafter reign in the kingdom of his Father even for ever and ever,—then must it not be said that we have at least *one* Palingenesia, or consummation most devoutly to be wished? The actual tendency of Bible principles to produce this consummation has yet been but feebly tried. But, doubtless, if even a second Pentecostal effusion were needed to give those principles their full efficacy, it is not out of the scope of fancy, nor beyond the expectation of those writers we are now speaking of, that such an effusion might be afforded. It is at least very clear, that up to this period what we might call the natural resources of that kingdom of Christ which was established upon earth at the day of Pentecost have not been fully tried: and *these might* be sufficient, if providentially awakened and called into force for all that we have hitherto described of a spiritual Millennial kingdom upon earth.

Such, in substance, are the statements of the most scriptural *Allegorical Millennaries* at the head of which we have placed our own countryman, Whitby and the foreign Vitringa. Whitby most largely and distinctly contends for the interpretation of the Millennium by a general and providential conversion of the Jewish nation. 'I believe,' says he, in chap. ii. of his treatise on the True Millennium, "that after the fall of Antichrist, there shall be such a glorious state of the church, by the conversion of the Jews to the Christian faith, as shall be to it *life from the dead:* that it shall then flourish in peace and plenty, in righteousness and holiness, and in a pious offspring: that then shall begin a glorious and undisturbed reign of Christ over both Jew and Gentile, to continue a thousand years during the time of Satan's binding: and that, as John the Baptist was Elias because he came in the spirit and power of Elias, so shall this be the church of the martyrs, and of those who had not received the mark of the Beast, because of their entire freedom from all the doctrines and practices of the anti Christian church, and because *the spirit and purity of the times of the primitive martyrs shall return.* And therefore, 1. I agree with the patrons of the Millennium in this, that I believe Satan hath not yet been bound a thousand years; nor will he be so bound, till the time of the calling of the Jews and the time of St. John's Millennium. 2. I agree with them in this, that the true Millennium will not begin till the fall of Antichrist; nor will the Jews be converted till that time, the idolatry of the Roman church, *being one* great obstacle of their conversion. 3. I agree both with the modern and ancient Millennaries, that then shall be great peace and plenty, and great measures of knowledge and of righteousness, in the whole church of God.—I therefore only differ from the ancient Millennaries in three things. 1. In denying Christ's personal reign upon earth during this thousand years: and in this both Dr. Burnet and Mr. Mede expressly have renounced their doctrine. 2. Though I dare not absolutely deny, what they all positively assert, that the city of Jerusalem shall be then rebuilt, &c. yet I deny what Barnabas and others contend, that the temple shall be built again. ' I saw *no temple* in this new Jerusalem,' Rev. xxi. 22. 3. I differ both from the ancient and the modern Millennaries as far as they assert that this shall be a reign of such Christians as have suffered under the Heathen persecutors, or by the rage of Antichrist making it only a reign of the converted Jews, and of the Gentiles then flowing into them and uniting into one church with them. This I believe to be indeed the truth of this mistaken doctrine.— He afterwards admits with favour the conjecture of Mede, that there shall be added, though not the personal reign, yet a *vision* of Jesus Christ to them; for saith God by Zechariah, I will pour out upon the house of David, &c. the Spirit of grace and supplication and they shall *look upon Him* whom they have pierced: see also Matt. xxiv. 30 and xxiii. 39. And from this and other texts he likewise considers, ' that there will be a full effusion of the Holy Ghost upon the church somewhat resembling that which was vouchsafed to the first ages of Christianity. To this period, in conclusion, he distinctly refers the whole substance of the prophecy contained in Rev. xxi. and xxii. as well as the resurrection of the souls, ver. 4 (or as he understands the expression the principles) of the martyrs, and their reign with Christ a thousand years as stated in chap. xx. whilst he admits that the rest of the dead lived not (ver. 5) in the literal and plain sense of a bodily resurrection.

But we proceed to Vitringa. Referring to Rev. xx. 1—15, ' Shall we,' he says, ' in admitting the whole current of early antiquity as well as the most approved moderns, in favour of the true period of the Millennium falling subsequent to the reign of Antichrist; also admit the less prudent and exploded notions of the ancient Chiliasts—notions of a magnificent earthly Jerusalem, furnished with a temple and Mosaic rites; Christ descending thither to reign in visible glory over the nations; the martyrs and saints of former ages really risen, and attached in person to the church; the face of the whole earth deflagrated and renewed and bringing forth spontaneous fruits from its renovated soil?' Certainly, from such *Chiliasm* I must entirely dissent. For I well know the kingdom of Christ to be spiritual, and his glory spiritual; nor, if ever to be exhibited in glory in this lower world, as I fully believe, will it change its nature and destroy itself. Then after asserting the conversion of the Jews as indubitable, and allowing the re-edification, &c. of Jerusalem, he proceeds,—

For the rest it will fully satisfy this, and all other like prophecies thus to explain their accomplishment; namely, that after the destruction of the great anti-Christian empire long spaces of time tranquil and peaceful will ensue, during which the church, embracing the Jews in its bosom; grounded and settled on Apostolical principles of doctrine and discipline, resplendent with the light of knowledge and purity, abounding in all spiritual gifts and graces, shall live and prosper in this earth under the care of pious rulers and prudent pastors— nay, shall spread its wings and diffuse its light and glory all around. Here is my hope: here are the prayers of the saints.—The more prolix consideration of these views he willingly declines; on the very ground of their full discussion by an antecedent writer, Whitby, to whose opinions upon the matter he yields his full assent, and under whose guidance he appears in his subsequent consideration of chaps. xxi & xxii. wholly and exclusively to appropriate those magnificent delineations of heavenly bliss to the promises of our terestrial and short-lived though glorious, Millennium.

Much of the same kind are the views of what may be called the modern school of Allegorical Millennarians. Dr. Bogue for example (see the review of his work on the Millennium in our volume for 1818, p. 744), describes, or as some persons would say " cools down" the prophetic Millennium the reign of Christ upon earth, to a period of Christian triumph, and general holiness and happiness extending throughout the great body of mankind, not to be brought about directly by a miraculous manifestation of Divine power, though doubtless preceded and accompanied by an enlarged measure of the enlightening and regenerating influences of the Holy Spirit; but in truth the result of measures already in progress, and greatly to be enlarged, for the conversion and happiness of an ignorant and perishing world. Dr Bogue indulges too much of imagination in descanting on the details of the supposed process, and may be thought by many persons to allow too little of miracle in his list of causes and "diagnostics,—such as Bible and Missionary institutions, books, tracts, education, reading clubs, peace societies, the progress of civil liberty and ecclesiastical equality, &c (to which, and the like, we conclude he has added in his second edition, just published, infant schools, mechanics institutes, joint stock companies for public improvements, &c.)—yet still whatever faults may appear in the details of such a scheme, it is at least a rational and probable, and we believe further a scriptural consummation of human history; and it has besides *this* advantage, which does not apply to the miraculous scheme of interpretation, that it tends to excite the Christian to exert himself with zeal, so far as lies in his power, towards co-operating in so glorious a result.

To return from the modern Allegorists to the modern literal Millennarians, under the guidance of Joseph Mede τὸ πᾶνυ, and his true second and most powerful compeer, Bishop Newton, we must be bold to say, as impartial reviewers, that neither the Millennarians of the present day nor their opponents, have added much light, though perhaps some warmth to this still dark question. We cannot, indeed, recede from our opinion that future events do not, from the very nature of prophecy, admit of the clearness of the past; or that after so much said by the wise on both sides, it cannot become either party to dogmatize, or even, without much of humility and deference, to assert, upon questions so remote from human ken. Least of all would we wish to see any one view of the case urged upon men as a matter of faith; being fully persuaded that no *interpretation* of prophetic events past, and much less future, is intended to be the object of *faith*, but simply the prophetic word itself. 'Thus it is written,' is to us a sufficient pledge that the prophecy will in some way or other, suitable to the Divine counsels, and to the views of Him who seeth not as man seeth, be fulfilled in its proper season and proper force; but of the exact nature of the events predicted, or the mode of fulfilment, we do not think ourselves warranted to form any very decisive opinion. Indeed, nothing can in that respect afford a brighter example or better omen for future improvement in this controversy than the language and temper of Joseph Mede himself, to say nothing of Bishop Newton likewise, and other leading assertors of the literal first resurrection. They evidently write as if hesitating to "rush in where angels fear to tread." And we cannot but strongly recommend the attention of those living authors who have the credit, or who make the avowal, of like works with 'The Messiah's Kingdom,' 'The Humble Expectant,' 'Palingenesia,' 'Basilicus,' &c. to study well such expressions as we shall give at the bottom of the page, from the altogether stupendous Mede.*

* In so great a mystery, says Mede, it will be enough to speak in generals, not too curiously to investigate particulars, lest a too great disposition to expatiate be saluted with that of Solomon, In the multitude of words there wanteth not sin! Yea reader, laying aside all prejudices, weigh the matter in the fear of God, and in the judgment of charity; if any where I have offended, pardon me. And having concluded his short hints,

—Millennial studies, we are afraid, have not advanced since his time at the rate they seem to imagine. And whatever improvement we owe (and it is much, under God) to such labours as those of Mede, on the one hand, or a Whitby &c on the other, we are far from thinking that either "Palingenesia" or the "Messiah's Kingdom," will tend materially to enlarge it. They had the Scriptures, as these moderns have: and we think the latter are not altogether in a disposition to profit by any increasing light to which perhaps they may appeal, in modern studies. Their tone of confidence in the truth of their hypothesis seems to be—we say it with great reluctance—their only step beyond the reach of their elder teachers: whilst we as frankly acknowledge, that some examinations of their writings may possibly fall short of embracing some points which the question, if it must be handled at all, seems to require to be noticed. Mr Jones, for instance (No 4 on our list), in his earnest and excellent sermon on the Last General Judgement, urges very strongly, and properly the danger of disuniting the resurrection and judgment of the righteous and of the wicked of carnalizing and temporalizing the reign of Christ, &c but he does not aim at reconciling the manifest allusions to such a temporal reign in Millennial prophecies *with* that inheritance ' reserved for the saints, as he properly observes, " in heaven. We do not, indeed, blame him for not wishing to puzzle himself and others with such a discussion, though Basilicus and his associates might perhaps fairly object, that till this is done all the necessities of the argument are not fully met. Mr Jones, however may as fairly reply, that he believes the hypothesis of his opponents to be both dangerous and unscriptural and that he can prove it to be so, without volunteering any counter hypothesis of his own and in this we are rather disposed to commend his modesty than to censure his reserve. The doctrine of these modern Millennarians extends as we understand it, to this that there is not a syllable in Scripture about what *we* call heaven that all that is said of heaven applies *only* to the Millennium that the state after the Millennium is an unrevealed blank. Now surely we may maintain that such a view is palpably erroneous, even if we should not pretend to unfold the *real* meaning of all the passages which are alleged to prove it.

Unwilling, then as we are to take any direct part in this difficult controversy, and confessing again and again that we neither offer to others, nor form for ourselves any decisive opinion respecting the interpretation of unfulfilled prophecy, we still feel ourselves called upon to pen some few observations, first, upon the particular scriptural arguments in the case under our consideration and, finally, upon its general bearing on the whole subject of prophecy and on the feelings of the Christian mind. We quite agree with the Millenna

> These things he says reader I have *suggested* not rashly *asserted*. But I defer the whole to be judged out of the word of God by the church [Basilicus is far less courteous for he says benighted church and lying in darkness] to whose verdict as is most fit I submit with all readiness those my sentiments respecting this *mystery*.—D Lawen who disputes much with Mede asserts *roundly* the same Millennial views as a quæstio nobilissima apprime necessaria &c to which Mede replies in *humble* thanks but with an implied check for agreeing with him only in that which was far the most paradoxical of all his opinions and in which he had *fewest* friends and supporters. Again replying to other strictures through a friend he remarks In my Apocalyptic comments I have said nothing as to the *particular mode* of the Millennium the then state either of the world or the saints these I have left *of set purpose* open and *in generals*.—So much for Palingenesia's censure of those who speak at large and in generals on this subject.— Then speaking of the restitution of all things he breaks out Sed quo abeo? Consilii mei memor Scripturaria isthæc cymbula altius non penetrabo in hoc mare —Poor Joseph Mede's little skiff! what is it compared with the Columbuses of Mr Bayford and Basilicus?

rian writers, that the appeal must be made to Scripture, and Scripture alone: and in the use of Scripture we agree with Basilicus, that

> merely to oppose 'passages of Scripture to one another instead of comparing them: thus observing their consistency and respective applications: we mutilate the character of both, cast them out of our hands as it were, and break them to pieces as Moses did the first tables of the Law: whereas by holding them up together we may find them to be as consistent as the two parts of the decalogue itself.—p. 56.

To this, however, Basilicus will in turn give us leave to add, perhaps a still closer and more apposite observation from the acute Dr. S. Clarke, who in his Sermon on the Justice of God remarks: 'It is an observation of great importance, and necessary to be attended to in this as in most other doctrines of religion, that obscurer passages of Scripture are always to be interpreted by the plain ones, and not the plain ones made doubtful by those that are more obscure. And the reason is plain: because that which is at present obscure may very easily, in the event of things, and in the unfolding of Providence, have the difficulties removed and make a final harmony and consistency of the whole: but if that which is once clearly and plainly revealed, in words express and full and without ambiguity, is ever in any wise to be shaken by any after discovery; or if a general perpetual rule can be made in any degree uncertain by the present difficulty of application of any particular case, then can there never be any certain assurance of the truth of any doctrine or revelation at all.'

But to come to the point. Following up these principles must we not be allowed to say, that if the conduct of the Anti Millennarians is, as is alleged, that of 'opposing passages of Scripture to one another, instead of comparing them,' the conduct of the Millennarians is unquestionably that of illustrating, or bearing down, the plain and palpable expressions of Holy Scripture by what is remote and obscure, rather than of explaining what is obscure by first attentively considering what is plain and undeniable. The future is necessarily, as we must again and again repeat, obscure, indefinite and shadowy: and yet it is exactly from those passages which seem to particularize and define what, after all cannot be distinctly known till the event has transpired, that the Millennarian begins and proceeds to model the rest of Scripture.

> After a considerable time spent in this examination, he can now say that till he saw the prophecies in the way he now sees them, he did not understand perhaps one chapter of them at least with any degree of clearness: nor till then understood or rightly valued many of the simplest blessings promised to the church and offered to her as objects of faith and lively hope. In making this assertion the writer does not stand alone, but is happy to say that many whom he must ever respect and esteem, some of them valuable ministers of the Gospel of Christ, and all of them persons of sound judgment and true piety, fully agree with him, and say that they now see a harmony and clearness in the Divine Book that they never did before.—Day of God, p. 4.

Doubtless, at the head of prophecies thus instructive to Millennarians stands the one only passage in Rev. xx., which distinctly or at all asserts the doctrine of a Millennial resurrection: and this *first* resurrection we have seen already to be one of the main points at issue between the contending parties. This, says Joseph Mede, and after him all his followers, is a true and literal resurrection: because "the *rest* of the dead *lived not again*, in a *literal* sense: and there must be a συστοιχια, or agreement, between the two expressions:" or, according to Basilicus,

> The living of the saints [souls of the saints] and the living of the rest of the dead, in this passage must obviously intend living in the same way, or the character of the resurrection is similar in both cases: it is bodily: for in this sense alone is any resurrection common to the saints and the rest of the dead or mankind in general—thus 'in Adam all die,' and thus truly 'in or by Christ shall all be made alive.' In a spiritual sense those who live and reign were already risen with Christ, and alive unto God by faith

and in that sense the rest of the dead whose bodies are raised at the end of the thousand years will never live at all—they were dead already in their souls and will receive their bodies only to be placed under the power of the second death. Basilicus pp 20, 21.

Now, not by "opposing" but by "comparing" Scripture with Scripture, that which is obscure with that which is plain, it appears to us that a συστοιχια, and an αντιστοιχια too, may be obtained here but of a very different nature from that which either Basilicus or his instructor Mede assumes. The very plain description of the final resurrection of 'small and great'— that is, as it would clearly appear at first sight, of ALL without exception—which immediately follows in Rev xx 11, &c leads to a strong supposition, *a priori*, that the former obscure 'first resurrection' could not be of the same nature with the latter event since those could not literally rise beforehand and live again, who were to rise from the dead at the general resurrection and hence we are immediately led at least to look for some other explanation. Now the *Allegorists*, as we have seen, find no difficulty whatever in applying the first resurrection of the souls of the martyrs to live and reign with Christ to a spiritual revival of their principles during the Millennial period and we would ask why are we not to grant to the Millennarian the συστοιχια he requires, by understanding "the *rest* of the dead *living not again* till the thousand years are finished, of a *figurative resurrection* also? That is, the prophet would intimate, we may suppose, that the *other* and *opposing* principles of vice and infidelity lived not again to disturb and defile the church of God or interrupt the harmony of millennial saintship during the whole period of the thousand years. As to the spirits of the saints, they lived, and they reigned with Christ in an earthly but purely spiritual dominion for a thousand years, what ever may be the limits of that prophetic period after this, also the rest of the dead rose, figuratively rose, under the personification of Gog and Magog, but only for greater and sorer judgments, preparatory to the grand final, and literal resurrection of small and great, good and bad, to be judged together, and sentenced together out of the books. Indeed, all the Millennaries, without exception, seem to us guilty of a great scriptural inaccuracy in denominating this "the *second* resurrection" a phrase never warranted in Scripture, and, we might perhaps say, rather pointedly avoided, as if to shew that they were by no means to be connected together, nor viewed as two parts of one great scene or as one great DAY of the Lord, but entirely distinct in nature, time, object, and circumstance the one, a resurrection of principles or souls the other, literally of bodies out of the grave the one, a re production of defunct influences and powers in the then existing state of the church the other an actual consummation of all things, a grand ceremonial conclusion to every preceding dispensation. And as it happens, we have a passage, by the very same inspired author, to somewhat of the same purport, or at least pursuing the self same order, with this prior spiritual, and that final and literal, resurrection. We turn to St John's Gospel, chaps v and xii "Verily, verily, I say unto you, He that heareth my word, and believeth on him that sent me hath everlasting life, and shall not come into condemnation, but *is passed from death unto life* Verily, verily, I say unto you The hour is coming and NOW IS *when the dead shall hear the voice of the Son of God and they that hear shall live* For as the Father hath life in himself so hath he given to the Son to have *life in himself* and hath given him authority to *execute judgment* also, because he is the Son of man Marvel not at this for the hour *is coming* in the which *all that are in the graves* shall hear his voice, and shall come forth they that have done good, unto the *resurrection of life;* AND they that have done evil, unto the *resurrection of damnation.* (John v. 24—29.) "Now is the judgment of this world: now shall the prince of this world be cast out." (John xii. 31.)—Other similar passages might be adduced: and do they not jointly lead to the view of a *first* spiritual resurrection, by conversion to God: and a *first* judgment, concurrent with the actual present reigning power of Christ: and a *final* and general recal from the grave, of the dead, small and great: when *all that are in the graves*—*all*, without exception—shall come forth: 'they that have done good, to the resurrection of life: and they that have done evil, to the resurrection of damnation?' —It does not interfere with the argument, that the Evangelist alludes only to the spiritual life in single converts to the Christian faith, and the Apocalypse (if the allegorical interpretation be right) to an aggregate resurrection of similar principles in the breasts of multitudes, or that the Apocalypse adds also the circumstance of the rest of the dead living not in *their* evil principles during the same period. The analogy of the two passages is so far clear: as containing in juxta position the two doctrines of a *first* and a *final*, or a *spiritual* and a *literal*, resurrection: and they occur, too, with a very remarkable affinity in some of their expressions and circumstances. The final resurrection in both cases is clearly and palpably the same: the spirituality of the prior resurrection, is likewise clear in the Evangelist (chap. v. 24*) and we cannot therefore but say, that we have some ground of analogy for assuming the spirituality of the first resurrection in the Apocalypse. We, however, wish to be understood as speaking only very generally: not adducing the passages in St. John's Gospel with a view of explaining what is meant in each instance by the terms *life, death, resurrection, judgment, &c.* but merely to shew that they are applied, and some of them even in the same passage, both spiritually and literally: so as to admit a fair presumption that they are not of necessity in every instance literal, when employed in other passages, and especially in the Apocalypse, by the same inspired penman.

Another most important series of prophecies, which follows in the twenty first and twenty second chapters of the Revelations, has shared the fate of what we must call 'private interpretation,' to a surprising degree. It is simply a representation of *heaven* to the Anti Millennarians: of whose use of it the Millennarians speak indeed in no very measured or respectful terms.* It is to Whitby nothing but *the conversion of the Jews*, perhaps re assembled in their new earthly Jerusalem. It is to the direct Millennarians a delineation of *their* splendid temporal *Millennial* Jerusalem: where each is pleased to revel in all the luxury of poetic invention: and temple, or no temple: death, or no death: marriage, or no marriage: carnal, or spiritual delights: for a longer or a shorter time: in a world either

---

* We may perhaps add ver. 25, which, from the expression 'and now is' many good expositors consider as referring to our spiritual resurrection from sin alluded to in ver. 24: and not to the final resurrection spoken of in the following verses. Doddridge in his Paraphrase applies it ambiguously to 'some dead bodies raised to life during our Lord's incarnation upon earth: and to 'many souls dead in sin quickened and made spiritually alive:' being doubtful he says to which of the two it really refers.

* It is a truly awful fact that in a pamphlet already referred to (a pamphlet respecting which every true friend to spiritual religion will have reason to lament that it ever saw the light) *going to Heaven* is more than once alluded to in a tone and manner which fall very little short of absolute contempt and ridicule. The author of these pernicious letters had the fullest ground for the apprehension which he himself expressed in the very outset that his views would give offence to serious Christians. Jones p. 31.

partially, or universally renovated are among the varieties to be found in this happy state but all at length to be terminated and dissolved, through certain intermediate conflicts of Gog and Magog, in that unfigured and " colourless void of the eternal state Happy should we have been to have found any thing like the attempt, in the several classes of writers before us, to reconcile those discordant opinions and properly to appropriate a prophecy, rather a promise, unquestionably among the most interesting and animating in the whole book of God It is remarkable, as Mr Bayford has observed, that all the considerable prophecies of the Old Testament terminate in a similar description all strongly pointing to an union of the Jews and the Gentiles, flowing in, in their fulness to Millennial blessedness How then shall we be taught to view this blessedness or, if not ourselves permitted to witness upon earth the fulfilment of Millennial predictions, still to find our share in those exceeding great and precious promises by which " we may escape the corruptions of the world through lust, and become partakers of a Divine nature ? The answer to these questions will we believe, be most readily found in that well known principle of prophetic interpretation, the *double sense* — an hypothesis certainly not without difficulties, but which at present we shall venture to take for granted, it being the current hypothesis of the best divines, especially of those who have most deeply entered upon such discussions as the present Bishop Horsley in a most remarkable manner lays down this doctrine in his Sermons on 2 Pet i 20 and confesses his own former error, in imagining that prophecy in order to be a complete vindication of the proceedings of Divine Providence should have but *one* direct sense and one direct fulfilment " Thus, says he, ' I reasoned, till a patient investigation of the subject, by God's blessing brought me to a better mind Then, having mentioned one particular instance, he proceeds ' The application of the prophecy to any one of these events bears all the characteristics of a true interpretation,—consistence with the terms of the prophecy consistence with the prophetic system Every one of these events, therefore, must pass, with every true believer for a true fulfilment * How then shall we apply the principle here, but as it is applied by almost all expositors in Matthew xxiv, in Mark xiii, in Luke xvii and xxi ? We have there a description of the Jewish wars and the judgments on the Jewish nation and these are regarded as significant of the events of Christ's coming, and of the end of the world As we cannot clearly sever these events from each other, in the close connexion which binds them together throughout the whole tissue of those remarkable prophecies so it is as difficult to sever the delineation of the triumphs in reserve for the church of Christ, as found in the twenty first and twenty second chapters of Revelation from a further mystic development, in the same chapters, of final judgment a separation of the good and the bad and a transfer of the good

* Basilicus refers to Horsley for this double sense of prophecy as also to Lord Bacon—we presume where he speas of its springing and germinant accomplishment throughout many ages though the height or fulness refer to some one age (Advancement of Learning book ii Historic Prophetica) also where in speaking of the literal histories of the Jewish church Lord Bacon regards them as pregnant of a perpetual allegory and a shadow of the work of redemption to follow (Confession of Faith) —We think Bishop Horsley has a little scrupled the application of his own rule in the explanation of the end of the world but we are still more sure that Basilicus fails in the proper use of *his* inchoate and complete accomplishment of prophecy (p 70) in driving the glorious promises of eternal felicity into the Millennial age and there finally burrying them

into an eternal and unchangeable bliss.

The whole system of prophetic revelation is considered, by many eminent divines, as a gradual figurative development of ulterior events, by the means and through the medium of lesser temporal incidents. Thus the triumphs in Canaan foretell the triumphs of the Gospel: the literal Babylon foreshews the spiritual Babylon, or Antichrist: the first coming of Christ foreshews, in some remarkable way, his second coming "in like manner:" the sabbath on earth exhibits beforehand the heavenly rest. It would fall in with such an analogy if a sabbatical millenary of years on earth, in all the peaceful triumphs of Christian purity (we say not directly miraculous, but in the accelerated progression of the principles of the Gospel under the especial influence of its Divine Author) should predict and shadow out that eternal rest which yet remains for the people of God. We do not assert that the fact will be so—we profess our utter ignorance on the subject—but we urge the possibility, we may say the probability, on Scriptural grounds, as an answer to those who tell us that *their* view is the only one that can for a moment be entertained, after fairly weighing the evidence on the subject. We have no *strong* opinion, and we do not think Scripture warrants us to have one, respecting the nature, the extent, or the duration of the Millennial glory: but if we must adopt some hypothesis, the above is the most probable we can at present form.

The fact however is, some will tell us, that no accomplishment short of a literal Millennial resurrection and the splendours of an earthly Jerusalem, will meet the magnificence of prophetic delineation on this subject. But the fact is *we* would reply, that no accomplishment short of an exceeding and eternal weight of glory, can possibly meet, either the supposed predictions of Millennial bliss, or the actual promises of the blessedness of the righteous: "They shall reign FOR EVER AND EVER." It seems to us that Millennial writers magnify the intermediate stage of prophetic progress into a grandeur by no means designed—and a grandeur, after all, short lived, earthly, sensible and entirely, we may say, non descript—instead, rather, of first reducing that which is limited in its very nature and essence, keeping it within the natural bounds of all temporal events, and then stretching forth their eyes and their desires to that eternal glory which is beyond, of which indeed these temporary, these momentary, triumphs of a Millennial day give the outline, but which is really to be filled up in the beatific and eternal vision of God himself. We may justly regard the 21st and 22d chapters of the Revelations as 'a little book' of events in the church during the preceding predictions of the 20th chapter: but when we remember that this chapter itself stretches far *beyond* the bounds of time and space, even beyond the judgment of the great day, to the final destiny of man, it is strange indeed, in our view of the case, to limit this little "book of the church" *within* those bounds which the very prophecy it was to illustrate had palpably outstretched and overleaped.

And we must here remark, in alluding to other comments of controvertists on this point—whether Whitby, on the one hand, or Basilicus, &c (for here extremes meet) on the other—that one of the most dangerous tendencies of their expositions is to be found in a perfectly unscriptural limitation, as before hinted at, of future duration in reference to 'the ages to come,' "the end of the world," and other Scriptural expressions indicative of an unseen and unlimited eternity. The *present* judgment of Christ going on in the church and in the heart we quite understand. We can comprehend the extension of *that* by means of spiritual, and even miraculous effusions of the Holy

Spirit. We can imagine overwhelming temporal judgments, individual and national. We can picture to ourselves a reign of Christian principles, in consequence of these providential orderings, which shall realize all that still remains to be realized of the promises made respecting the progress of the Gospel, as relates both to the Jew and the Gentile. In this sense we can understand even literally, that " The meek shall inherit the earth and that, in the ages to come God shall make known the mystery of his Gospel, in a way in which it has hitherto failed of its promised success and promulgation among the nations of the earth. We can conceive all this and further, that in spite of all those terrific portraitures of still remaining disease and vicissitude, and death itself, to which Dr Burnet so pathetically alludes, this state of things would still become a little picture of heaven upon earth; that it would be redolent of Paradise, and that, to those who shall be happy enough to view those peaceful Millennial glories, it may be most truly said, " Blessed are the eyes which see the things which ye see: for many prophets, kings, and righteous men have desired to see the things which ye see, and have not seen them; and to hear the things that ye hear and have not heard them." In a sense which we might feebly realize perhaps, in our purer moments of *present* Christian communion, it shall then be said, " The tabernacle of God is with men, and he will dwell with them, and walk with them: and they shall be his people, and he will be their God:" and every spiritual promise, which we now realize to our comfort and sustentation in the worst of times, may then (if indeed it should appear to be needed) be habitually brought home with a power and efficacy to the heart after which we can only now thirst and aspire. Then, with double force, may the Apostle's sense, even of his own existing privileges at that time, be kindled up in the soul. " Ye are come unto mount Sion, and unto the city of the living God, the heavenly Jerusalem: and to an innumerable company of angels: to the general assembly and church of the first born, which are written in heaven: and to God the Judge of all: and to the spirits of just men made perfect: and to Jesus, the Mediator of the new covenant."—" We *receive* a kingdom which cannot be moved."

But when all this is to be taken off from the ground of things as they at present are, and to be *literalized*, or mystified, into some unknown Palingenesia, some Millennial—we will not, from respect to the subject, say—Utopia,

> Some safe retreat, in depths of woods embrac'd:
> Some happier island in the watery waste:

when " a humbler heaven is to be brought down to earth, and saints are to rise again and converse with bliss, and sinners to lie prostrate in a direct literal sense—just as we are told in Scripture shall be the case with both classes in the eternal world to come—we then foresee, with terror, the very consequence which Basilicus and others contemplate without any visible uneasiness, namely, that nothing which Scripture has said of the eternal state will be believed, or can be understood. Both good and bad having had, at least to a considerable extent, their rewards or their sufferings " in this life," no sufficient ground, that we can see, will remain for their future and eternal sentence: and we shall only have to reduce what is perfectly palpable and plain, to what is absolutely evanescent and inexplicable: and we shall contemplate alike without hope and without fear, the solemn and unalterable declaration, " These shall go away into EVERLASTING punishment: but the righteous into life ETERNAL."

If, recurring to our former remark we may proceed upon the

generally received opinion of a primary and a subordinate fulfilment of prophecy, and regard Millennial events as typical of Heavenly happiness, we would place the subordinate and secondary fulfilment of the twenty first and twenty second chapters of the Revelation on the same ground with those events. If we compare the still subsequent revival of anti-Christian principles, considered to be personified by Gog and Magog in the twentieth chapter, with the following verses in the twenty second chapter,— 'He that is unjust, let him be unjust still, and he which is filthy, let him be filthy still; and he that is righteous, let him be righteous still; and he that is holy, let him be holy still. And behold, I come quickly; and my reward is with me, to give every man according as his work shall be,'—we think ground would appear for assigning secondarily many predictions in both the twenty first and twenty second chapters to this our punctual spot of earth. And so far we may concede equally to the ratiocinative Whitby and the imaginative Basilicus.* But this very concession, if made, we imagine should give the death signal to all the magnificent theories of a new heaven and a new earth as coincident, in their fullest sense, with the glories of the Millennial reign. For how, according to any common or consistent view of *such* a change, are we to find in this renovated heaven and earth, the spawn, so to speak, of a nefarious crew, who are again to rise, and threaten, from the four corners of the earth, the very camp and temple of Jehovah himself? We can readily imagine the long suppression of baneful principles in unwilling outward subjection to the Gospel of Christ, like winds long pent bursting out at the end of a thousand years and pouring on the earth a flood of overflowing ungodliness and demoniacal malice,—an outpouring to be met by the Messiah himself in the flames of judgment, and by Him to be repelled and rolled back upon itself till it shall subside for ever in the lake that burneth with fire and brimstone. But where is Dr Burnet to find *his* Gog and Magog in the renovated earth, except, as he does find them "bred, like Bishop Taylor's tadpoles, 'in slime, and mud of Nilus?' And where is Joseph Mede to find them, but in a most difficult invention, either surviving the Millennial fires or,—in short he knows not where. And where does Mr Bayford find them, but, as he charitably supposes, in a backsliding race of true Millennarian saints, who are to be brought back with rod and stripes from their transgressions? But the topic is *almost wholly* passed *sub silentio* by all modern Millennarians, especially, with small exception, by the fervid author of Palingenesia and of Basilicus's Letters, and by the Humble Expectant. That very omission is ominous. The placing this new irruption of blasphemy and crime after the Millennium by Scripture itself is ominous and portends, surely, the intention of the Spirit to establish a doctrine which neither reasoning nor silence can overthrow: namely, that the events of the Millennium are simply concurrent with the present constitution of God's providential government in his church, and but an increase and completion of the earthly kingdom and judgment of the Messiah established at his first coming in human flesh.

The same principles of inchoate fulfilment will very properly apply to the perpetual commentary on the 'ages to come,' 'the world to come,' &c. the αιων, αιωνες, and

---

* It appears by chap. xx. 9 that after the expiration of the thousand years Gog and Magog went up on the breadth of the earth and compassed the camp of the saints about and the beloved city. If this be that great city the Holy Jerusalem a church state on earth must be intended by the last chapters of the Apocalypse for how are Gog and Magog or any other enemies on earth to encompass the mansions of the blessed above? Basilicus, p. 45.

the αιωνιος, on which many have made ill favoured attempts in all ages. We consider these, in their fullest sense, applicable to eternity alone. In a secondary or subordinate sense, we will not say they may not be applicable to *other* ages, typical of the final consummation: and, amongst others, to the age of the Millennium itself: an age of triumph in the church, opposed to, but correspondent with, its previous age of sackcloth and sorrow.

But we hasten to another text, on which is built the Discourse on 'The Day of God' (No. 3 on our list), of which we may now perhaps find a sufficient ground laid for us to offer some illustration. Should any reader have travelled thus far with us, he will find we have endeavoured to establish (and it is all we have endeavoured to establish) two very plain and intelligible, and we are firmly convinced scriptural, notions—namely a grand spiritual extension of Christian principles during the course of the predicted Millennium (without pretending to define what length of time is comprised in that prophetic numeral, or when, or how, it shall commence or end) and a still subsequent era of *eternal* blessedness shadowed out perhaps by that former revival, but separated from it by the actual resurrection and final judgment. Now apply these two notions to the text of our Millennial discourser—taken however long before his time by Joseph Mede himself—from 2 Peter iii. 11—13. Seeing then that all these things shall be dissolved what manner of persons ought ye to be in all holy conversation and godliness, looking for and hasting unto the coming of the day of God wherein the heavens being on fire shall be dissolved and the elements shall melt with fervent heat, nevertheless we, according to his promise, look for new heavens and a new earth, wherein dwelleth righteousness. We have here, according to the discourse, a distinct order laid down. 1st, of the coming of the day of God. 2d, of the dissolution of this present frame of things by fire: and, 3d, the creation of new heavens and a new earth, wherein dwelleth righteousness. And the new heavens and new earth being assumed to be the Millennial period described in Rev. xxi. and xxii. the whole passage is used, to force upon us a notion, equally necessary to the literal Millennarians with the first resurrection itself, of *certain penal or purgatorial fires*, preparatory to a state of earthly blessedness in the new Millennial Jerusalem. But how does this appear when we apply the two notions above? why, simply thus: that as the Millennial type, if a type it be, *precedes* the fires of the last judgment: so the heavenly reality the eternal consummation of all things *succeeds* them: and whereas the new Jerusalem of the Apocalypse had been so described as to answer *both* the asserted type and the reality, the new heavens and earth of St. Peter are so constructed as to look more particularly to the reality, to heaven itself, the Christian's hope, the state of everlasting felicity and everlasting righteousness. We deny not however that, even *preparatory* to the Millennium certain strokes of judgment certain effusions of wrath may take place, themselves emblematical of the eternal judgment—just as the Jewish overthrow itself prefigured the end of the world. And we are not unprepared to allow, that in this case the order of the Apostle *could* be verified, according to the 'Discourser's own plan.

It must be acknowledged that our present search into the scriptural records of the unknown future, is necessarily, from the very principles we have assumed in this discussion, as well as from our limits, a bare suggestion of hints. We can scarcely expect to satisfy any party, on a subject in which we should even think it rashness to be satisfied ourselves: although on a review and a re-review of all the works before us we are not aware of overlooking any strength of scriptural appeal made with confidence on either side. We have taken especial pains to decipher, if possible, and enter into the mind of Basilicus, in his seven epistolary communications to the Jewish Expositor: and we must really say, that we are yet scarcely resolved whether he intends to assert any thing beyond ordinary Millennarianism, respecting the glorious epiphany, Titus ii. 13; the first resurrection, Rev. xx. 5; the end of the world, Matt. xxviii. 20; the world to come, Heb. ii. 5; the restitution of all things, Acts iii. 21; the kingdom of Israel, Acts i. 6;—which are his six palmary texts and topics—or whether his more prudent design is to throw out general scriptural hints in connexion with these *loci*, and to leave his readers to work their way as they can to their own conclusion. At the same time, it is very clear that he has a great objection to the *generally prevailing idea*, upon which we have attempted already to illustrate some of these favoured common places.

The most prevailing idea is that a great extension of the spiritual kingdom of Christ will take place towards the close of the Christian dispensation: at the end of which Christ will appear in person as the Judge of quick and dead: when the general resurrection; the dissolution of the material universe; the condemnation of the wicked; and the translation of the church to the glories of heaven will take place together—and these things are perhaps invariably viewed in connection with such expressions in sacred Scripture as 'the end of the world,' 'the world to come,' 'the day of judgment,' 'the kingdom of heaven,' &c. &c. Basil. p. 31.

And his own view, as opposed to this, appears to be that of referring to other more *distinct circumstances* in the *regal* dispensation of the Son of Man which had not been realized at his first advent: and these circumstances are

1st. The salvation of Judah and Israel. 2d. The restoration of the ten tribes. 3d. The gathering of the Jews out of all countries. 4th. The settlement of them in their own country to be pulled up no more. 5th. The universal establishment of Christianity. 6th. The entire destruction of the monarchies of the metal image and the enemies of the church. 7th. The unity of the doctrine and uniformity of Christian worship. Basil. p. 64.

If this be the main difference between us, we have thrown away much time and trouble to reconcile *agreements* made to our hands: for what discord is there between Basilicus and Whitby, and (except so far as respects a *literal* restoration of Israel and Judah) between Basilicus and every Millennary or Antimillennary, who reads his Bible, in the whole Christian world? But the truth is, our worthy disputant is not satisfied with that "*unity of doctrine and uniformity of Christian worship*" which are the essential and only assignable blessedness of any terrestrial Millennium, except he also be permitted to conjoin them with those outward and visible circumstances—an apparent Saviour, a resplendent throne, a golden city, a nightless day, a deathless body, renovated nature: and, in short, every attribute of the heavenly state itself,—which never can be, consistently with general principles of Scripture, attributed to this lower world. Take out these notions, eradicate their influence, in each remote ramification, upon the statement of the argument before us: and we should find comparatively little to reply to Basilicus, or he to us. Leave these lurking behind, and we have then lengthened grounds for a long, it may be a *millennial* discussion.

To these notions we have to attribute, what is sufficiently manifest, numerous perversions of Scripture, such as we have alluded to before, and such as those which follow:—

Who shall be punished with *everlasting* destruction from *the presence** of the Lord and from the glory of his power, applied to the *temporary* judgments of the Millennium, and to the temporary presence of Him " before whose *face**: it is said, ' heaven and earth fled away' at the final judgment, Rev. xx. 11 (§ 1 Glorious Epiphany, p. 9.)—

---

* απο προσωπ in both places.

"The dead in Christ shall rise first," made a distinction between the righteous and the wicked whereas in 1 Thess iv 16, 17, it is clearly a distinction between the *different servants* of God, those that "are dead in Christ, and those that "are alive and remain till the coming of the Lord (§ 2 First Resurrection, p 22)—In the same section, p 24, the intermediate blessedness is called "an exceeding and *eternal* weight of glory and "the righteous" are promised to "shine like the stars, but without the proper textual addition by the prophet, "*for ever and ever*, Dan xii —Also, in the same section, Matt xxv 31 & seq is properly applied to the last judgment, but against the opinion of a brother Millennary, who makes "Then shall the King say," "Then shall the King answer," to be *Millennial* acts (Day of God, p 15) and against his own in p 59, where the "coming of the Son of Man in his glory is made the same with his kingdom to come, or Millennial kingdom—Again 'Lo I am with you alway, even unto the end of the world, is allowed to be a spiritual not personal presence yet is *translated*, by mere assumption, to mean a personal as well as spiritual presence (§ 3 End of the World, p 35)—In the following section, angels are represented as worshipping the First Begotten only whilst seated on his mediatorial throne during the Millennium, during which time alone the address is considered applicable to him, "Thy throne O God, is for ever and ever whereas the angels are represented as adoring the Lamb previous to opening the seals nay, when God brought his First Begotten into the world at his birth, a multitude of the heavenly host attended and celebrated the event (§ 4 The World to come, p 39)—The figurative use of the new heavens and the new earth in Isa lxv 17 confessed to *appear* figurative, is yet distorted to a literal sense on the assumption that its use in 2 Peter iii is literal though the very contrary might have been far better assumed for the prophet with respect to the latter passage in St Peter (§ 5 Restitution of all Things, p 48).—In § 6, on the Kingdom of Israel, it is impossible to confine ourselves to one misconstruction of Scripture when the whole proceeds on an absolute denial, of what is absolutely *asserted* over and over again in Scripture, viz that Christ was exalted with great power to his kingdom in heaven at his ascension, to be a "Prince, as well as Saviour, of whose kingdom there shall be no end This kingdom is by Basilicus made to begin and end with the Millennium "*In the days* of these kings shall the God of heaven set up a kingdom which shall *never* be destroyed which is explained by Basilicus to be, *After the days* of these kings a kingdom is to be set up, which *they* shall not destroy (to be sure not), but which shall come to destroy them *upon* the utter destruction of the last p 60.—"*These* things, we are told, p 66, "the disciples understood not at the first nor any one we believe else only what *they* did not understand, nor Basilicus either, was *this*, the plain scriptural truth, "Fear not, daughter of Zion, behold, THY KING COMETH, sitting on *an ass's colt*, John xii 10

For ourselves, we shall only add, that as nothing can answer the visible display of "the King sitting on the throne of his glory, short of the grand ceremonial of the last day, when "before Him shall be gathered all nations so nothing can exemplify the *present* reign of Christ, and his judgment upon earth, so fully as that first figurative resurrection of his saints to reign with him on the earth shewing, as it will that he can master, even "on this plat of ground on this present earth, and with the natural resources of his kingdom, the great foe for a thousand years We once had hoped that Mr Bayford, in his Messiah's Kingdom, had meant no other than this in the following passage which we quote in our *own* sense with much approbation, but from which he soon digresses into all the maze of Millennial abstractions, never to return.

The Lord Jesus Christ, God over all, blessed for ever was manifested that he might destroy the works of the devil, and doubtless Satan's power over the mind, the will, the affections and the flesh of man is amongst the works to be destroyed. Unless this be accomplished before all flesh shall pass away how can the Lord be glorified in his saints? How can it be shewn what manner of persons the Lord's people ought to be, and shall approve themselves in all holiness of life and conversation?—Except during the period when our first parents dwelt in the garden of Eden and walked before their Lord in peace and in love blameless, the glory and perfection of man in the flesh or in his time state have never been seen in the beauty of their creation. Ever since the fall the flesh or mundane condition of man has been exhibited only as filthy, hateful to God, odious and defiled by sin, and under the power of the prince of darkness. The ground too cursed for man's sake hath brought forth thorns and thistles, and the very air he breathes conveys to him the seeds of pestilence, disease and death. The wicked of the earth rule over it, and all the desirable and pleasant things of creation which remain, seem left only to gratify the passions and to administer to the vices of the vilest and basest of mankind who not content with turning to evil purpose all the good things which have been provided for their use, with perseverance the most insidious and cruelty the most unrelenting have continually employed themselves in striving to pervert Jehovah's truth and to wear out and to destroy the saints of the Most High God. We might conjecture that our gracious Lord would not allow all flesh to pass away and to perish under the dominion of the evil one without bringing forth some better things than are to be seen under a dispensation like the present. His tender mercies are over all his works. And shall he not at length shew mercy and deliver man from the power of sin and Satan? Shall not man one day be brought to serve and to obey his Creator? If revelation were silent, reason might suggest an answer; but blessed be His name the question is not left for reason: the gracious purpose of the Redeemer is plainly declared in the words of unerring truth; for the times of the restitution of all things — the times of refreshing from the presence of the Lord, and the adoption, to wit, the redemption of the body are spoken of as amongst the blessings prepared for them that love him. In these glorious and happy days Jerusalem shall be made a rejoicing and her people a joy, the voice of weeping shall no more be heard, nor the voice of crying. They shall build houses and inhabit them, and they shall plant vineyards, and eat the fruit of them. They shall not labour in vain, nor bring forth trouble; for they are the seed of the blessed of the Lord, and their offspring with them. And Jerusalem shall be called a city of truth, and the mountain of the Lord of Hosts the holy mountain. The tabernacle of God shall be with men and he will dwell with them, and they shall be his people, and God himself shall wipe away all tears from their eyes. Messiah's Kingd. pp. 4—6.

Another very lamentable effect of this *material* Millennium, is the necessity it induces for professing to disregard *practical effects*. Of all unintelligible perversions of Scripture by Basilicus, the greatest surely is that which, under this head, makes the devil himself preach practical effects to Eve, as a lure to the forbidden fruit: 'and which is to be a warning to ourselves how we meddle with practical consequences' (p. 81.) The test established for the detection of false prophets by Him who came to destroy the works of the devil was this, "By their fruits ye shall know them"—a text acutely explained by the late Mr. Venn to mean, not so much the mere conduct of the prophet himself, as the conduct produced by his doctrine—and this test, after all, it appears that Basilicus is no less ready to adopt than his opponents, and indeed to enforce with no small urgency not only on ministers of the Gospel, but on the members of the church of Christ in general.

It is an observation suggested by a superficial view of human life and confirmed by common experience that, objects indefinite and distant do not affect the mind or influence the conduct of individuals: whereas distinctness of apprehension and proximity of attainment command immediate notice and excite practical exertion. The Christian church at large exemplifies the remark. The day of judgment, the resurrection of the dead, the world to come, even the recovery of Israel, and the latter day glory of the church, are subjects so confounded by indistinct conceptions of their nature and relative connection that hitherto they have rarely made a suitable impression on the mind, and some of them are placed at such an immoderate distance as to be scarcely perceptible to the eye of rational enquiry. Education, habit, and prejudice have concurred with a common understanding among men to leave these matters to their own generalities and supposed impenetrable obscurity. The general pleas of presumption, enthusiasm, self delusion, and the like, are advanced and admitted as sufficient to stifle at once any pretensions to nicer investigation and advanced discovery. Thus even believers remain in a state of nonage, babes for the most part in divine attainments, and have need to be taught again the rudiments of a science in which, considering the age in which they were born and the times in which their lot is cast, they ought to be instructors to their generation. Basil, p. 97.

This, then, may suitably introduce the very strong views of Mr. Jones on the opposite side, on this very head of practical consequences. After having alluded to the above sentiments from Basilicus, in his sermon on Matt. xxv. 31, 32, & seq. giving the plain and direct view of the general judgment from those words, in opposition to the Millennarian statements, he proceeds, in speaking of these last

They who do conscientiously subscribe to these views—for I am now supposing the case of a decided reception and an honest consistent avowal of them—must as decidedly dissent from views and sentiments which run directly counter to their own. As it is well known that these are not the expectations of the Christian Church, but only of a very small part of it, they cannot otherwise than believe that the bulk of professing Christians are deluding themselves with false hopes and expectations which can never be realized. These are not the doctrines of the Church of England, and accordingly her Creeds, Articles, Homilies, and Liturgical Services must surely appear to them at best mere amalgamations of truth and falsehood.—Lastly, their own views of the last judgment being so entirely at variance with the obvious and literal sense of the passage before us—this passage one would think must be considered by them much more calculated to betray ordinary Christians into error than to lead them into truth. Jones, pp. 26, 27.

And again

This system appears—

(1.) To give a weight to the arguments and a sanction to the opinions of those who deny or call in question the eternity of future punishments. And that such is indeed the case, who can remain in doubt after what has been already said? If the kingdom which believers will inherit at the second advent of Christ be a state of limited duration, then contradictory as it may seem, the everlasting fire prepared for the devil and his angels is limited also.

But let us beware how we thus any of us trifle with eternity. The doctrines of an eternal heaven and of an eternal hell are not to be trifled with, unless it can be proved that they are cunningly devised fables. Neither are they who maintain these doctrines to be almost regarded with contempt, unless it can be fairly shewn that they have no warrant in Scripture for doing so. Here, however, a question may easily be anticipated — Who even doubts respecting the doctrines in question? To which it is replied — Who is even charged with either denying or doubting them? But nevertheless, whatever be our own private views upon the subject, it behoves us to beware how either directly or indirectly we give our sanction to those who want not for inclination, if only the power and opportunity were offered them, to shake the pillars of Christianity, to undermine the foundation of our faith, and to pierce the very vitals of our holy religion.

(2.) There is also a tendency in this system to carnalize our views of heaven and of heavenly things, and in a great degree to bring these down to a level with the natural capacities of unregenerate men. Suppose now the case of a truly spiritually minded Christian, of one who has experienced some foretaste and earnest of that fulness of joy which is in God's presence and of those pleasures which are at his right hand for evermore; of one who has hitherto habitually contemplated Heaven rather as a state than as a place,—viz. as a state of absolute deliverance from all sin, of freedom from all sorrow, of nearness to God, and of complete conformity to his likeness; and who has accordingly considered such to be the happiness held out to believers in the Scriptures as the object of joyful hope and holy anticipation.—The very soul of such an one must surely revolt at the low and grovelling conceptions of the Millenarian respecting a temporal dispensation upon earth. Nor is it difficult to imagine how from his heart he would pity the man who has nothing better than a millennial happiness to constitute the sum and substance of his hopes, and the ne plus ultra of his expectations and prospects.

This leads me to mention another result and consequence necessarily arising out of this system, the last to which I shall now allude, and which of all others is the most to be deprecated.

(3.) It leaves us no solid foundation on which to build our hopes of immortal glory.—Millenarians represent the king dom of Christ upon earth as contra-distinguished from, and as absolutely opposed to, an eternal state. They represent it as strictly temporal and not only as limited but as specifically limited to an exact period, which the very word Millennium (the name by which they designate it) implies.

"To this strictly temporal state they continually apply without the least apology words and phrases expressive of eternal duration if indeed there are any words in language of this import — but if Millenarians are right there are not for their whole system goes to cut away even from Scripture itself the doctrine of eternity root and branch Jones pp 31—33

On this, and the perversions of Scripture to which Mr Jones proceeds, we have ourselves enlarged and, on a view of the whole, we must again express our own sense of the great hazard attending these opinions and *that*, however sanctioned by a few names of great men, who, perhaps by looking into past prophecies, and comparing them with past events, may have contracted a habit of looking into futurity with a view to similar analogies, which from the very nature of prophecy are absolutely inadmissible* Our feeling is plainly this, that, in regard to what is past, clear exposition of Scripture, and comparison of historical events with prophecy, are the points to aim at but in regard to things future, "indistinct conceptions of their nature and relative connexion are all that we can hope to obtain or that is necessary for Christian edification It is not for a moment to be imagined, as Basilicus so strongly insists, that St Paul derived any portion of his edifying exhortations from the dis-

* Joseph Mede e g and Bishop Newton whose tone of discussion however we have sufficiently exhibited Mr Faber we cannot but consider as a great exception whose sentiments with those of Mr Cuninghame we should scarely collect from their writings on this subject And when we consider such names as Scott or among living writers Simeon, Gauntlett, Cooper &c either keeping silence or speaking clearly though humbly against the literal Millennium we cannot too strongly censure the rash boldness of the opposite statements and wish at least it may proceed no farther

tinctness or proximity of the Millennium as apart from the general resurrection. The Jews, before Christ, had lamentably distinct conceptions of their own *carnal* Jerusalem in prospect of a reigning and a glorious Messiah and the first Christians, led by Papias, may have imbibed, and did imbibe, some pardonable but unsafe notions from those Apocryphal sources But to what of distinctness or proximity had St Paul to appeal in the Millennium, for encouragement or for warning (except only, as Mr Nesbit would exclusively have it, Christ s coming in judgment on the Jewish nation), which *we* have not, in our advanced period of the world, from the general resurrection?

If, indeed, the Apostolic converts did expect *any near* events, they were checked at once by the Apostle, for mistaking his word, or letter, to have meant that the day of Christ was at hand The result proves in that case their expectation to have been vain And were they *distinct* in their apprehensions? Then the question of practical effects (if from those we are to collect what it is they *did* apprehend) still reverts to this, whether the expectation of a heavenly happiness reduced and brought down to earth, and to a period of a thousand years, is likely to have been more operative upon those of old, and to be more operative upon ourselves, than the expectation of an eternal blessedness in heaven itself? What would there have been more encouraging to the ancient martyr, in the idea, that he alone was to rise, and reign for a thousand years on this earth, the scene of all his woes and tortures and temptations than in the hope that he should meet with *all* his fellow-creatures, and all his enemies, face to face, on one great and solemn day, to receive before each other, and *for ever*, their just and appropriate sentence? Surely, if this were still to be delayed, expectation would be yet suspended, and hope yet deferred Millennial blessedness, though far too short, would appear too long. We should have another cry from around the altar at Jerusalem "How long, O Lord, wilt thou not avenge the blood of thy servants which is shed? how long wilt thou not awake, and come to the consummation of all things, the very sentence itself of the eternal judgment?" "The eonian [not eternal] judgment," we still hear Basilicus reiterating that which shall last throughout the eon, or αιων, of the thousand years. Be it so: that this *present* judgment of the world by a Saviour invisible, yet reigning and judging amongst us, shall then be continued, enlarged, and verified. Let us but suppose it a judgment of principles, a prevalence of Christian principles throughout the world, for all that privileged and happy period, and what will not be its effect to present edification, and to present calls of duty? We have then, under this view, an assurance that the graces, now sparingly administered, in answer to our feeble prayers, shall one day be "poured out upon all flesh." We have then the hope, that the Divine word, now unhappily, even now, too closely bound, by the folly and inconsistency of Christians, shall at length go forth, free as air and lightsome as the sun, to every nation and kingdom under the whole heaven. We believe that then shall be made to appear the wisdom of those principles which men rejected, and the world despised, even as they had despised and rejected Him who gave them to the world. It shall be seen and felt, that the service of God is indeed perfect freedom and "wisdom shall be justified of all her children." Then may we expect the great mystery of godliness to be more fully expanded, and the secrets of the Divine counsels more brightly exhibited: men to walk more closely with God, and God to converse spiritually with men, as man talketh with his fellow. Then may we, doubtless, look for the more extended principles of a Divine charity: Christians, though of a different complexion of body, or cast of mind, yet meeting around one common altar, to worship their common God and common Lord: "the wolf and the lamb feeding together and "none hurting nor destroying in all the holy mountain of the Lord."—As sin removes, the curse removes: and it were difficult to say, how far the virtues of a temperate prime or of maturer life, the calm of passion, and the subjection of baneful appetites, might serve even to exhaust the remnants of bodily infirmity, and smooth the visage and the stroke of death.

With such prospects before us, which might be carried to an unlimited extent, can we but say, in Apostolic language "what manner of persons ought we to be in all holy conversation and godliness!" We may not live to see the glorious fulfilment: but we may help it forward with our labours and our prayers. We may not share on earth the blessings of a full development of Christian principles: but we may look down upon it, with holy and godlike satisfaction, from the higher elevation of the intermediate state of bliss and praise. We may even now be permitted to hail the dawning of that brighter day. We shall assuredly awake to behold its *setting* glories, as they yield to the still more rich and glorious brightness of the general resurrection. To this, as to a hope still higher and better, Millennial saints will be themselves aspiring. Heaven by them, will be only seen more brightly in its type: and enough of imperfection will still remain to invite their expectations to that "glory yet to be revealed:" till at length that glorious morn shall beam, when those who sleep in the dust shall *literally* awake: when the mystery shall be all revealed: when "we shall all be changed, in a moment, in the twinkling of an eye, at the last trump: when "the trumpet shall sound, and the dead shall be raised incorruptible, and we shall be changed"

We have but little space, and our readers of course less patience, for remarks, in conclusion, respecting the general bearing of the subject upon the aspect of prophecy, and the individual feelings of the Christian mind. Of the latter we have already, in a measure, spoken. In point of *prospects*, as furnishing a motive for exertion, we think we have made it clear, that a prospect of blessedness perfect and eternal *at once*, cannot be less encouraging to the Christian labourer, or Christian sufferer, than one of a thousand years duration, imperfect at first, and of *unknown* event at last. On the other hand, we think we have represented *certain* Millennial hopes as highly edifying, and as affording confirmation to the present wisdom of our choice, if Christians indeed, by assuring us that God will vindicate that wisdom in his own good time, nay, upon 'this plat of ground will shew it forth, and 'make his righteousness as clear as the light, his judgment as the noon day.' To imitate Millennial virtues, to help them forward by our own practice, and by our example, perhaps widely influential must be, doubtless, our high and happy and grateful endeavour, when we truly believe their promised accomplishment, and that 'not one of those good things will fail which God hath promised, all will come to pass.' The heathen poet himself makes his hero rejoice at the prospect of other souls rising again to enjoy a renovated country and more extended glories.

Has equidem memorare tibi atque ostendere coram
Jampridem hanc prolem cupio enumerare meorum
Quò magis Italia tandem *lætere* reperta
Æneid vi. 716

But there is one point, both with respect to the feelings of individual Christians and the general aspect of prophecy, to which, if our space allowed, we might have directed a short attention—namely, the due arrangement and proper application of Missionary efforts. "To the Jew first, and also to the Gentile* for there is no respect of persons with God" seems to be our stand

* This priority had reference chiefly to the first offer of the Gospel to the two classes, and will not, of course, by any person be construed as the rule for Christian exertions in the present or future ages. The Christian missionary will consider in every instance what is the most pressing case, and what are the most apparently favourable openings for his pious exertions, and will view these as Providential directions for his conduct, rather than any conclusions of his own, be they true or false, respecting the future designs of God, or the interpretation of unfulfilled prophecy. There is room enough in a world of sin and misery for all our efforts, and it appears to us to be little short of a snare of the tempter to set us speculating when we should be working, to be puzzling ourselves with questions of date and geography when we ought to be proceeding, in simple faith and humility to do good and communicate the Gospel, whether to Jew or to Gentile, as occasion offers and a sense of duty prompts. Some, it seems, will do nothing for the ignorant, the long oppressed and anti-Christian Jew, because, forsooth, according to their reveries (what better can we call them?) on God's secret dispensations, the time is not come. Others—we certainly do not include the chief friends of the Jews' Society, than whom none are more hearty in the cause of missions to the Heathen—but individuals there are who feel their active zeal for their Gentile brethren greatly diminished, from an opinion that the time is not come, on the other side, that the Jews are to be the chief appointed missionaries to the Gentiles, and that to labour for the latter till the former are called in, is of little use. We consider such speculations not only unfruitful but highly dangerous. In the minds of a few eminently religious men they may be and are neutralized by other principles, but to the great body of mankind they are fraught with various injurious practical consequences, of which harassing their minds, perplexing their faith, and impeding their benevolent efforts are among the number. During the late war, some Christians were in danger of losing their patriotism and loyalty by their prophetic speculations; and it has even been urged, and that not merely by sceptical slave traders or slave holders who took up the argument as a supposed excellent weapon to annoy those whom they chose to call "the Saints," but by some really sincere, though certainly not very enlightened Christians, whether the prophetic imprecations respecting Ham ought not to unnerve our efforts in the cause of the oppressed tribes of Africa. We surely need add nothing further on

and rule, our comprehensive duty, and, we must add, at this time our appropriate and hopeful call. If any thing is made out more clearly than another, by the concurrent voice of all prophecy, and of almost all interpretation of prophecy, it is the conversion of the *Jewish* nation to the Christian faith. "Again I will build thee and thou shalt be built, O virgin of Israel: thou shalt again be adorned with thy tabrets and shalt go forth in the dances of them that make merry." This surely may be food enough, and wholesome food, for the Millennarians to feed upon conceded by the most scrupulous and most able of their opponents, and strengthening the hands and hearts of all to join with them in their heartiest labours for the house of Israel. Divine Providence has innumerable resources, and varieties of working, of which our poor and low philosophy may have never dreamt. But in the signs of the present times there is nothing to discourage the hope that the peculiar resources of the Gospel kingdom may suffice to bring on that wished for, that earnestly looked and longed for event which shall be as "life from the dead" to the whole world. We are not now called to enumerate particulars, but we rejoice in placing only two interesting statements at the head of our article, indicative of the known disposition of Gentile Christians, and of corresponding dispositions in their elder brethren of the Jewish faith, well nigh already promising at no great distance of time, a union of both together in one bond as the children of faithful Abraham. From the North, at Manchester, we hear the Rev Mr Burton urging upon us, at the public baptism of 'a Jew and his two children,' and in concurrence with the views of "Newcome and Tillotson, of Horsley, Newton, Hurd, Mede, Lightfoot, Butler, and innumerable others," that of

'the conversion and universal restoration of the Jews there remains now no question. It admits neither conjecture nor hypothesis. We need not fear to develope every obstacle and difficulty with which the case is fraught and to look at the subject in its darkest attitude. We may admit the blindness and hardness of their hearts — their pre-eminence in guilt, wretchedness and infatuation —we may anticipate the cold reception to which we their despisers and scorners are entitled —we may calculate on the reproach the desertion and the persecution to which the converted Jew must be obnoxious — we may expect unbelieving timid bystanders to ask Can these dry bones live ?—But it is at once replied He who directs the gale of life and salvation says Prophesy. What is impossible with men is possible with God — The vail shall be taken away —Yea God is able to graff them in again.' Burton p 4.

From the West we hear, in corresponding strains, at Plymouth, a pleasing statement, by the Rev Mr Hatchard, of an open avowal and profession of Christian principles in baptism, made by 'a late Reader in the Jewish Synagogue.' An interesting document, appended to the sermon, contains the simple account of himself by this same "Israelite indeed," and abundantly indicates what might be expected should many such be awakened to testify to their brethren in the flesh the Gospel of the grace of God.

Times and seasons we have been earnestly desirous of considering as placed in God's hands, and at his bidding. This makes us careful, on the other hand, to impress on the minds of many sanguine writers, who, like Mr Faber (see his Anniversary Sermon for the Jews Society for 1822), have written and preached most strongly on the priority of Jewish conversion before the coming in of Gentile fulness, that the certainty, the point blank directness of prophecy, is not discernible *here*, which *had* appeared in the former case. It is a matter of calculation, on which calculators will and may differ, that the time is at hand. It

the subject to render every considerate reader careful not to injure himself or if not himself his less considerate neighbour by these worse than doubtful disputations is a matter of interpretation, on the details of which interpreters will and may be divided, that the Jews must bring in the fulness of the Gentiles: but it is matter of worse than doubtful disputation, whether that fulness must wait, and the labours for maturing it be suspended, *until* the time when all Israel shall have been saved. Here again we say, "Work whilst it is day." "Testify, both to the Jews and also to the Greeks, repentance toward God and faith toward our Lord Jesus Christ." Wherever a soul is to be saved, wherever a nation is to be called to the knowledge of the true God, and of Jesus Christ whom he hath sent, there does our calling as Christians extend: there it is the revealed "will" of God that "all should be saved, and come to the knowledge of the truth." In this line of remark we are not disposed to continue a single moment longer than to say, that all has been anticipated by one to whose encouragement no testimony of ours, though heartily offered, could add any thing beyond the peaceful reflections of his own conscience, the sunshine of the mind, or rather the abiding consciousness of an unceasing Providence over the sphere of his ever growing and ever pleasing labours in the cause of Christian missions. We allude to a little practical work on the subject of prophecy by the Rev. E. Bickersteth, whose concessions and whose monitions are equally appropriate, and doubly edifying from his own example.

It is to be feared, says he, that some who are warm friends to missions among the heathen have not sufficient faith with regard to efforts among the Jews and think it almost a hopeless undertaking. But is not this directly contrary to the plain argument of the Apostle on this very point: — They also if they abide not in unbelief shall be grafted in: for God is able to graft them in. For if thou wert cut out of the olive tree which is wild by nature and wert grafted contrary to nature into a good olive tree how much more shall these which be the natural branches be grafted into their own olive-tree? Rom. xi. 23, 24.

' The promised future conversion of the Jews with its effects on the world, should both encourage our hopes and excite our labours for them. This duty is brought before us in the statement of God's design in their present unbelief—

They have now not believed that through your mercy they also may obtain mercy. Rom. xi. 31.

There are other points respecting this subject on which Christians have been more divided and to which it may be desirable briefly to advert.

The priority of the general conversion of the Jews to that of the Gentiles has been much discussed. It appears to be left just in that obscurity in which it is in many respects desirable it should be, that Christians may not pay an exclusive attention to either or labour for the benefit of one to the neglect of the other. Plausible arguments have been urged on both sides of the question. Are they not concurrent events? Only let us consider the vastness of the scene of labour and the immense work to be accomplished and we shall see how easily both may be advancing at the same time and mutually promoting each other. Very small is at present the real church of Christ: a very large progress may be made in the purification of the church and the conversion of the world before the Jews are gathered into the fold of Christ: and yet quite enough may be left after their conversion to realize the assured hope that that event shall be as life from the dead to the world. On this point then le not the friend of the Jew or the Gentile use expressions which may have any tendency to damp that little flame of zeal which as yet far too sparingly and too partially burns for the salvation of either. Bickersteth pp. 15—17.

We are forced to conclude with only a most summary notice of those summary discourses on prophecy in general or on the Apocalypse in particular, which are placed at the head of this article under the names of Gauntlett and Davison. Of Mr. Gauntlett we must content ourselves with saying, that his endeavour has been to cause "the wise to understand the bearing of the Apocalyptic prophecies upon these times, when we are warranted, by every view of Scripture, in believing that their fulfilment is approaching." His object has been to bring them out of the abstruse didactic form in which they have been usually enveloped, and to shew them to an ordinary congregation in the familiar dress of consecutive discourses in doing which he has availed himself of the labours of all the great prophetic pioneers who have gone before him and has affixed practical notices, as well as given a general practical turn to speculations hitherto lost too much in abstraction while he has adhered very closely to that view of the Apocalyptic Millennium itself which we have feebly endeavoured to shew, in our remarks above, to be at least both scriptural and tending to edification. It may be a satisfaction to the readers on prophecy to know that Mr. Gauntlett has followed the usual interpretation of the Seals making them with Mede, Newton, and Faber, emblematical of the secular affairs of the church previous to Constantine not, with Wodehouse and Cuninghame, of the whole series of spiritual affairs from the first to the latest period of Christian history, terminated by the Millennium. And here, perhaps, the principle of *inchoate* or *secondary* fulfilment of prophecy, might serve his view and we might find, in the somewhat Millennial terms which close the sixth seal in chapter vii, a prediction of events at an early period calculated to *adumbrate* the fuller manifestation of Gospel blessings in the true Millennium, as that adumbrates in its turn the eternal glories of Heaven itself. Mr. Gauntlett knows nothing of a far more fanciful application, adopted, we observe, by Mr. Bayford, of the addresses to the seven churches in Asia as if *they* contained a series of prophetic admonitions in succession corresponding to the successive periods and supposed vicissitudes of the Christian church. We shall only mention further, that his view of the period of the Millennium brings it to nearly about the great millennial sabbatism of the world, in the two thousandth year of the Christian era and with much force and interest he suggests the arrangement of intermediate events, commencing with Mr. Faber's date of 1866 for the actual commencement of the destruction of Antichrist. In the anticipation of all that shall succeed—those notes of discord, that shall be necessary to introduce the grand Millennial chorus—we may well exclaim with the entranced prophet of olden time, "who shall live when God doeth this!"

The following extract may perhaps be acceptable to the readers of prophecy bearing upon our own politico religious prospect, as it regards times of trouble and depression yet to come. It is on the threatened death of the two witnesses to the Christian faith, which is made by Mr. Gauntlett and we believe by some others, still *future*, and nothing short of a threatened suppression for a time of all evangelical testimony previous to its triumphant resurrection and figurative ascent into the Millennial heaven.

No event has hitherto occurred of sufficient magnitude and importance and of apparent definitiveness to correspond with the terms of the prophecy which seem to announce a general death of the witnesses (Rev xi 7—10) in all parts of the western Roman empire. The testimony of the witnesses against idolatry and popery through the whole western empire for the space of 1260 years, is the immediate subject of the prophecy and till this testimony is generally suppressed, the witnesses are not slain. But it never has been so suppressed and therefore the witnesses have never been slain. The triumphs of persecutors at different times, in Germany Bohemia, England France, Spain and Italy do not amount to any thing which can be called slaying the witnesses so long as a public testimony against papal corruptions of the true Gospel has at the same time been abundantly borne in the western empire. Mr. Faber has indeed made two rejoinders to this objection neither of which, in my opinion is at all satisfactory. He observes that the prophecy cannot imply a general death of the witnesses because the broad street of the great city must signify a single Roman province. But assuredly such an interpretation is not necessary—the witnesses are restrained to *two* how then can it be said with propriety that the dead bodies of the *two* witnesses were lying unburied in *several* streets of the city? The reader will call here to mind, that the death of the witnesses, as well as their resurrection, is not to be considered physically but politically.* It does not follow that they will be all literally killed but only that they will be silenced, persecuted, and crushed.

Again the same learned and able commentator says that admitting the *general* death of the witnesses all the faithful witnesses of Christ from Europe Asia, Africa, America must be collected into the chief province of the Roman empire there to suffer a moral and political death. But, in the first place [the opponents] may not admit that the broad street *must* mean a single province of the Roman empire, and secondly they consider the whole prophecy as confined to the western empire and therefore, during the death of the witnesses there the Gospel in America, Africa the East Indies and other parts of Asia may be increasing and flourishing and hastening to its meridian glories. — Other reasons follow on to the conclusion that on the whole there appear insuperable difficulties and objections in admitting that the death and resurrection of the witnesses is a past event. But if it be not past, then the necessary consequence is that it must be future. — This subject has been considered in a more diffuse manner than many others as it is universally admitted to be an event of the highest importance to the Christian church. — Gauntlett, pp 160—163.

We should have subjoined to this extract another, in page 244, contained in a note expressive of Mr Gauntlett's decided opinion, in agreement with Mede, though formed prior to his 'having had that gigantic expositor in his possession, that the effusion of the *seventh* vial of wrath *alone* takes place under the *seventh* trumpet, the effusion of the six preceding vials having taken place under the sixth trumpet — an opinion contrary to Mr Faber, and most others, who consider the seventh trumpet as inclusive of the seven vials, just as the seventh seal has been supposed to be of the seven trumpets. The bearing of this upon the preceding extract, and its effect in placing the death of the witnesses immediately before the third woe trumpet, not yet supposed, in Mr Gauntlett's view, to have sounded, will be obvious to assorters of the Apocalyptic visions. But our limits forbid further enlargement on this subject. We must refer our readers to Mr Gauntlett's Exposition.

To Mr Davison's full and important abstract of the whole subject of prophecy we should have been glad, in ampler limits, to have done far greater justice than we shall now be able to afford. It is a work of much originality, depth of thought, and scriptural investigation but we can now principally view it only under one aspect as it confirms and illustrates much of what has been alluded to in the preceding pages, of the double sense and advancing fulfilment of prophetic records. Mr Davison's comprehensive plan, however, embraces a general view of the uses of prophecy, as an evidence of our holy faith and as a most important conveyance for the great lessons of religion and morality which, he teaches us to observe are always mixed up with the visions of futurity, and never could have obtained their full force and vivacity by any other method. After this, it proceeds to a very full and valuable summary of the prophetic records, from the Creation to Christ, given with a more especial view to their progressive development of the great doctrine of redemption. In this part we are glad to find he has co operated with Mr Faber, in disabusing the public mind with regard to some of the many crudities and self contradictions in Bishop Warburton's imposing, but imperfect, work on the Divine Legation of Moses. He might perhaps have improved his summary, if he had, with Mr Faber given the book of Job a more prominent place in his prophetic arrangements — Finally, he has interspersed certain dissertations, on the Moral Use of Prophecy given on Pagan Subjects on the Prescience of God manifested in his Predictions, as reconcilable with the free Agency of Man and on the Inspiration of Prophecy, as illustrated by a comparison of pre

---

* A very clear illustration and confirmation of the Apocalyptic hieroglyphics in speaking of the first resurrection and others not then living again, in a *political* not *physical* sense.

diction and event in the three great Christian prophecies, the establishment of Christianity, the dispersion of the Jews, and the reign of Antichrist and in three other series, embracing the fate of certain Pagan kingdoms, the decendants of Ishmael, and the four great empires To such a mass of matter and of remark it would require much space to do full justice Mr Davison has indeed scarcely done full justice to his own ideas It might, perhaps, have been well to have thrown the whole of his *disquisitory* matter into preliminary dissertations, and perhaps omitted altogether the disquisition on Divine Prescience *, which but loosely hangs on a dissertation upon express prophecies and to have either added the New Testament prophecies, at which he has only partially professed to arrive in the present work, or else to have drawn his concluding instances for the inspiration of prophecy from those Old Testament predictions which his summary included This, however, we only suggest with hesitation to the highly respectable author, whose work merits, and will repay the attention of every theological student

In reference to our own more immediate subject, could we have our wish of the present author and his work, we should be most happy to see the grand summary outline completed in something like the following order —First, the Scriptural predictions, if any, actually and absolutely independent of all reference to the Messiah and the affairs of his church their delivery and fulfilment being respectively brought to bear, upon principles *previously* laid down, on the nature, the use, and the inspiration of prophecy Next, the Scriptural predictions concerning the affairs of the church illustrated in the same manner This last department we should ther prescribe to be further divided, into predictions referring simply to the state and policy, the rise and fall of the Jewish empire, from Abraham downward to its last but not final dispersion And then, uninterruptedly the grand series of predictions, from the opening to the close of the sacred volume respecting the Redeemer and the church of the redeemed the progressive development of the first coming of the Messiah, and establishment of his kingdom upon earth the general principles of that kingdom their gradual manifestation through successive ages more especially during the predicted times of antiChristian apostasy their fuller expansion, upon the destruction of Antichrist, the recal of the Jews and the settlement of Jew and Gentile in one Millennial church and their absolute and complete perfection in the eternal kingdom of Christ and of God —Much of this,

---

* The subject of the Divine prescience would of itself fill a volume Mr Davison has failed of telling us how those writers who deny to God the knowledge of future contingent events reconcile the very idea of prophecy with such a denial It seems to us that the most obvious postulate to be demanded by a commentator on prophecy is that God is perfectly capable of doing what he essentially professes his own capacity of doing in every prediction he delivers As to the guilt or the worth of actions done by men and foreseen by God that seems to be an equally clear demand upon the reader of the prophetic writings and if we are to proceed further into practical questions on predestination it will be well for all sides to bear in mind the unanswerable dogma of the great Butler that if men s actions are predestined, the consequence of them in reward or punishment is predestined likewise In all these ultimate questions on which we who are of yesterday know nothing it is necessary for the deepest reasoners to *stop somewhere*

Whatsoever is done in the earth God doth it himself On this ground one man goes to the length of giving to God all the merit of what is good and all the blame of what is bad Another man stopping short of the latter gives to God only the merit of what is good A third stopping still shorter gives to God neither the blame of the bad nor the merit of the good The reason in each case may be philoophical but after all the grand scriptural doctrine remains quite clear of all doubt and uncertainty for the guidance and admonition of men So then every one must give account of himself to God

in other forms, will already be found in Mr Davison's valuable volume and we shall conclude with two or three extracts illustrative of the great principle, in reference to the Messiah's kingdom, of the *double sense* of prophecy, its *inchoate* and its *final* accomplishment. Of the enlarged views of Mr Davison on the subject of the earliest prophecies, the following passage will afford sufficient evidence.

I assume it as a principle which indeed has been sufficiently established upon Scripture evidence and vindicated by learned divines, that we are to consider the selection and appointment of a separate people to have been made for the custody and transmission of the Divine promises of that more general nature. It is not affirmed that the sense of Scripture on this head directs us to think that such was the only purpose to be served by the selection and appointment of the Jewish people, or that other great and material ends were not thereby promoted, but that the leading and most comprehensive design of the appointment was to introduce the Gospel by connecting and preserving the several revelations of God till they merged in the last, to which the whole Jewish economy is declared to have been subservient, the Law being described as "an elementary teacher to bring men to Christ," in respect of the imperfect knowledge of the Gospel and the preparatory discipline for it, which it contained, or as being the shadow of the good things to come; and the Prophets who were sent to that separated people having it as an eminent part of their mission to bear witness to Christ and announce his religion. For the benefit and privilege of the Israelite consisted in this chiefly, because to him were committed the oracles of God; and those oracles were a perpetual witness of the better dispensation. So that the hopes of the ancient believer may be said to have been always in a state of pilgrimage, travelling onward through successive periods of revelation, and finding no rest, till they had crossed the barrier flood which divided the Law and the Gospel, the first dispensation and the second. Davison pp 91 92

His caution will be no less demonstrated by what follows.—

I have been the more anxious to state precisely the twofold character of prophecy in respect of its subjects, and to fix the sense in which we ought to understand the proper subserviency of the whole of it to the attestation of the Christian faith on several accounts. First, By this partition of the subjects of prophecy we shall simplify our view of its structure and be carried to a truer idea of the use and intent of its several chapters of prediction as they may hereafter come to be examined. Secondly, we shall exclude a mistaken principle which has infinitely warped the interpretation of it, in the hands of persons of an excellent piety but an ill instructed judgment; the principle of endeavouring to expound almost every prophecy either immediately or typically in a Christian sense. This mode of explication, after all arts and temperaments have been applied to it, fails, and the credit of Divine prophecy loses by the detected unskilfulness of the interpreter. The error is one of an early origin in the Christian church, and the reproof of it followed, for it was soon observed to do disservice to the cause of truth; the adulterated interpretation of the Old Testament prophecies which did not express any thing of Christ, or his religion, throwing doubt and suspicion upon the genuine sense of those which did. The prophecies which unquestionably relate to the Gospel are numerous, full and explicit, and they require no support from equivocal or forced expositions to be put upon others. There are also mixt or typical prophecies which combine the Christian with some other analogous subject. But besides both of these there are portions of prophecy which must be granted to stop short in their proper Jewish or other limited subject, without any sense or application beyond it. Thirdly, we shall perceive at the same time how unnecessary it is to the honour of the Gospel to have recourse to that mistaken principle, since after all it is most true, that the Holy Jesus is the Lord of the Prophets, for they spoke by his Spirit and all that they spoke was but in subserviency to him. For when they ministered to the First dispensation which had its appendant services of prophecy, yet that dispensation and all its evidences are subordinate to his, and thereby Moses and Elias are witnesses and servants to his proper glory.

Lastly, I observe that the twofold design of the Divine economy was never divided, but there is an unity in it throughout. It was not the divergent course of two unconnected and independent dispensations, but there was a temporary disposition of things made in the one to prepare the way for the second and greater, that which comprehends in it the constant design of the counsels of God towards man; that which had been the first disclosed and was often confirmed, and which having been variously prefigured in the veil of types, or expressed in the clearer delineations of prediction, was finally brought to light by Him who is the Author and Finisher of our faith, and of the faith of all who have known him by the several communications of prophecy from the beginning. Davison, pp. 93—95.

Our next quotation will overleap many an ample page of prophetic history and disquisition, to give a specimen of Mr Davison's consistent use of his own principles.

"As an example of this symbolical prediction, founded upon the present scene of things, consider the following oracle of Zechariah. The prophet had been commanded to take silver and gold, and make crowns and set them, or set one of them upon the head of Joshua, the son of Josedeck the high priest, and then to deliver this prophecy. 'Thus speaketh the Lord of hosts, saying, Behold the man whose name is the Branch; and he shall grow up out of this place (or there shall be a growth out of his place,) and he shall build the Temple of the Lord: even he shall build the Temple of the Lord; and he shall bear the glory, and shall sit and rule upon his throne; and he shall be a priest upon his throne; and the counsel of peace shall be between them both. And the crown shall be for a memorial in the Temple of the Lord. And they that are afar off shall come and build in the Temple of the Lord; and ye shall know that the Lord of hosts hath sent me unto you. And this shall come to pass, if ye will diligently obey the voice of the Lord your God.'

"This oracle I think will justify and sustain the character I have assigned to it. Its mystic form, its sublime and emphatic spirit, its promise of glory, its union of the priesthood and the throne, its appointed memorial of the crown to be laid up in the Temple of the Lord, its assemblage of builders from afar, absolutely refuse to be confined to the literal idea of the present work of the Jewish restoration. But since the form of the prophecy is assimilated to that primary idea of the Jewish restoration in their national increase, their priesthood and their temple, the whole principle of the prophecy meets us in the face, first in its ground of analogy, and next in its proper extent, an extent where in it leaves the inferior subject from which it springs far behind. In truth there is both reason and sublimity in prophecy, and we shall scarcely understand it, unless we are prepared to follow it in both. Its sublimity is that it often soars, as here, far above the scene from which it takes its rise. Its reason is, that it still hovers over the scene of things from which it rose. It takes the visible or the temporal subject, as the ὁρμητήρ ὄν (if I may borrow the word) of its enlarged revelation, and yet by that subject it governs its course. In this method of it, I believe that men of plain unsophisticated reason find it perfectly intelligible, and that it is only the false fastidiousness of an artificial learning which puts the scruple into our perceptions either of its consistency or its sense. But when we consider that this structure of prophecy founded on a proximate visible subject had the advantage, both in the aptitude of the representation, and in the immediate pledge of the future truth, a sounder learning may dispose us to admit it, and that with confidence whenever the prophetic text or mystic vision is impatient for the larger scope and the conspicuous characters of the symbols and the fact, concur in identifying the revelation."—Davison, pp. 338—340.

The same line of observation follows upon the celebrated and mysterious prophecy concerning Zerubbabel, in Haggai ii. 21—23, where Mr Davison strongly repels the single secondary application of that noble passage to Zerubbabel, and concludes:

"But in all this why is Zerubbabel so distinguished in the prophecy, when it looks so far beyond him? Why is he characterized as the signet of God? He is so distinguished as being the representative of Christ; and his fitness to be that representative is most evident. Of his line and seed was Christ born into the world. When God, therefore, restored his people and reinstated them in their covenant and their land again by this prophecy, he designated Zerubbabel, and set his choice upon him, as the signet of his hand and purpose, in whom some work of his providence and mercy should be accomplished: but the time and period of that future work was to be measured by the circle of the new heavens and the new earth: and therefore it was to be in the ulterior system of God, after the great change of things in the new, the Christian dispensation."—Davison, p. 363.

The progress, and still future hopes, of the Christian dispensation, come properly under a further head—namely Predictions concerning Christianity—from which we gather a still progressive view of Mr Davison's conceptions respecting the advancing and the inchoate fulfilment of Christian prophecies.

Our last short notice will carry us as far as Mr Davison has hitherto carried us in our desired progress toward the ulterior stages of prophetic delivery and fulfilment. It respects the future restoration of the Jewish nation.

"We have cause from the Scripture oracles to expect that this people will one day be restored under the covenant of the Gospel to a happier and more honourable state and perhaps also to a public re establishment in their own land But this last event their national restoration is a point in which we wait for a clearer in formation of the prophetic sense Mean while so much is certain that till their conversion to the Christian faith pro phecy like the cherubim with the flaming sword guards the entrance of Canaan and forbids them the approach Davi son p 453

We shall conclude with not a word of our own but with a weighty practical admonition of Mr Da vison s, on the subject of Christian Missions

One point however is certain and equally important viz that the Christian church when it comes to recognize more truly the obligation imposed upon it by the original command of its Founder Go teach all nations, a command which having never been recalled or abrogated can never be obsolete will awaken another energy of its apostolic office and character than has been witnessed in many later ages in this most noble work of piety and charity combined and thereby begin to discharge an inalienable duty in further ing the clear design of the Gospel and perhaps also the consummation of pro phecy Whether belief shall be universal we know not but as to the duty of making an universal tender and communication of the Christian faith it is too clear to be denied and too sacred to be innocently neglected Davison p 431

LITERARY AND PHILOSOPHICAL INTELLIGENCE,
&c &c

GREAT BRITAIN

PREPARING for publication —A Display of the Manufacturing and Mechanic Arts of the Kingdom, by Dr Birkbeck — Poems by Mrs Hemans

In the press —Sermons preached in the Island of Barbadoes by the Rev W Shrewsbury late Missionary in that island —Twelve Sermons by the Rev George Hodson M A —The Life and Corre spondence of the Antiquary Dugdale — Sketches of Rio de la Plata

An interesting collection of manuscripts under the title of Johnsoniana, was re cently sold by auction, with the library of the late Mr Boswell Among the articles were the original plan of Johnson s Dic tionary in the writing of an amanuensis with copious interlineations by the author 8*l* The original draft of the same en tirely in Johnson s hand 17*l* The ori ginal MS of Pope s Life 16*l* A Diary in scribed Easter 1766, registering his self examination and preparation by prayer and fasting for the holy Sacrament 11*l* The portrait painted by Sir Joshua Reynolds for Boswell was sold for 76*l*

In consequence of the recent discovery of the Miltonian and other valuable manuscripts in the State Paper office his Majesty has appointed a commission to examine the documents in that repository with a view to print the most important of them

The magnitude of the local magnetic attraction in steam vessels owing to the quantity of iron in their construction has occasioned Government to employ Mr Barlow to make experiments on the devia tions of compasses thus exposed and so accurately is the principle of local at traction now understood that he was able before beginning to observe the compass s bearings to select a spot where the action of the iron was so exactly balanced as to leave a compass nearly as correct in its bearings as if no local attraction had been present

Mr C Bell the anatomist has pub lished several papers to prove that not only are our ideas formed by a comparison of the different signs presented to us through the senses but that there is a power in the body which though not called a sense is superior to all the senses in the precision which it gives to our per ceptions—bestowing on us ideas of dis tance of space of form and substance — that the muscular frame and the sense which we possess of the muscular frame in action give us this power —that, for example the sense of vision in the eye is imperfect until aided by muscular mo tion as the sense of touch in the hand would inform us of nothing without the motions of the hand —that hardness, softness smoothness and angularity are properties of matter not known to us merely by the sense of touch but by that sense aided by the motions of the hand — and that the entire and complete exercise of the sense of touch comprehends a comparison of the exercise of the nerve of touch with the consciousness of or the sensibility to the muscular motion which accompanies it

Prof Buckland states that hedgehogs prey on snakes. He saw one seize its prey, crack its bones at intervals of half an inch or more, and then placing itself at the tip of the snake's tail, begin to eat upwards till about half was consumed when it ceased from repletion, but during the night finished the remainder.

An Hygrometer has been contrived to ascertain the temperature at which dew is deposited from the atmosphere. It is simply a thermometer with a bulb of a flattened cylindrical form of black glass of considerable size, the lower end of which turns up and is exposed to the air the moisture of which is to be tried, the rest of the bulb is covered with muslin. To use the instrument, the covered part is moistened with ether, the evaporation of which cools the bulb and its contained mercury, so that in a few seconds dew begins to deposit on the exposed part, at which instant the degree of cold may be noticed on the scale.

The heat of bodies which do not shine will not pass through transparent glass. Heat thus afforded acts more on absorptive white surfaces exposed to its radiation than on smooth black ones, but the radiant heat of *shining* hot bodies penetrates and passes through glass and other transparent screens, and acts more on smooth surfaces than on absorptive white ones. The solar heat is of course of this latter transmissible kind. The principle is of importance to be understood in the process of warming and ventilating buildings.

A cabinet picture of the very highest class by Correggio representing the Virgin and Child has been purchased for the National Gallery in Pall Mall. There is said to be no other undoubted picture by that artist in this country except one in the Duke of Wellington's collection. The one in the National Gallery formerly called a Correggio is now acknowledged to be a copy. The present picture was in the Madrid collection, from which it found its way into the hands of a Dutch dealer, from him to M Perrier the banker, from whom it was purchased at a high price by the British Government.

A plan has been published for establishing a scientific school in Cornwall for teaching the mineralogical arts and sciences to the miners.

A prospectus has been circulated under the auspices of Sir H Davy for the formation of a society for introducing and domesticating new breeds or varieties of animals such as quadrupeds, birds, or fishes, likely to be useful in common life, and for forming a general collection in zoology.

Among the new associations advertised is a Telegraph Company, the object of which is stated to be to promote the interests of commerce by bringing London and Liverpool, which are 200 miles distant, within one hour's communication.

Government have ordered to be sent to the Tower of London the old relic shewn in Dumbarton castle as Sir William Wallace's sword.

Dr Granville in a paper lately read before the Royal Society, after giving a curious description of a mummy which he minutely dissected, draws the following conclusions respecting the preparation of mummies. The abdominal viscera were abstracted, the thoracic cavity was not disturbed, the contents of the cranium were removed sometimes through the nostrils and in others through one of the orbits. The body was then probably covered with quick lime to remove the cuticle, after which it was immersed in a melted mixture of bees wax, resin and bitumen, and, ultimately subjected to a tanning liquor. The bandages were then applied with the interposition of wax and resin, lumps of resin, myrrh &c having been previously placed in the abdomen. Dr Granville has prepared several imitative mummies by this process, some of which bear a close resemblance to the Egyptian and have withstood putrefaction for upwards of three years.

FRANCE

At a late meeting of the Institute M Costa read a memoir on the plague at Barcelona, in which in order to prove that the yellow fever is not contagious he offered to have the clothes of a person who died of the yellow fever in the Havannah or elsewhere hermetically sealed up and sent to France, and that he would put them on and wear them at a sitting of the Institute, a proof which was of course declined. The medical profession in France as among ourselves are zealously prosecuting their inquiries on the subject of contagion especially in relation to the plague.

A purse of several thousand francs has been made up by the Government and individuals for the first traveller who shall penetrate to Tombuctoo by way of Senegal and produce exact observations on the position and commerce of that town the course of the neighbouring rivers, and the country between Tombuctoo and Lake Tsaad. The Geographical Society has besides offered a gold medal of the value of two thousand francs to the traveller who, independently of the conditions already mentioned, shall satisfactorily study the country with a view to the various objects of science

ITALY

In addition to the palimpseste restorations of Cicero, by MM Angelo Mai and Niebuhr further fragments have been recently published by M Amédée Peyron from a palimpseste manuscript in the library of the university of Turin which belonged, like many rare monuments of antiquity to the monastery of St Colomban at Bobbio. The manuscript is a treatise of St. Augustin of the age of the twelfth century on which M Peyron has discovered the traces of the text of Cicero, going back to the third or fourth century The passages now first discovered or corrected are numerous and some of them afford valuable restorations

SWEDEN

Whether the earth possesses two or four magnetic poles is a disputed point which Professor Hansteen proposes to clear up by a journey into Siberia, to ascertain the site of the magnetic pole The King of Sweden warmly patronizes the object

TURKEY

A large folio work has been recently published at Constantinople entitled The Anatomy of Man This is the first work on this subject ever printed in Turkey the apathy and religious prejudices of the people and a law which prohibits the opening of the human body and coming in contact with blood having formed an insurmountable barrier to the Turks devoting themselves to the cultivation of anatomical science But a thirst for knowledge seems at last, to be gaining some influence even among the Turks for the author has been permitted to infringe upon a positive injunction of the Koran, by accompanying his work by a set of representations of the human frame The work is dedicated by permission to the Grand Seignor who is stated to have perused it with great interest.—The art of printing was not introduced into Constantinople till the year 1726 The first works which issued from the government press were

A History of the Maritime Wars of the Ottomans and the Arabo Turkish Dictionary of Vancouli A few other works occasionally appeared but in general the art was neglected till a printing commission was appointed in the year 1783, under whose management about fifty works were published from 1784 to 1820 Of these twenty one are grammars dictionaries &c three historical five on geometry &c eight on fortification and eight on Mohammedan theology Among the translations is Bonnycastle s Geometry

EGYPT

The late discoveries of the phonetic system seem to connect the present day with the infancy of the world The Egyptian sculptures continue as fresh and angular as when the graving tool of the sculptor quitted them 3000 years ago, and numerous learned antiquarians are now busily engaged in deciphering their hieroglyphics Among the names of the ancient kings of Egypt, Mr Salt discovered what he considered to be the heraldic appellation of Misarte the king who erected the obelisk now standing at Matarea and Thothmosis Thothmosis according to Josephus was the king who perished in the Red Sea These phonetic symbols were found on Cleopatra s Needle At Medinet Abu, Mr Salt deciphered, according to this system the name of Tirhaka, a contemporary with Isaiah whose existence many learned men have doubted but of whom it is said in the Second Book of Kings, Tirhaka, king of Ethiopia, came out to make war against Sennacherib king of Assyria. He was contemporary with Sethon the second king of Egypt who if the symbols are rightly deciphered has recorded in Vulcan s temple at Sais, the destruction of Sennacherib s army in the night, and his own deliverance from it The phonetic antiquarian every where beholds the pictured memorials of extraordinary national vicissitudes

INDIA

A magnificent work entitled The Seven Seas a Dictionary and Grammar of the Persian Language has been published by the King of Oude in seven parts, printed at his own press in the city of Lucknow, in seven volumes folio. No Asiatic prince it is said has for ages rendered such essential service to literature as an author as the Sultan of Oude by this publication which is stated to be the most complete of all Persian Dictionaries

A Society has been formed for bettering the condition of Indo-Britons and of children on both sides of European parents born in India, by affording them the means of acquiring a livelihood by professions and trades

UNITED STATES

Of the present members of the Congress of the United States three are from Ireland one from Scotland one from Wales one from France and one from Bermuda Of those born in the United States *all* the representatives of New England are natives of the eastern states and these states have besides the honour of having given birth to twenty one members for other states No one state is entirely represented by natives in New York for example only eighteen out of thirty four representatives are natives These facts illustrate both the migratory disposition of the people and the confidence reposed by the people of each state in their fellow citizens in every other quarter of the Union

David Brown a young Cherokee of promising talents is now engaged in translating the New Testament from the original Creek into his native tongue He has already completed seven chapters of St Matthew and expects to finish the whole at no distant period

A Missionary Gazetteer has been recently published by the Rev W Chapin of Woodstock, in Vermont, in a duodecimo volume of more than 400 pages It comprises a geographical description of all the countries and places where Protestant missionaries have laboured, arranged in alphabetical order with an alphabetical list of missionaries their stations &c

BUENOS AYRES

The Government, among their public improvements have made efforts to found a University and, considering the obstacles with which it has had to contend, the want of books of a literary community and the poverty produced by their long struggle for freedom it has made all the advances which could have been hoped for Various schools also are supported by the Government, under the inspection of the Chancellor of the University

PERU

Bolivar as Dictator of the Peruvian Republic has issued a Decree that there shall be established in the capital of each department a model school on the system of mutual instruction for the support of which the necessary funds shall be provided Each province shall send to the departmental school at least six children in order that they may hereafter extend the system to every part of the republic

---

LIST OF NEW PUBLICATIONS

THEOLOGY

The Semi-sceptic or the Common Sense of Religion considered by the Rev J T James M A 8vo 12s

A Letter to the Clergy of the Diocese of St David s on a Passage of the Second Symbolum Antiochenum of the Fourth Century by the Right Rev Bishop T Burgess D D 8vo 3s 6d

A Literal Translation of the Book of Psalms solely upon the authority of Parkhurst. 8vo

A Course of Nine Sermons intended to illustrate some of the Leading Truths contained in the Liturgy of the Church of England by the Rev F Close 12mo 5s

The Theology of the Early Patriarchs illustrated by an Appeal to subsequent Parts of the Holy Scriptures, in a Series of Letters to a Friend by the Rev Thomas T Biddulph M A 2 vols 8vo 1l 1s

The Gradual Development of the Office Titles and Character of Christ in the Prophets a Proof of their Inspiration by Allen Cooper A. M of Oriel College Oxford 8vo 4s

The Portrait of an English Bishop of the Sixteenth Century 1 vol 8vo

Christian Education a Sermon by the Rev R C Dillon M A

Manual of Family Prayer chiefly from the Common Prayer book by the Rev T Stevenson 3s

A Paraphrase of the First Epistle to the Corinthians by the Rev J G Tolley 1 vol 8vo

Dr Owen s Sermon entitled The Chamber of Imagery or an Antidote against Popery re-printed 1s 6d

The Life of the Rev J Braithwaite by R. Dickinson 6s

The Works of Arminius translated from the Latin with Brandt s Life of the Author and considerable augmentations by James Nichols

The Manchester Socinian Controversy 5s

The Cottage Bible Vol I to be continued monthly by T Williams

MISCELLANEOUS.

Memoir of the late John Bowdler Esq 8vo 10s 6d

Flora Conspicua by R. Morris, F L S No I 3s 6d to be continued monthly

Floral Emblems by H Phillips F L 21s coloured 30s

Lingard s History of England 4to. Vol VI 1l 15s 8vo Vols IX and X 1l 4s

The Lost Spirit, a Poem by the Rev J Lawson 4s

The State of the Jews in the beginning of the Nineteenth Century, from the Dutch of Van Hemert, by L. Jackson, 8vo, 2s. 6d.

A Tale of Paraguay, by R. Southey, LL.D., 1 vol. 12mo, 10s. 6d.

The Poetical Works, Correspondence, and Prose Pieces of A. L. Barbauld. With a Memoir by Lucy Aikin, 2 vols. 8vo, 1l. 4s.

The Rising Village, a Poem, by Oliver Goldsmith, a collateral descendant of the Author of The Deserted Village, 2s. 6d.

Proceedings of the Society for educating the Poor of Newfoundland, 1s. 6d.

The Chinese Miscellany, consisting of Original Extracts from Chinese Authors in the Native Character, with their Translations and Philological Remarks, by the Rev. Robert Morrison, D.D., 10s. 6d.

Selections from Horace, being Part I of Selections from the Latin Poets, with English Notes, for the use of schools, and for persons who may wish to renew their acquaintance with the Classics, 4s. 6d.

RELIGIOUS INTELLIGENCE.

SOCIETY for PROMOTING CHRISTIAN KNOWLEDGE.

The Society has recently issued an address to the following effect:—The importance of establishing schools for the diffusion, in the first place, of European, and ultimately of Christian Knowledge among Native children in India, must be admitted by all who have seriously reflected on the means of propagating the Gospel in the East. Little progress can be expected in this great work, unless the mind has been prepared for the reception of Christianity by some previous instruction. To make provision for such instruction has long been an object of the Society, which has, for a considerable time, had schools for that purpose, under the superintendence and direction of its agents. The success which has attended these exertions, particularly at Calcutta, has answered its warmest expectations. The schools are found to form a bond of union between the European clergy and the Natives, introducing the missionary to the people in the united character of teacher and benefactor. At the same time he himself thus becomes speedily and accurately acquainted with the language, manners, and opinions of the population at large; while by the communication of European knowledge the foundation upon which the superstition of the heathen rests is gradually undermined.

Strongly impressed with these considerations, the Society is anxious to extend and perpetuate the system; and with a view more effectually to provide the means of doing this, it has resolved to establish a separate fund for the maintenance of Native Schools in India; and has, for that purpose, voted the sum of five thousand pounds, in addition to an anonymous benefaction of 1000l. and another of 200l. Donations and annual subscriptions are respectfully solicited for the object.

BATH AND WELLS EPISCOPAL SOCIETIES.

The Diocesan Anniversary of the Bath and Wells Societies for Promoting Christian Knowledge,—for the Propagation of the Gospel in Foreign Parts,—and for the Education of the Poor in the Principles of the Established Church, took place in Bath last month. The company assembled at the Guildhall, whence they proceeded to the Abbey to attend divine worship, the Bishop of the diocese and the Archdeacon being at their head. After service the procession returned to the Town-hall, where the Bishop having taken the chair and prayers being offered, the Diocesan Report of the Christian Knowledge Society was read by the Diocesan Secretary. It presented a very satisfactory account of the progress of education in the diocese of Bath and Wells. It is calculated that there are at this moment not less than 22,000 children in the various National and Sunday Schools in the county of Somerset. The number of books, especially of Prayer Books, sold during the past year, was very considerable. It was announced that the Parent Society, at the suggestion of this Committee, had agreed to place works of a superior nature on their catalogue on the subjects of art and science, trade and manufactures, to meet the wants and wishes of our ingenious artizans and mechanics.

After the several resolutions relating to the Christian Knowledge Society had been disposed of, the Report of the Society for Propagating the Gospel in Foreign Parts was read by the Diocesan Secretary. It exhibited the recent proceedings of this Society in the British colonies and dependencies but more especially in the East and West Indies, and at the Cape of Good Hope. The report presented an increase of more than forty members in this diocese during the past year. The Archdeacon of Bath pointed out the claims of the Negro and the Hindoo of the follower of Mahomet and the worshipper of Bramah and concluded a very animated speech by calling on all present to lend their exertions to these useful undertakings. He was followed by R. B Cooper Esq M P whose speech related principally to the benefits to be derived by our West-India slaves from the diffusion of Christianity among them. He said It was impossible to attend a meeting of such a nature without imbibing a portion of the spirit under the influence of which those societies had been originally instituted and by which they were now conducted. He felt animated by the excellent reports he had just heard and convinced that in supporting an association for the Propagation of the Gospel in Foreign Parts on the sound principles of the Established Church, he was promoting the best interests and diffusing the genuine spirit of the Christian religion. When we looked to the West Indies the appointment of Bishops to Jamaica and Barbadoes was a circumstance of the greatest possible interest. They were not sent merely for the religious instruction of the colonists the planters and their agents but for the gradual conversion and tuition of the whole slave population. It had been found in various instances that when the Negroes had sincerely embraced the Christian faith either from the members of our own church or from prudent missionaries of other persuasions they had become comparatively quiet orderly and content. If the Negroes could be thus instructed and reformed if milder and more equitable laws were introduced and a more considerate treatment adopted would not the condition of the Black population be wonderfully improved?

The various motions being disposed of the friends of these Societies met at York House to partake of the usual ordinary the Bishop presiding. We do not wish to be fastidious but we suggest to the friends of religious charitable institutions whether giving them as toasts at a public dinner is the most decorous mode of entreating the blessing of God upon their exertions. The toasts however gave rise to some useful remarks from several speakers. Mr Whitehead the Diocesan Secretary to the Society for promoting Christian Knowledge said In every parish in which we have active members resident, the Bible and the Common Prayer Book must soon become the regular inmates of the dwelling of every poor parishioner. But more than all gentlemen the Sunday Schools of every parish must prosper where the spirit of our Society has taken root, and actuates a few zealous individuals only. Every person in fact, who belongs to this Association ought to consider himself as (*ex officio*) a visitor superintendent and occasional teacher of the Sunday school of his parish. And then when the influence and patronage of our Association become thus generally and diffusively spread through the diocese that active and interested aid of the higher and more especially of the middling orders of the laity might be obtained for the course of parochial religious instruction for want of which it now in many places so much and so mischievously languishes —On Prosperity to the National Schools being given the Rev Mr Grinfield the Bath District Secretary remarked My excellent friends who have preceded me have directed your attention—the one to our duty of diffusing the blessings of Christianity and civilization amongst our colonies abroad and the other to the state of the parochial schools in our country villages. It remains for me to call your notice to a less pleasing but not less important topic—the present state and condition of popular education in our towns and cities as regards the instruction of the people in the principles of the Established Church. It is in vain to deny my Lord, that however interesting it may be to contemplate the peace and retirement of a rural life yet that all great political and civil affairs are dependent chiefly on those who reside in towns and cities. Cast your eye over our towns and cities and you will acknowledge that the crisis has now arrived when the powerful effects of popular education are about to be developed. It remains for you gentlemen to discharge your duties at this important period by doing every thing in your power to give a salutary and beneficial tendency to these mighty operations. The adversaries of our present establishments in Church and State are using all their endeavours to turn the tide of education against us. They represent the friends of the Church and more especially the clergy as secretly hostile to the intellectual improvement of the working orders. Now it should be our great and unceasing endeavour to destroy this prejudice, and to correct this misrepresentation. Let it be clearly understood that so long as religion is made the groundwork we shall rejoice to behold the people rising in the scale of intellectual dignity; that we fear no increase of knowledge which is accompanied with moral improvement; and that we are anxious only to be their fellow workers and assistants in this goodly endeavour to extirpate ignorance and to illuminate their minds.

LANGUAGE INSTITUTION

We have perused with great pleasure the prospectus of a Society to be called the Language Institution, the object of which will be to assist in promoting the knowledge of Christianity by making the best practicable provision for teaching in this country the languages of the Heathen. In furtherance of this object every opportunity will be embraced of collecting information relative to the languages of Heathens and Mahomedans throughout the world, and to their manners, customs, and opinions; and of forming a library of such books, both printed and manuscript, as are connected with these subjects. Courses of lectures also are to be delivered, by the best teachers that can be obtained from time to time, in elucidation of the respective languages; to which lectures all persons concurring in the Society's object will be admitted, under due regulations.

The following are passages from an address issued by the promoters of this important object.

The commission which Christ gave to his disciples "Go ye and teach all nations" extended to the whole world. In order that they might be qualified to act under this commission with promptitude and effect, all the difficulties arising from diversity of language were miraculously removed; and, by the gift of tongues they were empowered to enter at once in this respect on the work of Missionaries in any country to which they might be sent. Although this supernatural qualification is not now to be obtained, yet the injunction of the Redeemer is still in force, and the knowledge of Heathen languages is still as indispensably requisite as it was in the days of the Apostles. It is the want of this knowledge which constitutes at the present day one of the most formidable impediments to the propagation of the Gospel. It is the want of this knowledge, and of the facilities for acquiring it, which deters many devoted servants of Christ from entering on the engagements of a Missionary Life; while the delay and difficulty in acquiring the language of the country in which he has arrived oppress more than any other obstacle the heart of a Missionary who finds himself surrounded by affecting displays of ignorance which he cannot remove and of wretchedness which he cannot alleviate. The anguish of heart, the eagerness of solicitude, the closeness of application to the study of the language, and the effects of a tropical climate have in some instances, brought to an early grave Missionaries whose estimable qualities gave the fairest promise of eminent usefulness.

But is it necessary, is it unavoidable that with these difficulties in all their appalling magnitude the Missionary should have to struggle on his arrival in a Heathen land? May not the elements of the language be acquired before he leaves his own country and has to contend with the debilitating influence of a vertical sun? Would not the knowledge even of its rudiments enable him to pursue the study with great advantage during his long voyage, and greatly accelerate the arrival of the day when his career of active and efficient service may commence?

In addition to acquiring languages, such a body of information may by degrees be collected relative to the manners, customs and opinions of the Heathen in all parts of the world as may prepare the Missionary—especially when communicated to him in lectures by living instructors who have themselves witnessed what they describe—to enter on his work with a degree of intelligence which may both preserve him from mistakes and greatly facilitate his progress.

The Language Institution has been formed on the principle of the co-operation of all sincere Christians. A knowledge of the languages, habits and opinions of the Heathen is all that will be communicated by the Institution; whatever else may relate to the due preparation of a Missionary will be entirely left to the body to which he may belong.

It is obvious that the great object in view will be obtained both more efficiently and at a less expense by one Institution concentrating all its efforts to this one point, than it could be by the separate exertions of the different Societies engaged in carrying the Gospel to the Heathen.

CITY OF LONDON INFANT SCHOOLS

At a meeting held at the Rectory-house Bishopsgate the Lord Bishop of Chester Rector of St Botolph s, Bishopsgate in the chair an institution was formed for establishing Infant Schools in the city of London, for the reception of the children of the poor from two to six years of age The Lord Mayor and the Bishop of London are patrons Mr Peel vice patron and the Bishop of Chester president, with a highly respectable list of vice presidents and other officers

The object of this institution the conductors state will be to provide for the care of the children during that portion of the day when by the necessary avocations of the parents they are unavoidably separated from each other to form the children to habits of obedience good order and attention and to give them such elementary instruction as may prepare them for entering with advantage into those schools where they may acquire useful knowledge and be taught the great truths and duties of religion Great inconvenience it is added is at present experienced in the National Schools from the number of children under the age of six years pressing for admission who having been taught no habits of discipline or good order, greatly embarrass and impede the process of instruction in the schools For this evil an effectual remedy will be furnished by an infant school out of which a regular supply of well trained children imbued with the rudiments of knowledge will be from time to time furnished to the National Schools It is no unimportant recommendation the committee add of such establishments that by promoting cleanliness and regular exercise on the part of the children they tend greatly to secure the health of the rising generation Those who are accustomed to visit the children of the poor best know how many cases of disease deformity and bodily incapacity are to be met with arising from confinement in crowded rooms with an impure atmosphere from other dangerous exposures and particularly from those distressing accidents by fire which are of such frequent occurrence

It is with the greatest pleasure we observe the extension of these highly useful establishments in various parts of the kingdom and we strongly urge our readers to consider the practicability of forming them in their respective neighbourhoods

GENERAL KNOWLEDGE SOCIETY

A provisional committee has been formed for establishing a Society to be designated the Society for promoting General Knowledge the object of which shall be the publication of approved works in the various branches of useful knowledge especial regard being had to their religious and moral tendency The price is to be so low as to bring them within the reach of the public in general There is reason to believe that a similar Institution will be formed at Paris The works to be published by this Society will include religious and moral historical scientific and miscellaneous Every thing exclusive whether in religion or politics it is stated will be carefully shunned Cheap reprints of standard and unexceptionable works will form a prominent part of the Society's labours In some cases however new treatises will be required

It is intended that extensive and varied knowledge shall be made subservient to the interests of religion and virtue and a powerful counteraction thus afforded to the pernicious publications at present in fearfully wide circulation The books of the Society it is added will be peculiarly adapted both in matter and price to mechanics institutes and, it is hoped will turn to good account the appetite for reading so widely diffused and so rapidly increasing

SOCIETY FOR PROMOTING EDUCATION AND INDUSTRY IN CANADA

At the meeting at which this Society was formed Lord Bexley gave the following details respecting the peculiar circumstances of Canada

The territory he remarked is of immense extent and the population thinly scattered over it It is a country as yet little known or explored and far from the means of instruction and civilization The inhabitants consist, 1st, Of the European settlers 2d The natives of Canada descended from the first settlers and 3d The native Indians

The first class have taken with them from this country their various religious creeds and there are Episcopalians Catholics and Dissenters of all classes Any schools therefore for their benefit must be founded on general principles, independently of particular creeds or forms of church discipline We must allow the respective clergy to lead their flocks in that which they think to be the right way. The venerable Society for propagating the Gospel in Foreign Parts, and the British and Foreign School Society in London are certainly doing much good; but there is still room and necessity for more.

The second class, being descendants of original settlers, often placed in situations which afford no opportunities of public worship, have in too many instances, almost forgotten their religion, or have been brought up without any, and are sunk into gross ignorance and vice. This is especially true with those in the back settlements.

As to the third class or native Indians, we owe them a debt which we ought now to pay. We have driven them gradually out of their own possessions, and reduced their numbers by compelling them to inhabit woods and swamps; several of the tribes are utterly extinct, and others hastening fast to decay. The intercourse we have hitherto carried on with them has been of a degrading and demoralizing character; we initiated them in the use of fire-arms and of spirituous liquors—at once giving them weapons of mischief, and stimulating their worst passions to the use of them. We must now endeavour to civilize these rude tribes, and instead of huntsmen or warriors, convert them into industrious and peaceable members of society, making them happier in this life, and fitting them for a better hereafter. Our schools, however, must be something more than seminaries of morality or religion. In the savage state each man is dependent on his individual exertions; he must know how to handle the axe, and build himself a house. Industry therefore must be combined with mental cultivation, and the best mode of inculcating such habits will be found in the principles of the Bible, which must form the basis of any system of instruction, carrying to all men the comforts of time, and the cheering hopes of eternity.

We are requested to state that, in addition to pecuniary aid, suitable books and tracts will be thankfully received by the Society.

LETTER FROM A NEGRO MISSIONARY IN AFRICA

An American Negro Missionary of the name of Carey, who is settled among his brethren in the colony belonging to the Colonization Society, on the western coast of Africa, in a recent letter to his friends, dated from Liberia, gives the following account of a native African in the vicinity of the colony who has recently been converted to Christianity. The writer himself was a slave till he was thirty years of age, and he never enjoyed the advantages of a common school education; circumstances which his friends justly consider a sufficient apology for any inaccuracies in the style of his letter. The extract shews how beneficial to their countrymen may be the ministrations of Christianized Negroes, even of humble attainments, as well as the advantages which are resulting to the natives of Africa from their intercourse with Sierra Leone.

The 13th of March, says the writer, being the Lord's-day, was blessed to us as a day of good news from a far country (a vessel having arrived with sixty colonists from America.) Early in the morning the church met to hear the relation of a poor heathen who was led to believe that God for Christ's sake had pardoned his sins. His name is John; he came all the way from Grand Cape Mount, about 80 miles down to Cape Mesurado to be baptized, having heard that here was a people who believed in Christ and practised baptism. The following is his own relation without being asked any questions:— When me bin Sa lone (Sierra Leone) me see all man go to church house—me go too—me be very bad man too—Suppose a man can cus (curse) me, me can cus im too—suppose a man can fight me, me can fight im too. Well, me go to church house—the man speak, and one word catch my heart (at the same time laying his hand on his breast)—I go to my home—my heart be very heavy and trouble me too—night time come—me fear me can't go to my bed for sleep, my heart trouble me so—something tell me go pray to God—me fall down to pray—no—my heart be too bad—I can't pray—I think so, I go die now—suppose I die I go to hell—me be very bad man—pass all turrer (other) man—God be angry with me—soon I die— Suppose man cus me this time, me can't cus him no more—suppose man fight me, me can't fight im no more—all the time my heart trouble me—all day all night me can't sleep—by and by my heart grow too big and heavy—Think to-night me die— my heart so big—me fall down this time— now me can pray—me say Lord, have mercy. Then light come into my heart— make me glad, make me light, make me love the Son of God, make me love every body.

This is his own relation, without being asked any questions. He appeared to be strong in the faith of the Son of God. While at Sierra Leone about three years ago he got the knowledge of his letters after about three months advantage of schooling his relations called him from Sierra Leone to Grand Cape Mount where he now lives. He however took along with him a spelling book, and he continued praying and trying to spell. Providentially while one of the men belonging to our settlement was on a trip up there in a boat, the boat got lost and the man himself was carried ashore by the waves and fell into the hands of this native man John who treated him with a great deal of hospitality and all he charged or asked him for, was a Testament which the man fortunately had, and gave him. Since that time which was about a year ago, he has learnt to read the Bible without any teacher (to explain it) except the Spirit of God and he has read and meditated on the different subjects of religion until he found it was his duty to be baptized when he came down to our place for that purpose and gave the relation which I have given you above. Accordingly on the first Lord's day after preaching in the morning I baptized the native man John and after preaching in the afternoon we had the honour to break bread in the house of God with our newly arrived brethren from America and our newly baptized brother. I need not tell you it was a day of joy and gladness.

VIEW OF PUBLIC AFFAIRS

FOREIGN

GREECE.—A variety of unauthenticated and contradictory reports have been current during the month, respecting the war in the Morea. It appears but too clear, that Ibrahim Pasha, with his invading army has been making an alarming progress into the interior of the country laying every thing waste before him with fire and sword. It is indeed, reported that the Greeks have permitted his incursion, with a view to entrap and separate his army in their difficult and dangerous passes, and to harass them with a straggling warfare to which it is added, that the invaders have already received a severe check, at a place called "the Mills," and are retreating towards the coast but this intelligence wants confirmation. It is understood that Lord Cochrane is about to sail for Greece, with several steam vessels and small vessels of war, to assist the Greeks by dismantling the Turkish fortresses, laying the inhabitants of the coast under contribution cutting off the supplies which the government are accustomed to depend upon from their maritime cities, and interrupting all commercial and military communications. It is thought that his Lordship's spirit of enterprise, and his long experience in a somewhat similar warfare in South America, may considerably assist the Greek arms.—We deeply lament, for the sake of our common humanity, the predatory nature of this afflicting struggle but the guilt of its mischiefs lies with the oppressor, much more than with the oppressed. It is one consolation, however, that, in proportion to the timely wisdom and vigour displayed by the Greeks and their friends, will probably be the brevity of this protracted contest.

MEXICO.—The treaty between this country and Mexico has been duly ratified by the Mexican Congress. The ultra-Catholic party seem to have been somewhat averse to it, as favouring religious toleration but, happily, the grasp of Popish despotism is rapidly relaxing throughout the newly emancipated colonies. The stipulations of the treaty are much the same with those concluded with Columbia, the United Provinces of La Plata, &c. Among the articles we notice the following.—British subjects are protected from persecution or molestation on account of their religion, provided they respect the laws and religion of Mexico. The Mexicans pledge themselves to co-operate with Great Britain for the total abolition of the Slave Trade and to prevent their own subjects being guilty of assisting in it. It is most equitably and humanely provided, that, in case of war, six months are to be allowed to merchants on the coast, and twelve to those in the interior to withdraw their property and settle their affairs that those who are settled may remain, subject to the laws and that debts due by individuals, and property in the public funds, shall not be detained.

HAYTI.—The French government has, at length, in consideration of the sum of 150 millions of francs, as an indemnity to the ancient proprietors of lands in the French portion of St Domingo, consented to acknowledge the independence of that country. Independent they have been, in point of fact, for a quarter of a century: we might say, from the time of the French revolution; and there was no reason to fear that either by arms or artifice they could be made to return to their servile condition; so that France may be considered as having received a most handsome and gratuitous boon for her acknowledgment, independently of the commercial advantages she will derive from the recognition, especially as the impolitic tardiness of our own Government has prevented our securing the commercial advantages, and perhaps preferences, which might have been our own, but which will now no longer be within our reach. The recognition by France has, however without doubt, been forwarded by the conduct of the British cabinet in respect to the South and Central American governments, and the general feeling in this country, that, after these precedents, our acknowledgment of the independence of Hayti could not be long delayed. Still the French acknowledgment is important, in many ways; it is a most serious innovation on the long cherished principle of colonial servitude, and affords a precedent for corresponding acknowledgments by Spain and Portugal; and it may thus, we trust, eventually stop up the avenues to much litigation. As respects the republic of Hayti, the measure will unfetter the shackled energies of that long persecuted country, and give to her agriculture and commerce the extension and activity which security alone can give, and the want of which has caused the enemies of freedom to turn round upon her with reproaches, for not having accomplished what in her circumstances was perfectly unattainable. The influence of the now acknowledged independence of Hayti upon her moral and religious condition, will also, we hope, be beneficial; and we recommend to the consideration of our various religious charitable institutions, whether under prudent regulations, they may not usefully employ a portion of their energies in this important field; especially now that the acknowledgment of Haytian independence, we may hope, will break down some of those jealousies and difficulties which have hitherto so seriously obstructed their progress.— Upon the West Indies in general, the acknowledgment must also be fraught with important consequences. It certainly holds out to the proprietors of the soil a pressing lesson to shape their way as speedily as possible to a safe and amicable extinction of Slavery, before the extremity arrives (as arrive it may, under various probable contingencies, especially in the event of another war), when the question may be, whether the mother country shall be forced either to abandon the planters to their fate, or to imitate the conduct of France in waging in defence of them a long, bloody, unpopular, and most ruinously expensive contest, to end only in degradation and defeat.

As we have alluded thus far to the subject, we shall subjoin a few particulars respecting what is stated to be the present condition of the country.

The island of St Domingo, it is well known, is of great value, both in an agricultural and commercial view. It is generally mountainous: but has many extensive plains and beautiful valleys. Its climate considering the latitude, is salubrious and delightful being tempered by the mountain breezes and trade winds. The immense wealth which it poured into France while in a state of colonial dependence, proves its fertility and great resources. The government is professedly framed on the model of the United States of America: the legislative and executive powers being vested in a President, Senate, and Chamber of Deputies. The deputies consist of two from the principal city of each department (Port-au-Prince sends three) and one from each district; and they are elected quinquennially by the people; all males of twenty-one years of age having a vote. The duties and privileges of all classes are defined by the constitution: the Code Napoleon is in substance the law of the land. Having hitherto been unacknowledged, and being obliged to keep on foot a large force both for achieving and maintaining their independence and having only their own arms to rely upon, for exemption from slavery or extermination the government has hitherto assumed chiefly a military aspect: but a standing army being now less necessary we may hope to view it under a more peaceful appearance especially as its constitution is opposed to a military government, and is founded on the modern system of checks and balances, and is not ill calculated to secure public and private liberty and prosperity. Since the union of the whole island under the present administration, great improvements are stated to have taken place: and for more than two years there has been the most perfect internal tranquillity. The Presi dent is popular and the government appeared to be quite stable, even before the recent recognition of its independence. Indeed all disinterested persons who have visited and examined the island, have stated that its fastnesses and mountains, the good discipline of its army, the spirit of liberty which animates the people, and the confidence of the public in a government which by a pure administration of justice, secures liberty and property, and guarantees to every human being who touches on its shores the rights of freedom, without distinction of clime or colour, rendered invasion an utterly hopeless project. The legislature appear to be acting upon principles of sound policy: they have recently equalized the duties on imports, lessened those on exports, and banished some remains of the feudal system in matters of property. The police is excellent, so that public crimes and outrages are far more rare than might have been expected considering that most of the elder and middle aged population, and the parents of the younger were born slaves, and must therefore have been but ill qualified for all the duties and dignities of freemen. The moral and intellectual taint hence derived is, however, still painfully visible, and years must elapse before many of the habits and vices engendered by slavery will have wholly disappeared. This serious disadvantage the Haytians inherit (and inherit, be it remembered from European hands) in common with the lately enfranchised vast regions of South and Central America; but they are taking the best means to check its perpetuation, by encouraging education, and according to the best ideas which their late masters saw fit to give them, religion. To promote the former, the government has established both colleges and schools of mutual instruction, in both which classes of institutions the public defray a great part of the expense. These excitements were absolutely necessary; for every person who has witnessed the general indifference of uneducated persons, even in our own country, for the education of their children, will easily infer that great difficulties must exist in instilling such a desire into the population of an island where, thirty three years ago, almost all were slaves, and, as such, prevented by a cruel policy, from being made acquainted with the simplest elements of mental cultivation. These remarks apply only, or chiefly, to those who were slaves before the revolution. Among those who have always enjoyed freedom there are many who are distinguished for intelligence and liberality of sentiment. Not a few were educated in France, and many of the children of both sexes are still sent to that country for instruction. There are several printing presses on the island, from which issue a few newspapers and one monthly publication.—With regard to the second point Religion, when it is recollected who were the late masters of the island and in what manner West Indian colonies were peopled it will not be wondered at that the Haytian population are not either very intelligent or very consistent Christians. The majority of them were African pagans torn from their homes, who acquired little of Christianity but the name, and not perhaps always even that, by their residence in a professedly Christian and Catholic colony. The present race have renounced their pagan for popish superstitions, or for a total disregard of all religious observances. A *Protestant* Sunday is unknown; for, though the public offices and generally the wholesale stores, are shut, yet the Sunday market still exists, and comparatively little attention is devoted to religious duties. The Catholic holidays are retained, and the churches are open and mass performed, on occasion of their recurrence; but they have the effect there, as every where else, of creating habits of idleness and vicious indulgence, rather than of strengthening religious sanctions. Many of the better-educated classes, we fear, have imbibed the infidelity of the French school. There is, however, on every hand, a visible and rapid improvement. The manners of the people are much less coarse than might have been expected and even partake, it is said, of great civility, having been modelled on the proverbially polished deportment of French society. Marriage, that almost unknown institution among West India slaves is beginning to be duly honoured among the poorest classes and we trust, that by the blessing of God, many years will not elapse before moral and spiritual improvements will have ensued, equal to those which have ameliorated their civil condition and that, being now blessed with temporal freedom and security, they will become increasingly partakers of the glorious liberty of the sons of God.

DOMESTIC

There is no article of Domestic Intelligence that appears to demand our notice. Profound tranquillity and public prosperity are at present our happy lot as a nation, and continue to demand from us the most fervent gratitude to God for his mercies. The public journals, during the month, are chiefly filled with the details of judicial proceedings throughout the country, and though, from the scenes of atrocity exhibited in some of these, and of gross and disgusting immorality in others, and the baneful avidity with which they are published and read, some persons are inclined to think we are retrograding in the scale of public morals and religion, we confess for ourselves we entertain no such apprehension. Our journals keep no secrets, and increased publicity has in some measure the effect of presenting an appearance of increase in crime, which we do not believe has in fact taken place. On the other hand, the augmenting anxiety of all classes for mental, and very widely for moral and religious, improvement, is a most hopeful symptom. We might allude also to the charitable institutions arising on every side, to which almost every number of our work reports some accessions. We might also notice many other indications, but we trust it is not necessary. The state of the working-classes, in particular, we view as fraught with hope and interest; this very month several new mechanics institutions and popular book clubs have been formed, and many circumstances tend to shew that very considerable changes are taking place in the moral and intellectual habits of these large and important bodies of our fellow-countrymen. We will not say that we have no shadow of apprehension mixed with our hopes, as we view the present train of affairs; but the latter in our minds, notwithstanding the dark auguries of some of our most respectable countrymen, greatly predominate; and the former will wholly vanish, if we can but see all our clergy and religious laity rising to the full level of their high duty under existing circumstances. With regard to recent combinations of workmen, and some other symptoms, which many view in a very gloomy light, we see nothing in them but the natural consequences of former unjust and impolitic laws and injurious habits, which will cease with the circumstances which gave them birth, and by the blessing of God, give place to a settled peace, order, and prosperity, which even this happy country has never yet known.

ANSWERS TO CORRESPONDENTS

THEOGNIS, C. R. H. A CONSTANT READER, E. R. and J. H. are under consideration.

We have received communications from several correspondents *pro* and *contra* relative to our Review of Admiral Sir C. Penrose's Remarks on the State of the Navy; but we do not think it necessary to go further, at present, into the subject, especially as the author himself considers, that we have brought the points in discussion very fairly before our readers, and as he is pleased to add, in a manner very flattering to himself.

We refer T. B. to a paper in our present Number.

We are much obliged to a correspondent at Lisbon for calling our attention to a statement, in our Review of Mr. Cooper's Crisis, that English Protestant churches have been permitted to be opened in the Portuguese dominions, and that, even in Lisbon itself, Portuguese churches had been appropriated by the Government for the purpose of Protestant worship. Upon further inquiry we find the fact to be that in Lisbon we have never had a Catholic church assigned us, but we have been allowed to build a place of worship for ourselves. In Madeira we had, for several years, the Jesuit church of that island for our use; we have since built a place of our own. That we are not allowed to have steeples and bells is only an application of the same rule which we apply to the Dissenters in this country. We believe that our correspondent is but too correct in asserting that there exists much bigotry and intolerance among the Portuguese, and especially among their priests; and most sincerely shall we rejoice in every well planned effort to diffuse the bright rays of Scriptural light over the moral and religious gloom.

We have very frequently and urgently called the attention of our readers to the melancholy fact of the tolerated Burning of Widows in India, as SCOTO BRITANNICUS will find by referring to our volumes. We agree with him, that a more decisive expression of public opinion on the subject might have a very beneficial effect.

ERRATUM

Page 443, col. 2, line 31, for *indifference* read *interference*.

THE CHRISTIAN OBSERVER.

SEPTEMBER 1825

RELIGIOUS COMMUNICATIONS

To the Editor of the Christian Observer

THE PHILOSOPHY OF THE ROMAN CATHOLIC RELIGION

No III

THE sovereignty of the Papal empire over human minds has, in every age been strengthened by its system of domiciliary espionage. From this arguing on the principle attempted to be developed and illustrated in these papers, have resulted the SACRAMENTS OF MATRIMONY AND EXTREME UNCTION *

* I am aware that in the following remarks I may seem to subject myself and my argument to a very obvious recoil for it may be asked Ought not then a Christian priesthood to concern itself for the spiritual welfare of mankind? Ought not ecclesiastical discipline to be intimately conversant with the current habits and practices of a professedly Christian community? Ought not the affairs of personal domestic and social life to be sanctified by religion and ought not the ministers of the Gospel of Christ to do all in their power to create and confirm this beneficial sanction? Does not our own church periodically lament the decay of the godly discipline among ourselves and is not the circumstance pointed out as a grievous defect in our Zion not only by Romanists but by some of our less relaxed Protestant establishments both North and South and very generally by our Dissenting and Methodist brethren among whom the system of inspection is often kept up very rigidly and with excellent effects? In a word ought a faithful pastor to suffer such an important occasion for suitable advice or admonition as the birth or baptism or marriage or death of an individual among his flock to pass by unnoticed? Are not his domiciliary visits at such seasons often among his best opportunities of doing good and for the neglect of which he would have seriously to account? And even supposing that his conduct is apparently open to the imputation of unworthy motives is he on that account to sacrifice positive duties and important benefits in order to guard

Wherever Popery is dominant, no man's house is his castle its ministers have the privilege of the *entrée* Now the most important events, in private life, are the circumstances of birth, marriage, and death They are the three centres circled by the most influential arrangements of private families In the first of these originated a sacrament, constituted such by Christ himself He appointed it as a visible means of grace and, with the exception of one very limited sect, the members of which consider the

against so unjust an apprehension?—I am aware I say that the Romanist may urge these and similar considerations in defence of the line of conduct adopted by his church especially when connected with the doctrine of the inherent efficacy of the sacraments and the benefits derived to the souls of men from actions not their own But my readers will I doubt not be able easily to draw the line of distinction between anxious spiritual disinterested and simply pastoral attentions, and those which are connected as is the basis of the Romish system with priestly power ambition and aggrandisement Let the ministers of Christ be as domiciliary in their spiritual attentions to their flock as their own time and the circumstances of modern life will allow—(usually a very stinted measure in the southern division at least of our island)—but let them prove to all men that they seek not their own but the things that are Christ's and that are for the use of edifying My complaint on this head against the Church of Rome is that it has gone far beyond this line and while professing to be anxious for the souls of its members has been mainly intent on its own sordid or ambitious ends —I have been the more anxious to notice this distinction obvious as it is because I should feel seriously concerned if my course of argument should seem to depreciate the value of pastoral attentions or to make the laity think lightly of the benefits to be derived from encouraging the ministerial visits and pious offices of a faithful spiritual guide.

injunction as purely spiritual, it has been adopted, and in its plain literal meaning by the whole of the Christian world. This initiatory sacrament became highly useful in the machinery of the Vatican. For, besides the advantage derived from an elaborate process at the baptistry, it domesticated, on the occasion, sacerdotal persons in houses not their own. It brought them into contact with families under circumstances peculiarly interesting to family feelings, and taught parents and relations unconsciously to connect the magic of priestly influence with the rising importance of the house. This point being gained, it became necessary to make another grand domiciliary visit at a moment when nuptial festivities and expectations opened human hearts, and when blessings from the priest might again be peculiarly welcome. To meet these emotions, marriage was elevated to the dignity and sacredness of a sacrament. It furnished a new source of intercommunion between the ruler and the subject, and a source not scanty in supplying the ecclesiastical government with augmented influence, and the governed with a deeper feeling of dependence. It increased the mysterious sensation, that the priest was a kind of presiding genius over the entire system of private life. It was felt that his sanction was essential to every movement of the house, and that only so far as the schemes of a family were connected with the awful institutions of THE CHURCH— I do not say of true religion—could they be regarded as promising the least success.

But, chiefly did the inventors of the *sacramental unction*, administered to the dying, discover the potency of a rite which should make an appeal inexpressibly tender and overpowering to human feelings, at a moment when the parent, the husband, the child, the friend, is retiring within the shades of the eternal world. It was a master stroke of policy, to ordain the presence and mystic ministrations of a priest (I speak not of really pious and pastoral offices, so endeared to the good and so important to the wicked at this juncture) as part of the indispensable attendance among the deepest solemnities of our nature, those which await us in the chambers of sorrow, pain, and death. If, at such times, the heart be most open to the impressions of true religion, it is also open to the gloomy influences of superstition, so that, under such circumstances, even irreligious indifference becomes alarmed at the sight of itself, and is glad, as it were, to find a sanctuary from its terrors in the presence of a minister of religion, who enters the chamber possessed, it is supposed, of an ability to communicate pardon and security. Bad men, in the hour of domestic calamity, are compelled to give themselves pause, amidst the hurry and thoughtlessness of life, and to stand aside, for an interval, from the crowd with whom they are generally intermingled. Catholicity improves the opportunity. It cannot make them true Christians, neither is this its aim. But it makes a timely effort to draw them into more intimate union with *the church*. When they gather round the bed of their dying relatives and friends, and take, at least, a passive share in the ritual of the Eucharist, and of the unction *in extremis*, they obtain from these ceremonies a more mysterious reliance than ever on the pretensions of the priesthood. They witness a member of that order allowing the VIATICUM—a word in ecclesiastical lexicography, of no trivial import—and accompanying the pilgrim in the last stage of his journey, even to the very confines of the unseen state, and the impression among the bystanders is, that the administrator of the unction has ensured to the departing soul a favourable acceptance at the tribunal of God. Bring me not volumes of controversy to prove the precise date of the various modifications of Papal imposture! The system is its own accuser, its own witness, its own judge. When a despot would enslave his subjects, he selects what are judged to be efficient instruments, as the exigencies of the moment rise; and if there be no counteraction, he succeeds. The usages of the Latin church in a sick chamber are nothing better than a splendid form of antinomianism—that universal and favourite heresy of mankind, which relieves our willing souls from the burden of responsibility, and permits the ordinary Romanist (for I speak not of the few pious and enlightened individuals who rise above and virtually reject the delusions of their own system) to transfer, as it were, his guilt to a sinner like himself; a sinner also, who adds to his other transgressions—not however, I would hope, in many cases consciously for the priest may believe as firmly in his own supposed power as the ignorant laic who seeks its efficacy — the crime of speaking peace where there is no peace. The eucharist and the unction, indiscriminately administered as they are, have a palpable tendency to hide the realities of eternity. They delude the dying with a persuasion of their final safety, and not only soothe the survivors with an impression that all is well with the dead, but that, when their own last hour draws on, they too shall be indulged with the same means of security, and enter the grave of a believer after having lived the life of a practical infidel. They calculate on the expectation, that their passport will, according to the invariable routine of the spiritual office, be duly signed and sealed; and though the bearer may be detained in a separate state of purgatorial anguish for a season, yet that the certificate may at length be confidently presented at the gates of Paradise. Well may the theologians of the school of the Vatican compose their dissertations on the power of the keys! Let it be added, well may those, who have been blessed with a scriptural knowledge of the Gospel, mourn and weep over the spiritual darkness and death of mankind, and breathe out, as the Spirit helps their infirmities, prayers and supplications with strong crying and tears—and these are the true *misereres* of the universal church—that God would bring into the way of truth all them that err and are deceived! Every feeling of contempt, disgust, abhorrence, and indignation (for all these are naturally awakened in the bosoms of those who wander among the machinations of Popery) should be absorbed into emotions of compassion, and into acts of intercession. 'Father, forgive them, for they know not what they do!'

But from an attitude of supplication for these victims of error and guilt, I must thus speedily retire, and re-embark on the current which has so far borne me in the progress of this painful discussion. I proceed to draw the attention of my readers to the subject of compensatory indulgences; and at this point I feel the need of their assistance to an extent not demanded by the previous topics. The doctrine of compensations is valued beyond all names of value in the divinity of the Sacred College. The Romanists, having drained from their votaries vast accumulations of silver and gold, precious stones, and every other article of value; having also required from them an implicit submission to creeds and confessions; and having further subjected them to external mortifications, amounting in some instances to self denial, and even self torture; the question arises, by what means does the church reconcile her adherents to this repulsive part of her discipline? How does she persuade men to endure actual anguish and pain? In more direct terms, how does she *repay* them—for there *must* be some compensation—for their severe losses? In attempting to think out a reply to these inquiries, I am driven to confess, that although it seems not very difficult to explain the principle on which men yield to moderate degrees of voluntary distress, yet my philosophy has found its line too short to fathom the depth of the fact, that immense numbers of persons among the Roman Catholics have deserted all the endearments of life, suffered almost all things, and done almost all things for the sake of what they considered to be the truth and this with the prospect of no recompence in the least adequate in a human sense, to afford a competent reward. I refer to the expatriation, poverty hunger thirst nakedness and exposure to death in its most appalling forms, endured for example by Jesuit missionaries and to the severities practised by some individuals attached to certain modifications of monachism. We understand the motive and the recompence of a patient who endures for instance the excision of a mortified member the prize is life the alternative, death. We sympathize with a parent who, to save a child from ruin consigns himself to indigence, and the world's oblivion. But where is any approach to proportion between the martyr life of a *Josephus à doloribus* in cloisters more gloomy than those of La Trappe, and the advantage proposed as the final result? Or if this measure of suffering—as the difficulty appears to class among questions of degrees—be capable of analysis, what enabled Sister Rachel and Sister Felicite to sustain the anguish of an actual crucifixion, nailed, as they were, through the hands and feet to two crosses for upwards of three hours during which they affirmed ' that they felt the most exquisite delight affecting sometimes to slumber as if in a beatific trance and sometimes addressing the spectators in the fondling and babyish language of the nursery? Let those who can furnish the natural history of the fact then proceed to explain the counter part system of torture and excruciation among the Hindoos. I will abandon this department of the inquiry with one remark, that if Catholicity be, as is contended, the only true religion, because it can inspire its disciples with a calm disdain of agony and death, Hindooism has equal, if not superior, claims upon human credence a circumstance not incapable of reducing a Papal apologist to very serious perplexities.*

In the mean time the doctrine of compensation is perfectly intelligible, when interpreted in connection with the minor and supportable sacrifices offered by the Papal populace, at the shrines of their divinities. A sensualist will fast, if you will allow him a carnival. He will abstain from meat on Fridays, if you will take no notice of a voluptuous life. He will wear a vest of sackcloth, and wallow in ashes during Passion week on condition of re assuming the purple and fine linen at Easter. He will even attend daily mass, if he may regularly retire from the wafer to the pursuits of avarice vanity and ambition. He will give the church his public homage on the Sunday, provided the church, in exchange, will grant him the rest of the week. In other terms, bad men may be persuaded to observe the outward services of religion, so long as religion

* See an account of the crucifixion of the sisters and of the practices of the *convulsionnaires* in the Quarterly Review for Oct 1822 in the criticism on Gregoire art I. The reviewer asserts that the women thus crucified were pitiable fanatics acting under the direction of consummate knaves the former were made to believe they were expiating their sins pleasing God and gaining a brighter crown of eternal glory by their sufferings while the latter made use of them as instruments for adding to the dignity emoluments or reverence paid to themselves or their order. I must here confess notwithstanding my remarks in the text that if pardon peace with God deliverance from the alleged pains of purgatory emancipation from eternal punishment and an entrance into eternal life *were* really procurable by self tortures as such devotees suppose the price were small indeed compared with the benefit and their conduct thus falls perfectly within the range of sufficient causes.

does not interfere with the routine of private life, or—what is, with them, exactly the same thing—the pleasures and gains of the world.——At this point indeed, I cannot but observe, in passing, that if Christianity itself considered entirely apart from all other schemes of religion, be capable of a concise definition, the most distinctive one would be that so often cited "*The Gospel is the religion of the heart.*" Catholicity and indeed nominal Protestantism, in all its ramifications, is satisfied with an external adherence to forms, and an indolent assent to creeds: and if this kind of allegiance be rendered, the beneficiary dues of the altar not left in arrear, and respect shewn to ecclesiastical officers, all is right. Priests and people sleep on, and take their fatal rest. But the Gospel considers all the public ministrations of religion only as means subservient to a practical effect in daily conduct. If such effect be not discernible, all the externals of the system are regarded as a cause barren of consequences: or, if productive at all, fertile only in delusion and guilt.

To recur to the topics more immediately under discussion: and to descend from the pure and elastic atmosphere we might inhale in the regions of Christianity, into the dark profound of its corruptions. I observe that the pontifical treasury distributes RELICS, as one article of remuneration, for its penances and mortifications. They are deposited in cabinets with fond and sacred devotion: as an officer locks up the epaulette of the uniform in which Nelson fell off Trafalgar: or they are exhibited, as we shew, at the Tower, the armour of a line of kings *, and the spoils of the Spanish Armada. They are to devotees what keep sakes are to our rustic swains. We, the children of the Reformation, laugh at the relics and their manufacturers, and have many a pleasant tale to tell about this department of imposture: but the sagacity of the Court of Rome here returns the laugh upon ourselves, and recognises in these precious baubles a value which no derision of a heretic can diminish. Is there no compensation to a Catholic mind in the possession of what once belonged, as he thinks, to a saint or a martyr?

But, leaving what may be considered a very inferior point of examination, let us advance to the grand machinery of ABSOLUTION.—No one needs long hesitate in ascertaining the super eminent importance of this movement in the compensatory apparatus of the Roman Catholic communion. Christianity has probably received her most cruel wound from this instrument of her enemy's power. The weapon thus formed against her has indeed prospered and will go on to prosper, so long as the evangelical prophecy is not more fully accomplished. Consciousness of guilt produces in human bosoms various degrees of uneasiness and alarm: and considerable sacrifices will always be willingly made to obtain composure. No fact in the history of mankind is more obvious than this. It was accordingly seen that a conscience disordered by a sense of sin demanded a cure: and Popery administered an opiate. This is a medicament which suspends irritation and pain, but leaves the distemper as it was found: or, rather, it increases its malignity, and, in some cases, superinduces new forms of disease. But what patient is there, who is not eager to soothe paroxysms of pain, and to obtain even a short respite from its bitterness, by whatever means he finds to be successful? He takes the tranquillizing draught and has the prospect of a few hours'

---

* There is more analogy between the reliqueries of the Catholics and the armoury in the Tower than is at first apparent. Dr Meyrick in his late splendid treatise on ancient armour has detected anachronisms and marks of modern manufacture in the line of steel clad monarchs such as might afford parallelisms to the treasures of a monastery.

repose. This is precisely analogous to the vulgar effect of remission of sins among the Papal populace. Their transgressions are not forgiven, but the consciousness of their existence, and of the punishment due on their account, is, from time to time, suspended. The opiate is administered, and they sleep. But who does not discern the incalculable value of having this medicament *at command?* The Church of Rome may amply repay the fines she exacts in the shape of fees, fastings, ceremonial observances, and restrictions, when she gives back, in return, to guilty minds, even an indistinct and unsatisfactory persuasion that their iniquities are forgotten. Now, in the indiscriminate and gregarious administration of absolution, the sacerdotal boon is bestowed, not when vice is forsaken—for this cannot be known—but barely when it is confessed. The confession may be insincere, yet the remission is plenary. It is *therefore* most grateful to the confessed, and *therefore*, also, the possession of the powers of absolution is numbered among the richest sources of pontifical influence.

Such is the machinery of compensation, as put into action by the religion of human nature under the name of the Roman Catholic Church. How despotic is its form of government, and yet how dependent, for its very existence, on the abjectness and degradation of its subjects! For the secret truth—part of the underwork of the whole system—is, that, while the hierarchy of Rome professes to be entirely independent of human opinion, it is, all the while, the veriest slave to those whom it affects to despise, and to rule with irresponsible right. Covertly it flatters men's vanity, confirms their universal self-righteousness, and (as before suggested) upholds, for their sake, a magnificent scheme of antinomian delusion. Does any Christian philosopher feel the possibility of doubting that Antichristianity has deluged the world with its doctrines by a skilful adaptation of them to the prejudices of a sinful race, by encouraging on the one hand what it professes to disallow on the other, and by reaching the climax of its guilt, when it succeeds ultimately in teaching its adherents the dreadful art of being satisfied with themselves, and with their deceivers? So that the superstition of the Romanists, when exposed in the nakedness of its character, is discovered to be nothing more than one division of a wicked world holding in captivity the rest, and by means of fetters forged by the very slaves whom they bind. It is the few, who have gained the ascendancy, domineering over the many,—the many, as in the instance of absolution, being more than willing to transfer to the few their own guilt and responsibility; and the few having the terrific power of assuring the majority, of their ability to sustain the pressure, and to effect also the removal, of the burden. It is thus that, by the ministrations of Antichrist, bad men gain what they want,—a regular licence to live as they please, and a provision against the alarms of death, by periodical acquittals at the bar of the assumed vicegerents of Heaven.

Whatever may be said of this statement, as being an unfair account of the matter, and a detail, not of the doctrine of absolution, but of its abuses, I answer that in all human concerns we must argue on them, not as they exist in the refinements of theory, but as settled down in practice, when a recurrence to original principles only suffices to prove that these tenets lie buried in obsolete statutes, forgotten and inefficient, derided and despised. Besides, I will venture to assert, almost without the fear of contradiction from Papists themselves, that if absolution were pronounced exclusively on sincere penitents—supposing such sincerity were ascertainable—the confessionals would be deserted both by priests and people; the popularity of the invention would be exchanged for undisguised hatred; the charm of the mighty sorcery would be dissolved; and the foundations of the 'eternal city' shaken.

(*To be continued.*)

FAMILY SERMONS.—No. CCI.

Job x. 12—16. *Thou hast granted me life and favour, and thy visitation hath preserved my spirit. And these things hast thou hid in thine heart: I know that this is with thee. If I sin, then thou markest me, and thou wilt not acquit me from mine iniquity. If I be wicked, woe unto me; and if I be righteous, yet will I not lift up my head. I am full of confusion: therefore see thou mine affliction, for it increaseth.*

IN these words Job addresses God as his Creator, Preserver, and Benefactor; and he seems to ask, why, knowing his weakness and frailty, he laid upon him such heavy burdens as those which he was called upon to bear. He appears to have felt some difficulty in reconciling the past mercies of God with his present afflicting dispensations; and he sometimes betrays almost a tone of reproach in his language, as if he had been sought out and punished with more than the ordinary strictness of God's righteous judgments. Yet, amidst all, he acknowledges that his Creator doubtless had wise, though to him unknown, reasons for his dispensations. 'These things,' said he, 'thou hast hid in thine heart;' they were planned in thine infinitely wise, holy, and beneficent, though unsearchable, counsels—"I know this is with thee: to me, indeed, it is a source of trouble and perplexity, but to thee it is plain; it was rightly though mysteriously devised; it is equitably though severely executed." And then, as though glancing at the righteousness of God's law, on the one hand, and, on the other, at the sinfulness of mankind generally, and in particular at his own personal transgressions, with a sense of the imperfection of his best obedience, he adds, "If I be wicked, woe unto me; and if I be righteous, yet will I not lift up my head. I am full of confusion: therefore see mine affliction, for it increaseth."

This affecting passage sets before us, First, Job's acknowledgment of his infinite obligations to God. Secondly, the judicial relation in which he stood towards Him, and his conscious guilt and confusion at the prospect. Thirdly, his appeal to Him to compassionate his affliction.

I. First, then, we have Job's acknowledgment of his infinite obligations to God. 'Thou hast granted me life and favour, and thy visitation hath preserved my spirit.' This acknowledgment is threefold; comprising the blessings of creation, preservation, and the additional mercies which through the 'favour of God' he had been permitted to enjoy.

1. The blessing of creation. "*Thou hast granted me life.*"—Job is supposed to have existed at an early period of the world, and most probably before the time of Moses; yet he was well acquainted with that fundamental doctrine, with which Moses opens the book of Genesis, that God created the heavens and the earth, and all that they contain. He does not attribute his existence to chance or necessity; but speaks of it expressly as a grant from the Almighty; a grant bestowed for the most wise, benevolent, and momentous purposes. Practical atheism is at at all times too common even among many who profess and call themselves Christians. How few, comparatively are accustomed, like Job, constantly to refer their being to God; and that not merely as an article of their belief, but with a deep impression of what they owe to him; with a practical conviction that they are not their

own; and with a due sense of their obligation to live to His glory. They do not, indeed, doubt in theory—for who can for a moment doubt it?—that 'it is He that hath made us, and not we ourselves:' but as concerns those feelings of love and gratitude, of duty and responsibility, which such a belief ought to inspire, they live as widely separated from Him "in whom they live and move and have their being," as though no such relationship existed. Yet it is certain that an habitual feeling of reverence towards God as our Creator, though not the whole of religion, is a necessary and indispensable part of it. The Gospel of Christ, in pointing out to us other truths, essential to be known by us as fallen and guilty creatures, does not overlook, but on the contrary uniformly takes for granted, and displays this first natural and unalterable bond of union between the Creator and his creatures. The grant of life was the first benefit we were capable of enjoying; and it opened the way to all that followed. Without it, we had been infinitely lower than the very beasts that perish: we could not have shared even the meanest enjoyments of the basest reptile: we had been as the dust on which we tread, without power or consciousness; a mere blank amidst those happy tribes of beings whom the all-wise and benevolent Creator designed to enjoy the blessings of his providence, or the higher delights of his eternal presence.

2. But to the benefit of creation Job adds that of preservation. "*Thy visitation hath preserved my spirit.*"—The same Almighty Hand that formed and animated the human frame, sustains it amidst the perils to which it is every moment exposed. We do not live by chance, any more than we were at first formed by chance. One moment's absence of that Divine visitation which preserves our spirit, would suffice to plunge us back—we know not whither,—all our capacities for happiness, all our hopes for this world, and those brighter expectations which, as Christians, we cherish beyond the grave, would be utterly extinguished. In vain would be all that has hitherto been done for us: in vain a frame fearfully and wonderfully made: in vain the hearing ear, the seeing eye, the expanding intellect, the cheering affections, the glowing heart. But such an abandonment—we cannot say, is not possible—but we are assured never has or will take place. For, said the Psalmist, "If I ascend up into heaven, thou art there: if I make my bed in hell, behold, thou art there also: if I take the wings of the morning, and dwell in the uttermost parts of the sea, even there shall thy hand lead me, and thy right hand shall hold me." This powerful and unceasing visitation of the Creator preserves all things in their appointed rank and order: and to it we are indebted for our continued capacity for partaking of the blessings to which our creation introduced us.

3. To sum up the whole, Job adds the mention of that Divine "*favour*" without which our creation and preservation had been but the commencement and prolongation of misery.—And here how widely might we expatiate! How profusely might we heap together the innumerable blessings which a merciful Creator has showered, like the manna in the Wilderness, around our path! How thickly, how interminably, do his benefits cluster around us! By night and by day, in infancy and in manhood, in childhood and old age, in our personal and social relations, in our families and in the world, in sickness not less than in health, in adversity not less than in prosperity, he pours into our cup blessings infinitely beyond our deservings,—all flowing from the favour which, as a Creator, he bears to his creatures: and which, notwithstanding we have forfeited all claim to it by our sins and provocations, he did not withdraw from us

in our hour of deepest necessity, for even when we were sinners Christ died for us. And here opens before us the most wonderful of all proofs of his favour. Here beams upon us the stupendous revelation of the redemption that is in Christ. Here we behold why even the sinner, to whom, as a sinner, no Divine approbation can be exhibited, is yet spared, and crowned with so many benefits, in order that he may turn to the God whom he had forsaken, seek the mercy which he had despised, and be won by the long suffering which he had perhaps profanely made a motive for a continuance in his sins. The temporal marks of favour, hitherto chiefly spoken of, are, in the case of the true Christian, but the scanty first fruits of an eternal harvest; while to the careless and impenitent they are so many proofs that it is not till after the most ample exhibitions of Divine patience that God at length "swears in his wrath that they shall not enter into his rest." It may not be clear exactly to what extent Job, and other holy men in the Patriarchal times, were made acquainted with the particulars of that highest instance of God's favour to mankind, which under the New Testament dispensation is fully revealed—namely, the redemption of the world by the death of Christ and our justification freely by faith in him. There are, however, several apparent references to it in the book of Job; and in the very chapter before that from which our text is taken, we find him expressing his consciousness of the need of a Mediator between God and man; where he says, "He is not a man as I am, that I should answer him, and we should come together in judgment; neither is there any day's man (that is, an umpire or mediator) that might lay his hand upon us both." But, whatever might be the exact degree of spiritual knowledge afforded by early revelations to Job and other Patriarchal believers, we who live since that blessed period when life and immortality were fully brought to light by the Gospel, cannot but perceive how inestimably great was the favour, that, "in the ages to come, God shewed the exceeding riches of his grace in his kindness towards us, through Jesus Christ." Whether we consider the awful magnitude of our guilt, or the costly nature of the sacrifice made to atone for it, or the freeness and amplitude of the pardon bestowed upon us, we shall see that this was indeed the climax of Divine favour, to which our creation and preservation were but preparative; and the issue of which, to all who humbly avail themselves of it, will be an eternity of happiness in the world to come.

II. Secondly. Having thus traced Job's acknowledgment of his infinite obligations to God, we proceed to consider the judicial relation in which he describes himself as standing towards him, and his conscious guilt, and confusion at the prospect. We might have supposed that his expressive description of God's past mercies would have been succeeded by the warmest language of hope and confidence. And thus would it have been, had no obstacle interposed. The angels in heaven, in reviewing the benefits conferred upon them by their beneficent Creator, blend with their emotions of love and gratitude no symptoms of apprehension or alarm. They are not 'full of confusion' while they survey the mercies of Him who "granted them existence and favour, and whose visitation preserves their spirit." The past manifestations of God's overflowing bounty, are to them a pledge for the present; and the present for the future. But not so with man, when duly conscious of the ungrateful return which he has made for the bounties of his Almighty Benefactor. His conduct towards God he well knows, presents a most condemning contrast to the conduct of God towards himself

For every relationship involves certain duties: and most of all, the relationship of a creature to his Creator. The very bond of this relationship on the side of man, was perfect love, confidence and obedience. He had a law given him to obey, and he was bound by every tie to obey it. This law was holy, just, and good: it was not less for his own benefit, than for the glory of his Creator: and its sanctions, were the approbation or the displeasure of God: and consequent happiness or misery, both here and hereafter. A creature, if guiltless, would not tremble for the consequences of his own conduct under such a law: but what are the actual circumstances of man? Job seems to exhibit them, in the text, under a three fold view—supposing, first, a case which may be considered as the ordinary average of human character, 'If I sin:' next, a case of peculiar atrocity, "If I be wicked:" thirdly, a case of unusual moral rectitude, "If I be righteous:"—and in all these he shews the condition in which we stand before God.

1 "*If I sin, thou markest me, and thou wilt not acquit me from mine iniquity.*"—No extraordinary degree of profligacy seems to be here supposed: nothing more is stated than what we all acknowledge to be applicable to ourselves: for who is he that sinneth not? Yet how stands our condition under this aspect? First we learn, that God "marks us:" his omniscient eye is upon all our ways: our iniquities, many of which we may think venial, he notes down in the book of his remembrance: there they stand awfully recorded: and that not as an idle memorial: but for the express purpose of his visiting them with a corresponding punishment. "Thou wilt not acquit me." How fearful the condition of a creature thus exposed by his own sinful conduct to the just wrath of his Creator! Well might Job exclaim: 'I am full of confusion.' For who shall stand before God when he is displeased? who shall stay his hand when it is stretched out to inflict punishment?

2 *If I be wicked, woe unto me.*—The degree of guilt marked by this expression seems to be more flagrant than that implied in the former: it appears to point out, not the general average, appalling as it is, of human delinquency: but a high degree of atrocity of conduct: as where he says in the seventh verse, "Thou knowest I am not wicked." The conclusion in this case is therefore most clear: for if *every* sin is marked, if *no* iniquity is followed by acquittal, then woe indeed to the hardened, the deliberate transgressor! And would that even under this darker shade were not to be found too many who have had ample opportunities for learning the requirements of their Creator, and their own bounden obligation to obey them!

3 "*If I be righteous, yet will I not lift up my head.*—Job cannot here refer to perfect and unerring holiness of heart and conduct—for to such a degree of sanctity no human being can lay claim: if he could, he might justly lift up his head.—but he doubtless speaks comparatively, taking man at his best estate: selecting the most moral, the most upright, the most amiable pattern of human virtue: then in this most favourable case, shewing the utter incompetence of man to stand justified in the sight of his Creator. Put the matter to the test: collect all that is fairest and brightest in our fallen and corrupt nature: and then examine whether no taint of sin or imperfection is found: whether the selected individual has adequately lived up to the law of his creation: whether with all his virtues, he has loved, honoured and served his Creator with all his heart and soul and mind and strength, or has loved his neighbour as himself. So imperfect are our best actions, so mixed are our purest motives, that far from challenging the rewards of merit we

must acknowledge ourselves, on an impartial survey to deserve the punishment of our aggravated disobedience. At best we are unprofitable servants: "to us belongeth shame and confusion of face;" and if, instead of abasing ourselves in the very dust before the Divine Majesty, we should proudly lift up our heads in his presence, what should we behold in his hand but the record of our sins and follies, our ingratitude and disobedience; what in his piercing glance, but the frown of his insulted justice; or hear from his lips, but the sentence of our own irretrievable ruin? The friends of Job thought that he wished to try this experiment, that he justified himself before God; but his affliction had taught him a lesson more suitable to his frail and fallen condition; so that, instead of lifting up his head, his language was "Whom, though I were righteous, I would not answer; but I would make supplication to my Judge;" or, in the corresponding sentiment of the text, "See thou mine affliction, for it increaseth." And this leads us

III. Thirdly, to consider his humble appeal to God to have compassion upon him.—He claims no merit; he proffers no gift. He had acknowledged God's mercies to him, and confessed his inability to stand before his justice. What, then, is his hope of escape? It is in substance the language of the Publican, and of every true penitent in every age, "God, be merciful to me a sinner." His affliction was increasing; nothing but despair lay before him; but in his extremity he applies where none ever rightly applied in vain, to the infinite Source of mercy and compassion,— "See Thou mine affliction." How excellent is the example which he here sets before us! In every exigency of life, or when weighed down with the burden of our sins before God, let us betake ourselves to Him who will compassionate our weakness, assuage our sorrows, and forgive our transgressions. Happy is it for us that he is not a God afar off, but is at all times, as it were within reach of our humble petitions; and that he has appointed for us a way of access to his throne through a Mediator who ever liveth to make intercession for us. Let us thus approach him with the language of Job,—with fervent acknowledgments of his goodness and of our own ingratitude; of his infinite justice and our own unrighteousness; with self condemnation on the one hand, and a humble trust in his mercy in Christ Jesus on the other—and then will he look with pity upon our affliction, then will he pardon all our iniquities. For no sooner had Job practically acquired this just view of himself and of God, no sooner had he said, "I have heard of Thee by the hearing of the ear, but now mine eye seeth thee, wherefore I abhor myself and repent in dust and ashes;" than it is added, "The Lord turned the captivity of Job." And thus will he continue to be gracious to every sincere penitent, through the infinite merits of his beloved Son. Only let us not neglect or reject his offered mercy by "ignorance, hardness of heart, or contempt of his word and commandment."

CHRYSOSTOM'S HOMILIES—NO II DE STATUIS

A Homily delivered in like manner (as the preceding) in the Old Church, when he was Presbyter, on the subject of the calamity which befel the city of Antioch for a sedition in which the Statues of the Emperor Theodosius were thrown down; likewise upon that saying of the Apostle (1 Tim. vi. 17), "Charge them that are rich in this world, that they be not high minded:" also against Covetousness.

WHAT shall I say? what shall I speak? It is a time for tears, not for words for lamentations, not for discourses for prayer, not public harangues. Such is the magnitude of these audacious crimes, the ulcer so incurable, so great the wound, it surpasses all medical skill and demands help from above. When Job after the loss of all things was sitting on the dunghill his friends heard of it and came to him, and as soon as they saw him at a distance, they rent their clothes, sprinkled themselves with dust and wept aloud. The same ought to be done now by all the cities around us; they ought to come to our city, and lament its misfortunes and sympathize with her.* *He* was *then* sitting upon a dunghill, and *she* is *now* sitting in a great snare; for as then the devil sprang (ωρχησατο, danced) upon the flocks and herds, and the whole family of this just man, so has he now raged against this whole city; but God gave (him) permission both then and now; *then*, in order to make that just man a more illustrious (example) through the greatness of his temptations; and *now*, in order to teach us sobriety by the heaviness of our afflictions. Allow me to weep over our present condition. We have kept silence seven days, like the friends of Job; permit me this day to open my mouth, and bewail our common misfortune. Who hath bewitched us, O beloved, who hath envied us? Whence has so great a change arisen? Nothing was more august than our city, now nothing is more wretched; a people so tractable, of so mild a disposition, ever pliant to the will of its governors, like a horse made gentle and familiar to the hand, has now on a sudden plunged into such extravagancies, committed such crimes, as it is not lawful for me even to mention. I now bewail and lament, not the magnitude of the impending threat, but the extremity of the past outrage; for if the Emperor were not provoked and incensed, if he would inflict no punishment whatever, still how should we be able to endure the infamy of these transactions? While I (attempt to) address you, my voice is obstructed by grief; I am scarcely able to open my mouth and part my lips, and give utterance to my words. Such is the oppressive weight of sorrow, it perverts and bridles my tongue and embarrasses my speech. Our city was before in the greatest prosperity; now she is immersed in gloom and sadness; the inhabitants, like bees humming round the hive daily thronged the forum, and all men observed how eminently blest we were with a thriving population; but now the hive is become desolate, for as *those* by smoke, so *these* are driven out by fear. What the prophet said when mourning over Jerusalem, that may we justly apply to the present occasion (Isa. i. 30.) Our city is become "as a pine tree which casteth its leaves and as a garden that hath no water" [" as an oak whose leaf fadeth" in our Translation; Chrysostom quotes exactly the Septuagint.] For as a garden when its irrigation has long failed, exhibits trees stript of their leaves and devoid of fruit, such is our city now become; assistance from above has failed her, and she stands deserted, stript of nearly all her inhabitants.* Nothing was

These fugitives are witnesses to the

---

* It appears from Gibbon chap. xxvii. that many sought refuge in the mountains of Syria expecting a massacre—an expectation verified in the case of Thessalonica about three years after, and therefore not entirely groundless at Antioch. The fact was that commissioners arrived twenty-four hours after the sedition, before whom some of the noblest citizens appeared in chains, and examination by torture was resorted to, and the houses of the criminals were exposed to sale, and their families reduced from affluence to abject distress, and Chrysostom says many were put to death; but at the intercession of the monks and hermits these two commissioners ventured to suspend the remainder of the bloody execution that was expected, and one of them went to Theodosius to consult the will of his sovereign. During the awful suspense of this journey some of these sermons were preached, but this second was before the going of Ellebicus to Theodosius.

more delightful to them than their own country but now she is become to them of all others the most bitter and calamitous they are all flying from the soil that gave them birth, as out of a trap they are deserting it, as if it were a gulf (ready to swallow them up) they rush out as from a conflagration. For as, when a house is on fire, not only its inhabitants, but all the neighbours, fly with precipitation, being in haste to save their persons, even in a state of nudity so it is now the imperial resentment being expected to descend like fire, every one is in haste to depart and save himself, stripped of all from this flame, before it overtake him in its progress. Our afflicted condition is an enigma no enemy, yet a flight no fighting, yet emigration and exile no capture, and yet captivity. We have not seen the fire of the barbarous nations we have not beheld the face of a foe, and yet we suffer as if the city was taken by storm.

All men are now informed of our calamity having received our fugitives from them they learn the consternation of our city. But I am not ashamed on this account, nor do I blush let them all be informed of the sufferings of this city that they may sympathize with their metropolis, and in every part of the land unite in lifting up their voice to God and supplicate with one consent the King of Heaven in behalf of their common parent and supporter. Our city has in time past been shaken by earthquakes but now the minds of its inhabitants are shaken then the foundations of the houses were shaken, now the very foundations of every heart are agitated. Daily do we all behold death before our eyes, and live in perpetual fear and undergo the punishment of Cain being in a more wretched condition than the inhabitants of a prison and sustaining a siege altogether strange and novel, much worse than a common one. For in this case, as men suffer from an (external) enemy, they are shut up only within the walls (of the city) but even the forum is inaccessible to us, and every man is shut up within the walls of his own house and as, in besieged places, it is not safe to go without the walls an enemy being posted there so neither is it safe for many of the inhabitants of this city to go out and appear in public, on account of the spies, who are in quest of the innocent as well as the guilty who snatch men from the forum, and drag them at random before the tribunal of justice. Men of generous extraction sit as prisoners in their own houses, in the company of their servants, anxiously inquiring, of such as are likely to be well informed, who has been apprehended to day, who has been committed to prison, who punished how, in what manner. Thus they lead a life more wretched than any death compelled, as they daily are to bewail the misfortunes of others, alarmed about their own security, and already levelled with the dead—for dead, indeed, they are with fear. But if any one, superior to such alarm, has a mind to repair to the forum, at the appalling sight he immediately retreats into his house, when he sees scarcely one or two and those bent towards the earth and with a dejected air pass over the vacant area so lately thronged with multitudes exceeding the confluence of (many) streams but now all these are chased from us and as a grove of oaks when many of them are cut down on every side or as a head entirely despoiled of hair presents an aspect ungrateful to the eye so now

---

reality of the danger and their evidence is much superior to Gibbon's who sneering at the monks and hermits who came to the city when others forsook it says that this courage of theirs was not attended with much risk. The risk at Thessalonica was however manifest by the many innocent who perished with the guilty and Antioch was certainly involved in a treasonable transaction of a similar nature though not so aggravated besides half the inhabitants of Antioch were still Pagans consequently no friends of monks and hermits

do the streets and pavements of this city, thinned of its inhabitants, having a few only scattered here and there, by the dismal aspect overspread the beholders with a dark cloud of despondency. And not only the ground but even the atmosphere, and the rays of the solar orb, appear to be obscured: not that the elements have changed their nature: the change is in our sight: our mental gloom has suffused the eye with turbid humours, and cast a mist before it, and intercepted* the pure rays of light. It was thus the Prophet spake (Amos viii. 9) in *his* lamentations: "Their sun shall go down at noon, and the day shall become dark:" and this he said, not as if the sun should be actually hidden, or the day light disappear: but because the people would be so dispirited as even at noon day to be unable to behold the light for the (internal) darkness of (their own) sorrow: which is now the case (with us). Whithersoever any one looks, whether to the pavement, the walls, the pillars of the city, or towards his neighbours, he seems to behold nothing but night and profound darkness: so universally does despondency reign, and a horrible silence, and utter desolation. Extinct is the animating busy hum of men: as if all were sunk into the earth. Silence pervades the city. They resemble stones: and, their tongues being fettered by their misfortunes, they preserve a solemn stilness, as at the near approach of an enemy wasting all things with fire and sword. Well may we now say, (Jer. ix. 17), "Call for the mourning women, that they may come: and the cunning women, that they may take up a wailing for us: that our eyes may run down with tears, and our eye lids gush out with waters. Take up a wailing for us, ye hills: and, ye mountains, a lamentation. Let us call upon the whole creation to sympathize with our affliction. A city so great, the metropolis of the East, in danger of being extirpated out of the earth! She had a multitude of children—suddenly she is become childless—and there is no one to help us, for he whom we have insulted has no equal upon earth: our sovereign is the head and summit of all earthly (power). Let us fly therefore, to that Sovereign who is above: on *Him* let us call for help: there is no remedy for what has been done, but by obtaining favour from above.

Here I could wish to close the subject: for the minds of the afflicted are averse to dilatory harangues: for as a dense cloud, intercepting the solar rays, rejects and throws back all the splendour, so a cloud of despair, overshadowing the mind, obstructs the entrance of exhortation and counsel: and chokes and suppresses them with much inward vexation. And this is the case not with speakers only, but also with the hearers: for as it does not permit the words to issue from the mind of the speaker with facility, so neither to penetrate the understanding of the hearers with their appropriate force. Wherefore, in former times, the Jews, when harassed with their clay and brick, could not bear to hear Moses speaking to them so frequently of their deliverance: dejection stopping their ears, and making their minds inaccessible to his words. For this reason I was myself desirous here to close this (painful) subject. But when I consider, that, though it be the nature of a cloud to obstruct the further progress of the rays of light: yet is it frequently otherwise—for when a hotter sun, by continually impinging, wastes a cloud, it often cleaves it asunder: and shining through (it) with condensed rays strikes the eye with a peculiar splendour—the same, I trust, that I shall this day effect: and, by the word being continually addressed

---

* See page 463 line 24 μηδ μ τατης αυτης διαθ σ ως—the *disposition* (to refract and reflect rays) *not being the same*. But I am uncertain about the true sense of these Greek words: therefore refer your readers to the page and line.

to you, and abiding with more constancy in your souls, I shall, I hope, break through the cloud of despondency, and diffuse, as before, the light of instruction over your minds. Surrender then your hearts to me; give me an attentive hearing; shake off this gloom for a little while; let us return to our former habits; and, as we have been always accustomed to attend in this place with alacrity and cheerfulness, the same let us do now, casting all (our care) upon God: and this will contribute to our deliverance: for if He see us diligently hearing his word, and not at all impaired in our devotion by the difficulties of the times, he will soon come to our relief, and make a calm, a happy deliverance from our present tempestuous condition. A Christian ought to be distinguished from an unbeliever by bearing all things with fortitude: winged with the hopes of futurity, he should ascend above the reach of mortal sufferings. The believer stands upon a rock: he is impregnable to the assault of waves; though the waves of temptation rise high, they cannot reach his feet: he is elevated above all such attacks. Then let us not despond, O beloved. *We* are not so careful for our own preservation as the God who made us. That we may suffer no very grievous calamity is not so much an object of concern to us, as it is to Him, who bestowed upon us the gift of an immortal spirit, and superadded so many other blessings. With such hopes let us elevate our minds and dispose them to attend to this discourse with their usual alacrity.

I have of late, my brethren, extended my discourses to a considerable length, and perceived that you were all attentive, and that no man withdrew. I return you thanks for your attention, and accept it as the reward of my labours. But I then requested of you another reward besides this: perhaps you know and remember (it); but what was this reward?—that you would chastise and admonish the blasphemers in this city; that you would restrain those who insult God himself with all the rudeness of a drunkard. I think that I did not then speak those words of myself, but that God, who foresaw what was coming, suggested them to my mind: for if we had punished those audacious offenders, the late events would not have occurred. How much better would it have been to have exposed ourselves to danger, yea, to have actually suffered, for admonishing and chastizing them (which would have procured us the crown of martyrdom), than to live in fear, as we do now, to tremble, and to be in expectation of suffering death for their sedition? Behold, the crime, which was committed by a few, is imputed to us all: see how they have now involved us in a general alarm, and we are expecting to undergo the punishment of their crimes: but if we had been beforehand with them, and expelled them from the city, and by reproof and admonition restored the diseased member to soundness, we should have escaped the present alarming crisis. I know that the inhabitants of this city are and long have been, distinguished for a liberal and ingenuous behaviour. Certain *strangers*, the refuse of mankind, vile and mischievous men who despair of their own salvation, (these it is who) have committed these daring crimes. Continually, therefore, did I cry aloud, and bear testimony (against them saying) 'Let us punish the madness of blasphemers, let us restore them to sobriety of mind; let us make some provision for their salvation: though we should die for so doing, it would (still) be great gain to us: let us not wink at insults offered to the Lord of all; to connive at such crimes will bring some great calamity on this city.' These things I spake some time ago: these things are now come to pass: we are (now) suffering the punishment of that supineness. You suffered God to be insulted: behold *He* has permitted your so vereign to be insulted, and extreme danger to be suspended over all our heads, that by this alarm we might pay the penalty of that sinful negligence. Did I not foretell these things, and continually trouble you (about them), all to no purpose? however, nothing more was done. But let something be done *now* being reclaimed by this present disaster, let us restrain their inordinate phrensy: let us stop their mouths as fountains of a poisonous and deadly quality, let us close them, and infuse opposite qualities: then will the evils that have assailed the city altogether cease.

The church is not a theatre, that we should hear for amusement: we ought to go hence improved: with some new, some great profit should we return (from these assemblies). In vain have we resorted to them, if it be only to have our minds beguiled and captivated for a moment, and depart without permanent edification. What good will these plaudits do me, these tumultuous commendations? Your actions are my praise, when they exemplify my precepts: then am I (truly) enviable and happy, not when ye receive, but when ye cheerfully perform whatever ye hear from us. Let every one admonish his neighbour, for so the Apostle speaks (1 Thess. v. 11) " Edify one another. If we neglect it, the guilt, being contracted by every individual, will bring down a public and grievous judgment upon the city. Observe, that we, who were not privy to the design, are as much alarmed as the perpetrators themselves, and tremble lest the vengeance of our sovereign should comprehend us all. It is not a sufficient excuse for us to say: "I was not present, I was not privy to these transactions, I had no share in them: for that very reason take thy share of punishment: submit, will he say to the rigour of the law, because thou wast *not* present: because thou didst not prevent (mischief), nor curb the disorderly, nor expose thyself to any danger for the honour of thy sovereign. Thou didst not participate in the crime: for this I commend thee: but neither didst thou hinder it: this deserves condemnation. And we may hear God addressing us to the same effect, whenever we pass by in silence the insults offered to *him*: for he who hid his talent in the earth, was not then accused concerning any thing secreted and reserved for himself, for he restored what was entrusted to him without any diminution: but because he did not increase it, because he did not instruct others, because he did not put the money to the exchangers —that is, did not exhort, did not counsel, did not reprove: did not [attempt to] reclaim the wicked and disorderly in his own circle— therefore, without any pardon, he was sent into those intolerable punishments. But though not before, that ye will *now* apply to this work of reformation, and no longer overlook the insults offered to God, I am fully persuaded: for the events which have befallen us are sufficient, without any exhortation, to persuade even the most insensible to secure henceforth their own salvation.

But it is time for us to set before you the usual portion of instruction from the writings of Paul: selecting the part which has this day been read. " Charge them that are rich in this world, that they be not high minded." 1 Tim. vi. 17.

By the expression " rich in *this* world," he intimates that there are rich persons of a different sort—those of the world to come. Such was Lazarus:—with respect to this present world, poor; but with respect to the world to come, rich—not in the wealth of gold and silver, or any substance of the same corruptible and transitory nature: rich in those unspeakable treasures which neither eye has seen, nor ear heard, nor has it entered into the heart of man (to conceive): and these are riches indeed, which are without alloy, and not susceptible of change. But as to the rich man who neglected him it was not so with him he soon after became the poorest of mortals, begging a drop of cold water, and not obtaining even that to such extreme poverty and destitution was he reduced He also called them rich in *this* world, for the purpose of reminding you that this abundance terminates with the present life proceeds no further does not accompany its possessors when they depart indeed often deserts them before their departure which he intimates in these words ' Nor trust in uncertain riches for nothing is so treacherous as wealth which as I have often said and will say it again is a fugitive slave without understanding a perfidious domestic Though loaded with chains it will soon escape dragging its chains with it Often have its possessors enclosed it with doors, and bars, and guards on every side but it seduced the guards themselves and took to flight along with them, drawing them as if they were enchained and all these precautions were of no avail What then can be more treacherous? And who can be more wretched than they who are devoted to the pursuit of it since with the utmost diligence they labour to collect things so frail and mutable and pay no regard to the Prophet who says [Ps xxxviii 10 is referred to in the margin but it should be xxxix 6 and in the Septuagint and our version also the former member of the sentence is differently translated], ' Woe to them that trust in their own power and boast in the multitude of their riches And for what reason did he pronounce this woe? (because) says he he layeth up treasures and knoweth not for whom he shall gather them so that the labour is certain but the enjoyment uncertain In many cases (may it be said) Thou art toiling and afflicting thyself for (the benefit of) thine enemies thy property will devolve after thy death upon those who injured thee and often plotted against thee it will be a source—to thyself, of sin—to others of enjoyment

But the question may justly be asked, Why did he not say, Charge them that are rich in this world to be rich no longer charge them to become poor, to divest themselves of their wealth instead of saying Charge them not to be high minded? He knew that a vain confidence and elation of mind are the very root and essence of riches * that there will be little zeal and application in amassing them wherever there is the wisdom of a temperate mind For tell me the reason why you go about with a large retinue of servants with parasites and flatterers and every species of pomp? It is not on account of any utility but vanity alone in order that you may attract a greater degree of reverence And besides the Apostle knew that riches were not forbidden, if a man use them as necessity and duty require for, as I said (on a former occasion) that not wine but drunkenness, is evil so now that not money, but the *love* of money, is ev It is one thing to be covetous, and another to be rich The covetous man is not rich, for he stands in need of many things and he who wants many things can never be said to be opulent The covetous man is the guard not the possessor of money the servant, not the master for he would sooner give a man a portion of his flesh than of his concealed treasure Just as if somebody had commanded him not to touch what he had laid up so does he preserve it all with the greatest exactness abstaining from his own as if it were another man's And indeed it does belong to another for as he would rather undergo the severest punishment than dispense it to others or distribute it among the poor, how can he imagine that it is his own? and how can he have

---

* Savile in a note thinks it should have been Riches are the root of vain confidence but Boisius more justly remarks that ἀπονοια is both a cause and effect of riches

the possession, when he has not the free use and enjoyment of it?

* Moreover, Paul does not usually lay injunctions upon all men indiscriminately, but condescends to the infirmities of his hearers even as Christ himself did: for to the rich man who came and conversed with him about (eternal) life, he did not (immediately) say, Go and sell thy property: but, passing over this, discoursed with him about the other commandments: afterward when he challenged him, by saying What lack I yet? even then he did not simply say, Sell that thou hast, but, "*If thou wilt be perfect*, go and sell that thou hast." I refer you to your own sentiments and leave you to choose without controul: I lay no necessity upon you. In like manner Paul also did not exhort the rich to poverty, but humility; on account of the infirmity of his hearers, and also because he well knew that moderation, and the mortification of pride, would soon liberate them from eagerness in the pursuit of riches.

Now (the Apostle) when he exhorts (the rich) not to be high minded, teaches them at the same time how they may be enabled to comply with this exhortation. How, then, may this be effected? By thoroughly considering the nature of riches: how very uncertain they are: how little to be trusted. Wherefore he added, 'Nor trust in uncertain riches.' The rich man is not he who possesses much: but he who gives away much. Abraham was rich, but not a lover of riches: for he did not look around upon this man's house nor curiously inquire into that man's substance: but he went out and looked round to see if he could find any stranger or any poor man, that he might relieve poverty: that he might lodge the traveller. He did not overlay his roof with gold, but patching up a cabin under an oak, was content with the shadow of its leaves,—illustrious and venerable abode, where even angels deigned to be his guests! for they were in quest of, not the splendours of a mansion, but the virtue which adorns the soul. Him let us imitate. O beloved, and bestow our goods upon the poor. His was a temporary dwelling slightly constructed: and yet more illustrious than the halls of princes. No king ever entertained angels: but the man who sat under that oak, and reared himself a hut, was counted worthy of that honour. Not for the meanness of his dwelling was he honoured: by the valuable qualities of his soul: by the riches laid up therein did he obtain this distinction. Let us not then, adorn our houses instead of our houses, (let us adorn) our souls. How great a reproach it is to case the walls with marble, while we neglect Christ as he walks on every side of us destitute of clothing! What need have you of a [splendid and ostentatious] house O man? Can you carry it away with you, when you depart? You shall not carry it with you, but your soul undoubtedly you must. You see what a dangerous condition we are in. Let your houses stand by you: let *them* rescue you from the impending danger: they are not able: and ye bear witness to it yourselves: for ye are leaving them empty and are taking your departure for the desert: as if ye feared lest some net or snare should entrap you. Let your money help you now: but this is no time for that. And if the power of money is proved to be unavailing against the wrath of man, much more will that be the case at the divine and impartial tribunal. If now, when it is a *man* who is provoked and full of indignation against us money is of no avail, how much more, when God's anger burns (who cannot need any thing of ours), will the utter impotence of wealth appear?

We build houses that we may dwell in them: not for ostentatious

---

* This is the third answer to the question proposed.

emulation that which is larger than we can make use of, that which exceeds the limit of usefulness, is even worse than useless Put on a shoe too large for thy foot but thou wilt not bear the inconvenience, because it clogs thee in walking so a house too spacious to be useful, is an incumbrance in our progress towards heaven

(*To be continued*)

To the Editor of the Christian Observer

I HAVE been much interested in the specimen, with which you have favoured your readers, of Chrysostom's Homilies for though the writings of this, as of the other Fathers, contain much that is inconsistent with modern ideas of logic, good taste, and pulpit discussion, and some things not perfectly scriptural yet I am persuaded that, notwithstanding these exceptions, there is in these neglected stores a mine of spiritual wealth which would well repay a more diligent working than is usually bestowed upon it The writings of the Fathers have stood the severe test of ages and it is not a mark of our theological wisdom that they are at present almost wholly laid aside It would confer an obligation on many of your readers, if the learned translator of the extracts from Chrysostom or some other correspondent versed in ecclesiastical studies, would point out what advantages are likely to accrue from the judicious perusal of the Fathers, to theological students, as well as to the private Christian Daillé, a learned French Protestant minister, published, in 1632, his treatise on the use of the Fathers in determining theological controversies which was translated into English and published in London about twenty years after And Reeves, an English clergyman in his preface to his translation of the "Apologies of the Fathers, published in 1709, has a dissertation on the same subject, in which he estimates the value and authority of the Fathers much more highly than Daillé was disposed to do Both these works, and some others, might be profitably consulted on the subject but the judicious theologian, in the present day, would probably incline to a middle view between them for if Daillé is considered by many persons as attributing too little to the Fathers, Reeves unquestionably attributes too much Keeping steadily before us the fundamental principle that 'the Bible, and the Bible only, is the religion of Protestants, we are not likely to err with the Church of Rome, in her blind veneration for these ancient worthies or to introduce them as arbiters in controversies which the Scriptures alone must be allowed to determine but, at the same time, they may be studied to great profit, especially by the Clergy and a brief exposition of their excellencies and defects would greatly oblige a constant reader,

R X

To the Editor of the Christian Observer

ON FAITH

CONSENT implies union which is an increment to assent, and the distinction I apprehend, subsisting between the two words Consent is agreement about something in union assent is agreement about something not in union Reciprocity is implied in the one, and not in the other The devils believe with fear and hatred they cannot believe with confidence and love they assent but cannot consent, to the truth because they never can be united with it their nature forbids the union, and is unchangeable 'God is love his nature is spiritual and unchangeable Union with the one nature is disunion from the other Human nature is changeable it was spiritual it may become so again it is the object of Christianity to make it so Whenever spiritual influence is *entirely* withdrawn, it becomes altogether sen sual, and 'at enmity with God and, *as such*, it can only believe, tremble, and hate.' Whenever spiritual influence is *fully* present, human nature becomes spiritual and at peace with God, and, *as such*, it believes, confides and loves. This nature retains the capacity of being spiritualized and changed, but not of spiritualizing and changing itself: it retains the capacity of *assenting* to the truth, but not of *consenting* to, and uniting itself with it. The change from sensual to spiritual mindedness, therefore, is entirely the work of God, and our union with him, his love and peace, is the effect of this work; for if God did not 'give this increase' to our assent to Gospel truth, no spiritual benefit could accrue from it, nothing spiritual could attach to it, we could not confide and love; and until it is given we are separated from him and cannot be joined to him. The planting of Paul, the watering of Apollos, the working of miracles, the accomplishment of prophecies, and the reading and hearing of the word of God, are the means appointed to produce *assent* to the truth of the Gospel on the human mind; but they cannot produce consent, for that implies *union* with God, and must be given by himself. The increase therefore given by God is that which changes our *sensual* assent into *spiritual* consent, and makes it *faith*, by uniting it with the Spirit.

The inference I would wish to draw from the above is, that the human mind is required and must give *assent* to the truths of the Gospel propounded to it by revelation, and that it is capable of investigating and being convinced by its evidences; but that it cannot give consent to them, and is incapable of deriving any benefit from them without Divine grace, because it cannot spiritualize and unite itself with them. If then human ability can only assent to Divine truth when propounded to unassisted reason, but cannot consent to it without preventing and assisting grace, it follows, that grace effects the union and the change from assent to consent, and gives *entirely* the spiritual increase; that 'no one can come to Christ except the Father draw him,' and that 'no one can say that Jesus is the Lord but by the Holy Ghost.' If this be so, the Scriptures enlighten the natural understanding by setting before it, and convincing it of, truths about which it must otherwise have remained in total ignorance, and are the appointed means of producing its assent to the Gospel; but I contend that this assent is not faith, which implies union with the Gospel; because, if the Spirit of truth does not unite itself with it and make it spiritual, it still remains sensual. For the same reason the assent of the natural will and affections which are effects of the assent of the natural understanding or reason, are not fruits of faith, because the same spiritual union is still wanting which makes them such. I conceive, therefore, that preventing and assisting grace must always go before and accompany human endeavours, to make them spiritual, pleasing and acceptable to God in Christ; and that they must always be interposed by the mercy of God, to give that spiritual increase 'without which nothing is strong, nothing is holy;' that without this grace of God by Christ preventing us, we can have no good will, and working with us when we have that good will, we can have no good affections, and bring forth no good* fruit, and that the implanting of this spiritual increase is the ordinary operation of the Holy Ghost upon our souls (on meeting with assent to the truth) which changes the assent of reason

---

* Good in Scriptural language means the same as heavenly and spiritual and refers to God; it is opposed to evil, corrupt, sensual, worldly, carnal. In this sense nothing is good but what comes from God and belongs to him; but what is of him and through him and to him to whom be the glory of it for ever.

into spiritual consent, makes it an actuating spiritual principle, unites us with Christ, and brings us under the guidance of the Spirit.

Hence I would define *faith* to be *spiritual consent to Gospel truth*, of heavenly growth and incorruptible seed, which necessarily engages all the faculties of the soul in its service; and I would leave *bare human assent*, or whatever falls short of *this consent*, as of earthly growth and corruptible seed, which can neither produce good fruit, nor lay up treasure in heaven. This broad line of demarcation appears to me to be laid down by St. Paul: "Whatsoever is not of faith is sin." I am, yours, &c. L. R.

To the Editor of the Christian Observer.

YOUR Correspondent, in his highly interesting account of the French Protestant Church, in speaking of Mr. Scott's Commentary, has these words: 'By his sober and devout criticism.' Now that Mr. Scott's criticisms and observations are always "devout," no one will dispute; but that they are always 'sober,' may well be questioned, even by his warmest admirers. One instance to the contrary just occurs to me, which I think it may not be unimportant to point out, in order to guard the reader against a system of Scriptural interpretation, from the effects of which even Mr. Scott is not always free, but which in less cautious hands has been carried to a most injurious excess, reducing the inspired and infallible page to a text book for far fetched analogies, and the exercise of fanciful ingenuity. I would ask then, is it sober, or judicious, or what was to have been expected from such a man as Mr. Scott, to bring forward Samson as a type of Christ? Without, however, entering upon the subject of types in general, or of this strangely supposed type in particular, I shall content myself with giving your readers the following extract on this very point from a contemporary commentator.—Dr. Adam Clarke. It well merits serious attention, not only in reference to the alleged type immediately in question but as bearing upon the general system of interpretation above alluded to, and which, I am persuaded, is equally at variance with sound scriptural explication, and the edification of the heart or mind of the Christian. It is very rarely indeed that we are warranted in discovering types or analogies, except where the sacred text itself points them out.

'A parallel, says Dr. Clarke, has been often drawn between Samson and our blessed Lord, of whom he has been supposed to be a *most illustrious type*. By a fruitful imagination and the torture of words and facts we may force resemblances every where; but that not one will *naturally* result from a cool comparison between Jesus Christ and Samson, is most demonstrable. A more exceptionable character is not to be found in the sacred oracles. It is no small dishonour to Christ to be thus compared. There is no resemblance in the *qualities* of Samson's mind; there is none in his moral conduct that can entitle him even to the most distant comparison with the chaste, holy, benevolent, and immaculate Jesus. That man dishonours the law of unchangeable righteousness, who endeavours to make Samson a type of any thing or person that can be called holy, just, and pure.'

THEOGNIS

MISCELLANEOUS

For the Christian Observer

The claims of the inhabitants of the enormous empire of China, and of the nations of Corea, Japan, the Loo Choo Islands, and Cochin China, where the Chinese language is familiar, to the sympathies and benevolent efforts of Christians for their spiritual welfare, are of such vast magnitude that it is most important that the British public in general, and especially the friends of religious missions, should become much better acquainted, than they at present are, with the actual circumstances of that large proportion—some writers say, one fourth!—of the human race. The difficulties of the language, and the still greater difficulties of access to the people, have doubtless been serious impediments in the way; but a still greater obstacle, perhaps, has been the ignorance or indifference of Christians to the unparelleled magnitude of the object. It is trusted, however, that the exertions which are now in progress for removing this ignorance and indifference, especially the indefatigable labours of Dr Morrison, will before long produce a most decided and powerful effect. With a view to assist this great object the following Memoranda of Chinese Literature, taken from Dr Morrison's elaborate researches, will, it is hoped, be found interesting and useful, and may be followed up, in a future communication, by some additional details.

R. S.

Knotted cords were, it is said, originally used in China to signify the intentions of rulers, and to be in some degree the signs of ideas. The next step towards improvement was made by Tsang hee, who is represented with four eyes, and who lived, they say, about 2600 years before Christ. He, observing the appearance of a certain constellation, the veins on the shell of a tortoise, and the print of a horse's foot, first conceived the idea of forming letters. Bamboos pared thin were first used to write upon; cloth, or silk, was next employed; and about the first century of our era paper was invented. The original pencil was the point of a stick, which was dipped in a liquid ink; hair pencils existed so early as 300 years B. C. About A. D. 600, solid squares of ink were invented; and during the tenth century the art of taking off on paper an impression from an engraving was discovered; and hence the Chinese wooden stereotype printing arose.

The following is a classification of the various branches of Chinese literature.

I. *The literature of China* consists first, of the writings or compilations of the moral philosophers of the age of Confucius (B. C. 500) with notes, and paraphrases, and controversies on the original text. The text of the *Woo king* which name denotes *Five Sacred Books* and of the *Sze shoo*, or *Four Books*, which were compiled by *four* of the disciples of Confucius, and from which circumstance the books receive their title, contain the doctrines and precepts which their master, Confucius, approved and communicated to them. In respect of external form, the *Five Books* (Woo king) of the Chinese correspond to the *Pentateuch* of Moses and the *Four Books* (Sze shoo) in respect of being a record of the sayings of a master, compiled by *four disciples* have a slight resemblance to the four Gospels. But the contents—how different! With the exception of a few passages in the most ancient part of the *Woo king* which retain seemingly something of the knowledge which Noah must have communicated to his children, the rest appears a godless system of personal, domestic, and political moralities, drawn only from the pride of the human heart, or the love of fame, or present expediency. The sanctions of the Eternal and Almighty God arrayed with every natural and moral perfection, wise and good, and just and merciful and the fears and the hopes of immortality and the grace of a Saviour are wholly wanting in these ancient Chinese works.

II. In the more serious parts of the Chinese literature may next be placed, *Histories* of China, and of its domestic and foreign wars especially with the Huns and the Tartars which are voluminous, and are generally written in a grave style, interspersed with remarks on the persons and occurrences which pass in review and occasionally an attempt is made to trace effects to the causes supposed to operate in the dual system of the universe, which they have gratuitously assumed as true and by which system of materialism they imagine both the physical and moral world are influenced.

The Chinese historians place their deluge about 2200 years B C, and carry back their antediluvian traditions concerning their great ancestor *Fuh he* (Fo hi), and *Neu wo* who melted stones, and repaired the heavens to about the year 3200 B C. Whether *Neu wo* was a man or woman, they know not for they say that although the character *woman* enters into the name, there were not at that time any letters and therefore the character now used proves nothing. Indeed in the time of Confucius the leaves of Chinese books were still rude slips of board having equally rude symbols marked with red ochre. Choo foo tsze and other Chinese historians, have not much confidence in the records of those remote times and consider all legends beyond that period as undoubtedly fabulous. There may be some truth in the traditions of great events and the existence of famous persons, anterior to the age of Confucius but certainly not much dependence can be placed on particular dates, or minute circumstances, which, as Choo foo tsze says subsequent historians have "pushed up to that period, for the sake of embellishment."

III. Historical novels constitute a favourite department of Chinese reading. other novels delineate the characters and manners of persons in private and domestic life which species of writing was originated by a desire of one of their monarchs, who could not mix with the people, to have their characters drawn, and their conversation and pursuits exemplified for his own use. Some of these compositions describe the vicious and profligate part of mankind in a manner that is offensive to decency. hence there are fathers in China who disallow all novel-reading. and the licentious novels are prohibited by law but, like the laws against gaming, and opium smoking, this law is very laxly executed and is not violated more by any class of the community than by magistrates, government clerks, and police runners. Very few of the Chinese novels are of the romance kind.

IV. The press of China produces also dramatic works which, like the novels, are generally published under fictitious names. Neither the one nor the other is considered a respectable department of literature.

V. The poetry of China consists chiefly in short compositions, expressing the tender or mournful feelings of the human heart. or descriptive of rural scenery. Of that poetry which is set to music their dramatic compositions contain a considerable portion and their popular songs come under the same class. The candidates for government offices are examined in the composition of verses which practice is opposed by some Chinese writers as useless, but defended by others, who argue, that poetry leads to an acquaintance with the passions or feelings of human nature, and as these must be consulted by every man who would well rule human nature, poetry is a proper study for the monarch, the minister, and the magistrate. This is in accordance with the precepts of the moralizing politicians of China, who always maintain that none can govern well or durably, but those who win the people's hearts by an adherence to the principles of equal rights, and a clement justice. The Chinese, we believe, have nothing that can be called epic poetry. The most ancient poetical compositions were a collection of popular songs made at the request of government, in order to ascertain the popular feeling, which, as has already been hinted, the Chinese monarchs have generally thought it right to consult. Although the ladies of China are not usually literary, there are exceptions; and in an educated family, the writing of verses from a theme given at the moment, by one of the party, is practised as an amusing trial of skill. The triennial odes composed at the public examinations, which obtain the prize of a certain rank, and eligibility to office, are usually printed and published. And these specimens of versification, together with the prize essays, written from themes extracted from the ancient books already noticed, are almost the only new publications in China at the present day. The literati of China now existing are either candidates for office, who go through the prescribed routine of studies, or laborious compilers of the sayings of others.

VI. The *collectanea* of appeals or remonstrances from public officers, and of the opinions of philosophers, and of the disputes of controversialists, and the endless *et cætera* of compilers, constitute another class of literary compositions.

VII. Geographical and topographical works are also abundant; the first named are very imperfect; the latter are voluminous and minute, marking every tomb and temple, and hill and dale, with the utmost exactitude; all of which detail interests the natives of China, but is tiresome to the inhabitants of Europe.

VIII. Medical books, containing the theory and practice of the healing art, are abundant in China. They have great confidence in the theory of the dual powers, which is introduced into this department of science and literature; and rely much on the recorded recipes of eminent practitioners. In works on medicine, the best notices of natural history, whether belonging to the animal, mineral, or vegetable kingdoms, are contained. In the medical works of China are to be found the doctrine of the circulation of the blood round the human system; the use of Glauber's salts, and of mercury, in ordinary practice; the last named of which medicines has now, however, fallen into disrepute. The theory of the pulse is in China carried by practitioners to a degree of exactness, which baffles the most careful attention of European surgeons to discriminate. When the Chinese and English practitioners have been seated at the same table and felt the pulse of the same patient, the one has professed to ascertain symptoms of which the other was unable to ascertain any thing. The Chinese are not at all convinced by the reasoning of the West, that, pulses being simultaneous in all parts of the body, the feeling of one pulse is therefore equal to the feeling of more than one; for they suppose that local disease may make a difference.

IX. Astronomical works in Chinese generally fall into the dreams of astrology, and state with wearisome minuteness lucky and unlucky, felicitous or infelicitous days and hours for bathing, for shaving, for commencing a journey, or beginning to sow, or to plant, or to visit a friend, or to make a bargain, &c &c. They can, however, without the aid of Europeans, foretell eclipses, and state, with considerable accuracy, other celestial phenomena.

X. A tenth species of composition in China, is the *Wăn chang*, or prize essays of many generations, which are preserved and published with care.

XI. Finally, the moral and religious essays of the *Three* sects, viz. those of the Confucian school of atheistical materialists, those of the visionary alchemic school of Laoukeum, and those of the Hindoo polytheistic school of Buddah, in addition to which may be named the essays of a sort of eclectic school, which picks and chooses from and sometimes blends the other three. The Mohammedan and Christian writers in China have been too few to produce any very sensible impression, beyond now and then a little scorn and philippic, such as is conveyed in the political sermons read by an official person, on the days of the new and full moon, in the several provincial imperial halls before the governors, deputy governors and magistrates in each province.

To the Editor of the Christian Observer.

It may not be unknown to your readers, that for some time past a warm controversy has been in progress between the Orthodox and Unitarian Dissenters, relative to the right of the latter, either in moral or legal equity to retain many of the places of worship at present occupied by them, but which were erected, and in some cases large endowed emoluments appended to them, for the exhibition of far other doctrines than those currently, but unjustly, because exclusively styled Unitarian. It is a well known and most melancholy fact, and one which affords a powerful argument for an Established Church and fixed formularies of doctrine and worship, that the Presbyterian chapels throughout England, founded, and at first frequented, by persons who though not agreeing with the Church of England in matters of ecclesiastical discipline, were strictly orthodox as respects all the leading doctrines of Christianity—men illustrious in their generation for their eminent talents, and many of them still known and revered by their lives and writings—have long since, in numerous instances, become the schools first of Arianism, then of Socinianism and its cognate doctrines. Of true Presbyterianism, even as respects matters of discipline, these societies retain nothing but the name, and in point of fact, except as these endowments are concerned, the Unitarians are publicly considered, and I presume generally consider themselves, Congregationalists. The recession, from the doctrines of the old Presbyterians to the present system was in most of these places gradual though now too deeply confirmed. The incursion of the new doctrines was usually accompanied by warm debates and in the end by the recession or gradual falling off of the orthodox members, after which the Unitarian managers retained the property, only numbering a few scattered converts to occupy the walls once crowded by the numerous and animated audiences of such men as Matthew Henry, and other worthies of the Presbyterian school. From the statements contained in the 'Manchester Socinian Controversy,' lately published, it appears that the Unitarians possess in this island, two hundred and twenty three places of worship of which no less than one hundred and seventy eight, four fifths of the whole, were originally orthodox. Taking England alone, they have two hundred and six chapels of which thirty six only, not one sixth, were built by Unitarians. It is stated further that one tenth of these chapels would probably contain the whole of the congregations which, though in some few instances large, are for the most part very thin and that in many instances the whole system is mainly kept up by the *bonus* of the endowments, which in some cases are very considerable

I restrain my pen from recording various remarks which occur to me on this painful subject one reflection only will I at present urge which is applicable to all classes of Christians —to work while it is called to day. Present good actually effected, even on a small scale, is so much rescued from the mass of contingency and disappointment. What may arrive on the morrow we know not and the records of all ages and churches testify that little dependence can be placed upon the best planned projects for futurity. No person can peruse the voluminous reports of the Commissioners appointed to inquire into the abuses of our national charities, without forming the melancholy conclusion that bequests, the most beneficially intended, may too probably become a positive evil, instead of a service, to succeeding ages. To day only is our own—let us make use of it as becomes the responsibility which we owe for the right use of our time, our property, and every other talent committed to our trust.

The above remarks are not applicable to the case of bequests to charitable societies not intended for the purpose of prospective accumulation, but for current or otherwise prudential use. Our Bible Missionary, and Educational Institutions lay up no pecuniary stores for an uncertain futurity they make no endowments or reserves except what may be considered reasonably necessary to meet their express or implied engagements and to prevent so far as human foresight can extend, their benevolent projects falling to the ground. They strictly "work while it is called to day," and therefore have a most powerful claim, not only on the life support, but the testamentary munificence, of those who have at heart the success of their momentous objects

X

To the Editor of the Christian Observer

YOUR Correspondent G in your last number, in his remarks upon the books commonly, but not very properly, called the Old and New Testament Apocryphas, has not mentioned two other books, which are necessary to make the apocryphal canon complete. I allude to the modernly discovered 'Book of Enoch' and 'The Ascension of the Prophet Isaiah.' A short account of these will form a fit supplement to the notice of the Old Testament Apocryphal books in your last number, and of the New Testament Apocrypha in your volume for 1822. They have both been published by the learned Dr Lawrence, Regius Professor of Hebrew at Oxford (since promoted to the Irish bench), and, though of no intrinsic value, possess a considerable degree of interest—one of them at least, from some collateral circumstances, which shall be briefly noticed.

The Book of Enoch was for ages supposed to have been lost but was discovered, at the close of the last century, in Abyssinia, and was first translated by Dr Lawrence, from an Ethiopic manuscript in the Bodleian Library, and published in 1821. For two centuries preceding, this book had furnished a prolific source for critical speculation, in consequence, chiefly, of its being supposed to be alluded to, or quoted, by the Apostle Jude, in his Epistle verses 14, 15. It was well ascertained to have been known from an early age of the Christian church, till the eighth century for the Fathers mention it, and quote from it but from that period it appears to have sunk into complete oblivion. Scaliger at length discovered a fragment of it, in a then unpublished manuscript, entitled, the Chronographia of Syncellus which fragment he gave to the world in his notes to Eusebius. It did not, however, contain the passsage alleged to have been quoted by Jude, and it continued to be controverted, among the learned, whether Jude had really seen this so called prophecy of Enoch, or whether he had only heard of it, or whether, in truth, the book itself had not been forged at a subsequent period, in consequence of the passage in Jude. Still, though no Greek copy could be discovered, it was conjectured as early as the commencement of the seventeenth century, that the lost Greek might be itself but a translation from the Hebrew or the Chaldee; and an idea prevailed, that an Ethiopic version still existed in Abyssinia. That distinguished Ethiopic scholar, Ludolph, accordingly searched for it, but in vain; and the pursuit was pronounced hopeless, till Bruce the traveller not only proved its existence, but brought with him, from Abyssinia, no less than three manuscript copies of it, one of which he presented to the library at Paris, another to the Bodleian, and the third he reserved for himself. It was from the second of these copies that Dr Lawrence made his translation.

The learned translator has proved that neither the Jewish nor the Christian church ever admitted the book of Enoch into the sacred canon. Tertullian, indeed, regarded it as an inspired composition, and from the pen of Enoch himself; but his opinion was contradicted by the uniform judgment of the Jewish and Christian churches, with the exception of the Abyssinian church, by which I believe it is, or was considered canonical. Dr Lawrence argues, from the internal evidence, that the book was the production of some unknown Jew, under the borrowed name of Enoch; that it must have been originally written in Hebrew, though the original is most probably lost; and that it was composed before the birth of Christ, about one hundred years before Jude wrote his Epistle. The passage alleged to be quoted by that Apostle is thus translated by the learned prelate — 'Behold, he comes, with ten thousands of his saints, to execute judgment upon them, and to reprove all the carnal for every thing which the sinful and ungodly have done and committed against him.' If the book was written at the era Dr Lawrence supposes, the source of Jude's quotation is abundantly clear; though his allusion is not any argument for the admission of it into the inspired canon, or even of his sanction to its contents—any more, for instance, than St Paul's supposed references to Aratus, Epimenides, Menander, or other heathen poets are proofs of his approbation of their compositions. Some sound scholars, however, still think, notwithstanding Dr Lawrence's arguments, that it is a forgery *subsequent* to the date of Jude's Epistle, and intended to meet that Apostle's allusion in verses 14, 15; and that Jude had in view some older written narrative, or, more probably, tradition. Perhaps some one of your learned correspondents could furnish the grounds of this opinion.

The subject of the Apochryphal book of Enoch is a series of visions respecting the fallen angels, their posterity, the giants which occasioned the deluge, the mysteries of heaven, and the place of the final judgment of men and angels; and several parts of the universe described as having been seen by the writer. Dr Lawrence has printed a Latin version of many chapters by Baron Sylvestre de Sacy from the Paris copy, of which professor Gesenius, of Halle, is, or was, preparing a transcript for publication, with a Latin translation.

The alleged "Book of Isaiah," like the Book of Enoch, had been lost for ages, till recently discovered in an Ethiopic form or translation. It contains a pretended history of the prophet Isaiah's ascension to the seventh heaven, with some fictitious prophecies, and an account of the prophet's martyrdom. As the early writers who have mentioned it furnish no evidence respecting its date, Dr Lawrence has resorted to the internal evidence, from which he concludes that it was written about the year of our Lord 68 or 69. It is doubtful whether it was written in Greek or Hebrew.

I cannot conclude these remarks without reminding the reader of the debt of gratitude which we owe to God, for the gift of his holy word in the form in which we at present possess it, separated from all human admixtures, in a well-ascertained, sacred, and exclusively canonical, text. Let us adequately value and duly make use of, this high privilege remembering not only the woe denounced against those who shall add to or take from the words of the inspired volume but also the guilt of those who possessing it, neglect it and the happiness, temporal and eternal of those who make it the code of their faith, and the directrix of their steps

Y

REVIEW OF NEW PUBLICATIONS

Christian Researches in Syria and the Holy Land in 1823 and 1824 in Furtherance of the Objects of the Church Missionary Society By the Rev. WILLIAM JOWETT M.A., one of the Representatives of the Society and late Fellow of St John's College, Cambridge. *With an Appendix, containing the Journal of Mr Joseph Greaves, on a Visit to the Regency of Tunis* London 1825. 8vo pp 515. 10s.

IT was only in the early part of the year before last that we introduced to the notice of our readers the former volume of Mr Jowett, containing his Christian Researches, most properly so called on the coasts of the Mediterranean. Its excellent author after a short repose from his fatigues embarked on another journey with a view to prosecute his intelligent and useful labours in that still more, we may say that most interesting portion of the globe Syria and the Holy Land and has accumulated fresh and truly important materials for examination, and new motives for urging on the momentous object of evangelizing the possessors of those countries, where were nurtured, and whence issued, the first Evangelists to others

By those who were apprized of the circumstance that Mr Jowett was engaged in this new work, and who knew what indeed his public life and labours amply testify the accuracy and soundness of his classical attainments, the tempered discretion of his zeal, and, above all, the simplicity and fervour of his piety—connected with many advantages for observation, with which his local knowledge furnished him—the present volume must have been anticipated with no ordinary expectations. The past history of that land, the scenes and inhabitants of which were to be the objects of his inquiries would necessarily awaken this interest and the confidence due to the tried wisdom, discrimination, and Christian character of the author could not fail greatly to augment this interest. The traveller of taste, the sentimentalist, the man of enterprize, the classic, the Orientalist, the Biblical reader (we mean the *mere* reader), have all gone over this field, and opened their communications and their conjectures on their return but the volume before us takes up ground nearly new, except as partially an ticipated by other recent Christian travellers especially the friends and agents of our Bible and Missionary institutions. Truly spiritually minded tourists are at all times so rare, that the journal of one who was proceeding to the Holy Land and Holy City in the real spirit of "a pilgrim and stranger upon earth, and with a view expressly to advance the eternal interests of their inhabitants could not fail to contain much information unanticipated by former writers, and of great importance to the Christian world. These expectations are fully realized and the information obtained by Mr Jowett from his journey is of a value amply sufficient to compensate for his toil, in the wisdom of those practical measures which it has enabled him to suggest and to justify the Church Missionary Society in the hopes which led to those Researches. We may justly deem it a favourable indication of the Divine blessing upon the labours of that invaluable institution, that such should be the character of its representatives.

The former volume of Mr Jowett was, in its arrangement, more systematic than the present. It contained the brief history of so many nations and churches, that such an arrangement was indispensable for the elucidation of their condition and opinions. The present is more in the detached form of a journal. There is, however, prefixed to the journal, an introductory section in which a compendious view is given of the chief classes of persons found in Syria and Palestine, compiled partly from the works of various authors who have written on the subject, and partly from Mr Jowett's own observations. Among these, the Jews and Samaritans, and the several *divisions*—the term is unhappily too distinctive—of professed Christians, hold the foremost place. These classes are tolerably well understood, but there are others of whose history less is known and respecting these we shall present to our readers some of the observations of the respected author.

The account contained in this prefix to the journal, of the belief and habits of the various sects in that part of the East, though short, is so distinct, and likely to be of so much use in assisting future missionaries, that we are surprised Mr. Jowett should have thought it necessary to offer an apology for its introduction. Many readers have doubtless yet to learn what are the creeds of the Sonnites and Metawálics, of the Druses, and Ansari, and Ismayly, and Yesidiens. The first two of these are Mohamedans, the other four are distinct classes. The Yesidiens are mentioned by Mosheim in his Ecclesiastical History (vol iv pp 252, 3). But they all affect the greatest mystery in their religious rites and observances, so that the attempts of travellers to penetrate the veil which conceals them have hitherto been next to fruitless. The Ismayly, or Ishmaelites, however, seem to be a most vacillating and unstable sect, conforming their views and professions to the religion of the people among whom they happen to dwell. All these classes are inferior, in point of numbers and influence, to the Druses, who are the most considerable people in Syria. Not only are their numbers greater than those of other sects, but their political situation on Mount Lebanon gives them there an authority of no mean importance. Their population and that of the Christians constitute nearly the whole population of the mountain. They also inhabit the mountains above Saide (or Sidon), and Balbec and the country of Jebaile, and Tripoli, and extend even to Egypt. The creed and the habits of this people greatly excited the attention of former travellers, particularly Niebuhr, the Baron de Sacy, and the more modern and most enterprizing traveller Burckhardt. Mr Jowett has quoted largely from the works of each of these in particular he presents us with translations of some very curious and interesting documents collected by the Baron de Sacy, in which are very evident traces of Biblical histories and allusions, or, at least, of prophetical declarations, clouded by that veil with which a corrupt tradition has invested them. Among these, the doctrine of the 'God manifest in the flesh,' the period of the Divine Saviour's sojourn on earth viz thirty six years, the future advent of the Almighty, to rule over all the earth throughout all ages, and the venerable 'charter written by Him to guide and prepare men for that period when all his enemies shall be depressed and overthrown, force themselves on the mind of the reader as springing from the common source of all truth, the fountain of Divine inspiration. It is remarkable, too, that these Druses seem to exclude from their creed the idea of human merit, and some passages are cited, in which an intimation is given of their expectations from a propitiating Mediator; but, notwithstanding all this, the prevailing character of their code is Deism, and the spirit of all false religions appears in their estimate of human ability "to do works well pleasing to God,"—all proceeding from the rejection of the doctrine that human nature is radically depraved by the fall of Adam and "fresh proof," observes Mr. Jowett, "is herein afforded of the tendency of mankind to corrupt pure revelation, and to fabricate a religion of their own, while the barrier of secrecy, with which they endeavour to surround it, is but a stratagem of the arch enemy to preclude the detection and overthrow of their errors." In the "Lettres édifiantes et curieuses," which is a collection of the statements made by the Jesuit missionaries of their proceedings in the Levant and the East, they speak without reserve of their want of success in preaching to this people, and even seem to regard their conversion as a hopeless experiment. We shall take another opportunity of referring to the probable causes of the want of success in these missions; but, so remarkably is this the fact, that the interest felt in missionary efforts in these quarters is most evidently and to a great extent, on the decline. The state of the convents is a proof of this; one of which, in particular, the convent of Harcessa, or Arissa, a spacious and extensive building, is now occupied only by Padre Carlo, the superior of a few students; and in other places the labour of the priests seems less the work of evangelizing the heathen, or unbelievers, than the maintenance of a position, which the Roman Catholic church, having once occupied, is unwilling to relinquish. Mr Jowett remarks, that it is impossible to survey these things without feeling that Rome is on the decline; her out works—her foreign boasted missions—being reduced to a mere shade.

But it is time to quit Mr. Jowett's introductory remarks—in which, however, there are so many other points worthy of attention that it is not easy to pass from them—to examine the journal of our author.

His journal opens on the 9th Sept. 1823, on which day he set sail from Alexandria to Beirout, or Berut, where on the 16th he was joined by Mr. Fisk, a missionary from America to Palestine, and Mr. Lewis, a clergyman in the service of the Jews' Society; the former of whom, as also Mr King another American missionary, who joined him at Antoura, proceeded with him throughout his journey. Mr King had left America with the intention of studying Arabic, in order to return, after three years as Arabic professor, to America, but had added missionary exertions to his studies. The route pursued by our travellers seems to have been shortly this. From Alexandria by sea to Berut, nearly the most northernly point which they reached; and the plain of which is exactly opposite to Mount Lebanon, rising at its eastern extremity from this range of mountains, through the whole pachalic of Acre, southwards, to the sea of Tiberias, Mount Tabor and Hermon to Sychem (now called Nablous), and Jerusalem, and Bethlehem. Having thus traversed the whole of Palestine, from north to south, they returned by the same stages to Beirout. We regret that we cannot follow our author step by step through these attractive scenes, but we shall invite the attention of our readers to some of the most important points.

At Antoura, which lies beyond the beautiful valley of Nahrel Kelb, and commands a fine view of the sea, and is a little more to the north than Beirout, is the college connected at the time of Mr Jowett's tour, with the London Society for the Conversion of the Jews. There our author met with that well known and valuable servant of the Jews Society Mr Wolff, to whose services and character he bears high testimony. The circumstances which led, about 100 years ago, to the first establishment of this college at Antoura, are given by Mr Jowett, from the 'Lettres édifiantes' of the Jesuit missionaries. The narrative exhibits a specimen of a missionary spirit, kindled (with many errors it may be, but perhaps with much of the true spirit of the Gospel) in an European resident Monsieur Lambert one of the five principal merchants who were directors of the French congregation established at Saide.

This person having learnt from the missionaries the necessity and advantages of a mission to Ispahan the capital of Persia conceived the design of devoting himself to this service having put his affairs in order and drawn up his last will and testament he quitted Saide with the intention of joining the missionary fathers in Persia. After many vicissitudes he landed in India, near to Meliapor. Here he visited the tomb of St Thomas and took counsel with a religious of the order of St Augustine who having fully considered what might be the nature of his vocation advised him to go straight to Rome and there apply to the superior general of the Jesuits. He did this and was accepted. After two years of noviciate he was ordained priest and appointed to Palestine. He quitted Rome with two young Jesuits, who earnestly desired to accompany him. They all three embarked in a vessel destined for Saide or Tripoli but Providence which had thus far conducted Father Lambert and designed to use him for the establishment of a mission to the Maronites suffered a violent tempest to cast his vessel on the coasts adjacent to a little village called Antoura. The inhabitants seeing a vessel approach their coast took it for a corsair and without particularly examining what it was ran and seized Father Lambert, his two companions and some other passengers and conducted them before the commandant of the country.

This commandant was Abunaufel a Maronite the most respectable of his nation. The fame of his probity was so great, that Louis XIV of happy memory chose him although a subject of the Grand Seignior to be consul of the French nation and sent him his brevet to that effect.

It was before this person that Father Lambert and his two companions appeared. Abunaufel interrogated them. In their answers they declared what they were shewing him the patents of the Reverend Father General.

Abunaufel readily perceived that these supposed corsairs were missionaries sent him by Providence. He gave them the best reception possible and lodged them in his house. Their arrival and the intercourse which he had with them suggested to him the idea of establishing a mission in his country in order to give the Maronites of Mount Lebanon that spiritual assistance of which they are so often deprived. He made the proposition to Father Lambert and offered him a settlement in his own domain situated in a part of Mount Lebanon called Kesroan.

Father Lambert, after having consulted the superiors of our Syrian missions and received favourable answers accepted on their part, the offers of Abunaufel. This person kept his word with the missionaries appointing them a lot of ground sufficient to build a small house with a chapel he even bore a share of the necessary expenses. Father Lambert was the man chosen by God to be the founder of the mission of Antoura. He opened it with an extraordinary concourse of people who assisted at the first exercises of the mission. Aided by his two companions he continued his exertions till death with indefatigable zeal. pp 70 71

At the town Deir el Kamr which may be called the capital of Mount Lebanon, as being the residence of the Emir Bechir, prince of the mountains, to whom Mr Jowett paid a visit of respect, our author's lodging for the night was at the house of a respectable man, to whom he had letters of introduction and who appears to have given the party a hearty welcome. But we notice their visit chiefly from its having afforded an instance, the only one Mr Jowett ever personally met with, of an attention to the comfort of the traveller which prevailed in ancient times, and which was selected by our adorable Lord to convey almost the last assurance of his own condescending care to his people.

Before supper the master of the house directed the servant to bring in a large brass pan full of warm water in which for the first, and indeed the only time that I ever experienced such attention he illustrated the ancient custom of washing the feet of strangers and no compliment could have been more seasonable. p 79

This part of the pachalic appears to be the residence of the Druses and Mr Jowett obtained, in his conversations with the Emir, some additional information respecting them. But there is much of mystery purposely thrown around their worship and ceremonies. None but the perfectly initiated are the depositaries of their secrets. Their sacred books, like the alleged "Secreta Monita of the Jesuits, are never shewn to others the punishment is capital for such an offence and probably some of their instructions are like one in the above code "to disavow the authenticity of the copy if it should ever get abroad.

'Yet there are many manuscripts shewn about purporting to be of this description procured furtively and when they are lent or sold it is done under promise of secrecy. A set of these books was put in our way some days ago for purchase and the enormous sum of five thousand dollars asked for them! I for my part, felt sufficiently content with the account given of them in De Sacy's Chrestomathie Arabe and in Niebuhr's Travels. Were I to be as a missionary in the midst of them I should probably make no attempt to penetrate into their mystery so far as it might hinder the reception of the pure Gospel I should consider it as so much of Satan's ground, and not go upon it but should invite them off from it to walk with me in a plainer path. I entertain no doubt but that God would bless this method eventually in His own time and when converted, the Druses would probably, of their own accord, imitate that memorable act of the new converts at Ephesus— bring their books together and burn them before all men—even though the price of them should be more than fifty thousand pieces of silver. p 82

Mr Jowett found on the premises of the Emir a young native Abyssinian he was in his childhood carried as a slave to Egypt, but had endured all the persecutions of a Mohamedan master and remained a Christian Mr Jowett narrated to him the circumstance of the Amharic translation of the Scriptures. Of Abu Rumi he seemed to have some knowledge, and M Asselin he had seen in Egypt. Mr Jowett was informed by him that the Abyssinians sometimes *compel* the Mohamedans to turn Christians the latter are known to act with the same compulsion towards the former in each case the character of the convert must be of the most doubtful kind. The mere outward reformations of some of the Druses are little better. We subjoin the excellent, though obvious, explanation which Mr Jowett gave of them, in a conversation with Monseignior Gandolfi, the Pope's apostolic vicar at Antoura.

One thing noticed by Monseignior Gandolfi seemed to the company an inexplicable wonder in their character. You shall see he observed, a young man among them dissolute in the highest degree given to every vice and altogether unbridled yet, on his becoming initiated, in an instant his character is changed to sobriety and even rigid virtue instead of drinking wine freely he drinks water only his passions are curbed his vices seem to drop off from him and he is as strict as before he was licentious. This description struck the hearers with amazement nor did they seem to know how to account for it. Some secret principle in the religious theory of the Druses was what their minds were evidently turning to as the operative cause of such miraculous conversions. I endeavoured therefore to explain them upon a principle which every man who examines his own heart may easily descry. Admitting the fact, as stated to be true yet it may be nothing more than a change from the indulgence of the lusts of the flesh to the more dominant tyranny of the lusts of the spirit —the dæmon of pride expelling the dæmon of licentiousness. The unclean spirit as our Lord describes is gone out of the man but, ere long seven other spirits, still more wicked enter in, and take up their abode in the restless unhumbled heart; and the last state of that man is worse than the first. All assented to this view; but, with it, the conversation on this topic dropped. pp. 100, 101.

In Deir el Kamr Mr. Jowett witnessed one among many painful proofs of the undue influence of the rule of the Church of Rome.

"Conversing with my Arabic reader, I said, Mr. King and myself wish to sell as many of the Scriptures as we can. Copies for this purpose were in the house. He said he was aware of this; but that the sale of them had been prohibited by the Pope. In this country, said he, whatever the Pope tells us we do. But, I said, God commands men to read the sacred Scriptures. I know that, he replied, and I cannot comprehend why the Pope should forbid it—especially as the book is the same version as ours, and so very cheap; perhaps it is that these holy books may not be torne or dirtied by children—they are therefore kept in churches. But, said I, in this family there is your father; you are five brethren; thus there are six who know how to take care of a book; and in some families there are no children, or they are grown up. True, he answered; but the people at large are taught to refuse them. Well, I said, God has given us the sun; if Satan put up his hand before it to turn the day into night, would you not think it an act worthy of Satan? He readily acknowledged this. I bid him apply the comparison to all who would prohibit the reading of the sacred Scriptures. I added—While you remain willingly under this yoke of ignorance, do you not feel as if you deserved to remain under the Turkish yoke?" p. 92.

In another conversation with an Armenian priest, the expediency of the monastic vows and the celibacy of the clergy came under consideration. To the objections of the priest Mr. Jowett made the usual replies, urging with success the unscriptural character of these practices. The Armenian was then compelled to argue on the advantages afforded in the convent for study and seclusion, its freedom from worldly distraction and its leisure for the service of God. To this Mr. Jowett answered,

"In what way now, we asked, do these converts promote the active service of God? Do the priests here preach the Gospel at the hazard of their lives? Is it to this that their young men are trained? Does their unmarried state, which would give them an opportunity of more easily escaping if their life were sought for, encourage them to stand out boldly on behalf of the Gospel? What, for example, is the state of the converts in Mount Lebanon? What converts are they in the habit of making among the Mahomedans?

"Are you then, he asked, come to preach to the Mahomedans? I replied, I will go with you and preach to them; but from this answer he manifestly drew back. He asked what ground we had for supposing that all countries would become Christian—expressing it as his opinion that the promises of sacred Scripture do not go to prove that all the world will be Christian, but that there will be some Christians in all countries, a sufficient number to stand as witnesses of the truth and examples to their Heathen or Mahomedan neighbours. Is there then, I asked, a sufficient number of converts to Christianity in Mount Lebanon and Syria? To this he principally answered, that he thought the call to preach the Gospel applied fully to Pagan nations; but that in these countries nothing could be done without protection; that the moment any one should begin to preach generally out of the line which he was known to occupy he would be put down by the Government. Here he at once came to their *magnum gravamen*. We dwelt on the obstacles opposed to the first entrance of Christianity and its triumphant success in spite of them; endeavouring to shew how much we all need the revival of the faith and zeal of the primitive times." pp. 111, 112.

While at Beirout, which was the head quarters of our travellers for some time, and from which they made excursions to various places adjacent, for the purpose of disposing of the Arabic and Armenian Scriptures, their principal means of usefulness, it was the daily practice of our author's little company to read the Arabic Scriptures in their family circle; and in the evening frequently some neighbours would come in, and often very interesting conversation would ensue on what was read. We observe, in reading the journal, that the Saturday evening in each week was devoted by them to united and earnest prayer for the Divine blessing on the work of missions; and every first Monday evening in the month for the same purpose, in reference to an enlarged effusion of the Holy Spirit. Chris tians in the quiet enjoyment of their domestic blessings might perhaps usefully imitate this practice such united prayer is certainly calculated to bind together the spirits of religious persons in all countries and, we may humbly trust, to draw down the fertilizing dews of the Divine blessing, and to minister to a spirit of enlarged zeal and affection, as well as to personal edification. And what a contrast must the simple, fervent devotions of our pious traveller and his friends have afforded to the formal and unintelligent services of the neighbouring convents and the general spirit of worldliness of their occupants!

How many temptations to sloth trifling and sin does this monastic system furnish! In the performance of their multiplied rites it is to be feared the mind can enjoy very little pure and heavenly delight from the genial influence of friendly and social prayer they are in a manner debarred for every thing must be done by rule and form and according to book the office of preaching not being practised by them or at the most very rarely they are deprived of that powerful impulse to cultivate habits of furnishing and improving their minds and of cherishing and pouring forth their best affections toward all around them. On those festivals which lead them more peculiarly into contact with the Frank residents of the principal towns an easy convivial temper is found to be a greater recommendation than spirituality of mind and conversation. The holy rest of the Sabbath is moreover universally profaned to purposes of visiting and amusements of every description. If to all this it be added that the spirit of infidelity in its gradual course from the west and south of Europe into the Levant finds not much purity of manners to discountenance or power of learning to refute it, we shall have a tolerably complete picture of the melancholy condition of this region

The decay of the Romish missions is certainly opening the way for the labours of Protestant Christians but how loudly does it teach the members of all our rising institutions to fear lest they in their turn should become secular corrupt and inefficient! It is indeed a solemn call upon us to look well to our motives and our measures—to endeavour to approve ourselves in all things as the ministers of God by pureness by knowledge by long suffering by kindness by the Holy Ghost by love unfeigned by the word of truth by the power of God, by the armour of righteousness on the right hand and on the left. pp. 123, 124.

We must pass over, with regret, the interesting remarks which our author makes on his visit to Sour, or modern peninsular Tyre. They are chiefly intended to verify, and render more intelligible, from a minute and careful examination of the coast, that fearful prediction of the *utter* overthrow of ancient Tyre, contained in the Prophecies of Isaiah and Ezekiel. Mr Jowett had seen before the ruins of Athens, and the memorials of Egyptian glory in Thebes and there, he remarks enough survives to expand the mind with wonder, or to sadden it with regret but of ancient Tyre there just remains so to speak that *utter nothing* which prepares the mind to imbibe the spirit of the prophetic language — I will cast thee to the ground I will bring forth a fire to devour thee thou shalt be a terror and never shalt thou be any more. We must content ourselves with referring our readers to the journal itself, for the reasonings by which the author endeavours to reconcile various expressions in the prophecy with the appearances of the site of its fulfilment such solutions, however ingenious or probable can only be conjectural but in the instructive lessons which he appends to his remarks we most fully agree with him and shall extract his allusion to our own land

The Lord hath purposed it to stain the pride of all glory! Surely if there be on the face of the earth at this moment one nation pre eminent above the rest in ships in colonies in commerce this is the spot from which the voice of the Judge of Nations should be heard by her—warning her not to be lifted up with pride or debased by luxury and selfishness but to devote her merchandise as holiness unto the Lord — liberally embarking her wealth and powerful influence in every benevolent and religious enterprise. Gratitude demands it and this will be her surest protection. p. 142.

With a mind capable of appreciating all the claims to natural beauty in the scene before him, and enriched by the various combi nations of thought and feeling associated with the very names which met his ear how fair must have been the dawn of the morning which opened on our author in sight of Mount Carmel

The first hour of our journey we spent nearly in darkness—wanderers as it seemed to me among the mountains both guides and animals however with instructive sagacity keeping the track At length the pleasant light covered the sky and not long after we arrived at the height which commands the ample plain of Acre The elegant and lofty minaret of the city appeared at a distance of seven or eight miles directly before us in the back ground far off twice as distant as the city was a noble scene—Mount Carmel dipping its feet in the western sea and to the east running considerably inland entirely locking up from our view the vale of Sharon which lies to the south of it In the horizon on the left the sun was rising over the milder mountain scenery which lies on the road to Nazareth

Here though already three days within the confines of Palestine I first felt myself on holy ground We were leaving the glory of Lebanon and before us was the excellency of Carmel As I descended the mountain and entered on the plain I was often constrained to give utterance to my feelings in singing a favourite air of which the words are Emitte Spiri um tuum—et creabuntur—et renovabis faciem terræ ! It was the anniversary of my first landing in Malta eight years have I now been on the Mediterranean mission and I can truly say Hitherto the Lord hath helped me and preserved my going out and my coming in Then I and my family were alone in the Mediterranean since that time more than twenty missionaries have entered on the field of whom the greater part yet continue in it pp 143, 144

On the Sunday following Divine Service was conducted by our travellers, in the midst of a small but singular assembly

The individuals who composed it were a British consul—his dragoman a native of the country—a Maronite priest—a Roman physician—one Greek—one Jew—an English captain of a merchant vessel then in port—my servant who is under French protection—an American brother missionary—and myself of the Church of England Mr Fisk conducted the prayers and I afterward preached from 2 Cor v 17 Therefore if any man be in Christ he is a new creature old things are passed away behold all things are become new The whole service was in Italian Toward the close of my sermon quoting the verses following the text I dwelt briefly on the importance of the right exercise of the Christian ministry pointing out that, till the work of preaching is revived there is no hope that these countries will be raised from their present degradation and misery and that this is manifestly the calling and office of the ordained ministers of the country

This was particularly intended for the ear of the Maronite priest Don Giuseppe and it was well taken I believe by him he remained after the service and conversed very affably He bears a very respectable character and has had a superior education to many having spent several years in early life in study in the college at Rome He appears now to be nearly fifty years old He has under his pastoral care all the Maronite houses in Acre but they are not numerous pp 145, 146

In the mosque at Acre to which our author paid a visit he appears to have been struck with the Mohamedan ablutions the fountains playing in basins of marble the trees waving their branches, with a softness and coolness most congenial to tranquil thought and the Turks and Arabs with venerable silvery beards performing their cleansings with an air of solemn enjoyment and religious precision Such a scene we may well imagine was calculated to make a thoughtless spectator forget that there is in Turkey and the East generally amidst all these ceremonial purifications not only literally much offensive filthiness but far deeper moral stains than those which the lavatories of the most venerated mosque can cleanse But if it be true that

Ev n from the body s purity the mind
Receives a secret sympathetic aid

still we cannot forget the tendency of these strict ceremonial observances to impede a better sort of purification and which called down from a Higher than the poet s Authority, that rebuke on the men of like mind in His day Ye fools, and blind cleanse first the inside of the cup that the outside may be clean also

for the thoughts from within, they defile the man but to eat with unwashen hands defileth not the man

The superior of the convent at Nazareth having forbidden our tra veller's servant to sell any more copies of the Scriptures, and having told them that all the books should be burned when they were gone, Mr. Jowett encouraged him with this thought "Giuseppe, there have been *men* put into the fire, who nevertheless came out unharmed, and so it will be with the Scriptures some may be burned but good will come, on the whole. We mean no disregard to the superior under whose roof we are living, but this Book is the master of us all." "Very true he replied 'and all buy it.'" "Then continue to sell, and fear nothing, for it is the will of God." He did so, adds Mr. Jowett, and no evil came of it, and he was much encouraged.

Mr. Jowett points out the spot from which the men of Nazareth are traditionally reported to have intended to cast our Lord down after his memorable address to them and from his personal observations he thinks the account sufficiently probable, and correspondent to the sacred text, although the distance is as much as two miles from the city. Maundrell has not hazarded a conjecture on the subject. Mr. Jowett suggests several reasons for the supposed bad reputation of the town of Nazareth. *Nathanael*, in reference to whose question, "Can there any good thing come out of Nazareth?" being himself a man of Cana of Galilee, would not be likely, we may suppose, to have quoted unless perhaps ironically, as the current reproach of others, the scornful proverb of the Jews, that out of Galilee ariseth no prophet. Mr. Jowett thinks allusion is made not to this adage, which is generally adduced by commentators in illustration of the passage but to the circumstance that Nazareth was a resort for persons of vile character.

The very position of this town might in some measure account for its ill character. It was a kind of frontier town. It was frontier in three directions—toward Samaria to the south a region notorious for iniquity and frequent revolts—toward the land of the Philistines on the south west—and, on the west, toward the maritime city peopled by heathens, Acre. Between these three regions and Nazareth there is little more than the broad sweep of the plains of Esdraelon and Acre. These plains lie more or less at the feet of the mountains of Nazareth although the plain of Acre does not so nearly approach them as the plain of Esdraelon. In the rear of Nazareth northward and eastward are the peaceful towns and plains of Galilee. Now in addition to the bad character of the Samaritans the inhabitants of all the sea-coast were notoriously flagitious. They were left, as we are expressly told (Judges iii 1—6) to prove the Israelites and that the generations of the children of Israel might learn war. An evil neighbourhood this for Nazareth! The men of Nazareth might in such a vicinity easily be ensnared into heathenish affinity (Judges iii 6.) Their worst characters fleeing from justice or revenge would easily find the nearest asylum at a distance of from twenty to thirty miles in Nazareth. In every quarrel or war between Galilee on the one side and on the other side either Samaria or the Philistines and the inhabitants of the coast, Nazareth would stand the foremost. In commerce with the maritime towns Nazareth would lie constantly exposed to the temptations to break the Sabbath mentioned in Nehemiah xiii 16. Thus by degrees might this frontier town become a nest of the very worst characters and addicted to the worst sins and its condition would probably be the more notorious from the contrast which it would form to the better protected and more peaceable inhabitants of the interior of Galilee. pp 168—170.

We cannot forbear to add that if there be truth in these conjectures, and they are in a degree confirmed by Whitby in a note on Matt ii 23 in which he quotes the authority of Buxtorf and Abarbinel respecting a celebrated thief called Ben Nezer, in allusion to whom Jesus Christ was in contempt called the "Man of Nazareth" how conspicuously does the circumstance display the condescending love of Him, who though he was rich, not only became *poor* for our sakes, but consented to expose himself to the contumely and scorn merited by others fulfilling that word "The reproaches of them that reproached Thee fell on me." Most truly was it written of him, as Mr. Jowett remarks, that He made himself of no reputation and this in reference even to the temporal circumstances of his condition.

After a visit to the Baths of Tiberias, Mr Jowett, feeling himself too unwell to proceed with his fellow Christian traveller to the south of the lake, where the river Jordan issues from it, retired to seek a little shade by the side of a small fragment of ruins. Here he writes with equal piety and tenderness of emotion.

The composure which came over my feverish spirits at this hour was inexpressibly refreshing. I laid myself down upon the ground, and resting my head upon a stone near me drew a little coolness from the soil; while the simple train of reflections which naturally sprung up from the scene around me added much to my enjoyment. At a great distance to the north was the mountainous horizon, on the summit of which stands Safet glistening with its noble castle; it is not improbably supposed that our Saviour had this spot in his eye and directed the attention of his disciples to it when he said, A city that is set on a hill cannot be hid; for it is full in view from the Mount of the Beatitudes as well as from this place, and indeed seems to command all the country round to a great extent. Tracing at a glance the margin of this simple lake on the opposite or eastern side, the eye rests on the inhospitable country of the Gadarenes—inhospitable to this day, for my guide, after long silence, perceiving my attention directed that way, begins a long tale about the dangers of that part, the untamed and savage character of the mountaineers and the extreme hazard of attempts to visit them; few travellers in fact venture there; but seeing that his account is not very congenial to my feelings at this moment, he has dropt his story. Close above my head an Arab is come to spread upon the ruins his tattered clothes which he has just washed in the lake that they may dry in the sun; and at a distance just perceivable is another indolent peasant sauntering by the water's edge and singing at intervals a poor Arab song, which though not most musical has nevertheless the charm of being most melancholy. But that which awakens the tenderest emotions on viewing such a scene as this is the remembrance of One who formerly so often passed this way and never passed without leaving by his words and actions some memorial of his Divine wisdom and love. Here or in this neighbourhood most of his mighty works were done; and, in our daily religious services we have read with the most intense interest, those passages of the Gospel which refer to these regions. However uncertain other traditionary geographical notices may be, here no doubt interrupts our enjoyment in tracing the Redeemer's footsteps. This and no other is the Sea of Galilee—in its dimensions as I should judge resembling exactly the size of the Isle of Malta, about twenty miles in length, twelve in breadth, and sixty in circumference. Here Jesus called the sons of Zebedee from mending their nets to become fishers of men. Here he preached to the multitudes crowding to the water's edge, himself putting off a little from the shore in Simon Peter's boat. But there is not a single boat now upon the lake to remind us of its former use. Yonder on the right must have been the very spot where, in the middle of their passage from this side toward Bethsaida and Capernaum the disciples were affrighted at seeing Jesus walk upon the water—where he gently upbraided the sinking faith of Peter —where he said to the winds and waves Peace! be still; and the sweet serenity which now rests upon the surface is the very same stillness which then succeeded. Here finally it was that Jesus appeared the third time after his resurrection to his disciples, as is related by St John (chap. xxi.) and put that question to the zealous backslidden but repentant Peter— Simon son of Jonas lovest thou me?— one question thrice repeated plainly denoting what the Saviour requires of all who profess to be his and followed up by that solemn charge. Feed my lambs— Feed my sheep! While I gaze on the scene and muse on the affecting records connected with it, faith in the Gospel history seems almost realised to sight, and though I cannot comprehend that great mystery of godliness God manifest in the flesh, yet believing it, all my feelings of wonder and adoration are called into a more intimate exercise. pp 174—176.

Mr Jowett's indisposition continuing, Capernaum and Bethsaida were visited by Mr Fisk alone. Bethsaida exists in little more than in name; ' and Capernaum, which was exalted to heaven, has now scarcely a relique to attest its former existence.'

The visit to the Mount of the Beatitudes is too interesting to be omitted.

Saturday Nov 15 1823.—At early dawn we set off from Hattyn to ascend the Mount of the Beatitudes. The road was steep but very shady and refreshing, and as we went we read aloud the first twelve verses of the fifth chapter of St Matthew and the thirteenth chapter of the First Epistle to the Corinthians. Our minds were raised to the enjoyment of those heavenly truths. We could not but feel how infinitely inferior all the maxims of sages and philosophers are, to those brief and simple descriptions of the graces of humility, meekness, gentleness, purity of heart, and patience, of faith, hope, and love!

"Why is it, I asked, that the very scenes become endeared to us as we read the portions of sacred Scripture relating to them, so that they are rendered much more lovely than mere scenery could make them? My companion illustrated the feeling of religious association aptly by putting the case of two amiable persons, for both of whom he said, we might conceive a very warm affection; but if one were pious and the other not, how far more congenial would our attachment be to him whose heart was one with ours in the love of God! He is, in the truest sense our friend—a friend in common with us of God—a friend for eternity! We may know him only for a short space of time on earth, but we shall know him hereafter for ever. So to compare inanimate things with spiritual, our attachment to this spot is heightened by the remembrance of the Divine discourses once uttered here, and which seem to make it hallowed ground: there are other scenes equally or more lovely in the various countries which we have visited, but to this we are united by a kind of religious endearment.

With such reflections we entered the plain of Galilee at its east end. Being arrived at this elevated plain, we find that the Mount of Beatitudes, which closes as it were a kind of barrier on the east, is not on this side so high as on the other side it appeared to be. The plain in fact rises at the end by a gentle slope into two small hills, on either of which it is probable enough that our Saviour sat when he delivered the sermon on the mount. They are nearly close together, and would take a person not more than five minutes to ascend them. The plain itself abounded in flowers; and although we were not able to say that among these we could discern the lilies of the field to which our Saviour directed the thoughts of his hearers, yet my eye was particularly delighted by the sight of a flower not very common in England, the purple autumnal crocus. I have observed it flourishing at this season in every part of Mount Lebanon, and here at this moment it was expanding its beautiful petals to as bright a sun as ever lighted up the blue firmament. And if our Heavenly Father so clothe the grass of the field, will He not much more clothe us? Have not we that same evidence of His care exhibited to our senses on this unexhausted soil which the Apostles themselves had? It was impossible supposing this to be the spot or near to it where these words were uttered, not to seek some collateral proof which however faint might serve to illustrate the topography of the scene. pp 186—188

At Nablous (or Sychem), the city of the Samaritans, Mr Jowett visited the Samaritan priest. But it was not without considerable difficulty that he obtained from him a sight of the celebrated Samaritan MS of the Pentateuch. Dean Prideaux, in his Connection, has condensed most of the conjectures of the learned in reference to this precious document: we refer to Mr Jowett's journal for any additional information. The priest pointed out the spots on the Mounts Ebal and Gerizim where the curses and blessings were pronounced; and with reference to the imputation of the Samaritans worshipping the dove (noticed by Prideaux and others) the priest declared it to be a falsehood and calumniation of their enemies.

After a short stay in Samaria, Mr Jowett at length proceeded, through Bethel, on his journey to the holy city. We may naturally suppose that his expectations were excited to the highest pitch, as the uncultivated state of the hilly tracts from the rocky height of Beer announced it as not far distant. He appears to have been much struck in common with almost all other travellers with the exceeding beauty of its position and the glories which yet remain of that once exalted city. The scenery around is unchanged. Mount Zion and the Mount of Olives are yet beheld by the traveller. No lapse of time has plucked up from their base the everlasting hills. *They may not* be removed but abide fast for ever, and furnish to the traveller the vivid emblem of that security which Jerusalem had before she cast off His protection who had promised. As the mountains stand round about Jerusalem, even so to compass round his people for ever.

But the distant view of Jerusalem is all the glory which it now retains and even in that view the elegant proportions, the glittering crescent, and beautiful green blue colour, of the mosque of Omar, which is its present prominent beauty, form the most forlorn features in the scene, as occupying, or rather usurping the place unoccupied by the "temple of the Great King" and appearing, to use Mr Jowett's application of the prophetic figure, the 'abomination of desolation standing in the holy place, where it ought not'

Mr Jowett, on first entering the city, seems to have been suffering greatly from fatigue, and those un pleasant exactions which attend the employment of the Arab guides, and it was some time before he could realize the emotions which his si tuation was calculated (except from the impoverished and debased state of the city itself) so strongly to excite —

When however the evening had closed and the hour for retirement de votion and repose arrived all that I had ever anticipated as likely to be felt on reaching this place gradually came into my mind and filled me with the most lively consciousness of delight at being in Jerusalem This — I thought — is no other than the City of David Hither the Queen of the South came to hear the wisdom of Solomon Isaiah here poured forth strains of evangelic rapture which will glow with unspent warmth till the end of time Here the building of the Second Temple drew from the beholders mingled shouts and tears and here was that very Temple made more glorious than the first by the entrance of the Desire of all Nations the Messenger of the Covenant! Here after he had rebuilt the temple of his own body he began the wondrous work of raising a spiritual temple to his Father shedding abundantly upon his disciples the gift of the Holy Ghost for which they waited in this very city and then sending them forth as His witnesses to the uttermost parts of the earth

Such were the principal thoughts with which I had for some months associated this visit and now all were gradually presented to my mind pp 209 210

We cannot omit the following remark respecting the holy places because it appears to us the precise feeling which should occupy the mind of the Christian in reading the author's own narrative Mere sentimentalism is far out of place amidst scenes and recollections like these

I felt, I confess no particular anxiety to see what are called the holy places. Many have hastened to offer their first devotions at the Sepulchre of our Lord: so far from having this desire I feel somewhat of repugnance at the idea it is enough for me to know that I am not far from that scene—that Gethsemane, and Calvary and the place where the Lord lay are all so near to me that I can truly say I am dwelling in the midst of them All this too my heart can better conceive in the stillness of the night-season than by the light of day And He, who suffered here still lives— Jesus Christ the same yesterday to-day and for ever! Spiritually He is as near to me as he would have been had I seen him this very day at the ninth hour expiring upon the cross the blood then shed is still fresh in its efficacy and cleanseth us from all sin If to have come hither should prove the means of raising me one degree higher in love to this adorable Redeemer I would be thankful but let me remember that He desires us chiefly to view him with the eye of faith and that although we see him not in the flesh yet believing we may rejoice in him with joy unspeakable and full of glory pp 210 211

Our author's time at Jerusalem was occupied chiefly in visiting the various convents * and monasteries in conversations with the patriarchs and ecclesiastics in the distri bution of the Scriptures and in noting (which he must have done with great diligence, and we doubt not fidelity and accuracy) the state of the population † in reference to intellectual and religious matters Of these, at the close of the journal he furnishes a lengthened and most melancholy account He also employed himself in the com position of a tract, more imme diately for the use of the people

* The number of these is stated in a note at the end of the journal to be thus thirteen Greek convents of which some are for monks and others for nuns three Armenian two for monks and one for nuns two Coptic one Abyssinian one Latin with another religious house at- tached to it In all twenty one

† Professor Carlyle had stated the population of Jerusalem at 15,000 con sisting of 9000 Mohamedans 3000 Jews, 2000 Greeks 600 Latins 200 Armenians 100 Jacobites or Syrians and two or three families of Copts or Maronites Mr Jowett disputes the accuracy of Hassel quist's estimate of 20 000 and confirms the former

around him, on the Holy Spirit, which—contrary to the plans of most travellers, who would have left a sedentary work like that till their return—Mr Jowett felt it more important to compose in the midst of the scenes and people where its distribution was intended, and where the impression of the value and necessity of the Divine influences would be peculiarly vivid. The Poet Gray justly remarks, in one of his letters to West, "One line writ ten on the spot, is worth a cart load of recollections."

Many of the conversations with the Greek monks and higher ecclesiastics must have been highly interesting, but that with the Bishop of Nazareth, at the convent of the Holy Cross, we cannot omit.

The Bishop was inquisitive to know of what rite my servant was. I gladly availed myself of the opportunity of explaining to him in what light I regarded these differences. The youth I told him is by profession of the Latin Church but I did not, in taking him into my service inquire into that matter but merely desired him in the morning and evening to come to us when we read the Bible and pray together to which he never made the least objection but on the contrary, seems to be pleased with it.

The Bishop was very attentive and spoke little so that, as I feared to appear to trespass on his feelings the conversation was often suspended. Indeed I thought I perceived a great degree of dejection on his countenance.

Presently it being three o clock our attention was roused by the voice of the Mowedden from one of the minarets calling the Mahomedans to their usual prayers of that hour. The Bishop mournfully turned to me and exclaimed ἕως πότ.

How long? His few and simple words quite sunk into my heart. I said it was truly painful to hear that voice in the Holy City and that I viewed with sincere sympathy the present distresses which they suffer. Our sins! he slowly replied. The measure of our punishment is not yet filled up! I could only assent by the motion of my head.

I then acquainted him that I was writing a tract, in which I wished to address his nation in as consolatory a manner as I could but added. It will not all of it be consolatory. He plainly took my meaning as one who saw that it was impossible to speak agreeably to truth of a suffering nation, without also saying something concerning their sins. Yet I never felt more, than I did at this interview a desire to address them with tenderness and that verse (Isaiah l 4) was brought with fresh feeling into my memory. The Lord God hath given me the tongue of the learned, that I might speak a word in season to him that is weary. How difficult to do this! It is easy to chide with justice but it is a high attainment, learned only in the school of suffering to reprove with a merciful spirit. Neither may we rebuke an elder and the tract must speak to many bishops and dignitaries whom I am bound rather to entreat as fathers.

To his expression which he would ever and anon sigh forth—How long! Lord, how long!—I at length made some reply drawn from the interpretation of prophecy. He listened with great interest for on no topic is it more easy to gain an eager ear in the East, than on the mysterious and unknown future. I limited myself however to general allusions to the period of 1260 years now apparently drawing to its close and endeavoured to exhibit also some of those signs of the times which indicate the approach of an important crisis—particularly mentioning the Bible Society and the system of general education. As I described the convulsions which shake the continent of Europe from the west to the east he mentioned the affairs of Spain as being settled and seemed, therefore to infer that no good had resulted from that movement. After noticing that the revolutions in the West had been conducted very much by men who disbelieve the Christian Religion I asked whether it might not be part of a merciful dispensation not to suffer such men to attain all that they grasp at, lest they should overthrow Christianity. He entered into this view and seemed fully sensible that change without Christian principle was always to be mistrusted. I seized the moment to press again the unspeakable advantage of the labours of the Bible Society—filling the world with Divine Light at the moment when the nations appear restless for innovation. On this topic it is peculiarly grateful to find the Greek Church favourable.

I retired from this interview with spirits unusually depressed. I had felt, throughout the whole conversation that my heart was drawn in contrary directions—on the one hand by emotions of pity for these suffering Orientals and, on the other by a view, every day augmenting of their sinful blindness and unchristian superstitions. While humanity pleads for them Christian faithfulness cannot acquit them as innocent. pp 240—242

We could willingly accompany our author to the Pool of Siloam and the Garden of Gethsemane, and "as far as Bethany" but we can only glance at these interesting scenes. He quitted the city on the 15th of December, after a stay of about a month. The questions which he addressed to his own heart, on taking his last view of its towers from the hill over against it, are such as should conclude every Christian's undertakings.

While the servants went on, I rode to a fair green spot and turned my horse's head round, that I might enjoy a few moments' solitary meditation in the view before me. Surely no traveller would fail to snatch such a moment! With little bodily strength and through a variety of scenes in which troubles had been anticipated, though none had been experienced, I have thus succeeded in accomplishing the pilgrimage to the Holy City. What good, I thought, has my visit done here? Who will be the better for it? Here—where the Saviour bled—how have I requited his love? These thoughts rapidly passed through my mind, raising such pensive feelings as I am no stranger to. I feel that I have done almost nothing; and even if humanly speaking I had done much, yet I must before my Master acknowledge that I am an unprofitable servant. But it is now too late to amend this visit, for the time is past, and I must bid farewell to Jerusalem. The noon day sun shines strong and bright upon the city, and seems to mock its base condition. What a contrast between its aspect at this distance and its actual state! Here the smaller objects not being minutely discernible, the glowing strains of David seem as true and lively as they were when they first answered to the touch of his instrument of ten strings—

Beautiful for situation, the joy of the whole earth is Mount Zion. Still there seem to be her towers, her bulwarks, and her palaces challenging our admiration. But I have now for more than twenty days known that these are not the towers or the temple of ancient times. At every step coming forth out of the city the heart is reminded of that prophecy accomplished to the letter, Jerusalem shall be trodden down of the Gentiles. All the streets are wretchedness, and the houses of the Jews more especially (the people who once held a sceptre on this mountain of holiness) are as dunghills.

While I gazed my eyes filled with tears till I could look no longer. The frequent ejaculation of the Bishop of Nazareth came into my mind— Lord how long! I thought too of those Brethren from whom I had just parted, and for whose sakes I had an additional motive to pray, Peace be within thy walls! I then suddenly broke off from this multitude of thoughts, which was growing too painful for me, and pursuing my journey I felt by degrees as though my present mission was in some sense accomplished, and began to indulge more warmly the hope of returning to my family in peace. pp. 269—271.

We have left ourselves no space to comment on the Biblical Illustrations which our author could not fail to collect in these scenes. Some of them involve nice criticism; but we still think him, in common with most if not all Oriental illustrators, fanciful in the application of some texts—a circumstance which we noticed in our review of his former volume.

We must also content ourselves with merely noticing the Journal of Mr. Greaves, who while Mr. Jowett was engaged in his visit to Palestine, was proceeding for a similar object to Tunis, Biserta, Suse, and other parts of the Barbary states, and engaged in those investigations which might be calculated to assist the operations of the Church Missionary Society in that quarter, as well as in dispersing the Scriptures. We regret to find what however, was naturally to be expected, that in many instances the Sacred Book was rejected, the modern Jews like their forefathers 'judging themselves unworthy of everlasting life, and dashing the cup of salvation untasted from their lips. The slave market there and also the violations of the Sabbath by those of the European residents whose religious creed ought to have taught them better things cannot but be noticed with grief. There is one bright exception to this latter evil, in the case of the British Consul, who is said to close his doors on the Sunday to every visitor. He experienced many difficulties in consequence of his religious habits, and of his care to preserve his family from the evil of bad example. He would not permit his children to learn the language of the country, in order to preserve their minds untainted by the oaths, and indecencies of expression, to which they would be exposed. With this exception, and a few more, which are rather inferred than stated, the region visited by Mr Greaves appeared dark indeed, and uncheered by any consolatary prospect. Would that his journal might be the means of leading some Christian Marius to re-visit the ruins of Carthage, with the self-devoting zeal of an apostle and martyr, to plan and execute deeds worthy of more than classic fame, for the spiritual benefit of millions yet unborn!

One third of the volume before us contains a most valuable body of Remarks and Suggestions, which the author offers to the Society whose representative he is, and to the Christian public at large, as presenting, in a condensed form, the impressions made on his own mind with regard to the natural, civil, and religious state of Syria and the Holy Land: the past measures which have been adopted for the illumination of the natives, and those which, if encouraged for the future, may with great probability, be crowned with eventual success. He has availed himself of some of the excellent instructions issued to the Catholic missionaries on many of the plans acknowledged in common by the Catholic and Protestant churches—such as the education of youth, and the strictest attention to personal holiness, that branch of it particularly which involves purity of life and manners—and has quoted passages from the Rules of the College established in Mount Lebanon (entitled Regulæ Seminarii erecti in Monte Libano ab Urbano P. P. VIII. dat. die 30 Julii anno 1625) to the value of which we cannot but give our tribute of most cordial approbation, with the addition only of the fervent wish ' O si sic omnia!'

And above all, would that the zealous missionaries from the Church of Rome had given the Scriptures to their converts! Then, by the blessing of God, very different had been the issue. Our readers will not regret the introduction of one extract on the recommendation of Spiritual Exercises.

Since neither he that planteth is any thing, nor he that watereth, but God who giveth the increase, it is necessary that the missionaries seek to obtain from Him both the spirit of apostolical labourers, and likewise the good success of their labours. Let them therefore always walk before Him. To Him let them frequently lift up their hearts. Especially once in the year, let them for the space of several days withdraw themselves from every other business* and give themselves to spiritual exercises, exclusively occupied in the contemplation of things heavenly. If not at too great a distance, they are to observe this sacred leisure in the nearest monasteries of their residence, those especially pertaining to the congregation of Mount Lebanon. In the year of their electing the Prefect, let them come together into one place, and let these spiritual exercises precede their election. And that they may continually grow in the Spirit, let them twice at least daily be occupied in mental prayer and in the reading of holy books. pp. 340, 341.

Mr Jowett's Suggestions generally display a very observant mind, and have been formed from a careful comparison of the state of things in the countries he last visited with those of which he had enjoyed previous opportunities of acquiring a correct knowledge. There are, of course, some points on which all his readers would not be able to speak their opinion in his words.

Without, however, entering upon any of these dubious points, we ardently hope that his valuable suggestions may have the effect of stirring up many to undertake the work of missionary enterprize. He notices in his preface various countries which still need an investigation like that furnished in the present journal. Modern Greece, Turkey in Europe and Asia, Arme-

---

* This is a very interesting practice provided for by the Church of Rome. Persons would thus retire from worldly cares for ten, fifteen, or twenty days or longer, paying a sum of money sufficient for their maintenance to the guardian of a monastery. An establishment of this nature existed in former times in Malta, at the south-west part of Florian: the building still remains.

nia, and the neighbouring regions, Persia, Arabia, Egypt and Nubia, Abyssinia, Barbary, and the *Papal States themselves.* May such intelligent and truly Christian travellers as our author, be raised up to view these lands and missionaries as duly qualified be found to follow them into the fields of sacred labour! But among all the spheres of exertion which he has mentioned, no one surely from its past history, and from every association of thought and feeling and obligation with which it is connected can be so deserving of attention and effort as that where Mr Jowett has recently led us

The present spiritual condition of what was once the 'holy Land' is most affecting and deplorable. This once highly privileged country has become one of the darkest spots on the face of the globe—a real 'Bochim,' "the place of tears." The equity of that Divine administration which has poured forth for Jerusalem the dregs of so bitter a cup, no Christian will for a moment impugn: it is but to point to the great national sin of her children, to shew the justice of every infliction of God's displeasure upon her. But to refuse to feel the deepest sympathy in the condition of that most glorious and most favoured but now most abject and degraded, city is impossible. The winds of heaven have long howled in mournful anger on her once fair but now desolate, places. Its lightnings have riven, and its thunders rolled over, her once peaceful and goodly structures and the visitations of Divine Providence have left, in the spiritual, even more than in any other sense of the term, "not one stone upon another which has not been thrown down." The words of her most evangelical Prophet have been amply and affectingly illustrated, and we may with truth acknowledge, "This is a people robbed, and spoiled" "They are all of them snared in holes, and hid in prison houses." The iron hand of the earthly oppressor* has in many cases united with the still more despotic influence of the god of this world, in blinding and bowing them down to the dust and added to this is the more grievous and more criminal *neglect* of *Christendom* so that ' they are for a prey, and *none delivereth* for a spoil and *none saith, Restore!*' It is in such visits as those of Mr Jowett's and the attempts for their spiritual welfare to which they lead that the reproach begins to be wiped away

The Christian church has indeed, as we have before observed, made occasional efforts for the relief and recovery of " the seed to whom the promises were made" but they have been for the most part tainted by the errors of the particular community with whom they originated. The one principal error which has, in a very great degree, impeded the utility of the Catholic missions, has been already noticed—their not freely granting the Scriptures to the people—for although the Romish church did allow a translation of the Bible to be made into the universal language of Mohamedanism, the Arabic yet that work was intended solely for the clergy of their missionary establishments, and not for general distribution

But it has appeared to us that another cardinal error of the Romish church and one to which their want of success in their missions has been mainly attributable, is the peculiar character which the Gospel, as delivered through their authorized interpreters of it, must assume in the eyes of their people. There is so much in the services and ministrations of that church (and we may add, of the Greek church also) calculated (unintentionally no

* There are in the volume before us many proofs in the exactions of the governors and the oppression of the Jews of the threat in Deut xxviii 66 "Thy life shall hang in doubt and thou shalt fear day and night and shalt have none assurance of thy life"

doubt) to avert the thoughts from Him who is *the one Mediator* between God and man, so divided a homage and so broken a reliance produced from the continual appeals to the auxiliary intercessors whom that creed has felt itself bound to invoke—to say nothing of the questionable character of some of its saints—that, when we find an exclusive and continual exaltation of the Crucified One, not in symbolic representation but in fervent and affectionate but simple words, language addressed not to the eye but to the heart, made the sole condition of the promised blessing, we cannot wonder at the small measure of success which has hitherto attended most of the Catholic missionary efforts in Palestine and its vicinities. Surely it is not marvellous that the beating storm is still felt, and the desolations of her spiritual captivity are yet mourned over by Zion, if He who is the sole "hiding place from the wind, and the covert from the tempest," He who alone "bringeth the captive out of the prison house, and comforteth all their waste places," has not yet been undividedly and fully proclaimed. This is the true secret of Missionary success; this is the direction in which our Lord's own declaration points. "And I, if I be lifted up from the earth, will draw all men unto me."

We have been struck with the coincidence of testimonies to this truth from all the labourers in the field of missions. The journal of Mr Jowett adds one more to the number. I find, he says in his journal at Deir el Kamr, where he had been explaining the simplicity of the Gospel scheme of salvation, "that the more simply this truth (the death of Jesus Christ) is told, the stronger the case appears to them, and the more strongly does it affect my own mind. This grand view throws all controversial matter into the back ground."—May, then, this affecting truth be the simple but sublime and efficacious, theme of all future missionaries! Within the very walls of Zion may her children look on Him whom their forefathers pierced, and mourn! There is Jerusalem in her desolation: there are the remnants of the family of Abraham "attainted and despoiled of its heritage, but not extinct"; still lingering, a part at least, upon the paternal estate, anxious to be found on the spot at the moment of the appearance, daily and hourly expected, of their Deliverer and Restorer; or, in the event of their death, fondly deeming it meritorious to be gathered to the grave of their fathers. May the time soon come when this attainder shall be purged away; when, what Mr Jowett in the fine exordium of his book, beautifully calls the "Divine nobility of the race," as energetically sketched by the Apostle (Rom. ix. 4—6), that majestic train of titles, such as no master of heraldry ever pronounced before, that splendid record of privileges and distinctions such as no country, not the proudest, can present, may be again restored, and it may again, in the New Testament signification of the term, be said of them. They *are* Israelites; to them pertaineth the *adoption*, and the *glory*, and the *covenants*, and the *giving of the Law*, and *the promises*; theirs are the *fathers*, and of them, as touching the flesh, Christ came, who is over all God, blessed for ever. Then, though long "trodden down of the Gentiles," Zion will arise and shake herself from the dust, and be beautiful as "a dove that is covered with silver wings, and her feathers like gold."

Practical and internal Evidence against Catholicism, with occasional Strictures on Mr Butler's Book of the Roman Catholic Church; addressed to the Impartial among the Roman Catholics of Great Britain and Ireland

By the Rev. J. BLANCO WHITE. London, 1825. 9s. 6d.

THE subject of Popery has within the last year been agitated, with a vigour not perhaps to be paralleled at any period since the Reformation. The opposition of the Catholic priests in Ireland to the promiscuous circulation of the Scriptures among their flocks, and the proceedings in Parliament relative to that long divided country—and we may add perhaps, the publication of Dr. Southey's Book of the Church—have been among the more prominent causes of this renewed controversy, the result of which we would trust may, by the blessing of God produce new accessions of triumph to the cause of pure and undefiled religion, for which, and not for the mere name and honour of any sect or party, the true Christian will ever be mainly anxious.

Respecting the true character of the ecclesiastical and theological system which has given rise to the present and to innumerable former controversies, Protestants of every name and rank ought to be well informed. The actual power, the possible though we hope not very probable extension, and the very existence of Popery ought to be viewed by them with feelings the farthest removed from concurrence or indifference. The best of men, the most staunch friends of the Reformed churches may indeed differ, and differ conscientiously, as to the actual state of the Roman Catholic church, its augmented or diminished potency, its moderated or acerbated spirit, and the best means for rescuing the world from its withering grasp: they may discuss among themselves with a fair latitude the relative merits of perpetuating or abolishing, of extending or abridging penal enactments and civil disabilities, as instruments of repression or conversion: but respecting the evil effects, doctrinal and practical, social and political, temporal and spiritual, of the system of Popery, there ought to be but one opinion and one voice. We will add, as little difference ought there to be as to the duty of cherishing, towards those whose errors they oppose a spirit of candour, of conciliation, and of good will: which, we regret to say has not always pervaded the litigants on either side.

The late controversies have been of a very mixed character: they have extended to numerous ramifications of fact and fiction, of history and chronology, of doctrine and discipline, of duty and policy with we know not how many more points of zealous litigation. We had meditated preparing for our readers a brief view of some of the chief points more immediately brought under examination by the contending parties in the late and pending controversy: but after reading some dozen or fifteen of the publications on the subject and making a list of perhaps as many more, we gave up the search—we will not say in despair or in disgust: for our duty requires that we should not spare a little pains, especially on such a subject, if the result would be profitable or interesting to our readers—but from a conviction that reams of controversy are not necessary to a sufficient understanding of the real merits of all that is religiously important in the great questions at issue between the Catholic and Protestant churches. A scripturally educated people, a people able to read and to think, and permitted to have free access to the word of God for instruction are not in any great danger from the worst errors of Popery. Indeed, the Catholic priesthood themselves give the most convincing attestation to this conclusion from their avowed zeal in order to retain the laity within the trammels of their church, in forbidding the indiscriminate right of Scriptural reading, private judgment, and free discussion.

Under this general impression we shall at once cut short the whole controversy, and spare both ourselves and our readers a long list of title pages, and a galaxy of opinions and quotations and present to their notice one work only on the subject, from the mass of publications with which the press has lately teemed, so as to cause both readers and reviewers to "toil after it in vain." Some of these works are merely ephemeral: others, we ought in justice to state, have been compiled with considerable research and ability, and may be perused with interest, for their facts or arguments, even if the reader should not coincide in their conclusions: but, to our minds, far the most important of them all is that which we have selected for the present notice, and to which we should have devoted a somewhat lengthened article, had not the extent of our Review of Mr. Jowett's Researches rendered it impracticable within our present limits, and the popularity of the work itself made it unnecessary. Such an exposure of Popery from the pen of one who was once a Catholic clergyman, is a document of great interest; and, we would trust, will be of extensive utility, not only in confirming Protestants in their holy faith, but in opening the eyes of many who have hitherto blindly followed the dictates of a supposed infallible church. Our readers will thank us for promising that our notice shall consist chiefly of extracts from the work itself.

The arguments in Mr. White's publication being closely connected with his own personal experience and testimony, it may be proper to premise that he must have had ample opportunities of becoming acquainted with the merits of the system which in no feeble terms he reprobates and explodes; for to his name is appended a list of degrees, titles, and appointments *, which prove, that, in listening to his remarks, our information is at least derived from an authentic and authoritative source: so that, unless we disbelieve his testimony, which there is not any ground for doing (and indeed it is indissolubly bound up with facts and arguments which cannot be questioned), we must come to the conclusion that the " practical and internal evidence against Catholicism, without one word of further argument, is utterly fatal to all its loudly boasted claims." To some of our readers it may be an argument in favour of the book, and to others against it, that the writer is hostile to what is currently called Catholic Emancipation: but to both classes its theological and ecclesiastical bearing is important, however much they may differ as to this much agitated question. The following is the substance of the author's auto-biographical detail.

I am descended from an Irish family whose attachment to the Roman Catholic religion was often proved by their endurance of the persecution which for a long period afflicted the members of their persuasion in Ireland. My grandfather was the eldest of three brothers whose voluntary banishment from their native land rooted out my family from the county of Waterford. pp. 2, 3.

My father combined in his person the two most powerful and genuine elements of a religionist—the unhesitating faith of persecuting Spain, the impassioned belief of persecuted Ireland. He was the first of his kindred that married into a Spanish family; and his early habits of exalted piety made him choose a wife whom few can equal in religious sincerity. pp. 3, 4.

Such were the purity, the benevolence, the angelic piety of my father's life, that at his death, multitudes of people thronged the house to indulge a last view of the dead body. Nor was the wife of his bosom at all behind him, either in fulness of faith or sanctity of manners. The endeavours of such parents to bring up their children in conformity with their religious notions may therefore be fully conceived without the help of description.

No waywardness of disposition appeared in me to defeat or obstruct their labour. At the age of fourteen all the

---

* M.A. B.D. in the University of Seville: Licentiate of Divinity in the University of Osuna: formerly Chaplain Magistral (Preacher) to the King of Spain in the Royal Chapel at Seville: Fellow and once Rector of the College of St. Mary a Jesu of the same town: Synodal Examiner of the Diocese of Cadiz: Member of the Royal Academy of Belles Lettres of Seville, &c. &c.: now a Clergyman of the Church of England.—Author of Doblado's Letters from Spain.

seeds of devotion which had been assiduously sown in my heart, sprung up as it were spontaneously. The pious practices which had hitherto been a task were now the effect of my own choice. I became a constant attendant at the congregation of the Oratory, where pious young men intended for the church generally had their spiritual directors. Dividing my time between study and devotion, I went through a course of philosophy and divinity at the university of Seville, at the end of which I received the Roman Catholic order of sub-deacon. By that time I had obtained the degrees of master of arts and bachelor of divinity. Being elected a fellow of the college of St. Mary a Jesu of Seville, when I was not of sufficient standing for the superior degree of licentiate of divinity which the fellowship required, I took that degree at Osuna, where the statutes demand no interval between these academical honours. A year had scarcely elapsed since I had received priest's orders, when after a public examination in competition with other candidates, I obtained the stall of magistral or preacher in the chapter of king's chaplains at Seville. Placed so young in a situation which my predecessor had obtained after many years service as a vicar in the same town, I conceived myself bound to devote my whole leisure to the study of religion.—pp. 4—6.

Shortly after this period he began to doubt the truth of Christianity, till at length he verged to the very precincts of Atheism. We shall transcribe this part of his narrative at length, chiefly for the sake of the solution appended to it. The Church of Rome incessantly accuses Protestantism of being the magna parens of infidelity; but we believe that the direct reverse is the fact, and that in a given number of educated individuals, in a tolerant Protestant or an intolerant Catholic country, though more may confess themselves to be Deists in the former than in the latter, a larger number really exist in the latter, having for their wretched excuse not only the current arguments common to both parties, but the superadded and deeply rooted impression of Popish error, superstition, and mummery, identified from their childhood with Christianity, from which source of prejudice the Protestant is free. The unexpected and appalling disclosures produced by the French Revolution are the strongest corroborations as to this fact.

That immorality and levity are always the source of unbelief, the experience of my own case and my intimate acquaintance with many others enable me most positively to deny. As to myself, I declare most solemnly that my rejection of Christianity took place at a period when my conscience could not reproach me with any open breach of duty; but those committed several years before, that during the transition from religious belief to incredulity, the horrors of sins against the faith deeply implanted by education in my soul haunted me night and day, and that I exerted all the powers of my mind to counteract the involuntary doubts which were daily acquiring an irresistible strength.—pp. 6, 7.

If my case were singular, if my knowledge of the most enlightened classes of Spain did not furnish me with a multitude of sudden transitions from sincere faith and piety to the most outrageous infidelity, I would submit to the humbling conviction that either weakness of judgment or fickleness of character had been the only source of my errors. But though I am not at liberty to mention individual cases, I do attest, from the most certain knowledge, that the history of my own mind is with little variation that of a great portion of the Spanish clergy. The fact is certain. I make no individual charge; every one who comes within this general description may still wear the mask which no Spaniard can throw off without bidding an eternal farewell to his country.

Now let us pause to examine this moral phenomenon, and since I am one of the class which exhibits it, I will proceed with the moral dissection of myself, however unpleasant the task may be. Many indeed will dismiss the case with the trite observation that extremes generally produce their opposites. But an impartial mind will not turn to a common place evasion, to save itself the labour of thinking.

When I examine the state of my mind previous to my rejecting the Christian faith, I cannot recollect any thing in it but what is in perfect accordance with that form of religion in which I was educated. I revered the Scriptures as the word of God, but was also persuaded that without a living infallible interpreter the Bible was a dead letter, which could not convey its meaning with any certainty. I grounded therefore my Christian faith upon the infallibility of the church. No Roman Catholic pretends to a better foundation. I believe whatever the holy mother church holds and believes is the compendious creed of every member of the Roman communion. Had my doubts affected any particular doctrine, I should have clung to the decisions of a church which claims exemption from error; but my first doubts attacked the very basis of Catholicism. I believe that the reasoning which shook my faith is not new in the vast field of theological controversy. But I protest that, if such be the case, the coincidence adds weight to the argument, for I am perfectly certain that it was the spontaneous suggestion of my own mind. I thought within myself that the certainty of the Roman Catholic faith had no better ground than a fallacy of that kind which is called reasoning in a circle: for I believed the infallibility of the church because the Scripture said she was infallible, while I had no better proof that the Scripture said so, than the assertion of the church that she could not mistake the Scripture. In vain did I endeavour to evade the force of this argument: indeed I still believe it unanswerable. Was then, Christianity nothing but a groundless fabric, the world supported by the elephant, the elephant standing on the tortoise? Such was the conclusion to which I was led by a system which impresses the mind with the obscurity and insufficiency of the written word of God. Why should I consult the Scriptures? My only choice was between revelation explained by the church of Rome, and no revelation. Catholics who live in Protestant countries may, in spite of the direct tendency of their system, practically perceive the unreal nature of this dilemma. But wherever the religion of Rome reigns absolute, there is but one step between it and infidelity. pp 7—10.

The state of his feelings, believing that religion was a fable, and yet compelled daily to act as its minister and promoter, was indescribably painful, and he would have fled from his country, but for fear of the distress which such a measure would have cost his parents. In this state of mind he continued for ten years, till the approach of Bonaparte's troops to Seville enabled him to banish himself without suspicion of his motives. He retired to England, where he first learned the nature of Protestantism, and discovered new and irresistible arguments for the truth of Christianity.

It was the general opinion in Spain that Protestants, though often adorned with moral virtues, were totally deficient in true religious feelings. This was the opinion of Spanish Catholics. Spanish unbelievers like myself were most firmly convinced that men enlightened as the English could only regard religion as a political engine. Our greater acquaintance with French books and with Frenchmen strongly supported us in the idea that belief in Christianity decreased in proportion to the progress of knowledge in every part of the world. As to myself, I declare that I did not expect to find a sincere Christian among educated Englishmen. Providence however so directed events, that some of my first acquaintance in London were persons whose piety was adorned with every good quality of the heart and mind. It was among these excellent friends and under the protection of British liberty that the soreness and irritation produced by ten years endurance of the most watchful religious tyranny began to subside. I was too much ashamed of being supposed a Roman Catholic to disguise the character of my religious opinions, but the mildness and toleration with which my sentiments were received made me perceive, for the first time, that a Christian is not necessarily a bigot. The mere throwing away the hated mask which the Inquisition had forced me to wear refreshed my soul; and the excellent man to whom, for the first time in my life, I acknowledged my unbelief without fear, was able to perceive that I might yet be a Christian, provided I saw religion divested of all force but that of persuasion. pp 12 13.

Paley's Evidences produced considerable effect upon his mind, sufficient at least, he adds, 'to make me pray daily for Divine assistance.' Now it is indubitably certain that God will give his Holy Spirit to them that ask Him, that the meek will he guide in judgment, the meek will he teach his way, and that 'whoso will do the will of God, shall know of the doctrine.' We cannot therefore, after his declaration of his constant and submissive application for Divine instruction, but feel prepared for what follows, namely that his mind became enlightened, his judgment convinced, and his affections conciliated. After a period of a year and a half—namely in 1814—he resumed his clerical functions as a Protestant Episcopal minister, subscribing the Articles of the Church of England, and retiring to Oxford for the quiet and exclusive study of the Holy Scriptures. He gave the result of his inquiries and confirmed convictions to the world, in a volume published anonymously in 1817. He ingenuously adds that before his mind was fully settled he had nearly been seduced into Socinianism; but prayer, humility, and an honest search after truth were his safeguards

"What was the real state of my faith in this period of darkness, God alone can judge. This only can I state with confidence,—that I prayed daily for light: that I invariably considered myself bound to obey the precepts of the Gospel: and that, when harassed with fresh doubts and tempted to turn away from Christ, I often repeated from my heart the affecting exclamation of the Apostle Peter— to whom shall I go? thou hast the words of eternal life." p. 24.

Here our author's personal narrative somewhat abruptly concludes: we must therefore follow him from his private journal to his general facts and arguments, which are presented to us with a vividness and interest for which the previous circumstances amply prepare us.

The Second Letter discusses the question of the real practical extent of the authority of the Pope. Mr. White affirms, that, whatever may be the modified opinions of those Catholics who have mixed freely with Protestants, the Church of Rome is still domineering and intolerant in its spirit: that it approves and enjoins persecution: and that, though it does not actually inculcate the doctrine that faith is not to be kept with heretics, the working of the system virtually amounts to that enormity, in consequence of the blind obedience which the church exacts, and the duty of all its members to endeavour to extirpate heresy. Our own view, on the whole of this matter, is, that neither individuals nor bodies of men are accustomed voluntarily to concede their powers, prerogatives, or immunities: that the Church of Rome follows, with remarkable skill and pertinacity, the usual practice of mankind in this respect: and that therefore little thanks are due to the conductors of its policy for any actual or prospective ameliorations of its rule. But, on the other hand, there is a counter spirit at work throughout the world—a vast extension of principles, some good, some evil: but all at variance with the despotism of a pretended infallible church: a wide diffusion of education, of Protestantism, of true and of false principles of liberty, of indifference to ecclesiastical usage and precedents, and of impatience under all unnecessary, and even some very necessary, restrictions. As to practical effect, therefore, it is not so much what Rome wishes or inculcates, as what the spirit of the times is willing to admit: and when we find so staunch a Catholic as Mr. Butler calling intolerance, which is an undoubted tenet of his church "detestable," we indulge a hope that matters are gone too far to allow of a practical resumption of all that a bishop of Rome or a bigoted priesthood, or even their ignorant lay devotees may consider within the limits of pontifical or priestly power. At the same time, in judging of principles we must view the system not where, as in this island, it exists with numerous checks and counteractions, but as it is seen in Spain, or Portugal, or Italy: of which Mr. White gives us the following most painful illustration:—

"Believe a man who has spent the best years of his life where Catholicism is professed without the check of dissenting opinions: where it luxuriates on the soil which fire and sword have cleared of whatever might stunt its natural and genuine growth,—a growth incessantly watched over by the head of your church and his authorized representatives the Inquisitors. Alas! I have a mother: outweighed all other reasons for a change in a man of genius [Pope] who yet cared not to show his indifference to the religious system under which he was born. I too had a mother: and such a mother as, did I possess the talents of your great poet tenfold, they would have been honoured in doing homage to the powers of her mind and the goodness of her heart. No woman could love her children more ardently: and none of those children was more vehemently loved than myself. But the Roman Catholic creed had poisoned in her the purest source of affection. I saw her during a long period unable to restrain her tears in my presence. I perceived that she shunned my conversation, especially when my university friends drew me into topics above those of domestic talk. I loved her, and this behaviour cut me to the heart. In my distress I applied to a friend to whom she used to communicate all her sorrows: and to my utter horror I learnt that suspecting me of anti-catholic principles, my mother was distracted by the fear that she might be obliged to accuse me to the Inquisition if I incautiously uttered some condemned proposition in her presence. To avoid the barbarous necessity of being the instrument of my ruin, she could find no other means but that of shunning my presence. Did this unfortunate mother overrate or mistake the nature of her Roman Catholic duties? By no means. The Inquisition was established by the supreme authority of her church, and under that authority she was enjoined to accuse any person whatever whom she might overhear uttering heretical opinions. No exception was made in favour of fathers, children, husbands, wives: to conceal was to abet their errors and doom two souls to eternal perdition. A sentence of excommunication to be incurred in the fact was annually published against all persons who, having heard a proposition directly or indirectly contrary to the Catholic Faith, omitted to inform the inquisitors upon it. Could any sincere Catholic slight such a command?

Such is the spirit of the ecclesiastical power to which you submit. The monstrous laws of which I speak do not belong to a remote period; they existed in full force fifteen years ago; they were republished under the authority of the Pope at a later period. If some of your writers assume the tone of freedom which belongs to this age and country, if you profess your faith without compulsion, you may thank the Protestant laws which protect you. Is there a spot in the universe where a Roman Catholic may throw off his mental allegiance, except where Protestants have contended for that right and sealed it with their blood? I know that your church modifies her intolerance according to circumstances, and that she tolerates in France after the revolution the Hugonots whom she would have burnt in Spain a few years ago, and whom she would doom to some indefinite punishment little short of the stake at this present moment. Such conduct is unworthy of the claims which Rome contends for, and would disgrace the most obscure leader of a paltry sect. pp. 61—64.

The Third Letter examines the title to infallibility, spiritual supremacy, and exclusive salvation, claimed by the Roman Catholic church, and exhibits strong internal evidence against that church, in the use which she has ever made of her assumed prerogative. As Protestants writing for Protestants, we think we need not at present embark upon this section of the controversy. The haughty claims against which Mr. White points his weapons are so obviously irrational, unscriptural, and absurd, that the wonder is, not that they should be easily refuted, but that they should for one moment be entertained, at least by any individual one degree removed above the most unexpanded intellect and ignorant credulity. And even those who cannot reason *à priori* on the subject, may have such ample evidence *à posteriori* that their dearth of argument is abundantly made up by superfluity of condemning fact, as we find to have been the case in the first stages of the Reformation when the eyes of many were opened by the obvious venality, cupidity, and ambitious domination of the Church of Rome, by her gainful system of relics, holy images, indulgences, and absolutions, who might not have been able to weigh the abstract dialectics of a theological warfare. Mr. White's third letter is, however, important not only for its arguments, but in bringing down the painful narrative of Catholic peculations (for what else can we call them?) to the present era, and shewing, from a personal knowledge of facts, that the trade in relics, indulgences, and rites of human invention but pretended sanctity, still continues, to the utmost extent to which the manufacturers of the staple can find a market for their wares.

We pass on to Letter IV., which gives us a specimen of the unity exhibited at Rome, examines the well known distinction between infallibility in doctrine and infallibility in conduct, with the consequences of this distinction, and shews that the alleged unity and invariableness of the Church of Rome is a delusion. The author then presents us with his own views of what constitutes the unity of the church of Christ, and in so doing gives us both a rational and scriptural account of the matter. We quote the passage the rather as it is a more favourable specimen of the pious feeling of the writer's mind, than is apparent in mere controver sial arguments. We may just add, with regard to his style, that for a foreigner, he appears to be a very considerable master of our difficult language, though there is an occasional obscurity in his sentences which may require a slight indulgence. The passage is as follows:

If mere controversy were my object, I should feel satisfied with having demonstrated that the system of Roman Catholic unity is but an arbitrary contrivance, a gratuitous assumption of a supernatural privilege which is nowhere clearly asserted in the Scriptures, an endeavour to produce certainty by a standard conceived and planned upon conjecture. A more Christian feeling, however, induces me to dwell still on this subject and propose to you what I conceive to be the true scriptural notions on the unity of the church of Christ.

In reading the New Testament with a mind carefully freed from the prejudices of school divinity, it is impossible not to perceive that the assemblies of men who are called to obtain salvation through Christ cannot either singly or collectively constitute that church whereof the Roman see has tried to appropriate the qualities and privileges to herself. Wherever men assemble in the name of Jesus, there he has promised to be by means of his Spirit, and certainly the works of that Spirit are more or less visible in the Christian virtues which never yet failed to spring up in these particular churches, though mixed with the tares and other evils which are not separable from the kingdom of heaven in this world. But there is a structure of sanctity in perpetual progress, towards the completion of which the Christian churches on earth are only made to contribute as different quarries do towards the raising of some glorious building. The churches on earth partake in various proportions of the attributes of the great church of Christ, which is his body, the fulness of him that filleth all in all. But the church to which the great privileges and graces belong has characteristic marks which cannot be claimed by any one of the churches on earth, for it is that church which Christ loved and gave himself for it, that he might sanctify and cleanse it with the washing of water by the word, that he might present it to himself a glorious church, not having spot or wrinkle or any such thing, but that it should be holy and without blemish. To become members of that church we should indeed endeavour to keep the unity of the spirit in the bond of peace; but such unity is proposed as the effect of endeavour and consequently of choice and judgment, not of blind submission to a silencing authority, which is the Roman bond of union. The true unity of Christians must arise from the one hope of our calling. There is indeed for us one Lord, one faith, one baptism; but that faith is a faith of trust, a confidence which hath great recompence of reward, not an implicit belief in the assumed infallibility of men who make a monopoly of the written word of God, prescribe the sense in which it must be understood, and with a refined tyranny which tramples equally upon Christian liberty and the natural rights of the human mind, insult even silent dissent and threaten bodily punishment to such as in silence and privacy may have indulged the freedom of their minds. Yet such is the saving faith of the Council of Trent! How different from that proposed by St Paul! pp. 109—112.

Whatever might be the effect of the prejudices which the first reformers brought away from their Roman captivity, whatever the necessity which Protestant churches still acknowledge of preventing internal feuds by proposing formularies of faith to their members, they have never so misunderstood what spirit they are of as to deny salvation to those who love their common Lord and Redeemer. Their churches indeed may differ on points which the subtilty of metaphysics had unfortunately started long before the Reformation and even before the publication of Christianity; they may observe different ceremonies and adopt different views of church hierarchy and discipline, but their spirit is the only one which deserves the name of Catholic in the genuine sense of that word, the only spirit indeed which can produce even on earth an image of the glorious church which will exist for ever in one fold and under one Shepherd. pp. 113, 114.

The Fifth Letter describes some of the practical enormities of the system of the Church of Rome, under the heads of moral character, celibacy, and nunneries. The details in this painfully interesting and affecting chapter fully confirm what many Catholic writers affect to consider the more popular prejudices of Protestant countries on these subjects. The evils resulting from monastic vows and imposed clerical celibacy are so notorious and appalling that the Church of Rome evinces a most culpable pertinacity in still clinging to these restraints, especially as such points of discipline might be altered without prejudice to her doctrines, or disparagement of her claims.— In no part of his work does our author speak with more poignant feelings, or with a more painful testimony from personal knowledge, than in this letter. The concluding paragraph is deeply affecting: we quote it, however chiefly for the sake of shewing the cruelty and tyranny of monastic vows imposed often in tender youth and never to be broken. The moral evils of the system have been often exposed, and we need not dwell on them; but second only to these are the inflictions of suffering which it often involves.

Cruel and barbarous indeed must be the bigotry or the policy which rather than yield on a point of discipline sees with indifference even the chance, not to say the existence, of such evils. To place the most sensitive, innocent, and ardent minds under the most horrible apprehensions of spiritual and temporal punishment without the clearest necessity, is a refinement of cruelty which has few examples among civilized nations. Yet the scandal of defection is guarded against by fears that would crush stouter hearts and distract less vivid imaginations than those of timid and sensitive females. Even a temporary leave to quit the convent for the restoration of decaying health is seldom given and never applied for but by such nuns as unhappiness drives into a disregard of public opinion. I saw my eldest sister at the age of two and twenty slowly sink into the grave within the walls of a convent, whereas had she not been a slave to that church which has been a curse to me, air, amusement, and exercise might have saved her. I saw her on her death bed. I obtained that melancholy sight at the risk of bursting my heart when in my capacity of priest, and at her own request I heard her last confession. Ah! when shall I forget the mortal agony with which, not to disturb the dying moments of that truly angelic being, I suppressed my gushing tears in her presence; the choking sensation with which I forced the words of absolution through my convulsed lips; the faltering steps with which I left the convent alone, making the solitary street where it stood re-echo the sobs I could no longer contain!

I saw my dear sister no more; but another was left me, if not equal in talents to the eldest (for I have known few that could be considered her equals) amiable and good in no inferior degree. To her I looked up as a companion for life. But she had a heart open to every noble impression—and such among Catholics, are apt to be misled from the path of practical usefulness into the wilderness of visionary perfection. At the age of twenty she left an infirm mother to the care of servants and strangers, and shut herself up in a convent where she was not allowed to see even the nearest relations. With a delicate frame requiring every indulgence to support it in health, she embraced a rule which denied her the comforts of the lowest class of society. A coarse woollen frock fretted her skin; her feet had no covering but that of shoes open at the toes that they might expose them to the cold of a brick floor; a couch of bare planks was her bed, and an unfurnished cell her dwelling. Disease soon filled her conscience with fears, and I had often to endure the torture of witnessing her agonies at the confessional. I left her when I quitted Spain dying much too slowly for her only chance of relief. I wept bitterly for her loss two years after, yet I could not be so cruel as to wish her alive. pp 140—143.

The concluding letter, the Sixth, points out the obstacles which the Roman Catholic doctrine and discipline present to mental improvement, and the tendency of the Catholic Breviary and Prayer book to cherish credulity and adulterate Christian virtue. These are heavy charges, but we fear they are but too well founded. This long and miscellaneous letter does not admit of abridgment, and our limits forbid quotation. If any of our readers have a taste for absurd stories and fictitious miracles, they may largely indulge their appetite in Mr White's citations from the Breviary and other accredited formularies. While such idle legends are made the subjects of faith and religious reverence, well may the Church of Rome prohibit the miscellaneous perusal of the Scriptures; well may she forge trammels to confine the expansion of the human mind, and to render the nineteenth, and all succeeding centuries, as exact a counterpart as possible of the darkness and superstitions of the middle ages.

From the foregoing remarks and extracts it will be seen that Mr Blanco White has exhibited an appalling, and, it may possibly be said, in some instances an exaggerated, picture of the Church of Rome yet with every abatement, if abate ment be necessary—but, on the other hand, with some important additions to the catalogue of evils, including several doctrinal errors, which are but slightly alluded to by our author—what a spectacle is presented to us of a professed, *the* professed church of Christ, once the arbitress of all Christendom, and still boasting a larger numerical census than any other section of the Christian church! But let us not think it enough to exhibit either our grief or our indignation, or both, at the melancholy exhibition. As Britons, as Christians, as Protestants, we have a responsible part to perform as respects this corrupt church. First, we must in heart, as well as in name, renounce its unscriptural doctrines and practices, some of which are but too ready to cling around our common nature, under every variety of sect and persuasion. Next, we have a duty to perform towards the members of this corrupt community itself; not, indeed, to imitate their example, by attempting to convert or subdue them by force and persecution, but 'in meekness to instruct them that oppose themselves'—to offer to them the sacred Scriptures, and by charity and conciliation endeavour to win their attention to their life giving message; and, when all other means fail, to pray for them to Him who alone can enlighten the understanding, and correct the pravity of our fallen and guilty nature.

LITERARY AND PHILOSOPHICAL INTELLIGENCE, &c. &c.

GREAT BRITAIN

PREPARING for publication.—Four Sermons by Dr Doddridge, directed in his will to be published, but hitherto retained in manuscript.—A translation of the Existing Fragments of Proclus, by T. Taylor.—Letters of Marshal Conway.—The fourth vol. of Grant's History of the English Church and Sects, bringing down the narrative to 1810.

In the press.—Sketches of Rio de la Plata.—The Proceedings in Parliament for the Session of 1825.—Essays on the Evidences and Doctrines of Christianity, by J. J. Gurney.—A Practical Illustration of the Book of Psalms, by the Author of the Family Commentary on the New Testament.—The Turkish Testament incapable of Defence, and the true Principles of Biblical Translation vindicated, by the Author of the Appeal.

A remarkable feature of the age is exhibited in the mass of works published for children and young persons; as an illustration of which we give the following list of little works in a single department only, namely Juvenile Religious Periodical Publications:—Youth's Magazine, price 4d; Youth's Instructor, 4d; the Juvenile Friend, 4d; the Religious Instructor or Church of England Sunday School Magazine, 4d; the Sabbath School Magazine for Scotland, 6d; the Children's Friend, edited by the Rev. W. Carus Wilson, 1d; Sunday School Magazine, 2d; Teacher's Offering, 1d; the Tract Magazine, by the Tract Society, 1d; the Child's Companion, by ditto, 1d; the Child's Magazine, Wesleyan Conference edition, 1d; the National School Magazine, 1d; the Christian Gleaner and Domestic Magazine, 2d.

The English language contains twenty four letters, to which, if we add j and v consonants, there will be twenty six; the French contains twenty three; the Hebrew, Chaldee, Syriac, and Samaritan, twenty two each; the Arabic twenty eight; the Persian thirty one; the Turkish thirty three; the Georgian thirty six; the Coptic thirty two; the Muscovite forty three; the Greek twenty four; the Latin twenty two; the Sclavonic twenty seven; the Dutch twenty six; the Spanish twenty seven; the Italian twenty; the Ethiopic and Tartarian each two hundred and two; the Indians of Bengal twenty-one; the Baramese nineteen. The Chinese have properly speaking no alphabet, except we call their whole language by that name; their letters are words, or rather hieroglyphics, amounting to eighty thousand.

In addition to the intended improvements at Charing Cross, the equestrian statue of Charles I. is to be replaced by one of the most magnificent monuments of antiquity, Cleopatra's Needle. Government have been for some time past in treaty for the transport of this stupendous colume from its present situation to London.

The rare library belonging to Messrs. Nicoll the printers has been lately sold. Among the most curious articles were the original Scottish League and Covenant, a MS. on parchment, and a very ancient Hebrew MS. of the Pentateuch on vellum, for the latter of which it is said a learned Jew offered 1,200l. Neither of these articles were sold. A French MS. Poem of the fourteenth century, illuminated, was bought for 43l. The Mentz or Mazarin Bible printed on vellum by Guttemberg and Faust was bought for 480 guineas. The Duke of Sussex bought a Latin Bible without date, place, or name of the printer, but undoubtedly from the press of Ulric Zell, for 44 guineas, and the Latin Bible printed at Nuremburg 1475 for 48l.

By an official report of the business of the various offices for fire insurances in England it appears that there are forty-six offices or companies, and that the amount of duty paid to Government for insurances effected by them, for the last year, amounts to 659,377l. The duty being three shillings for every 100l. insured, the total amount of property insured is in round numbers about 439,585,000l.

A statue of Dr. Cyril Jackson, by Chantrey, has been placed in Christ Church, Oxford.

Comparative Heights in English feet of the highest Edifices known in the World.

Pyramid of Gizeh in Egypt	543
Steeples of the Cathedral at Cologne	501
Steeple of the Minster at Ulm	431
Steeple of the Cathedral at Antwerp	476
Steeple of the Minster at Strasburg	486
Pyramids of Cheops in Egypt	452
Steeple of St. Stephen's at Venice	442
Cupola of St. Peter's at Rome	431
Pyramid of Cephrenes in Egypt	426
Steeple of St. Martin's at Landshut	422
Steeple of the Cathedral at Cremona	396
Steeple of the Minster at Friburg	395
Cupola of the Cathedral at Florence	384
Steeple of St. Persina in Saxony	382
Cupola of the Cathedral at Milan	357
Steeple of the Cathedral at Utrecht	356
Pyramid of Sackkarah in Egypt	356
Steeples of Notre Dame at Munich	348
Cupola of St. Paul's at London	347
Steeple of St. Ascharius at Bremen	345
Steeples of the Cathedral at Magdeburg	335
Steeple of St. Mark's at Venice	328
Cupola of the Jesuit's Church at Paris	314
Assinelli Tower at Bologna	314
Cupola of the Invalids at Paris	295
Steeple of St. Mary's at Berlin	202

PRUSSIA

A royal edict has been issued in Berlin forbidding the publication of all works against the established religion, at the same time ordering that in all discussions on these subjects invectives and personalities should be avoided. Defamatory writing is forbidden. The author is obliged to send copies to the Berlin library, to the university, and to the censor as before. No foreign work must be sold without express permission.

POLAND

The following information is extracted from the report of the Minister of the Interior Count Mostowski as to the state of affairs during the last four years. In consequence of the number of the Reformed, sixteen extra parishes have been created, and the people have already commenced building houses for their Lutheran ministers. The regulations for the Jews have been newly modelled, and inspectors have been established to watch over the affairs of the ecclesiastics. The funds allowed for public instruction have amounted to 6,536,509 florins, and the profits arising out of the schools amounted to 896,784 florins, which sum has remunerated the temporary class masters, and purchased a great addition of books, mathematical instruments, &c. The botanical garden contains 10,000 species of plants. The university library has 150,000 volumes, among which are many rare and curious works. The Institution for the Deaf and Dumb supports twelve of this unhappy class of persons, who are taught various works. Sunday schools are open in various parts of the kingdom. Limits have been made to civil procedures, so that in the last four years 15,908 causes have been determined by justices of the peace. Iron rail roads have been constructed from Kalish to Brezesc, sixty German miles in uninterrupted length. Numerous high roads have been constructed, and 523 bridges. The country has ceased to be tributary to foreign nations in many important points. The manufactory of cloth is sufficient for the wants of the people. More than 10,000 foreign manufacturing families have peopled new towns. The mines of Poland produce independently of silver, copper and lead, large quantities of iron, zinc and pit-coal. The report exhibits a great improvement in the manufactures and general prosperity of the country.

UNITED STATES

Professor Everett in his oration at the celebration of the landing of the Pilgrim Fathers at Plymouth says. I can truly say that after my native land I feel a tenderness and a reverence for that of my fathers. The pride I take in my own country makes me respect that from which we are sprung. In touching the soil of England I seem to return as a descendant to the old family seat, to come back to the abode of the aged, the tomb of a departed parent.

I am not, I need not say I am not the panegyrist of England. I am not dazzled by her riches, nor awed by her power. The sceptre the mitre and the coronet, stars garters and blue ribbons seem to me poor things for great men to contend for. Nor is my admiration awakened by her armies mustered for the battles of Europe, her navies overshadowing the ocean, nor her empire grasping the farthest East. It is these and the price of guilt and blood by which they are maintained which are the causes why no friend of liberty can salute her with undivided affections. But it is the refuge of free principles though often persecuted, the school of religious liberty the more precious for the struggles to which it has been called, the tomb of those who have reflected honour on all who speak the English tongue, it is the birth place of our fathers, the home of the pilgrims,—it is these which I love and venerate in England.

CEYLON

A novel scene lately occurred at Kandy in the presentation to the Governor's lady of the ladies of the principal Kandyan chiefs. The usual seclusion of Asiatic females of rank is rather strictly adhered to in this part of the island, but it was still customary for the families of the chiefs to pay their respects to the king and queen. Lady Barnes having expressed a wish that the Kandyan ladies should be introduced to her, the chiefs gave their ready assent. They came in palanquins attended by numerous domestics, and accompanied by their respective husbands. The Governor, his staff and other officers in Kandy came into the room and entered into conversation with each of them for some minutes.

MECCA

Great as has been the defalcation in our more Western continent of Catholic pilgrims to the sacred city on occasion of the late Jubilee, there seems to be no dearth of votaries in the Eastern continent at the Mussulman shrine of Mecca. A letter from Singapore states that a vessel had touched there with no less than 286 pilgrims on board returning to the various islands of the Malayan archipelago after their pilgrimage to that city. Nearly a thousand individuals from those islands alone were calculated to have visited Mecca during the last year.

LIST OF NEW PUBLICATIONS

THEOLOGY

A Key to the Book of Psalms. By the Rev T Boys A M 8s 6d

Different Sentiments on the weekly Sabbath. By R Burnside A M 5s

A Paraphrase on the First Epistle to the Corinthians. By the Rev J G Tolley

Christian Sympathy, a Sermon preached to the English Protestants at Rome on occasion of a collection for the Vaudois. By the Right Reverend J H Hobart D D Bishop of New York

Hymns. By John Bowring 3s

Two Letters to the Archbishops and Bishops on the defective State of Ecclesiastical Discipline

Sermons. By the Rev R Gordon 10s 6d

The Portrait of an English Bishop of the sixteenth Century

Boyle's Treatise on the Holy Scriptures. By Panter 8vo 7s

A Sermon preached at Abergavenny at the Visitation of the Bishop of Llandaff. By the Rev C Michell 1s 6d

A Dissertation on the Seventy Weeks of Daniel the Prophet. By the Rev J Stonard D D 8vo 15s

Anti Apocryphal Observations upon the King's College Letter to Lord Teignmouth. By J Wickliff 1s

The New Testament arranged in chronological and historical order (in such manner that the Gospels, the Epistles and the Acts may be read as one connected history). By the Rev G Townsend M A 2 vols 8vo 40s

The Works of James Arminius D D translated from the Latin. To which are added Brandt's Life of the Author with considerable augmentations. By J Nichols Vol I 8vo with a fine portrait

MISCELLANEOUS.

Universal History and Literature from the German of Professor Bredow. By Major Bell. Royal folio. 1l 10s

The Complete Servant. By Samuel and Sarah Adams. 12mo. 7s 6d

Civil Architecture. By J. Burridge

Antiquities in Westminster. By T. Moule

Classical Bibliography. By J. W. Moss, 2 vols 8vo. 1l 10s

The Life of the Rev. J. Braithwaite. By R. Dickinson. 12mo. 6s

RELIGIOUS INTELLIGENCE

CHURCH BUILDING COMMISSION

The Fifth Report of his Majesty's Commissioners for building and promoting the building of additional Churches in populous Parishes announces that twenty churches and chapels have been completed since the last Report, by which accommodation has been provided for 13,631 persons in pews and for 17,287 poor persons in free seats, making in the 45 churches and chapels now completed a total provision for 72,578 persons (including 44,313 free seats for the use of the poor). The Report goes on to state that 30 churches and chapels are now in progress and that 20 of these churches and chapels will be completed in the course of the present year.—Exchequer bills already issued to carry the object into effect amount to the sum of 645,900l.

MISSIONARY SEMINARY AT BERLIN

Respecting the present state of this Seminary the Rev Mr Jænicke writes in the following terms:— There continue to be twelve dear brethren in our seminary at Berlin ready to go forth to the work of their Lord. In literary education they are advanced further than any of the former students, and in piety they yield to none of their predecessors. If the Lord should incline to us the hearts of one of the Missionary Societies in England to promote some of our dear young brethren to the harvest amongst the heathen we confidently trust that the believers in Germany would be willing for still greater offerings and that in future Missionary Societies in Britain will not have to complain of the want of agents, nor those in Germany be able to excuse themselves by the want of opportunity to take part in the most sacred of causes.

SCRIPTURAL EDUCATION ON THE CONTINENT

The following details relative to the progress of education, chiefly of a Scriptural kind and by means of the system of mutual instruction, on the continent of Europe are given in the last Report of the British and Foreign School Society.

On the continent of Europe France first claims attention. The Committee deeply regret that their Report must again be unfavourable. The Executive Government has withdrawn its assistance, hostility to Scriptural instruction seems lamentably prevalent, and in consequence the aid hitherto derived from benevolent individuals or the municipal authorities in large towns is materially diminished. There is reason to believe that this opposition is greatly encouraged by the ecclesiastics. The schools in France are not so numerous as before, it is thought that there may be still from 600 to 800. The schools in Paris which are 22 in number and are supported by the city contain 5000 scholars, they are reported to be going on well.

The accounts from the Netherlands are very encouraging. Two large model schools are now in preparation at Brussels with suitable residences for the master and mistress. Several cities and towns have been supplied with masters who have been regularly trained in the system and the Scripture Lessons in French are permitted to be used. His Excellency the Baron de Falck, the minister of public instruction, zealously promotes education among the poor. His Majesty the King of the Netherlands and the Prince of Orange patronise the object, under whose auspices the system of mutual instruction will undoubtedly prosper.

The British system has been introduced into Denmark in the villages of which country education has been long enjoyed while the inhabitants of the large towns were surprisingly neglected. In several of the old schools the plan of mutual instruction had been adopted. The expense of preparing the writing lessons was defrayed by a donation from the King who with the Queen is represented as highly pleased with the system.

Mr. Gerelius is prosecuting his labours in Sweden, if not with splendid success, yet not without beneficial results. There are several schools in Stockholm, some of which are so crowded that many children are waiting for admission: these schools contain about 500 scholars. There are upward of 80 schools in different parts of Sweden, and the British system is said to be encouraged by all branches of the community.

By the persevering exertions of the Russian Bible Societies, great progress is made in the design of supplying all the nations and tribes of that immense empire with the sacred Scriptures. The general establishment of schools will be a necessary appendage to these efforts; the Committee trust that the importance of this measure will not be overlooked. Application has been made to Mr. Heard by General Ballashif to organize a model school at Riazan, with a view to the introduction of the British system into the five provinces of which he is the governor, and which are situated in the centre of the Russian dominions.

The School for Foreigners has been eminently successful; the numbers thronging for admission were so great that a larger building was found requisite, and a fine hall capable of accommodating 600 children has been engaged; the former school room is to be appropriated to the instruction of 150 girls. Some striking anecdotes have been communicated to the Committee, shewing the happy effects of Scriptural Education both on the pupils and on their parents.

Though no direct information has reached the Committee from Tuscany, the schools there, upward of thirty in number, superintended by the active friends who form the Education Society at Florence, continue to thrive and bear fruit. At Naples one of the large schools which had been suppressed has been re-opened, with promising indications of efforts being made for the opening of others.

Very little intelligence has been received from Spain. That the progress of education has been in some instances at least checked by recent occurrences it seems impossible to question. The flourishing schools at Seville were suppressed on the approach of the French army; it is not improbable that a similar disaster has occurred in some other places. But when it is considered that the British system was introduced into Spain before the late disturbances and under the royal sanction, it may be hoped that it will not be suffered to wither and die: this hope is further justified by the fact that the central schools in Madrid are prospering, assisted by the direct patronage and personal superintendence of the Duke del Infantados.

NAVAL AND MILITARY BIBLE SOCIETY.

The following passages contain the substance of the last Report.

In one part of the field selected for your labours certainty and system have taken the place of diffidence and difficulty and doubt, and the arm of God has deigned to use the arm of princely power to carry into effect its measures of mercy. While in the other part an extended and still widening space is courting the culture of your industry, and crying to the sincerity of your professions to remove from it the 'reproach of barrenness.'

The first point on which your Committee appeal to you, not for your approbation alone, but for your unqualified and grateful concurrence, is that involved in the code of Regulations for providing the Army with Bibles and Testaments, recommended by three prelates who have long held distinguished patronage in your Society, and approved by his Most Gracious Majesty himself. It is proposed that the following arrangements shall be made for providing the army with Bibles and Testaments through the medium of the Chaplain general only.

1. That a circular letter shall be addressed by the Adjutant general to the different regiments throughout the service, acquainting them that the Commander in Chief has deemed it expedient to cancel all orders which gave a sanction to direct communications and correspondence between the Naval and Military Bible Society and commanding officers of corps, that such correspondence can only be held with the Chaplain general of the army, who will obtain from the Naval and Military Bible Society and other sources the means of complying with all requisitions of this description which commanding officers may address to him.

2. That commanding officers shall be directed by the Adjutant-general to send to the Chaplain general an immediate return of the number of Bibles, Testaments, and Books of Common Prayer in the possession of the men, and of the number necessary to furnish one to every man who can read.

3. That exclusive of the requisitions which may follow this circular instruction the Chaplain general will procure from

the Naval and Military Bible Society and other sources such number of Bibles and Testaments and Books of Common Prayer together with such Religious Tracts as he may think sufficient, to be lodged as a depôt in the orderly room of each corps in order that recruits and others wanting such books may be provided from time to time as they may require them. That these Bibles &c shall be kept in a chest and that the state of this depot of books shall be inspected at the half yearly inspections and the number of Bibles &c in store inserted on the back of each half yearly return transmitted to the Adjutant general the Adjutant general will furnish the Chaplain general half yearly with a return of what is required to keep these depôts of books complete

4. That the expense of furnishing these books to the soldiers now in want of them as well as to all the recruits who may from time to time join their respective corps shall be borne by the public. But that each man who is found upon the usual periodical examination of his necessaries to have lost or disposed of his books shall be again provided from the depot of Bibles Testaments &c at his own expense and commanding officers of corps will address to the Chaplain general a return every six months of such deficiencies. (Signed) C CANTUAR
D EBOR
London Feb 1825. W LONDON

The consequence of this regulation had been that a communication had been entered into with the Very Rev the Dean of Carlisle Chaplain general of his Majesty's forces in which it was understood that the Bibles necessary for completing and keeping complete the supply for the whole British Army would be drawn from the depository of this Society the price not exceeding that at which Government had already been offered a supply which would leave a charge of about two shillings per volume to be made up from the funds of this Society. The Committee were in daily expectation of a requisition for seven thousand copies

The Committee state that they feel it unnecessary to make any comment upon the attainment of a measure so replete with the fulfilment of the best wishes of the Society. They add that they exult in an order so reasonable and wise in all its bearings and most fit to stand written in characters of durability in the regulations of a Christian army

The second point to which the Committee call the attention of the subscribers is the extension of the space sought to be occupied by the Society and consequently a modification of some of its original laws —that whereas the objects to whom the bounty of this Society was restricted were the British Navy and Army that restriction should cease and that the objects coming under the naval denomination should include the sailors in the service of the Honourable the East India Company and fishermen and all mariners whether connected with inland or general navigation. This modification contains nothing more than the application of the Society's operations to a body of men already partially connected with it and not adequately provided for by any other specific institution. The Committee confidently expect that it will be followed by a large accession of auxiliaries in the different seaports. It is also hoped that in time it will have the effect of opening wider the door of communication with the Royal Navy an object which the Committee regret to say is yet but very partially accomplished —The issues of Bibles and Testaments this year have exceeded the last one by nearly seven hundred copies amounting to six thousand and forty nine Bibles and Testaments making the total issues of the Society a hundred and seventy five thousand four hundred copies. The debt under which the Society stood at its last anniversary has been paid off

ROMAN CATHOLIC MISSIONS IN CHINA

The following recent intelligence is contained in a letter from M Fontana Bishop of Sinite and Apostolic Vicar of Suetechura in China we need make no comment upon it — Persecution which raged with great violence five years ago and which has never entirely subsided had nevertheless gradually diminished but in 1824 it was renewed in several places on account of a conspiracy formed against the Emperor by a sect of pagans but happily discovered. The examinations relative to this affair served as a pretext to call the Christians to an account. Most of them escaped by giving money a few yielded to fear and placed superstitious tablets in their houses others however resisted with great courage and made a noble profession of the faith for which they suffered

Among the latter the Christians of two towns called Lo Tcha hien and Tchoung Kin hien distinguished themselves by their constancy Efforts were made to constrain them to apostatize but nearly all both men and women shewed themselves disposed to suffer death rather than renounce their faith. This conduct drew upon them all sorts of insults ill treatment, and vexations at length they were left quiet but nine Christians of Lo Tcha hien who by their exertions encouraged others were conducted before the governor who omitted neither caresses nor punishments to induce them to renounce their faith. These noble believers throwing themselves upon their knees declared that they would voluntarily suffer death for the sake of their religion. The viceroy affected by their firmness did not condemn them to death but perpetual banishment in Tartary. The Emperor confirmed the sentence and the nine Christians departed for the place of their exile in May 1824 with their wives who resolved to follow them. The Christians of the other town Tchoung Kian hien were likewise ill treated and here also there were nine who distinguished themselves by more courage than the rest.

Notwithstanding these occurrences and although the Christians were extremely ill treated in many places the exercises of religion were no where interrupted and the missionaries were able to visit almost all the Christian institutions and administer the sacrifice to the faithful. The Christians who at the beginning of the persecution had been condemned to carry the cangue until death constantly displayed the same firmness. The Emperor upon his accession to the throne remitted the punishment of those under condemnation. The Christians condemned to the cangue were also to return home but upon condition of renouncing their religion. In 1824 all those who carried the cangue were brought before the governors and urged to make abjuration in order to enjoy the grace promised. All of them except one confessed the faith anew and consequently continued to carry the cangue voluntarily. Monsieur Thadee Lieon a Chinese priest was strangled for having refused to renounce the Christian religion and having confessed that he was a priest and preacher of the said religion.

In 1824 the establishment of a seminary was commenced in which are collected twelve pupils who study Latin and are formed in the practice of piety under a Chinese priest. Many others solicit admission but the difficulty of the times and the poverty of the mission prevent the reception of a greater number. The number of the Chinese priests is twenty six of whom five are infirm and can no longer visit the Christians. In the course of 1824 there were in Sutchaen 29,342 annual confessions and 335 adults baptized. There are moreover 1,146 old catechumens and 401 received this year without reckoning many other adults who have determined to embrace religion but who have not yet been classed among the catechumens. Baptism has been administered to 837 children of Christians and to 6,280 children of infidels in danger of death. The number of Christians is 46,287 including the catechumens and children but not the apostates there are twenty seven schools for boys and twenty five for girls.

PROGRESS OF CHRISTIANITY IN TAHITI

Messrs Tyerman and Bennet missionary inspectors make the following report respecting the progress of the people of Tahiti.

We visited these kind and interesting people in many of their dwelling houses and were every where treated with some little refreshment placed on a neatly covered table while we were seated on a sofa in the English manner all which tables and sofas are of their own manufacture. Many of them also dress on the Sundays in good English clothes and all would do so if they could obtain the means and for which they are striving. We were favoured with a delightful opportunity of witnessing the advances which these people are making in civilization at a feast which they obligingly made for us upon the Patu which is a noble stone platform of very great extent formed upon the spot and with the stones of a vast idol temple or Murae Here as it Raiatea and Huahine all the congregation assembled in families each having its sofa or sofas its table or tables and these neatly covered with a table cloth. An awning of native cloth screened them from the sun. Men women and children were comfortably dressed. They all partook of a dinner in the English manner each family generally speaking having provided their own dinner. With great delight we went from family party to family party and rejoiced to see so much neatness and comfort and so much manifest happiness.

We had during the day many excellent speeches from various chiefs and others and every one in some part or other of his speech adverted to the wonderful change and benefits that receiving the word of God has produced, and then in various ways contrasting their former degraded with their present elevated and happy condition, and generally closing with an exhortation to be grateful to God and diligent to improve their great privileges.

NEW YORK EPISCOPAL SEMINARY

The foundation stone of the General Theological Seminary of the Protestant Episcopal Church of the United States has been recently laid at Greenwich near New York. Numerous clergymen of the Episcopal Church, the trustees, professors and students of the seminary, together with deputations from the vestries of several Episcopal churches, the junior students and several bishops attended on the occasion. A short address setting forth the objects of the intended building and the hopes and views of those who were about to erect it, was delivered by Bishop White. A prayer was put up by him for the blessing of God on it and its founders and on the labours of those who should be called to teach or to learn within its walls. A box was then handed to the bishop in which were separately placed the Bible, the Book of Common Prayer, Homilies of the Church and the documents relative to the seminary. These were enclosed in the corner stone prepared for the purpose—the bishop receiving from the architect a hammer with which he struck the stone and dedicated it in the name of the three persons of the Trinity. The same ceremony was repeated by the other bishops.

OHIO EPISCOPAL THEOLOGICAL SEMINARY

It will be gratifying to those of our readers who have interested themselves in the proposed Episcopal College in Ohio to learn that its incipient operations are already in progress. The preparatory departments of the institution are for the present opened at the residence of the president, Bishop P. Chase, near Worthington in Ohio. Two instructors of ability have been engaged to assist the president and the course of study is the same as in the most approved American academies and colleges. The students will reside under the same roof with the president and instructors and be continually subject to their inspection. The terms will be for tuition in the collegiate studies (per annum) 20 dollars, academical studies 10 dollars, board per week one dollar, incidental expenses 25 cents. Candidates for Orders will receive instruction gratis.

POOR PIOUS CLERGY SOCIETY

We have so often detailed the plan and proceedings of this truly benevolent and useful institution that in bringing its last Report before our readers, we need only copy a few extracts from recent letters received from the objects of its bounty.

1. I still remain the curate of ——. My income in the last year was 135*l*. I have nine children dependent on me for support—my hearers may amount to 500. There is a charity school on the public plan, and thank God there is not the least want of Christian education for the poor—

2. At present I am in want of a situation as a parish minister in consequence of the death of the incumbent. The total income which I have been in the habit of receiving from clerical sources is 60*l* per annum, but during the last twelve months in consequence of my furnishing supplies to neighbouring clergymen who have wanted assistance it has amounted to 80*l*. Fifty pounds of it from the superintendence of the school. I have a wife and five children all dependent on me for support, in addition to a female servant whose services are indispensably necessary to us.

3. I have lately been removed to the parish of —— at a salary of seventy five pounds with an aged mother of 87 and an infirm wife of 70 to provide for, and am myself 63 years of age, having nothing but my bare salary for our support. If you are of opinion that my case will meet the attention of the Committee, which the Almighty knows is distressing enough, I will thank you to lay it before them.

4. I beg leave to say that my circumstances are nearly as they were the last time I addressed the Society, save a few additional troubles, being four in family. My salary sixty pounds a year. We have been visited with illness which occasioned us to have recourse to medical aid, the bill for which I have not yet received. My poor wife is hardly recovered. I must not omit to mention that although we have to contend with a few earthly troubles, spiritual consolation is administered to soothe them, not a little of which I reap in my feeble labours in the ministry. I have the sacrament now in my two churches administered monthly, which before was only four

times a year. I now serve another church for the Rev. Mr. —— a truly pious man, who has been confined these six weeks, being only a poor curate like myself, and having three motherless infants, I feel it my duty to do it entirely gratis. After the three duties are over, to which I travel on foot, 1 attend the Welsh school till eight o'clock.

5. When I last addressed the Committee my trials were numerous. Since that period they have been complicated and severe! Poor Mrs. ——, confined of her ninth child, never left her bed after much suffering for nearly five months, until she was removed a corpse! In her death six surviving children have lost a tender mother, and the unworthy writer a faithful companion.—Had it not been for kind and liberal friends, my embarrassments must have been extensive. Thus circumstanced, you will see that my case is a strong one, especially when I inform you that my curacy does not amount to fifty two pounds per annum, and that I am entirely destitute of any other means of assistance save charitable institutions and sympathizing friends!—I have never yet been able to get any commentator on the Bible, nor other publications, which I find a great disadvantage to me.

ECCLESIASTICAL PREFERMENTS.

Rev. Wm. Maddock Williams, Dom. Chap. to Marquess of Londonderry.

Rev. Dr. Butcher, Minister of Chap. Royal, Brighton, Dom. Chap. to Marchioness of Hastings.

Rev. Edw. Chaplain, to be Morning Reader and Evening Preacher at Gray's Inn.

Rev. Edwards Hannam, Chaplain to Royal Horse Guards.

Rev. Henry Blayds, Chaterhouse Hinton P. C. Somerset.

Rev. Edw. Bullen, S. C. L. Gunby near Spilsby R. Lincolnshire.

Rev. Francis Dyson, Dogmersfield R. Hants.

Rev. Miles Formby, Cothelstone P. C. Somerset.

Rev. Thomas Gatehouse, North Cheriton R. Somerset.

Rev. John Gathorne, Tarvin V. Cheshire.

Rev. Wm. Greene, Aboghill R. diocese of Connor.

Rev. Robt. Harkness, Stowey V. Somerset.

Rev. Jos. Haythorne, Congresbury V. Cum Week St. Lawrence Chapelry, Somerset.

Rev. Bennett Michell, Winsford V. Somers.

Rev. And. Quicke, Newton St. Cyres V. Dev.

Rev. R. S. Robson, Rancliffe P. C. co. York.

Rev. T. Wharton, St. John's Wood Chapel, Mary le bone, vice Parke dec.

Rev. Geo. Wood, Holy Trinity R. Dorchester, Dorset, vice Richman dec.

Rev. Matthew Irving, B. D. Prebendary of Rochester, Chaplain in Ordinary to the King, vice J. R. Deare dec.

Rev. Jeremiah Smith, D. D. one of the four King's Preachers in Lancashire.

Rev. L. P. Baker, B. D. Medbourne cum Holt R. co. Leicester.

Rev. Wm. Clark, Wymeswould V. co. Leicester vice Sheepshanks resigned.

Rev. F. Godfrey, Newbourne R. Suffolk.

Rev. G. Haggitt, Soham V. Cambridge.

Rev. Adolphus Hopkins, Clent V. cum Rowley Regis Chap. annexed co. Stafford.

Rev. Benj. Robert Perkins, to a Chaplaincy in Christ Church, Oxford.

Rev. J. C. Prince, St. Thomas P. C. Liverpool.

Rev. Wm. Henry Quicke, Ashbrittle R. vice Andrew Quicke resigned.

Rev. James Royle, Stanfield R. Norfolk.

Rev. Peter Roe, Odogh, Doughnamore and Kilcormuck united VV. and Coolchahur R. and V. co. Kilkenny.

Rev. Charles Tynte Simmons, East Lambrook R. Somerset.

Rev. H. R. S. Smith, Little Bentley R. Ess.

Rev. David Smith, Stone Wilton Perp. and Augmented Cur. vice Cliffe resigned.

Rev. John Thos. Trevelyan, Milverton Prima V. cum Langford Badville Chap.

Rev. T. Nayler, Dom. Chap. to Duke of York.

Rev. E. J. Crawley, Chap. to Household of Duke of Clarence.

Rev. J. Sandford, Chaplain to Marquess of Queensbury.

Rev. E. J. Keane, Chaplain to the Colony of New South Wales and Dependencies.

DISPENSATIONS.

Rev. Thos. Newcome, Rector of Shenley, Herts, to hold Tottenham High Cross V. Middlesex with Shenley R.

Rev. W. Hardwicke, to hold Lavington R. co. Lincoln with Outwell R. co. Norfolk.

Rev. John Bouden, to hold Farmington R. co. Glouc. with St. Mary's V. Warwick.

Rev. Jeremiah Jackson, to hold Elm cum Emneth V. co. Cambridge with Swaffham Bulbeck V.

VIEW OF PUBLIC AFFAIRS

FOREIGN

SPAIN.—This country continues in a wretched condition. The French vainly endeavour to preserve a superficial peace by obliging the government in its opposition to the constitutional party to refrain from the counter extreme of encouraging the madness of ultra royalism. The result is, that no party is satisfied: the ultra royalists in particular are disappointed at the failure of their hopes, and are endeavouring to make the absolute king still more absolute, and also to restore the despotism of the church. Bessieres, a leader in this project, has been taken at the head of his little band of associates, and shot with seven of them after receiving the last rites of their religion. The French government have been collecting a military force on the northern side of the Pyrennees, apparently to keep the contending parties in Spain in awe, and to be in the vicinity to act as circumstances may require.

GREECE.—The intelligence from Greece states that the Turks have made a powerful assault both by sea and land on Missolonghi, but have been obliged to retreat with great loss. Some interest has been excited by the intelligence that the Greeks have determined to place themselves under British protection. A manifesto has been published in the name of the Greek Nation, but probably by a few individuals, in which after urging the inherent justice of their cause, the impediments thrown in their way by some of the continental powers, and the strict neutrality of Great Britain, they place their liberty, their independence, and their political existence, under the absolute defence of this country. Our neighbours, and allies if we may judge by the public journals, seem to be greatly offended at this proposition. No notice appears to have been taken of the matter by our Government, nor is it clear that they could with any propriety interfere even if the appeal to them was really national. At the same time it must be admitted that Great Britain by her influence and resources has it in her power to do much safely and honourably to terminate the existing sanguinary warfare, and to secure to the Greeks the enjoyment of their civil and religious liberties, and we trust that no timid policy or systematic prejudices will prevent our attempting at least to achieve this act of humanity and duty with a magnanimous rejection of all interested or ambitious views.

PERU.—Bolivar has issued a decree superseding some restrictive regulations to which foreigners trading in or with Peru were subject. A letter has also been published, written by him to Mr Joseph Lancaster, expressing his admiration of the system of mutual instruction, and placing in his hands twenty thousand dollars, with a promise of a larger sum if necessary, towards establishing schools in Peru. The Government of Peru he adds has been generous to him in a thousand ways, and among other things has placed at his disposal a million of dollars for the service of Columbia, in the distribution of which sum public education will receive his first attention. The whole conduct of this extraordinary man has for years been characterized by a combination of splendid qualities, which place him in the foremost rank of patriots, heroes, philanthropists, and legislators.

BRAZIL AND BUENOS AYRES.—The only hostile indication at present of any importance in South America is a dispute between the empire of Brazil and the Republic of Buenos Ayres respecting the right to the possession of Monte Video. The people of Buenos Ayres with the approbation and promised assistance it is stated of the other new republics threaten an invasion of Rio Grande if the emperor persists in his claim. Their first measure in such an extremity they add, will be to proclaim liberty to all the slaves who shall join their standard—a most formidable menace considering the vast numbers the recent importations and the abject condition of the slave population in the Brazils. And yet while every nation can see the political infatuation of the system of slavery in neighbouring states it continues to be widely upheld and almost fondly clung to both by mother countries and their colonies as if it were the very strength and life's blood of their existence.

UNITED STATES.—Our readers are aware of the solemn festivity with which the 4th of July the date of American Independence is celebrated throughout the Union. Contrasted with these proud national scenes, and the speeches and sermons, breathing the warmest spirit of liberty, annually delivered on occasion of their recurrence, the Americans have been often and not unjustly, reproached with the existence of slavery on a large portion of their soil. We are most happy to learn that this incongruity is beginning to be more widely felt among our transatlantic brethren especially since the anti slavery discussions in Europe. The following extract from a discourse delivered on the 4th of last July in one of the churches of Newark by the Rev Mr Russell breathes, we would hope the spirit of a large and widely increasing portion of his countrymen especially the clergy of all denominations

"I tremble for my country on finding that the utterly indefensible practice of slavery is far more extensive and popular in this independent Republic, than in any other civilized nation of the earth. It is indeed the great political sin of the American people and it has already fixed upon our national escutcheon a deep and indelible stain. Thanks to the superintending providence of God and to the wisdom of our legislators the disgraceful traffic in slaves is for ever hereafter prohibited in our commonwealth and soon the last vestige of slavery will be hunted from among us. But there are comparatively few states within the middle and southern sections of our Union that have attained to the same elevated rank in the patriotic enterprize of African emancipation. In the south especially slavery still exists in all its horrors and is rather on the increase. There fifteen hundred thousands of the descendants of Ham are uttering their fruitless wailings and panting for release. There is a bitter groan issuing from the anguished bosoms of a million and a half of bondmen in the south it cries for redress and if this be long withholden it will pierce the highest heaven, and call on God for vengeance!"

We have seen extracts from other addresses at the late anniversary the forty ninth of American Independence to the same effect particularly a discourse by the Rev Mr Todd of Andover Theological Seminary in which he shews that slavery must and will soon be removed from the earth. In proof of this position he adduces arguments from the following sources 1 The progress of enlightened freedom over the earth at the present day 2 The Christian feeling awakened in behalf of Africa throughout the world 3 The Book of Prophecy, as illustrated by the events of the day

Such a theme well befitted that great national festival, and we hope will continue to be dwelt upon till the occasion for it shall cease. We are happy to learn that even in the slave states among the younger and more liberally educated members of the community, a spirit hostile to slavery is beginning to spring up as a proof of which we might mention the pleasing fact, that voluntary emancipations are occasionally taking place, and some of them to a considerable extent, and with great pecuniary sacrifice. One most honourable recent instance we cannot forbear noticing. A gentleman of Virginia Mr David Minge has emancipated upwards of eighty slaves and made provision for colonizing them in Hayti. He chartered a brig and put on board eighty seven Coloured People of different ages from three months to forty years, being all the slaves which he owned except two old men whom he has likewise manumitted but who being past service he retains and supports. The value of these Negroes is estimated at *twenty six thousand dollars!* and Mr Minge expended previous to their embarkation about 1 200 dollars in purchasing articles of husbandry for them, besides providing them with clothes provisions and every thing which he supposed they might require for their comfort during the passage and for their use after their arrival in Hayti. He also paid 1,600 dollars for the vessel. As they were about to go on board, he had a peck of dollars brought down to the bank of the river and calling them all around him under a tree he distributed the sum among them. With but a very few such individuals as this scattered throughout the world, slavery cannot long exist. Let us hope the next bright precedent will issue from our own colonies

DOMESTIC

We have little or nothing to report under the head of domestic intelligence, but that the accounts from the seat of war in the East though they announce the progress of our arms in the Burman empire are very far from consolatory. Our losses from disease and casualties have been large, and our work is still unfinished

A report had been widely prevalent of the immediate dissolution of Parliament. The Cabinet has recently decided against the measure

In Ireland the Biblical discussion still continues, and has called forth much ardent controversy. Dr Doyle, in particular, has circulated on the occasion a most remarkable letter, in which he says —

"I need not remind you, dearest brethren, of what is ruled by the supreme authority of the Church with regard to individuals, unauthorised thereto by their bishop not entering into public disputations with persons maintaining heretical opinions. your own good sense and the very nature of divine truth as deposited by Christ with his Apostles and their successors shew to you that whatever relates to faith morals, or discipline, should be regulated by those whom the Holy Ghost has appointed to govern the church. As the obedience you owe to me is a reasonable one it is just that I should state the grounds upon which I require of you to exercise it in this matter and they are—First, because the character of the Christian religion is peace and the end of it, to establish peace and good will upon earth, as the means of fitting men for heaven. Secondly, St Paul says, 'if any one be contentious or fond of disputes we have no such custom nor the church of God. Thirdly, because all experience has proved the justice and truth of Tertullian's remark, that disputes with heretics weary the weak create anxiety in the mind of others, and that the only thing we obtain by them is to have our anger excited by their blasphemy. Fourthly because no general principle, to which the questions to be discussed could be finally referred, can be agreed upon between the parties for this reason, that the members of the Bible Society do not admit our creed nor have they any creed of their own Fifthly you are to avoid these disputes because by entering into them you appear to call in question those truths which are already defined by the Holy Ghost and by us that is, by the bishops the successors of the Apostles! Sixthly, you should not dispute with these men in the manner proposed, because there is no tribunal on the earth competent to try the issue between you. Lastly, you should not contend with men, over whom a triumph could be productive of no permanent advantage as individuals, they may be learned and respectable, but as religionists they are deserving only of your unmixed pity. They profess to be seeking for truth—this can only be found in the Catholic Church."—We have quoted these remarks of this celebrated Roman Catholic prelate not so much to shew—what is, however but too apparent—the dogmatical and overbearing spirit of the Church of Rome, and its horror of free Biblical reading and discussion as to exhibit the evident anxiety which pervades the Roman Catholic hierarchy for the consequences of the rapid progress of education and religious inquiry. If Dr Doyle is a fair sample of the opinions of his brethren, we may well conclude that the spiritual despotism under which large portions of the world have so long groaned is verging to its downfal. It is very unlikely, that in the presence of liberal inquiry, men can long or widely, consent to be governed by a system so purely arbitrary,—a system which admits no argument but the mere dictum of a self assumed infallible church. As one proof of this inference we may notice the fact of the largely increased sale of the sacred Scriptures in Ireland since the late Biblical discussions. Let then, Protestants rightly judge where their true strength lies not in the arm of temporal power not in a return of evil for evil or railing for railing but in educating the illiterate, instructing the ignorant, communicating the Scriptures to all who will receive them—in a word banishing darkness by light, error by truth, misrepresentation by charity and superstition by pure and undefiled religion

---

ANSWERS TO CORRESPONDENTS

A——a A Villager A F A J G G Johannes S R C J W Theognis H H J M B Christian Cosmopolite and M A C are under consideration

THE CHRISTIAN OBSERVER.

No 286] OCTOBER 1825 [No 10 Vol XXV

RELIGIOUS COMMUNICATIONS

To the Editor of the Christian Observer

THE PHILOSOPHY OF THE ROMAN CATHOLIC RELIGION

No IV

IN pursuing the melancholy course marked out for an inquirer into the system of Popery, I shall remind the reader, that it can survive only so long as the governors and the governed reciprocally obey each other There must be a perpetual interchange of despotism and submission Of all mankind, Papists are the most consistent patrons of the doctrines of passive obedience and non resistance and necessarily are they so because the plebeians, so to speak of their church yield their submission on a certainty that the aristocracy will support, and must support, the course of policy already established Their loyalty has nothing in it of the dignity of an unbought and patriotic obedience A loyalty of principle can sustain, without murmuring, the opposition of a legislature to many an expression of popular wishes It can also blame the measures of the same legislature, without indulging a spirit of sedition On the contrary a Catholic populace are at once enslaved and feared by their despotic ecclesiastical government They are Catholics just while the pope of the day ratifies the plans of his predecessors The head of the papal empire is spiritually to his adherents what Napoleon was to the military population of France The latter was the idol of the army because he led them to plunder and martial glory They adored him as a genius of extraordinary address in directing and completing their own selfish projects But had he, in the full career of his success, abandoned the lust of conquest, declaimed against the criminality of unprovoked war fare, and invited his invincibles to retire with him to the quietness and useful arts of peace, he would probably have soon come to his end, and there would have been none to help him Let the generalissimo of the papal armies make a parallel experiment Let him issue a bull, under all the talismanic authority of the fisherman's ring tending to reduce absolution and the power of the keys, within the severe restrictions of the first Apostles let him hint a suspicion of the efficacy of relics indulgences, and rosaries and *his* infallibility would doubtless disappear ! The philosophy of inspiration describes indeed, with the plain emphasis of Scripture, the compromise which will invariably take place between the teachers and the taught, in all religions not truly modelled upon the word of God ' The prophets prophecy falsely, and the priests bear rule by their means *and my people love to have it so* A collection of correspondent texts would readily detect the causes and consequences of such combinations and would vividly illustrate the fact asserted in a former paper that the proudest pretensions of infallibility rest on no foundation more favourable than an abject subserviency to human passions

Such is an attempted specimen of the history of the rise, progress, and establishment of the Roman Catholic religion If the writer has been, in any degree, correct in the analysis of his subject, he is anxious, in closing the discussion, to illustrate, with at least equal truth, the virtual identity, with Popery, of every form of nominal Christianity. He has been hitherto silent on one leading tenet of the Vatican namely, the authority of TRADITION, considered, as it is, to be a necessary commentator on the side of the Church, upon the holy Scriptures. It has been said on certain occasions of political jealousy, that there was something behind the throne greater than the throne. This paradox has a parallel in the circumstance common, though in different degrees to the Papal and Protestant divisions of the Christian church. There is too often, with many who profess to reverence and appeal to, the Scriptures something practically greater in its influence than the Scriptures themselves. A *mere* Papist, and a *mere* Protestant—meaning, by the epithet to designate men who know nothing of religion, but as partisans of rival sects,—will always find the Bible an obstacle, which both of them cordially wish to be removed at least as to its real spirit and design. It blocks up the progress of every kind of sectarianism and intolerance. I am aware, at this point, of the difficulty of avoiding a revival of the now quiescent controversy on the Bible Society. Extremely thin partitions in some instances, divide the debates between various members of the Reformed Church, from the standing dispute on the exclusive authority of Revelation, between the general body of the Reformation and the defenders of Papal tradition. A cardinal who forwards a rescript against the indiscriminate circulation of the Bible among Papists in a Protestant kingdom is, *to all practical purposes** the ally of such Protestants as write pamphlets against the diffusion of the Scriptures among the subjects of the British crown. In either instance, the effect would be to restrain mankind from discovering religious truth, otherwise than may subserve the interests of an exclusive church. Anti-biblists whether transalpine or cisalpine are afraid of trusting the Bible *alone*. If abandoned as it were, to itself, without a guard or corrective, they dread its exposure to the world, lest the world should injure it, by undue familiarity or it should injure them by its alleged obscurity and liability to perversion. Such is the essence of all the apologies ever offered for the detention of the sacred volume in ecclesiastical custody. The defence assumes the language of reverence with regard to revelation and of affectionate caution in reference to the people who are *not* to read it. But as there were judaized Christians in the earliest period of the church, so at all times there are papalizing Protestants in the very heart of the Reformation. A centre of union is found where the nominalists of every communion meet. Even the Unitarians, and the followers of Swedenborg sects utterly opposed to each other, are yet so entirely dissatisfied with the New Testament in a plain simple version that the first have given the world an 'Improved Translation,' with cautionary notes and the second declare it to be unintelligible, unless by the commentary of a Scandinavian baron. What an unintentional satire is this upon the magnificent pretensions to traditionary power at Rome and, I may add, on the determina-

* I say *to all practical purposes* because justice requires it to be remembered that all who oppose the Bible Society do not necessarily profess to object to the free circulation of the Scriptures. They ground their hostility on the instrument and not on the act. I think them quite wrong and cannot but consider that a truly *adequate* persuasion of the necessity and value of the universal diffusion of these life giving records ought to make them and *would* make them abate somewhat of their scruples as to the means but still they are not to be confounded with those who in the very bosom of Protestantism really deprecate the indiscriminate circulation of the book itself at least without a very decisive human comment.

tion of those among ourselves who would forbid the circulation of the Scriptures, unless their progress be accompanied by an interpreter

The transition is natural, from this portion of the subject to the identity of feeling which exists between our insular and continental adherents to the infallibilities of their respective modifications of priesthood. The moderation of the Anglican Church, illustrated for example, in her Nineteenth Article, has long been a source of almost undissembled irritation among those who have wished to invest her with an authority, which she disclaims, corresponding with that of the triple crown. They have languished, but in vain, to find in the *lex scripta* of the Church of England, a scaffolding capable of supporting their own opinions on the height of spiritual intolerance.

Whoever charges these remarks with harshness, or even novelty, must have read ecclesiastical history to very little purpose. Especially, he must have consulted the *scriptural* records of the church without gathering the instructions they obviously inculcate. Let him, for a moment, contemplate the character and deeds of the Jewish Sanhedrim of the chosen council of the chosen people headed by the high priest and the rulers yet *these* crucified the Lord of Glory! Then again, among the first twelve authorities of the Christian church, one of them had a devil and in every subsequent period experience has perpetually confirmed the dictum of the fathers of the English church, that 'in the visible church of Christ the evil be ever mingled with the good and sometimes the evil have chief authority in the ministration of the word and sacraments. Neither are the extravagant claims of the sacerdotal order preferred only by priests attached to affluent and influential establishments but they exude, in subordinate degrees from the ministers and patrons of the minor sects. Luther said, that every man had a pope in his own heart. The love of exclusive authority is inherent, by nature, in every human bosom. Hence a papalizing Episcopalian of the present times would repose on the decisions of a convocation, were it allowed to sit, as devoutly as if it held its sessions in the apostolic chambers of the Vatican *because* he would find or think he found in such decisions an echo to his own prejudices. By a similar process—*mutatis mutandis*—a papalizing sectary would cling to his own peculiar forms or favourites. I am not discussing the merits or demerits of the decrees of convocations conferences, or other ecclesiastical authorities which doubtless, like other expressions of human opinion, have their respective virtues and vices—but my object is to illustrate the slavish and selfish make of those minds which submit to these several decrees, simply on account of the acts in question having been passed by their own legislatures. How many mere victims of prejudice without any true knowledge or practice of genuine religion marshal themselves under the standards of Protestantism! which they prefer to the banners of the Holy Father or of Mohammed, only because their native soil was not within the territories of Rome or Constantinople.

Many writers have shewn the parallelisms which exist between the ancient and modern modifications of Roman idolatry and the goddess of the Dunciad, written by a member of the Church of Rome, describes with poignant satire the universal empire of ignorance in Europe during the middle ages and the transfer of the machinery of Paganism to the use and benefit of its heir and successor on the seven hills *. But

---

* See the cirque falls the unpillar'd
   temple nods
Streets pav'd with heroes Tiber chok'd
   with gods
Till Peter's keys some christen'd Jove
   adorn
And Pan to Moses lends his pagan horn
See graceful Venus to a Virgin turn'd
Or Phidias broken and Apelles burn'd
&c &c

we are less familiar with parallelisms observable nearer home, and even at our very doors. I shall endeavour to explain this farther by a graphic exhibition of character, whence, it is hoped, may be deduced a lesson, not indeed of novelty, but of high importance to every denomination of Christians.

Pertinax was the son of parents educated under the discipline of the Established Church. Externally they were consistent members of its communion: but gliding through life at a period when the ecclesiastical world was generally quiescent, they took little interest in the controversies occasionally awakened; and, at such times, gazed at what was done by others, as incurious and idle spectators. Their son passively succeeded to their principles, as he did, in after years, to their mansion and estate. In his childhood, he was regularly taught the catechism: and, at the usual time, passed onward, in *his* religious life, to the rite of confirmation. In those days, and in such a family, the act of confirmation was generally regarded pretty much as an *opus operatum*, as something which rivetted the beneficial process of baptism: while little or nothing except what was merely superficial and common place, was said as to the conduct of the catechumen since his baptism, and also with respect to the spiritual responsibilities attached to the rite next to be performed. Pertinax therefore went for imposition of hands, not as to a means of grace, through which a Divine blessing might be communicated to sincere candidates: but as if about to undergo an undefined and mystic spell, such as might secure the receiver from evils equally undefined and mysterious. The routine of the family soon after introduced him within the circle of communicants: and, at the sacramental table, the entire value of the ceremonial seemed to be comprized in a certain feeling of satisfaction, that now he had accurately complied with the requisitions of Christianity and the Church: and that a periodical repetition of the act would be a current source of merit and security.

In this course, Pertinax approached the autumnal season of life, and had never been sensible of any *painful* suspicion as to his fitness for eternity. He had attended the death beds of both his parents: had seen them quietly receive the sacrament of the Lord's Supper, much as a Catholic receives the *viaticum*, and depart in all apparent composure: but neither they nor himself had examined the evidences of their claim to everlasting happiness. I know not how to express their views on this solemn subject more definitely, than by saying that *they looked upon their salvation as a matter of course*. There was no inquiry: and there was no doubt. Their lives had not been vicious: their dispositions were amiable: their passions not vehement. The family was regular in its habits: their attendance at church and at the holy communion ostensibly exemplary. They were able to name other families, who were almost utter strangers to public worship, and also to many of the established decorums of the world. The religion of Pertinax was hereditary, both in essence and in form. If, for a moment, he paused in the career of self satisfaction, under the shadows of hesitation, he recovered his progress by the recollection of his parents' lives and deaths: and especially by a cherished remembrance of the *devotion* with which, *in extremis*, they offered, as he said, the eucharistic sacrifice. On these occasions there had been a great attendance of the household: the communion plate was brought from the parish church: and the ceremony was closed by tears, and

---

Whatever else the writer of these lines might be, he *professed* to be a Catholic, and formally declined the overtures of Bishop Atterbury, who endeavoured to allure him within the pale of the Anglican Church.

by encomiums, on the part of the domestics, on the patrons who were leaving them. I am not objecting to such solemnities: very far from it: but the evil was, that, from circumstances such as these Pertinax gathered materials towards completing an edifice, always in progress, the temple of a human soul admiring its own virtue: and the building was to receive its top stone, when at the termination of his own life, he should close its " well spent hours by a death bed sacrament.

So rolled away forty or fifty years of his probationary state. But as he lived on to times when neither the political nor religious world was slumbering, he deserted the tranquil position occupied by his fathers, and took a decided share in the busy polemics of the day. He became a strenuous believer, not indeed verbally in the infallibility of his church: but in something which, although not called such, appeared to claim the attributes of pontifical sovereignty without the name. He shewed himself to all other divisions of the Protestant community exactly in the attitude which a rigid Romanist assumes towards the Church of England. Under the keenest feelings of exasperation, excited by hearing a neighbouring Roman Catholic gentleman pronounce our Establishment to be a church without an altar and without a priesthood, excluded from the privileges of the covenant of God, and abandoned to a desperate reliance on some extraordinary exertion of Divine mercy,—he yet told precisely the same tale, point by point, to a Dissenting minister, who made incursions into his vicinity: denouncing *him* and *his* party as a church without an altar, without a priesthood: and so on according to the technical phraseology employed against himself. Yet no one frowned upon the papal system with darker hostility. It was observable also, that, in proportion as he declaimed against Popery, he seemed eager to approximate the ceremonials of his own church, even to its decorations, to those of that corrupt community: and this in direct opposition to the opinions of his venerable and old-fashioned rector: who had much to say in self defence, about the relics of Popery, the simplicity of the Reformers, and of the inconsistency of a layman disputing the authority of his own spiritual guide.

If the question should be asked, where was the specific, definite, difference between Pertinax and his Catholic neighbour, who unchurched the hierarchy of these dominions: no sagacity of mine can bring it towards a satisfactory answer. I can tell where they met, but not where they separated. They both defended outward and visible signs, without any serious reference to an inward and spiritual grace. Their signs varied in conformation but not in intrinsic value. The symbolic bread of the national church was to Pertinax as darkly mysterious and efficient as the wafer alleged to veil the real presence. The Liturgy was his missal: and beyond the respect and attachment justly due to devout and holy men, of whatever name or church the prelates and clergy of England were his conclave: although, among these, he had his peculiarly orthodox favourites, as distinguished from all enthusiasts. In the Canons, Articles, and Homilies, and especially in the first of these: for in sooth of the other two he knew little but the name, he found his Tridentine decrees. He seemed except in the moment of heated controversy, to be perfectly unconscious of the existence of other divisions of the Reformation: and supposed that his own communion were in exclusive possession of all theological erudition, and the sole depositaries of pulpit eloquence. All the while he slumbered on, in melancholy ignorance almost of the simplest doctrines and certainly of the practical influence, of the Gospel of

Jesus Christ. He was, it is true, aware of the advent and birth of the Messiah, because the institutions of his country brought these events to annual remembrance. He observed, with outward strictness, the periods of the ecclesiastical year, and was not a little irritated, if his rector neglected to deliver discourses appropriate to them. It was at once pleasant and painful to watch the skill with which he, at the same time, unspiritualized the subjects in question, and celebrated the festivals of the Christian world, with little apparent consciousness of their origin, or at least of their real spirit. The Epiphany, for example, brought to him no grateful sensation, that among *us* Gentiles were preached the unsearchable riches of Christ. Passion week was, in his estimation, the most important period of the year; but the subject uppermost in his mind was the consideration of the actual passion, the personal sufferings of Jesus Christ, without any due corresponding reference, beyond a vague heartless recognition, to their cause in human guilt, especially his own guilt, and their consequences in the salvation of believers. He was affected, sometimes to tears, by a detail of the events in Gethsemane, and on Calvary; but practically he went no further. The crucifixion was contemplated by him very much as the performance of a tragedy, with the mournfulness and the scenery of a painful death. Easter was a season of unintelligible triumph, not of spiritual gratitude. And, to add one example more of nominal churchmanship, Trinity Sunday had a large share of impressiveness; but Pertinax held the Athanasian doctrine only as a series of metaphysical positions, sanctioned by ecclesiastical power; also connected with what *he* most admired and cherished, namely, a denunciation of error and heresy opposed to the sectarianism of Arius and Socinus, and forming a line of demarcation between orthodoxy and the corruptions of Christianity; but with no appropriate reference to the agency of the three Divine Persons in the work of human redemption; with no practical, personal desire to obtain and enjoy the grace of the Lord Jesus Christ, or the love of God, or the communion of the Holy Ghost. Yet there was an ample space of neutral ground where Pertinax cordially shook hands with the practical irreligionist, whether Catholic, Arian, Socinian, or of whatever other species; for, differing as they might in other respects, they were firmly united in pursuing, with avidity, the things of this world. They severally returned from the church, the chapel, or the meeting, to the central point of pleasure and profit from which, for a moment only, they diverged, when public worship or party doctrines demanded their retreat from the direct pursuit of avarice and vanity. At the Monday morning's assemblage in the county hall, to expedite the concerns of a canal or a mine, (of course there was nothing wrong in the engagement itself—I speak only of the spirit of the individual) and at the evening party and ball, there was a perfect identity of feeling. On the race course, and in the chace, all *religious* dissension was merged in the pleasurable sensations of the hour. If they did not cement their union by an attendance at the gambling table, or the cock pit, they did not abstain on purely Christian principles. The occupation did not suit their taste, or was too low, too gross for *their* department of the world. No question was asked how it stood with regard to the Divine law.—Now what does this tale unfold, but that such men were unbelievers in masquerade, whether concealing their anti-Christianity under the visor of Catholicity, or dressed in various costumes of Protestantism! They never contemplated the Gospel in the abstract, or considered forms of ecclesiastical polity valuable, only in proportion as they bring men personally acquainted with the religion of Jesus Christ. Pertinax was not aware that the majority of mankind, and himself among the rest, were *nihilists* practically indifferent to every thing, except to the secularities and perversions superinduced upon the Gospel by human frailty or contrivance. Such is the papal system—such the religion of the Reformation—as too frequently exhibited by the adherents of either scheme to the gaze and compassion of a genuine Christian.

And here I close this lengthened discussion. If it confirm the devout reader in the faith once delivered to the saints, by contrasting with the true religion of Jesus Christ the perverse superstitions of his merely nominal adherents, it is well. Grace be with all them that love our Lord Jesus Christ in sincerity!

CHRYSOSTOM'S HOMILIES.—
NO II DE STATUIS
(*Concluded from page* 551.)

WOULDST thou build spacious and splendid houses? I do not forbid thee only not upon *earth* build mansions in *heaven*, such as may enable thee to receive others such as shall never be taken down. Why dost thou madly pursue things fickle and fugitive, and not removeable from this world? Nothing is more mutable than wealth to day with thee, to morrow against thee it arms the eyes of envy on every side it is an enemy within thy tent a foe in thy household and ye that possess it bear me witness, for ye are endeavouring in various ways to conceal it under ground. Riches make the present danger more grievous and insufferable to us for you see the poor free from encumbrances at their ease and prepared for all events, but the rich in great anxiety going about, searching for a place to bury their gold in, or for some person to take care of it for them. Why dost thou seek thy fellow servants O man? Christ stands ready to receive and keep for thee thy deposit and not only to keep but increase it, and restore it with a great addition from his hand no one can wrest it. But he does not merely preserve what thou committest to his care, he also delivers thee from dangers on this very account, [for having reposed confidence in him]. With men, indeed, they who take charge of any thing valuable, think they have done us a favour, by guarding what they received but with Christ it is otherwise for he, whenever he receives thy deposit, says he has not granted but received a favour he does not demand from thee, but he bestows upon thee a reward for the care which he takes of thy property how inexcusable then and unpardonable should we be if we pass by him that is able to secure that property and [so to speak] will be obliged to us for the custody of it, and will give us in return unspeakable rewards to put it into the hands of men who cannot secure it, who will think that they do us a favour, and after all, restore us no more than they receive!

Thou art a stranger here, thy country and thy home are in heaven thither remit all that thou hast, that even before thy full possession, even *here* thou mayest enjoy (some earnest of) thy reversion for he who is sustained by a good hope he who looks into futurity with confidence, he by that hope and confidence has already a foretaste of the kingdom (of heaven) for nothing does usually recreate and improve the soul so much as a good hope of the (joys of the) world to come, if thither thou transfer thy wealth, and take care of thy soul with becoming assiduity. They who waste all their care and diligence in adorning their houses while they are rich in external things neglect the internal and suffer the (mansion) of the soul to be dark and unfurnished and full of spiders webs would they (but) disregard external things, and spend their zeal upon their own minds collecting ornaments for *them* from every quarter, the souls of such men would (then) become an habitation of Christ (through the Spirit), and what greater felicity can there be than to possess such an inhabitant? Wouldst thou be rich? make God thy friend, and thou shalt be of all men the most affluent. Wouldst thou be rich? be not high minded this is necessary not (only) for thy future but thy present welfare for nothing is so much the butt of *envy* as a rich man,—and, if haughtiness be superadded, his pre eminence then becomes a doubly dangerous and slippery precipice, his conflict with all men far more arduous but if thou knowest how to be moderate and self-denying (in the midst of wealth) by that humility thou wilt undermine the power of envy, and whatever thou dost possess, thou wilt possess in safety for such is the nature of piety and virtue, not only are future benefits conferred by them the rewards are also present and immediate

Let us not then be elated by wealth, nor indeed by any thing else for if he that is proud of spiritual things is undone and perishes, much more (he that is proud) of things temporal Let us consider our nature, let us compute our sins, let us learn what kind of persons we are, and this will furnish us with sufficient materials for every species of humility Do not tell me that you have so many years rents laid up, ten thousand talents and fresh profits coming in every day What ever grounds (for confidence) you may allege they are all unfounded often in a single hour, in a moment, like dust whirled by the blast, are all such things dislodged and dispersed Life abounds with instances of this nature and histories are full of these instructive examples to day rich, to morrow poor Wherefore I have often laughed when I read wills, devising the property of house or land to one man, and the use or tenancy to another for we are all tenants, none of us proprietors should we preserve our possessions undiminished, even throughout our whole lives, still, whether we will or not; we shall leave them to others at our decease, after having been (all the while) usufructuaries only even that (temporary) ownership * we are entirely stript of at our departure out of this life It is manifest, therefore, that they only are the real (and permanent) proprietors (of wealth) who despise the use, and scorn the enjoyment, of it for he that casts away his wealth by distributing it among the poor, has had the use of it for all necessary purposes, and when he departs, still retains the property of it he is not turned out of this possession even by death itself, but recovers all (and much more) at that time when he most wants its protection, in the day of judgment, when an account of our affairs will be demanded of us all Wherefore if any one wishes to have the full possession and property of things as well as the use, let him (now) divest himself of all his substance since he who does not do that, will, at his death, separate himself from it altogether, and often before death, in the midst of dangers and various afflictions, will (be obliged to) cast it away And that this change is both summary and complete is not the whole of the evil for a *rich* man comes with a mind unpractised unprepared for enduring the hardships of poverty but it is otherwise with the poor man, for *he* trusts not in silver and gold, those lifeless substances, but in God who bestoweth all things liberally, so that the rich man is in a much more precarious state than the poor man, as he must be (ever) expecting a succession of changes (for the worse)

But what does this (expression) mean Who giveth richly all things? God bestows all things liberally things far more necessary than riches,

---

* Δ σπο7 α he here uses in a sense inconsistent with his former assertion δ σπο7 ν δ ς χ 4, therefore I insert temporary though a somewhat inconsistent epithet to ownership

such as air, water, fire, the sun, and all others of the like nature; it cannot be said that a rich man enjoys more and a poor man less of the sun's rays, nor can it be said that the rich man breathes the air more freely than the poor man, but these things are provided for all men alike and why then, it may be said has God made those greater gifts common which are necessary and even essential to life, but the inferior and less valuable gifts (wealth I mean) not common? What is the reason? That our life might be provided for and secured, and (also) that there might be an arena for the exercise of virtue for if those necessary things had not been common, perhaps the rich, actuated by their usual avarice, would have extinguished the life of the poor for if they do it (now) about money, much more would they have done it about these (other more necessary) things On the other hand, if wealth had been common to all, had lain open and exposed for general use, almsgiving would have been superseded and there would have been no opportunity for beneficence Wherefore, that we might live without fear, he has made those things common on which life depends On the other hand, that we might have an opportunity of obtaining (higher degrees of) celestial honour and glory, wealth was not made common in order that we might, by hating covetousness, pursuing charity, and distributing our substance among the poor, obtain by this method some consolation respecting our own personal sins or some palliation of them [for so the original I think implies though the sentiment inclines towards doctrines of a dangerous tendency] *God has made thee rich why dost thou make thyself poor?* God has made thee rich that thou mightest relieve the necessitous that thou mightest unbind (the burden of) thy sins [λυσης τα ἁμαρτηματα τα σεαυτȣ] by liberality to others he gave thee wealth, not that thou shouldst shut it up to thy destruction, but disperse it to thy salvation and for this reason also he made the possession of it precarious and inconstant, that he might thereby abate the intenseness of (our) frantic passion for it for if the possessors of wealth, notwithstanding they are unable to have much confidence respecting it, and even see many snares arise out of it, are thus inflamed with avaricious desires (what would have been their devotion) if no such instability had attached to riches, whom (then) would they have spared, from what (victims) would they have withheld their talons, what widows, what orphans, what paupers?

Think not then that wealth is any great benefit a great benefit it is to possess, not wealth but the fear of the Lord, and perfect godliness Were there any righteous man (among us) who had much confidence towards God, though he were the poorest man in the world *he* would be sufficient to deliver us from the present calamity for he need only stretch out his hands towards heaven, and call upon God, and this cloud would blow over (whereas) our treasures of gold are no better than so much clay for any power they have to avert the impending evils.—And not in *this* danger only, at the approach of disease and death, or any severe affliction, the inefficacy of wealth becomes apparent for out of its own resources, no relief can it produce for the changes and chances (of this mortal life) There is one thing in which riches seem to have the advantage of poverty in daily luxury, in the perfect enjoyment of convivial pleasures nevertheless (I aver that) this (pleasure) is (more) conspicuous at the tables of the poor, and that they enjoy it in a greater degree than the rich Be not surprized nor think this assertion a paradox for I will prove it by facts It is universally acknowledged that the pleasures of the table depend not (so much) on the quality of the viands as the tem perament of the guests, for example, the most ordinary fare, when a man sits down to it with an appetite, will be more grateful to the palate than any meat or confectionary, or the greatest variety of high seasoned ingredients. But he who sits down to table without waiting till necessity induces him, and does not previously sustain (any degree of) hunger (which is the case with the rich) will derive no pleasure from the *delicacies* that are set before him, for want of a due excitement of appetite. Your own experience clearly confirms these observations: but let us also hear the testimony of Scripture, (Prov. xxvii. 7.) 'The full soul loatheth an honey comb, but to the hungry soul every bitter thing is sweet.' What is sweeter than the honey comb? yet it is *not* sweet to the man who is not hungry: and what more distasteful than bitter food, yet is it sweet to them that are oppressed with hunger: and it is manifest to every one that the poor are urged to take their repasts by necessity and hunger, but the rich wait not (for these urgent demands of nature) consequently do not enjoy the genuine pleasure. What has been said of food may be applied to drink also; for as hunger contributes more to gratification than the quality of the aliments (which relieve it), so thirst makes a draught most grateful, though it be a draught of water only; which is illustrated by those words of the prophet, "He fed them with honey from the rock, Psal. lxxxi. 16.* Although we no where read in the Scriptures that Moses brought honey out of the rock, but in several passages, (that he brought) rivers, and waters, and cooling streams: what is it then which is here asserted, for the Scripture does not give false accounts? [It amounts to this, that] since they fell in with those cooling streams at a time when they were thirsty, and in great distress, (the prophet) meant to express the delight which drinking would in such circumstances impart, and therefore called the water honey:* not that the element was changed, but the state of the persons who drank it made the water sweeter *to them* than honey: so you perceive how the pleasantness of the draught arises from the thirst of them that take it. Wherefore, it has frequently happened that the poor, when worn out with labours and hardships, and parched with thirst, have derived from water only the gratification I am speaking of— while the rich, though they drank wine of the most excellent quality, sweet and fragrant, have not derived the same delight [from it as the poor did from water only.]

The same may be said of sleep: not the softest down, nor couches enchased in silver, nor the stillness that reigns in the apartments, nothing of this kind can produce such sweet and gentle sleep as they enjoy who, after labour and fatigue, sink down upon their beds, oppressed with drowsiness and the want of rest. Besides the testimony of experience, we may here also allege the declarations of Scripture: for Solomon, who was no stranger to a luxurious life, confesses as much in these words,—"The sleep of a labouring man is sweet, whether he eat little or much." (Eccles. v. 12.) Wakefulness arises both from emptiness and repletion: the one exhausting the moisture of the body, making the eyelids rigid, and suffering them not to close: the other contracting and weighing down the mind, and producing many pains: yet such is the benefit of labour, that whenever either (of these extremes) occur, the labourer is notwithstanding able to sleep: for since he is running about in various directions the whole day, upon his master's business, worn out with

---

The Septuagint and the Vulgate give this sense: but in our two translations it is *not* an assertion of a fact but is *merely hypothetical*. I would have fed, &c.

* But I presume the knowledge of the Hebrew tongue would have obviated this error.

toil, and having scarcely any respite, for these labours he receives an ample recompence, the refreshment of (profound) sleep. Such is God's gracious appointment, that (the best) pleasures should be procurable not by gold and silver, but by labour, and fatigue, and indigence, and the severities of a life of self denial. As for the rich it is not so with them, they enjoy not this satisfaction, but frequently lie sleepless on their beds during the whole night, haunted by the multiplicity of their schemes and occupations whereas, the poor man who had his limbs wearied with daily labours before he lay down, rises up refreshed by a sound, and sweet and genuine sleep, and even in this gift (alone) receives no small recompence for his honest labours.

Wherefore, since the poor man sleeps and eats and drinks with greater pleasure (than the rich man), what further grounds can remain for any high estimation of wealth stript as it is even of that plea which seemed to give it an advantage over poverty. Wherefore, from the very beginning (of the world) God appointed man to labour, not [altogether] as a penalty and a punishment, but as a salutary discipline. When Adam lived a life without labour, he fell from paradise when the Apostle lived a laborious life, and could say we "wrought with labour and travel night and day," (2 Thess. iii. 8) then he went to paradise, and ascended to the third heaven. Let us not then vilify labour nor cast contempt on the work and toil of our hands, for even before (we reach) the kingdom of heaven (even here) we derive from it a very great recompence, extracting enjoyment from the occupation itself, and, what is superior to any pleasure, the most perfect health. But the rich, besides a fastidious disrelish, are assailed by many actual diseases whereas the poor are kept out of the hands of physicians, or, if at any time they fall sick, they recover speedily, being free from indolence and delicacy, and having a sound and firm constitution. Poverty, to them that bear it with pious (submission) is great wealth, a treasure inviolable, a strong staff a possession unassailable, an inn secure from ambush.

It may be objected that the poor man is oppressed—but the rich man is plotted against still more the poor man is despised and insulted—but the wealthy is envied the poor man is not so much exposed to attacks as the rich man, who presents various handles on every side, both to the devil and to insidious men and, owing to the wide circle of his affairs, is obliged to be subservient to all men he who needs the attendance of many is forced to flatter many, and to humour them with much servility but the poor man cannot be subdued, even by Satan himself, if versed in the wisdom of true godliness wherefore Job, though strong before, after the loss of all things, became much stronger and obtained a more glorious triumph over that adversary. Besides, the poor man *cannot* be insulted, if he be a pious man, and "wise * unto that which is good for what I said concerning the pleasures (of the table), that they did not arise from the costliness of the viands but the temperament of the guests, the same I also say of insult,—that not upon the intention of them that offer the insult but upon the disposition of them that receive it, does it depend whether that insult (shall) take effect or be defeated for instance, (suppose) any one has cast upon you all kinds of reproaches if you derided his attack, if you did not admit his words [into your mind] if your [soul] was too elevated to receive the wound (intended for it), then you have *not* been insulted just as if the body were invulner

* Αἴδη φιλοσοφείν By philosophy Chrysostom manifestly means the knowledge and practice of piety as the very frequent recurrence of the phrase and its various connexions with other subjects prove clearly

able, then, though assailed by showers of arrows, it would receive no wound, for wounds arise not from the hand that shoots the arrows, but from the bodies which receive them in like manner insults and the dishonour attending them have their subsistence, not in the madness of those persons who offer them, but in the weakness of those who receive them. If then we are influenced by that wisdom which is from above, we cannot be insulted, we cannot yield to (the impression of these external) evils. Such a one insulted you, you did not feel it, it did not grieve you, (that is) you were *not* insulted instead of being wounded yourself, you have on the contrary inflicted a wound for when the injurious person perceives that the blow which he aimed does not reach the heart of those for whom he intended it, he is greatly mortified and while they who are assaulted hold their peace the stroke rebounds of its own accord from them upon the man from whom it came.

Wherefore my beloved, let us on all occasions study and practise this divine philosophy [of invincible meekness], then poverty will not be able to hurt us, it will even become a great benefit it will render us more glorious than we could ever have been without it, and richer than the richest of the sons of men. What could be poorer than Elijah? yet he surpassed all rich men on this very account because he was so poor, and had chosen that condition by reason of the affluence of his mind for he embraced such extreme poverty because he considered the greatest abundance of wealth unsuitable to the elevation of his soul, beneath the dignity of his ascetic life thus, if he had highly esteemed the things of the present life, a mantle made of sheepskin would not have been the whole of his property but to so great a degree did he condemn all the vanity of this world—looking upon all (its) gold as so much worthless clay—that he possessed nothing but that external garment [the leathern mantle]. Wherefore a king* was desirous of meeting with this poor man, and he who had much gold hung on all he spoke, though he was owner of nothing but a leathern mantle so much more splendid was that rough garment than a purple robe, and the cave of the righteous man than the palace of a king. Wherefore, when ascending to heaven he left nothing to his disciple but this sheepskin with this, he said, I have wrestled with the devil take and arm yourself with it against his assaults for poverty is a strong shield an impregnable shelter a tower that cannot (be undermined and) shaken. Elisha received the mantle† as a very great inheritance and a very great inheritance it really was, more valuable than abundance of gold and from that time he was invested with a double portion of his master's spirit and Elijah though ascended on high remained still below (in the person of his successor). I know that you have a peculiar veneration for this just man and that you each of you wish that his case were your own but what if I can convince you that

---

* I suppose he means Ahab who searched for him throughout his dominions and took an oath of the inhabitants of cities that he was not concealed among them

† This mantle is five times mentioned. The prophet wrapped his face in it when God spoke to him in the still small voice he threw it over Elisha when he was at plough and thereby called him to the prophetic office. Twice it divided Jordan and, falling from Elijah as he went up, was caught by his disciple and successor—this μ λωτης [adareth in Hebrew which Bishop Patrick says means also a splendid and furred vest] was like the rod of Moses an appendage to his prophetic office—and might not be altogether a rude and homely dress nor does it appear to be all he possessed for he had a servant, in which circumstance other accommodations are strongly implied.—still the hardships and severities of Elijah's life will in general justify Chrysostom's observations abating some exaggeration which is a prevailing fault of his oratory

we who have been initiated in our sacred mysteries, have all received something much greater than this? For Elijah indeed left his mantle to his disciple but the Son of God, when *he* ascended, left us his own flesh, and Elijah (left his gift) by divesting himself of it: but Christ carried *his* along with him when he ascended, and yet left it behind him for us. Let us not then be dejected, nor give way to grief, nor be alarmed at the present difficult and dangerous crisis of our affairs, for he that did not refuse to shed his blood for (us) all, he who made us partakers of his flesh and of that same blood again, what is there that *He* will refuse to do for our preservation? Animated by such hopes as these, let us then invoke (his aid) continually, let us be urgent in prayers and supplications, and fulfil all our other duties with the greatest exactness, that we may escape this danger that now hangs over us, and may be accounted worthy of the blessings of the world to come which may we all obtain, through the grace and goodness of our Lord Jesus Christ, by whom and with whom be glory unto the Father with the Holy Spirit, now and for ever and ever. Amen.

FAMILY SERMONS.—No. CCII.

Jeremiah ii. 11. *Hath a nation changed their gods which are yet no gods? but my people have changed their glory for that which doth not profit.*

THE records of all ages exhibit to us the strange obstinacy with which the heathen usually cling to their evil customs and superstitions. If we except the triumphs obtained over Paganism by the Gospel of Christ from the Apostolic age up to the present moment, some of which even in our own day have been most signal and consoling, the idolatrous nations of the world still perpetuate the absurd, and cruel, and unholy practices transmitted to them by their fathers. Human sacrifices, voluntary tortures, ceremonies the most preposterous, opinions the most irrational, are handed down from generation to generation as their best birth right, their highest privilege. Long and widely must knowledge and civilization extend their influence before they subvert even the grosser rites of heathenism; nay we find that the most polished and classical nations of antiquity wandered as far from truth and righteousness in their idolatries, and were as tenacious for their fabled gods, as the most barbarous tribes of savages.

Most urgent then is it upon all who profess themselves to be Christians, to feel pity for their fellow-creatures sunk in the darkness and guilt of heathenism, and to exert themselves to the utmost of their power in their various spheres of life to assist in sending to them the word of God and Christian teachers, to rescue them from their fearful condition.

But there is also another practical consideration connected with a survey of the obstinate blindness and superstition of the heathen, and their devotion to their idolatrous worship, namely, the contrast which it affords to the conduct of too many who consider themselves worshippers of the one true God, and of Jesus Christ whom he hath sent. Such persons may not indeed have professedly thrown off the Christian faith, or bowed down before lifeless images for to these particular sins they have no temptation but viewing the expostulation in the text in its full meaning and spiritual application, may it not too truly be said, "Hath a nation changed their gods which are yet no gods? but my people have changed their glory for that which doth not profit." The justness of this application will but too clearly appear if we compare their conduct, as to its real spirit, with that of the Israelites addressed in the words before us; in which the prophet in the first place shews a twofold sin of the people, in *forsaking God*, and *choosing idols* and in the second, a threefold aggravation of their conduct, in *its sinfulness, its ingratitude*, and *its folly*.

First, then, we have set before us the evil conduct of the people which consisted in two particulars forsaking the worship of the true God, and joining themselves to idols as is expressed in most striking imagery in the thirteenth verse "My people have committed two evils they have forsaken me the fountain of living waters, and hewed them out cisterns, broken cisterns, that can hold no water God is the author of all blessings, both for the body and the soul and whatever else men prefer before him, be it, as in the case of the Israelites, the idols of the heathen, or, as in the case of too many who call themselves Christians, the sins and vanities of the present life, or the uncertain possession of mere worldly blessings, they are guilty of the twofold sin here described

1 The first step in the career of evil, is "forsaking God This is the fountain and root of all other sins If men lived as always in his presence, seeking to do his will, and placing their highest enjoyment in his favour, they would be preserved by his grace and protection, as with an impenetrable shield, from the power of sin and temptation While the prodigal son remained contented and dutiful under his parent's roof, he knew nothing of the want, the poverty, the hunger, which he afterwards experienced, and the keen feeling of which convinced him of his folly in forsaking the duties and comforts of his paternal mansion His first sin, and that which led to all the evils which overtook him, was his neglect towards his parent, his indifference to his approbation, his carelessness as to incurring his displeasure, his wish to cast off the duties he owed to him, and to live in utter selfishness and independence of paternal restraint. If then we would guard against evil, if we would not expose our immortal souls to certain ruin, we must watch over our hearts, and beware of forsaking God The more gross and open violations of his law, are readily discovered, and they are apt to startle us by their enormity while perhaps we think little or nothing of that great sin which is the foundation of all others Yet who is there that has not been guilty of this sin? who is there that can say, that he has not neglected the service of God refused him the tribute of his affections, been indifferent to his glory, and disobeyed his commands? "I know you, said our Saviour to the Jews, "that ye have not the love of God in you and this still continues to be the great offence of all mankind

2 But this sin leads to another for we are not content, when we forsake God, that our hearts should continue a mere blank we seek to fill up the void which his absence has made, and to find our satisfaction in other objects which can never afford us true repose Having forsaken God, we choose to ourselves idols for, in the language of Scripture, every thing is an idol which usurps, in our affections, the throne to our Creator alone Whether we place our chief delight in the desires of the flesh, that is, in sensual indulgences or in the desire of the eye, that is, in a thirst for riches and temporal possessions or in the pride of life, that is, in ambition, vain glory, and the love of human applause, we commit the sin of spiritual idolatry we break the first and great command, " Thou shalt have none other gods before me we prove that we do not love God "with all our heart, and soul, and mind, and strength and we incur the just displeasure of Him who has declared " I will not give my glory to another Thus are all mankind proved to be guilty before God In the words of the Almighty

in the chapter before us, "they are gone far from me, and have walked after vanity, and become vain they even refuse his offers of peace and reconciliation they reject his promises of grace and mercy, they despise the sacrifice which he has provided for their sins they will not come unto Christ that they may live they grieve his Holy Spirit they are not willing to be born again and sanctified, and made new creatures in Christ Jesus in a word, content with the world, satisfied for a time with the broken cisterns which they have substituted for the fountain of living waters, they choose their portion in this life, and overlook the concerns of the life to come

Secondly Such is the universal offence of mankind against God we proceed now to shew *the sinfulness the ingratitude*, and *the folly*, which are involved in it, all of which are distinctly pointed out by the prophet in his solemn expostulation with the people of Israel and Judah

1 *Its extreme sinfulness*—Persons are apt to speak and to think of these subjects with the most careless indifference they admit indeed that they are not so good as they ought to be, or hope to be they own that they have too often failed in their duty to God they do not profess to be perfect and they trust that God will forgive them for the sake of Jesus Christ but beyond this customary acknowledgment they proceed not a single step in the path of humility and sincere repentance They do not consider themselves as virtually addressed in such words as those in the chapter which precedes our text, where Jehovah says by his prophet, "I will utter my judgments against them, touching all their wickedness, who have forsaken me, and have burned incense unto other gods Except perhaps as respects a few special transgressions their conscience is little burdened with a sense of the enormity of their offences against the Most High They do not open their eyes to the aggravation of their crime, as pointed out even by our natural sense of obligation to our Creator, of which the very heathen are examples for, says the Almighty, "hath any nation changed their gods, which are yet no gods? The light of natural reason taught them that they ought to obey their Creator, their Preserver, and their Benefactor, though their ignorance, their superstition, and their vain imaginations had profanely changed his glory, " the glory of the incorruptible God, into an image made like to corruptible man, and to birds, and four footed beasts, and creeping things

But the proof of our sinfulness in forsaking God, and in placing our trust and happiness in the things of this present life, does not depend upon the mere light of natural conscience for we have in our possession a revelation from himself, in which he plainly declares to us his own unerring decision upon the subject When he chose the people of Israel to be peculiarly under his protection, he made with them this solemn stipulation " Ye shall walk after the Lord your God, and fear him, and keep his commandments, and obey his voice and ye shall serve him, and cleave unto him The same obligation applies to all mankind and we are told throughout Scripture, that " the wrath of God cometh upon the children of disobedience When the Jews had neglected to obey the laws of God given to them in his word it was said, " Great is the wrath of the Lord that is kindled against us, because our fathers have not hearkened unto the words of this book to do according to all which is written concerning us And so great was the sinfulness of such conduct, that, in the verse which follows the text, the heavens are called upon to be " astonished and horribly afraid that a feeble and sinful creature should thus set himself as it were in systematic opposition to the will and the commands of his Creator.

2. But the sinfulness of forsaking God, and preferring other things to his service, is greatly aggravated by the *ingratitude* involved in the offence. The chapter before us contains the most affecting expostulations on this subject. The Almighty reminds his rebellious people of the miracles of mercy which he had performed in their behalf; how he had brought them out of the land of Egypt, and led them through the wilderness, through a land of deserts and pits, through a land of drought and the shadow of death, through a land that no man passed through, and where no man dwelt; and "I brought you, he continues, "into a plentiful country, to eat the fruit thereof, and the goodness thereof." He gave them his law to guide them, and pastors to teach them; and he challenges them as it were to point out any instance in which he had acted unjustly or unkindly towards them: "what iniquity have your fathers found in me?" And does not this representation exhibit to us the tender mercies of God towards ourselves? Has he not given us existence and food, and clothing, and all the endearments and blessings of life? has he not preserved us amidst all the dangers temporal and spiritual to which we were exposed: has he not bestowed upon us an understanding capable of knowing him, and a soul capable of enjoying his presence for ever in heaven? Above all, has he not given his Son to die for us? and if we avail ourselves of his mercy, and place our faith in that sacrifice for our sins, will he not with him also freely give us all things? Have we found him a hard master? Did he ever command any thing injurious to our happiness? Is not his service perfect freedom; his love our highest privilege and reward? How great then the ingratitude of forsaking so good and merciful a Creator; of denying him our affections; of preferring to him the most senseless trifles; of offending him by our neglect or disobedience to his laws!

3. But there is still another consideration dwelt upon by the prophet in reference to this sinful and ungrateful course of conduct, namely, its unparalleled *folly*. The very heathen had not changed their gods, though they were no gods: they would not give up their vain hope of benefit from the supposed protection of their images of wood and stone: yet the professed worshippers of the one living and true God are too often willing to sacrifice the inestimable blessings of his favour, for the most trifling gratifications of a frail and sinful life. "My people have changed their glory, for that which doth not profit." The glory of man is the protection and favour of God; and a life of devotion to his holy laws; this, and this alone, is really profitable either to the body or the soul; for godliness only hath the promise of this life, as well as of that which is to come. To follow the evil example which has been described, is both debasing and injurious: we sacrifice, by so doing, both our true "glory" and our highest "profit." What earthly honour is of any avail if the Infinite Source of all glory condemn us at the last day to eternal shame, and confusion of face? What profit would it be to us, if we could gain the whole world, and lose our immortal souls? No! it is the height of folly, thus to choose the worldly mammon before the true riches; to forsake God for the creature; and to prefer earth to heaven, and time to eternity.

In conclusion, let us bring this subject home to our own hearts by humble self examination. Are we not conscious that we have been guilty of the sin of forsaking God? Have we not neglected to cherish a due sense of his presence; to reflect with lively gratitude upon his goodness, especially that highest instance of it in the sufferings and death of Jesus Christ his Son for the pardon of our offences have we not forsaken him as respects studying his word, keeping his laws, praying for him in our necessities, praising him for his benefits, and living to his glory? Let us further consider the extreme folly, as well as the guilt and ingratitude of so doing For we are wandering from Him who alone can make us truly happy We are weak and we refuse to repair to the infinite source of strength for help and protection We are sinful and justly exposed to the displeasure of God yet we slight his invitation to return to Him for pardon we reject the salvation freely offered to us by his infinite mercy Let us be convinced, and may the Holy Spirit convince us, before it be too late, of the greatness of our loss, the aggravation of our guilt, and the awful risk we incur by this sinful and unhappy course Who but that gracious Being whom we thus ungratefully neglect, can support us in the hour of severe trial, bestow on us a hope full of immortality and glory when we walk through the valley of the shadow of death, and be our exceeding great reward in the eternal world? All other things may, and must disappoint our hopes but God can never fail us If we make him our portion, he will supply whatever is necessary or beneficial for us, for the body and the soul, for time and for eternity Let then the rich count his favour their most valuable possession let the poor seek it as that which can infinitely compensate for all their short lived troubles let the young return to him in youth let the aged cleave to him in age for to all persons, and under all circumstances, to walk humbly with God, and to enjoy his fatherly approbation in Christ Jesus, is the highest honour, the most splendid reward

MISCELLANEOUS

To the Editor of the Christian Observer

AT this period of widely diffused Christian charity, when the minds of all who " wish well to Zion, and would desire yet to see her fallen bulwarks again built up, are more than usually excited in behalf of the wandering sheep of the house of Israel at a period when, if we adopt the opinion of a late writer, we are arrived at that point in prophetic development, when Michael is standing up for the children of his people I have thought that the relation of a visit to that portion of the scattered tribes dwelling in Rome, during a late residence in that city, might not be uninteresting to some at least of your untravelled readers My chief desire in sending you this leaf from my sketch book is to excite a further interest for the Jewish people, whose wants call as loudly to us, as did the man of Macedonia to the Apostle in his vision, " Come over and help us

I am &c

CHRISTIAN COSMOPOLITE

I had with natural interest on a first visit to the ' city of the seven hills, wandered immediately on my arrival to the Forum The aspect of nature gave no indication of the severity of winter although it was still February The atmosphere was clear, and glowed with the warm rays of a very cheering sun, shining forth from a cloudless sky This brightness of nature was strikingly contrasted with the ruins around me A falling portico rose on my sight, the melancholy remains of a temple once dedicated to Fortune, whose fabled smiles have been long withdrawn from this her seat and from the descendants of her ancient adorers. Further on stood the still beautiful columns which once adorned the temple of Jupiter the Thunderer, and close to me the ruins of the Comitium, where once from the rostrum had been heard the eloquence of a Tully, and other so called 'great men,' whose name and deeds history has handed down to the world's admiring gaze. But now all was silent; the voice of man scarcely met my ear, or his image crossed my path. It was a scene to speak to a Christian mind sermons very different from the speculative emotions which the mere moralizing sentimentalist delights to indulge in, and fondly calls elevating his soul to nature's God. I never felt more powerfully than at that moment the truth and the strength of the Psalmist's words. Man is as grass, as a flower of the field so he flourisheth. For the wind passeth over it, and it is gone, and the place thereof shall know it no more. Over the once fair scene before me had fearfully passed the shafts of war and famine and pestilence, and every blast of the storm came fraught with a curse; the place where the boasted glory of man once reigned supreme now "knows it no more."

Nor were my feelings less excited when turning from this scene of ruin and devastation a few steps brought me to the triumphal arch of Titus, the conqueror of the anciently favoured people of God, a ruined monument of ruin. First fell Jerusalem to the very dust, and then fell her haughty conquerors. The idea that this trophy was erected in the pride of victory on his return from that scene of mourning lamentations and woe which brought the daughter of Jerusalem to the ground, and made all that passed by her say, 'Is this the city that men call the perfection of beauty, the joy of the whole earth?' cannot but deeply affect the mind of a Christian visitant. I approached to take a nearer survey of the bas reliefs of the interior, on which are sculptured the trophies taken from the temple. The six branched candlestick, which Moses was commanded to make of pure gold that its lamps might burn before the Lord continually is still distinctly to be traced. On the other side I saw the spot where the ark of the covenant had been traced, but the sculpture is completely effaced; the arch itself was rapidly sinking into decay, and seemed to echo the monitory memento—

———— That all of man must fade and die
Passing his pride, his glory but a dream

But not to delineate further a monument so familiarly known from the numerous descriptions and prints of it, I shall only add, that it could not fail to bring vividly before me the picture of the captive Israelites bowed down by every species of sorrow, the unwilling spectators of the triumphs of their conqueror contemplating the spoils of their magnificent temple profanely carried in his pagan procession. Who that has read the account of the horrors of the siege of Jerusalem, the sufferings which entered her very palaces, but has felt some respondent emotion to that which caused the afflicted Prophet to exclaim, 'Oh that my head were waters, and mine eyes a fountain of tears, that I might weep day and night for the slain of the daughter of my people!'

In the distance rose on my view the magnificent amphitheatre erected for the entertainment of the Roman populace by the hands of these captives of Israel, and I felt a strong desire to visit the dwelling place of those of their descendants who are now inhabitants of this proud city. Turning from the silent and deserted forum I bent my steps to the more frequented part of the city, hoping to meet with some person to shew me the way to their dwellings. A crowd filled every avenue to the capitol on the side of the city. Inquiring of a group of idle monks, whom I first encountered, what was the occasion of this unusual circumstance, I was reminded that this was the first day of the carnival, the festivities of which open by a senatorial procession to the capitol, where the principal senator (the present father of the senate, a shadow of what that office was,) receives the homage of the Jewish rabbi, and lays his foot on his neck in token of superiority over him and his people. The scene was humiliating in the extreme for the unhappy Jew. My newly made acquaintances, the monks, who had left their convent to see the show, added to this information, that the prizes given at the carnival horse races were all paid by the Jews, as a species of tribute money; but they could not answer my further inquiries, being too good and too ignorant Catholics to know any thing more respecting the heretic Jews, though they had indeed some slight association floating in their minds between the arch of Titus and the inhabitants of the "Ghetto, as the quarter of the town they inhabit is called; for they know this much, that no Jew will pass under that arch. Finding them too much amused with the masks who began to parade the streets in senseless disguises, to wish to be diverted from the object of their attention, and being myself more than usually disposed to be disgusted with waxen faces, and chattering harlequins, I quickly bade them a good day, and returned to my lodging, questioning the meaning or object of such a ' farewell to the flesh' as this " carne vale" of Rome.

I deferred my visit to the Jews to another day, not doubting that they too, as well as their enemies the monks, had found their way to the one street where all Rome seemed anxious to assemble. On the following Saturday I set forth on my journey, and those who know this renowned city will recal to mind that it is a real journey to penetrate through the streets, the filthiest perhaps in the world, to the ' Ghetto degli Ebree.' To arrive at the Jews quarter the traveller must cross the very filthiest of those filthy streets; approach the precincts of the fish market, which sufficiently warn the passenger to stear clear of it by a most sensibly affecting appeal to his olfactory perceptions. As I entered the Ghetto, the air seemed to me almost infected with unfragrant odours. The gate under which I passed at its entrance was guarded by a soldier, whose business it is to close it upon the inhabitants every night at dusk; when by the closing of a second gate at the opposite extremity of the long narrow street assigned them, they are shut out from all communication with the rest of the city.

I have said that it was Saturday —the Hebrew Sabbath. The Jews, as I passed their doors, were standing or sitting in crowded groups; their shops were shut, and an air of idleness rather than of rest seemed diffused over the whole scene. These were the only circumstances to remind me of this being their holy day; that Sabbath, which they were to observe " throughout all their generations, for a perpetual covenant; which was to be " a sign between the Lord and the children of Israel for ever." They appeared indeed to keep within their gates, and to carry no burdens; but no observance of dress, no neatness of appearance, marked the day. I traced my way through these groups, amongst which many a fine and expressive countenance might be distinguished. They all saluted me as I passed, and directed me with humble civility to the synagogue, where they were about to repair themselves. The building was plain, and dirty in the extreme on the outside; but how much were my feelings shocked, when, on entering, I found the rabbi reading the Law at one end to a large congregation, and, at the other, stalls laid out with goods of various descriptions for sale, where the buyers and venders carried on their bargains during the time of service. How truly was I reminded of our Lord's remonstrance, "My house shall be called a house of prayer, but ye have made it a den of thieves!" I could almost have felt disposed to turn out "those who bought and sold, and to have overthrown their seats and tables." I left the synagogue; and as I turned my steps from the door, and wandered out of the Ghetto, absorbed in melancholy and commiserating reflections, I found myself before a church, built at its very gate, on which the inscription in Hebrew and Latin arrested my attention. All day long have I stretched forth my hands unto a disobedient and gainsaying people.

A woman sitting on the steps with a distaff in her hand rose, and imagining I wished to see the edifice, of which she acted as the keeper and show-woman, came forward to tell me that this was the church where the annual sermon for the conversion of the Jews is preached by a Catholic priest, at which the inhabitants of the Ghetto are all obliged to attend. She further added, that converts are baptized every Easter eve, at the baptistory of Constantine; respecting which, by the way, the exhibitor says, that some drops of the water in which that imperial convert was baptized still remain in the fount. The supposed converts are very usually represented by an old man and woman, reproduced every year in order to support the power of the Church over the souls of the poor Jews, who in truth are seldom or never really converted to Catholicism; which is certainly not a matter for astonishment when we view the nature of that religion as professed by those around them. Would that some really affectionate and scriptural instruction could be afforded to these wanderers from the fold! That the neglected habitations of the Ghetto might resound with the grateful intelligence that "Messiah is indeed come," and that many voices might join in declaring, "Now we believe, for we have heard him ourselves, and know that this is indeed the Christ, the Son of God, the Saviour of the world."

Passing strangers have but little opportunity of doing much for the spiritual welfare of any class of persons in this land of gross darkness. Superstition and ignorance rise as thick mists to prevent the bright rays of the unsophisticated Gospel beaming forth to gladden her sons and daughters. But if the hands are bound, and the lips often sealed, as it regards spiritual subjects, the heart may still be open: the benevolent solicitude of Christian charity may prepare the way for more direct religious ministrations; and at least, and with humble confidence, the visitant may "pray with all prayer and supplication" for those whom he sees 'sitting in darkness and the valley of the shadow of death.'

To the Editor of the Christian Observer.

I BEG leave to call the serious attention of your readers to a practice which does not appear to have been noticed with the reprehension which it deserves. I allude to the gross profanation of the Sabbath by country feasts, or wakes; and especially to a custom which obtains, in some parts of England, of holding the feast in the church yard, and on the Lord's day. I had lately an opportunity of witnessing the celebration of such a parish feast in a country village. While advancing towards the church yard, individuals and groups, comprising persons of every age, from the imbecility of infancy to the imbecility of second childhood, were seen moving along to the scene of festivity, decked out in holiday style; the females with a profusion of trifling decorations, common on such occasions;

Occasionally were seen persons carrying baskets full of various wares, to sell in the common mart of profanation and impiety. In the church yard itself the scene was most incongruous. Divine service had been celebrated in the morning at in early hour, followed by the administration of the Holy Communion, as if it was advisable to give a practical exhibition, on the same ground and in the same day, of the readiness with which human nature can blend the extremes of vice and of religious formalities; having first, by familiarity with both, contrived to remove from vice the mask which it generally wears, and unnaturally disguised with it the fair features of religion. Two parties against different sides of the church tower were, with full eagerness and activity, playing at balls; around were stands of various commodities exposed for sale, chiefly heaps of fruit, pastry, and confectionary, and a few toys; gambling tables were scattered in different situations, and various games of hazard were displayed upon the ground; while the unhallowed breath of those miscreants who gain a debasing living by practising upon the simplicity of ignorance, and the inexperience of youth, was employed in vociferating yells of invitation to "try the luck," where, by long practice imposture had become dexterous and chicanery adroit. To a visitant from a more moral or less heathenish portion of the empire, such a display must be most painful and offensive. A heart, not hardened by accustomed familiarity with it must recoil at such a glaring defiance of all authority, human and divine; but in the instance to which I allude, on almost every countenance there sat a perfect and most pleasant tranquillity, almost as if the people had felt themselves safe in disobedience to God, because in the very precincts of his temple, and had walked with confidence in hostility to him upon consecrated ground, and skipped with impunity over the graves of their ancestors, relatives, and friends, and fellow-villagers, from whose tombs, on this privileged occasion, issued no voice, such as generally in the solemn abode of death, strikes upon the startled conscience to warn the sinner from those evil deeds which will assuredly make him, at last, " to lie down in sorrow."

If any thing additional were wanted to make such a scene still more painfully affecting, it is supplied in the consideration that it takes place at regular periods, in a country which acknowledges Christianity as part of the law of the land, under the eyes of Christian ministers and magistrates, and upon ground devoted by the solemnities of religious consecration, and secured by the strong mounds and fences of legal sanction, to the worship and service of God. With what indignation must that just and holy Being, who says, "Vengeance is mine—I will repay," look on while such insults are offered to his despised authority! and how great must be his anger against those whose capabilities and influence, if not employed to encourage such mal practices, are not exerted to prevent them!

THEOGNIS.

To the Editor of the Christian Observer

I AM very anxious to obtain the matured opinions of some of your senior correspondents, on a subject which has of late called forth much of the serious feeling of myself and others, who are earnestly seeking after that consistency of conduct which becomes the Christian character. I allude to the subject of Oratorios performed in behalf of charitable institutions, which have now become prevalent in various parts of the kingdom, and which seem to engage a large *attendance* from the religious world. In order to maintain the testimony of a good conscience, the Christian must not only be assured that he has a right object in views, but ought also to be fully persuaded in his own mind, that he is using lawful means to accomplish it. Judging upon this principle, while I readily admit the powerful effect of these performances, in the excitement of highly devotional feelings, I would still ask, whether this *end* can justify the *means* which are employed to promote it and whether the various circumstances, connected with such performances, are not such as ought to induce the Christian to forego his own gratification, rather than give his sanction to consequences which he cannot contemplate without serious concern? The subject of musical performances has indeed been often touched upon in your pages (particularly in your volume for 1821) but I am convinced that what are called the religious world have not yet come to a clear understanding upon the subject and therefore a few well weighed suggestions respecting it, will still be acceptable.

H. H.

To the Editor of the Christian Observer.

HAVING noticed in your publication for August, the judicious remarks of one of your correspondents on indiscriminate charity to persons apparently distressed, I beg leave to offer a few additional observations on the same subject, founded on my own experience, hoping they may be useful to some of your readers, who may be disposed to the exercise of benevolence, but are restrained by the fear of imposition and on the other hand, that they may tend to check in others that profuse liberality which too frequently gives a sanction to indolence and vice.

To benevolent and pious minds, there cannot be a greater luxury, if with the will they have likewise the power of "*doing good*." The page of inspiration, exhorts us to be rich in good works, ready to distribute, and willing to communicate it also assures us, that with such sacrifices God is well pleased. Our Lord declared, "The poor ye have always with you" and in his own preeminently charitable conduct, for he went about doing good, "he has left us an example that we should follow his steps." But while the duty is enjoined, proper caution is needful as to the manner of performing it. In particular, a careful selection of suitable objects should be made, lest the stream of benevolence should flow in a wrong direction, and ' the children's bread be cast unto the dogs;' in other words, lest vice should be encouraged, and worth of character disregarded.

It is a lamentable truth that much of the misery of the poor too generally arises from their own imprudence or misconduct and it is almost a certain criterion to judge by, in visiting a case of distress (with the exception of sickness,) that if the habitation has the appearance of extreme destitution and filth, there is something in the character of its inmates that will not strictly bear the light cleanliness should always be a strong recommendation in its favour and it would be well for those who are in the habit of visiting and relieving the poor, to notice this point particularly, and not to pass over what tends so essentially to their health and comfort.

Persons unaccustomed to visit the habitations of the poor generally act from the impression they receive at first sight of the extreme wretchedness of the case and from this momentary impulse, they relieve the objects of their bounty with a liberality that would perhaps be better bestowed in a quarter where cleanliness and decency were more observed. Were they fully to investigate the case, they would find, that notwithstanding their liberality, affairs continued from day to day much the same as at first. Persons of this description often subsist wholly on the bounty of benevolent individuals in succession, by keeping up a miserable appearance for very few persons comparatively take the pains thoroughly to investigate either real character or circumstances

Imposition in many instances would be prevented, were families to forbid their servants receiving petitions promiscuously at the door. Unless a petition is drawn up and taken in hand by respectable individuals from a full knowledge of its relating to a case of real distress it is seldom worthy of notice or relief. Petitions drawn up and presented by the parties themselves are always to be regarded in a suspicious light, and it is injudicious in the extreme to relieve such cases indiscriminately. It is not unusual for those who adopt this hackneyed system of obtaining money, to use the names of individuals known to the persons whose aid is requested, and thus the unwary and unsuspicious are not unfrequently imposed upon.

In giving recommendatory letters to persons for the various benevolent and religious institutions the same caution is usually needful as to the character of the applicant. If a case of sickness, it should be ascertained, as far as possible, whether the sickness is real or feigned, or whether it proceeds from intemperate habits, which is often an unsuspected cause of ailment; and even where real sickness prevails, care should be taken that *two* societies are not visiting the same individual, a species of imposition which is too frequently practised by designing persons.

It would take up too much of this paper, to state at length all the cautions requisite to avoid or detect imposition. The object of these remarks is simply to impress on the minds of your numerous readers, (a large portion of whom are no doubt engaged in the laudable and important duty of ministering to the wants of the necessitous in their respective neighbourhoods,) the urgent necessity of thoroughly investigating the merits of the cases that may come under their notice. In so doing, each should pray earnestly for that wisdom which is profitable to direct us in our intercourse with our fellow creatures. But at the same time, the "wisdom of the serpent should be blended with the "harmlessness of the dove," and though, even with all necessary caution offences of this kind will come, the genial current of Christian benevolence must not be checked on this account. We are still "not to be weary in well doing," nor are we to relax our exertions in the cause of suffering humanity. The affliction that befals our neighbour may at some period be our own, for in this uncertain state of existence, who can tell what a day may bring forth?

There cannot be a more pleasing or profitable employment, either for male or female, than visiting the sick and afflicted. It is frequently in seasons of sickness and deep affliction, that the mind is softened and prepared to receive Divine instruction. The truths of the Gospel at such periods often reach the soul with a power hitherto unknown, and an opportunity thus afforded of stating them should never be lost sight of by the visitor. Here lies indeed the grand responsibility of those engaged in such a work, that while ministering to the temporal wants of the necessitous the eternal interests of the soul should not be disregarded.

In the Epistle of St. James, i. 27. we read, that "pure religion and undefiled before God and the Father is this, to visit the fatherless and widows in their affliction." Aged widows, without children to render them assistance, and single females unprovided for, are a class of persons too generally overlooked; they seldom obtain relief with that facility that persons do with large families, and many of them, it may be, having formerly been in better circumstances retire from rather than attract observation. The

known several persons of this description who live upon a very small and uncertain pittance, who nevertheless are clean, creditable, and contented such persons should be preferred as objects of benevolence, delicately administered, before those who are more clamorous and querulous. In cases of extreme sickness, even when the character of the sufferer is *doubtful*, application should be made for parochial relief, and other necessary assistance obtained, so that no one should perish for lack of food, or care, under such circumstances.

In conclusion let each bear in mind that after the most active exertions in the cause of benevolence, we are still but unprofitable servants and that no works can be acceptable or well pleasing to our heavenly Father but as they proceed from faith in the atoning sacrifice of his beloved Son

A—A

REVIEW OF NEW PUBLICATIONS

1. *Osric, a Missionary Tale with the Garden, and other Poems* By CHARLOTTE ELIZABETH Dedicated by permission to Mrs Hannah More Dublin pp 134 & 53 8vo
2. *Hints on Missions* By JAMES DOUGLAS, Esq Edinburgh 1822 pp 118
3. *The Advancement of Society in Knowledge and Religion* By the same Author Edinburgh 8vo 1825 pp 383
4. *Thoughts on Missions, written after a Perusal of Douglas's Hints on Missions* By a Missionary London 8vo 1825 pp 19
5. *The Moral Dignity of the Missionary Enterprize,* a Sermon delivered before the Boston (United States) Baptist Society By F WAYLAND, Jun Pastor Boston 1825

It is not our intention, in placing these works in our review department, to discuss at large the nature of Christian missions, and their imperative claims on the regards of all professed Christians These topics are not new either to ourselves or our readers Our pages have borne repeated testimony to the value and the importance of the measures which are in active operation at the present time, for widely diffusing the "glorious Gospel of the blessed God We feel especial pleasure in witnessing the successful part which our own church has long borne in this hallowed enterprize, and in observing the calm and undisturbed manner in which the "Free Thoughts, and the Protests, and "Addresses, and "Defences of Protests, which were directed in particular against one most valuable institution, conducted by members of that church, have been sustained and survived The cause of missions in our Establishment, like, we would trust, the cause of that Establishment itself, is now resting on a basis of increasing security and strength The very agitations which have pressed upon it have contributed to its stability, and we doubt not that any new and yet untried resistances will prove equally impotent to subvert its foundations In noticing, however, the movements of a power like that of our missionary apparatus as it directs its efforts against the altars of idolatry in one quarter of the globe or the bulwarks of superstition in another we see persons of various gradations of rank, intellect and principle, directing their attention towards its operations and expressing in many diversified forms their surmisings or their approval Even the dislike of opponents is compelled to pause in its denunciations, while the augmenting resources which from unexpected springs are rising to sustain it cannot but cheer its immediate friends and agents with the brightest omens of eventual success

The general opinion now entertained in this country respecting Christian Missions is very distinct from what it was only a few years ago. Of the countenance afforded to these benevolent enterprises by some of those whose rank and talents have placed them in the most responsible situations of life, we cannot speak but with gratitude and satisfaction: but while we allude to this source of influence, and generally to all the co-operation received from every quarter in aid of missionary objects, there is one class of individuals whose notice seems at last to have been drawn to the societies and their operations, who appear to have been long standing as observant of them at a distance watching the movements of these alleged "wandering fires," till at length they have been induced to come forth and yield their testimony to the value of the object pursued mingled, however, with many sage and cautious directions for its attainment. Some of the individuals to whom "in class, and not to any one in particular, we refer, would appear desirous of being thought not merely the approvers but the advocates of missions, and have actually employed their talents and their pens on its behalf: but we own it appears to us that the few valuable suggestions which have proceeded from them have been so clogged and embarrassed by the theory out of which they originate their speculations, that we are inclined, perhaps over carefully, to hesitate in admitting their soundness and utility. We doubt not that the object of such persons is good—is the extension of Divine truth and wisdom: but there is an error very prevalent among them, that the best, nay the only efficient, precursors of the Gospel in heathen lands are *civilization,* literature, and science.

The cultivation of intellect and the arts of civilized life are said to be indispensable for preparing men to understand or to receive, with any hope of advantage, the instructions of Christian teachers. This theory appears to us quite incorrect, and calculated seriously to mislead the friends of missions. True it is that barbarism and ignorance are a bad soil in which to plant the doctrines of religion, and the amelioration both of the intellectual and civil condition of mankind will be the certain and immediate result of the introduction of the Gospel; and, in some degree, letters and the arts may conduce to the same ends: but we cannot for one moment view these as necessary preliminaries to the reception of the Gospel. "Unlearned heathens received the truth, and were made "wise unto salvation," while to the learned, civilized, and polished, it was "foolishness." The reasonings of those who would maintain these conjectures appear to us to proceed upon a very inadequate view of the true character of the Gospel itself, of fallen man as addressed by it, and of that spiritual condition to which it is its ultimate design to elevate him. Of the Gospel itself it must be remembered, that it was, by its Divine Promulgator, declared in its spirit and its tendency to be essentially "not of this world." Of the state of those to whom it is addressed there are abundant testimonies, both in the Divine record and in the outward developments of their character, that it is altogether "earthly;" and the object which is to be attempted is the conversion of their souls; an object as distinct from the *mere* gratification or expansion of the intellect, as it is from the growth of the bodily powers or animal capacities.

The two works of Mr Douglas now before us may be considered as chargeable with a proportion of this inverse reasoning which we the more regret as his pages are distinguished by great strength, acuteness, and very considerable research

In his geographical dissertations he displays extensive reading, and has accumulated more hard names in some of his pages than Johnson ever accused Milton of boastfully heaping on his similes in the Paradise Lost. He stands forward too as the avowed advocate of missionary exertion, though he does not always occupy the high ground which might be chosen for the basis of his reasoning. Many of his arguments are striking and powerful, and we do not think that full justice has been done to his work on missions, in the reply to it which we have placed upon our list; but in the sentiments of that reply, in the main, we cannot but agree. We shall, in the course of our remarks, introduce to our readers some valuable extracts from Mr Douglas's "Hints." But of his two works generally we cannot think otherwise than that he has been somewhat entangled in the perplexities of his own powerful mind, and too much busied in amusing speculations.

In proof or illustration of these remarks we might notice the anxiety apparent throughout Mr Douglas's book, so to construct the plans and operations of missionary enterprize as to render them acceptable in the eyes of philosophers and men of taste, and the sneer with which he condemns the missionary's journal "filled too often with the experiences of particular converts which have often more connexion with the body than with the soul," and the suggestion that he proposes as a far preferable object of pursuit, namely, that "Christians would shew what Christian benevolence can do for the comforts and embellishments of this transitory life, and that thus there might be some common feeling between two parties who might gain much by mutual intercourse." In addition to recommending for study, as is most necessary, the languages of heathen nations, he adds to them their national music and songs, their tales and superstitions and besides this, the physical localities of the country, the order of the rocks, the soil, the vegetables, the animals, the aspect of nature, and the events of history. He would have a register kept of the weather, and the direction of the winds; regular observations made of the thermometer, and, if possible, of the barometer, and all this in order that those philosophers, who, as he confesses, would be scared at the mention of the soul or a future state, and who consider missionaries as ignorant fanatics, may be forced to read through these returns, and acknowledge them, what Mr Douglas has no doubt they would become in time, the most magnificent range of experiences that has ever been made to science!

Now, without denying, and indeed strenuously maintaining, that the Christian missionary may and ought to endeavour to enlarge his sphere of knowledge, for the sake of the important work in which he is engaged; believing also that, in many instances, without any sacrifice of higher duties he may greatly benefit the physical condition of those among whom he labours; that he may greatly promote civilization and the arts of social life, and even in some cases transmit home, at little expense of time or labour, various miscellaneous *memoranda* of value in different departments of knowledge; we think it cannot be too strongly inculcated that a missionary should be most emphatically a man of one object and of one book—and that whatever really diverts him from that object and that book, however laudable in itself, is to him a dangerous diversion. Mr Douglas needs not be reminded that an attempt to conciliate the favour of 'the wise and prudent' towards the cause and the doctrines of the Cross, has ever been amongst the most infelicitous and unsuccessful of experiments. It was so even before our Saviour's first advent made them known more clearly than by type and prophecy; it has been increasingly so since. "Have any of the rulers or the Pharisees" adopted these plans?' is a question which overpowers the cursory inquirer and " Art *thou also* of Galilee?' is the assault made, too often with success, by the opponents of religious activity upon any more happy spirit of their own fraternity who has had light and zeal and decision enough to ' come out and be separate from his former habits and companions Our author seems to be a little too anxious as it respects wordy assailants of this character otherwise he could not, we think, so largely sacrifice at the shrine of mere literary taste, and so far mistake the character of the Gospel, and the arduous duties of its heralds, as to exact from the latter a register of every variation of heat from Greenland to the Cape, and from Siberia to New Zealand the direction of the winds and the fluctuations of the atmosphere from Benares to Astrachan, and from Astrachan to the mouth of the Columbia and deem the improved state of civil society and natural fertility so beautiful a part of the fulfilment of the prophecy which employs these figurative delineations, as almost to lead his readers (for certainly he does not really do so himself,) to look with but a secondary glance on the moral and spiritual amelioration in the view of which all else is really " less than nothing and vanity He would have done well to have very explicitly stated, that the want of a more absorbing sense of the truth of this moral renovation leaves ' many wise men after the flesh, (how graphically does the conciseness of Scripture delineate them!) in the utmost " bewilderment on these subjects The simple duty of the Christian teacher, we conceive to be, to employ the most *Scriptural*, and apparently efficacious, methods of leading men from their idols, whether material or spiritual to the one living and true God The suggestions of philosophy have no connexion with this object The first charge of the Saviour, when he sent forth the first missionaries, contained no allusion to philosophical researches, and when they were sent forth, they interpreted that charge in its simple and obvious import. The missionaries of the present day must do the same, remembering the solemn injunction of the great teacher of the gentiles " Give thyself wholly to these things."

We have already stated, that it may often be advantageous, (and, when so, the judicious teacher will embrace the occasion,) to gather up hints from an attentive observation of character, opinions, superstition in its diversified forms, the natural aspect of the country, and other points which may eventually prove beneficial in the prosecution of missionary objects His mind ought, in short, to be prepared to turn every thing within the sphere of his observation, whether of a moral, intellectual, or physical description, to some useful account, in strict subserviency, however, to the great object of his pursuit—the diffusion of the light of the Gospel But much beyond this will, in most cases be an intrusion on the time and efforts due to the direct objects of a Christian mission and that teacher will surely suffer in his own religious zeal and affection, and in the success of his ministrations, who should be moved, by any deference to the false standard of this world's judgment to depart, in the construction of his diary or in the habits of his life and conversation from the simplicity that is in Christ At the same time we freely admit, that there have been many missionary diaries presented to the world which it would have been a great benefit to the cause of religion to have entirely suppressed

Into these observations we have been led chiefly by the smaller work of Mr Douglas on Missions In the exciting contemplation of " the advance of society in knowledge and religion in his large and more recent publication, we find him expatiating on various schemes for the production of those two blessings, and calculating their results and processes. What will our readers think of his suggestion of a few new pyramids, the erection of which in this country would, he says, be far more corresponding to the greatness of the nation than all such tame (but to be sure somewhat more useful) works as our canals, or the mole which protects our navy against the violence of the tempest?

There are many truly excellent observations in Mr Douglas's books, a few of which we must now, in justice to him, extract, that our readers may have a higher opinion of his talents and his views than our remarks may have hitherto led them to entertain. The following passage is on the duty which devolves on British Christians, from their possession of their mighty Indian empire. The duty is now widely acknowledged, but it is impressively defined by our author.

We know not whether God intends the stability of particular nations, but we know that he makes all revolutions subservient to the introduction of his own kingdom, that the appointed years of delay are now elapsing and that the time to favour the Gentiles is at hand. A great improvement in the moral condition of Hindostan is therefore certain in the natural course of events and still more certain in the interruption of those events by which God breaks in pieces the obstacles to his designs, whether in a political calm or storm the mustard seed which has been sown will become a great tree and spread wide the shadow of its branches, and any changes in the body politic will ultimately accelerate that great change from darkness to light by which Hindostan will become full of the knowledge of the Lord. Nothing was ever more beyond all human calculation, than that England should become the mistress of India, that an island thinly peopled with barbarians the prey of every roving pirate should, after so immense a navigation, far as the sea-fowl in a year can fly, subdue the empire of Sandracottus, overcome that hostile array that terrified the soldiers of Timour and with handfuls of men put myriads to flight. That such events did not happen without the Divine will and guidance even heathens would acknowledge: it is thus that God casts a stain upon all human glory—by the weak things overcomes the strong and baffles all the conjectures of human prudence. But if Britain thus holds India, it holds it by an imperative condition, that of being subservient to the designs of Providence, and when that condition is not complied with the possession ceases along with its infraction. The Portuguese and the Dutch have already been our forerunners but the one pursued the course of its own cruel bigotry and the other its gain, and neither of them did the work of the Lord. If we follow, instead of avoiding their example, and neglect to make known so great salvation the empire will be taken from us and given to another nation, our conquests will pass away like a dream and the time of our benefitting India will be closed for ever. But let us hope better things of Britain and that the nation and the government will at length co-operate in spreading every blessing in ameliorating the temporal and spiritual condition of the Hindoos in fulfilling to the uttermost the sacred trust reposed and in securing to themselves the perpetual gratitude of India. pp 264—266

The objection to missionary efforts in India, from the alleged hopeless obstinacy of the Hindoo character, and their tenacity to their own creed, is met as follows:—

The Hindoos are the thinking people of eastern Asia, their doctrines have spread to Siberia and Japan and the new system which has been transplanted from Hindostan has overshadowed and nearly rooted out the native superstitions of central Asia, as well as of China, and has spread itself with the Malay colonies over the islands of the southern ocean. Thus, India has already changed the religion of the East and may well change it again if Christianity had once taken possession of India. Missionaries in abundance would be found among the Hindoos, who would carry the Gospel along with them to nations who already look to India as the fountain from which spiritual light has streamed out to them. It has been objected (for to what will men not object which is contrary to their inclinations?) that the character of the Hindoos will not admit of change and that it is impossible to convert them but this is an objection which is alike refuted by history by reason and by religion. The Mohammedan conquerors have left behind them abundant traces of the possibility of changing the faith of the Hindoos though their method of conversion was not likely to be the most successful, as the courage and the enterprise which marked the beginning of their dynasties soon changed into effeminacy, the intolerance with which they assailed the Hindoos at first ended in religious indifference nor was there any interval between persecution and acquiescence, which they filled up by commending the reasonableness of the unity of the Godhead to the conviction of the Hindoos. Still Mussulmans abound in India, not merely the descendants of the Mogul conquerors, but multitudes of those who have been won over from the native creed. The religion of the Hindoos has frequently changed without any foreign impulsion: the early worship of the elements has yielded to the complexity of the Braminical Polytheism. Polytheism for a time seemed to bend under the Pantheism of the Budhists and then by a new revolution regained its former ascendency even within that Polytheism itself rival sects are ever rising and decaying and the slightest acquaintance either with the present or past state of the Hindoos may shew that the human mind with them has not changed its character or lost its desire of change and that if it is prone to error it is also prone to novelty Reason also might demonstrate that no forms of opinion can be perpetual except those that are founded upon immutable truth All errors have arisen from a combination of circumstances; and when that combination is dissolved, and the causes which gave birth to them cease to operate the errors gradually lose their hold over the mind and fall to decay Again from religion we have the sure word of prophecy that every idol under heaven shall be broken and as this has been fulfilled with respect to Greece and her idols so it shall soon be fulfilled with respect to India and her idols. pp 257—260

In both his works Mr Douglas suggests a new arrangement of the geography of the globe, classing the sections of it by a moral, instead of an artificial or physical, division Our readers may remember an attempt at this in a little chart prefixed to Dr H Pearson's prize essay, on the Propagation of Christianity in the East, and also given in the third volume of the Missionary Register, and in several maps on similar plans

The following is the author's view of those advantages which an over ruling Providence may eventually compel the wickedness of man to produce for wretched Africa

Out of the very depth of the calamities of Africa, a prospect arises of ultimate relief the slave trade which heightened all the evils to which that devoted country is subject has brought a portion of the African race into close contact with men who are civilized Europe and Africa have been dissevered in their fate from each other, but they have met together in the colonies of America; and the rising prospects of that new world afford the means and the hopes for the improvement and civilization of Africa. While the Europeans from the climate were prevented from settling in Africa, and the Africans had no means of acquiring the knowledge of Europe, an unpassable barrier seemed raised between them but now that both have been brought to inhabit a third country, it is comparatively easy to educate and train those Negroes in America, who will be able to introduce into Africa the first rudiments of amelioration The rapidity with which the Negroes are increasing in America, and the peculiar circumstances in which they are there placed, insure a return of numbers of them to their original continent, carrying with them the languages, and not unfurnished with the acquisitions of Europe In a century there will be more Negroes in the United States alone than exist in Africa itself at the present moment and an emigration like that which is now carrying the Europeans to America, or the African slaves to the coast of America, will restore the descendants of those slaves to their native countries Africa is the natural resort of the Blacks that are emancipated by their White masters placed in the new world in an ambiguous situation between the freemen and the slaves, they can scarcely taste the sweets of liberty while they are still considered as a degraded race and looked upon with an evil eye as persons who have no ascertained situation in society but in Africa a new career awaits them and, while they are slighted by the Whites and every impediment thrown in their way they will be hailed by their kindred race across the Atlantic as the introducers of whatever is useful, and the instructors of nascent empires What is wanting is a landing place some settlement to receive them on their first touching the coast, from which in time they would spread from one tribe to another till they diffused themselves over the interior of the continent and when that returning emigration to Africa has once begun, it will every year widen and extend as one race of emigrants will smooth the passage for others, and prepare a more eager reception for those that are to follow pp. 270—273

Such a landing place as our author deems so desirable, has in truth been formed in the colony of Sierra Leone The deduction which the unhealthiness of that settlement demands in reference to Europeans, is not necessary in respect to native Africans and the hope may justly be cherished of its becoming at some future period the gate of life to Africa, in addition, we would add, to the American colony of Liberia, formed on similar principles. We may certainly anticipate much from the introduction of writing and education among the natives, who are known to possess the greatest reverence for written characters. The stream of emigration which our author anticipates from the United States is at present diverted towards Hayti, where a Black skin is no civil disqualification or source of daily mortification, as is the case in our Christian colonies. The freedom conferred upon all classes in the South American Republics will also render emigrations to Africa less numerous.

In his reasoning on the case of the Jews, Mr Douglas suggests the direction of learning and talent towards an exposure of the rabbinical traditions and writings (see p 281) In this suggestion, however, he is at variance with Mr Jowett and the converted Jew Mr Wolff, who both agree that it is better to quit all discussions with them on the Talmud or the rabbinical writings, and to confine them to the simple ground of Scripture. In this conclusion we agree, for this among other reasons, that the Jew is likely to prove the more able disputant when argument is drawn from the former sources and the latter appears to us the legitimate and available weapon—a weapon, not as the other 'carnal but 'mighty through God to the pulling down of strong holds.'

In another suggestion also, is Mr Douglas at issue with the dictates of experience. He recommends the pursuit of trades and professions in the missionaries. But with one voice all whose opportunities of observation entitle their opinion to the greatest weight on this subject enter their protest against the secularizing tendency of this permission in the missionary himself, and the diminution of his influence, which is the strongest where raised far above all suspicion of interested motives. See Mr Jowett's last volume of Researches, and Mr Marsden's Hints respecting the Australasian Mission, in the last Church Missionary Report, p 101

We must now proceed to notice the other works at the head of our paper, and in dismissing for the present this elaborate work of Mr Douglas, we cannot but acknowledge that we have enjoyed considerable gratification in the perusal of it. He is a writer of a bold and original character he reasons with the spirit and confidence of one who knows he has surveyed the globe in all its parts, who may challenge a disproof of his acquaintance with its statistics and its phenomena, who delights to trace up the history of the past to all its secret springs in the heart of man, and expatiates with a glowing rapture in the anticipations of the future, and is not afraid to define the aspect and the influence of European and Asiatic society on all the rest of the world, as that period when " the oak which was planted yesterday shall have reached its full maturity

The unpretending but pleasing volume of Poems which we have placed at the head of our list, is dedicated to Mrs More, the long tried friend and advocate of those principles out of which alone missionary exertions must spring, and on which alone they can depend for support. It is the production of a lady who veils her family or marital name from view the title page presents only names which are the common property of many. In the Preface we slightly glance at the motives of its authoress in sending the volume to press* it is described to be like herself, " one of the weak things of the world, but sent forth

* We are informed that the publication of this volume is looked to with some anxiety as it is hoped to contribute to the support of an aged parent of the authoress. We sincerely wish it may prove successful

with fervent prayer for the Divine blessing. Well had it been for the world had some of our loftier bards met their muse on ground like this. It would at least have purified their lays, if not exalted their poetical merit. We take the present Tale as we find it, having often expressed our opinion on the use of the imagination in the service of religion. It is evidently a fiction, and we are not informed whether any part of its groundwork has been fenced off from actual occurrences. It is very simple in its construction. Osric, the hero of the tale, is the last survivor of a shipwrecked crew on some part of those icy regions which cool the northern summit of "Columbia's mountain throne." The precise spot is not named, but our readers will understand it when they hear of icebergs floating in all directions. After recovering from the effect of his calamities, and paying the tribute of a tear to the memory of his companions, he is found by Indians: signs of friendship are exchanged, the rites of hospitality displayed, and Osric accompanies the band through pathless woods, where the incision of the Indian's knife on the bark of the sapling is the only guide to their distant kraal. In the cabin of their chief, Osric is received and entertained. He whiles away his weeks and months in the pursuits of hunting and fishing, conforming to all the native habits, when an incident occurs which, like the first smoke of a volcanic flame, warns him of the hollowness of that soil on which he has so confidently planted his feet. A visit is paid to the chief of the valley by a deputation from a distant tribe who, with their wampum belts of doubtful hue, relate the report which has reached their river of this hospitality to one from the White man's land, and they declare the purport of their three suns journey to be the investigation of its truth; when the insidious Ayuta, (the chief,) from his matted seat, in a dialect unknown to Osric, who surveys the assembled tribes with deep and unconscious interest, disavows the motive of hospitality, and in proof declares that moment to be the occasion for which his victim had been lured and nourished, and he then offers him to their united fury. Unable to resist the number of his enemies, and more than vanquished by the surprise which this treachery occasions, Osric is seized, and his death as a sacrifice to their fury and their appetite is determined on, but is deferred till the tribe of the mountain, returning with the calumet of peace, shall have regained their home, to "hide their hatchet and to plant their tree, and feed it with the White man's blood." The midnight feasting and revelry succeed, and Osric is placed in one of the cabins, with a guard of his enemies, Ayuta, at the head stationed in the open side. All hope of deliverance fails the victim; the vigilance of the Indian, he believes, can keep "at wondrous bay the leaden wand of sleep." But at length the flickering flame betrays the effect of the night's carnival on the whole party; though as they are stretched across the cabin's mouth, escape is impossible. We must now inform our readers, that an aged chief, who dwelt among this tribe of the valley, has an only daughter. The "Last Minstrel" would have said,

Her ebon locks to shame might bring
The plumage of the raven's wing.

Of course Osric's soul has been a long time captivated with this maiden who is not insensible to his feeling but Osric is as yet no Christian, except in name, and Zaila had heard a British teacher in a distant missionary settlement, and had become converted to the faith. She hoped therefore to have heard from Osric's lips that theme which White man knows, but is disappointed. Yet she loves him and contrives his escape through the aperture in the roof of the cabin. In safety, but not without peril, the maiden conducts him through the woods to the river's brink, where a boat is waiting with an Indian guide to receive him. He parts with Zaila, not altogether "con amore," but is entrusted to the care of his new conductor, who loosens his boat, and speeds his way all night, and continues it partly on land and partly in the canoe, till they are overtaken by violent snow-storms and frost, which bind up the rivers; a thaw however succeeds, and the result is, that Osric—whose soul becomes deeply affected by the communications of his guide, once a warlike chief, but then a disciple of peace, his tomahawk exchanged for the Gospel panoply, in the settlement whither he aims to conduct him—is compelled to witness the death of his instructor in an icy creek, where worn with toil and broken on the rocks, he breathes out his soul in Christian love. Deserted and lonely, Osric pursues his way, reaches the settlement of the missionary, and enters it on their Sabbath. There he again hears an English voice employed in the worship of God. He hears too a particular prayer for one who had been sent to guide a wanderer to their abode. It is *his* guide; he can communicate nothing but the tidings of signs, in the girdle and the vest. The settlement is overwhelmed with grief, and it is seen that they had lost a brother. His body is sought, and committed to a more honoured grave, and his character detailed, and Osric becomes the future resident and bright ornament of the Christian colony.

'This is an outline of the tale; we shall present a few extracts from it, that our readers may judge of the poetical powers of the authoress. The character of Osric is drawn in the following passage. He will stand for a large class. Strong in mind, probably in body also—a victim of others' ingratitude, but possessing himself a generous heart, best of the bold and noblest of the brave—a reader moreover, and a reasoner, and also a religionist—but such a one only as the dim light of nature, and an historic acquaintance with the Gospel, are able to compound.

Osric had felt the arrow in his heart,
And proudly rose superior to the smart
Still, in the glances of his eagle eye,
Shone inward peace, and calm philosophy
By temperance nurtured on his native soil
His hardy frame defied disease and toil—
Oft when luxurious viands steamed around,
The hermit's fare his simple meal had crowned
He knew the wants of nature to supply
Those wants unsatisfied to smile and die
What lacked he yet?—he lacked the heaven taught lore,
Prospering to bend, and chasten'd to adore
His pliant mind in philosophic schools
Was warped to systems formed by specious rules,
With Reason's dim, unaided eye he saw
Creation swayed by one unchanging law
Evil and good promiscuously he found,
Rapture and woe trod their alternate round
Man seemed the sport of fortune, made in vain,
His life a bark launched on the treacherous main
Reason his pilot, fickle Chance the breeze
Death the sole port on those uncertain seas
Thence landing on an undiscovered shore
The disembodied spirit might explore
Regions in more than earthly splendour bright,
Or scenes of darkness and eternal night
But all was wrapped in one mysterious shroud
Nor reason's keeenest gaze could pierce the cloud
'Yet deemed he not but some Eternal Cause
Formed the high scheme, and fixed the wondrous laws
Wheeled the round earth, upon her viewless pole
And gave the planetary spheres to roll,
Called Nature blooming from her annual grave
Swelled the dark tide and curbed the rising wave;
Gave man the soul that sparkles in his eye
And formed that soul for immortality
Creator infinite, and Judge alone
This God should summon them before his throne
And speak a doom of bliss or woe on all
Equal and just, and fixed beyond recal
Yet more he knew that, pitying mortal woe
God's Son incarnate had sojourned below
Had lived in poverty and guiltless died,
For wretched man some blessing to provide
But darkly were these living truths impressed,
With dubious outline upon Osric's breast

What marvel, then, God's work so faintly
  known,
Osric should rest his hope upon his own,
And build a towering castle on the sand,
And glory in the labours of his hand?
But clouds unlooked-for veil his summer
  skies
The rain descends the stormy winds arise
And wave succeeding wave must yet
  assail,
Ere the strong fabric of his hope shall fail,
Shew him the vengeance of a righteous
  God
And leave him shelterless beneath the
  rod
While the stern voice of Justice from the
  sky
Proclaims The soul that sinneth it
  shall die   pp 10—12

This last description may suit the creed of many professed Christians They acknowledge a Deity and the fact of the incarnation, combined with an indefinite expectation of good to arise out of it But there is nothing distinct in their conceptions The Gospel is beheld like a distant mountain landscape, when a passing wind has separated for a moment the misty veil which conceals its summit, and discloses enough of beauty to inspire regret at its quick concealment

The following is an account of Osric's repose on the sea shore, followed by his aching morning recollections.

———————— Slumber spread
Her darkest, dreamless mantle, o'er his
  head
Till morning's ray gleamed o'er the gilded
  wave
And cheered the rude apartment of his
  cave
The sunbeam resting on the sleeper's eye
Roused him once more to life and memory
He felt that strange mysterious waking
  pain
That thrills the heart and presses on the
  brain
When some deep anguish of the former
  night,
But half remembered floats before the
  sight
The sickening soul turns inward from the
  view
Of deprivations terrible and new—
A loved-one whose expiring sigh is o'er,
Or living parted—to return no more
            pp 13, 14

The "natural religion" of Osric had, in common with that of some others, led him to turn disgusted from the hypocrisies and deceits of men in *civilized life*, and to resolve that, if simplicity and truth are any where to be found, they must be in the unspoiled native excellence of the savage This beautiful dream has deluded finer minds than Osric's and it was perhaps the basis of the celebrated delineation penned by Pope, and inserted in so many children's extract books, in praise of

  The poor Indian whose untutor'd mind
  Sees God in clouds and hears him in
    the wind

The incident of Ayuta's treachery, therefore, is usefully introduced to convince our hero of his mistake. It shews that by nature, as nature exists since the fall of Adam, the heart of all the children of men, whatever be the colour of their skin, the tone of their speech, or the meridian of their abode, is, in the main alike the seat of guile—
" Qua terra patet, fera regnat Erinnys We doubt not, however imaginary the tale of the poem before us, that stratagems of policy and sins of expediency are as abundant in the conferences of the tribes of the mountain and the tribes of the vale as in the tactics of any European administration and that, if the interior of many a savage kraal were correctly analysed, it would present as deep and hollow intrigues as the secret councils of any continental cabinet, or the corruptions of its court The christianized conductor of Osric effectually reasons with him on this point as they pursue their way together We are obliged to pass over their communications but they are such as, united with the recollections of Zaila's counsels, soften and humble his heart His haughty spirit had once shrunk back from such instructors Should he
' Who thro' the world defying and defied,
Bore high the banner of unvanquish'd
  pride
Before such puny arms that banner furl
A praying savage and a preaching girl?

But at length he allows his guide to question his high pretensions to religion, founded on no better basis than the church's rites, and his compliance with them,

"The Cross once signed upon his infant
    brow,
Whose riper judgment ratified the vow."

The Indian's narrative of his own conversion contains a specimen of the preaching that found its way to his heart.

"'Go,' he would say, 'and in the forest near
Plant the dry polished shaft of yonder
    spear
There bid the rootless stem to life expand
And wave luxuriant branches o'er the
    land
The hope were vain—closed is each pliant
    pore
The circling juice revisits them no more
By guilt dissevered from the living tree
Through Adam's fault, so dead and dry
    are we
Nor profitless alone; for tainting sin
Pollutes our lives, defiles our hearts
    within
Jehovah's purity our race disclaims
His justice dooms us to eternal flames
But mercy hath revealed an open path
A covert from the tempest of His wrath
And day by day the oft-repeated strain
We heard, Repent, believe, be born
    again.'" p. 61.

The following are the authoress's reflections on the power of death as an instructor, as she describes the distress of Osric in viewing the dead body of the Indian.

"If thou wouldst blunt the edge, and
    calm the smart
Of disappointment's fang and sorrow's
    dart
Quell mortal fear, disgrace and want abide
Shame thy rude lusts, controul thy daring
    pride
And still the war of passion's angry breath
Go gaze upon the leaden brow of death
It is a book of wisdom, written plain
By Him who never traced a line in vain
Deck as thou wilt that stern and ghastly
    hue,
Disguise with laurels or with roses strew
In silken gear the rigid limbs enfold
O'ertop with waving plumes, and crisp
    with gold—
Tis yet the face of death, and yet must
    thrill
Through thy cowed spirit with a boding
    chill
The sweetest tongue that ever knew to
    pour
The flood of eloquence from learning's
    store
In all the flow of breath could never speak
So well, so wisely as a clay cold cheek,—
And when the glance of morning chill
    and pale
Pourtrayed in livid lines that awful tale
On the fixed traits of death, and feebly
    shone
To light the earthly house whose guest
    was gone
That scene so deeply stamped, in Osric's
    thought,
The seal of life on every truth he taught,
It seemed as though his heaven appointed
    guide
Who lived to teach had to enforce them
    died." pp. 110, 111.

The climax of the poem is the reception of Osric in the missionary settlement, and the communication there made to him of the character of his deceased guide, in whom religion had acquired such dominion, that, though he was the lover of Zaila, he had concerted with her the plan which conducted his unconscious rival in safety from his foes.

"Nor did a deed or word or glance betray
One jealous pang upon their lengthened
    way
This last great triumph over self was given
To crown the fight, and ripen him for
    heaven."

The moral of the poem is an appeal to the reader, whether his "talents have been devoted to the furtherance of Christian Missions in a degree at all proportioned to their just claims on his exertions." Those claims are so forcibly set forth in the last of the publications on our list, that we pass on at once to refer to it. The sermon preached by Mr. Wayland, on "the moral Dignity of the Missionary Enterprise," is distinguished by a bold manly eloquence, and displays a mind full of the magnitude of its subject, a brilliant warmth of imagination, and, what is more to be desired than all, a truly scriptural view of the motives, means, and obligations to missionary exertion. If there is a degree of impetuosity occasionally discoverable it is but the heat of his own rapid *fervidæ rotæ*, which he cannot restrain, arising from the contemplation of the scene presented by the glowing volume of prophecy. It is a source of great satisfaction to us to witness the frequent union of intellectual power and moral worth in the writers and preachers on the other side of the Atlantic. So long as the rising energies of the new world are under the restraining and governing influence of a sound and scriptural piety; so long we feel confident in the application of their augmenting vigour to hallowed purposes: but without such a conductor the electric influence of talent may descend with uncertain force alike on friends and foes. We will endeavour to give our readers a faint outline of this powerful sermon.

From the words " the field is the world," after a spirited exordium on the true character of sublimity, Mr Wayland describes the *grandeur of the missionary object*,—namely, the conversion, not nominal, but spiritual, to Christianity, of seven out of the eight hundred millions of whom the population of the globe consists. The darkened degraded state both in morals and religion of these millions with the multiplied species of suffering endured by Asia's superstitious, and Africa's enslaved children, is spread over the canvas in glowing colours, and the supremacy of the missionary enterprise rises into a brightness before which patriotism and conquest and the honours of fame all fade away, as he describes the work of missions, and seizes with a strong grasp on the temporal and eternal destinies of the whole family of man. The *arduous* character of the work is the next feature considered by the preacher. It is the conversion of "the world." That of an *individual* is described, and shewn to be a miracle. What then is that of the world? The difficulties and impediments are glanced at: those particularly which arise from diversity of tongues, forms of government, and insalubrity of climate: and the features of a true missionary's character are added, uniting the qualities of wisdom, perseverance, self denial, courage, and faith. We do not quite admire the arrangement of these constituents. Had the last been first, and the second last, we should have seen more of propriety and system; but in developing these characteristics, we find the requisites of a good missionary placed fearfully high. They are such as without the special grace of God, would be quite unattainable.

The means by which the moral revolution of the world is to be effected is the next subject of consideration, and this is at once declared to be the *preaching of Christ crucified*. The *simplicity, benevolence*, and *efficacy* of these means are severally examined. On this last point, we cannot withhold the following animated passage which meets the fears of such as apprehend a decline in these labours and successes:—

Never did the people of the saints of the Most High appear to be going forth in such serious earnest, to take possession of the kingdom and dominion and the greatness of the kingdom under the whole heaven as at this very day. We see then nothing in the signs of the times which forbodes a failure, but every thing which promises that our undertaking will prosper. But, secondly suppose the cause did seem declining, we should see no reason to relax our exertions, for Jesus Christ has said, Preach the Gospel to every creature. Appearances whether prosperous or adverse, alter not the obligation to obey a positive command of Almighty God.

But, suppose all that is affirmed were true. If it must be, let it be. Let the dark cloud of infidelity overspread Europe across the ocean and cover our own beloved land. Let nation after nation swerve from the faith. Let iniquity abound, and the love of many wax cold, even until there is on the face of this earth but one pure church of our Lord and Saviour Jesus Christ. All we ask is that we may be members of that one church. God grant that we may throw ourselves into this Thermopylæ of the moral universe.

But even then we should have no fear that the church of God would be exterminated. We would call to remembrance the years of the right hand of the Most High. We would recollect, there was once a time when the whole church of Christ, not only could be but actually was gathered with one accord in one place. It was then that place was shaken as with a rushing mighty wind, and they were all filled with the Holy Ghost. That same day three thousand were added to the Lord. Soon we hear they have filled Jerusalem with their doctrine. The church has commenced her march. Samaria has with one accord believed the Gospel. Antioch has become obedient to the faith. The name of Christ has been proclaimed throughout Asia Minor. The temples of the gods, as though smitten by an invisible hand, are deserted. The citizens of Ephesus cry out in despair, 'Great is Diana of the Ephesians!' Licentious Corinth is purified, by the preaching of Christ crucified. Persecution puts forth her arm to arrest the spreading superstition: but the progress of the faith cannot be stayed. The church of God advances unhurt, amidst racks and dungeons persecutions and death: yea, 'smiles at the drawn dagger and defies its point.' She has entered Italy and appears before the walls of the eternal city. Idolatry falls prostrate at her approach. Her ensign floats in triumph over the capitol. She has placed upon her brow the diadem of the Cæsars!

"After having witnessed such successes and under such circumstances we are not to be moved by discouragements. To all of them we answer, 'Our field is the world.' The more arduous the undertaking, the greater will be the glory. And that glory will be ours; for God Almighty is with us."

We trust our readers have now a tolerably clear view of the purport, and the mode of forwarding it, adopted in the works before us. It cannot but be interesting to them, as it is to ourselves, to witness these several writers uniting in the endeavour to extend the progress and the influence of the missionary work; to see the philosopher and poet, as well as the ministers of Christ, all combining their energies to accelerate its triumphant progress. Should the reader think that in the writings of Mr Douglas there is an appearance of too great a dependence on secondary causes; that he calculates with too much certainty upon the employment of mere earthly agents, and the adoption of the plans of human wisdom, and without sufficiently urging the necessity of the unseen, but real and exclusively effective agency of the Divine Spirit, to further the work of Christian missions, he will be pleased to find that the author has not really lost sight of this important subject, but has reserved it for separate consideration. We may therefore look for another volume from his pen. The present is intended only to describe that active procedure which, in the course of human probabilities, would be crowned with success. Mr. Douglas, with ourselves, would esteem it unwise to omit in any dissertation on such a subject, the avowal of human insufficiency, and would augur ill of those measures, however zealously advocated or sagaciously planned, which do not tend to prostrate all earthly energies before the secret but powerful influence of the Holy Ghost without which, as our own church has simply but emphatically stated "nothing is strong, nothing is holy;" the most brilliant intellectual power will be employed to no purpose, the planting and watering of even an apostle will be without increase. This applies also to the experience of each individual teacher. It is true that the missionary, (as one of our modern bards has expressed it,)

"Unwearied, like the camel, day by day,
Tracks through unwatered wilds, his doleful way;
Yet in his breast a cherished draught retains,
To cool the fervid current in his veins."

But this is the very living water of which we speak: this secret well of consolation is the refreshing of the 'indwelling Spirit;' and the soul that does not possess it will find its graces on the decline, drooping as the leaves of a water-plant, whose running brook has been dried up by the scorching rays of a summer's sun.

Grounded on this basis of the promised influences of God's Holy Spirit, we urge the adoption of every practical measure recommended in the volumes before us. Great as have been the exertions made in the cause of missions by our countrymen generally, or by the members of our own church in particular, they are most inadequate to the necessities which give them birth. Great encouragements have been afforded to perseverance and sanguine hope. We might point to the surprising state of the West African Missions. Where once not fifty persons could be found willing to hear the Gospel, now *thousands* of liberated Africans are assembled with gladness to receive the tidings of salvation, and these of different nations, and some of the most savage tribes. We might also point to the hitherto unattainable translation of the Chinese Scriptures; but the single fact of the success in the South-Sea Islands is sufficient for our purpose. The prophet's question, once addressed in the certainty of a negative reply, "Hath a nation changed its gods?" is no longer to be thus met in despondency, for a nation *hath* changed its idols. They are cast as loathsome abominations into the depths of the sea. Let British Christians then rise with redoubled energy to the hallowed work: great as their efforts are, there are, we feel convinced, unnumbered energies yet slumbering that need to be aroused. Cromwell's project of 10,000*l.* a year would be smiled at in an age of thirty times its amount raised annually for this purpose: but what is even this last sum compared with the wants which it desires to meet, or even with our own resources? If Britain do not, other nations in whom the light of Divine truth is blazing strong, may advance before her, and occupy in privileges and glory the post now offered to her. Without admitting the sentiment of many who think, with devout Herbert, that as the course of the light of day is from east to west, so will it be with Divine truth, and that

"Religion stands on tiptoe in our land
Ready to pass to the American strand;"

we believe that, if an adequate sense of the value of the light of revelation is not entertained, and that light is not transmitted to the utmost of our power through the dark regions of the earth, the torch will be snatched from our unworthy hands, and placed in others which shall lift it high and carry it far, and rejoice the eyes of the benighted with its cheering rays. Thus has it been with other nations among whom the light shone for a long season, but at last set in terrible darkness. Where are now the Apocalyptic Churches? What is the state of the once "holy city?" Where are Chorazin and Bethsaida, and Capernaum, "once exalted to heaven?" We trust the spirit and the works of the Gospel have taken too deep a "fixity," as Mr. Douglas would call it, in our country, ever to suffer such an eradication; yet if a neglect of those known obligations for which England holds her privileges in trust, be the consequence of her unprecedented prosperity; if, while she is seated on a couch of ivory and listening to the sound of the harp, she should become forgetful of the misery of the Gentile, or be less "grieved for the affliction of Joseph," or should content herself with an acknowledgment of the duty, without an augmenting effort for the furtherance of its fulfilment, she may be made an example of that vengeance which is now heaped upon desolate and darkened Africa. The case of that unhappy people is so powerfully delineated by Archbishop Sharp, that, with his pathetic lamentation, we shall close our remarks.

"That Africa (said he) which is not now more fruitful of monsters, than it was once of excellently wise and learned men—that Africa which formerly afforded us our Clemens, our Origen, our Tertullian, our Cyprian, our Augustine, and many other extraordinary lights in the church of God—that famous Africa, whose soil did thrive so prodigiously, and could boast of so many flourishing churches—Alas! how is it now a wilderness! How have the wild boars out of the wood broken into the vineyard and devoured it, so that it bringeth forth now nothing but briars and thorns!"

A Charge delivered to the Clergy of the Diocese of Bath and Wells, at the Primary Visitation of that Diocese, in July, August, and September, 1825; by G. H. LAW, D.D. Lord Bishop of Bath and Wells.

THOUGH the publication before us is his lordship's primary charge at

Bath and Wells, it is not the first episcopal charge delivered by him, or reviewed by us. In our volume for 1815, p. 177, is noticed at large his lordship's primary charge at Chester; and, on other occasions, his lordship's publications have been referred to in our pages, especially his sermon before the Society for promoting Christian Knowledge, and his discourse on "communion with God," from both of which some valuable and interesting passages are respectively extracted in our volumes for 1814 and 1820. From our acquaintance, therefore, with his lordship's writings, and his well known amiableness and benevolence of character, we were prepared to find the charge before us marked by a truly kind, devotional, and ingenuous spirit; by an earnest desire to cultivate friendly relations with his clergy, and to excite them to a conscientious and cheerful discharge of their pastoral duties. In none of these respects have we been disappointed, as our readers will perceive by the following analysis of the charge: but at the same time we think there are some allusions, and also some omissions, which with equal frankness we ought to specify, with a view to a just estimate of his lordship's publication.

The charge opens with the customary compliment to the memory of his lordship's deceased predecessor, Bishop Beadon, who for more than twenty years had exercised the episcopal superintendence of the diocese. The only points, however, alluded to in the character of "that late amiable prelate," are "his mildness and urbanity of manners, and his wish to promote the interest and comfort of his clergy;" excellencies which all who knew Dr. Beadon will cheerfully acknowledge to have been conspicuous in his character.

But we would respectfully ask, whether to assert *no more* than this of a Christian prelate, (we do not mean to say that more might not have been asserted in the present instance,) is not in effect a reproach rather than a panegyric. Would St. Paul, or would a greater than St. Paul, have been satisfied with these merely gentlemanly and professional qualities in one whose high office it is to watch over "the church of God which he hath purchased with his own blood;" whose character is required to be not only amiable and decorous, but eminently devout, and holy, and spiritual; and whose necessary qualifications are summed up with an appalling elevation, both in the sacred Scriptures and in the consecration service of our own church? We have just observed, that we intend no disrespect to the memory of the particular prelate whose virtues are thus succinctly narrated; much less do we mean to intimate what we are quite sure from Bishop Law's own writings is not the case, that his lordship would himself be satisfied with so very inadequate a testimonial: but we fear that the frequent recurrence of such meagre attestations to the memory of deceased prelates has a most injurious effect in lowering in the minds both of our clergy and laity the estimate which they ought to form of the true character of a bishop of the church of Christ. If to be courteous in his manners, and attentive to the secular interests of his clergy, be all the virtues requisite in a bishop, then we can only say that the sacred writers and their most pious uninspired followers have most strangely overstated the matter: but if, on the other hand, the higher estimate be correct, then we could earnestly wish the abolition of a custom which in expected courtesy obliges every new or translated bishop to utter the eulogies of his predecessor, even though the object of the eulogy should have had no higher claim to the episcopal office than some powerful personal or family interest, and have exemplified few or no qualities which could be related as justly characteristic of his exalted station. We, a third time repeat that we do not intend any individual allusion but we have often contrasted in our own minds such scanty measures of episcopal encomium with the striking lineaments of departed prelates of former days. Let our readers take the following as examples.

"He was a bishop,' says Burnet of Archbishop Leighton, 'that had the greatest elevation of soul, the largest compass of knowledge, the most mortified and most heavenly disposition that I ever saw in mortal: that had the greatest parts, as well as virtues, with the most perfect humility, that I ever saw in man: that had so sublime a strain in preaching, with so grave a gesture, and such a majesty, both of thought, of language, and of pronunciation, that I never saw a wandering eye when he preached, and have seen whole assemblies often melt in tears before him. And of whom I can say with great truth, that, in a free and frequent conversation with him, for about *two and twenty years*, I never knew him say an idle word, or that had not a direct tendency to edification. And I never once saw him in any other temper, but that which I wished to be in, in the last moments of life.

Of Archbishop Usher it was remarked by one of his chaplains, that "though in himself an Apollos, an eloquent man and mighty in the Scriptures, yet in his sermons and especially those delivered at Oxford, he did much deny himself that Christ might be the more glorified. When in the work of labouring for souls you might perceive, that, like Paul at Athens, his spirit was stirred within him. One who knew him well said of him, that such was his earnestness in the cause that, like his Lord, only in an inferior degree, '*the zeal of his house did eat him up.* For though like Moses his temper was naturally meek and gentle, yet such was the longing of his soul for the everlasting welfare of the people. that his words were not unfrequently like thunder and his countenance glowing like the flashes of lightning ...As his preaching was thus fervent, so was it constant. Even to the close of his life, and that life extended to seventy-five years, he constantly preached once a week and many times oftener. No preferments, no business, nothing but sickness stopped him in this labour of love. Though his places and his offices were such as might have excused him from the toil of preaching, yet he never made use of them as indulgences.

We might quote numerous passages of a similar kind but these will be sufficient to shew the sanctity of character which we could ever wish to find in the description of those who hold the episcopal office and where this most appropriate praise cannot be justly awarded, whatever may be said of them as men, the less that is said of them as bishops the better.

The object of the charge before us is "to recommend that line of conduct which, from the circumstances of the times, the clergy are peculiarly called upon to adopt. This object will be allowed by every serious person to be highly important for every age has its own characteristic topics of advice and instruction, and a zealous prelate will avail himself of his high influence to urge these prominently upon his clergy. We would, however, venture to suggest, whether the almost exclusive attention so often devoted to this part of episcopal charges has not incidentally had the effect of too much keeping out of sight those more general and fundamental topics on which the pastors of Christ's flock, in every age, need most urgently to be addressed. It was the well known, though somewhat quaint, remark of one who was reproached for not preaching as it was phrased, "to the times, that "while so many eminent ministers were preaching to the times, one poor brother might surely preach for eternity. An episcopal charge ought, we think, to embrace both these points. While the more special duties or topics of the age require due attention, the broadest basis should be laid for them all, in a distinct recognition of the infinite value of the souls of men; the high responsibilities of the clergy, not merely as moralists, or customary ecclesiastical functionaries, or enlightened benevolent residents in a parish, but as "ambassadors for God, "ministers of reconciliation,' men on whom will lie the blood of those committed to their charge, if they are not faithful in teaching them their need of salvation, and the only way of obtaining it, as well as the conduct which befits those who hope for this invaluable but gratuitous boon. To say the truth, an episcopal charge, however excellent in other respects, appears to us defective, if the more *spiritual* considerations connected with the Christian ministry are too much lost sight of in the press of other, though in their degree highly important, matters. The habit of taking for granted that the clergy of any church are, as a matter of course, all religious and conscientious servants of God, is calculated to produce effects the most unhappy on the more thoughtless and worldly minded members of the "profession." The broad line which separates the merely official ecclesiastic from the faithful devoted minister of Christ, should never be lost sight of, nor can too great attention be exerted to prevent the habit so common and so fatal among the majority of the members of all churches, of being satisfied with the forms of religion without its true spirit and power. May not, for example, almost all the duties and offices described in the following interesting sketch be gone through, as a mere matter of custom and routine, without any really spiritual or moral effect either upon the administrator or the recipient? and if they may, is it not most important that the danger of merging piety in formality should be often and distinctly pointed out, both to the laity and to their instructors? Our Right Reverend author will fully agree with us, that it is not what is done "for" persons, either in infancy, "before they know what is done for them," or after death, "when earth is to be returned to earth, and dust to dust, but what is done practically IN them by the hallowed effects of the ministrations of the messengers of God, under the sacred influences of the Holy Spirit, that will at the last day constitute the real efficient value of the pastoral relation.

The ties which bind the pastor to his people are of a sacred and a hallowed nature. The connexion between them begins at their birth, and ends but with their death. Before they know what is done for them they are initiated by him into the fold of Christ, are thus made the children of God, and may become inheritors of the kingdom of heaven. As their reason expands his care of them grows with their growth, instructs the child and forms the future man. From his hands they afterwards receive the tenderest of human connexions sanctioned by all the ceremonials of religion. Through life his precepts tell them what they should do, whilst his example shews them how it may be done. And when at length as all things must, their years are drawing to a close, when the soul is fleeing away to him who gave it, then the messenger of the Gospel attends with healing on his wings, commemorates with them the last Supper of our Lord, and offers up the dying prayer of penitence and hope. Nor does his mournful office end here, when earth is to be returned to earth, and dust to dust, the minister accompanies their remains to the last receptacle of all the living and repeats over them the sublime service of our church in sure and certain hope of the resurrection to eternal life. pp. 28, 29.

Our author divides his charge into three parts, the first relating to clerical residence, and the discharge of ministerial duties; the second to the necessity of avoiding the extremes of lukewarmness on the one hand and enthusiasm on the other, and of "delivering from the pulpit the peculiar and saving doctrines of the religion of Christ;" the third to "the line of conduct which the clergy are called upon to adopt towards their Roman-Catholic brethren."

Under the first head his lordship

stated, that 'residence, where it can properly be required, will be his primary object in the administration of the affairs of his diocese.' On this subject he most justly and feelingly remarks

'A non-resident minister is little better than no minister at all. He who would secure an interest in the poor man's heart, must enter his cottage. He who would lead him into the right path must gain his love and esteem. Sunday we allow to be the most important day of the week; but it is only one day out of seven. The lot of the minister may not be cast on fair land, but *there* is a flock of Christ; there are souls destined for immortality; souls of which he has undertaken the care and of which he must one day render a full and fearful account. That he may present every man perfect in Christ Jesus should be, as it was with St. Paul, his hope and crown of rejoicing. But how can he who has abandoned his flock dare to think on that memorable declaration of our Lord, I am the good Shepherd, who know my sheep and am known of mine? With what emotions must he even read these awful words, 'of those whom thou hast given me, I have lost none!'" p. 10.

His lordship's exertions in promoting residence he states will be directed " to procure for each parish, wherever it can justly and fairly be enforced, the personal residence of an incumbent *or curate*." This we believe is about the utmost extent of what the most anxious and zealous prelate can at present perform, as respects this main point of ecclesiastical administration; but let our readers reflect for a moment on the fearful list of exceptions still allowed by our laws and usages. It must never be forgotten that in official language a non-resident incumbent may be construed to mean only a *delinquent*, or, as we might say, a run-away, non-resident, and not an incumbent who has legal cause for absence from his benefice almost throughout the year. It is the baneful system of pluralism—that necessary physical bar to non residence, unless a clergyman had as many bodies and souls as he happens to hold places of preferment—that is the real hydra to be slain; and we must say, though we would not wish to say it uncandidly, that much as we rejoice in the efforts of late made by so many of our prelates to enforce legal residence, we cannot think the governors of the church so seriously anxious as they ought to be on this vital subject, till we see some due attempt made to abolish the system of pluralities, and to lay the foundation for a plan that shall secure, in every part of the kingdom, resident efficient incumbents respectably provided for, who shall confine their ministrations to a fixed local spot, (whether comprising one parish, or two small contiguous ones, or a section of one of our overgrown large ones), from which they cannot remove to another living without vacating with it its emoluments as well as its duties. We are told again and again, that in the present state of things many of our parishes cannot suitably maintain an incumbent; which is very true, and the evil ought promptly to be remedied; but true as it is, it is no sound argument for the system of pluralities, for it is notorious that this system seldom avails for the benefit of the poorer clergy; our duplicate, triplicate, and multiplicate preferments falling usually to the lot of those who have interest to command them, rather than of those who have no plea but that of necessity: but besides this, the argument is suicidal; for if a living will not maintain one clergyman, how is it to maintain two? We greatly applaud the intention of our Right Reverend author to see that in every parish, abating all "just and fair exceptions," there shall be a resident " incumbent *or curate*," but if the curate can live respectably on the cure after the non resident incumbent has subtracted his share, perhaps the larger part, of the profits, there can be no reason why the law should not say at once, that such a parish shall have a resident rector or vicar without any proviso for a stipendiary substitute except in cases of obvious charity or necessity, and if the curate cannot live thus respectably, may it not be as great a hardship to confine him, under the name of a curate, to the parish with but a part of its emoluments, as it would be if he had the name of rector, and enjoyed the whole? To our minds, all little nibbling schemes for cutting off some stray twig of pluralism, while the main root and stock are suffered unmolested, and almost venerated, to flourish in rank luxuriance, are little better than acts of legislative hypocrisy to satisfy complainants without abating the evil. Every enlightened and religious man in the country, and every true friend of the church, have long and loudly complained of the system: the public voice denounces it throughout the land: we hope therefore that it will not be long before some really efficient remedy will be contrived and enacted by our authorities, civil and ecclesiastical, to meet the evil. Much that has been done on the subject is worse than useless, especially the degree of discretional power given to individuals to decide in so many cases upon the claims of applicants for this so-called privilege of clerical absence. While prelates are but men, and men of like feelings with others, it is not wise to allow of private discretion, where the law might provide a specified scale of adjustment. But it is not the discretional exercise of power by our bishops, but the legal undisputed *right* of non residence, occasioned by pluralities and unnecessarily privileged exemptions, that we chiefly lament. While this exists, much as we are indebted to individual prelates, who, like our Right Reverend author, wish to curtail the evil, it will and must exist in scarcely diminished magnitude.

Connected with the duty of residence, his lordship expresses his deep regret that in the larger number of churches in his diocese there is but one service on the Sunday, and his wish and expectation that there should be two services with a sermon at each. He justly states, that every person, anxious respecting his soul's health and his eternal condition, has a right to expect that the doors of the church shall be open to receive him, and that "the word and the will of his Creator and Redeemer should be faithfully explained and enforced for his edification." "If the church be shut, adds the Bishop, he will repair to any place, *and we blame him not*, where he hopes that Divine knowledge may be imparted to his soul." His lordship will find it more easy, we suspect, to reconcile this candid admission, with true Christian charity and a paramount anxiety for the welfare of the souls of men, than with the opinions of some who profess themselves exclusively the true sons of the Church, and would prefer an ignorant, and irreligious, and profligate self called member of their own community, to the most modest, and pious, and amiable, and conscientious Dissenter, who ever sought for " Divine knowledge, and his "soul's health, and the interests of " his destiny through the endless ages of eternity, within the walls of an unconsecrated edifice. We are strongly sensible of the evils of Dissent, and should be most glad to retain all our fellow countrymen within the precincts of the Established fold, and to have them therein plentifully supplied with the most wholesome and abundant pastures: but where the pastures are miserably scanty, or clearly deleterious, is it to be wondered at, that seceders are to be found? and in *these* cases, at least, must we not allow with the Bishop of Bath and Wells, that the " blame rests elsewhere than with the reluctant wanderers? His lordship states, " from a personal visitation of the churches in two very important dioceses that " where the parishioners enjoy the benefit of a resident and a zealous minister, and where there is double duty, [two services,] Dissent has not dared to approach their dwellings." We are not sure that this is always the cases, but his lordship's experience should at least influence all who call themselves the friends of the Church, and most of all those who profess themselves to be the only sound churchmen, to see well that they duly use that powerful anti secession instrument which is furnished in the faithful ministrations of a pious and affectionate pastor.

His lordship is equally zealous in urging upon his clergy the duty of visiting the sick, administering frequently, he would wish monthly, the holy communion, and establishing Sunday schools. These three items of advice are highly seasonable and important, and we trust that his lordship's suggestions respecting each of them will meet with the cordial response of all his clergy. In reference to the last of these points, the Bishop remarks, that

"A Sunday school is an easy, a cheap, and an unmixed good. Education unless grounded upon religious principles may be a curse instead of a blessing. Education, with religion is the greatest boon which man can confer upon man." pp. 16, 17.

His lordship, we believe, well knows the truth of these remarks, not only from reading and observation, but also from his own personal and affectionate exertions in the instruction of a Sunday school. We wish that all our clergy would lay this important matter to heart. Thousands of our parishes, to this hour, possess no Sunday or other parochial free school. The Dissenters, "and we blame them not, but we severely blame ourselves, far surpass us in their attention to Sunday school instruction. Much of the difficulty in establishing these incomparably useful institutions arises from the want of a regular system, the knowledge of proper books, and other practical details. If a society somewhat on the plan of the National Society, supported generally by our bishops, clergy, and pious public spirited laymen, were formed for the purpose of promoting Sunday schools in the Established Church, the effect, we are convinced, would be most important. To our own knowledge, at this moment, there are numerous parishes in which nothing is wanting in order to the establishment of Sunday schools, but a few necessary suggestions for commencing the plan, a list of suitable books, and an easy channel for cheaply procuring them, with, perhaps in some cases, a slight outfit by way of encouragement. In default of a new institution for the purpose, the National Society itself would perhaps do well to open a separate fund for this object, and might, on strong grounds, solicit the special contributions of the public to it. There has been, we are aware, for many years, a Sunday school Society in existence but it does not seem to be generally known or applied to by the clergy. All we desire is an institution generally recognized by the leading members of our church, so as to secure the requisite degree of confidence and operative communication. A circular issued from such a body, and duly sanctioned in each particular diocese, would, we doubt not, prove of the greatest utility. The pecuniary expenses would be very moderate.

We pass on to his lordship's second general head—the necessity "of avoiding the extremes of lukewarmness and enthusiasm, and of delivering from the pulpit the peculiar and saving doctrines of the religion of Christ." This advice is most wholesome and seasonable but it will not be easily settled among our clergy what these extremes are, or what line of preaching best tallies with the admonition. We do not ourselves quite understand the exact drift of our Right Reverend author, in his opening sentences on this subject, in which he says,—

A zealous but well tempered attention to this point is now particularly requisite in this age of religious inquiry and discussion. Many prefer theory to practice and trust more to delusive feelings than to that faith which worketh by love. All wish to be saved but all will not make those sacrifices which true religion

> *demands. Hence the preachers of more easy and accommodating doctrines, have acquired an alarming degree of popularity, and have withdrawn many from the safe and steady paths of the church.* p. 17.

We have said that we do not fully comprehend the bearing of this passage, for who are "the preachers of easy and accommodating doctrines who have acquired an alarming degree of popularity, and withdrawn many from the safe and steady paths of the church?" To no class of religionists can we fully apply the description. The Unitarians, for example, may preach an "accommodating doctrine," but they are not by any means a "popular" sect. The Methodists are popular, but their doctrines and practices are generally considered the very reverse of accommodating. The same may be said of the great body of those who are currently called "the Evangelical party," whether Episcopalian or Dissenting, whether Calvinistic or Arminian: for the great outcry against them is, that their lives and doctrines are of an "*un*accommodating cast:" not that they are, as a body, remarkably conformed to the usages and opinions of the world, but, on the contrary, that they are unnecessarily rigid and precise. Nor are we fully aided in our researches on this point by his lordship's succeeding observations, the object of which is "to lay before his reverend auditors the opinions of each party:" for what are the opinions which his lordship specifies? They are respectively noticed as follows:—First,

> *The Calvinists maintain that God from the beginning of the world pre-ordained some of his creatures for everlasting happiness and doomed others to eternal perdition—irrespectively, without any regard to what they might do. Good works they say are not required of necessity for final salvation: our doom is appointed independently of them. Regeneration also or conversion is described as being instantaneous and perceptible conferred through grace upon a chosen few who hence can never fall away finally. These are the elect: the rest are vessels of wrath fitted for destruction.* pp. 17, 18.

Again, secondly,

> *Equally erroneous and unscriptural are the opinions entertained by this sect, under whatever title denominated, respecting justification and faith. We are justified or accounted righteous before God, only for the merit of our Lord and Saviour Jesus Christ, by faith: yet still, good works are pleasing and acceptable to God in Christ. We are required, throughout the whole of the apostolical writings to add to our faith virtue. Jesus Christ came down from heaven not to save us in our sins, but from them. Justification therefore is through faith alone: final salvation through faith with works.* p. 19.

Then, thirdly, follow some rather desultory remarks, respecting the influence of the Holy Spirit, but without any express statement of the exact error which his lordship considers this "sect" as maintaining, though it would seem to be the doctrine of perceptible Divine influences. These three specifications form the list of exceptionable points: and "such," adds his lordship, "appear to me to be the opposing tenets of Calvin and the Scriptures." Such then, we conclude, are the alleged "accommodating doctrines," but if this be the case, we think there is much to diminish his lordship's "alarming apprehensions." We arrive at this inference, as follows:—

With regard to the first point, the doctrines of election and reprobation, his lordship must be aware that all the Wesleyan "Methodists," whether professing to be in or out of the church, reject *both* these doctrines as zealously as his lordship himself: so that, however much they may "draw men from the safe and steady paths of the church," they do not at least do it by these alleged "accommodating doctrines." A large part also of what are called the Evangelical Clergy (if these are meant to be included in the censure) are equally explicit in their disavowal of them: and of the remainder, who believe, with various modifications, in personal election, few, almost none, admit the doctrine of reprobation. Again, of those who believe in election, it would be difficult to find any, except perhaps a very few isolated Antinomians, who preach that "good works are not required of necessity for final salvation," for though they probably would not choose this particular phrase for the expression of their opinions, they yet maintain that those who are elected to salvation are equally "appointed unto good works, that they should walk in them." And we think further, they would not greatly differ from our prelate, that to all practical purposes, as a test of character, ' the elect are they, and they alone, who obey the law of their God.'

With regard to the second point, we do not think it Calvin's doctrine, but the doctrine of the Bible and of our own church, that not only is our justification but also our final salvation wholly gratuitous: our works subsequent to our justification by faith being not a meritorious claim, but rather a test of character, as our Lord himself intimates when he speaks of the cup of cold water given to a disciple *in the name of a disciple* not losing its reward. We fully agree with our author and the church, that "good works (and what is meant by good works is plainly specified in the Article) "are pleasing and acceptable to God in Christ," we believe, also, that at the last day we shall be judged "according to the deeds done in the body;" but this is a very different doctrine from what is currently meant by ' final justification through faith with works,' which, as too often expounded, (we mean not by our respected author,) involves a sentiment that by no means runs commensurate with the reasoning of St. Paul in " excluding boasting."—But our limits are so rapidly diminishing, and we have so often discussed these subjects at large, that we must forbear entering upon the controversy on the present occasion. On one point, however, we may venture most fully to reply to the anxious forebodings of the Right Reverend prelate, by stating that the way in which this doctrine is exhibited by what are called "the Evangelical Clergy,' and we may add by the "Evangelical Dissenters, is opposed the farthest possible to an "easy and accommodating system of doctrine or course of life," and certainly is by no means calculated to withdraw persons from the "safe and steady paths" of a church whose formularies are most explicit as respects the perfectly gratuitous character, not only of our redemption and justification, but of our whole salvation and final entrance into the kingdom of heaven.

We must be still more concise in our allusion to the third point under this second head; indeed, we know not that we need allude to it at all: for who but a few most ignorant and wild enthusiasts looks for special, sensible, overpowering manifestations of the Divine Spirit? We fear that the error has been found too generally on the other side: that the *promised* influences of that sacred Agent have been too little expected or implored and that an Episcopal Charge, inculcating the importance of doing more adequate honour to the official relations of this Divine Person to mankind in the scheme of human redemption, might be to the full as salutary as a caveat against a fanatical abuse of the doctrine. We, however, concur most heartily in the conciliatory tendency of his lordship's concluding remarks under this general head. May the amiable and Christian spirit which they breathe be widely diffused among all who have really at heart the common cause of promoting the glory of God and the highest good of man.

These however, and similar differences in the religious world, must inevitably injure the cause of our common Christianity. A spirit of mildness and conciliation would do much in allaying the heat which controversy has excited. We have of late approximated nearer to each other. Equally admitting the first truths of Christianity all lesser discrepancies might surely be removed by a mutual good understanding and by sincere and friendly explanations. At least let all suspicion and reproach and evil-speaking be done away and let us bear in mind, that we are bre-them, brethren in Christ; created by the same almighty Father, redeemed by the same atoning Saviour, and journeying onward to the same home—the mansions, as we hope and pray of eternal happiness and glory." p. 22.

The third general head relates to the conduct of the clergy as respects what is called Catholic Emancipation. His lordship's view of this subject is, that further concessions to "our Roman Catholic brethren," as he denominates them, would be injurious to our civil and religious liberties; and that the clergy ought quietly to express their opinions, and to petition Parliament on the subject, but to avoid inflaming the popular mind, and not to allude to the topic in the pulpit, or allow petitions to be signed in their churches.

Such is an outline of the Charge before us, on which we have very frankly expressed our opinions, both in approval, in explanation, and in dissent. The general tone of his lordship's remarks is so much in the spirit of moderation and kindness, that we are far more inclined to find points of agreement than of difference with him.

To the great Arbiter of all truth, and the Bestower of every good gift, we would humbly look to "send down upon our bishops and curates, and all congregations committed to their charge, the healthful Spirit of his grace, and the continual dew of his blessing," that, duly taught by their preaching, and animated by their example, their flocks may advance in true faith and godliness, and in the end arrive at life everlasting.

LITERARY AND PHILOSOPHICAL INTELLIGENCE,
&c. &c.

GREAT BRITAIN

PREPARING for publication.—Biography of Dr. Parr by E. H. Barker;—Sketches of the United Provinces of Rio de la Plata.—The Secret Correspondence of Madame de Maintenon, from the original MSS. in the possession of the Duke de Choiseul.—The English Gentleman's Library Manual, or a Guide to the Choice of useful modern Books, by William Goodhugh.

In the press.—Eighty six Family Lectures on the Principles and Practice of the Christian Religion, by J. Pridham, M. A.;—An Historical View of the Hindoo Astronomy, by J. Bentley;—The first part of a new work, entitled 'Laconics or the best Words of the best Authors;—Antediluvian Phytology by E. J. Antis,—Outlines of Truth by a Lady.

A letter from Dr. Richardson, the associate of Captain Franklin, dated Penetanguishene, on Lake Huron (the most advanced naval station on the Lakes) April 22, 1825, gives the following intelligence respecting the Arctic expeditions.

"We start to-morrow in two large canoes, and thirty two in party for Sault St. Marie and Fort William on Lake Superior. From the latter place we proceed in four north canoes towards Methye Portage, and the Athabasca country. On the Methye Portage, or at the farthest at Chepewyan we expect to overtake the boats that left England last summer. Nothing of importance has hitherto occurred on our journey, nor have we made any scientific observation worth mentioning. We hope to reach our winter quarters about the end of September and the whole party are at present in good health and spirits."—Another letter from Captain Franklin, dated June 2, states that he was 700 miles in advance of Cumberland House and that circumstances were favourable for his enterprise.

In consequence of the loss of one of the vessels under Captain Parry, the naval branch of the expedition has returned home without accomplishing its object, just it is stated at the time when, to all appearance a North West Passage was actually open before them. This failure, it is feared, may disarrange the plans of the land expedition.

A monument is being erected in Glasgow to the memory of John Knox. It is to be a Doric column, sixty feet in height

He is to be represented as preaching leaning a little forward, his left leg advanced and holding in his right hand a small pocket Bible. In the energy of speaking he has grasped and raised up the left side of the Geneva cloak and is pointing with the forefinger of his left hand to the Bible in his right.

Mr. Wayland, in his missionary sermon reviewed in our present Number estimates the number of spiritual as distinguished from merely nominal Christians at perhaps only one hundred out of the eight hundred millions of which the globe consists. We must leave to the omniscient Searcher of hearts alone to determine this point: but with regard to *nominal* Christianity the following is the current estimate. If the inhabitants of the world amount to 800,000,000, its Christian population will be 200 millions, namely the Greek and Eastern Churches, 30 millions; the Papists 100 millions; and the Protestants, 70 millions. The pagans are estimated at 461 millions; the Mohammedans at 130 millions; and the Jews at nine millions.

FRANCE.

A French journal has furnished an estimate of the number of children in the several countries of Europe, who are educated at public schools, compared with the whole population. According to this table the pupils of the public schools in the circle of Gratz, is one in nine of the whole population—in Bohemia, one in eleven—in Moravia and Silesia, one in twelve—in Austria, one in thirteen—in Prussia, one in eighteen—in Scotland, one in ten—in England, one in sixteen—in Ireland, one in eighteen—in France one in thirty—in Poland one in seventy eight—in Portugal one in eighty—and in Russia, one in nine hundred and fifty four.

There are born at Paris about 22,000 children annually: about two-thirds of these are sent out to nurse in the country: of these, the mortality, during the first year, is three out of five; while of the 7,000 to 8,000 nursed in Paris, more than half die within the year. In populous quarters of Paris, the mortality is about nine in ten in the first year. In the country when good air cleanliness and comfort are united as in Normandy, the mortality during the first year is only one in eight. At the Foundling Hospital at Paris it is stated, that of the immense numbers received annually there only remain 180 at the age of ten. The Academy considering the importance of these facts has communicated them to the *Société Maternelle*, and similar institutions. Hitherto these societies have invariably recommended mothers to nurse their children; but in consequence of the mortality, bad air and other circumstances, it is now urged to be more charitable to aid them to send their children to nurse into the country. As a *general plan*, however we much doubt either the wisdom or benevolence of this scheme.

NETHERLANDS

The Dutch papers contain an account of a new discovery in lithography for reprinting foreign journals, by which it is calculated that the postage and stamp will be saved. The reprint will be executed by a chemical process. It is to appear two hours after the arrival of the mail.

A Philosophical College has been founded at Brussels, and the Government spare no expense, that it may be answerable to its destination. All the courses of lectures are gratuitous; the expense of board is only 200 florins; and stipends will be granted to promising pupils who are not able to pay even so moderate a sum.

SPAIN

The Pope has lately pronounced the beatification of a Spanish Franciscan named Jubern. Among the numberless miracles attributed to this monk is one of having resuscitated several couple of half-roasted fowls, which at his command took wing from the spit and flew away with miraculous velocity. This ignorant and wretched country teems with pretended miracles at the present moment.

RUSSIA

The emperor has sanctioned the project of a Technological Institution at Moscow, for the propagation of the arts relative to manufactures. Youths of *free condition* may be admitted from sixteen to twenty four years of age and their instruction is afforded gratis.

GREECE.

The National Assembly at Argos has declared that public instruction shall be under the immediate superintendance of the legislative body by whom it has been decreed, that a central school of arts shall be established at Argos, and the minister of the interior be entrusted with the execution. An inspector general of instruction is named who is to inform the Government of the state of the schools already established, to propose the establishment of others; to examine the capabilities of the instructors, and to superintend the institution of libraries and museums.

UNITED STATES.

A city law has been passed in Charleston against riding or driving by places of public worship on the Sabbath, at any gait faster than a walk.

Proposals are in circulation for making a *carriage road* from the top of the bank on the Niagara river, below the falls, down to the water's edge on both sides of the river. If this undertaking should be carried into effect, the traveller may pass the tremendous chasm below the cataract in safety, sitting in a carriage.

As an illustration of the progress both of population and of education in the United States, it may be mentioned that the Boston Free Schools, which contained in the year 1758 only eight hundred and fifty-six pupils, have now five thousand six hundred and fifty-one.

From the following curious address issued by one of the candidates for the shrievalty of Schuylkill county, Pennsylvania, we may judge that the violation of the boasted freedom and purity of election is not confined to our own worn out monarchial section of the globe:—

"In making this application I wish it to be understood that it is not my intention to take the rounds of the county—to go from house to house with a view to corrupt your morals by what may be termed a liberal course of bribery—shaking those hands I never shook before and which I do not intend again to shake after the election—handing round a capacious snuff box well filled with scented snuff—carrying with me a pair of saddlebags stuffed with chewing tobacco cut to convenient lengths to distribute in all directions,—treating to whisky on all occasions,—swearing white is black and black is white, and making promises I never intend to perform, and by some fabricated story to excite your sympathy and extort promises of votes and favour which you would be base to fulfil. I leave this course to other candidates. If you think me worthy of your support and confidence elect me."

A gentleman having occasion to pass through some parts of the State of New York most destitute of religious instruction, purchased about 15,000 tracts in assorted packages. These packages he committed to the care of benevolent individuals in as many different towns, with a request that every head of a family might have one tract, provided he would agree, after reading it, to exchange with his neighbours for theirs. It is the purpose of the donor to continue these deposits.

CANADA, &c.

There are now not less than thirty-nine provincial publications in the British North American provinces, whereas fifty years since there were only two newspapers in the whole of that vast territory.

SOCIETY ISLANDS.

A sugar manufactory has been established at Otaheite, where sugar is made from the native cane, and a building designed for a cotton manufactory has been erected at Eimeo, the machinery for spinning and weaving has been imported from England, and is to be put in motion by water power. Cotton grows spontaneously in great abundance.

LIST OF NEW PUBLICATIONS.

THEOLOGY.

The Gospel of St. John in German, with an analytical and interlineary Translation. By George Hamilton. 4s 6d.

Jesus Christ the True God and Eternal Life. By T. F. Churchill, M.D. 8vo. 6s.

A Course of Catechetical Instruction. By the Rev. Harvey Marriott.

The Protestant Reformation Vindicated from the Misrepresentations of William Cobbett. By the Author of "The Protestant."

The Parish Church, or Religion in Britain. By Thomas Wood. 10s 6d.

Affectionate Advice to Apprentices and other Young Persons. By the Rev. H. G. Watkins. 6d.

Tolley's Paraphrase of the First Epistle to the Corinthians, with Notes. 1 vol. 8vo.

Williamson's Reflections. 2 vols. 8vo. 1l 1s.

Evangelical Rambler. Vol III. 3s 6d.

Catechism of the Evidences of the Bible in Rhyme. By W. F. Lloyd. 4s.

MISCELLANEOUS.

The Slave Colonies of Great Britain, or a Picture of Negro Slavery drawn by the Colonists themselves, being an Abstract of Papers recently laid before Parliament.

Engraved Specimens of the Architectural Antiquities of Normandy. By J. and H. Le Keux, after Drawings by Pugin. Part I. 1l 11s 6d.

Historical Notices of the Collegiate Church of St. Martin le Grand, London. 8vo.

A Voyage towards the South Pole performed in 1822-24. By J. Weddell. 8vo. 18s.

Wanderings in South America, &c. By C. Waterton, Esq. 4to. 1l 11s 6d.

The Session of Parliament for 1825, containing a full and faithful delineation of every thing done by or relating to, the

British Senate during that most interesting Period. 8vo 16s
The Fruits of Faith a Poem By Hugh Campbell. 1 vol 6s

Martin Luther a Poem 6s
An Essay on the Chinese Language. By T Myers
The Mirven Family 6s

RELIGIOUS INTELLIGENCE

SOCIETY FOR THE PROPAGATION OF THE GOSPEL

From an interesting appeal lately issued in behalf of this earliest of our missionary institutions we copy the following passages The whole of the appeal is drawn up in a truly excellent spirit

The duty of endeavouring to spread the light of that Gospel under which it is our highest happiness to live among those who are strangers to it must be acknowledged by all who have any reverence for the commands of their Lord and Saviour Go ye into all the world and preach the Gospel to every creature was his last solemn injunction to his Apostles and it is painful to reflect how imperfectly from the supineness of Christians that Divine command has as yet been obeyed

From such inexcusable indifference to the spiritual welfare and eternal salvation of their fellow creatures it is high time that Christians should awake and blessed be God! there are many who have long been labouring to wipe away so foul a reproach upon the Christian name

It was under a strong sense of this obligation and for this noble and truly benevolent purpose that the Society for the Propagation of the Gospel was originally instituted and it is with the same views and for the same end that it now earnestly calls for the support of all the friends of religion—all indeed who name the name of Christ—especially those who worship him in the communion of the Church of England Acting in strict accordance with the principles and under the regular and chartered superintendence of the heads of that church the Society has for its object nothing less than the universal diffusion of Christianity in its purest form and in its most perfect conformity with the faith which was once delivered unto the saints

The Society's general designs are far from being confined to one portion of the globe they embrace every part of it to which British power and British benevolence have access and nothing but the want of adequate means stands in the way of their more extended accomplishment and more beneficial effects Unwilling to reject the pressing applications which have been made for its assistance the Society has enlarged its bounty to the impoverishment of its funds and the material diminution of its capital but the increased exertions of its friends and the inexhaustible liberality of the public when the claims of the Society shall have become as extensively known as they deserve are resources which are looked to with the most sanguine confidence

Let not then this appeal to a Christian nation be made in vain Let not those who partake of the bread of life in abundance withhold that charitable aid which is absolutely necessary for the communication of the same spiritual food to the multitudes who are perishing with hunger Freely they have received freely let them give They pray constantly that the kingdom of God may come—let them prove the sincerity of their prayers, by contributing according to their several abilities to the maintenance of those missionaries the business of whose lives it is to extend that kingdom upon earth Let the members of the Church of England in particular come forward to support, by all the means in their power a society which is engaged in disseminating the Gospel, according to their firm persuasion as the truth is in Jesus

The operations of the Society extend over the vast provinces of Upper and Lower Canada Nova Scotia, New Brunswick Prince Edward's Island Newfoundland and the Bermudas

Of late years the population in those colonies has increased to such an extent, that the Society has deemed it necessary greatly to increase the number of its missionaries The spiritual wants of those countries cannot be adequately supplied without such an addition to the ministers of religion as would triple the number that was employed even at so late a period as the year 1816 The actual number of missionaries now in the service of the Society in the North American colonies alone, is one hundred and three; and, in addition to these, more than one hundred schoolmasters are partially supported from its funds.

"With a view to the formation of a body of native clergy for the service of the colonies, the Society has contributed largely toward the support of King's College Windsor, Nova Scotia, by an annual grant and by the endowment of divinity scholarships and exhibitions. The Society is also called upon to make frequent grants, in aid of the erection of churches in the infant settlements and has been the great instrument of introducing the National System of Education in the capitals of Canada, Nova Scotia, and New Brunswick, and of extending it through every part of the North American colonies.

"Another source of expenditure has been opened to the Society by the extended colonization of the southern parts of Africa and the interior of New Holland where it will form an object of great and important interest, to carry forward the same plan of religious instruction and general education which has been found so effectual in the North American colonies so soon as the funds of the Society will admit of such an extension of their operations.

"To meet these great and increasing demands the resources of the Society are found to be utterly inadequate notwithstanding the liberal aid which they have obtained from parliamentary grants. The average annual expenditure of the Society has for the last four years exceeded its income to the amount of 6000*l.* an excess which if continued for a few years more must bring inevitable ruin on the Society's funds.

The collections under the authority of the royal letter granted in 1819 have been appropriated to the exclusive uses of Bishop's College Calcutta and the establishments connected with it and will be found unequal to answer the increasing demands from that quarter. The buildings there though not yet completed are so far advanced as to admit of the residence of the principal two professors a limited number of students and the Society's missionaries on their first arrival in India.

The lamented death of the late Bishop of Calcutta could not fail to check for a time the progress of the Society's operations in the eastern peninsula but they look forward to the happiest results from the co-operation of the present diocesan and the zealous exertions of their missionaries, who are diligently engaged under the direction of the principal of the college, in those studies which will enable them to carry on with effect the ultimate designs of the Society. In the mean time, and in addition to the main object of their present occupations the attainment of the native languages and the acquisition of a general knowledge of Indian rites and customs, the missionaries are actively employed in superintending several institutions for the education of the native youth.

"The formation of a college library has been commenced at a considerable expense; it will, however require many additions to render it efficient. At the meeting of the Board in March 1822, it was resolved to endow twenty theological scholarships for the purpose of forming a body of missionaries catechists and schoolmasters.

The Society has recently been enabled to make an important addition to its establishment in the East. In order to extend its operations in that quarter and give union and strength to the missionaries it has undertaken the superintendance and management of the missions in Southern India which have been hitherto maintained by the Society for the Promotion of Christian Knowledge and which that Society consented to resign in consideration of the benefits which the missionaries must derive from an intimate connexion with Bishop's College Calcutta.

Five European missionaries and six native teachers devoted to the instruction of the native congregations in the neighbourhood of Madras have thus been added to the Society's establishment and there is an urgent demand for more labourers in the same field.

Under these circumstances the Society feels justified in expressing a conviction that the British public will not fail to aid its labours. Its friends are therefore entreated both to form themselves into committees for this purpose in concurrence with the ecclesiastical authorities and to circulate authentic details of the nature and extent of the Society's operations which will be furnished to them from time to time.

SOCIETY FOR THE CONVERSION OF THE JEWS

The following is an abstract of the Seventeenth Report of this Society read at the last annual meeting.

The Committee state that the cause

of the Society is gaining ground, and obtaining increased attention from the Christian world. Various new auxiliary societies have been formed. Ireland has contributed to the Society the sum of 1150l. since the former anniversary. The whole contributions of the year amounted to 13,715l. exceeding those of the preceding one by the sum of 1289l. It is stated that there are some symptoms of an increasing attention to religion and of a less hostile feeling than formerly towards the Society among the Jews of this country. The continued attendance of Jews and Jewesses at the lectures on the Old Testament types is adduced in confirmation of this statement.

Two rabbies have during the past year been frequent writers in the Jewish Expositor and have proposed their objections and stated their arguments in a manner until lately altogether unknown in the annals of this controversy. During the same period a Jew has published a history of his own nation in English, avowedly with a view to call the attention of his brethren to the Scriptures.

The number of copies of the holy Scriptures issued by the Society has not been more than about 1200. This has in some degree arisen from a more rigid economy in the distribution of them, but is chiefly to be attributed to the various stations having been so abundantly supplied. Of Hebrew and foreign tracts about 12,000 have been issued.

The Committee have ventured to undertake the printing of an edition of the whole Scriptures of the Old and New Testaments in Hebrew.

Respecting the schools of the Society the Committee present a favourable report. The number of children in them is thirty-six boys and forty-seven girls.

Six missionary students have been admitted into the Society's seminary in the course of the last year, four of them (of whom one is a converted Jew) are foreigners, the other two are members of the university of Cambridge. Six missionaries have gone forth from the seminary since the last meeting, Messrs. Wermelskuk and Reichardt to Poland, Mr. Stockfeld to Holland, Mr. Banga to Basle, Mr. Bergfeldt to Posen, and Mr. Nicolayson to visit his friends in Denmark previously to his proceeding to Palestine, whither also Dr. Dalton an Irish medical gentleman has proceeded as a missionary agent from the Society. The number of students now in the seminary is six, and the number of the missionaries in actual employment is twenty-five.

The Committee next proceed to give some account of the Foreign Operations of the Society. Beginning with France, they state that even in that country some anxiety is manifested, and some exertion used to promote Christianity amongst the Jews. A large chapel has been opened at Paris, under the sanction of the British Ambassador, for the use of the English residents and visitors, by the Rev. Lewis Way of which he himself is the minister, and where the cause of the Jews is not likely to be forgotten. After two sermons by the Rev. Mr. Simeon and Mr. Way, above sixty pounds were collected.

With respect to Holland the Committee state that a Ladies Association had been formed in aid of the Society at Amsterdam. The Rev. A. S. Thelwall still continues his labours at that place. He writes, I have seen four Jews baptized, all of whom I have good reason to hope are truly converted and have passed from death unto life. We have one family, and those of superior rank, in which there are six Jews and Jewesses, over whom we may rejoice and bless the God of all grace.

The Second Report of the Frankfort Society for promoting Christianity amongst the Jews, states that the cause is prospering in that place. The better informed Jews are described as ready to receive any thing that can enlighten their understandings and as eager to read the Society's tracts and New Testaments. Nine baptisms are reported to have taken place. The Committee having heard that into an institution at Dusselthal under the direction of Count Von der Recke twenty Jews have been received, have agreed to contribute towards the maintenance of a minister in the institution. Two similar institutions were about to be established, the one at Weimar and the other at Berlin. From Detmold Baron Blomberg states that several young Jewish teachers in that neighbourhood were examining into the truth of Christianity, and that one of considerable talents and hopeful piety had been baptised and has begun to preach Christ crucified to his brethren. At Dresden fourteen have been baptized.

Prussia.—An account was given in the last Report of two young Jews of Berditchef who had travelled 1300 miles to Berlin for the purpose of obtaining Christian instruction, and that after a due course of religious instruction they had been there baptized. Having for more than two years given proofs of their sincerity and manifested the requisite qualifications the Berlin Society have determined to prepare and send them forth as missionaries. Professor Tholuck carries on his periodical publication, The Friend of Israel, which it appears is read by a considerable number of Jews as well as Christians. He is engaged in preparing a work on the prophecies which relate to the Messiah.

Poland.—The accounts received from this station have been, it is stated, of an encouraging nature. The German services which the missionaries are permitted to hold in the Lutheran church have been attended by many Jews, and several have been publicly baptized. Public sanction has been given to the missionaries by the government.

Mr Moritz, a converted Jew, hitherto employed as a missionary in Russian Poland, testifies that the younger Jews have begun generally to lay aside the fables and traditions of the rabbies in the Talmud, and diligently to search and study the Scriptures of the Old Testament.

Various interesting discussions have been carried on between the Society's missionary, the Rev C Neat, and the Jews at Gibraltar. Mr Neat is pursuing the object of the Society on the shores of the Mediterranean.

The Society at Malta has been engaged in the dissemination of the holy Scriptures and tracts. The translation and printing of many tracts of the Society are in progress.

Palestine.—At the last annual meeting the Committee presented an abstract of Mr Wolf's interesting journal up to the date of November 1823. He was then at Damascus with the Rev Mr Lewis diligently labouring to impart instruction and consolation to his afflicted brethren who were at that time suffering unusually from the tyranny of their Turkish oppressors. He left Damascus for Aleppo. His visit to that place in the autumn of the preceding year and his providential escape from the ruin which he witnessed are already known to our readers. Of the population whom he found on his former arrival, and amongst whom he had preached the Gospel, five sixths had been overwhelmed in the earthquake and left either dead or maimed. When I entered Aleppo the first time, says Mr Wolf, the Franks lived in houses like palaces richly furnished with all the luxuries of the East. We heard the exclamation of the Turkish watchman from the tower of the mosque—God is very great, there is God and nothing but God and Mohammed is his prophet. Prayer is better than sleeping. But it is a truth that except the Lord keep the city the watchman waketh but in vain. An earthquake ruined their palaces, and happy those fathers who counted the number of their families and found them safe. Seven hundred Jews now go about deprived of their eye-sight, no longer able to read Moses and the Prophets! The Sultan's first care was to send a company to Aleppo to take the money of the slain families. Happy England! under the wings of the Gospel and the laws of thy land. Mr Wolf had afterwards an opportunity of preaching to several respectable Jews in the house of the British Consul. The Jewish Consuls, says Mr Wolf, thanked me after the sermon was over, and then he adds, I am the first Protestant preacher who has preached at Aleppo for thirty four years. I have daily conversations with Jews, often till after midnight.

More recent letters had been received from Mr Wolf dated at the British residency at Bushire in the Persian Gulf, where he arrived after having visited Bagdad and Bassora. He speaks with much thankfulness of the blessing which has invariably attended all his recent labours near the Persian Gulf. A request has been made by the British and Armenian inhabitants at Bushire that a person may be sent them from England to superintend the establishment of schools for the Armenian, Persian, and Jewish children, upon the plan of mutual instruction. A subscription had been raised amongst the more opulent inhabitants towards the expense of this object. The British residents are also anxious to have a missionary to instruct the children in the principles of the Gospel and to undertake a regular ministry there on the Sunday.

Mr Lewis the Society's missionary in Palestine, after leaving Mr Wolf at Damascus, returned to Jerusalem. The account which he gives of the state of the Jews in that city is most distressing. That class of Jews who first began to assemble in Jerusalem about eighteen years ago and who have come to die in the land of their fathers, he represents as being shamefully and inhumanly oppressed. Their firmans are disregarded, and they know not where to apply for relief or protection. Mr Lewis sold forty Bibles, five of which were bound with New

Testaments, besides twelve copies of the Prophets and Testaments ninety of the Prophets alone, and 1065 Psalters. 'I endeavour,' he says, 'to put the Prophets as much as possible into the hands of the Jews though they are not so acceptable to them.' Events however had occurred during the year to check that free circulation of the Word of God in Palestine which had been so happily begun. The opposition of the public authorities had been very strongly manifested and accounts had been received of attempts both on the part of the Turkish and Roman Catholic power to prevent the circulation of the Scriptures. Bulls from Rome as our readers are aware, and firmans from Constantinople had been simultaneously issued for that purpose, which directed amongst other things the seizure and burning of all the books of Scripture which had arrived or which might arrive within the Ottoman dominions. Mr Lewis in consequence of the violent measures adopted by these opposers of missionary efforts, had been under the necessity of surrendering the premises at Antoura, originally taken by Mr Way and afterwards made over to the Society by Bishop Hannah Marone, the Vicar Patriarchal.

The Society's schools in India are conducted by Mr Michael Sargon, a converted Jew under the superintendence of the Madras Committee. He has 109 scholars under his care.

In conclusion the Committee once more call upon their friends to unite with them in humble thanksgivings to God for the success which he has already vouchsafed to the exertions of this Society, and in fervent prayer that he will finally render them effectual by the abundant effusion of his Holy Spirit on the house of Israel.

THEOLOGICAL SEMINARY IN OHIO

We have received the journal of the proceedings of the Episcopal Convention of Ohio held last June, from which we copy the following portions of Bishop Chase's highly interesting address relative to the theological seminary.

The cause of our seminary set forth in the appeal in behalf of the diocese of Ohio has continued to gain ground in the best affections of our English friends. Considerable accessions to the fund have been made and the spirit of good will and Christian fellowship which it was our object always to promote was daily increasing. Scarcely a post has past without bringing some good tidings of great joy to our infant seminary. The most encouraging words and deeds have been recited to me in letters from persons most eminent for private virtue and public station. Would that their loved and respected names could be here recited! But you know them and will embalm their kindness in your memories.

To determine the great question where our seminary is to be established I always considered as a right belonging to the Convention, for by that body I understand an assembly of men acting in the fear of God for the diocese in general, free from prejudice, partial views and local interests—in short an assemblage of the wisdom of the whole diocese—of the bishop—of the clergy—and of the laity. As an integral part therefore of this body I have thought it my duty to give this subject all the investigation and deliberation in my power, the result of which the same sense of duty now compels me to lay before you.

Before we enter on the consideration of any particular place the proposals for the seminary divide themselves into two classes, namely those for town and those for country places. 1. In the country we can have the choice of a site most eligible for health, which is not always the case in our towns as experience abundantly proves. 2. Wherever in the country our seminary is placed the lands for many miles around will greatly increase in value, and if they should be in a state of nature that increase in the opinion of good judges would be more than doubled. 3. By placing our seminary on lands of which itself is the owner for some distance round we might possess and if we chose we might exercise a power as effectual as salutary—a power by right of soil to prevent the evils which otherwise often the best of collegiate laws cannot cure. Such is the nature of our civil government that it must be employed rather in punishing than in preventing vice. Thus of necessity the woe falls more on the seduced than on the seducer. The tempted is punished while the tempter often too often escapes unhurt. In schools and colleges placed in cities and receiving students from abroad these evils are most alarmingly apparent. Young men are often disgraced by punishment and sometimes ruined by expulsion, whilst when compared with their seducers they are innocent—and those who enticed them from the paths of rectitude chiefly ought to suffer

"There is a time in youth when the body not the mind has attained maturity—a time when amid the storms of passion, reason's feeble voice is scarcely heard—a time when inexperience blinds the eye and pleasure like an opiate lulls the conscience fatally to sleep—a time when the paths of sin, though they end in death are by the arts of Satan strewed with flowers—a time when all restraint, though imposed by Mercy's self seems hard and galling;—there is in youth a time like this and this is that which is commonly spent at college when for the want of means to prevent temptation they are most exposed to the seducements of wicked and designing persons This is so true and so frequent that through a life of half a century and for the greater part of this spent in being taught or in teaching others there has been no one subject on which my mind has dwelt with deeper and more melancholy regret than this—namely that there were not in our seminaries of learning some way invented or some power reserved by which temptation might be suppressed and thus vice prevented or at least the tempter for example's sake more severely punished—some way I say by which our youth when removed from the guardian eye of their parents might contend with vice on more equal terms—might be taught at least the use of weapons of self defence before they are brought as in our city colleges to contend unarmed with the worst enemies of their happiness—those who find it their interest or malicious pleasure to seduce them from their studies into vice and dissipation And here—may God be praised both for the suggestion and the way to accomplish it—this much desired means of preventing evils which no collegiate laws can cure (till that cure come too late) is now before you Put your seminary on your own domain be owners of the soil on which you dwell and let the tenure of every lease and deed depend on the expressed condition that nothing detrimental to the morals and studies of youth be allowed on the premises This condition whiles it secures good men for the first settlers will ensure them such for ever and in so doing will close up the greatest widest and most fatal avenues to vice

With regard to our affairs in England it becomes my duty to state that besides the permanent fund now upwards of 5000 guineas, there remained at the last advices, a large collection of books still in London, given by different most benevolent individuals also the stereotype plates for our Prayer book and a separate fund for a most complete set of printing types to carry into effect an essential part of our plan

We have already stated in our last Number the incipient operations of the college held for the present at Bishop Chase's residence at Worthington The Bishop concludes his address in the following language of earnest devotion and dependence upon the blessing of God

I have been through necessity speaking solely of outward things let us now speak of those things which concern the heart and the spirit I mean our prayers to God for his blessing on all we do Pray ye then for the good of our loved Zion Till very lately a cloud dark and heavy hung over her infant head and even now the light which by God's mercy has broken in upon us from the east, serves but to discover how weak we are and though on the bosom of the tempest which surrounds us British benevolence has painted the rainbow of hope yet that hope must be cherished with faith and that faith must live by the breath of prayer O pray we then to Him who ordereth the storm for our trial and sendeth the rain for our comfort Though in ruins cast us not off for ever O God of mercy Raise up thy power and come amongst us lift up the light of thy countenance upon us and give us peace both now and evermore *Amen*

SCOTTISH MISSIONARY BISHOP

During a residence of five years in France the attention of Dr Luscombe (Chaplain to his Royal Highness the Duke of Cambridge) was directed to the state of religion among his countrymen settled in that country the number of whom actually resident is calculated at no less than 50 000 and he observed with regret the great inconvenience and danger to which this large body of British subjects were exposed from the absence both of teachers episcopally licensed and visited and of the regular administration of the holy sacraments

He was advised to lay the case before the bishops of Scotland and to seek that assistance from them which circumstances rendered it improbable he could obtain in England After a long correspondence they determined to consecrate him as their missionary bishop to his British fellow subjects abroad. He was accordingly consecrated at Stirling, last March, for the purpose of representing the Scotch Episcopal Church on the continent of Europe He is stated to have met with a cordial cooperation among all ranks of British residents at Paris On the 23d of June, he confirmed 120 young persons in the French capital eight clergymen attended on the occasion and the sermon was preached by the chaplain to the embassy

PRAYER-BOOK AND HOMILY SOCIETY

We lay before our readers with great pleasure the substance of the last Report of this highly useful Church of England institution

The most prominent feature in the Society's proceedings among our own countrymen at home during the year has been a series of endeavours to supply the crews of trading vessels in the port of London with the formularies of our church Not less than 100 000 men upon a moderate calculation are annually employed in these ships besides 16,000 lightermen and watermen, and very many others engaged in the fishing trade In prosecuting this object, the Society's agent met with many difficulties but he has, on several occasions witnessed a very strong desire on the part of the young to embrace the advantages so unexpectedly offered them Among the seamen, there has been marked at times the appearance of strong compunction and desires of amendment. One seemed particularly thankful for the book of Select Homilies regretting the idle manner in which he had spent the last Sabbath and expressing a hope that by the blessing of God a good use would be made of the book presented to him And upon another occasion the mate of a vessel said I seldom hear a sermon but when I do it makes me shudder I shall read the Homilies and I hope they will make me a better man In some cases the uninstructed have shewn a wish to learn Upon some occasions very pleasing instances have occurred of piety and candour The Homilies have been universally well received Among 8,560 men visited only forty had before seen them but when read they have always appeared to give great satisfaction One captain said I find them plain excellent, and very good matter The mate of a ship on board which a copy had been left addressed the agent on a subsequent occasion in these words Sir I have read the Homilies which you left in the summer they are truly excellent sermons, very plain but very good —In one case, also, they seem to have been greatly blessed in alarming the conscience of a careless individual, and bringing him to a better mind.

The number of ships visited by the Society s agent in the course of eight months, as opportunities have occurred, is 853. The crews of these ships amounted to about 8,560 persons of whom 1,474 were previously provided with Prayer books, and 7 086 were unsupplied. Among these, 766 Prayer books, and fifteen copies of the whole Book of Homilies in duodecimo, have been sold at reduced prices. One or more of the little books of Select Homilies having been left for the use of the ship s company on board each vessel which has been visited, it not unfrequently happens that the Bible Prayer book and select Homilies are now given out to seamen on the morning of the Sabbath for their religious instruction in the course of the day

Application has been made to the Society also, by zealous individuals at other ports for assistance in pursuing a similar course

A new edition of the Prayer book has been completed in Irish consisting of 1 500 copies. A correspondent writes

The demand seems to increase the people certainly like the book and after their manner of expressing themselves consider it to be fine Irish He farther says that he knows of a Roman Catholic priest who possesses a copy of the Prayerbook has kept it by him for several years, and values it highly

From the foregoing account of the operations of this society at home the Committee pass on to a brief statement of their efforts abroad

Prayer books and Homilies have been sent, in the course of last year, to a colony of English residing in Normandy, who assemble on the Sabbath to worship God according to the customs observed in the land of their fathers Upon similar principles, as well as with a general view to the spiritual advantage of those who should receive the books the chaplain of a ship stationed off the coast of Africa the chaplain of the Blonde going to the Sandwich Islands and other clergymen filling similar offices or going to minister in foreign stations have been supplied with copies of the church formularies The writer of a letter lately received expresses himself to the following effect —

I have taken every opportunity of supplying with your books both soldiers and sailors who have visited this colony I have frequently sent Prayer-books and Homilies to Barbadoes and other islands as well as to British America. To a Roman Catholic who called upon me I have given a Common Prayer Book and some Homilies, particularly recommending the Articles of the Church of England to his notice. To a fellow overseer I gave a Prayer book and some Homilies; and two Prayer-books and some Homilies to the mate of a ship who was teaching two boys to read. Some have also been given to prisoners in the jail. A friend of your society having furnished me with four copies of the Book of Homilies I presented two in a respectful manner to clergymen and a third to the missionary. I keep one copy to lend. Some time back I lent this to the soldiers of the fort.

Many of your books have been put into the hands of Negroes whom we have taught to read. I have presented about thirty to Crown Negroes and have distributed Homilies wherever I could. Having given notice that I would sell Prayer books at a guilder each I sold nine the next day. Upon another occasion I sold three Prayer books to a young man of colour from Barbadoes the steward of a schooner he said he wished to read good books only. He then had no Bible but shortly afterwards he bought one for himself and another for his sister and I gave him some Homilies. An elderly woman bought a Bible and also a Prayer book to send by this person to her daughter in Barbadoes.

A coloured man bought of me four Prayer books to send to some relations two or three of whom are slaves. I gave him some Homilies. I have sent a Prayer book and some Homilies to a young woman, who had formerly been in our school and who having removed to Demerara, refused to live with a White gentleman, and married a person of her own colour.

"Some weeks since I was much pleased with an old Mulatto a slave to the Crown named Gabriel I heard him in prayer use the confession at the beginning of your service. In conversation with him afterwards I found he had learned perfectly all the sentences of Scripture preceding morning and evening prayer he repeated correctly some of the prayers and spoke of some of the collects and parts of the communion service as passages from which he thought he had derived benefit. He told me that he reads part of the evening service every evening and on Sunday afternoons, in his house I encouraged him to learn as many of the collects as he could, and pointed out to him some of the excellencies of the Litany and of the prayer for the King. The religious Negroes in general have a great veneration for the King. They often pray heartily for him and many of them have an idea that through him they have the Gospel. Gabriel is a very old man blind of one eye but has learnt to read easy parts of the Bible.

The Committee next proceed to the Society's foreign operations. These we purpose to notice in a future Number.

SUNDAY SCHOOL SOCIETY FOR IRELAND

The conductors of this Society state that under the circumstances of Ireland during the last year it could not be expected that they should be enabled to report unvaried prosperity some schools have been discontinued, and there has been a reduction in the attendance on others but several new schools have been added to their list, and the conductors and teachers in all parts of the country express the strongest assurances of unabated zeal and unchanged resolution to persevere. The Society's total receipts for the last year amounted to 2 653l. of this sum 394l were the produce of books and quarterly extracts sold at the depository. Gratuitous assistance has been afforded to 534 schools of which 352 had received similar assistance in former years. A considerable increase has taken place in the sale of books at reduced prices and principally of Bibles the sale of which has been trebled as compared with that of the preceding year.

In Ulster there has been a decrease of scholars which the Committee attribute chiefly to the general establishment in the past year of schools held on Sundays in the Roman Catholic chapels which measure has withdrawn from the neighbouring Sunday Schools many of the children of that communion. In Leinster there has been a small increase in Connaught, a decrease. In Munster in two counties there has been some decrease but in four others an increase.

The Committee have received information that in their schools there are 22 256 adults above the age of fifteen years in attendance—62 993 scholars reading the Scriptures—and that the number of males and females in the schools is nearly equal. A large proportion of the adults consists of those who have been for some time attending the schools, and continue to do so for the purpose of receiving religious instruction. The Committee corroborate, by the experience of the past year the testimonies which have been given in former Reports as to the effects produced generally by Sunday school instruction. The disinterested zeal and perseverance manifested in general by the conductors and gratuitous teachers have frequently produced their full effects on the children and their parents. The information diffused by means of lending libraries and above all the Scriptural instruction given in the schools produce the most happy results. The Sabbath is applied to its peculiar and sanctifying occupations—public worship is more numerously and reverently attended, and the irreproachable conduct of the young people when they enter on the duties and responsibilities of mature life, and the comfort which they have received and communicated in times of affliction, sickness and of death have in many instances been the fruits of Sunday school instruction.

VIEW OF PUBLIC AFFAIRS

FOREIGN

GREECE.—No well authenticated specific details have been received from Greece, but the general complexion of the accounts is favourable to the arms of the patriots. The Egyptian army appears to be dwindling away under the vexatious harassings of a skirmishing warfare. The Greeks in Candia have raised the standard of liberty.

SPAIN.—The king has appointed a junta for improving the finances of the country, and suggesting any other measures that may be desirable; but it appears to consist of individuals wholly addicted to the most bigotted principles, civil and ecclesiastical, and to afford not the slightest prospect of producing any public benefit. Numerous executions are still taking place for political offences, and the whole country appears to be one scene of anarchy.

HAYTI.—The French recognition of independence has been received with the most lively joy by all classes of the people. The first step of the government, upon the receipt of the intelligence, was to disband their large standing army, by which measure it is stated there will be an accession of nearly 50,000 able men to the agricultural interests, and a consequent diminution of the public expenses, with an increase of revenue.

SOUTH AMERICA.—A feeling seems to exist in the minds of some religious persons that the influence of Popery is greatly on the increase: our own opinion we have repeatedly stated, tends the contrary way; and almost every succeeding month we are happy to add, confirms us in this more encouraging view of the subject. We might advert even to Ireland itself; we might further refer to the vehement complaints of the Roman Catholic clergy in Holland, in consequence of a recent ordinance of the King, for shutting up certain seminaries of education, to prevent the extension of the influence of the Jesuits; we might mention the not less urgent remonstrances of the Catholic clergy of France (see for example a pamphlet on the subject, just published by the Abbé de la Mennais,) that they have lost all political power; that they are placed only on the same footing as the most obscure sect; and that they must be indebted for whatever influence they can acquire to their personal character and exertions, instead of to their unalienable rights as the divinely appointed depositaries of the true faith, the only persons who ought to be allowed to conduct the education, or minister to the spiritual wants, of the people. We might refer, in the very heart and stronghold of the Catholic portion of Germany, to a circular of the Archbishop of Cologne, just issued, forbidding the clergy to celebrate the ancient holy-days, suppressed by the Concordat forced upon the Pope by the French Government; which holy days the Archbishop says, in language perfectly true and familiar to the ears of Protestants but quite new in the Church of Rome, far from contributing to true religion, " very generally give occasion to idleness, intemperance, and useless expenses." But we turn to the new world, where still more strikingly the influence of Popery seems verging to its decrepitude. The Government of Buenos Ayres has formally recommended to the House of Representatives of that province the establishment of the liberty of Divine worship in the broadest and most unrestricted manner by the adoption of the following simple but comprehensive law:—" The right which every man has to worship the Divinity agreeably to his own conscience is inviolable in the territory of the province.

In the note accompanying their proposition, the Government say that the term toleration is too tame and ought not to be introduced into any law which shall be framed on this subject. "The province, say they, " would appear to descend from the point of civilization which it has attained, if it were to establish a law of toleration or to pretend to grant a liberty which the public authority was always obliged to protect; but since the laws that formerly governed render necessary an act to abolish them, and give a solemn guarantee to persons who may wish to live in our society, the Government has found no other way to do it with dignity than by the proposed law, which it has the honour to transmit for the consideration of the honourable representatives. This act, which will complete the liberty of the citizens, will not be less glorious than that which solemnly declared the independence of the Republic."

And even in Mexico, which has been usually considered as more under the influence of the Papal power than any other Spanish colony on the Western continent, the supremacy of the Bishop of Rome is now publicly and solemnly renounced. The constituent Congress of Mexico has just issued a long and spirited address to its constituents, in reply to a circular from the Pope, from which, as being a very important ecclesiastical document, we think it right to copy some of the most material passages. We apprehend that our readers, after the perusal of this document in connexion with the many other " signs of the times,' will be of opinion that there is upon the whole far more to fear from a latent but widely spread spirit of infidelity than from the exploded claims of the hierarchy of Rome; though against both evils we ought to be on our guard, and to oppose to them their best remedies, the universal circulation of the holy Scriptures, the extension of Christian missions, and the promotion of Scriptural education throughout the world. The following are extracts from the Mexican document.

The Congress would do a manifest injury to your religious feelings, and your advanced knowledge, if it for a moment suspected that a document of that kind [the Pope's circular] could affect your adherence to the religion which you profess or the liberty and independence which you have purchased at the price of your blood and of twelve years of sacrifices and sufferings. The time has passed when a bull forged in Rome could throw into combustion empires and nations and in which they saw themselves under the necessity of breaking off their connexion with the Roman See, or becoming the puppets of the intrigues of its courtiers. The moderation and knowledge of this philosophic age have succeeded to that exaltation of the passions which characterised the ages of barbarism. We now know enough to fix with precision and clearness the limits between the rights of the Church and of its visible head, and those of the nation in which it is established. The controlling power which belongs to governments used with care and circumspection, has avoided those tumultuous schisms which never began without bloodshed, nor ended without bringing scandal on religion and good morals.

"The religion which you profess is nowise opposed to the liberty and independence which you have adopted as the basis of your government; that the ecclesiastical authority neither interferes, nor can interfere in that kind of affairs, and that the civil government is sufficiently authorized by justice and the laws to repress all the excesses which endanger the public tranquillity and which are committed under pretext of religion.

" Whoever has read the Gospel with attention will comprehend the spirit with which it is animated, and the plan which the holy and wise Founder of Christianity proposed respecting civil governments. Jesus Christ assures us in the most direct manner that his kingdom is not of this world—that the mission which he received from his Heavenly Father was only to establish the empire of holiness and the doctrines of faith. He constantly refused, though pressed by the Jews, to exercise any civil function. He abstained from meddling with governments not because he would authorize their vexations and injustice, as some unjust censors of his conduct calumniously pretend, but because his mission was simply limited to the establishment of the church which had nothing to do with them, and because that was the only object of his cares and his labours. Finally He was so circumspect and delicate in this point that He even refused to give his opinion respecting the Roman dominion exercised over the Jewish people, in spite of having been provoked to do so by the Pharisees. The principles of doctrine and conduct adopted by Jesus Christ to place civil governments apart from all ecclesiastical interference being so clear, solid and luminous, what have such governments to fear from authorities which not only have no power to intermeddle in such affairs, but even have no right to express an opinion if they wish to follow the example of their Divine Master?

'Inhabitants of the State —you see clearly that to profess the religion of your crucified Redeemer, you are so far from being required to renounce your liberty and independence that you are called upon to repress the excesses of some wicked ministers, who pretending to decide on points beyond their competence, dishonour the religion which they preach, by infringing its precepts. Neither the dogmas of Christianity nor its worship nor the jurisdiction of its ministers which is purely spiritual, and has nothing of physical power—nor the means of supporting this religion, which are reduced to exhortation good example, patience and the exercise of all the virtues have any thing to do with the form of government under which the nations in which it exists are constituted. It has no right to dictate whether they shall be subject to a foreign chief or not — whether or not they shall maintain relations with the other parts of the world or whether they shall have juntas or assemblies to prescribe their respective fundamental laws. What then shall we say of the encyclic which embraces the decision of such points? The kings who took the title of Catholic, such as Ferdinand the Catholic, Charles V the Defender of the Church,' Philip II the Pious, would have characterized the document as they did so many others as being turbulent and seditious but your congress guided by the principles of moderation which animate it, see only in it a monument of that human weakness from which even the successor of St Peter unhappily is not exempt

From the 5th and 6th centuries of Christianity a scandalous struggle has been maintained between the priesthood and civil authority

Happily the morning of light and knowledge which followed the dismal night of the 13th 14th, and 15th centuries enlightened nations on their true rights and taught them to reduce within its natural limits the respect due to sacerdotal authority. Governments gradually desisted from agitating questions foreign to their functions and began on the other hand to protect themselves from the consequences of bulls and excommunications. The heads of the church on their side have been receding gradually from their pretensions over civil affairs so that in the last three centuries the successors of St Peter could scarcely be called a shadow of the popes in the middle age

DOMESTIC

We have great pleasure in stating, that the quarterly accounts of the revenue continue to afford a gratifying proof of the vast resources and prosperity of the country. The receipts for the quarter ending this month exceed those of the same quarter last year, by the sum of 137,594*l* and the increase for the year above the revenue for 1824, is 1,863,695*l* and this notwithstanding the recent diminution of taxes

We lament to find that most extensive naval and military operations are considered necessary for prosecuting the Burmese war. The expenditure in this unhappy war has been enormous and the waste of human life most appalling and all for no object that the public is acquainted with which can justify either the cost or the bloodshed

Among the numerous and many of them highly interesting papers recently laid before Parliament is a voluminous series of documents on the subject of Colonial Slavery. Most of these papers were printed at too late a period of last session to allow of much use being made of them before the prorogation of Parliament and to the public at large their contents and even their existence, are scarcely known. We are most happy therefore to find that an abridgment of them has been drawn up and printed under the title of 'The Slave Colonies of Great Britain or a Picture of Negro Slavery drawn by the Colonists themselves with the very appropriate Scriptural motto Out of thine own mouth will I judge thee. The pamphlet is printed for the Anti Slavery Society and may be had at our publishers. We trust it will be very widely circulated and perused. The picture which it exhibits of slavery is so fearful and revolting that we might hesitate to credit the existence of the reality were it not that the statements are official and emanate from the Colonial Authorities themselves and what renders it peculiarly deserving of public attention is that it is not a narrative of atrocities long forgotten, and we would hope deeply repented of 'a tale of days by gone' furbished up anew to excite the feelings of the British public but a delineation of the actual state of our Slave Colonies at the present moment a narrative which tells us of stripes yet unhealed of groans which still echo around our plantations of tyranny to this moment unchecked in its deeds of cruelty and crime of injustice oppression, and inhumanity, both private and legislative, bearing date not in dark ages or Pagan lands but in British Colonies, and with the ink scarce lydry upon the record. Our extracts must necessarily be brief, and for the present shall be confined to the conclusion and postscript of the pamphlet. The editors remark

"Having now brought the proposed analysis to a conclusion, we beg to offer a few observations upon it.

'The first impression, which its perusal is calculated to produce is a feeling of surprise and horror at the extraordinary state of society which it develops, as existing in a considerable portion of his Majesty's dominions. In the present analysis as in Mr Stephens Delineation of Colonial Slavery the colonists are made to describe their own system the proofs of its iniquity being drawn from the colonial laws, from other colonial records of unquestionable authority, or from the evidence of colonial proprietors. In the ameliorated slave-codes now brought before them, the public will find the proof, the irrefragable proof of the determined pertinacity with which the colonists cleave to the worst errors, and most revolting deformities of their system —That such would be the result of a reference of this great question to the decision of the colonial assemblies, we never doubted for a moment. Our opinions on the subject have never been more admirably or accurately expressed, than they were by Mr Canning, in a speech on the Slave Trade made by him in 1799. 'Trust not, says that enlightened statesman, making the sentiment of a previous speaker his own, '*trust not the masters of slaves in what concerns legislation for slavery. However specious their laws may appear depend upon it they must be ineffectual in their operation. It is in the nature of things that they should be so*'— LET THEN THE BRITISH HOUSE OF COMMONS DO THEIR PART THEMSELVES. LET THEM NOT DELEGATE THE TRUST OF DOING IT TO THOSE WHO CANNOT EXECUTE THAT TRUST FAIRLY. *Let the evil be remedied by an Assembly of freemen, by the Government of a free people, and not by the masters of slaves.* THEIR LAWS CAN NEVER REACH COULD NEVER CURE THE EVIL. *There is something in the nature of absolute authority, in the relation between master and slave which makes despotism in* ALL *cases, and under* ALL *circumstances an incompetent and unsure executor even of its own provisions in favour of the objects of its power.*

"It appears from the papers we have now had under review, that the Order in Council for Trinidad was framed (with the exception of one point, that of the evidence of slaves,) on the suggestion of the West-India body in England. The plan, therefore, was theirs it was adopted on their recommendation, and was supported in Parliament by their concurrence. It has been contumaciously rejected, however by the colonists and now neither Parliament nor the West-India body can, with propriety, decline the only means of carrying their own propositions into effective operation.

"We have hitherto confined our remarks to the single point of legislation and we think it has been shewn that it is the very height of fatuity to continue to look to the colonial assemblies for any adequate improvement of the state of the slave law.

"But the papers which we have analysed exhibit a view not only of West Indian legislation, but of the administration of West India law. Here a new field of horrors opens upon us. And here again we derive our proofs of the radical iniquity of the system, exclusively, from the recorded testimony of the colonists themselves. They are our witnesses. We do not confine this remark to those domestic punishments of which we have so curious an exhibition in the returns from Trinidad and of which neither law nor justice but mere individual caprice is the arbiter. We allude rather to their criminal slave-courts —to the nature and imperfections of the judicial returns from the fiscal of Demerara —to the trials of the insurgents in that colony in 1823 (which, however, are not comprehended in the returns that form the subject of the preceding analysis) —to the impunity of the White insurgents of Barbadoes —and, above all, to the reports of the trials of the alleged Black conspirators in Jamaica, in which every species of judicial irregularity appears to find a place,—and to the barefaced oppressions exercised in that island towards some of the People of Colour. Let these things be fully weighed, and neither the Government nor the Parliament can hesitate as to the imperative necessity of radically reforming a system which produces such abominations as have been detailed such perversions of the very forms of law to purposes of cruelty and oppression, as can only find their parallel in the execrated proceedings of Judge Jefferies, or in the practical jurisprudence of Constantinople, Morocco, or Algiers

'These things must come to an end and that speedily. They must come to an end, because neither the government, nor the parliament nor the people of England can tolerate them much longer and even if the government and the par liament and the people of England should be so lost to a sense of their obligations, as to suffer them to continue, they must find their close in one of those convulsions which will involve White and Black, master and slave, the oppressor and the oppressed, in one common and undistinguishing and overwhelming calamity

"We are at the same time well aware of the preponderating influence which the West-Indian proprietors possess in both houses of parliament This alone could have prevented, for twenty long years, the abolition of the slave trade This alone could, for fifteen years more, have paralyzed every effort which was made to rouze the attention of the government and the parliament to the enormities of the slave system and to the utter worthlessness and inefficiency of all the pretended improvements adopted by the colonial assemblies To this cause must we also ascribe it, that almost every public functionary in the slave colonies, is either a proprietor of slaves, or the known partizan of the slave system —that not only many governors and judges and attorney generals and fiscals and registrars are taken from the class of slave holders and their friends but that, even under the new order of things, this class has been made to supply protectors and sub protectors of slaves—the very officers on whose zeal, fidelity, and disinterestedness its whole efficiency depends —that we should be burdened with imposts and our commerce fettered by impolitic and injurious restrictions in order to enable the colonists to perpetuate their demoralizing and murderous system ,—that the interests of one hundred millions of British subjects in India in addition to those of Great Britain herself, should be sacrificed to about two thousand planters and merchants —and that all the benefits which would have flowed to us from establishing international relations with Hayti should have been contemned her overtures rejected and her offered favours scorned until she has at length been driven to throw herself again into the arms of France

In a postscript to the pamphlet, is given an analysis of the official Report of the Proceedings of the Fiscals of Demerara and Berbice, in their Capacity of Guardians and Protectors of Slaves, with their Decisions in Cases of Complaint of Masters and Slaves against each other This document was ordered by the House of Commons to be printed last June These returns, though very defective, are highly important as admitting us into the interior, the very penetralia, of the slave system, which they exhibit in all its deformity It is out of our power, however, to do more than select a very few examples from the mass

The first complaint on the list we are sorry to say, is against a lady, Mrs Sanders Nine Negro men, on the 1st of February 1819, complain of a great want both of food and clothing One man produces a bolt and shackles with which the Negro women were often confined, the ancles and wrists crossways, by which they are bent double and says he was twice confined in that way himself He and three others went on one occasion to complain of hunger Mrs Sanders ordered them to be tied down and flogged by two drivers It was on a Sunday supposes he had sixty stripes They are made to reap cassava, and get firewood, every Sunday, till the greatest part of the day is spent The women and children have no allowance and the men are obliged to share their allowance, which is also a very scanty one, with them These charges are denied by the lady They are in part admitted, but in part denied, by her overseer The Fiscal's judgment is not given Mrs Sanders appears before the Fiscal on several other occasions, to answer to similar complaints on one of which the son of this lady, undertaking to defend his mother, says,

The Negro is a very bad character My mother will not allow him to be flogged, because *he bears the marks of former punishment so very evidently* he did receive a slight punishment for running away this punishment was inflicted by two small boys with tamarind rods and it was to endeavour to shame him My brother brought him to town five days ago to cook and why he has run away I do not know *he was flogged by said boys under his feet with tamarind rods on account of* HIS BACK BEING CUT UP

The following is the next case —

Nettelje Julia Lea and *Mietje* each with an infant in arms complain that no time is allowed them to nurse their children that during the crop an equal quantity of coffee is expected and required of them as from other women having no children or of the men that a similar task is given them in weeding grass with the rest of the gang which they are not able to perform in consequence of carrying their children on their backs if they fail they are beaten in the manager's presence with the handle of the whip by the driver Esperance Nettelje and also Mietje were flogged the day before yesterday by the carpenter La Fleur they with others, were weeding the dam they had made a fire to drive away the sand-flies they were seen by Mr Toel the manager, suckling their infants he inquired if they had no work to do they replied they had just taken their children up, who were crying they were laid down and flogged their coats were stained with blood Mr Toel took the fire up and threw it in the trench Julia was locked up in the stocks because she did not keep with the rest of the gang and threatened to be flogged next morning she is a young girl with her first child Lea complains that she is not allowed to suckle her child during her work she was threatened to be flogged next day by Mr Toel at same time with Julia

Complaint of the woman *Minkie* belonging to Thomas C Jones —Says Mr Jones took her out of the barracks on Tuesday after I got home he sent me to Mr Henery he would not buy me He sent me to another gentleman I do not know his name but he lives in town they both said my master asked too much money for me and sent me back I begged for a pass to look for an owner he said no he would put me down and would give me more than the law gives I was then laid down and tied to three stakes and Chance flogged me with a cart whip I got a severe flogging I saw Mr Layfield at his door with another gentleman and Mr Kerschner the baker saw it from his window Mr Jones bought me for Mr Logie of Demerara I have marks of severe punishment visible on me old and recent floggings all inflicted by Jones Exhibits her person which is apparently lacerated to that degree that the court judged it expedient to direct her not to uncover the wounds Mr Jones said he *had* flogged her, and broke her mouth for her insolence He had thirty nine laid on her, and *they were well inflicted* When he sent for her, he had no intention of flogging her but after sending her to three persons for sale, and not succeeding, he told her she had often deserved a flogging he then directed her to be flogged, and that they should be well laid on, which was done

Felix, belonging to Plantation Scotland, states

That he has had a Black woman upon the estate for his wife now two years and the reason of his coming to complain is that the manager of the estate takes her from him although he has a wife of his own He is always taking the Negroes wives particularly his wife (Felix s) for she has had a child for him and since the child has been born the manager is always punishing him and his wife without a cause Some time ago ten of the gang came to complain to their master (Dr Broer) to report to him that the manager had connexion with their wives their master promised to them that he would remove the manager from the estate and place another one there Upon this promise the Negroes returned to the estate but since that they have never heard of another manager Felix and his wife are daily punished which has compelled him to come to your Honour for redress He calls upon the whole gang of the estate to prove his assertions to be correct On hearing this complaint the acting fiscal proceeded to the estate accompanied by Dr Broer the owner and on questioning the manager and Negroes in presence of each other on the subject-matter of the complaint it appeared that Felix had neglected his work and was told he would be punished if he did not finish his task the next day which he did not do and therefore supposing the manager would punish him he went to the fiscal to complain This being proved *Felix was punished for his misconduct and the manager severely reprimanded for taking improper liberties with the women on the estate which it was evident he had done* and Dr Broer was therefore strongly recommended to discharge him from his employ

That Felix should be the person punished for misconduct, will appear very extraordinary to all who have not imbibed their notions of justice in slave colonies and it is the more surprising that the fiscal should pursue this course in the present instance as some time before he had addressed a letter to Governor Beard then president of the court of justice, in which he charges these very persons, Broer and his manager, specifically first with greatly over working the Negroes secondly, with severe flogging repeated on successive evenings, and with illegal instruments of punishment thirdly with making them work on Sunday and fourthly with considerably underfeeding them The case was so gross that, notwithstanding an attempt on the part of the owner and manager to deny the charges the fiscal ordered them to diminish the tasks of the Negroes, and to increase their food forbad their being worked on Sunday *threatened* the owner with prosecution and told the Negroes if their wrongs were not redressed they should complain again

The next case is that of a father who complains in consequence of being flogged by the manager of Providence plantation for refusing to give his consent to the prostitution of his child The manager of this estate on another occasion, laid a Negro on the ground with two drivers over him who gave him 100 lashes His innocence being afterwards proved, the fiscal *reprimanded* the manager for punishing a Negro on such slight grounds.

Four Negroes belonging to Cotton tree plantation, the property of the Hon. W. Katz complain of various severities. The charges are denied by the manager and overseer, the persons, in fact who are accused, and on their denial the fiscal finds the complaint unfounded and orders three of the complainants to be punished with seventy five lashes and one with fifty, in his own presence, in the market place. There are complaints also against Mr Katz from his estate of Philadelphia. Among others Murphy came to the fiscal to complain, instead of going to Mr Katz, because three Negroes had gone to complain to Mr Katz, and without sending for the manager, they were flogged and sent back, and the next day one of them was flogged again by the manager.

Mr Grade, the manager of plantation l'Esperance is charged by the slaves with various delinquencies. A pregnant woman, named Rosa was picking coffee with some other women. Thinking they did not pick enough or well, Mr Grade ordered the driver Zondag to flog them. The driver did so. Rosa had previously objected to working, as being unable to stoop, but the manager over ruled the objection and she went to pick coffee on her knees. Zondag explained to the manager her condition. The manager replied " Give it to her till the blood flies out.' She was flogged with the whip doubled. This was on a Friday. She was sent to the field on Saturday. The result of this melancholy case is too horrible for us to relate. It beggars all our former conceptions even of West-India inhumanity.

A Negro woman named Laura belonging to plantation Reliance, with a very young child at the breast complains that she is not allowed to take her child to the field to give it the breast now and then but is obliged to leave it with an old woman at home. When she steals from her work to the child and is discovered the manager flogs her. The child is of a weakly constitution and requires a mother's care which she is not able to bestow. The manager does not deny any of the above facts, only says that *the women with young children are not required to come out till half past six in the morning and they quit the field at half past ten, return to the field at half past one, and leave it at half past five*.

The complaints are more frequent from Sandvoort formerly one of the crown estates, than from any other plantation.

' *Carolus* says he is sick and swelling and that he cannot work, though willing. When he complains of sickness the manager licks him instead of helping him Yesterday he was twice licked. —' *Amsterdam* says he is afflicted with pains in his bones. He does his best, but cannot work as others who are healthy. Mr Cameron licks him with a horse whip curses him and when he goes to the hospital drives him away. — *Mietje* says she is willing to work when healthy. She went yesterday sick to the hospital. Instead of getting physic she received a flogging. She is still sick and has come to complain. — *Lambert* had a bad disease and the manager would give him nothing. He ran away. He is admitted to labour under disease but is directed by the fiscal to be punished.

Jenny complains of her mistress, Elizabeth Atkinson, that *she beats her unmercifully kicked and trampled on her belly locked her in the stocks, and beat her on the back. In half an hour she miscarried.* Her child Philip is extremely ill treated and is never allowed to come near her. *The child is exhibited marks of severe flogging over the whole body*.

General Murray, the late governor of Demerara, well known by the share he had in the prosecution of Smith the Missionary, has two estates in Berbice, Resolution and Buses Lust, from which there are numerous complaints. For example, *Hopkins* complains that

He has been flogged severely by the manager on account of complaining he was sick three different times once 12 another time 39 and again 25 lashes have been inflicted shews marks of severe flogging and much neglected —*Michael* says that they work from morning till late in the evening picking coffee and when he comes home between six and seven in the evening instead of going home to get some victuals he is ordered to work till twelve at night, bringing mud from one place to another. Also on Sundays they are ordered to work and if they should refuse they would be flogged. *Philip* makes a similar complaint — *Thomas* Says he is an old man and the work that the manager gives him to do is impossible for him to complete from the weakness of his body and state for which he is always punished and kept continually in the stocks.

The result of the complaints made to the fiscal is seldom given. In this instance it is given in very laconic terms and will doubtless surprize our readers

Two directed to receive SEVENTY FIVE *lashes*. Again on the 17th November 1823 at the very time when Smith's trial was proceeding we have a complaint from ten *women* belonging to the same plantation. Among other things, they say

"If any of the women be pregnant, no attention is paid to them: they are wrought as hard as the others; for that reason there are no children, manager says—*he does not come to mind children.*

The Negroes of Culcaim plantation make bitter complaints against their manager. Their complaints are referred by the fiscal to a burgher officer. His letter of instructions on the occasion throws no small light on the principles on which justice is administered to complaining slaves. After stating the heads of complaint, the fiscal observes,—

Although I am perfectly satisfied that Mr Ross would not permit his slaves to be oppressed by the manager, yet some of the charges of complaints may require redress, and in such case I certainly shall recommend Mr Ross to afford instant relief. I am also well aware and fully confident that such recommendation would be needless if the complainants had not lost sight of a duty incumbent on them, to have sought redress in the first instance from Mr Ross their proprietor.—The Negroes distinctly say they had complained to Mr Ross and were refused redress.—In case the officer considers the complaints groundless the fiscal says, *I would then recommend you to direct the said Negroes to be exemplarily punished in presence of the gang; and one of them having asserted that ——— was the one who induced them to come to town to complain, he ought to receive fifty lashes, and the others thirty-nine each well applied, and cautioned to refrain from further wanton behaviour on pain of more severe punishment.*

'*Ness* states, That he is the driver over the women, and the manager asked him last Sunday why he did not go to work, and he answered that he had not been ordered to do so, or he would have gone to work as he did not wish to do any thing without the manager's order. The manager then offered to flog him, but he made his escape and came to your Honour for redress.—*The complainant in this instance was punished by the acting fiscal for having left the estate and come to town to complain without any cause;* and when he had been guilty of disobedience of orders and neglect of duty, and the manager was *warned of the impropriety and illegality of working the Negroes on Sunday.* The manager is not punished for so flagrant a breach of the law, but warned of its impropriety! The poor Negro is punished!

But we have done. We have not given a tithe of the atrocities brought before the fiscal of the small colony of Berbice, containing about 20,000 slaves! What a mass of horrors should we have had before us, could we have had a similar return from all our colonies, containing altogether upwards of forty times that number! Only three, however, of these colonies have fiscals or any analogous officers, to record, in any manner, however imperfect, such transactions. Last year Mr Baring facetiously observed, that "what might be called our stock stories" were worn threadbare. He was tired to hear of nothing but Huggins and Carty, and Kitty and Thisbe: they were repeated in every speech and pamphlet, till they were fairly worn out, proving also the absence of any new facts of the same kind. The fresh importation, of which we have given a specimen, will prevent, in the next session of Parliament, the offence to good taste of which Mr Baring so sensitively complains. His commerce connects him with Berbice, the scene of these atrocities: and yet Mr Baring, with all his assumed knowledge of the subject, was as ignorant of these transactions as the child unborn, and would have been perfectly incredulous of them had they come, not from the fiscal of Berbice himself a planter, but from some of those persons whom he unfairly and ungenerously represents as fabricating such stories in order to curry favour with their employers. He complains too of the assiduity with which petitions are got up on this subject. And does he suppose that such transactions as these, when they come to be known, will not rouse the public to petition? The people of great Britain cannot remain unaffected by such enormities perpetrated on their helpless fellow-subjects, nor can they continue to tolerate those fiscal regulations by which they are made to pay, in bounties and protecting duties, for the cost of this bloody and murderous system.

ANSWERS TO CORRESPONDENTS

S D, J M W, W W, Nazarenus, H D, ΨΨ, G S F, A Constant Reader, are under consideration.

We are much obliged to our correspondent R for his offer to translate a further portion of Chrysostom's works for our miscellany; but the two Homilies already inserted, with another prepared for press, will probably be sufficient to content most of our readers as a specimen. Our learned correspondent will perhaps turn his attention to some other neglected Father.

We are sorry we cannot give L M the address of the correspondent respecting whom he inquires.

THE CHRISTIAN OBSERVER.

No. 287]   NOVEMBER 1825   [No. 11 Vol XXV

RELIGIOUS COMMUNICATIONS

For the Christian Observer

MANKIND RESPONSIBLE FOR THEIR RELIGIOUS OPINIONS

A FEW years since it would have been thought quite a superfluous proposition to have enunciated, that men are responsible for their religious opinions. The certainty of human accountableness was till recently a settled part of the creed of all who professed to believe in the existence of the soul, or the doctrine of a future state; and indeed must ever be the firm belief of all who seriously credit those fundamental articles of religion. It is notorious however, that of late years, an hypothesis has widely gone abroad, that men are *not* responsible for their opinions. The anti Christian physiologists on the continent, followed by some of their disciples among ourselves, have been among the warmest patrons of this dangerous sentiment. Mankind, it is alleged, merely obey their destiny; they follow certain unalterable laws of organization, affecting the mind as much as the body, and are no more answerable for their opinions, than for their physical conformation. The brain, these professed philosophers teach us, secretes thought just as the liver secretes bile; and it would therefore be as absurd to suppose that a man is blamable for being an Atheist, as for being afflicted with an attack of jaundice. They in fact broadly lay down the principle, that it is utterly impossible that any human being, exposed to the particular influences which it has been his chance to encounter, could be otherwise than he is, either in body or mind. He grows like a vegetable, or accretes like a chrystal, or is attracted and repulsed like a particle of iron exposed to magnetic affections; and taking the aggregate of all the circumstances that assail him, combined with the primordial tendencies of his organization, he comes out what he is, good or bad, virtuous or vicious religious or irreligious, a blessing or a curse to himself and others according to circumstances over which he himself has no control. The reader has but to open Mr Lawrence's Lectures on Physiology, or Sir Charles Morgan's Treatise on the 'Philosophy of Morals,' or any other book of this class, to see that the above statement is not in the least exaggerated.

The theory has descended from these physiologists to certain of our professed philanthropists, of whom Mr Owen, late of New Lanark, may stand as the most prominent example. The disciples of this school maintain not only, what is very clear, that education most powerfully moulds and modifies the human character; but that, combined with other extrinsic accidents, it so *necessarily* and *irresistibly* directs it, that the individual is not in fact a responsible agent; that he cannot be judged by the Almighty for his opinions, be they what they may, having no power either to originate or to bend them otherwise than the destinies of his location have decreed.

But passing over these schools of physiology and philosophy so called, it is to be feared that this most dangerous latitudinarian opinion is making way in other and still more influential circles; and if we may credit the newspaper statements, something very like it has been, by more than one speaker, expressed within the walls of Parliament itself. Mr. Brougham, for example, on presenting a petition from Mr. Richard Carlile, is reported to have said, that "if a man was an atheist or an infidel, it was his misfortune not his fault," that "he should look upon an atheist or an infidel, if any such there were with pity, not with blame."—On another very solemn occasion, in which the warmth of politics cannot be supposed to have prompted the expression of an opinion for mere party purposes (the election of a Lord Rector of the University of Glasgow) we find the same learned and eloquent gentleman stating, in his inaugural speech on his appointment to that office that ' the great truth has finally gone forth to all the ends of the earth, that man shall no more render account to man for his belief, OVER WHICH HE HIMSELF HAS NO CONTROUL. "Henceforward, continues the Lord Rector, "nothing shall prevail upon us to praise, or to blame any one *for that which he can no more change than he can the hue of his skin, or the height of his stature**

* The conductors of a widely circulated journal, the Morning Chronicle, remark that Mr Brougham's inaugural address having been printed at the request of the principal professors and students of the University of Glasgow is to be considered as adopted by that learned and highly respectable body and they add that it is the more meritorious in Mr Brougham and the University of Glasgow to adopt so liberal a principle, that the nation in general is, we believe, far from being ripe for it. It is some consolation at least to learn this fact for woe to the nation that shall be ripe for the dogma that men have no controul over their opinions and therefore are not morally responsible for them. The University of Glasgow it is to be presumed are as little worthy to share in this left handed compliment as the nation at large in deed one of its members of the highest grade the Rev Dr Wardlaw has exonerated himself and without doubt the large majority of his academical associates from the charge of so unchristian a sentiment in two excellent discourses just published, and which well merit extensive circulation. It may be necessary to state that Dr Wardlaw's line of argument and remark is quite distinct from that of the present essay, the substance of which was written several years since and a few copies printed and circulated under a somewhat different form. Justice also requires it to be added that Mr Brougham's oration contains many very valuable passages and that the dangerous sentiment that men have no controul over their opinions is adduced only for the purpose of grounding on it the duty both of enlightening the ignorant and of abstaining from every species of religious persecution. But the sentiment itself as Dr Wardlaw justly observes goes further than this, inculcating the principle not merely that man is not responsible to his *fellow-men* for his religious opinions but that he is not responsible to *God himself* any more than for the hue of his skin, or the height of his stature.

This principle of virtual fatalism and the total moral irresponsibility of men for their religious opinions, thus widely espoused, thus warmly advocated, thus diligently inculcated, it surely needs not be said, to any who make the word of God their guide, is both fatally detrimental to the best interests of mankind, and utterly opposed to the first principles of religious truth; and a few pages devoted to the subversion of so dangerous a position may therefore not be inappropriate to the object of a religious miscellany. It will not, however, be the purpose of the present remarks to enter into the question in all its bearings; but simply

* It is necessary to add the epithet *moral* because the assertors of the doctrine animadverted upon do not deny that the interests of society require a *judicial* amenableness where the opinions of an individual practically interfere with the well being of the community. In truth the opinion of this school as freely expressed in various publications (Sir Charles Morgan's "Philosophy of Morals" for example) is that public utility is the only test of virtue that according to Horne Tooke's fanciful etymological definition what is right means only what is ordered by law or custom that there is no abstract good or bad in human conduct and that moral responsibility is a mere dream or at best means only not acting contrary to what is the current standard of our age or country. The will, the law, the very being of an Almighty Governor and Judge are wholly set aside in this system.

to discuss one simple but very important point connected with it,—namely, the influence which the affections have upon the understanding in matters of religion; the reflex action of the life upon the judgment in short the intimate connexion between what a man *is* and what he *believes* The result of this discussion will clearly be, that we are fearfully responsible for our belief that the infidel and atheist are not only to be "pitied (which most deeply they are) on account of their awful delusions, but that, in the sight of God, they are also deserving of "blame and punishment for them that in truth mental obliquity in religion is almost invariably connected with delinquencies of heart and life which amply account for, but cannot excuse, the adoption of anti Christian or unchristian principles

It will not indeed be denied that there is a portion of truth mixed up with the erroneous opinions above adverted to Children, for example, usually follow a prescribed or conventional creed ignorance and irreligion propagate their kind and the majority of every nation, in every age, walk in the beaten track of their forefathers The Scriptures themselves teach us, that children wickedly educated will usually prove wicked that others trained up in the way they should go will not depart from it and they shew us that in the decision of the last day, our relative circumstances will be taken into the account in balancing the awards of Eternal Justice that the Searcher of all hearts will judge according to what a man hath, and not according to what he hath not The heathen will be judged by the law of nature and those who have better opportunities of knowing their Lord s will by the more complete code prescribed for their observance But to the extent of their knowledge of their duty or their opportunities for acquiring that knowledge, all will have to account for 'the deeds done in the body But let us take up the subject from the beginning it may be in a manner somewhat too 'theological for the taste of some "moral reasoners but not on that account the less rationally or usefully

In tracing the origin and progress of religion in the human soul it is impossible to reduce it to a series of precise and invariable operations, and to allot to each of our faculties and powers its definite share in the general process It seems indeed to be the ordinary course of the Holy Spirit, in his agency on the heart and mind of man, first to illuminate and convince—then to convert—then to sanctify or, in other words, first to lead men to a perception of their natural condition and of the character of the Gospel to teach them their sinfulness and spiritual inability and to pour into their hearts the grace of contrition and penitence then to guide them as conscious transgressors to the Great Sacrifice of Calvary, to repose by faith in the death and merits of the Saviour alone for pardon and acceptance with God and then to bestow upon them that peace which accompanies a true and lively faith—to sanctify them by his gracious influences—and to render them fruitful in every good word and work, as becomes those who being bought with a price are not their own, but are bound in point of duty, and are also anxious, in conformity with their renewed nature, to live no longer unto themselves, but unto Him who loved them, and gave Himself for them But the successive stages of this spiritual process do not always follow each other in the strict order assigned to them by artificial systems of theology sometimes the understanding, sometimes the will, sometimes the affections, seem to take the lead The graces of love, joy, faith, zeal, humility, vigilance, knowledge, though co existing in the heart of every true Christian, do not always unite in equal proportions, or follow each other at accurately defined intervals. They mutually act and re-act, augmenting each other by their reciprocal influence; so that what was originally an effect, becomes in its turn a *cause*, and gives birth to new causes and effects in perpetual succession.

These remarks apply in an especial manner to the three Christian graces of *Knowledge*, *Faith*, and *Obedience*. Strictly speaking, there must be some degree of knowledge before there can be faith: " he that cometh to God must first know that He exists, and that he is a rewarder of them that diligently seek Him." There must also be faith before there can be genuine obedience; for faith is the only true source of Christian virtue. Yet, on the other hand, our Lord teaches us, that "if any man will *do the will of God*,—that is, will commence a course of humble and ingenuous obedience,— " he shall *know* of the doctrine:" his practical attention to duty shall prove the harbinger to new accessions of spiritual information; and not of information only, but of faith also: for the Scriptures accurately trace up the want of faith to a moral as well as merely mental obliquity; they speak of "an evil *heart* of unbelief,"—an expression which, however peculiar it may seem, will, upon investigation, be found perfectly philosophical, and consistent with the phenomena of daily fact and experience.

I shall endeavour to illustrate the subject under consideration, by a series of remarks bearing upon the two following propositions:—

First, That unholiness either of heart or life has a powerful influence in depraving the judgment in matters of religion: and,

Secondly, That a humble and conscientious endeavour to "do the will of God," is eminently conducive to the progress both of faith and spiritual understanding.

These two propositions I purpose to discuss in two future papers; concluding my remarks for the present with a few appropriate passages from the publication of Dr. Wardlaw:

" That infidelity—and not infidelity only, but even atheism itself—is to be regarded by us as a man's *misfortune* and not *his fault*, is, in my mind, a licentious extension of charity beyond all scriptural and all reasonable bounds. That an atheist is to be *pitied*, I grant. There is not, amongst all on earth that can claim compassion, a more truly pitiable being. Oh the dreary wretchedness of that soul, if such a soul there be, that has quenched to itself the light of creation, and divested the universe of a presiding and pervading Deity! But amongst the grounds of my pity, I must be permitted to include the state of the man's *heart*, as well as of his *understanding*. A blameless atheist—an atheist that has arrived at his miserable conclusions without the perverting influence of *moral pravity*, under one or more of its various modifications—is a character, I honestly confess, of which I am unable to form the conception.

" When the Apostles announced their testimony, in the name of the God of truth, they knew nothing of that philosophy which would now release men from the obligation to give it a believing reception, and exculpate them from all guilt in the refusal of it. When they ' went into all the world, and preached the Gospel to every creature,' they subjoined the authoritative assurance, ' He that believeth shall be saved, and he that believeth not shall be condemned.' According to *their* declarations, the difference between faith and unbelief was of no trivial import. It was all the difference between safety and destruction, between the blessing and the curse of God, between heaven and hell. We do not find them saying to their hearers,—' We are aware that you have no controul over your belief; that it is a thing altogether involuntary; that your believing or not believing what we testify can therefore have no influence whatsoever upon your prospects of retribution as accountable creatures; for it is as unconnected with your will, as is the hue of your skin or the height of your stature. We recommend our testimony to you, knowing it to be from God, and persuaded of its beneficial tendency: but, if the evidence we set before you of its truth does not produce conviction in your minds, we are far from meaning to insinuate that on this account it will fare at all the worse with you in the end. They proceeded on no such principles: but, in direct and unqualified terms, connected *salvation* with the *acceptance* of their message, and *perdition* with its *refusal*.

"We must lay it down as a position which will not admit of controversy, that in as far as *opinions* are influenced by *disposition*,—*belief*, by *inclination*,—the *decisions of the understanding* by the *state of the heart*,—they are fair and legitimate subjects of *moral responsibility*. There may, in this view of the matter, be no absurdity in affirming, that moral evil may attach to an opinion—virtue or vice, to belief or unbelief—and a just imputation of sin to an intellectual decision.'

"A revelation from our Creator *must* be desirable—supremely desirable. I will not reason with a fellow-creature that can question this. His intellect must be disordered; and disordered, there is reason more than to fear, by the power of a perverted conscience and a vitiated heart. And in proportion as such a revelation *is* desirable, should the importance be felt of our not being deceived,—of our neither being, on the one hand, the dupes of a witless credulity, nor the victims, on the other, of an incredulous obstinacy. Oh how inexpressible the folly and the impiety of the man, who has in his hand what professes to be a communication from the Sovereign and Judge of all, and who does not think it worth his while either to acquaint himself with its contents, or to inquire into its authority! Here surely, if any where, there is guilt without apology. The conduct that incurs it is neither *accidental*, nor *involuntary*, nor a matter over which there can be *no controul*. It is, in all respects, wilful and therefore, on no just principle, capable of vindication.

"There are *three things* which appear to be necessary to the guilt of unbelief: these are, *capacity of understanding, opportunity of knowledge*, and *sufficiency of evidence*."

"With regard to the last of these, *manifestation* and *evidence* may be *sufficient*, and *even superfluous*, and yet those to whom they are presented be neither enlightened nor convinced by them. The cause of the failure may lie *in themselves*: and it may be evil,—deeply evil,—and the just ground of condemnation.—It is admitted, that, to be a legitimate ground of moral responsibility, the unbelief must be affected by moral causes; and that it can involve guilt, only as springing from an evil heart. That, in regard to the discoveries of the Gospel, it must be influenced by such causes, is evident from the very nature of those discoveries. The Gospel is not a merely speculative doctrine. It is not, in this respect, of the nature of abstract propositions in geometry or metaphysics. It is, in its substance and tendency, moral. The very *facts* of the Gospel may be truly denominated *moral facts*; inasmuch as they contain in them the display of the purest and most sublime *moral principles*, and the enforcement upon the conscience of the highest *moral motives*. Now, whatever is thus, in its nature and tendencies, moral, *must* either harmonize on the one hand, or conflict on the other with the moral state of the heart. The latter is peremptorily affirmed in Scripture, to be the case between the discoveries of the Gospel and the principles and feelings of the natural or unrenewed man. This opposition is, without exception or qualification, declared, by the lips of the gracious Author of the Gospel himself, to be the cause of the rejection of his testimony.

'There are three general sources, to one or other of which unbelief of the Gospel may fairly, I conceive, be traced. These are *profligacy, thoughtlessness,* and *pride*:—the last subdividing itself into various kinds, of which the chief are also three—the pride of *worldly distinction,* the pride of *wisdom,* and the pride of *self-righteousness.*

"Now, the question is, Are these things so? And if, in any case, they be so, do they constitute *a right state of mind.*—a state of mind that is free of moral culpability?"

(*To be continued.*)

To the Editor of the Christian Observer.

YOUR correspondent R. X. (in your Number for September, p. 551.) wishes to have some account of the benefits to be derived from the study of the Fathers. Should the present communication suit the purpose of your work, and seem likely to meet his desires, it is much at your service.

I. My general view of the degree of importance which attaches to the writings of the Fathers, I would briefly state as follows.—

We receive them not, as being *in the abstract* infallible propounders of true doctrine: for the privilege of *infallibility* we limit to direct inspiration. But, as *witnesses,* both to the train of thinking, to the mode of explaining Scripture, and to the statement of doctrines which prevailed at the times during which they severally flourished, we justly deem them invaluable.

II. Your correspondent seems to me to have expressed himself very inaccurately respecting a matter of much importance; and the pointing out of this defect will enable me the better to exemplify what I esteem the true and legitimate use of the Fathers. He recommends, that we should steadily keep before us the fundamental principle, that *the Bible, and the Bible only, is the religion of Protestants:* and he asserts, that *we ought not to introduce the Fathers, as arbiters in controversies which the Scriptures alone must be allowed to determine.*

I must always regret, when propositions are set forth thus nakedly and generally: for they can serve no end, save that of exposing us to the attacks of our brethren of the Latin Church.

1. Doubtless, in the *legitimate* sense of the words, *the Bible, and the Bible only is the religion of Protestants:* but I greatly fear, that these words are very commonly used in a sense which they are by no means intended to convey. The Bible, and the Bible only, is certainly our religion; if, by such an expression, we mean to intimate that *we will receive nothing, save what can be clearly proved from Scripture:* but, if we mean to say, that *the Bible only is so the religion of Protestants, that each crude interpreter, depending solely upon his own unassisted judgment, is thus arbitrarily to strike out a theological system for himself;* we make an assertion, whereof it is difficult to determine, whether the folly or the mischief be the greater.

After rejecting what cannot be *proved from Scripture,* we have still to learn *what Scripture actually teaches.* Now, this is obviously *a matter of interpretation:* and, before our faith can be fixed, we must have, not only *the Bible itself,* but also *such an exposition of the Bible, as, on solid grounds, may be thought to propound its genuine sense.* When it is said, therefore, that *the Bible, and the Bible only is the religion of Protestants,* we are not to fancy that *each individual is arbitrarily to frame a system for himself:* for, in that case, we may well nigh have as many religions as there are expositors. But we are to understand by the apophthegm, that *it is a principle with Protestants to receive nothing save what can be demonstrated from the Bible.* Thus, on the broad Protestant principle, I am *bound to reject* the invocation of saints; because no such practice can be demonstrated from Scripture; but, on the same broad Protestant principle I am *not bound* to reject the doctrine of transubstantiation because, whether that doctrine be or be not the mind of Scripture depends purely upon a point of interpretation, respecting which (as we all know) there may be a very considerable diversity of opinion

2. Your correspondent proposes, that *the Scriptures alone, with a studied exclusion of the Fathers, must be allowed to determine controversies.*

He writes, I fear, without fully considering the amount of what he writes. When a controversy respects image-worship, or any other matter which cannot be *scripturally* established, *then*, no doubt, the Bible *alone* can determine the controversy because, either its total silence or its marked reprobation, more or less strongly *condemns* the practice. But the matter assumes a very different aspect, when *the controverted point itself* professes to be *built* upon Scripture.

In the Socinian controversy respecting the Godhead of Christ, or in the Romish controversy respecting transubstantiation, how will your correspondent manage to make the Bible *alone* determine the question? Such controversies respect, in truth, the *very meaning* of the Bible. Whence it is evident, that, if two men differ as to *the meaning* of the Bible, the Bible *itself*, to which they equally appeal, cannot possibly *alone* determine their controversy. Can the Bible *alone*, for instance, determine the controversy between the Trinitarian and the Antitrinitarian, or the controversy between the Transubstantialists and the Antitransubstantialists? Clearly it cannot for the two sets of opponents severally appeal to it with equal confidence; and, when they have argued from Scripture until they are all heartily weary, all still contend, that Scripture is manifestly on the side which they have respectively espoused. I may err in my view of this matter but, if your correspondent will explain HOW *the Scriptures alone must be allowed to determine controversies*, I shall better understand the principle on which he refuses to introduce the Fathers as arbiters.

III. My *present* difference from him on this point is so great, that I really know not how we are to decide many of our doctrinal controversies, save by calling in as arbiters those very individuals whom *he* would reject and, in truth, this if I mistake not, is the proper use of the Fathers. I receive them not, as being *abstractedly* and *per se* irresistible *arbiters* but I receive them, according to their several degrees of antiquity, as *witnesses* to that system of doctrine which the primitive Catholic Church universally maintained as having received it immediately from the hands of the inspired Apostles.

Take, as a specimen of the mode in which I would use the Fathers, the two controversies to which I have just alluded

1. Between Trinitarians and Antitrinitarians, the dispute is, whether Scripture teaches the Godhead of Christ and the doctrine of a personal Trinity on the one hand or whether it teaches the bare manhood of Christ and the doctrine of an impersonal Unity, on the other hand. In prosecuting the dispute, the difference between the parties respects the interpretation of a variety of texts and, so far as the Bible *alone* is concerned, each is quite positive that it is clearly in *his* favour. What then is to be done? Must we, with your correspondent, call upon the Bible *alone* to determine the controversy, when the very controversy respects *the true meaning of the Bible itself*? Or must we confer

the office of arbiter upon primitive antiquity? The latter is the plan which I would venture to recommend; nor do I see, what reasonable objection can be made to it. They, who lived nearest to the Apostles, must best have known the mind of the Apostles. If then the Apostles were humanitarians and antitrinitarians, so must the primitive church have been: and, consequently, if the reverse, the reverse. And now let us see how the matter actually stands.

With respect to the texts litigated between the Trinitarian and the Antitrinitarian, not an instance can be brought, so far as I know, from any Father of the first three centuries, in which any one of those texts is expounded as Dr. Priestley or Mr. Belsham would expound them. From my own actual examination I speak with confidence, that the Fathers invariably understand the litigated texts as the Trinitarian still understands them. Now, if the Apostles had been *unanimous deniers* of Christ's Godhead, this remarkable circumstance, so far as I can judge, would have been physically impossible. In *that* case, Scripture, in the primitive church, *must* have been universally expounded as Antitrinitarians *now* expound it. But the primitive church, in her exposition of litigated Scripture, universally *differs* from Dr. Priestley and Mr. Belsham. Therefore, since the system of those writers is *not* the system of the primitive church, it *cannot* have been taught by the Apostles, and consequently *must* be false.

Take another mode of adducing witnesses. Justin Martyr bears the following testimony to the worship and doctrine of the primitive church.

" *Him*, the Father, *and the Son, who came forth from him and who taught us both respecting these things and respecting the army of the other good angels who follow him and resemble him; and the prophetic Spirit: these three* WE *worship and* WE *adore, honouring them in word and in truth, and unjudgingly delivering to him who wishes to learn, as* WE OURSELVES HAVE BEEN TAUGHT." Justin. Apol. i. vulg. ii. p. 45. Wurceburg 1593.

Justin flourished only forty years after the death of St. John. His use of a plural phraseology shews, that he speaks not merely of his own individual practice, but of the practice of the whole church. And his intimation, that he and his contemporaries were willing to teach others as they themselves had been taught by their predecessors, demonstrates, that the ecclesiastical generation, which preceded Justin, believed and worshipped exactly in the same manner as himself. If then such worship were the worship of the church only forty years after the death of St. John, and if the church had learned this worship from the church of a yet earlier period, chronological necessity will compel us to admit, that this identical worship must have been the worship of the catholic church even in the life time of that Apostle. I cite Justin only *as a witness to facts*: but then the facts, which he *attests*, are of such a nature as to involve the inevitable Trinitarianism of the Apostles. He bears witness, that John and the contemporaries of John taught to their successors the worship of the Father and the Son and the prophetic Spirit: and that the worship, thus handed down, was the worship of the catholic church only forty years after the death of John; which worship the catholic church was ready to *teach* to others as she herself had *received*.

Evidence of the same description is afforded by Irenèus. This eminent person taught the Godhead of Christ and his joint worship with the Father and the Spirit. As he *taught*, so he professed to have *received* from Polycarp, who similarly professed to have *received* from St. John: and, that he himself taught the identical doctrines of Polycarp, he appeals to the churches of proconsular Asia, among whom

Polycarp had sat as bishop of Smyrna for the long space of half a century from his consecration by John. Iren. adv hær lib 1 c 2 § 1, 2, 3, lib. iii c 3. § 3.

2. So much for one of the two controversies adverted to: let us next see the use of the Fathers in the other.

It is disputed between Transubstantialists and Antitransubstantialists, whether the words employed by our Lord in the institution of the eucharist ought to be understood *literally* or *figuratively*: that is to say, whether the bread and wine, by virtue of consecration, experience a *physical* change into the *literal* body and blood of Christ: or whether they experience only a *moral* change from secularity to sacredness.

Such is the subject of dispute. That the Antitransubstantialists are in the right may, I think, be inductively proved even from Scripture itself: but the scriptural arguments, which convince *me*, do not convince a *Transubstantialist*. Hence, again, it becomes nugatory to contend, that the Scriptures *alone* must be allowed to determine controversies: for here, as before, the *very meaning* of the Scriptures themselves is the point disputed. Under these circumstances, where can we find a more unexceptionable umpire than the primitive church, speaking through those ancient accredited writers whose works have come down to us? For, though we claim not *infallibility* on behalf of the Fathers; yet they are unexceptionable *witnesses* to the doctrine of the primitive church: and the doctrine, *held* by the primitive church, whatever it might be, must, I think, inevitably have been *received* from the Apostles. What then say the Fathers respecting the present controversy?

Our Latin brethren quote them in great abundance, as teaching the doctrine of a change in the consecrated elements: but quotations of this sort will do nothing toward determining the controversy, unless we can ascertain, whether the Fathers speak of a *physical* change or of a *moral* change. Would we learn their *meaning*, therefore, we must hear them *explain* themselves.

Now, with respect to explanation and specification, they are full and explicit *against* the doctrine of Transubstantiation.

They compare the change, produced in the elements by consecration, to the change produced in an individual by ordination: when ceasing to be a layman, he becomes a priest. They compare it, moreover, to the change, effected by consecration, in oil or in buildings intended for altars and churches: by virtue of which, these several objects cease to be common or secular, and henceforth become holy or appropriated. They furthermore compare it to the change effected in our fallen nature by the mighty efficacy of spiritual regeneration. Now all the changes, to which they thus avowedly compare the change produced in the bread and wine by the prayer of consecration, are purely *moral*, not *physical*, changes. Therefore, the only change in the consecrated elements, which they can have acknowledged, must have been purely *moral*.

With this their avowed explanation, perfectly agrees their language of specification. They declare, that the consecrated elements are only types or symbols or figures or allegorical representations of the true body and blood of Christ. They contend, that the bread and wine pass not out of their own nature by virtue of consecration, but that physically they still remain what they ever were. They assert that, as no physical change takes place in the water of baptism, so neither does any physical change take place in the wine of the eucharist. They even pronounce, in express terms, that, in partaking of the consecrated elements we do NOT eat the *literal* flesh, and that we do NOT drink the *literal* blood of our Saviour Christ.

Nor is even this the whole of the

evidence which they afford us when the novel doctrine of a *physical* change was first started by the Eutychians, in the fifth century, it was immediately opposed by direct arguments. The Fathers of that period deny and argue against a *physical* change, and contend that the Catholic Church acknowledges no change, except a *moral* change only.

Your correspondent will now perceive the utility of the Fathers in determining controversies. If, by their evidence, the Catholic Church, down even so late as the sixth century, not to say yet later, denied the doctrine of a *physical* change, it is quite clear, that she can never have received from the Apostles the doctrine of transubstantiation, as the doctrine taught by our Lord when he instituted the eucharist.

For the satisfaction of your readers, I subjoin references to establish what I have said.

Iren. adv. hær. lib. iv. c. 34. § 6. Cyril. Hieros. Catech. Myst. iii. p. 235. Uom. de corp. et sang. Christ. in Hieron. Oper. vol. ix. p. 212. Gregor. Nyssen. de baptism. Christ. Oper. vol. iii. p. 369. Clem. Alex. Pædag. lib. i. c. 6. p. 104, 105. lib. ii. c. 2. p. 151, 156, 158. Tertull. adv. Marcion. lib. i. § 9. p. 155. lib. iii. § 12, 13. p. 209. Tertull. de anim. in capit. de quinque sens. p. 653. Cyprian. Epist. Cœcil. lxiii. p. 153, 154. Cyril. Catech. Mystag. iv. p. 217. August. cont. Adimant. c. xii. Oper. vol. vi. p. 69. Enarr. in Psalm. iii, xcviii. Oper. vol. viii. p. 7. 397. Athanas. in illud evan. Quicunque dixerit verbum contra filium hominis. Oper. vol. i. p. 771, 772. Vacund. Defens. Concil. Chalced. lib. ix. c. 5. p. 144. Gelas. de duab. Christi natur. in Biblioth. Patr. vol. iv. p. 422. Theodor. dial. i, ii. Oper. vol. iv. p. 17, 18. 84, 85. Ephrem Antioch. cont. Eutych. apud Phot. cod. 229.

G. S. FABER.

To the Editor of the Christian Observer.

In the passage quoted by THEOGNIS, in your Number for September, from the commentary of Dr. Adam Clarke, that annotator asserts, that "*it is most demonstrable not one resemblance will naturally result from a cool comparison between Jesus Christ and Samson*." He does not merely say that the history of Samson might be read without any such resemblance being perceived; but that it cannot naturally be discovered even on a deliberate comparison! He goes on to explain the ground of this assertion—"Samson, he remarks, "was a very exceptionable character, and it is a great dishonour to Christ to be thus compared." But I suppose that no commentator ever thought of instituting a comparison between the moral conduct of Samson and that of "the chaste, holy, benevolent, and immaculate Jesus." It is certainly only in the character which he sustained as a *judge and leader* of the tribes of Israel that any thing analogous to the spiritual King of Israel—the Divine 'Leader and Commander to the people'—is to be discovered; and surely without any "torture of words and facts," a resemblance may be seen (as far as earthly things can resemble spiritual) between the signal deliverance which Samson by the prowess of his arm wrought for the heritage of God, and that effected by Him who "by his own arm brought salvation to his people, and triumphed over all their enemies."

And again, is there no similitude in the circumstances of their departure from life? Is there nothing that reminds us of Christ when we read of Samson just before his death, being brought out, degraded and blind, from the prison house to be mocked and made sport of by his persecutors? And in the voluntary sacrifice which he made of himself, and by which it is said "the dead which he slew at his death

Samson a Type of Christ

were more than they which he slew in his life, can there be nothing found that is typical of the death of Christ? Here, remarks Matthew Henry, "Christ was plainly typified. He overthrew satan's kingdom, as Samson did Dagon's temple, and, when he died, obtained the most glorious victory over the powers of darkness. Then when his arms were stretched out upon the cross, as Samson's to the two pillars, he gave a fatal shake to the gates of hell, and, through death, destroyed him that had the power of death, that is the devil: and herein exceeded Samson, that he not only died with the Philistines, but rose again to triumph over them."

I have before observed, that no person endeavours to justify many of the actions of Samson's life; but that he was called of God to accomplish an important work for the service of his people, cannot be doubted: and it is certain that the Apostle, in the xith of Hebrews, ranks him in the list of those illustrious servants of the Most High, 'who through faith subdued kingdoms, wrought righteousness, and obtained the promises.' Yet Dr. Clark says, "that man dishonours the law of unchangeable righteousness, who endeavours to make Samson a type of any thing or person that can be called holy, just, and pure." If none can be a type of Christ, but such as resembled him in purity of life, then David and Solomon, and various other persons mentioned in Scripture, must be deprived of the honour which in every age of the church has been conferred on them in being thus considered, and in several cases on direct scriptural authority. The high priest also under the Levitical economy, who so strikingly prefigured the great "High Priest of our profession," must no longer be viewed in that light, for "the law made men high priests which had infirmity," and who were obliged "first to make atonement for their own sins." The whole difficulty imagined by Dr. Clark vanishes by considering these persons simply in their public and official character. Were a perfect accordance necessary between the type and the antitype, the sacrifice of animals could not set forth the atonement of the Son of God, nor the various rites of the Jewish temple "serve to the example and shadow of heavenly things." A number of other instances might be adduced, in which the meanness of the symbols employed, or other points of difference, are evidently overlooked where they possess sufficient significancy to answer the purpose of a type.

That Mr Scott, in the remarks alluded to, has not gone beyond the latitude of exposition which even the Holy Spirit appears to justify, may I think be inferred from St Matthew's application of the passage in Hosea, "out of Egypt have I called my Son:" though it may be urged in reply, that in this and many other scriptural references, especially in the Epistle to the Hebrews, the connexion would not have been clear, and could not have been soberly adduced by an uninspired commentator, had not the sacred writers themselves, under the express guidance of the Holy Spirit, pointed out the analogy.

I am far, however, from being an advocate for forced and unnatural interpretations of Scripture: only in avoiding these, let us be careful not to deprive the sacred page of what Melancthon calls "that secret manna and food of the soul to which St Paul alludes when he speaks of *spiritually discerning it.*"

D.

Another correspondent, who signs himself NAZARENUS, in urging a similar line of argument, has sent us an extract from a treatise on the types by an old writer, Dr Thomas Taylor, of Aldermanbury, who, in his ninth chapter, entitled "Samson a Type of Christ," adduces four spe

[...] proofs of his position. It is not our practice to interfere between our correspondents, and we shall not do so in the present instance, but we are very sure that Mr. Scott, though considering, as he did, that Samson was a type of Christ, would have been very far from commending the minute search after fanciful, and to our minds not always reverential, analogies displayed in the following extract. We make this remark for the sake chiefly of younger students in divinity, who are often in great danger from an indulgence of the imagination in the explanation of Scripture and who will in this respect do well to imitate that general caution and sobriety of interpretation for which, not less than for his piety, Mr Scott is so extensively valued as a commentator, both in this country and beyond the Atlantic. His interpretations of prophecy, in particular, are usually characterised by a most laudable spirit of Christian caution.

Dr Taylor considers Samson a type of Christ,—1st, in his person and condition; 2d, in his actions; 3d, in his sufferings; 4th, in his stratagems and victories.

I. In his *person* and *condition*. 1. In his miraculous annunciation and birth, and the declaration of his office as a Saviour. 2. Both must be *Nazarites*, sanctified (to God's service,) from their birth. 3. Samson grew, and the spirit waxed strong in him, so that he became a saviour of incomparable strength. Both were great deliverers; the one from great thraldom and temporal misery; the other from a greater spiritual and eternal thraldom under sin, the law, satan, and hell.

II. Samson was a type of Christ in *actions*. He went among the enemies of God for a wife; which might seem a sin in him but that the text says, "it came of God." This was a type of Christ's love to the Gentiles, casting his love on her that was not beloved; to make his despised and dispersed of the Gentiles his spouse and wife. Hosea ii. 23, where the whole contract on both sides is set down at large. Samson put forth his mind in parables and riddles; so did Christ, in his doctrine to the Pharisees.

III. In *suffering* they were very like in many instances. 1. Both sold for money; both betrayed by their most familiar; both under pretence of love; both apprehended, led away, bound, brought forth at a great feast; blinded, scorned, fastened to a post. 2. As Samson offered himself freely to death among wicked men, as a most valiant captain, being called the revenger of God's enemies; and therefore it is said he died (not as a self murderer, but) in faith; so Jesus Christ, voluntarily offered himself to death, and went out to meet apprehenders, and was content to die among wicked men, and to be hanged between two thieves, that he might destroy and scatter the power of the enemies of the church's salvation.

IV. In *victory* and *fortitude*. 1. His first stratagem (which was a preludium to his calling) in which he assayed his power, was, that he overcame a stout lion in the desert, and slew him with his own hand, and tore him as one would have rent a kid; so the first powerful work in which our Samson shewed himself, was the conquering of the devil, that roaring lion, hand to hand, who assaulted him in the wilderness by three horrible and hellish temptations. 2. Samson slew with his own hand (being alone) above a thousand men at once, having nothing but the jaw bone of an ass; a weak, base, and insufficient weapon for so great a war and victory; and as it was unfit, so it was an unclean weapon, of an unclean beast by the law, which his strict profession of a Nazarite should not have touched, had it been out of a case of necessity; so our true Samson, by as weak and vile instruments, and as contemptible in the eyes of flesh, conquers thousands daily; while by the foolishness of preaching, by the doctrine of the cross, by weak earthen vessels, he subdues whole countries and kingdoms unto him,' that the work may be known to be his own hand and power, and not the instrument's. 8. Samson slew more of God's enemies *at his death* than in all his life. (This needs no application.) 4. Samson being in Gaza at night, and the gates fast barred, was thought to be secured by his enemies: so when satan and sinners had buried Christ, laid a stone on him, sealed it, and watched him, thinking they had him sure enough never to molest them more, he, like another mighty Samson, rose in his might, while it was yet dark, and carried away the gates and bars of death from himself and all his members: all the bands of death and sin with which he was bound in our stead, he shook off, as Samson did the seven green cords, and broke their power as tow is broken when it feeleth fire.

The author then urges the following " practical uses of the analogy.—1. Not to judge of the piety or impiety of God's children by their calamities. Samson had many enemies. Jesus Christ was beset with enemies, as the sun with motes. 2. God can, and usually does, use strange, weak, and unexpected means to overthrow his enemies and the enemies of the church. 3. The greatest victory against the enemies of the church is by suffering affliction, and by patience. Thus did Samson officially, and our Lord morally, overcome their enemies, when they seemed most overcome by them. 4. Comfortable reflections. As Samson officially revenged the wrong offered him in his wife, so will Christ in respect of his spouse the church. " Ye did it unto these little ones: ye did it unto me." And, availing ourselves, as the sacred writings do, Heb. vii. 23, 24, of the *imperfection* and insufficiency of a type contrasted with its antitype, we may reflect, that ' though Samson's wife may be taken from him, and given to another, Christ's spouse cannot. ' None shall pluck them out of my hand.' A greater deliverer is here for Israel than Samson: he might abuse his strength, as he did, but Jesus Christ used all his strength for God, against sin and his enemies. Samson by disobedience might lose his strength, but Christ could not lose his obedience. Samson, though not slain by force, was slain by policy, but Christ neither by policy, more than by power, can be overcome: for in him are hid all the treasures of wisdom. Samson overthrew his enemies: but that was *his own* overthrow, but Christ's conquest was his most glorious exaltation. Samson *only began* the deliverance of the church, but could not perfect it, but Christ perfected its deliverance and salvation. 5. In both learn to contemn the greatest and most extreme peril in God's cause. As Samson, so did Christ, *offer* himself unto death: so learn not to love thy life to the death. For a man to thrust himself in hazard, or venture his life without warrant from God, or by his own private motion, is rash; but, God calling, in standing against the enemies of the church, it is honourable.

Our correspondent remarks, that ' more might be added, but here is sufficient to shew the *cui bono* of such a comparison.' This *cui bono* we must leave our readers to estimate for themselves: our own estimate of it, we confess, is not very flattering.

To the Editor of the Christian Observer.

Quamvis agminibus me mala densius
Omni ex parte premant, quam super horridos
Montes grando sonat, quam mare verberat
   Raucis littora fluctibus
Tu me si placido lumine videris
Cedent tristitiæ nubila tetricas
Mœroris tenebras discutiet mihi
   Lucis dulce jubar tuæ.
       Buchan. in Psal. xlii.

It is a remark of Lord Bacon, that " a little philosophy inclineth man's mind to Atheism, but depth in phi-

[...] bringeth [...] about [...] religion. A similar observation may be made in reference to the disposition or habit of mind selected for the topic of this essay. A small portion of piety is apt to produce melancholy, but a large measure is calculated to produce unspeakable joy. If this observation be well founded, it may serve to elucidate some instances of apparent gloom, associated with the possession of Christian principle. Many persons, it is to be feared, have religion enough to make them miserable, but not enough to make them happy. That there is an adaptation in religion to create emotions of the liveliest pleasure can be denied only by those who are alike unacquainted with its nature and destitute of its influence. While it prohibits every gratification which is not consonant with the will of God, with the dictates of reason, and with our own interest and welfare; and while, at the season when first its power begins to be felt, remorse for past offences, and a foreboding apprehension of the Divine wrath, may occasion for a time considerable distress and anxiety, the direct and immediate tendency of religion is to render the mind happy, to heal the disorders of our nature, and to dissipate those clouds of obscurity and gloom which are apt to overshadow our prospects of eternity. The intention of this paper, however, is not to answer the objections which may be urged against religion, on the ground of its supposed aptitude to excite a spirit of melancholy, but to notice some of the characteristic qualities of religious joy, and to enforce on every Christian reader the cultivation of this delightful temper of mind.

The causes then, by which it is produced and invigorated are spiritual objects. It arises from the consideration of what God is, and of what he has done and is engaged to do on behalf of those who put their trust in his mercy. Accordingly, it is denominated in Scripture, "rejoicing in the Lord." In this particular, it is essentially distinguished from the joy of the worldling and the hypocrite. The pleasures of which such persons are at any time partakers arise from earthly and perishing objects. They feel a kind of happiness because they are perhaps advancing in the world to the utmost of their wishes, are attaining the honours and riches which it offers, or else have opportunity for the indulgence of their appetites and passions. Their delight in that is altogether of a sublunary nature, originating in sources which are entirely distinct from every thing divine and heavenly. 'The lust of the flesh, the lust of the eye, and the pride of life, which are not of the Father, but of the world, occupy their thoughts and affections and communicate to their minds all the satisfaction which they ever experience. But the pleasure of the Christian is derived from objects of a different, and of an infinitely superior, description. He feels happy, not because he is learned, or wealthy, or high in the estimation of mankind, but because he possesses an interest in the love and attributes of God. He enjoys inexpressible felicity when meditating on the character, the operations, or the word of the Most High; when he reflects, for instance, on his omnipotent power, and considers that it is adequate to his security amidst danger, and his defence from every foe; when he thinks also of his unsearchable wisdom, which can impart to him all necessary information, and "lead him by a right way to a city of habitation;" or when he calls to remembrance the immutability and faithfulness of God, which create in his mind the assurance that God will not forsake him in the darkest hour, and will at length introduce him to "the inheritance of the saints in light." Especially does the joy of the Christian spring from meditation on the character of God, as he is represented in the Gospel of Jesus Christ, as devising for the fallen children of men a plan of salvation, as commissioning his Son to redeem and his Spirit to sanctify our souls. In this wonderful exhibition of the goodness and mercy of the Almighty, as well as of his justice and holiness, the believer discovers ample matter for the exercise of every affection which communicates delight to the heart. In short, the pleasure of the Christian is of a nature entirely spiritual, because it originates in God himself, who is the most spiritual Being in the universe.

Another feature in religious joy is calmness or placidity. I do not mean to deny that some Christians are occasionally indulged with a tone of religious feeling which may border on exultation, and which is not owing to a disordered state of the physical system, or to the influence of imagination rendered wild by enthusiasm, but to a scriptural unwavering reliance on the merits of the great propitiatory Sacrifice. In ordinary cases, however, the pleasure experienced by the believer is of a less elevated and transitory nature. That it is free from violent or boisterous emotions will be evident on a recollection of its causes which have been shewn to be the perfections and works of the Supreme Being. Now the joy which springs from the contemplation of the abstract attributes of Jehovah must necessarily be distinct from every state of feeling that resembles tumultuous agitations or commotions. The benevolence and mercy of God which are the perfections of his nature most calculated to encourage our confidence are still blended and tempered with the severity of his justice and purity. Could the former be regarded as affording too great licence for the indulgence of exultation, the latter are suited to check every rash or precipitate emotion, and to awaken in the mind sentiments of veneration and awe. The condescension of God, therefore, exhibited in connexion with his majesty, is adapted to excite not the sensations of unreflecting rapture, but the calm silent feelings of acquiescent joy. If we also advert to the exercise of the perfections of God towards the human race, we shall perceive that the pleasure which the consideration of this exercise is calculated to impart to the Christian is of a thoughtful and placid description. In that exercise the Deity is represented as offended on account of our sins, though "*so* loving the world, that he gave his only Son, that whoso believeth in him should not perish, but have everlasting life:" at the same time, we are exhibited as depraved, and guilty, and rebellious; as unable to redeem our souls from destruction, or to perform any good action of ourselves; as well as dependent on God for the continuance and consummation of that spiritual life which has been commenced in the heart. Accordingly we are commanded in Scripture to "rejoice with trembling:" and if we entertain proper views of ourselves, and of the relations which we sustain to the Almighty, our joy will no doubt be moderated or intermingled with a deep consciousness of our numerous imperfections.—Besides, rapture is that agitation or excitement of mind which cannot, according to the constitution of our nature, be of long duration, and which cannot therefore be accordant or intended to be combined with the general circumstances of the Christian in the present state. But a peaceful joy is what may be not only attained, but preserved amidst every vicissitude and trial. Rapture we are not required to cherish; but "the peace of God which passeth all understanding," is what we are frequently directed to seek, and it is promised to an unwavering dependance on the Saviour. Peace is the legacy which Christ left to his disciples, in the immediate anticipation of his sufferings and death; but rapture is reserved for that world where no sin is felt, where no temptation is known, where no

...darkness overspreads the prospect with gloom. But where death, and the curse are done away, and the Lord God himself is an "everlasting light and glory."

The joy of the Christian is also marked by its solidity, and its satisfying influence. In this respect, it is incalculably superior to every other species of pleasure. Ask the sensualist whether his career of dissipation has afforded him any real or lasting enjoyment; and if he make a candid acknowledgment, he will confess that the gratifications which he so eagerly pursues, never yet communicated to him one particle of rational or solid satisfaction, that pleasure still recedes from his grasp, and vanishes from his view. Ask the man of ambition, if the honours at which he has even successfully aspired are able to sooth his mind, and repay him for the toil and anxiety he has undergone for the sake of his present elevation. If he is truly honest he will readily admit that " the honour which cometh from man,' is incapable of yielding substantial felicity, and that exaltation above others, whether obtained through the medium of opulence, of literature, or of any other circumstance, is inadequate to the production of one peaceful hour, or of one elevated sensation. Of the truth of these remarks, we have a memorable confirmation in the experience, and the testimony, of Solomon. He was favoured with access to all the advantages and gratifications which earth could afford, yet he was nevertheless dissatisfied, disconsolate, and unhappy; and after a calm deliberate review and estimate of all sublunary good, he was compelled to make the mortifying confession, " All is vanity and vexation of spirit." " Even in laughter, says he, " the heart is sorrowful, and the end of that mirth is heaviness.—True religion however, an interest in the favour and love of God, grounded on faith in the atonement of Christ, is able to cheer the soul, and to impart to the mind unutterable satisfaction. The man who has God for his portion, experiences a felicity " which the world knoweth not," " a joy which is unspeakable, and full of glory." He possesses a richer patrimony than the most wealthy or elevated of mortals; he enjoys that which is preferable to the whole universe besides; he is the heir of " an inheritance which is incorruptible, undefiled, and that fadeth not away." When a person is the subject of the pleasure which we are now considering, his desires are perfectly satisfied, he longs no more for the joys which worldly amusements or sinful gratifications can afford; but possesses within himself the elements of happiness produced by the diffusion of the love of God through his soul. His former thirst for the delights of sin is now quenched by that water which Christ gives to every fainting soul, and which is " in him a well of water springing up unto everlasting life."

It is hoped that, in the remarks which have already been made, the more prominent and characteristic features of religious joy have been, in the main scripturally, however faintly and imperfectly, delineated. The remainder of this paper shall be devoted to the specification of a few considerations adapted to impress on the mind of the Christian the importance of cultivating this excellent disposition.

One very powerful reason which presents itself on this point is that which is derived from the intimations of the will of God, furnished by his general nature and diversified operations. The character of the Deity is that of pure benevolence. The whole of his perfections are comprised by an Apostle, in that beautiful definition, " God is love." Even his justice, which appears to sustain but a remote affinity to love, is only a slight modification of that attribute; for it is never exercised but with a view to promote the ultimate and general happiness of his creatures, and a greater portion of enjoyment will, without doubt, on the whole, be secured by its operation, than could possibly result from its neglect and infringement. From this scriptural representation of the Divine character, the accordance of that state of mind which has been recommended with the general intentions and will of God, may be inferred with the strictest accuracy. The same conclusion may be drawn from the manifestations of the Divine benevolence observable in the system of creation, and especially in the complicated structure of the human frame. All the indispensable functions of life might have been performed, so far as we can perceive, without the perception, on our part, of any pleasure from the performance. Our bodies might have been so constituted that food would have contributed effectually to their nourishment without affording us the least grateful sensation. The eye might, no doubt, have been constructed in such a mode as to receive the rays of light, and to discriminate colours and objects while nothing which we beheld should have been capable of gratifying the sight or of yielding us pleasure, through the medium of our visual organs. In like manner the ear might have been so formed that it should distinguish, with perfect correctness, every variety of sound and yet be unsusceptible of delight from any tone, or from any combination of tones.* Let it be recollected, that he has made this beneficent arrangement for beings who deserve his severest displeasure, and that the specimens of his goodness here mentioned are selected only from an immense variety of similar instances which the universe supplies, and which fully establish his claims to the character of the most disinterested benevolence. But, in the most impressive manner, has he displayed the infinite goodness of his nature, by sending his only begotten Son to die for our transgressions, to purify our hearts, and to fit us for a state of inconceivable dignity and bliss and if we have rightly accepted of the salvation offered in the Gospel, the Almighty regards us with the complacency of a Father, and is willing that we should appropriate to ourselves all the consolation and joy which an interest in his paternal love can warrant.

The positive commands of God in the sacred oracles are accordant with the preceding view of his character and enforce the obligation to religious joy. To this purpose may be cited numerous passages, both in the Old Testament and the New. At the beginning of the thirty third Psalm David says, " Rejoice in the Lord, O ye righteous for praise is comely for the upright. In another of his devout and beautiful compositions, he says, " Let the righteous be glad let them rejoice before God yea, let them exceedingly rejoice. A variety of other passages of a similar nature may be found in the Old Testament. In the New the same sentiment is frequently conveyed, and the same duty explicitly enjoined. While the disciples of our Lord were forbidden to rejoice on the ground of " the

---

* The reader is referred to Dr Paley's very ingenious illustration of this subject in his Principles of Moral and Political Philosophy. The following passage besides being connected with the argument above noticed possesses so much intrinsic merit, that I trust no apology is requisite for the quotation. When God created the human species either he wished their happiness or he wished their misery or he was indifferent and unconcerned about both. If he had wished our misery he might have made sure of his purpose by forming our senses to be as many sores and pains to us as they are now instruments of gratification and enjoyment or by placing us amidst objects so ill-suited to our perceptions as to have continually offended us instead of ministering to our refreshment and delight. He might have made for example every thing we tasted bitter every thing we saw loathsome, every thing we touched a sting every smell a stench and every sound a discord."

devils having been made subject to them, they were, at the same time, exhorted to rejoice that their names were written in heaven. Of course if we possess a scriptural hope that our circumstances are in this respect analogous to theirs, that our names are inscribed in the Lamb's book of life, it is equally our privilege with the Apostles to cultivate a spirit of perpetual joy. In the First Epistle to the Thessalonians, St. Paul directs Christians to "rejoice evermore"; and in his subsequent Epistle he says, "Finally, my brethren, rejoice in the Lord." And as if these injunctions were not sufficient, he afterwards delivers a command to the same purpose, and enforces it by a very emphatic repetition "Rejoice in the Lord alway, and again I say, Rejoice." In short, the portions of Scripture which inculcate on believers the duty of religious joy, are too numerous to be specified in the present essay. It is therefore incumbent upon them to aim at the acquisition of habitual serenity and cheerfulness of mind. Their obligations to this duty rest on the same foundation as their obligations to be honest, to be humble, to be spiritually minded, or zealous in the service of God. The same Divine and Glorious Being prescribes all the duties in question.

The argument receives additional strength from a consideration of the evils which the absence of religious joy implies or produces. In reference to the persons themselves, it argues ingratitude and unbelief, as well as unfits them for the performance of incumbent duty. When we are habitually disconsolate and sorrowful, we tacitly declare that we feel little or no gratitude for the past tokens of the Divine goodness we have experienced. And surely a desponding ungrateful temper of mind is a very improper return for the various mercies, temporal and spiritual, of which every true Christian is made the recipient. Such a disposition must certainly be displeasing to God; and, if treated according to its desert, would be visited with a discontinuance of his benefits. Were we to confer special obligations on one of our fellow-creatures, who, instead of appearing delighted or thankful, shewed that he was still dissatisfied and ungrateful, we should regret the bestowment of the alleged advantages, and be careful to avoid a repetition of them in future. How equitably might the infinite Jehovah thus reward those professed Christians, who, notwithstanding all the sources of enjoyment to which they have access, seem as it were to cultivate a spirit of depression and gloom! Besides, this absence of religious joy indicates, not only ingratitude for past favours, but distrust for future blessings. God has assured us as plainly as language can declare it, that he "will never leave us nor forsake us," and has appealed to our common sympathy and apprehensions by saying, "He that spared not his own Son, but delivered him up for us all, how shall he not with him also freely give us all things?" This appeal ought to be irresistible, because it is founded on a fact which evinces in the strongest manner the love and mercy of God to our souls. Now when we cherish gloomy forebodings, and dark anticipations, we distrust the testimony which God has given of his own character, as well as his declarations of regard for our welfare. We thus charge him, as it were, with falsehood, for "he that believeth not God hath made him a liar." The criminality attached to the neglect of a cheerful state of mind, is therefore obvious, since it involves ingratitude and unbelief.—It has also a tendency to unfit the individual for the active and profitable discharge of his duties. When the soul is cast down and disconsolate, the energies are paralyzed, the mind is enfeebled, and the individual rendered incapable of those zealous efforts which otherwise he could make with facility and success. This disposition of mind also, if indulged to a considerable extent, may even prevent the subject of it from devoting a sufficient degree of attention to the lawful and necessary avocations of life. The evil consequences of this habit are too evident to require specification. As we then value the right performance of duty, let us diligently cultivate a spirit of perpetual cheerfulness. This will communicate ardour to all our efforts for the glory of God, and impel us forward in the way to eternal happiness. Thus shall we find that ' the joy of the Lord is our strength,' both for the discharge of commanded duty, and the suffering of allotted trial.

Nor are the evil effects of the want of this disposition, confined to the person himself; they extend their pernicious influence to unnumbered individuals, and operate in an incalculable variety of modes. All men are certainly engaged in the pursuit of happiness; and in a qualified sense it may be affirmed, that we all ought to seek happiness. This being the case, persons in general will judge of the obligations of religion, by its apparent tendency to promote the felicity of those who comply with its dictates. Many persons are incompetent, and still more disinclined, to investigate the abstract evidences of religion; but the greater proportion of mankind, whatever may be the complexion of their moral or intellectual character, are able in some measure, to ascertain whether or not religion makes its professors happy. Now, if they perceive in these persons nothing but the symptoms of gloom, dissatisfaction, and anxiety, they will be furnished with a pretext for refusing obedience to the requisitions of Christianity. On the other hand, nothing tends so much to recommend religion to the esteem and acceptance of mankind as a disposition, in those who profess it habitually cheerful or serene. When we are not only correct in our deportment but grateful and happy in the temper of our minds, we shew that we delight in the service of God, that his commandments are not grievous, that the "yoke of Christ is easy, and his burden is light." We shew that we love God and his ways in sincerity, and that we do not observe any precept of Scripture merely from constraint or compulsion, but from a principle of attachment to the service of God. In this manner, we may be the instruments of winning souls to Christ; and though the providence of God may not call us to advocate the claims of religion in an official capacity, we may speak to all around us in language not less intelligible or persuasive. At all events, we shall take away the ground for an objection which is frequently adduced against true piety, and shall exhibit to the world a practical proof, that religion has a salutary influence on the present, as well as the future happiness of those who obey its sacred dictates.

But as we cannot, notwithstanding all the provision which God has made for our comfort, anticipate perfect felicity in this state of imperfection and trial, our highest source of repose should be in looking forward to that world where joy will be complete and eternal. There the sky is ever bright and cloudless, and the prospect irradiated with the beams of the Sun of Righteousness. There no sin obtains admission, and consequently no sorrow. There the beatified spirit of the righteous, admitted to the presence of his God and Saviour, without the intervention of a single cloud, will enjoy pleasures unmingled with pain, and eternal as their all bountiful Author. "The ransomed of the Lord shall return, and come to Zion with songs, and everlasting joy upon their heads; they shall obtain joy and gladness, and sorrow and sighing shall flee away."

C.

FAMILY SERMONS—No. CCIII.

James i. 12.—Blessed is the man that endureth temptation.

TEMPTATION means, in Scripture, either an enticement to what is sinful, or an affliction by which God is pleased to try the faith and patience of his servants. St James, in the chapter from which the text is taken, uses the word in both these senses. "My brethren," he says, "count it all joy when ye fall into divers temptations," that is, chiefly, into afflictions and persecutions for the sake of Christ, "knowing that the trial of your faith worketh patience." These painful dispensations were divinely permitted, in order to exercise the Christian graces of faith, perseverance, and acquiescence in the will of God. But there were trials of another kind; trials not so much of the Christian's patience, and constancy under affliction, as of his renovation of heart, his holiness and his aversion to sin. Of these last, St James says, in the verses which follow the text, 'Let no man say when he is tempted," that is, to evil, " I am tempted of God: for God cannot be tempted with evil, neither tempteth he any man: but every man is tempted when he is drawn away of his own lust, and enticed.' In either case, however, whether the trial of our patience, or the trial of any other virtue of the Christian character, ' blessed is the man that endureth the temptation;' that is, who remains unconquered by its assault, coming out from the furnace like gold seven times refined. There is no blessedness in the mere circumstance of being called upon to suffer affliction; still less is there any thing desirable, but, on the contrary, much that is most perilous and awful, in being exposed to the allurements of evil: but the blessedness mentioned in the text consists in surviving the conflict, and in the proof which is hence derived of the reality and firmness of those principles which enabled the tempted person to withstand the dangerous encounter: to which the Apostle adds that "he shall receive the crown of life, which the Lord hath promised to them that love him." Whether tempted to evil, or called upon to bear suffering, the remembrance of this crown should excite us to " endure hardness as good soldiers of Jesus Christ," in the exercise, as the case may require, either of the passive graces which lead us to bear trouble, or the active graces which lead us to repel the allurements to sin. The text from its connexion with each of these kinds of temptation, as described in the verses that go before and that follow it, may perhaps refer in a measure to both of them; but chiefly to that which arises from a state of affliction, and to temptations to evil only as they spring from that source; as was the case with the first Christians whose persecutions for the cause of Christ operated as powerful temptations to forsake him, and to go back to their former state of worldliness and irreligion. In the present remarks, however, we shall confine our attention to that species of temptation from which our greatest danger arises; namely, that against which we daily pray, in the words which our Lord himself taught us, ' Lead us not into temptation, but deliver us from evil.' And here we shall consider,—First, The sources of temptation; secondly, How we may be enabled to overcome it; and thirdly, The blessedness of those who thus endure.

First, then, what are the sources of temptation? These are briefly and scripturally pointed out in our baptismal vow and in the catechism of our church; in both of which we are taught to renounce ' the devil and all his works, the pomps and vanities of this wicked world, and all the sinful lusts of the flesh.' And accordingly in the litany, we constantly pray against " the deceits of the world, the flesh, and the

days. We ought therefore to be well acquainted with the nature of these deceits, in order that we may not be overcome by them.

1. One source of temptation is from the world. We are exposed to danger from the false opinions and evil practices of too many of those around us; from irreligious conversation, from persuasions to what is sinful, from the vanities of life, from a desire for the honour that cometh from man, more than the approbation of God; from the snares of riches or pleasure; in short, according to the language of St John, from "whatever is not of the Father, but of the world." This is a source of temptation from which it is impossible to escape, so long as we remain in the present life. Whatever may be our temporal condition, whether we are rich or poor, young or old, in prosperity or adversity, in sickness or in health, the world, in some one or more of its forms, will continue to surround us, and to draw us to what is evil. This source of temptation we are earnestly to avoid; for "Christ gave himself for our sins, that he might deliver us from this present evil world;" so that if we are following its wrong courses, however plausible or attractive they may appear, we are none of his.

2. We are to avoid temptations arising from ourselves, from those enticements to what is wrong which spring from our own evil hearts, or our depraved passions and desires. We are by nature so selfish, and so ready to indulge our corrupt inclinations, even though we know that they are forbidden by the law of God, that the greatest watchfulness and prayer are necessary that we may be on our guard against this inlet to evil. Even if the world should cease to tempt us, we should still be in danger from ourselves; and what renders this danger the greater is, according to our Lord's own warnings, that we may commit sin in the heart, even though we should not proceed to any open act of transgression. The temptation to envy, to covetousness, to anger, to immorality, may be secretly listened to, and we may be involved in the guilt of cherishing it, and thus be condemned by the great Searcher of hearts, at the very time when, before our fellow-creatures, our conduct is free from suspicion or reproach. Especially in this class of temptations, arising from ourselves, ought we to include the danger of forgetting God, of being insensible to his mercies, of repining at his providence, of not submitting ourselves to his will, and of preferring our own ways to the requisitions of his law.

3. The third source of temptation is the secret agency of satan, "who as a roaring lion walketh about, seeking whom he may devour." We cannot, indeed, distinguish between his evil promptings and those of our own hearts; but we may in general include among them those sins which he is spoken of in Scripture as particularly suggesting. Thus our Saviour says to the Jews, "Ye are of your father the devil; and the lusts of your father ye will do: he was a murderer from the beginning, and abode not in the truth, because there is no truth in him: when he speaketh a lie, he speaketh of his own, for he is a liar and the father of it." Here we are taught to trace the sins of fraud and falsehood, of envy and hatred and revenge, to the temptations of the devil. So again Elymas the sorcerer is called by St Peter the "child of the devil, because he was full of subtlety and mischief," an "enemy of all righteousness," and 'did not cease to pervert the right ways of the Lord.' The temptation to pride is further spoken of by St Paul, as 'the condemnation of the devil.' Envying, strife, vain glory, and "lying against the truth," are denominated by St James as devilish as well as 'earthly and sensual.' These and other passages of Scripture should teach us to be aware of the tempta-

tions of our spiritual enemy, who ever finds in our own hearts, and in the corrupting influence of the world around us, the most powerful aids to allure us into the snares which he spreads for our destruction.

Secondly. We are now, in the next place, to inquire how we may be enabled to overcome temptation. The following directions may, by the blessing of God, be useful for this purpose, whatever may be the source from which the temptation comes.

1. We should cherish an habitual consciousness of our own weakness. "A haughty spirit, says Solomon, 'goeth before a fall;' and never are we so likely to be led astray as when we put confidence in our own ability to resist temptation. We see this illustrated by numerous examples in Scripture. Hazael said, "Is thy servant a dog that he should do this great wickedness?" yet he almost immediately committed it. St. Peter said, "Though all men should deny thee, yet will not I;" yet before the cock crowed twice he thrice denied his Divine Master. Warned, therefore, of our frailty, even at our best estate, let us constantly mistrust our own hearts, and thus avoid the delusive influence of a proud and dangerous self security.

2. We should shun, as much as possible, the sources of temptation. We cannot, indeed, "go out of the world," but we should seek to be kept from its evil; we cannot be divested of "the body of sin and death," but we must strive to mortify its affections and lusts; and we should also be ever on our guard against plunging ourselves into circumstances of which our spiritual enemy may take advantage to draw us into a snare. We are not sincere in our professed wish to walk in the way of God's commandments if we do not avoid whatever might draw us aside from them. We cannot live safely in the atmosphere of temptation; voluntarily to breathe it is to perish; our only safety is in a knowledge of our danger, and in instant flight from the scene of peril.

3. We should be armed beforehand against the approach of temptation. For this purpose we should practise self examination, to know where our chief weakness lies, and there especially we should keep a vigilant guard over ourselves. We should be habitually prepared with the whole armour of God, in order to resist the wiles of the devil. We should seek to grow strong in holy principles and devout affections; we should cherish a constant sense of God's presence, and a holy reverence for his laws; we should reflect upon the guilt and the folly of provoking him to wrath; and we should call to mind the love of Christ in dying for the sins of the world, and the base ingratitude of offending against it. This habitual state of mind will be a powerful check against the incursions of temptation.

4. We must resist temptation when it comes. The same considerations which are to fore arm us against its approach should be earnestly made use of upon its arrival. Temptation is harmless when prepared for and strenuously resisted; but we are in danger the moment we listen to the evil suggestion. We must therefore use, without delay, all the means which God has mercifully presented to us for repelling it; and above all, conscious of our own weakness, we must earnestly seek for his assistance, that we may be enabled to overcome the violence or resist the insidiousness of the assault.

5. We are thus led to the last means which will be mentioned for overcoming temptation, namely, casting ourselves upon the protecting grace of God, in earnest prayer for his assistance. In vain, without this would be all our wishes or efforts; but with this we are safe amidst every danger; for "he will not suffer us to be tempted beyond what we are able to bear; but will, with the temptation, make a way

for our escape." He has given us numerous promises to this effect: and, above all, he has provided for us "a merciful High Priest, "who can be touched with the feeling of our infirmities, having been tempted in all points like as we are, yet without sin." Fixing the eye of faith steadily upon him, both as our example and our strength, we shall find his promise to St. Paul fulfilled in our behalf: "My grace is sufficient for thee:" and shall be enabled with the same Apostle to reply, "When I am weak, then am I strong:" 'I can do all things through Christ that strengtheneth me.'"

Thirdly. Having thus spoken of the sources of temptation, and pointed out some assistances for overcoming it, we are to shew the blessedness of those who do so. The Scriptures abound with promises to those who by the grace of God, thus endure to the end: "Be thou faithful unto death, and I will give thee a crown of life." In particular, in numerous passages in the Book of the Revelations are promises made to 'him that overcometh.' Thus it is said, "I will give to him to eat of the tree of life;" and again, "he shall not be hurt of the second death;" and again, "I will give to him to eat of the hidden manna;" and again, "I will make him a pillar in the temple of God, and he shall go no more out;" "I will grant to him," says the Saviour, "to sit with me in my throne, even as I also overcame, and am sat down with my Father in his throne;" "he shall inherit all things, and I will be his God, and he shall be my son." It is no trifling interest, then, that is at stake: it is our immortal soul, our eternal welfare in the world to come. If we follow the temptations of the world, the flesh, and the devil, we forfeit all that is most valuable,—the favour of God, our own salvation, and the glories of heaven: and we incur all that is most awful,—his righteous displeasure, and our own eternal ruin. Which portion then are we seeking: the vain short lived pleasures of this world, or the never ending blessedness of those who resist the temptation to yield to its attractions, and live upon earth as candidates for heaven? The inspired Apostle, in our text, pronounced those to be blessed who, for the sake of Christ, endured the most grievous persecutions, because "when tried, they should receive the crown of life, which the Lord hath promised to them that love him." No sinful temptation offers to us any enjoyment that can for a moment be put in competition with this unspeakable reward of glory. Let us then, through the promised assistance of God's Holy Spirit, reject every bribe presented to us by the world, the flesh, and the devil, to allure us from the path of love and obedience to God: and let us press onward in faith, humility, and true devotion of heart to the service of our Creator and Redeemer, towards the prize of our high calling of God in Christ Jesus. The conflict, however arduous, will soon end: and its issue will be an eternal triumph to all who have fought the good fight of faith, under the banners of the Captain of their salvation: and who, having endured the trials, and surmounted the temptations, of this mortal life, shall receive, through the free mercy of God in Christ Jesus, an abundant entrance into that blessed world, where sorrow and temptation are for ever unknown.

MISCELLANEOUS

For the Christian Observer

ON INFANT EDUCATION, AS PRACTISED IN SOME INFANTS SCHOOLS.

INFANTS' schools are formed for the purpose of the preparatory education of as many children, under the age of seven years, as may be regulated by two individuals, a master and a mistress. The circumstances must be peculiarly favourable, where more than one hundred and fifty children can be educated in such an establishment.

The principal object in an infants school, is to form the moral and religious character of the children and this is proposed to be done by the prevention or cure of those evil dispositions which are incident to that tender age, and by the communication of the more simple principles of religion in that form in which they are most likely to commend themselves to their understandings and their hearts. It is hoped to effect to a considerable degree the prevention of immoral habits, by withdrawing the children for a few hours of each day, from the influence of that promiscuous example which too often presents itself in the neighbourhoods of the poor and by forming, in a room of sufficient dimensions, a little society which is constantly under the eye of a religious and intelligent, as well as affectionate, individual, who may use his utmost endeavours to discover amongst them, and to correct the earliest appearances of what is wrong.

Beyond, however, this negative effect of the system of infants schools, it is found that if the business of the little society be always connected with that which is pleasurable to the infant mind, children will almost insensibly form their habits of thinking and feeling from what they see around them. While the vices of the human mind which most early unfold their evil tendencies, (I mention for the present only three—falsehood, dishonesty, and revenge,) are thus almost imperceptibly corrected excellency of conduct becomes desirable by becoming the source of real gratification.

In such an institution it will obviously appear, much will depend on the dispositions and characters of the master and mistress. If they have not a real love for moral excellence and the pure and reasonable principles of religion they will be unprepared to communicate those principles and habits to the children for, after all, where books and other artificial instruments of instruction are but partially used the teachers must be themselves the fountain of every influence which they wish to communicate. At this early age, knowledge of every kind presents itself in a more especial connexion with the senses, and unobstructed by prejudice, or habit, or any abstract mode of inquiry obtains an almost immediate reception, and exercises an almost immediate influence. The teacher then must be the moral book of his school and the great precept of our religion must be imprinted on every action, and on every change of his countenance. "Love one another." He may successfully endeavour to build upon this every other principle which may have relation to the character of a good neighbour, a good citizen, and a good subject such as order, obedience, loyalty but the foundation of all his moral instructions and the declared principle of all his own actions, must be *Christian charity*.

In the farther prosecution of this part of his duty, the teacher must inform the minds of the children, who are supposed to be of too early an age to receive instruction by books on the subject of morals and religion, by *familiar conversation*. The great principles and the more prominent precepts of religion, all imply the previous acknowledgment of certain simple and original truths. These preliminary truths, or, if I may so express myself, these axioms of a religious life may in this manner be successfully impressed on the mind of an infant. I will endeavour to give an instance of what I intend to express.

The duty of prayer is incumbent on every man and it is perhaps one of those duties the obligation to which we should wish at the most early age to impress on the mind of a child. On what principles, then, does the duty of prayer rest? Amongst many others, on the following:—God is present every where. God knows all things. God sees me. God can understand the thoughts of my heart. God can do all things. God is merciful. All good things come from God. God will give what is good, if I pray to him.

It must also be manifest, that, previously to the attainment of the art of reading, the histories and examples of Scripture, connected with the various subjects of religion, may be effectually impressed on the memory and the heart of an infant, by conversational instruction and by graphic representations. First of all, the life of the Saviour may be set before him; and, in succession, that of those persons whose character is handed down to us in the sacred volume, in illustration of any particular precept of religion. It will not, moreover, be without an immediate good effect, if, after having deeply infixed on the minds of the little pupils the idea of the sacred character of the volume of inspiration, they are taught to commit to memory, in the words of the Bible, some of the more simple precepts, or even doctrines, which are there to be found. It must however, here especially, and also in relation to every part of the instruction of infants, be borne in mind, that it is desirable, in such an attempt, not to exercise the memory to weariness. They must be taught by reiteration but it is not necessary to complete the lesson at one time. To say over, or to repeat a sentence, may be made an amusement: to learn a task must be an effort which, in the great majority of instances, at so early an age, will be accompanied by painful, and therefore repulsive, sensations.

The principal aim, then, of the system of infant education is, by congregating into one society a certain number of children under seven years of age, to throw around them a moral influence, and, by connecting the practice as well as the knowledge of that which is excellent with pleasurable emotions, to induce, as far as may be possible, a predisposition to that which may tend to the formation of a good character, and to the obedience of the mind to the principles of religion.

Having thus, however, laid the foundation of the education of the human mind in morals and religion, very much may also be done in order to dispose it for the action of life. The mind may be prepared for knowledge, and led forward into some of the subjects of general instruction in common schools whilst at the same time, under judicious regulations, certain of the earlier difficulties which attend the attainment of some of the more simple and necessary arts of life, may, with a little perseverance, be overcome.

It is obvious, that there are many subjects of *general information* to which the mind of an infant may be very easily directed. The book of creation, for instance, lies at all times before him. He has already received the idea of a horse, or a cow, or a dog, or perhaps of most of the animals around his dwelling. He knows the more prominent characteristics of a tree, and perhaps the names of some of its parts

Now these, and a multitude of other things, may be made the sources of knowledge to him. He may be taught to recognize the representation of them, to observe their various parts, to describe their culture, and their uses in connexion with the arts of life. And this mode of instruction may be carried forward to any extent, and may derive its sources from all the varied circumstances by which a child must be supposed to be surrounded.

With relation to those points of the education promoted in an infants' school, which are more especially prospective of the subsequent instruction of the child, much care is requisite.

I shall here suppose that it is intended to prepare the infants for instruction in arithmetic, reading, and writing.

Arithmetic.—Now the system of infant education regards the combinations of numbers as the foundation of arithmetic; and, without immediate regard to the art, we attempt to lay the foundation of it by directing our attention first to those efforts of mind which are connected with these combinations. When, for instance, the children have accurately accustomed themselves to the following modes of combination, through any range of number which may be thought requisite, it will be believed that they may proceed with every hope of success, to the earlier efforts in the arithmetical art.

Addition.—72 and 9 are 81. 81 and 9 are 90.

Subtraction.—9 from 90 leave 81. 9 from 81 leave 72.

Multiplication.—9 times 8 are 72. 9 times 9 are 81. 9 times 10 are 90.

Division.—9 in 72, 8 times. 9 in 81, 9 times. 9 in 90, 10 times.

Fractions.—9 is $\frac{1}{8}$ of 72. 9 is $\frac{1}{9}$ of 81. 9 is $\frac{1}{10}$ of 90.

This habit having been acquired, the children may proceed to the more useful tables; and when they have attained the power of reading figures, before they can with facility write them, the master may practise them in some simple efforts in the arithmetical art, by himself describing the figures with chalk, either on a sufficiently large slate, or on a black board prepared for that purpose.

Reading.—In the next place, the system of infant education regards the combination of certain sounds, as the foundation of the art of reading; and therefore, in the communication of this art, directs our attention first to those sounds. On this principle, we teach the children first to enunciate the alphabet. When this has been learned with accuracy and distinctness *by the ear*, the letters are then presented separately to the eye, and the children are taught to recognize them as the forms and representatives of that with the sound of which they have already been made familiar. We proceed in the same manner with syllables and words. A selection is made of the words which most frequently occur, and of the more common primary and final syllables. These the children are taught, first by the ear, to spell; so that they become acquainted with the combinations of sound which form most of the common words of the language, before they have been presented to their eye. In order to this further step, the same words and syllables are printed on cards, or impressed on pieces of tin, each of which is from time to time placed in the hand of the child; to whom, having previously learned the separate letters, and their combined sound in the word, the art of reading is become altogether a simple effort. It is needless that I should add that the progress from these cards to the use of books is easy, as the knowledge of the words which most frequently occur has thus been already acquired.

Writing.—It is not necessary to detain the reader long on the subject of the acquirement of the art of writ ing. It must be regarded, in the first instance, as a system of forms and the child should be accustomed to read writing, and describe the parts of a letter, before he is suffered to commence the attainment of the art which is done by the imitation on a slate of a letter, or part of a letter, described by the master on the large black board.

In proceeding to another point in the subject of infant education, I may be permitted to express a regret, that education in general has not been more universally connected with the action of human life. Had it been made to bear more immediately upon the duties and the necessities, as well as the pleasures, of the station in which the life of the individual is to be thereafter passed, its beneficial effects would, I am persuaded, have been more manifest, and more universal.

We have been able to introduce into our infants schools several works of industry. The children soon acquire a moderate proficiency in the arts of sewing, and of plaiting straw for bonnets and hats. While this prepares them in some small measure for the business of after life, it tends also to fix their attention and is at the same time a means of real pleasure and amusement.

I have thus endeavoured to describe some of the principal parts of the education, and some of the more important subjects of instruction, in well conducted infants schools. Bearing in mind the preceding remarks, the reader will readily follow the attempt which I am about to make, to unfold some of the operations which take place in them.

The Infant School at Walthamstow, which I will take as an example, is divided into three principal parts:—the body of the larger room, around which all the several classes are arranged in order; the class room whither one or more classes occasionally retire for examination and individual instruction, and a certain space in the larger room, where the more advanced children practise mutual examination in those things which are more immediately connected with the instruction of the schools, to which they are afterward to be removed.

In the large room, the progress of instruction is twofold. All things which are addressed to the ear alone, such as the combinations of numbers, the easier tables, spelling, hymns or precepts of Scripture, the children there learn by reiteration in one class, standing in their respective places round the room. They receive the lesson from one of the older children, or from the master himself, standing in some conspicuous place, to whom they unitedly respond. In the large room also, the school is divided into classes each of which is watched and instructed by an older boy, who teaches them by the eye that which they have already learned, in one class, by the ear. Figures, letters, and words, are learned in this manner.

In the class room, the examination and instruction become individual. There reading is pursued to a greater measure of accuracy, there arithmetic is taught and there also the histories and narratives of Scripture are communicated, and its precepts explained and enforced.

The space set apart in the larger room for the exercise of the more advanced children, is used by them occasionally for mutual examination in Scripture history, mental calculation, or spelling.

In establishing an infants school it is of the utmost importance not to indulge at first too high an expectation of immediate success. Persons who have witnessed one in full operation are in considerable danger of subjecting themselves to disappointment in this respect. The progress of such an institution must under even the most favourable circumstances, be gradual if not slow, but, where sufficient pains is exercised, the event is certain. It is far better to begin the operations of such a school with not more than fifty children. When these are reduced to any measure of order, their example will aid the teacher in giving efficiency to the system over any larger number which it may be thought right to introduce. The first few days, or even weeks, will be well spent in arranging the school, in teaching the infants to imitate the master; to clap their hands, or stamp with their feet, when he does so; or to move their arms in the same manner as himself. He may teach them to step to the beat of a tambourine; to be silent when he rings his bell; to whisper when he uses some other sign. Something of a moral character will be attained when he has proceeded even thus far; obedience, attention, order, rhythm, all of which will be important aids to the future success of his plans.

The course of intellectual instruction must be regulated by circumstances; but it must always be the endeavour of the instructor rather to do a little well, than to make an appearance of improvement, without its substantial qualities.

The final result, I have said, is certain, and in this I speak in a great measure from experience. An infants' school will perhaps never present that uniform appearance of silent order and exact formal arrangement which offers itself in those for older children. It is perhaps hardly desirable that it should do so. Whatever destroys the pleasurable feeling which is encouraged in these institutions, must also throw a shade over the moral influence which it is the principal aim to promote in them. A considerable measure, however, of even silent attention may be secured; and although it is impossible to keep so large a body of children at so early an age, from the occasional influence of that variable state of feeling to which the infant mind must be expected to be subject, the elements of *general* order may always be effectually preserved,—the order of time, of lessons, of manner, and of place.

A good education is said to be that which teaches the human mind " to derive pleasure and pain from the right sources." Such is the undeviating purpose of the system which I have thus endeavoured, very briefly, to unfold; and, so far as they have fallen under my own notice, the results have been in every respect satisfactory. Moral evil has been removed. Brotherly love has been called into action. The incipient forms of an excellent and useful character have made their appearance; and the love of knowledge has been promoted. It is only left to us to desire that these institutions may meet with that countenance and support which they so eminently deserve, and that the system by which they are at present regulated may receive additional improvements under the yet more extensive observation of those who, from the experience which they have attained in the education of the human mind, at other periods of life, may be justly supposed to be the persons most competent to conduct it to its perfection.

W. W.

To the Editor of the Christian Observer.

THE inclosed extract from Mr. Carey's "Journal of a Tour in France," relative to the state of religion in that country, appears to me so generally interesting that I solicit its insertion in your pages.

H. D.

" We had observed in our journey from Avignon, all through Provence, and as far as Carcassonne, in Languedoc, a great number of crucifixes standing by the side of the roads; and in the towns and villages some had lately been erected, and old ones replaced. The churches were repaired and newly ornamented, and attended daily by crowds of both sexes. From Carcassonne to Bourdeaux we did not see a single new cross, or any others, except now and then one broken and lying on the ground in decay. The churches in the towns too, appeared neglected, and sparingly decorated, and the majority of those who frequented them were women. The Catholic religion is calculated so strongly to impel its votaries to manifest their piety by these outward and ostensible symbols, that wherever it is sincerely professed, they must of necessity appear; therefore, in all Catholic countries where they are not to be found, it may be fairly considered as indicating an absence of religious feeling in the community. French people themselves always speak of their defection from Christianity as being the work of the Revolution; but the mischief was of an older date. The higher classes had not for years attempted to conceal their infidelity; they affected to consider religion merely as an engine of state, to keep the common people in order; and it cannot be a matter of wonder, that by degrees the common people should adopt the opinion, that they were as well able to do without religion as their superiors. Scraps of infidelity, sarcasms on the priesthood, and sneers at revelation, were disseminated amongst them with indefatigable industry; and unfortunately they had no armour to repel these insidious attacks. Ignorant of the grounds of their belief, they scarcely knew the contents of the Bible, but by the ridicule that was levelled against it. Wherever the Bible is in the hands of the people (which it may truly be said to be when it is printed in the language of the country, sold openly in the shops, and read publicly in the churches,) Christianity stands on its own basis: the waves may beat, and the winds blow, but it is built on a rock not to be shaken. The Bible is in itself a tower of strength; and although individuals may be drawn aside, yet it appears almost impossible that a whole nation should lose their faith, supported by such a bulwark. The French had it not, and their faith had given way. Sapped by degrees, no apparent change took place in their morals. The power of habit, the long established rules of society, originally grounded on Christian principles, the restraint of public opinion, and the fear of the laws, prevent any great aberrations in individuals whilst these ties remain undisturbed; but put them in a moment aside, break through established habits, the curb of opinion, and the fear of the laws, and then the mischief will stand bare and naked. The Revolution did all this; and the horrid and unexampled atrocities that ensued, proclaimed the people devoid of Christianity as loudly as they did themselves when they renounced their Saviour, and bowed the knee to the goddess of reason.

"We were in Paris in the year 1802, soon after the Government had deemed it expedient to re-establish the forms of Christianity; and I observed a curious inscription on the door of the church of St. Roch, purporting, that on such a day, the French nation would recognize the immortality of the soul. It appeared to me, then that a total indifference to religion discovered itself even in the very act of resuming its ceremonies. The eyes of the people had been opened to the errors and superstitions of the Church of Rome, which had been exposed and ridiculed. If a religious sentiment had really actuated the rulers of the land, they would have considered, while it was yet in their power, whether a creed more enlightened and conformable to the doctrine of the Scriptures might not be adopted. I have been told that the Directory had it once in contemplation to establish some form of Protestant worship; but a man of great weight, La Reveillère, opposed the measure strenuously for being, unhappily, a bigoted Deist, he was very anxious to impose his own dogmas on the nation. The rest were afraid of a second edition of the goddess of reason; and therefore to cut the matter short, voted for the restoration of the ancient church with all its imperfections on its head,—a most unfortunate decision! Not only religion itself had been vilified in the eyes of the people, but its ministers had also been rendered odious, not as being bigots, superstitious fools and blind professors of a blind faith, but as being impostors, impostors by trade, who, for worldly purposes, promulgated, and endeavoured to impose on the belief of others doctrines which they themselves held to be false. Now, there were unprincipled men amongst them, who, by boasting of their infidelity and past hypocrisy, justified the accusation and the notoriety of its truth, in these acknowledged instances, gave countenance to the opinion that it was true in all. The priesthood was thus deprived of the accumulated respect of ages, and loaded with obloquy, nor could the people be easily brought to listen with reverence to a body of men, whom they had been so sedulously taught to regard with distrust and abhorrence. Under these disadvantages, it is not so surprising that religion should be slow to revive in France, as that it should revive at all; however, it has revived, though partially. In some provinces the whole population display a spirit of devotion that might shame their more enlightened neighbours; whilst, in others, the men appear to take no interest in the subject, but to consider it as an affair of the clergy, whom they employ as agents to settle their accounts with Heaven in the best manner they can, without their own personal interference; but the women discover every where a pious zeal that does honour to their sex, and the leaven in their hearts may, perhaps, be mercifully designed to spread by degrees, its kindly influence through the whole mass.

REVIEW OF NEW PUBLICATIONS

Sermons du PERE BRYDAYNE, *Missionaire Royal. Publies sur les Manuscrits Autographes.* 5 Vols. Avignon 1823.

THE editor or editors of these volumes not having favoured the public with any narrative of their author, we shall, before we enter upon them, lay before our readers a few particulars respecting that extraordinary man.

Jacques Brydayne (or Bridaine) is well known as one of the most powerful of the preachers of France. According to the accounts furnished by his biographers, particularly the Abbe de Carron, in his work entitled, Modele des Pretres, he was the son of a surgeon in the village of Chuselan, department of Gard, and belonging to the diocese of Uzes, which was a bishop's see until the Revolution. Brydayne was born in 1701, and appears first to have studied at the Jesuits College at Avignon, and then removed to the seminary of the congregation of the royal Missionaries of St Charles de la Croix in that town. During his noviciate he was employed as a catechist in the various churches there, and very early evinced those powers of elocution and that peculiar talent of engaging and rewarding the attention of those who heard him, which distinguished him in so remarkable a manner in after life, and during a course of very prolonged and zealous labours

Almost as soon as he had taken orders he was, unexpectedly to himself, deputed to go to the town of Aigues Mortes, and preach there during the then approaching season of Lent. He went accordingly in a humble manner, and entered the town on foot and it seems that the inhabitants of that place who had probably been accustomed to at least more imposing appearances in their priesthood, at once "despised his youth" and indicated, by their manner of receiving him, that but little expectation was excited by his visit, and no confidence reposed in his talents. This was an inauspicious introduction to his labours but his discouragement must have been not a little increased when, on entering his church on Ash Wednesday, he found no one worshipper in attendance and the lapse of some considerable time, during which he waited in hope of a congregation, convinced him he was to be left to his own devotions, at least for that day. Brydayne on this critical occasion, when so much was depending on the part he should take, adopted one of those singular expedients to which he several times afterwards had recourse in his public ministrations when he had any particular object in view. He went out of his church habited in his surplice, and carrying with him a little bell, and without saying a word rang it at all the crossings of the streets. He soon, as might be expected gathered a crowd about him every person stopped to know the reason of so remarkable a proceeding, and followed him till he had led the multitude to the church, where, after a little hesitation, they all hurried in after him. He ascended the pulpit immediately and commenced the service by giving out and singing in the French custom a psalm on death while the sole responses of his hearers were rude bursts of laughter. But the missionary persevered. To each of these their responses, he presently added a paraphrase of the terrible subject in terms so solemn, and with a vehemence so impassioned, that he soon exchanged their jeering and derision for silence, attention, and awe. From that time, the greatest respect was shewn him his ministry was fully attended. He was afterwards summoned to preach at St Sulpice in Paris, before a most distinguished auditory, as we shall have occasion hereafter to notice, and secured till his death the esteem and regards of his superiors, as well as the love of those among whom he ministered. His life was one of incessant labour. He performed two hundred and fifty six missionary tours. He was the Bernard Gilpin or Whitfield of France and scarcely a city, town, or village of that country, (the northern provinces excepted,) but witnessed the fruits of his zealous labours. He was on a tour to Villeneuve les-Avignon, when death seized him, at Roquemaure, on the 22d December, 1767. The chapter of Chartres wished to preserve his memory by striking a medal of him and shortly before his death, Pope Benedict XIV had permitted and exhorted him to extend his missionary labours to any part of Christendom.—Of the character and effect of Brydayne's eloquence, the Cardinal Maury (the text writer on that subject in France) appears, by his lavish encomiums, to have entertained the highest opinion They were contemporaries and while the zealous missionary was occupied at his various posts in the country, with a humility as unpretending as his powers were brilliant, the polished cardinal was recording his fame as the foremost of living orators. Ranging in pursuit of the traces which might yet survive of the nervous eloquence of former days, that eloquence which he defines with brevity and beauty as the "instinctive voice of nature, imitated or improved by art" the cardinal points is to the almost exclusive depositaries of it in his day, to the importance of his church. "Behold," he observes, "those men of apostolic minds, the true instructors of the people, endowed with a bold and vigorous imagination, and talents of the first order, yet knowing no triumph or success but the conversion of souls, no applauses but the tears of repentance. Wherever they move, the people follow them; they force their way at once to the consciences of their hearers; they are listened to with rapture; and to them the orator of this world might repair to trace with advantage the operations and achievements which he is in quest of, as the result of refined art."

Among these men, Maury selects Brydayne as the most conspicuous. His eloquence was a natural gift, eminently popular in its character, and full of energy, and those quick and clear comparisons which a vigorous imagination conceives and develops to the life. No one could more entirely possess the attention of his audience, which was generally composed of a vast multitude. His voice was so clear and powerful that it recalled the prodigies related of the declamations of former times; and it was no greater effort to him to make himself heard by ten thousand persons in the open air, than if he had been addressing a small assembly under a well turned arch. His whole preaching was distinguished by an ease which appeared to spring, without solicitation, from the resources of his own genius; brilliant sallies, whose native force discovered more of genius and talent than the most refined polish of art; natural turns of real oratory; the boldest metaphors; thoughts new, vivid, and striking; an elocution of the simplest kind, but noble in its popularity, fully equal to excite the attention it desired, and to sustain the interest which it had awakened; ingenious apologues, deeply affecting, and sometimes sublime; the secret of appearing to amuse his hearers, and then returning to compel their

tears or violence, joined with the sudden vehemence with which he broke through his usual link of eloquence with those passages, which had been elaborately prepared, and wrought with a care which restrained his imagination, and in which the regularity of his composition had weakened his ordinary force.

One of the happiest efforts of his eloquence was the celebrated exordium to the sermon which he preached in the church of St. Sulpice, at Paris. His fame had there spread so as to have attracted to the highest circles of the capital to hear him; and when he ascended the pulpit he saw before him many prelates, a great number of individuals of rank, and a vast body of the clergy. The first feeling of intimidation having passed away, was succeeded by an energy of effort which inspired an address not unworthy of Bossuet or Demosthenes. We think our readers will easily forgive our translating it in this place. We advise those of them who would judge of Brydayne's eloquence to refer to the original; but we translate our extracts for the sake of those who have not the opportunity of consulting it. The following passage is taken from Maury; we cannot find it in the volumes before us.

"At the sight of an audience so new to me, it seems, my brethren, that I ought to commence by imploring your kindness in favour of a poor missionary, destitute of all those talents which you require in one who comes to discourse with you on the subject of your salvation. But I experience at this moment a sensation of a very different kind; and if I feel deeply humbled, do not, I beseech you, imagine that it is with the wretched disquietudes of vanity, as though I were accustomed to preach *myself*. God forbid that one of *his* ministers should ever think that he needs to be excused by you; for whoever you may be, you are all like myself, in the judg ment of God, but miserable sinners. It is then solely in the sight of your God and mine that I feel myself at this moment compelled to smite upon my breast. Until this moment I have been accustomed to proclaim the Gospel of the Most High in lowly temples, covered with thatch. I have preached the severities of repentance [penance!] to unhappy beings, the greater number of whom have at the time wanted bread. I have announced the most fearful truths of our religion to the simple villager. Unhappy man! what have I done? I have made sad the poor, the dearest friends of my Lord! I have filled with apprehension and grief those simple and faithful souls whom I ought rather to have condoled with and comforted. It is, *in this place*, where my eye meets only the great, the wealthy, the oppressors of suffering humanity and bold and hardened offenders — ah! it is here alone, in the midst of so many scandals, that I ought to echo, with all its thunders, the Divine word, and summon to me, in this pulpit, on the one hand, Death, which threatens you all, and on the other, the great God who comes to be your Judge. I hold even now your sentence in my hand. Tremble then before me, ye proud and scornful men! The thankless abuse of all the means of grace, the necessity of salvation, the certainty of death, the fearful uncertainty of its arrival, final impenitence, the last judgment, the small number of the elect, hell itself, and above all, eternity! eternity! these—these are the subjects on which I am about to enter, and which I should have reserved for you alone! Ah! how I need your help—you who will condemn *me*, perhaps without saving *yourselves*. May God touch your hearts while his unworthy minister speaks. He surely will, for I have acquired a large experience of his mercies. He, He alone can reach the depth of your consciences. Then, struck with alarm, smitten with distress at your past iniquities, you will come and cast yourselves in the arms of his love, pouring forth tears of compunction and grief. Then, and then only, will you think me eloquent enough."

It was generally supposed that all Brydayne's pulpit compositions were of the "improvisatore" kind. Of the above exordium there has never been a question that it was so; but the appearance of the volumes before us clearly proves, that he was in the habit of at least writing before he went into the pulpit, although he may not always have carried his manuscripts with him; and for many striking passages he was, without doubt, indebted to the excitement of the occasion. His biographers have stated that on his first going to Aigues Mortes he had but five sermons, and that, being driven to rely on his impromptu powers and resources, he succeeded so well that he was ever afterwards induced to depend on them, and that they were never known to fail him. But had he done so we should not now be engaged in our present review. The supposition may have originated from his not carrying his manuscripts into the pulpit, and gained strength from their having been considered lost to the world for many years after his death; but the recent discovery of them, in autograph, at Avignon, has established the op-

Maury adduces the following as a fine specimen of the preacher's spirited illustrations; we give it briefly. If a criminal on being adjudged to the scaffold should find an innocent man ready to substitute himself in his place, but when the fatal spot was reached no executioner could be found, what if the real criminal instead of being thankful should offer himself as the executioner and should actually perform the dreadful ceremony, how should we abominate such conduct? Yet this is the act of every one who by living in sin crucifies his Redeemer afresh and opens up his bleeding wounds. This it must be owned, is a striking thought; but in volume ii Brydayne ingenuously acknowledges that he had it from St Bernard.

posite fact.* That occasional brilliant digressions from his written discourse were the inspirations of the moment we have already said we believe, because those which the Cardinal Maury has retained, and some reported by Mad. Necker, and by La Harpe, in his 'Cours de la Literature,' are not to be found in his five volumes. In these are many felicities of expression, and vigorous thoughts; but they are often allied to conceptions of a grotesque character,† which a few moments of preparation would have enabled the preacher to modify according to the dictates of his own better taste.

Our own impression of Brydayne's style, from the perusal of the sermons which are preserved, is, that he excels rather in the terrific than in the pathetic—rather in those deep and glowing descriptions of the fearful and the sublime which overpower the understanding, than in those softer appeals which melt the heart. He seems to us to have known this, by selecting oftener for contemplation such features of the Divine character as display more of majesty than mercy, and represent God as "the high and lofty one who inhabiteth eternity, whose name is Holy," rather than as delighting to "dwell with the poor and contrite spirit that trembleth at his word."

Brydayne must have displayed considerable vehemence of manner in the delivery of his sermons. We know the importance that belongs to the suitable action of an energetic public speaker; and we have often

---

The editor's preface informs us that the original autographs were in a most mutilated state when discovered, and that the greatest care and labour were requisite in order to render them legible. We very much regret that a slight sketch of the author's life was not prefixed to the volumes. It would have greatly added to their interest.

† One in particular we were amused with as sounding very oddly to an English ear. It occurs in the 5th volume where he speaks of repentance as making the *amende honorable* to God for past sin.

---

wished to thaw or shake some of our still divines of modern times into something like an activity, sympathetic of the themes on which they are descanting. But rather than be compelled to witness the unnatural, and studied, and ill-graced gesticulations of some declaimers, we would a thousand fold prefer the most unrelaxing muscular sedateness. In Brydane, however, as in Whitfield, very much of the effect of his appeals depended on his manner; and he had the happy art of varying and accommodating it with perfect readiness to the subject matter of his address; but in many instances he must have carried it to an extreme. Mad. Necker relates, that one day when preaching on the eucharist, before a large company of the clergy, who appeared quite unmoved, he suddenly raised his voice and exclaimed, "O my God I [almost] determine from this time to renounce the ministry of thy word. I have preached before the voluptuous, and they have abandoned their irregularities. I have addressed the avaricious, and they have given to the poor; but those who daily celebrate thy holy mysteries I cannot move." Then seizing a pyx which was at hand, he dashed it to the ground, and exclaimed, "At least this shall no longer be profaned."

At another time, he was addressing the people, and for a short time rested his body forward on the pulpit with great apparent calmness, and observed, 'My brethren, some judges have endeavoured to discover a culprit by making him, among others, pass before the corpse of him whom he had murdered, and watching the movements of his countenance. Here then, for you is the corpse! Behold it!' and he at the moment drew from his garment a crucifix. "Which of you has been the betrayer and murderer? (qui l'a tué?) Look, ye licentious, ye ungodly, &c. &c. (See les Nouveaux Melanges de Mad. Necker, tom. 2.)

But these *stratagems* (for they

really deserve the name, and would suit, we apprehend, the French nation much better than our own) were not confined to his sermons. They were adopted by him (always, we are sure, with a good design,) in his general ministrations. One instance shall suffice. He was once at the head of a procession, when he pronounced, with a loud voice, a spirited exhortation founded on the shortness of human life, and concluded by saying to the multitude who followed him, ' I will now conduct you to your homes, and then led them to a cemetery.

Our readers will now be anxious to learn something for themselves of the contents of the published volumes, and we propose to lay before them rather copious extracts, though many excellent passages must still be passed over. The first volume consists chiefly of sermons on death, the death of the ungodly, first dying as they had lived, and then in despair: on the general judgment, on particular judgment, and on hell. Were it not for some fragments on retirement, and a closing sermon on paradise (which by the way is truly excellent), this volume, presenting such a terrible table of contents, would be like one continued peal of thunder. There is, indeed, enough of the solemn and awful, but there is a little also of the encouraging. in describing the value of retirement particularly, some of our readers may regard as rather hyperbolical the assurance that *three* days spent in it would infallibly end in the conversion of the most hardened profligate. (See p 11.)

The French language presents a construction favourable to the impressions which the first class of subjects in this volume are calculated to excite, and the preacher has fully availed himself* of its interjectional exclamations, even to an extent to be deprecated. In such a solemn address as that of Harreaux's celebrated sonnet, the " Grand Dieu! is not objectionable: but when that, and " O Ciel! and ' Oh mon Dieu! and many more, are breaking forth in every tenth page*, we cannot pass them over in silence.

The second volume, which appears to us the best of the five, contains several sermons on wilful and venial sin, with the usual addition of fragments to each: some detached remarks on the aggravation of sin in professed Christians: a sermon on the small number of the elect, and another on repentance.

All these are treated with great spirit and discrimination. It is on practical subjects of this kind that our author excels. We feel generally that we can go the whole length of his admonitions: but in treating the various points of Christian doctrine, on which, however, there are fortunately but few sermons in the whole series of volumes, we are often compelled to withhold our assent. There may be truth in the main points: but there is so great and frequent an unsoundness developed in some of the other sermons, that we have not felt the same pleasure in perusing them ourselves: nor can we, with the same warmth, commend them to the attention of our readers.

The first two sermons in this volume are on Wilful Sin. Matt. xxiv. 15, 21, is applied in a sense of accommodation to the nature and effects of sin. The exordium is very striking.

What is this, my brethren? This abomination of desolation in the holy place which is to be followed by the terrible vengeance of Almighty God and the most calamitous of trials? What, but sin? Is there any thing more frightful or more abominable than sin in a soul which God has created in his own image, formed by his heavenly hand, purchased with his blood, consecrated by his presence, and a

---

* Our readers may form some idea of their abundance from the following cluster at p 229 vol 1. O regrets! O repentirs! O larmes! O fureur! O desespoir! O rage! feux et flammes de l'abîme! &c

See vol 1 p 32, where these exclamations occur not less than three times within a short distance of each other

thousand times sanctified by his grace, a soul which is intended to be the temple the throne, and the sanctuary of God himself? What can be more strange or more atrocious an abomination than sin, and what desolation can be more fatal and terrible than that which its infection produces in the guilty soul? No brethren all the appalling calamities which the Divine Saviour announced to the ungrateful and perfidious Jews, all the heavy penalties which have fallen on and overwhelmed unbelieving Jerusalem, present but a faint picture of the miserable state of that soul which is polluted by sin. Hence the saints and servants of God, who form their estimate of sin by the eye of faith, have hardly found words sufficiently energetic to express their horror at it. Some have termed it the cursed seed of satan transforming the children of men into the offspring of the wicked one. Others have described wilful sin in a Christian soul as a loss of beauty and even of vitality or at least of worth and reason and an entire overthrow of the whole character. This is Saint Augustine's idea. Tertullian declares it to be an execrable preference of the devil to the sovereign majesty of the Creator. Saint Anselm pourtrays it as a sacrilegious seizure of the crown and sceptre from the hands of God himself. St. Paul formally designates it as *crucifying the Son of God afresh*. All agree that wilful sin is an entire extinction of grace the death of the soul the corruption of human nature, the shame of angels the disgust of heaven, the misery of the world an infinite evil, the sole and exclusive evil the parent of all other evils in the world and, in short, the sovereign evil and antagonist of God, the capital enemy of man at once *an abomination and a desolation* "And when ye see this abomination of desolation in the holy place then shall there be great tribulation." pp 5, 6.

The exordium to his sermon on venial sin is also very impressive indeed, his introductions are often particularly excellent but in these brilliancies he appears to us with a high hand to violate some of the most accredited rules of the orators. It is the direction of both Tully and Quintilian that the exordium should ever be simple, quiet and unpretending.* But in some of Brydayne's openings he delivers out his

* "Proemium decebit et sententiarum et compositionis, et vocis, et vultus *modestia*."—Quintil Instit lib iv c 1

In exordienda causa servandum est ut usitata sit verborum consuetudo ut non apparata oratio esse videatur —Cic ad Heren 1. 7

whole plan at once the ideas of his mind seem to have reached their full maturity, and break forth in all the perfections of their combinations. The evil is this, that when so many rich thoughts fly out at the first opening, scarcely a hope remains that the unexhausted subject can afford materials to sustain the interest, and minister to the edification of the reader and in many of the sermons which begin so well we have had to regret a disproportion of excellence of this kind. We must add, however, that it is not so in all. But we promised our readers the exordium of the sermon on venial sins. The text is from that chapter in St. John's Gospel which describes the case of Lazarus —

This sickness is not unto death. My brethren are not *we* in the daily habit of applying this description given by the Saviour of the sickness of Lazarus, to the spiritual maladies of our own souls? Do we not say of the greater part of our transgressions that they are little sins trifling errors venial faults in a word sicknesses not unto death? With the pretext that they affect not the root of the matter in our souls, the fundamental principles of grace we commit them without reluctance we live in them without remorse, and consider them as of little moment it is even possible that we may suspect in ourselves scruples and weaknesses of mind to fear them. This sickness not unto death? Ah! what state can be more terrible or more fatal to our safety? Yes Christian souls, this state of lukewarmness in which you pretend you can be saved and yet live in the indulgence of these venial sins without hesitation is a very doubtful state a state in which no one has ever yet attained true holiness a state of which the saints afford no example and of which Jesus Christ does not hesitate to assure you that with all your specious pretences to devotion you will *infallibly be damned*. p 225

We extract his enumeration of a great proportion of these venial sins

I have only in view at present those faults which Christians who live in a lax and lukewarm state are accustomed deliberately to commit, and out of which they form habits which they make no conscience to correct. Such are my brethren to give you some general idea slight resentings of injuries trifling irri tations, secret envyings, scornful words, slanders in matters of no moment, railings, falsehoods, irreverent deportment in sacred things, unchecked distractions in prayer, distaste in the service of God, confessions and communions without fervour, and almost without fruit; slowness to cast out evil thoughts, love of human applause, a prying disposition, undue love of taste in dress, a fondness for ornament, self-love and self-will, idleness, carelessness of time, self-complacency, slight excess in food of either sort, and every kind of particularity therein: in a word all those negligencies in the various departments of duty, whether the instruction of servants or the right education of children or of any other kind—these are some of your venial sins: these and a thousand others which I will not specify; but of whatever sort, wherein the exciting cause is slight, and whose characteristic is rather inconsideration than design. I assure you, Christians, that all these faults, especially when they are often fallen into and indulged in without scruple and continued in without distress and become habitual and are not striven against and checked, are indeed serious evils. Take I pray you, in this first part of my discourse, these three considerations to shew you the guilt and enormity of these venial sins: their guilt in relation to the Being whom we offend in them; their guilt in reference to the cause or occasion which gives rise to them; and their guilt in reference to the measure in which we offend.—p. 231.

After describing at some length the greatness and majesty of God, and ascribing our feeble conception of the heinousness of sin in his sight to the incorrect views we entertain, or try to realize, of the infinite holiness of the Divine nature, he proceeds with the following passage. In quoting it, however, it is necessary to notice the unscriptural and anti-Protestant complexion of the distinction between sins that only *partially* and others that *greatly* offend God, sins that expose the offender to *risk* and others that expose him to *ruin*. The whole distinction between mortal and venial sins, in the Roman Catholic view of that distinction, is most unsound. The writers of that communion teach that some sins, though offences against God, and violations of his law, are so slight that they deserve only temporal punishment (meaning by the term *temporal* punishment, either in this world or in *purgatory*, as distinguished from *eternal* punishments in hell,) and may be expiated by penance or devotion, or the communication of the super-errogated merits of others. But, as Bishop Burnet justly observes, "The Scripture no where teaches us to think so slightly of the majesty of God or of his law. Under the Old Testament dispensation a curse was pronounced upon every one that continued not in all things which were written in the book of the law to do them: and the same curse must have been upon us all, if Christ had not redeemed us from it: for 'the wages of sin is death.' St. James teaches that there is such a connexion both between all the precepts of the law of God among themselves, and between the observance of them and the authority of the Lawgiver, that "He who offends in one point is guilty of all." The Roman Catholic Church seems in this, as in various other points, rather to regard the outward action than the motive or the principle from which it springs: but though Brydayne falls in some measure into the error of his church, on this subject, his view is much nearer the scriptural doctrine than that of many other writers of the same communion. There is a sense in which the term "venial" is retained by many Protestant divines, in allusion to sins of ignorance and infirmity: and our church seems to admit of the distinction by its use of the epithet "deadly" or "mortal" in the Sixteenth Article: but while we make the just distinction between the *degrees* of transgression, let us never forget that *all* sin is sin, that all sin deserves God's wrath, and to us, who know of no purgatory, there is no medium between full forgiveness and eternal punishment. Having premised these explanatory remarks we proceed to translate the extract.

I acknowledge however my brethren with you that venial sin may not absolutely draw down upon you the enmity and hatred of God, but is it nothing to you to incur even his displeasure? It may not render you altogether unworthy of his mercy, but is it nothing to you that it exposes you to his formidable justice? It may not cause the entire loss of his love but is it nothing that it should chill his favour and that it deprives you of certain special favours and certain peculiar gifts which would have infallibly guided you to salvation? It may not have absolutely deprived you of the title to that salvation in his eternal glory but is it nothing to commit a sin which can delay the possession of it, till a course of penitentiary expiation is accomplished? It may not deserve eternal punishment, but it may merit very severe chastisements. Yet once more, it may not, I concede effect absolutely an entire rupture with God destroy his grace in your souls, quench his Spirit in your hearts but is it nothing to live in coldness with your God, to be in continual danger of losing his friendship, and to be ever grieving his Spirit, by your resistance and your abuse of his most precious gifts? p. 236

"Venial sin is an evil greater than all the evils of the natural world and wherefore? because it is essentially opposed to God, which all the evils of the natural world are not and what follows from this? Attend I beseech you while I adduce some of those astonishing consequences from this principle, which will give you a most terrible, but yet just, conception of the heinousness of venial sin. It follows my brethren that God may for example command his creatures to do many natural evils as he commanded the exterminating angel to kill all the first-born of the Egyptians and Saul to destroy all the sinners the Amalekites and to spare neither women, children, nor cattle: but he cannot command, nor counsel, nor even (expressly and positively) permit any creature to commit *a single venial sin*, not even the slightest deviation from truth It follows then my brethren that God may nay he does command us to endure with patience all the ills of life, that he may excite us to desire and even to love them (in consideration of their beneficial effect on the mind); but as to venial sins there is not one which he can direct, or tolerate, or approve not one even which he must not forbid, however small and inconsiderable it be. God may then be the author of all the evils which afflict man on earth want, disgrace reproach destitution pestilence war famine sickness death all these may be the effect of his mercy or his justice but almighty as he is he cannot be the author of a single venial fault not even of the least imperfection It follows also that the Son of God in becoming man may have been able to assume all the miseries of our nature may have become mean weak and mortal may have suffered and did suffer in his body, poverty, hunger thirst, reproaches, sufferings, the thorns, the nails the cross, and death but that he could not ally himself to sin. I speak not of mortal sin, but of sin in general whatever it be and this, by reason of the essential and irresistible opposition which exists between sin and God p. 241

Our author however, is not content even with this affecting representation of the evil of sin, as committed against God but, in order to strengthen that representation, he supposes a case which never can exist, and draws deductions from it, which, instead of aiding his argument, have a directly contrary effect

But I stop not here my brethren taking with me the principles above mentioned that sin is a greater evil than all natural ills, I will suppose myself for a moment in a situation where I should be threatened at once with pains the most acute and ruin the most complete, which I could experience all that want has most desolate suffering most overwhelming and shame most abasing to inflict and I say that it is not permitted me by a single venial sin to escape from these troubles This is not all I suppose the entire overthrow of a family of a state of a world and that in order to arrest the desolations which are sweeping away families provinces states and kingdoms, there requires only but a single venial sin to be committed but once and a moment after to be atoned for by a brilliant expiation I maintain that it is better that families perish states dissolve kingdoms depopulate and decay that the universe, earth and heaven be annihilated than a single venial sin be committed however slight and small it may appear Yet more my brethren count the multitude of sinners on earth who walk in the ways of perdition, and are for ever condemned of the righteous who walk in the paths of life and are saved of the reprobate who suffer in eternal flames of the blessed who rejoice in their everlasting reward souls beloved by God so precious that he bought them with his blood and suppose for a moment that a single venial sin would suffice to convert all the sinners on earth, and bring them back to God, and to uphold all the saints to final perseverance and preserve them from an otherwise inevitable fall that this single venial sin would avail to lift the condemned from the pit, and raise them to the realms of glory; would confirm to the blest, the full beatitude of heaven and prevent for ever a return to woe I maintain brethren, that were the alternative proposed to you you would be bound without a moment's hesitation to consent to the condemnation of the impenitent and the reprobate;

yes, even to consent to the eternal ruin of all the righteous in earth, and all the blest in glory, rather than wilfully to allow one sin (even one venial sin,) against God! And why? for the same simple reason because the ruin of angels and the damnation of men, is after all but the sorrow of the creature: but sin is the grief of God, a grief therefore of a far higher order than that of all creation itself.—pp. 243, 244.'

Forced and unnatural, and even extravagant and revolting, as this statement is, we nevertheless recommend it to the attentive consideration of fair and accommodating religionists, of "borderers" who are ever changing their relative position in the church of Christ, of conforming, temporizing Christians seen often "in the garb of Egypt, while speaking the language of Canaan," as at least exhibiting their slight estimation of sin in powerful contrast. The subject of this discourse is so useful, that we shall continue our examination of it. The argument which is framed to meet a palliation of the sin on account of its inconsiderableness, is the next branch of our author's subject, and is not quite so well illustrated or enforced. Much light has been shed on this point by the powerful sermon of Dr Chalmers on Luke xvi. 10 "He that is unjust in the least, is unjust also in much." That admirable writer turns the argument of triviality into an energetic reproof of the extenuator, who might have reasoned it before he yielded to a temptation, the unresisting compliance with which, while it has occasioned the loss of so much, has procured for him little or nothing in return. The devout George Herbert also felt and applied the same reasoning

The cheapest sins most dearly punished are
Because to shun them also is so cheap
For thou hast wit to mark them and to spare
Oh *crumble* not away thy soul's fair heap

Brydayne supplies his remonstrance from the complaint in Ezekiel's prophecy, and points out as the remunerating price of the sinner's compliance with temptation, "a handful of barley and a piece of bread." Miserable inducement and wretched compensation! Yet too sweet a morsel to be foregone even for the love of Him in whose favour is life. But his application of the case of Naaman we consider without point. It was not the love of an indulged sin, which prompted the Syrian captain to turn from the prophet in a rage but the revolt of pride against the simplicity of the means which the prophet prescribed for his cure. "Had the prophet bad thee do some great thing wouldst thou not have done it?" The latter part of the same scene might have afforded a better illustration of the love of little sins, when the converted leper pleaded for his *unavoidable* comformities in the house of Rimmon at least our author would have had the greater part of commentators on his side in this interpretation "Is it not a little one?" is the character they usually give of Naaman's last conference with the prophet.

In exposing the danger of these little sins, their very obvious tendency to greater and heavier and mortal ones, is forcibly described in the sermon under consideration, together with the fearful state of the soul, when the Almighty withdraws the communications of his peace in the retrospect of the past, and his grace for the future time of need

Sin, my brethren of every kind, even venial sin is a work of darkness, which always brings some obscurity with it These little ones may in truth at first be only light vapours which raise themselves by degrees from an impure conscience but which, uniting in greater numbers form at last a cloud so thick, as to eclipse altogether the Sun of Righteousness; and then comes on that bewildered state of understanding in which all discrimination of good from evil is lost sins and graces mortal and venial transgressions are comprised together and the soul is filled with deadly disquietude. I will explain myself I know ye loose and lukewarm professors of religion that at certain times when your passions are excited, or youthful pride rising and animosity rankling and a thousand other impulses that you stop not to examine any thing but blindly

You cannot tell whether Divine love has not been sorely wounded: for the consent of your mind may have accompanied the word but not the deed. You may have passed the limits of poverty of spirit. Humility and purity and charity, may all have been wounded. This opinion which you have given, this look which you have assumed, this word which you have dropped, this example which you have set, this complacency which you have felt, may they not all be advancing towards a mortal sin? Will they not at least all draw after them a train of venial consequences for which you must be responsible before God? Such a state of mind, unless the fear of God be in lively exercise, will raise a thousand doubts, scruples, perplexities, and alarms, and will become so intolerable, that at length to get rid of them, the man would shake off the yoke of religion altogether. But not only does God in consequence of our little sins refuse his graces of peace and consolation, or spiritual light and discernment, but also his graces of preservation and support and without these it is impossible to avoid wandering in the path of perdition. Your venial sins, Christian brethren, may be I admit at present in reference to your soul, but as a small hurt which makes but little progress. But if you apply not some prompt and efficacious remedy, it will spread its poison throughout, and soon reduce the frame to dust. They are but as the small drops of rain which insinuate themselves beneath the basement of the edifice scarcely worthy of regard: but unless some means of defense be prepared they will soon sap the foundations, and the building will crumble into ruins. They are but as small sparks; but if instead of making the most vigorous efforts to quench them, you fan them still more they catch and spread and light up at last a flame which it is not possible to put out. wait but a little, and the effect will convince you. Continue brethren to commit all these little sins familiarize yourselves with them yield yourselves to them without scruple and without remorse and you will see that when an occasion presents itself of committing greater sins, you will have the greatest toil to escape from the commission of them. Such an occasion comes, a critical and perilous moment what need have you of the sovereign grace of God to sustain you. O Lord if thou sustain not this soul by some extraordinary help, it is lost for ever. But, oh the fearful judgment of God! provoked by so many offers of grace despised. In

The writer then delineates the sickly state of soul, which by oft repeated yielding to small temptations, and the indulgence of little sins, begets: its proclivity to evil, its growing disinclination to the self denial of the Cross: its feeling the burden and the yoke of Christ, first to be heavy, then irksome, and then insupportable, it bows under it, and drags it along in a languishing and weary manner and he then invokes the testimony of the backslider on earth, and the apostate spirits in hell, to bear witness to his assertion, that all their defilements and all their desperation have originated in some small deviation from the path of godliness, some relaxation of vigilance, or some neglect of prayer. He then adduces the following examples from Scripture:—

'Who does not know how much a slight act of disobedience cost Lot's wife? She only turned her head contrary to the command of God to observe what was taking place in the terrible conflagration of Sodom, and immediately by one of the most fearful punishments, she lost the power to turn again, and became a pillar of salt. Who needs to be told how much a slight murmur cost Miriam, the sister of Moses? She blames and complains of the conduct of her brother and the same hour a frightful leprosy seized her whole frame. Who needs be told what a small distrust cost Moses himself? He smote the rock with his rod twice, as if he thought once would not have sufficed, and for no other crime was he excluded from the land of promise and died when just about to enter it. Who knows not what it cost an Israelite to violate slightly the Sabbath day? He was gathering a few sticks and the Lord commanded Moses and Aaron that he should be stoned to death by the congregation. What did not a vain curiosity cost the Bethshemites? Seven months had the ark been kept by the Philistines when they recovered it but because they regarded it with lightness the Lord slew more than fifty thousand men; whilst Uzzah on the other hand for not sufficiently preserving it when in danger of falling, is also struck to death.* What did not a trifling

---

* We presume this is the accredited interpretation of Uzzah's crime among

fession which he made to David, fully referred to his choice, one of the three evils of war, pestilence, and famine and when the humbled prince referred back the selection to God, he lighted up a pestilence in Israel which, in the space of three days, destroyed seventy thousand souls. What did not a trivial conformity cost the prophet who yielded to the solicitation of another prophet to eat and drink with him? What did not a slight disrespect cost the two and forty children? The one was destroyed by a lion, the others by two bears all severely punished by the Lord to shew an example of his justice, as well against unfaithful ministers, as against those who fail in a due reverence for them when faithful. And what under the dispensation of grace, did not a small equivocation cost Ananias and his wife? They were under no strict obligation to give their goods to the church but they brought a part to St Peter and kept back the rest. This reserve was dissimulation because they wished to persuade the Apostles that they had surrendered all. On this the Apostle in the name of the living God, pronounces upon them sentence of death, and without delay the sentence was executed and they both fell dead at his feet The Scripture adds that a chastisement so summary and so severe threw a fear on all the church and made them dread the least offences Ah, my brethren all these terrible punishments, and many others which are recorded in the sacred word but which I do not now refer to, may well inspire in you the same terror, and teach you what a serious evil it is to offend God, even by the smallest faults. Vol ii p 292.

We cannot follow our author in his next argument, where he attempts to draw aside the veil which conceals from mortal view the world of spirits, and depicts the sufferings of *purgatory* as endured by a soul, which, although renewed on earth after the Divine image, and reinstated by the blood of the covenant in the favour of God, is yet doomed, for the stain of some " venial sin yet cleaving to it, to the endurance of those sufferings, the horrors of

the French divines We have been accustomed to view it in the light of an irreverent meddling with things sacred Yet in the sermon in the fourth volume on Frequent Communion Brydayne alludes to Uzzah's case as rash sacrilege p. 117

which our author seems to quake as he details. His imagination is at full stretch while he pictures those " penetrating and scorching ' flames, whose intense heat is not approached at even a moderate distance by the furnace of Nebuchadnezzar, though in its " seven times hotter state. We feel our strongest regrets awakened at this pitiable view of that productive error of the Romish Church. And while our indignation rises at the bearing which every increase in the temperature of these imaginary flames must have had on the coffers of the clergy, an increase to be effected or restrained at pleasure and at a price, though we do not wish to cast any imputation on our author, with whatever zeal he may have described his fiery limbo, we yet feel strong regret at the introduction of this doctrine in such a sermon as that under consideration, especially as no one discourse in these volumes is more calculated to shew the necessity and the value of the Saviour's complete atonement We cannot but see the tendency of this purgatorial purification to impeach the full efficacy of the Redeemer's sacrifice, by which, and by which alone, he "hath himself *purged our sins*,' leaving none to cleave to us unatoned for, or uncancelled, and it is when we have the exceeding sinfulness of sin forcibly set before us, that we feel we can less than ever dispense with the conviction, that " the blood of Jesus Christ cleanseth us from *all* sin," and that by a daily application of this blood to the conscience, " they who are washed, but who, while walking through this defiling world, need continually " to wash their feet may also attain this perpetual purifying, and " be clean every whit Really this fancy of the Roman Catholic priesthood is most appalling, and it is humiliating and affecting to hear so enlightened a man as Brydayne declare, that the soul pardoned of its heavier and mortal offences, may yet for one little sin be condemned for ages to the dismal abode of purgatory. It is a horrible conception, and as unscriptural as horrible. The true Christian will, indeed, *in this world*, be made for his inconsistencies to feel the chastisements of that heavenly Father who "scourgeth every son whom he receiveth;" but at the grave all his sorrows cease. There will be an end of all chastisement and unmixed joy and full redemption are from that period his happy lot. The line of separation is finally drawn at death. "He that then is filthy, will be filthy still; he that then is holy, will be holy still." There are no middle characters. None are *half born again*, whose regeneration the processes of purgatory are to perfect. The supposition is as detrimental to the progress of the divine life in the soul, as it is derogatory to the honour of Him of whom it is said, "Ye are in him *complete.*"

Altogether apart from the doctrines of purgatory, we can, however, join heartily in Brydayne's practical exhortations to contrition and watchfulness, the two duties which he urges on his hearers as the conclusion of his discourse, and in the fragments which are attached to it; in one of which last he addresses with great spirit those who are ever floating between the smaller peccant indulgencies of every day, and the larger transgressions of particular temptation, or those who are steering as closely as they can to deadly sins to comport with final salvation. And he asks them, "who has revealed to them the limits of the sins that may be forgiven, the sins "not unto death;" and how they "can accurately tell how deeply the devouring blade of this two-edged sword has plunged in their soul? It may be up to the very hilt. We still regret to find, however, even in Brydayne, the prevailing tendency of the Romish creed, to build up another righteousness than that of faith. In his enumeration of the *expiatory* plans which "the church recommends, and the preservatives from future falls, alms, and the visiting of the sick, and fasting, and holy water, and some holy supererogatory works ("quelque sainte œuvre de surérogation"), hold a more considerable place than faith and prayers; indeed the former is once) honoured with the passage now under consideration; and the latter is only called some short supplication—"quelque petite prière."

The following are, however, two very admirable passages which occur not far from each other, among the fragments at the close of this second volume. The first is on the rapid but imperceptible progress of crime, and the subtle approach of temptation, illustrated by the case of Judas.

"Behold says the Apostle James, how great a matter a little fire kindleth! Judas thirsted for money. To gratify this desire he became unjust and sacrilegious, a hypocrite, a calumniator, a traitor, a Deicide! He became unjust and a thief when he retained for himself a part of the money which Jesus Christ had confided to him; a knave and a hypocrite in pretending a zeal for the comfort of the poor when he meditated his own interest; a railer and slanderer when he blamed the use which the unhappy Mary Magdalene had made of the ointment which she shed on the feet of Jesus, and accused both her and the Saviour himself of a criminal prodigality; sacrilegious and profane when he had the hardihood to receive the body of Jesus Christ in that fearful state.* Traitor towards his Master and of a heart black enough to say to the Pharisees, 'What will ye give me and I will deliver him to you?' and at length manifestly reprobate and an object of execration to the whole world in ending his life in despair! What was the first step which conducted him to this? *A step which we ourselves take every day when we feel the least undue attachment to the interests of the present life.*" Vol. ii. pp. 304, 305.

The second is an alarming address to the negligent and relapsing Christian.

"Oh how deplorable is this state of lukewarmness! Nothing excites and arouses you. The ordinances which you

---

* Among the other errors of the Romish Church the doctrine of transubstantiation is so incorporated with the writings of our author that we cannot present our extracts entirely free from allusions to it.

attend leave you in the same languid frame in which you approached them. The same holy terror fell upon our soul as rain upon the barren earth: your unbelief yet prevails, and throughout your duties and your affections reign the same coldness, indolence, and torpor. You draw near the Throne of Grace, and you retire with no increase of fervour, of determination, or of strength. What you were yesterday you continue to-day; not a step have you advanced in excellence. Ah! I fear lest the Lord angry with this supineness, should at length abandon you to the chastisement you deserve. I have no wish to distress your conscience; but I must tell you that your state is any thing but safe. I must tell you that you are much more an object of the hatred than the love of God; that this languor cannot long exist without degenerating into absolute crime; that a lively piety gives tokens of its vitality, that it is constantly taking wing; and that graces so dumb, inert, and ideotic, are not Christian love. Alas! perhaps the priest to whom you open your case and who traces in you no improvement, may tell you that you *sleep* as the disciples said of Lazarus. He may excite you to vigilance, and encourage you to hope that this relaxed and torpid condition may consist with safety. But Jesus Christ, who judgeth not as man judgeth, says at once, that you are *dead*. He said unto them plainly, *Lazarus is dead*. Vol. ii pp 319—321.

We pass now from this to the third volume, which contains a "conference" or discourse on *alms giving*, with several fragments on the same subject, and on that other duty equally allied to the Confessional, the duty of *restitution*, a very long but excellent sermon on *prayer* with some additional detached remarks on that comprehensive part of Christian practice; two sermons on the *love of God*, and some hints relative to the sacrifice of the Mass, and the means of joining in it with advantage.

The first and last of these contain about 170 pages of gross error and heresy. The ample basis which they present for the construction of self righteousness, their unqualified avowal of the expiatory nature of almsgiving, of its forming the best part of the purchase money of conversion, the mummery of the Mass, the mischiefs of the Confessional, and the almost entire exclusion of that adorable Redeemer who is the only hope of the trembling penitent, admit of but poor compensation from the ingenuity and force with which some of the preacher's exhortations are pressed home on the consciences of his hearers. With one mode of address, to which Brydayne resorts in his discourse on alms, we were somewhat amused: it is at least more innocent than those to which we have above adverted. He dwells on the uncertainty of success which attends all the preacher's exhortations on other subjects, and reasons to this effect: "If we preach to you on salvation, and demonstrate its deep importance, how shall we know that you labour to work it out with fear and trembling? If of repentance, how shall we know that you cordially fulfil it? If of the horrors of sin, you may promise us to avoid it with care; but this is all—this occasions us grief. But on the present subject it is otherwise. You may this very day assure us to our conviction and comfort of your sincerity, and give the most substantial proofs of the effect which our ministry has had upon you. Set no bounds then to your liberality."

We pass by the unscriptural views which these sermons present, in order to proceed to the sermons on prayer and the love of God: bestowing on the former, however, but one remark,—namely, that it is observable that the unchristian doctrines which we have had occasion to notice in our author's writings are developed chiefly, perhaps solely, on those subjects which find their main support in the peculiarities of the church of which he was a minister. We would trust, therefore, that the errors belong rather to that corrupt church than to its servant; for where Brydayne feels himself more at large on other topics, such as prayer, it is curious to notice how he seems to exult in the opportunity of declaring boldly his more enlightened views, and to magnify the grace of that Saviour whom, we doubt not, with all his errors, he

The fragments on almsgiving contain this passage:—

"What joy must it afford to think that God is not using to content himself with so little as this (charity to the poor) to grant you the pardon of all your sins and to discover to you, notwithstanding your niceties, in these superfluous temporal possessions the means of purchasing the rewards of eternity."—Vol. iii. p. 151

The sermon on Prayer presents the following contrast in describing salvation as the crown of final perseverance.

"You know how well how often this pulpit has resounded with this astonishing truth that this blessing is not infallibly attached to innocence of life—that it is a gift purely free and gratuitous from the Sovereign Arbiter of our eternal state—that we can neither purchase nor merit it by the sanctity of our works—that no fastings, no mortifications, no tears, no charities, no alms-deeds—no innocence of manners, no abstinence from sin—no separation from the world, nothing in short, is able to render us worthy of this inestimable gift."—Vol. iii. p. 164.

What could Luther, in all the glow of his indignation against indulgences, or Calvin, in his zeal against legal self-dependencies, have uttered more explicit than this passage, which Bridayne employs to introduce his considerations on the value of prayer, as opening all the exhaustless stores of wisdom and grace which are treasured up in Christ Jesus.

His sermon on this subject is grounded on the 23d and 24th verses of the xvith chapter of St John. He considers at great length, in the first part, the obligations to the duty, one class of those which he enumerates being the encouragements given to it, though this would rather appear to form a separate branch of his subject; and in the second, the character of our petitions, and the frame of spirit in which they must be offered up to be suc-

cessful. But what, exclaims he, of our obligations to the duty of prayer. Christ from our sinful wants and weaknesses. He thus alludes to the case of St Peter.

"How astonished must Peter have been at his own defenceless state. Three times had he been invited and entreated by Jesus Christ to watch and pray with him; but the presumptuous Apostle would not. Behold him then taken in the toils of the enemy; he struggles, and resists, and hesitates for a short moment, but the temptation is strong. Peter is weak and he is vanquished. What was the cause of this fatal and remarkable fall? It was that Peter had first abandoned the duty of prayer."—Vol. iii. p. 181.

He thus most hyperbolically marks the efficacy, or, to use his own term, the "infallibility of prayer:

"Nothing appears to me more surprising than this infallibility of prayer. It has force enough to render (in one use) the word of man as powerful and even more powerful than the word of God. As powerful, because as the Lord by his word made all things (He spake, and they were made,) so man has but to speak and to ask, and all things are granted to him. Ye shall ask what ye will, and it shall be done unto you; and more powerful if I dare to express it, because if the Lord be himself obeyed it can be but by created beings, whilst God, with all his attributes and powers, by the efficacy of prayer is brought according to the expressions of Scripture, to obey the voice of the man who prays. Joshua x. 14. The Lord obeyed the voice of man."—Vol iii. p 187

Then follows a list of the worthies whose names are recorded in holy writ, whose experience has in some remarkable way attested the value and efficacy of prayer—from the victory of Israel over Amalek, obtained by the prayer of Moses, the breaking of St Peter's chains, effected by the prayer of the church, and the conversion of the church's persecutor into a faithful disciple of Christ; and the effusion of the Holy Spirit on the collected disciples, and on the apostles previously to their first ministerial labours. He also instances the remarkable expression used by the Almighty to Moses, when interceding for the

But what, exclaims the preacher, on these words "Let me alone? What hinders thee, O Lord? Where is the obstruction to the accomplishment of thy will? What stays thy hand? What a spectacle does this present! Moses, who prays on the Mount, arrests the arm of the Almighty, and obtains for prayer the glorious testimony that it divests the Lord of hosts of the power to arise and avenge himself.

In the second part of this sermon he considers the spirit in which we should pray, if we would obtain our desires; and his remarks on the cold and careless supplications of some (what Brydayne expressively terms "la sécheresse de nos prières"), and the contrast between the prayers and the lives of others, the spirited rebukes also with which he censures the superstitions of his own communion, and his view of God answering prayer in anger, and sometimes denying in mercy, are deserving of a very attentive perusal. The following passage concludes his discourse on prayer.

"Pray then, my brethren, be instant therein; nothing is more important for all of you. If you are yet in a state of sin, by prayer you will obtain your conversion; if you are among the righteous, and have a reasonable hope of your living in the grace of God, prayer will procure you the inestimable gift of perseverance; if you are in the state of neither, but sometimes righteous sometimes sinning [or, as Dr Chalmers would with more of theological precision describe it, hovering so near the line of demarcation as hardly to be known to which side you actually belong] like thousands of lax and unwatching Christians, prayer will obtain for you those particular helps which will attach you more to grace and duty, and sustain you therein. Again, I repeat it, you have but to ask to obtain. If you are tempted, prayer will give you a triumph over temptation; if weak, prayer will be your strength; if sick, your consolation; if persecuted, your support; if athirst, it will become a springing well of living water, which whoso tastes shall never thirst again. Oh, my brother, what a joy, what a consolation is it to find in the Lord, by means of prayer, an all

sufficient ——— ——— ——— ——— a Benefactor, who ——— ——— ——— a Father, who listens to our grief; a Physician, who heals our wounds; a Judge ——— ——— ——— ——— himself ——— as ——— ——— in this sacred exercise, ——— which can alone soothe our grief; a beloved hand which dries our tears; a secret light which shews our path; a sovereign remedy and a resource in all our ails, and all our woes. Pray then, brethren, but pray often; be instant in prayer; at evening, at morning, at night and day; in your churches, in public, and in the privacy of your houses! Alas! you live constantly in the midst of such perils, in such darkness, on the edge of so few ——— precipices, pursued by so many ——— assailed by so many fatal passions, that it is surprising you neglect so ——— ——— recourse you may have to God; ——— from him protection and help. Pray then brethren, but pray in a suitable frame of mind, and ask only of the Lord what you ought. To this end, return without delay to his favour; renounce the ——— ——— and then seek great things from the Lord in prayer. Ask of him the blessings of grace, blessings for eternity, and for the soul, far more than any advantages for the body; an enlightened mind to know the path in which you ought to tread, and the means you should adopt to walk therein with confidence; a spirit of penitence to weep over your past wanderings, and to resume from them a spirit of love to animate you in the service of God and in the practice of Christian virtues; strength to sustain you in your conflict with the corruptions of your nature, and the temptations of the world, and the devil; submission in the various trials of life; and a spirit of holiness to lead to perfect and Christian ——— fulfilling all your obligations, whether generally those of men and Christians, or particular in the various stations in which it has pleased God to place you, and by which he is conducting you, as by so many paths, to a joyful eternity. Pray then, brethren, but pray as you ought through Jesus Christ, and even with him—let your supplications ascend from your understanding and heart and not merely from your mouth and lips; let them be animated by faith, sanctified by humility, and sustained in perseverance, that they may end in eternal joy." Vol. ii pp 228—231

The fourth volume is chiefly occupied with two very long sermons on true piety; the former of which is entitled its "eloge," or commendation; the latter, its "apologie," or defence. There are likewise some "instructions" and a sermon on frequent and fervent *communion*

As in the former volumes, various *fragments* are appended to each of these. Brydayne's view of the sacrament of the Lord's supper is just what might be anticipated from a zealous minister connected with the Roman Catholic Church. His invitations to it are universal, but at the same time his warnings against a profanation of it are perfectly appalling, and derive much of their high colouring from that painfully preposterous doctrine of his church which has introduced itself into this symbolic rite. His lively imagination is in full exercise on this subject: on one occasion he exposes the unworthy communicant by a sorry conceit, which, by the way, places the transubstantiators in an awkward predicament. "Other shepherds," he says, "nourish themselves by their flocks, but ye (oh the malice and ingratitude!) devour your Shepherd." But after severing these, and many other passages, which originated in the "*church's*" gross ideas of this simple and affecting ordinance, and which transform it into an "august mystery," there are many very fine and powerful passages, and impassioned appeals to his hearers. His ejaculatory and occasionally lengthened addresses to the Saviour, appear to us objectionable. To have produced any effect, they must have been accompanied by a manner and gestures suited rather to the stage than the church.

In the sermons on true piety, or devotedness to God, we find much to admire. They surely could not have been framed by an undevout mind. Brydayne's heart must itself have experienced the pleasures which, with so much fulness and freshness, he spreads before the eyes of others. It is only matter of regret with us, that in these and also the sermons on prayer, when in the immediate contemplation of that subject which brings the soul at once before God, and which lays open all the exhaustless stores of infinitude to the prayer of the petitioner, Brydayne could not for once have so far lost sight of the nugatory succour of the saints, as to exclude all reference to the intercession of the Virgin. But in these, as in the other sermons, the exordia are not considered complete without her succours, for his prefatory remarks customarily conclude by Ave Marias. When, however, he is fairly launched on his subject, nothing can be finer than the stately movement and swelling majesty of some of his periods. The best breath of Heaven, that hallowed wind which bloweth where it listeth, seems to fill his sentences, and to carry himself and his hearers past every "wave of this troublesome world, safe into that haven of true religion, where alone is real peace."

From that short but affecting sentence uttered by the good Shepherd, in Luke xii. 22, "Fear not, little flock, it is your Father's good pleasure to give you the kingdom;" our author undertakes to shew, that nothing is so entirely worthy of our regard and pursuit as true religion,—and that nothing, on the other hand, is more unjust and impious than to censure those who profess and practise it. The former of these positions is established in his "eloge," the latter in his "apologie." In the following passage, the zealous father presses, with evident emotion, the important union with the people of God from a view of the sacred pleasures to which it is introductory.

Come, behold and taste for yourselves these pleasures. See what is experienced by the pure souls who yet remain among the inhabitants of this world, but who have received the grace of God. Behold their fidelity, their zeal in the service of their Lord; and above all, what a joy in the Holy Ghost they experience in the midst of all their exercises and devotions. You esteem the church as a burning bush; approach it, and you will see that it burns, but is not consumed. Expressive symbol this of the bright and sacred flame which the unction of real piety kindles in a believing soul, producing no other injury than the destruction of its lusts. Enter this desert which appears to you so dry and barren, and where you discover only monsters quick to devour all that dwell therein; this thorny path of true religion, which terrifies and alarms you; and you will astonished, find the most delicious manna covering the earth, streams of milk and honey flowing in every direction, and even the hard rocks breaking forth in peaceful and refreshing waters, making the echoes murmur with the delightful sound. Examine as closely as you will, what in religion you call crosses and thorns, and you will find beneath these crosses a sacred unction which softens them, and beneath these thorns, roses which remove their sting." Vol. IV. pp. 184, 185.

In the general view given by our author of the Divine favour resting on the people of God, and the preservation of this their earthly abode, with all its incidents, solely for the accomplishment of that period, when all the elect shall be gathered in, there is much in which we cannot but agree. We might quote some beautiful passages; but throughout his remarks on this subject there runs much of the author's unscriptural, and merely oratorical exaggerations, in the course of which he seems to forget the Divine declarations that the mercies of God are over all his works, and, that he maketh his sun to rise upon the evil, as well as upon the good; and almost to give to the godly what belongs alone to the sole Mediator between God and man.

In the following sermon Brydayne gives an admirable summary of the useless creeds and practices of the religionists of his day; we may add of every day.

"First," he says "comes the religion of *ostentation*. This comprises those who would have no religion but for the glory which accompanies it. They will subject their bodies to austerities and penances and become the instructors of the poor: they will remain we may say *dwell*, for whole days in churches and abandon their former religion in quest of new and higher modes: but all this is to attract observation and to make a glittering display of piety. Hence hence ye self righteous souls! will the Sovereign Judge at last say to them. Depart from me ye *have* received your reward.

Then comes the religion of *party* (Devotion intrigante et dominante.) This will not endure the ordinary modes and the uniform sentiment and habit of their fellow-Christians. A badge of distinction is sought in peculiarity of outward appearance, in more frequent communions and an intemperate zeal for the interest and ease of a particular teacher, whose flock they wish to increase. Some one heard to say 'I am of Paul,' and others 'I of Apollos,' said, cry those of the intestine war which is often kept up with the flames of religion, and which proves that neither the one nor the other are truly of Christ.

"Then comes the religion of *false zeal*. Martha, Martha, said Christ to the sister of Mary, you are careful and troubled about many things; a reproach which might with great reason be applied, to those hasty spirits who do nothing with sound judgment, and whose zeal is the effect of a heated temper. It is the work of God say they; woe to him who performs it negligently. But I say also, woe to him who does it precipitately.

"Next is the religion which is all *severity for others*, but all *indulgence to self*; because you have raised the standard of religion, you esteem yourselves impeccable, but others incorrigible. For offenders, you have no eye of pity; but only of scorn; far from being affused with compassion for their state, you are angry with the forbearance of God towards them; you would even ask for fire from heaven to consume them; but all the while, with an astonishing obliquity you perceive not your own corruptions. Ah, my brethren, the prophet described his zeal as consuming himself; yours finds its enjoyment in devouring others.

"The religion of *caprice* is another form of fruitless profession. Persons of this character are perpetually passing and repassing between the two extremes. Now they are religious, now they are worldly. Sometimes they are cold, sometimes fervent. One day given up to the indolence of pleasure, the next concealed in the obscurity of retirement; continually changing their system in the practice of piety, and hurrying from preacher to preacher, and from guide to guide, to discover one more to their taste. This is not to seek a teacher to govern you, but to seek by a teacher to govern and please yourself.

"The religion of *accommodation* is another error. Many wish to be religious but they cannot deny themselves; they cross their own wills in nothing but live in the utmost self-enjoyment. As for me, will one of such professors exclaim, in embracing religion I aspire to serve God quite smoothly without torturing myself as some do; provided I confine myself to an honest conversation, retrench my flagrant crimes, inflict no injury on any one and frequent the sacrament God will demand nothing more. What an error and delusion is this! A truly religious life will ever be one of labour and self denial.

An *ill-regulated religion* is the last we shall notice. In this essentials are forgotten and the chief regard paid to what is accidental and accessary; plain precept is abandoned for the adoption of questionable

couldst the man wishes to be religious, but ... Christian. What fruit will you derive from religion which leaves no subordination on side? The most deplorable consequence is that these, to all appearance, good men, have the greatest scruples in omitting a sermon, a communion, a form of prayer, but their conscience slumbers over the ... which they spread, and their palpable neglect of primary and relative duties. Is it not to such that the Saviour addresses those threatening words of his Gospel, 'Woe unto you who pay with sound exactness your tithe of mint, anise, and cummin, but forget the weightier matters of the law, judgment, mercy, and truth; who strain out a gnat and swallow a camel? These ought ye to have done, and not to leave the other undone.' Vol. iv. pp. 225—229.

In the application of the Scriptures cited in the above extract, there is a deviation from the immediate intention with which they stand connected in the sacred text, but it is not so considerable as to induce us to omit a passage so useful and practical. With equal strength does our author in the sequel of this discourse, describe and condemn that spirit of captious enmity which preys upon the healthy and consistent graces of the true Christian, and by the distorting powers of its own misrepresentations converts them into its own disease. The men of the Saviour's and of the Baptist's day were the same. The straight appeared to them crooked, the plain rough. This enmity begets in those who feel it, a reluctance to resemble, in the remotest degree, the objects of their censure, and locks them up therefore in the security of a self-confidence, which unhappily may terminate only when the unsealing of the spell will be of no avail.

Brydayne's description of this spirit, and his exposure of its tendency, are full of point, but we cannot quote them, nor is it necessary; for such a state of mind almost carries its own folly and sinfulness on its very surface.

The last of the volumes contains various shorter papers, which the author, or the editor*, has denominated, Exhortations, ... Fragments, and Prayers. There are likewise some exordia of sermons, a homily for the fourth Sunday in Advent, a letter to one young female, and some regulations for another as to the profitable employment of time.

The principal subjects of the former of these letters are purity of heart and life, marriage, the cross, (considered more, we regret, in its visible appearance, as an object of sense, than in the clear development of its vital doctrines), and some excellent remarks on the perils attendant on relapsing into sin, and on occasioning scandals in the church or the world, with the inevitable effect and influence which every individual example must have, in a direct or indirect manner, on the heart and conduct of others. "No man liveth unto himself."

We have no space for any extracts from this volume, and indeed feel the less inclined to make them, since although occasionally there are fine passages in it, many of them are either quoted, or adopted with some slight alterations, from the fathers for whose writings, particularly those of St. Augustine and St. Bernard, Brydayne appears to have entertained a warm and reasonable partiality. We have another reason for passing over this volume with slighter notice than the others, that it is more fully impregnated with the exceptionable peculiarities of Rome. The faults of Brydayne's style of oratory are also brought into greater prominence, one in particular, of which, from its repeated adoption, he seems to have been by no means conscious as a fault, but which obscures and weakens some of the brightest and strongest passages in his sermons. we allude to his selection of some brief sentence

---

* It is rather surprising that the editor has not given the public any particulars respecting the discovery or the authenticity of Brydayne's manuscripts, which had long been considered as lost. There can be no doubt, we think, of their authenticity, but the circumstances of their discovery ought to have been mentioned

condemning probably several of the thoughts in his own mind; and he opening or closing his paragraphs with it, not once or twice, which is often done with great effect, but with a wearisome repetition, as many as nine or ten times, till his sermon quite echoes with it. The reader will discover, among other examples, three instances of this blemish, where it has peculiarly impaired the best parts of his composition. One occurs in vol. ii., where Brydayne is describing the deep agony of David on account of his lamentable fall, an agony of mind which could be assuaged neither by the glories of his kingdom, nor the pleasures of his court, nor altogether renounced even by the consolatory voice of the prophet declaring his pardon. This passage is in other respects forcible and striking, but is weakened even to puerility, by the often repeated exclamation, "Thy sin ever before thee!" with the continual and close recurrence of the expression "What prince!"

Another occurs in vol. iv., where *sixteen* pages are occupied with a sort of running comment on these few and simple but majestic words, which reveal, while they shroud in solemn obscurity, the incommunicable name of the self existent and eternal Jehovah,—"I am that I am." The sublimity of this passage is altogether frittered away by the fault of the orator. This last volume furnishes another instance of the same kind, where the statement of St John, "Even now are there many antichrists," is made the ten times repeated motto for an exposure of the evils of modern days, which is by no means written with the author's usual spirit.

But all these are *trifles*—our quarrel with Brydayne, in this last volume particularly, but which extends more or less to them all, is the display which he makes amidst all his exhortations to the "caritas, spesque, fidesque of the Gospel which he preached, of the intolerent spirit of his church. He brands the two chief reformers of Germany and France, as the two arch-heretics (*ces deux fameux hérésiarques*) who had spread so much misery, and caused such abounding and eternal ruin, (see the sermon on *scandals* or offences), vol. v. p. 448. He even advances against Martin Luther, (not specifically on account of his marriage, but generally against his character), a charge of licentiousness, and classes him with the most abandoned profligates of his age. Surely this is an awakening specimen of the possible excitement of temper, in some at least, of the most enlightened of the ministers, and missionaries too, of the alleged "true church," when any secession from its ranks, or any assault on its tenets, or any inquiry into its discipline, or any doubt of its authority, is avowed, or even indicated.

In short, the principles which pervade many of his reasonings are such as to compel those who adopt them to a habit of persecution towards the members of other religions, and of indefatigable proselytism as respects their own. This fact has recently been illustrated by the statements of Mr Blanco White, and we need not enlarge upon it. But there is one little specimen in Brydayne of this exclusive spirit, which we deem too curious for its logic, and too explicit in its temper, to be passed over. He enumerates four points of faith as indispensable in every saving creed. The first is the being and unity of God, comprehending all his attributes and perfections; the second, that as there is but *one God*, so there can be but one religion; the third that that religion must be the religion of Christianity, because God has revealed it: so far all is well; but then comes the fourth, that that single available religion, being the Christian, cannot be any other than the *Catholic*. All others are excluded, and in them none can be saved.' (See vol. iv. p. 382.)

But while we justly censure the

intolerant spirit of the Roman Catholic Church, let us not forget that intolerance is not the vice of that church alone, but of human nature itself. Has our own church been always free from this antichristian spirit? and do we not owe it far more to the growing freedom of our political institutions, than to the liberality of some churchmen, that we have not in this age to lament the scenes which darkened the days of Charles the Second, of Laud, and even of Elizabeth? Have we not heard divines of our own times attributing to the Church of England prerogatives little short of those claimed by Rome, and charitably consigning the Dissenters from it to "the uncovenanted mercies of God"? And are we sure that in the temper and conduct of that party which in this and the sister kingdom assumes to itself emphatically the designation of Protestant, there have not too often been displayed the worst fruits of that proud, exclusive, and persecuting spirit which constitutes the lasting reproach of Popery?

LITERARY AND PHILOSOPHICAL INTELLIGENCE,
&c &c

GREAT BRITAIN

PREPARING for publication.—Bibliotheca Biblica, by the Author of Biblical Gleanings;—Heads of Lectures in Divinity, by the Rev J B Hollingsworth—Devotional Exercises by the Rev R Morehead;—The Cottager's Family Altar, with Scriptural References for Daily Reading,—(by subscription) Narrative of a Tour, by a Party of the Missionaries in the Sandwich Islands, around Hawaii, by the Rev W Ellis.

In the press.—A Parting Memorial, consisting of Sermons preached in China, Singapore, &c., by the Rev. Dr Morrison,—Moral Hebrew Tales, translated from ancient Hebrew Works, by H Hurwitz,—Limborch's History of the Inquisition, re-modelled and enlarged, by C Mackenzie,—Essays to illustrate the Mode of Education pursued in Sunday Schools, and to remedy their most important defects, by A H Davis.—A Book of Martyrs for the Young, by the Rev Isaac Taylor illustrated with upwards of fifty engravings.

Professor Barlow has found that the magnetic power may be imparted merely by rotation. Circular plates made of iron copper zinc, and other metals being set in rapid revolution all possessed more or less influence in deflecting a needle from its true position but the iron plate in a much greater degree than the other metals.

A patent has been taken out, both in London and Paris for a process for reducing straw into pulp for making paper, and in extracting from it the colouring or other matter. The straw is boiled with quick-lime and water to extract the colouring and separate the fibres. The fibrous substance is then submitted to the action of hydro-sulphuret, to get rid of the mucilaginous and silicious matters. The fibrous material is then washed, pressed, bleached, and introduced into the ordinary rag-engine employed for making paper.

Cambridge.—The Seatonian prize for the present year has been adjudged to the Rev J Overton, M A of Trinity College, for his poem on 'The Building and Dedication of the Second Temple.'

Captain Manby recently arrived in Europe is stated to have brought a report supported by presumptive evidence, that the spot where La Perouse perished forty years ago, with his crew, is now ascertained. An English whaler it is said, discovered an island between New Caledonia and New Guinea, at nearly an equal distance from each of these islands. The inhabitants came on board the whaler and one of the chiefs had a cross of St. Louis hanging as an ornament from one of his ears. Others of the natives had swords on which the word Paris was engraved and some were observed to have medals of Louis XVI. One of the chiefs aged about fifty, said, that when he was young a large ship was overtaken in a violent gale and total ress, and that all on board perished, and that his cross, some books, one chest which contained the cross of St. Louis and other things. During his voyage round the world, Captain Manby had seen several medals of the same kind, which La Perouse had distributed among the natives of California. It is added that the cross of St. Louis is now on its way to Europe.

An institution has been formed in Edinburgh, through the bequest of a lady, amounting to some thousand pounds for the purpose of endowing an Episcopalian Theological Professorship to be filled by a Master of Arts of Oxford or Cambridge subject to the control of the Scottish Bishops.

FRANCE

At the last annual sitting of the French Academy the prize of 10,000 francs for merit and virtue was awarded to Pierre Martin, a poor day labourer, who having married a poor girl who had three blind brothers, and an infirm father, maintained them by his labour, and would suffer none of them to ask alms, though he had three children of his own to support. He worked night and day, depriving himself of sustenance, that they should not want, till he frequently fell down from over exertion and want of food. The second prize, of 3,000 francs, was given to a poor girl named Hermitte, who took a poor deaf and dumb child under her protection and, without any knowledge of the methods in use succeeded in teaching her little protegé to read and write. Various other rewards were distributed on similar grounds. The prizes for publications conducive to morals and virtue were awarded to the Baron de Gérando for a work " On Moral Improvement or Self-Education,' and to the work of the late Madame Campan On Education.

RUSSIA

In the Russian empire, there are six Universities namely, in the cities of Moscow, Petersburgh, Kasan, Dorpat, Charkow, and Wilna. The subjects of that empire are not suffered to go into foreign lands for education till they have studied at least three years in one of these institutions. The professional chairs are few; many branches of learning are entirely interdicted and a jealous watch is kept even as respects those that are allowed. The emperor has prohibited the schools throughout the empire from using any foreign linen or cloth, and has established annual markets for the sale of native woollens.

SARDINIA

A royal edict, it is stated, has been lately issued, directing that in future, no person shall learn to read or write who cannot prove the possession of property above the value of 1500 livres, about 60l sterling.

NEW YORK

A steam-boat, composed wholly of sheet-iron, intended for a passage-boat, is being constructed at New York. It is intended to be much lighter, and at the same time stronger than if built of wood.

BRAZIL

Orders have been issued in Brazil for the establishment of botanic gardens in all the provinces and the attention of the planters has been called to the cultivation of the tea-plant, of which one proprietor has already 4,000 on his estate.

INDIA

At a late meeting of the Asiatic Society of Calcutta various articles from Nipal were laid on the table. The Secretary read a paper by Mr Hodgson on the literature of Thibet. Some progress has been made in the collection of Bhoteea works and Mr Carey is about to give to the world a grammar of that language. Five works, procured by Hodgson, are from the archieves of Swogoombhoc Nath various others were procured from poor traffickers and monks who annually visit Nipal. It is a matter of surprise that in such a region as Bhote literature should be so widely diffused as to reach persons covered with filth, and destitute of any of those advantages which usually precede the luxury of books. Printing, however, is in general use among the Bhoteeas. They make use of wooden blocks for types, which are often beautifully engraved.

LIST OF NEW PUBLICATIONS

THEOLOGY

Essay on the Writings of St Luke from the German of Dr Schleiermacher with an introduction by the translator, containing an account of the Controversy respecting the Origin of the three first Gospels since Bishop Marsh's Dissertations 1 vol 8vo 13s bds

Man responsible for his Belief, two Sermons occasioned by a Passage in Mr Brougham's Glasgow Inaugural Address by the Rev R Wardlaw D D 2s

A Review of Notices formerly in a Discourse by the Rev. J. Ely.

Divinity, or Discourses on the Being of God, the Divinity of Christ, and the Personality of the Holy Ghost, and on the Sacred Trinity; being Improved Extracts from a System of Divinity; by the Rev. W. Davy. [For some curious memoranda respecting this publication see C. O. for 1823, p 654.]

Wesleyana, a Selection of Extracts from the Writings of the Rev J Wesley arranged to form a Body of Divinity 6s

Bagster's Comprehensive Bible (Parts I and II) adapted for Pulpit, Study and Family Use is now in the course of publication with Notes philological or explanatory 1 vol 4to

The Ordinance of the Lord's Supper illustrated by W. Orme, author of the Life of Dr. Owen.

MISCELLANEOUS

The Poor Man's Preservative against Popery by the Rev B. White 3s 6d of a cheap edition 1s 6d or 16s per dozen

Cottage Comforts, with Hints for promoting them, gleaned from Experience, by Esther Hewlett 2s 6d

The Amulet, or Christian and Literary Remembrancer 12s

The Literary Remains of Lady Jane Gray by N H Nicolas Post 8vo 7s 6d Royal 8vo 15s

The Life of the Right Hon R B Sheridan by T Moore 4to 3l 3s

An Attempt to establish the First Principles of Chemistry by Experiment by T Thompson M D. 2 vols 8vo 30s

---

RELIGIOUS INTELLIGENCE

SOCIETY FOR THE PROPAGATION OF THE GOSPEL.

THE last Report of this Society recently distributed among its members contains many interesting facts, the substance of which we shall lay before our readers confining our attention in the present Number to that part of the Report which refers to India.

We cannot however avoid adverting before we proceed with our extracts to the manner in which the Society's Reports are drawn up which with a little care might be rendered much more inviting The style of printing also is much too expensive The names of the twelve members by charter, for example, occupy two whole pages; two benefactors by legacy of 100l each engross two more; the short list of "incorporated members" occupies twelve, and the other subscribers one hundred and thirty The whole volume is at once redundant and deficient. No list of Vice Presidents is given District Committees are put down which do not exist; and Subscribers are inserted in as many places as they have livings Dr. Gaskin's name for example appears no less than five times in pp. 195, *53, *60, *66, *86; Dr Walmsley four times, Archdeacon Browne twice in one page, &c. &c.

We regret to observe the very little public interest excited by the anniversary sermons preached before the Society and that no collection is made on those occasions Might they not be rendered more attractive to the well disposed part of the public and be made also a means of increasing the funds of the Society? One of the best measures perhaps for rendering the Society better known and more highly valued would be either to throw open its committee room to all its members; or, if that were inconvenient, to appoint a representative board elected by the subscribers at large At present its affairs being conducted by a self-elected, and irresponsible though most highly respectable and venerable, corporation the public take far too little interest in them The sister Society for promoting Christian Knowledge most wisely fixes no restriction as to the number of its members all who wish to subscribe a guinea annually to its objects, if their character will stand the ballot, may be elected members, and attend and vote at the monthly board In most other societies where this 'universal suffrage' would be inconvenient, a representative system is adopted the subscribers annually electing their own committee and other officers, and virtually voting through them But in the Society for the Propagation of the Gospel the great body of the subscribers have no voice either personal or representative in the procedings of the institution or the administration of its funds a circumstance which we fear greatly weakens the interest of the public in its behalf Could no remedy be discovered to obviate this inconvenience?

We feel ourselves called upon to add that we cannot wholly approve of the spirit in which the Report is drawn up

missionary efforts were not so much to make men Christians, as to prevent their becoming sectarians. We shall quote but one passage as an example. "It is of great importance," says the Report, p. 141, "to provide this part of the province [Lower Canada] with resident clergy, as the Methodists have for a long period used their efforts to secure an ascendency in the township of St. Armand." We should be greatly rejoiced to see resident episcopal clergy both in Canada and elsewhere, and to learn that they were subverting the Methodists by "out-preaching and out-living them:" but merely to spar with Methodism in foreign parts is a very paltry motive for all the toil and anxiety, the heavy expense and the unwearied prayers of the patrons of Christian missions. We are convinced that the best friends of the Society would deeply lament if any of its agents should so far forget the nature of their momentous province as to be more anxious in a mere party spirit, to stave off Dissenters, than to "bring home Jews, Turks and Infidels to Christ's flock."

But we proceed to the more pleasing task of extracts from the correspondence of the Lord Bishop of Calcutta, dated June and August, 1824.—

"I am happy to acknowledge the safe arrival of the library and communion plate destined for Bishop's College, as well as of Mr. Townsend the printer and his necessary stores, and the power of attorney. For all these I should have taken an earlier opportunity of offering my thanks to the Society for the Propagation of the Gospel had not they arrived when I was much occupied in preparing for the journey in which I am now engaged, and which it is in my purpose by God's blessing, to pursue through the greater part of this diocese.—His lordship proceeds to account for the slow progress which had been made in the erection of the college, and adds that it was with difficulty that the principal was enabled last Christmas to take possession of his lodging. He continues, "Since that time the progress of the work, if not more rapid has been more perceptible. The ground has been cleared and drained, the pools filled up, walks of pounded brick constructed round the quadrangle and to the river. The offices are finished, and the dwellings for the native teachers and the printer are in some degree of advancement. The rooms are to a certain extent furnished. The library, which is a very beautiful apartment, has received, and shews to great advantage, the books which it owes to the munificence of the Society, and some other benefactors, among whom the principal himself is most conspicuous. It was with no common emotion that I first heard a well-toned bell calling, amid those teak and cocoa-nut trees, the inmates of the building to morning prayers, though as yet, unfortunately, not in the chapel. The latter is still empty and unglazed. The wood work of the stalls has been some time under the workmens' hands, but from such hands no speedy result can be expected. The hall is sufficiently furnished for the present number of its inmates; but its walls have a naked and unadorned appearance, which may perhaps be one day removed by a portrait of the distinguished and excellent prelate who designed it. The printing press is setting up in one of the lower apartments of the east wing. A separate building would be now most desirable, and will ere long be absolutely necessary, but the funds are at present unequal to such an undertaking. The organ is for the present in one of the recesses of the library. With regard to the expense incurred, I beg leave to assure the Incorporated Society that no single item has been allowed by me which both the principal and I have not agreed in thinking absolutely necessary, or respecting the usual price of which I had not obtained the best information in my power.

The college now contains two students on the foundation of the Incorporated Society, Mr. James Dunsmure and Mr. Daniel Jones; a third, Mr. William Addison Godfrey on the foundation of the Society for promoting Christian Knowledge, and from the archdeaconry of Madras; and a fourth, a non-foundation student, supported and to be paid for by the Diocesan Committee of the Church Missionary Society. The Rev. Christian David, long a native catechist in the employ of the Society for promoting Christian Knowledge, and lately ordained by me deacon and priest as one of the colonial chaplains of his Majesty's Government of Ceylon, has been an inmate within its walls during the time of his residence in this archdeaconry. The Rev. Mr. Tweddell, one of the Incorporated Society's missionaries, is prosecuting his studies there also; and Mr. Townsend, the printer, is, as a matter of necessity, admitted on the same footing.

The college is a beautiful object, in a singularly picturesque and sequestered scene. And, above all, it is already in active and efficient auxiliaries as a place of oriental, classical, and Christian education in which its excellent principal is labouring, though single-handed, with a patient and persevering ability which, to be duly appreciated, must be witnessed. Both he and I, however, look forward with anxious earnestness to the arrival of one, if not both, of the professors who are to share in his toil."

"The Society's two elder missionaries Mr. Christian and Mr. Morton are employed, I believe most usefully and I trust in a manner not contrary to the Society's intentions, in superintending two excellent circles of Bengalee schools, supported by the Diocesan Committee of the Society for promoting Christian Knowledge. They are both men of good talents, and much zeal and diligence. Mr. Christian is every thing, as I conceive, which a missionary ought to be; devoted to, and delighting in, his work; endearing himself to the natives by his kind, condescending and cheerful disposition, and to his countrymen and brother clergy by his modesty and propriety both of behaviour and doctrine."

Additional communications state that Mr. Morton has undertaken, with the approbation of the principal of the college, the preparation and publication of a Manual Bengalli, and English Dictionary, including the Bengalli Synonyms, to be succeeded or accompanied by a Bengalli Grammar. The Bishop has marked out the present Dutch settlement of Chinsurah, thirty miles up the river, for a missionary station.

In the north circle Mr. Christian superintends six schools, which contain nearly five hundred children. The establishment of these schools was a great undertaking and no doubt will effect a material change in the religious and moral principles of the rising generation. By the active zeal and attention of the Secretary to the Society for promoting Christian Knowledge, religious tracts in English and Bengalli have been introduced into all the schools of his circle and the New Testament in English into two of them which is read and understood tolerably well.

Mr. Christian has found the appearance and manners of the children since he came among them, greatly improved. Distinguishing marks of red and yellow clay, which were then common on their faces and which served to impress the mind with the strongest idea of their superstition, are now laid aside; the Parables of our Lord, which were read in schools, he has prevailed on them to commit to memory so that they can now repeat any of them in their own language with readiness, and they have received from him the Gospel of St. Matthew in Bengalli to copy out as a profitable exercise which when finished is to be bound and returned to them as a reward for their industry. It is to be hoped that many of these children will be brought up in the Christian faith; certainly they will be very different from the generation before them. The difficulty with adults is great. Caste it is added is found to be one of the chief obstacles to the progress of Christianity, for were that difficulty removed, many would avow their attachment to it.

CHURCH MISSIONARY SOCIETY

The Twenty-fifth Report of this Institution delivered at the last annual meeting which is now passing through the press contains a highly interesting account of the Society's proceedings during the last year. We purpose on its publication to lay before our readers our usual annual abstract; in the mean time we give, by anticipation, the following general particulars:—

Five new Associations have been formed during the year, besides four Branch and sixteen Ladies' Associations; with six Associations in aid of the Hibernian Auxiliary—making a total in the United Kingdom of thirty-one.

The income amounted without deducting expenses and including the contributions to the Institution at Islington to more than 45,000l. The net income of the year, available for the general purposes of the Society, has been upward of 40,500l.; being an increase, on the net income of the twenty-fourth year, of nearly 6,000l. The expenditure of the twenty-fifth year has amounted to nearly 38,000l. The Committee are anxious, however, to have it distinctly understood that the surplus of the income over the expenditure has not arisen from any inability on their part to expend a larger sum on missionary objects but on the contrary, from a prudent desire to restrict the Society's expenditure within the limits of its probable income. The calls for assistance are now so urgent from all parts of the heathen world, that were the income of the Society twice as large as the sum to which the exertions and contributions of its friends have raised it, there would be no difficulty in making an efficient appropration of the whole amount. In north and south India, in Ceylon, in Australasia, and in Africa, much of the field of toil which has already been entered upon remains, comparatively, uncultivated, for want of labourers; while in various parts of the globe, to which, hitherto, few or no missionaries have been sent, opportunities are continually opening for exertion. The total number of missionaries, including those of every country and of every religious denomination is utterly inadequate to supply the wants of the hundreds of millions of heathen who are *perishing for lack of knowledge*.

The offers of service during the past year have been more numerous than during the year preceding sixty persons have expressed their readiness to labour in the work of the Society. Of this number the services of sixteen have been accepted those of twenty nine have been declined and the cases of the remaining fifteen are under consideration. There are at present, twenty students in the Society's Institution, under preparation for missionary labour of whom five are Lutheran clergymen from the seminary at Bâsle.

After reporting the opening of the Institution at Islington, the Committee add—

There is one important feature connected with these proceedings which must not be overlooked. The first institution which the Established Church has witnessed in our own country, for the specific purpose of training up missionaries for the heathen, has been opened, with every prospect, if adequately supported, of extensively promoting the great object for which it has been set apart. The Rev Professor Lee had undertaken the superintendance of the Oriental studies of the students.

The survey of the Society's proceedings in its missions occupies nearly 150 pages in the Report a table is given in the introductory sheet, of the missions, stations labourers, schools, and scholars and at the close of the Report, appears the following summary —

In the nine missions of the Society there are forty five stations with which are connected 296 schools

These stations and schools are occupied by 440 labourers of these 119 are Europeans including a few females born of British parents in India and 321 were born in the respective countries chiefly where they are employed. The number of scholars under the Society is 14,090 of whom 10,457 are boys, 2957 girls and 676 youths and adults. In connexion with the principal missions, printing presses are established, and are coming in some places into very active and beneficial operation.

In conclusion, the Committee avow their full conviction, with thankfulness to Him who guides all things to the advancement of His kingdom that, amidst numberless and augmenting difficulties, that kingdom is steadily advancing. Severe trials indeed, continue to attend the servants of God, in their combined exertions to fulfil His will. of these trials, particularly in that most interesting of all the scenes of Christian labour among the liberated Africans, a large portion has befallen the Society, and still exercises the faith and patience of its friends. Not only, however, is countervailing success granted in other quarters, but, as the Committee rejoice to witness the Reports of the Associations throughout the United Kingdom indicate the prevalence of a spirit so truly Christian, in reference both to the trials of the Society and its own duties and those of its members that the Committee cannot but hail this as a manifest token for good

LADIES SOCIETY FOR THE EDUCATION OF NEGRO CHILDREN

We have in our possession a large mass of interesting papers and publications connected with the proceedings of Anti-slavery Societies, and the present condition of the slaves and people of colour in our West India islands; some of the most important extracts from which we hope in future Numbers to lay before our readers. For the present, we must content ourselves with announcing the formation of a Ladies Society for promoting the early education and improvement of the children of Negroes, and of People of Colour, in those colonies. The Society is under the patronage of a number of benevolent ladies of high rank and distinction, and we trust it may be of service, if not in its more direct efforts for the objects of its humane care, at least in exciting an additional interest in the minds of the British public, especially among persons of influence, in behalf of the most degraded and oppressed portion of the human race; more degraded and oppressed in the nineteenth century of the Christian era, under professedly Christian masters, the subjects of the British Crown and enjoying themselves the ample liberties of Britons than were the helots of Sparta, or the slaves of Rome in far less enlightened ages, and under the obdurate institutions of Pagan despotism. It is well that our countrywomen should seriously pledge themselves to the prosecution of the important object of educating the children of the slaves and coloured population, who in a vast majority of instances, are scarcely more regarded as fit objects for mental culture than brute animals reared for the market or the plough. And if the benevolent individuals who patronize this object should not find our plantations generally open to their exertions, and not be able to establish efficient schools for the education of a future race of well instructed, well ordered Christian labourers, but from the present unhappy condition of West-India Society should find obstacles to impede their efforts, the difficulty will at least afford a new argument to prove the necessity for the authoritative interference of the mother country to place our colonial system on a more wise and liberal and humane basis.

The following is the Society's address:

The Society now announced originated in a conviction that while much has been effected for the benefit of heathen nations there yet remain thousands of human beings who are spending their strength to supply us with luxuries, but whose ignorance and depravity though we have often lamented, we have yet done little to remove; and whose peculiar situation as slaves renders them incapable of promoting their own improvement, or that of their children. Even those Negroes whose masters have been the most compassionate have, except in a few instances, enjoyed rather the happiness of the inferior animals than that of rational and immortal beings; for whatever may be the case with regard to their food and clothing, it is an acknowledged fact, that no adequate provision has been made for their instruction in the duties of morality and religion.

In confirmation of this statement it has been estimated, by persons well acquainted with the subject, that the whole number of Negro children now under instruction does not amount to 10,000 while on the most moderate computation there are not less than 150,000 of the slave population under ten years of age in our West-India Colonies, so that only one child in fifteen is receiving the blessing of education, in a country where from the depraved habits of the parents it is so peculiarly needed.

Surely then a vigorous effort ought to be made. The responsibility rests in a great measure with ourselves, for no one will any longer deny, that Africans are capable of improvement and civilization. In the actual state of Sierra Leone, we have the most gratifying testimony to the admirable effects of Christian instruction upon this neglected race. The opinion of the late Sir Charles M'Carthy on this subject is worth recording. When he was asked by a naval officer (connected with one of the West-India Islands) what method had been pursued to bring them from the deplorable condition in which they were received from the slave ships to such a state in so short a time. No other he replied than teaching them the truths of Christianity; and believe me, he added, if you admit Christian teachers into your island, you will find your slaves soon become affectionate and faithful servants to you. The evidence of Captain Sabine of the Engineers, an unprejudiced eye-witness who resided there six weeks and who closely and repeatedly inspected the state of the liberated Africans, is also most satisfactory. He has declared in reference to the largest assemblage of them at Regent's Town, that he is persuaded there is not to be seen upon earth a community of equal size so truly exemplary. *See Quarterly Review* No. 63, p 34.

Such indeed has been the happy result wherever the experiment has been made. The governments of different colonies where missionaries have been stationed bear the most favourable testimony to the influence of their labours on the state of society; and wherever insurrections have taken place *the instructed Negroes have invariably been found the most faithful to their masters*. It is not surprising that these facts, confirmed as they have been by the reports of other individuals, and now become notorious, should have contributed to remove the prejudices that formerly existed against Negro education. Many applications have accordingly been made to the Committee of the Church Missionary Society, by proprietors of estates, to supply their slaves with teachers; and liberal offers have been made for their support. There also exists among the Negroes themselves, an ardent desire for instruction. In some places those children who are not allowed to go to school have waited for the return of their more fortunate companions, and by offering some little bribe prevailed on them to impart the instruction they have just received.

The claims of another numerous class of destitute children the free children of colour are also most urgent; many of them are in a lamentable state of poverty and wretchedness, and stand peculiarly in need of Christian instruction. But every effort for their improvement is impeded by want of funds; and without liberal contributions from this country they no less than the slaves will remain in their present state of ignorance and degradation.

'Under these impressions a Ladies Society has been formed, the object of which will be to establish schools and further to assist such schools already established as may be approved of by the Society and sanctioned by the owners and superintendants of estates. In all its proceedings, the Society will consider the latter condition indispensable. The Society will thankfully avail itself of the counsel and assistance of the established ecclesiastical authorities wherever it can procure them; and, aware of the importance of a regular system of inspection, will endeavour to engage those authorities specially in this service; and where this is not practicable, will place their schools under the superintendance of the agents of the Church Missionary and other Societies. In making grants to institutions already established, the Society will always deem such of them as are connected with the Church of England to have the first claim, but will not refuse their aid to those which are under the care of Christian Missionaries of other denominations. They hope especially, in the prosecution of this importat undertaking, to have the co-operation of ladies connected with the West Indies, from whose influence and local knowledge they expect much valuable assistance. Above all, they would depend entirely on the Divine blessing, without which no human efforts can be of any avail.

Individuals disposed either to subscribe to the Society in London, or to form Associations in the country, may forward their names to the Treasurers, the Hon. Miss Calthorpe, 41 Lower Grosvenor Street; Miss H. G. Sperling, Highbury Hill; the Secretaries, Mrs Rich, 42 Cadogan Place; Miss F. Maitland, 11 Bryanstone Square; Mr Nisbet, Berners Street, Oxford Street; Sir C. Scot and Co., Holles Street, Cavendish Square; Messrs. Coutts and Co. No 59 Strand; and Messrs Hoare and Co. 62 Lombard Street.

PRAYER-BOOK AND HOMILY SOCIETY.

In our last Number we abstracted that portion of the Society's Thirteenth Report which refers to the distribution of the Church Formularies in the vernacular tongue: we shall now lay before our readers an account of its proceedings in procuring translations into other languages, and distributing them in foreign countries.

On this subject the Committee adopt the language of a foreigner who says

The distribution of the Liturgy in the languages of Roman Catholic countries is most important with a view to proving, to those who will read it, that Protestants are Christians as well as themselves; and that they agree in many fundamental articles of faith. The Church of England being, like the Church of Rome, governed by bishops, and having priests and deacons: the principal doctrines of the Christian faith being also distinctly expressed in the Liturgy, it is probable that the Book of Common Prayer may be acceptable to Roman Catholics; and that many may cease from that prejudice which causes them to consider Protestants as little better than Jews or Heathens, by shewing them that there exists a church besides their own which is neither Arian nor Socinian. Illustrations of this are afforded in the correspondence of the Society.

But in distributing the Liturgy, and some of the Homilies in foreign languages, the Committee have by no means an eye only to the religious benefit of Roman Catholics. To conciliate and edify any *Protestants* is an object equally important in their view. The state of Protestants here, writes a resident in a very distant land, is most lamentable. The great body of them is apostate from the faith, and consequently unholy in their life and conversation. From this you may conceive what a blessing our simple and scriptural prayers are likely to be; and what a contrast they make to every thing else here. This is felt by the inquiring Jews, who express their approbation of our service in strong terms.

In a subsequent letter the same correspondent says Your Prayer-books are used in Divine service in places where there are no ministers to conduct it. The burial service, which is also used in such cases, is much admired. As to the translated Homilies, we have distributed a great number; and it is peculiarly pleasing to us to know that the people make the best use of them. They have been so long without spiritual food that they are literally hungering and thirsting after it."—Additional testimonies to a like effect, might be produced from the letters of correspondents.

The Society in the course of the year have printed in one of the languages of the continent, four short selections from the Liturgy. As the Society's funds may allow, the Committee hope to publish similar portions in other languages.

The translations of the Prayer-book and Homilies already procured have been found very useful in visits paid by the Society's agent to foreign ships on the river Thames. In one month he visited one hundred and forty German, Dutch, and Danish ships, the crews of which consisted of five hundred and seventy men, and distributed among them German Homilies, and both Homilies and a Selection of Prayers and Thanksgivings from the English Liturgy translated into Dutch. These were for the most part very thankfully received, especially by the Dutch: some of the more respectable captains expressed their willingness to reciprocate acts of kindness towards English sailors who should visit their ports; and in more instances than one, expressions uttered by the seamen, signifying, "My mother tongue!" testified the peculiar pleasure with which these tokens of good will were accepted. The sailors on board a Greek ship (the Amphitrite) seemed particularly grateful for some copies of the first Homily in modern Greek. A foreign sailor understanding the object of the agent's visit, said with great earnestness, "Pray sir, leave me one of your books; a Hamburgh captain once gave me one of those Homilies, it was very good, but I have lost it." His gratitude on being presented with a selection of German Homilies was very great. The Society's agent having been informed by the chaplain of the Grampus frigate, which is stationed at Greenwich as a seaman's hospital ship, that on board that vessel not only natives of England and Wales, but also French, German, Italian, and Spanish sailors were confined by sickness, some Prayer-books and Homilies in each of those languages were sent to him.

The morning and evening services and the Psalter translated into Malay by Mr. Thompson, have been printed at Singapore, and the prayers in Malay are read every Sunday.

In Chinese, the Committee had reason to suppose that two thousand copies of the morning and evening services and Psalter had been printed in the course of the last year. They had also received, from Dr. Morrison, a manuscript copy of the Second Homily, "On the Misery of all Mankind by Sin," translated by him into Chinese. On this subject Dr. Morrison remarks: "I agree with you in considering the Second Homily very appropriate for distribution among the Chinese, whose moral and religious teachers all feed the vanity and pride of the human mind by the most unfounded assertions concerning the meritorious efficacy of their deeds. Mistaken men under the idea of reforming the people here have drawn up a scale of virtues and vices, and have stated what sort of virtues and how many will make amends for so many and what sort of vices. The true knowledge of ourselves and the right knowledge of God are equally removed from this people. I pray and hope that the excellent discourse to which this letter refers, and which I have endeavoured to translate faithfully and perspicuously in Chinese for your Society, may become a means amongst others of good to China."

The Committee had undertaken on behalf of the Society to print the whole of the Book of Common Prayer in the language commonly called Indo-Portuguese. It is estimated that forty thousand people at least, inhabiting the island of Ceylon, understand this language. Part of this version, made by Mr. Robert Newstead, a missionary in Ceylon, was submitted by him to the inspection of the late Rev. Dr. Twistleton, Archdeacon of Columbo, who highly approved of it; and it has been used with acceptance by the translator in native congregations. The decency and good order which pervade the whole of our national worship are considered by Mr. Newstead as features which render it peculiarly suitable for introduction into congregations newly formed among the heathen, to whom regularity and decorum in religious rites are quite unknown. He states that he has observed with delight the effects which the use of it has produced, where untutored heathens have been disciplined into outward reverence and sober deportment in the house of God.

The number of bound books—that is Prayer-books, Psalters, and Homilies in the entire volume—issued by the Society during the last year has been nine thousand seven hundred and ninety-four: this is larger by five hundred and forty-nine books than the issue of the preceding year while the number of Homilies as tracts sent out from the depository or printed abroad during the same period has been one hundred and thirteen thousand eight hundred and seventy five being an increase of more than eleven thousand beyond the issue last reported

No additional charge is now made for the Ordination Services which are inserted in every Prayer book which this Society issues In addition to this a very considerable reduction has been lately made in the prices affixed to several Prayer books on the Society's list

We deeply regret that the funds of this highly useful Church of England institution continue to fall very far short of what is necessary to give due effect to the operations of the Society New prospects of benefit, especially in the article of foreign translations are widely opening but the state of the Society's funds necessarily limits its exertions within much too narrow bounds We strongly recommend the Society to the best wishes and prayers and liberality of our readers

RELIGIOUS TRACT SOCIETY

A circular has been issued by the Committee of this Society relative to its foreign objects in which they state that since the year 1808, the Society has printed tracts in no less than forty two different languages They add the following among other very interesting notices on this subject —

The Missionaries in China write —

It will gladden your heart to hear that many both Chinese and Malays have lately called and entreated for the word of life We sent lately to Cochin China, nearly three thousand volumes of Chinese books They were eagerly read by the Cochin Chinese and many of their great men came to the college with a great body of servants and requested books As a proof that the books sent to that country have been read and understood we may state that they had copied the names of many of them in order that they might be supplied with books of the same kind Indeed there appears an increasing desire in all classes to obtain our books Our weekly tract is continued and is much sought after by the Chinese Animated by this information the Committee placed the sum of 300l at the disposal of Dr Morrison and the missionaries at Malacca which though a liberal grant considering the Society's very limited funds is but a small sum towards the instruction of three hundred millions of a reading heathen population

A correspondent in India writes to the Society We want English tracts, paper and pecuniary assistance to print tracts in the Bengalee and Hindoostanee languages Had we funds, we could do much in the circulation of tracts new fields are opening before us daily Pious officers and gentlemen in the Upper Provinces when they leave Calcutta for their destinations wish to furnish themselves with tracts As an instance I can state that a military conductor has distributed in a few months four thousand tracts and requests more. —The American Missionaries at Bombay write,—

The thousands of tracts which we have already distributed have only shewn us, that tens and tens of thousands more are needed which we cannot supply for want of pecuniary means The demand for tracts in the Mahratta country and the facilities for distributing them appear to us to be almost unlimited

With a view to the benefit of South America, the Committee notwithstanding the narrowness of their means have devoted about 300l to the publication of various tracts in pure Spanish Other tracts are also translated, and only wait for funds to be published

From Germany Dr Leander Van Ess writes — For the sake of the kingdom of the Lord and the everlasting salvation of our brethren purchased at so infinitely high a price I repeat my most earnest request for a fresh supply to my little tract fund The Committee have made a grant of 100l to assist his object

FEMALE EDUCATION IN INDIA

In our Number for March we announced the formation of The Calcutta Ladies Society for Native female Education In December last an examination of the children took place in the presence of numerous ladies of the presidency The girls divided into four classes had been previously assembled in an adjoining room about 100 in number one class of which beginning at the lowest was conducted into the room as soon as Lady Amherst and her suite had arrived The children were examined by the Rev Mr Wilson Mrs Wilson and the Rev Dr Carey The whole of the examination was in Bengalee and the classes were successively questioned on the Gospel of St Matthew, Watts's Catechism Pearce's Geography and a very useful work defending and stating the benefits of female education, written by a learned native. Specimens of writing and needle-work were also exhibited. The children have given general satisfaction to those friends who are most actively engaged in promoting their welfare.

It appears that in less than three years, thirty native female schools have been formed and between 500 and 600 girls are under instruction in the different schools supported by the Ladies Society for Native female Education. Several of these have made rapid progress in reading the Bible: the first classes can all write, and many of them can perform interesting specimens of needle-work. An Association has been formed in Calcutta in aid of the Ladies Society. The ladies who form the Committee of this Association have undertaken to superintend Native-female Schools in their own neighbourhood, and to collect funds for the enlargement of their plans.

In reference to this Association and to the general progress of female education Mrs. Wilson thus writes:—' I hope that we may get at least six schools formed in the European Town, which will be supported and superintended entirely by ladies of the Association. Several young ladies are learning to read the Bengalee: many already understand it. Thus in a month or two, they will be perfectly qualified to take charge of a school or two each. Mrs. Reichardt has taken charge of ten of my first schools, and is very happy in her work. The Ladies Society has now thirty small schools, and we have opened two this morning for the Association.'

VIEW OF PUBLIC AFFAIRS

FOREIGN

FRANCE.—The chief subject of public interest in this country at the present moment seems to be the struggle which is taking place between the intolerance of the Catholic priesthood and the general feeling of French society. The church, with a most impolitic zeal, is urging its long exploded claims, and endeavouring to reduce the people to the yoke of the ancient ecclesiastical discipline: for which end the decrees of the legislature and the arm of the police, are called in as auxiliaries. There can be no doubt that the doctrines and discipline of the Church of Rome have of late, and principally by means of the Jesuits, made considerable progress among the people at large, a vast proportion of whom, being educated in the infidel school of the Revolution, had their religion yet to choose, and might be easily captivated, at least the more unenlightened part of them, by the sophistries and spectacles of the papal creed and worship; but, to the large mass, the verities of religion, as well as the superstitions appended to it, are matters of such perfect indifference, and even of distaste and repulsion, that we cannot think the French public by any means ripe for the adoption of the principles and habits which the priesthood, in conjunction with the ultra royalists, seem determined to impose upon them. A crisis may be impending which shall, before long, bring the question to a decision, and lead, like the events which followed the restoration of our Second Charles, to another and more benignant revolution.

SPAIN.—The late revolution in the Spanish cabinet has not hitherto given rise to any measures of much public importance. One truth however, is very clearly to be inferred from the whole train of proceedings in that distracted country, that neither the efforts of Ferdinand and the native priesthood, nor the arms of their French allies, can eventually perpetuate the dominancy of civil and ecclesiastical tyranny, which have long since received their mortal wound, protracted as may be their expiring struggles.

GREECE.—There is no intelligence of a decided nature from the Morea; but the general complexion of events, we fear, has of late been in favour of the invading army.

UNITED STATES, &c.—The religious and philanthrophic portion of the inhabitants of the United States, we are happy to learn are becoming greatly interested in the cause of the unhappy Negroes and their descendants in that country. Emigrations both to Africa and to Hayti are widely encouraged. The affairs of Hayti at present occupy much of the attention of the public and politicians of the United States, in consequence of the late recognition of its independence by the French cabinet and both their own Government and ours are freely animadverted upon in some of the journals for not long since acknowledging the independence of Hayti. It is stated, that the commerce of the United States with that country has been of greater advantage to them than half their joint commerce with the nations of Europe of the greater part of which they expect to be deprived by the commercial advantages given by the treaty of recognition to French merchandize. With regard to this country, it is added, that the French will imitate the English style of goods for the Haytian market with the advantage for six years of paying but half the scale of duties imposed on other nations by which, to a great extent, they will gain a monopoly of the market. The Slave States in the American Union seem to feel as sensitively as would our own West-India colonies in the prospect of receiving Black or Coloured official agents—the very thought of such a contamination revolts their imagination. Yet, amidst all this narrow and invidious prejudice, not a single charge of bad faith or improper conduct is adduced against the Haytian Government notwithstanding the protracted course of oppression and injustice which has attended its efforts in the cause of liberty. The following circumstance, related in the American journals, evinces at once the wisdom, the integrity and the patient firmness of their conduct. It is stated as a well known fact that a large sum of money has been appropriated for many years, and now lies useless in a vault for the payment of the balance of claims which American citizens hold for losses of property in their transactions with Hayti. The Haytian Government has repeatedly acknowledged that a large balance is due to American citizens but that they could not and would not pay it until the amount was settled by a convention to be adjusted by commissioners of the two nations duly accredited. 'The claimants,' add the American journalists, 'have been kept out of their dues for many years because our representatives have deemed it inexpedient to acknowledge a nation of a little darker complexion than some of their constituents, lest it might give offence to the gentlemen of the South.' Whatever excuse may be urged as respects the line of policy adopted by Great Britain in reference to Hayti and we have heard of none which has any weight there is still less for the American Union, which had so recently achieved its own liberties by similar means, which had indeed some of the same difficulties and prejudices to contend with which impeded the course of our Government, but which from a feeling of sympathy as well as from policy, ought to have been the first to enter into relations of amity with their sister republic, rescued from a state of vassalage infinitely more painful and degrading than that mild colonial dependence which they themselves so zealously threw off. We conclude our observations on this subject, with the following remarks from a letter lately written by a resident in Hayti to a correspondent in the United States. We trust they will at least have the effect of exciting British and American Christians to consider what degree of reparation can be made to that injured people for their sufferings by devising judicious measures for promoting their best and eternal welfare

" I thank God that I have lived to see this worthy people take their seat among the nations of the earth. For the last twenty-seven years I have been an inhabitant of this island and am now the oldest White resident in Hayti. During that period I have been an eye witness to all the bloody and ruinous revolutions which have taken place and have seen with what devoted patriotism untiring perseverance, and unfailing bravery the Haytians have broken the iron arm of slavery which for a century and a half had bound them down to the dust of oppression and bondage. It is true France has at length done an act of justice, and awakened the Haytians to joys hitherto unknown. For this proceeding she will command the approbation of all who value the blessings of liberty, and who are capable of estimating the deserts of a people who have unaided by any power but their own moral courage literally severed their own bonds driven from the land the tyrants who oppressed them and rising from actual servitude, established a liberal form of government, and a system of laws the best calculated to promote social order and rational and elevated character. But when I call to mind the innumerable evils France has inflicted upon the Haytians, it seems but a poor reparation that she should be the first to recognize their political independence History will transmit to posterity a tale of long continued misfortunes and of horrible, disgraceful, and iniquitous tortures endured by the Haytians while under the colonial system with which no parallel can be found, and for which no commensurate atonement can be made.'

A paper, issuing from New York, has been widely circulated, and some interpreters of unfulfilled prophecy seem inclined to attach an importance to it which, in that light at least, we should not have thought it deserved. It is entitled a Proclamation to the Jews by Mordecai Noah, ' Citizen of the United States, late American Consul at Tunis, High sheriff of New York, and [self elected] Governor and Judge of Israel,' by which the Jews throughout the world are invited to emigrate to a tract of land in the State of New York, called Grand Island, on the Niagara river, where Major Noah intends erecting a city of refuge to be called ' Ararat,' for the revival of the Jewish government, after the dispersion of that people for nearly two thousand years. The proclamation does not dwell much upon theological considerations, but addresses the Jews by the tangible arguments of a salubrious climate, a rich soil, extensive trade and commerce, inexhaustible resources, equal political rights of a land, says the circular, "where industry is encouraged, education promoted, good faith rewarded, a land of milk and honey, where Israel may repose in peace under his vine and fig tree, and where our people may familiarize themselves with the science of government and the lights of learning and civilization as may qualify them for that final restoration to their ancient heritage which the times so powerfully indicate.' The Jews, we imagine, will pay little attention to the decrees of this self-elected dictator, who commands a census of the people and imposes a capitation tax on them in every part of the world; but undoubtedly to a Jew of liberal mind the Western world with its free apportionment of rights, citizenship and freehold soil, affords attractions which are not to be found in countries where he must continue for life an alien, subjected, whatever may be his moral character or public virtues, to various inconvenient and degrading restrictions and disqualifications. But we will not dwell upon these and other considerations which occur to us on perusing this singular proclamation; we will only remark that it is most harsh and inconsistent for Christians to reproach the Jews, as for ages they have done, for their sordid venality, their attachment to mere money-getting, their alleged dislike for the occupations of pasturage and agriculture, their preference for corrupt towns and cities, above the boasted purity of rural life, when the policy of all Christendom for more than a thousand years, with only a few modern exceptions, has been to force them from all the more reputable and dignified scenes of industry, and even to forbid their occupation of a single patrimonial acre.— To those of our readers who may have adopted the opinion of various writers, and particularly of Dr Boudinot, that the North American Indians are the descendants of the ten dispersed tribes, the following passage from Major Noah's address may appear worth transcribing.

' The Indians of the American continent, in their admitted Asiatic origin, in the worship of one God, in their dialect and language, in their sacrifices, marriages, divorces, burials, fastings, purifications, punishments, cities of refuge, division of tribes, in their high priest, and in their wars and in their victories, being in all probability the descendants of the lost tribes of Israel which were carried captive by the king of Assyria, measures will be adopted to make them sensible of their origin, to cultivate their minds, soften their condition, and finally to re-unite them with their brethren, the chosen people.'

BRAZIL.—A treaty, we are most happy to state, has been ratified by the mediation of Great Britain between Portugal and her late colony of the Brazils, by which the king of Portugal acknowledges the independence of the empire of Brazil, reserving only the honorary title of emperor to the present sovereign of Portugal. This treaty, besides its direct advantages, will, we trust, be useful as a precedent for the imitation of Spain. The whole South American continent is rejoicing in the stability afforded to its independence by the late recognitions, and is most warm in the praise of Great Britain for its wise and liberal policy, in this important respect.

DOMESTIC

Scarcely any subject of domestic interest calls for notice, unless it be the visible decline of the system of unlawful combinations among various classes of mechanics, and a decisive check which has been given to the wildness of speculation in joint-stock companies by some recent exposures of the futile or fraudulent manner in which some of them were constructed.

On the first of January will come in operation the new act for regulating weights and measures, the provisions of which are as follow.—

1. The standard inch, foot, yard, acre and mile, remain the same as at present. There is no change therefore in what is called long measure, and the measures deduced from it. 2. The pound, ounce, and pennyweight troy, and the pound, ounce and dram avoirdupois, also remain the same as at present. The pound troy is declared to be the unit from which all others are to be derived. It contains 5,760 grains; and the ounce troy 480 grains. The pound avoirdupois contains 7000 troy grains; and the ounce avoirdupois 437½. Thus we have still two different pounds, and two different ounce weights, an inconvenience which we could have wished that the act had remedied. As a means of restoring the weights, if they should be lost the cubic inch of distilled water is declared to be equal in weight to 252.458 grains—the barometer being at 30 inches and the thermometer at 62°. 3. The sole difference between the new system and the old is in the gallon and the measures deduced from it. The new or imperial gallon is declared to contain ten pounds avoirdupois of distilled water—the temperature and pressure being as above. It contains 277¼, or more correctly 277.27 cubic inches. The present wine gallon contains 231, and the present ale gallon 282 cubic inches. It follows that the new imperial gallon is to the old wine gallon as 6 to 5, and to the old ale gallon as 47 to 48, neglecting minute fractions. To convert wine gallons into imperial gallons deduct one sixth; to convert imperial gallons into wine gallons add one fifth. To convert ale gallons into imperial gallons add 1.47 part; to convert imperial gallons into ale gallons, deduct 1.48th part. The new pint and quart being declared to be respectively the 8th and 4th part of the new gallon bear the same proportion to the old pint and quart as the new gallon does to the old gallon. Two gallons are declared to be a peck, and eight gallons a bushel as at present. But the proportions here are not the same as in the case of the pint and quart, because the old gallon for dry measure is neither the wine nor the ale gallon, but a gallon of 268.8 cubic inches. The imperial peck and bushel are therefore to the old Winchester peck and bushel as 268.8 to 277.27. Hence to convert Winchester bushels into imperial bushels deduct one 33d part; and to convert imperial into Winchester add one 32d part. This is sufficiently near for practical purposes: the sum to be added is correctly 1.31.73. The old Winchester bushel contains 2150.42 cubic inches; the new contains 2218.16. The new or imperial quarter has the same ratio to the old quarter, as the new bushel has to the old bushel. The standard measure of capacity for coals, culm, lime, fish, potatoes, or fruit, and all other goods and things commonly sold by heap measure is to be the aforesaid bushel containing 80 pounds avoirdupois of water, being made round with an even bottom and being 19 inches and a half in diameter; the goods to be heaped up to the form of a cone of the height of at least six inches. Three bushels shall be a sack, and twelve such sacks a chaldron. It is not obligatory on persons to buy and sell by these measures; they may use the old measures, but when this is done the ratio which the measures used bear to the new standard measure must be specified, otherwise the contract of agreement is void. This will render it necessary to refer to the new measures in all written bargains. Bargains made without a special reference to some other measures are held to be made according to the new measure. The existing weights and measures may be used if marked, so as to shew the proportion they have to the standard measures and weights, but not otherwise. All weights and measures made after the first of January 1826 are to be conformable to the new standard.—The act will be of great use in regulating this hitherto confused branch of public economy.

ECCLESIASTICAL PREFERMENTS

Very Rev. Vesey Fitzgerald Dean of Emby, Rector of Castleraghan, co. Cavan, to the Deanery of Kilmore vice Magenis deceased.

Rev. Dr. Holland, Rector of Poynings, to be Precentor of Chichester Cathedral vice Toghill deceased.

Rev. Marcus Beresford, Kildallen R. vice Magenis deceased.

Rev. Wm. H. Dixon, Wistow V. co. York.

Rev. James Hoste, Barwick V. Norfolk.

Rev. W. C. Madden, Christ's Church Woodhouse P. C. near Huddersfield, co. York.

Rev. K. C. Packman, Langdon Hills R. Essex.

Rev. George Norman Gale, Corse C.
Rev G Palmer Parham R. Sussex.
Rev G. Pearson, B D Castle Camps R Camb.
Rev Benj. Pulleyne Sherringham V Norf.
Rev J Arundel Radford, Nymet Rowland and Lapford RR Devon
Rev W Russell Chiddingley R. Sussex
Rev Adam Sedgwick Woodwardian Professor Shudy Camps R Camb
Hon and Rev Adolphus-Augustus Turnour Garveston R Norfolk
Rev Dav Williams S. C L. St Mary's Church C Brecknock
Rev W Corbett Wilson jun Bozeat cum Strixton V Northamptonshire
Rev J Wood, Santhorpe V Norfolk
Rev J W Worthington, Evening Lecturer at All-Hallows, London
Hon and Rev Dawson Massy to be Dom Chap to his brother Lord Massy
Rev J Brown Chap to Nor County Gaol
Rev Henry Fielding Chaplain to Salford New Bailey Prison
Rev Samuel Paynter Clerk Domestic Chaplain to the Right Hon the Earl of Cassillis
Rev Dr Lawrence Adamson to the Church and Parish of Cupar, Kirk of Scotland vice Dr Campbell, dec
Rev N M'Leod Church and Par of Campsie co Glasgow vice Lapslie dec
Rev Edw Hyde Cosens Chap to Shepton Mallett House of Correction
Rev J Baldwin Leyland V Lanc
Rev Wm Buckland, B D F R S P G S Stoke Charity R Hants
Rev Geo Chandler, D C L All saints R Mary le bone
Rev J Corrie Morcott R. Rutland
Rev G Dixon Tynemouth V Northumberland
Rev P Felix, Easton Neston V Northamptonshire

Rev W Harlee, Angelli Pymbroke
Rev Jas Robertson Holcombe Steventon V Bucks.
Rev Lanc Ch Lee Wootton R. Oxford
Rev R. Churchman Long Swainsthorpe, R Norfolk
Rev Alex. Macarthur Minister of Dairsie
Rev Dav Fred Markham Addingham V Cumberland
Rev J Hollier Stephenson, Dengie R. Essex vice Faithfull, resigned
Rev Ric Bohun Tomkyns, B C L. Saham Tony R Norfolk
Rev Fred Twisleton Broadwell cum Addlestrop R. vice Hon Dr Twisleton, dec
Rev G Williams, Sedgberrow R. Worcestershire
Rev J W D Merest, Dom Chap to the Duke of Grafton
Rev Thos Prince D. D elected Chaplain to the British Residents at the Hague
Rev J B Byers, Curate of Carmarthen to the Vicarage of Nantmel, with Llanyre vice Wm Hewson, to St David s
Rev R. W Bamford, Bishopstone V Durham
Rev Chas Bowle Milborne Port V Somerset vice Bp. of Hereford, res.
Rev Sam Carr Little Eversden R Cambridge vice Heaton, dec
Rev Cobb Burmarsh V Kent
Rev Miles Coyle A M Monnington on Wye R Hereford
Rev Julius Deeds M A Orlingbury R Northamptonsh vice Whitehouse
Rev Wm Creasy Drew Sandringham R. with Babingley annexed Norfolk
Rev R Duffield B D Impington V Cambridge vice Baker res
Rev Thomas Hawes Thorndon R. Suffolk

ANSWERS TO CORRESPONDENTS

Capitan J T Clericus G C G M S A Constant Reader Ecclesiae Rector C T and a correspondent who signs himself Amator Veritatis, are under consideration

We have often considered the plan suggested by a Country Curate but upon attempting to reduce it to practice have found it attended with considerable difficulties

We were acquainted with one at least of the publications alluded to by S C but our publisher could not procure a copy of it It does not appear to us necessary at present to renew the discussion

In reply to two or three correspondents we have to state that we do not insert anonymous Reviews and still less pledge ourselves to admit them before we see them

G B s direction shall be attended to

S. Z had better propose his difficulty to some judicious friend

The Committee of the Language Institution will find that the substance of their Address has already appeared in our pages, with cordial approbation of the Society's object

ERRATUM

Page 613 col 1 line 7 instead of *for* read *to*

THE CHRISTIAN OBSERVER.

RELIGIOUS COMMUNICATIONS

MANKIND RESPONSIBLE FOR THEIR RELIGIOUS OPINIONS

(*Continued from* p. 666.)

It was proposed, in a former paper, to shew the responsibility of mankind for their religious opinions, by a series of remarks bearing upon two propositions: the consideration of the former of which will form the subject of the present communication; reserving the discussion of the second to another Number.

The proposition now to be examined is, that immorality or unholiness either of heart or life has a powerful influence in depraving the judgment in matters of religion.

The effect of unholiness of heart and life, in producing false judgment in matters of faith, will be most conspicuously though by no means exclusively, seen in the case of *professed infidels*. Among those who have rejected the evidences for the truth of the Gospel, where shall we find an individual who has conscientiously submitted to its allowedly excellent moral restraints? If we except a very few persons, whom literary habits, or a virtuous education, or self respect, or an ostensible station in society, or a natural inertness of temperament, or a secret misgiving of conscience, may have restrained from the grosser excesses of vicious indulgence, where shall we discover a professed infidel who does not prove by his conduct that his rejection of the Gospel is so closely connected with laxity of principle, or immorality of life, as to furnish the strongest reason to conclude, that the one is the chief cause of the other,—that he has discarded religion precisely because he disrelishes its inhibitions and commands? The mere circumstance of the co-existence of two facts does not indeed necessarily prove their connexion as cause and effect; but where this connexion is frequent and striking, it furnishes a strong *primâ facie* presumption; and that presumption is increased, we may say, to certainty, when as in the case under consideration, powerful *à priori* reasons may be assigned why that effect *ought* to follow, which we find in point of fact *does* actually follow, such and such causes. In the late inundation of irreligious writings, for example, we saw infidelity joined in striking and intimate union with a spirit of detraction, sedition, blasphemy, and numerous other things " contrary to sound (that is, to Christian) ' doctrine." And can we doubt that these evil propensities were among the exciting *causes* of that infidelity which, in its turn, would naturally give birth to a new progeny of vices? Is it a circumstance peculiar to theology, that what men dislike, they easily persuade themselves to disbelieve? Is it extraordinary that immorality should nurture irreligion? Would it not even be difficult to believe that extreme wickedness could exist without eventually *generating* infidelity, even if it did not find infidelity already at hand to assist its efforts, by blotting out the fearful prospect of a future retribution?

But we need not resort to *extreme cases* in proof of the powerful effects of unholiness of heart and life in inclining men to a rejection of the Gospel; for as there are crimes of less malignant aspect than treason and murder, so also there are various approaches towards infidelity of a more specious character than the revolting blasphemies of a profligate Atheism. There is not an anti-christian or an unchristian principle, which may not lead to a corresponding anti-christian or unchristian creed. All the *malignant passions*, for example, may have this effect: as we find from Acts xiii. where we are informed (ver. 48), that the Gentiles were glad, and glorified the word of the Lord, and *believed*; but the Jews (ver. 45), " being *filled with envy*, spake against those things which were spoken by Paul, contradicting and blaspheming." The *selfish* passions also may produce the same effect. Thus " the Pharisees, *who were covetous*, heard all these things, and derided him." (Luke xvi. 14.) The *proud* and *vain* and *ambitious* passions also may have the same effect. " They did not confess Him, lest they should be put out of the synagogue; for *they loved the praise of men* more than the praise of God." " How can ye *believe* that have honour one of another?" Thus enmity, covetousness, vain glory, to which various other evil principles might be added, are proved by scriptural testimony to be capable of subverting faith, and even of conducting men to the awful extremes of contradiction, derision, and blasphemy.

It would be easy to proceed to shew still more specifically, both by Scripture and fact, the injurious influence of sinful dispositions and habits in alienating the mind, not only *from the love* but also from *the understanding* as well as *the belief*, of the truth. To these sources may we also usually trace up those less glaring species of latent infidelity which often display their existence in the form of Antinomianism, Socinianism, or kindred heresies. Even where there is no temptation to palliate the enormities of a profligate life, there may be secret sins, sins of a somewhat decorous kind, sins of the heart or sins of the intellect, which may greatly impede the spiritual perceptions, as well as vitiate the spiritual taste. In casting a glance over the names of the most celebrated persons who have enrolled themselves among the abettors of heterodox principles in religion, we shall discover in one a stubborn pertinacity which renders the admission of unwelcome truth into a mind under its influence morally impossible; in another, a hardihood which shrinks at no consequences, even though the declarations of God himself should be disputed and traduced before the bar of human presumption; in a third, a levity; in a fourth, a self conceit; in a fifth, a petulance; in a sixth, a fearless self confidence; in a seventh, a proud dictatorial dogmatism;—in all, a mental aversion to Divine truth, which must inevitably prevent a devout submission to scriptural authority, and the establishment of just and sober conclusions from scriptural premises.

Nor are such dispositions and habits less really culpable in the sight of God than those sins which men of the world look upon with greater abhorrence. *Pride*, in particular, in all its shapes, is one of the most offensive and injurious of evils; and in no form more so than when it wears the semblance of intellectual imperiousness. This species of pride has, from the first ages of the Gospel to the present moment, been always averse to " the truth as it is in Jesus." The Scribes and Pharisees, confiding in their boasted attainments, and exclaiming, ' Are we blind also?' preferred remaining among those self sufficient " wise and prudent" to whom the Gospel was hidden, to being numbered among those " babes" in simplicity to whom it pleased God to reveal it. Saint Paul alludes to the same evil disposition of mind, when, in writing to the Corinthians, he says—"The preaching of the Cross is to them that perish foolishness; but unto us which are saved it is the power of God. For it is written, I will destroy the wisdom of the wise, and I will bring to nothing the understanding of the prudent. Where is the wise? Where is the scribe? Where is the disputer of this world? Hath not God made foolish the wisdom of this world? For after that, in the wisdom of God, the world by wisdom knew not God, it pleased God, by the foolishness of preaching, to save them that believe." A *humble and conscientious* use of the powers of the human understanding, and of the best aids of literature, is indeed eminently serviceable in the cause of truth; for Christianity has nothing to fear from the most rigid scrutiny: but the *misdirection or perversion* of the intellect—and no misdirection or perversion is more baneful than that which springs from self sufficiency—is one of the most frequent causes of false judgment in matters of faith. How often do we find, even in the case of persons who are not vicious in their lives,—nay, who perhaps preserve a respectable decorum of conduct—that *the heart* is prejudiced against a practical admission of Divine Truth, at least of its more peculiar and mysterious doctrines, on account of the Scriptures not making their appeal to mankind in such a manner as to gratify the pride of *the intellect.* They find themselves required to believe promptly and implicitly upon the strength of a Divine declaration: they are enjoined to admit, without hesitation or scruple, many things that they cannot fully understand; and they are invited, yea commanded, on pain of eternal condemnation, to embrace exactly the same faith which has been professed by thousands of the most illiterate of mankind,—in common, it is true, with men of the highest order of thought, and the most extensive range of literature,—but still a faith which owns no submission to human intellect, and refuses to bow its lofty claims before the tribunal of any created mind, however wide its grasp or exalted its powers. A mind vain of its intellectual superiority, and unsubdued by the grace of God, will not easily be persuaded to submit to this; it will recoil from such an unreserved self dedication: it will demand something more conciliating to the pride of the human heart, and will venture peremptorily to denounce as false, whatever cannot be inferred by the deductions of uninspired reason, or, at least, which, *when revealed*, cannot be fathomed or fortified by human philosophy.

To illustrate the subject by an example—To what but to this cause, combining indeed with some other subordinate ones, must we attribute the vehement opposition which has always been carried on against that fundamental article of the Christian system, and of our Protestant Church, the doctrine of *justification solely by faith?* The humble practical Christian, whether poor or rich, illiterate or learned, discovers no moral danger attending this doctrine: so far from it, he feels it to be in his own case, and observes it to be in the case of others, not only " very full of comfort, but a powerful motive to love, to gratitude, and to good works, and he is perfectly convinced, that if any persons would so far abuse it as to say " Let us sin that grace may abound," they understand not its real nature—much less are they among those who have a scriptural right to take to themselves the blessings which it exhibits. But the mere intellectual reasoner, experiencing nothing of the practical effects of the Gospel in his own soul, recoils, or professes to recoil at such a doctrine. It is not enough to prove that it is revealed in the sacred Scriptures: it must also comport with his warmly cherished prejudices and prepossessions; or, as he considers them, his reasonable deductions; he must see that it has some other basis to rest upon than mere authority, even though that authority be the authority of God himself; for till he can fully demonstrate the propriety of this Divine arrangement and solve every difficulty which a presumptuous intellect may consider as flowing from it (which he is least of all likely to do while he remains in his present attitude of mind), he will not submit to the doctrines of the Cross of Christ, or adore that "mystery of godliness" which is involved in this and every other part of the disclosures of Revelation.

But *gross vices* on the one hand, and *mental sins* on the other, (to which two classes of impediments the preceding remarks have been chiefly confined,) are not the *only* forms of moral evil which may cloud our judgment in matters of faith: for, in fact, even *the widely tolerated habits in which the great body of mankind pass their lives; the love of worldly company and the fashionable gratifications of the age*, slight as such causes may seem, powerfully exert the same influence. The votaries of the world in all its forms, the more decent as well as the disreputable, plainly perceive that the doctrines and precepts of Christianity, if admitted and acted upon *in their real spirit*, would cut up, at the very roots, their most cherished habits and predilections; and hence a species of practical infidelity is gradually suffered to steal over the mind till the judgment itself is at length incapacitated for the office of piercing through the thick veil of passions and prepossessions which have accumulated to intercept the rays of celestial Truth.

Nay, we may go yet farther; for even the sincere Christian himself may too often discover within his own bosom a decisive proof of the powerful effects of unholiness of heart or life in obscuring the spiritual understanding and weakening the faith. No sooner does he relax in his Christian vigilance, no sooner does he become secularized in his temper,—no sooner does he grieve the Holy Spirit by pride or lukewarmness, by the neglect of prayer, by inattention to any known duty, or by indulgence in any known sin,—than he finds that he cannot bring home to his feelings, as at more devout moments, the sentiments which become his holy profession: he is perhaps even almost inclined to harbour a secret wish that he may have too strictly construed the self-denying character of the Gospel. His mind may begin at such times to waver respecting some of its essential truths; if not under the influence of temptation, to venture for a moment to bring into dispute its Divine authority. No Christian, however advanced, stands so firmly as not to require to "take heed lest he fall:" and though there may seem to be a wide interval between incipient sins of the heart, and such a lapsed state of the mind and affections as amounts, for the time at least, to little short of infidelity; yet upon further reflexion it will be evident that this interval is more easily passed over than at first sight appears probable, and that in truth there is *a very close connexion* between such a state of the heart as makes it a man's interest that the Gospel, or any of its doctrines, should be false, and the temptation to believe that very possibly they *are* so. Certain at least it is, that sinful habits or affections of whatever kind, have such a deadening effect upon the soul, that even where they do not open a direct way to professed infidelity, they greatly impede the operations of faith, and cause every Christian grace to wither and decay; so that whether the man become a *speculative* unbeliever or not, he at least for the time, becomes a *practical* one.

In thus illustrating the fact that

unholiness, either of heart or life, has a powerful influence in depraving the judgment in matters of faith: some of the causes of this unhappy effect have been incidentally mentioned. It may, however, be useful to consider these causes somewhat more definitely.

It is obvious, then, in the first place, that where the life is allowedly unchristian, there cannot possibly exist *any serious wish to be right on the subject of religion*, and such a *defect of will* is always a powerful cause of obliquity of judgment. The Scriptures constantly attribute both doctrinal and practical error to a corrupt state of the moral and spiritual volitions. "Ye *will* not come unto me," said our blessed Lord, "that ye might have life." Had the wish existed, the power would not have been withheld. "If any man be anxious to do the will of God, he shall know of the doctrine:" but where such a disposition of heart does not exist, there will always be a threefold barrier to the attainment of truth; namely, *a want of suitable application, a want of aptitude to learn, and a want of Divine instruction.*

1. *There will be a want of suitable application.*—A correct knowledge of the Christian scheme of faith and duty is not an intuitive endowment: it can be acquired only in an attentive perusal of the sacred Scriptures; in frequent meditation upon their contents, 'comparing spiritual things with spiritual;' in the conscientious use of every subordinate assistance, and in earnest prayer for the Divine illumination and guidance. But where there exists no adequate desire to know and practise the will of God, such an application of mind, and such a devotion of heart to sacred studies, are not to be expected; and consequently we cannot hope that a right judgment should be attained in matters of faith, except indeed so far as an orthodox education, or other advantageous circumstances, may have operated, unsought for by the individual, to enlighten his understanding, even while they failed of converting his heart.

2. *A want of aptitude to learn* was further mentioned as an unavoidable concomitant of wilful unholiness of heart or life; for not only is a mind under the influence of sin rendered averse to the humble study of Divine subjects, but the necessary prerequisites for studying them aright are wanting. We constantly perceive, in ordinary life, and on points quite unconnected with theology, the powerful influence of particular habits in producing an inaptitude for the perception of truth on subjects which, to all but the parties thus prepossessed, appear sufficiently plain. The arguments which would fully convince an unprejudiced person of the criminality of importing or vending illicit articles of merchandise, would have no effect upon the mind of a practised smuggler. The most elaborate dissertation upon the atrocity of a piratical life, would be lost upon the callous perceptions of an Algerine corsair. And without adverting to such extreme cases, do we not perceive in the daily occurrences of civilized society, that a familiarity with certain practices, and the frequently recurring, though scarcely noticed temptations arising from them to shut the eyes and harden the heart against the truth, have the effect of gradually raising the most powerful impediments to a right judgment on these particular points; and this, perhaps even where there is no distinct consciousness, in any individual instance, of a wilful opposition to the force of evidence? We see this observation forcibly exemplified in the conduct of ardent party men of all sects, ages, and countries. We may also observe, in almost every profession and avocation of life, the prevalence of particular practices, which, to all but the individuals concerned, bear an undeniable character of moral delinquency; but the sinfulness of

which the offenders themselves, even though in other respects virtuously inclined, do not perceive, because they have lost, in that particular point, the moral discrimination which is necessary to render the most powerful evidence and suasion, effectual to produce conviction and amendment.

And thus it is in the case under consideration: for how is it possible that a dispensation of which the prominent feature is "righteousness and true holiness," should approve itself either to the judgment or the heart of an individual whose perceptions are clouded by moral prejudice and the love of sin? For example, the Scriptures every where exhibit to us the excellency of the law of God; but how can this excellency be duly felt by one who regards that law with abhorrence, on account of the restraints which it imposes upon his unbridled appetites? The Scriptures again constantly speak of the happiness of a life of devotion to God; but how can this be admitted by one who places his happiness exclusively in earthly gratifications? The Scriptures declare, that "to be carnally minded is death, but to be spiritually minded is life and peace:" but how can this be credited by one whose whole practice proceeds upon quite a contrary estimate? The Scriptures speak throughout of sin, in all its modifications, as an evil of enormous magnitude: but to such a person no evil is apparent, except indeed so far as the temporal interests of society are concerned. The Scriptures describe the equity of God in visiting every breach of his laws with the severest infliction of judgment: but to a man in the state of mind we are describing, such a proceeding appears far from equitable: he even ventures perhaps to think it nothing short of tyranny to inflict punishment upon men for what he thinks fit to call the "innocent propensities of the human character." The Scriptures further speak of whatever is holy, whatever resembles God, as excellent and lovely: but the individual in question perceives no loveliness in any thing of the kind; on the contrary, he views a life of piety as morbid and misanthropical, and would gladly prefer the vain pleasures of a sinful, as well as a transitory, existence to what he considers the gloom and austerity of scriptural devotion. In short, while his whole constitution remains under the dominion of sin, there must necessarily be a corresponding inaptitude for attaining a right judgment on religious subjects: for such subjects, it must ever be remembered, are not, like the deductions of mathematical or physical science, merely speculative —they powerfully affect the life and actions, they involve the operation of the will and affections, and therefore the study of them, can be entered upon with advantage only where there is a suitable "preparation of heart;" and such a preparation, it is obvious, can never exist where a preference for the ways of sin is deliberately cherished.

3. *The absence of Divine instruction* was also mentioned as a most important reason why those who have no wish to "do the will of God," are not likely ' to know of the doctrine,' at least in a way conducive to their salvation.—The Scriptures every where teach us, that Divine instruction is essentially necessary to a right understanding in matters of faith: and this instruction, we are further informed, is bestowed only upon the humble and the contrite. "Evil men understand not judgment: but they that seek the Lord understand all things." ' A scorner seeketh wisdom, and findeth it not: but "the secret of the Lord is with them that fear him." Those who persist in wilful impenitence, the Almighty consigns in equitable retribution to the suggestions of a misguided understanding and a hardened heart. Such was strikingly

the case with the idolatrous heathen "As they did not like to retain God in their knowledge," God gave them over "to a reprobate mind, to do those things which are not convenient." Likewise of those who "have chosen their own ways, and whose soul delighteth in their abominations," Jehovah says, "I will choose their delusions, and will bring their fears upon them because when I called, none did answer when I spoke they did not hear but they did evil before mine eyes, and chose that in which I delighted not." And to the same effect the Apostle St. Paul, speaking of "the deceivableness of unrighteousness in them that perish," adds, as *the cause* of this delusive influence, "because they received not *the love of the truth*, that they might be saved."

(*To be concluded in the Appendix.*)

To the Editor of the Christian Observer.

THE following letter to a literary friend, which has lately fallen into my hands, appears to me so useful and interesting that I should be glad to see it inserted in your pages. The subject to which it relates is the most important which can occupy the attention of a rational and responsible being; and it is to be feared that there are too many persons, in this intellectual but too sceptical age, to whom the remarks contained in the letter are quite as important as to the individual to whom it was originally addressed.

PASTOR.

LETTER TO A LITERARY FRIEND.

My dear sir,—Though in many of our interviews, any particular sentiments I entertain on the subject of religion may not have been introduced, I believe you know so much of these, as to be fully aware of my attachment to the Christian Faith—that I profess to hold Christianity to be a Divine revelation; and that, as such, it ought unquestionably to secure the attention, and command the faith and obedience, of all who have an opportunity of becoming acquainted with it. This conviction has not been superficially adopted. It is not the result of early prejudice, but of a deliberate examination of the grounds on which the New Testament claims to be received, as a communication of the will of God to the human race.

While I then am convinced that just views of the great leading doctrines of Divine truth, and a belief in that gracious Saviour who came into our world to proclaim the way of acceptance with our offended Creator, are essentially necessary to our well grounded peace, you will surely not be surprised, that I feel a strong desire to direct your attention to a subject which I conceive to be of such unspeakable moment. I have often looked with eagerness for a tract suited to such a mind as yours, that I might put it into your hands, and beg of you to consider its contents. But, not finding exactly what in this respect I could wish, I thought a few lines from one who, I trust you are convinced, entertains for you a most sincere regard, and who would feel it a source of the highest satisfaction to be of any service to you, might be fully as likely to gain your attention as any thing in another form which I could bring under your notice. I should be happy indeed, if I could clothe my sentiments in that vigorous and eloquent language in which I know you are capable of stating whatever you wish to express; but I cannot allow my inability to do this, to prevent me from thus addressing you; and I trust you will accept of the kind intention which dictates my letter, as some compensation at least for the absence of those qualities which I feel myself incapable of imparting to it.

After this preamble, I can easily conceive you asking with some surprise (I hope there is no other emotion, as I would not willingly

.... What is the drift of
this communication? I hope my
friend does not suppose that I am
a downright infidel; and that he is
not so narrow-minded as to think
that nobody is right but himself?
Religion is a subject on which men
have thought differently in every
age, and will do so, I believe, to
the end of the chapter —No, my
dear sir, I do not address you as a
downright infidel. I have often
heard you speak with much respect
of revelation in general,—I have
heard you warmly express your
admiration of the moral precepts it
contains and I believe you are
quite aware, that nothing tends so
much as the observance of these to
promote the peace and good order
of society. But will you excuse
me, if I express my fears that you
have not examined this interesting
subject with that degree of attention which its importance demands?
I consider Christianity as containing
a great deal more than a number of
moral precepts, however useful and
excellent these may be. As a revelation of the Divine will, it appears to me to give certain views of
the character of that Great and
Glorious Being with whom we have
to do—of the state and character
of man as a creature of God—of
the relation in which he stands to
his great Creator, as a being who
has violated his law, and is thus exposed to his displeasure. While
Christianity represents all men as
exposed to the most imminent danger, on account of their transgressions, I view it at the same time as
pointing out a remedy. It tells us
of an Almighty Deliverer from that
guilt we have contracted, while it
expressly states that it is only by
seeing our need of this Deliverer,
and personally relying on Him, that
we can be found in a state of safety
at the great future day of trial.
Along with this I may add,—it
speaks of a certain change that
takes place on the heart and character of all who truly believe in
the only Saviour; and that this
change is essentially necessary, before we can be interested in the
blessings and hopes which he reveals.

Now, remark, I am not wishing
you to take these representations
on my authority. What I wish is,
simply to fix your thoughts on this
very interesting subject, that you
may examine for yourself, whether
or not this revelation actually contains such statements as these I
have now suggested. In short, my
earnest desire is, that you treat that
Book as it ought to be treated, if it
be really true that, according to
the solemn declaration of Jesus
Christ, the word which he spake
is that by which every man is to
be judged at the last day.

Many, I know are apt to think
that any interference with their
religious sentiments is very officious
and improper. "Let every one,
they say, "judge for himself on
these subjects no one is entitled
to dictate to another." From what
I have already said, I trust you are
convinced that any attempt to dictate is out of the question. But I
put it to yourself, if you could at
all reconcile it with consistency—
if it could be supposed in any degree compatible with genuine friendship, for me to entertain such views
as I have stated of the great leading
truths above mentioned, without
endeavouring to bring them under
your review nay, I will go farther,
and say,—without most seriously
and earnestly begging your attention to them.

What I fear is, that, amidst your
various literary and professional
pursuits, this subject may have been
in a great measure overlooked, or,
that you, like many others, have
rested satisfied with some vague and
general admission of the truth of
Christianity as a whole, without
ever particularly inquiring what it
is, or how, according to its own
statements, we are personally interested in the hopes it reveals. I
have certainly met with not a few,
distinguished for extensive know-

ledge on other subjects, who allowed this one, which, if seriously considered, must be admitted by all to be of the very first importance, to pass unexamined and disregarded. Now, if you have never seriously considered the testimony of revelation on the topics above referred to, you must admit, that it is possible at least, that I may be in the right: and if I be, reflect, I beseech you, my dear sir, on the deeply eventful consequences which this supposition involves. Your safety and happiness in the world to come, according to my view of this revelation, are essentially connected with your receiving its doctrines—your experiencing that transforming effect on the heart and character without which, we are assured, we cannot enter the kingdom of heaven—and your resting your hopes on that foundation which it teaches us is the only one on which we can build with safety for eternity.

As I firmly believe that according to the declarations of Scripture, the Almighty orders the various circumstances in our history, I cannot contemplate this truth, and reflect that it is under the arrangements of this overruling Providence that we have become acquainted, without being impressed with a strong feeling of deep responsibility, when I look forward to the future scenes which Christianity unfolds. While it points us to a day when all the unnumbered millions of our race shall stand before the tribunal of the Son of God, I should tremble to look forward to that interesting period, if it should then be found, that, with my sentiments of the necessity of personally embracing the Gospel of Jesus Christ, I had so frequently enjoyed the pleasure of your society, and thus had an opportunity of calling your attention to that which I was convinced to be essential to your everlasting peace, if that opportunity had all along been neglected.

I must again then, my dear sir, beg you will not be offended with me for bringing the subject of this letter under your notice. In whatever light you may view this address, or whatever use you may make of it, I trust you will not for a moment entertain a doubt of the purity and sincerity of the motive by which it is dictated: and that it is with the warmest affection, and most cordial esteem, I subscribe myself

Your friend and servant

To the Editor of the Christian Observer.

DURING a recent visit to the Low Countries, my attention has been drawn to a very beautiful essay on the important duty of the reading of the holy Scriptures, which is the more interesting as having been written by a *Roman Catholic*, and as being prefixed to an ' authorised version' of the New Testament. At the present moment when the circulation of the Divine word among the Romanists occupies the public attention, in several important points of view this document may be an acceptable contribution to your pages. I have therefore inclosed a translation. I shall only add, that the edition * of the New Testament to which the following " preface" is annexed, was translated into the French from the Vulgate, and printed at Mons in 1667: it was sanctioned by the " privilege" of his Most Catholic Majesty, Charles, King of Spain, dated at Bruxelles, 24th July, 1666.—I am, sir, yours, &c.

G. C. G.

* I have not met with the original edition: my translation is made from an *extract* of the preface to the Mons New Testament, contained in an interesting pamphlet entitled, Conversion de Familles Catholiques Romaines dans le Grand Duché de Bade au Christianisme Evangelique. This work, originally written in German by Dr Tzschirner, has been translated into French and published at Liege with notes 1825, (I believe by M Vanderbanc a Protestant pastor in that city but the name is not given.)

PREFACE TO THE FRENCH TESTAMENT, MONS, 1667.

It is so essential to all Christians to love and venerate the New Testament, that it may be said that they cannot allow these sentiments to be extinguished, without forgetting the name they bear, or renouncing that to which they belong. We are the children and disciples of Jesus Christ: if we then really love these two amiable titles, and consider them as constituting all our dignity and glory, how precious ought that sacred book to be to us, since it is an assemblage of the Divine instructions of our Master, and the Testament which ensures to us the heritage of our Father! It is true that the new law which St Paul calls the law of the Spirit of life, and which he always opposes to the old law, as a ministration of death, is not the simple *letter* of the New Testament, but the *love of God*, which the Holy Spirit writes in the hearts of Christians as a *living* and *inward* law which renders them properly children of the new covenant, as they are called by St Augustin. But it is also certain that that inward law has such a union with the outward law contained in the book of the New Testament, that the saints have always considered the Word as the chief means of which God made use to write in their hearts that law of love and grace. It is for that reason they have always made one of the principal duties of the pious Christian to consist in meditating without ceasing on the truths which God teaches us by that Divine book: for they have not considered the Word as separated from the Holy Spirit, but as being filled with his fire, with his unction, and with his influence, which renders it capable of producing in every well disposed mind the same gracious effect which it has uniformly produced throughout the world in the conversion of mankind.

We must not then be surprized that the holy fathers so frequently complain of the negligence of the faithful in the discharge of this important duty. The Gospel, say these holy men, is the mouth of Jesus Christ. His abode is in heaven, but he speaks continually on earth. How then can he dare call himself the servant of Jesus Christ, who takes no pains to know his will, and how can he be ready to obey him, if he neglect to listen to him?

"*The precepts of the Gospel*, says St Cyprian, "*are the foundation of our confidence, and the nourishment of our souls: in reading them we find the light which conducts us, the power which supports us, and the remedies which cure us.*"

This holy man then shews, and the other fathers after him, the great advantage which the Gospel has over all the books of the Old Testament: for though Jesus Christ is the end of the law, and has there been prefigured in a variety of ways, nevertheless he is so concealed that there are few persons found who have sufficient light to discover him, especially in these latter days, in which the sacred Scriptures are so little read.

But in the Gospel He who was foretold by the Prophets presents himself to us. God descends from heaven to conduct us thither, says St Cyprian: and we no longer receive, as formerly, the oracles of God by the word of his saints; but we adore the truth of God spoken by God himself.

"The life of Jesus Christ which is there described, says St Augustin, "is a continual guide for the regulation of our own. "We there see, in the sick and the possessed whom he cured, all that occurs in the diseases and the cure of our souls. And it is a sufficient motive to forsake sin and to live godly,' adds the same father, "to consider the good things which he renounced, and the evils which he endured: for we only sin in two ways, either in wishing for that which he despised, or in avoiding that which he was content to suffer

"If God formerly commanded his people to read continually the Law which he gave them, and to meditate thereon day and night, how can we neglect to read the Law of Jesus Christ, the words of which are spirit and life; since, having entered by baptism into the Catholic faith, of which Jesus Christ is the founder, we ought to regard the Gospel as our rule, which teaches us his will, which assures us of his promises, which is our light in this world, and which will one day judge us in the other. It is that which made St. Cesaire, Bishop of Arles say, that "even those who know not how to read are not excusable, on that account, for being ignorant of what they might learn by reading the Gospel: for if the most ignorant and the lowest of the people, not only in towns but in villages, find means, says that saint, 'to have read to them, and to learn, profane and worldly songs, how will they pretend after that to plead ignorance as their excuse for having never learned any thing from the Gospel? "You have invention enough, adds he, " to learn, without knowing how to read, what the devil teaches you, that you may be lost, and you have not enough to learn from the mouth of Jesus Christ the truth, by which you may be saved.

It would be endless to mention all that has been said by the holy fathers, respecting the excellence of the Gospel. All their works are full of marks of veneration, not only for the sacred history of the life of Jesus Christ, but also for all the other books which compose the New Testament. We might shew in what manner they have spoken of it; but as we have made some observations at the commencements of these books, we shall only say here, that the *Acts* are the accomplishment of the Gospel, since we there see the descent of the Holy Spirit, which Jesus Christ had promised, the formation of the church, and the charity, the patience, and the perfect union of the primitive Christians,—that St. Paul is the first interpreter of the Gospel; that he explains all the mysteries of Jesus Christ, and that he instructs us in all the rules of Christian morality and virtue. The *Epistles of St. Peter* and the other Apostles are filled with the fire and unction of the Holy Spirit. The Apocalypse, in its divine and prophetic obscurity, has sparks of light which strike the heart, and deeply impress the humble soul with the majesty of God.

It is hoped that not only the most enlightened, but even the most simple understandings, might here find what will be necessary for their instruction; provided they read with entire simplicity of heart, and that they humbly approach the Son of God, saying with St Peter, "Lord to whom shall we go? thou hast the words of eternal life, and it is thou alone who canst teach them to us!" We must approach him, as those did of whom it is said in the Gospel, they came to hear him, and to be cured of their diseases; for "curiosity," according to St Augustin "is a wound of the mind, so much the more dangerous as it is more concealed; and if we think only of satisfying it in reading the words of our Saviour, it would be to nourish our disease by the remedy which ought to cure it. He who seeks only for *salvation* in the Gospel will find it, as well as the knowledge which he sought not; and he who seeks only to satisfy a vain desire after *knowledge* is in danger of becoming more ignorant and blind, in becoming more presumptuous; since according to the saying of a great saint, "pride shuts the eyes of the soul, as humility opens them."

To make the obscurities of that study an obstacle to our perseverance in it, would be the means of our losing all the fruit which we might gather from so holy a pursuit. St Augustine, the most enlightened of all the holy fathers, fails not to acknowledge that the Scriptures are full of wisdom so exalted, and so profound, that there is much more beyond than within our comprehension. And after this, shall we be surprised that what has happened to other saints has happened to us, and that we cannot penetrate what has remained concealed to the most enlightened of men?

"The holy Scriptures," says St. Gregory, "are like a great river, which has always flowed, and will continue to flow to the end of time." The great and the little, the strong and the weak, there find that living water which springs up to heaven. It offers itself to all, it is proportioned to all, its simplicity condescends to the meanest capacity, and its height elevates the most exalted. All may partake indifferently, but far from exhausting by supplying ourselves from the fountain, we leave always depths of wisdom and knowledge, when we adore without comprehending.

But what ought to console us in this obscurity, is according to St. Augustin, that the holy Scriptures offer to us, in an easy and intelligible manner, all that is necessary for the conduct of our lives: that they explain and elucidate themselves by declaring plainly in some parts what is mentioned obscurely in others: and yet even the obscurity which we find is very useful, if we view it with the eye of faith and piety: as pearls and precious stones are so much the more valuable, as they are the more rare, and as they are found only with much trouble. For the same reason, silver, in the time of Solomon, was as much despised as stones, as the Scriptures inform us, because it was so common. Thus it is, according to St. Denys and Augustin, that the majesty of God and the excellence of his wisdom, are, as it were, surrounded with a cloud, and concealed under shadows and figures, which we can only penetrate by much meditation and labour, in order that they may impress the hearts in a more lively manner with that religious fear and profound reverence which they claim.

It was also necessary to man, in the state into which sin had reduced him, that God should declare his truth in such a manner as to humble his pride by the difficulty he should have in penetrating its mysteries. This serves to rouse his indolence, to oblige him to ask, that he may receive; to seek, that he may find; and to knock long at the door, that it may be opened. It shews him also, that the Spirit of God alone knows the mind of God, and that it is by the Spirit, and not by his own understanding, that he must learn what God teaches him. It is to cure him of that indifference which makes him too apt to despise what he obtains without difficulty. Its effect is constantly to renew his admiration and love of the wisdom of God in presenting it to him under different ideas and by fresh types. Finally, when he shall have understood one of those hidden truths which the prophet terms diamonds, it enables him to taste a joy, which is the greater in proportion as it had formerly appeared to him obscure, and as he had had difficulty in discovering it. St. Augustin assures us, that this joy is so lively and pure, in one who fears God, and who only seeks to know him in his word that he may obey and love him, that there is nothing on earth comparable to it, and that it is the greatest consolation of those who are still in the wilderness. It is what this holy doctor has comprised in these excellent words which merit well our consideration: 'There are, says he, "in the holy Scriptures profound mysteries which God keeps concealed in order to render them more highly estimated: which he permits us long to seek, in order to exercise and humble us by this labour: and which he discovers to us when it pleases him, in order that they may be the joy and support of our hearts."

This same saint (whose mind as humble as it was exalted, penetrated with more light than any other into the spirit and meaning of the sacred Scriptures, which St. Gregory calls "the mind of God,") adds to what we have said another very important truth, and which affords much consolation to minds not fully enlightened. It is, that that multiplicity of precepts and mysteries which is spread in so many different ways through these holy books are all in conformity to that one commandment, "to love God with all our heart, and our neighbour as ourself. "*For holy Scripture*, says that great doctor, '*forbids but one thing which is covetousness and love of the creature, and it commands but one thing, which is charity and the love of God. Upon this double rule is established all Christian morality.*

On this hang, according to the words of Jesus Christ, all the Law and the Prophets and, we may add, all the mysteries and instructions of the new law: for love, as says St. Paul, is the fulfilment of the law. 'It is that love,' adds Augustin, ' which is the root: all the truths are as the branches and fruit.' "If you cannot understand, says he, "all these branches which have so great an extent, content yourself with the root which contains them all. He who loves knows all, for he possesses that to which they all tend. Say not, then, that you cannot understand the Scriptures. Love God, and there is nothing which you shall not comprehend. When Scripture is clear, it *plainly* points out the love of God: and when it is obscure, it points it out *obscurely*. He then knows what is clear and what is obscure in Scripture, who knows how *to love God*, and whose life is regulated by *that love*. It is with this disposition that we ought to read the word of Jesus Christ and it is this love which, purifying our heart, will dissipate by degrees those obscurities which we find, and which will increase our light more and more. According to the assurance of the same father, when he says, ' It is love which asks: it is love which seeks: it is love which knocks at the door, and causes it to be opened; and it is by love that we shall remain stedfast in those truths which the Spirit of God has revealed to us.'

Let us never separate the word from the Spirit of Christ. Let us invoke his Spirit whilst reading his word, that it may not be to us a dead and barren letter, but living and efficacious, being accompanied by the unction and influence of his grace.

But that which is a great consolation to us, and which ought to give us a peculiar love for the word of Jesus Christ, is, that in whatsoever state we are, it is always salutary and profitable. The word of Jesus Christ may be read profitably by those even who are still in sin; provided they make use of it to discover their maladies, to have a fear of the judgment of God, to hope in his mercy, and to place themselves in the hands of him who can heal them. Thus it is not only the food of healthy souls, and of those established in grace, but it is also the consolation of sinners, the light of the blind, the remedy of the diseased, and life to the dead.

The meditation of evangelical and apostolic truths may be continual. At *all* times, in *every* condition however weak, we may nourish ourselves with this bread of life, which is " the food of the blessed," as says St. Augustin. we may have the law of God in our hearts, in our minds, and in our mouths, and draw from his Scripture, according to St. Paul, [see Romans xv. 5.] the 'comfort which will confirm us in "patience" and 'hope' of good to come.

To the Editor of the Christian Observer.

' THEY also are to be accursed, as serts the Eighteenth Article of our Church, " that presume to say that " every man shall be saved by the " law or sect which he professeth ' so that he be diligent to frame his " life according to that law and the "light of nature. For holy Scripture doth set out unto us only the name of Jesus Christ, whereby men must be saved." It is not my intention to enter upon the discussion of this celebrated article, which, in spite of the Scriptural proof of its truth which itself adduces, has been more cavilled at than most of the Thirty-nine, but only to point out what appears to me to be a mistake in its interpretation, under which many of its advocates have laboured. Not to trouble your readers with quotations from the various pages which have fostered this criticism, I will content myself with the words of that exposition to which in this case, I believe, (as well as in many other) succeeding commentators have been indebted. "They are here condemned," says the excellent Bishop Burnet, "who think that every man shall be saved by the law or sect which he professeth. Where a great difference is to be observed between the words saved *by* the law and saved *in* the law: the one is condemned, but not the other. To be saved *by a law* or sect, signifies that by the virtue of that law or sect, such men who follow it may be saved; whereas, to be saved *in a law* or sect, imports only that God may extend his compassion to men that are engaged in false religions. The former only is condemned by this article, which affirms nothing respecting the other."

Minute verbal criticism (especially in the English language) is very apt to mislead an inquirer after truth; and I confess that, on reading the remarks above quoted, my mind recurred to a well known example of an error arising from this source, in the interpretation once put on the phrase "*very far gone* from original righteousness." Remembering further, that that error was refuted by means of the Latin version of the Articles, which is contained in the preface of Burnet's book, accompanied by the remark that both the Latin and English are *equally authentical*, I turned to that version, and found the words "IN lege aut secta."

Surely, then, the real meaning of the compilers cannot be doubtful; and whether their doctrine be scriptural or otherwise, an interpreter ought at least not to adapt it to his own views by a false gloss upon their words. All writers, whether sacred or profane, ought to be construed in their expressed or clearly implied meaning; and those who revolt from their conclusions ought not to mutilate their text. Nothing can be more injurious to the cultivation of true Christian sincerity than the too frequent practice of signing formularies "cum grano salis," while professing to adopt them in their literal grammatical meaning. If the document be faulty, let it be amended; but let not minute criticism be called in to make it contravene its own design.

Ψ Ψ

To the Editor of the Christian Observer.

THE authorised English translation of Heb. vii. 18, 19, appears very incorrect and awkward: for the addition of the word "did," in the 19th verse, grammatically requires the words 'make nothing perfect' to complete the sentence, which brings out a meaning the exact contrary of that intended both by the Apostle and the translators, and intimated by the disjunctive '*but*.' The translators, however, doubtless intended the added auxiliary "did" to convey the sense of "made something perfect." Still the question remains, What was perfected? which the sentence cannot be brought to answer. The French translation of Martin runs thus: "Il se fait une abolition du commandement qui a précédé, à cause de sa foiblesse, et parce qu'il ne pouvait point profiter. Car la loi n'a rien amené à la perfection; mais ce qui a amené à la perfection, c'est ce qui a été introduit par dessus, savoir une meilleure espérance, par laquelle nous apprehends de Dieu." This has avoided the difficulty that hangs over our translation by bringing in the sentence "ce qui a amené à la perfection;" but I do not see what authority it has for doing so. The Italian of Diodati appears still farther from the mark, and the introduction of the words "si bene" does not make the passage more clear. If the following reading be, as it appears to me, consistent with the genius of the Greek language, it would remove the difficulty. "There is verily a disannulling of the commandment going before for the weakness and unprofitableness thereof, (for the law made nothing perfect,) but *there is* the bringing in of a better hope by which we draw nigh unto God." By this the words "Αθετησις προαγουσης εντολῆς" are put into direct opposition to "επεισαγωγη κρειττονος ελπιδος" and "το αυτης ασθενες και ανωφελες" to "δι ἡς εγγιζομεν τῳ θεῳ, and the unprofitableness of the first covenant is put into strong and striking contrast with the life giving privileges of the second. I do not see any objection that can be made to the supposition that "Ουδεν γαρ ετελειωσεν ο νομος" is a parenthesis accounting for the epithets "ασθενες" and "ανωφελες" which had been applied to the law and that being granted "γινεται" is the only word that can be understood in connexion with "επεισαγωγη."

A CONSTANT READER.

FAMILY SERMONS.—No. CCIV.

Ephes. v. 30.—"*For we are members of his body.*"

How different is the character given in Scripture of true religion, from that mere form and profession which often pass current in the world, under its name! It is not a few ceremonies, a course of outward observances, or even a decent regard to the common duties of morality that constitutes true religion: it is a union to Christ, such a union as insures both our justification and our sanctification; in other words, the pardon of our sins, and our acceptance with God for the sake of the infinite merits of the Redeemer, and that renewal of our minds in true righteousness and holiness, by which we are enabled to bring forth fruit to the glory of God. Religion thus viewed is a state of the highest happiness: it is that which alone can support us amidst the troubles of life, give us solid peace in death, and unfold to us the glories of the eternal world. It is also a state of the highest exaltation: for what can be more ennobling than to be members of Christ, children of God, and inheritors of the kingdom of heaven? Yet to this dignity does every true Christian arrive: he is a member of the body of Christ; he is one with Christ, and Christ with him; in the language of the Apostle, "Christ is formed in him the hope of glory:" he is Christ's, and Christ is God's; and hence flows to him, through this inexhaustible fountain, whatever is necessary for his best and eternal welfare.

The declaration in the text will lead us to consider,

First, The nature of the union to Christ here mentioned.

Secondly, The privilege of those who are partakers of it.

Thirdly, Some marks by which we may judge whether we are united to him.

First, then, we are to inquire into the nature of the union to Christ mentioned in the text.—The Scriptures illustrate this union by various comparisons. Thus he is spoken of as the good Shepherd, and we as his sheep, guided, defended, and fed by his hand. Again he is the Corner stone, and his members are the building: he unites and supports the whole spiritual edifice, all the parts of which aptly fitted together, grow up a holy temple to his glory. He is also a King: and all true believers are his subjects: he rules over them by his righteous laws, he keeps them in peace, and he pro

...... them from their enemies while they, on their part, being made willing in the day of his power, submit themselves to his sway, and yield him a true, though imperfect, allegiance. So also, He is the vine, and they are the branches: they are engrafted into him, and derive from his fullness, every supply of spiritual vigour and nourishment: they bring forth fruit, only by means of their union to him, and without him can do nothing. This union and participation are still more fully illustrated, under the emblem of food, by which the body is supported and kept in health for the performance of its various functions. Our Lord describes himself as the true manna which came down from heaven, of which whosoever should eat, should live for ever: "I am the bread of life," said he "he that cometh unto me shall never hunger, and he that believeth on me shall never thirst." This spiritual participation, he further teaches, is not a matter of little moment, but is absolutely necessary to salvation. "Verily verily, I say unto you, Except ye eat the flesh of the Son of man, and drink his blood, ye have no life in you: whoso eateth my flesh, and drinketh my blood, hath eternal life, and I will raise him up at the last day." Again, this union is represented in Scripture under the emblem of marriage, which shews us the duty of a willing devotion of our heart and affections in the service of Christ, while from him we receive support, protection and the enjoyment of his love and favour. It was this particular illustration which the Apostle had immediately in view, in the words of the text, which are introduced in the course of his exhortations on the duties of the marriage state. And he sums up the whole by adding, "we are members of his body:" an illustration which he also uses in other epistles, to shew the close union between Christ and his church. "We being many, says he, in the Epistle to the Romans," "are one body in Christ, and every one members one of another." Christ is the head, "from which all the body by joints and bands having nourishment ministered, and knit together, increaseth with the increase of God." All mankind indeed have a relationship to God as his creatures, formed by his hand, and designed to live to his glory: but, having failed in this great obligation of their existence, they do all in their power to forget the ties which bind them to their Maker and all merciful Benefactor. Still they are his, by this first and unalienable right; for he hath made them, and not they themselves. But the true Christian is united to Him in a closer and more endearing union by the blood of Christ: he is his by the right of redemption, as well as of creation, by the indwelling of his Spirit in his heart, and by a willing dedication of himself to his service. By nature he was dead in trespasses and sins and alienated from the life of God through wicked works; but by means of his union to Christ, he begins to live a new and spiritual life, according to the language of the Apostle, "Christ liveth in me and the life which I now live in the flesh, I live by the faith of the Son of God who loved me, and gave himself for me."

Here then is expressed the closest possible union: a union so important and necessary, that as well might it be expected that the members of the natural body could live and grow separated from the head, as a man be a Christian, or bring forth the fruits of true Christianity, severed from Christ.

But we shall see the nature of this union more plainly if we consider the manner in which it is effected. This is, on the part of man, by means of a true and lively faith in Christ, wrought in the heart by the power of the Holy Spirit: and on the part of God by the gift of that Spirit, to dwell in us, and to make us new creatures in Christ Jesus.

First, then, there must be faith as the bond of union. Faith leads us to renounce ourselves, and, disclaiming all merit of our own, to depend wholly upon the Saviour for pardon and acceptance with God. This fundamental grace of the Christian character lays hold, as it were, of the Redeemer in his various relations to mankind in the covenant of mercy. It is not enough that the understanding is convinced: there must be also a personal application of the truths of the Gospel to our own particular case. We must feel our individual weakness and sinfulness, and have recourse to the redemption that is in Christ as a full remedy for all our wants. Faith thus embraces the promises of God, made to the true penitent: it "receives Christ Jesus the Lord:" it gladly accepts of "the righteousness of God in Christ:" it thankfully prostrates itself at the foot of the cross of Christ: it introduces the believer to a state of adoption into the family of God, in place of his former alienation from him: it is the instrument of his justification: and in proportion as it is in vigorous exercise it brings peace into his soul. It looks to Christ, it feeds on him with thanksgiving, it reposes on him for the supply of every necessity.

But besides faith, there is the gift of the Holy Spirit dwelling in us, as a bond of union to Christ. The Scriptures bear witness to this truth in numerous passages: as, for example, "If a man have not the Spirit of Christ, he is none of his." "Hereby know we that we dwell in him, because he hath given us his Spirit:" and again, "He that is joined unto the Lord is one spirit." Our union to Christ is a union of love: now, "the love of God is shed abroad in our hearts by the power of the Holy Ghost which is given unto us." It is also a union of holiness, and in this respect also the Holy Spirit dwells in our hearts as his temple, his chosen seat, there shedding abroad the graces of faith, humility, meekness, heavenly mindedness, and whatever else is lovely and of good report. He presides over the whole man, regulating the will, the understanding, and the affections, and bringing every thought into willing captivity to the obedience of Christ. These graces of the renewed life are both proofs of union to the Saviour, since they shew the operation of his Spirit in the heart, and are in part the essence of that union itself, which is holy, spiritual, and heavenly. The Christian is not allied to Christ merely in that outward sense in which all mankind have a bond of union to him, by his having become partaker of our flesh; but he is also united to him by being raised in some measure to a participation of his Spirit. The presence of Christ in his heart is shewn by an imitation of the example of Christ. The union, in a word, is of a two fold kind, that by which he receives pardon, justification, and peace, and that by which he becomes renewed in the spirit of his mind. Without this union he would, on the one hand, remain for ever exposed to the anger of God for his transgressions; while, on the other, he would never feel any desire to forsake them, and to return to his justly offended Creator. But now, being united to Christ he not only is justified by faith, and has peace with God, but the love of his Saviour constrains him to present himself body and soul to the service of his infinitely gracious Creator, Redeemer, and Sanctifier.

Secondly. Having thus considered something of the nature of this union, we are now to inquire into the privileges attendant upon it. These will, however, be apparent from what has been already stated. In truth, all the blessings of religion flow from union to Christ. By virtue of it, our natural state of sin, and guilt, and death, is exchanged for a new state of pardon, and holiness, and eternal life. As transgressors against God we were under the sentence of his righteous law, but "there is now no condemnation to them that are in Christ Jesus," his infinite merits being made available for their pardon and reconciliation with God. Hence he is called their righteousness, the end of the law for righteousness; by his blood they are cleansed, by his stripes they are healed. Under his protection they remain in perfect safety; even their afflictions are turned into blessings, and all things are made to work together for their good. Instead of being exposed to the wrath of God, they, in consequence of this union, become partakers of his love and favour according to the prayer of our Lord himself for his disciples, 'that the love wherewith thou hast loved me may be in them, and I in them.' Thus joined to the Redeemer, they are not only interested in the benefits procured for them by his holy life and expiatory death upon earth, but also in his intercession for them in heaven: he appears in the presence of God for them; he is their Advocate with the Father; he pleads their cause as their High Priest, entered into the holy of holies; he sends down the Holy Spirit, the Comforter, to abide with them; he opens to them a way of access to the throne of God; he accounts them his brethren; "he gives them power to become the sons of God; and 'if sons then heirs, heirs of God, and joint heirs with Christ.' They have communion with him, already begun during the short period of this mortal life; they live as constantly in his sight; they enjoy the communications of his grace; they draw nigh to him, and he to them; to promote, though with much remaining imperfection, and innumerable sins and failures, his glory is their supreme object of desire; their constant cause of pain and humiliation is, that their union to him is not more practically operative in its effects upon their hearts and lives; yet still they view it as constituting their highest privilege; they feel the value of it amidst their deepest sorrows; and they often 'rejoice with joy unspeakable and full of glory,' under circumstances which, to the mind of one whose whole portion was upon earth, would present nothing but grief and disappointment. United to Christ, God is their portion, their unspeakable reward; they are pardoned by his mercy; they are regenerated by his grace; they are comforted by his promises; they are covered from danger under the shadow of his wings; and they look forward to the eternal consummation of their happiness in the enjoyment of his presence for ever in heaven. Compared with blessings like these how worthless is all that the world accounts great or privileged! This truly is heaven commenced upon earth, and a foretaste of the heaven of heavens above. And what heightens and secures the whole is, that it is not a benefit enjoyed only for a short time, or secured by a doubtful tenure. The Apostle Paul therefore, after showing what it is to be in Christ, and the results of that union, the deliverance which it brings from condemnation, and the spirituality of life to which it gives birth, most sublimely concludes his argument by saying, 'I am persuaded that neither death nor life, nor angels, nor principalities, nor powers, nor things present, nor things to come, nor height, nor depth, nor any other creature, shall be able to separate us from the love of God which is in Christ Jesus our Lord.'

Thirdly. In proportion then to the importance of being united to Christ, and to the value of the benefits which flow from this union, is the care which we ought to exercise, that we be not deceived in judging whether we are thus united. In bringing ourselves to the test, we must bear in mind, that far more is necessary than a mere outward appearance of union. The Jews of old were ever ready to boast of their high religious privileges; they had Abraham to their father; many of the most eminent servants of God were of their nation; they had the appointed rites of Divine worship, the visible presence of God in their temple, his lively oracles in their hands; yet in spirit a large proportion of them were living as much "without God in the world" as the Gentiles who had never heard of his name. Thus also under the Christian dispensation, many deceive themselves with the outward forms of religion; they have been baptized in the name of Christ; they call themselves his followers; they perhaps even partake of the emblems of his body and blood; they observe many forms of devotion and duties of morality; and this is all that they consider requisite, if indeed they reflect upon the subject at all, to constitute that union to Christ, which the Scriptures point out as of indispensable necessity to salvation. But with all this they may still fall far short of a truly spiritual union. The sacraments themselves, upon which perhaps they place a large share of their dependence, are but visible signs and seals of this union; they do not of necessity confer this grace upon the partaker; for there may be true union to Christ, where unavoidable circumstances have prevented a participation in either of them; and there may be an utter disunion where they have been outwardly and visibly received, the latter of them perhaps often and under circumstances the most solemn.

Not indeed that either of these sacred institutions is of slight importance; the true servant of Christ is very far from thinking them so; he views baptism as the divinely appointed visible sign and seal of his cleansing by the blood of Christ, of his burial with him to the deeds of the flesh, and his resurrection to newness of life; he is "baptized into Christ;" the supper of the Lord also he estimates as another divinely appointed sign and seal of this union. 'The cup of blessing which we bless, is it not the communion of the blood of Christ? the bread which we break, is it not the communion of the body of Christ?' but inestimably valuable and important as they are, our participation of them is not in itself a proof that we are savingly united to him. Again and again must we remember, that the only sure proof of union to Christ is to have the Spirit of Christ. We must love him, we must place our whole dependance upon him for salvation, and we must walk in his steps. The proud man, the vain, the selfish, the worldly, the self righteous, the impenitent, the unholy, have no evidence of being in this state of union; their dispositions and conduct shew the fact to be quite otherwise; for union with Christ ever produces conformity to his image. If the heart be void of the spiritual graces which characterise the true Christian, it is self deception to be contented with any other pretended mark of union. "If any man be in Christ, he is a new creature; old things are passed away, and all things are become new." With this simple test then ever at hand, and with humble prayer to the Searcher of all hearts to guide us in the use of it, we cannot fail to ascertain what is our true character in the sight of God; and oh! that we may duly feel the importance of the inquiry, and make no delay in coming to a decision on a point of such infinite importance!

MISCELLANEOUS.

To the Editor of the Christian Observer.

ONE of your correspondents has lately touched upon the behaviour due from Christians towards their domestics and dependants, and the subject is most worthy of attention and that not only for the sake of the servant but also of the master for every Christian is required to bring forth "the fruits of the Spirit," many of which are called into constant exercise in domestic life. It becomes the faithful follower of Christ, to be watchful to see whether or not he possesses that important proof of Christian sincerity which arises from the habitual exhibition of a spirit of meekness, gentleness, forbearance, and due consideration towards those who are placed under his controul. The following passage, from Paley, describes the relative situation of master and servant in so just and interesting a manner, that it deserves to be familiar to the mind of every Christian master, as a guide for the examination of his own behaviour.

"A party of friends setting out together upon a journey soon find it to be the best for all sides, that, while they are upon the road, one of the company should wait upon the rest another ride forward to seek out lodging and entertainment a third carry the portmanteau a fourth take charge of the horses a fifth bear the purse, conduct and direct the route not forgetting, however, that, as they were equal and independent when they set out, so they are all to return to a level again at their journey's end. The same regard and respect the same forbearance lenity and reserve in using their service the same mildness in delivering commands, the same study to make their journey comfortable and pleasant, which he, whose lot it was to direct the rest, would, in common decency, think himself bound to observe towards them ought we to shew to those who, in the casting of the parts of human society, happen to be placed within our power, or to depend upon us. I do not perceive any foundation for an opinion, which is often handed round in genteel company that good usage is thrown away upon low and ordinary minds, that they are insensible of kindness, and incapable of gratitude. If 'by low and ordinary minds are meant the minds of men in low and ordinary stations, they seem to be affected by benefits in the same manner as others are, and to be no less ready to requite them and it would be a very unaccountable law of nature, if it were otherwise.

"Whatever uneasiness we occasion to our domestics, which neither promotes our service nor answers the just end of punishment, is manifestly wrong were it only upon the general principle of diminishing the sum of human happiness. By which rule we are forbidden, 1. To enjoin unnecessary labour or confinement, from the mere love and wantonness of domination. 2. To insult our servants, by harsh, scornful, or opprobrious language. 3. To refuse them any harmless pleasure. And, by the same principle, are also forbidden causeless or immoderate anger habitual peevishness, and groundless suspicion.

The above passage may not be unworthy the notice of 'Christian observers.' It is written with that delicacy of feeling which, under a certain coarseness of outward manner, Archdeacon Paley possessed in a great degree. We are brought in contact with our domestics every hour of the day and occasions are constantly arising which prove considerable trials of temper Besides, towards them, there is less restraint than towards equals or superiors and therefore harshly to express what we feel, is too often a "sin which most easily besets us" But if it be, as it undoubtedly is, a duty to try to bring all within our influence to the faith and fear of God how careful ought we to be, that we do not, by unchristian dispositions, lead them to believe that our own professions of religion are vain! A true delicacy of feeling, independently of a higher principle would teach us, in all the commands we give and in all the duties we require to keep back as much as possible the feeling of superiority, at least not to obtrude it without necessity It must make a great difference to the happiness of a domestic, whether he is every moment made to feel that he is your dependent or whether your kindness leads him to serve you, ' not, by constraint, but willingly No person needs complain that he has not sufficient opportunities of exercising a Christian disposition, when there is occasion for doing this, throughout the day, within his own doors

A CONSTANT READER.

To the Editor of the Christian Observer

I FEAR your correspondent's "cautions in affording relief to the destitute," in your Number for August, may unintentionally produce effects prejudicial to the spirit of charity To prevent all impositions is impracticable but we are not on that account to curtail the exercise of beneficence The perversion of charity has, no doubt, a tendency to weaken our sympathies, and to chill our best feelings, but this tendency does not generally take effect except on minds which are more influenced by the dread of evils than by the noble and powerful impulse of genuine benevolence

Your correspondent, in answer to "the trite observation, that it is better to relieve ten worthless impostors, than to suffer one deserving object to pass by unassisted, says, "that we profess a religion which teaches us, not to do evil that good may come How this bears on the subject, appears to me a mystery Who ever relieves a poor object under the *impression* that he is an impostor? How then can the relief afforded be doing evil on his part? But suppose the donor to be in an uncertainty is it a sin for him to relieve such as are apparently distressed? To detect imposition is certainly our duty, if practicable but to deny relief, even when the real character of the applicant is uncertain, if labouring under evident distress, is, in my view a neglect of duty, in no way to be justified If I understand the drift of your correspondent's observations, they lead to this, that no relief should be afforded except to persons whose case the benefactor is thoroughly acquainted with and that, if he have no time to examine or means to ascertain their character, he is to grant no relief Now, I prefer "the trite observation, as your correspondent terms it, to this 'It is very necessary to ascertain, if possible, the character of such as ask charity but when we are solicited, the duty is so plain and peremptory, that we cannot deny it, without really "doing evil The applicant may be an impostor Very true then let him be examined But "I have no time"' That lies with you and not with the poor object He presents himself to you as one distressed Your great and obvious duty is to relieve him Your duty also is to prevent imposition but this is inferior in its importance to the other If you *must* neglect either of the two, let it be the latter

I have some faint recollection of reading, some years ago, of a gentleman, who deeply regretted having in one instance denied relief to a poor man, under the idea that he was an impostor The poor fellow died from want, shortly after and so deeply affected was the gen tleman at the event, that he determined never afterwards to deny relief to an apparently distressed applicant. There are, no doubt, impostors, but there are also, notwithstanding the changes of the times, many really distressed mendicants. With some such I have on several occasions met. Their prompt answers to any questions proposed to them, their right forward tale of woe, and their heart felt gratitude when relieved, convinced me that they were so. It is not difficult, in most instances, to detect an impostor. His answers are shuffling and evasive. He manifests a dislike to be minutely interrogated. His story is plausible. He contradicts himself if he is asked many questions. He shews much shrewdness and cunning. But at times there are characters to be met with respecting whom nothing satisfactory in either way can be made out. They excite suspicions and yet afford something that may lead to a belief that they are real objects of charity. Two young fellows, not long ago, called at my house in the dusk of the evening, requesting a place to lie down during the night. The account they gave of themselves was not very satisfactory. Their evident fatigue was the strongest reason that induced me to grant their request. I was not without fear of dishonest intentions on their part. They rested, left in the morning, and were very thankful; and I felt thankful too, that I had been induced, notwithstanding some suspicious appearances, to shew kindness to two very poor and distressed fellow creatures. They might, it is true, have abused my kindness; but had they done so, I should not have repented of my resolution, because the impression that they deserved relief was stronger than my suspicions, and therefore what I did resulted from a sense of duty.

M. S.

To the Editor of the Christian Observer.

IT is with much satisfaction that I have perused some remarks in your pages on relieving the destitute, because the subject is of very great practical moment. I fear, however, that the real bearings of the question are not likely to be soon settled, unless some preliminary positions are first agreed upon. In conversing with many individuals as prompt in works of charity as enlightened and judicious in the mode of administering it, I have found them lay down almost as a maxim, that the large mass of applicants for relief are *not* really distressed persons, and that there is incomparably far less danger of doing evil on the side of extreme caution in indiscriminate almsgiving than from hasty profusion. They argue also that the commands in Scripture to charity have no reference to this question, the very point being whether it *is* charity to bestow alms on casual applicants. Other benevolent individuals lay down as *their* maxim, that the majority of applicants need relief, and that a few only are impostors or otherwise improper objects. Now, it is clear, that the two parties can never determine on the same uniform line of conduct till they can come nearer together in theory. What then is the right view of the case, under the existing circumstances of society? Are the injunctions of Scripture, not to turn away from any poor man, to be literally and indiscriminately applied to all who *profess* themselves to be in distress, or is an enlightened spirit of Christian inquiry to induce us to pause till the necessity is ascertained? It would be well if all the friends of humanity could come to some common understanding on this subject; but as that does not appear to be immediately probable, the next best course is for each to exercise a sound judgment as respects each individual application; taking care that he does not allow his own feelings of charity to become blunted, or find excuses for indulging a cold hearted selfishness: and, on the other hand, that he does not condemn his Christian neighbour for a line of conduct which may be to the full as conscientious as his own.

C. C.

To the Editor of the Christian Observer.

In your Number for September last a correspondent inquires, what advantages are likely to accrue from the judicious perusal of the Fathers. I shall not undertake to answer this question, or follow up the line of argument commenced by another correspondent Mr. Faber in your last Number; but will only endeavour to state the question fairly, and inquire by what measures it might possibly be answered.

I cannot think this object will be attained by referring, on the one hand, to the writings of those who depreciate the Fathers, or to their eulogists on the other. With regard to Daillé's Treatise de l'Emploi des Saints Peres, alluded to by R. X. it is known that he wrote it when he was only thirty-four years of age: now, what is it that this celebrated theologian had so early in life learned to despise? In Rivington and Cochran's Catalogue I find a collection of all the Fathers 126 vols fol. 4 4to 7, 8vo together 137 vol., price 315*l*.! Is it probable that those who depreciate the Fathers have studied seriatim all these massy tomes? yet bare justice requires that the works of an author should be *first* read, and *then* appreciated. By reference to a copious index, by making an extract here and there on our own favourite topics, by culling out absurdities or by selecting brilliant passages, a writer may attain the reputation of a learned theologian, deeply read in the Fathers; and so, without much fear of detection he may act as a dictator in this department: and, if his general attainments are known advantageously to the public, may disseminate and establish his own ideas on the subject, while all the while his judgment is grounded on very partial evidence and a very cursory examination. The excellencies and defects of this long series of theological writers are to be fairly estimated by actual and laborious examination, and in no other way. I conjecture that your correspondent's remark is a very just one, that there is in these neglected stores a mine of spiritual wealth; but it is a mine that is *neglected* and not worked: little therefore can be said with certainty of the depth and value of the ore. I only assert that there is prima facie evidence to encourage us to re-open this deserted mine. The question therefore is, where—to speak the language of the present day—shall we find capital and skilful engineers, and above all hard working miners, willing to delve in these dark regions, where the sun of patronage is never likely to penetrate, where meteors of fancy and flashes of eloquence can seldom be expected to beguile the mind, and where the steady light of solid argument is still more rare? To be plain, are there any who, from regard to the Christian religion and the interests of piety, would be willing to take a share in a work so laborious as this, which is productive neither of honour nor profit, but yet must be allowed by every reflecting mind to be of considerable importance?—for these writers are the principal links of that chain which connects our own age with the age of the Apostles; and even their defects as well as excellencies, as parts of the history of human opinions, bear some relation, and no very obscure or remote relation either to the welfare of the church of Christ: they probably contain many unnoticed historical [*] re-

[*] Though Lardner has laboured in this line so admirably, yet it is probable he has not exhausted the subject; and his well-known heterodoxy makes it very desirable that the ground he has gone over should be retraced by men of better principles.

schemes would be the external observances of religion, where they find examples to direct and animate us; yet, at the very worst, they are beacons to warn us, they are memorials of past generations which may throw light on the transactions of the present or of those yet to come for many a heresy, and many a folly that has risen and set, will rise again

But I may seem chargeable myself with that ignorant and rash anticipation which I have been condemning. What the Fathers are, remains in a great measure to be proved though not entirely, yet in a great degree they are a terra incognita. I therefore repeat the question, where shall we find the means of setting on foot a journey of discovery, in which principle and not profit must be the inciting cause, in which many a dreary desert must be passed with only here and there an oasis to relieve and refresh the weary traveller, and all the merit even of that discovery often be forestalled by an idle index student?

I pause before I proceed to answer this question, because I am aware that my suggestions may appear Utopian however, if I were to form a conclusion upon this subject, it should be this, that since, as before remarked, all authors, whether ancient or modern, to be treated fairly, should be judged by those who really read them through, and collect their doctrines and principles from the whole of their works, and not from garbled extracts and since in the present instance, this is confessedly beyond the powers or inconsistent with the avocations of individuals, I would invite a sort of joint stock company of Biblical students, to contribute their proportion of labour to this object, and to give the results occasionally to the public. Small efforts, like rays of light, feeble when scattered might be of great power condensed to a focus Such contributions, preserved and concentrated in your pages, would amount in time to a solution of many doubts and diffi-

culties relating to the ancient Fathers, and afford frequent illustrations and valuable hints respecting the canonical Scriptures themselves for the study of the canonical Scriptures in the original languages, the devout and diligent study of them, should be the paramount duty of every theologian and it is in subordination to this great and leading object, that my remarks respecting the Fathers are to be understood. Had a very small department of your work, twenty years ago, been devoted to these voluminous and venerable authors, upon a discreet and regular plan, considerable progress might have been made, and many elucidations of the Fathers have been interspersed in your volumes, which would have been no discredit to their contents It is one of the uses of a periodical publication, that it affords a repository for the labours of numerous students, who, though unequal to the task of instructing the public by a distinct work of their own, could, if their efforts were combined with others—the parts being judiciously distributed,—effect together, what no one could effect singly The most obvious plan would be to proceed chronologically with the series to translate the best pieces, to make an abridgment of inferior ones, and a very brief abstract or mere table of contents of the worst Wake has translated some of the apostolic fathers a revision of his work with the best of the notes of Cotelerius and Leclerc might be sufficient to begin with, adding a brief dissertation on the merits of the author, as compared with the canonical Scriptures

S

To the Editor of the Christian Observer

Your amanuensis, in copying the appellation of one of the new churches in the parish of Mary le bone in the list of Ecclesiastical Preferments in your last Number has written "All Saints" for "All Souls" His error was very natural and I wish the patron, who fixed on this name, had made the same mistake; for it is a strange anomaly, that the founders of a Protestant church, in this "most enlightened age," and in the largest and most wealthy parish in the world, should have been able to find for it no better name than the most popish and superstitious of all dedications to which any church has been subjected in the darkest ages. The intention of our old churches known by the name of "All Souls," was, as their muniments attest, for the repose of all Christian souls departed out of this world, with a view to their deliverance out of purgatory, by means of the prayers and masses there to be offered. All-Souls' college at Oxford founded by Archbishop Chichley, the persecutor of Wickliffe, is an imperishable record as well of gross superstition as of literary munificence.

If we are to have new "All Souls" churches, I see not why our church should have banished "All-Souls Day" from the calendar, where it stands, in the popish prayer-book, on the second of November, as conspicuously as our own "All-Saints" does on the first. Let Wheatley tell the rationale of the commemoration.

'The second of November, he says, "is called [in the Romish calendar] All Souls Day, being observed in the Church of Rome upon the following occasion. A monk having visited Jerusalem, and passing through Sicily as he returned home, had a mind to see Mount Ætna, which is continually belching out fire and smoke, and on that account by some is thought to be the mouth of hell. Being there he heard the devils within complain that many departed souls were taken out of their hands by the prayers of the Cluniac monks. This, when he came home, he related to his Abbot Odilo, as a true story, who thereupon appointed the second of November to be annually kept in his monastery, *and prayers to be made there for all departed souls*; and in a little time afterwards the monks [finding the trade gainful] got it to be made a general holyday, by the appointment of the pope, *till in ours and other reformed churches* [excepting, I suppose, the new church in Langham place] it was deservedly abrogated.

At a time when so many new churches are being erected throughout the country, and some difficulty seems to be felt in giving them characteristic designations, I trust these remarks on "the unfortunate church in Langham place" may not be deemed useless, if they excite a just degree of attention to this not unimportant subject.

I will only add, that no blame applies to that highly respectable clergyman Dr George Chandler, whose appointment to the preferment your ecclesiastical list announces, for this unhappy dedication, any more than for the equally unhappy style of architecture which has called forth the most severe remarks, both in parliament and among all persons of taste who have visited the structure. It is strange, that in "this age of good taste" such miserable specimens of ecclesiastical architecture should be growing up on every side. But let this pass—the architecture of this church cannot now be altered, nor, I presume, its name; but at least let it be understood that that name is meant only in its *Protestant* sense, and in *that* respect, if I could divest myself of purgatorian associations, I confess that it might be made to point out a very edifying lesson.

ACADEMICUS

To the Editor of the Christian Observer

IT has afforded me much pleasure to see in your columns an account of the formation of a Ladies Society for the education of Negro children. British ladies have thus at length so far done an act of jus tice, in attempting to deliver British slaves from the dark ignorance in which they have so long continued; and, by this proceeding, they will command the approbation of all who value the blessings of religion: but when I call to mind the innumerable evils which England has inflicted upon her slaves, that they are still in bondage, the most cruel and tyrannical the world ever witnessed, surely this attempt to shed light on their benighted minds is not *the only aid* that British ladies intend to bestow upon them? I entreat you, Mr. Editor, as a Christian observer, to let them know they are doing but little towards discharging the vast debt they owe the African race, by forming a society for the education of infant slaves; and that what they are doing, in the present state of our colonial system, will be of little avail. Place before them, Mr. Editor, those parts of Scripture which command us *all* to defend the poor—to rid them out of the hand of the wicked, and not to remain passive spectators of cruelty and oppression. Urge them to study the narrative of Esther; Prov. xxiv. 11, 12; Isaiah lviii.; Psalm x., lxxxii.; and Heb. xiii. 3; and then perhaps they will begin "to remember those in bonds as bound with them, and those that suffer adversity as being themselves also in the body;" they will then perhaps begin to see that they should follow the example of Queen Esther, and plead for those who cannot plead for themselves, for those who have been worn down with cruel bondage, to furnish them with luxuries.

I would beg you also to lay before them the following quotation, from the Cries of Africa; and may it teach them how much they have yet to perform, and what little chance of success awaits their labours, till they apply *their whole strength* to raise the fallen African, instead of merely stretching out, as it were a finger, to aid him to rise and say, "I am a man and a brother!"

"Of all countries in the world, we should least think of a conversion to Christianity there." The author is speaking of our European colonies: "The hatred which the poor slaves must naturally bear towards their masters, must almost force them to despise the Christian religion. They are placed in an unnatural state of society—in a state which almost forbids *moral improvement*. You wish, for example, to teach them to be honest; but hunger calls upon them, perhaps at the same moment, to be thieves: you read them lessons of fidelity and submission; but, ground down by hard labour and severe punishments, they retain a sense of their injuries, and are perhaps at that very moment awakened to revenge. It is not, therefore, to be expected that they can make any great proficiency in religion, while their *very condition* forces them into crime."

Can schools for our slaves teach chastity to females while our present system of slavery exists? If they are taught it, it must only add to their misery and anguish, when they are under the power of lawless overseers, who, as we see from the official accounts of the fiscals of Demerara and Berbice, printed by order of the House of Commons, may act towards them with impunity in the most licentious manner, and flog the wretched father who attempts to keep his child from prostitution. Englishwomen must know these things; for British female Negro slaves have to endure them in order to furnish us with luxuries. And shall Englishwomen leave them, as too many propose to do, in this state, polluted and debased by our colonial system, in order *that we may educate them first?* Let us indeed unite in educating them wherever we find an opening for so doing; and I rejoice that it is to be attempted; but let us not deceive ourselves by thinking that education is the first best gift we can at this time bestow; let us assist in delivering them from their cruel bondage which reduces them to the brutish and demoralized state, in which we find them. Do not, I conjure you, Mr. Editor, join with those who think it is of no use to release them till they are *first amended*—while all the time, the same debasing and abominable system is *creating* the evils which education is to cure. The iniquity of the present tyrannical and degrading system takes away all time for education on most estates. God says, 'Six days shalt thou labour:' the planter says, "Seven days shalt thou labour: if not for me, for thyself." God says, 'Keep holy the Sabbath day:' the planter says, "Profane the Sabbath day: *thou shalt not keep it holy.*" I know there are many honourable exceptions, but I am speaking of the system: a system which prevents all lawful marriages, causes Negro women to be lashed naked by men in public, and then it is said these women are without decency! and their morals cannot be cured "by a mere cessation of slavery:" and thus the system is perpetuated, because education is to cure their faults! This kind of doctrine, which is too widely circulated, would paralyze the arm that is stretched out to redress their wrongs and give a fatal blow to the cause of Negro emancipation. It neutralizes the efforts of many otherwise noble minded advocates: it prevents many a conscientious female from using the means which are in her power of assisting these unhappy women, by diffusing information, and making their cause heard: and it prevents British ladies joining hand in hand to break their bonds. But what says the Almighty? see Prov. xxiv. 11, 12, already alluded to. I entreat you, Mr. Editor, to shew British women their duty.

B T W L

REVIEW OF NEW PUBLICATIONS.

De la Religion, consideree dans ses Rapports avec l'Ordre politique et civile. Par l'Abbé F. DE LA MENNAIS. Premiere Partie. Seconde edition. Paris. 1825.

THIS is a pamphlet which, we understand, has excited some attention upon the continent: nor should we be surprised were it to find many more readers in that quarter. The subject of it is philosophically, as well as religiously, interesting and important. It may be supposed to speak the sentiments of a large party in France, who are unceasingly endeavouring to establish and augment their power. It supplies, also, abundant matter for reflection upon the probable destiny, religious and political, of that great and powerful empire. It is, in short, one of the most singular and spirited pamphlets which of late years have issued from the presses of either France or England. When we call it *spirited*, we allude of course only to its tone and manner. When we term it *singular*, we refer to the doctrines which it promulgates, and to the reasoning by which those doctrines are attempted to be established. It is written in the characteristic style of French genius, with great vivacity and great confidence, with some very eloquent declamation, but with little solid reasoning; not without vigour and acuteness, but with more of the appearance of those qualities than the reality. It has more pretension than power, and is calculated to impose on the simplicity of those readers (not a few in number) who are apt to mistake subtlety and adroitness for wisdom, and the boldness of paradox for the force of truth.

The subject of it is "Religion

considered under its civil and political relations, with a close and constant reference to the present state of affairs in France. The author professes to have left his work incomplete, and promises a second part, should the reception of the first be such as to encourage him to proceed. The part, however, already published, presents a sufficiently distinct picture for the eye of the reflecting critic, and still more the reflecting Christian, to rest upon and examine. The pamphlet is divided into four chapters. The first is on the actual state of society in France. The second attempts to prove, that, in that country, religion is at present totally unconnected with the civil and political order of things, and that consequently the state is no better than atheistical. The third goes a step farther, to shew that atheism, concentrated in the government, has thence diffused itself throughout the walks of private and domestic life. The fourth and last shews that religion has come to be regarded, in the eye of the law, as only one of the many subjects that fall under the regulation of the executive power, being placed in the annual budget upon the same footing of rank and dignity with the fine arts, the gaming houses, the theatres, and the haunts of vice and infamy. This would be indeed an appalling picture, could it be deemed a perfectly correct one, and our author's statements would be calculated to beget great apprehension, did not some of the very circumstances which most excite *his* fears, give strength and encouragement to *our* hopes of better times.

We must begin with exposing one error or false principle which pervades this treatise, and forms the sole basis of much of the reasoning it exhibits. Whenever Mons. de la Mennais speaks of religion *in the abstract*, he annexes any thing but a liberal meaning to his words. By religion he understands, solely and exclusively, the Church of Rome—

that one holy, undivided catholic apostolic see, out of whose communion no salvation is to be obtained: all other churches, all other sects and denominations of Christians go with him for nothing. Their tenets may be error and absurdity, under a thousand forms; but they are not entitled to be called religion. Thus he *virtually* places the whole of Protestant Europe (the Greek Church is accounted by the Latin as schismatical, but not heretical,) upon the same footing, and under the same ban of proscription, with the aggregate community (how many soever they be) of professed deists, sceptics, and atheists. He knows but of two distinctions, Religion and Atheism. The one comprises the Romish communion; the other all the rest of the world besides. This is—we do not say the deliberate and intentional but—certainly the real and virtual basis upon which much of his reasoning and most of his observations are built. Remove this prop, and many of his arguments and remarks fall to the ground "like the baseless fabric of a vision," without leaving a wreck behind.

We shall not deem it necessary to follow the author minutely through the several chapters of his publication. The attention of our readers will be best rewarded, by our seizing upon and examining some of his main facts and positions. Whoever attentively peruses this pamphlet, of only one hundred pages, will find himself almost overwhelmed with the quantity of matter which it yields for reflection on topics historical, political, moral, and religious. If the author have not thrown much additional light on these topics by his own remarks, he has at least the merit of laying open within a small compass, a mine of inexhaustible speculation for the exercise of every reflecting mind. Statesmen, moralists, divines, and philanthropists may all glean something suited to their respective views and occupations, and derive, if they will, some profitable hints of the direction of their future conduct, and of whose apostolic see out of whose bosom—

The author's first chapter can hardly be said to answer to its title. It contains much a view of the state of society in France, as a view of the present constitution of the government, and of the probable results of that constitution on the opinions and manners of the people. 'Quel genre de gouvernement a remplacé la monarchie Chrétienne?' is the subject of our author's first speculation. He begins with informing us, that, wherever the *pretended* Reformation gained a footing, it was followed, either by arbitrary government, or by anarchy. He then goes on to tell us that Great Britain can boast of nothing more than the fiction of a monarchy, and is in reality "an aristocratical republic," a singular phrase, which confounds ideas that ought always to be kept distinct. France, it seems, by the constitution of the Charter, intended to follow closely in the steps of England; but, in consequence of the previous overthrow of all her privileged orders, has in reality sunk down into a pure democracy, headed by the pageant, or rather the ghost, of a king; for he is said to be only "un souvenir vénérable du passé." The chapter concludes with a spirited, and most portentous sketch of the genius and complexion of democratical power. We give the concluding paragraph of his frightful predictions.

'Cependant la raison s'affoiblira visiblement. On contemplera avec surprise et comme quelque chose d'étrange les plus simples vérités; et ce sera beaucoup si on les tolere. Les esprits s'en iront poursuivant au hasard dans des routes diverses les fantômes qu'ils se seront faits. Les uns s'applaudiront de leur sagesse qui n'admet rien que de *positif*, c'est à dire ce qui se voit, ce qui se touche, ce qui se laisse manier avec la main; les autres se passionneront pour des rêves; et plaignant le genre humain de son opiniâtre attachement à des idées qui ne durent après tout que depuis six mille ans, voudront pour son bonheur le forcer à vivre de leurs immortelles abstractions. Tous, quelles que soient leurs pensées, leurs opinions particulières, s'accorderont pour rejeter

l'ancienne........ ..... Il sera convenu que rien de........ peut plus être, que le monde doit changer, qu'il faut à ses lumieres présentes une nouvelle morale, une religion nouvelle, un Dieu nouveau. En attendant qu'on le découvre, nous allons faire voir qu'en France l'état a cessé de reconnoître l'ancien. pp. 46, 47.

But the preceding topics of this chapter are too extraordinary to be passed over without some notice.

We were not ignorant that the Reformation in some degree affected the *civil* and *temporal*, while it shook, in a far greater measure, the *ecclesiastical* polity of Europe. But we had yet to learn, that wherever this grand revolution of opinions took place, "on vit naître aussitôt ou le despotisme ou l'anarchie." Of this our author is quite sure, because there happened to be some tyrants and many disturbances in the Protestant states of Europe during the course of the sixteenth century. Of course the examples of Henry VIII and of the Great Rebellion under Charles I are adduced as illustrations of his doctrine; as if (though we should allow all he says about them to be true, which we are far from doing,) the *merits* of the great question of religious reform depended in the least degree on the political characters and convulsions of those periods of our history. The arbitrary government of the Tudors, who, whether Popish or Protestant, were all despotic, and who began to reign some time before the æra of the Reformation, is to be traced to causes totally unconnected with that glorious event. They were a race of able and resolute, but domineering, rulers who having been elevated to the throne soon after the civil wars of York and Lancaster, availed themselves of the depressed and miserable state of the country for the advancement and increase of their power. This, we think, is the only reason which can be given why the English as Hume remarks, were, during that period, more like the slaves of an eastern despot than the subjects of a constitution in which the elements of freedom were to be found. "En embrassant le Calvinisme," says Mons. de la Mennais, "les Provinces Unies formèrent une république turbulente, avare, cruelle." Undoubtedly the Dutch of the seventeenth century were but too notorious for avarice and cruelty, in their distant possessions; and had this last propensity been confined to *them*, some plausible pretext might have appeared for connecting their cruelty with their Calvinism. But *cruelty* they might have learnt from the Spaniards in the new world, and from those monsters of barbarity and bigotry Philip and Alva, who deluged their territory with the blood of martyred Protestants; and, after their best experiments in this line, they might still have found it a difficult matter to have outdone their masters. With respect to the Dutch government at home, during the whole of the seventeenth century, it deserves any thing rather than the appellation of anarchy. It was no doubt exposed to occasional disturbances; but it presented the animating spectacle of a people inconsiderable in numbers, but strong in liberty, who, having nobly conquered their independence, knew how to consolidate and preserve it, and to make themselves respected by the rest of Europe: could anarchy accomplish this? But our author, as he confounds all religious faith, but that of Rome, with *concealed Atheism*, gives to every popular form of government the title of anarchy.

While we are upon this subject, we may just notice another of his remarks (at p. 48). "La Revolution Françoise, he tells us, "ne fut qu'une application rigoureusement exacte des dernières consequences du Protestantisme." This likewise is news for *us*, and we doubt not will prove such to many of our readers. We do not mean to deny that this irreparable breach of Romish unity was the means of introducing great freedom and variety of opinion in matters of religion; nor that this liberty of thinking, constantly blended, as every thing human will be, with a large mixture of error, infirmity, and corruption, might prove one source of those sceptical and infidel speculations of the last century which, along with many other co-operating causes, prepared the way for one of the most alarming political convulsions that ever shook the world. All this is undeniable; but what, we ask, has all this to do with the merits of the great question of religious reform? We would suggest another genealogy for the horrors of the French Revolution, which appears to us far more probable. The gross errors, absurdities, superstitions, and corruptions of the Church of Rome, had long disgusted all thinking persons who were not interested in the support and continuance of her abuses. Viewing Christianity in the mirror held up to them by Rome they beheld it stripped of all its beauty and comely proportions, and distorted into an image of mingled odiousness and folly. Mean while they refused to be at the trouble of either examining Scripture for themselves, or inquiring into the state of those churches which exhibited a purer and more faithful model of the Gospel. The consequence was, that they became decided unbelievers, or at least reckless sceptics themselves, and most assiduously and successfully propagated their pernicious doctrines through the medium of their writings. These writings, though by no means the sole cause of the French Revolution, were powerfully instrumental, not only in accelerating and promoting that event, but in aggravating its horrors when it arrived; nor have they ceased to prolong their pernicious influence, now that it has passed away.

Some of our readers may, perhaps, think that we have given ourselves useless trouble in refuting the absurd positions here advanced. But we cannot think so. The most extraordinary and untenable positions, when, as here, soundly and happily expressed, confidently affirmed, and perseveringly repeated, are but too apt to gain credit with the inconsiderate and superficial reader, who is influenced more by the tone and manner of the writer than by the merits of his argument.

We now proceed to notice our author's account of the British Constitution. There are many, he says, who believe " que l'Angleterre est une monarchie, par ce qu'il y a dans cette terre natale des fictions politiques et de toutes les déceptions modernes, un homme qu'on appelle roi."

" La monarchie Anglaise, he says, expira sous le glaive des bourreaux avec Charles Ier Son fils n'en reproduisit qu'une vague et triste image Jacques II, doué d'un sens droit, mais dénué du génie nécessaire à l'exécution des desseins qu'il avoit conçus, voulut la rétablir, il succomba. L'esprit du Protestantisme, incompatible avec l'existence de la véritable royauté triompha de tous ses efforts. En cessant de reconnoître l'autorité suprême, et même toute autorité réelle dans l'ordre religieux, le peuple avait perdu la notion de la souveraineté dans l'ordre temporel. Il ne pouvoit plus comprendre ce que c'est qu'un monarque, il ne pouvoit surtout plus souffrir un pouvoir au dessus du sien. Le trône pour lui ce fut un fauteuil comme l'autel n'étoit plus qu'une table. Par la force même des choses, on vit recommencer en Europe le gouvernement républicain. Il ne resta de la monarchie et de la religion Chrétienne que des mots vides de sens. L'Angleterre devint en effet une véritable république selon l'acception rigoureuse du mot, mais la souveraineté qui suivant les principes in troduits par la reforme appartient de droit à la nation entière se concentra de fait entre les mains d'un petit nombre de familles propriétaires du sol et qui seules possèdent les emplois et forment les deux chambres c'est en elles que le pouvoir réside essentiellement. Le parlement est le vrai souverain puisqu'il peut tout selon Blackstone tout sans exception même changer la dynastie, même changer la religion, et ces deux choses il les a faites la loi c'est sa volonté. Il gouverne par des ministres responsables envers lui et non envers le roi qui ne peut jamais en choisir d'autres que ceux désignés par la majorité des chambres ou que cette majorité consent à soutenir. De royauté à peine en existe-t-il une vaine apparence elle est nulle en réalité. Les affaires sont discutées, décidées dans le parlement, celles que la constitution paroit abandonner au roi dépendent entièrement des ministres, que le parlement fait et défait à son gré. Le refus des subsides arrêteroit sur-le-champ le monarque, si sur ce point comme sur tout autre, il essayoit de s'opposer à ce que veut le parlement.

" L'Angleterre est donc réellement une république aristocratique. Aussi a-t-elle tous les caractères qui appartiennent toujours à ce genre de gouvernement une administration forte mais à qui tous les moyens sont indifférents pour arriver au but proposé des conseils suivis et soutenus d'une action qui ne se relâche jamais un système d'agrandissement progressif et continuel, qui, portant au dehors les pensées du peuple et son activité assure la tranquillité intérieure une grande prospérité matérielle la soif des richesses, l'estime de l'or des croyances vagues, des mœurs foibles, et dans les classes inférieures une sorte de licence qu'elles prennent pour la liberté pp 21—23

This is a passage too extraordinary to be left unnoticed Admitting, as we do, the constitution of our country, and deeming it, under its present form and operation, though assuredly not perfect, yet perhaps the finest specimen of political wisdom the world has ever seen, we cannot hear it thus traduced without a few remarks tending to correct the misrepresentation We conceive that, in estimating the merits of the British Constitution, our author has fallen into two grand mistakes which, though they would be very excusable in a mere foreigner, are less excusable in a writer for the public eye In speaking of the power vested in our two houses of parliament, he quite overlooks the check arising from the expression of *public opinion* a check of the utmost importance in this intelligent and free country, which will be found to exercise, upon all questions connected with the vital interests of the country, no inconsiderable control over king, lords, and commons It is therefore not true, as Mons de la Mennaís says that the sovereignty is with us concentrated in the hands of a few great landed proprietors who seize upon the administration of affairs and compose the two houses of parliament. Doubtless, hereditary rank, opulence, and borough interest work many a wheel of the machine: but they have not yet displaced the impulse of the genuine popular voice, nor do we think that they are ever likely to displace it. And in those instances, not a few, where popular suffrage and public opinion are left to display their more unfettered tendencies, we firmly believe that they often come in as a kind of regulator, and prevent much of the abuse which might otherwise ensue, from the operation of the above named influence. Again, in denying all real power to the crown in this country, our author has, we think, overlooked the constitutional rights of the king, as the sole fountain of honour, and as the owner and manager of all that vast influence which is necessarily connected with the executive branch of the government. By being the sole fountain of honour, he almost certainly attaches to himself the majority of one chamber of the legislature, the House of Peers, whose prepossessions and interests always dispose them to lean to the side of royalty. Through the influence connected with the executive, the king may, under favourable circumstances, even become so formidable as to disturb, in his single person, the balance of the constitution. It is true, indeed, as our author observes, that the executive is itself in some degree, under the controul of the two houses as, by withholding the necessary supplies, they may compel the king to change his ministers. Still, the sole circumstance of his being the head and organ of the administration inevitably throws much real power into the hands of the crown. For an executive there always must be, and it is the tendency of this, more, perhaps, than of any other kind of power, to promote and propagate itself. The sovereign, who for some time exercises it with only common prudence, gradually builds up for himself a rampart of influence under which he may find shelter from many a rude shock of popular aggression, if, indeed, he be not able to make many a successful inroad on popular rights.

These are considerations which our author has quite overlooked. He will tell us indeed, that our remarks are nothing to the purpose; for that we must not confound this indirect, and, as it were, accidental influence of the crown with those *droits fixés* which are the substance of constitutional rights. But what does he mean by his *droits fixés?* He means neither more nor less than *the claims and privileges of irresponsible power.* Of this we must admit that the British Constitution knows nothing; and may it always continue in this respect unaltered! While the person of the prince is held inviolate, he is made responsible through the medium of his ministers.—Upon the whole, Mons. De la Mennais may give our constitution what title he pleases: we style it, and we think it deserves to be styled, a limited monarchy, constituting the happy mean between despotic rule on the one hand and republican anarchy on the other. Our king is possessed of real power: he is far more than "une vaine apparence."—" un souvenir venerable du passé.' If his power be rather indirect than otherwise, this is a circumstance which does but contribute to shield it from much odium, without at all affecting its reality and extent. On the contrary, by laying asleep the suspicions of the people, it may even tend to increase the actual power of the prince. It seems the peculiar excellence of our constitution, that it makes his power very much dependent on the discharge of his proper duties as a sovereign; on his enlightened and beneficent regard for the true welfare of his people. And hence has it been observed, that a king of Great Britain, limited as his prerogative may appear, possesses the means of becoming virtually the most powerful ruler in the world.

One short observation will, we

published what are our author's
sentiments on the subject of
royalty, and will serve to expose
the inconsistency of the opinions
he does most evidently avow, both to
a representative legislature and to
the responsibility of the executive
while at the same time he professes
to be an enemy to despotic sway.
Yet, if these two grand checks be
removed, what is to prevent kingly
government from merging eventually in arbitrary power? We defy
Mons. de la Mennais to find any
medium betwixt downright despotism and the responsibility of the
king's advisers. But is then nothing
short of despotism entitled to the
name of "véritable royauté?"

We hope that our author's vigorous description of the effect of
what he calls our Aristocratical
Republic on the measures of government and the manners of the
people, is not a correct one. Perhaps there have been periods since
the Revolution of 1688 when it was
more accurate than it will be found
at present: at all events we may
glean from it some useful hints.
We have certainly " une administration forte," but we trust not
one " a qui tous les moyens sont
indifferents pour arriver au but proposé." We have " des conseils
suivis et soutenus," but not, we hope,
" un système d'agrandissement progressif et continuel." If we are
regularly increasing our power, we
would fain believe that this is to be
attributed rather to the unshackled
energies of a free and happy people
than to any deliberate system of
encroachment upon the rights of
other nations. There may be
amongst us much " soif des richesses," and " estime de l'or," but
we hope that there is also much
love of benevolent exertion from a
sense of duty and much application of our wealth to the mental,
moral, and religious benefit, not
only of our own population, but of
mankind at large. We may have
" des croyances vagues, des mœurs
foibles, et dans les classes inférieures

une sorte de licence qu'elles prennent pour la liberté;" but it is to
be hoped that under all our varying shades of opinion, we have so
much real and substantial Christianity that our morals are not more
corrupt than those of the subjects
of papal and despotic sway, and
that the abuses of our liberty, much
as they are sometimes to be deplored, bear no proportion to the
amount of good which accrues from
its legitimate operation and effects.
The Abbé ought to have studied
the luminous letters of his countryman the Baron de Stael, on England, before he ventured to publish
his incorrect and undigested opinions.

But it is now time for us to cross
the Channel, and to observe what
is the state of affairs in a neighbouring country. Our author's views
of the existing government of France
will be found condensed in the following short sentences.

Reprenant donc les questions posées
précédemment, qu'est ce que les chambres? qu'est ce que le ministere? qu'est-
ce que le roi? nous répondrons sans
hésiter.

Les chambres sont une assemblé dé-
mocratique divisée en deux sections qui
délibèrent a part assemblée dans laquelle
réside avec la souveraineté toute la
puissance du gouvernement.

Le ministere est l'action publique
des chambres leur agent responsable en
tout ce qui tient a l'administration.

Le roi est un souvenir vénérable du
passé l'inscription d'un temple ancien
qu'on a placée sur le fronton d'un autre
édifice tout moderne. pp. 32, 33.

The grand and, as he judges the
sole material difference between the
actual constitutions of France and
England is this, that the former
wants what the latter possesses, a
substantial and permanent order of
nobility to restrain the influence
and progress of democratical principles and power. 'Chez nous,'
he observes ' les pairs ne repre-
sentent point une aristocratie qui
n'existe pas, et que le tems même
ne sauroit former sous l'empire des
loix qui nous regissent.' There is
doubtless much truth in this remark. For, though there is a

chamber of peers and an order of nobility in France, it should seem as if they could never rise to any high degree of influence and importance, under the present system. The spoliation of their estates at the Revolution has made them poor, and will probably long keep them so; while the existing laws, which controul testamentary devises and favour the equal division of property strike at the root of hereditary grandeur, the ancient claims of primogeniture, and the preservation of great opulence in the same families. What will be the end of this system we do not venture to predict; but certainly it is a system which, however it may tend to a more general diffusion of property, and of the comforts connected with property, among the lower classes, is calculated to excite serious alarm in the minds of all who, like our author, are exclusively attached to the old claims of rank and royalty, and who dread a republican government as teeming with the seeds of anarchy and atheism.

We consider it of importance to rectify one mistake into which Mons. de la Mennais has fallen respecting the British Legislature, though we do not deny that his remarks may be more justly applicable to the two chambers in France. He tells us, that these two chambers, though distinguished by a sort of political fiction, are altogether one as to purpose and effect, *like the Parliament of England.* Again, he says (page 26), that ' our two houses, having both precisely the same interests to uphold, and representing both but one class of the community, are in truth but one and the same body, in which is vested the real sovereignty of the realm.' We shall not stop to inquire how far the account is consistent with his own definition of the British Constitution, by which he makes it to be compounded of the two very distinct ingredients of aristocratical and democratical power. To us he appears to contradict himself in this particular. But certainly it is an error to suppose, that our two houses are either composed entirely of the same class of society, or are governed entirely by the same interests. It is well known that these assemblies frequently differ on minor questions of policy, and sometimes on questions of vital importance to the country. Those frequent contests between the crown and the commons in which the weight of the peerage has been thrown into the scale of royalty sufficiently disprove his statement. He might have learnt from the history of the Great Rebellion what support the crown derived from the upper house: had that been preserved entire and inviolate, it would certainly have prevented the execution of the king, and perhaps might have ensured his ultimate restoration to power. The composition of our two houses is therefore essentially different. The upper house has a general and very natural leaning to the support of the power whence it derives its hereditary rank and dignity. The lower house, though it contains many sons and relatives of peers, receives them in the sole capacity of commoners; while the larger proportion of its members is composed of the gentry of the landed and monied interests, individuals who are generally (in point of fact and in spite of many apparent incongruities), representatives of the bulk of the nation, and guardians of the rights and liberties of the people.

The French charter has unquestionably assimilated the government of that great empire, in some very important particulars, to our own. The Revolution, amidst the mighty ruin which it occasioned, had swept away some of the worst abuses of the old regime; but, through its excesses it merged eventually in the vigorous, but hard, despotic rule of Bonaparte. The French still wanted the elements of a free constitution. The charter would have applied some remedy for this defect, if its provisions were respected and reduced to practice

This, however, is but very imperfectly done at present; and while in the charter there are many valuable abstractions capable of being wrought out into a more improved form of government, yet the practical power of the crown is so large, the controul of public opinion so slender, the influence of ministers in the election of representatives so overwhelming, the right of free discussion, even in the legislative assemblies, so hampered by arbitrary rules, and their means of direct interference with the conduct of the executive so inadequate to any efficient purposes of check and responsibility, that France can hardly be said to have yet attained a free constitution. Yet the Revolution with all its evils has left some great and beneficial changes—The abolition of exclusive privileges, the equality of taxation, the very existence of an elective assembly where consent is necessary for the imposition of any public burden and for the making of any new laws, the recognition of responsibility in the executive, however ineffective in the present circumstances, the institution of trial by jury, though shackled by regulations which deprive it of much of its utility, and the tendency of the press to escape from the restraints which the jealousy of the state has imposed on its unfettered movements; these are all indications, germs as it were, of the commencement of a rational and enlightened system which will hereafter rise into life and vigour. May neither the influence of popish bigotry, on the one hand, nor the growth of scepticism and irreligion, on the other be permitted to defeat the beneficial tendency of these changes, and disappoint the best hopes of the nation!

We should weary both our readers and ourselves, were we to examine, in succession, all the bold paradoxes with which this pamphlet abounds. We cannot, however, dismiss the present chapter, without briefly adverting to one of the most extraordinary positions we have ever encountered. "Le Christianisme," says our author, "avoit créé la veritable monarchie inconnue des anciens; la democratie, chez un grand peuple detruisoit infailliblement le Christianisme." We cannot but believe that there are many ultra royalists in France who, on reading this, will be disposed to think that Mons. de la Mennais has made a very grand and happy discovery and is as much entitled to his Ευρηκα as the old philosopher who jumped in triumph out of a bath at the unexpected solution of a problem in mathematics. True monarchy unknown to the ancients! Was then the single arbitrary rule of an individual, which in our author's vocabulary means the same thing, unknown to the nations of antiquity? Again, ' True monarchy is the offspring of the Christian religion!' Yet how can this be, when that religion, according to its only genuine record, the New Testament, has left the question concerning modes of civil government completely open and untouched, only enjoining submission to the powers established, whatever they may be. But perhaps what is meant is, that the genius of Christianity is favourable to monarchy. We will not determine this knotty point. It is sufficient for us to know, as Paley has well remarked, that it is the tendency of Christianity to make men better, and that it is easier to govern good than bad men, under every variety of political institutions. But it seems that, in large states, democracy will infallibly operate to overturn the Christian religion. If by democracy our author means any thing else than a republican form of government, we do not comprehend him; and if he mean a republic, we think that the case of the United States of North America is alone sufficient to refute his doctrine. We are by no means partial to republics, strictly so called; and independently of their political defects, we are not disposed to think them the best possible forms of government for upholding and preserving the Christian faith in its purity, or for counteracting the tendency to needless and pernicious separations. At the same time, there is assuredly nothing in them which renders them incompatible with the authorised profession and practical influence of our holy religion. But we are favoured with a reason for the opinion here given. In democracies, observes our author, power is continually liable to change hands, and this exposure to fluctuation and turbulence in the *state* cannot well consist with one supreme unchanging authority in the church. We perfectly understand him here. *Where there is no monarchy there can be no pope; and without a pope there can be no true religion!*

We now proceed to the second chapter, the object of which is to shew that, in France, religion is at present totally unconnected with the civil and political order of affairs, and that consequently the state is no better than atheistical. Ecclesiastical matters, he tells us, still remain on precisely the same footing on which they were left by Bonaparte, to whom he is willing to allow some little credit, in the *Concordat*, by which an end was put to the persecutions of the Directory, and the free exercise of the Roman Catholic worship was restored: still he maintains that the state, as a body, remains to this day as irreligious and atheistical as ever. In support of this position, he adduces several topics of illustration. From the first which he mentions our own legislature might derive some salutary instruction, and be taught to adopt a better tone of speaking in their deliberative assemblies.

Combien de fois n'a-t-on pas remarqué que l'on cherchoit en vain le nom de Dieu dans nos codes, seul monument de ce genre où l'homme apparoisse pour commander à l'homme en son propre nom? Si ce recueil d'ordonnances humaines passoit aux siècles futurs, sans qu'aucun autre souvenir de notre temps leur parvint, ils se demanderoient avec effroi si l'idée de la cause suprême, du souverain législateur, s'etoit donc perdue chez ce peuple; et méditant l'oubli profond dans lequel il est tombé, ils s'efforceroient de jeter encore un voile plus épais sur sa mémoire. p. 50.

His next illustration is derived from the tenor and provisions of the Charter. The Charter declares, in words, the Romish religion to be the religion of the state; but he considers that it virtually nullifies its own decree, by affording equal protection to every kind of worship, by allowing salaries to ministers of all persuasions, by setting apart an annual fund for the support of their churches, nay by treating heretics in some respects with more favour than subjects of the true church. This indeed we were not aware of; and we apprehend that the privations, difficulties, and distresses under which many Protestant communities, particularly in the south of France, still labour, will amply disprove his assertion. At the same time there certainly is at present no established church in France, if by an established church, we are to understand one with fixed revenues, preeminently recognized and guaranteed by the state, to the support of which the members of all other communions are required in some degree to contribute. We shall not now discuss the expediency of such an establishment, or how far the interests of religion may suffer in the United States of America, for example, from the want of it. Much however must depend on the nature of the establishment. It is true that many candid and enlightened Dissenters, both in England and Scotland, have admitted the benefits accruing from the respective national churches of these countries, in their bearings upon the general interests of religion. But would they have made the same concession, had the church been Socinian or Roman Catholic? And with respect to France, supposing the ruling power of that country to tolerate, freely and fully, all other denominations of religionists, it would be no fair subject of blame that it shewed a marked preference for the faith and ritual which it considered best; but to denounce it as atheistical because it does not give any peculiar political predominance to that particular form of Christianity above the rest, or endow it with large revenues drawn from all classes alike, is not a little extravagant on the part of the Abbe de la Mennais. Those indeed who are acquainted with the usurpations of the Romish church, her hostility to the diffusion of the holy Scriptures, her hatred (sufficiently indicated in the work before us) of civil and religious liberty, will not sympathize with those who lament that the state of her establishment in France does not give her that overwhelming ascendency which she covets. On the contrary, they will rejoice in any arrangement which operates to restrain her power, not indeed with the prospect of the reign of scepticism and infidelity being introduced in its place, but with the hope that any change short of this result will be better than the errors, the corruptions, and the spiritual tyranny of Rome.

As another proof of the alleged irreligious spirit of the present government of France, our author proceeds to comment on the recent law against sacrilege. The following statements do indeed display an unhappy specimen of French levity on the subject of religion. It seems that before the present year (1825) the tribunals had no power to punish robberies committed in churches, because, according to the language of the laws, *the house of God was to be considered in the light of an uninhabited dwelling.* In 1824, however, the government, in consequence of the number of sacrilegious thefts committed, proposed to place churches and chapels on the same footing with *places of shelter for domestic animals;* as the Archbishop of Troyes observed, they determined to *raise them to the dignity of a stable.* More recently, however, as all the world knows, they seem to many to have passed into an opposite extreme, by the law constituting sacrilege a capital offence.

Our author differs from those who hold it an abuse of power, in the civil government, to punish sacrilege with death; still he affects to be tender towards offenders. The church, he says, sets her mark upon the crime of sacrilege, but decides nothing as to what ought to be its punishment. This is the old hypocritical subterfuge of the Church of Rome, to avoid the imputation, while she incurred the guilt, of cruelty and blood. She condemned the heretic, but delivered him over to the secular power for punishment. The civil authority was to issue the writ "de heretico comburendo," while the ecclesiastical tribunal, that had fixed the doom of the victim, professed to weep over his fate, and even to entreat the lightest punishment with which his alleged atrocities, blazoned out by the church in the most exaggerated colours, might safely be visited. The church, however, had full power to screen the victim in more ways than one, if his rescue better suited her purposes than his death. Perhaps our worthy Abbe himself is not unwilling to remind good Romanists of what, in these heretical days, they are much in danger of forgetting—*the ancient rights of sanctuary.* "The church, we are told, 'extends her mercy to all penitents, even to those whose impunity would be utterly incompatible with the safety and well being of Society." The meaning of this we suppose may be, that Popery, while she has exercised the greatest cruelties upon persons whose sole offence was the denial of her supremacy, has manifested a most pernicious tenderness for others stained with the most enormous guilt, provided they did but flee to her bosom for protection. Is it not a fact that, for ages this corrupt church made the house of God not merely ' a den of thieves,' but an asylum for murderers and assassins? Did she not set open the doors of her temples to harbour the vilest of mankind, without any proof of their repentance, or rather in defiance of all real proof of it, till the civil power could no longer tolerate the abuse, but was compelled virtually at least, to sacrifice the doctrine of the church to the welfare and security of the public.

But we return to the recent French law against sacrilege. Our author states a remarkable fact attending the progress of this law, which is, perhaps, not generally known. In 1824, nothing was said about sacrilege, as it bore upon the churches of *Protestant* congregations. The proposed law was then to be enacted solely with a view to the inviolability of Romish altars, with an understanding that a subsequent statute, attended, of course with milder penalties, would be framed for the security of property in other places of worship. Thus, a clear line of distinction was drawn, in this respect, between the rights of Protestants and Papists. But let our readers mark the very important alteration which took place in the course of one little year. When the recent law was brought forward, by which sacrilege is made capital, not a single voice was raised in the chamber of peers, proposing the revival of the above distinction, though that chamber counts as many as thirteen Catholic prelates within its walls.

De sorte, says Mons. de la Mennais, qu'il a été legalement reconnu, sans la moindre opposition, qu'enlever dans un prêche Calviniste une table, un banc, une nappe, où une Bible, dans une synagogue étoit un véritable sacrilege; par consequent, que les objets employés à ces divers cultes ne sont ni plus ni moins sacrés que ceux à l'usage du culte Catholique; que dès lors l'état considère tous ces cultes comme également vrais, ou plutot comme également faux, c'est-à-dire que l'état s'est de nouveau déclaré athée. pp. 56, 57.

We consider this little fact, trifling as it may appear, of much importance. For, while it does not, like too many other facts, imply a total indifference to religion, on the part of the French legislature, it has an aspect unfriendly to the exclusive pretensions of the Church of Rome, and seems to announce the progress of liberal opinions, with regard to the Reformed churches. This result, however, was clearly not contemplated by the framers of this absurdly impolitic and unreasonably severe enactment, which it is impossible not to regard as a strong symptom of the revival in France of popish bigotry, and of the desire of the hierarchy to increase their power; and it was a severe mortification to them, to have the same protection extended, by an amendment, to Protestant places and rites of worship, which it was their aim to appropriate exclusively to those of the Catholics. It must be observed, however, that the law, as it applies to Protestant chapels, can be little better than a mere nullity; for what is to be found in a 'prêche Calviniste,' (as it is here contemptuously styled,) that is worth stealing, at the risk of the offender's life? The costly and splendid gewgaws of popish worship, are the things which excite the cupidity of 'robbers of churches,' and call for a law against sacrilege.

Our author proceeds to illustrate his own views of the present state of France, by extracts from a speech of Mons. Royer Collard, 'Est-ce qu'on croit, par hazard, que les états ont une religion comme les personnes,' observes this gentleman, 'qu'ils ont une ame, et une autre vie, ou ils seront jugés selon leur foi et leurs œuvres?' "Voila certes," as Monsieur de la Mennais justly replies, 'une bizarre demande.' We can so seldom agree in opinion with the writer of this pamphlet, that we are glad to do so as often as we can, and here undoubtedly he has answered well. It would be evidently nothing better than solemn trifling, were it not at the same time something worse than trifling, to dress up a man of straw, under the abstract idea of *the state*, and then pretend that the state was to be held incapable of religious duty and responsibility, because, forsooth, an abstract idea can admit of neither. Mons. R. Collard should know that governments are composed of *individuals*, who are accountable beings, and who will be judged hereafter each one according to his works. And happy indeed would it be for all the individuals who compose cabinets and legislative assemblies, did they reflect far more than they do upon the extent and incalculable importance of their public functions; did they uniformly consider that *of those to whom much has been given much will be required*; and act continually under the solemn apprehension that they will have, not a lighter, but a heavier account to render than they whose sphere of exertion, and opportunities of usefulness are circumscribed within more narrow bounds.

In the following short passage our author would class, with atheists, those legislators who would place all modes of religious faith and worship on precisely the same footing of encouragement, without proclaiming their preference for any particular system. Little as we are disposed to favour latitudinarianism in religion, the views of our worthy Abbé are somewhat too strong for our taste:

Si l'état *peut* avoir une religion il *doit* en avoir une, et par conséquent la vraie. Que si au contraire l'état n'adopte aucune religion *si la vérité n'entre pour rien dans la protection que nos lois accordent aux différents cultes si ces lois ne consacrent n admettent comme vraies aucunes croyances* j en adjure tous les hommes qui entendent la valeur des mots ces lois sont *athées.* p. 60

The very maintenance of religious faith and worship, of whatever kind, or in whatever degree, proceeds upon the assumption of the acknowledgment of a Deity, the Creator, Preserver, and Governor of the world. To call such conduct atheistical is an abuse of terms. At the same time we cannot view, with any degree of favour, a line of conduct in any man, or set of men, which would argue an indifference to the truth or falsehood, the beneficial or malignant tendency, of different systems of religion, or who would refuse encouragement to true religion, from a fear of encroaching upon the principles of liberty. The spirit and language of public men in the present day, have, it must fairly be admitted, a strong tendency to this issue. But we certainly are very far from thinking at the same time, that the cure for this evil is to be found in the maintenance of civil and political disabilities, grounded on the peculiarities of a man's belief. Such a system may exclude, from a participation in the common rights of citizenship, men of true loyalty and eminent talents for usefulness, who happen to differ from others in their speculative opinions and creeds; while it opens wide the door to men of no creed or principle whatever, nay, who are enemies to all creeds.

We would next direct the attention of our readers to the following curious description of Popery. Short as it is, it will be found accurate, so far as it can be understood, and it proceeds from an authority which Mons. de la Mennais will not be disposed to cavil at:

'Dans cette invariable religion aucun individu ne *crée* la vérité ou ne la détermine par son jugement mais il la reçoit sans discussion d une autorité toujours vivante et parlante spirituelle par sa nature et infaillible *même humainement* puisqu il n en est point de plus élevée sur la terre p. 61

Whether the author means here to represent the pope or the church, as the authority which is always in activity, and always, humanly speaking, infallible, is not quite clear. But in either case the argument is not a very logical one. If the pope, or the church over which he presides, were the highest ecclesiastical authority upon earth, this would not prove either to be infallible, because fallibility is the universal lot of man. Nothing is more certain than that popes and councils, in all ages, have borne their full share of the errors, frailties and corruptions of our fallen race.

Having seen the author's account of Popery, let us now look at his picture of Protestantism.

"Dans le système Protestant, au contraire, chaque individu crée la vérité ou la détermine par son jugement : d'où il suit que *les vérités les plus contradictoires entre elles sont la vérité au même titre la vérité immuable absolue* ou qu'il n'existe aucune vérité et la même chose a lieu pour l'etat." p. 62.

Again,

"Le système Protestant ou philosophique détruit, pour les individus comme pour les états, toute vérité sans exception et que l'atheisme absolu qui en est la suite inevitable en est aussi le fonds essentiel." p. 62.

In the former of these sentences we encounter another jumble of ideas which it is difficult to marshal into any orderly array. What our author means by *creating truth*, or *how truth can ever be created under a system, such as he supposes, a system admitting truths that are contradictory, or subversive of each other*, are questions we must leave to the decision of wiser heads than our own. The *truth* is, that the Abbé has given a very absurd account of Protestantism. *Protestantism tolerates a variety of opinions in religion, but the toleration of such variety does not confound truth with error.* Protestants as to what regards *human authority* in matters of faith and practice, hold themselves fully and finally amenable to no control but that of their own reason and conscience. But does it thence follow that religious truth is no where to be found, and that absolute Atheism must be the result? Does it follow that, because some amongst us may be grievously in the wrong, many are not in the right, or that it is not the fault of each individual, if he finally miss the way of life, or wander out of it and perish? Mons. de la Mennais may draw these inferences, if he pleases, but he must excuse us, when we tell him that we cannot comprehend either their force or their propriety. In short the whole puzzle of his declamation about Protestantism,—not ill calculated to produce an effect upon the superficial reader—proceeds from this, that *he confounds a full toleration of variety of opinions in religion, with the impossibility of distinguishing truth from error, two totally distinct topics.* His method here is not very *philosophical*, though, for aught we know, it may be very *popish*.

Proceed we now to another important subject, the determination of the French government, (and we may add of most other Roman Catholic governments) with respect to monastic vows and establishments. This is his next illustration of the atheistical tendencies of the civil power. It is well known that the present government of France refuses to sanction or legalize the vows of monastic seclusion, celibacy, mortification, and obedience, and thus restrains the church from enforcing these obligations which have occasioned so much idleness, so much vice, and so much misery in the world, and have proved in all ages one of the firmest props of papal delusion and imposture. Our author quotes the minister as declaring with regard to these matters "L'état ne s'en mêlera pas : ce sont là des choses d'un ordre plus élevé qui se passeront entre la conscience et Dieu." This, at least, is not impiety but true wisdom. The government does not prohibit individuals from taking upon themselves, or from keeping, as many religious obligations as they please. It only witholds the priesthood from perniciously tampering with the consciences of men, from practising upon the easiness or ardent feelings of the young and inexperienced, especially among the female sex, and from rendering men generally useless as members of society, often miserable, and sometimes guilty to a greater extent, than a more unrestrained commerce with the world would make them. We would seriously ask every intelligent Roman Catholic, has not the pretended solitude of the cloister been witness to as much real wretchedness as the scenes of public life,—to as much secret guilt as much spiritual—aye, and actual, substantial wickedness? Have not deeds of darkness and horror been perpetrated there which can scarcely find their match, amidst the broad glare of day light, and the awful corruptions of the busy world? As for those habits of contemplative devotion, for which some pious minds seem better adapted than others, far be it from us to speak of them without the utmost reverence. It was, we believe, the opinion of the excellent Archbishop Leighton, who in his own person exhibited the rare union of a high degree of contemplative piety with a high degree of active usefulness that Protestantism might have derived some advantage from the continuance of monastic establishments, but under a very different form from that in which they had so long existed. On this we shall hazard no opinion. Of one thing, however, we are quite sure, that such establishments should in all cases be not only apparently, but purely, strictly voluntary; this is what the spirit of Popery abhors and condemns, and what the French government wisely determines to maintain.

Another subject of our author's bitter complaint, another proof of French Atheism, is the spoliation of those dignities and emoluments, which the church of France enjoyed, antecedently to the Revolution of 1789. He here draws a contrast between that church in its present condition and as it appeared under the monarchies of ancient Christendom, when it stood forth as the first and highest of public bodies. He compares it also with the state of our own ecclesiastical establishment. "The clergy in France," he observes, "receive annual salaries; but their order can boast of no permanent endowments. In England, on the contrary, the national church is enriched with immense revenues." *Not immense*, we reply, nor scarcely adequate, as compared with the number to whose maintenance those revenues might be applied. He adds, "Its bishops are members of the Upper House of Parliament, and a large proportion of legal suits and causes are referred to their tribunals." But is our author ignorant, that our Court of King's Bench can revise and controul the decisions of our Spiritual Courts? Is he ignorant that our canon law now exists rather by sufferance than by right, and that not a few enlightened friends of our excellent church are of opinion that she would lose no substantial power, but might conciliate some public favour, by the removal of these shadows of ancient ecclesiastical dominion? With respect to the spoliation of the French Church, at the period of the Revolution, we can no more excuse it than we can the spoliation of our own church by the Eighth Henry. At the same time, we cannot contemplate the spoliations of the Revolution, so far as they may tend to promote the downfal of papal sway, without adoring the wisdom of that Providence which deduces good from evil and makes the wrath and wickedness of man subservient to the praises of God.

Our author's concluding illustration of the irreligious and atheistical tendencies of the present government of France, is drawn from the state of the law respecting births, marriages, and deaths. The civil power looks at these events without the slightest reference to religion. No rite of Christian baptism, no marriage ceremony at the altar, no burial service over the dead, no certificate of a minister of religion is in any case required before the tribunal of the magistrate. The people may omit the religious rites, connected with the several events above mentioned, without suffering the least loss or inconvenience as to what regards the validity of their temporal claims or the security of their temporal interests. "Un enfant naît, on l'enregistre, comme, a l'entrée de nos villes, les animaux soumis a l'octroi. Rien, dans ce

que l'état présent, née rapide, ni naturelle, cet être fait à l'image de Dieu, sans devoirs, qui l'attendent, mi des destinées qui lui sont promises?.... Chez toutes les nations, même les plus barbares, le mariage eut toujours un caractère sacré." "Pour nous, peuple sans Dieu, nous avons chargé un adjoint de village d'accomplir, loin de l'autel, l'œuvre de la toute puissance." "De consolations, d'espérances, la loi n'en connoit pas; hors de la terre il n'y a rien pour elle. Un officier public vient constater la mort. Il déclare qu'appelé à tel lieu, il y a vu un cadavre; on écrit dans un registre le nom du décédé; deux fossoyeurs font le reste." Such is Mons. de la Mennais' account of the utter separation of all civil transactions from the interference of the priesthood, and from those rites and ordinances of religion with which, till the revolutionary period, they had always been associated. There is, however, a distinction to be made between a voluntary and a mere legal association. We do not feel quite so much shocked as our author, that the events of the birth and death of individuals should not be connected by positive legal enactments with religious rites. We should think it very hard if the law in this country compelled every man to have his children baptised, or rendered a burial service an indispensable part of interment. The practice, in either case, in this country, is not enforced by law. It is perfectly voluntary. And why may it not be so with our neighbours in France, without involving a charge of Atheism? Marriage indeed, in this country, stands on a different footing. In Scotland it is entirely at the option of the parties whether it shall be accompanied by any religious ceremony whatever. In England, however the case is different; and the religious rite, except in some cases as that of the Quakers, is indispensable to the validity of the contract. A great variety of inconveniences, however, are found to result in the case of Dissenters from the present state of the law on this point: still we think it of the very highest importance to connect the sanctions of religion with the solemn obligations which are involved in the marriage contract, and we lament therefore any tendency to break down the barrier of ancient usages which may contribute, though but in the smallest degree, to keep alive a sense of religion in the minds of the people.

We have dwelt so long on the many important topics of our author's second chapter, that our readers must be satisfied (if indeed they are not wearied already) with a very brief survey of the remainder of his pamphlet.

The object of the third chapter is to prove, that the alleged infidel and atheistical spirit of the government has descended into the walks of private and domestic life. It seems that there are many well meaning, and some able Catholics in France, who think differently on this subject, and fancy that they perceive in the active and zealous exertions made by numbers for the support and increase of Catholicism, traces of the permanent triumph of a religious spirit over the infidelity and impiety of the revolutionary period. As a proof of this, M. le Vicomte de Bonald refers, in his speech on the law respecting sacrilege, to the efforts of the Greeks in the East, and those of the Irish in the West of Europe; to the restoration of the episcopal dignity in France; to the *concordats* negociated with the see of Rome; and above all, to the voluntary enlistment of no less than eighteen hundred *sisterhoods* and a proportionate number of *fraternities* in defence of the church, and for the propagation of her doctrine and authority. 'l'esprit religieux, he maintains, "est le caractére particulier du nouveau siecle." Still our author is not convinced. He finds little ground for consolation in all this display of zeal and activity.

If religion, he observes, be considered with more than common vigour, by true Christians, that is, only because it has become an object of more bitter hatred, and more persevering attacks than ever. He quotes the opinion expressed in the French Legislature, on passing the recent law, that carelessness, forgetfulness, and indifference with regard to religion, were the main characteristics of the present "perilous times." The repose of the Christian Sabbath is no longer respected.—*When*, we ask, was it respected in Roman Catholic countries? The army and navy, it seems, continue as they were in the worst periods of the Revolution, without a priest, without an altar, without any opportunities of regular worship. Corruption of manners is on the increase, especially with regard to licentious immoralities.— Such is our author's picture of the present state of society in France. But what he considers the most hideous and alarming feature of the whole remains to be mentioned. This is the establishment of public schools for the education of the poor, founded substantially on the plan of Lancaster, and admitting Papists, Protestants, and children of all persuasions without distinction or preference. This he considers as one of the most fearful auguries in his church. We can bear witness indeed to the correctness of the fact here alluded to. In the Netherlands, where Popery has, perhaps, a firmer hold upon the common people than in France, schools of the above description are gaining a firm and rapid footing. They are to be found in villages as well as in great towns, and in spite of all the efforts of the priesthood, the people are forward to encourage them. We cannot, indeed, praise these schools for the sufficiency of their instruction. For instance, in a large seminary of *enseignement mutuel* at Liege, the only Scriptural instruction appeared to us to consist of moral sentences taken from the Bible, and pasted upon paste boards, like any common lessons. The children, it is to be feared, were left to collect, as they were able, the character of the source whence these extracts were derived, and might, perhaps, for any thing they heard to the contrary, regard a precept of Solomon, as on the same footing of authority with any given morsel selected from Æsop's fables. We do not say that even such teaching, though grievously defective, is not infinitely better than the darkness in which they would continue plunged without such means of instruction. What we wish to observe is, that, where such institutions find encouragement, Popery must be on the decline, whatever may be eventually substituted in its place.

Nothing has more forcibly struck us, in the perusal of this clever and spirited pamphlet, for such assuredly it is, than the tone of alarm, and sometimes passionate invective, which pervades the pages of the writer. His concluding chapter is little more than an animated declamatory sketch, in which he touches upon much that he had before advanced, and vents his indignant rebukes upon those whom he considers the enemies of religion, or rather of the Romish hierarchy. Whence can all this fire and ferment proceed? Our author is not one likely to be terrified without reason; and we doubt not but that his terrors are those of the great body of stricter Catholics on the continent? The cause, we think, is obvious; Popery is on the decline—is in real danger; though we venture not to predict, with any exactness, how much longer her reign may last. Much that we observe around us tends to confirm us in this opinion. The progress of education and knowledge, steady in its march, and sure in its operation as to what it will *beat down*, if not as to what it will *build up*; the diminished influence of Papal authority in *all*, and the virtual renunciation of it in *some* Catholic countries; the very extent

the abolition of monastic communities, and the suppression of the regular clergy, once the strongest pillars of the Church of Rome; the partial abrogation of festivals and holidays, those props of idleness, ignorance, and superstition; the mitigated opinions expressed by the well-educated and also by the less instructed part of the Catholic laity with regard to some of the most objectionable doctrines of their church; the decay of sacerdotal influence in the case of all but the most ignorant;—these, and various other causes, now in operation are strong indications of the actual decline, and approaching fall of Popery. In short Catholics must necessarily partake of the impulse given to the world, by the changes and advancements of society; and those changes and advancements are manifestly at variance with every article of their creed, as far as it differs from the creed of Protestants. The Church of Rome therefore, we think, trembles to its foundations; and the momentous question is,—what *will be reared upon its ruins?* We know that the true church of Christ must eventually triumph; but nevertheless it may still have to encounter many a severe struggle with the "powers of darkness."

And here, we confess with pain, we cannot altogether concur in opinion with many excellent persons, as to the religious character of the present times. We think that they are apt to look too exclusively on the bright side of the prospect; and that they suffer themselves to be too much dazzled by splendid and specious appearances. The increased support given to Bible Societies, Missionary Undertakings, and Religious Charities, by the noble and the opulent, may be a proof of great easiness, great good humour, and great liberality of sentiment; but it is no proof of strong moral principle, or genuine piety. It is very compatible with the prevalence of a lurking scepticism,

which those who are the subjects of it perhaps hardly themselves perceive. We see much in the tone and language of public men, especially in both houses of Parliament, that indicates great laxity of opinion in matters of religion. An impatience is manifested with regard to sacred subjects, and a tone of lightness adopted, very ill becoming persons who profess themselves Christians. There is no bold or presumptuous impiety in their lips, nothing acrimonious, nothing violently offensive, but there is often a playful levity of remark which shrewdly denotes the state of the speaker's mind; and which is the more dangerous, as it appears under the insinuating forms of good humour and politeness. The maxim that religion is out of place every where but in the church, seems acted on more than ever; and how many thousands, who will not find it elsewhere, never resort to church to seek it! We may notice a few other bad symptoms of the times. In legal instruments, such as wills and testaments, we no longer meet with those pious exordiums and commendations of the soul to God which were customary not an hundred years back, and which, though in many, perhaps most cases, a mere form, were also not unfrequently indications of a religious frame of mind. At all events, the practice was decorous, and little deserved to be exploded; still less ridiculed as we fear it would now too often be. At the period we allude to, commercial transactions bore the outward stamp of piety. A bill of lading was often made out, with some reference to the Divine blessing and protection. How would such a bill be satirized by the custom house wits of our day! Much gross inconsistency, much secret hypocrisy, were no doubt often mixed up with these pious details. The master of a slave ship, for example, would sometimes be found solemnly invoking the blessing of the Almighty on his voyage of the middle passage. This, to be sure, was monstrous;

But any notion, indeed, of hypocrisy, or rather our forgetfulness of God, has been silly betraying us into opiate error? Morning and evening family prayer, and grace before and after meals—these good old customs, so well adapted to keep alive a spirit of piety in the serious, and to solemnize, at least, if they failed of spiritualizing the careless and irreligious—had fallen into sad decay, though we trust that, with respect to both practices, a visible improvement has of late years taken place. These things some may call trifles. But they are not. They are symptomatic of the moral and religious feeling of the times in which we live, as slight alterations in the pulse of a sick person are of importance, for judging of the increase or abatement of his disorder. And, "Eheu! quam minimis pendent ingentia causis." The great revolutions of human opinion and human conduct are usually not the work of any single agency of overpowering force but the result of a great variety of petty agencies and operations, all converging to one centre, and terminating in one point. If even in our own country, favoured as it is, the sceptical and irreligious spirit appears to gain ground in some quarters, what must we suppose to be the case in a country like France, where the Revolution has left behind it a thousand "roots of bitterness," all too strong to be speedily eradicated?—As another proof of the scepticism of the age, and of the effect of Popery, as it exists under its most forbidding form, in producing that scepticism, we may quote the authority of Blanco White, who tells us that the better informed ecclesiastics in Spain are generally tainted with infidel, if not atheistical, opinions. And how few of them are likely, after the example of that excellent individual, to pass from the gloom of infidelity into the light of a truly scriptural church!

But we have done. "Magna est veritas, et prevalebit." The signs of the present times, strangely diversified and opposite as those signs may be, are not of a nature to disturb our confidence with regard to the final issue. Monsieur de Bonnais speaks of the genius of infidelity as though it were now more actively and effectively at work than ever. It may be so, but when, we ask, was the great enemy of souls idle, or not partially successful? He has assumed various forms in different ages; but he has never slumbered. At one time he has blinded men by the darkness of ignorance, credulity, and superstition; at another, he has led them astray amidst the mazes of wild enthusiasm; at another, he has wielded the sword of bitter, unrelenting persecution. He would now deceive principally by the flattering doctrine of *the equality of all religions on the score of safety and importance.* Let us but "resist him, stedfast in the faith, and without carnal weapons, and all will be well." Let us unceasingly disseminate the pure word of God. In dealing with sceptics and unbelievers, let us, though without the smallest compromise of principle, display knowledge, temper, and moderation, as well as zeal and firmness. And, what will eventually outweigh a thousand arguments, let our lives speak for us, and shew that true Christianity is adapted to form a character of excellence which will be sought in vain, under any other system of religion.

Bishop BUTLER's *Analogy of Religion natural and revealed, to the Constitution and Course of Nature, with an introductory Essay,* by the Rev. Daniel Wilson, A.M. Vicar of Islington. 1 vol. 12mo. 1824.

AMONG the works now in a course of publication by Messrs Chalmers and Collins, under the title of "Select Christian Authors,"—some of which, by the way, is neither the most happy choice. We have much pleasure in introducing to our readers the celebrated treatise of Bishop Butler, with an elaborate preface nearly half as long as the work itself, from the pen of the Rev. Daniel Wilson.* Bishop Butler's Analogy is so familiarly known to every sound theological student, that a mere reprint of it would not call for our notice; but Mr. Wilson's dissertation upon it contains so much, not only of new, but of highly useful and interesting matter, that we feel it a duty to lay some extracts from it before our readers. We would hope that this preface may in future become a current appendage to the work: the cheapness of the present edition will, at least, secure it a wide circulation.

Mr. Wilson possesses that primary qualification for a commentator, a most zealous admiration for his author. He describes as follows, and he can scarcely describe too warmly, the high value of Bishop Butler's great work:

"It has fixed the admiration of all competent judges for nearly a century, and will continue to be studied so long as the language in which he wrote endures. The mind of a master pervades it. The author

---

* Mr. Wilson has lately published a third edition of his Tour on the Continent, with such numerous alterations and additions, as to render it nearly a new work. Among the most interesting additions are a detailed account of the disgraceful persecutions in the Canton de Vaud and a sketch of the life of Cardinal Borromeo, with some extracts from his writings. The Protestant reader will be glad to be made better acquainted with that celebrated and remarkable man, a model of ardent devotion and exuberant charity in a dark era, a licentious country and a corrupt church. We must not omit to mention the addition of a copious preface, in which the author in reply to some objections urged against his work defends not only the doctrine, but also the practical application of the doctrine of a particular Providence, followed by an earnest and eloquent vindication of some other Scriptural principles as connected with the daily affairs of human life, in answer to those who would both dismember the Gospel of some of its essential principles, and restrict it to the precincts of temples and the solemnities of holydays.

---

of a theme so infinitely important had treated his subject with a force, sagacity and talents which few students on the whole have equalled; and he almost exhausted his subject. And a genius which never oversteps the line of prudential caution, united with a penetration which nothing can escape. There is in all his writings a vastness of idea, a reach and generalization of reasoning, a native simplicity and grandeur of thought, which command and fill the mind. At the same time, his illustrations are so striking and familiar as to instruct as well as persuade. Nothing is violent, nothing far fetched, nothing pushed beyond its fair limits, nothing fanciful or weak; a masculine power of argument runs through the whole. All bespeaks that repose of mind, that tranquillity, which springs from a superior understanding, and an intimate acquaintance with every part of his subject. He grasps firmly his topic, and insensibly communicates to his reader the calmness and conviction which he possesses himself. He embraces with equal ease the greatest and the smallest points connected with his argument. He often throws out, as he goes along, some general principle which seems to cost him no labour, and yet which opens a wide field of contemplation before the view of the reader.

"Butler was a philosopher in the true sense of the term. He searches for wisdom wherever he can discern its traces. He puts forth the keenest sagacity in his pursuit of his great object, and never turns aside till he reaches and seizes it. Patient, silent, unobtrusive investigation was his forte. His powers of invention were as fruitful as his judgment was sound. Probably no book in the compass of theology is so full of 'the seeds of things,' to use the expression of a kindred genius (Lord Bacon) as the Analogy.

"He was a man raised up for the age in which he lived. The wits and infidels of the reign of our Second Charles (Butler was born in the year 1692,) had deluged the land with the most unfair and yet plausible writings against Christianity. A certain fearlessness as to religion seemed to prevail. There was a general decay of piety and zeal. Many persons treated Christianity as if it were an agreed point amongst all people of discernment, that it had been found out to be fictitious. The method taken by these enemies of Christianity was to magnify and urge objections more or less plausible against particular doctrines or precepts which were represented as forming a part of it, and which, to a thoughtless mind, were easily made to appear extravagant, incredible and irrational. They professed to admit the being and attributes of the Almighty, but they maintained that human reason was sufficient for the discovery and establishment of this fundamental truth, as well as for the development of those moral precepts which the conduct of life should be regulated; and they boldly asserted, that sundry objections and difficulties might be urged against Christianity, as to exclude it from being admitted as divine, by any thoughtful and enlightened person.

These assertions Butler undertook to refute. He was a man formed for such a task. He knew thoroughly what he was about. He had a mind to weigh objections, and to detect, and silence cavils. Accordingly, he came forward in all the self-possession and dignity, and meekness of truth, to meet the infidel on his own ground. He takes the admission of the unbeliever, that God is the Creator and Ruler of the natural world, as a principle conceded. From this point he sets forward and pursues a course of argument so cautious, so solid, so forcible, and yet so diversified, so original, so convincing, as to carry along with him almost insensibly those who have once put themselves under his guidance. His insight into the constitution and course of nature is almost intuitive; and the application of his knowledge also surprisingly skilful and forcible, as to silence or to satisfy every fair antagonist. He traces out every objection with a deliberation which nothing can disturb, and shews the fallacies from whence they spring with a precision and acuteness which overwhelm and charm the reader.

Accordingly, students of all descriptions have long united in the praise of Butler. He is amongst the few classic authors of the first rank in modern literature. He takes his place with Bacon and Pascal, and Newton, those mighty geniuses who opened new sources of information on the most important subjects, and commanded the love and gratitude of mankind. If his powers were not fully equal to those of these most extraordinary men, they were only second to them. He was, in his own line, nearly what they were in the inventions of science and the adaptation of mathematics to philosophy founded on experiment. He was of like powers of mind, of similar calm and penetrating sagacity, of the same patience and perseverance in pursuit, of kindred acuteness and precision in argument, of like force and power in his conclusions. His objects were as great, his mind as simple, his perception of truth as distinct, his comprehension of intellect nearly as vast, his aim as elevated, his success as surprising. pp. v—viii.

"It may afford consolation to those students who depend more on diligence than on native talent for their acquirements, while it holds out a salutary lesson to more mercurial spirits, whose whole staple is ability without application, to state, that Bishop Butler's Analogy was in effect the labour of a whole life of persevering effort. As the year 1843, in the age of twenty-one, we find that his mind had begun to apply itself to this great subject, and afterwards, from the year 1718, when he was appointed preacher at the Rolls chapel, till he published a volume of Sermons in 1726, the "Analogy" was still uppermost in his mind, as appears from these discourses which contain the germ of his great work. That work itself appeared in the year 1736; and in all his subsequent publications, the commanding theme of his life continued to occupy his attention. Thus a long course of forty years was devoted by this extraordinary man, with a depth of knowledge and a strength of mind exactly suited to his theme, to the illustration of the truth of Christianity from the order of God's providence in the natural creation.

This elaborate work has been read, praised, and commented upon beyond most books of abstruse reasoning; but it has never been refuted. It stands, and must ever stand unanswerable. Still there are two defects in it: the one is, a difficulty and obscurity of style which perplex the course of the writer's powerful argument, at least to an inexperienced student; the other, a coldness of manner, not to say a defectiveness of statement, as respects the character of Christianity itself. He proves the truth of religion, but he does not make us love it; he marks well the bulwarks of our spiritual Zion; but he does not, at least adequately, introduce us to the interior of its palaces; he does not go through the good land in the length thereof, and in the breadth thereof; he does not dwell upon the love of God, the grace of Christ, the communion of the Holy Spirit, the life of faith, the consolations of hope, the delights of obedience, and other topics not only peculiar to Christianity, but inseparable from it. Such indeed was not his theme; but Mr. Wilson thinks, and not unjustly, that his numerous references to the scheme and object of revelation

these interesting subjects. Our preface is at a loss to ascertain whether the deficiency, allowing it to exist, arose from the nature of the writer's argument, and the character of his opponents, or from his own turn of mind, addicted rather to close argument than to vivid description, or from the languor now so generally and most justly complained of in the theology of the era in which Bishop Butler wrote. We presume that all these causes might concur to produce the alleged effect certain, at least, it is that the deepest metaphysicians have not always been the most glowing biblical expositors, and least of all at a period when truly evangelical preaching, (we use the phrase in no narrow or invidious sense,) was at nearly the lowest ebb to which it has ever declined since the Reformation, in the ministrations both of our own national church, and among various classes of our dissenting brethren.

These two defects of style and of statement, Mr Wilson applies himself in some degree to remedy not however with any view of disparaging, much less superseding, his author, but only to introduce him more advantageously to the general reader. Nothing, he remarks, can give a just impression of Butler, but Butler himself and bold as Mr Wilson's attempt may appear it is impossible not to admire the modesty, the delicacy, and judiciousness with which he undertakes and pursues it.

With a view then in the first place, to elucidate his author, Mr Wilson devotes more than seventy pages to a very masterly analysis of his work. For us to endeavour to abridge this abridgment, would be both impracticable and superfluous. We will only say of it, that to those younger students who are entering upon the study of the Analogy, it will be of great service

ment which awaits them, and will facilitate their investigation of a subject of very great moment and importance, and highly interesting to every inquiring mind, though arrayed in what is to many persons the repulsive form of deep abstraction. Nor, even to those who are familiar with the original, will the perusal of Mr Wilson's outline be unwelcome, as it will bring before them in condensed form the rich treasures of this magnificent work, and perhaps afford them a clearer view of the whole chain of reasoning than it is possible to obtain without a more elaborate analysis than most readers have the time or the patience to form for themselves. It would also be of great service to the cause of truth, if the unbeliever and sceptic, who might shrink from the direct perusal of Butler, should have their attention arrested by this ratiocinative table of contents, which it is impossible, we think, to read without wishing to become acquainted with the great original.

But it is not for the sake of the first part of Mr Wilson's dissertation, in which he condenses his author's argument, but of the second, in which he addresses himself to supply the theological deficiencies of his treatise, that we chiefly bring before our readers the present notice. The scholiast has annotated upon his classic with equal reverence and discretion, and has been very successful in pointing out some of the prominent defects of a school of theology highly respectable for eminent talent and moral excellence, but not as we venture to think commensurate in its doctrines and their practical application with the very marked and peculiar statements of the Divine Record, especially the complete disclosures of the New Testament. We shall endeavour to give our readers a view of Mr Wilson's argument in his own words, adding little to our extracts but our general con-

[top lines illegible]

In entering upon the second main branch of his disquisition, Mr. Wilson begins with shewing the connexion of the analogical argument with the other branches of Christian evidence. For the argument from analogy does not stand alone; it is closely connected with those two leading branches of evidence, the external and the internal. Mr. Wilson offers some very striking and original remarks, both upon the connexion and the distinctness of these three branches of argument, and upon the unreasonableness of demanding à priori arguments for the truth of the Gospel, to the rejection of its actual and irrefragable proofs.

"The external evidences are those which should be first studied. Indeed they are the only ones that can be considered in the first instance as essential, because they undertake to shew the credentials of the messenger who professes to come with a revelation from Heaven. Christianity claims a Divine origin. I have therefore a right, indeed I am bound, soberly and impartially to inquire what proofs she brings of this high claim. And when she refers me to the holy Scriptures as containing all her records, I have a right to ask what evidence there is of the genuineness and authenticity of these books, and what footing they place the religion upon, which they wish to inculcate on mankind. The answer to all these questions is found in what we call the external evidences of Christianity. pp. lxxxvi, lxxxvii.

"We have no right to go further than this in the first place. The moment the messenger is sufficiently proved to have Divine credentials we have but one duty left, that of receiving and obeying his message, that of reading and meditating on the revelation itself in order to conform ourselves to it with devout and cheerful submission. pp. lxxxvii, lxxxviii.

"Great mischief has been done to the Christian cause by taking another method. Men have allowed themselves to be entangled with discussions on the possibility and credibility of a revelation being given to man, on the nature and tendency of the Christian doctrine, on the reasonableness of its particular injunctions—questions every one of them out of place in examining the evidence of a Divine religion. Let it fairly be made out to come from God, and it is enough. More than this is injurious. We are sure indeed, that the contents of it must be most worthy of its perfect Author; but we are no adequate judges of what is worthy or what is not worthy of an Infinite Being." p. lxxxviii.

"The danger of acting in the way which I am now venturing to condemn, is greater because the door being once opened to such reasoning it is quite certain that the minds of men will too often employ it amiss. The infidel is the person just the least capable of acting aright in such a case. The pious well-trained judgment of a sincere Christian, might indeed form a better estimate of the internal character of a revelation from Heaven; but the unsubdued mind of an unbeliever can only come to a wrong decision upon it. He wants all the preparation necessary.

"But although the external proofs of Christianity are thus all that, in the first examination is required; yet the internal evidences may afterwards be profitably most profitably studied. Christianity shrinks from no scrutiny. She courts the light. When the outward credentials of the heavenly messenger have once been investigated and the message been received on this its proper footing, then if it be asked, whether the contents of the revelation seem to confirm the proof of its Divine original; whether the sincere believer will find them adapted to his wants; whether the morals inculcated, the end proposed the means enjoined, are agreeable to man's best reason and the dictates of an enlightened understanding and conscience; whether the character of Christ be worthy of his religion; whether the influence of grace said to accompany Christianity may be obtained by prayer; whether the lives and deaths of Christians as compared with those of professed infidels illustrate the excellency of their faith; whether in short the promises and blessings of Christianity are verified in those who make a trial of them by submitting to the means appointed for their attainment; when such questions are put with candour by those who have embraced Christianity we answer them by referring to the internal evidences of Revelation. pp. lxxxix, xc.

"The third branch of the evidences in favour of Christianity is that arising from the analogy between this religion and the constitution and course of nature. We have no right indeed, (for the idea is too important not to be repeated,) to call for this species of proof any more than we have a right to call in the first instance for an examination of the internal character of Christianity or rather to call for it at all. All we have any fair right to ask for is the credentials of the ambassador who professes to come to us in the name of our absent though ever present Sovereign and Lord. p. xciii.

"Still, after we have sincerely embraced

the Gospel, we may humbly enquire whether the difficulties which are raised against it by unbelievers, or which occur to our own minds, may be relieved by an appeal to the works of God in nature, and his order and government therein. This is the argument from analogy, which rises still a step above the two preceding branches of the subject, not as in itself necessary to the first reception of Christianity, but as furnishing the subsequent confirmation of it, and removing scruples and objections arising from the ignorance and presumption of man. It is indeed, a glorious thing thus to discern the harmony between Christianity the greatest of the Almighty's works and all the other known productions of the same Divine Architect.' p. xciv.

After a series of additional remarks upon this threefold species of evidence, Mr Wilson proceeds to offer some observations upon Bishop Butler's particular view of Christianity, and on the adaptation of his argument to religion in its full extent. Mr Wilson's objections to his author,—we had almost said his idol,—are of the following kind.

'His references to the precise nature of our justification before God—to the extent of the fall and ruin of man by sin—to the work of the Holy Spirit in regeneration and sanctification—and to the consolatory, cheering, vivifying effects of peace of conscience and communion with God, and hope of rest and joy in heaven, do not correspond with the largeness of the case. They are partial and defective. They might and should have embraced incidentally at least, some intimations of the peculiar structure and design of spiritual religion. The powerful argument in hand should at times have been carried out to its consequences. The inexperienced theological student would not then have been in danger of drawing erroneous conclusions, on some practical points of great importance.' p. cvi.

We shall endeavour to detach and weave together a series of passages illustrative of Mr Wilson's view of the nature of these deficiencies. Separated from their context our extracts will not appear with the requisite proofs and qualifications; but we think that every spiritually minded Christian will feel their force and importance. After shewing the very subordinate sense in which only the expression natural religion can be justly used, and that Butler uses it only

knowledge and humility require. We add this restricted application Mr Wilson goes on to remark

'Whilst we thus claim for natural religion what the Scriptures clearly imply or rather inculcate, and defend Butler on this point, we must cautiously avoid the dangerous error of attributing to it a power, which in the fallen state of man it does not and cannot possess, and which may militate against what the same Scriptures teach of the extent of man's depravity, and the necessity of Divine grace, in order to his doing any thing spiritually good. And therefore the language which occurs in some parts of the Analogy on the nature and powers of man may appear to be too strong too general, too unqualified. We speak here with hesitation, because, considering the line of argument pursued by this most able writer and the class of persons he addressed, it may be doubted whether this remark is applicable in fairness or not. Still we cannot but think that he sometimes attributes too much to the unaided nature of man, allows too much to his moral sense and feeling, dwells too largely on his tendencies to virtue and goodness, and speaks too ambiguously on the ground of his justification before God.' pp. cxiv, cxv.

The language used by our author in speaking of the Almighty finally rendering to every one according to his works, and establishing the entire rights of distributive justice is open to objection. Perhaps, if taken alone it might admit of a favourable interpretation, but when joined with the over statements already noticed, on the powers of man and the remains of natural religion, it becomes decidedly dangerous. The great doctrine of our justification before God, not by our own works and deservings but only for the merits of our Lord Jesus Christ is too fundamental, and too important, to be undermined, even incidentally. We refer to such expressions as the following.

'The advantages of Christianity will be bestowed upon every one in proportion to the degrees of his virtue. — Divine goodness may be a disposition to make the good, the faithful, the honest man happy. — We have scope and opportunities here for that good and bad behaviour which God will reward and punish hereafter. —

Religion teaches us, that we are placed here to qualify us by the practice of virtue, for another state which is to follow it. — Our repentance is accepted to eternal life. These, and similar statements occur throughout the work. In the second part where the leading features of revealed religion are delineated, they ought by all means to have been accompanied with those modifications which the superinduced scheme of the Gospel and the necessities of man, and the glory of the cross of Christ, and the ends of self knowledge and humility require. We say they should have been accompanied by such modifications, because they are so accompanied in the holy Scriptures. The doctrine, that every one shall receive the things done in the body, that they that have done good shall rise to the resurrection of life, and they that have done evil to the resurrection of damnation, is most true and most important. But the doctrines which accompany and modify this fundamental truth, should never be wholly lost sight of, even in a treatise on evidences, when any reference is made to the subject. We are taught in the New Testament, that these works must spring from faith and love to our Saviour Christ and must be renounced in point of merit on account of the inherent evil which defiles the very best of them and must be accepted only through that sacrifice which is the real footing of a sinner's dealings with a holy God and must be regarded by those who perform them with that deep humility and almost unconsciousness of having done them which is so strongly marked in the conduct of the righteous in our Lord's account of the last day. Now these modifications are so essential that the language of our author however undesignedly becomes really dangerous when stripped of them.— pp. cxvii cxviii

These observations lead me to notice a general defect, as it seems to me in our author's representation of the stupendous recovery of man provided in the Gospel. For if any doubt could be raised on the inexpediency of the above language, all such doubt would be removed when we find, on further examination that our Bishop's allusions to the whole doctrine of redemption and salvation as revealed in the New Testament, are not sufficiently clear and comprehensive to agree fully with the Scriptural statements of our natural corruption and of the operations of grace as adapted to it. Let us not be misunderstood. Bishop Butler is far from omitting altogether the peculiar scheme of the Gospel. He states distinctly the insufficiency of repentance alone to restore us to God's favour. He speaks with admirable clearness on the mediation and sacrifice of Christ. He quotes the passages in Scripture which teach the vicarious nature of Christ's sufferings and insists on the benefit of those sufferings being something much beyond mere instruction or example. On these subjects at least on some parts of them no complaint can be alleged against his brief statements they are luminous and adequate for an elementary treatise. Still the general idea of the scheme of the Gospel as a dispensation of grace which would be gathered from the whole of his representations and suggestions, would be erroneous. He calls Christianity a moral system he speaks of it as teaching us chiefly new duties and new relations in which we stand he describes it as 'an additional order of Providence.' These expressions are cold and inadequate. But we object most of all to the following passage. 'The doctrine of the Gospel appears to be, not only that Christ taught the efficacy of repentance but rendered it of the efficacy which it is by what he did and suffered for us that he obtained for us the benefit of having our repentance accepted unto eternal life not only that he revealed to sinners that they were in a capacity of salvation and how they might obtain it but moreover that he put them into this capacity of salvation, by what he did and suffered for them put us into a capacity of escaping future punishment, and obtaining future happiness. And it is our wisdom thankfully to accept the benefit by performing the conditions upon which it is offered, on our part, without disputing how it was procured on his.' (Part II chap V § vi.) Surely this is plainly deficient. Surely the salvation of Christ proceeds on a different footing, and includes much more than this. Surely the great sacrifice of the Cross not only obtained for the sincere believer that his repentance should be accepted to eternal life (a phrase unscriptural in its very terms,) not only put him in a capacity of salvation not only proposed certain conditions to be performed on his part—all which places the stress of salvation upon ourselves makes the reception and application of it to depend on our own efforts and leaves to our Lord merely the office of removing external hinderances affording us some aid by his Spirit and supplying our deficiencies—but purchased also salvation itself in all the amplitude of that mighty blessing, procured pardon reconciliation justification adoption acceptance the gift of the Holy Spirit, and the promise of everlasting life. Surely salvation brings men from darkness unto light, reverses the sentence of condemnation and makes them the righteousness of God in Christ it places them under a new covenant and confers the grace necessary for repentance towards God and faith towards our Lord Jesus Christ it puts them on the footing not of the Law but of the Gospel—not of works but of grace not of obtaining acceptance for their repentance but of receiving 'the gift of God which is eternal life.' Let Butler's summary of the benefits of Christ's death be compared with such summaries as the Apostle gives —' We have redemption through his blood even the forgiveness of sins. — By grace are ye saved through faith and that not of yourselves it is the gift of God not of works lest any man should boast for we are his workmanship created in Christ Jesus unto good works which God hath before ordained, that we should walk in them.'

With this defective view of the fruits of our Lord's propitiation, is allied a corre-

from his coldness in pressing the particular course of his argument, is to lead the reader to suppose that the effects of Christ's redemption are enjoyed by all who profess the Christian religion and live a moral life; that is, by all who have that general belief in the doctrine of Christianity which springs from education and rational conviction, if they are free from gross sin, cultivate virtue and set a good example to others by a decent reputable conduct. All these things are indeed included in the acts and fruits of a true and lively faith, but they reach not those peculiar effects and properties of it which prove it to be spiritual and salutary." pp. cxxi—cxxiv.

"Faith includes besides the general reception of Christianity a particular conviction of our own sins, a particular apprehension of our own lost estate, a personal application for ourselves of the offered blessings of the Gospel, and a distinct and spiritual reliance for our own salvation on the death and merits of our Saviour Christ—and some reference should have been made to all this by our author; at least no expression however brief should have been inconsistent with it." p. cxxv.

"The same kind of inadequate statements seem to be chargeable on our author's remarks on the doctrine of the Holy Ghost. Indeed we are not sure if serious omissions are not to be found here—more serious than on most of the preceding topics. Bishop Butler allows indeed distinctly that the Holy Spirit is our Sanctifier, and that the recovery of mankind is a scheme carried on by the Son and Spirit of God. He speaks frequently of the aid which the Spirit affords to good men. He acknowledges that man is a depraved creature, and wants not merely to be improved but to be renewed, and he quotes the striking text, 'Except a man be born of the Spirit he cannot enter into the kingdom of God.' We would wish to give the full benefit of these admissions in favour of the Bishop and against what we are about to state. Nor do we doubt that this remarkable man implored the operations of the Spirit in his own case, experienced his consolations and ascribed every thing to his grace. Still we conceive his general language in his Analogy on this fundamental subject does not come up to the Scriptural standard. He does not give even that prominence to it which he does to the mediation of Christ. He speaks of the Spirit as aiding, but scarcely at all as creating anew: he describes his assistances but hardly ever his mighty operations, in changing the whole heart: he talks of his presence with good men, but seldom of that of his regeneration and power to renew the wicked. He allows occasionally, but not prominently and most certainly not distinctly, as the Scriptures teach, and as the importance of the case requires; he dwells on the help of the Spirit in subduing our passions, and qualifying us for heaven, but passes over slightly the illuminating influences of the Spirit in opening the understanding, and his transforming power, in 'taking away the heart of stone and giving an heart of flesh.'" pp. cxxv, cxxvi.

"If men are not taught the necessity of a new creation in Christ Jesus, in consequence of the blindness of their understanding as well as the disorder of their affections, they must and will begin, and we find in fact they do begin, their religion, in a proud self dependent temper; in ignorance of their own wants, and of the mighty change which must take place in them." p. cxxvii.

But in truth all these deficiencies, if we are right in our judgment about them, spring from an inadequate view of the fallen state of man. We know the controversies on this mysterious subject. We allow that statements have too often been made which go to annihilate man's moral nature and his capacity of restoration, which weaken his responsibility and unnerve the exhortations and invitations which the Scriptures address to him; which extinguish the faint light of natural conscience, and repress effort and watchfulness. But we cannot but know at the same time, that the errors on the side of extenuating and lessening the Scriptural account of man's spiritual state since the Fall are equally dangerous and more prevalent. We cannot therefore conceal our conviction that Butler's view of human depravity does not fully meet the truth of the case as delineated in the inspired writings, and confirmed by uniform experience. He speaks we allow occasionally of men "having corrupted their natures, having lost their original rectitude, and as having permitted their passions to become excessive by repeated violations of their inward constitution." He avows that mankind is in a state of degradation however difficult it may be to account for it; and that the crime of our first parents was the occasion of our being placed in a more disadvantageous condition." Yet notwithstanding these expressions, the sincerity and importance of which, so far as they go, we do not for a moment call in question, he dwells in the course of his work, so copiously on man's powers and capacities—on his favouring virtue—on his having within him the principle of amendment,—on its being in his own power to take the path of life—on "virtue being agreeable to his nature"—on vice never being chosen for its own sake, that we cannot but consider the result as dangerous. If these expressions were qualified as they are in Scripture by other and explanatory statements, [illegible] standing as they [illegible] convey the idea that man is not that weak, corrupt, perverse, depraved, impotent creature which the word of God teaches us he is. The consequence of slight impressions of this great truth infallibly is, that men not being duly instructed on their real state before God, cannot feel that humility, nor exercise that penitence, nor sue for that renewal, which all depend on the primary fact of a total moral ruin; and which form the adaptation between the real grace of the Gospel and the actual wants of man Thus all the great ends of Christianity are missed and inferior benefits only are derived from it Neither conversion on the one hand nor real obedience to God on the other, can be attained; and the arch, deprived of its key-stone, as it were loses both its beauty and its strength pp cxxx—cxxxii

"His standard of the effects of Christianity in the holy happy lives of real Christians is far too low It could not indeed be otherwise The spiritual life is a whole If the glory of the Saviour and the operations of his Spirit and the total ruin of man as requiring both are not first understood it is impossible that the blessed fruits of all this in the new life and happiness of the renovated pardoned and sanctified heart should be produced There is however such a thing as the love of Christ constraining a man to live no longer to himself but to Him that died for him and rose again there is such a thing as the inward experience of the grace of Christianity there is such a thing as a holy, happy spiritual life, which dif[illegible] [illegible] from his coldness in [illegible]

After these ample extracts we must lay down our pen, though unwillingly, as there remains another topic of great interest discussed by Mr Wilson,—namely, the application of the principle of analogy to the peculiar disclosures of Christianity in their most exalted bearings. The argument is novel and striking; and, we think, in the main just, though not equally applicable to every part of the Christian system We must refer the reader to Mr Wilson for the details

We cannot, however, part from our respected author without expressing our great pleasure, that in the midst of almost overwhelming engagements, and almost from the bed of sickness, he has found leisure and strength to give to the public this new token of his anxiety for the spiritual benefit of mankind May he find his best recompence in the blessing of Divine Providence, which we trust, will largely attend his truly Christian exertions!

LITERARY AND PHILOSOPHICAL INTELLIGENCE

&c &c

GREAT BRITAIN

PREPARING for publication —Memorials of the Nineteenth Century by the Rev A. Bishop,—Four Vols of Sermons by Dr Doddridge left by his will to the late Mr. Orton with a desire that they should be published for the benefit of the author s family,—A weekly publication entitled "The Spirit and Manners of the Age by the Author of the Evangelical Rambler —An enlarged edition of Deism Refuted or Plain Reasons for being a Christian by the Rev. T H Horne being an Analysis of the first volume of his Introduction to the Study of the Scriptures —Vindiciæ Christianæ a comparative Estimate of the Greek Hindu, Mahometan and Christian Religions by the Rev J Alley,—Proceedings of the Expedition dispatched by Government in 1821 to explore North Africa by Capt Beechey,—Mission from Bengal to Siam and Cochin China by G Finlaison with an Introduction, by Sir S Raffles —Life of Erasmus by C. Butler —Memoirs of the late Miss Jane Taylor by J Taylor —Mexican Memoirs

In the press —Short Discourses from the MSS of eminent Ministers,—Hints for Ministers and Churches; by the late Rev Andrew Fuller —Selections from the Works of Dr John Owen, by the Rev W. Wilson D D —Howe's Redeemer s

Dominion over the Unseen World, with an Introductory Essay, by the Rev. Robert Deluce.—Lord Clarendon's Papers, illustrative of the History of Ireland during the Years 1670 to 1700, and Debates in the House of Commons during the Interregnum, from the original manuscripts in the possession of W. Upcott; with Notes.—History of Europe during the last Twenty-five Years.—A Treatise on Education, by Madame Campan;—The Conway Papers from the collection of the Marquis of Hertford;—Constitutional History of England, by H. Hallam.—Papers of Sir R. Wilmot Bart.—Recent Discoveries in Africa, by Major Dixon Denham.—Voyages of Discovery, to survey New Holland between the Years 1817 and 1822, by P. P. King.

OXFORD.—The following is the subject for the Theological Prize: "The operation of human causes only will not sufficiently account for the propagation of Christianity." This subject for an English essay is proposed on the following conditions:—The candidate must have passed his examination for the degree of B.A. or B.C.L. He must not have exceeded his twenty-eighth term, on the first of this present December. He must have commenced his sixteenth term on or before the first of February next. The essays are to be sent under a sealed cover to the Registrar, by Wednesday in Easter week.

The following are the Chancellor's Prizes for the ensuing year, viz.—Latin Verses—"Montes Pyrenæi." English Essay—"Is a rude or a refined age, more favourable to the production of works of fiction?" Latin Essay—"Quibus præcipue de causis in artium liberalium studiis Romani Græcis vix pares, nedum superiores evaserint." Sir Roger Newdigate's Prize—Trajan's Pillar.

CAMBRIDGE.—The Seatonian Prize was adjudged to the Rev. John Overton, of Trinity College, for his poem on 'The Building and Dedication of the Second Temple.' The subject of the Norrisian Prize Essay for the ensuing year is—"The Mosaic Dispensation not intended to be perpetual."

A course of lectures in the Chinese language, has commenced at the house of the Language Institution, 27 Bartlett's Buildings, Holborn, which will be continued every Monday, Wednesday, and Friday, at eleven o'clock, during the months of January and February next. A similar course of lectures, in the Bengalee language, has also commenced. Missionaries, missionary students, clergymen, and other persons, and students for the ministry will be graciously admitted. To the public the terms of admission are, course of Chinese, five guineas; do. the course of Bengalee, three guineas.

Since the discovery of the Milton manuscript in the State Paper Office, Mr. Lemon, jun. has found an entire translation of "Boetius de Consolatione Philosophiæ," by Queen Elizabeth. Walpole mentions that the queen had translated this work, but no vestige of it was known to exist. Nearly the whole is in her majesty's own hand-writing; but there are parts written by her private secretary and by the secretary of state. It is stated that there are letters discovered which identify this translation to have been made by the queen. The public is to be gratified with the publication of this literary curiosity.

A novel class of publications has recently started into life, with a suddenness almost as great as that of the birth of twopenny works,—namely, annual works of expensive embellishments, and some of them of literary merit, designed as New Year's presents. Two or three of them are of a religious cast.

At a recent meeting of the Society of Antiquaries a paper was read on the remains of the sub-church of Edward the Confessor, in the cellars under Westminster Abbey. The most important remain is the vault where the pix was deposited and which it is thought, was formerly the treasury of the kings of England. The altar-table and piscina remain. On the upper slab of the altar is a concavity, used perhaps to contain the oil for anointing the kings. This sub-church is more than four feet below the present level of the Abbey Church which is 2 feet 4 inches above the level of the cloisters. It appears that in the course of ages, the level of the city of Westminster has been raised from four to six feet. At every entrance to the abbey from the street is a descent.

FRANCE

Baron Charles Dupin's lectures on mathematics (in their application to the arts) delivered last winter to the artizans of Paris are in a course of publication, and the minister of marine has ordered the royal professors at forty-four sea-ports, to repeat them to the youth training up for the public service.

A memoir was lately read before the Asiatic Society of Paris by M. Schulz respecting a very remarkable and hitherto unnoticed Oriental MS. in the library of the king of France; namely, a Persian translation of the Sanscrit poem

Maha Bharata, performed by command of the Emperor Akbar, it consists of 784 leaves, in large folio. The first twelve pages contain the eulogies of Shah Akbar, preceded by ascriptions of praise to God. The followers of Mahomed and the worshippers of Brahma, although subject to the same government, were in the reign of Akbar, in a state of religious animosity, and the emperor it appears, wished to reconcile them, by making each party better known to the other,—an example of tolerance extraordinary on the part of a Musulman prince; represented as holding the Koran in one hand and the sword in the other. Grounds however exist for distrusting the Musulman orthodoxy of the great Akbar; for example his placing in the same rank the faithful along with heretics. It is observable besides that in nearly all his letters he has omitted the customary formula of benedictions of Mahomet. But the most irrefragable evidence of his heresy is furnished in a letter addressed to the king of Portugal, found in two MSS. in the royal library of France; in which he avows that 'he has followed the plan of frequenting the company of wise men of all classes, profiting by the precious words and sublime ideas of each of them;' and with a view of deriving more information respecting the Christian religion, he requests a Persian and Arabic translation of the Evangelists, the Psalms, and the Pentateuch. There is in the royal library a translation of the Four Evangelists, made, as the catalogue states, by command of Akbar.

M. C. De Perceval, in an Arabic grammar lately published at Paris, gives a characteristic illustration of the mock sublime in language, and the mixture of secular business and religion, for which the Orientals are distinguished, in an Arabic certificate of the noble birth of a race horse.

"Peace be to him that reads these characters, and who possesses good sentiments! We, humble servants of the most high God, certify and declare by our good fortune, by our fate, and by our girdles, that the sorrel colt, aged three years—Here follows the description and pedigree at large, tracing up the animal's descent to those horses which God created by the breath of the winds, and presented to the prophet (may the Lord shed upon him his benedictions!) and which the prophet distributed to his companions. It is in their praise that the prophet hath said, &c. &c."

Chain bridges having begun to be adopted in France, a committee of public safety, have decided, that the thickness of the chains should be so calculated, that the weight should not exceed eight tons per square inch of the sectional surface, and that, before use, they should be subjected to a proof weight of double that power without sensible elongation. The best iron it was found supported, without breaking, twenty-six tons per square inch, but, began to elongate with about sixteen; bad iron gave way under fourteen tons to the square inch, and did not elongate materially before it burst.

ITALY.

The Academy of Sciences at Leghorn has proposed a prize for the solution of the following problem. To determine the influence useful or hurtful, of different states of memory on the understanding and its utilities with regard to the other faculties, &c. and to shew by what educational means it may be developed, strengthened, or recovered.

RUSSIA.

The expedition to Siberia for the purpose of determining geographically the coasts of the Frozen Sea, and the north-eastern part of Siberia has returned to St. Petersburgh. The results have not yet been given to the public.

UNITED STATES.

An elaborate work has lately been published at Vermont, by the Rev. W. Chapin entitled 'The Missionary Gazetteer, comprising an account of the places where Protestant Missionaries have laboured alphabetically arranged, and so constructed as to give a particular and general history of Missions throughout the world, with an Appendix, containing an alphabetical list of missionaries, their stations, and other particulars.

The American Sunday school Magazine states, that a strong effort was lately made to have the reading rooms of the Athenæum in Philadelphia kept open during certain hours on the Sunday. Various addresses were delivered on the occasion, but one from a distinguished civilian Mr Duponceau, produced the greatest effect. He urged among other considerations apart from religion, "that the strict observance of Sunday is peculiar to the United States and that, the sacred manner in which this day is kept, so very different from its observance in any country in Europe as to make it a striking feature in the character of the nation should, as such, independent of all other considerations, be most carefully cherished as a national trait. The American traveller in other lands would remember his country with affection, while he said to himself—" They do not keep Sunday so at home:" and he would love his country for the very peculiarity. Only thirty-five voters could be found to resolve on a public violation of the Sabbath: the number on the other side, amounted to between eighty and a hundred.

PERSIA

At Cochom there are preserved, some leaves belonging to a koran of the most magnificent dimensions perhaps in the world. These leaves are formed of thick paper, and when opened out measure from ten to twelve feet long by seven or eight broad, the letters are beautifully formed as if made by a single stroke of a gigantic pen. Few of the leaves are perfect, as they have been mutilated for the sake of the ornaments or the blank paper of the immense margin.

INDIA.

The following are moral maxims of the Malabars as given in a native work. "Spend no day without offering prayers to God; Have nothing to do with witchcraft. Go not where you have no invitation; Ridicule not the absent; Shew not your back to the enemy. Contend not with the poor. Abuse not any without a cause. Criticize not the faults of others; Satirize not a virtuous woman. Contemn not the divinely inspired sages. Treat not the learned contemptuously. Carry no tales of detraction. Become not security for another. Have no intercourse with gamblers. Reside not where there is no temple. Utter not a lie though death be near you. Never regard your enemy as a friend. Associate not with mountebanks. Second not a new custom. Travel not by a solitary route."

LIST OF NEW PUBLICATIONS

THEOLOGY

A Review of the Conduct of the Directors of the Bible Society relative to the Apocrypha, with an Answer to the Rev. C. Simeon, by R. Haldane, Esq.

A Plea for the Protestant Canon of Scripture with an Account of the Bible Society Controversy respecting the circulation of the Apocrypha, with a History of English Translations. 4s.

Sabbath Meditations, in Prose and Verse for 1826, by the Rev. J. East.

A Voyage to Immanuel's Land, in the ship Hopewell. 2s. 6d.

A Companion for Pilgrims on their Journey to Canaan. 2s.

A Treatise on the Necessity of being born again, by the Rev. H. Gipps. 1s. 6d.

Christian Characteristics, by the Rev. T. Lewis. 5s.

Fifteen Select Sermons, printed by the Religious Tract Society. 2s. 6d.

The Lollards, or some Account of the Witnesses for the Truth in Great Britain, for 1400 to 1546.

MISCELLANEOUS

Stranger's Elements of Hindu Law. 2 vols. royal 8vo. 1l. 15s.

English Stories, third series, illustrating the Reformation under the Tudor Princes, by Maria Hack. 7s.

A System of Punctuation on fixed Principles, by C. J. Addison. 4s.

Maria's Reward, or a Voice from the Dead, by the Author of Jane and her Teacher. 2s.

The Causes and Evils of War, by T. Thrush, late Captain in the Royal Navy, intended as an Apology for withdrawing from the Service. Part I.

An Encyclopædia of Agriculture, by J. C. London, F.L.S. with 800 engravings. 2l. 10s.

The Amulet, or Christian and Literary Remembrancer for 1826. 18mo. 12s.

A Manual of the System of Instruction pursued at the Infant School, Meadow street, Bristol, with engravings considerably enlarged, by D. G. Goyder. 12mo. 5s.

The Analytical Part of Principia Hebraica, with introductory Lessons, by T. Keyworth. 8s.

Historical Sketch of the Origin and Progress of the Art of Printing, by T. C. Hansard. 8vo. 3l. 3s.

RELIGIOUS INTELLIGENCE

BRITISH AND FOREIGN BIBLE SOCIETY

We have not hitherto noticed the inquiry which has been for some time in progress among the friends of this invaluable institution respecting the circulation of the Apocrypha, being unwilling to foment a controversy which we could not hope to decide. We are happy however at length to announce that this important question has been determined in the manner explained in the following circular and resolution. We will not revive the discussion, and shall therefore only say that our opinion is, that the Committee have come to a most wise and judicious conclusion and we trust, that by the blessing of God the discussions which have taken place on this subject, and which might have led to serious differences of opinion in the Society will be found to have terminated only in renewing the ardour of all its friends in its cause The following is a circular from the Secretaries dated November 28.

The earnest attention of the Committee having been solicited, by certain members of the Society and also by many of the Committees of its Auxiliaries to the propriety of affording aid, from the funds of this institution to the circulation of foreign editions of the Scriptures which contain the Apocrypha, the subject was referred to a Special Committee appointed for that purpose from which, as well as from the General Committee it has received the most mature consideration The result we are instructed to transmit to you in the subjoined Resolution

It is our fervent prayer that the harmony which has hitherto subsisted among the members and friends of this institution both at home and abroad may be preserved to the latest age and that the Society may long continue to prove a blessing to the Christian Church and also to the World at large

ANDREW BRANDRAM }
JOSEPH HUGHES } Secretaries
C F A STEINKOPFF, }

November 21 1825

The Committee in accordance with the spirit of the recommendation in the Report of the Special Committee adopted the following Resolution —viz

That the Funds of the Society be applied to the printing and circulation of the Canonical Books of Scripture to the exclusion of those books and parts of books which are usually termed Apocryphal and that all copies printed either entirely or in part at the expense of the Society and whether such copies consist of the whole or of any one or more of such books be invariably issued bound no other books whatever being bound with them and further that all money grants to societies or individuals be made only in conformity with the principle of this regulation — At a subsequent Meeting of the Committee this resolution was read and confirmed

We have prepared an abstract of the Society s last Report which we purpose to lay before our readers in the Appendix.

FUND FOR THE RELIEF OF THE WALDENSES.

We have frequently had occasion in former volumes to bring before our readers the past and present condition of the Vaudois or Waldenses and their claims on the sympathy and charity of their fellow-Christians and fellow Protestants in this country We are most happy to learn that the circumstances of these interesting people are beginning to awaken a very general interest in their behalf and that a highly respectable Committee has been formed for receiving donations and subscriptions for their relief We have intended to lay before our readers some interesting recent particulars respecting them and the plans in progress for their benefit in reviewing the Rev S Gilly s Excursion in the Mountains of Piemont but have delayed our notice of that work till we could combine with it two others on the eve of publication the one a Description of the Valleys and their Inhabitants by the Rev T Sims the other a posthumous work from the pen of the late Moderator of the Waldensian Church J R. Peyrani which we understand will supply many new and interesting details respecting the history of his venerable church and countrymen*

M Peyrani (or Peyran) is described as a man distinguished for profound erudition acute powers of reasoning accurate judgment, and a clear and vigorous style It is stated in a note to Mr. Gilly s work that his MSS have been entrusted to the Rev Thomas Sims to be published for the benefit of his family These MSS consist of dissertations and letters on a variety of theological philological philosophical and historical subjects For the present it is intended to publish a single volume in the original (French) containing pieces of an argumentative nature against the errors of the Church of Rome The author undertakes to prove from the testimony of even Roman Catholic writers That the Waldenses and Albigenses were not two distinct bodies but one body under different names that their faith was similar to that of Protestants that though stigmatized as Arians and Manichees they opposed the errors of those heretics more successfully than the Church of Rome did that, to ascertain their origin we must recur to the first ages of the Christian church that the Waldenses have both adhered to true doctrines and opposed the novelties of Rome and that, with the exception of the primitive church no Christian people have been more distinguished for their virtues and morals or have shewn more zeal for the propagation of the Gospel or greater fortitude and constancy under affliction

In the summer of 1823, the Rev T. Sims and Mr Plenderleath paid a second visit to the valleys of Piedmont, accompanied by Mr Durbin Brice, for the purpose of inquiring minutely into the temporal and spiritual wants of the Waldenses and more especially with respect to the state of education amongst them. Having explored their villages and hamlets they were fully persuaded that one of the greatest benefits that can be conferred is the establishment of schools for girls, under the care of schoolmistresses, who shall instruct the children in needlework, knitting &c as well as in reading the holy Scriptures. This plan received the cordial approbation of the ministers of the Waldensian Churches, as females competent to undertake the instruction of the girls are to be found in the valleys. The population of the valleys amounts to between eighteen and twenty thousand souls, who inhabit fifteen villages (in which thirteen ministers officiate) and one hundred and three contiguous hamlets. Fifteen schools are wanted for the villages for the greater part of the year at an expense of ten pounds each, and one hundred and three small schools are wanted during five winter months, in the hamlets at an expense of three pounds each. The necessity for establishing so many small schools it is stated, arises from the nature of the country. To each parish five six or more hamlets situate on the declivities of the mountains are attached. In the winter the season when these smaller schools are kept, the hamlets are surrounded by deep snow that covers such tremendous precipices and ravines that the lives of the children would be in imminent danger if they were to go from one hamlet to another. A school is therefore wanted if there are only twelve or fifteen children in the hamlet but frequently we find twenty thirty and more. In the smaller hamlets a schoolmistress may give instruction to little boys as well as girls. We would suggest the utility of forming circulating schools where fixed ones cannot be supported. Amongst other inducements for extending relief to the Vaudois there are three particularly mentioned, in an address which has been printed on their behalf namely their poverty—the danger of apostasy to which they are exposed—and the magnitude of the benefits to be conferred by means of a comparatively small sum of money. The inducements are detailed as follows —

'Their poverty and privations are extreme. The hardships they endure in procuring the necessary food for their families are such as we rarely witness. Compelled to raise walls even to prevent the scanty portions of soil on the sides of the mountains from being washed down by torrents obliged to break up that soil by manual labour since no cattle can be used to plough it forced (women as well as men,) on account of the steepness of the ground to carry hay corn &c on their backs to a great distance, and thus undertake the drudgery assigned to horses in England; and after this excessive labour, obtaining in the generality of instances, only coarse buck wheat, chesnuts and potatoes for their subsistence;—none can feel surprised that they are not able to pay for the education of their children however desirous—and they are ardently so—that they may be instructed.

The Waldenses still maintain, as their forefathers did, a strong attachment to those great truths of the Gospel which prevailed among the primitive Christians and were revived at the Reformation but education is particularly requisite because their temptations to apostatize are very great. Snares are in fact, continually laid bribes are perpetually offered to seduce them to conform to the Church of Rome especially when obliged to seek employment as servants in Roman-Catholic families and removed from home. This circumstance alone may well induce those who really love the Protestant religion to assist in promoting education that, being well instructed in the truths of the Gospel, the females may be still preserved from fatal errors and enabled under every temptation to persevere in an unshaken attachment to the truths bequeathed to them by their ancestors.

The magnitude of the benefits conferred by means of a comparatively small sum is likewise a strong additional reason for aiding them, and it is proposed as a desirable way of proceeding, that one individual should kindly undertake to collect from a few friends small *annual* contributions of five shillings from each person, to make up either the sum of ten pounds for a village, or three pounds for a hamlet school

A Committee has been formed in London for their relief and sums of money remitted either for the school-fund, the hospital their ministers or churches the

---

The price of the volume is not intended to exceed 10s. The profits will be placed in the hands of a committee for the benefit of M. Peyran's family. Subscribers may transmit their names to our publishers

poor, or any other specific object, will be appropriated to that object, according to the wish of the donor.

The Committee consists of the Earls of Clarendon and St. Germains; the Bishops of London and Winchester; Sir G. H. Rose; Sir T. D. Acland, Sir Thomas Baring, Sir Robert Inglis, and several other clergymen and gentlemen. Communications may be addressed to the Secretary, the Rev. H. S. Gilly, 2, Tavistock Place, Russell Square, London.

From another address on the subject we copy the following statements.

"When Piedmont was under the late Government of France the Vaudois were put in full possession of all the privileges common to other subjects; but on the restoration of the Bourbons in the year 1814, they were again united to Sardinia; and though they never murmur, they are subjected to the most grievous restrictions: for instance, they cannot purchase lands out of the confined limits assigned them; they are obliged to desist from work on the Roman Catholic festivals which are almost perpetual, under penalty of fine or imprisonment; they are forbidden to exercise the professions of physician, surgeon, or lawyer; and these people, together with their ministers, are compelled to serve as private soldiers without possibility of advancement: all religious books are prohibited except the Bible, which is subject to such a high duty as almost to place it beyond their reach. Schools are indeed allowed on the old system; but on Bell and Lancaster's they are not permitted. The Scriptures and Catechisms have sometimes been circulated leaf by leaf, as the only means of obtaining a perusal of their pages: they are not allowed to multiply their places of worship, though they may rebuild and enlarge their old ones.

In the time of Oliver Cromwell collections were made throughout England on behalf of the Vaudois, amounting to 38,241l., which after affording them considerable relief left a fund of 16,333l. which Charles the Second on his restoration used for his own purposes, assigning as a reason that he was not bound by any of the engagements of an usurper and a tyrant. William and Mary restored the pension; but during the reign of Napoleon the British government from political motives withheld it; and the Vaudois Pastors, thirteen in number, are for the most part living in a state of poverty. Efforts are now making to recover this lost aid, and thereby enable the Pastors to surmount their difficulties, to assist in the establishment of schools, and the education of their ministers, and especially in building a hospital among them. His Majesty George the Fourth has presented them with a hundred guineas: several of the Protestant States on the Continent are interesting themselves for these suffering people; and it is hoped that a favourable moment has arrived for their relief."

NATIONAL EDUCATION SOCIETY.

The thirteenth and fourteenth Reports have just been published together; the former having been postponed with a view to annex to it the returns of sums collected in the several parishes of the kingdom under the royal letter. The Committee advert with great satisfaction to the impulse which has been given to the feelings of the public on the subject of national education, by the circulation of this letter. The increase of schools during the present year has been going on with great rapidity and vigour. In the thirteenth year 116 schools were received into union; and, in the fourteenth 112—making a total of 2095. The total number of scholars, including 50,000 in schools which follow the plan of the Society though not formally united, is estimated at 360,000. We are happy to learn that National Schools have been established in connexion with many of the new churches erected by his Majesty's Commissioners.

In reference to the training department, it is stated that in the thirteenth year 80 schools, and in the fourteenth 98, were assisted by permanent or temporary masters and mistresses, or by monitors sent out to communicate the knowledge of the system.

The sum of 28,225l. has been received from 9943 parishes in consequence of the king's letter. In the thirteenth year, grants amounting to 5060l., were made to 54 places; and, in the fourteenth 7355l. to 75 places. These grants varied in amount, from 10l. to 800l. The net income of the thirteenth year was 2615l., and its expenditure 3013l. The income of the fourteenth year was 2615l. and its expenditure 2154l.

Circulars having been sent to 530 schools, in order to obtain reports of their state and progress, returns have been received from 330. The Committee remark that their anticipations of the blessings diffused by the National System derive additional strength from the communications which they continually receive from all parts of the country. In particular, they are gratified with learning, on the authority of numbers of the parochial clergy, that the children who are examined for confirmation in parishes where National Schools have been established, exhibit, in a most marked manner the good effects of the instruction there received in the increased measure of religious knowledge which they bring with them for that solemn rite.

FEMALE EDUCATION IN INDIA

We have laid before our readers many interesting details respecting the commencement and progress of female education in India, chiefly however in Calcutta and its neighbourhood. We copy the following particulars from the communications of the Church Missionary Society's missionaries in the Madras station, as proofs that the benefit is not confined to one part of India, but that all that is wanted is sufficient funds to extend the boon throughout the whole peninsula. Mr Schmid thus traces the rise of this promising enterprise.

As soon as we arrived at Palamcottah we directed our attention to the object of native female education, and neglected no opportunity to admonish the natives, especially the native Christians to care for the education of their daughters, which had the effect that two of our central school boys requested me, with the consent of their parents, to give them Tamul alphabets and spelling cards in order to teach their sisters to read. But after it pleased God to bless our labours among our pupils in the seminary to the conversion of many, we were induced to establish at once a similar institution for native girls. The boys induced not less than twenty five, mostly their own sisters, cousins and nieces, to wish to come to Palamcottah. A building having been prepared for their reception Mr Schmid says— It was a pleasing scene to see our little girls walking to church in great order, cleanly dressed, and with cheerful countenances. many of them are attentive to Divine things their countenances have such an expression of satisfaction and happiness.

The number was soon increased, as appears from the following appeal, which Mr Rhenius makes in their behalf.

This female institution is an important undertaking. It will be a new era for this part of India. May Europe not be slack to answer this call upon its bounty! Ladies I think must feel particularly interested and I trust that their hearts will be open to promote it. Let them reflect on the fact in all its bearings that thirty native females who were by the common usage of the country destined to be slaves to ignorance superstition irreligion and vice—and who would be neither able nor willing to fulfil the important duties of wives and mothers in such a manner as to ensure or promote true happiness—will now be brought up on the contrary in the light of the Gospel—will learn to be cleanly and orderly in their persons and in their houses—will receive proper ideas on right and wrong on God and the Saviour and on the present and future worlds—will learn to become sober faithful and affectionate wives and mothers—will be in the way to receive that change of mind and that true holiness through the Spirit of God without which none shall see the Lord. Let then our Christian friends in Europe rejoice in this small though in its consequences vast beginning! The female children are readily susceptible of kind instructions and these instructions have not been bestowed without an early blessing and reward. Mr Schmid gives the following pleasing view of the female children — Although the evil practices of the natives and the bad inclinations of the human heart, especially envy vanity and covetousness, were often visible in several of our girls yet the change which both their exterior and interior have undergone in the short time that they have been with us is very great. The evil inclinations of many of them disappeared quickly and their very countenances formerly so unmeaning and wild, became soon very sweet and lovely and expressive of the happiness which they enjoyed.

VIEW OF PUBLIC AFFAIRS

FOREIGN

FRANCE.—We have alluded in another part of the present Number to the struggle which is going on in this country between ultra royalism and religious bigotry on the one side, and almost every shade of opinion and party on the other and have expressed our conviction that the issue must be the triumph of liberal principles, (blended we fear in too many instances, though by no means intrinsically connected with infidel ones,) over the civil and religious despotism which would equally enthral the body and the soul. The events of each successive month increase our expectation of this crisis. We might mention, as an illustration, the tokens of veneration which have just been shewn for the memory of that well known opposer of ultra-royalism and priestly domination General Foy, and which seem to have been almost ostentatiously obtruded as an indication of the national sentiment. But a more important proof of the resistance which is likely to be made to the encroachments of bigotry and arbitrary power, is afforded in the acquittal of the conductors of the Constitutionnel and Courier François journals, who have been for some time under a state prosecution for a libel, consisting of a series of articles 'tending to disparage the Jesuits and missionary priests.' Our readers are aware that the present administration, at an early period of their power, procured an act which placed the administration of the law of libel not in the hands of juries, but of a court composed of judges removeable at the pleasure of the crown; at the same time extending the definition of libel to a succession or collection of writings, each perhaps innoxious in itself, but *tending* in their cumulative series to offend the ruling powers. The alleged libel in the present case was, in substance, a charge of disparaging religion by frequent attacks upon the Jesuits and ultra-Catholic clergy. M. Dupin, the advocate of the accused, exposed with great energy the doctrines and practices of the missionary priests; and the judges decided that it was no abuse of religion, or of the press to oppose the introduction of associations unauthorised by law, or to denounce ultra-montane doctrines, which France had long since indignantly rejected, and which were alike hostile to the public liberties and the independence of the throne. The result of this trial has been hailed with a burst of public acclamation, and we hope indicates the limited range of that bigotry and superstition which the Jesuits in particular were beginning to revive.

Russia.—The autocrat of this mighty empire—so well known and who was so popular in this country for his conduct at the conclusion of the late war, and still more so among the friends of religion and humanity for the plans of benevolence which he patronized, particularly the Bible Society—is now no more. His once well-earned popularity had been long on the wane, and was at length well-nigh extinguished, at least among Englishmen, from his adherence to the arbitrary policy of the mis-named Holy alliance, and the contemporaneous decline of his zeal for religious and beneficent objects. He has been for several years a most formidable opposer of just principles of public liberty; and to him, more than perhaps to any other individual, Spain, Naples, and other parts of the continent, owe their present degradation. In extenuation, however, it must be allowed that looking at the events of the last five and thirty years, he may have honestly feared the encroachments of a spirit of anarchy, and have honestly, however erroneously, thought he did service to mankind by throwing the weight of his power into the opposite scale. He certainly has done much for the strength and internal improvement of his own empire, though of late he seems to have shrunk from the natural effect of his own measures. What change, if any, his demise may make in the political state of Europe, remains to be seen; but we should hope it will be found to remove a formidable barrier to the extension of those just principles of national happiness, of which our own country is so eminent an example, and which it is so honourably her present line of policy to promote among the great community of nations.

DOMESTIC.

The present month has proved a month of extraordinary agitation and of peculiar alarm and disaster in the commercial world. Some of the first banking establishments in the metropolis have been driven by the extreme pressure of the moment, to suspend their payments; and numerous country banks have been reduced to the same painful necessity, spreading dismay, and consternation and distress around them. The remote cause of this tremendous commercial crisis is doubtless to be found in that rage for speculation combined with the very low rate to which interest had fallen in the public funds of the country, which led so many persons to embark in schemes connected with foreign loans and foreign adventures, in the hope of adding to their income. To these operations the liberal issue of bank notes, for a considerable space of time, afforded great facilities. These facilities the high state of general credit, and the desire of beneficially placing their deposits, induced many bankers to make advances, in the way of discount, for far longer periods than had been customary. Besides this, in the course of the last spring, a great and sudden rise having taken place in the price of many articles of very wide and general consumption, speculation was carried to an enormous height: but the rise of price, in some articles at least, proving of short duration, a calamitous re-action took place, and large failures ensued. At the same time the Bank of England is said to have felt such a drain of its gold as made it prudent somewhat to contract its issues. However that may be, the mercantile world began, in the month of October, to experience a change in the state of the money market. Bank notes were obtainable with greater difficulty, the interest of money rose, and the pressure continued gradually to advance until the beginning of the present month, when it threatened to involve a great part of the commercial world in one common ruin. The immediate and proximate cause of this state of things, was, without doubt, a scarcity of bank notes. Not that the bank had materially lessened its circulation, but that those who were anxious to fortify themselves against coming difficulties, were eager to possess a larger quantity of its notes. The apprehension of a run, on the part of the eight hundred banks scattered throughout the country, led to an immense transmission to all parts of the kingdom, both of gold and bank notes, which were necessarily subtracted from the currency of the metropolis; and thus the evil was greatly aggravated. In such a state of things, producing as it did a strong, though unreasonable panic, the policy of the Bank should have been, boldly to have met the pressure by very free issues of their notes, proportioned in some degree to the new and unprecedented demand to which the panic necessarily led. That they might have done this with safety, provided only they took care to obtain valid securities for their issues, is unquestionable, because, during the whole continuance of the alarm, the foreign exchanges were favourable, and bank notes were at a premium as compared with gold: the market price of gold 3*l*. 17s. 6d. being 4½d. less than the Mint price. The Bank, we are told, were extremely liberal in their issues. Their liberality, however, came too late. Had it been exercised a fortnight earlier, as it ought to have been, much of the evil that has taken place would, without doubt, have been prevented. At the same time it would not be fair greatly to blame the directors, if at such a crisis they should have partaken of the panic, and acted on erroneous views of the subject. Their conduct shews, however, in what a fearful predicament the stability of the whole commercial world is placed by its being left, as now, to the determination of twenty-four men, acting without public responsibility, whether or not it shall be in the power even of the very wealthiest individuals to make good their pecuniary engagements. The tremendous crisis through which we have passed, must lead, as we apprehend, to some more secure and salutary arrangement than that of our present monetary system: and must have the effect of doing away that monopoly enjoyed by the Bank, which raises its directors, however excellent and worthy they may be in their private capacities, to a situation for which they are wholly unfit, that of being the arbiters of the supply of the very life-blood of our whole immense commercial system.

These are the economical views of the present state of things which have occurred to us. To the moral bearings of the question, which are many and important, we cannot now advert.

The meeting of Parliament is prorogued to the second of February. Among the subjects which are likely to excite an early and powerful interest in the proceedings of that august assembly, there is one to which we feel it a duty to direct the early attention of our readers: we mean, the necessity of abolishing colonial slavery. Petitions are already in preparation, and are likely to be poured in in vast numbers, and with an overwhelming mass of signatures, on this great question, of which the public are, we trust, at length beginning to feel the importance. The subject is of such powerful and pressing interest that, though the limits of our present Number are exhausted, we cannot withhold from our readers the statements made in a special Report, at a meeting of the Anti-slavery Society held on the twenty-first instant, for the purpose of petitioning Parliament for the abolition of colonial slavery, Mr. Wilberforce in the chair. The powerful conviction excited at this meeting, both by the Report and by the addresses delivered, by Sir James Mackintosh, Messrs. Brougham, Buxton, Denman, Lushington, and others, has already led to a most numerous and respectable signature of the petitions intended to be presented to the legislature. We insert the Report entire. It was as follows:—

"Since the publication of the Second Report of the Society, made on the 30th April last, a large mass of most important information, on the subject of Colonial Slavery, has been laid before Parliament. A digest of the most material parts of these parliamentary documents has been published, under the title of the 'The Slave Colonies of Great Britain, or a Picture of Negro Slavery drawn by the Colonists themselves' (See Christian Observer for October, p 655) As this pamphlet has been largely circulated, it will not be necessary to enter into a detail of the statements which it contains, or of the fresh horrors which it develops It has admitted us to a near view of the interior of society in one of the slave colonies, Berbice, where the Fiscal had been so attentive to his duty as to preserve some record, though an imperfect one, of the causes of complaint, on the part of the slaves, which came before him We are not to suppose that the slave system in this colony is marked by features of peculiar atrocity The presumption, on the contrary, is rather in favour of its comparative lenity, because it is one of the few slave colonies in which the population does not diminish We have unfortunately no similar disclosures from any other of those colonies But when we consider what a mass of suffering is laid open to our view in the account which has reached us from this single colony, containing only 23,000 slaves, being about a fortieth part of the whole slave population, how frightfully would that mass have been augmented had we received a similar report of the remaining 800,000! Over *their* sufferings the veil of oblivion has been drawn Of *them* no record has been preserved We may imagine, indeed, what they must have been, from the glimpse which has been afforded us in the returns from Berbice; but the full amount of their horrors can now be known only to Him whose eye makes inquisition for the blood of the innocent and by whom not one sigh of the oppressed is disregarded

"Revolting, in every point of view, as is the delineation, contained in these papers, of the state of British colonial slavery, as it exists in law and in practice, there is at least this advantage attending the melancholy detail, that it serves amply to confirm the view of the nature and effects of that cruel system which has been sanctioned and circulated by this Society, making *their* statements to appear even cold and tame in the comparison

"These parliamentary documents are particularly valuable as exemplifying the unchanged spirit of colonial legislation on the subject of slavery The local legislatures have refused, without a single exception, to comply even with the moderate requisitions of his Majesty's Ministers, as these are embodied in the Order in Council for Trinidad, and the colonists, generally, exult in the refusal, encouraging each other to persevere in the same contumacious course Their tone of secure and triumphant irony is remarkable. 'We beg you to observe,' says the editor of one of their newspapers—and we give the passage only as an illustration of the prevailing spirit— 'We beg you to observe, that not one of the unconquered colonies' (meaning the colonies having legislatures of their own) 'have had the *civility* to comply with Earl Bathurst's wishes, notwithstanding he informed them, *in the most earnest and feeling manner, of the serious extent of the disappointment which his Majesty's Government would experience if they rejected his application We sympathize most sincerely with his Lordship on this unexpected event*

"Attempts, it is true have been made, by several of the colonial legislatures, to ameliorate their slave codes and they boast of their new laws as models of wise and beneficent legislation But it has been shewn, by the digest of these laws already laid before the public that, vaunted as they have been, they are nevertheless an outrage on every just principle of legislation and afford, at the very moment they profess to protect the slave, a decisive proof of his utter want of effective protection, and of the depth of his legal degradation And if such be the character of their recent enactments, deliberately framed in the strange hope of satisfying the expectations of the parliament and people of this country,—if the colonial legislatures can have so egregiously misapprehended the whole current of British principle and feeling,—would it not be the height of fatuity to continue to look for any useful reforms from that quarter? The work must be undertaken and executed by the British Parliament They alone are competent to it In no other way can a reasonable hope be entertained, either of effectually mitigating the rigours of colonial bondage, or of finally abolishing that opprobrious state of society

"It cannot be supposed, that, in the hands of the men who framed, and who boast of having framed, such enactments, the administration of the slave laws should manifest any remarkable traits of lenity and forbearance, or indicate any peculiar respect for Negro life or Negro comfort On the contrary the parliamentary papers exhibit many atrocious cases of judicial oppression, which have taken place in the colonies, and which may possibly become the subject of early parliamentary investigation If so, we trust they may lead to the institution of some adequate securities against the effects, on the lives and happiness of the Negro and Coloured races, of the blind and irrational alarms, and headstrong and ungovernable passions of the dominant party, who exclusively act as judges and jurors

"But of all the harsh features of the colonial slave laws, none is more revolting to every feeling of humanity and justice, than that which makes the very act of complaining a crime in the slave In him, even the murmurs of suffering nature must be suppressed We may see this lamentable perversion of all established principles of just legislation fully and strikingly illustrated in the recorded proceedings of the fiscal of Berbice who, at the same time, appears to be a person of a mild disposition.—Four Negroes, belonging to the Hon Mr Katz complained to the fiscal of harsh usage by the manager On the mere denial of the party accused, the fiscal punished three of the complainants with seventy-five lashes and one with fifty.—Again three Negroes belonging to General Murray late Governor of Demerara, complained to the fiscal of overwork, and want of food, and severity of treatment Two of them were selected by the fiscal to receive the torture of seventy five lashes each

"But it is needless to proceed Similar instances might be multiplied without end Nay the very laws of all the colonies provide that, in the case of a slave complaining of ill treatment the magistrate may if he deems the complaint unfounded, punish the complainant with the cart whip at his discretion And yet be it remembered that, as Negro evidence is not admitted in proof of the complaint, the complainant has no possible means, should the accused deny it, of establishing the most undoubted fact

'Since the publication of the abstract to which we have been hitherto referring another official document, of considerable importance has been made public namely, 'A Report on the Civil and Criminal Justice of the West Indies by the only surviving commissioner, Mr Dwarris, employed to inquire into that subject

"This gentleman, it appears, is the proprietor of a considerable sugar estate in Jamaica cultivated by about 220 slaves, and although we have no doubt that it was his purpose fairly to represent the case which he was employed to investigate yet we must lament that it should have been found necessary to select a person in his peculiar circumstances for this delicate and difficult task It surely never can be expedient to place any public functionary in a situation in which private interests, early prepossessions and the most cherished associations and attachments, may be found unavoidably to clash with the uncompromising claims of public duty If his Majesty's Ministers have felt it incumbent on them to determine that henceforward no governor or judge or fiscal or protector of slaves shall be the owner of a plantation cultivated by slaves, it surely is still more indispensable that the persons who are expressly delegated to inquire into the abuses of a particular system should not be chosen from the very class whose interests, as well as whose strongest prejudices, are deeply involved in its maintenance We have been almost involuntarily led to this reflection by the manifest anxiety which Mr Dwarris evinces to prevent his exposure, of the many evils in the judicial administration of the West Indies from producing an impression adverse to West-Indian planters, or to that system of Negro slavery which as planters, they are naturally solicitous to accredit

"The general view of the condition of the Negro slave which the commissioner has in this case gone out of his way to give is, without doubt, widely different from that which a consideration either of general principles or of the facts of the case, would permit any disinterested and unprejudiced individual to form.—' The poor slave,' he says, ' if left to himself, —But here in the very outset we must stop to remark, that ' a slave left to himself' is not we apprehend, a state of ordinary occurrence in West-Indian life A slave ' left to himself is in fact no slave — But ' left to himself' the Reporter informs us the poor slave is generally contented and happy Possessing a spot to which he is commonly attached —(we shall presently see by what tenure he holds this spot)—' Possessing a spot to which he is commonly attached, looking to his master (a master be it recollected, generally 4000 miles off whom he never sees, and cannot therefore look to but) looking to his master for support in health, care in sickness, and advice and help in distress and difficulty, the improvident

Negro, far from pining in misery, dances and sleeps, trifles and dreams away life thoughtless, careless, and happily ignorant of his own unprotected condition and of the impotent fury of the laws. This, be it remembered, refers more immediately to Barbadoes, the very colony where, a few years ago, hundreds of Negro lives were sacrificed with breathless dispatch, by the operation of laws which the Report represents as only *impotently* furious.—' A little more time and a little less work form,' adds the Reporter, ' the narrow boundary of the wants and wishes of the Negro.'—And what has reduced the Negro to this abject and brutish state of existence, a state which this gentleman strangely considers as a subject even of satisfactory contemplation?—But, supposing such a picture as this to be realized on the estates of a few of the few, resident planters, yet in what respects does it differ from that which might be given, by many an English gentleman, of his stud of horses, or of his kennel of hounds? The comforts and enjoyments of the Negro, on the shewing of this Report, are like those of the horse and the hound, exclusively of the animal kind. Are we then to shut out of our view that the Negro is a human being, born with the power of looking afore and after, possessing the capacities of thought, intelligence, reflection,—that he is endowed with desires, affections, cares, passions, responsibilities, and—may we dare to add—RIGHTS,—in common with ourselves? Shall we forget that the poor Negro was formed like his master in the image of God, has shared in the same moral ruin, has been redeemed by the same blood, and is an heir of the same immortality? If then the delineation of the Reporter were as generally true as it is notoriously the reverse, still, to level the Negro's highest enjoyments with those of the brutes that perish, to make his whole existence, its comfort and even its duration, to depend like theirs on the will, the caprice, the prudence, the health, or the life of another, to put it in the choice of that other not only to be himself the sole arbiter of the destinies of his slave, the food he shall eat, the clothes he shall wear, the labour he shall undergo, the stripes he shall receive, the indignities, nay the tortures, he shall suffer, but even to delegate these tremendous powers to third parties—what is all this but an impious usurpation, for which nothing can compensate, an insult to the Majesty of Heaven itself?

" Some idea of the wretched insecurity of the tenure by which slaves enjoy even the spot to which the Report tells us they are attached, together with all the dearest ties and charities of life, may be obtained from the case of a Mr Padmore, who was driven to the necessity (a necessity of common occurrence in the West Indies) of selling his estate to satisfy his creditors. 'The slaves, it is stated, he *could* have sold separately (detached from the estate) at a much higher rate, but they came to him in a body, with most distressing cries, and threw themselves on the ground before him, when a spokesman appointed by the rest fell down at his feet and implored him, in all their names, not to separate them both from himself and the estate. They were ready to follow him to the other end of the island, but if he could not retain them about himself, if his necessities compelled him to sell them, they besought him not to part friends and relations, husbands and wives, parents and children, not to tear them from their houses and gardens, but to let them go with the land. He could not resist such an appeal, and he lost at least forty pounds a head by it.' (p 22.) This occurrence says much, it is true, for the ruined individual who had the courage and the feeling to make this sacrifice;—but what does it say for the system? for that state of society, that state of law, which can for one moment tolerate and sanction such enormities? Even Mr Dwarris admits, that, by the law of Barbadoes, there is no express direction that families shall be sold together, nothing in any Act prohibiting the separation of husband and wife, parents and children. He endeavours however to palliate the effect of this statement by remarking, that many of our other islands had adopted with the best effect a humane provision to prevent the separation of families. In venturing to make this statement, in which however, we believe him to be mistaken, he ought at least to have named the islands in which such a provision has been adopted, especially as, in the case of the only two other islands, Tobago and Grenada, whose laws he speaks of, he himself distinctly tells us that ' unattached slaves are ordered to be sold one by one, except mother and child under twelve years of age.' (pp 81 and 103.) We find him indeed even becoming the apologist of the general principle of separating the slaves from the land, which destroys root and branch even that miserable semblance of property which a slave can be said to possess in his house and garden. However desirable it may appear, he observes ' to prevent the slave from being torn from his home and garden, it would be found very difficult, *consistently with a due regard to the interests of creditors* (the paramount consideration of course, in the minds of colonial legislators) 'to provide any remedy for the evil.' 'It would be unsuitable to a state of things in which the support of credit, and the security for borrowed capital form the *first* object of attention and even of legislative care and provision.'—The first objects of attention therefore are not human life and human comfort—at least in cases where the skin happens to be darkly tinged—but the security of credit and capital and that even in the estimate of this Report.—a Report which while it affords some curious illustrations of the regard paid to the Negro, as an article of the *master's* property one of *his* chattels one of *his available securities* exemplifies no less strikingly the utter disregard of all his *rights* and *feelings*, as a man as a rational and sentient being.

We shall say nothing of the scandalous abuse of those forfeitures to the Crown by means of escheats by which the name of the King is abused to purposes of oppression and wrong in a manner altogether unconstitutional as well as most disreputable, but let us take a view of the proceedings of what are called Slave Courts in Barbadoes.— In cases of capital offences by slaves, and these are very numerous, 'the court is composed of two justices and three freeholders of the neighbourhood of the place where the offence is committed. These five compose the court, and are all judges of the law and the fact. They are not appointed to meet at any fixed time, but only as occasion requires. When the court is assembled, no indictment is preferred or bill found by a grand jury. The magistrate before whom the complaint was made is taken to have decided that there is sufficient ground to put the slave on his trial and this magistrate sits upon the trial. The evidence may consist of the evidence of slaves, but not upon oath unless they have been baptized.

They are sometimes sworn on grave-dirt according to a superstition. A Negro's wife's evidence is admitted (against him) because it is in general a nominal and not a legal marriage. In the case of false evidence given by a slave, the justice or the court, before which the false evidence is given, directs the offender to be (forthwith) flogged. There is no regular record, the magistrates who try the case keep an account of the proceedings. These are not returned to any public office, and after the lapse of a few years it would be difficult to procure evidence to prove a former acquittal if a slave were to be apprehended a second time for the same offence, while neither the slave nor the master has any remedy for the malicious prosecution of the slave. If the five members of the court are agreed, a conviction takes place. Upon conviction *sentence of death must be passed.* An appeal may be brought *by the owner* (but by him only) to the governor and council. If there is no appeal, no copy of the trial is laid before the governor or report made to him or any other superior authority before the execution takes place. The warrant of execution is directed to the constable who attends the trial, and he executes it *without delay.* There is no fixed time or appointed place for the public execution of slave malefactors. That the owner may not be discouraged to detect and discover the offences of his Negroes a condemned slave is always appraised and the value paid to the owner out of the public treasury, but if the master has not duly provided for the support of the slave and necessity might have compelled the Negro to commit the offence the whole appraised value is to be paid to the party injured, and nothing to the master. And yet the execution of the slave may still proceed!' The trials of slaves in this island, the Report goes on to remark in duly measured terms, 'are very unsatisfactory.' We heard them pronounced disgraceful. 'The judges,' it is said, 'are ignorant, the proceedings are slovenly, the charge being unwritten shifts with the case. A disposition to favour, (and the Reporter might have added, a disposition to condemn,) where it exists receives no check from the want of publicity. There being no assigned place or appointed time for the execution of slave malefactors, the wretched convict *as soon as sentence is passed, is fastened to the nearest tree* unless, which frequently happens, the owner of the soil is at hand to prevent it. In such case, *the miserable culprit is dragged from tree to tree from estate to estate and in one case of then recent occurrence the constable was at last forced to throw the exhausted sufferer off the town bridge securing the rope by a lamp post.*

'Is it necessary to add a single word more to these sickening statements? Yet we cannot forbear touching upon another subject.—After the eulogy pronounced by Mr Dwarris on the general treat ment of the slaves in Barbadoes, the Meeting will scarcely be prepared for the following representations of the same gentleman in the very same Report

Slaves in this island he says are 'without legal protection or redress for personal injuries' The slave has no remedy in case of the greatest oppression by the master or his delegate or the grossest injury by third persons though the *master* (in case of his slave being assaulted or robbed) may have reparation in damages for *the loss of service* or *the injury to his property in the slave* The murder of a slave *wilfully maliciously wantonly and without provocation* is now a capital crime But there is no other legislative provision restraining the absolute power of the master over the slave, or inflicting punishment upon the owners or others, in case of mayhem, mutilation dismemberment or cruel treatment No other act of assembly has been framed for the protection of slaves no tribunal is specially appointed for inquiry into their wrongs A slave who is or thinks himself, aggrieved looks in vain in this island, for a proper quarter in which to prefer his complaint *It can no where be received* Murder is the only case in which the law interferes *For the punishment of general oppression and maltreatment of a slave there is no provision by any law of Barbadoes* If inflicted by the master it would be *dispunishable* If perpetrated by a third person the *owner* would have *his* remedy by civil action but the slave would still be without redress 'There is not,' in Barbadoes, any law regulating the quantum and kind of punishment, the hours of labour and rest the provision of food and (except nominally) of clothing These are dependent on the performance of moral duties, of which good men feel the obligation, but of which the breach is not cognizable before any earthly tribunal A wicked and cruel master or delegate (so that he do not kill or maim * a slave) may inflict on him ANY degree or severity of punishment *No man, or set of men has legal power to call him to account for working his slave as long as he likes for whipping him as much as he pleases for chaining for starving him A master has uncontrolled, undefined, and absolute power* Where, then asks Mr Dwarris very justly however inconsistently, ' where then, is the protection of the slave and where in case of accident,

To except maiming is inconsistent with the whole of Mr Dwarris's statement

the justification of the master? In a case even of very grievous bodily injury inflicted upon a slave by a manager, the sufferer himself, or his slave brethren who were present, cannot give evidence, even though all the free persons on the premises should have been *designedly* sent out of the way In such a case, a slave is not allowed to be a prosecutor *Maimed mutilated disfigured, dismembered* (I am putting says Mr Dwarris, the most aggravated case,) his wounds must be the only tongue permitted to relate his wrongs These however will speak for him here, if they do not speak for him in the colonies

But to proceed It is generally held says the Report, 'as a principle in slave colonies, that slaves cannot acquire property except for the benefit of their owners By law, they cannot, but only by indulgence p 111 Again, the slave has not any means of acquiring his freedom without the consent of the master There is no redemption of the slave in this island by force of law (nor in Tobago and Grenada, nor indeed in any of the islands,) and 'every Negro is presumed to be a slave, unless he can legally prove the contrary

"To much the same effect is the view given of the legal rights of slaves in Tobago and Grenada In the former island, the chief justice, Mr Pigott testifies as follows A manager sent all free persons out of the way, and then gave a Negro 150 lashes The Negro was brought, in a state of which he might have died to us, the sitting magistrates We had no means of proving it I proposed a bill to admit slave evidence or to make the accused purge himself on oath The bill was not approved The testimony of the attorney general of Tobago is to the same effect *I know* he says, ' *as a magistrate, cases of extreme cruelty that have passed unpunished for want of slave evidence It is very common when they wish to be cruel,* to send free persons out of the way *I have known many such cases* I think it a very common cause of discontent among the slaves, that, when they have been ill treated, and bring their fellow slaves as evidence, such witnesses cannot be received They go away with a feeling of injustice The same gentleman has since expressed an opinion that, by the *new* Tobago Act, ' the power of the master has been limited in almost every point essential to the well being and comfort of the slave This opinion only shews how easily some men may be satisfied with the shew of reform Lord Bathurst has wisely dis allowed the very act which the attorney-general thus commends

'The Report from Grenada, though varying in a few points is not more favourable than that from Tobago. Some of the Grenada laws are extremely harsh and even manifest what may be properly called a wantonness of severity. And as for the appointment of guardians of slaves, of which we have heard so loud a boast, it is admitted by the present report to be inefficacious. No independent men, we are expressly told, can be found to fill the situation, but it is filled by overseers or managers, who cannot be expected to denounce their employers; and 'in all cases between Black or Coloured persons and Whites, observes the attorney general 'the prejudice of juries is very strong in favour of Whites.'

"Neither in Tobago nor in Grenada are there any public institutions, by which infant or adult slaves are instructed in religious principles and useful knowledge. There are no Sunday schools. The Wesleyan Methodists alone have given any instruction to the slaves of these islands. In Barbadoes only one school is said to exist for Black or Coloured children though the Black and Coloured population is about 90,000.

"Such are some of the material *facts* brought to light in the most authentic form, by this recent report, in which, however, we must admit that many *opinions* are expressed which it is exceedingly difficult to reconcile with those facts, or indeed with the notorious realities of the case. Take an example.— Mr Dwarris states it to be the *only just ground of complaint against the present inhabitants of Barbadoes* that they had not repealed a certain act which inflicts the punishment of slitting the nose and burning the face with a hot iron, on a *Negro* who strikes *a Christian* a second time. But when Mr Dwarris thus sweepingly cleared the Barbadians from every other charge, had he not yet heard of the atrocities of 1804 reported by Lord Seaforth? of the wholesale massacres of slaves in 1816? of the destruction of the Methodist chapel and the expulsion of the Missionary in 1823? or of their new slave law of 1824? And is it not this very gentleman whose report of the Barbadoes slave courts, and of the summary and brutal executions of their convicts, and of the unprotected state of the whole slave population is of so sickening a kind? How are we to explain such strange incongruities as these?

But it would require far too detailed a statement, were we to go through all the inconsistencies and incorrectnesses which might be pointed out in this, in some respects invaluable Report. On the whole, however we are extremely thankful for its appearance and we cannot doubt that it will do much to open the eyes of the public to the multiplied abominations of this unchristian and merciless system.

'Never however, let the people of England forget, that of this unchristian and merciless system they will continue to be the criminal upholders if they now refrain from lifting up their voice against it or if they silently acquiesce in contributing as they now do largely and directly to its support. On this part of the subject however we mean not now to enlarge. In the Second Report of the Society the question of bounties and protecting duties was amply discussed and not only their impolicy but their malign and wasting influence on the happiness and increase of the slave population, as well as their pernicious effects even on the interests of the masters, were fully, and as we believe most incontrovertibly established. We will therefore now content ourselves with remarking that it is absolutely vain for us to be hoping to succeed in abolishing slavery, or to expect that by the vehemence of our speeches, or by the strength of our resolutions, or even by the severity of our enactments we shall be able very materially to abate this evil, if we continue as we now do, to extend to the slave holder those solid marks of our favour which are conveyed to him in bounties and protecting duties thus supplying to him the very means of maintaining his iniquitous system against the united wishes of the parliament and people of England.

"And now, after the statement which has just been given, combined with all our previous information, are we not entitled to call upon the people of England to come forward to strengthen the hands of the government, in the righteous work of carrying into effect the hitherto abortive resolutions of Parliament on the subject of Colonial Slavery? We call upon them therefore to assemble in every county, and city and town and even village of the United Kingdom in order to testify their abhorrence of this impious system and to implore of the Legislature respectfully indeed, but most earnestly, to relieve them from its guilt and its burden. Let no man in this free and happy country, where the voice of the very manner has its appropriate weight in Parliament, imagine that he can discharge himself from the performance of this solemn duty or—should his application to Parliament fail of its effect—from adopting every other expedient in his power, such as abstinence from slave-grown sugar, the promotion of cultivation by free labour, &c. for wiping away this foul stain from the national character. And we would address this call to men of all political parties in the state. Those of every party who have sympathized with the victims of despotism in Spain, in Italy and in Greece have now an opportunity of combining to deliver 830,000 of their own fellow subjects from a still more grievous despotism. The friends of the Government are bound to see its orders respected, and to repress that insubordinate and contumelious spirit in the colonists which would set them at nought. The members of the Opposition are bound by all their professed principles to unite heart and hand in undoing the fetters of our own fellow subjects. Above all (to avail ourselves of the language of one of the ablest advocates of this cause)—above all, we would call on Christians of every name to come forward to lend their aid as one man to deliver their country from this great national iniquity—to reform this cruel and impious system which shuts out the light of the Gospel, which violates in the grossest manner all its precepts, which keeps, in a cruel thraldom, the minds as well as bodies of its unfortunate victims, and which adds to its other enormities the fierceness of antichristian persecution. There would surely be an inconsistency in the charitable efforts now making to convert our fellow creatures in the most distant regions of the globe, while we suffer our fellow subjects to be kept in pagan darkness, and the vilest moral degradation, not by choice but by compulsion, through a domestic tyranny, which our own power within our own territories, alone upholds. To all then we would say, in conclusion, in the words of the same eloquent writer, ' Come forward with your petitions. Instruct your representatives. Give or withhold your suffrages for the next Parliament, and use your personal influence throughout the country, all in such a manner as may best promote the success of this great and sacred cause. If you succeed, you will give a new triumph to the British Constitution. You will exalt the glory of your country in that best point, her moral elevation, and recommend her to the favour of Heaven. If you fail, you will at least have the inestimable consolation that you have done what you could ' to undo the heavy burden, and to let the oppressed go free, and that the sins and calamities of your country, however pernicious in their consequences to yourselves or your children, were evils which you could not avert.'

"One word more. we rejoice to be able to report that the number of associations, and especially of Ladies associations for the abolition of slavery, has been increasing of late. We trust that they will be largely multiplied both in the metropolis and in the country at large.

The present meeting for the purpose of petitioning Parliament has, we are also happy to say, been anticipated in several places by the impulse of that popular feeling which furnishes the best pledge of our ultimate success. In this important line of service Norfolk has taken the lead, and has been followed by the city of Norwich, by Birmingham, by Hull, by Beverley, by Derby, and by Ipswich; as it had been preceded, though not for the express purpose of petitioning, by Edinburgh. In all these places our cause has been advocated with remarkable power and effect, and has happily united the general suffrage. The Corporation of the City of London has signalized itself by its zeal in the same cause, and we are anxious to record the high sense we entertain of the advantage which has accrued from the nearly unanimous and energetic declaration of the chief authorities of the first commercial city in the world, against the principle of colonial monopoly, and in favour of the claims of injured and outraged humanity. The influence of their high example will, we trust, induce the mercantile and manufacturing classes throughout the kingdom to come forward to vindicate the commercial character of this country from the discredit, and its commercial interests from the injury, caused by the prolongation of the existing colonial evils.

' It would be ingratitude in this connexion to withhold our warm acknowledgments of the great services which have been rendered to our common cause, since we last met, by the able, zealous, indefatigable and successful efforts of Mr Cropper of Liverpool.

These various indications of the general sympathy in our labours are strong incentives to perseverance. And we must all feel it as not among the least cheering and encouraging circumstances, which we are called to acknowledge with gratitude to the Giver of all good, that we should once more behold among us, and in the chair of this assembly that loved and revered individual dear to all to whom the interests of humanity are dear who, having consecrated the strength and flower of his days to the vindication of the wronged and degraded African, and having at length signally triumphed in the protracted and painful conflict now, though bending under the weight of added years, still marshals our way, as we trust to victory, in a no less arduous struggle—in the endeavour to break the yoke of the oppressor and to achieve the rescue of the oppressed, in every corner of the British dominions May it please God to spare him to witness the final consummation of this labour of love and mercy!'

The resolutions unanimously adopted, were to the following effect —

That, highly approving of the resolutions moved by Mr Canning in 1823, and of the subsequent efforts of Government to reform Colonial Slavery, they deeply lamented that the opposition of the colonial authorities had hitherto succeeded in almost wholly frustrating their benevolent efforts That the additional and incontestible evidence received from the colonies, fully confirms the injustice and cruelty of the slavery prevailing there, and the hopelessness of its extinction, or even of its effectual mitigation, without the direct interference of the Imperial Legislature That the Colonial Legislatures had either treated the wishes of Parliament, and the recommendations of his Majesty's Government with neglect or met them with decided opposition and that even where attempts have been made to frame an ameliorated slave code, the new enactments manifest the same disregard of justice with the old that the existing laws afford no effectual protection to the slaves, and have been made, on recent occasions, an instrument of the most grievous judicial oppression and that the general treatment of the slaves continues to exhibit the same harsh and disgusting effects of domestic despotism which first excited the indignant feelings of the British public, and which should now lead to a fixed determination, on the part of every individual who values British freedom, or the blessings of Christianity, to do his utmost to prevent their continuance That they are convinced that this unjust and immoral system derives great support from bounties and protecting duties on the produce of Slave Labour, enhancing its price, increasing the miseries of the slaves and rendering their liberation more difficult That, if called upon to contribute to the same amount, for the purpose of extinguishing slavery which they now pay for its support they would cheerfully obey the call but that to the existing regulations they entertain insuperable objections because while those regulations violate the principles of sound policy, and impose on the nation a heavy burden for the maintenance of slavery they serve to aggravate and perpetuate its evils and they involve the people of this country still more deeply in the guilt of upholding it That they hold it to be their bounden duty, and that of every individual who acknowledges the claims of humanity and justice, to lose no time in petitioning both Houses of Parliament, to take the work of colonial reformation into their own hands and in accordance with their own resolutions, and the wishes and prayers of the nation at large, to bring slavery itself to the earliest practicable termination in every part of his Majesty's dominions

A Petition to both Houses of Parliament, grounded on the above Resolutions, was adopted and his Royal Highness the Duke of Gloucester was respectfully requested to present the petition to the House of Lords and Mr Fowell Buxton that to the Commons

The meeting embraced the opportunity of presenting their heartfelt acknowledgments to their revered Vice President, William Wilberforce, Esq, for his gratifying attendance and of testifying their deep sense of the services, which, during a long and arduous parliamentary life, he had rendered to his country and to the world at large and especially of that indefatigable, but tempered zeal, with which he had so unceasingly and successfully consecrated his powerful talents and fascinating eloquence to the vindication and relief of suffering humanity

ECCLESIASTICAL PREFERMENTS

Rev F Lockey Blackford P C parish of Wedmore co Somerset

Rev H V Rishes M A Hill Bishops P C vice Codrington dec

Rev Alex Nivison to the Church and Parish of Roberton Presb and co of Selkirk vice Hay dec

Rev C A Sage St Peter Brackley V co Northampton

Rev S Lloyd Horseley V co Glouc

Rev F Woodforde Weston Banfylde R. Somerset

Rev Jas Hooke LL D Deanery of Worcester

Rev J D Coleridge a Prebend in Exeter Cathedral

Rev J Lonsdale a Prebend of Lincoln Cathedral

Rev T Gaisford 2d Prebend of Worcester Cathedral

Rev G S Evans Temple Crafton V co Warwick

Rev J Gordon Bierton V co Lincoln

Rev H Hubbard Cheriton R Hants with Kilmaston and Tichbourne Chs annexed

Rev Wm James East Sambrook R co Som

Rev J Johnson Houghton V Notts

Rev Wm Marsh Gwenap V Cornwall

Rev J B May St Martin R. Exeter

Rev R B Paul Long Whitenham V Berks

Rev Sam Paul Tetbury V co Glouc

Rev G S Penfold Christchurch R St Mary le bone

Rev B Puckle Graffham R Hunts

Rev Wm Pyne Pitney R co Somerset

Rev C T Simmons Shipham R co Somerset

Rev G W Smith Bawdsey V Suff

Rev H Strangways Rowe V Devon

Rev C Tripp D D Kentisbeare R Devon

Rev E W Wakeman Claines C co Worc

Rev A Ward Eastrington V co York

Rev G H Webster All Saints with St Julian R Norwich

Rev Jos Algar Chaplain to Lord Clinton

Rev Thos Douglas Hodgson East Woodhay R Hants vice Herbert

Rev Sam Lee Professor of Arabic in the University of Cambridge to the Perp Cur of Bilton with Harrogate vice Mitton

Rev James Thomas Matthews Priors Lee Perp Cur Salop

Rev Mr Oakley the valuable stall of Wenlock Barns in St Paul s Cathedral vice Parr deceased

Rev T C Percival Horseheath R Camb

Rev J Sergeant, Doddington V Northamptonshire

Rev H G Talbot, Mitchell Troy cum Cymearvan R Monmouthsh vice Tomkins

Rev G Wood Holy Trinity R. Dorchester with that of Cam St Rumbold.

Rev Richard Meredith Curate of Hagborn Berks domestic Chaplain to the Earl of Rock Savage

Rev Edwin J Parker Dom Chap to Lord Braybrooke.

Rev C Taylor D D, Head Master of the College School Hereford, to the Chancellorship of the Diocese vice Rudge

Hon and Rev Hugh Percy Dean of Canterbury Cathedral vice Andrews dec

Rev J Timbrell D D Archd of Glouc with Dursley R vice Rudge

Rev Geo Vanburgh Rector of Aughton Prebendary in Wells Cathedral

Rev John Booker Killurm V diocese of Ferns vice Travers res

Rev T Brooke Wistaston R Cheshire

Rev J W Butt Southerey R Norfolk

Rev J Hutchins Telscomb R. and Piddinghoe V Sussex vice his father

Rev J Ion Hemingbrough V Yorkshire

Rev Rich Johnson Lavenham R Suffolk

Rev T Mackereth Halton R Lanc

Rev J Mavor Hadley R. Essex

Rev R Montgomery Holcot R. Northamptonshire

Hon and Rev Ed Pellew Christowe V Devon

Rev J Richards Wedmore V Somersetshire vice Richards deceased

Rev J Roby Austrey V Warwickshire

Rev R Smith First Minister of the Church of Montrose vice Molleson, deceased

Rev H Thursby Isham Inferior R North

Rev J Rudge D D F R S to be Chaplain to the Duke of York

Rev Wm C Wilson Whittington R Lanc

Rev Samuel Paynter of Trinity College Cambridge to the Rectory of Hatferd Berks

Dr John Banks Jenkinson Dean of Worcester promoted to the See of St David s

Rev Chas Pilkington Prebendary of Eartham in the Cathedral of Chichester a Canon Residentiary of that Cathedral, vice Toghill

Rev W Hewson Chancellor and Canon Residentiary of the Cathedral Church of St David s

Rev W Barter Burghclere and Newtown RR Hants

Rev E G A Beckwith to be a Minor Canon of Westminster Abbey

Rev T Clarkson Acton Scott R. Salop

Rev Rob Cobb, Burmash R Kent, vice Carpenter

Rev G Coke Marston and Pencoed CC. co Hereford

Rev Gaven Cullen Balmaclellan Church in Presbytery of Kircudbright.

Rev Chas Champnes St George s and St Botolph Billingsgate RR London

Rev D Clementson Chap to Doch Goal

Rev J Hodge, Bolnhurst R co Beds

Rev W H Dixon Chaplain to Abp of York

Rev P Gurdon, Chaplain to Lord Bayning

Rev C. D Wray Chaplain to Lord Balcarras

Rev J Hill Archdeacon of Bucks

Rev R Cockburn a Prebend of Winchester Cathedral

Rev J Allport Atherstone P C Warwickshire

Rev J H J Chichester Loxhore R co Devon

Rev E Hardman Wesport C Ireland

Rev J Jervois Ballinadee R Ireland

Rev F C Johnson Whitelackington V co Som

Rev W Johnson Bilsby V co Lincoln

Rev J Knight Huish R co Devon

Rev Mr Knox, Ballimodan V Ireland

Rev R. H Leeke Longford R Salop

Rev W Moore Spalding P C co Linc

Rev D Nantes Powderham R Devon

Rev H E. Head Bromfield P C Kent

Rev R Pretyman Alverstoke and Havant RR. Hants

Rev J Stewart, Lislee R co Cork

Rev S Barker Chapl to the Duke of York.

Rev H Jones Northop V Flintshire

Rev Thos Dixon Tibbenham V Norfolk

Rev R F Elwin St Margrave of Westwick R. Norwich

Rev T Frere Burston R. Norfolk

Rev T Guy Howden V Yorkshire

Rev R Greenside Seamer P C Yorksh

Rev D Arcy Haggit St Andrew V in Pershore with the Chapels of Holy Cross &c annexed co Worcester

Rev W Ives Caddington V Bedfordshire

Rev T A Melhuish St Mary Steps R Exeter

Rev Geo Millers Hardwicke R Cambridge vice Millers res

Rev Henry Morgan Withington P C Salop

Rev T G Roberts Dolgellan R Merionethshire

Rev O Sergeant St Philip s Salford

Rev E B Shaw St Matthew s Manchester

Rev W Tanner Bolnhurst and Colnworth RR Bedfordshire,

Rev Wm Twigg M.A Pickhall V Yorks

DISPENSATIONS.

Rev Charles Turnor M A prebendary of Lincoln to hold Milton Ernest V Bedfordshire, with Wendover V Bucks

Rev R Roberts D D to hold Wadenhoe R with Barnwell All Saints and St Andrew RR. co Northampton

Rev M W Wilkinson to hold Harescombe cum Pitchcombe R with Uley R co Gloucester

Rev A Stapleton to hold Halwill R with that of East Budleigh Devon

Rev C S Miller Vicar of Harlow Essex, to hold the living of Matching, Essex

ANSWERS TO CORRESPONDENTS

CORNUBIENSIS Μικρος, W M X Y Z S J S A Ομικρο T D E M B C L. are under consideration

If CLERICUS had made due inquiries he would have found that the demand he mentions was not exorbitant Is he aware that one third goes to Government?

In reply to several inquirers respecting the Index to our first twenty volumes we have to express our great regret, that, from circumstances which we could not control it should have been so long delayed It is however now in a course of revision and we have reason to hope will be ready for press in the month of March We have before stated that it will be numbered Vol XXI for the convenience of making the numeral of our volumes and the unit of the date of the year correspond The volumes from 1821 have been thus numbered. This will solve T M s query

A friend in announcing to us a new edition of Mrs H More s Hints on the Education of a Princess expresses regret that this admirable work should be less known than perhaps any other of the revered author s publications which may have arisen from an idea that it was applicable only to royal female education Except however in a very few particulars it is equally adapted for general education male and female in the middle and higher walks of life and we strongly recommend those of our readers who value the author s [other works especially Christian parents, to add this highly useful and interesting publication to their collection

ERRATUM

Page 724, col 1 lines 40, 41 for All saints read All souls

APPENDIX

TO THE

CHRISTIAN OBSERVER,

VOLUME THE TWENTY FIFTH

FOR 1825

RELIGIOUS COMMUNICATIONS

MANKIND RESPONSIBLE FOR THEIR RELIGIOUS OPINIONS

(Concluded from p. 731.)

HAVING considered in my last paper the powerful effect of unholiness of heart and life in depraving the judgment on religious subjects, I proceed secondly, to shew, that a humble and conscientious endeavour to *do the will of God* is eminently conducive to the progress both of faith and spiritual understanding.

In pursuing this second line of the discussion, we need only employ the converse of the arguments urged under the first with a view to shew that an ingenuous obedience to the will of God is conducive to a right judgment in matters of faith, First, because it supposes conscientious application to the subject Secondly, because it shews a suitable preparation for instruction and, Thirdly because God will not withhold from the humble and conscientious inquirer the secret guidance of his Holy Spirit, by whose aid alone we can ' have a right judgment in all things,' or in any thing necessary to our salvation.

And, first it is a very important advance towards a correct understanding in religion, when the mind is honestly *disposed for serious investigation*. The Bereans " searched the Scriptures daily whether the things which were told them by the Apostles were so ' and " *therefore* many of them believed" While the heart is enslaved by sin, there can be no taste for the practical study of the word of God religion, of all subjects, is least likely to attract suitable attention and hence, the very circumstance of entering upon those inquiries which concern our eternal destination, with a seriousness and zeal proportioned to their importance, is always an auspicious symptom.

Nor can we doubt that a cordial desire to do the will of God *will* thus lead to diligence in investigating it. In human society, a sincere wish on the part of an individual to oblige a friend whom he respects and loves, or to conform to the rules of an institution to which he has voluntarily attached himself, naturally induces him to make diligent inquiry into the means of so doing in order that he may not offend by negligence or ignorance those whom he would not alienate by wilful misconduct. A similar effect takes place in religion so that a conscientious wish to do the will of God will not only operate in a constant endeavour to perform his commands, *so far as they are hitherto understood*, but it will also, under the guidance of his Holy Spirit, operate *still farther*, in leading to such a devout study of the word of God such earnest prayer for his blessing and direction, and such a diligent use of every means of instruction, as can not but issue in a competency of knowledge and faith, as well as of practical obedience.

Again this desire to obey the known commands of God, is of essential service to a right knowledge in matters of faith, because it indicates a suitable *preparation of mind* for coming to the knowledge of the Divine will. We have already seen how fatal an influence is exerted, not only by habits of gross vice but by every unholy thought and temper, in blinding the judgment as well as hardening the heart. In like manner on the other hand, every incipient desire to obey the commands of God, opens the way for new accessions of faith and spiritual information. It was a wise and truly religious, though but apocryphal, apophthegm, 'he that keepeth the law of the Lord getteth the understanding thereof and the perfection of the fear of the Lord is wisdom' (Ecclus xxi. 11.) The *sacred* text is equally explicit. 'The fear of the Lord is the beginning of wisdom a good understanding have all they that do his commandments.' 'With *the heart* man believeth unto righteousness.' 'He that doeth the will of God, shall know of the doctrine.'

The fact, thus scripturally asserted, is conformable to what we might naturally expect from a due consideration of the circumstances of the case. For, in the first place, a person who advances to the study of the sacred oracles with a humble determination to obey the will of God avoids most of those *sources of error* which have been mentioned in a former part of these remarks. Not having any wish to render his religious scheme subservient to the indulgence of "the lusts of the flesh, the lust of the eye, or the pride of life," he is not biassed by a false self-interest to explain away to his own conscience the awful declarations of the word of God relative to sin and sinners. His researches not being conducted with a view to any sinister or merely secondary object, he is not tempted "to wrest the Scriptures to his own condemnation." His paramount desire being to know the mind, and to obey the commands, of God, he will be content, in simplicity and godly sincerity, to follow wherever the Scriptures of truth may lead. His moral endowments, his humility, his integrity, his fear of error, his love of truth, will prove a constant panoply to guard him from the insidious wiles of his spiritual enemy, and from the suggestions of those evil minded men whose quarrel with the Gospel is more an affair of the heart than of the understanding.

The parable of the Sower affords an interesting illustration of the foregoing remarks. The seed sowed was but of one sort; the hand that sowed the different portions of it was the same; yet in some instances it sprang up and bore fruit abundantly, while in others it was either devoured by the fowls of the air, or withered away after a short and unserviceable shew of vegetation. Whence arose the difference in these cases? The narrative itself informs us. In the former, it was sown in 'an honest and good heart'—a heart prepared by the Holy Spirit, through penitence, faith, humility, and an earnest wish to obey the will of God, for its reception: while in the latter, it fell either upon a superficial or a rocky soil, or among briars and thorns,—the cares of the world and the deceitfulness of riches, which choked it, so that it brought forth no fruit to perfection.

The third and chief reason why a humble and ingenuous inquirer will attain to a right understanding in religion, while those whose immorality of heart or life proves their practical indifference to the subject are left to the natural blindness of the human understanding, is intimated in that inspired promise "The meek will He guide in judgment; the meek will He teach his way." It is not enough that there be diligence in study; it is not even enough that the heart be in a state of preparation: for in addition to this, the Divine blessing and guidance are still requisite to prevent our being deluded by plausible error or misconception. Not only must the organ of vision be opened and turned towards the object, but there must be light from above in order to discern it. And hence we are taught, both in Scripture and by our church to pray for the illuminating influences of the Holy Spirit; not indeed the sensible impulses claimed by the enthusiast, but that ordinary and unseen agency by which God is pleased to "work in us both to will and to do of his good pleasure." This sacred guidance is promised to all who diligently seek it; so that to every Christian we may apply, at least subordinately the words of the Apostle, "We have received not the spirit of the world, but the spirit which is of God, that we might know the things that are freely given to us of God." "Ye have an unction from the Holy One, and know all things."

The narrative of Cornelius, the Roman centurion, furnishes a striking corroboration of the preceding arguments. He is described as "a devout man, one that feared God with all his house, who gave much alms to the people, and prayed to God alway." Conscientious in his character, and doubtless guided, though unknown to himself, by the secret influences of the Holy Spirit, he endeavoured to act up to his imperfect knowledge of the Divine will, at the same time earnestly wishing for a clearer discovery of it than he had hitherto enjoyed, or than his profession and opportunities of instruction seemed likely to afford. Thus devoutly disposed, he was keeping a solemn fast, and was occupied in prayer at the hour of the evening sacrifice, when an angel was divinely commissioned to appear to him, and to direct him in what manner to obtain those instructions which issued in his plenary information and baptism into the faith of Christ.

The case of the Ethiopian Eunuch is somewhat analogous. He evinced his sincere desire to obey the will of God, and his preparation of heart to receive the doctrine of the Gospel, by taking a long journey in order to worship at Jerusalem; by diligently perusing the holy Scriptures "which were able to make him wise to salvation;" and by gladly accepting the proffered instructions of Philip, who had been expressly commissioned by an angel to meet him on his way.

In both these instances we see the promises before cited of Divine guidance to the humble and obedient inquirer, fulfilled not only in a very remarkable but even a miraculous manner: yet the very circumstances which exclude these cases from the rank of ordinary precedents, prove most forcibly the general truth under consideration; for we find from these narratives, that sooner than a heart prepared and disposed to receive religious instruction should be left finally destitute of it, an angel was commissioned from Heaven and an apostle or other special messenger appointed to convey the necessary intelligence.

The circumstances of these two memorable instances will further supply a satisfactory answer to some of the chief objections which may possibly be alleged against the views contained in the preceding pages.

Should it be urged, for example, on the one hand, by a mere systematic doctrinalist, that an endeavour, however ingenuous, to obey the commands of God, while there remains great doctrinal ignorance in the mind, is not likely to lead beyond formalism or pharisaism; nay, is even less favourable to a humble reception of the Gospel, than a state of allowed vice: these remarkable instances, in which the Almighty was pleased to honour such a teachable disposition of mind with peculiar approbation, and to gratify the desires of these penitent inquirers by miraculously sending to them the knowledge of the truth, will prove the fallacy of so unscriptural an hypothesis. The case of the Scribes and Pharisees, of whom our Lord said that publicans and sinners should enter the kingdom of God before them, was of a very different kind. In those haughty self-justiciaries there was no disposition conscientiously to perform even the ordinary duties of morality: they subverted the Divine Law by vain traditions and superstitions; and, far from exhibiting any tenderness of conscience, any disposition to practise what they already knew, and to look humbly for further instruction, they were perfectly contented with their own attainments, and even made use of their knowledge in order to relax, by disingenuous glosses, the obligations of the system which they professed. It is obvious that such characters possessed nothing in common with the devout and diffident inquirer to whom exclusively the promises of Divine illumination are made.

Or should it be urged, on the other hand, by a far more numerous class of objectors, that moral conduct is all that is necessary for human salvation; should it be said in contradiction to the declarations of Scripture, and the language of our established church, that "every man shall be saved by the law or sect which he professeth, so that he be diligent to frame his life according to that law, and the light of nature"; we have here two remarkable cases in which God saw fit in a most conspicuous manner to evince the necessity of Divine revelation in general, and particularly of faith in the atonement of our Lord Jesus Christ*, and the other distinguishing doctrines of the Gospel, by sending chosen servants expressly to instruct Cornelius and the Ethiopian Eunuch in points of this nature, notwithstanding their previous devoutness and moral deportment.

In short, should it be argued, that, upon the hypothesis which it has been the object of these pages to enforce, any point of Christian faith or practice is rendered unnecessary, we may confidently appeal to the two examples under consideration to prove the contrary. Should it be doubted, for example, whether an ingenuous desire to obey the will of God, even before we are fully acquainted with it, is an important and characteristic mark of incipient conversion, we may adduce the history of Cornelius and the Ethiopian Eunuch, to shew how conspicuous a place such a disposition occupied in the first stages of *their* religious inquiries. Or should it be urged, that if practical obedience be of so much importance, there is no great necessity for prayer or sacred study, the objector may be reminded that it was while the Roman Centurion was fasting and praying, and the Ethiopian Treasurer was diligently reading the Scriptures, that God was pleased to mark his approval of their conduct by sending to them the means of further instruction. Or should it be objected that the preceding remarks would reduce religion to mere ingenuousness of principle, thus superceding the necessity for correctness of religious doctrine and faith, these very narratives teach quite a different lesson: for Philip expressly said, " *If thou believest with all thine heart, thou mayest be baptized*. and he answered and said,

* The doctrine of the atonement and the chief points connected with the person and offices of the Divine Surety seem to have been the especial subject of Philip's conversation with the Eunuch: for it is said, The place of the Scripture which he read was this: He was led as a sheep to the slaughter, and like a lamb dumb before his shearers, so opened he not his mouth: in his humiliation his judgment was taken away: and who shall declare his generation? for his life was taken from the earth. Then Philip opened his mouth, and began at the same Scripture, and preached unto him Jesus:—doubtless in the capacity in which this and other prophets represented him, as a sacrifice for the sins of the world.

I believe that Jesus Christ is the Son of God." And lastly, should it be urged that if practical obedience has such a tendency to lead to scriptural knowledge, the agency of the Holy Spirit is rendered unnecessary, it is obvious to reply from the same narratives, that it was the Holy Spirit who, unseen by mortal eyes, implanted and fostered the rising graces of Cornelius and the Ethiopian Eunuch, who further provided the means for their instruction, who opened their hearts to receive it, and who is expressly mentioned as having been present by his Divine influences with both these devout men at their baptism thus shewing throughout the whole process of their conversion the need of his own all powerful agency, even while he saw fit to employ the ordinary means of prayer, and fasting, and preparatory dispositions and the study of the Scriptures, and the Christian ministry and sacraments, to effect his gracious purposes

While thus alluding to some of the principal arguments which may be urged against the main propositions which have been attempted to be established it may be well to advert to another objection which at first sight appears somewhat plausible namely, that, in point of fact, we often find, in the current phrase, ' a weak head joined with an honest heart so that the doctrine contended for cannot be generally true To this it is only necessary to reply, that we have no sufficient proof of the alleged fact that an ingenuous desire to know God, and to obey his will, is not *always* able in due time, by means of the appointed assistances and means of grace, to overcome any obstacles which may arise from want of vigour of understanding provided, of course, the inaptitude be not of such an extent as to render the individual incapable of exercising the ordinary mental functions of a rational and responsible agent Indeed, we not unfrequently observe persons of very confined intellect, and with but feeble means of instruction, acquainted, in a surprising degree, with religious subjects, and able both to reason and to act in spiritual concerns with a propriety which ought to put to the blush many learned and intellectual, but only nominal, Christians Besides all which, we must never forget to add the promised assistance of God s Holy Spirit, who will not suffer those who humbly and diligently seek instruction, to perish for want of it. " If thou incline thine ear unto wisdom, and apply thy heart to understanding if thou seekest her as silver, and searchest for her as for hid treasures, then shalt thou understand the fear of the Lord, and find the knowledge of God for *the Lord giveth wisdom and out of his mouth* cometh knowledge and understanding Such is the Divine promise and sooner than it shall fail, a Peter shall be sent to instruct a Cornelius or a Philip be commissioned to seek out a remote Ethiopian stranger And if such miraculous interpositions are not to be expected in our own day (as of course they are not,) it is only because they are no longer necessary for the fulfilment of the Divine promises The Almighty can and will render the ordinary means of grace, by the blessing of his Holy Spirit, amply sufficient for the instruction of all who are really solicitous to learn Their progress in Divine knowledge may, in many cases, be slow and their views, after all their efforts, may never become very expansive or elevated but of thus much we may rest assured, that they shall be preserved from every essential error, and " be kept by the power of God through faith unto salvation in that narrow road which leadeth to life everlasting " A highway shall be there and a way, and it shall be called the Way of Holiness the unclean shall not pass over it but the way faring men though fools, shall not err therein It is not necessary to salvation to be initi mately acquainted with every topic even in theology much less is it essential for our knowledge to be collected at the first glance by the intuitive sagacity of a perspicacious intellect. The most humble and teachable penitent may for a considerable time find his mind distressed or disturbed he may wander long in doubt or difficulty but he shall not wander fatally or finally Implicit self dedication to God prayer for the Divine direction avoiding pride, obstinacy, and levity on sacred subjects and conscientiously seeking every opportunity of instruction, constitute a far surer road to Christian knowledge, as well as to faith, than the laborious triflings of a powerful but self sufficient understanding

Another objection which may be anticipated to the position laid down in these pages, and the last to which we shall allude, is, that the doctrine contended for is unfortunately too well founded for that in truth the devout admission of the peculiarities of Christianity is only a pious prejudice and that such a state of mind as has been described is therefore a very suitable preparation for it The infidel notoriously urges this argument and many who assume to themselves the title of rational Christians occasionally employ it, at least in a modified form 'What connexion it is asked 'can moral sensations have with intellectual verities? If a man is not likely thoroughly to understand and believe the Gospel till he is prepared to obey it is it not a proof that prepossession rather than argument effected his conversion? Ought not every doctrine professing to come from God to carry with it such irresistible evidence that a man *must* understand and believe it whatever may be his secret wishes, or however strong his natural prejudices?—To this it may be fairly replied, that Christianity *is* demonstrable—irrefragably demonstrable—by argument a point on which it is surely not necessary here to enlarge after the many invaluable treatises which have appeared on the subject But however demonstrable Christianity, or any of its peculiar doctrines, may be proved to be, still moral, and indeed spiritual, dispositions are required for investigating its claims for where such dispositions do not exist, there will not even be the taste or capacity for such an investigation any more than a person destitute of musical perceptions would be likely voluntarily, and for no purpose, to devote himself to the study of Handel, or a man singularly averse to mathematical reasoning to the Principia of Newton It is not therefore derogating from the demonstrable character of the Gospel, to admit that though its Divine Author *might* doubtless have rendered its evidences irresistible, even to the most careless or hardened opponent, he has seen fit to connect the whole of Revelation with a system of moral discipline, and to render an obedient heart the surest guide to a perception of its character and evidences In truth we may fairly contend that had the Gospel been a system appealing merely to abstract reasoning and as susceptible of being correctly estimated by a proud and vicious, as by a humble and dutiful inquirer, it would have lost one of its strongest evidences namely, its wonderful adaptation to the actual habits of mankind, whose reasonings are almost in every instance strongly affected by their personal character and feelings and who could never have been induced, without a direct miracle, generally to embrace Christianity even as a system, had it been presented to them in the aspect which the advocates for abstract reasoning unconnected with moral obedience contend that it ought to have assumed

But this is a large field, into which it is impracticable in the present papers to enter Let it suffice to have suggested the topic for the consideration of those who have not duly reflected upon the eminent wisdom displayed in the divinely appointed connexion between Christian faith, Christian knowledge, and Christian obedience or who may have thought the arguments for the Gospel weakened rather than strengthened by this union of appeal to the heart and the understanding. It may be consoling also to the diffident Christian who perhaps finds his faith sometimes endangered, when he hears of persons of alleged powerful minds and great attainments rejecting the Gospel, or any of its essential peculiarities to reflect that they could never have examined into its claims and character aright for that, even if they applied their intellect to the investigation, they were deficient in those teachable dispositions those conscientious efforts to obey the known will of God and those earnest aspirations for the instructions of his Holy Spirit which the all wise Founder of Christianity has rendered absolutely necessary for appreciating its merits a circumstance quite consistent with our views of the character of God, and in full accordance with the fact of mankind being in a state of spiritual discipline and probation

Where is there to be found a deliberate infidel, or a confirmed advocate for any grossly heterodox doctrine, who, by the union of a spirit of prayer and devotion of reverential fear of God a conscientious dread of misinterpreting any alleged statement of his will, a humble distrust of his own judgment and a determination not to be swayed by his passions or preconceived opinions, is really qualified to decide upon the doctrines of holy writ? But how stands the case with such an inquirer as has been before described? Does he hear of mysteries in religion? He knows that the world is full of mysteries and he is too well assured of the unsearchableness of God, and the narrow limits of his own understanding to view the mysteries of the Gospel, as a just obstacle to his belief indeed, he would rather be inclined to distrust a professedly Divine Revelation which should contain nothing beyond what was fathomable by the feeble powers of a short-lived and imperfect being like himself. It does not therefore shock his mind to believe, that though there is but "one living and true God, yet that "in the unity of this Godhead there be three persons of one substance, power and eternity,—the Father, the Son, and the Holy Ghost. Convinced again by daily experience of the powerful tendency of his own heart to gravitate to the world and its vanities of the manifold temptations to sin which beset him, and of the feebleness of his best unassisted endeavours to resist them he is prepared to understand and to admit, that "man is very far gone from original righteousness, and is of his own nature inclined to evil that "this infection of nature doth remain yea in them that are regenerated that we are at our best estate 'miserable sinners that "there is no health in us that "we have no power of ourselves to help ourselves and that we cannot "turn and prepare ourselves by our own natural strength and good works to faith and calling upon God Thus penitently convinced of his real condition by nature, and disposed to receive the testimony of God as it unfolds itself to his understanding and conscience, such an inquirer will gratefully perceive the close adaptation of Christianity to the necessities of those for whose benefit it is revealed and will find a powerful incidental argument for its truth and Divine origin, in that consolatory doctrine, that ' the Son, which is the Word of the Father, begotten from everlasting of the Father, the very and eternal God, of one substance with the Father, took man's nature and in this nature " truly suffered was crucified dead, and buried, to reconcile his Father to us, and to be a sacrifice not only for original guilt, but also for the actual sins of men;" and, further, that "we are accounted righteous before God only for the merits of our Lord Jesus Christ by faith, and not for our own works and deservings.' (2d Art.) At the same time, anxious to obey the will of God, and prepared, by holy dispositions of heart and moral habits of life, to make a disinterested judgment in those matters of faith which relate to our submission to the Divine commands, he perceives nothing to lead him to suppose that this fundamental tenet of Scripture, this foundation-stone of our own church, has any licentious tendency or that it is otherwise than " a most wholesome doctrine, as well as " very full of comfort." Far from feeling inclined to take advantage of it with a view to sin in order that grace may abound, he is conscious from his daily experience of its sanctifying tendency; his faith, in proportion as it is "true and lively,' he finds to be " necessarily productive of good works; so that he perceives the wisdom of the Divine arrangement in securing the interests of morality by means of that very dispensation which reveals free and unmerited pardon, justification, and salvation to every true believer, in virtue of the obedience unto death of his all sufficient Surety

W

PROCEEDINGS OF RELIGIOUS AND CHARITABLE INSTITUTIONS

SOCIETY FOR PROMOTING CHRISTIAN KNOWLEDGE

In presenting the Report of its proceedings during the last year, the Society for promoting Christian Knowledge begins with returning thanks to the Giver of all good for continued support and an increasing sphere of usefulness

The number of books and tracts delivered from the Society s stores for the year amounted to 1,474,067 being an excess of 5,712 Bibles, 8,377 Testaments and Psalters, 7,028 Common Prayer Books, 15,705 bound books, and 119,570 half bound (a total of 156,292) above the preceding year The receipts for the year have been 62,387l. from ordinary sources, unassisted by large donations or legacies ; the expenditure also consists of payments in immediate prosecution of the Society s designs which circumstances prove that the increasing exertions of the Society produce increased demands upon its funds, and that even its present large income is not more than sufficient to meet its unavoidable expenses

The removal of the office from Bartlett s Buildings to Lincoln s Inn Fields, has been attended with many advantages and among others an increased attendance of members at the monthly general meetings

During the year, much attention has been devoted to the revision of the Society's books and tracts. On this subject, the Report states, that the length of time which has elapsed since many of these works were adopted, and the changes which have subsequently taken place among all ranks of society, have shewn both the necessity of some alteration, and the extent to which such alteration should be carried Those works which, after mature examination, are considered unsuited to the present wants of the people will be suffered to remain out of print, while others which are partly of a similar description, will be offered in an abridged form for the especial use of the Society Thus it is hoped without any sudden or violent change, the Society will be gradually disencumbered of works which have served to swell its catalogue to an inconvenient bulk, without producing a corresponding advantage to the public. It is calculated that a fourth part of the books and tracts have been submitted to this revision, and that the task will be completed in the course of two or three years. In the mean time the Society will gladly avail itself of the best new tracts which may be submitted to its choice, especially of short and plain expositions of Christian doctrine and duty.

We think it of great importance to call the attention of those of our readers who are members of the Society to the foregoing statement. There can be no doubt that a general revision of the Society's tracts has long been needed; some may be well spared, others require alteration or abridgment, and new ones may also be desirable; but judging both on sound principle and by past experience, it is not without apprehension that we contemplate a measure of the kind now in progress, at least till we are assured that the individuals selected for the important office of revision are so chosen as fairly to represent the general voice of the friends of the Society, and that the most scrupulous care will be taken to admit no change in a spirit of party, or with reference to those differences of opinion which are known to exist among the members of the institution and of our common church. We should especially object to unacknowledged changes of a doctrinal kind in some of the older tracts, especially where the name and authority of the writer are a guarantee for the sentiments contained in his works; a licence most justly complained of in the Society's Family Bible. We are also alarmed at the idea of superseding any of the Society's standard publications by such modern specimens of divinity as in some instances have unhappily found their way upon its list. We however, speak only hypothetically for a revision well and impartially executed would be a benefit; but we trust that the members will demand, or rather that the committee of revision will spontaneously present, a full and specific report of the exact nature and amount of the changes which they propose for the Society's adoption. The painful discussions, a few years since, respecting baptism and regeneration, shew the necessity of a full explanation on the subject, to prevent a division of opinion which might be fatal to the best interests of the institution.

Additions have also been made to the books of amusement and instruction upon the supplemental catalogue. The great demand for scientific and mechanical information has induced the Society to adopt two well known works upon these subjects, Conversations on Chemistry, and Conversations on Natural Philosophy. It is intended to follow up this step by the circulation of other books of a similar description. We are not convinced of the expediency of a very extended enlargement of this part of the Society's plans as the funds of the institution are specifically subscribed for promoting—not scientific, but Christian knowledge and the former may be equally well or better obtained through other channels.

Two editions of the New Testament in Welsh have been adopted, and a third is in preparation with the Welsh and English in parallel columns. An edition of the first five homilies in Welsh has also been procured. Welsh translations have also been published of various other tracts.

Gratuitous grants of books to the amount of 690*l.* have been sent to New South Wales, the Cape of Good Hope, to Demerara, and other foreign stations.

The Society has great pleasure in noticing the important and liberal measures which have been taken for supplying the religious wants of the army. His Majesty's Government, as our readers are aware, have resolved to furnish every soldier who can read with a Bible and Book of Common Prayer, and at the request of the Chaplain general, the Society most readily consented to co-operate in this good work. Very large supplies of Bibles and Books of Common Prayer suited for the use of soldiers are now in a course of delivery.

The proceedings of the Society in London have been zealously seconded by the Diocesan and District Committees, and, with their assistance, a very considerable progress has been made in many branches of the Society's undertakings. The sale of books and tracts to the public has been adopted in many parts of the kingdom with great success. In every diocese in the kingdom, the circulation of the Society's books has increased.

No branch of the Society's proceedings partakes more largely of the general prosperity than the Parochial Lending Libraries. It is supposed that about 800 of them are now regularly established, of which more than a third have been instituted since the last Report. Every week brings intelligence of additions to the number.

New committees have been formed during the last year, at Uxbridge, Mortlake, Wandsworth, Harrow, Lyme Regis, Warrington, Ross, Sawley, Antigua, Grenada, and St. Kitt's.

After this sketch of its domestic proceedings the Society next advert to the foreign occurrences of the year, the most important of which relate to the East India Mission. The Board having taken into consideration the present state of this mission, and being desirous of adopting measures for providing more effectually than could be done by this Society for the extension of missionary objects in British India, have resolved that the management and superintendence of the Society's mission in Southern India be transferred to the Society for the Propagation of the Gospel in Foreign Parts. It appears from the earliest proceedings of the Society, that its constitution was not considered fit for the establishment of extensive missions, to meet which difficulty its principal members obtained a charter of incorporation for the institution just mentioned. Subsequently the Danish Mission College at Copenhagen established a mission, for which this Society received and transmitted benefactions. The mission gradually extended to Vepery, Tanjore, Trichinopoly, Tinnavelly, Cuddalore, Madura, and Ramnad. And this Society's connexion with it became more and more intimate, until eventually several of the missionaries were adopted as missionaries of the Society, and the mission stations at Vepery, Tanjore, Trichinopoly, and Tinnavelly, were made over to it by the Danish College. Such was the origin of the Society's India Mission. The undertaking has been blessed with no ordinary measure of success. Several of the missionaries who have been employed are famous throughout the Christian world. The congregations of native Christians in the neighbourhood of Madras, estimated upon good authority at 20,000 souls, owe their existence in a great measure to the Society; and the appearance of their villages, when contrasted with that of the pagan towns by which they are surrounded, is described by an eye witness as a most affecting proof of the good that has been actually accomplished, and as an encouragement to persevere in missionary labours. But still the establishment of this mission was an experiment upon a comparatively small scale, and the Society did not feel itself enabled even by success, to extend its care to the whole of Hindostan, although it resolved not to relinquish the work in which it had been engaged. The Society considered that they could not do more, while no public countenance was given to Christianity, and even the European inhabitants of Asia were most inadequately provided with religious instruction. But by the erection of the See of Calcutta, a vast field was opened to the missionary labours of the Church of England. Soon after the arrival of Bishop Middleton in the East, the establishment of committees, under his lordship's sanction, placed the Society in direct communication with every part of India. the Society's mission in Southern India was enlarged; and, subsequently, the Society for the Propagation of the Gospel founded and endowed, on the bishop's suggestion, a mission college at Calcutta, towards the erection of which this Society contributed the sum of 5,000l. together with a grant of 6,000l. for the endowment of scholarships on the plan of the late Bishop Middleton. The consequences have been highly satisfactory. Bishop's College has been completed, and is now in action under the patronage of the bishop of the diocese. A principal and two professors have been appointed; the former is already employed in the assiduous discharge of his duties, and the latter have departed for their destination. Missionary stations are selected. European missionaries and native catechists and teachers are engaged; others are under education in the College; translations of Scripture and various works in the Oriental languages have been begun; and the institution, even in this early stage, may be considered the greatest Protestant establishment that has been formed for the conversion of the East. The Diocesan and District Committees of this Society have also been very successful. They have distributed the Scriptures and the Liturgy in large numbers. They have established schools on an extensive plan; and they are regularly employed in translating tracts into the Eastern languages, and printing them for the use of the native scholars.

The union now adopted will concentrate the missionary efforts of the two societies, and ensure to the mission in the South of India a regular supply of missionaries, catechists, and schoolmasters educated at Bishop's College.

So convinced is the Society of the importance of native schools in India, that it has determined to establish a separate fund for their support, and has appropriated the sum of 5,000l. to that purpose. An anonymous benefaction of 1,000l. has been added to this fund, and several other handsome contributions have been subsequently received.

The Calcutta Committee have continued to supply all the European stations in the East, their churches, schools, hospitals, and prisons with Bibles, Prayer books, and religious tracts. Captains of ships, and other marine officers, are also frequently supplied with the word of God and other books from its depository at the reduced prices or gratuitously, for the use of their crews. The Committee, it is added, "are not without instances of good derived by various persons, in a spiritual point of view, from its public services." With regard to its second object the education of the heathen, the Calcutta Committee have pursued the plan of Bishop Middleton, who maintained that the inculcation of Christian principles on the natives would be the only safe and certain measure of securing to Britons their Oriental possessions. In this department of its labours the Committee experience an increasing satisfaction; and, in reference to it, they remark, that much good has already been accomplished to an amount exceeding their most sanguine expectations. Parents are every where perceptibly laying aside their prejudices, and growing more and more anxious to have their children educated. The morality of the Gospel is now at length regularly inculcated in the minds of the scholars, who read, with the permission and concurrence of their parents and religious guides, as their daily task, selections from the New Testament, translated into their own tongue. The full benefit of such a system of instruction can hardly be appreciated in the course of a single generation: but in the children who frequent these schools a moral and intellectual improvement is already discernible,—the regularity of their attendance,—their readiness in acquiring knowledge, their hand writing, and the accuracy with which they are enabled to answer arithmetical and other questions, exhibit a proficiency, such, it is stated, as few parochial schools in England have, in a similar space of time, exceeded.

The Society next advert to the state of its affairs in North America and the West Indies. The importance of the former increases daily in consequence of the increasing emigration from the mother country: and the latter, it is added, 'present a field for the promotion of Christian knowledge which has never before been seen in that quarter of the globe.'

In the diocese of Quebec, the schools have been maintained both at Quebec and Montreal with great success. Two sums of 500*l* each have been granted by the Society for the use of the diocese of Nova Scotia: the first of which is placed at the disposal of the bishop, to be employed at his discretion in aid of the Society's designs: the second to be applied to King's College, Nova Scotia, and to be employed in providing two or more tutors, to superintend the morals and the religious instruction of the students, under the direction of the bishop.

In the West Indian Islands, now divided into the dioceses of Jamaica and Barbadoes, the prospects of the Society, it is stated, are of the brightest kind. A report had been received from the Jamaica Committee, informing the Society that, with the approbation of the bishop of the diocese, they had invited the different rectors of the island to explain the constitution, nature, and objects of the Committee to the proprietors in their respective parishes, and to solicit their assistance in promoting its views by donations of money or books. The clergy who are members of the Society had been requested to make an annual collection at their churches in aid of the designs of the institution. Large supplies of books have been requested and forwarded both in Jamaica and Barbadoes.

The Report concludes as follows: "Upon a review of the proceedings detailed in the foregoing pages, the Society has again to thank God for the blessing which has attended its labours: and to express a hope that such encouraging results will be followed up by increased exertions. An immense field now opens before it: and it is not too much to entertain a humble confidence that the same Almighty Hand, which has raised the church from small beginnings to her present flourishing condition, will in like manner enable the Society for promoting Christian Knowledge to diffuse the principles and enforce the practice of the Gospel, as long as the name of England endures, and as far as its empire extends."

BRITISH AND FOREIGN BIBLE SOCIETY

In opening the Report of the proceedings of the past year, France is the first point to which the Committee direct their attention. The Society's foreign agent, Dr. Pinkerton, was requested to undertake a journey to Paris, to inspect the foreign editions of the Scriptures printing at the expense of the Society; and to inquire as to the best means of assisting the French Protestant Bible Society at Paris. The Turkish Bible he found advanced as far as the Book of Job. Professor Kieffer continues his indefatigable exertions in editing the work. It appeared advisable that 2000 additional New Testaments should be printed, which the Committee ordered. The Syriac and Carshun editions of the New Testament have been expedited the Persian and Coptic versions are in progress the modern Armenian Testament is completed and copies were preparing to be forwarded for the use of the Armenians, at Constantinople and in other parts of Turkey

The Paris Bible Society has continued to receive many testimonies of the utility of its labours to the Protestant communions in France The Associations have gone on increasing The Scriptures have been received in many instances with lively joy and their perusal is reported to have produced beneficial effects Among the works completed by the Paris Society during the past year has been Ostervald's Bible, stereotyped Extensive distributions of the Scriptures take place from the Society's depot at Paris An application, from an island in the Mediterranean, for 300 Bibles and 3000 Testaments, for the use of schools, has been met from this source

In Spain, Portugal and Italy, little can at present be done towards disseminating the holy Scriptures

The Report of the Netherlands Bible Society states, that there have been put into circulation, during the year, 5837 Bibles and 6490 Testaments The same document contains a letter from the Dutch East-India Bible Society, communicating the Report of a special Committee appointed to examine the Chinese version of the Bible, by the Rev Drs Morrison and Milne, which states that the translation was ascertained to be well executed in consequence of this Report, the Committee of the Netherlands Bible Society have ordered a number of copies to be forwarded to the Dutch settlements in the East Indies

In Switzerland the Zurich Society has just completed its edition of 7500 copies of a large Bible The Bern Society writes, "Our Piscator's Bible is finished, and has already found its way into the cottages of the poor, as well as into our schools, both in town and country and our Ladies Associations, ever mindful of their founder (the late Mr Owen), continue with unabated zeal to labour with us to promote the good work The Geneva Committee have contributed towards supplying the Waldenses with the Scriptures The Lausanne Society, besides an edition of 10,000 Bibles in quarto, have printed an edition of 4000 French Testaments and have made an agreement for a second edition of 4000 copies From the Basle Institution Antistes Falkeisen writes —' The blessing of God has rested in a particular and even wonderful manner upon our Bible Society in the year past, for which we cannot be sufficiently thankful Many Roman Catholics have applied to us for Bibles and, as they are too poor to pay for them in money, they bring different kinds of produce, which is afterwards sold

The last Report of the Hamburgh Altona Society mentions the completion of an edition of 12,000 Bibles and 15,000 Testaments

In consequence of the desolations which have occurred by the late inundations in the kingdom of Hanover, the Committee have voted 1000 German Testaments for the sufferers The King of Bavaria has given the royal assent for the establishment of a Central Bible Society at Nuremberg, and some Auxiliaries are already formed around this central institution To the Saxon Society assistance has been afforded by several grants The last anniversary meeting of this Society was addressed by the venerable president, Count Hohenthal ' On this very day, said he, " nay, at this very hour, ten years ago, twenty-seven persons who took delight in the Bible, met at my house, and, under the direction of Dr Pinkerton, formed a Society for the sole object of circulating the holy Scriptures. He then recited their names, and added—' Of these twenty seven, fifteen have departed this life, one resides in Berlin, another in Budissen, and a third in Prussian Lusatia so that only nine of the first founders can be present with us this day. From these comparatively feeble beginnings a circulation has ensued of 38,490 Bibles and 7,767 New Testaments. Since these documents arrived, Count Hohenthal has himself been added to the number of the departed.

The Frankfort Society's distributions have been during the past year 928 Bibles and 5470 New Testaments. Among these have been more than 1000 New Testaments to pilgrims, who received them with the greatest readiness. The Society in the kingdom of Wuertemberg has distributed on its own account during the past year, 5570 Bibles and 3009 Testaments; making a total of 102,432 copies since it commenced its labours. The desire, however, for the Scriptures is by no means abated. The King of Wuertemberg has renewed his donation of 500 florins. Some prisoners, who had received copies of the New Testament, made a collection among themselves, and remitted it to the treasurer; and, though it had been feared that the disastrous floods which had occurred, would have prevented the regular payment of the smaller subscriptions, one of the correspondents of the Wuertemberg Society writes, " I was agreeably mistaken not a single member withdrew himself, and some whose houses were absolutely swept away by the inundation, continue their subscription with joy and thankfulness of heart.

Every letter that has been received from Dr Leander Van Ess has borne testimony to the prevailing desire for the holy Scriptures, notwithstanding the difficulties which have arisen in the way of their circulation. He had been supplied with 10,000 German Testaments of his own edition and 2000 of Gossner's, 1000 Lutheran Bibles, besides some smaller quantities in the Hebrew, Greek, and other languages. An opportunity of supplying the Roman Catholic schools in the kingdom of Wuertemberg having occurred, the Professor had applied for 10,000 Testaments for this important purpose, which the Committee readily granted. The zeal of this individual has stirred up others and the Committee had heard with pleasure, that another professor in the Roman Catholic communion had prepared a version of the New Testament, which has been approved by some ecclesiastical authorities in that church. The Minister of Finance in the Grand Duchy of Darmstadt, has waved the duties in favour of the Bible Society, as well as of the professor himself, and other individual distributors and duties previously paid have been returned.

The secretary of the Prussian Central Bible Society, writes,— ' During the last year, ending October 1, 1824 we have put into circulation 3874 Bibles and 976 Testaments, and during the last ten years 78,247. Within the same period, a far larger number of copies of the Scriptures have been circulated by the Branch Societies in Prussia so that at present there is not a poor man in the whole country who may not, if he please obtain the Bible or Testament at a very reduced price, or even gratis. This Society has superintended an edition of 10,000 Bohemian New Testaments.

In the Report of the Silesian Bible Society the following interesting statement occurs —" The numerous difficulties and attendant anxieties with which many of our fellow Christians have had to struggle, in consequence of the pressure of the times, have driven many to seek for consolation, where alone it can be truly found, in the Book of Life. In many families the long neglected Bible has at length been brought forward again. Where in reality it was most wanted, no Bible was to be found. In this situation the parties would have been left, had not Bible Societies in different places stepped forward, and supplied them with the word of God. It is with thankfulness we add, that we have been able to satisfy every demand made upon us for copies of the holy Scriptures.

The Ninth Report of the Bunzlau Bible Society records the following pleasing fact "We have never been obliged, from want of the means, to send any one who applied to us for a Bible empty away. In this benevolent work, the clergy and schoolmasters here have not a little assisted us during the last year."

"To every clergyman," states the Fifth Report of the Kreuznach Bible Society, "who applied to us Bibles have been given for the purpose of presenting every newly married couple with a copy on their wedding-day. All without exception, have received this present, offered to them on one of the most important days of their lives, with demonstrations of gratitude and joy and many have in return made handsome donations to the Bible Society." The Berg Bible Society, is about to print an edition of 10,000 New Testaments for the supply of schools. "We had no conception," the secretary writes, "that the want of Bibles would be found so great in this country. The same spirit which has been awakened in England, has, God be praised, found its way to us."

The Danish Bible Society, in connexion with its Auxiliaries has been successful in distributing about 60,000 Bibles and New Testaments.

From one of the branches of the Bible Society in Norway, at Bergen, the secretary writes,—"Even here among Norwegian rocks, the long slumbering desire after the Divine Word has been at length awakened in the souls of our fellow Christians even here do Christian brethren unite in contributing towards the great and glorious work which so many others are engaged in carrying on."

In an interesting address, delivered by Count Rosenblad, at the anniversary of the Swedish Bible Society, it is observed, that, from calculations which have been made of the copies of the Scriptures in existence in Sweden, and of the number of persons who ought to be presented with them, but who may be supposed not to have the means of supplying themselves, at least 30,000 annually will be wanted for many years to come. There have been printed at this Society's press 96,700 Bibles and 118,600 New Testaments. The Ladies Association says "If the members of the Ladies Bible Society in Stockholm can claim any merit for the sincerity of their intentions to co operate in the accomplishment of so grand and desirable an object, and if they have already witnessed instances of a happy result of their exertions, it is a duty which they cheerfully discharge to own that they are indebted to the British and Foreign Bible Society for the example, the counsel and the means, which have guided and facilitated their labours."

With mingled feelings of regret and delight the Committee next turn to Russia regret at the difficulties which had arisen in that quarter, and delight at the retrospect of the labours of the Russian Bible Society. Prince Galitzin having resigned the office of president, Archbishop Seraphim had been appointed his successor. At the first meeting of the Committee, at which his Eminence presided, he expressed a lively hope that the Lord would be pleased to shower down his blessings on the united and important labours of the Committee, and vouchsafe to them his Almighty aid. Prince Galitzin had written a letter expressive of the interest felt by him in all the operations of the Bible Society in every part of the world notwithstanding he has resigned the situation which he before occupied

By the Russian Society a periodical monthly paper has been issued during the past year. In the first number a general review is taken of the operations of the Society since its commencement from which it appears that, in the space of eleven years, it has purchased or printed versions of the entire Scriptures or the New Testament or parts thereof, in forty one different languages or dialects, and distributed 448,109 copies and has collected and received 3,711,376 rubles and that there are in different parts of the empire 289 Committees who mutually co operate, and, in union with the St Petersburg Committee, dispense throughout the whole extent of the Russian dominions the bread of life. Among its most important versions, that into the Modern Russ deserves to be mentioned 50,000 of the Modern Russ and Slavonian New Testament have been published and 20,000 of the Modern Russ alone. These journals contain many pleasing testimonies of the good produced by the labours of the Society. The Committee have availed themselves of the central situation of Malta, to send out supplies in different languages, to be in readiness to meet the wants which may occur in those quarters of the world. The last Annual Report of this Society states that 10,486 copies of the Scriptures, in fifteen different languages, had been distributed making a total with those distributed in former years, of nearly 40,000.

The secretary of the Ionian Bible Society reports, that in the first three years and a half of the Society's existence 841 Bibles and Testaments had been issued by it, and within the last two years 2201. Some hundreds of copies of the Greek Testament have been sent to different parts of Greece, where they have been received by the people with eagerness and many of them it is said while encamped and expecting the enemy, employ themselves in reading the word of God. The revision of the entire Albanian New Testament is completed and the Gospel of St. Matthew has been printed and put in circulation.

In the Turkish empire, for the benefit of the Greeks who speak the Turkish language, the New Testament is preparing in Greek characters. The Jewish Spanish New Testament has been revised for a third time, and is about to be printed at Malta. The translation of the Modern Greek Bible has been finished and the entire copy is in the hands of Mr Leeves. The New Testament is about to be printed in London. "To a Sciot lady (Mr Leeves writes), who had lost her husband and part of her family in the recent calamities which befel that island, but who, through Christian exertions, has had the happiness to be redeemed from slavery, and to recover two sons and a daughter from the same unhappy condition, I gave Greek Testaments for herself and all the members of her family and I have the satisfaction of knowing that these books are diligently studied, and supply a constant source of instruction and comfort to these individuals, united once more as a family, after their many sufferings and perils. Mr Leeves has had the happiness of introducing the Scriptures into several schools the masters agreeing that a portion of the time which is now devoted to the study of Æsop's Fables Lucian's Dialogues, Homer, and Sophocles might be profitably employed in giving the youths an acquaintance with the charter of a Christian's duty, privileges, and hopes. The issues from the depository at Constantinople had amounted in the whole to 2959 more than half the number were Greek Testaments. From Smyrna there have been circulated 350 Bibles and Testaments, with 44 copies of the Proverbs of Solomon. From Aleppo, Mr Barker writes that at Lattakia, a place which he visited, 112 copies of the Armenian

Scriptures had been disposed of, and that he had been assured by a Syrian prelate, that the holy Scriptures now preparing in the Carshun language will prove a most acceptable present to the Christians for whose use they are designed. The Scriptures had been sent to Jerusalem, Tyre, Sydon, Tripoli, and Damascus. Many demands are reported to be made for the Arabic Bible, and Mr Barker had supplied 78 out of 80 boys belonging to an Arabic school, with the book of Psalms in the Arabic language at ten paras a copy. During the course of the year, Mr Barker has made two tours in Asia Minor and Syria. He received an assurance from one of the British consuls, who assisted him in various ways, that the Scriptures distributed were read.

In the Persian language, the Pentateuch had been completed, in the revision of which Professor Lee is engaged, while the translators are advancing with the historical books. In a letter received from a missionary, it is observed,—"In our journeys we have frequently met with Persians who were partly acquainted with the New Testament and ardently desired to read the Old Testament, remarking, We cannot remove into a new house unless we have found its foundation to be strong let us have the Old Testament that we may see whether the Gospel is well founded upon it.

The Committee next call the attention of the Society to the gratifying reports received from Calcutta, Bombay, Madras, and Ceylon.

At Calcutta, three new auxiliary institutions have been formed and 11,000 copies of Bibles, Testaments, and single books, have been sent from Calcutta to these infant societies. The Hindoostanee Testament, by the assistance of the Rev Principal Mill, has been printed as far as the Acts. Mr Bowley's Hinduwee Testament is completed. The Book of Genesis in Hindoostanee is about to be published separately, it having been much approved. The demand for the single Gospels in Bengalee, for the use of schools, is so great that a large impression of the Gospels and Acts is ordered, instead of completing the whole of the New Testament as had been before determined. Dr R Heber, Bishop of Calcutta, has greatly aided the Society by his counsel and influence.

At Bombay, the Old Testament with the New, in the Goojurattee language, are now completed. The missionaries write, ' Nearly the whole of the numbers, amounting to about 6,000, are gone among the people. Few days pass without some one calling for parts of it and we frequently have persons from villages at a considerable distance applying for Testaments. When out among the people, I am frequently called to explain parts to them.

At Madras, the version of the Scriptures in Malayalim, under the superintendence of the Rev B Bailey, had proceeded to the eleventh chapter of Hebrews. It is in contemplation to print the four Gospels without waiting for the completion of the whole, as the Syrian Christians are very anxious for some part of the Scriptures to be printed in their native language. The Syriac Bible has been completed, under the superintendence of Professor Lee. The version in the Malayalim dialect for the northern parts of Malabar had been advanced, as also the revision of the Tamul New Testament. A translation of the Pentateuch into the Carnatica, by the Rev W Reeve, has been presented and approved. The printing of 1000 copies of the Old Testament in the Tamul language has proceeded as far as the Prophets. In a letter from the secretary of the Madras Auxiliary, the writer, after mentioning the observable change now taking place in the minds of the natives, with regard to their former superstitions and after lamenting their deplorable ignorance observes, " that the influence of Bible Societies, in accelerating the evangelizing of the country, will be highly important, whenever it shall please God to excite a spirit of research and inquiry and that till then they are usefully employed in efforts of preparation, in endeavouring to improve existing translations, and in giving them as wide a circulation as possible among the nominal Christian population, and such of the heathens as may desire to have them

The Colombo Auxiliary has made large distributions in the English, Dutch Malay and Cingalese languages The demand for the Books of Genesis, Psalms, and Proverbs, has been such, that, though extra impressions were provided, they have been all exhausted Mr Newstead has brought to England the manuscript copy of the Indo Portuguese New Testament, of which he is the translator A version of the New Testament has been made into the Pali language

A letter from the South Sea Islands accompanied the Acts of the Apostles in the Taheitan language, 500 copies of which have been circulated in thirteen different islands In six of these missionaries are stationed, and four have renounced idolatry and embraced the Gospel The writer of the letter says, I apprehend that our edition of the sacred Scriptures must be at least 10,000 copies to satisfy the demands of the Leeward mission alone In the name of my brethren, and in the name of the surrounding islands, I therefore entreat the Bible Society to send us an adequate supply of paper The labours of the Bible Society (he adds) have been already blessed in these seas, and I trust they will increase more abundantly, even unto the coming of the great day In a short time I hope to print the Epistles, together with the Book of Psalms a new edition of the Gospel of St Luke is also loudly called for

Dr Morrison having stated that all the Chinese who live in the islands of the Malayan Archipelago, are capable of receiving the sacred Scriptures without difficulty, as far as the governments are concerned; and that their probable number is from two to three hundred thousand, and that through them, the Scriptures may and will find their way into China itself, the Committee have determined to employ a special agent in promoting the objects of the Society in this quarter The missionaries at the Anglo Chinese College write that "many, both of the Chinese and the Malays have lately called and begged for the word of life Many hundred copies have gone from hence, and there appears an increasing desire among all classes to obtain our books'

With regard to Africa the Society returns thanks to the Church Missionary Society, for a valuable present of ten volumes of Ethiopic manuscripts containing among others the entire New Testament, an edition of which is now preparing for the press under the direction of the librarian

The King of Madagascar sent to this country, a few years since, three youths for the purpose of receiving an European education while here, they became converts to the Christian faith, and were baptized. To each of them an English Bible was presented on their departure from England

From the Mauritius, intelligence has been received, that 362 Bibles and 400 Testaments in the French language have been already distributed, and that scarcely a day passes without persons calling upon him to know if he had any Bibles to give them

The South African Bible Society s Report proves that the circulation of the Scriptures has done, and is still doing, much good. A missionary writes, " You cannot conceive what joy sat on each countenance, when it was published in our church, that Bibles and Testaments had arrived To the Namacquas it was a day of gladness The friends of the Bible will rejoice to hear that the poor Namacquas, whose days were formerly spent in roaming over mountains and deserts, have learnt from the sacred Scriptures to assemble together to worship the true and living God. A translation of the New Testament has been undertaken in the Namacqua language, and four Gospels have been already finished.

Every opportunity that has offered of sending the Scriptures to the Northern shores of Africa, has been embraced. A gentleman on a visit to Tunis, has taken with him 500 copies of the Scriptures in the Arabic and other languages.

Passing to South America, the Committee rejoice in stating, that all the information from this quarter continues to afford the pleasing hope of a still more extensive circulation of the Scriptures. They have, in consequence, ordered very large impressions of the Spanish Bible, and have accepted the offer of the Rev. Mr Armstrong, to visit South America on the Society's account. His principal employment will be to discover channels in which they may hereafter be advantageously sent.

At Lima, the Monthly Extracts have proved acceptable, and fit individuals are found here and there willing to assist in distributing the Scriptures. There have, however, been efforts of an opposite tendency for information has been received of the landing of infidel publications on the shores of South America. The translation of the New Testament into the Peruvian language is completed. "I am convinced, writes a correspondent, 'that the Testament is in general considered a treasure for with pleasure have I seen, in passing through the streets the shopkeepers, and poor people who have stalls read in the Gospel and had I had ten times as many I could have sold them all. The Bishop of Durham having received from one of his clergy, a chaplain of a ship of the line, a statement that ' the Spaniards on the Western coast are hungering and thirsting for the Bible in their own language, and anxiously wish for a few hundred copies, no time was lost in placing at the disposal of this gentleman 100 Spanish Bibles. Another communication has been received, from Rio de Janeiro, relative to the Portuguese Scriptures. When the distributor published that he had Bibles and Testaments to dispose of, the former were all sold in three hours, and the latter within three days, and he was often asked when more would arrive. Five hundred Bibles and 500 Testaments have in consequence been dispatched.

From the Jamaica Eastern Auxiliary a remittance has been received of 150*l*. In the letter announcing it, the Secretary observes,—" In these eventful times it will rejoice our friends to hear that the Bible cause has not suffered loss, notwithstanding the distracted state of the public mind. On the contrary, its interests are fostered by many respectable individuals, whom Divine Providence has raised up to watch over them. By this Society upwards of 700 copies of the Scriptures have been issued in two years. From the Auxiliary Society of the People of Colour, in the parish of St Thomas in the East, a donation of 30*l*. has been remitted. From Barbadoes also the People of Colour have remitted 25*l*.

The American Bible Society continues to prosper. At the publication of the last Annual Report, its distribution of the Scriptures had reached 309,062 Bibles, Testaments, and parts of the New Testament. The more it labours, the more it finds the need of its labour. In the city of New York, where Bible Societies were established at an early period, and where many thousand copies have been distributed, it was found on an examination of one ward during the past year, that 264 families containing 513 persons who could read, were without the Scriptures and in another ward, that 324 families, con taining 1265 individuals, likewise able to read, were equally destitute. This statement is accompanied by several others of a similar import. The net receipts of the treasury, during the eighth year, have been greater than in any preceding year.

The Auxiliary in Nova Scotia has remitted 188l. and the secretary announces the establishment of a Ladies Association, from which much good was augured. At Montreal, a Roman Catholic minister, on being presented with a copy of De Sacy's New Testament, remarked that he had never before seen a French New Testament complete, but merely a part of one of the Evangelists. Gaelic Bibles and Testaments have been sent to New Brunswick. At Miramichi the Society requests some Hebrew Testaments, "for some of the descendants of Abraham." "It is pleasing to see the people of this place (writes the secretary), while suffering many privations in their attempts to form a new settlement in the wilderness, desiring to enjoy the word of life to cheer and comfort them amidst their toil."

From Labrador the Committee report the progress of the translation into the Esquimaux language. The New Testament and the Psalms have been translated. The people peruse the New Testament daily in their houses and tents with the greatest earnestness, delight, and edification. Their understanding of the word of God has greatly increased, and its influence upon the moral conduct is manifest. Those things which were formerly practised among the Esquimaux, by their sorcerers and angekoks, are at present hardly ever heard of.

In Greenland, we are informed, "the New Testaments have been distributed and read with manifest blessing. The joy of the people, Greenlanders, in receiving this generous gift is not to be expressed in words."

Among the domestic occurrences of the past year, the Committee record, with peculiar satisfaction, his Majesty's gracious acceptance, for his private library, of a set of the different versions of the Scriptures printed by the Society.

The net receipts of the Society for the year have been 93,285l. and its expenditure 94,044l. The number of copies of the Scriptures issued from the depository has been 116,539 Bibles, and 164,116 Testaments, making a total of 3,722,987 copies of the Scriptures issued in this country by the Society in twenty one years.

Such is an outline of the Report of this invaluable institution. May the Society continue to be one of the instruments of the providence of God in hastening that day when every creature which is in the heaven and on the earth, and such as are in the sea, shall say "Blessing, and honour, and glory, and power, be unto him that sitteth on the throne, and unto the Lamb, for ever and ever, Amen."

AFRICAN INSTITUTION

Deeply anxious as we feel on the whole subject of slavery, believing, to use the words of Mr. Justice Best, in a recent memorable judgment that 'the law which recognises it is an anti Christian law and one which violates the laws of nature and ought not to be recognized in this country,' and convinced that the utter extinction of it is the most decisive, if not the only death blow to the slave trade, we still view it necessary not to lose sight for a moment of the actual enormities of the latter, or to remind our readers that the existing state of this brutal commerce still calls for the most vigilant measures of repression on the part of every friend of religion and humanity. If from whatever cause any such individual should be disposed to sink into any degree of apathy on this painful subject, he has but to read the Report now before us to awaken anew his warmest ardours in this truly Christian cause.

The observations in this Report are classed under the following heads—First on the point to which the different countries of the world have up to the present time, brought their laws respecting the slave trade; next, on the state of the slave trade as actually existing and lastly some particulars regarding the colony of Sierra Leone, and European intercourse with the interior of Africa

The Report of the last year contained a detailed account of the legislative measures, more or less effectual which Foreign Governments had respectively pursued, for the Abolition of the Slave Trade Unfortunately but few steps have since been taken There has been hitherto no opportunity of advantageously resuming the conferences on the slave trade which were adjourned from Verona to London No general regulation therefore has been adopted for its repression but some progress has been made in two instances by individual treaties, towards affixing on this traffic its proper name and character as a violation of the law of nature, and of nations, and of the common rights of humanity All dealing in slaves by British subjects from the 1st of January of the present year has been declared Piracy by Act of Parliament The Swedish Government had previously published an ordinance putting her subjects engaged in it out of the protection of the law and a treaty has since been concluded between his Majesty and the King of Sweden which provides the necessary measures for carrying the above declaration into execution

A treaty of a similar description, founded on the same reciprocal recognition of the piratical nature of the trade was negociated between this country and the United States Some difficulties arose in respect of its ratification, but every modification which could possibly be admitted in order to meet the views of that power having been adopted by this country a new treaty had been arranged accordingly, and sent out to America

Portugal still remains a melancholy exception to the concurrent authority of the rest of Europe. She alone of civilized nations, continues to class the purchase of our fellow creatures among the ordinary modes of lawful commerce, having only restricted herself by treaty, to carry it on to the Southward of the Line and because the English Government has been reduced to plead with the different courts of Europe for the interests of mankind almost as for a matter of personal favour she persists in professing to regard this honourable interference as a mere manœuvre of some selfish policy of our own

The conduct of the French Government, although less open and explicit than that of Portugal is perhaps on this account only the more prejudicial It perseveres in maintaining at the lowest possible point of practical effect, its co operation with those humane and enlightened declarations the verbal subscription to which it had not declined France is the single government, which, proclaiming the trade to be unlawful, and well aware that its profits are in themselves an ample insurance against the mere risk of simple confiscation refuses to adopt the only system which other States have found effectual and to affix an infamous punishment to the offence The consequence is that wherever the French flag floats on the coast of Africa, it is the signal for devastation nor is it merely a cover to its own adventurers for the supply of its own colonies but it extends a flagitious security to the outrage on the laws of the respective governments which the smugglers of other countries are enabled to perpetrate under its protection France remains the great slave carrier of the world

Government, has declined to legislate on the quality of the offence, although it has been recently employed in amending its code of navigation and maritime commerce. The captain, who without necessity throws overboard the goods of his employers is visited with the whole vengeance of the law; but if he takes on board a greater number of Negroes than his vessel can conveniently transport to her place of destination, and, as has lately happened, quietly casts the supernumeraries into the sea, the crime becomes alleviated, and he escapes with comparative, nay with almost entire, impunity. Public opinion however under the exertions of the Abolition Committee and other enlightened individuals in France appears gradually to be acquiring a firmer and louder tone on this subject. A petition against the slave trade had been presented to both chambers. It is the first movement of the kind which the French public has manifested; and when we remember the small beginnings among ourselves and the magnificent result which followed, too much importance can scarcely be attached to it. The signatures comprised the names of some of the very first merchants and bankers in Paris. The necessity of prompt and decisive measures by the French government is proved from the horrible fact that thirty slave-ships had recently sailed from Nantz alone.

It is gratifying to observe that the rising Republics of South America continue to identify their interests and their own emancipation from political slavery with the restoration to personal freedom of the still more degraded members of the human family the Negro slaves. By a decree of Mexico every ship whether national or foreign arriving in their ports with slaves is confiscated; a punishment of ten years imprisonment is inflicted and all the slaves on board are *ipso facto* declared free. The United Provinces of Rio de la Plata also engage to prohibit, in the most effectual manner, all persons residing in the United Provinces, or subject to their jurisdiction from taking any part in the traffic.

The bill for consolidating the Abolition Laws had passed into a law. One of its most important provisions our readers are aware is the termination of the inter-colonial slave trade. The removal of slaves from island to island is permitted only until 1827 and that under very definite and limited restrictions, and with permission upon application by the King in Council, on proof that their removal is essential to the welfare of the slaves.—The Court of King's Bench has pronounced a memorable judgment the ultimate consequences of which may be scarcely less important than the celebrated decision which gave freedom to the slave the moment that he touched the soil of England. Some slaves the property of an English subject resident in East Florida, where slavery is tolerated by law, escaped on board an English ship; their late owner brought an action in this country against the commanders Sir Alexander Cochrane and Sir George Cockburne for harbouring them after notice. The Court held, that no such action could be maintained; the broad intelligible principles and emphatical language of Mr Justice Best were worthy of the cause and of the tribunal from which it proceeded:—
'The Legislature of this country has given judgment upon the question. They have abolished the trade in slaves: they have even bought up at a great price the right of other countries to carry it on. There is no statute recognizing slavery which operates in the part of the British Empire in which we are now called upon to administer justice. It is a relation which has always in British Courts been held inconsistent with the constitution of the country. It is matter of

pride to me to recollect, that whilst economists and politicians were recommending to the legislature the protection of this traffic, and senators were forming statutes for its promotion and declaring it a benefit to the country, the judges of the land, above the age in which they lived, standing upon the high ground of natural right, and disdaining to bend to the lower doctrine of expediency, declared that slavery was inconsistent with the genius of the English Constitution, and that human beings could not be the subject matter of property and if indeed there had been any express law commanding us to recognize those rights, we might then have been called upon to consider the propriety of that which has been said by the great commentator upon the laws of this country that ' if any human law should allow or enjoin us to commit an offence against the Divine law we are bound to transgress that human law for upon the law of nature and the law of revelation depend all human laws : that is to say, no human law should be suffered to contradict these —Now if it can be shewn that slavery is against the law of nature and the law of God it cannot be recognized in our Courts If slavery be recognized by any law prevailing in East Florida, the operation of that law is local It is an anti Christian law, and one which violates the rights of nature, and therefore ought not to be recognized here Sir George Cockburn having in the first instance received these Negroes into his ship he could no more have forced them back into slavery than he could have committed them to the deep

With regard to the trade itself the Directors have no ground whatever for indulging a hope that any material or permanent diminution has taken place With the exception of three vessels two under French and one under Spanish colours captured by the French flag it does not appear that the French squadron have offered any effectual interruption to the traffic During the whole of 1823, there were never at any one time less than three or four vessels under the French flag, trading for slaves, at the Gallinas and Shebar This must have been well known to the French authorities on the coast, civil military and naval but, during all that time not a capture was made Within the short space of two months the boats of a British vessel the Maidstone visited nineteen vessels, all carrying on the trade yet not one of whom, from the present state of our relations with France or from the inefficiency of our treaties with other powers was she authorised to touch Ten of these were under French colours furnished with French papers and belonging to French ports The object of the voyage was openly avowed and gloried in by some of the masters

But the French slave trade is not confined to regular voyages It is stated that every coasting vessel belonging to the French settlements of Goree and Senegal is accustomed regularly to purchase two or three slaves in each successive ship, and to import them into these settlements that the inhabitants may buy slaves whom they have only to take before the mayor to be registered and that the French government itself is in the habit of making purchases from the inhabitants and training the persons so purchased to serve in their garrisons Captain Pince commanding a merchant ship belonging to Liverpool, during a short stay in the river Bonny saw about twenty slave-vessels under French colours, one or more arriving every two or three days among others three first class brigantines direct from Nantz each destined to take upwards of 500 slaves It was generally understood by the French ships there, that their cruizers would not meddle with them on this head they seemed to entertain no fears Captain Pince passed under the stern of the Hebe a French frigate, whilst three French slave-ships were in sight, but the Hebe took no notice of them

The Report goes on to detail a variety of cases illustrative of the deep atrocity as well as the lamentable extent, of the trade as at present conducted. We extract a few specimens.—

The Victor fell in with a schooner-boat called Piccaninny Mena. Though only of five tons burthen she had taken on board in the Gaboon besides her crew water provisions, and some cargo, twenty-three slaves six of whom had already died. The Negroes were in a state of complete starvation and approaching dissolution: one died the day the boat was seized. The space allowed for them was no more than eighteen inches between the water casks and the deck.

The Maidstone it has been mentioned in two months, boarded nineteen slave ships, ten of which were French. The Bann, in four months, boarded ten, two of which only were taken, the rest therefore will have succeeded in carrying off about 3000 slaves.

The Diana a captured vessel had 143 slaves on board of whom she afterwards lost 23 on her passage by the small pox. "Of all the vessels I was on board of," says Captain Woolcombe the captor, "this was in the most deplorable condition: the stench from the accumulation of dirt joined to that of so many human beings packed together in a small space (the men all ironed in pairs) was intolerable. To add to the scene of misery the small pox had broken out among them: nine died before we took possession, and one almost immediately after our first boat got alongside. The Two Brazilian Friends another captured vessel, had 257 slaves on board: she was one of thirteen which sailed about the same time from Bahia to Badagry on the same errand. She had been previously boarded at different times both by the Maidstone and Bann but in vain, as the slaves, though then assembled on the beach, had not been on board. Commodore Bullen, who visited this ship, says "Its filthy and horrid state beggars all description: many females were far advanced in pregnancy and several had infants from four to twelve months of age, all were crowded together in one mass of living corruption; and yet this vessel had not her prescribed complement by nearly one hundred."

The Aviso another captured vessel had 465 slaves on board of whom 34 died after their capture notwithstanding every attention. Such was the filth and crowd that not half could have reached the Brazils alive. Commodore Bullen put the crew on shore in Prince's Island. These wretches as soon as they found that they must be boarded, had stove in her boilers as a last malignant effort to add to the misery of those whom a few minutes would place beyond their power. At the date of her capture she had scarcely twenty days provisions for the slaves and less water. How they intended to subsist them till their arrival at Bahia (says the Captain) is to me a problem unless they calculated on a great decrease from death."

The Bella Eliza cleared out for Molemba, but took in her cargo at a place known only to slave dealers by that fraudulent designation but which is, in fact the western bank of the river Lagos. She also had been twice boarded by the capturing ship before by embarking her victims she had become liable to be detained. According to the tonnage, as stated in her passport she was privileged to take 368 slaves: she had taken on board 381 being thirteen more even than this allowance of whom twenty two died before they reached Sierra Leone. The passage lasting seven weeks the suffering from want of water and provisions was so great that in two days more all hands must have perished

Upon an accurate inspection of these four vessels, to ascertain whether they answered the description in their papers, a remarkable discovery was made of the corrupt and cruel connivance of the official authorities of the Brazils. The tonnage of every vessel is entered in the royal passport and permission is given to carry a cargo in proportion to that tonnage, at the rate of five slaves for every two tons. On admeasurement the real tonnage was found, in every one of these instances to be so much less than the tonnage stated in their passport, that the Diana according to its passport was in fact authorized to take five to each ton, the Two Brazilian Friends four to each ton, the Aviso above five to each ton, and the Bella Eliza at the rate of nearly seven to every two tons. The men's slave room in the first was only two feet seven inches high, in the second two feet, and in the third two feet three inches. Taking into calculation the size of the women's room and the number shipped, little more than three and one fourth square feet was allowed to each adult. Indeed, had they attempted to put on board the number to which according to the false description thus sanctioned by the Brazilian authorities they would have been entitled, they could not literally have been stowed although they are stated to have been packed under deck, on deck, and in boats like beasts. Some of these vessels had on board fierce dogs of the blood hound species, natives of the Brazils, trained to sit watching over the hatches during the night lest the wretched beings below should rise either for resistance or for air.

One Oiseau, commander of a French slave ship called Le Louis, having completed his cargo on the old Calabar, thrust them all between decks (a height of only three feet) and closed the hatches on them for the night. Fifty were found dead in the morning. As a matter of course, he only immediately returned on shore to supply their place. Captain Arnaud, of the Louisa, arrived at Guadaloupe with 200 Negroes, the remainder of an original cargo of 265. Having by mistake purchased more than he could accommodate he had thrown the odd 65 into the sea.

On board a captured vessel was found a letter from a French slave-agent to Messrs Bannaffe and La riviere of Guadaloupe which furnishes an edifying specimen of West Indian correspondence. It is a sort of circular, soliciting for custom and evidently drawn up in the current language of the trade, language calculated to make all except these consignees of human beings, shudder at the depth of moral debasement to which it seems our nature may be reduced. The following is an extract from it:—

Under the auspices of Mr Couronneau of Bordeaux our friend we have the honour of tendering to you our services at this place. You know gentlemen that the advantage which our market offers for the disposal of *ebony* gives it a great preference over any other of our colonies and it strikes us that it would suit you to send to it a few shipments of that sort. We have received this year a great many cargoes of that article, on account of merchants of Nantz and towards the end of January we expect here other ships that have sailed from the last-mentioned port. All our sales have been attended with favourable results. The last cargo sold here was that of the Harriett of Nantz 328 *logs* were disposed of on their landing (those that were damaged excepted) at 225 dollars each. This merchandize was of a very ordinary nature, and had suffered much by getting rid of the article at once you may make a much better thing of it. After some particular instructions it proceeds. The commandant who is devoted to us would deliver a letter of instructions for the captain when once the cargo is on shore all risk is at an end.—We have this day to communicate to you a circumstance that will no doubt afford you as much interest as it does to us. The brig, Two Nations, Captain Pettier, which had lately been captured by an English cruiser (at the moment when she appeared before Uragua with a cargo of ebony) and carried to Kingston, has been released, the admiral having declared that no one had the right of capturing the French flag. in consequence of this the brig returned to Uragua where she landed 456 logs. Had the wood been good it would have had a fine sale, but owing to the bad state of the bulk of the cargo, which had suffered much, it is of the smallest kind. The liberation of this vessel offers to us the assurance that our flag will henceforth be respected. The three vessels that were cruising upon our coast were immediately recalled to Jamaica. As to the Dutch, there is only one English vessel of war in our latitude commissioned to capture them, the others are altogether interdicted that right. We consider therefore that there is no longer any risk upon our coast, and that vessels may present themselves with all safety before Uragua, where we constantly keep a pilot. The sales meet with no opposition and are carried on in some measure publicly.

We turn from these sickening details to the statements in the Report respecting Sierra Leone, from which we copy the following particulars:—

The mortality of 1823 at Sierra Leone though of a most distressing nature has been much exaggerated. The fever which prevailed did not attack a Black or Coloured person, but out of a White population of 110 the deaths were 25. Serious injury arises to the interests of the colony from the occasional prevalence of severe sickness, and in no respect more than by the temporary interruption to which the advancement of education and religious instruction has been exposed, in consequence of the death of their principal instructors, among whom the mortality was unusually great. The effect of these unexpected losses was that for a considerable period both properly qualified school masters and also chaplains had been wanting. But the Church Missionary Society, which has now taken off the hands of Government the burden of supplying to the colony the means of religious instruction, has been making great efforts to supply the requisite number of teachers; and their zeal and that of their missionaries, has only been rendered more remarkable and praiseworthy by the difficulties with which they had to contend.

The regular attendance on public worship consists of nearly the whole population of the colony, and the schools are attended by the whole of the young and even by not a few of the adults.— Sierra Leone contains about 18,000 inhabitants, of whom, about 12,000 consist entirely of liberated Africans, who for the most part occupy the parishes in the mountains and nothing can be more gratifying than to know that the almost impenetrable woods which were the haunts but lately of wild beasts have been replaced by villages with comfortable habitations, and surrounded by tracts of ground under cultivation, and containing school houses for both sexes. In one of these it is reported that, out of 103 children 64 can read the Scriptures; in others that out of 1079 scholars there are 710 persons who can read and so on in different proportions. The churches erected among them are said to have crowded congregations; one in Regent Town usually assembling a congregation of from 1200 to 2000 souls.

In addition to the labours of missionaries it seems highly important, that persons should be placed over these liberated Africans qualified to discharge the duties of magistrates to form and preserve those habits of order by which a rising society must be bound together and to direct its labour to those objects of industry which may be most useful and advantageous

In speaking of the progress of civilization in Africa it is in Sierra Leone itself that a rational inquirer can alone expect to find that improvement has taken root up to the present time Beyond the borders of the colony, whilst the slave-dealer, the missionary of barbarism is in the field there is little or rather no possibility of a harvest for the missionary of peace How could a native however curious and intelligent occupy himself in acquiring knowledge when he may not stir out of his village but at the risk of being seized and sold?

The civilization of Africa never can proceed until the slave trade is put down beyond a hope or possibility of return To suspend it to alternate between a year of repose and a year of plunder to give the bud just time to germinate, and then to tread it under foot is little better than a machinery for adding to the growth and the number of the victims and for rendering by the contrast their sufferings more intense The appearance of a slave-ship demoralizes a whole neighbourhood

The Directors close their Report with calling the attention of the public to the precise point which they have reached in this great cause and to the nature of the difficulties with which for the future they have to contend Our own slave trade is extinct But a state of things, such as at the institution of this Society never could have been anticipated, has arisen since the peace a new disturbing force is introduced which we have not the power of controuling and the enemies of humanity have rushed in between us and our object and threaten to bear it beyond our reach As in the abolition of the slave trade we originally sought the mitigation of slavery so we are now driven to consider whether any other efficient means are left us than that of reversing our course of proceeding and whether we must not look henceforward to the mitigation and extinction of slavery as our only security for the abolition of the slave trade We cannot, it is true compel other nations to abandon it it seems too probable that they are not to be persuaded but, by a determined encouragement of free labour we may make it not worth pursuing

ANTI SLAVERY SOCIETY

The Second Report of this Society brings down the intelligence on the subject of slavery to the date of the last annual meeting

Since the former meeting of the Society little or nothing had occurred which affords any satisfactory indication of progress in the great work for which the Society has been instituted *the Mitigation and gradual Abolition of Slavery in the British Dominions* In the colony of Trinidad, indeed an Order of his Majesty in Council, containing many salutary regulations though greatly defective in some important respects, had been promulgated Against the imposition of this Order, the White planters of the island have universally and strenuously remonstrated alleging that it was pregnant with inevitable ruin to all their interests The Governor's instructions, however were peremptory and in June 1824, the Order was promulgated, and became the law of the island — A committee of planters was subsequently appointed, who complain that the Order in Council " has made an entire revolution in the system under which slaves were heretofore managed and governed that ' nothing but the force of habit, and a brutish indistinct idea of the superiority and fixed power of their masters, keep them in awe and subjection that one great source of discomfort to the *slave* is the change produced by the Order in Council in the *old mode* of punishment, ' so well established, recognized, and understood by the slave (alluding of course to the abolition of flogging as it respects the women, and of the driving whip as it respects both sexes) " By those, they remark, " who have most considered the subject in this colony, the use of the whip is believed to be identified with the existence of slavery This and much more equally condemnatory of the West Indians and their system, is said not by any enemy of slavery, but by West Indians themselves

In the various resolutions, remonstrances, and representations of the planters of Trinidad, the Committee rejoice to learn that the free Blacks and People of Colour with few if any exceptions, have taken no share They possess, it is said, a full half of the property of the island but they have not chosen to set themselves in opposition to the wishes of Parliament and of the public on this occasion The civil degradations which they themselves are doomed to sustain are many and galling and the Committee believe they are sufficiently enlightened to have at length attained a just and settled conviction that the slavery of their colour is the real root of the evils they experience and that while that slavery is perpetuated —while the Negro continues a " brutish outcast from the pale of society " deprived of his natural rights a mere beast of burden a mere instrument of profit —they who partake of his colour must of necessity partake of his debasement *His* brand will cleave to *them* and neither wealth nor distinguished talents nor eminent moral worth, were they all to meet in one individual will suffice to efface it

It was stated in the last Report to be the declared intention of his Majesty's Ministers, to extend the provisions of the Trinidad Order in Council to Demerara, Berbice, St Lucia, Mauritius, and the Cape of Good Hope but the purpose had remained still unexecuted, probably from the opposition of the planters of those colonies to reforms which they in common with the planters of Trinidad, profess to "regard with dismay and horror as a dangerous invasion of their most sacred rights

On the concurrence of the slave holders, the resident slaveholders especially, in any effective plan for controuling their own power, and for raising their wretched bondsmen in the scale of being, the Committee have never placed any strong reliance Indeed, they are persuaded that the aversion which prevails, in the West Indies, to conferring upon Negroes the common rights of human nature, is too deep rooted and general to be overcome except by the direct and authoritative interference of a higher power

The spirit and temper which the Committee attribute to the colonists, have been the most clearly manifested in those colonies where the movement of the popular mind among them is the most free and unfettered In Barbadoes, for example, two sessions had been consumed in debate and deliberation, and nothing had yet been done towards the reform of the Slave Code The very mover of the proposed reform seemed to feel that he could not expect a hearing without the most unmeasured abuse of the Abolitionists and their ' *hellish designs* But all the violence of this vituperation was insufficient to secure the slightest degree of popular favour in Barbadoes, to the man who had dared to innovate however sparingly, on the sacred institutions of its slave code The speech was followed by upwards of two months of deliberation in the Assembly on the bill which it introduced but during this time the mover of it appears to have been assailed, out of doors, by every species of clamour and invective

Our readers will recollect the outrages which were perpetrated in Barbadoes, by the lawless destruction of the Methodist Chapel at Bridgetown and the expulsion of the Missionary Shrewsbury. These outrages have been followed by others of a similar description. Mr Rayner, another missionary, went from St Vincent's to Barbadoes: he applied in the first instance to the Governor for protection, but his application was very coldly received, and no hope of effectual protection was afforded to him. Mr Rayner therefore did not dare to land, on account of the threats of the leaders of the former mob. "One zealous man, it is stated, "sat on the shore a whole night with a loaded pistol, to shoot him had he left the vessel. The vessel itself was menaced with an attack of boats, and was obliged to seek protection under the guns of a ship of war. The congregation also, which Mr Shrewsbury left behind him, and which continued to meet in a private house for the purposes of worship and mutual edification, were threatened with violence. The former mob announced their purpose of celebrating the anniversary of the destruction of the chapel, by razing the obnoxious house to the ground. This was prevented by the interference of the governor and the magistrates, but the latter have forbidden any more meetings to be held. In short the whole account which has been given to the public, by the Methodist Mission Society, proves the existence, in Barbadoes, of a state of disgraceful lawlessness and a deep and settled hostility to the religious instruction of the Negro and Coloured population, of whom the Methodist congregation was chiefly composed

That a similar feeling should be represented to prevail in Demerara where, the same Report tells us, a hostile spirit against missions of every kind has continued to be manifested, will be no subject of surprize. In Jamaica also, a like spirit had shewn itself at different parochial meetings, where resolutions were agreed to, recommending the expulsion of the missionaries. In the other West India colonies there appears considerably less hostility to missionary exertions and in some, they are even encouraged

The proceedings of the Legislature of Jamaica have been no less instructive than those of the Barbadoes Assembly but we must refer our readers to the Report itself for the details

The Committee cannot learn that any effective measures of reform have yet been adopted in consequence of the recommendation of his Majesty, by any of the other colonies except Tobago. In that island, containing a population of 14,000 slaves the Legislature have, in one point, gone even beyond the provisions of the Trinidad Order in Council for they have admitted slave evidence in the very case in which the Order in Council has rejected it,—namely, in the case of the wilful murder or mayem of a slave by a White or free person. Clauses are also introduced for securing the personal property of the slaves for abolishing Sunday markets and substituting Thursday for allowing to the slaves thirty five week days in the year for their provision grounds and for limiting arbitrary punishments to twenty stripes and, if more than twelve are given, providing that it shall be in the presence of a free person besides the person who inflicts the punishment. These are undoubtedly improvements, though they fall far short of the recommendations of his Majesty

With this single exception the Committee cannot discover that during the year any enactments had been framed by the Colonial Legislatures which tend to the mitigation of Slavery so that the in terference of the imperial Parliament is imperatively called for to ameliorate and finally abolish this unjust and wicked system.

It is not, however, merely by the interference of Parliament, in the internal legislation of the colonies, that the mitigation and final extinction of slavery may be effected: the abolition of the West Indian monopoly would tend, perhaps, even more certainly to that end.

That monopoly is at present supported, first, by a bounty of upwards of six shillings per cwt. on the export of refined sugar, and which necessarily raises the price, not only of all the sugar exported, but of all the sugar consumed at home, to the extent of the bounty;—and secondly, a protecting duty of ten shillings a cwt. more on East Indian, than on West-Indian sugar, which favours sugar grown by slave labour, in preference to that grown by free labour, to the extent of about 50 per cent. on the cost of the article, and tends to exclude the latter from our consumption, and to force us to consume the former. On coffee also, the West Indies have a protection of 28s. a cwt. Now, to say nothing at present of the degree in which prices are raised by the operation of the protecting duty, the cost of the West Indian monopoly arising from the sugar bounty alone, is estimated at about 1,200,000l. annually. And it is this large sum, (in addition to whatever enhancement of price may be produced by the protecting duty,) paid by the people of this country to the growers of sugar, over and above what that sugar would otherwise cost, which does in fact chiefly maintain unimpaired and unreformed the wretched system of colonial bondage. The people of England are therefore the real upholders of Negro slavery. Without their large contribution to its support, it could not fail to be rapidly mitigated, and eventually extinguished. It is absolutely vain therefore, to be hoping to abolish slavery or to expect that by the vehemence of our speeches, or the force of mere parliamentary resolutions, or of royal recommendations, we shall be able to abate this evil, while we are extending to it such solid marks of our favour, and thus affording to it its great and principal means of support.

If it were proposed in Parliament to give to each of our 1800 West Indian proprietors, pensions varying in their amount from 500l. to 5000l. a year, according to the quantity of sugar which each might extract, by means of the cartwhip, from the labour of his slaves and forming a total aggregate of one million two hundred thousand pounds, what reception would such a proposition meet with? Would it be tolerated for a single moment? And, yet, wherein does the actual state of things differ substantially from the case which has been supposed except that, in this last, the transaction would stand forth to the public view in all its flagrancy, while, in the other, it is more concealed from observation. The payment is not the less real on that account.

It will not be alleged that the West Indians have any claim to levy such a contribution upon the people of this country for merits or services of their own. They are themselves sensible of this. They allege it to be necessary not so much on their own account, as with a view to the well being and comfort of their slaves. But no notion, the Committee maintain, can be more fundamentally erroneous than this and they shew, that whatever tends to raise the price of the slave grown produce of our colonies tends in the same degree to rivet the chains, and to add to the labour and misery, of the slave while the depression of its price operates beneficially both in relaxing his bonds, abating his toil, and enlarging his comforts. Our readers will find a most convincing argument on this subject in the Report before us.

The Committee do not, however, mean to argue that slaves may not be wretchedly used, and cruelly oppressed, when prices are low, and their labour comparatively unproductive It is not in human nature that the possession of such an uncontrolled despotic power as that which is possessed by the colonial master over his bondsman should not be abused under whatever circumstances or system

But still it will be argued, that the abolition of the bounties and protecting duties must issue in the ruin of the planters If, with all the support which these afford them, they find it scarcely possible to keep themselves from sinking their utter ruin must be the inevitable consequence of withdrawing that support Now, although it is too much to require that the pecuniary interests of 1600 or 1800 sugar planters should be allowed to come into competition with the comfort, the health, the liberty and the lives of seven or eight hundred thousand human beings, and with the clear interests of the whole community of the British Empire and although the facts of the case leave no room for hesitation as to the expediency, nay as to the absolute necessity, of putting an end to this most impolitic, inhuman, and unchristian system yet the Committee meet their opponents, even on this ground The system of bounties is a system of pauperism on a large scale, attended with all the evils of pauperism But for this, would it have been possible that the West Indies should have continued in that low and wretched state of improvement which they now exhibit,—that the miserable hoe, raised by the feeble hands of men and women driven forward by the cartwhip, should still be their only instrument in turning up the soil, to the neglect of cattle and machinery —that all modern improvements in husbandry should be almost unknown that one unvarying course of exhausting crops should be pursued without change or relief —and that in a climate congenial to them the population should continue progressively and rapidly to decrease? These and many other points that might be mentioned are fatal anomalies, which can only be accounted for by the withering influence of slavery and of the factitious aid by which it is upheld in all its unmitigated malignity How different would have been the state of things in our colonies had a different course been pursued! Nothing short of the removal of all protection of the produce of slave labour, against competition with the produce of free labour, can effectually banish the evil

The cultivation of sugar is at present a forced cultivation, which must ever be a hazardous and expensive process, and can only be supported by a monopoly price, both high and permanent The first effect of the removal of restrictions would be, that the colonist would be induced to withdraw from sugar cultivation (which is at once the most exhausting to the soil, and the most oppressive to the slave of any) his inferior soils, and to employ them in pasture, or in the growth of other articles of a less onerous description By reserving his best soils only for sugar, its remunerating price would be lowered and his profits of course raised But the necessity of the case would force upon him other improvements He would be obliged to become resident That curse of the West Indies, a non resident proprietary, would cease the heavy cost of agency would be saved the ruinous effect arising from the unfaithfulness and disobedience of agents, frustrating every designed amelioration, would be stopped the plough and various other articles of machinery would then be brought into use, and would both lessen the expense of culture and lighten the labour of the slaves Cattle would be more generally employed a change of crop, a better system of manuring and a better system of general management would follow The women would be relieved from that con

...and oppressive drudgery of field labour which unites them with barrenness, and abridges their lives. The population would increase, and as they increased their condition would gradually approach to that of free labourers. The West Indies would then be able to compete in the sale of their produce with any other country in the world, and the West Indian planter would find the improvement of his income to keep pace with the progress of those reforms, which would, at the same time, most effectually promote the happiness, and exalt the moral and social condition, of his unhappy bondsmen.

It is vain, however, to expect, that, while the West Indies maintain their monopoly, and are thus protected against the competition of free labour, a single effectual step will be taken in this career of reformation. Other expedients therefore must be resorted to, if Parliament should refuse to abolish the restrictive system; such as the competition of free labour, and the substitution of the use of the produce of free labour for that of slave labour. In the mean time, however, the slaves are suffering and perishing. The depopulation of our colonies is proceeding at a rate which can be explained on no principle but that of the severity of their treatment. They still labour under the whip without wages. They are still chattels. They are still not the subjects of law, but of individual caprice. They are still without any civil or political rights. Even their marriages are still unsanctioned and unprotected by any legal recognition. Their evidence is still generally inadmissible. Their manumission is still obstructed; and, even after being made free, they are still liable to be reduced again to slavery if unable to produce proof of freedom. The master may still sell or transfer them at his pleasure, without any regard to family ties. He alone still regulates the measure of their labour, their food, and their punishment. He may still brand them, whether men or women, in any part of their bodies, with a heated iron; confine them in the stocks; load them with chains; strip them naked and cartwhip them at his pleasure. He may still deprive them of half their night's rest, and leave them no alternative, with respect to the employment of Sunday, but that of toiling for their subsistence, or carrying their produce to market; and he may still shut them out from the means of religious instruction. He may thus, and in a variety of other ways, make " their lives bitter with hard bondage." Is it possible, under these circumstances, that the nation can consent that the present system should be continued?

But it is said that the Negroes, when they become free, will not work; that the exports from the West Indies will therefore greatly diminish; that all industry and exertion will be at an end; and that they will merge again into the state of savages. In reply the Committee refer to Hayti. There the slaves were to the full as depressed as our slaves now are, and much more ignorant. They have been engaged also in a struggle for liberty, through a long protracted period of blood and desolation, of confusion and anarchy. Twenty years of sanguinary conflict of the most barbarizing description, sometimes with foreign, sometimes with domestic enemies, were little calculated to train them to habits of industry, or to the arts of peace. And yet what do we witness in their case? They have contrived, in the period which has since elapsed, at least to maintain themselves without any foreign aid. Though it was necessary to keep a large portion of the ablest and most active labourers under arms (who are of course sustained by the labour of the rest,) their own exertions have alone ministered to their subsistence as well as defrayed the entire expenditure of the state

They have not only abundantly supplied their wants by their own labour, but they have nearly, if not more than, doubled their numbers in twenty years. And while they have done this, they have been advancing in intelligence, respectability, and wealth. Schools have been multiplied among them: knowledge has been widely diffused: the arts of civilized life have been cultivated: the reign of order and law has been established: security has been given to property: and industry, having its reward, has been progressively extending its boundaries: so that the value of foreign merchandize imported into Hayti in the year 1822, and consumed there (the whole of which must have been paid for by the produce of Haytian labour), amounted, by the official returns of that island, to three millions sterling.

After adverting to these and various other topics, the Committee remark, that they have said enough to convince the Meeting that the labours of the Society are far from being at an end. As yet, in truth, little or nothing has been done beyond enlightening, to a certain degree, the public mind on this subject, and awakening, they trust, the national conscience to a sense of the enormity of the evil they have associated to remove. It remains for the friends of the African race to employ their best endeavours to induce Parliament to redeem its solemn pledge on this subject, by adopting effectual measures for carrying the resolutions of 1823, disregarded and resisted as they have been by the colonies, into early and full effect. It will also be an important part of their duty to obtain, if possible, the abolition of those fiscal regulations which protect the produce of slave labour against the competition of free labour—regulations which, in fact, render the people of Great Britain the main upholders of this vicious system. And it will be further incumbent on them to aid every scheme, which may hold out a fair prospect of success for attaining the same desirable end, by bringing the produce of free labour into competition with that of slave labour. They must even be ready, if necessary, to make large pecuniary sacrifices to accomplish their great object. By the appropriation of less than a third of what we now pay in bounties and drawbacks, we might redeem from their bondage the whole of the female population, and thus extinguish slavery in a single generation.

The Committee before they close their Report, remind the friends of their cause throughout the kingdom, of the indispensible necessity of funds to the performance of the duties they have undertaken to execute. The diffusion alone of information by means of the press, necessarily occasions a considerable expenditure. The press, however, is the grand instrument of success, because it is the only effectual means of enlightening the public mind. They therefore earnestly impress upon the minds of their friends, throughout the kingdom, the importance of their exerting themselves, each in his own sphere, to procure subscriptions and active co-operation, and to diffuse information, by means of the books and tracts of the society among every class of the community. On the degree in which the public feeling is kept alive on this subject depends, under God, mainly, if not entirely, the final triumph of their efforts.

The substance of the speeches delivered at the general meeting, together with an Appendix, containing documents, notes, and illustrations, are added to the Report, and will well repay the perusal of all who are interested in this cause of humanity and religion.

PRISON DISCIPLINE SOCIETY.

The Sixth Report and Appendix of this Society's transactions, forming a closely printed volume of several hundred pages, well deserves to be in the hands of all who are practically concerned in the administration of justice or prison discipline. We shall condense for the information of our readers the chief particulars.

The former Reports of this Society bear ample testimony to the improvements that have within the last few years taken place in most of the county gaols throughout the kingdom. There is yet however much to be accomplished before they shall be what the laws intend them to be the instruments of just punishment and fear and at the same time the medium of moral reformation and religious improvement. The prisons under local jurisdiction continue in a very deplorable state. In England alone there are about 140 places of confinement of this description. To many of them capital offenders are occasionally committed and it has been ascertained that about 8,000 persons pass through them in the course of the year. In several there is no effectual separation of the sexes in some the keeper does not even reside in others the insecurity of the building renders it necessary that irons should be used and other illegal and unwarrantable means of detention be adopted for security. In the greater part of them, the sick are not separated from others. The consequence of such defects is, that these gaols are so many establishments for the encouragement and growth of crime. There is no employment no reflection, no moral nor religious instruction.

The Committee adduce several most revolting illustrations of these remarks but we are happy to state that steps have been taken by the Legislature towards the reformation of gaols under local jurisdiction. The measures necessary for this purpose, however, involve many difficulties.

In their last Report the Committee stated that an opinion was entertained by the magistracy in one of the northern counties, that the law did not authorize the maintenance of any prisoner before trial, otherwise than by his own labour; and that acting on this conviction, they had proceeded to place the untried at the tread wheel. On a refusal to work, the ordinary allowance was withheld, and a scanty fare of bread and water was substituted. This measure involved a very important principle. The common law of England has uniformly regarded imprisonment before trial as the means of safe custody only and, independently of the injustice of a practice which would confound the accused with the guilty, its impolicy was also evident for nothing can tend more effectually to weaken the character of punishment in the mind of the criminal than the consideration that the unconvicted share alike the same penalty. It is therefore, very satisfactory to find that the question is now set at rest it having been enacted that no untried prisoner shall be employed at any work without his own free consent.

It is highly gratifying to observe the favourable disposition which prevails in Parliament, and the readiness that exists on the part of his Majesty's Government to promote the improvement of prisons. The attention of the Legislature has hitherto been very beneficially directed to the investigation of the county gaols and to the measures best calculated to insure their proper regulation. These measures cannot be too highly appreciated as well for their own value as for the promise which they afford of further legislation on other subjects connected with the administration of prisons, and the prevention of crime.

Of these subjects, there is none which more earnestly demands the attention of Parliament, than the delay which occurs in the administration of justice, from the want of a more frequent gaol delivery. It is a fine principle of the jurisprudence of our country that every person is presumed innocent until proved to be guilty; but the long period of imprisonment before trial, especially in the present condition of the gaols, is in effect directly opposed to this just maxim. A great proportion of those committed are in confinement before trial for a longer period than that to which, if guilty, they are ultimately sentenced; and a considerable number who undergo this preliminary confinement are acquitted of the crimes with which they are charged. From papers laid before Parliament, it appears that throughout England and Wales, not including Middlesex, one sixth of the prisoners had suffered confinement from six to eight months, and nearly the half from three to six months, before it was known whether they were guilty, or whether their offences, if even proved, were such as to merit that extent of punishment.

There is another object, connected with the administration of justice, which does not, in the opinion of the Committee, attract the attention that it merits. They refer to the expediency of taking bail in a greater number of cases than is at present the practice. Whatever will diminish the number of persons committed for safe custody is of great importance in the defective state of many of our gaols; and the extension of bail in certain cases, would greatly facilitate the classification of convicted prisoners, and essentially promote the ends of justice. Nothing can be more erroneous or more impolitic than to give a detention which is avowedly for safe custody only, the character of a punishment for crime. All that is contemplated, is the appearance of the accused in court, to answer the charge alleged against him. If this appearance can be obtained by the intervention of sureties, instead of throwing the individual into gaol, the ends of justice are answered, the prison is relieved from an unnecessary burthen, and the accused himself is not exposed to the influence of bad example. The law has very properly declared that the higher offences shall be unbailable; not that the previous imprisonment is intended as a portion of punishment, but because the motive for absconding is too great to be restrained by ordinary sureties; the security of the person can be answered for only by the walls of a gaol. But it is very different in many cases of inferior crime.

The Committee, in adverting to an opinion which is prevalent, that, notwithstanding the efforts making for the moral and religious welfare of society, crime continues to increase, state that it is not founded in fact. An official return has been laid before Parliament, from which it appears that the number of offenders committed for trial was considerably augmented from the year 1816 to the year 1819; but this increase was only proportionate to what might have been anticipated from peculiar causes; and it is gratifying to find that since that period the number of persons committed for trial has been gradually declining; in some districts, indeed, in a much greater proportion than was its previous increase. Generally speaking also the offences have been of a less guilty character than those of the former period.

For a detailed description of the improvements that have taken place in the several prisons throughout England we must refer to the Appendix to this Report, which records the actual results of a great variety of experience; its perusal cannot fail to give rise to reflections of deep interest. It will be seen by these statements, that considerable alterations are now in progress in the construction of various gaols and houses of correction; but the Committee do not think that the importance of inspection has been adequately appreciated; in many instances it has been altogether neglected.

The various statements in the Appendix also shew the great extent to which the labour of the tread-wheel has been introduced into the houses of correction of the several counties. If it be inquired upon what grounds the Committee continue to advocate this description of prison labour, they reply, because it possesses in their opinion, many of the primary requisites of efficacious punishment. It is corrective; it is exemplary; its application is not inconsistent with humane feeling, and interferes in no way with the inculcation of moral and religious impressions. It has received the approving sanction of the community at large; its penalties are felt by those who are subject to its discipline, and it operates to deter from the commission of crime — "I will never come here again," is the language of the prisoner on quitting confinement. Still it is known to have excited the warm opposition of several enlightened friends of humanity; and the controversy occasioned by this circumstance has given rise to much valuable discussion, and been productive of great good. The Committee state that they have discovered no reason to alter the opinion they have hitherto entertained, as to the nature and effects of this species of prison discipline. Further experience has, on the contrary, strengthened their conviction that the labour, when under proper management and restriction, is prejudicial neither to the health nor limbs of the prisoners. From the introduction of the tread-wheel the country has derived great benefit; and so general is the impression in its favour that in a short time there will probably be few county houses of correction throughout England in which this description of labour will not have been adopted.

The Committee notice some ingenious improvements in the construction of tread wheel machinery, consisting of a moveable reel, or cylindrical wheel substituted in the place of the hand-rail by which prisoners hold when on the tread-mill. The object of this small wheel is to remove an objection which has been urged against this kind of prison labour, namely, the inert position of the arms while the individual is at work. This wheel is connected with the other machinery; and when put in motion the prisoners work with their hands at the same time that the feet are kept in constant action; and thus a more general degree of exercise is afforded to the body.

The Ladies Committee who have devoted themselves to the care of the female department in Newgate, continue their labours with an assiduity worthy of their high character and of the distinguished cause in which they are engaged. The benefit resulting from their unwearied exertions has been more permanent and extensive than could possibly have been anticipated, from the absence of proper classification, and the confined limits of this badly constructed prison. Availing themselves of the public interest which their plans have excited, they have established a society for the encouragement and formation of committees similar to their own in the principal gaol towns throughout the kingdom; and many such associations are now in operation, conducted with unostentatious yet ardent kindness. In some places where associations could not be formed, very beneficial effects have been produced by the exertions of ladies who have, alone and unsupported, engaged in the arduous work of visiting female prisoners. At one prison, visited by a lady of high respectability, six young women who had abandoned their homes to lived in habits of prodigacy were restored to their respective families, and have since afforded the most satisfactory proofs of reformation

In turning to Scotland, the Committee quote a remark of Howard, that the prisons are 'old buildings, dirty and offensive without courts, and also generally without water." Since that period but little alteration has taken place in the condition of these gaols and there is no part of the United Kingdom in which prison discipline is so neglected as in Scotland. It is somewhat surprising when the magistracy in other parts of the kingdom are actively engaged in the amendment of their gaols, that the discharge of these important duties should generally have escaped the attention of the authorities in Scotland It surely cannot be said that the defective condition of the gaols in that country is unknown the well known work of Mr Gurney renders ignorance on such a subject impossible

The second annual Report of the inspectors-general of Ireland is framed on very enlightened views and replete with interesting facts. Since the former Report important improvements have taken place in the Irish prisons In many counties either new gaols are in progress or are about to be erected or such additions will be made to those already in use, as are best calculated to provide a suitable remedy for the great evils which the want of sufficient prisons has occasioned The valuable aid which the regulation of prisons has received from the superintendence of the parochial clergy cannot be too highly estimated The law has imposed upon them a duty in the local inspection of bridewells situated in their respective parishes, without any remuneration whatever and the wishes of the Legislature have been realized by the discharge of this office with benevolent and disinterested zeal

Prison schools have made great progress within the last year a male and female school are now established in almost every prison The valuable influence of "Ladies Associations" is also felt throughout many counties, in visiting and instructing female prisoners

In calling the attention of the public to the consideration of the second leading object of the institution—the reformation of juvenile offenders—the Committee advert, with peculiar pleasure to the establishment of infant schools The Committee dwell with much earnestness on the merits of these institutions because they are in an especial manner applicable to the most indigent classes and to a vast proportion of those whose welfare and reformation form one of the leading objects of the Society

But great as is the importance that attaches to the education of the poor, and to measures calculated to insure the prevention of crime, they do not supersede the necessity of other exertions to arrest the course of juvenile delinquency The Committee therefore recommend the establishment of a large Penitentiary to which upon conviction for repeated offences, boys might be sentenced for long periods, and in which punishment could be inflicted on the refractory and habits of restraint imposed But there are others whose slight offences would not warrant such a punishment and whose destitute condition gives them strong claims on public sympathy Many hundreds of these lads have either lost their parents or have been deserted by them Thus abandoned they live from day to day by preying on the property of others at night they usually sleep in the open air Their minds are in a state of the darkest ignorance, and the grossest vice They are very frequently brought up before the magistrates for petty offences They are committed for short periods, and when liberated are very sent again to prison. One boy but nine years of age, who has been under the notice of the Committee, had been eighteen times committed to the different prisons in the metropolis. On their discharge they have no other resource than the work house: they continue pilfering, increasing in guilt as they advance in years, until their career is terminated by transportation or death. In the application of their funds on behalf of distressed boys, the Committee state that their object has not been personal relief, but moral reformation; and they have the pleasure to state that the lads admitted into the Temporary Refuge whose cases were formerly reported, continue to give the most satisfactory proofs of amendment. Several are now filling respectable situations with great credit and usefulness, and afford unquestionable evidence of the benefit that has resulted from the establishment of the institution. During the past year a further number of distressed boys discharged from prison have been admitted. Many of these cases are of a most affecting kind. We quote a single specimen.

W— F—aged seventeen. His father and mother are dead. He was five years engaged in the commission of crime, and has been in all the prisons of the metropolis and its neighbourhood. He formed one of a gang of the most desperate juvenile thieves who infest London. He was severely flogged in Newgate, and discharged on the same day. After remaining three months in the Temporary Refuge he was admitted into the permanent establishment, where he is now learning to be a shoemaker. It is hardly possible to conceive a human being more degraded in a moral point of view than this lad appeared to be on his admission. He has now been in the Refuge upwards of twelve months and has made considerable progress in his trade. He evinces much good feeling, and has been a monitor for more than two months, discharging the duty of that office very much to the satisfaction of the superintendant.

To enable the Committee to extend the plans upon which they are now acting for the prevention of juvenile delinquency they strongly and most justly appeal to the public liberality.

The Committee at the conclusion of another year's labour indulge in those gratifying reflections which the further amendment of prisons is calculated to excite. The recent provisions of the Legislature are now in a course of gradual operation; and although there are exceptions to the zeal that is generally manifested—although a great proportion of the borough gaols are yet in a condition that constitutes them at once a public grievance and a national disgrace—yet improvements are visibly advancing; and there is reason to hope that further remedial measures will, if necessary, be adopted by Parliament. If indeed we may anticipate the progress of the future by the retrospect of the last few years, there is ample ground for encouragement; and we most warmly recommend the object to the best wishes, prayers, and liberality of our readers.

CHURCH MISSIONARY SOCIETY

In reporting the proceedings of its twenty fifth year, the Committee acknowledge with gratitude to God that amidst partial discouragements they have abundant ground for thanksgiving and praise. They can discover, in various parts of the earth, evident proofs that the cause of 'pure and undefiled religion' is, notwithstanding the opposition which it encounters in various ways, steadily advancing.

The leading general statements

of the Report respecting the Society's funds and proceedings, have already appeared in our Number for November, p 714 we therefore proceed to a few particulars connected with each particular mission

The Committee commence the account of their proceedings with the

West Africa Mission

In reporting the death of Sir Charles MacCarthy, the Committee notice the address of the acting Chief Justice of the colony, which while it bears testimony to the exertions of that individual on behalf of the temporal and spiritual welfare of those entrusted to his charge, demonstrates by an appeal to witnesses on the spot that these exertions were rewarded by abundant success 'Gratitude, he remarks, 'is due to Sir Charles and will always be paid to his memory but the appeal is to facts Look at the state of the colony when he arrived and look at it now Look at the difference in Freetown—in the inhabitants, in the resources in the importance of the colony but, above all, look at the liberated Africans and their villages Could the gentlemen present, who have themselves seen it have otherwise believed the change which has taken place? To say nothing of the churches the houses, the cultivated fields, which are every where occupying what was previously a dark and impenetrable forest look at the change in the man Is the man who is now worshipping his God as a Christian, who daily performs all the duties of civilized and social life as a duty for which he knows himself answerable, and many of whom are now in this room as constables and as jurymen—are these the debased, degraded, ignorant beings, scarcely equal to the brute whom British philanthropy rescued from destruction—from the hold of a slave ship—from slavery both of body and mind? The change has been miraculous! The finger of God is here!"

The arrangement between his Majesty's Government and the Society, for the supply of Christian teachers for the colony of Sierra Leone, has been finally adjusted By this arrangement, the preparation and maintenance of all the clergy employed in the colony, whether stationed at Freetown or in the country parishes, will devolve on the Society The colonial school at Freetown, and the Christian Institution at Regent, will be supported at the pecuniary charge of the Society while the expenses incurred by the instruction of the children in the country parishes and by the erection of habitations for the teachers and of suitable buildings for education and religious worship, will be defrayed by Government. In order to meet, more effectually, the pressing demand for labourers in this mission, it has been deemed expedient to invite clergymen of piety and zeal to offer their services to the Society for a limited period and the Committee trust that this appeal, for immediate aid in the important and interesting stations at Sierra Leone, will not be made in vain.

Our readers are already acquainted with the many bereavements which have left several important stations in this mission in a state of comparative destitution - and which had been attended with their natural consequence in impeding for a time the progress so auspiciously commenced, of the liberated Africans, in civilization and Christian piety and morality Preaching and the administration of the sacraments have been necessarily very irregular, and far from commensurate to the spiritual wants of the people It is therefore a source of thanksgiving to God, that amidst a population recently extricated from the very depths of heathen pollution and superstition, the evils which have crept in have not been more serious The Committee feel anxious to do all in their power to supply the wants of this mission. They are sensible that to maintain what is actually possessed is as important as to enter on new conquests. They contemplate with gratitude the conquests already achieved by the Gospel over the superstitions of a part of the native population, they feel that a promising commencement has been made in the work of evangelizing Africa. They are impressed by the conviction, that the discouragements which have lately arisen in the African Mission are chiefly and naturally to be referred to the loss of missionaries and they confidently anticipate the removal of those discouragements, under the Divine blessing, when these losses shall be adequately supplied.

Mediterranean Mission.

We are particularly anxious to invite the attention of our readers to this mission, because we are not sure that its importance is in general sufficiently understood or appreciated, and from the circumstance of its operations being hitherto chiefly preparatory and prospective, they do not force themselves upon public observation so conspicuously as the Society's labours in some other quarters. For a general view of the momentous objects contemplated by means of this interesting mission, we must refer our readers to the various notices of it in our volume, and especially to Mr Jowett's last volume of Christian Researches, recently reviewed in our pages.

On the arrival of the Rev John Hartley at Malta it was determined that he should proceed to Corfu, and spend some time in that and the neighbouring islands, and that his subsequent measures should be regulated according to circumstances. His report of his visit is highly encouraging. He finds the greatest readiness among the Greeks, both to promote the circulation of the Scriptures and to attend to addresses from the pulpit. He says, "It was a spectacle highly gratifying to observe an archbishop a bishop, and a considerable number of laymen, listening to an English minister addressing them in the language of Greece. I have heard of no sermon addressed to them, to which they have not resorted with eagerness. And it is not a few obscure individuals who have been present on these occasions; but the heads of their church and the heads of their nation."

Mr Jowett, after his return from Syria, had been fully and most usefully occupied in the superintendance of the press and in the preparation of the second volume of "Christian Researches." He had also several tracts, both in Italian and in Arabic, ready for the press and he was preparing to commence a small periodical publication in Modern Greek, which would probably have considerable circulation but some unavoidable circumstances had retarded the execution of his measures.

The table of contents of Mr Jowett's Researches, which is extracted in the Report before us, contains a wide and interesting notice of the field of Christian exertion contemplated by the Mediterranean mission. It may be said to comprise the Papal States with the nations in relation with them—Modern Greece—Turkey in Europe and Asia—Armenia, and the neighbouring regions—Persia—Syria and Palestine—Arabia—Egypt and Nubia—Abyssinia—and the Barbary States. The attention of the Committee has been of late directed to two portions more particularly of this wide field—Greece and Abyssinia. For the benefit of the latter the British and Foreign Bible Society has prepared the Scriptures both in the Ethiopic as the ecclesiastical language of the country and in the Amharic as the chief vernacular dialect. The Four Gospels in Amharic, from the translation of Abu Rumi procured for the Society by Mr Jowett in Egypt have been printed, and forwarded to Abyssinia. The Ethiopic

Scriptures are under preparation: and in aid of this work, the Church Missionary Committee have presented to the Bible Society some Ethiopic Manuscripts, purchased by Mr. Jowett at Jerusalem among which was a valuable copy of the entire New Testament. The Committee had also made preparations for a mission, at the earliest practicable period, to Abyssinia. On the arrival from Basle of the five Lutheran clergymen before mentioned, three of them were destined to this service and the other two to such stations in the Mediterranean as might appear most eligible, in reference to a connexion with Abyssinia.

The great questions at issue between Christians and Mohammedans have been fully exhibited in a volume of "Controversial Tracts" recently published by professor Lee, containing a translation of Mirza Ibrahim's Arabic Tract in defence of Islamism, the three Tracts of Mr. Martyn in reply, the Rejoinder of Mohammed Ruza, with much valuable matter from the pen of the editor. This volume, it is hoped, will be of great service to Oriental missionaries.

EAST INDIA MISSIONS

The Society's proceedings in India are too numerous and miscellaneous for us to detail them at length, and many of them especially those which respect the commencement and rapid extension of female education, have already been noticed in our pages. We shall therefore content ourselves with a few cursory extracts from the Report before us.

The Calcutta Committee congratulate the Society on the accession to their numbers of the Right Reverend the Bishop of Calcutta. The personal attention paid by his Lordship to the interests of the Society, not only adds greater efficiency to its operations, but also affords additional security that their measures will be pursued in strict conformity with the principles which the Church Missionary Society has always maintained. The Society's missionaries episcopally ordained bear a relation to their diocese similar to that of the clergy to their respective bishops at home.

The Society's missionaries at Calcutta are diligently pursuing their labours and in some branches of their work, under circumstances of great encouragement. They are fully convinced that there is no obstacle in the way of general education, but the want of agents and of increased funds. With a view to meet the feelings of the respectable natives of India, and to improve more extensively the opportunities opening for female education, a Society had been formed as our readers are apprised entitled the Ladies Society for Native Female Education in Calcutta and its vicinity of which Lady Amherst is patroness. A most interesting examination took place of the Society's Native Female Schools. Many of the women and children, it is stated, evinced a proficiency truly astonishing, considering the obstacles which they had to surmount. The first classes read the New Testament, not only with facility, but with an evident understanding of its meaning, and answered several questions put to them with a degree of intelligence and pertinence little to be expected. Mrs. Wilson had introduced the New Testament into her schools. When we bear in mind, that the project of communicating instruction to the Native Females of the East which till recently was regarded as hopeless is now in active operation and daily extending its range, we cannot but consider the facilities afforded for this important purpose by the rapid diminution of prejudice as opening a most cheering prospect. The Society express their grateful acknowledgments to God, that an entrance on this interesting path of missionary labour has been so unexpectedly and happily effected; and we are happy to learn, that while Native Females are making progress in the elementary branches of education, the higher aims of the Society for their spiritual welfare have also, in several cases been successful

On the gradual diminution of prejudice among the natives of India a missionary remarks—'I spoke a few months ago to an intelligent Hindoo of the Merchant caste who said We are no more so prejudiced against Christianity and the customs of Europeans, as we were twenty years ago and some few years hence we shall be still less so I am not so superstitious as my father, and my son is not so much prejudiced as myself' This is the sentiment of a native himself and I can testify, from what I have daily opportunity to observe and to hear that he spoke the truth The Brahmins are still a strong barrier against the introduction of Christianity into this country though their influence is rapidly declining

The national system of education has been found productive of much benefit, so far as it has been practicable to adopt it in the Bengalee schools The order and harmony which attend this system are every where apparent and have excited the admiration of many intelligent Hindoos

The Native Missionary Abdool Messeeh continues faithful to his profession In a letter to the Archdeacon of Calcutta after referring to the loss of the use of his limbs and his extreme weakness he adds 'The palsy has not wholly left me but I can move about in a carriage, and God grants me the faculty of speech Through his blessing I trust I shall be permitted until death to declare the truths of the Gospel When at length this sinful body of mine is dead, and shall have put on immortality, may I be found among the least of the blessed!'

The field of exertion among the Syrian Christians and their neighbours required additional missionaries especially as domestic afflictions and sickness have interposed many obstacles to the present ones, in the full discharge of the duties in which they are zealously engaged Mr Bailey, with the Syrian clergy and in the care of the press—Mr Fenn, in the college—Mr Baker in charge of the schools—and Mr Norton, at Allepie—have, however, with some interruptions, proceeded in their work The Report on the state of the Syrian college mentions that the number of students was 51 and that their punctuality in attendance and application to study have borne testimony to their desire for improvement Fresh applications have been made for parochial schoolmasters in different places and in two instances the requests have been accompanied by offers, on the part of the people to bear the charge of one half of the schoolmaster's stipend The schools bear a good character among the people Two new churches are being built The translation of the Scriptures advances Two improvements have been effected among the clergy—the abolition of celibacy and the purifying of some of the festival solemnities from the heathenish admixtures by which they were degraded but the Missionaries still lament the corrupt state of the Syrian Liturgy the low condition of the females and the want of due regard to the Sabbath

CEYLON MISSION

There are now in service at the four stations, six English missionaries of whom five are married They are assisted by 34 natives and have 29 schools of which 7 are at Cotta, 5 at Kandy 6 at Baddagame and 11 at Nellore The return of scholars is as follows —Cotta 193 boys Kandy, 42 boys (the number being much reduced by sickness) Baddagame, 192 boys 77 girls and Nellore 411 boys 73 girls—making a total of 838 boys and 150 girls.

Mr. Lambrick's translation of the Bible into Cingalese had proceeded to the Book of Exodus in the Old Testament and to the middle of St. John in the New. The missionaries continue to preach, and to visit and converse with the natives. They had also introduced female schools, and had also entered on the plan of taking native children into their families. Their hopes are very high with regard to the benefits, which, by the blessing of God, may be derived from these schools.

One of the Society's missionaries gives the following general view of the mission — "The Reports of the respective stations will make the Committee acquainted with the existing circumstances and future prospects of this mission. We consider ourselves as settlers in a wild country thickly covered with forests and jungles our business is as it were to bark the trees and burn them—thus preparing the way for future cultivators a patch here and there may indeed be cleared and a few handfuls of seed thrown in which by the Divine blessing may produce a crop to encourage us amidst our labours but we cannot expect to see a large harvest that will be the privilege of those who come after us." Further help is required at the present stations and there are favourable openings for new ones. The missionaries write — 'Here is a useful field for ten additional missionaries and if it should please God to put it into the hearts of his servants to provide as many more they will all find employment among the heathen here.'

AUSTRALASIA MISSION

In reporting the state of the Australasia Mission, the Committee express their gratification in the unremitted favour which Sir Thomas Brisbane has shewn not only to the Society's proceedings and designs but to the native population within the influence of his authority. The Society has felt, from the commencement of its efforts in these seas, greatly interested in the protection of the natives from insult and injury, by unprincipled Europeans; and they congratulate the friends of humanity on the passing of an Act which enables the colonial authorities to try individuals for crimes against these unoffending natives. Colonel Arthur, the lieutenant-governor of Van Dieman's Land, affords every practicable assistance to the Society's exertions in these seas. An archdeaconry has been established in the colony, and the present archdeacon the Ven T H Scott who is well acquainted with the circumstances of the mission, has assured the Committee that he will render it every assistance in his power.

Mr Marsden was confirmed, by what he observed in his fourth visit to New Zealand in his views of the importance of a seminary in New South Wales for the instruction of young natives of New Zealand and determined therefore, on his return, to renew the attempt to form such an establishment and with the further view of providing education therein for the European children of the mission now fast increasing in number "I purpose he says to have the New Zealand youths taught shoemaking tailoring, weaving flax dressing and spinning with gardening and farming If the chief's sons are educated with the children of the missionaries they will become attached one to another and the work of the mission will be promoted thereby I have six New Zealanders with me now all young men of chief's families they rejoice to see the foundation of our institution laid' The missionaries in New Zealand are stationed as follows —Mr Hall and Mr King at Rangheehoo, Mr Kemp and Mr Clarke, at Kiddeekiddee Rev H Williams at Pyhea, and Mr Davis and Mr C Davis, whose place of settlement had not been determined all of these are married except Mr C Davis Several others have been attached to the mission from New South Wales. Meetings are statedly held, for conducting the business of the mission, for united prayer, and for studying the native languages.

On a general view of the mission, it appears, in reference to the natives, that with a few exceptions their behaviour has been generally less peaceable and friendly than in former years. It ought, however, to be considered, that their violent conduct has usually been connected with their notions of retaliation for some imagined injury or insult. The resort of shipping to the bay leads to consequences not a little injurious. Within the year, not less, it is supposed, than a hundred men had fixed themselves among the natives. In the present state of the natives, great firmness is required on the part of the missionaries.

The warlike spirit is still cherished, to the great injury of the people and of the attempts to benefit them. Wherever the missionaries go among them, it is observable that those who abstain from war live in comparative comfort, while those who make a practice of accompanying the war expeditions live in penury and wretchedness. The state of the natives however under various alleviating circumstances does not deter the missionaries from contemplating the formation of other settlements among them. Shunghee though avowedly hostile to Christianity, is generally on friendly terms with the missionaries, and will frequently stand up in their defence. The difficulties attending the support of schools are very great, and food must be provided for the scholars. Cultivation has been on the increase in all places. In reference to this mission Mr Marsden writes—'I observed with much pleasure that the natives in every place were much improved in their appearance and manners since I last visited them; and that notwithstanding the misconduct of some of the Europeans, the work was gradually going on, and the way preparing for the blessings of the Gospel to be imparted to this people.'

Sir Thomas Brisbane also says,—"I have already expressed my favourable opinion in regard to the progress of the mission in New Zealand and I am happy to say, that length of time tends only to fortify me more strongly in this sentiment.'

WEST-INDIES MISSION.

The Society has in the island of Antigua fifteen schools, connected with sixty-three estates, and containing about 2,000 Black and Coloured men women, and children. They are Sunday schools but instruction is given on other days also, as there is opportunity. The schools continue under vigilant inspection and their general progress is very encouraging. Mrs Thwaites writes,—"The prayers of the converted Negroes are peculiarly striking and affecting. The schools are never forgotten; they express their gratitude to God that they were instituted, as by that means the poorest slaves may be taught to read God's word."

NORTH WEST AMERICAN MISSION

The Rev. David T Jones, the Society's missionary at Red River Settlement has met with countenance and support. He gives the following view of the progress of religion:—"The church has been crowded all the winter by Europeans, half bred natives and native Indians. Two half breeds have, I trust, been added to the number of those that shall be saved. The influence of religion has shewn itself in the observation of the Sabbath by many who had been accustomed to pay no regard to it. I could particularize many very pleasing instances of what I hope is the beginning of the work of Divine grace.' The increased attention to religion among the settlers has rendered a second church necessary. A num ber of the half-breeds attend the Sunday-school in the afternoon, and the Indian boys come in the evening to say their catechism and to sing. The average attendance in the Sunday School for the year was 102.

In giving a summary view of the Society's proceedings, its efforts for the diffusion of Divine truth among the heathen may be thus stated.— In the nine missions of the Society, there are forty-five stations with which are connected 296 schools. These stations and schools are occupied by 440 labourers of these, 119 are Europeans, including a few females born of British parents in India, and 321 were born in the respective countries, chiefly, where they are employed. The number of scholars under the Society is 14,090 of whom 10,457 are boys, 2,957 girls, and 676 youths and adults. In connexion with the principal missions, printing presses are established, and are coming in some places, into very active and beneficial operation.

We have not space at present to notice the Appendix, &c to the Report, which contain several interesting documents, particularly the Rev Bird Sumner's sermon before the Society, and the address of Mr Pearson the principal of the institution at Islington on opening that important establishment.

UNITED STATES DOMESTIC MISSIONARY SOCIETY

This institution is formed, we presume, on the plan of the 'Home Missionary Society in England, but with this radical difference, that in the United States of North America, there is no Established Church which extends its ministrations to every village and hamlet in the kingdom, and only needs to be quickened in every quarter into full activity of zeal and exertion, to supply with no scanty stream, the religious wants of the whole population. We have before us the Third Report of this Society, from which we copy the following passages, which place in an affecting light the religious necessities of many parts of the Union as well as the active zeal of the friends of religion in every quarter to supply them. No allusion is made in this Report to the labours of the members of the Episcopal Church but we are happy in believing that, in proportion to their numbers and opportunities of doing good they are by no means behind other bodies of their fellow Christians in home missionary exertions.

"The whole number of missionaries employed the last year is 123—the number of churches aided 130. This Society has thus upon little more than 11,000 dollars, preached the Gospel to 80,000 persons. Our field of labour is greatly enlarged during the past year. Many of the best friends of the missionary cause looked with deep solicitude upon the great experiment, unexampled, we believe in any country, of a society which should in its first year employ fifty-seven missionaries—in its second, seventy eight. They scarcely dared to desire more than that we should hold fast what we have so speedily acquired. But we have gone beyond the hopes of many and feel that efforts need only be made under the blessing of God, with steadiness and judgment to find a ready and efficient co operation in the members of the one household of faith. Except in peculiar cases, our missionaries are supported for one whole year some upon fifty dollars, many upon seventy five dollars, few upon more than one hundred dollars. This is performed by leaving to the towns and congregations helped the selection of their own ministers and by adding our gift to what their utmost efforts can effect for his temporal maintenance. Abandoning the system of itineracy which is comparatively very expensive and obviously little effectual, this Society seeks to build up permanent churches

"The Committee would earnestly press upon the friends to education, and all who favour our theological seminaries considerations suggested by the experience of this year. The need of ministers, spirited, able, enlightened is greater than most will believe who have taken only a cursory survey of the country. From intimate knowledge, we can name counties and towns on every hand which open stations of vast importance. In our growing country such young men are needed by hundreds. Along the line of the State Canal new towns are rising, on our lakes new ports opening, on the banks of our rivers new edifices of worship erected, the steeples of which shew to the traveller the signals of want, not of supply. In some of our old counties, half the population is without the Gospel, the whole line of division between the States of New York and Pennsylvania is one vast waste, the State of Vermont even, is scarcely more than one half supplied. Indeed, we have but to run through the old States on the seaboard, from this city to St Mary's, to say the same of them all. Ohio ought to have a hundred ministers to settle at once. Michigan is opening a field for domestic missions, fertile as its own fallow ground. That territory contains, probably 14,000 inhabitants and but one Presbyterian minister, who is our missionary. The State of Indiana contains 170,000 and but 79 preachers of all kinds. The St. Louis Presbytery has but five ordained clergymen and one licentiate, with eighteen churches under its care and extends over a country almost 300 miles square and embraces a population of 160,000. Indiana, Illinois Missouri, Louisiana, with the States which are clustering fast upon our Union, by which a mass of human beings are to be consolidated from the Mississippi to the Pacific, into one scene of life, and duty, and responsibility—all call loudly for the embassage of peace. At our present ratio of increase, we are to be in 1850 twenty two millions of people and in 1875, forty four millions. Let any man calculate what ought to be the ratio in the increase of the ministers which the church should train for this teeming population."

Many of our readers feeling greatly interested in the valuable plans of Bishop Chase for the spiritual benefit of the State of Ohio, we copy the following passage from the Report illustrative of the pressing necessity for such exertions. A correspondent writes "Infidelity, universalism and irreligion of every kind have exerted and still exert a powerful influence in this country, and especially in this county, and can only be counteracted by learned, pious and able defenders of 'the faith once delivered to the saints.' Respecting the counties around, I would say, that they are all in need of assistance though probably there is no one in a worse condition, nor even so bad as this. I have no doubt that twenty and even more ministers might be immediately settled on the Connecticut Western Reserve alone if they could have a little assistance at first from your Society. Throughout this state there is one vast field for missionary labours. One summer I spent riding over the state in various directions and preaching the Gospel at my own expense, and often my heart was pained by witnessing the moral desolation that every where abounded. But most of the inhabitants are too poor, or too wicked, or too indifferent about religion to make much effort to obtain the preaching of the Gospel. The few pious, in connexion with some others who feel the worth of the Gospel make such sacrifices and pay such heavy subscriptions for the support of preaching as would make some in New England give over in one year

The pious in this country generally, where a minister is settled pay at least five times as much to have preaching *half* of the time, as the people of New England pay for the whole of the time

RECEIPTS OF CHARITABLE SOCIETIES

We close our volume with an interesting and appropriate document namely, an alphabetical list of the Receipts of various Missionary, Bible Education and Tract Societies for the year. The amount exceeds that of last year by nearly 70 000*l*. In two instances the contributions include government grants the Society for the Propagation of the Gospel, 20 281*l* 5*s* and the Irish Education Society, 22 000*l*. In estimating the income of the American Societies, the dollar has been reckoned at 4*s* 6*d*.

African Institution	£883	13	8
American Bible Society	10462	14	0
American Board of Missions	10683	13	6
American Colonization	985	10	0
American Education	2127	7	6
American Jews	3114	4	6
American Methodist Missionary	931	10	0
American United Foreign Missionary	4719	7	6
Baptist Missionary	£15995	11	2
British and Foreign Bible	93285	5	2
British and Foreign School	2114	19	3
Christian Knowledge	60225	2	6
Church Missionary	45383	19	10
Church-of England Tract	649	14	2
Continental	2133	15	10
Gospel Propagation	27622	15	0
Hibernian	8143	3	11
Irish Sunday School	2653	7	1
Irish Education	36560	11	2
Irish Society of London	363	15	7
Irish Tract and Book	3659	4	10
Jews Society of London	14183	18	6
Ladies Hibernian Female Society	2422	3	0
London Missionary	40719	1	6
Merchant-Seamen's Bible	911	4	7
National-Education	2615	7	0
Naval and Military Bible	2615	2	0
Newfoundland Education	701	0	6
Port-of London Seamen s	283	3	7
Prayer book and Homily	1781	12	10
Religious Tract	12568	17	0
Scottish Missionary	8257	4	3
Slave Conversion	3038	9	8
Sunday School Union	4253	12	2
United Brethren	9864	5	8
Wesleyan Missionary	38046	9	7
Total	£474,960	18	0

ECCLESIASTICAL PREFERMENTS

Rev C B Clough Rector of Llanferris Denbighshire Domestic Chaplain to the Marchioness Cornwallis.

Rev Walter Fletcher to a Prebendal Stall in York Cathedral

Rev James Johnson to the Prebendal Stall of Hampton in Hereford Cathedral

Rev C Nixon to a Prebendal Stall in Southwell Collegiate Church Notts

Rev J Cross to be Precentor and Rev W Miller a Minor Canon of Bristol Cathedral

Rev J Brown Bottisham V co Camb

Rev R R. Faulkner St Sepulchre s P C Cambridge

Rev R Edmonds Woodleigh R Devon

Rev Morgan Evans to the Benefice of Builth, and Llanddewir cwm, co. Brecon

Rev J Tapp Griffith Great Elme R Somerset

Rev W B Leach Sutton Montague R. with Lovington P C Somerset

Rev G A Legge Bray V Berks

Rev ——Hume Melksham V co Wilts

Rev T Musgrave St Mary the Great P C Cambridge

Rev Dr Spry Mary le bone R Middlx

Rev J Stratton Halston V Kent also a Minor Canon of Canterbury Cathedral

Rev H Tripp Blackborough R Devon

Rev V F Vyvyan Withell R Cornwall

Rev C Ward, Moulden R. co Bedford

Rev John West, Evercreech V Somerset with Chesterblade Chapelry annexed

Rev W B Whitehead, Chard V Somerset

Rev G E Whyley Eaton Bray V Beds

Rev T Wynter Daylesford R co Worc

Rev R. Richards Domestic Chaplain to the Duke of Sussex.

Rev G G Smith Domestic Chaplain to the Duke of York

Rev John Langley of Worcester Domestic Chaplain to the Earl of Stirling

Rev P Gurden Reymerstone R Norfolk

Rev Chas Rich Sumner (now D D)

Ecclesiastical Preferments

Librarian to the King and Prebendary of Worcester, to a Prebendal Stall in Canterbury Cathedral vice Percy

Rev T Gaisford a Prebendary of Worcester Cathedral vice Sumner

Rev Wm Potchett, to be Prebendary of the Cathedral of Sarum vice Smith

Rev J Chamberlayne Eastwick R Herefordshire

Rev T Crick, Little Thurlow R. Norfolk

Rev S Davies, Bringwyn R. Radnorshire

Rev R. Edmonds, Church Lawford R. and Newnham V co Warwick

Rev C Davies Chancellor of Down Cathedral

Rev G Townsend, Preb of Durham

Rev G Vanburgh, Preb of Timberscombe in Wells Cathedral

Rev C H Hodgson Vicar Choral of Salisbury Cathedral

Rev J Ackroyd, Egmere R. with Holkham V co Norfolk

Rev W W Aldrich Butley P C Suffolk

Rev R. Allan Church and Parish of Little Dunkeld, co. Perth

Rev W Annesley North Bovey R. Devon

Rev Jas Baker, Nuneham Courtney R Ox.

Rev Edw Barnard Alverstoke R. Hants.

Rev W Clark, Guisley R. Yorkshire

Rev George Day Bedingham V Norfolk

Rev J Ellicot, Horn R. co Rutland.

Rev Dr Goddard, Bexley V co Lincoln

Rev T Hollway Partney R and Spelsby P C co Linc

Rev R. Jefferson South Kilvington R co York

Rev R. Mountain, Havant R Hants.

Rev G Osborne Stainby with Gunby R. Linc

Rev R. Pretyman Elingdon Wroughton R. Wilts

Rev J Randall, East Stonehouse R. Devon

Rev E Montagu Salter Swanton Nowers R. cum Woodnorton Norfolk

Rev R. Sheppard Thwaite R. Norfolk

Rev J Surtees, St Augustin R. Bristol.

Rev H Tacy Swanton Morley R with Worthing Chapel annexed, Norfolk.

Rev A. A Turnour Besthorpe V Norfolk

Rev H F Vaughan Myshall R. diocese of Leighlin and Ferns Ireland

Rev R Meredith Hayborn V Berks

Rev C P Vivian Wellingborough V Northamptonshire

Rev R. Warner Timberscombe V Somerset

Rev C Woolcombe, Minster and Forrabury CC Cornwall

Rev C Moore Rev Dr J Sleath and Rev W Strong Chaplains in Ord. to the King

Rev H Wetherell, Prebendary of Gloucester Cathedral

Rev C Barnwell Barnwell, Mileham R. Norfolk

Rev G W Butler St Nicholas R. co Nott

Rev T Chambers Studley V co Warwick

Rev E Coleridge Monksilver R. co Berks

Rev G H Curtois, East Berkwith R Linc

Rev R. Eden Hortingfordbury R. co. Herts

Rev J Edwards Finningham R. co. Suff

Rev J Couch Grylls Saltash Ch Cornwall

Rev H Watts Harries Prendergast R Pembrokeshire

Rev J Jones, Bodedeyrn P C Anglesea.

Rev T Kilby St John s P C Wakefield

Rev C S. Leathes Ellesborough R Berks

Rev S Madan Twerton V Somerset

Rev J F Parker Bentham R. Yorkshire

Rev W W Quartley Heynsham V Somer

Rev M Scott, Slawston V co. Leicester

Rev J Senters St Augustine R. Norwich

Rev T L Shapcott, St. Michael s V Southampton

Rev R. Walsh Six-mile-bridge R. Ireland

Rev W Waters, Rippingale R. co Lincoln

Rev —— White St. Andrews R. Hertf.

Rev E Wilton Christ Church C. Wilts

Rev Dr Crane and Rev W Walker to be Chaplains to the Earl of Carlisle

Rev W Moore Chaplain to Earl of Donoughmore

Rev T Randolph, Chapl in Ord. to the King

DISPENSATION

Rev T Brown Rector of Conington, Cambridgeshire to hold Westow R Hurtingd

INDEX

TO THE
ESSAYS, SUBJECTS, INTELLIGENCE, OCCURRENCES,
&c &c

	Page
ABSOLUTION	537
Act of Uniformity	116
Advent of Christ	432
African Institution	816
Algiers	323
All Souls Church	748
Alphabets	585
America	450
Amiableness without Piety	51
Analogy of Religion	769
Anglo-Saxon Church	35
Animal Heat	389
Answers to Correspondents 64 126	200
264 332 396 460, 532, 596	660
	724, 796
Antediluvians	26
Apocrypha Character of the	480
Apocryphal Books of Enoch and Isaiah	558
Arctic Expedition	123 640
Atheism	47 662
Australasia	826
Autograph Letters	123
Bartholomew Massacre	133
Banwell Cave	56
Berlin Missionary Seminary	588
Bible (see Scriptures)	
Biblical Criticism 14, 212, 274, 348	406
	480 738
——— Studies, Importance of	141
Bishops Character of	634
Breda, Declaration from	115
Brazil	711, 722
British Constitution	755
——— Ladies Address to on Slavery	749
——— Museum	191, 321
Buenos Ayres	523
Burmese War	128 200 262, 460
Burning Widows	388 450 532
Calcutta (see India)	
Calvinism Doctrines of	202 640
Calvinistic Archbishops	109
Calvinists	108
Cambridge 55, 123 191, 448 710	778
Canada	454 644
Catholics (see Church of Rome)	
Catholic Emancipation	351
Ceylon	587
Character and Writings of Lord Byron	79
	151 214 281
——— of Women	216
——— of Bishop Butler	770
——— of Miss Jerram	161
Charge Bishop Law s	633
Charity on administering 486 618 745	746
——— Oratorios for	617

	Page
Charitable Societies (see Society)	
Children susceptible of Religion	118
Chinese Literature 251 504	778
China 57 251 554 718,	719
——— Catholic Missions in	590
Christ Genealogy of	338
——— how betrayed	211
——— Advent of	432
——— Union with	739
Christian Church Unity of	138
——— Obedience	476
——— Temple	279
——— Watchfulness 275	344
——— Missions Remarks on 327	620
Christianity Excellencies of	2
——— Character of	249
——— Evidences of	773
——— Definition of	11
——— Estimated Extent of	643
——— Healing Effects of	819
——— How corrupted	400
——— Temporal Benefits of	69
——— Defective Views of	774
Churches Consecration of	415
Church building Commission	588
——— Gallican (see French Catholic Church)	
——— of England when founded	31
——— of Rome Doctrines of	120
——— Demands implicit Obedience 581	596
——— Declining Influence of	653
——— Missions of 33	590
——— not uniform 16,	582
——— opposes Circulation of Scriptures 62	231
——— Philosophy of the	398
——— 461, 533	597
——— Persecutions by the	103
——— Recent Efforts of the	230
——— 720,	751
——— Superstitions of 42	233
——— 235 352	584
——— Worship of	350
——— Psalmody	225
——— Protestant of France (see French Protestant Church)	
Circumspection 275	344
Classical Parallelisms	359
Cleopatra's Needle	586
Clerical Studies 213	387
——— Sporting	488
——— Residence 293	630
Commercial Embarrassments	785
Consecration of Churches	415
Columbia	199
Commandments the	65

INDEX

	Page
Communion on administering to Criminals	21, 159
Confession	13
Conservateur Chrêtien, Work so called	333
Corn Laws	331
Corporal Punishments inexpedient	363 443
Counsel extending Benefit of	331 357
Creed of St Gregory	407
Deluge Tradition respecting the	252
Denmark	322
Destitute on relieving the	486 618 745 746
Dew	57
Diorama	450
Druses	561
Easter on making it a fixed Festival	87
Ecclesiastical Dry rot	18
———— Preferments	332 593 723, 795 843
Edict of Nantes	204
Edifices Heights of	586
Edinburgh Review	152
Egypt	323 522
Eighteenth Article	787
Elijah's Mantle	608
England Character of	587
Enoch, Apochryphal Book of	558
Enthusiasm	47
Episcopacy	312
Episcopal Floating Chapel	456
———— Seminary New York	592
———— Ohio	592
Evidences of Christianity	773
Extreme Unction	534
Faith Definition of	15
———— Justification by	90, 727
———— Nature of	551
Family Sermons	11 73 137 207 275 344 402, 475, 539 609, 680 739
Fatalism	662
Fathers on the Study of the	551 666, 717
Ferney Voltaire	125
Fiction, on Works of	163
France	57 60 123 129 198 201, 252 261, 265 330 333 393 450 521 643, 688 711 720 778 784, 817
Free Labour Benefits of	149
French Charter	758
———— Protestant Church History and Condition of	129 201 259 265 333 762
———— Catholic Church	330, 688 720 751
Gallican Church (see French Catholic Church)	
Georgia	459
Genealogies	358
Geneva Pastors	334
Gentleman's Magazine on H More	321
Glastonbury Abbey	388
Gospel (see Christianity)	
Grace, Definition of	11
Greece and Greeks	61 252 331 393 459, 529 643 653 720
Guiana	323
Hayti	530 653 721 828
Heart Wickedness of the	402

	Page
Heathen obstinate Superstition of	609
Hebrew Learning Importance of	144
Hints for a Princess H More's	796
History of French Protestant Church (see French Protestant Church)	
Holy Orders Preparation for	213
Homilies of St Chrysostom	408 460, 543 603
House of Reform	261
Hygrometer	521
Immorality Effects of, on the Judgment	664 725 797
Immoralities in Navy	366 441
Imperial Measures	722
Impressment	366 441
India	192 195 196 197 200 252 324, 327 388 450 522 711, 780 813, 837
———— Female Education in	197 453 784
Infant Schools	396, 527, 684
Infidelity how generated	664
Ireland	128 200 235 318 331 395 460 651 652 823
Isaiah Apocryphal Book of	558
Italy	323 522 779
Java	192
Jerusalem Modern	570
Jews Conversion of the	513 626
———— in Rome	613
———— Proclamation to the	722
Johnsoniana	520
Joy Religious	246, 673
Judas Character of	207
Juggernauth Car	323
Jury Bill	200 331 460
Juvenile Publications	585
Justification by Faith	90 727
Kent Loss of the	435
King's Speech	126
Laity to read the Scriptures	16
Language Institution	527 724
La Plata	331
Law of God complete	9
Letter Sheppard's to Lord Byron	83
———— to a Literary Friend	731
Letters, Cowper's	24
'Let us Pray' meaning of	78
List of New Publications	57 124 192, 254 324 389 451 523 587 644 711 780
Literary and Philosophical Intelligence	56, 123, 191 251, 321 387 448 520 585 642, 710 777
Literary Property	449
Locusts	388
Lollards Defence of the	93
London University	395 449
Lord's Supper on administering to Criminals	21, 159
Love of our Neighbour	66
Madagascar	452
Malabar Maxims	780
Mankind responsible for Opinions	661, 725 797
Mass	463
Mecca	587
Mechanics Institutions	56, 192

INDEX

	Page
Memoir of B White	578
———— Brydayne	690
Menai Bridge	388
Methodist Protest on Slavery	63
Mexico	61, 325, 529
Missionary Gazetteer	779
———— Seminary at Berlin	588
Millennium Opinions respecting	426, 489
Missions Remarks on	327, 620
———— in China, Roman Catholic	590
Monastic Institutions	566, 583, 764
Moravian Missions	33, 58
Mummy	56, 521
Nantes, Edict of	204
National Gallery	521
Navy State of the	360, 441
Negroes (see Slaves)	
Netherlands	643
New York	711
———— Episcopal Seminary	592
Nonconformists	116
Non residence of Clergy	293
North America	252, 327, 389
Oaths	91
Obituary Rev W Reid	263
———— W Richmond	64
Ohio, Theological Seminary in	197, 592, 649
Oratorios for Charity	616
Original Sin	310
Oxford	55, 321, 337, 778
Parliament, Proceedings in	126, 200, 262, 331, 394, 449, 460
Penang	124
Persecution	103
Persia	780
Peru	199, 525, 595
Philosophy of the Roman Catholic Religion	398, 461, 533, 597
Plague, whether contagious	521
Poetry	29, 419
Poland	261, 393, 586
Popery (see Church of Rome)	
Portugal	458
Prayer, Archbishop Laud's	113
Prophecy Remarks on	227, 422, 489
Prison Discipline	258, 830
Prussia	586
Protestantism Defence of	764
Protestant Church in France (see French Protestant Church)	
Psalmody	225
Psalms, Value of the	146
Public Affairs	60, 126, 198, 261, 330, 393, 458, 529, 594, 653, 720, 784
———— Buildings	191
Publicity, Benefits of	365
Purgatory	464, 701
Puritans Character of the	107
Pulpit Eloquence	690
Quarterly Review	234, 536
Radiant Heat	521
Reformation Defence of the	98, 751
Reformed Church (see Protestant Church)	

	Page
Relics	42
Religion, false Shew of	707
Religious Controversy	301
Religious Intelligence	58, 125, 193, 254, 324, 390, 452, 524, 588, 645, 712, 780
———— Joy	246, 673
Responsibility of Man	661, 725, 797
Revelation (see Scriptures)	
Review of Reviews	441
Righteous, why afflicted	465
Rochester Cathedral	123
Roman Catholic Chapels	123
Rome Church of (see Church)	
———— Visit to Jews in	613
Russia	192, 643, 711, 779, 785
Sabbath (see Sunday)	
Sacrament (see Lord's Supper)	
Sailors, Observations respecting	360, 441, 456
Saints Worship of	42
Samson whether a Type	553, 670
Sanctification, Nature of	405
Sardinia	711
Scientia Biblica Work so called	387
Scottish Missionary Bishop	650
Scriptures (see Bible Society)	
———— Circulation of opposed	62, 231
———— Completeness of the	8
———— distributed at Confirmation	78
———— on Studying the Original	141
———— the Guide of Life	1, 65
———— should determine Controversy	667
———— to be read by all	15, 734
Scriptural Education, Progress of	588
Seamen (see Sailors)	
Senses, the	520
Serampore College	196
Servants Conduct towards	485, 744
Sierra Leone	256, 625
Sin the Parent of Infidelity	664
———— Venial and Mortal	696
Slave Colonies (see West Indies)	
———— grown Sugar	64, 146, 826
———— Trade, State of the	816
Slaves	643
———— Emancipation of	199, 595, 818
———— Schools for	59, 715, 840
Slavery	459
———— Effects of on Free Children	224
———— on Petitioning against	792
———— Enormities of	173, 222, 288, 374, 655, 786, 828
———— Dr Johnson on	293
———— Proceedings respecting	63, 823
———— Address on Female	749
———— (see also Anti Slavery Society)	
Slave Trade defended by Boswell	158
———— French Petition against	330
Societies Bible Benefits of	60
———— Progress of	260
———— Bath and Wells Episcopal	524
———— Charitable Receipts of	843
Society Anti Slavery	146, 174, 374, 655, 823
———— Asiatic Calcutta	252, 711
———— London	191, 322, 387
———— Paris	60
———— Bible American	454
———— Bern	809

	Page		Page
Society, Bible, Bunslow	811	Society, United States Domestic Missionary	541
——— British and Foreign	790	——— Islands	451
	808	South America	126, 199, 455, 655, 815
——— Ferney Voltaire	125	Spain	61, 128, 252, 393, 543, 655, 720
——— Frankfort	810	Spanish America	456
——— Hamburgh-Altona	809	Steam Engine	123
——— Ionian	812	Sugar, Slave-grown	64, 146, 826
——— Naval and Military	589	Sunday, Violation of	89, 616, 779
——— Netherlands	809	Swearing	56
——— Nuremberg	809	Sweden	323, 522
——— Paris	259, 452, 808	Syria, Jowett's Travels in	560, 836
——— Prussian	810		
——— Russian	811	Tahiti	124, 591
——— Silesian	810	Tartary	57
——— Swedish	811	Temptation	680
——— Wuertemberg	810	Theology, Science of	815
——— Zurich	78, 809	Tracts, Strictures on	23, 77
——— Calcutta School	196	Transubstantiation	44
——— Ladies Female School	197	Turkey	522
——— Church Missionary	256, 324, 452, 714, 834	Uniformity, Act of	116
——— Episcopal Floating Chapel	456	Unitarian Chapels	557
——— for Education in Canada	454, 527	United States	61, 124, 199, 451, 459, 460, 523, 587, 648, 720, 779, 841
——— poor pious Clergy	592	——— Slavery in	288, 595, 643
——— promoting Christian Knowledge	254, 360, 390, 524, 804	——— Prosperity of	262, 294
——— Propagation of the Gospel	193, 524, 645, 712	Upas Poison	123
——— Female Education in India	719	Vaccination	448
——— General Knowledge	527	Vaudois (see Waldenses)	
——— Hibernian	330, 396	Venial Sins	697
——— Female School	392	Voluntaries	21, 226
——— Infant School	396		
——— for London	527	Wakes	613
——— Ladies', for Negro Children	715	Waldenses	89, 781
——— London Missionary	591	West Indies	58, 63, 147, 173, 331, 373, 393, 655, 715, 786, 808, 823
——— London Jews	646	——— Episcopacy in	193
——— National School	524, 783	Widows, Burning of	388, 450, 532
——— Prayer book and Homily	125, 651, 717	Wilful King in Daniel	227
——— Prison Discipline	830	Will of God, on doing the	476
——— Religious Tract	719	Women, Character of	216
——— Royal, of Literature	56	Works, not Meritorious	90
——— Spanish Translation	455		
——— Sunday School for Ireland	652		

INDEX TO THE REVIEWS

	Page		Page
ADAM's Private Thoughts	242	Catholicism, B. White on	576
Advent, Stewart on the	422, 489	Charge, Bishop Law's	683
Alleine's Alarm	242	Christian Researches, by Jowett	560
		Cooper's Crisis	226
Bayford's Modern Millenarianism	422, 489	Crisis, by Cooper	226
Basilicus	422, 489	Cunningham's Sermons	47
Beche on Negroes	373		
Bickell's West Indies	173	Davison on Prophecy	422, 489
Bickersteth on Prophecy	489	Day of God	422, 489
Book of the Catholic Church, Butler's	30, 89	Douglas's Advancement of Society	620
Book of the Church, Southey's	30, 89	——— Missions	620
Brydayne's Sermons	690	Dwight's Theology	294
Burton's Sermon	422, 489		
Butler's Analogy, by Daniel Wilson	769	Gambold's Works	242
Butler's Book of the Catholic Church	30, 89	Gauntlett on the Revelations	489

	Page		Page
Hatchard's Sermons	422, 489	Penrose on the Navy	360, 441
Howe's Redeemer's Tears	242	Prophecy, Works on	422, 489
		——— Bickersteth on	489
Jamaica, Bèche on	378	——— Davison on	422, 489
Jerram's Parental Affection	161		
Jones on the Judgment	422, 489	Religion by Abbé Mennais	751
Jowett's Christian Researches	560	Revelations, Gauntlett on	489
Judgment Jones on	422, 489	Romaine on Faith	242
		Select Christian Authors	242
Kent Loss of the	435	Serle's Remembrancer	242
Law, Bishop Charge of	633	Sermon by Burton	422, 489
Letters by Basilicus	422, 489	——— by Hatchard	422, 489
Letter to Jones, Bayford's	422, 489	——— by Wayland	620
		Sermons, Brydayne's	690
Mennais De la Religion	751	——— Cunningham's	47
Missions Works on	620	Southey's Book of the Church	80, 89
——— Douglas on	620	Stewart on the Advent	422, 489
Negroes Bèche on	373	Theology by Dwight	294
		Thomas à Kempis	242
Observations on the Navy Penrose's	360, 441	Wayland's Sermons	620
Osric, a Tale	620	West Indies Bickell's	173
		White B on Catholicism	576
Palingenesia	422, 489	Wilson's Butler's Analogy	769
Parental Affection by Jerram	161	Witherspoon's Treatises	242

INDEX TO THE PRINCIPAL NAMES

	Page		Page		Page
Abbot Abp	109	Barrow	220	Brownlow	831
Abdool Messeeh	838	Ball St.	17, 428	Brydayne	690
Abel Ramuset	60	Bathurst, Earl	176, 288	Buchanan, Dr	322
Abernethy	449	Baxter	118, 402	Buckland	56, 521
Adam	242	Bayford	422, 489	Burdett Sir F	200
Adams, Pres	199, 262	Beadon, Bp	634	Burleigh Lord	109
Africanus	338	Bèche	373	Burnett Dr	490, 494
Alban St	31	Bell, C.	520	——— Bp	100, 430, 635, 738
Alexander	422	Belsham	668	Burton	422, 489
——— Emperor	785	Benet	521	Bussonet	131
Alleine	242	Becket, Thomas à	39	Butler	30, 89, 576, 551
Alfred	34	Beza	267	——— Bp	769
Amyraut M	202, 267	Best Justice	816, 818	Buxton	394, 786
Amherst Lady	197	Bicheno	239	Byron Lord	79, 151, 214, 281, 464
Angelo M	421	Bickell	173, 373		
Apollinarius	428	Bickersteth	489		
Anselm	37	Billerme	123	Calamy	115
Armstrong	815	Birkbeck	56, 192	Calvin	131, 132, 265, 267
Arrowsmith	450	Bloomfield Bp	254, 527	Campian	106
Arthur, Col	176	Bogue	495	Canning	394, 656, 794
Athanasius	17	Boleyn A	100	Carey	192, 688
Atterbury, Bp	17, 600	Bolivar Gen	262, 523, 594	Carlisle Lord	153
Augustine	17, 44, 429, 734	Bonaparte	206, 228, 237, 266	Caulker	258
		Bonner, Bp	103	Chabrand	271
Bacon Lord	501, 673	Boswell	121, 158, 520	Chalmers, Dr	242
Back	123	Boudinot	722	Chandler Dr G	749
Bailey	226, 813	Boughton	97	Chappin	523
Bakewell	834	Boyd	407	Charles II	115
Bancroft	109	Bradwardine	92	——— I	867
Baring	660	Bran	31	——— IX	132
Barker	812, 813	Brisbane, Sir T	839	Chase Bp	197, 592, 649
Barlow	520, 710	Bridges	385, 394	Chénévière	835
Barnes, Lady	587	Brougham	394, 622, 786	Chesterfield	86
Barrett Dr	339	Brown, D	523	Christian David	195

INDEX

Name	Page	Name	Page	Name	Page
Christian	714	Galitzin, Prince	811	Kempis, T a	242
Chrysostom, St	15 17 408, 465 543 603, 660	Gallard	269	Kenney	276
		Gambold	242	Kidd Dr.	450
Cicero	521	Gauntlett	489	Kieffer, Prof	808
Clarke, Dr A	553, 670	Gerelius	589	King	562
Clarendon, Lord	111	Gibbon	544	Kotzebue	232
Claude	267	Gilgrass	177	Knox	642
Clement XI	122	Gilly	781		
Clifford Capt	388	Gilpin	101 112	Lainé Viscount	330
Closworthy	113	Gordon	242	Lambert, Father	563
Cobb	430	Goulburn	128	Lardner	428 430 747
Cobham Lord	93	Granville, Dr	521	Latimer Bishop	101
Coligni	132 134	Gray	572	Laud Archbishop	103
Collins	28	Greaves	573	Law Bishop	633
Confucius	554	Green	114	Lawen	497
Coombs	21 128 159	Gregoire, Abbé	536	Lawrence Bishop	558
Cooper	226 375 422, 532	Gregory	32	—— Mr	661
—— R B	525	—— Thaumaturgus	407	Leclerc	131
Corregio	521	Grinfield	525	Leeves	391
Corrie Archdeacon	325	Grotius	489, 492	Lee	321 715
Costa	521	Grosseteste	92	Leigh	226
Cowper	23, 283			Leighton Bishop	635 765
Cranmer	100	Haldane	335	Lescesne	393
Crespel	450	Haubroe	391	Lewis	562 648, 812
Cribb	448	Hall, Bp	111	Lissignol	271
Cunningham	47	Hastings Marchioness of	325	Lightfoot	338 341
		Hatchard Rev J	422 489	Liverpool Lord	331
Daillé	202 267, 551 747	Hayley	283	Lollard	130
Dallas	79 153, 215 286	Heath	105	Love	119
Davenant, Bp	111	Heber, Bp	195 324 713 813 837	Louis XIII	202 648
Davison	422, 489			Luther	99 131
Davy, Sir H.	521	—— Mrs	197	Luscombe Dr	650
De la Chaise Pére	203	Henry II	131	Lushington Dr	394 786
Denman	786	—— III	136	Lynam	370
Desmarets	267	—— IV	136 201	Lyon Captain	389 464
Doyle Dr	535	—— Matt	671	Lyttleton, Lord	220
Dionysius	429	Heylin	113		
Doddridge Dr	212, 213	Hilary	130	MacCarthy Sir C	257 835
Douglas	620	Hill	24	Macknight	213
Droz	333	Hoare Sir R C	192	Mackintosh, Sir J	456 786
Drummond	321 335	Hodson, Dean	590	Mœstrezat	202
Dubois, Abbé	195 234, 327	Hodson A	222	Maio A	523
Dubosc	202		711	Malesherbes	205
Dunstan St	85	Hohenthal	809	Manby Captain	710
Dupin	124 778 785	Hohlenberg	322	Marbois Marquis de	330
Duponceau	779	Horne Bp	146	Marignan	452
Dwarris	788	—— T H	297, 480	Marot	131 132
Dwight, Dr	294	Horsley	111 492 501	Marsden	226 626 839
		Howe	242	Martin	200
Elizabeth Queen	201 778	Humboldt	450	—— P	711
Ellerton Dr	587	Hume	395	—— General San	253
Erskine	242	Hunt, L.	221	——	259 265
Erasmus	16, 99			Maury	691, 693
Escoffery	393	Innes	387	M Gregor Major	436
Everett Prof	587	Irving W	819	Mede	427 430 489 492, 494, 496
Eusebius	428	Irenæus	668		
				Medwin	79 219 221 282 285 287
Faber	56, 513 666	Jackson Dr	586		
Falck	588	Jœnické	588	Melancthon	3, 92 98
Faucher	202	Jamaica Bp of	394	Melville Lord	457
Fearon	439	Jean d Albert	133	Mennais Abbe de	751
Fenelon	252	Jebb, Bp	406 480	Meyrick	536
Fisk	562 569	Jerram	161	Middleton Bishop	807
Fontana, Bp	590	Johnson Dr	28 80 121 156 158 220 282 286 293 520	Mill	252 226, 813
Franklin Capt	123 642			Milne	809
Fraunce	29	Jones J E	122 489, 497	Milner	32, 44 90 93 130 333
Foy	785	Jowett	258 322, 560, 626 836	Milton	220 282
Fox	101	Jullerat	273	Minge	595
Fuller	108 109, 111	Justin Martyr	343, 427, 668	Monod	270, 271 273

INDEX

Name	Page	Name	Page	Name	Page
Moorcroft	57	Ranken	480	Suffield Lord	260
More Sir T	103	Rayner	825	Sully	135 136 201
—— Mrs H	321 620 626 796	Read	263		
Morgan Sir C	661	Reeves	551	Taylor Dr T	671
Morice	101	Rhenius	784	Tertullian	428 489
Moritz	648	Rich	321	Theodosius Emperor	643
M rrison Dr	57 191 251 554 718 809 814	Richardson Dr	123 642	Thelwall	647
		Richelieu Cardinal de	202	Thomas St	322
		Richmond W	64	Thomson	242
Mosheim	112 121	Ridley Bishop	103	Tillotson, Archbishop	34
Mostowzki	586	Rieu	333	Todd	321 595
Musculus	98	Robinson	391	Tylsworth	97
		Romaine	242	Tyerman	591
Necker Madame	694	Rose Sir G	184	Tzschirner	733
Newall Col	226	Rosenblad	811		
Newton	24	Ross	660	Usher, Archbishop	342 635
—— Bishop	496	Rousseau	439		
Noah Major	722	Russell	595	Van Ess	810
Nix	97			Venn	508
Nylander	256	Sacy Baron de	561 564	Vesey D	282
		Salt	258 522	Vitringa	430 494
Oberlin	270	Sanders, Mrs	660	Voltaire	125
O Connell	61 396 460	Sargon	649	Vincent	452
Olivetan	131 132	Saumarez Sir J	443		
Osgood	455	Saurin	267	Waddington	25
Ostervald	259 265	Savery	332	Waldo	130
Owen Dr	117	Schmid	784	Walker Col	329
—— Rev J	269 270 809	Scott	212, 213 272 296 553 671	Warburton Bishop	112
—— R	661			Wardlaw	662
		Segur Count de	330	Way	649
Padmore	789	Seraphim Archbishop	811	Wayland	620 643
Paley	580 677 714	Serle	242	Wellesley, Lord	329
Parker, Archbishop	109	Shakespeare	282	West G	220
Parry Captain	642	Shelley	221	—— Rev Mr	252, 327
Patrick, Bishop	608	Sheppard	83	Whitby	213 427, 430 494 497 502
Payne	242	Shillibeer	223		
Pearson Dean	625	Shrewsbury	394, 825	White J Blanco	577 709
Peel	20, 331 460, 527	Shute	293	Whitehead	525
Pelagius	44	Sims	781	Whitgift Archbishop	109
Penrose Sir C.	360 441	Skelton	370	Whitmore	263
Perkins	402	Silliman Professor	306	Wickliffe	92 121 130
Perceval	779	Smith Dr	335	Wilberforce	242, 394 786 794
Perouse	710	Southey	29 30 82 89, 229, 577		
Peschier	327			Wilson, D	242 769
Peyron	522	Spalato	108	Wilson Mrs	197 329 454 720, 837
Peyrani	781	Stael Baron de	125, 757		
Pinkerton	808	Stapfer	273	Winter J	160
Platt	322	Stephen	656	Witherspoon	242
Pomare III	124	Stewart	422, 489	Wolff	563, 626, 648
Poole	213	Steinkopff	78	Wren Sir C	56
Pius IV	46	St Etienne R de	205	Wright	391
Priestley Dr	668	Stobwasser	59		
Pulley	117	Story	104	Yardley	841

INDEX TO THE TEXTS

ILLUSTRATED OR REFERRED TO

Reference	Page	Reference	Page	Reference	Page
LEVITICUS xxii 12	339	JOB xxxviii 14	359	PROVERBS xxvii 7	609
DEUTERONOMY xxviii 66	575	PSALMS i 1	406 480	ECCLESIASTES v 12	606
		xxvii 4 5	73	EZEKIEL xii 13	359
1 KINGS xxii 8	359	lvii 1	359	JEREMIAH ii 11	609
JOB ii 3	467	lxxxi 16	606	iv 14	402
x 12—16	539	cxxvii 3 5	359	xvii 9	14

INDEX

	Page		Page		Page
JEREMIAH xxxi 19	359	ACTS xiii 48	15	EPH v 15, 16	275
DANIEL ii 12	359	xvi 13	77	v 30	739
xi 36	227	xix 19	359	2 THESS iii 8	607
xii 1	230	xix 21	473	1 TIM i 5	77
MATTHEW i	338	ROMANS iii 4	78	v 23	498
xxiv 15—21	695	ii 20	78	vi 17	548, 548
MARK xiii 37	344	iii 24	78	TITUS ii 11—13	11
LUKE i 32	339	ix 4—6	576	HEB vii 18 19	738
iii	338	xv 5 6	137	xi 1	15
xi 21 22	54	1 COR ii 9	212	JAMES i 12	680
xii 22	767	xv 19 32	468	i 27	619
x i 10	699	2 COR v 14	212	ii 10	77
xxii 48	207	x 2	51	ii 14	77
JOHN v	499	xii 7	465	v 17	469
xii	499	GAL ii 16	78	REV xx 1—15	495
xiv 2	55	EPH i 2	274, 348	xxi	500
ACTS iii 19	77	ii 8 9	78	xxii	500
ix 6	475				

INDEX TO THE SIGNATURES
IN VOLUME TWENTY FIVE

	Page		Page		Page
A	146	G C G	733	Pastor	731
A—A	620	G F	480	Penrose	448
A B C	89, 225	G K	275	Philodemus	18
Academicus	749	G S Faber	670	P M M	21
A Constant Reader	488 739			Ψ Ψ	738
	745	H D	688	P S O	226
An Abolitionist	293	H H	618		
A O	348	H W	421	R	78 408
A Reader	226	H W Y	420	R L G	480
				R P B	21 281
B C	159	J	264 349	R S	554
B. L. W T	78	J C	16	R X	551
B T W L.	751	J S H	213		
		J Winter	160	S	15 79 288 748
C	407 679			S M W	421
C. A L.	29	K G	73	Spes	89
C C	747				
Christian Cosmopolite	613	Lydias	421	Theognis	553, 617
C V Penrose	448			Tiro	420
		Monitor	23	T S	419
D	671	M. S	486 746		
D G L S	294			W	804
		N J B	707	W D	23
E R	553			W W	688
		Olbius	214		
F	288	O U A	488	X	558
Faber	670	Out s	359		
				Y	560
G	421, 480	P	415		

END OF THE TWENTY FIFTH VOLUME

www.ingramcontent.com/pod-product-compliance
Lightning Source LLC
Chambersburg PA
CBHW081836230426
43669CB00018B/2728